INFOTAINMENT SYSTEMS ON FAST FORWARD

INFOTAINMENT SYSTEMS ON FAST FORWARD

PT-135

Edited by
Ronald K. Jurgen

Published by
SAE International
400 Commonwealth Drive
Warrendale, PA 15096-0001
U.S.A.
Phone: (724) 776-4841
Fax: (724) 776-0790

The Engineering Meetings Board has approved this paper for publication. It has successfully completed SAE's peer review process under the supervision of the session organizer. This process requires a minimum of three (3) reviews by industry experts.

For permission and licensing requests contact:

SAE Permissions
400 Commonwealth Drive
Warrendale, PA 15096-0001-USA
Email: permissions@sae.org
Tel: 724-772-4028
Fax: 724-776-3036

SAE®
Global Mobility Database®

All SAE papers, standards, and selected books are abstracted and indexed in the Global Mobility Database.

green press INITIATIVE

SAE International is committed to preserving ancient forests and natural resources. We elected to print *PT-135 Infotainment Systems* on 30% post consumer recycled paper, processed chlorine free. As a result, for this printing, we have saved:

9 Trees (40' tall and 6-8" diameter)
3,606 Gallons of Wastewater
1,450 Kilowatt Hours of Electricity
397 Pounds of Solid Waste
781 Pounds of Greenhouse Gases

SAE International made this paper choice because our printer, Thomson-Shore, Inc., is a member of Green Press Initiative, a nonprofit program dedicated to supporting authors, publishers, and suppliers in their efforts to reduce their use of fiber obtained from endangered forests.

For more information, visit www.greenpressinitiative.org

For multiple print copies contact:

SAE Customer Service
Tel: 877-606-7323 (inside USA and Canada)
Tel: 724-776-4970 (outside USA)
Fax: 724-776-0790
Email: CustomerService@sae.org

ISBN-13 978-0-7680-1943-8
Library of Congress Catalog Card Number: 2007931382
SAE/PT-135

Positions and opinions advanced in this paper are those of the author(s) and not necessarily those of SAE. The author is solely responsible for the content of the paper. A process is available by which discussions will be printed with the paper if it is published in SAE Transactions.

SAE Order No. PT-135

Printed in USA

INFOTAINMENT SYSTEMS ON FAST FORWARD

Other SAE books in this series:

Object Detection, Collision Warning and Avoidance Systems, Volume 2
(Product Code: PT-133)

Adaptive Cruise Control
(Product Code: PT-132)

Electronic Braking, Traction, and Stability Controls, Volume 2
(Product Code: PT-129)

Multiplexing and Networking, Volume 2
(Product Code: PT-128)

Automotive Software
(Product Code: PT-127)

Electronic Engine Control Technologies, Second Edition
(Product Code: PT-110)

Sensors and Transducers, Second Edition
(Product Code: PT-105)

Electric and Hybrid Electric-Vehicles
(Product Code: PT-85)

Electronic Transmission Controls
(Product Code: PT-79)

Multiplexing and Networking
(Product Code: PT-78)

Navigation and Intelligent Transportation Systems
(Product Code: PT-72)

INTRODUCTION

Infotainment Systems on Fast Forward

In-vehicle infotainment systems cover a wide variety of digital applications, including internal connectivity, entertainment, external communications, navigation services, and radio. The first infotainment systems introduced in production automobiles were modest in scope compared to those now emerging. Future systems promise to provide drivers with ever more complex capabilities. A Strategy Analytics' January 2007 study predicts that the semiconductor demand from OEM and aftermarket infotainment systems in North America, Europe, and Japan will grow from $2.9 billion in 2005 to $5.0 billion by 2013.

An announcement at the 2007 Consumer Electronics Show in Las Vegas, Nevada, in January is an example of the growing trend in complexity of new infotainment systems. XM Radio displayed the XM Infotainment Vehicle. It includes the company's new personal weather tracking system and other information and entertainment services. The vehicle features the company's voice-recognition software, which includes controls for the radio, weather, traffic, stock quotes, and sports scores. A parking spot locator is integrated into the GPS navigation system.

The infotainment engineering developments covered in the 89 papers in this book, published from 2000 through 2007, are presented in several parts. After this brief introduction, the first part covers overviews on many aspects of infotainment systems. The next part presents basic enabling technologies—software, communications, voice recognition, speech synthesis, displays, and radio systems. The driver assistance systems part covers a variety of systems, including navigation, lane departure warning, and parallel parking. The importance of human factors is emphasized in the papers contained in the part on driver/vehicle interfaces. The last part, on future trends, includes papers on future security needs, virtualization architectures, operating system requirements, network architectures, and data-reduction protocols.

Here are a few insights from the papers herein:

- "It is widely accepted that one IVIS [In-Vehicle Information System] design does not fit all users. First, driving tasks vary depending on the driving context; therefore, it is desirable to make the IVIS able to adapt to the environmental context. Second, different drivers have different driving habits and cognitive ability, which must be accommodated when they are sharing the same vehicle." (2007-01-1739)

- " . . the lifecycle of software is generally shorter than the lifecycle of cars. To resolve this issue, new telematics software should be able to be added and upgraded into a car during the lifecycle of a car." (2007-01-1778)

- "Vehicles have to authenticate each other and verify that they are participants in IVC [Inter-Vehicle Communications] networks before exchanging safety-critical information. Besides vehicle authentication, IVC networks must provide mechanisms to guarantee that the contents of safety-critical information are authentic, unalterable, and not outdated. If the mechanisms are not provided, then the contents of safety-critical information can be forged, which may cause accidents and damages." (2006-01-1493)

- "Color can be used as an information carrier. PDA size display (3.5"–3.8") is sufficient to present all cluster information to a driver. Color scales are visually appealing. Time needed for a driver to receive qualitative information can be significantly decreased. A driver can choose from several options of fonts, hues, shapes, and screen location of scales, but not predetermined symbols, such as phone, etc. Display area sharing between elements that do not have to appear simultaneously enables a significant decrease of the display size and consequently price." (2006-01-0951)

- "Current LDWS [Lane Departure Warning Systems] implementations that rely on microprocessors to process image data perform well, but costly hardware reduces their practicality. In order to implement a low-cost hardware design, algorithms used in proven lane departure systems must be modified to run in hardware rather than software. This study investigates the implementation of a set of such algorithms on an FPGA [Field Programmable Gate Array]." (2007-01-1736)

- "Searching the Location-Based Service (LBS) on the Internet, such as Yellow Pages, has the advantage to have the most updated information, for free (at least for the moment). Due to a number of limitations, mobile users still encounter many troubles when they use wireless devices to perform online LBS searching. Providing a convenient access to the online LBS information for those wireless users is a challenging problem and also a business opportunity." (2007-01-1107)

- "The brave new world of future intelligent vehicles promises another level of vehicle performance in the area of safety, traffic management, highway guidance, remote repair, and driver convenience. However, these improvements open the door for attacks not just on inter-vehicular communications, but also with the rest of the communication and information system." (2006-01-1426)

* * * * * * * * * *

This book and the entire Automotive Electronics Series are dedicated to my friend Larry Givens, a former editor of SAE's monthly publication, *Automotive Engineering International.*

Ronald K. Jurgen, Editor

TABLE OF CONTENTS

PART I - INTRODUCTION

PART II - OVERVIEWS

PART III – ENABLING TECHNOLOGIES

SOFTWARE

COMMUNICATIONS

VOICE RECOGNITION, SPEECH SYNTHESIS

DISPLAYS

RADIO SYSTEMS

PART IV - DRIVER ASSISTANCE SYSTEMS

PART V – DRIVER/VEHICLE INTERFACES

PART VI – FUTURE TRENDS

PART II
OVERVIEWS

2007-01-1739

Adaptive In-Vehicle Information Systems and Their Usability Evaluation

Cui Li, Blair Nonnecke and Judi McCuaig
University of Guelph

ABSTRACT

In-Vehicle Information Systems (IVIS) provide vehicle travelers with a range of useful information, including road condition, weather broadcasting, GPS maps, and city navigation. It is widely acknowledged that a single IVIS design does not fit everyone as users can have different interface and content preferences. These preferences are often related to age, gender, experience, and other demographic, social, and psychological characteristics. IVIS need to be capable of adapting to the context. This paper reviews adaptation techniques found in user-adaptive systems and develops a mapping between adaptation techniques and the characteristics of the system being adapted. This mapping is then used to show that adaptation techniques for user-adaptive systems can be applied to the design of IVIS. As IVIS become popular and their functionalities become more diverse, driver distraction will increase due to increased cognitive load. Since inappropriate adaptation can lead to user confusion and distraction, the usability of adaptive IVIS need to be carefully evaluated.

INTRODUCTION

In-Vehicle Information Systems (IVIS) provide drivers with a range of useful information. There are few standard definitions or categorizations of IVIS. In this paper, the term IVIS includes any in-vehicle communication and electronic technologies which provide drivers with a range of useful information, including vehicle information, driver information, www, email, phone, movie, music, games, weather report, traffic report, safety information, and navigation [1], [2]. As the cost of these systems rapidly decreases and as the automobile market competition becomes fiercer, more and more car manufacturers are including IVIS in their new models

The effect of using IVIS is twofold. On the one hand, IVIS equipment provides enormous benefits to driving safety, convenience, and entertainment. For example, navigation systems with voice instructions allow drivers to safely travel in unknown areas, mobile phones provide rapid access to emergency services from almost anywhere across the country, email and web access allow drivers and passengers to be more productive while on the road, traffic, and weather information systems provide useful information to drivers in a timely manner. On the other hand, complex IVIS user interface and integrated information output can overload drivers, compromising safety and usability. Statistics from crashes in several countries have shown that crashes are more likely to happen when the driver is interacting with an IVIS interface (e.g., dialing or answering a call, and looking at the navigation screen) [3]. Experiments on human cognitive performance also demonstrate that human can process a limited amount of information effectively. All these research results make it a difficult task to design usable IVIS.

It is widely accepted that one IVIS design does not fit all users. First, driving tasks vary depending on the driving context; therefore, it is desirable to make the IVIS able to adapt to the environmental context. Second, different drivers have different driving habits and cognitive ability, which must be accommodated when they are sharing the same vehicle.

Adaptive IVIS have a range of advantages over traditional IVIS. For example, navigation systems identify the vehicle location and remind the driver of the next turn; adaptive cruise control systems could detect nearby vehicles, be aware of external traffic data, and detect speed signage.

One approach to designing usable IVIS is to regulate information flow to the driver based on the current driving demand, the availability of remaining visual and mental resources to process in-vehicle information, and the priority of each task. However, little research has been conducted on summarizing adaptation techniques appropriate for IVIS. As a result, IVIS designers do not have a guideline to follow when designing adaptive IVIS. In contrast, adaptation techniques have been widely investigated in other user-adaptive systems. Some of these adaptation techniques should be reusable in adaptive IVIS; some may be adjustable to the characteristics of IVIS, while others may not be applicable to adaptive IVIS.

This paper maps adaptation techniques to system characteristics, and in summarizing the characteristics of IVIS, it shows which adaptation techniques are appropriate for IVIS. The next section introduces IVIS, and discusses why adaptation is needed in IVIS. The section after that summarizes adaptation techniques in user-adaptive systems and maps adaptation techniques to system characteristics. The next to last section investigates the system characteristics of IVIS and summarizes adaptation techniques for IVIS. The last section concludes the paper and discusses future work.

ADAPTIVE IVIS

Systems capable of adapting to the environment and user context are the goal of most modern information systems. First, adaptation is needed to create portable systems that can autonomously configure and run on different operating platforms, in various locations, and under different environmental context without human intervention. Second, for tasks requiring continuous human-computer interaction, adaptation is needed to provide accurate information based on changing user goals and requirements. Thirdly, adaptive displays can be customized precisely to user preferences and needs, based on user information and direct request.

IVIS are typical of systems that need adaptation. In this paper, we refer to adaptive IVIS as systems capable of detecting the context using sensors and of changing information and/or presentation by applying adaptation techniques based on a context model. The context here refers to the user (driver), the usage data as accumulated during user-system interactions, and the environmental contextual data such as temperature, geographical situation, weather, and road condition.

As suggested by Brusilovsky [4], the process of an adaptive system consists of three stages: data collection, model building/updating, and adaptation; however, Brusilovsky's process model of adaptive hypermedia systems only considers user data collection and user modeling. Kobsa [5] further suggests that an adaptive system should adapt to not only user characteristics, but also usage data and environmental context. Based on this understanding, we created a process model of adaptive IVIS, as illustrated in Figure 1. This figure also briefly depicts the three main components of an adaptive system: location tracking component, map database, and user interface. From the driver's point of view, the adaptation functionality is primarily represented in the user interface; but from the viewpoint of the adaptive IVIS, the main tasks are adaptive information retrieval and adaptive content and link presentation [6].

Example scenarios of adaptive IVIS behaviors include: adjusting on-screen color and font setting for different drivers, knowing the vehicle location by GPS sensing; detecting lane usage through cameras and sensors equipped on the vehicle; being informed of traffic situation of current and upcoming road segments by accessing the real-time traffic broadcast; automatically adjusting gaps with nearby vehicles through intelligent cruise control system; being warned of extreme weather conditions by subscribing to weather network web services.

In-vehicle tasks, such as reading navigation maps and entering a destination address, are visually and cognitively demanding; and the complexity of these tasks can depend on the driving context. For example, when driving in the dark, it may become more difficult to read on-screen maps and text. As a result, it is desirable to make IVIS automatically adapt to the ambient light levels by changing map and text colors. Research has been conducted on creating a workload manager to regulate and adjust information flow to the driver based on momentary driving demand, the availability of visual and mental resources to process in-vehicle information, and the priority of each task [3]. A workload manager adapts the information load based on various attributes of the driving context, including vehicle location, road geometry, traffic, speed, weather, time of day, and in-vehicle task. Because portable IVIS can be used in different cars, the demand for them is also growing [7]. These portable IVIS may require additional adaptive abilities based on their current vehicle.

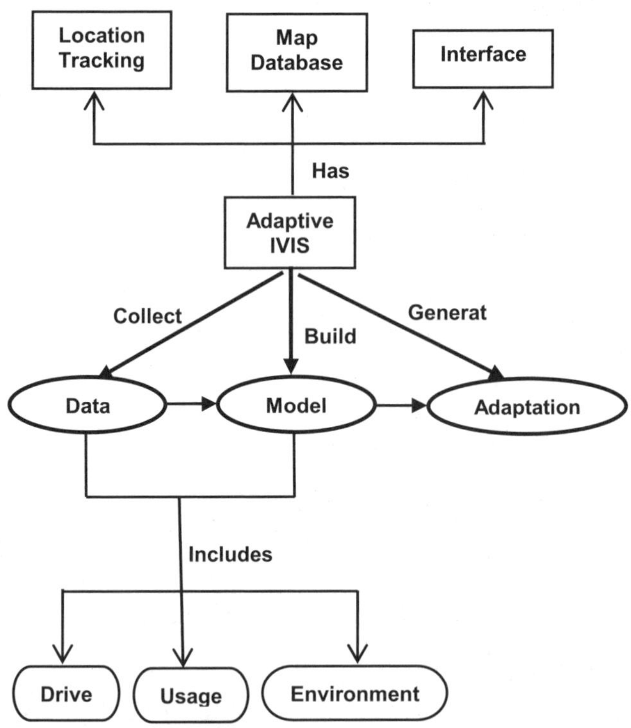

Figure 1: Components and process model of adaptive IVIS

Although adaptive IVIS is a research area requiring innovative thinking, the design of adaptive IVIS must not violate the fundamental design guidelines of traditional IVIS. In order to guide the design of IVIS, various organizations have published standards and design guidelines, such as the SAE J2364 recommended practice [8], the AAM recommendation [9], and the JAMA guideline [10]. The general research practice for IVIS is to apply prototyping, car simulation, user testing, and user survey in order to evaluate the safety and usability of IVIS, and to propose guidelines of performing common in-vehicle tasks. For example, Stevens et al. [11] investigated the use of occlusion for evaluating the distraction of operating IVIS, in [12], Stevens et al. proposed detailed design guidelines for IVIS, Young et al. [13] conducted lab-based static load test to predict on-road driver performance and to assess the safety and usability of IVIS while driving.

By studying the design guidelines and by surveying the literature of IVIS, we can summarize the fundamental characteristics of IVIS for guiding their design:

- Variety: a number of IVIS functionalities are expected to be available, including vehicle information, driver information, www, email, phone, movie, music, games, weather report, traffic report, safety information, and navigation. Drivers do not want to be restricted to the music on the radio and CD, or movies on DVDs, so on-demand music and video are expected to appear in vehicles.
- Integration: since there are so many components in IVIS, it is not feasible to have a separate interface for each component. Various information outputs need to be integrated into several user interfaces, leading to potential driver confusion. Some manufacturers already use in-car LANs to integrate different IVIS. Portable IVIS components will be expected to be plug-and-play.
- Ubiquity: information provided through IVIS needs to be ubiquitously available.
- Safety: the top concern for IVIS. Intensive user testing is needed to understand the efficiency, effectiveness, learnability, and memorizability of an integrated IVIS.
- Convenience: ease of use affects user satisfaction and thus determines whether IVIS will be widely adopted.
- Entertainment: last but not least, IVIS may need to be entertaining.

These system characteristics of IVIS have to be kept in mind when considering the design of IVIS, even for adaptive IVIS.

A number of researchers have been investigating adaptive systems, including IVIS. Kovordanyi [14] studied the impact of an Adaptive Cruise Control (ACC) system on driving safety. Kovordanyi and Ohlsson [15] investigated adaptation based on monitoring the driver's cognitive processing of visual information. Baus et al. [16] presented a navigation system that adapts the presentation of route directions to different output devices and modalities. Console et al. [17] investigated adaptation and personalization techniques on in-vehicle tourist information systems, and presented an architecture for providing adaptive in-vehicle services based on the driver's preferences/interests and the context of interaction [18]. Trivedi et al. [19] developed a Human Centered Intelligent Driver Support System (HC-IDSS) to support driver attention management, perception, decision-making and control. Anguilo [20] identified and summarized the most appropriate information presentation formats in IVIS, and proposed guidelines for designing IVIS presentation interfaces. Vidales and Stajano [21] developed context-aware automotive telematics providing cooperation and adaptation capabilities in IVIS.

The above research focused on a specific in-vehicle feature (e.g., Cruise Control or tourist information system) or was restricted to a specific adaptation technique (e.g., context-awareness or HCD). No work was done on identifying existing adaptation techniques from other domains and applying it to adaptive IVIS. However, user adaptive systems and context awareness are well-researched fields, and there are well-established adaptation techniques, user models, and design guidelines. As a result, it is important that this research be taken into consideration when understanding and designing adaptive IVIS.

We argue that existing adaptation techniques, which have been successfully proposed and applied in user adaptive systems, can be categorized along two dimensions, adaptation and triggers for adaptation. Categorization along these dimensions will clarify which adaptation techniques should be used for IVIS by matching the system characteristics of adaptive IVIS to what they are adapting to. In this paper, we present a mapping and a summary of adaptation techniques for adaptive IVIS.

ADAPTATION TECHNIQUES

User-adaptive systems have been an actively researched field for the past decade. The objective of user-adaptive systems is to personalize the system by providing appropriate services to users based on dynamically collected user models, user preferences, and historic data.

A significant number of adaptation techniques have been proposed in the past decade, and many of them have been found effective in user-adaptive systems. Adaptation techniques can be categorized by various criteria, including the goals of the user, the features of the user to which the system adapts, the features which the system adapts, and the adaptive application domain. In this section, we classify adaptation techniques into two categories: 1) adapt to what, and 2) what to adapt.

ADAPT TO WHAT

This classification considers what features the adaptive system can adapt to. The features considered are centered on the users. We consider five user features and discuss the adaptation techniques correspondingly (features: goal, knowledge, background, preferences, and environment). These features are based on the classification of methods and techniques in adaptive hypermedia systems [4] and adaptive user interfaces [22].

Goal: This feature cares about what the user wants to achieve by using the adaptive system. The goal-oriented approach starts with collecting the goals of the user. User goals can be statically collected using user surveys, or dynamically retrieved by detecting the interacting between the user and the system. Since user's goals can change frequently, it is important to make the system adapt to the changes. Goal-oriented adaptation can take advantage of existing research result of goal-oriented analysis and modeling [23], [24], [25].

Knowledge (or experience): user knowledge or experience of the subject. Since user knowledge changes constantly (due to variants against learnability and memorizability), the system has to identify the change and update the user model accordingly. For example, IVIS interfaces presented to a novice user should be different from those to an experienced user.

A simple technique for understanding the user knowledge/experience is to apply stereotype user models to categorize users. For example, users can be categorized as novice, beginner, intermediate, or expert; and different type of users can be presented with different kinds of content. Another user knowledge/ experience model is called the overlay model. The overlay model uses binary values to represent the user knowledge (e.g., know vs. not know), or use qualitative measures (e.g., good, average, or poor knowledge), or apply quantitative measures (e.g., the probability of knowing a concept) [4]. In some situations, a hybrid of overlay model and stereotype model can also be used.

User knowledge/experience can be initially gathered by informal interviews or relatively formal user surveys. Both general-purpose questionnaires [26] and specific-purpose questionnaires [7] can be applied. As the user continues to interact with the system, his/her knowledge/experience grows gradually; therefore it is essential for the system to dynamically identify the momentary user knowledge and adjust the adaptation model accordingly. This can be a difficult task.

Background: Background information includes the user's experience with similar technologies, the user's professional, viewpoint, and perspective. For example, for IVIS users, background information can be the user's previous experience with WWW, touch screen, high-definition display (HD), and keyboard since the user's experience with these related technologies can affect his/her performance in using the adaptive system. Background information is almost always static, and it can be collected by user interviews. Stereotype models are often used to identify background information. For example, a user's background may be categorized by *((WWW, experienced), (touch screen, novice), (HD, intermediate), (keyboard, experienced))*.

Preferences: Preferences reflect the habits and desires of a user while interacting with the system. Preferences are user-dependent. Different users with similar background and knowledge can have very different or even opposite preferences. Like backgrounds, preferences can be initialized by conducting user interviews or surveys. Another way of collecting user preferences is to apply data mining on historic usage data and identify the user's usage patterns [27].

Individual traits form another part of user preferences that are sometimes treated as a separate set of user features. Individual traits include the personality, cognitive factors, learning styles, and other psychological characteristics of the user, which can only be retrieved by psychological tests. Privacy is a big concern in collecting individual traits [28], [29], and are outside the scope of this paper.

Environment: Adaptive systems adapt to location, platform, network bandwidth, GPS signal, and other environmental parameters. For example, an IVNS should be able to run in different modes depending on whether GPS signal is available or not; an ftp client can apply different download modes depending on the network bandwidth. Environmental parameters can be detected through various kinds of sensors, such as a GPS receiver for detecting global location and a thermometer for sensing temperature.

Table 1 discusses the mapping between adaptive characteristics and what to adapt. The purpose of this table is to identify the starting point of applying an adaptation technique. Adaptation techniques vary based on different emphasis on "adapt to what". If the system needs to adapt to user goals, then further modeling techniques need to be employed to understand the lower level user goals. For example, the usability goal can be decomposed into efficiency, effectiveness, learnability, memorizability, and satisfaction subgoals. Based on the decomposed goals and subgoals, the system can determine which adaptation technique(s) to apply. If efficiency is the most critical concern, then the system interface needs to be presented simply and clearly, which means removing/hiding/disabling techniques are applied to omit unnecessary information. If learnability is the top user goal, then either inserting/generation or removing/hiding/disabling can be applied based on the level of experience of the user (i.e., a novice user should be hided from advanced features, while an experienced user should be presented with more short-cuts and hot-keys).

Similarly, if preference is the user feature to be emphasized, then further modeling techniques need to be used to acquire the user preferences. Based on different user preferences, the system can choose suitable adaptation techniques. For example, sorting can be employed if the user prefers information to be displayed in an order other than the default one. Inserting/generation can be applied if the user prefers to a range of groups of information in a single group (i.e., a PDA may presents calendar, email, address book as different applications by default, but can combine them in a single application if the user prefers).

The applicability of techniques for each user feature is briefly discussed using simple scenarios. By using a goal-oriented approach [23, 25], the user's goals can be hierarchically structured, and the appropriate adaptation techniques for each goal or subgoal can be further studied.

ADAPT WHAT

The previous section summarized what features the adaptive system can adapt to. This section discusses what system features are context-dependent and can be adapted.

Presentation: Presentation adaptation refers to the adaptation of the interface presented to the user [4]. The task is to adapt the interface accessed by a particular user to the user's current knowledge, goals, background, preferences, and personal traits. Presentation adaptation can be further categorized into adaptive text presentation and adaptive multimedia presentation.

System Characteristics	Adapt to What
- variety (functionality) - integration - ubiquity - safety - convenience - entertainment - portability	**Goal:** Different goals of user determine different adaptation techniques. **Examples:** - If efficiency is the most critical concern of the user, then removing and hiding should be applied as much as possible to make the user interface interaction as efficiently as possible. - If clarity and learnability are the more important user goals, then annotation and explanation variants should be applied.
- personalization	**Knowledge/Experience:** Different adaptation techniques should be applied based on different level of user knowledge/experience. **Examples:** - For knowledgeable users, customization of the user interface is highly expected. - It is important for novice users to learn the user interface in a stable fashion, so it is preferable not to use either insertion or deletion much.
	Background: Different adaptation techniques should be applied based on different level of user background. **Examples:** - Similar to user knowledge/experience, adaptive insertion or deletion can be frequently used for users with enough related background, but should be seldom applied to users without related background.
	Preference: Different adaptation techniques should be applied based on different user preferences. **Examples:** - It is expected to insert more content and navigational links for topics preferred by the user, and to remove or hide content and links of no interest to the user.
- context-aware	**Environment:** Different adaptation techniques should be applied based on different environments. **Examples:** - Alteration is a commonly used technique to adapt to environmental change. For example, the system can change working mode when the network bandwidth changes.

Table 1: Identification of adaptation techniques based on what user features the system adapts to

The purpose of adaptive text presentation is to adjust the size, color, font, layout, and other properties of the text displayed on the user interface. Adaptation techniques of text presentation include insertion/removal of text fragments, alteration of text fragments, sorting of fragments, stretchtext (that extends a hypertext word to a detailed explanation or collapses an explanation back to the original word [4]), conditional text, explanation variants, and frame-based techniques. For example, an adaptive web browser can analyze the historical navigation history of a user and hide or minimize the contents the user is not interested in. Similarly, commercial web sites, such as CNN.com, have different versions customized for visitors from different continents.

Adaptive multimedia presentation concerns the adaptation of other formats of information presented to the user, including sound, music, video, animation, and static or motion picture. An example (which may not be practical) is to configure the voice direction of an IVNS to change to a native natural language as the vehicle crosses the border of two countries, which is common in Europe.

Link: Link adaptation is also called adaptive navigation, and it adapts the presentation of links in order to help users find their solution paths. For example, a portable PDA normally presents the users with a full menu of possibilities upon system startup, making it difficult for the user to navigate through different icons to find the functionality needed. By sorting the icons in an expected order, or by hiding some icons not needed in the current context, the remaining functionality can be navigated more easily.

There are a few adaptation techniques for adaptive navigation. Direct guidance points the user to the next system resource directly. Examples include a blinking arrow shown on the IVNS screen or the voice directions from the IVNS speakers, or the "NEXT" and "PREVIOUS" buttons during a series of steps. Adaptive link sorting is a technique to sort a list of links in a user-friendly way (e.g., put the most frequently visited links at the top). Adaptive hiding of links hides links unwanted by hiding, disabling, and removing links. Adaptive annotation of links puts textual annotations or visual cues (icons, highlighting, and different font type or size) on links. Adaptive generation of links automatically creates links unavailable on the original interface.

Common adaptation techniques are summarized in Figure 2 based on the system features adapted. The mapping between content adaptation techniques and link adaptation techniques shows that these techniques are very common across different adaptation domains. In the following discussion of adaptation techniques, we will combine presentation adaptation techniques and link adaptation techniques.

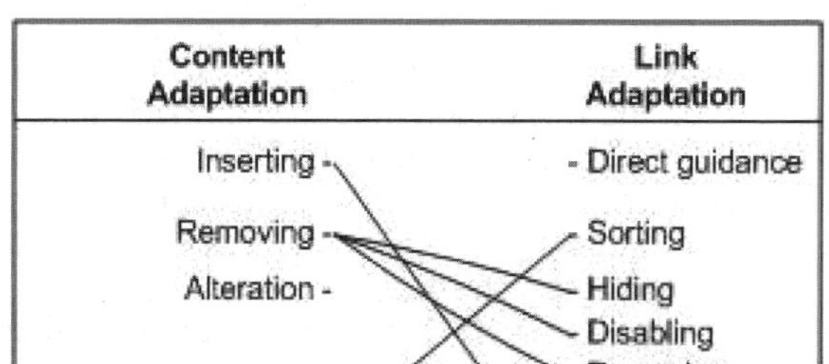

Figure 2: Summary of adaptation techniques based on what system features are adapted

ADAPTATION TECHNIQUES FOR IVIS

Table 2 summarizes adaptation techniques for IVIS based on "adapt to what". Since different components of IVIS have different interfaces, it becomes difficult to provide the summaries for all aspects (functional and non-functional requirements) of IVIS; instead, we create the summary by focusing on the user interface for IVNS.

There are three columns in Table 2. The first and second columns are based on the mapping between "adapt to what" and adaptive characteristics summarized in Table 1. The third column lists adaptation techniques summarized from Figure 2. For example, in response to the user's preferences regarding the gender and accent of the voice instruction or the color usage on navigation maps, alteration can be a suitable technique (e.g., IVIS give male voice instructions for female drivers and vice versa). As another example, if the user's goal concerns learnability, then for novice users, advanced functionalities can be adapted by removing, hiding, or disabling.

We need to emphasize that the application of adaptation techniques in IVIS must satisfy the fundamental system characteristics of IVIS summarized in section 2.1: variety, integration, ubiquity, safety, convenience, and entertainment. Note these requirements can be conflicting. For example, extending the variety of services may potentially increase distraction, therefore affecting safety; integration of multiple services together can decrease the simplicity of the user interface, thus affecting convenience. It is difficult to find a solution to resolve all the potential conflicts. Simulation, prototyping, and user testing can be extensively applied to evaluate the IVIS with respect to these six requirements.

Modeling techniques are not discussed in Table 2, though they are important for collecting each feature of "adapt to what". For example, if IVIS need to adapt to the goals of the user, then interview, survey, and questionnaire can be applied to elicit the user goals. NaviQ [7] can be an effective questionnaire used for this purpose. Interactive user interfaces can also be designed to dynamically collect and update the user goals. For example, an IVNS can prompt the driver to input the trip's purpose each time the device is turned on so that the IVNS can present adapted interfaces to the driver based on different goals (i.e., if the driver's goal is to find a restaurant, then points-of-interest (POIs) can be highlighted on the navigation map. If the driver is heading for a long distance journey, then highway entrances and exits should be highlighted). In addition, context-awareness techniques can be used to automatically and dynamically update the user goals without user intervention, but special care needs to be taken in applying this technique because inappropriate adaptation may lead to safety concerns. Keith et al. [30] indicated that it can be desirable to provide both the "pull" mode and the "push" mode and let the user decide whether to enable automatic adaptation or to manually select what information to present.

Adapt to What	Adaptive IVIS Characteristics	Adaptation Techniques
Goal - Safety - Usability (Efficiency, Effectiveness, Learnability, Memorizability, Satisfaction)	- Variety - Integration - Ubiquity - Safety - Convenience - Entertainment - Portability	- Removing - Hiding - Disabling - Sorting - Annotation - Explanation variants
Knowledge /Experience	- Personalization	- Inserting - Generation - Removing - Hiding - Disabling - Sorting
Background		- Inserting - Generation - Removing - Hiding - Disabling
Preferences		- Inserting - Generation - Removing - Hiding - Disabling - Sorting - Alteration - Stretchtext - Annotation - Explanation variants - Direct guidance
Environment	- Context-aware	- Inserting - Generation - Removing - Hiding - Disabling - Alteration - Direct guidance

Table 2: Summary of adaptation techniques based on what user features the system adapts to

Interview/survey/questionnaire is a common technique for collecting user features on "what to adapt". The NaviQ questionnaire [7], which was designed for IVNS, can be reused or modified for this purpose. NaviQ incorporates questions concerning the driver's background, experience, learnability, memorizability, and satisfaction. Most of the questions are not only suitable to IVNS, but also applicable to IVIS. For example, a driver's previous experience with IVNS (e.g., how many IVNS have been used for how many years), and familiarity with HDD, touch screen, and other common information technologies, are important information to build the user model.

HEURISTICS FOR ADAPTIVE IVIS

Heuristic evaluation is an efficient and effective method for detecting problems of a user interface. Nielsen pioneered heuristic evaluation by proposing ten heuristics to guide the design of user interface [31, 32], and these heuristics have been adapted by various researchers to evaluate systems in specific problem domains.

Mankoff et al. [33] changed Nielsen's heuristics to evaluate ambient displays and reported that the adapted heuristics found more usability problems than Nielsen's heuristics. A later study by Consolvo and Towle [34] confirmed that these adapted heuristics are effective at finding usability problems. Since both ambient displays and adaptive IVIS can be sub-areas of ubiquitous computing, and both possess characteristics that the system needs to adapt to the environmental context, the adapted heuristics for ambient displays may be reused for adaptive IVIS. Another similarity between ambient displays and adaptive IVIS is that both have the same goal of serving the users without distraction or cognitive burden.

Other modifications of Nielsen's usability heuristics are also known in the literature, including a modified version of heuristics to evaluate safety of medical devices [35], adapted heuristics to evaluate adaptive learning environments [36], and modified heuristics for evaluating paper-based Web pages [37].

Our objective is to build a set of heuristics for evaluating the usability of adaptive IVIS. While we can take advantage of previous research on heuristic evaluation, we need to acknowledge the characteristics specific to IVIS (and adaptive IVIS). The system characteristics of adaptive IVIS summarized in this paper can be helpful for this purpose. The expected system features of IVNS summarized in [7] can also be studied and adjusted in order to reach a complete understanding of the system characteristics of adaptive IVIS.

Twelve heuristics for the usability evaluation of adaptive IVIS are summarized in Table 3. These heuristics are based on Nielsen's heuristics, the modified heuristics for evaluating ambient displays, and the summarized IVNS expected features. The effectiveness of these heuristics for evaluating adaptive IVIS remains to be verified through future empirical studies.

CONCLUSION AND FUTURE WORK

This paper reviewed adaptation techniques for user-adaptive systems and summarized the relationship between adaptation techniques and the characteristics of the system being adapted. The paper suggests that adaptation techniques for user-adaptive systems can be applied to the design of adaptive IVIS. A set of twelve heuristics were proposed to evaluate the usability of adaptive IVIS. Future research will focus on applying these heuristics to evaluating adaptive IVIS.

ACKNOWLEDGEMENTS

We would like to thank Auto21, the University of Guelph, and the OGS committee for their generous support of this project.

Characteristic	Heuristics for Adaptive IVIS
Adaptability Variety	**Useful and relevant Information** Information presented should be useful and relevant to the drivers.
Safety Integration Convenient	**Efficient and effective in-vehicle device operations** Every in-vehicle task should be performed efficiently and effectively (e.g., following the 15-second rule).
Safety	**"Peripherality" of display** For safety reason, the user interface should remain unobtrusive and operations on the user interface should be quick and easy.
Integration	**Match between design of adaptive IVIS and environments** IVIS devices should be made an integrated part of the whole interior of the vehicle.
Variety Safety Integration Convenient	**Sufficient information design** The interface should convey "just enough" information. Too much information adds distraction, decrease safety, affects integration of multiple interfaces, and is not easy to use. Too little information makes the system useless.
Convenient	**Consistent and intuitive mapping** Operation of IVIS devices should match human intuition and follow the daily usage habits of the driver.
Ubiquity Adaptability	**Easy transition between minimum and in-depth information** If the interface adapts its content and presentation to the user knowledge, experience, and preferences, then the transition should be made quick and easy.
Safety	**Visibility of state** An adaptive IVIS should make the state of the vehicle noticeable.
Entertaining	**Aesthetic and pleasing design** The display should be entertaining when it is displayed in the intended setting.
Ubiquity	**Working in various driving contexts** An adaptive IVIS should work under all types of driving conditions, and the interface should seamlessly adapt its content and presentation to different contexts.
Safety	**Error recognition, diagnose, and recovery** An IVIS system should detect errors quickly, provide meaning error messages, and recover from error smoothly. Errors should not generate panic on drivers and should not cause safety concern.
Variety Integration Convenient	**Technical manual and online help** Operations on IVIS devices should be easy to learn by following the technical manual and online help.

Table 3: Heuristics for Adaptive IVIS

REFERENCES

1. *User Acceptance of ATIS Products and Services: A report of qualitative research*. 1997, U.S. Department of Transportation's ITS Joint Program Office and Volpe National Transportation Systems Center.
2. Lappin, J., *Advanced traveler information service (ATIS): What do ATIS customers want?* 2000, EG&G Services/Volpe Center, Sponsored by the US Department of Transportation's ITS Joint Program Office.
3. Green, P., *Crashes Induces by Driver Information Systems and What Can Be Done to Reduce Them*. In *2000 SAE World Congress*. 2000: Detroit, USA.
4. Brusilovsky, P., *Methods and Techniques of Adaptive Hypermedia*. User Modelling and User-Adapted Interaction, 1996. **6**: p. 87-129.
5. Kobsa, A., *Generic User Modeling Systems*. User Modelling and User-Adapted Interaction, 2001. **11**(1-2): p. 49-63.
6. Brusilovsky, P., *Adaptive Hypermedia*. User Modelling and User-Adapted Interaction, 2001. **11**: p. 87-110.
7. Li, C., B. Nonnecke, and L. Trick. *NaviQ - A User Satisfaction Questionnaire for IVNS*. In *SAE 2006 World Congress*. 2006. Detroit, MI, USA.
8. SAE, *SAE J2364: Navigation and Route Guidance Function Accessibility While Driving*. 2004, Society of Automobile Engineers.
9. AAM, *Statement of Principles, Criteria and Verification Procedures on Driver Interactions with Advanced In-Vehicle Information and Communication Systems, Draft Version 3.0*. 2003, Driver Focus-Telematics Working Group, Alliance of Automobile Manufacturers.
10. JAMA, *Guideline for In-Vehicle Display Systems - Version 2.1*. 2000, Japan Automobile Manufacturers Association.
11. Stevens, A., et al., *Occlusion as a Technique for Measuring In-Vehicle Information (IVIS) Visual Distraction: a Research Literature Review*. 2004, Transport Research Laboratory.
12. Stevens, A., et al., *Design Guidelines for Safety of In-Vehicle Information Systems*. 2004, Transport Research Laboratory.
13. Young, R., et al. *Road-to-Lab: Validation of the Static Load Test for Predicting On-Road Driving Performance While Using Advanced In-Vehicle Information and Communication Devices*. In *3rd International Driving Symposium on Human Factors in Driver Assessment, Training, and Vehicle Design*. 2005. Ocean Rockport, Maine, USA.
14. Kovordanyi, R. *When will Advanced Driver Support Systems be User-Adaptive? The Case of Adaptive Cruise Control*. In *2005 AAAI Spring Symposium*. 2005.
15. Kovordanyi, R. and S. Ohlsson. *Toward adaptive support: Modelling drivers' allocation of attention*. In *the Thirty-Fourth Annual Congress of the Nordic Ergonomic Society*. 2002.
16. Baus, J., A. Krüger, and W. Wahlster. *A resource-adaptive mobile navigation system*. In *the 7th international conference on Intelligent user interfaces*. 2002. San Francisco, California, USA.
17. Console, L., C. Gena, and I. Torre. *Evaluation of an on-vehicle adaptive tourist service*. In *The UM 2003 Workshop on Empirical Evaluation of Adaptive Systems, at the 9th International Conference on User Modeling (UM'2003)*. 2003. Johnstown, USA.
18. Console, L., et al., *Personalized and Adaptive Services on Board a Car: An Application for Tourist Information*. Intelligent Information Systems, 2003. **21**(3): p. 249-284.
19. Trivedi, M.M., et al., *Human Centered Intelligent Driver Support Systems: A Novel Multi-Modal "Driving Ecology" for Enhanced Safety*. 2001, University of California at San Diego La Jolla.
20. Aguilo, M.C.F., *Development of Guidelines for In-Vehicle Information Presentation: Text vs. Speech*, in *Industrial and Systems Engineering*. 2004, Virginia Polytechnic Institute and State University: Blacksburg. p. 172.
21. Vidales, P. and F. Stajano. *The Sentient Car: Context-Aware Automotive Telematics*. In *the First European Workshop on Location Based Service (LBS-2002)*. 2002. London, UK.
22. Dieterich, H., et al., *State of the Art in Adaptive User Interfaces*, in *Adaptive User Interfaces: Principles and Practice*. 1993, North-Holland. p. 13-48.
23. Ebnenasir, A., B. Cheng, and S. Konrad. *Goal-Oriented Modeling of Requirements Engineering for Dynamically Adaptive Systems*. In *14th IEEE International Requirements Engineering Conference*. 2006. Minneapolis, MN, USA.
24. Shen, Z., et al. *Goal Oriented Modeling for Intelligent Software Agents*. In *IEEE/WIC/ACM International Conference on Intelligent Agent Technology (IAT'04)*. 2004.
25. Dardenne, A., A.v. Lamsweerde, and S. Fickas, *Goal Directed Requirements Acquisition*. Science of Computer Programming, 1993. **20**: p. 3-50.
26. Harper, B.D. and K.L. Norman. *Improving user satisfaction: The questionnaire for user interaction satisfaction version 5.5*. In *Mid Atlantic Human Factors Conference*. 1993.
27. Holland, S., M. Ester, and W. Kiessling. *Preference Mining: A Novel Approach on Mining User Preferences for Personalized Applications*. In *7th European Conf. on Principles and Practice of Knowledge Discovery in Databases (PKDD '2003)*. 2003. Dubrovnik, Croatia.
28. Lederer, S., et al., *Personal privacy through understanding and action: five pitfalls for designers*. Personal and Ubiquitous Computing, 2004. **8**(6): p. 440-454.
29. Shoji, T. and T. Nakajima. *Privacy-Concern for Context-Aware Environments*. In *Second IEEE Workshop on Software Technologies for Future Embedded and Ubiquitous Systems (WSTFEUS'04)*. 2004.
30. Keith, C., et al., *Using Context as a Crystal Ball: Rewards and Pitfalls*. Personal Ubiquitous Computing, 2001. **5**(1): p. 8-11.

31. Nielsen, J. and R. Molich. *Heuristic evaluation of user interfaces*. In *CHI 1990*. 1990: ACM Press.
32. Nielsen, J. *Finding usability problems through heuristic evaluation*. In *the SIGCHI conference on Human factors in computing systems*. 1992. Monterey, CA, USA: ACM Press.
33. Mankoff, J., et al. *Heuristic Evaluation of Ambient Displays*. In *CHI 2003*. 2003. Ft. Lauderdale, FL, USA: ACM Press.
34. Consolvo, S. and J. Towle. *Evaluating an Ambient Display for the Home*. In *CHI 2005*. 2005. Portland, Oregon, USA: ACM Press.
35. Zhang, J., et al., *Using usability heuristics to evaluate patient safety of medical devices.* Biomed Inform., 2003. **36**(1-2): p. 23-30.
36. Magoulas, G.D., S.Y. Chen, and K.A. Papanikolaou. *Integrating Layered and Heuristic Evaluation for Adaptive Learning Environments*. In *Second Workshop on Empirical Evaluation of Adaptive Systems*. 2003. Pittsburgh, USA.
37. Allen, M., et al., *Heuristic evaluation of paper-based Web pages: A simplified inspection usability methodology.* Journal of Biomedical Informatics, 2006. **39**: p. 412-423.

2006-01-1509

Infotainment System Immunity Characterization Via Bulk Current Injection

Vipul Patel and Laura Ball
General Motors

ABSTRACT

The proliferation of entertainment and communication systems in vehicles has led to increased concern as to the performance of these systems in an electromagnetic environment. One methodology used to assess radiated immunity performance on a component level is bulk current injection (BCI). In BCI a current probe is used to inject lower frequency radio waves (RF) onto the harness of an automotive device under test. This is an indirect methodology given that on a vehicle level a direct radiated field is impinged on the vehicle rather than a coupled current such as in BCI. Because of that, important considerations need to be taken into account to replicate the vehicle coupling phenomena on a component test. This paper examines setup issues and assesses the effectiveness of the BCI methodology for immunity testing of infotainment systems.

INTRODUCTION

With increased pressures to be quicker to market, automakers have sped up vehicle development times. A key to faster vehicle development in the electrical and electronics area is effective component level tests. These bench tests offer the chance for the component supplier to assess their parts' performance long before vehicle properties are available. In the area of electromagnetic compatibility (EMC), there are many component level tests in the various areas of electromagnetic compatibility, such as radiated emissions, radiated immunity, electrostatic discharge, and conducted transients. The challenge with component level tests is to simulate as close as possible the vehicle level environment. One of the most challenging areas for developing this correlation is component level radiated immunity. There are many methodologies available, each with its own advantages and disadvantages. A popular methodology is the bulk current injection methodology. Since this uses a coupled current to simulate a vehicle radiated field, it is important that all parameters are well understood when using this methodology, especially for infotainment systems.

MAIN SECTION

VEHICLE RADIATED IMMUNITY

Vehicle level testing of radiated immunity consists of two types of tests. One is the off board transmitter test, used to simulate off vehicle radiated sources such as, television towers, radars, and other fixed base type transmitters. The other type of testing is on board transmitter tests, used to simulate on vehicle transmitters such as fleet users, amateur radio transmitters, and more prevalent now, cellular phone users.

For the vehicle off board testing, a semi-anechoic chamber is used. The frequency range of interest can be from Kilohertz to Gigahertz. The field strength transmitted varies, but the range is typically from 25V/m to 200V/m for non-radar bands. For the radar bands the field strength goes up, but is a pulsed field rather than a continuous wave. The exact requirement depends on the type of device it is, such as a safety related device or an entertainment only device. Even though entertainment devices are allowed a lower performance requirement for functions, they are held to the same requirement for any permanent loss of function.

On-board transmitter testing is different, given that it can be performed in outdoor test sites. The frequencies are not continuous, but are spread out because of spectrum allocations. Interestingly, the transmitted power is not in V/m, but rather watts that range from a few watts to more than a hundred watts. It might appear that this test would be more benign that the off board tests, but actually is similar in the field intensity. This is because the on board transmitters are within a few feet of the electronics (in the case of hand held devices, within a few inches), so even a few watts can produce relatively high field strengths.

COMPONENT TESTS OF RADIATED IMMUNITY

As is evident from the previous discussion, the component test for radiated immunity has to encompass two vehicle tests, and has to be compact and cost efficient enough for component manufacturers to use. Because of this, there are many challenges and thus variants for these tests. There are direct radiation methodologies, such as strip-line, tri-plate, and transverse electromagnetic (TEM) cell, and there are indirect methodologies, such as bulk current injection and direct pin injection. Bulk current injection and direct pin injection are indirect given that they do not have a field radiation similar to that on a vehicle. In bulk current injection a current is induced onto the harness through a current injection probe, and in direct pin injection, RF energy is injected directly onto the wire of a device.

BULK CURRENT INJECTION

As discussed, in BCI the current injection probe is wrapped around the DUT (Device Under Test) harness (see figure 1). Typically the whole harness is routed through the injection probe, except for the differential mode method. In differential mode, typically for low frequencies, the power return wire is routed outside the injection probe. Also, for BCI there is the substitution method and the closed loop method. In the substitution method, a calibration fixture is used to generate the current, and that same input power is repeated for various DUT's. In closed loop, a monitor probe is used to feedback induced current, and based on that value, the input power is adjusted. When using the substitution method and using differential mode injection, it is important that multi-ground devices be setup properly. Vehicular receivers that have a coaxial wire for antenna feed are of this class. The coaxial cable shield typically becomes another current return path when grounded on the antenna side. This is standard for AM/FM receivers but is not necessarily true for higher frequency antennas such as GPS antennas.

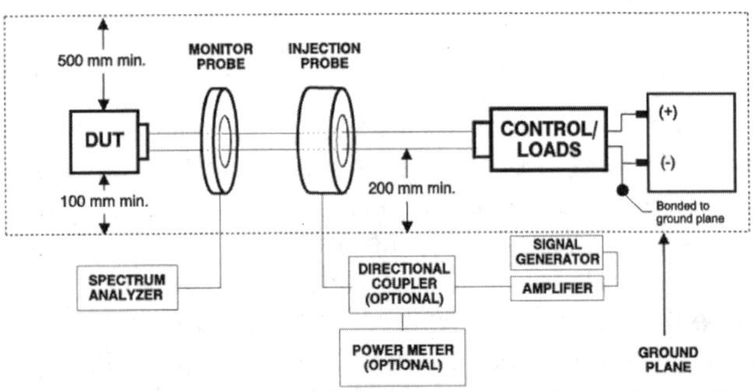

Figure 1

Coaxial Ground Effects

To understand the influence of the coaxial ground as related to induced current on non coaxial wires of the receiver a series of tests were performed. Utilizing a BCI bench, measurements of induced current were made to understand current levels with and without coax in the harness bundle. The measurements were of current induced on all other wires, i.e. audio lines, signal lines, etc., except the coax wire. Figures 2-4 show test results. As can be seen from the results there is not a significant difference noted for the exposure of current on these wires whether the coax is in the injection probe or not.

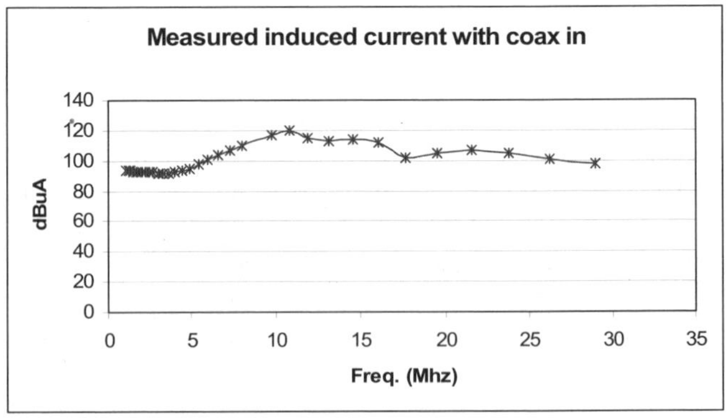

Figure 2

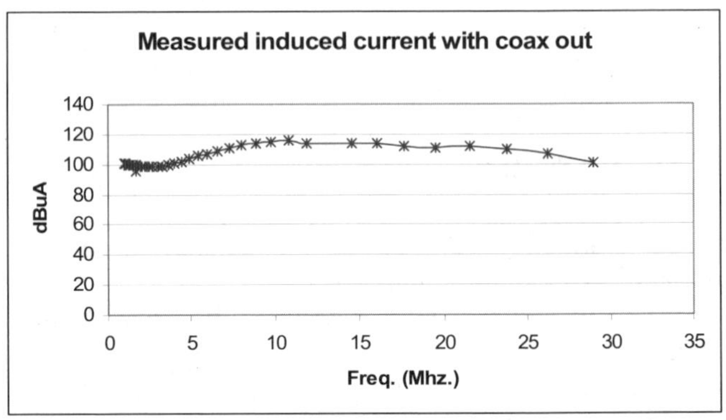

Figure 3

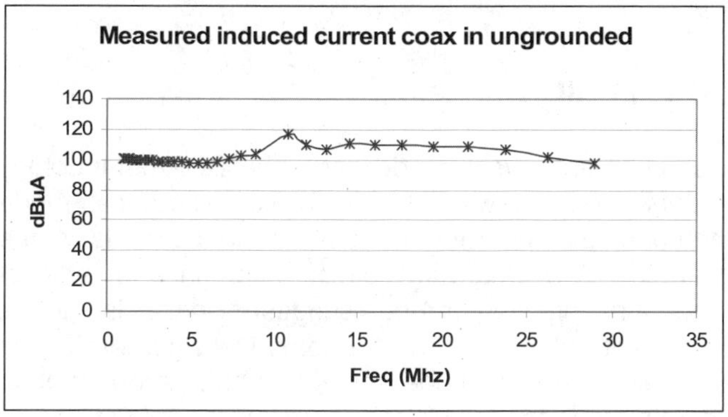

Figure 4

"Front-End" Immunity

When testing an AM/FM receiver, another aspect of the testing is the verification of the "front-end's" ability to perform in an electromagnetic field. The last section focused on the "back-end". This generally refers to all the lines that are not related to the tuner function. While the tuner is at the end of the coax, in the testing described in the last section, the center wire is not part of the injection point. This is true because the shield on the coax is grounded both at the receiver end and also at the termination point to simulate the dual ground it has in a vehicle application. In vehicle applications the center wire will also have electromagnetic energy imposed on it, both intended and unintended. Desired electromagnetic energy on this line will be the intentional AM and FM signal from off the air broadcast. Unwanted energy will be all other out of band energy that is present. This could be from either an on board transmitter located in close proximity to the mast part of the antenna or an off board source. In the case of the mast type AM/FM antenna, the receiver will receive all this energy.

Active antennas are another element that needs consideration. Different than the mast antenna, active antennas themselves need verification in BCI testing. There are generally two types, in glass and active whip type. The in glass antennas have traces on glass elements, typically rear glass on cars and side glass on crossover and sport utility vehicles. Active whip antennas are shorter than their fixed mast counterparts, but require electronics to compensate for impedance mismatch loss. The "back-end" testing of these antennas would be very similar to receiver "back-end" testing. Wires in these test setups would be typically power and in some cases select and diversity antenna control lines. The "front-end" testing would be similar to testing of receivers with fixed mast antennas "front-end" testing. Testing of receivers that are mated with active antennas should be limited because the active antenna would couple in the electromagnetic energy first and would be the equivalent "front-end" for the receiver.

The challenge, as discussed with BCI and front-ends is that it is not a direct test methodology. It uses current drive to simulate an electromagnetic field. Interestingly, there is a radiated field in the chamber, because the harness under test takes the current excitation and radiates it like any antenna would. Since there is no electrical termination on front-ends that can be driven by current, one could rely on the radiant field in the chamber. Studies were done to look at the radiant field in the chamber utilizing a field strength measurement probe. A field strength probe is placed adjacent to the DUT to measure these fields as they would be seen by a wire draped in the vicinity to simulate an AM/FM antenna. Figures 5-7 show the measured field strength. As can be seen, the field strength generally follows the induced current profile, Figure 8. However, there are frequencies where the field strength exceeds the expected field from the current profile. This indicates resonances in the system. Additionally, the field strength is not uniform across the band, as the vehicle requirement would be.

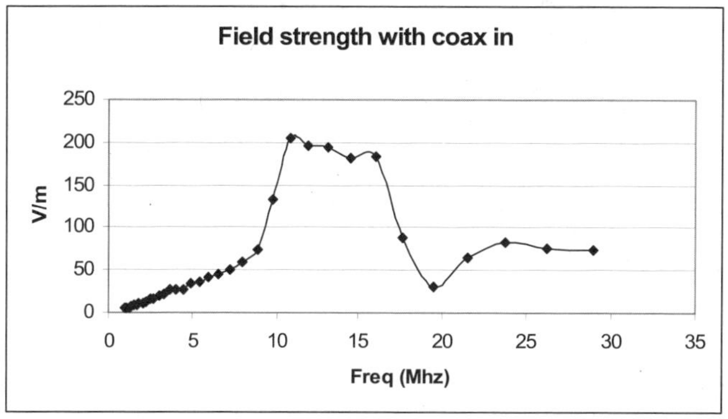

Figure 5

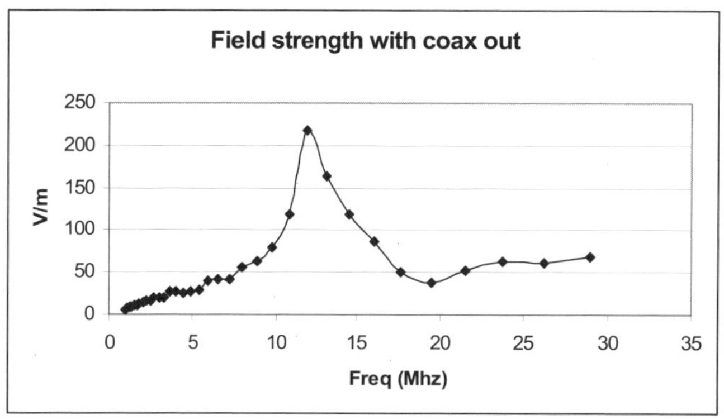

Figure 6

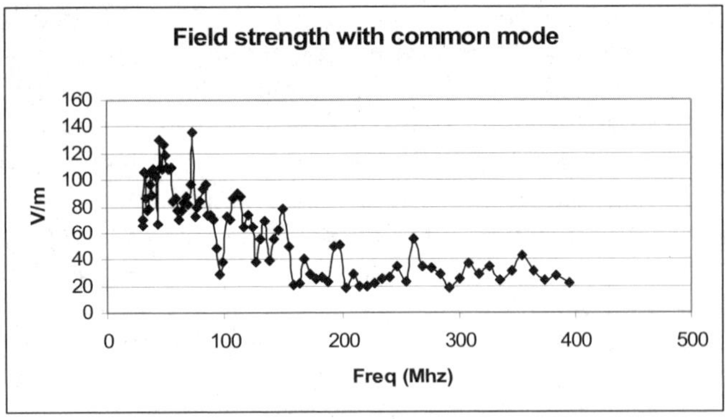

Figure 7

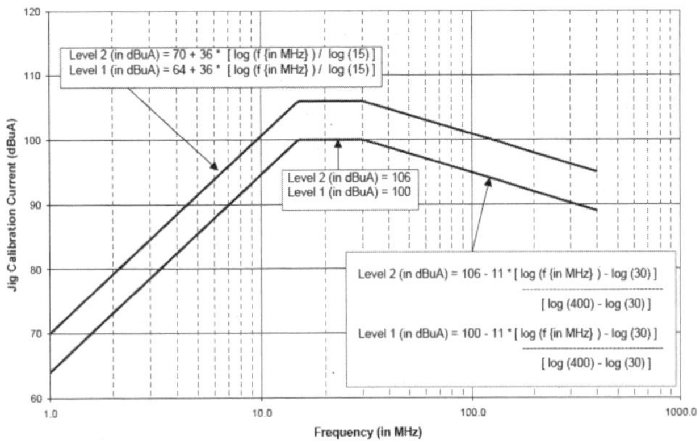

Figure 8

While this appears to be a discrepancy, it does have a general correlation because the AM/FM antenna also has resonances in the vehicle. One way to supplement BCI data would be to use a direct test methodology, such as tri-plate, strip-line, or TEM cell. Also another possibility is to use direct pin injection. Since the parameter, length, of the antenna is well understood, using calculations or simulations, a transfer function can be developed and used to inject in the appropriate terminal voltage.

CONCLUSION

Measurements were made using the BCI methodology to look at coax wire effects in the differential mode methodology and radiant electromagnetic fields in the chamber. The data with coaxial insertion and removal from the injection probe suggests there is not a significant influence from the coax. Data gathered from the field strength probe measurements suggest that, depending on the frequency, there can be field strengths higher and at times lower than those expected to be encountered on a vehicle for the front-end of a receiver or antenna.

REFERENCES

1. SAE J551 series
2. SAE J1113 series
3. GMW3097 component emc test procedures

CONTACT

Vipul Patel
EMC
M.S. 483-340-111
3300 GM road
Milford, MI 48380
Vipul.patel@gm.com

Laura Ball
EMC
M.S. 483-340-111
3300 GM road
Milford, MI 48380
Laura.l.ball@gm.com

2006-01-0814

Incorporating Hard Disks in Vehicles- Usages and Challenges

Vivek D. Bhise
University of Michigan-Dearborn

ABSTRACT

With recent advances in microprocessors and data storage technologies, vehicle users can now bring or access large amounts of data in vehicles for purposes such as communication (e.g. e-mail, phone books), entertainment (e.g. music and video files), browsing and searching for information (e.g. on-board computers and internet). The challenge for the vehicle designer is how to design data displays and retrieval methods to allow data search and manipulation tasks by managing driver workload at safe acceptable levels. This paper presents a data retrieval menu system developed to assess levels of screens (depth of menu) that may be needed to select required information when a vehicle is equipped with the capability to access audio files, cell phone, PDA, e-mail and "On-star" type functions. Implementing the basic principle of "7 plus or minus 2 magic number" to account for human information processing limitations -- to retrieve information in tasks such as selection of a data source, selection of a function within the source, and further selection of required tasks -- can easily lead to a 5-6 levels or steps of menus. Studies reported by the author and others in the literature using driving simulators suggest that such tasks, when incorporated in visual screens, will require the drivers to make over 5-8 glances. In performing the tasks of such levels of difficulty can increase lane position variability (e.g. increase in lane position standard deviations by about 50%). Thus, new approaches are needed to reduce driver distractions. The paper discusses some solutions and challenges in overcoming the data retrieval problems.

INTRODUCTION

With the increasing availability of large data storage capabilities and at decreasing costs, the demand for inclusion of data storage and retrieval devices in vehicle will steadily increase over time. The answers to the questions related to how we will use the increased data storage capabilities will also provide a rich list of possibilities for incorporation of future features in vehicles. Some possible usages include:

- E-mail (e.g. retrieving and reading stored messages)
- Internet (e.g. storing and accessing websites)
- PDA (e.g. reviewing a stored calendar)
- Telephone (e.g. searching a number from the phone book, dialing, etc.)
- Navigation (e.g. following instructions/route to a stored destination)
- Reports (e.g. retrieving/storing reports through text-to-voice and voice-to-text interface)
- Digital Books (e.g. listening to stored books via text-to-voice interface)
- DVD Entertainment/Radio/TV/CD/DVD (e.g. selecting a music file/station, etc.)
- Vehicle diagnostics/Engine system measurements (e.g. recording inputs from engine control module for diagnostics/service functions)
- Warning signals and vehicle state histories
- Real-time parameter modifications in vehicle control computers (e.g. reprogramming electronic controls modules in various systems)
- Fluids (Lubricants, coolant, fuel, etc.) consumption and state histories

The data can be downloaded from various sources (e.g. CD/DVD, PDA, cameras, portable hard drives, flash drives) and storage in the vehicle can be accomplished by considering many possible storage media such as traditional or upgraded hard disks, flash memory, etc. The data handling (storage and retrieval) interfaces include: hand controls (keys/buttons, rotary controls, sliders, touch controls, joy-sticks, etc.) and voice operated controls.

PROBLEM

The problem addressed in this paper began with the question of how to provide a hard disk interface and what kind of data can be handled in an automotive audio system. The constraints in addressing the problem assumed that the hard disk will be incorporated in an existing audio product by creating interchangeable electronic modules, software, and faceplates (i.e. user interface) with many of the common controls and displays. The hard disk was assumed to be used for: a) storing audio/music files, b) cell phone book and dialing, c) PDA storage files, d) e-mail, and e) On-star/emergency assistance system.

RESEARCH APPROACH

A multi-function team consisting of audio products planning and engineering, instrument panel design engineers, industrial designers, electrical/computer engineers and human factors engineers brainstormed a number of possible issues related to implementation of the hard disks in automotive products. The following section provides a summary of issues.

Product Planning Issues:

1. Design the audio products for "upgradeability" and "brand differentiation/reconfigurability." The "upgradeability" involves ability to incorporate new audio/electronic features without making the current design obsolete. This was considered possible by: a) allowing the user to install new software that can change functionality of programmable/ reconfigurable buttons in the radio faceplate, b) disassociate the audio interface faceplate from the chassis of audio components (e.g. radio, storage media), and c) organize and arrange electronic hardware such that modules containing new features can be easily plugged into existing electrical/electronic interfaces somewhat like the integrated circuit boards in desktop computers.

2. Design hardware interfaces such that they could be easily changed to create different "brand perceptions" by changing operational and ergonomic characteristics such as types of controls and displays, their layout, appearance and feel (using colors, materials, lighting, haptic/tactile characteristics, etc.). This will allow keeping the same basic hardware but create a different "look and feel" to meet a different brand image.

Human Factors Issues:

1 Develop interfaces that can be operated with minimal eye (reduce driver's time away from the road scene) and hand involvement (reduce number of hand finger/motions).

2. If a hierarchical menu systems is used, make sure that breadth and depth of menus well within capability of most operators (i.e. minimize cognitive workload; no more than 5 to 7 number of items per screen).

3. Allow for "hands-free" operation (e.g. consider voice controls).

4. Locate reconfigurable displays high on the instrument panel (i.e. reduce down angle. See Bhise and Dowd (Ref. 1) on high mounted instrument cluster evaluation).

5. Provide compatible association features/cues (related spatial, locational, direction of motion, etc.) in locating and designing controls with respect to their displays.

Packaging and Craftsmanship Issues:

1. Make space to allow location of centerstack displays high on the instrument panel. (Note that disassociating the driver interface from rest of the audio product electronics makes this possible).

2. Find space for locating disassociated electronic hardware.

3. Design faceplate and controls with minimal "gaps" (i.e. mechanical separation between different adjoining/mating surfaces) for improved perception of craftsmanship.

DESCRIPTION OF A POSSIBLE INTERFACE

User Interface:

Figure 1 below shows a picture of the user interface developed for the research. The layout of the radio was "traditional" with a center display, two rotary controls (placed near two ends of the display) and six preset buttons located below the display. This layout was selected because the preset buttons can be easily assigned different sub-functions depending on a selected function/operational mode in the previous step. The labels for each of the preset buttons can be easily changed and displayed in the lower portion of the display just above the buttons as shown in Figure 2 below.
A heading label was provided on each screen to identify the operational mode.

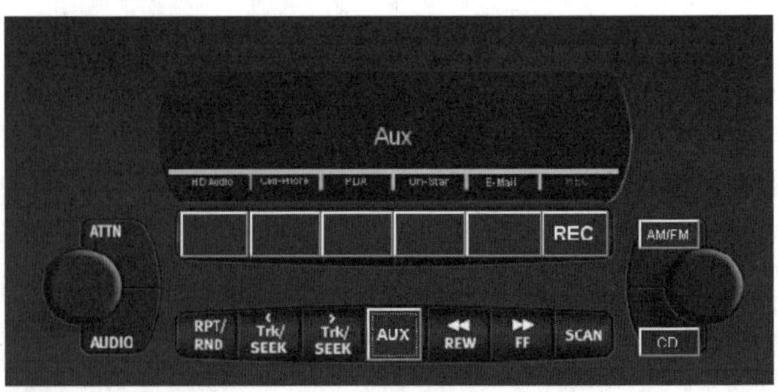

Figure 1. Traditional Audio Interface with Six Changeable Label Push Buttons

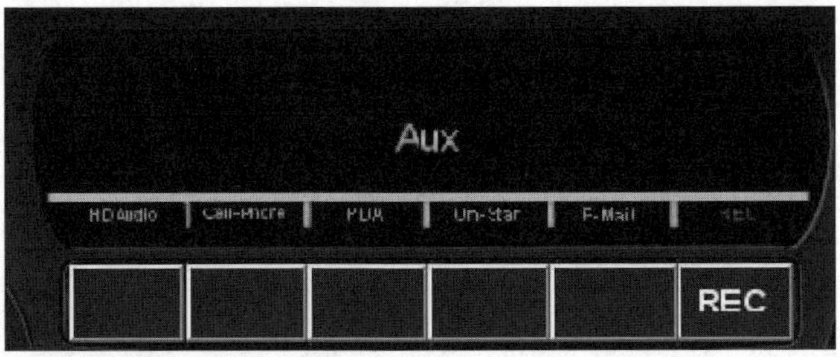

Figure 2. Display showing labels of the six buttons when AUX button (see Figure 1) in the middle of the second row of the buttons is pressed

If the first button (labeled "HD Audio") is pressed when the radio is in "AUX" mode (Figure 2), the screen will switch to the "HD Audio" mode as shown in Figure 3.

Figure 3. Display showing labels for the buttons when the "HD Audio" button in previous step (Figure 2) is pressed.

When the button below the "Music" mode is pressed, the screen will switch to the music mode and display the screen as shown in Figure 4.

Figure 4. Display showing labels for the buttons when the "Music" button in previous step (Figure 3) is pressed.

The last button REC was made available in all the screens to allow for recording of the output in the selected mode (e.g. it will record radio output if the music is being played, or it can record the phone conversation if a call was in progress when the cellphone mode was selected).

Menu Structure:

Figure 5 shows an example of a menu tree developed to incorporate the following features within the AUX menu: HD Audio, Cellphone, PDA, E-mail, On-Star and Satellite Radio.

Figures 6A and 6B show displays corresponding to each of the selected modes.

Observations from the Menu Structure:

From the menu tree shown in Figure 5, the following observations can be made on the breadth and breadth of the menu:

1. Breadth of the menu: The breadth (number of items displayed in a menu) were limited to five items in each screen (excluding the REC button which was placed at the same last (right) location in every screen).

2. Depth of the menu: The depth of the menu (i.e. the number of levels that one needs to reach to get to a required function) is shown in columns of Figure 5 (see labels on the top of the columns). The "menu depth" is an important consideration as it directly affects the driver distraction.

References (1, 2, 3, 4, 6 and 7) provide results of a number of studies and data related to operation of in-vehicle devices during driving, performing a number of common driver distraction tasks, and guidelines for designing driver interfaces. Based on such available data, the amount of time a driver would need to get to a given function in the above menus will depend upon: a) distance of the button from the steering wheel, b) button size, c) number of buttons, d) the number of levels or button pushes a driver needs to make, e) number of items (e.g. words) displayed on each screen (breadth of menu) in each step/level, f) ease of readability of the labels (font size, font type, label contrast, display luminance, viewing distance), g) screen identification, h) ability to go back to a previous screen (by use of the arrow buttons in the second row—see Figure1) or to a different device by use of the "AUX" button in Figure 1 (always available as a hard key function in the middle of the second row), etc.

As a first simple estimate of the hand movement time to reach to a button from the steering wheel, the well-used MTM (Methods Time Measurement) model used in the industry (Konz and Johnson. Ref. 5) was exercised.

Figure 7 presents hand movement time predicted from "Reach (of type D)" of MTM for typical reach distances (from the steering wheel hand placements from 3:00 to 11:00 clock positions to a radio button mounted in the center stack area) of 200 to 600 mm. Adding 0.4 sec time to account for a single eye-fixation to read a label, the total time as shown in the top line in Figure 7 can reach about 0.8 to 1.2 sec. This suggests that each simple step or level of button pushing should take approximately 1.0 sec of eye involvement time. Thus, if a driver has to push six buttons to reach to a given function, total time required could be more than 6.0 secs.

LEVEL 1	LEVEL 2	LEVEL 3	LEVEL 4	LEVEL 5	LEVEL 6
Aux					
	HD Audio				
		Music			
			Up		
			Down		
			Playlist		
				1	
					Up
					Down
					Select
				2	
					Up
					Down
					Select
				3	
					Up
					Down
					Select
				4	
					Up
					Down
					Select
				5	
					Up
					Down
					Select
			Select		
			Sort		
				Up	
				Down	
				Select	
					Up
					Down
					Select
			Add		
				1	
				2	
				3	
				4	
				5	
	Cell Phone				
		Phone Book			
			Up		
			Down		
			Select		
				Edit	
					Next
					Del Contact
			Add Contact		
			Store Number		
		Call Log			
			Dialled		
				Call	
				Call Time	
				Delete	
			Missed		
				Call	
				Call Time	
				Delete	
			Received		
				Call	
				Call Time	
				Delete	
		Messege			
			Voice		
				Read	
				Create	
			Text Msg		
				Read	
				Write	
		Conference			
	PDA				
		Planner			
			Calender		
			Appointments		
			Alarm		
		Address Book			
			Search		
				First Name	
				Last Name	
			Store		
		Phone Book			
			Search		
			Edit List		
				Add Contact	
				Del Contact	
			Service Nos		
		To-Do List			
			Read		
			Write		
		Memo			
			Read		
			Write		
	E-Mail				
		Inbox			
			Read		
		Compose			
			Reply		
			New		
		Address			
			Search		
				First Name	
				Last Name	
	OnStar				
		Emergency			
		White Dot			
		Navigate			
	Sat Radio				
		Up			

Figure 5. Illustration of a Menu Tree with Different Levels

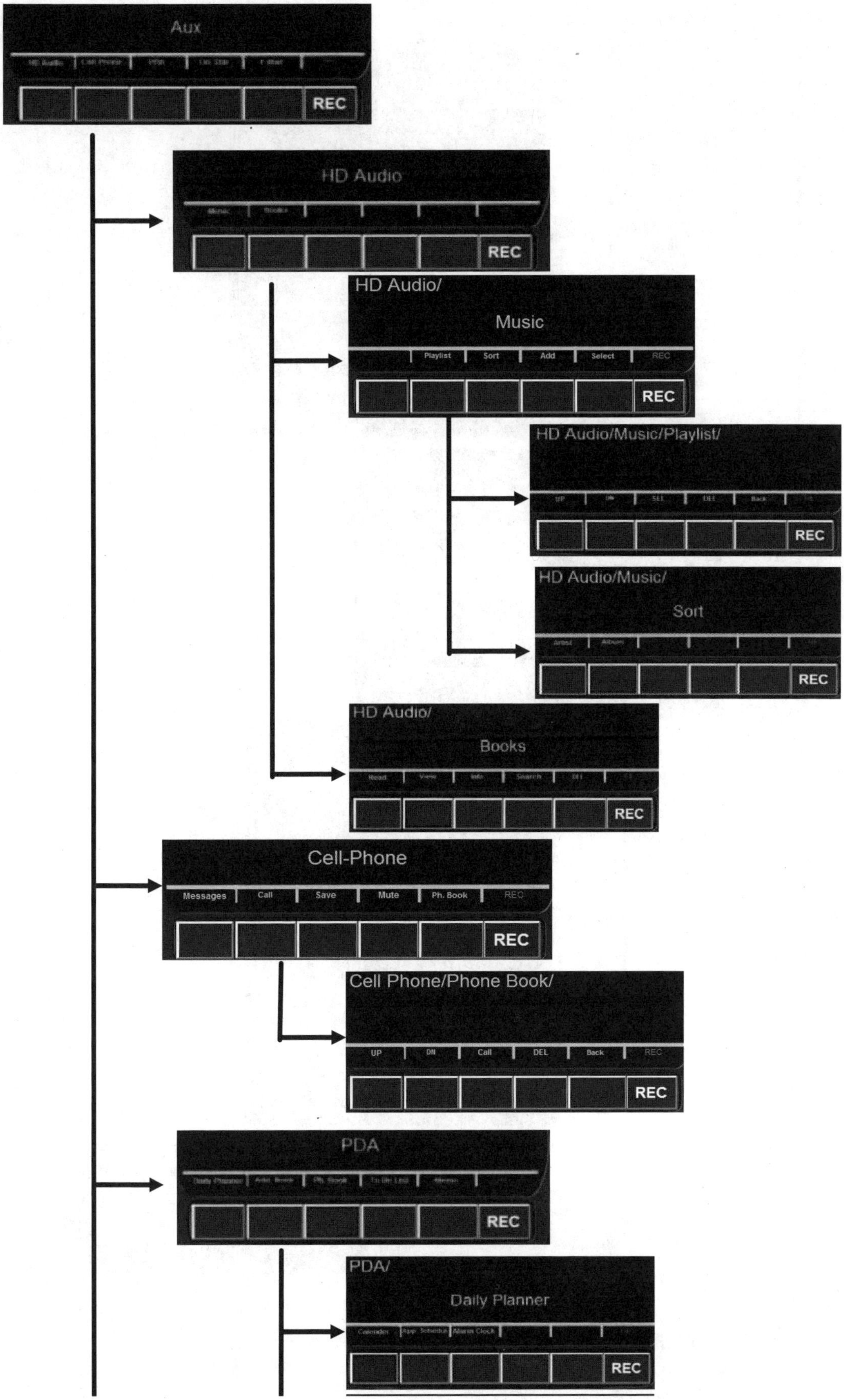

Figure 6A. Illustration of Displays for the Menu Structure (continued on Fig.6B)

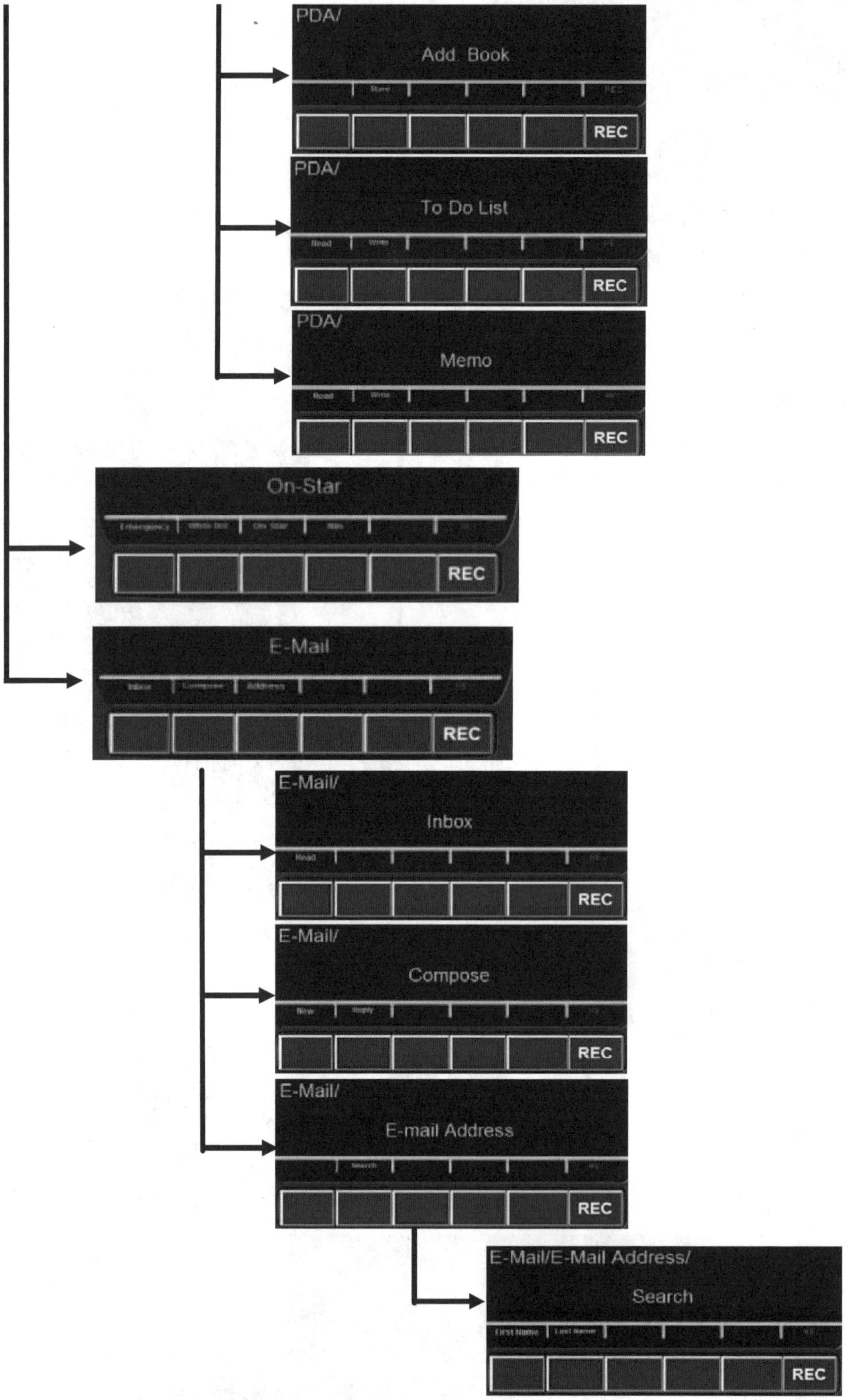

Figure 6B. Illustration of Displays for the Menu Structure

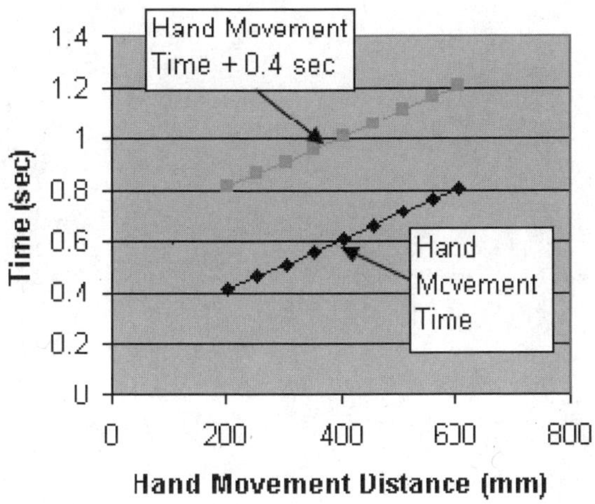

Figure 7. Hand Movement Time Predicted using MTM.

Results of several studies reported in the literature can be also be used to estimate the time required by the driver to operate to a given level in the menu.

Chaing et al (Ref. 6) measured eye movements of ten drivers while entering destinations using touch screen display of a navigation system while driving an instrumented vehicle. They reported about 2 sec entry time/keystroke and 0.6 sec increase in display fixation time for each additional keystroke entered, for both city streets and the freeway driving.

Green & Shah (Ref. 7) summarized data available from 11 research studies involving radio tuning tasks. Their data summaries show that: a) the number of glances for radio tuning ranged from 3 to 15, b) mean glance durations ranged between 0.5 to 2.5 sec with an overall glance duration of about mean of about 1.25 sec., c) total time tuning a radio ranged between 8 to 30 sec, and d) the time to tune a radio was affected by the driver's age, leading to estimates of 7.2 sec for a 24-year-old driver and 21.0 sec for a 70-year-old driver.

Based on the analysis of eye glance data obtained in driving simulator studies, Bhise (Ref. 4) has shown that total visual involvement time (TVT) was a linear function of number of glances (N). The resulting regression line was: TVT = -0.712 + 2.40 N with R-square = 79%. Lambert, Rollins and Bhise (Ref.3) have also shown that for more demanding tasks, those requiring more than 3 eye glances and more than 10 seconds of total distraction time on average, the standard deviation in lateral position increased by 60 to 100% over their baseline driving (when the driver was not asked to perform any other tasks).

DISCUSSION

While it may be easy and possible to store files from many features such as of music, phone books, etc. in a hard disk, the depth and breadth of menu screens can very quickly reach to a level that can create potential driver distractions. Therefore, other possible methods to advance through the menu structures must be considered. Voice controls are often considered as a possible solution. However it has many drawbacks such as: a) accuracy and response time of voice recognition system within the noisy road/traffic environment, b) need for a redundant control system in case the driver is unable or does not prefer to use the voice controls, and c) limitations of subjects to remember many functions and their identifying words (like those in figure 5) in the menu structure. Other possibility is to incorporate direct access function keys that can be preprogrammed by the user. For example, if two additional "store" and "retrieve" key functions are incorporated, then the six available preset keys can be used to store and retrieve user selected six functions anytime by pressing two keys (retrieve plus a preset).

CONCLUSIONS

This paper has pointed out several human factors issues that can limit integration and use of many features that can be possible by availability of large hard disks in vehicles. Developing a menu system and a user interface that will be preferred by the drivers and that will allow the driver to access any required function with very few keystrokes or developing alternate methods that can limit driver distraction need further work.

ACKNOWLEDGEMENTS

The author wishes to thank Collins & Aikman and Sanyo Automotive USA for sponsoring the research project presented in this paper. The author also wants to acknowledge the software and menu systems development support provided by student assistants Rashad Hammoudeh, Roshini Bhalla and Nitin Joshi during the early stages of the project.

REFERENCES

1. Bhise, Vivek D. and Dowd, James D. ""Driving With the Traditional Viewed-Through-The-Steering Wheel Cluster vs. the Forward-Center Mounted Instrument Cluster." Proceedings of the Human Factors and Ergonomics Society 48th Annual Meeting in New Orleans, Louisiana, September 2004.

2. Bhise, Vivek D. "Designing Future Automotive In-Vehicle Devices: Issues and Guidelines." Proceedings of the Annual Meeting of the Transportation Research Board, Washington, D.C., January 2002.

3. Lambert, S., Rollins, S. and Bhise, V. "Effects of Common Driver Induced Distraction Tasks on Driver Performance and Glance Behavior." Presented at the 84th Annual Meeting of the Transportation Research Board of the National Academies in Washington, D.C., January 9-13, 2005. Also published in the Compendium of Papers CD-ROM of the meeting.

4. Bhise, V. D., Dowd, J. D. and Smid, E. "Driver Behavior while Operating In-vehicle Devices." Presented at the 82nd Annual Meeting of the Transportation Research Board of the National Academies in Washington, D.C., January 12-16, 2003. Also published in the Compendium of Papers CD-ROM of the meeting.

5. Konz, Stephan and Johnson, Steven. Work Design: Occupational Ergonomics. Sixth Edition. Holcomb Hathaway, Publishers, Scottsdale, Arizona, 2004.

6. Chiang, Dean P., Brooks, Aaron M., and Weir, David H. "An Experimental Study of Destination Entry with an Example Automotive Navigation System. SAE Paper no. 2001-01-0810.

7. Green, Paul and Shah, Reshma. "Task Time and Glance Measures of the Use of Telematics: A Tabular Summary of the Literature." SAVE-IT (Safety Vehicles using adaptive Interface Technology) Task 6 Report, University of Michigan Transportation Research Institute, December 2004.

CONTACT

Prof. Vivek Bhise
Department of Industrial and Manufacturing Systems Engineering
4901 Evergreen Road, 2280 EC
Dearborn, Michigan 48128-1491
E-mail: vbhise@umich.edu
Tel: (313) 593-0365

2004-01-0236

The Many Faces of Security

Mark Krage and Laci Jalics
Delphi Research Labs

ABSTRACT

There are many analogies between physical security and information security. Both are concerned with protecting something of value, and both have many aspects that need to be considered to ensure the development of cost effective security practices. Repositories for items of value become targets for theft, and the transport of items of value increases the risk for theft. Some major differences between physical security and information security are the higher risk of malicious attacks with information networks, the exposure of wireless information during transmission, and that information can be stolen without being physically removed. This paper highlights the many faces of security and provides concrete examples from the literature of common security breaches, security problems and security solutions that are relevant to vehicle information systems, and tradeoffs. Emphasis is placed on the need for the development of security policies, the important role of economics in the business of security, and the recognition that security by its nature is evolutionary and not absolute.

INTRODUCTION

The concept of security is typically applied to something of value such as an expensive physical item, or something abstract such as personal well-being or intellectual property. For a physical item of value, security may consist of protecting the item from theft. One possible approach is to hide the item of interest. This can be highly effective but runs the risk of someone discovering the item or even someone observing the act of hiding the item. Alternatively, the item can be locked inside a theft resistant cabinet. If the item is very valuable, a thick vault with a closely guarded combination lock located inside a building patrolled by guards may be appropriate. In general, the level of security depends on the value of the item. However, higher levels of security may lead to inconvenience and added cost. Someone needs to pay for the vault and the guards, and one's identity needs to be verified to gain access to the vault. This concept also applies to information systems as well, where security measures take the form of firewalls, proxies, passwords, etc.

In general, repositories for items of value are targets for theft. This applies to information as well as physical items. In some cases, a thief may use a brute force approach and attempt to break the lock or container. However, if the lock and container are known to be very strong and well guarded, a more sophisticated approach such as bribing a person who has access to the storage may be preferred. Frank Abagnale, a former thief, states: "Only amateurs hack into computers. Professional criminals 'hack' people.[1]" There is no such thing as absolute security. One can only hope to raise the level of difficulty enough so that the act of breaching security is not attractive for most potential thieves. Information theft can be insidious since it can be stolen while it still resides in the repository. Without proper logging, information can be stolen unnoticed.

Things get complicated when the information or items of value are to be transferred from one location to another. The mere act of taking an item out of storage makes it vulnerable to theft. If an external agent is used to move the item, means need to be provided to positively identify the agent and for the agent, in turn, to positively identify the intended recipient. Typically, external agents have credentials, such as a badge, to verify their identity. The process of verifying identities in the IT world is known as authentication. One also needs to ensure that the vehicle (or the network in the case of information) used to transfer the item has adequate anti-theft measures and that agent follows proper procedures. In the information world, this is the primary role of encryption, digital signatures and established protocols. In many cases, a receipt is desired as proof that the agent successfully transferred the item to the correct party. There need to be ways of tracking transactions or what is referred to as accountability. Also, it may be necessary to prove that a person who initiated a transaction indeed has completed the transaction; this is known as nonrepudiation. Agents who can demonstrate that certain aspects of their security procedures are better than their competitors may be able to command a higher price for their services. Obviously, one would expect to pay more for an agent using an armored vehicle with armed guards than for someone using a standard van. Of course, the guards could be convicted felons, but an armored vehicle and uniforms give the impression of security. In the case of IT, 256-bit encryption is definitely more impressive than 128-bit encryption and should provide better protection. However, it is possible to misuse encryption so that the effective protection is much less than one thinks.

The prevention of malicious tampering of information and unauthorized access to information are important aspects of information security. An indication of the severity of these problems is the large number of viruses (with more being generated constantly) that are scanned by anti-virus software. Such viruses can cause a lot of damage before effective countermeasures are put in place. While there software practices that can reduce the susceptibility of software to viruses, these measures are often ignored. On the other hand, anti-virus software is a profitable business for a number of companies. In many cases, information system practices focus more on curing problems instead of on preventing them. In the following, we present a brief overview of the many faces of security and some insights from the literature on best practices for improving information security as they relate to vehicular information systems.

THE SCOPE OF THE SECURITY ENVIRONMENT

The scope of the security environment for internet-based vehicular applications is illustrated in Figure 1. It is clear from the diagram that wireless security is just one aspect of the overall security environment. In order to provide a proper context for understanding the requirements for wireless security, it is necessary to look at the enabling infrastructure, the security policy environment for the applications of interest and the software execution environment of the vehicle. Many tools are available that can provide high levels of security for specific links in the communication chain. However, high security of a specific link does not ensure high end-to-end security. A primary reason that information security is so difficult is that a single weakness anywhere in the chain can compromise the security of the chain.

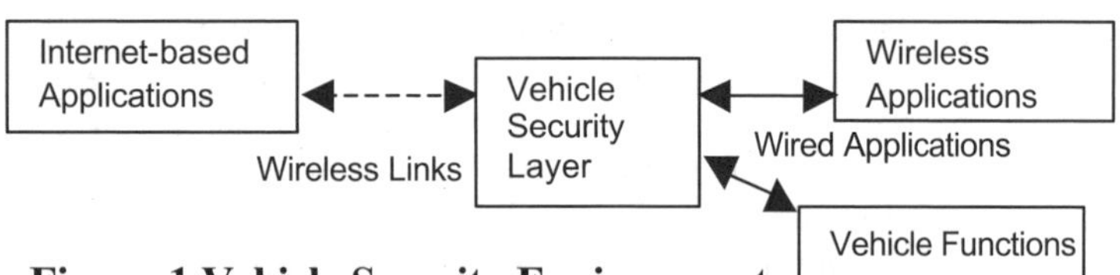

Figure 1 Vehicle Security Environment

The level of security required in a given exchange depends on the potential consequences of theft or corruption of the information to be exchanged and the possible effect of malicious downloads on vehicle systems. As an example, if one is trying to download weather information from a public website to the vehicle, there is no real consequence if the information is stolen by an eavesdropper; there is little consequence, in most cases, if the information is corrupted (it might cause the driver/passenger to change his or her plans in some circumstances); but, there can be some serious consequences to the vehicle information system if the information stream from the website is used to download a malicious application, e.g. a virus, along with the weather information. If the virus can propagate to a safety critical system, it is possible that the safety of the vehicle could be compromised. A proposed solution to this problem is the use a vehicular firewall to restrict the information that can be sent to critical vehicle buses. Some OEMs (Original Equipment Manufacturers) would also like to restrict the information that can be received from vehicle buses. Things get more complicated when the information to be sent or received is of a sensitive nature, such as a private e-mail or a credit card or social security number. In this case, it is generally important that the downloaded (or uploaded) information be received by only the desired parties, that the information be received without modification, and that the information cannot be viewed by undesired parties. This brings into play the need for authentication, encryption and digital signatures. A third important case is that of downloading software applications and updates to the vehicle. As previously mentioned, it is imperative that downloads to the vehicle cannot interact directly with safety-critical systems. If safety-critical software is to be updated, techniques must be in place to ensure that the downloaded software is not corrupted and is free of malicious content. In addition, provisions should be made to monitor the download for proper operation before accepting the download as permanent.

SECURITY BY DESIGN

Vehicular systems security designers have a very difficult task. While they may have many security tools at their disposal, the challenge is to provide both security and performance in a cost effective manner. The authentication process (e.g., passwords, digital certificates or biometrics) takes processing time, a supporting infrastructure, and, in the case of biometrics, additional hardware; encryption sometimes requires additional hardware for acceptable performance, can introduce processing delays and can add a variety of costs; virus/worm/Trojan horse software detection can be large and complex, leading to processing delays, and a need for regular updating. The costs of these tools need to be weighed against the risk of providing less security. The human factors impact of these tools on the usability of operation also need to be considered. If the security requirements make the user interaction difficult, the usability while driving will be decreased, and the user may be tempted to bypass the desired security measures. Due to ongoing advances in processing power and constant efforts to defeat security measures, security tools that were effective yesterday may not be effective today. As systems become more and more connected, hackers from far away places can affect software in many arenas. It is possible today for a hacker in Germany to break into a computer in an Ohio university. Soon, everyone's connected vehicle or refrigerator may become vulnerable. This is why "security is an evolutionary process[2]." "If you implement absolutely bullet-proof security, you're probably going to throw an unreasonable amount of financial and computing resources at the problem[2].” Knowing that bullet-proof security is unreachable[3], accepting a given level of risk is necessary. For example, encrypting only sensitive data instead of all the data can significantly improve efficiency in many cases.

An issue that has become evident in the light of recent virus attacks is the trend toward intertwining data and code. “Because the distinction between data and code is vanishing, malicious code may be introduced, without a conscious decision on the part of a user to install executable code, whenever data is imported into the system. For example, malicious code could be introduced with a Java applet or by viewing apparently benign data that, in actuality, contains executable code[10].” This is especially apparent in e-mails and web pages. E-mails started out as purely text messages that had little or no possibility of containing a virus or causing harm as a program. However, software companies added “improvements” to allow short scripts to execute along with sending the text message to provide a richer interface. Now we have very powerful scripts that execute themselves along with showing the e-mail. This enables a rich e-mail environment, but also enables a very insecure execution environment. By requiring separation of data from code, very strict requirements can be placed around the installation of the code so that accidental installations do not occur. Thus, even though the data may contain sensitive information, it does not contain potentially damaging executable code. Web pages have followed the same pattern. Initially web browsers could only parse the HTML data and generate a display screen. Now several varieties of executable code coexist with HTML data. While this provides a rich display environment, it also provides hackers with a route to access user’s resources.

The privileges provided to various applications need to be restricted to the minimum required. The Windows operating system has had particular trouble with hackers because programs execute with system level privileges. Once a program is installed, it can access very sensitive operating system files. Operating systems that execute programs at a particular user level can’t maliciously affect sensitive operating system files. Embedded scripting languages within office documents, called macros, are often written in Visual Basic, a very powerful language that is closely tied to the Windows operating system. A seemingly innocuous MS Office document can contain a very powerful program in macro form.

Security tools and software design should be deployed as a part of a “security policy” for a given application. In some cases, the security policy is a de facto policy that amounts to a collection of tools developed for general use. In applications where the information being exchanged has little value, this is probably sufficient. However, if the confidentiality and integrity of the data being exchanged are important, a well thought out security policy is a necessity.

SECURITY POLICY

Organizations with large number of computers that communicate over local area networks and the Internet typically have well established IT security policies. These policies consist of a set of security goals and a corresponding set of rules, procedures, and standards that are designed to achieve the desired goals. In general, a security policy determines what types of information can be accessed by individuals and groups, what types of information can be sent by an individual or group to others within and outside the organization, how the information is to be tracked and protected, how individuals and groups are to be authenticated, how new threats are to be handled, and what groups are responsible for various security aspects. To be effective, the rules must be enforceable, and their effectiveness measurable. The rules should also be flexible enough so that they are not hardware or software specific.

The starting point for the development of an effective security policy is the development of a set of security objectives. This can include the desired level of security for supported applications and ease of use versus level of security. The next step is to assess the risks of the various supported applications and their associated computer environments and the cost effectiveness of various tools and procedures to provide the desired security goals. This assessment needs to be compared to the goals to determine what tools will be supported. The resulting policy needs to be communicated to all parties responsible for developing and maintaining the IT applications and their operating environment.

A security policy is needed for vehicle-based information systems that have wireless access to local area network, e.g., through 802.11 type communications, or Internet access. While there are no comprehensive security policies for vehicle IT systems today, some pieces have been developed. For example, it is generally accepted that some type of firewall is needed to protect communications with critical vehicle buses. Also, to minimize development and implementation costs of the vehicle system and to increase interoperability with existing applications, it is expected that existing protocols and standards should be used when they are appropriate to the computational resources of the vehicle system and meet the desired security objectives. This is the approach being taken by the Automobile Multimedia Interface Collaboration (AMI-C)[4]. There are many other decisions that will need to be made. For example, comprehensive virus/worm/Trojan horse protection software can be complex and difficult to implement in a vehicle environment. How are vehicle systems to be protected? Legacy code, while functional in many cases, may be marginal in terms of performance or security. Should the code be modified to improve security, replaced, or should one simply live with it until some time in the future? Since vehicle owners are rarely computer administrators, mechanisms must be in place to remotely manage vehicle information systems with wireless connections. The Open Services Gateway Initiative (OSGi) [5] provides many services that can give a vehicle Service Provider managerial access to the vehicle information systems. An effective security policy for vehicle information systems should provide guidance for resolving and managing such issues.

THE COST OF SECURITY

There can be many difficult tradeoffs in determining the level of security needed in some applications. One example mentioned in the previous section was ease of use versus level of security. Requiring mobile users to remember sufficiently random multiple passwords that change every month leads to the need for a supporting infrastructure to assist the user when the password is forgotten. In general, passwords associated with specific applications should be the responsibility of the application provider. However, there may also be a system password that is the responsibility of the OEM or the vehicle system developer. In general, the cost of providing a password-reset service needs to be balanced against the threat of someone guessing user passwords and the potential for wrongful gain.

There are a number of standards for encryption as well as different levels of encryption. 256-bit encryption is generally regarded as more secure than, say, 64-bit encryption, but requires more computer resources to process the information in a timely manner and requires sending more bits over the air for a given message. The vehicle system impacts of providing a more secure encryption algorithm are on vehicle system hardware (and its associated cost), potential processing delays, and possibly on airtime usage charges (if they apply). Processing delays due to more complex encryption and decryption are important in that, if they are long, the user may be tempted to bypass higher levels of encryption if given the choice, effectively defeating the available security. Also, when higher levels of encryption are employed, it is essential that they be employed in a manner that does not compromise their effectiveness. Netscape at one time used 256-bit encryption to send passwords to users. However, the net entropy of the encrypted passwords was equivalent to 64-bit encryption, making the passwords easy to decipher[6].

A common view is that information security is primarily a matter of applying the proper security tools. However, a white paper by Ross Anderson[7] makes a number of points about the importance of understanding the role of market economics in achieving effective security. One point is that the party that is in a position to protect the security of an application should be the party that suffers the economic consequences of a security failure. If this is not the case, desired levels of security may never be properly implemented. A reference cited by Anderson suggests "that the costs of distributed denial of service attacks should fall on the operators of the networks from which the flooding traffic originates; they can then exert pressure on their users to install suitable defensive software, or, for that matter, supply it themselves as part of the subscription package." Another point is that, due to the large cost associated with switching technologies and the value of being in common with the rest of the world, there is a strong "first-mover" advantage that supports the practice of selling software as soon as possible followed by updates with fixes. While people may criticize Microsoft's software scruples for this practice, it is a practice that makes economic sense in markets where "network economics" apply. A third point made by Anderson is that the hacker has a distinct advantage when it comes to attacking the security of complex software applications. Complex software with millions of lines of code typically requires many thousands of hours of pre-release and beta testing to minimize the number of bugs. However, some large number of bugs will almost surely remain, some of which may never affect normal operation. Basically, the developer has reached a point of diminishing returns. However, a hacker only needs to invest enough time to find just one of the bugs that the developers did not catch. This has important implications on how much effort should be expended on perfecting software. The interested reader is encouraged to read the paper.

THE HACKER AND HACKER DEFENSE

Security is a chain, and malicious users will look for the weakest links in this chain to exploit the system. If the weakest link of a system is stronger than those of comparable systems, the malicious users will likely attack the easier to exploit comparable systems first. Hackers, in many cases, view breaking the security of a system as a challenge. In fact, encryption algorithms are often published to challenge the security community to find a method of cracking the code. This, perhaps, is a counter example to the argument that higher levels of security will deter people from trying to attack a given system. On the other hand, the motives of hackers are often altruistic. Unfortunately, some hackers have taken it upon themselves to expose the weaknesses in systems by publishing attacks that succeed. While this practice may be motivated by the desire to force the security provider to strengthen their security practices, it exposes current users to less security.

Due to continuous increases in computing horsepower, yesterday's daunting computational challenges are now readily solvable exercises. Clever programmers with advanced computers can quickly check millions of keys. A few years ago, this would have been considered almost impossible. In a few more decades, it may be possible to check billions of keys. The security community, thus, is faced with developing increasingly complicated cipher algorithms to maintain the same level of security. Hackers, in many cases, are able to use system complexity to their advantage. "Any sufficiently complex system will have failure modes – failure is unavoidable.[8]" What's even more telling is that a hacker can write an agent program to search on its own for susceptible servers or electronic backdoors. This way a few people can attack on millions of computer systems.

Hackers focus on possible flaws and overlooked security holes. A common flaw in security software is the buffer overrun problem. As an example, a program may require the user to enter a name or string, to gain access to a system. The hacker will attempt to put in a name that is much longer than what the program expects. If the program expects 10-20 characters, the hacker may try putting in 400 characters! If the program doesn't check the length of the string, the computer can copy the 400-character string into memory. The hacker inserts a code snippet (a brief program) in the string after the 256-th character, corresponding to the buffer size. If the program tries to execute any of the memory containing the hacker's snippet, the program loses control and the hacker's program is running. A similar approach can be exploited with embedded systems but, in this case, using an abuse of (operating) system calls. Operating systems control access to system resources. "A malicious program can use that access to alter I/O settings, disable system interrupts, or alter memory pointers.[9]" Alternatively, one can "launch a process that allocates memory until that resource is exhausted," or use interprocess communications to send invalid messages to valid destinations. There are solutions to all of these[9], but all of them have associated costs and tradeoffs.

Another common flaw is the use of random number generators to generate secure passwords or keys. Computers are deterministic machines and any "random" number generated by a computer is only a pseudo-random number. Generally, only physical phenomena produce random events or numbers. If the inputs to a computer pseudo-random number generator can be guessed or computed, then, by knowing the algorithm, the number generated by the computer can be calculated. In 1999, Cigital discovered that the seed for the random number generator for an online gambling site was based on the number of milliseconds (32 bit) since midnight. In a deck of cards, there are 2^{226} unique shuffles. By using a 32 bit seed, 2^{226} was reduced to 4 billion (2^{32}). Using the number of seconds since midnight reduced the number of shuffles to 86 million. By synchronizing their clock they reduced the number to 200,000 possibilities. After seeing the 5th card and searching the 200,000 possibilities, every card from that point forward was known. From a programmer perspective, the solution used seemed reasonable. From a security perspective, it was a terrible solution[6].

Java is an example of a language that was designed from the start with security in mind. The Java Virtual Machine does byte code verification, there is a security manager with policy files that restrict Java application from certain resources, and so on. From a hacker's perspective, however, "a significant portion of the Java system is in the form of native methods that are implemented as object code and are not subject to the JVM's type-safety checks. The JVM is not able to protect itself from tampering by other applications.[10]" So the hacker exploits a potential weak point that has nothing to do with the design of Java or the JVM, but the environment in which the JVM is running. In this case, an insecure operating system can allow a virus or malicious program to destructively affect the operation of the JVM and the code within it. This example illustrates how "operating system security mechanisms play a critical role in supporting security at higher levels.[10]"

Corporations, small businesses, and recently homeowners have been using firewalls to prevent viruses from causing damage, and thieves from stealing private or sensitive information. Although firewalls can be an important security tool, they are far from foolproof. For example, many of the viruses that have plagued the IT community have come through e-mail that is not affected by firewalls. Microsoft's corporate firewall was breached through a corporate user's home computer that had less stringent security measures. It is clear that "firewalls provide no protection against malicious insiders[10]." Given a large enough company with thousands of access points to their internal network, there are many opportunities to bypass a strict firewall.

There are many ways to attack a "secure" system. "No single technical security solution can provide total system security; a proper balance of security mechanisms must be achieved.[10]" One way to increase the level of security against attacks is to use a layered approach to security. For example, layer one could be onsite access only for administrators, layer two could be username and password, and layer three could be time of day (certain administrators can only gain access during 8-5). With security layering, multiple successful attacks are needed to compromise the security of a system. One strategy with this type of approach is to have the system fail in such a way that there is no access to information if two or more attacks succeed. This requires software that tracks unsuccessful attacks and software that responds to such attacks.

COMMON THREATS TO WIRELESS SERVICES

Wireless information system interconnections have a distinct security disadvantage over wired information communications in that information is broadcast over an open-air link to and from a wired network or another wireless user. People with knowledge of wireless communication systems and cryptography can easily intercept radio transmissions and possibly decode the information. The typical areas targeted for message interception are airports, hotels, and business areas, and both voice and data communications can be monitored. While this type of snooping leads to a lot of useless data and chatter, it may take only a few useful hits to make this process of value to an eavesdropper. Wireless information systems are vulnerable to attacks that usurp wireless communication channels through the generation of excessive communications (denial of service attacks, which also includes jamming), and various spoofing ("man-in-the middle") attacks that imitate the interactions of a legitimate service provider.

The open-air exposure of wireless communications requires heavy reliance on encryption to ensure the security of the transmitted information. The encryption procedures used with early 802.11 wireless local area networks (LANs), known as Wired Equivalent Privacy (WEP), received a lot of criticism for their vulnerability to hacking. This problem was traced to the use of "weak" keys, and many techniques have since been proposed to enhance the encryption security of such networks. Another concern in wireless networks is being able to restrict LAN access to specified clients. One possible way of doing this is to base client authentication on the Media Access Control (MAC) address, a globally unique address programmed into the 802.11 card at the factory. Thus, authentication is tied to the hardware being used and not the identity of the user[11].

As mentioned earlier, malicious users generally look for the easy way to gain access to things of value, and there are often subtle details that they exploit to their advantage. As an example, keys for encryption are often stored in volatile memory with the assumption that turning off the power erases the keys. However, latent charge on the memory may leave a partial memory image that can be used to recover the keys. This requires physical access to the memory, i.e. temporary or permanent theft of the unit. This problem can be avoided by writing over the sensitive areas of memory as a part of the shut-down process. Since a power failure could be used to preempt the shut-down process, an internal battery may be needed to ensure that shut-down is completed properly. Separate encryption chips are sometimes useful in speeding up the information processing, and have the advantage of storing keys internally[12]. Malicious users can also use chip number information and board layouts to reverse engineer encryption/decryption signal processing data flows. The reverse engineering process can be made more difficult by scratching out part numbers, potting components, and adding false traces. Potting also makes the process of reverse engineering tamper-evident.

Software is typically a prime area of vulnerability. When malicious users have access to the source code, they can examine the code for weak spots. As discussed previously, buffer overflows can allow a bad guy to bypass programmed security measures. Despite widespread knowledge of the frequency of this type of attack and known techniques for counteracting this type of attack, malicious users continue to succeed.

CONCLUSION

Absolute security is unobtainable. Effective security requires setting forth the desired security goals, examining of the risks associated with the desired application(s), and assessing the cost effectiveness of available tools and procedures to manage these risks.
Some operating systems are inherently safer than others. Microsoft Windows has many more security holes than Linux, for example.
Even though Java is a "secure" programming/execution environment, the use of an underlying operating system that is not secure can expose the application to various security attacks.
Separating data from code greatly reduces the risk to certain types of attacks (viruses).
Good software design practices, e.g., eliminating buffer overflows, can help to minimize the susceptibility to common hacker attacks.
Security needs to be looked at from a systems perspective A weak link in the chain of security can compromise other security measures. The security practices used with early WiFi(802.11) networks are known to be weak. Virtual private networks(VPN) and other measures can be used to plug those holes.
The cost of a security breach should be the economic responsibility of the security provider. If not, a perverse economic condition exists where there is no incentive for a security provider to provide adequate security measures.
Due to constant advances in computer power and the ongoing development of new security attacks, security is an evolutionary process that needs to be managed.

REFERENCES

[1] Frank Abagnale, "Former Thief gives dealers security tips", Automotive News, February 24 2003, p. 20

[2] Dennis Eaton, "WiFi stands guard", Electronic Business News, January 13, 2003, page 22.

[3] Randall K. Nichols and Panos C. Lekkas, Wireless Security Model, Thread and Solutions, McGraw Hill, 2002

[4] AMI-C, http://www.ami-c.org

[5] OSGi, http://www.osgi.org

[6] John Viega and Gary McGraw, "Building Secure Software", Addison-Wesley, 2002.

[7] Ross Anderson, The University of Cambridge, UK, ("Why Information Security is Hard – An Economic Perspective,"

[8] John Viega and Gary McGraw, "Failing Safely", www.sdmagazine.com, February 2003.

[9] Robert Monkman, "Enhancing embedded security," EDN, October 17, 2002, p. 62.

[10] Peter A. Loscocco, Stephen D. Smalley, Patrick A. Muckelbauer, Ruth C. Taylor, S. Jeff Turner, and John F. Farrell, "The Inevitability of Failure: The Flawed Assumption of Security in Modern Computing Environments", National Security Agency, 21st National Information Systems Security Conference, pages 303-314, October 1998,

[11] Jan Haagh, "Protective Coats -Layers of Security Plug Holes in Wireless LANs," Converge, 2002.01, p. 35-38.

[12] Nicholas Cravotta, "Prying Eyes," EDN, September 26, 2002, p. 42-54.

2003-01-3365

Multi-user Infotainment System

A. Mazhei
Scientific-Engineering Enterprise "Belautotractorbuilding"

A. Uspenskiy
Belarusian National Technical University

ABSTRACT

The paper develops a concept of a multi-user infotainment system , taking its application in a tourist bus as an example. It has a specific feature that every passenger is able, by means of a personal remote control console, to access the choice of a TV program or play computer games on a general display. Hardware analysis and an example of interface are given.

INTRODUCTION

In modern public transport the use of information and entertainment systems (which are shortly named infotainment systems) is growing up progressively. Today, passengers of tourist or regular buses, trams, trains and subways may expect to get entertained during the trip by reading the news, watching movies or making use of other multimedia facilities.

Interaction of a passenger with the infotainment system (ITS) may be either passive or active. The passive interaction implies that a passenger has no opportunity to affect the ITS. An example of such ITS is a display module installed in the front of a bus passenger compartment, connected to video player or receiving TV programs. An advantage of this service is a relatively low equipment cost; however, the passengers have a limited choice. Since the overall length of a bus makes about 12 meters, to improve the visibility for the passengers taking rear seats another display is usually installed in the middle of the bus. A further development is installation of small (about 12-inch) personal display modules into seat backs. But in this case, apart from increased cost of the system, some technical problem arise, such as a limited cable length between the central processing unit, which receives the TV-signal and processes graphic information, and display modules in the passenger seats. The maximum length of this cable is about 20 meters. And anyway, a passenger has no opportunity to choose a TV program, a serious drawback of such type of passive ITS.

An active interaction of a passenger with the ITS requires great expenses and is used when satisfaction of passengers' demands is the top priority, for example, in aircrafts, high-speed trains and tourist buses. In this case display modules, control consoles and processor units are installed into passenger seats. An aggregate of a computer and a digital display is known as a panel PC. In this case the above limitations of the cable length and the number of displays are eliminated. Furthermore, the passenger ceases to be a passive viewer; he or she may choose a TV program, read news or play games. Even access to Internet is often possible. Such version renders the passengers the most advanced set of services. However, this technical solution has, besides obvious expensiveness, a number of other essential disadvantages, which may result either in a complete failure of the whole system, or in excessively high operation and maintenance costs. The disadvantages of a multiple panel PC-based ITS are as follows:

1. Increased overall dimensions of panel PCs compared to display modules.
2. Low reliability of every single unit and the system in general due to a great number of critical components with low service life and the overall complexity of units.
3. Low resistance to outer external effects, such as increased vibration and shocks, temperature variations, humidity, electromagnetic interference, etc.
4. Dependence of functional parameters on the type of the operation system used.
5. A necessity to make license deductions for every copy of the operation system and other software, installed on every single panel PC.
6. Complexity of cable connections and a necessity to use additional components, such as concentrators, routers, etc.

In view of the aforesaid, an attempt was made to offer a concept of an ITS to combine the advantages of active and passive ITS and to take an intermediate position of these two.

CONCEPT OF A MULTI-USER INFOTAINMENT SYSTEM WITH A GENERAL DISPLAY

The offered ITS comprises a large display and a central processor, installed in the front part of the passenger compartment, and control consoles kept by the passengers. The control consoles are connected with central processing unit via a multiplex bus, CAN for example. The block diagram of the ITS is given in Fig. 1.

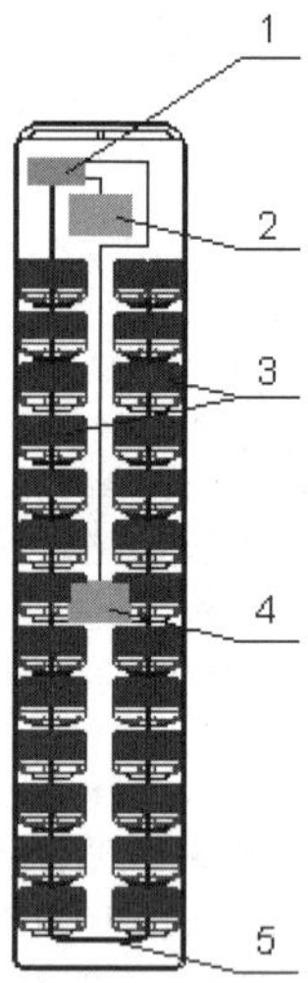

1 – Central processing unit;
2 – Front display module;
3 – Passenger seats with control consoles;
4 – Rear display module;
5 – Multiplex bus

Fig. 1

CONTROL CONSOLES

Since the offered ITS implies that each passenger has a control console only, the cost of the latter should be minimal. It is desirable also to minimize the number of keys. The design of the control console should comply with the requirements of electric safety, dust and moisture resistance. A malfunction or failure of one or several control consoles should not lead to a failure of the whole ITS, for instance when using the CAN multiplex bus such console is cut off the network. Constructively, the control console may looks as a game pad for a game box with a minimum number of keys (Fig. 2). 1 – Game pad; 2 – Key; 3 – "Sleeping mode" LED; 4 – "Active mode" LED; 5 – Case with a corresponding color scheme.

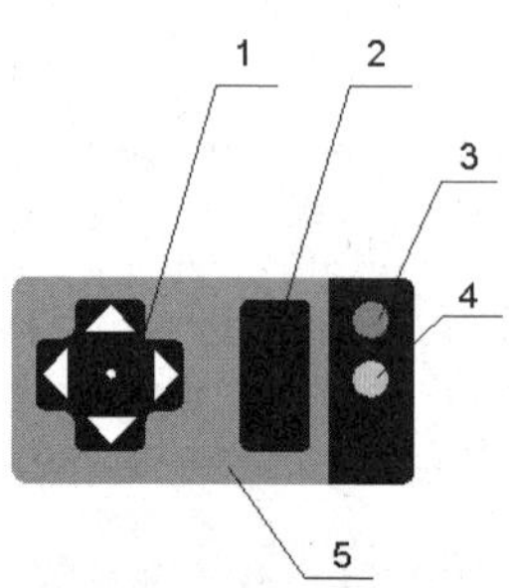

Fig. 2

With such design of the control console menu navigation is possible with the help of a cursor only.

DISPLAY SCREEN INTERFACE

An example of a possible screen interface is given in Fig. 3.

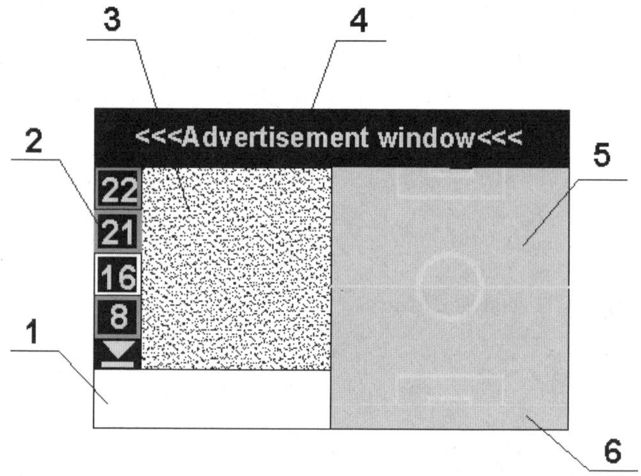

Fig. 3. Display screen interface

In the display screen shown in Fig. 3 we may identify the following zones: 1 – Main menu window; 2 – Queue window; 3 – TV window; 4 – Ad window; 5 – Game window; 6 – Game status window. Now consider them in more detail.

Menu window

The menu window may look as follows (Fig. 4):

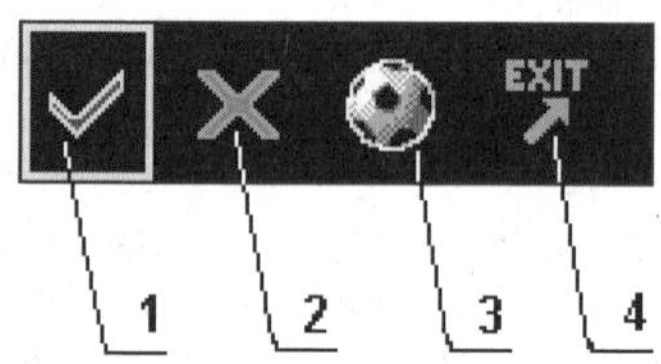

Fig. 4. Main menu window

The main menu has the following icons: 1 – Vote for the TV program, 2 – Vote against the TV program, 3 – Switch to game, 4 – Exit. Menu navigation is made with the help of a frame-shaped color cursor. The color (blue in Fig. 4) is required to enable the passenger to identify his or her "own" cursor (see pos. 5 in Fig. 2), when the latter appears in the menu bar. There is no need to appoint a color for each passenger, for instance eight colors are enough.

In the menu, the passengers are able to express their attitude to the TV program, which is shown in window 3 at the moment. To eliminate the situation when one passenger is able to choose among TV channels against the opinions of other passengers, the voting system is applied. A user should only vote for the present TV program or against it. The algorithms of voting results processing may be various. For example, it may summarize plus or minus results, accordingly, and multiply by coefficients. The later the result, the higher the coefficient and its influence on the final outcome. In this way we may track the rating of the present TV program. Fig. 5 gives an example of such algorithm. The criterion function of passenger's desire to change the TV channel is calculated by the following formula:

$$F = \sum_{i=1}^{n} vote_i \cdot \frac{time_i}{time},$$

Where:

n – number of passengers of the bus, $time_i$ – the time elapsed from the moment of switching on the current channel till the moment of voting of the ith passenger, time – the time elapsed from the moment of switching on the current channel, $vote_i$ – the result of voting of the ith passenger of the bus. The variable $vote_i$ equals to 1, if the ith passenger has voted against the current channel and equals to –1, if the ith passenger has voted for the current channel. If the ith passenger has not voted, the $vote_i$ equals to zero.

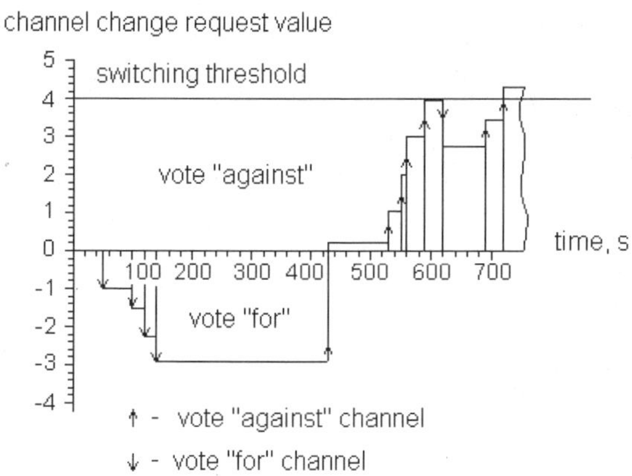

Fig. 5. Results of the TV rating estimation algorithm

Fig. 5 clearly shows how the aforesaid algorithm takes into account the time and "actuality" of voting. In the given example the TV program at first takes four votes "for", but after the lapse of time they ceased to affect the result greatly, and only one vote 400 seconds after switching on the TV program has a stronger impact on the evaluation function. If after another voting "against" the processing program makes a conclusion that the present TV channel is unpopular, then channel selection menu becomes available and appears instead of the main menu (Fig. 6).

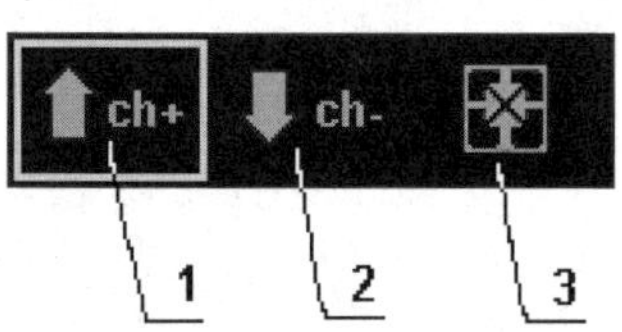

Fig. 6. Channel selection menu

The channel selection menu has the following icons (Fig. 6): 1 & 2 – Channel review; 3 – Channel select. After selection of the most attractive channel (to the opinion of the passenger, who is currently in the menu), the main menu re-appears, but the voting icons are now unavailable. If the current user does not want to enter the game, he or she only has to select the "Exit" icon. The control console switches into the "sleeping mode", and the next user in the queue enters the main menu. Since a user may suddenly lose the interest to the menu and to the infotainment system in general, it is necessary to envisage a transfer of an inactive control console into the "sleeping mode" (in case the user is in the menu system at the moment), in case it remains inactive, say, for one minute.

Queue window

If after a control console activation, there is already a user in the main menu, the passenger is placed on the queue, and the queue window shows in the cursor frame of the respective color the number of his or her place (see pos. 2 in Fig. 3). The queue advances gradually, as the menu liberates. The console LEDs 3 and 4 (Fig. 2) are flashing in turn. The flashing rate increases, as the cursor approaches to the head of the queue. When the user gets into the menu, LED 4 becomes constantly on, and the "sleeping mode" LED 3 is out.

Game window

A possibility for a dozen users to play simultaneously on one display is an interesting feature of the offered ITS. The game acquires the network character, but the cost of the infotainment system does not rise remarkably, because single central processing unit and two large display modules are used and only simple terminal units are in multitude. However, a necessity is to keep all the players in the same game screen. A suitable variant is football.

The playing procedure is clear. The kick power is adjusted by pressing key 2 in compliance with the ever-changing indicator in the game screen. Exit from the game into the "sleeping mode" is achieved by a long pressing key 2. Here too, it is necessary to provide for switching off the inactive control consoles.

HARDWARE SUPPORT OF THE ITS

Multiplex bus

As already mentioned above, to connect the control consoles of the passengers to the central computer it is expedient to use a multiplex data transfer bus. The CAN multiplex bus is most widely used in motor vehicles. The maximum bit rate via CAN reaches 1 Mb/s at the bus length of up to 40 meters. The maximum message size q makes 114 bits, of which maximum 64 bits contain the data for exchange with the central computer. The necessary number of nodes is equal to the number of control consoles (or seats), therefore, to the capacity of bus N. The latter value does not usually exceed 50 (Neoplan Starliner – 26 passengers, Mercedes-Benz O560 Intouro – 46 passengers). To avoid a passenger's feeling that the ITS is too slow to react to a key pressing, the maximum message transmission time should be less then t = 0.1 s. Thus, the required minimum bit rate of the CAN bus:

$S = N \cdot q / t = 50 \cdot 114/0.1 = 57{,}000 = 57$ Kb/s.

To reduce the effect of external interference on the data transfer via the CAN bus, in case the bus capacity is N=50 persons, it is expedient to program not to 1 Mb/s, but to another generally adopted value of 100 Kb/s.

Display modules

Today's digital LCD display modules are the best solution for the offered ITS. The image quality of large flat 21-inch TFT-monitors guarantees a clear saturated picture at an absolute absence of twinkling and broad viewing angles. Compared with CRT-based monitors they are smaller and stronger, contain no high-voltage circuits, emit no radiation and high-frequency noise, thus they may be installed practically in every place. As mentioned earlier, if we take a rather big tourist bus having capacity of 50 passengers as an example, two display units are required. One is installed in the front of the passenger compartment; the second - in the middle of it. However, to transfer graphic information from the computer to the display in the serial mode, we need an exclusively high bit rate: graphic in XGA graphic mode (resolution 1024x768, 16 bit per pixel and vertical scanning frequency 60 Hz) requires the bus capacity of about 1 Gb/s. If we use a standard 40-bit TTL interface, such physical effects like miphasing, front jitter and reverberation will restrict the maximum length of a flat multiple-strand cable by 30 centimeters. To connect the display unit, situated in the middle of the passenger compartment, to the central processing unit a special engineering solution is required, for example: the GigaSTaR high-speed serial backbone link, which has a 36-bit parallel interface. The data from the parallel bus are converted into the serial flow by the GigaSTaR INGT165B transmitter and transmitted via STP-cable to the GigaSTaR receiver, where it is re-covered into the parallel code. This technology allows to move the LCD displays up to 100 meters away from the video controller (equipped with the GigaSTaR transmitter) when using the copper cable without any repeaters and amplifiers, and up to 500 meters when using the multimode fiber optic. Thus, the installation of a universal multimedia video card is required, for example, ICP-MMEDIA, from Inova Computers, which has a built-in GigaSTaR transmitter and two outputs: STP and a common interface for the display module, installed beside the central processing unit in the front of the bus passenger compartment.

CONCLUSION

Information and entertainment systems, called "Infotainment", are finding their broader and broader application. Their purpose is the most possible satisfaction of demands of the users under a reasonable cost. Various existed infotainment systems are able to establish active dialogue with every user and to account his or her interests, but the cost remains high. It may be radically decreased by means of the above-offered concept of a multi-user ITS, which is based on some changes in the structure of the Infotainment system and certain functional limitations. The article considers an example of installation of a multi-user ITS in a tourist bus. Other applications of the above system may be offered: waiting halls of railway stations and airports, mobile training buses and TV systems in bars.

REFERENCES

1. A. D. Sysoyev, "Built-in Computers, Entertainment and Advertisement", "PC Week", No. 16-17 and 19, 2002.
2. Robert Bosch GmbH. CAN Specification Ver. 2.0, 1991.
3. Inova Semiconductors, GigaSTAR Transceiver ING165B_DS Data Sheet, 07/2001 – rev. 1.6.
4. Inova Semiconductors, Display Link Application Note, 07-2001 – rev. 1.2.

2002-01-0144

Reconfigurable Vehicle

Karen M. Parnell
Xilinx

ABSTRACT

When we envisage automotive electronics we automatically consider electric windows, central locking systems, safety systems, climate control and electronic ignition systems, all of which require stringent qualification, temperature cycling and certification. The new emerging automotive electronics boon has now shifted from under the hood or bonnet to in-cabin multimedia applications. The trend towards mobile offices and entertainment on the move has meant a large portion of the electronic or semiconductor content has moved into this expanding area.

Xilinx programmable logic devices can enable the automobile to be a more entertaining, informative and a more productive environment with the added benefit of reconfigurability.

INTRODUCTION

When we envisage automotive electronics we automatically consider electric windows, central locking systems, safety systems, climate control and electronic ignition systems, all of which require stringent qualification, temperature cycling and certification. The new emerging automotive electronics boon has now shifted from under the hood or bonnet to in-cabin multimedia applications. The trend towards mobile offices and entertainment on the move has meant a large portion of the electronic or semiconductor content has moved into this expanding area.

Car manufacturers are striving to differentiate themselves from their competitors by offering high tech infotainment items such as GPS navigation, DVD players and in-car PCs. In this paper we will explore new market trends in automotive applications and consider how consumers are driving the need for enhanced telematics and more comprehensive infotainment. We will then move on to look at the differences in the qualification for in-cabin components versus those in the harsher under bonnet/hood environment. Finally we will look at actual application examples and how Xilinx® Field Programmable Gate Arrays (FPGAs) and Complex Programmable Logic Devices (CPLDs) are helping to change the way we think about automotive designs and how they reduce time to market in this new era of fast moving in-cabin automotive electronics. Figure 1 shows both where electronic systems are present in the average vehicle and highlights those areas where Xilinx devices can be used.

We will be concentrating on how Xilinx can enable the automobile to be a more entertaining, informative and a more productive environment.

Increasing the amount of information and entertainment provided within a car is not without limitation or restriction; we are now seeing the automotive governing bodies introducing user guidelines. For example, the European Union and several U.S States are considering prohibiting the use of cell phones while driving. An alternative solution would rely on speech recognition for dialling instruction. Global Positioning Systems (GPS) radio frequency (RF) or smart card technologies are being explored and implemented for electronic toll collection in order to reduce congestion. These hot new features are driven by consumer demand, vehicle manufacturers trying to differentiate themselves from their competitors but also by governments around the world dedicating resources to researching and developing ways to address safety concerns. This momentum creates a favourable environment for deploying more electronics into vehicles.

Due to time to market and cost pressures the increased electronics content can only be achieved by integrating electronics with electrical and mechanical systems. Additionally car manufacturers are increasingly reliant on independent electronics system suppliers or third party suppliers to provide these new functions. The third party suppliers have to produce a different model of system for each different OEM. This leads to different PCBs, new front displays and mouldings, different connectors and wiring and dedicated software. The trend therefore for these third party suppliers is to base every model they produce on a common platform which can be 'tweaked' through minimal changes for each OEM. This has lead to programmable logic not only being used for prototyping systems but being also used in full production to allow for system personalisation. Motorists and 'early adopters' through the booming after market are already using many of these new technologies. These after market products such as GPS navigation units, in-car TV systems and DVD players are fitted after the car has been manufactured.

XILINX DEVICES

In the digital world, there are two types of electronic chips: memory and logic. Memory chips are used to store information. Logic chips are used to manipulate, or interface with, the information contained in memory. Programmable Logic Devices (PLDs) are "off the shelf" logic chips that the customer, rather than the chip manufacturer, programs to perform a specific function. With the ability to program their own chips, customers realize two key benefits: product design flexibility and faster time to market. With today's shorter product life cycles, both of these factors can be critical determinants of a product's ultimate success.

Electronic equipment manufacturers rely upon PLDs to make fast design changes, accommodate uncertain production volumes, and accelerate their product's introduction to the marketplace.

In the future, it is expected that programmable logic technology will play a bigger role in automotive applications. This will come as a result of its ability to provide advanced network centric features, such as Xilinx Internet Reconfigurable Logic (IRL). By using IRL, the automotive manufacturers can build-in upgradeability and reduce risks. For example you can upgrade or enhance the performance of your car for the weekend by paying for your engine management system to be 'race' tuned to enhance the performance of your car. This will give you the ability to purchase a 'racing car' for the weekend in your standard family vehicle. The reconfigurable logic based engine management system would be reprogrammed via a wireless Internet connection to change the car's 'personality' and at the end of the pre-paid time period re-programmed back to its original settings.

Xilinx high-volume Field Programmable Gate Array (FPGA) and Complex Programmable Logic Devices (CPLD) provide system designers with cost effective solutions that retain the traditional PLD time to market advantage. Today, Xilinx programmable logic devices are employed by a large number of telematic and infotainment product manufacturers, who recognize the added flexibility and time to market benefits achievable through the use of programmable logic solutions.

TELEMATICS AND INFOTAINMENT

The intelligent vehicles market offers a new breed of automotive engineering and a whole New World of electronics systems, computers and software applications. These systems applied to vehicles will affect the vehicle in three basic functional areas: the basic vehicle, safety/security and telematics (the merging of communications and computing technology to provide driver information, communications and entertainment). Below are some of the features the next generation of vehicle will have as standard equipment, all of which are encompassed in telematics or infotainment systems:

- Navigation and route guidance
- Real-time information (traffic, news, business directories, internet/email)
- Entertainment (broadcast, onboard)
- Automated transactions (tolls, purchases)
- Position reporting (via GPS)
- Communications (broadcast, two way)
- Stored onboard information databases
- Services on demand (voice activated systems, vehicle tracking and recovery)

Auto-industry participants also use the term "infotainment" to describe devices such as stereo systems, navigation systems, cell phones and others. The graph in figure 2 shows the huge growth in car navigation, multimedia and emergency only systems, this market is predicted to grow from just over 2 million units in 1999 to over 12 million units in 2004.

Figure 3 shows the elements that make up a typical infotainment system. These functional blocks are:

- Global Positioning System & GSM wireless receiver
- Digital Radio (Digital Audio Broadcast – DAB decoder & Analogue to Digital Converter – ADC)
- Television
- Audio entertainment units such as Tape, CD & MP3 player
- Digital Versatile Disk (DVD) Player
- Graphics controller to interface to the in-car display for entertainment (e.g. games console) for the passengers & information for the driver
- Sound system controller for audio front and rear
- Digital Signal Processing (DSP) for processing sensor & gyro data and for processing the digital audio and video
- CODEC for coding and decoding audio to and from the Human Machine Interface (HMI) e.g. voice recognition system

Xilinx devices can be used to perform the interfacing functions between the main functional blocks. Most of the functions can be considered as chipset glue logic, memory decoders and interfacing logic.

We will study each functional block in Figure 3 that could potentially contain Xilinx programmable logic in turn:

1. GPS Receiver - Programmable logic can be used as part of the GPS receiver to process the output from a GPS chipset and format it for the microprocessor being used in the system

2. Gyros & Sensors - Xilinx devices are ideal for high speed digital signal processing and signal conditioning on the outputs from sensors and gyros. The processing may not need to be exceedingly fast, but where programmable logic could add benefit is if there are multiple channels to process. Multiple channels even at a slow data rate can equate to high Digital Signal Processing (DSP) Multiply and Accumulate (MACs) operations. Where DSP MAC operations are in the billions per second offloading this process from a standard Digital Signal Processor to an FPGA may be beneficial. A common DSP function is a filter and the more MAC operations that are applied to the incoming signal, the higher the accuracy of the filter. The latest Virtex® II FPGAs from Xilinx can perform 600 billion MACs per second.

3. Digital Audio Broadcast (DAB) - Xilinx high density FPGAs, such as Virtex devices, have been instrumental in bringing this technology into the vehicle by providing a reprogrammable platform for research and design proving. In this design-proving phase they were used to perform the main DSP functions. As the technology has matured these functions have been integrated into Application Specific Standard Product (ASSPs) and standard chipsets to reduce costs by reducing redundancy. We are now seeing Xilinx low cost FPGAs & CPLDS, such as Spartan® II, XC9500 and Coolrunner® devices, being used as the "glue logic" between these chipsets.

MULTIMEDIA PLATFORM

As more and more information and entertainment systems are added to automobiles, we're seeing the inevitable conflict of digital standards and protocols. A bewildering array of emerging standards and protocols are being tried and tested for use in the latest in-car systems. These new standards and protocols include:

Bluetooth™, BlueCAN, MP3, Java™, AutoPC, AMIC (Automotive Multimedia Interface Consortium with JINI interface), WAP (Wireless Application Protocol), HTML, XML, MOST (Media Oriented System Transport), FireWire, CAN (Controller Area Network), TCP/IP, and more – but which one(s) will prevail?

OVERCOMING THE DESIGN CHALLENGES

Designers of the new wave in-car multimedia systems must include traffic information systems, Internet/Web access, electronic game consoles, MPEG music download capability, digital radio reception, and mobile commerce services. They must also have the flexibility to provide all or just a few of these functions.

Other challenges faced by the designers are:

- Small physical space available to place these products in the dash or seat backs
- Low cost units that can fit into more than one model of car
- Aesthetically pleasing look and feel
- Ease of driver use
- The ability to upgrade the unit when Automotive standards change

Designers must now also ensure that the in-car multimedia system can "talk" to the other devices introduced into the cabin space. For example, if a mobile phone is brought into the car environment, it should be automatically detected and able to communicate with the car's communications network. This automatic connectivity could also include connection of PDAs, portable PCs, MP3 players, and other personal portable electronic equipment to provide a truly connected and functional in-car environment.

Some 'after market' product manufacturers have provided short-term solutions to some of these problems by producing audio systems based around MP3 technology. When in the cabin, the MP3 player is seated in the car audio system, but when you leave the vehicle it can be removed to become a handheld portable MP3 player.

THE NEW WAY OF DESIGNING

As in-car and consumer functions converge – and new automotive and consumer standards and protocols emerge –manufacturers are starting to prototype multimedia platforms that can provide as much, or as little functionality, as required. Such multimedia platforms can be best realized by designing reconfigurable hardware.

Reconfigurable hardware can be programmed late in the production flow to provide custom functionality on a "standard" hardware platform – and can also be configured to accommodate new and emerging in-car standards.

Figure 4 shows the automotive multimedia platform design approach. This concept will also allow hardware upgrades throughout the lifetime of the car – these upgrades can be implemented remotely by utilizing the wireless communications/Internet connectivity provided by the unit. Xilinx terms this remote hardware upgrading process Internet Reconfigurable Logic (IRL) via the Xilinx Online program.

The Xilinx Online program is designed to enable, identify, and promote network upgradable systems, hence "future proofing" a system and avoiding product obsolescence.

These are systems that can be upgraded, modified, or fixed long after they have been deployed in the field. While many designers have been building upgradable devices based on Xilinx technology for years, the explosion of networked devices has dramatically increased the demand for these user configurable and adaptable applications. For example, an engineer can use the existing wireless communications/Internet infrastructure to reprogram an in-car multimedia system to include extra functionality such as adding an MP3 player or upgrading the system to take advantage of the latest protocol or standard.

MULTIMEDIA SYSTEM DESIGN FLOW USING FPGAS

The multimedia platform ideally should be based around one Human Machine Interface (HMI) to allow for all functions to be accessed via one colour menu-driven touch screen. As the functions are implemented in software and reconfigurable hardware, the system can be upgraded even after the car has been purchased and driven away.

The new way of developing in-car systems is to prototype using FPGAs in a generic development environment. The elements can then be developed quickly and easily without the need to fix specifications. This initial prototyping phase can be realized using Virtex®-II Platform FPGAs. At this early stage, the different standards, protocols, and functions can be tried, tested, and debugged utilizing the headroom that a large FPGA gives.

As the design firms up, the specifications are “chilled” or “frozen,” and the boards are “productionized.” In other words, the specific standard, protocol, or function is chosen from the many tested. This move from prototype to production enables the design to be optimized and fitted into a smaller, low cost FPGA, such as a device from the Spartan® IIE family, while still allowing for system upgradability. Once in production, the FPGA can be used to aid total printed circuit board (PCB) testing using JTAG techniques. If necessary, designs can be ‘tweaked’ or enhanced at this stage.
The final stage is the look and feel or aesthetics of the product, which can be designed for each car manufacturer to fit into their specific dashboard (or fascia). All of the production multimedia units are built up around the standard FPGA-based platform. This standard platform can be programmed with its “personality” late in the production flow to accommodate last-minute design changes, or end-user preferences. Having a common platform cuts down on inventory and takes advantage of the cost saving associated with producing one platform for all units. The benefits of using this reconfigurable hardware-based multimedia platform approach are:

- Easier control of software and hardware development
- Re-use of components, be they software or hardware (design re-use)
- Increase in the time developers can spend on creating value as opposed to creating system interconnect structures
- Reduction of risk through clearer understanding of the basic components
- Choice of standard or protocol can be deferred and simply reconfigured
- Increased productivity through the application of modern development tools
- Increased openness of the system, supporting the use of standards and integration of third-party components.

THE XILINX IN-CAR MULTIMEDIA SOLUTION

We predict the heart of the reconfigurable multimedia platform will be a Xilinx programmable logic device. The common platform approach enables one PCB to be produced for all customers – with the only change being to the style, shape, and color of the interface to satisfy the need for product differentiation.

Xilinx is the leading provider of complete and innovative programmable logic solutions. Our products help minimize risks for manufacturers of in-car electronic equipment by shortening the time required to develop products and in taking them to market. You can design and verify your proprietary circuits in Xilinx PLDs (programmable logic devices) much faster than you could by using traditional methods, such as ASICs and ASSPs. Xilinx builds programmable ICs, develops software, IP (Intellectual Property) cores, and other tools to provide complete solutions to our customers. We also provide application support and design services to customers developing their own proprietary designs.

To “drive” the in-car digital convergence revolution, Xilinx recommends the Spartan-II FPGA family and the CoolRunner and 9500XV CPLD families. The Xilinx CPLD families are qualified to the automotive temperature range parameters. The Spartan-IIE FPGA family is based on the very popular Virtex family. Spartan-IIE extends the legacy of the Spartan series, with more gates, better performance, and enhanced features. The Spartan-IIE family offers digital delay locked loops, programmable I/Os, on-chip block memory, and densities up to 300,000 system gates.

These features and densities, coupled with enhancements to software and an increased number of available IP cores, provide a reduced time-to-market and increased time-in-market at a much lower cost. Xilinx also has a range of IP cores such as memory controllers, system interfaces, DSP, communications, networking, and microprocessors.

DIGITAL RADIO

Digital Audio Broadcast (DAB), Radio Data broadcasting Systems (RDS), and the Traffic Message Channel (TMC) are set to change car stereo systems as we are witnessing massive innovations toward telematic applications. Until recently analogue radio signals such as FM have been subject to numerous kinds of interference between the transmitter and the radio. Mountains, high rise buildings and atmospheric conditions can cause these problems. DAB uses these effects as a reflector creating multi-path reception conditions to optimise receiver sensitivity. Since DAB always selects the strongest regional transmitter automatically the in-car receiver will always be the focal point of incoming radio signals. DAB is broadcast on terrestrial networks and is received using a small non-directional stub antenna. The reception is CD-like quality without the annoying interference or signal distortion. DAB is not only able to carry audio but can also carry text, pictures, data and video. In this application time to market and price is a key factor when selecting components to perform such tasks as decoding the incoming data stream. Xilinx CPLDs are an ideal fit in this product as they are low cost and easy to design with. By completing a design in the Xilinx WebPACK™ software designs can be input, simulated and programmed into a device in a matter of hours.

Passenger entertainment and on-board interactive information systems are just around the corner. Newer vehicles will have multiple display terminals, and personal audio sets will become available for passengers.

Although DAB/RDS systems are starting to be very popular in Europe, they are not in demand yet in other regions. Video and gaming systems are starting to ship in significant numbers in Japan, but not in other regions yet.

These new multimedia products are thought to have the effect of entertaining passengers and reducing driver interruption, allowing these solutions to be marketed as new entertainment, convenience, and safety systems. Some of the latest technologies, such as DVD (Digital Versatile Disk), are already finding their way into the in-car entertainment market. DVD players are replacing CD-ROM (Compact Disk – Read Only Memory) players in car navigation systems, mostly being used to replay pre-recorded video, interactive video games, and other such high-density software titles. The evolution of in-car entertainment continues at the same pace as development in consumer entertainment markets.

Motorola has designed and developed a new in-car Internet radio prototype called iRadio, a revolutionary concept in in-vehicle information and entertainment via wireless Web access.

IRadio will enable drivers to capture music on demand; listen to real time traffic reports; download audio books; access voicemail; receive the latest news and weather reports; get updated stock portfolio information and access Email. These off-board mobile multimedia features will be delivered wirelessly via Web access, satellite, digital cellular, and FM sideband technologies.

A number of infotainment system manufactures are designing Multi-Media Platforms (MMPs) that integrate functions such as DVD, DAB radio, MP3 player and other functions. The MMP is a building block for future enhancements and technological advancements in in-car infotainment. Many of these platforms are based on FPGA technology to allow for future growth and enhancements and also accommodate new standards and interfaces. These platforms have the potential to be updated and upgraded in situe to provide new emerging audio and visual pleasures such as MP3 audio.

CAR DRIVER ASSISTANCE

Car safety is one of the primary concerns in the automotive industry and we have seen over the years the addition of airbags, seat belt pre-tensioners, side impact beams and other structural enhancements. We are now seeing the emergence of car driver assistance systems to augment the more 'physical' safety enhancements. The latest car driver assistance system is based around a video processing system located in the rear view mirror and dashboard of the vehicle. The system processes data from both inside and outside the car. It analyses erratic road movements or leaving the lane if the driver has fallen asleep and automatically corrects and brings the car to a gentle stop. The system also analyses outside light levels compared to road conditions, such as curves, and adjusts the headlamp luminosity and direction accordingly. This driver assistance system also measures distance to the car in front and if an accident is imminent it will ensure activation of the airbag systems. The distance sensors can also aid when parking your vehicle. Xilinx FPGAs are ideal for implementing complex imaging and DSP functions and have been used in car driver assistance systems.

AUTOPC

Choosing how large your hard-drive will be and how much RAM you require may soon be as common as choosing what colour your vehicle will be in the list of car options. It is predicted that the AutoPC will become an integral part of the make up of your vehicle by integrating all audio, visual, internet connection, cell phone & navigation functions into one small PC; which will fit into the dash board where the typical car radio usually fits.

This addition to the average family car will enable an office on the move along with playing DVDs for the rear passengers and downloading the latest MP3 file to pipe through to your car speakers. This addition will allow you to purchase items advertised on the radio by reading your credit card details and authenticating it via the dash mounted smart card reader; dialing up the appropriate website from details provided by the RDS function of your radio and then transacting an on-line purchase via wireless internet connection.

Internet traffic is doubling every 100 days so it is conceivable to imagine this technology migrating to standard in car equipment very soon. At Visteon, Ford's auto electronic business, a Pentium and Microsoft CE based Information; Communications, Entertainment and safety (ICES) platform contains numerous features. It includes a CD player for audio, a DVD player for movies (displayed via a LCD screen), a cellular telephone, Internet access for e-mail and information and a global positioning system. The company plans to add MMX features in its second generation system. For safety purposes and to keep the driver's attention on the road all system commands are voice-activated.

A similar system was developed at GM's Delphi subsidiary. GM worked closely with IBM, Sun Microsystems, and Netscape to come up with a system that offers essentially the same tools and features as the Visteon unit. GM and IBM took the client-server approach in their system development. In a prototype, the car (client) was connected to a satellite, which provided access to the Internet and geo-graphic positioning. Data was beamed at a rate of 400K baud from a satellite to an antenna built into the roof of the test car. Digital audio from an Internet broadcast was beamed at the rate of 80K baud, producing CD-quality sound.

IBM also is working on a system for Mercedes-Benz in which an embedded PowerPC chip performs as a server, and other electronic systems—climate control, entertainment, information, and communication units—are the clients.

Typical services offered are:

- Entertainment - audio CDs, DVDs, Games etc
- Communications - Internet access, Cellular phone, GPS navigation, IR link to PDA/laptop
- Information - news, weather, traffic, email, engine diagnosis etc
- Navigation - route finder, maps etc
- All under voice control, commands given verbally and feedback from the unit in digitized voice.

Some of the major in-car audio system designers are producing their own version of the AutoPC that fit into the dashboard. These multi-functional in-dash systems are available as aftermarket products, but will be installed as standard or optional features in high-end vehicles beginning in late-2001 or 2002. As the price of electronic systems declines, they will be placed in mid-priced cars and eventually, all vehicles.

Because the AutoPC is designed to fit into the space usually occupied by the standard audio system the electronic design has to be highly integrated. Many manufacturers of these products are looking to system-on-a-chip technology but with short time-scales to meet consumer demand. FPGAs lend themselves very well to this environment having the ability to absorb interface logic, decoding, encoding and Digital Signal Processing (DSP) functions. Ball Grid Array (BGA) packaging techniques allows many millions of system gates to occupy very little space on a Printed Circuit Board (PCB). FPGAs can offer a great advantage over ASIC equivalents by reducing time to market and can by upgraded in-dash using Internet Re-configurable Logic (IRL). IRL can be used to great advantage in this fast moving area as the Internet connection is already there in the AutoPC. If the hardware needs to be upgraded to implement new functions or standards then this is achieved by Internet based FPGA re-configuring.

NAVIGATION AND GLOBAL POSITIONING SYSTEMS

Navigation semiconductor content is the third fastest growing sector – in fact it is predicted to reach the same growth rate in terms of semiconductor consumption as the consumer market place by 2001 (according to Dataquest figures).

GPS technology offers immense capabilities for navigation systems with its accurate location tracking systems. The accuracy of the location systems also make them very suitable for vehicle tracking applications, and these systems have therefore been designed into fleet control and car security systems. While GPS is widely used in Japan for navigation systems, in the United States, roadside assistance and emergency calling are expected to drive the first wave of GPS use in cars. Table 1 illustrates some GPS applications.

GPS lets you and your car know exactly where you are at any time; this can be used for:

- Geographic based advertising
- Fleet car management
- Toll road direct billing
- Automatic Emergency calls
- Route finding and mapping

As you are driving and listening to your favourite digital radio station and the advertising break is reached a personalised geographic based advert could be played to you. For example if you are driving past a restaurant you could be offered money off meals or told about the latest meal deal. Estate agents, hotels, and car dealerships could use this adverting technique (especially if they receive information from your car about its make and model as you pass), basically it can be used by anything you drive past to advertise and inform.

GPS could also be used to track fleet vehicles so that the fleet manager knows exactly when and where anyone of the vehicles goes. This information could be useful for planning more efficient routes and also diverting vehicles if there is an accident or road works.

Volkswagen plans to produce future versions of its Passat model with a built-in server that will let owner's track the location of their car and analyze its services and maintenance records using GPS and wireless Internet connection.

MULTIMEDIA DATA BUS

Today's vehicles contain hundreds of circuits, sensors, and other electrical components. Communication among these electronic modules is usually handled via a dedicated wire through point-to-point connections. If all possible combinations of switches, sensors, motors, and other electrical devices in fully featured vehicles are accumulated; the resulting number of connections and dedicated wiring is enormous. Multiplexing systems together (in other words, putting the systems on a network) is more efficient for today's complex in-vehicle communications. Multiplexing technologies are networked cabling and communications techniques designed to eliminate the multiplicity of wiring found in the typical vehicle, brought on by the proliferation of electronic systems.

In Europe the CAN bus has been used to connect the vehicle sensors and safety systems. Controller Area Network (CAN) has been used to implement car busses to reduce wiring loom size, weight and cost and also provide a standard serial bus that can be used to connect devices from many 3rd party suppliers that make up the total vehicle. As more and more electronic equipment is added to the average vehicle more and more wiring has been added. CAN offers the ability to reduce the amount of wiring in the car using multiplexing techniques. Multiplexing is a method for transferring data among distributed electronics modules via a serial data bus.

The emerging Intelligent Transport System (ITS) data bus could allow communication among audio, video, and computing devices. A gateway could transfer required diagnostic information among the multiple networks. Figure 5 illustrates how networks may be configured in the future.

Because ITS products are considered "consumer" items, a widely open ITS data bus standard is critical. An open ITS data bus would allow consumers to select products and features for their vehicles in much the same way as they select their home audio/video equipment. This development would enable a larger market and probably more rapid adoption rates, as ITS products designed to the standard could potentially be used in any vehicle. Also, with a standard bus architecture, manufacturers could use a colour LCD display not only for route guidance and maps, but also for emergency call service, environmental control, personal calendar, phone directory, and ultimately as a "PC" monitor.

Bluetooth, meanwhile, is working on a wireless scheme to connect PCs, cell phones, pagers, PDAs, and other devices for data sharing. Bluetooth in a vehicle could be the easiest way for an occupant to link a handheld computer or an external network via a cell phone to the ITS Data Bus (IDB) through a wireless gateway. Using a Bluetooth connection allows for short range (less than 10m) wireless connection of many devices in a small area. This would facilitate hands free cell phone operation with out the need for mechanical contact and speaker and headphone reception without wires! Xilinx programmable logic devices have been used in Bluetooth application areas such as screen phones and prototyping PSTN networks for home use. Further details about Xilinx and Bluetooth can be found at the emerging Standards and Protocols (eSP) web portal (www.xilinx.com/esp).

Other standards the Telematics Suppliers Consortium (TSC) may pursue could link cars to cars, cars to road infrastructure, or cars to services at businesses, such as petrol stations. TSC foresees a day when you can pull up to the fuel pump and download a digital movie or e-mail over a short range wireless link while you fill up your tank.

CAN INTELECTUAL PROPERTY

As we have seen CAN is the dominant automotive data bus in European cars and is being evaluated by the US automotive sector. The functionality of the CAN interface can be embedded within Xilinx FPGAs by using an 'off the shelf' core also known as Intellectual Property (IP) cores.

Xilinx offers the industry's largest selection of intellectual property (IP) cores, which serves as the foundation for accomplishing complex system-on-a-chip designs. Xilinx cores are pre-defined, tested, and verified to ensure correct functionality. In addition, Xilinx Cores utilize Smart-IP technology to predetermine the implementation providing optimal and predictable performance and utilization. The broadest selection of industry-standard solutions offered by Xilinx comprise two IP sources:

LogiCORE™ and AllianceCORE™. The LogiCORE program being the most successful in the industry offers cores exclusively for Xilinx FPGAs. These cores are sold and supported by Xilinx. The AllianceCORE program provides a broad selection of third-party cores customized for use with Xilinx FPGAs and CPLDs.

The need for design reuse has been apparent for many years; no company likes to put many man-years of effort into a design that can be used only once. Today, thousands of designers are creating intellectual property (IP) on a huge scale, targeting the widely popular Xilinx FPGA families, which are ideally suited to support design reuse.

The AllianceCORE CAN bus interface (R3.0) from Sci-worx can be used in many automotive applications. This core can be embedded in an FPGA which can perform the CAN2.0B interface functions and also integrate discrete logic and other functions in one re-configurable device.

CONCLUSION

We have seen that there are a number of factors effecting the way vehicles are evolving, consumer demand for a safer more entertaining and a productive in-car environment. Government legislation has also been dictating items such as voice recognition systems for hands free device operation and emerging in-car bussing standards.

Consumers are demanding home comforts on the move such as DVD players, Internet access digital radio reception & constant telephony services. In-car bussing systems have been developed to decrease the amount and hence the cost of wiring in the car and also to allow interfacing to equipment from 3rd party sources. Changing international standards for in-car busses are driving the need for re-configurable test and diagnostic equipment, which can be transformed to suit any bus standard. All of these factors are increasing the in-cabin semiconductor content. We are also seeing the time to market pressure reducing car cycles times from 5 years down to 2 years. Time to market pressures can be alleviated by using programmable logic by providing shorter development time scales over traditionally used ASICs.

Xilinx high-volume FPGA and CPLD devices provide system designers with cost effective solutions that retain the traditional PLD time to market advantage. Today, Xilinx programmable logic devices are employed by a large number of telematic and infotainment product manufacturers, who recognise the added flexibility and time to market benefits achievable through the use of programmable logic solutions.

In the future, it is expected that programmable logic technology will play a bigger role in automotive applications. This will come as a result of its ability to provide advanced network centric features, such as Xilinx Internet Reconfigurable Logic, IRL. By using IRL, the automotive manufacturers can build-in upgradeability and reduce risks. For example you can upgrade or enhance the performance of your car for the weekend by paying for your engine management system to be 'race' tuned to enhance the performance of your car. This will give you the ability to purchase a 'racing car' for the weekend in your standard family vehicle. The engine management system would be reprogrammed via a wireless Internet connection to change the car's personality and at the end of the pre-paid time period re-programmed back to its original settings.

Bussing standards are in a state of flux. Most in-car systems designers can not wait for this to settle on a particular standard so are looking to programmable logic to give them the flexibility to change their hardware in-system to meet existing and future standards.

ACKNOWLEDGMENTS

Prep for a multimedia future, EDN, Maury Wright

Automotive Semiconductor Application Markets 1998 – 2003, Dataquest

Automotive Electronics (2000), IC Insight

Xilinx European Automotive Applications, Margit Tischler

CONTACT

Karen Parnell is the European Marketing Manager for Coolrunner, XC9500 CPLDs and Spartan, Virtex FPGAs within the European marketing group. In 1999 she joined Xilinx from Philips Semiconductor where she was Marketing Manager for Coolrunner devices in Europe. Her responsibilities as European marketing manager include regional market analysis, European product introductions and promotions as well as customer sales support and training on the high volume product lines.

Parnell's prior experience includes business development manager and field applications engineer at a leading semiconductor distributor and sales & engineering positions at British Aerospace, Defence.

Parnell holds a bachelor's honours degree from the University of Hertfordshire in electronic and electrical engineering and is a Chartered Engineer and member of the Institution of Electrical Engineers.

ADDITIONAL SOURCES

www.xilinx.com

DEFINITIONS, ACRONYMS, ABBREVIATIONS

ADC: Analogue to Digital Converter

AMIC: Automotive Multimedia Interface Consortium

ASIC: Application Specific Integrated Circuit

ASSP: Application Specific Standard Product

CAN: Controller Area Network

CD: Compact Disk

CODEC: Coder-Decoder

CPLD: Complex Programmable Logic Device

DAB: Digital Audio Broadcast

DSP: Digital Signal Processing

DVD: Digital Versatile Disk

eSP: Emerging Standards and Protocols

FPGA: Field Programmable Gate Array

GPS: Global Positioning System

GSM: Global System for Mobile communications

HMI: Human Machine interface

HTML: Hyper Text Markup Language

IRL: Internet Reconfigurable Logic

ITS: Intelligent Transport System

JINI: Java network technology of Sun Micro Systems

LCD: Liquid Crystal Display

MAC: Multiply Accumulate

MMP: Multi-Media Platform

MMX: Multi-Media Extensions

MOST: Media Oriented System Transport

MPEG: Multi-Media Extensions

PC: Personal Computer

PDA: Personal Digital Assistant

RDS: Radio Data Service

TCP/IP: Transmission Control Protocol Internet Protocol

TSC: Telematics Suppliers Consortium

WAP: Wireless Application Protocol

XML: eXtensible Markup Language

APPENDIX – TABLES AND FIGURES

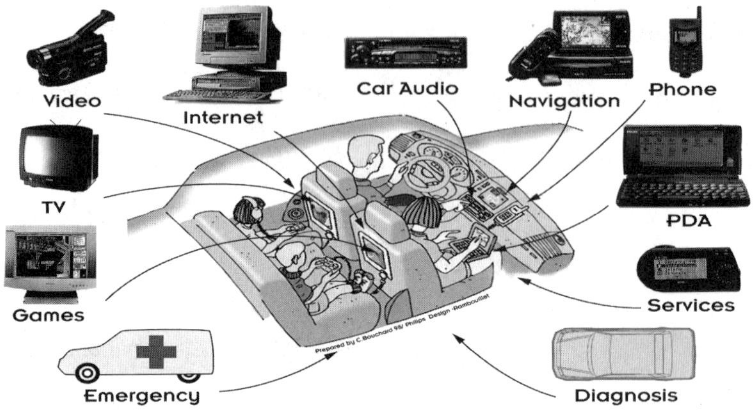

Figure 1 – Emerging In-Car Systems

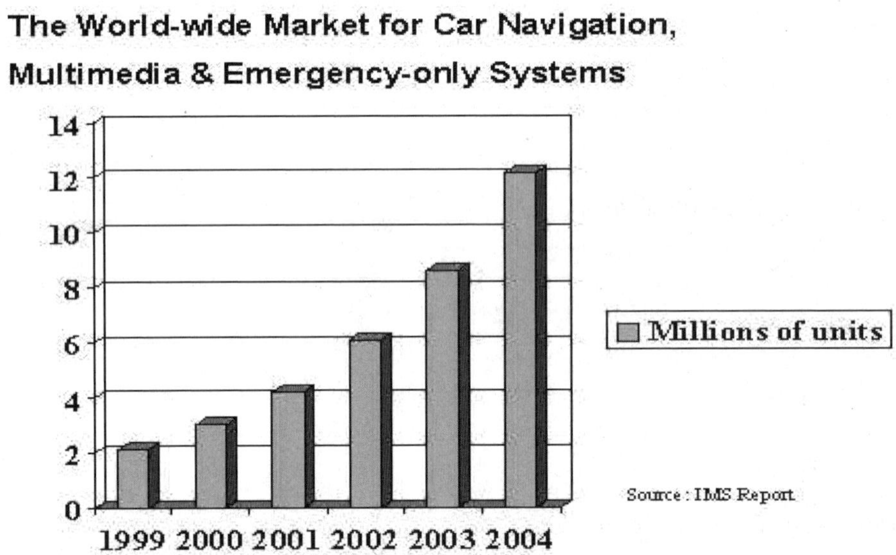

Figure 2 – The WorldWide Market for Car Navigation, Multimedia & Emergency Systems

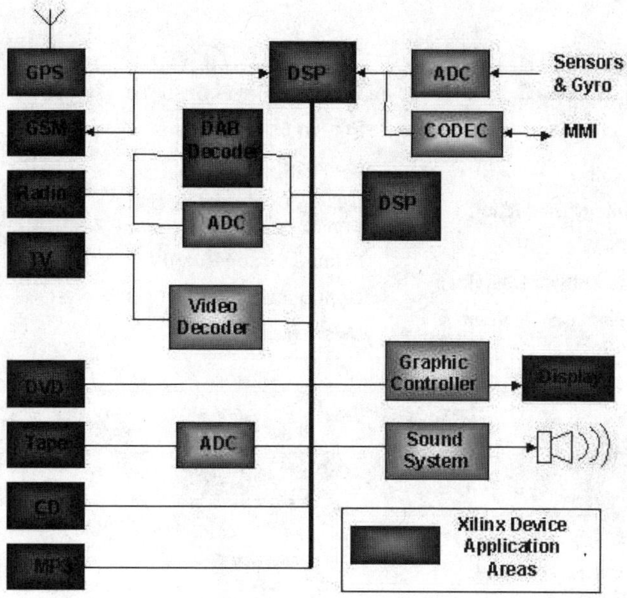

Figure 3 – Typical Elements of an Infotainment System

Table 1 - Key GPS In-Car Applications

GPS Combined with:	**Provided Feature**
Electronic maps (CD, DVD, Internet or GSM), LCD monitors	Route guidance
Electronics maps, LCD monitors or head up displays, up to the minute travel information (via FM radio data system (RDS)), road information (speed limit and conditions)	Advanced navigation systems
Telephony (cell phones or GSM), phone directories (in either personal databases or via Internet)	Advance reservations, roadside assistance, emergency calling
Air bags, seat belt control, accident data recorders	Automatic emergency calling
Electronic vehicle identification or GSM	Automatic toll payment (cashless)
Ignition control and GSM	Stolen vehicle recovery
Speech recognition	Hands free operation
Infrared sensors, radar, CCD cameras	Collision avoidance, warning systems

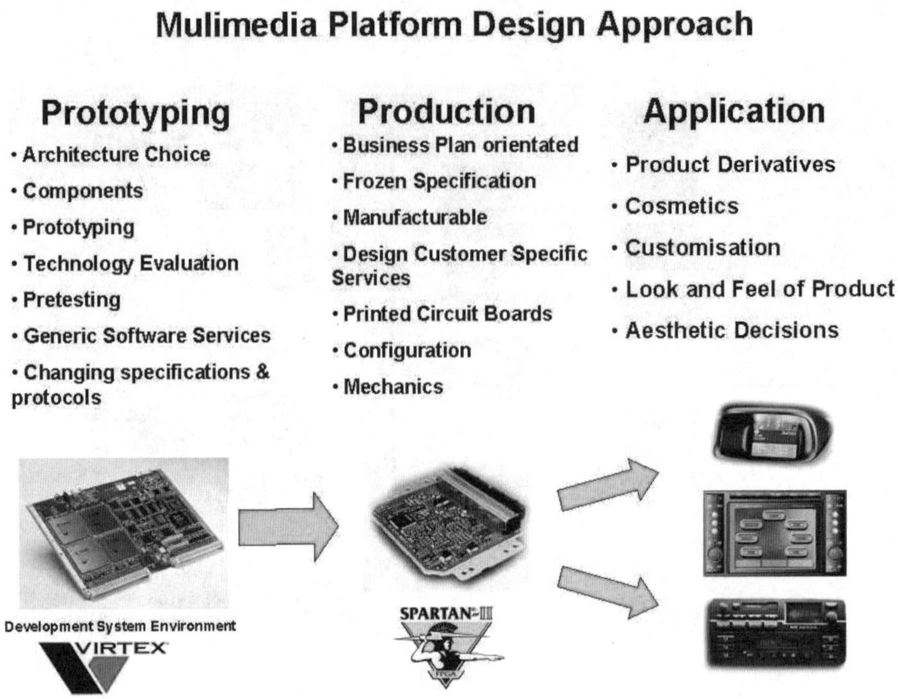

Figure 4 – The Muti-Media Platform Design Approach

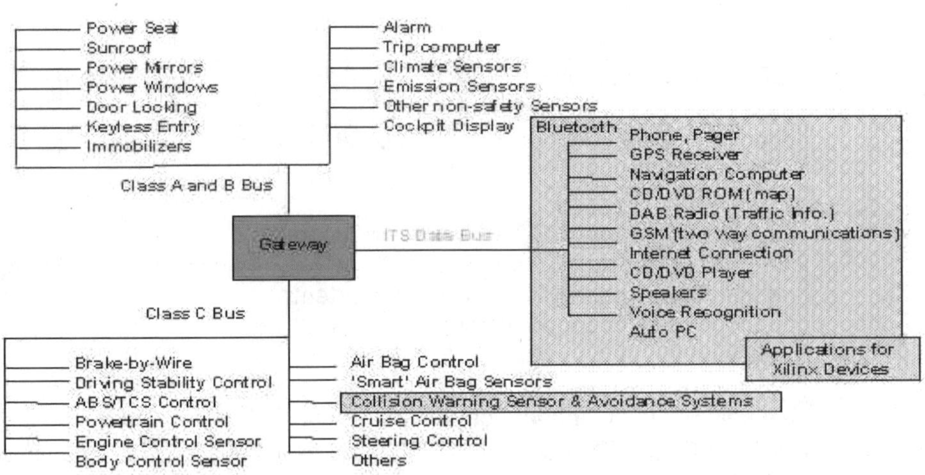

Figure 5 – Multimedia Data Bus

2001-01-0809

Mobile Multi Media Open Computing Platform

Phil Motz, Arch Wills, Jill Hersberger, Mike Laur
Delphi Delco Electronics Systems (DDES)

ABSTRACT

Under the brand name "Communiport," Delphi has been introducing many new products into the mobile multi media infotainment market. To date, each of these products have been uniquely designed with software tailored to the specific application. To meet the rapid time to market requirements, to develop the myriad of new products while keeping development resources to a minimum, to maximize reuse, and to establish an open architecture demanded by our customers, DDES is developing an open computing platform (OCP) for its next generation "Communiport" products. This paper describes the OCP, from both a hardware and software perspective; how we got there and where we are heading. Included for reference is an analysis of eleven systems from various customers.

The heart of the OCP is the Hitachi SH-4 computer and companion IC, the QSSL QNX Neutrino operating system, the Win CE operating system, and the Hewlett-Packard Chai Java Virtual Machine. Because the architecture is open, application programs from within DDES as well as third party vendors are accommodated.

INTRODUCTION

Mobile Multi Media (MMM) is advanced communication, information, and entertainment in vehicles. MMM leverages advancing technologies such as wireless communications, internet, PC and multimedia technology to enable features and functions for the driver and passengers including navigation, telematics, internet access, multiple video and audio sources, hands free cell phone use, with voice recognition and text-to-speech.

Under the brand name "Communiport" a broad product portfolio representing four distinct product lines is being developed. First, Smart Radios integrate radio and audio controls, navigation, cell phone access, e-mail and internet browser functions using large full color flat panel displays, voice recognition, and text-to-speech. Second, Advanced Audio includes satellite digital audio reception, MP3 playback, and digital audio broadcast, incorporating reconfigurable displays. Third, Telematics systems combine GPS functions with a cell phone to provide functions like GM's On-Star system. And fourth, Rear Seat Entertainment provides TV, DVD, and games on large screen displays with headsets. Figure 1 shows a "Communiport" product.

Figure 1 "Communiport" Smart Radio

Today, these products all have unique designs. Although the central computers and much of the application software may be common, the electrical designs, the circuit board layouts, and the software architectures including operating systems, are uniquely designed for minimal system cost and with little regard for reuse. Because all the product lines have similar requirements of the core computers (with varying memory needs) and have similar I/O needs, and because there is a great need for fast time to market with new systems, it was determined there was a need for a common, open computing platform.

OPEN COMPUTING PLATFORM HARDWARE

A request for quotation was sent out to the computer industry with the requirements listed in Table 1. The platforms evaluated included superscalar architectures, MIPS machines, RISC processors as well as traditional microcomputers. The Hitachi SH-4 was chosen along with a companion chip to be defined in conjunction with the selected supplier.

Software requirements	Hardware requirements
WinCE & Java compatibility	Microprocessor & Companion IC
POSIX compliant RTOS	200 – 500 MIPS
Navigation	Memory to 128MB SDRAM & 128MB Flash
Speech or Voice Processing	EMC compatibility
Video Processing	Algorithm processing capability
Vehicle Communications	Display capability (.25VGA to VGA+)
Busses	Computer generated graphics
Telematics	ATAPI for CDROM & DVD
	MPEG interface
	Power down modes
	I2C, I2S, RS232, IrDA, CAN, J1708, MML, PCMCIA, PCI, USB, AC97, SPI, & others

Table 1 OCP RFQ

By this time, a dozen system request for quotes had been received at DDES for various systems in the "Communiport" family of products. Eleven of these were tabulated (Appendix A) to understand the memory requirements, the I/O needs, and the application software. This data was then used to guide the development of the companion IC, the operating systems, and the application software. The companion IC was meant to cover the middle 80% of those system applications without overburdening the bottom end systems with cost or sacrificing performance of the high end systems.

{In parallel with this process, Hitachi was working with a tier one European supplier on a similar program. These two programs were combined to build one companion IC, and thereby positively affect the open nature of the computing platform.}

Figure 2 in a system block diagram of the OPC implemented with the companion IC now named Amanda. Amanda combines a graphics engine, various serial and parallel I/O ports, an interface to the SH-4 MPX bus, and a unified memory controller for SDRAM. The serial I/O content, two CAN channels, four I2S channels, two I2C channels, three UART channels, and one each IrDA, SPI, and SPDIF, were the direct result of the analysis of the contents of the eleven systems. The timers (input capture, output compare) and PWM outputs stemmed from the general need in automotive systems for timer functions, such as interfacing with GPS receivers and controlling display brightness. AC97, USB, ATAPI, and the parallel expansion port capable of interfacing to the MOST interface chip, were required for Auto PC compatibility. The digital panel display output is a direct 6-6-6 color output to a digital panel. The Video Input Processor is a direct interface to an MPEG decoder.

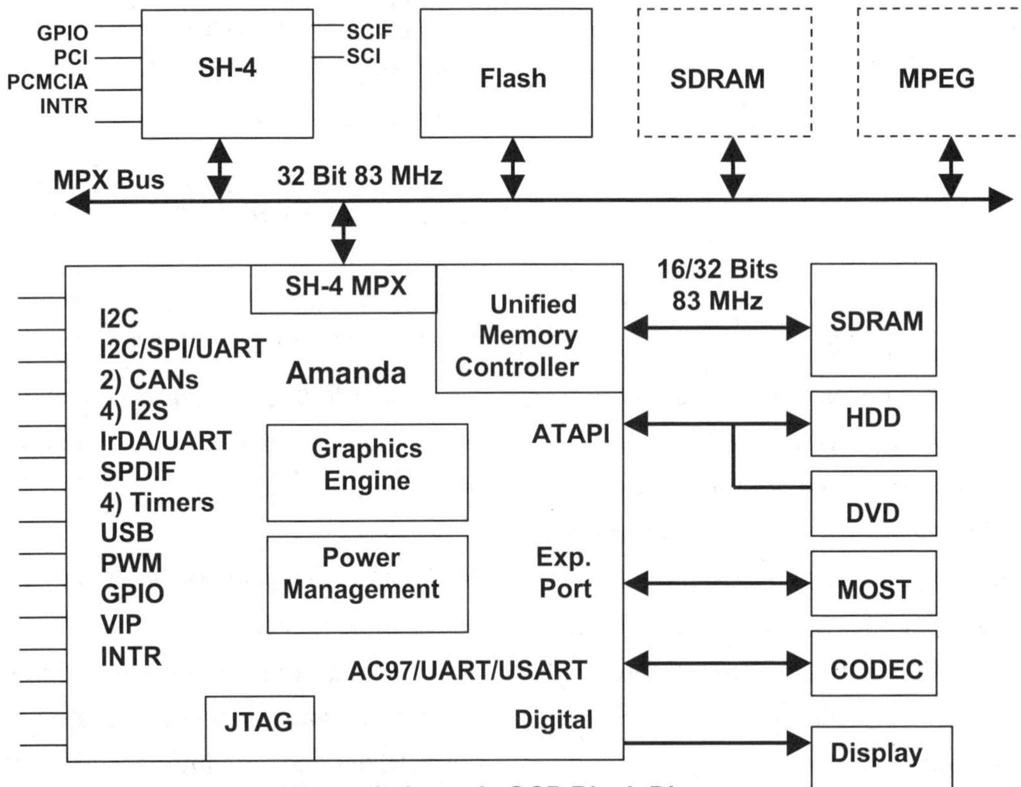

Figure 2 Amanda OCP Block Diagram

Figure 3 shows the internal architecture of Amanda. Note the two separate buses: the very high speed pixel bus, and the medium speed register bus. All data going to/from the graphics engine passes on the pixel bus. Data to/from the other I/O passes over the slower peripheral bus. FIFOs are sized to maximize unified memory bus bandwidth.

Each of the modules on Amanda can be powered on/off under software control. This allows for optimal power consumption and power dissipation, in standby as well as operational modes. For example, all the modules on Amanda, save one CAN interface, can be powered down. When a message comes in over CAN, the CPU (via an interrupt) and the appropriate Amanda modules (via software) can be energized for the correct system response.

The unified Memory Controller allows SDRAM to be attached to Amanda and be directly accessible by either the SH-4 via the MPX bus, or the internal DMA controller on Amanda. Additional SDRAM, optional based on system needs, plus the Flash memory, reside on the MPX bus. SDRAM on the Amanda unified memory bus will contain 1) SH-4 program memory downloaded from the Flash memory; 2) screen data for the digital panel; 3) scratchpad for the graphics engine; 4) data files from/to the various I/O channels. The SH-4 has an internal 8KB instruction cache and 16KB data cache. Amanda has a 32 byte write data cache between the MPX and unified memory buses plus additional FIFOs on all I/O channels. For smaller Integrated Navigation Radios, and medium sized telematics systems, only memory on the unified memory bus are envisioned. Only the very largest, up-scale systems, are

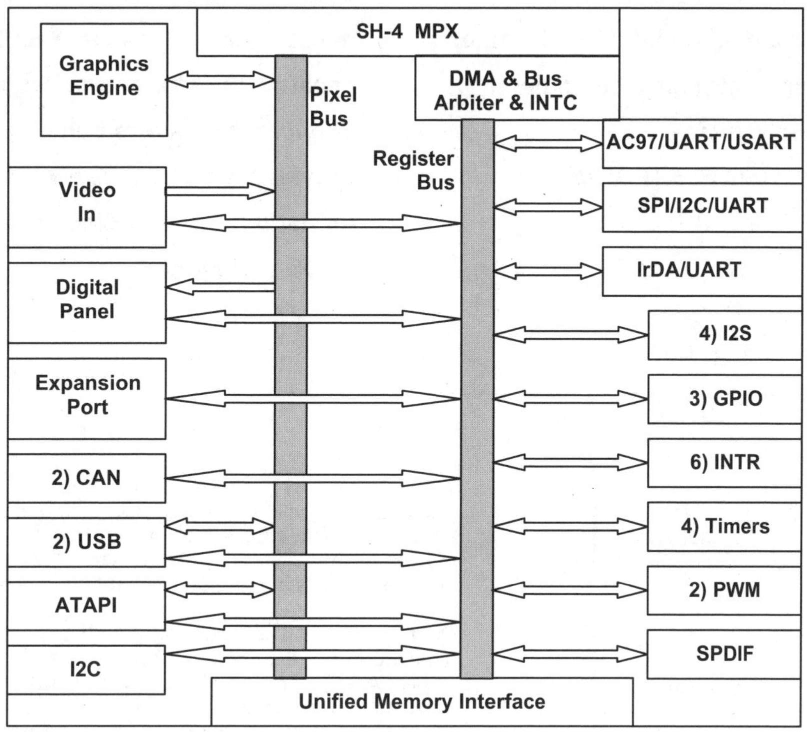

Figure 3 Amanda Internal Architecture

envisioned to require additional SDRAM on the MPX bus.

The main idea behind the common, open computing platform is for the SH-4, Amanda, SDRAM, Flash, and MPEG decoder to form an electrical block that is reused across the entire “Communiport” product line. The reuse module would actually be a circuit board or ceramic substrate layout with known EMC capability and a defined interface to other reuse modules controlling the actual interface to the vehicle.

OPEN COMPUTING PLATFORM MIDDLEWARE

OPERATING SYSTEMS

There are several "layers" for middleware (see Figure 4). The first layer is the operating system. It was decided that Delphi needed to be able to offer two types of solutions - one based on WinCE and one based on a hard Real-Time Operating System (RTOS). The selection process for the Real-Time Operating System began before the final selection of the microprocessor. This was possible because the characteristics of the class of microprocessors being considered provided sufficient hardware definition for early rounds of discussions with the RTOS suppliers.

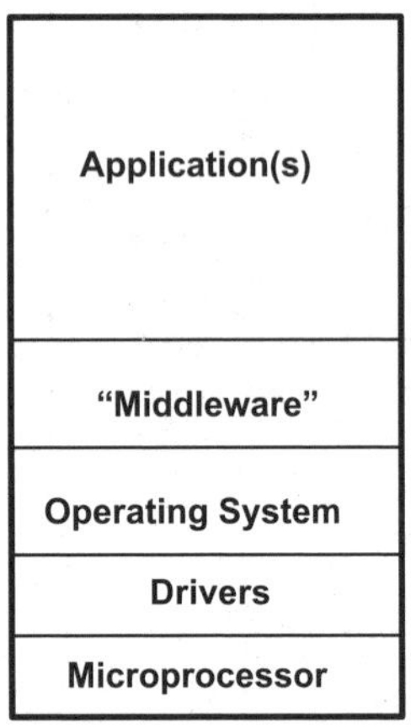

- The “classic stack” - a level of abstraction to isolate the application software from the hardware.
- The more abstract, the more reusable, but at a price.
- *“Middleware”* - all software between the application and the operating system.
- *“Operating System”* - a collection of useful services to organize and execute algorithms.
- *“Real Time Operating System”* - an operating system in an environment with time constraints.
- *“Drivers”* - All software that touches the hardware.

Figure 4 Stack Diagram

The key requirements for the RTOS are 1) POSIX conformance, 2) memory management and memory protection capability, 3) be modular, scalable and flexible, 4) must support a process model, i.e., must allow multiple processes, each with multiple threads, and 5) and be able to execute in place.

The POSIX requirement is very key to the overall design strategy of the Open Computing Platform. POSIX is the

Portable Operating System Interface - produced by the IEEE and standardized by ANSI and ISO. The goal of POSIX is the source-code portability of applications, i.e. to be able to move an application from one operating system to another by simply recompiling it. The overall design strategy of the Open Computing Platform is to have well-defined layers that are bounded by documented Application Programming Interfaces (APIs). This will allow a given layer to be modified, replaced, upgraded, etc. with little or no affect upon the adjacent layers and no affect at all to non-adjacent layers. (See stack diagram.)

The QNX Software Systems Ltd.'s QNX Neutrino RTOS has been selected to be the RTOS for the Open Computing Platform. QSSL's QNX® real-time platform will support Hitachi's SuperH microprocessor architecture, providing embedded application and network appliance designers a dynamically upgradable and fault-tolerant operating system. The QNX platform is targeted for network appliances, telecom equipment, and automotive multimedia applications, including in-vehicle email and navigation systems. The QNX platform can recover from software faults without having to reboot, since every driver, OS component, and application runs in its own memory-protected address space.

With Hitachi's SH-4 driving the QNX real-time platform, Delphi customers can be sure they are getting one of the most stable operating systems as the foundation for efficient, highly reliable products, with fast time-to-market. By combining Hitachi's leading embedded microprocessors with QNX's mission-critical OS technology, Delphi will have a highly scalable, dynamically configurable, and fault-tolerant real-time platform for their Mobile Multi Media Open Computing Platform.

JAVA VIRTUAL MACHINE

The Java Virtual Machine (JVM) was the next layer of the middleware to be selected. The key requirements for the Java Virtual Machine are:

1. The JVM shall be compatible with Sun Microsystem's JDK v1.1.7 or higher.
2. The JVM shall support remote software and thread debugging through the Java Virtual Machine Debug Interface (JVMDI) as specified by Sun Microsystems.
3. The JVM's garbage collector shall be incremental, pre-emptable and compacting.
4. The capability for dynamic class loading and verifying shall be configurable.
5. The JVM shall fully load, resolve and link a class upon instantiation.
6. The JVM thread support shall be mapped directly to the underlying operating system's thread support.
7. The JVM's execution of bytecodes shall be deterministic such that the execution time is either constant or the time can be calculable or predictable given a set of pre-conditions.

8. The JVM shall have a configurable heap manager that allows for an initial and maximum heap size.
9. The JVM shall employ a hardware abstraction layer in order to isolate microprocessor dependencies.
10. When hosted on a Posix RTOS, the JVM shall only use Posix compliant calls to access the RTOS services.
11. All non-Posix calls should optimally be isolated through an operating system abstraction layer such that the JVM and OS do not become tightly coupled.
12. When hosted on Microsoft WinCE, the preferred method of implementation is to isolate the JVM from the OS through an operating system abstraction layer that would be modeled after Posix compliant calls.

Hewlett-Packard's ChaiVM has been selected for the Java Virtual Machine. HP's ChaiVM provides a small-footprint, scalable environment for running Java applications on intelligent devices. ChaiVM offers superior Java application performance using HP's TurboChai compiler and the smallest memory footprint using HP's ChaiFreezeDry technology. ChaiVM will be available for both the WinCE and QNX Neutrino operating systems on the Hitachi SH-4 microprocessor.

Because of the minimal hardware support requirements for applications running on the HP ChaiVM, a huge variety of mobile communications and multimedia applications can now be supported cost-effectively in the automotive market. Examples of such applications include telematics systems that reach specialized call centers with cellular voice communications combined with data from global positioning satellite systems; rear-seat entertainment systems that access Web-based full-motion video and streaming audio applications; and advanced Web-based navigation systems that support voice-recognition and text-to-speech capabilities.

HP's ChaiFreezeDry technology delivers a compelling advantage to developers seeking to build appliances that can host Java applications with minimal memory resources. The technology is both a new format for representing Java class files more efficiently and a new class loader that transforms standard Java class files into the new format without removing any information from the files. By consolidating and running Java applications in a concentrated form, ChaiFreezeDry technology reduces the memory footprint required by an application by up to 50 percent.

The HP TurboChai ahead-of-time compiler also plays a critical role in providing the strong application performance advantage for the HP ChaiVM virtual machine, enabling up to a twenty-fold speed increase for Java applications. The compiler is designed to take advantage of all the powerful resources available on an application-development system to optimize code performance, while the TurboChai run-time environment is tightly integrated with the HP ChaiVM virtual machine to provide optimal performance. The result is Java execution performance that is close to applications written in C or C++.

SOFTWARE ARCHITECTURE / APPLICATION SOFTWARE

GENERAL

The software architecture and application concepts began before the selection of the actual operating system. This was appropriate because it was necessary to ensure that there would be portability between different operating systems. Not knowing which OS was to be used reinforced this requirement. POSIX compliance, which was an overall design strategy, dictated certain constraints that allowed the development of only a very thin layer of abstraction from the OS. If a Non-POSIX compliant OS were used, this layer would expand to accommodate the new requirements without affecting the layers above.

The architectural guidelines used to develop the system were efficiency, portability, modularity, reusability, and scalability. Modules within all layers would also need to accommodate a Java or C++ solution. These guidelines, being somewhat in conflict, were accommodated by coding guidelines and the choice of an efficient JVM.

The Advanced Engineering Java Group at Delphi Delco Electronics Systems has demonstrated that Java can be efficient from the driver level to the application level. Java is very important for accommodating the emerging strategies from several groups such as AMIC and OSGI. Java solutions are very seriously being examined as viable methods of enabling remote services. C++ enables code usability and the availability of open source software.

ARCHITECTURE

The basic software architecture, shown in Figure 5, is divided into multiple layers. From the bottom are the hardware, operating system, physical device drivers, model device drivers, managers, Interfaces, and application layers. Native or Java components can reside at any level.

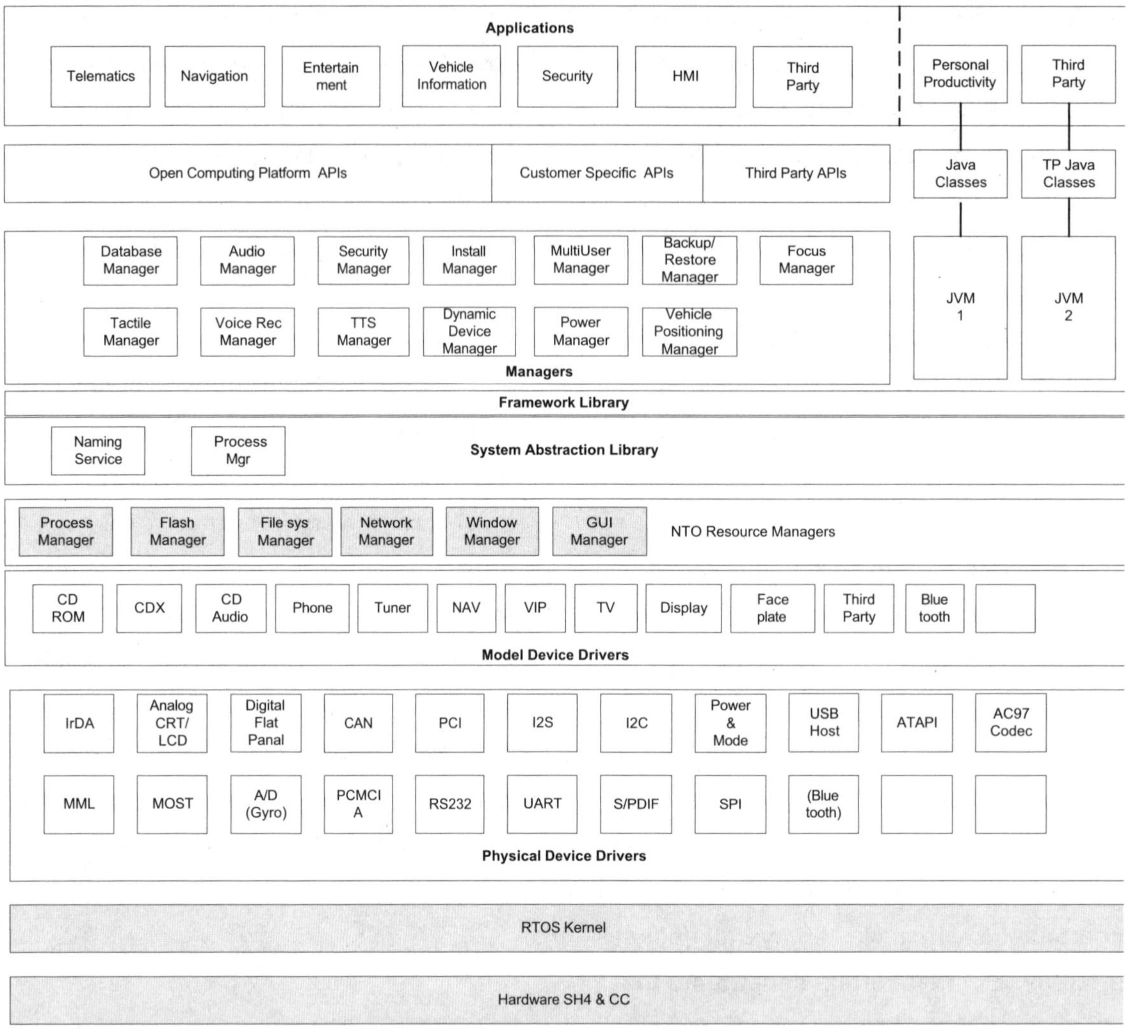

Figure 5 Software Architecture

SYSTEM ABSTRACTION / FRAMEWORK LAYER

This very thin system abstraction layer in combination with POSIX compliance abstracts the OCP software from the details of the operating system. It also encapsulates two manager components that need to be built as platform dependent QNX Neutrino Resource Managers. By encapsulating all platform dependence in a single layer, there is not the need to recode at the manager or application layer if the OS changes. This layer also allows for a faster migration to a non-POSIX compliant OS if ever required.

The resource managers that are encapsulated are the naming service and the process manager. The naming service allows an object in one process to advertise itself to other objects in the system or to find another object in another process. This is how an application process would identify a manager process. The process manager handles creation and lifetime management of processes.

The difference between the System Abstraction Layer (SAL) and the Framework layer is that the SAL wraps up simple system services while the Framework wraps up more complex system services such as client server communications.

DEVICE DRIVER LAYER

To provide for either distributed or local devices, the driver layer is divided into two sections as shown in Figure 6. Applications or managers requiring access to devices connect to the same model device driver independent of how the device is actually attached. For instance, in some systems the CD-ROM may be attached directly to the ATAPI interface of the Companion Chip. In other systems, the CD-ROM may be attached to the MOST bus. In this way, an application would always access the data at the same location without having to know how the device is actually attached to the system (See Table 2 for more examples).

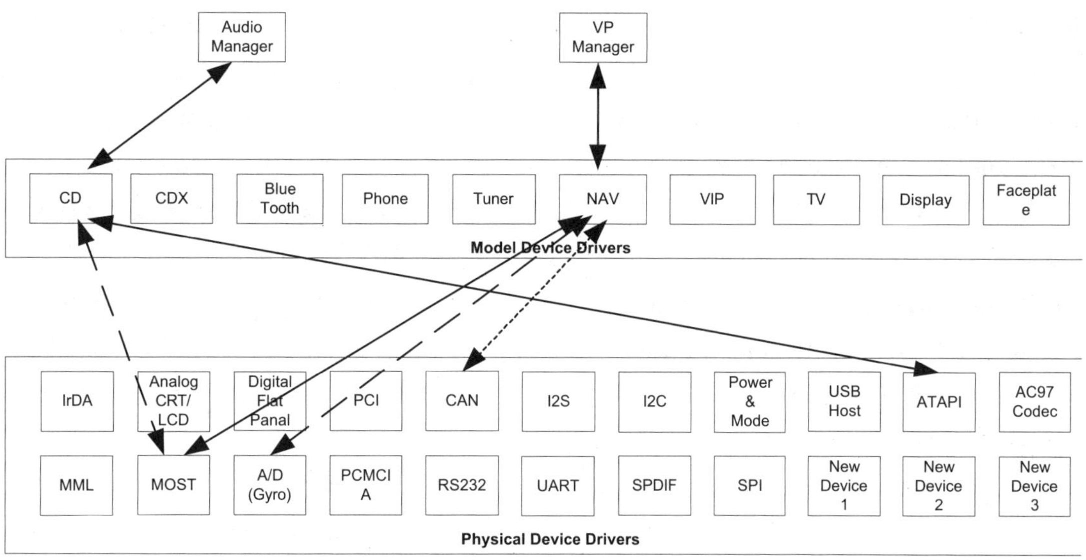

Figure 6 Driver Layer

	MOST MML 1394	IDE	USB	GPIO	Codec	I2C	I2S	SPI	SCI	CAN	Blue tooth	PCMCIA	UART
CD ROM	×	×											
CDX	×	×	×										
Bluetooth			×	×				×					×
Phone	×		×		×						×		×
Tuner	×					×	×						
NAV	×									×			
Vehicle Gateway	×		×					×					×
TV	×												
Faceplate	×					×				×			×
A/D								×	×				
3rd Party	×		×								×	×	

Table 2 Device vs. Device Driver Potentials

MANAGER LAYER

The manager layer can be considered to be the application enabling modules within the architecture. They either provide services or they provide interfaces to services that are available to all applications. As an example see Figure 7. In this example, an application registers its grammars at startup with the speech manager. The speech manager then uses rules and communications to the focus manager to determine which grammars are active and which applications are delivered the recognition results. The speech manager provides an interface to the L&H ASR 1600 recognition engine. Applications only see a generic interface between the application and the speech manager. The speech manager maintains the L&H specific interface between the manager and the ASR 1600 engine. This allows for the replacement of the recognition engine to only affect the manager layer and not the application layer.

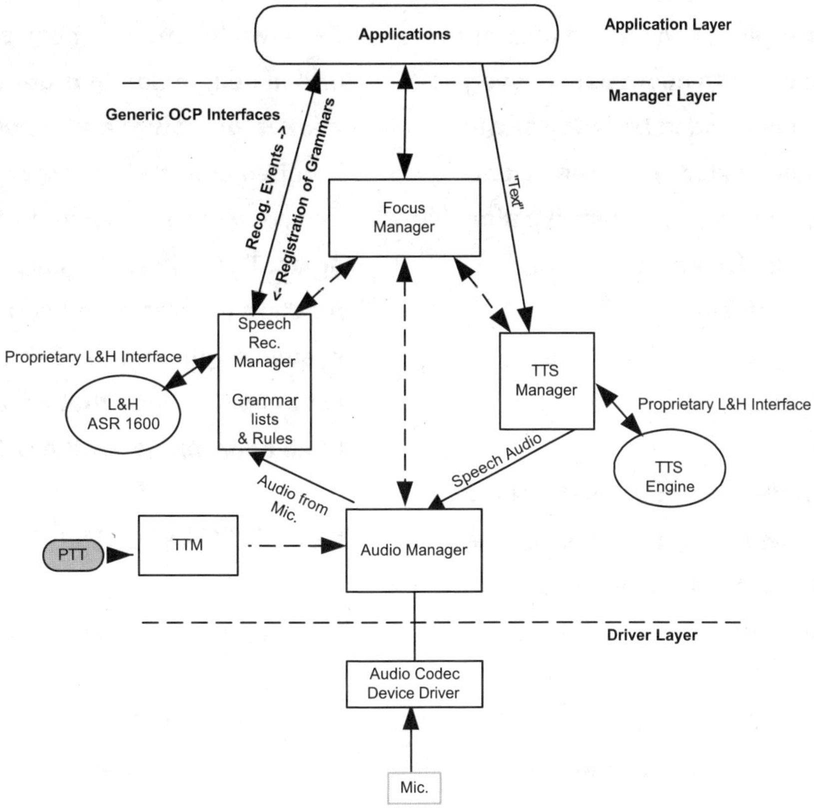

Figure 7 Manager Layer

INTERFACE LAYER

Applications have access to managers through well-defined but not closely coupled interfaces. The method of establishing a communications channel is performed by a base class which all applications and managers derive from. The base class independently maintains communications to system components for common functions such as stay – alive. Extensions to the base class allow the managers and applications to expose interfaces required for the their specific functionality.

The base class communication mechanism utilizes the Observer Pattern. For instance, an application and manager make up an observer / subject pair. The manager or subject may have any number of dependent observers or applications. The application is notified whenever the manager undergoes a change in state. In response, each application will synchronize its state with the manager's state.

This method says nothing about the type of communication that is used to maintain the channel. That is a function of the requirements. High bandwidth requirements might use shared memory while low bandwidth might use message queues. That is decided by the user when the channel is created. The Framework implements a variety of communications mechanisms to accommodate application requirements.

APPLICATION LAYER

The Application Layer follows the Model Controller View design (MCV). Customer independent components are in the Model while customer dependent components are in the View. This division allows for maximum reusability and minimum time for adaptation of different Human Machine Interface (HMI) requirements. The design allows for single as well as multiple View Architectures. The single View approach utilizes a Browser that all applications use for displaying their HMI components. The multiple View approach requires applications that implement specific Views. These specific Views can be developed as Java or native components.

Application requirements typically come from two locations. Those are marketing and the customer. In order to survey the market for feature and function requirements a study was made involving substantial input from both areas. The generated feature and function list was then used to determine system requirements. Table 3 shows a list of applications that were determined to be appropriate for the OCP.

MEMORY MANAGEMENT

Neutrino will use the Memory Management Unit (MMU) of the Hitachi SH4 Processor. This protects process address spaces from each other, preventing coding errors in a thread on one process from damaging memory used by threads in other processes or even in the OS. While the thread executes, it uses memory addresses much as it would in a non-MMU system, except that the page tables managed by the OS control how these addresses are "mapped" onto the physical memory attached to the processor.

Application	Make/Buy	Description
Navigation	Make	Navigation Application utilizing Navigation Technology Navtools and SDAL. Route guidance, geocoding, map display, vehicle positioning, route calculation, and dynamic services.
Web Browser	Buy	Java Browser
Address Book	Make/Buy	Java component in sourcing stage.
Agenda	Buy	Java component in sourcing stage.
Message	Make/Buy	Java component in sourcing stage.
Voice Memo	Make/Buy	Java component in sourcing stage.
Phone	Make/Buy	Java component in sourcing stage.
Office Viewer	Buy	Plug into Java Browser in sourcing stage.
Database	Buy	Native component in sourcing stage.
Speech Recognition	Buy	Native Recognition engine. ASR 1600 from L&H
Text to Speech	Buy	Native text to speech engine from L&H.
Text Input	Make	Java front end. T9 like backend is a buy.
T9 like Algorithm	Buy	Native component in sourcing stage.
Audio Toolkit	Buy	MP3, PCM, CODEC
Manager Components	Make	All manager level components. These are the application enablers.
Interface Components	Make	Complex system service wrappers.
Abstraction Layer	Make	Simple system service wrappers.
Palm Synchronize	Make	Native
JVM	Buy	HP Chai
Operating System	Buy	QNX Neutrino
Audio Driver	Buy	ALSA driver with extensions ported to NTO.
Vehicle Information	Make	Alarm, logbook, compass, preferences, trip computer.
Security	Make/Buy	Encryption (Buy), User authentication, Theft alert, Smart card.
Entertainment	Make	DVD, Mini disc, DAB, Games, TV, Radio, CD

Table 3 Applications List

Memory partitioning of a typical system is shown in Figure 8. It is made up of compressed, non-compressed and non-compressed file system regions. The Initial Program Load (IPL) is located in a non-compressed memory save area that can not be accessed by applications. Image 1 comprises compressed core components that are not subject to modification unless of an error condition. Image 1 components are Operating System, Graphics Subsystem, and OCP Managers. Image 2 is an alternate compressed image that is called when new system components are to be loaded into memory. The section under Image 2 shows an area of memory that can be loaded with new components without having to reload an entirely new core component Image. These components can be compressed or non-compressed. The uncompressed flash file system on the bottom is used for dynamic data that is produced and destroyed during runtime. This would include data such as customer preferences, error information, and navigation routes. Components which need to be executed out of flash need to be stored as non-compressed images.

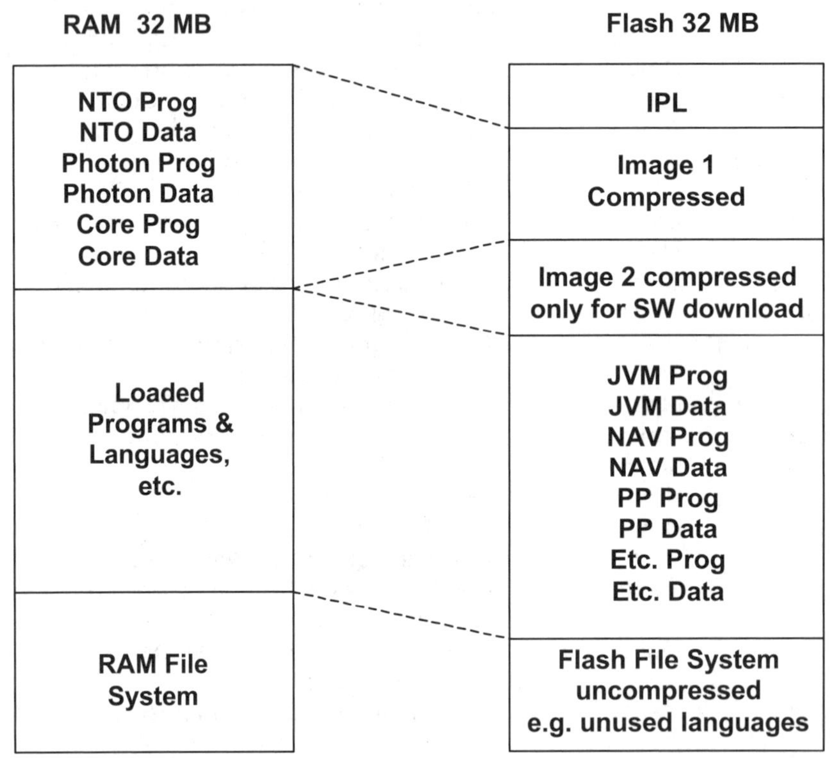

Figure 8 Memory Partitioning

CONCLUSION

The Mobile Multi Media Open Computing Platform is being designed as an open system architecture, utilizing an industry standard hardware platform, standard operating systems and a Java Virtual Machine. Applications software is being developed by the best source available, be that internal to Delphi or from the external software industry. Considering the dynamics of the computer industry, a roadmap to a higher performance platform is already under development using the SH-5 and a second generation companion chip.

CONTACTS

Arch Wills arch.c.wills@delphiauto.com

Technical Fellow

Program Manager, Open Computing Platform

Delphi Delco Electronics Systems, Kokomo, IN

Phil Motz phillip.r.motz@delphiauto.com

Technical Fellow

Open Computing Platform, Lead Systems Engineer

DDES, Kokomo, IN

Jill Hersberger jill.g.hersberger@delphiauto.com

Staff Development Engineer

Open Computing Platform, RTOS & JVM Development

DDES, Kokomo, IN

Mike Laur michael.h.laur@delphiauto.com

Staff Development Engineer

Open Computing Platform, Software Architecture & Applications Development

DDES, MMM Design Center, Bad Salzdetfurth, Germany

Appendix A

					MMM Systems						
Data	**A**	**B**	**C**	**D**	**E**	**F**	**G**	**H**	**I**	**J**	**K**
Software Environment											
OS	WinCE	WinCE	RTOS	WinCE	WinCE	RTOS	WinCE	RTOS	RTOS	WinCE	WinCE
JVM		No	Yes	TBD	Yes	No	No	No	No	Yes	Yes??
Applications											
1. Telematics											
Phone	Yes	Yes	Yes		Yes	No	Yes	No	Yes	Yes	Yes
Telematics Services		No	Yes							Yes	Yes
Theft protection		Yes	Yes			Yes	Yes	Yes			
Breakdown Service		No	Yes								
Mayday Package		No	Yes					No		Yes	Yes
Bluetooth		No	Yes			No		No		Yes	Yes
2. Navigation	Yes	Yes	Yes	Yes	Yes	Yes	Yes	Yes	Yes	Yes	Yes
3. Entertainment											
Audio Disc	CD	CD	Yes		DVD	CD	CD	DVD	CD	CD	CD
CDX Control	Yes	Yes	Yes			Yes	Yes	Yes		Yes	Yes
DAB		No	Yes			Yes	Yes	Yes	No		
DVD Video		No	Yes		Yes	No	No	Yes	No		Yes
TV		No	Yes		Yes	Yes	No	Yes	No		Yes
Radio	Yes	Yes	Yes		Yes	Yes	Yes	Yes	Yes	Yes	Yes
MP3 audio		No	??		Yes	No	maybe	No		Yes	Yes
Rear Seat Entertainment		No	Yes			Audio	Audio	Audio			Yes??
RDS		Yes			Yes	Yes	Yes	Yes	Yes		
4. Personal Productivity											
Address Book	Yes	Yes	Yes	Yes	Yes	Yes	Yes	Yes	Yes		
PDA			??			Yes		Yes			
Browser/WWW		No	Yes	Yes	Yes	Yes	Yes	Yes	Yes		
Messages		Yes	Yes			Yes	Yes	Yes	Yes		
Voice Memo Record		Yes	Yes			Yes	Yes	Yes	No	Yes	Yes
Traffice Info Record		Yes	Yes			Yes	No	Yes	No	Yes	Yes
Office --applications such as or similar to MSOffice		No	Yes	TBD	No	No		No			
File Manager			Yes	Yes	No	No		No			
Agenda --similar to calendar		No	Yes	TBD	No	No		No			
Fax		No	Yes	No	No	No		No			
Personal Profile		No	Yes	Yes	Yes	No		No			
5. HMI											
Speech		Yes	Yes			Yes					
Voice recognition	Yes	AutoPC	Yes	Yes	Yes	Yes	AutoPC	Yes	No		Yes
Nav voice	Yes	AutoPC	Yes	Yes		Yes	AutoPC	Yes	Yes		Yes?
Text to speech	Yes	AutoPC	Yes	Yes	Yes	Yes	AutoPC	Yes	No		Yes?
Digitized speech		Yes	Yes								
Local Display Manager		Yes	Yes			Yes	Yes	Yes	Yes		
Root Application Process		Yes	Yes			Yes	Yes	Yes	Yes		
GUI		Yes	Yes	Yes	Yes	Yes					
Device control --s/w for control of volume, CD, comms -- local/global		Yes	Yes	Yes	Yes	Yes					
Sound	Yes	Yes	Yes	Yes	Yes	Yes	Yes	Yes	Yes	Yes	Yes
6. Vehicle Information											
Vehicle Info		No	Yes			Yes	Yes	Yes	No		
Service		No	Yes			Yes	Yes	Yes	No		
Feature Programming		No	??			Yes	Yes	Yes	No		
Compass		Yes	Yes			Yes		Yes			
Trip Computer		Yes	Yes			Yes	Yes	Yes			
Customer Settings		Yes	Yes			Yes	Yes	Yes			
Logbook		No	??			No		No			
7. Security											
User authentication		No	Yes					No			
Encryption		No	Yes					No			
Smart Card		No	Yes			No		No			
8. Third Party											
Application interface		undecided	Yes	Yes		No	Yes??	No	No		
Application device		undecided	Yes	Yes		Yes	Yes??	Yes	Yes		
SDK		undecided	Yes	Yes			Yes??				

Hardware Requirements											
1. Data Busses											
IDB-C		No	No		Yes	Yes	Yes	Yes	Yes?		
CAN1		No	Yes	No	No			No		Yes	Yes
CAN2		No	Yes	No	No	No	No	No	No		
Class 2	Yes	Yes	No		Yes	Yes	Yes	Yes	Yes		
E&C	Yes	Yes	No			No	No	No	Yes		
VICS Class 2		No	TBD			No	No	Yes	No		
PCI	Yes	Yes	No	Yes	Yes		Yes	No			
Local Bus	Yes	Yes	Yes	Yes	Yes	Yes	Yes	Yes	Yes		
I2C	Yes	Yes	Yes	No	Yes	Yes	Yes	Yes	Yes		
I2S1	Yes	No	Yes	Yes	Yes	No	No	No	No		
I2S2 / SPDIF		No	Yes	not used	?	No	No	No	No		
MOST		No	Yes			No		No			
Parallel		No	Yes	No	??	No	No	No	No		
UART1	Yes	Yes	Yes	Yes	IrDA	Yes	Yes	Yes	Yes	Yes	Yes
UART2	Yes	Yes	Yes	Yes	Yes	Yes	Yes	Yes	No		
UART3		Yes	No	Yes	No	No	Yes	No	No		
USB1	Yes	AutoPC	No	Yes	Bluetooth	No	AutoPC	No	No		
USB2	Recommended	No	No	Yes	AutoPC?	No	?	No	No		
J1587/J1708 (similar to Class 2)		No	No	Yes		No		No			
J1939 (similar to CAN)		No	No	Yes		No		No			
High Speed Bus		No	MOST	115k bps serial b	IDB-C	No	No	No	No		
2. Interfaces											
ATAPI	Yes	Yes	Remote	PCI-IDE Controller	PCI-IDE Controller	Yes	Yes	Yes	Yes		
Bluetooth		No	No		Yes	No		No			
IrDA	Yes	AutoPC	No	Yes	Yes	Yes	AutoPC	Yes	Yes		
PCMCIA	Yes	Yes	No	Yes	Yes	No	Yes	No	No		
RS-232	Yes	Yes	No			Yes	Yes	Yes	Yes		
MOST I/F		No	Yes	No	No	No		No			
VSS		Yes	No			Yes	Yes	Yes	Yes		
3. Audio											
CODEC	Yes	Yes	No	Yes	No	Yes	Yes	Yes		Yes	Yes
CarDSP (CASP)		Yes	No		Yes						
Mic input A/D	Yes	Yes	No		Yes	Yes	Yes	Yes		Yes	Yes
Audio Amplifier		Yes	No		Yes	Yes	Yes	Yes		Yes	Yes
4. Memory											
Memory - SDRAM total avail	Yes	16MB	32MB	32MB	32MB +2MB video	512K	32MB	512K		??	??
Memory - Flash total avail	Yes	12MB	32MB	16MB	32MB	16MB	16MB	16MB			
Memory - DRAM or SRAM (other than on Local bus)	Yes	Yes - xMB		Yes - xMB		16MB	Yes - xMB	16MB	Yes - xMB		
5. Timers											
Timer1		No	TBD	TBD	?	?	?	?	Yes		
Timer2		No	TBD	TBD	?	?	?	?	Yes		
Timer3		No	TBD	TBD	?	?	?	?	Yes		
6. Video											
MPEG decoder		No	Yes??	No	Yes??	No	No	DVD	No	Yes	Yes
AC3 support		No	Yes	TBD	No			DVD			
CSS support		No	Yes	TBD	??						
OSD support		No	Yes	TBD	No			DVD			
Display support		No	Yes	TBD	Yes						
NTSC/PAL/SECAM baseband input		No	No			Yes		TV			
MPEG decoder input port		No	Yes??	No	Yes			No			
A/V Link		No	Yes		??			No			
Video I/F processor		No	Yes	No	??	No	No	No	No		
7. Devices											
CDROM	Yes	AutoPC	Remote	Yes	No	Yes	AutoPC	No	Yes	Yes	Yes
DVD		No	Remote		Yes	No	No	Yes	No		Yes
DVD ROM		No	Remote		Yes	No	No	Yes	No		
Hard drive		No	No		4GB, IDE	No		No			
Display	Yes	Yes	Yes	Yes	Yes	Yes	Yes	Yes	Yes	Yes	Touch screen
technology		AMLCD	AMLCD	Electroluminesce	AMLCD	AMLCD	AMLCD	AMLCD	AMLCD	Dot matrix	AMLCD
size		5.8"	5.8"	24mmx96mm	5.8"	7.0"	7.0"	7.0"	5.8"		5.8" or 7"
pixels	256x64	400x234	400x234	320x80	400x234	480x234	480x234	480x234	400x234	256x64	256x64??
GPS	Yes	VIB	Remote	Yes	??	Yes	Yes	Yes	Yes	Yes	Yes
Modem		AutoPC	Remote			No	AutoPC	No	No		
Dimming PWM		Yes	Yes			Yes	Yes	Yes	Yes		
Gyro (A/D)		Yes	Remote			Yes	Yes	Yes	Yes		Yes
Battery (backup, KAM, etc.)	Yes	Yes		Yes			Yes				

PART III
ENABLING TECHNOLOGIES

SOFTWARE

2007-01-1778

Development of Telematics Software Platform using WIPI for Service-based Applications

Young Woo Choi and Nam Kwon Jung
Hyundai Motors R&D Center

Jun Seok Choi
KTF Corporation

Kyong Won Moon
Geotel Corporation

ABSTRACT

Telematics is about delivering electronic services to "connected" devices. This includes more than showing web content in a browser: It should be able to download and upgrade new services in a wireless environment. To this end, auto makers have applied an "open architecture software platform" in a car so that hopefully fast-moving software can be supplied to customers and a new business model can be created after a car release.

WIPI (Wireless Internet Platform for Interoperability) is a set of standard specifications for the mobile platform made by the Mobile Platform Special Subcommittee of the Korea Wireless Internet Standardization Forum (KWISF). These are standardized for providing an environment for mounting and implementing application programs downloaded via the wireless Internet on the mobile communication terminal. These features make it possible for WIPI to be a solution for the telematics software platform. WIPI has already been adapted to more than 14 million handset devices in Korea (as of June 2006) and has verified the stability of the front/back-end system.

This paper reports on the development of a telematics software platform currently being pursued as a collaboration between Hyundai Motor Company and KTF (Korean Telecommunication Company) that has commercialized WIPI in the hand-set environment. As a result, WIPI was adopted as a telematics software platform for the device developed by HMC. In this paper, the features for an open architecture software platform like downloadability, upgradeability, interoperability, security were also verified.

INTRODUCTION

There have been some evolving issues in telematics software. The first is the lifecycle issue. The conflict between the lifecycles of vehicles and their telematics software is a constant headache to the automotive industry [1], because the lifecycle of software is generally shorter than the lifecycle of cars. To resolve this issue, new telematics software should be able to be added and upgraded into a car during the lifecycle of a car. The second is the interoperability issue. If the software applications are not interoperable, the automaker should develop and test those software applications that have the same features every time when a new car is released. This issue creates the huge cost of developing software applications.

Therefore, automakers have adapted an open architecture software platform in a car [2]. The following lists the objectives to be attained by using the telematics software platform [3].

- Providing an up-to-date software application
- Software development cost reduction
- Adding a new business model after car release
- Improving customer satisfaction

To meet the above objectives, the telematics software platform should be designed with the following requirements:

<u>Downloadability</u>

The software platform should be able to download a new software application in a wireless environment.

Upgradeability

The software platform should be able to replace the existing software with the new one.

Expandability

In order to perform a new application program that is downloaded, the software platform should be able to expand its functionalities by adding and managing the APIs.

Interoperability

The software platform should be able to use the application programs that are provided by software developers regardless of its device model.

Backward compatibility

The upgraded software platform should be able to operate application programs that are developed for the previous versions of the platform

Security

The software platform should support a mechanism to prevent a malicious attack for the purpose of modifying, degrading, corrupting or otherwise intentionally disrupting normal operation by the owner.

Modularity

The software platform should be able to have standardized interfaces so they can be modified, upgraded or replaced without requiring a change to the other elements in the system

The OSGi-based platform is widely used by automakers [4] because it satisfies the above requirements. However, its weak point is in execution speed like other Java-based platforms: the telematics user requires the execution speed to be faster than PC-based environment.

WIPI's strong points are security like Java-based platforms and fast execution speed like C-based native platforms. Furthermore, as of June 2006, more than 14 million handset devices have adapted this platform and more than 2000 application programs have been developed for the Korean market [5] so that its stability has already been verified. Therefore, little additional investment is needed to build and test the back-end system. This means that telematics service providers are able to provide services by modifying the existing system and application programs.

This paper discusses the application of the WIPI platform in a telematics device. At first, the paper describes the conceptual structure and key functional specifications of a WIPI platform. After that, the paper deals with the strong points of a WIPI platform compared with a Java-based platform – how to guarantee platform security and how to improve the application program execution speed. Finally, the paper presents the implementation of a WIPI platform in a telematics device and verifies whether the proposed platform satisfies the features of the telematics software platform.

MAIN SECTION

CONCEPTUAL STRUCTURE OF A WIPI PLATFORM

Figure 1 shows the conceptual structure of a WIPI platform. [6]

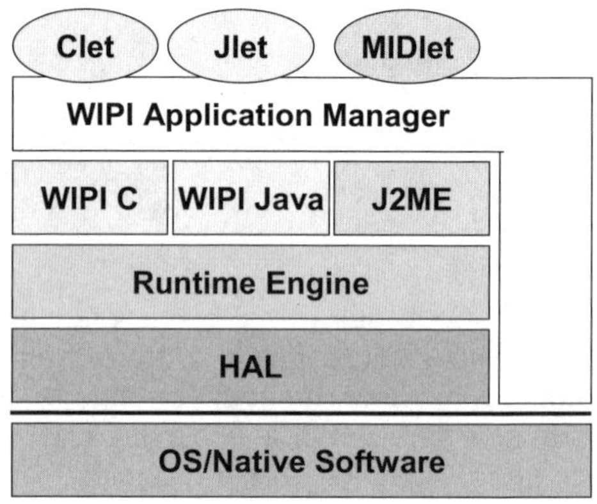

Figure 1. Conceptual WIPI structure

The lowest layer consists of hardware, OS and native software such as device drivers. This layer depends on the device manufacturer.

HAL (Hardware Adaptation Layer) is a layer used to support hardware independence in platform porting. Through this layer, abstraction for the device is performed. This means that the platform is configured independently from the hardware. HAL provides high portability for the above layers such as the Run-time Engine, WIPI-C, WIPI-Java and WIPI application programs. HAL hides the complex operation of the underlying hardware devices and simplifies the access and control of them.

Run-time Engine provides the execution environment for WIPI application programs like Java Virtual Machine (JVM). The main difference is that JVM loads and executes Java class files, while the WIPI engine takes and executes platform-specific machine code. Run-time Engine consists of a linker/loader, a memory manager, a garbage collector, a thread manager, a synchronization manager and a run-time library for supporting the converted code. An event handler and an exception handler are also needed for preserving the semantics of the Java language.

The API Layer provides both C libraries and Java libraries for developing application programs like Clet,

Jlet, or MIDlet. Clet is a program written in WIPI-C and Jlet is written in WIPI-Java. the WIPI also provides compatibility with MIDlet. MIDlet is a small application program written in CLDC/MIDP of the J2ME platform.

Each WIPI application program has an event handler and life cycles such as start, pause, destroy and resume. The WIPI application manager (WAM) installs, deletes, lists, or searches applications.

KEY FUNCTIONAL SPECIFICATIONS OF WIPI

Supported Programming Languages

The platform supports both the C and Java language. The C language is useful for those application programs that need high performance, like multimedia applications. However, in most cases, the developers use Java for applications development because of easy usage and high security features. In this paper, therefore, a WIPI application program means the application program implemented by WIPI-Java.

Specifications for the Binary Code of Applications

The platform should download and execute binary code of WIPI application programs. The C-based application programs are compiled by the developers as a type of binary code. However, for a Java application program, the binary code is created from Java byte code through AOTC (Ahead of Time Compiler). More details will be explained in the subsection: Improving the application program execution speed.

Executing Multiple Application Programs

The platform supports an environment where several application programs can be loaded to memory for concurrent execution. When several application programs are running concurrently, each application program should be executed independently. A method of transmitting shared memory and events should be provided to support communication among independent application programs. In addition, the platform should be able to manage the life cycle of an application program written in a programming language supported by the platform

Managing the Application Program

The startup of an application program should be determined based on the setup of limitations on the date and number of executions of application programs. Install and Uninstall functions of the application program should also be provided. Likewise, the Suspend function of an application program may be offered. The Suspend function deletes only the execution program, thus leaving the corresponding data files intact. Existing data can be utilized when the program is installed again. In addition, the platform should enable the Add/Override API function and the forced termination function of an application program.

The platform should support the downloading of application programs. In case of error during the download, the application program should be restored to its default state.

Managing Memory

The platform has restricted memory size and supports the execution of multiple application programs. Therefore, effective management of memory is required. The memory that allocated to the application programs is managed as follows.

- Automatic Release of Memory
- Memory Compaction
- Java Garbage Collection
- Java Stack
- Support for Shared Memory

For more information about memory management, refer to the WIPI memory management specifications [6].

Support for Adding/Overriding the API

The platform can add/override APIs via the wireless network, and Add/Override is carried out using DLLs. DLL is a method by which the platform adds new APIs and overrides the existing APIs. A DLL can be divided into implementation and interface. To manage the outcome of the DLL implementation, the platform should possess version management and Install/Delete functions required for adding and overriding APIs. The DLL user (application developer) can use the specific DLL functions (libraries) of DLL through the interface. The platform should equally apply the API security level policy to added or overridden APIs (See more details about security in the subsection: Platform Security). The DLL/Interface can either be installed as a basic embedded item in the device or downloaded according to the specification of an application manager or the user.

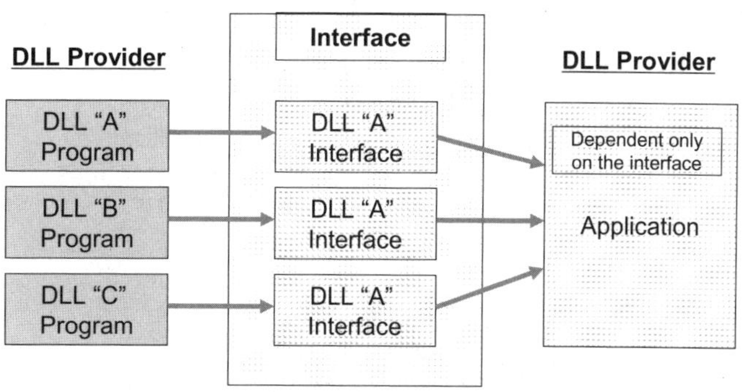

Figure 2. DLL service and use scenarios

PLATFORM SECURITY

Platform security means a policy and related technology against the actions of an application program when it affects the operation of other entities such as other application programs, platforms where these application programs operate, devices where such platforms are mounted, and the network/server system with which those devices are interlinked [7]. The platform should be able to control the access of these entities to platform resources in accordance with the security specifications.

Security Level

Basically, platform security techniques should be based on the access right to the platform through the security level defined for each resource and on information on the security level of each application program. In WIPI, there are three security levels – **Public**, **CP** and **System**.

Among the security levels existing on the platform, **Public** denotes the least reliable level or one with the most restrictions. When an application program of this level is executed, the platform should not allow access since it may cause security problems such as those affecting the system or allowing access to personal information.

At the **CP** level, some or all restrictions placed on resources at the **Public** level are removed, because the platform trusts the application program either fully or to some extent.

At the **System** level, which is a subset of the **CP** security level, access to all resources is automatically allowed, because the platform regards the application program as completely trustworthy

API Security

The platform categorizes the APIs as the security groups to control API access.

- NO ACCESS : Access is not allowed
- READ ONLY : Only READ access is allowed
- WRITE ONLY : Only WRITE access is allowed
- READ/WRITE : Both READ and WRITE access are allowed

Access Right to Resources by Security Level

There should be a table that defines the access right to the resources of the platform by security level. Likewise, the security level should be specified according to the application program. Table 1, showing the access right to resources by security level, can be located either in the device platform or in the server hosting the application program.

	Graphic	Sound	Personal Info	System Property
Public	Allowed	Allowed	Not allowed	Not Allowed
CP	Allowed	Allowed	Requires user permission	Not Allowed
System	Allowed	Allowed	Allowed	Allowed

Table 1. Access right to resources by security level

IMPROVING THE APPLICATION EXECUTION SPEED

Despite a lot of advantages of a Java-based platform, sometimes the execution speed does not satisfy the customer's needs for an embedded system. Fast execution speed is especially important in a car environment. A WIPI platform uses AOTC to resolve this problem.

HOW TO COMPILE THE WIPI CODE

WIPI has adapted an AOTC (Ahead of Time Compiler) for compiling WIPI-Java application programs, while a Java-based platform generally uses a just-in-time (JIT) compiler that turns Java bytecode into binary code. After writing a Java program, the source language statements are compiled by the Java compiler into bytecode rather than into binary code. The AOTC compiles bytecode into binary code before program execution. This makes heavy optimizations possible compared with a JIT compiler so that it can improve the program execution speed. Figure 3 shows how to make binary code in a WIPI platform.

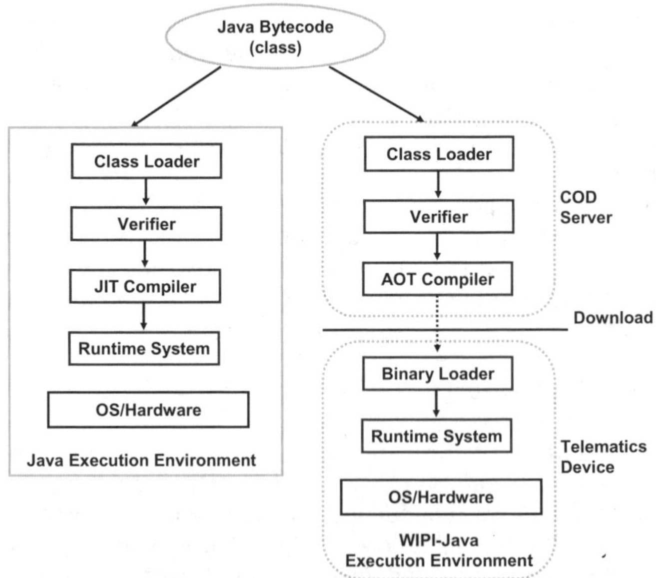

Figure 3. WIPI-Java Compiler

WIPI-COD

A Java-based software platform like OSGi, as mentioned above, executes bytecode using the VM (virtual machine) which needs more resources than a native based platform. Therefore, Using a Java-based software platform causes the slow execution speed especially in the embedded computing environment like a telematics device which the CPU and memory resources are limited. However, a VM-based platform has a strong point in system stability and security.

A Native binary based platform, on the other hand, support high executing power without interpreting bytecode. Programming languages for developing native binary applications are C or C++. However, a malicious developer can access the memory, and this is a risk factor for system stability.

A WIPI platform has mixed the strong points of these two controversial platforms. In other words, the execution performance is almost equal to the native-based platform, while the system stability and security satisfy the level of a Java-based platform. This is possible by using a COD (Compile On Demand) server that interprets bytecode into binary code remotely (in a server environment).

COD

COD is a framework including AOTC technology. When a user wants to download an application program, COD compiles the WIPI-Java bytecode to binary code and sends the code to the device.

Security Issue with Binary Java

Java is called an 'internet language'. This means that Java guarantees security and system stability by verifying the code before running [7]. However, since code written in C/C++ cannot be verified before running, malicious developers are able to attack the system including personal information.

Although a WIPI platform does not cover the verification of bytecode, a COD server will perform code verification before running. This means a COD server compiles the byte code appropriate for each CPU and sends the compiled binary code to the device when requested, instead of compiling byte code in a device. This is similar to the class loader in the Java platform. The only difference is that a WIPI platform loads the binary image, not class files. So the platform should confirm that the binary image was loaded in a certified gateway.

Execution Speed

As noted above, the program execution speed of WIPI applications is faster than Java applications and almost same as the C native-based application programs. Table 2 compares the program execution speed of WIPI-Java applications compiled in a COD server with native-based application programs and Java application programs.

Test	Test case	Native	WIPI	Java
Array copy	Execute 2-dimentional array of [50][100] size 5100 times	0.13	0.18	1
Loop test	Calculate Fibonacci sequence with size 1000	0.12	0.14	1
Function call	Call two functions recursively 200 times	0.17	0.24	1

Table 2. Comparison of execution speed

APPLYING WIPI IN A TELEMATICS DEVICE

Software Architecture of the Front-end System

Figure 4 shows the software architecture briefly adapted in a telematics device.

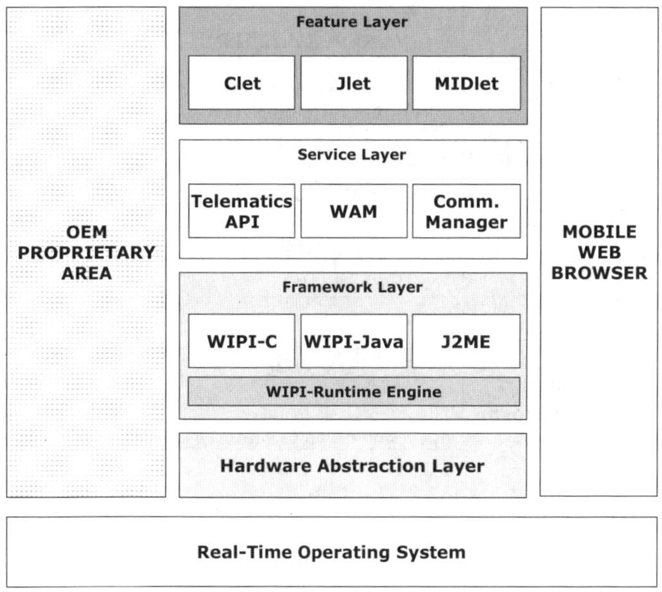

Figure 4. Software architecture of a telematics device

The software architecture is divided into 3 parts – the OEM proprietary area, the WIPI platform, and the mobile web browser.

The OEM Proprietary Area contains the OEM-specific and built-in applications that do not need to be downloaded or upgraded. This area also represents the distinctiveness of a product.

Although the concept of a WIPI platform was already explained above, there is an additional component in a WIPI platform: the communication manager that communicates with the OEM proprietary area and the mobile web browser to send data and receive data. That is, the role of communication manager is to link the WIPI platform to other parts of the software components.

The Mobile web browser is used for acquiring data from the server side. The device user can browse the information about application programs to be downloaded. The detailed usage of a web browser in a WIPI platform will be explained in the next subsection.

Security Check by the COD server

A security check by the COD server for the telematics software applications was tested and verified. The tested application is developed in a class file and entered in the COD server with application information. After that, the COD server compiles the class file to the binary file and sends it to the telematics device when application download is requested. In this process the COD server checks the security, so that the binary code can be ensured the Java-level security.

Downloading a WIPI application

Figure 5 shows the WIPI application download sequence.

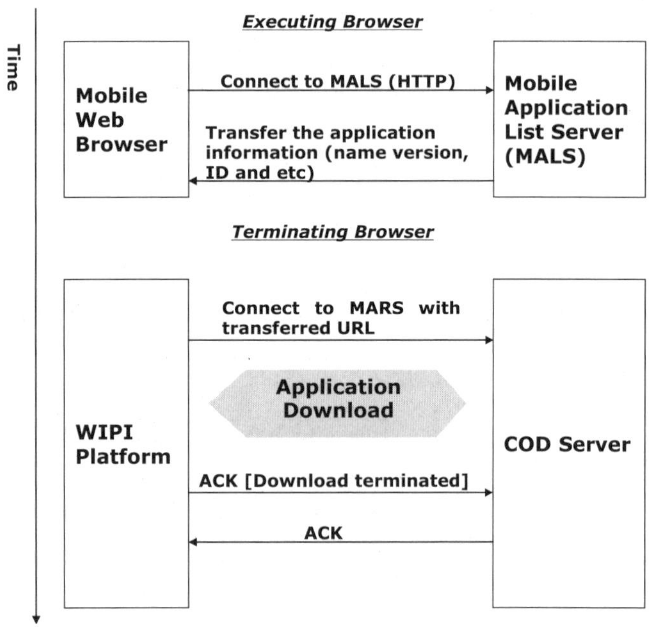

Figure 5. WIPI application download sequence

To download an application program, the developer should enroll it in the COD server with application information such as program name and version number. After that, the application information file is sent to the Mobile Application List Server (MALS) that manages all entered application lists. When the device user wants to download a WIPI application program, the mobile web browser is connected to MALS and shown the list of application programs.

The above application download sequence was tested and verified in the telematics environment.

Verification of Interoperability

Interoperability of the WIPI platform for the telematics device was confirmed by operating the existing WIPI application programs that were developed for hand-set devices. However, the application programs for hand-set devices are not appropriate for telematics devices because of the difference of HMI features, such as display size and operating keys. Therefore, a new WIPI standard for telematics is required.

Checking Expandability and Upgradeability features

Expansion of the WIPI platform was tested and verified in the telematics device. For a new service after device release, the platform expands its APIs through wireless internet while downloading an application program that needs new APIs.

Likewise, the Upgrade feature was also confirmed in the telematics device. When the user wants to download a new version of the application, the WIPI platform would check the version of an existing application and determine whether the platform supports execution of the application program. If the platform does not support execution of the application, it automatically expands its APIs and then downloads the application.

Backward Compatibility Check

The Backward-Compatibility feature was tested and verified in the telematics device. When the platform is up-versioned by expanding APIs, the existing applications in the platform should be operated.

CONCLUSION

In this paper, a new telematics software platform was introduced and the basic concept of the platform was explained. It was also verified that the proposed software platform satisfied software features like expandability, downloadability, upgradeability, security, interoperability, and backward compatibility. In addition to these features, it was made sure that the program execution speed of WIPI platform is 400~500% faster than a Java-based platform.

In Korea, WIPI is a standard software platform for hand-set devices, and 14 million hand-set devices were already using it. Therefore more than 2000 application programs have been developed for a handset environment.

Nevertheless, this was the first test adapting WIPI in the telematics environment, so lack of applications for telematics is a weak point of this platform. However, as the number of devices applying a WIPI platform is growing, it is expected that the number of applications will grow as well.

REFERENCES

1. Jae Hyun Woo, Young Woo Choi and Jung Min Kim. "Software Architecture for A/V combination Telematics Unit," Journal of Korea Location Based Service Society Vol.4, pages 55~60, December 2004
2. Andrew L. Kun, W. Thomas Miller, William H. Lenharth, Brett J. Vinciguerra, Michael E. Martin. "An open architecture supporting telematics and the integration of in-car devices," ITU Workshop on Standardization in Telecommunications for motor vehicles, Geneva, November 2003
3. Automotive Multimedia Interface Collaboration. "AMI-C System Requirements," Version 1.0, January 2003.
4. Open Services Gateway Initiative. "OSGi Service Platform Specification," Version 3.0, March 2003.
5. WIPI Forum. October 2006 [online] - URL: http://www.wipi.or.kr
6. Korea Wireless Internet Standardization Forum. "Wireless Internet Platform for Interoperability: Part 1. Structure and Function of WIPI," Version 2.0.1, September 2004
7. Scott Oaks. "Java Security 2nd edition," O'Reilly Media, May 2001

2007-01-1711

Real Multi-Partitioning for Optimized Distributing and Allocating Software in Vehicle Networks

Stephan Brummund, Christian Steup and Uwe Kiencke
Institut für Industrielle Informationstechnik, Universität Karlsruhe (TH), Germany

ABSTRACT

In this paper two new approaches are presented how to partition an amount of functions distributed in automotive electronic systems. In contrast to common partitioning algorithms as Kernighan-Lin, Best-Gain-First, Simulated-Annealing, a.s.o., these algorithms are real multi-partitioning ones. With respect to ECU (electronic control unit) characteristics, the software functions to be partitioned will be allocated automatically onto the available hardware. Main motivation is the reduction of the resulting bus-load which is provoked by the communication between such functions. Moreover these algorithms optimize the final partitioning solution to achieve a reduced number of ECUs. Reducing bus-load and the number of ECUs can lead to significant cost reduction. In order to validate partitioning results, a CAN as well as a FlexRay model was developed in Matlab/Simulink determining the bus-load over time. Therefore system engineers can assess the performance of the partitioned system during design process and decide for the best implementation before test stage.

INTRODUCTION

Due to increasing electronically controlled functionality in cars and hence increasing demand of computational resources in vehicle networks [1] recent development focuses on splitting software and hardware by placing an operating system in-between as done by the AUTOSAR project. This split enables developers to concentrate on programming the functionality and opens up the problem of assigning functions to standardized ECUs [2]. As external communication between ECUs via a bus is crucial in this scenario this approach aims at minimizing these communication costs by partitioning the functions to be implemented. Given several dozens of ECUs and hundreds of software functions in a car this approach uses real multi-partitioning.

Normally multi-partitioning is based on iterative bi-partitioning like Kernighan-Lin, Best-Gain-First, Simulated-Annealing, a.s.o. This leads to a high computational effort for complex systems. Furthermore, these algorithms often stuck to local minima [3]. An alternative would be clustering algorithms realizing real multi-partitioning. However, with geometric partitioning used input data has to be transformed into n-dimensional space first which always provokes a loss of information [4] and provokes huge computational effort. In this paper two new heuristics are elaborated realizing real multi-partitioning using directly the adjacency matrix [5, 6] describing the communication network. The first one is mainly based on the distances to a node's neighbors and to its neighbors' neighbors to decide whether two nodes should be placed on the same ECU or not. The second one partitions distributed systems based on similar communication properties of different functional objects determined via correlation. In addition to the communicational behavior of the functions represented by the adjacency matrix some feature vectors are needed describing the computational demand and supply of the functions and the ECUs respectively.

Finally the approaches will be valuated using formal criteria as well as two bus models, a CAN as well as a FlexRay model. It will be shown that partitioning results concerning the bus-load are much better than using common algorithms. Furthermore, our methods allow to determine an optimized number of ECUs needed. Both achievements will allow for cost reduction and better placement or accessibility of ECUs in vehicles.

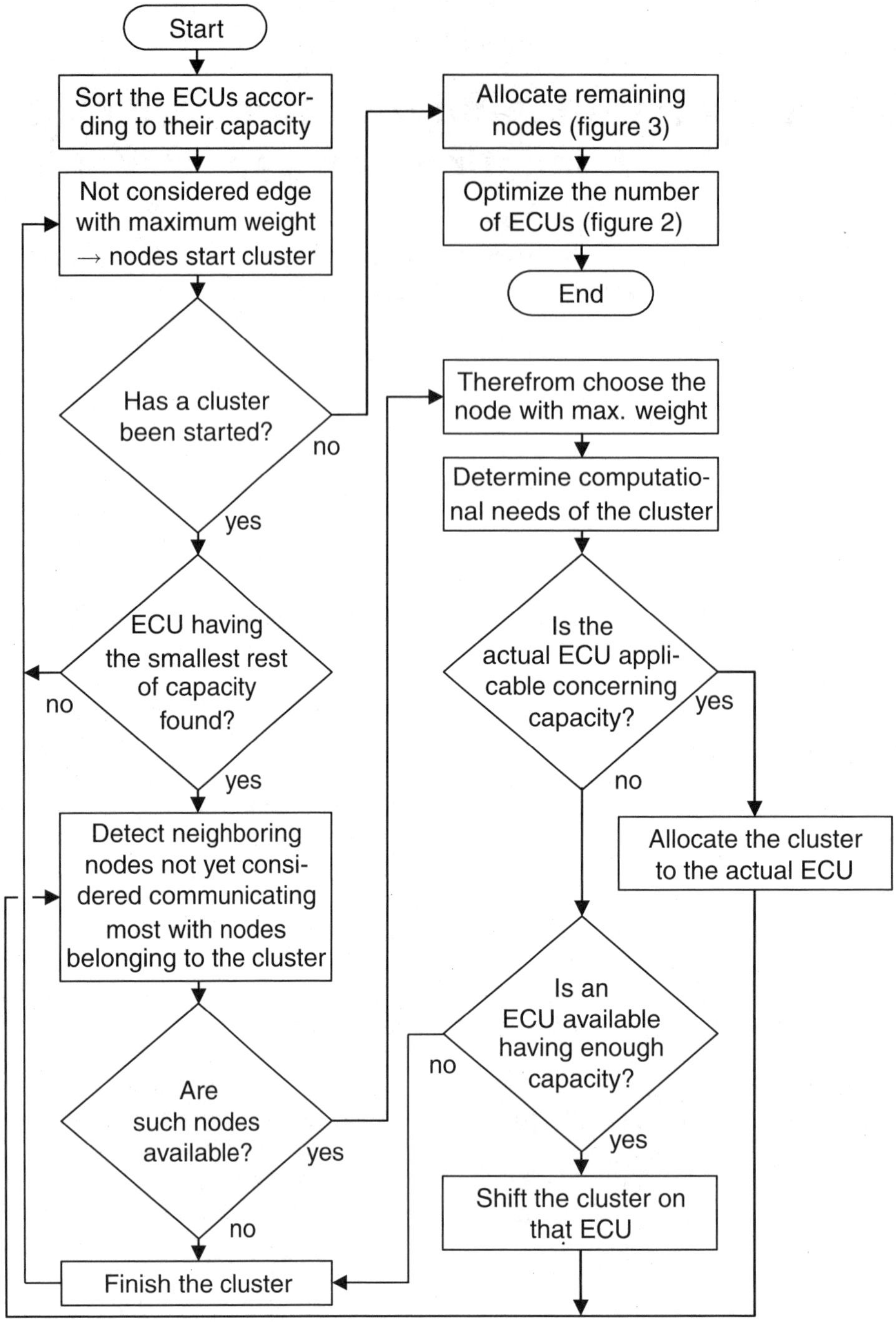

Figure 1: ISAT algorithm

ALGORITHM - ISAT

The ISAT algorithm (Iterative Self-Allocating Technique) was developed in this project partitioning distributed automotive electronic systems. Common partitioning algorithms such as Kernighan-Lin, Best-Gain-First, Simulated-Annealing, a.s.o are based on several bi-partitionings. First the system engineer has to pre-define the number of clusters and pre-partition the system for example randomly. Due to the fact that multi-partitioning will be realized by iteratively computed bi-partitionings, such algorithms stick to local minima and results depend on the initialized partitioning.

The ISAT algorithm is a pure multi-partitioning algorithm. Moreover the final solution is independent of initializations, so that system engineers do not need to pre-partition the system first. In [3, 4] an approach was presented realizing real multi-partitioning using geometrical-based clustering algorithms. Compared to common partitioning algorithms results were much better. However, the adjacency matrix of the system has to be transformed into a geometrical matrix in n-dimensional space first. Besides high computational effort for large systems it also leads to a loss of system information. Therefore, an algorithm was needed using the adjacency matrix of the system, realizing multi-partitioning without initialization, leading to a lower bus-load than common

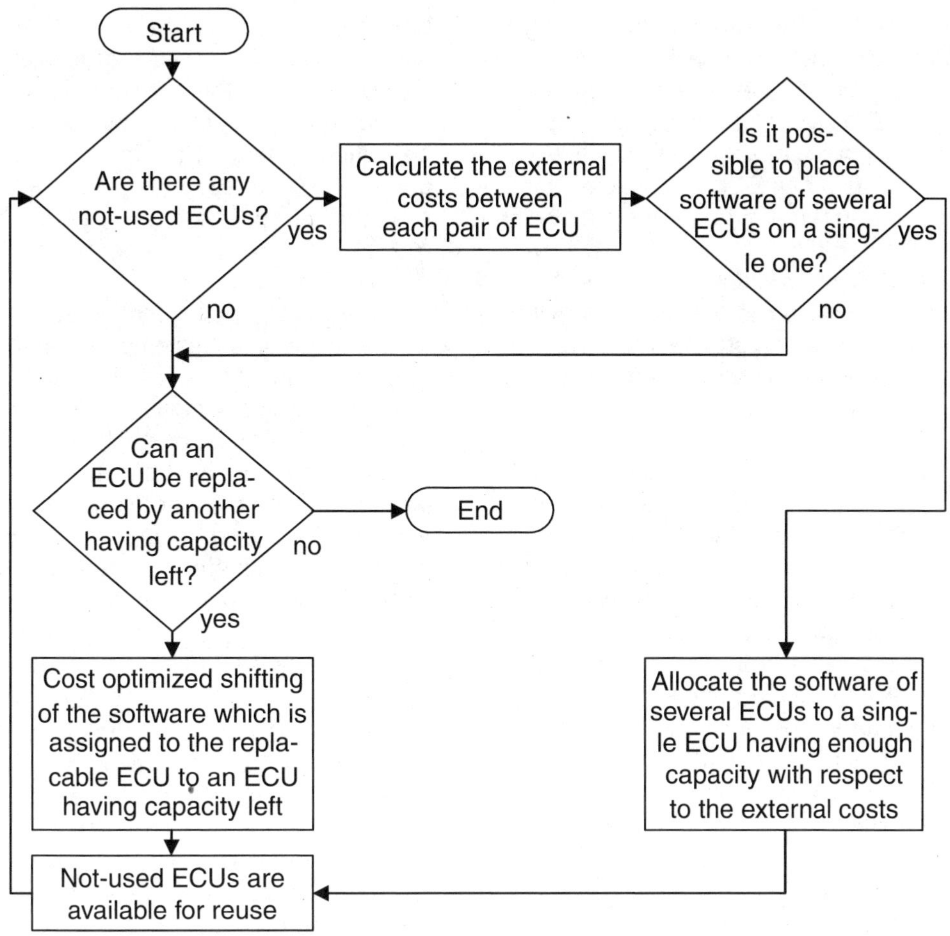

Figure 2: ISAT Algorithm - Optimization of the number of ECUs

algorithms and also optimizing the number of clusters representing the later used ECUs of the system. Well elaborated clustering helps to stop the costs for in-vehicle networks from rising. Resources set free can be used to enable future technologies like X-by-wire.

In order to partition a distributed system its adjacency matrix is used. Furthermore available ECUs representing the clusters have to be characterized by feature vectors. In this paper, ECUs available will be characterized by their calculation capacity in order to solve functional modules in real-time. For example this could be the number of MIPS (Million instructions per second). However, this algorithm can be simply extended for further feature vectors as ECU resources for instance. The specialty of this approach is the fact that the algorithm chooses the number and type of ECUs needed from an available range. Hereby, the engineer pre-defines the number of each type of ECU which would be available when implementing the network. On this basis the algorithm will determine the optimal number of each type to be used in order to reduce bus-load and the number of ECUs within the network. Besides these vectors, further feature vectors are needed characterizing the software functions. So vectors can be build, describing computing effort, resources needed, a.s.o.

In figure 1 the flow-chart of the ISAT algorithm is illustrated. First of all, the ECUs have to be sorted according to their computing capacity in ascending order. Of course, they can also be sorted by price or other features. Nevertheless, the algorithm will regard the ECUs according to the order of that list. Therefore it is possible to prefer cheaper types sufficient for calculation.

The main part of the algorithm then consists of two loops. The first loop seeks repeatedly for two nodes to initialize a cluster. The second loop then iteratively adds other nodes to the started cluster until certain abort criteria is met. In the first loop to start a cluster the graphical system representation described by the adjacency matrix will be analyzed in regard to the maximum communication weight between two different functional objects. This can be found taking the maximum of all matrix elements of the corresponding adjacency matrix. This communication weight refers to two nodes communicating with each other. These two nodes build up the first cluster.

The two nodes starting a cluster will be allocated theoretically onto the first ECU of the sorted list fitting the corresponding features. Then iteratively neighboring nodes not yet clustered have to be detected. If these nodes are communicating stronger with nodes of the actual cluster than to other ones, they are candidates to be added to the actual cluster. That one communicating most to a node of the actual cluster will be added. Afterwards the features of the ECU and the software modules are checked. If the actual ECU fits the software demands, further neighboring nodes will be searched iteratively. If not and in case of fitting other ECUs available, the cluster will be transferred on the first of them listed and the algorithm continues iteratively looking for new neighboring nodes. In case of no fitting ECU available, the current node will not be added to the cluster which will now be finished and implemented theoretically on the actual ECU. The actual ECU will be listed for further iterations with a certain rest of capacity.

After each finished cluster, the rest of capacity describing the available hardware will be updated and the algorithm looks for new clusters to start. If all nodes already have been considered during partitioning, it is possible that not all nodes are allocated to certain clusters. Such remaining nodes will be assigned according to the flow-chart of figure 3. Iteratively the external communication costs between such a node to all clusters fulfilling the functional features will be calculated adding the corresponding communication weights listed in the adjacency matrix. Finally the corresponding node is assigned to the cluster leading to a minimized bus-load.

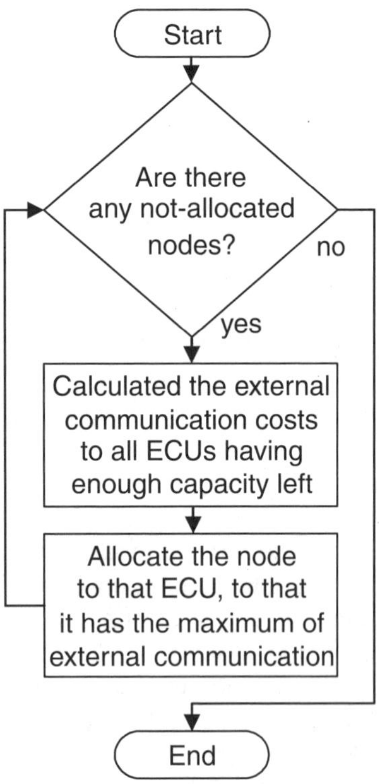

Figure 3: ISAT Algorithm - Allocating not-assigned functional objects

In figure 2 the last step optimizing the number of ECUs is shown. Maybe one ECU has enough capacity left in order to compute the software modules of a second one. Then the software functions of the second ECU will be shifted to the first ECU so that the second ECU can be removed from the network. This way space and cost limitations can be fulfilled. Moreover, in case of powerful ECUs not used, the partitioned system will be analyzed for clusters which communicate strongly and which can be shifted on that ECU simultaneously. Besides reducing problems due to space limitations this optimization leads to a further reduction of bus-load in combination with reduced costs.

Using this algorithm for partitioning distributed automotive electronic systems, engineers have a powerful tool optimizing the most important factors concerning in-vehicle network design: bus-load, costs and space. Solely the features of each available ECU as well as the requirements of the software modules have to be pre-defined. A further advantage is the simplicity of this algorithm. It is easy to implement and extendable for features to be considered. In contrast to common partitioning algorithms it is much more flexible and effective.

CASA - ALGORITHM

The CASA-algorithm (Correlate And Soak Allocation) developed in this project is a real multi-partitioning algorithm. According to the ISAT algorithm of the preceding paragraph it is meant to partition distributed automotive electronic systems. However it can not be described using commonplace classification as it is neither a geometric nor a graphic method.

The CASA-algorithm is a two step method. In the first step it calculates all $\frac{n\cdot(n-1)}{2}$ correlation-like indices between the the n nodes and sorts them in descending order. In the second step the partitioning is done in a specific way according to the sorted list. To calculate the correlation CASA considers two different features. One feature is the way two nodes communicate directly between each other. The second feature is the way they communicate with the rest of the whole network. Before the flow-chart in figure 4 will be explained in detail, the following paragraph describes how to determine the correlation values used for partitioning.

CALCULATION OF THE CORRELATION VALUES

Calculating the according values, sending behavior as well as receiving behavior of each functional object is relevant. Sending and receiving behavior is named the communication profile. To consider both sending and receiving the rows as well as the columns of the adjacency matrix will be analyzed. The number of functional objects, described by FO_i, is n. In the first step, for each functional object or node of the graphical system representation the expectation value of its communication behavior is determined. Due to the fact that the sending behavior of FO_i is described by the i-th row and the receiving behavior by the i-th column, the expectation value of the communication $E(c_I)$ of FO_i has to be determined using

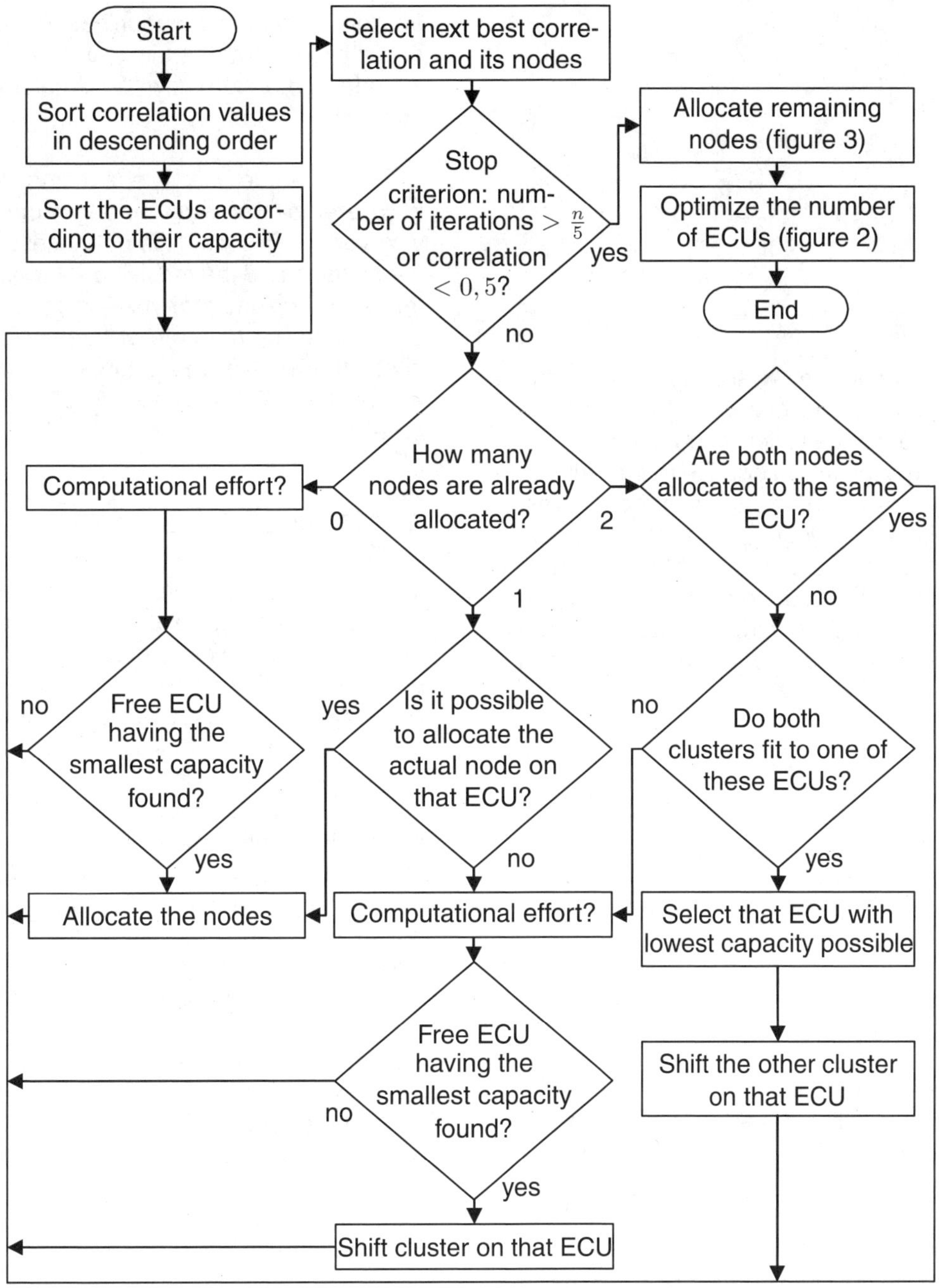

Figure 4: CASA algorithm

$2n$ elements.

$$E(c_I) = \frac{1}{2n}(\sum_{i=1}^{n} c_{iI} + \sum_{j=1}^{n} c_{Ij}) \quad (1)$$

Subsequently the variance

$$var(c_I) = \frac{1}{2n}(\sum_{i=1}^{n}(c_{iI} - E(c_I))^2 + \sum_{j=1}^{n}(c_{Ij} - E(c_I))^2) \quad (2)$$

of the functional communication behavior can be calculated. To this point the method is perfectly known from the correlation. The calculation of the covariance corresponds to the communication of FO_i and FO_j to the rest of the network. The covariance

$$\begin{aligned} cov(c_I, c_J) &= E(c_I \cdot c_J) - E(c_I) \cdot E(c_J) \\ &= \frac{1}{2n}(\sum_{i=1}^{n} c_{iI} \cdot c_{iJ} + \sum_{j=1}^{n} c_{Ij} \cdot c_{Jj}) \\ &\quad -E(c_I) \cdot E(c_J) \end{aligned} \quad (3)$$

can be derived from the classical one with a crucial change. This change takes into account the direct link between two nodes which is the second feature to be considered as mentioned above. Considering the communication matrix

$$\underline{C} = \begin{pmatrix} 0 & \cdots & c_{1i} & \cdots & c_{1j} & \cdots & c_{1n} \\ \vdots & & \vdots & & \vdots & & \vdots \\ c_{i1} & \cdots & 0 & \cdots & c_{ij} & \cdots & c_{in} \\ \vdots & & \vdots & & \updownarrow & & \vdots \\ c_{j1} & \cdots & c_{ji} & \leftrightarrow & 0 & \cdots & c_{jn} \\ \vdots & & \vdots & & \vdots & & \vdots \\ c_{n1} & \cdots & c_{ni} & \cdots & c_{nj} & \cdots & 0 \end{pmatrix} \quad (4)$$

we can see that calculating the covariance between the rows i and j as well as the columns i and j, direct communication links would not be taken into account. The reason is the main diagonal set to zero due to the fact that functional objects do not communicate with themselves. Therefore the correlation between such a zero element and an element c_{ij} would be canceled. In order to take direct links into account, the according zero elements are swapped with the elements describing the intercommunication, as it can be seen for the calculation of the rows in equation 5.

$$\underline{C} = \begin{pmatrix} 0 & \cdots & c_{1i} & \cdots & c_{1j} & \cdots & c_{1n} \\ \vdots & & \vdots & & \vdots & & \vdots \\ c_{i1} & \cdots & 0 & \cdots & c_{ij} & \cdots & c_{in} \\ \vdots & & \vdots & & \vdots & & \vdots \\ c_{j1} & \cdots & 0 & \leftrightarrow & c_{ji} & \cdots & c_{jn} \\ \vdots & & \vdots & & \vdots & & \vdots \\ c_{n1} & \cdots & c_{ni} & \cdots & c_{nj} & \cdots & 0 \end{pmatrix} \quad (5)$$

Considering the rows in equation 5 0 and 0 is multiplied as well as the direct link c_{ij} and c_{ji} as seen. In addition to the swapping the correlation describing the direct link is weighted by a weighting factor as the direct link is an important indicator to reduce the bus-load. In our approach, the weighting for the direct link was set to $dL = \frac{n}{5}$. Changes to this weighting factor may provoke changes in the clustering.

After having calculated the elements of the modified covariance matrix for each combination of FO_i and FO_j according to equation 3, the elements of the correlation matrix will be determined.

$$cor(c_I, c_J) = \frac{cov(c_I, c_J)}{\sqrt{var(c_I)} \cdot \sqrt{var(c_J)}} \quad (6)$$

These correlation values filling a $(n \times n)$-Matrix are sorted in descending order. This list contains both the correlation value and the functional objects FO_i and FO_j responsible for it. According to that list the objects will be clustered.

VARIANT OF CALCULATING THE CORRELATION

In addition to the method to determine the correlation values described before another variant was implemented as well. So far the communication profile was considered consisting of both sending an the receiving behavior of a node. Therefore rows and columns were taken into account.

One can argue that the sending behavior of a node is covered by the receiving behavior of the other nodes or vice versa. This way it is not necessary to consider both the sending and the receiving. Mathematically this means that either columns or rows in the adjacency matrix are considered but not both of them. So this variant covers either the rows or the columns. However the swapping of the direct link between FO_i and FO_j in c_{ij} and c_{ji} remains valid.

CLUSTERING WITH CASA

In figure 4 the flow-chart of the algorithm is depicted. In the first step the correlation values between all functional objects have to be calculated as described in the previous paragraph and sorted in descending order. According to the ISAT algorithm ECUs are only sorted in ascending order due to their capacity. Other features as resources and price for example will not be considered. However, feature vectors describing further ECU characteristics are easy to implement into that algorithm. In the next step the values of the correlation list are considered top-down and the two corresponding nodes are clustered. This principle will be repeated iteratively as the number of iterations is smaller than $\frac{n}{5}$ or the correlation value is larger than $\frac{1}{2}$ which turned out to be good criteria to abort.

Considering the entries in that list starting from the top three cases can occur. Either none of the nodes is yet clustered or one of them is clustered or both of them are already clustered. In the first case the smallest possible unused ECU is searched and both FOs are placed on the ECU. If there is no free ECU large enough to host the FOs the entry is ignored.

In the second case the unclustered FO is tried to be placed on the ECU hosting the clustered FO. If the ECU's capacity is not big enough for this another unused but larger ECU is searched. With such an ECU existing the whole cluster is shifted to that one. If not the list's entry is ignored.

In the third case both FOs can be clustered on the same ECU. This case is trivial. If they are clustered on different ECUs it is tried to combine both clusters on an ECU big enough to host both of the clusters.

As already described in the paragraph of the ISAT algorithm, remaining nodes have to be allocated according to the flow-chart of figure 3. Moreover, the number of ECUs has to be optimized at the end. If some ECUs of low capacity are used, it might be better to swap the clusters on a large one left. This will be realized implementing the flow-chart of figure 2 as already seen.

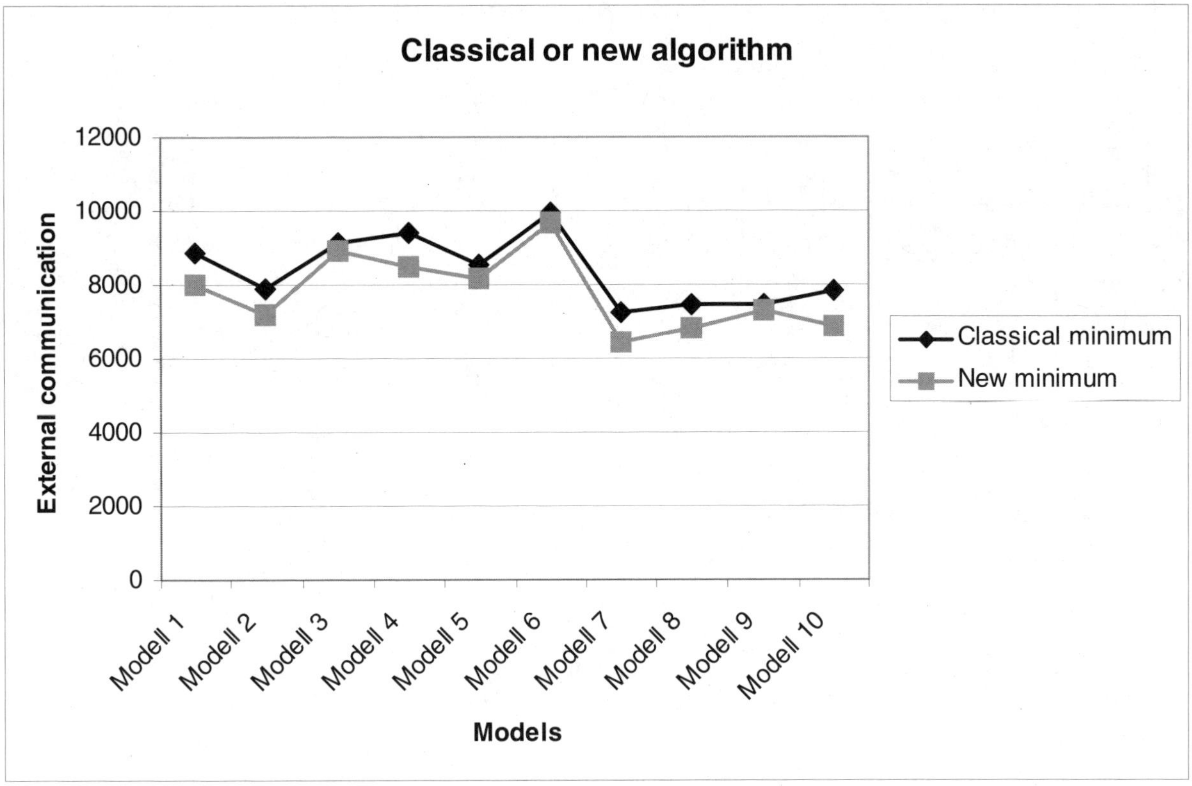

Figure 5: The best new algorithm vs. the best classical one

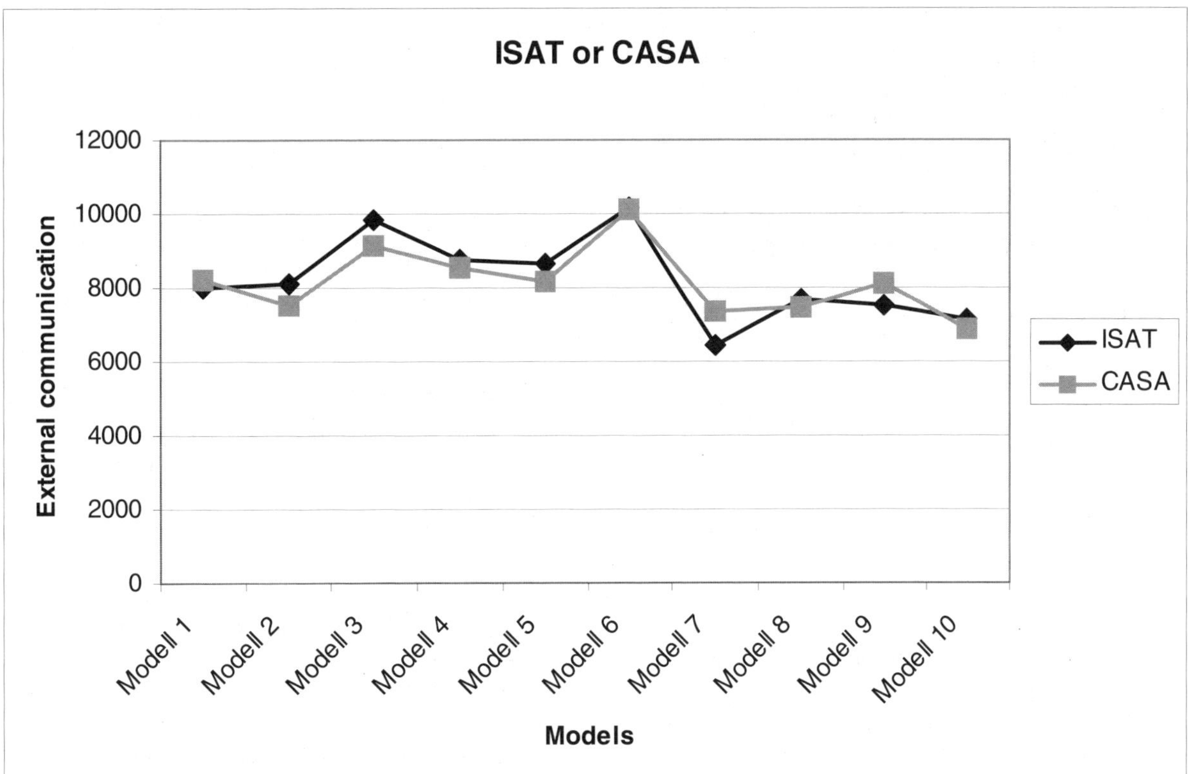

Figure 6: ISAT vs. CASA

RESULTS

In order to validate the partitioning results of the newly presented algorithms, example systems were taken and partitioned with common algorithms as well as with the presented ones. First of all, the two algorithms are validated using various models. The models to be partitioned were generated randomly in Matlab. They consist of 25 by 25 adjacency matrices with 40% of the entries not zero. These elements are chosen randomly

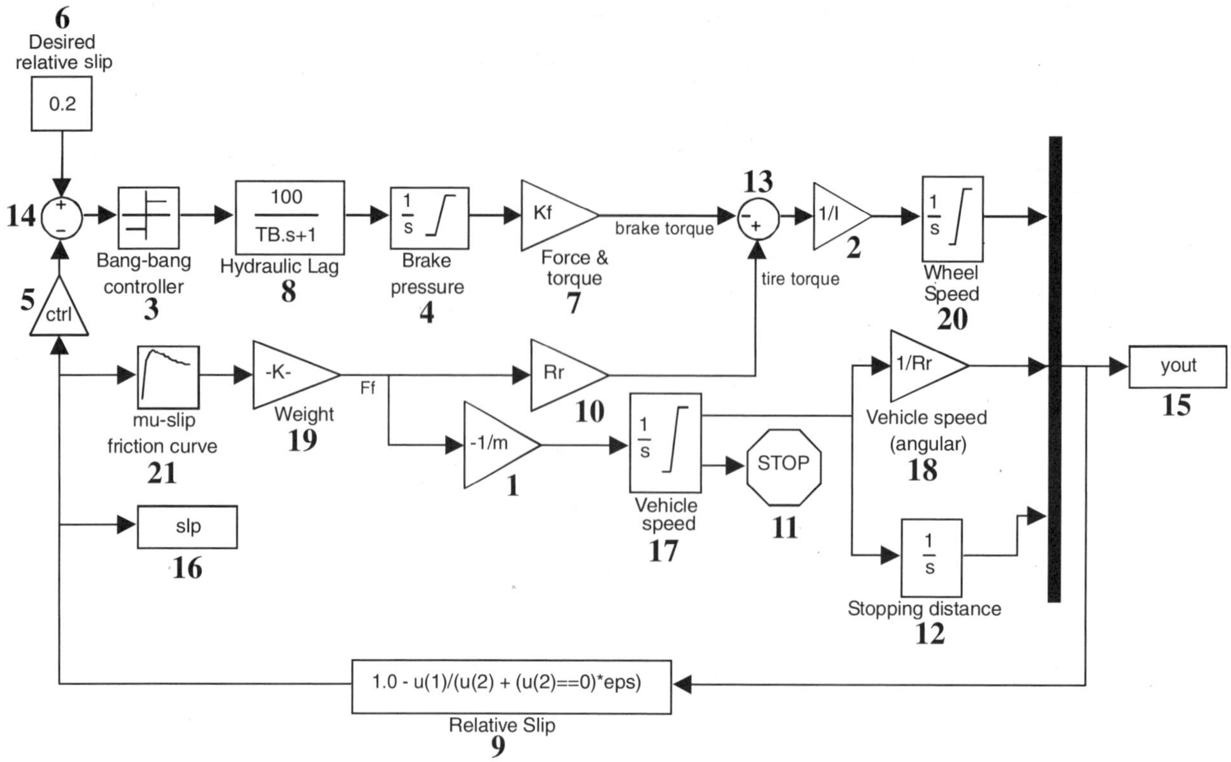

Figure 7: ABS Simulink Model

between 1 and 100 indicating the communication load between different functional objects. Moreover six ECUs are assumed to be available with capacities between 100 and 600 whereas the computational efforts of the functional objects are set randomly within 1 and 100. As we can show the newly presented approaches lead to much better partitioning results concerning external communication compared with the classic methods.

Considering figure 5 the results of the best classical algorithm (Best-Gain-First, Ford-Fulkerson, Fiduccia-Mattheyses, Jarvis-Patrick, Kernighan-Lin, Simulated-Annealing) are compared to the best partitioning solution obtained using the new approaches (ISAT, CASA). Tests lead to a global improvement of 12.41% considering the reduction of external communication over the bus system. This improvement is an average over 12 randomly chosen models.

In figure 6, it can be seen that the CASA approach leads to better solutions in respect of the external communication than the ISAT algorithm. However, ISAT often is more effective. In the figure both algorithms are compared partitioning 10 models. The external costs are minimized taking the ISAT algorithm in case of three models (model 1, 7 and 9). Their characteristics are less loops and less direct communication links between different functional objects. As an example system, the Simulink ABS model of figure 7 will now be partitioned. It can be seen that this model has only less intercommunication. Most of the blocks only have one input and one output signal. Using Matlab, the adjacency matrix of this

Algorithm	Busload
ISAT	$8,14\%$
CASA	$13,47\%$
Best-Gain-First	$21,23\%$
Ford-Fulkerson	$26,51\%$
Fiduccia-Mattheyses	$20,02\%$
Jarvis-Patrick	$15,03\%$
Kernighan-Lin	$16,23\%$
Simulated-Annealing	$23,19\%$

Table 1: Busload using the CAN-bus model

model can be determined automatically as described in [7]. Partitioning this model and testing the partitionings on the CAN-bus and FlexRay model lead to a minimized bus-load taking the solution of the ISAT algorithm. Simulating the bus-load of FlexRay the functional objects were assigned to the dynamic segment. The reason is that the static segment is time-based and therefore the bus-load is already reserved for the different functional objects. Taking the dynamic segment using priorities, we can simulated bus-load according to CAN.

In table 1 the bus-load of the CAN-bus model is depicted using different algorithms partitioning the ABS model of figure 7. The model is taken from the Matlab examples which come with the software package.

As it can be seen, ISAT algorithm is leading to the best bus-load. The second best solution is obtained using CASA allocation. However, we have to state that the weighting dL was not only set to $\frac{n}{5}$ as used for the rest of the models. In case of models with less intercommunication as the ABS model, the weighting has to be raised in order to weight direct communication links between neighboring functional objects instead of the communication behavior in general differing in such cases. In this example dL was set to $dL = n$.

Shortly, we can say that ISAT and CASA lead to better results than the classic methods. Nevertheless the more nodes a network has and the more edges there are to link the nodes the more effective CASA turns. This shall be no surprise as correlation-based approaches need a certain amount of data to work out.

CONCLUSION

In this paper two new algorithms for partitioning distributed automotive electronic systems were presented. The first one called ISAT algorithm (Iterative Self-Allocating Technique) allocates software onto distributed hardware. Hereby the maximum intercommunication not yet considered leads to an effective partitioning approach also optimizing the number of ECUs used. This may lead to reduced costs and to less failure of in-vehicle networks.

The second algorithm presented is the so-called CASA algorithm (Correlate And Soak Allocation). This technique considers besides intercommunication between neighboring functional objects the communication behavior of each functional object to the whole system. In case of software having much intercommunication this approach is extremely effective and leads to less bus-load than ISAT. However, taking models like the Simulink ABS model of figure 7 ISAT is more powerful due to the fact that the communication behavior analyzed by correlation differs between each functional object. Therefore a weighting dL weights the direct link between two functional objects is used.

Recapitulating the two newly presented algorithms lead to much better partitioning solutions in general compared to common approaches like Best-Gain-First, Ford-Fulkerson, Fiduccia-Mattheyses, Jarvis-Patrick, Kernighan-Lin and Simulated-Annealing. We can state that an improvement of 12.41% in respect of the external communication was reached on average. Results of the new approaches have not been worse than the classic methods in no case. Engineers therefore only have to try these two algorithms in order to decide for a partitioning solution. In case of much more functional objects having only one input and output link than multiple partners communicating ISAT turned out to be more adequate. Otherwise CASA is more outperforming due to its correlation based method including the direct link between nodes.

Both methods provoke low computational effort with respect to today's computer hardware. All calculation and simulation has been done on standard desktop computers. Results have been returned instantly.

REFERENCES

[1] Ross Bannatyne, "Microcontrollers for the automobile", in *Micro Control Journal*, 2004.

[2] Paolo Giusto, Luciano Lavagno, Alberto Ferrari, Massimiliano Chiodo, and Jean-Yves Brunel, "Electronic-system design in the automobile industry", in *IEEE Computer Society*, 2003.

[3] Stephan Brummund, Natalja Kehl, Philipp Nenninger, and Uwe Kiencke, "Isodata clutering for optimized software allocation in distributed automotive electronic systems", *SAE, 2006-01-1053, Detroit (USA)*, 2006.

[4] Stephan Brummund, Philipp Nenninger, Simmi Saxena, and Uwe Kiencke, "Design of automotive's complex electronic system based on som clustering", in *Workshop on Self-Organizing Maps (WSOM)*, 2005, pp. 33–40.

[5] Francois Baccelli, Guy Cohen, Geert Jan Olsder, and Jean-Pierre Quadrat, *Synchronization and Linearity: An Algebra for Discrete Event Systems*, Wiley & Son, 1992.

[6] Uwe Kiencke, *Ereignisdiskrete Systeme: Modellierung und Steuerung verteilter Systeme*, German, Oldenbourg Verlag, 2006.

[7] Philipp Nenninger, Thomas Rambow, and Uwe Kiencke, "Clustering of complex electronic systems with self-ordering maps", *SAE, 2005-01-1286, Detroit (USA)*, 2005.

2007-01-0509

The AUTOSAR Standard – The Experience of Applying Simulink According to its Requirements

Anila Mjeda, Gabriel Leen, and Eamonn Walsh
University of Limerick

ABSTRACT

Software has become the driving force behind innovation in the automotive industry. According to a recent Frost & Sullivan market research report, "Strategic Analysis of the European Market for Software in Passenger Cars", the software for passenger cars in Europe accounted for 5.8% of the cost of vehicles in 2004. The same report projects an annual growth rate (CAGR) of 15.5% until 2011, when software is expected to represent 11.0% of the cost of vehicles.

This paper discusses the emerging AUTOSAR standard (AUTOSAR release 2.0), which aims to address the need for more efficient E/E (Embedded Electronic) automotive architecture solutions. The paper also provides a review of the mapping of a few key AUTOSAR concepts to their Simulink counterparts, which should help designers using Simulink deliver AUTOSAR compatible solutions.

Finally the paper features a component of an experimental engine management system that has been remodeled in Simulink to conform to the AUTOSAR requirements.

INTRODUCTION

The automotive industry has a history of each supplier developing its own proprietary automotive software and of high confidentiality surrounding this development. Currently there is growing awareness of the need for customization and common solutions.

AUTOSAR (Automotive Open System Architecture) is a partnership of major players in the automotive industry formed with the objective to establish an open standard for automotive E/E architecture.

According to the AUTOSAR official website *(www.autosar.org)* its vision is "...to improve complexity management of integrated E/E architectures through increased reuse and exchangeability of SW modules".

AUTOSAR aims to achieve modularity, scalability, transferability and re-usability of functions in automotive software.

Heinecke [1], reports that the main focus for AUTOSAR is to provide a layered architecture (see Figure 1), which allows for abstraction from hardware on the lower interface and abstraction to application layer software on the upper interface. This is complemented with the provision of specifications for "compatible functional interfaces and the design of a coherent methodology based on standardized templates and data exchange formats".

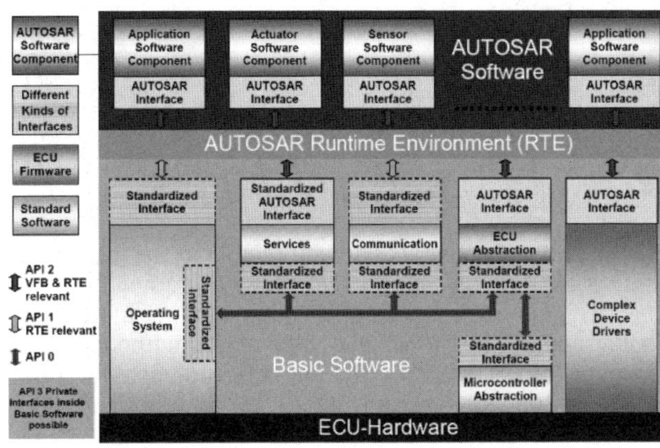

Figure 1 AUTOSAR Architecture Overview (www.autosar.org)

AUTOSAR supports the C, C++ and Java programming languages and identifies the driving forces behind the standardization as follows [2]:

- "Manage the increasing E/E complexity associated with the growth of functional scope

- Improve flexibility for product modification, upgrade and update
- Improve the scalability of solutions within and across product lines
- Improve the quality and reliability of E/E systems
- Enable the detection of errors in early design phases."

AUTOSAR PROJECT OBJECTIVES

AUTOSAR aims to achieve a number of project objectives (PO-s). The following table provides the full list of these objectives as documented in AUTOSAR Release 2.0.

No	Project Objectives	Abbreviation	Priority
1	Consideration of availability and safety requirements	AUTOSAR PO1	1
2	Redundancy activation	AUTOSAR PO2	2
3	Scalability to different vehicle and platform variants	AUTOSAR PO3	1
4	Implementation and standardization of basic system functions as an OEM wide Standard Core solution	AUTOSAR PO4	1
5	Transferability of functions throughout the network	AUTOSAR PO5	1
6	Integration of functional modules from multiple suppliers	AUTOSAR PO6	1
7	Maintainability throughout the whole product life cycle	AUTOSAR PO7	2
8	Increased use of commercial off the shelf hardware (COTS)	AUTOSAR PO8	3
9	Software updates and upgrades over vehicle lifetime	AUTOSAR PO9	2

Table 1 AUTOSAR Project Objectives [3]

where the priority levels have the following meaning:

- 1 = High, Required
- 2 = Medium, recommended
- 3 = Low, optional

LAYERED ARCHITECTURE

AUTOSAR features a layered architecture with standardized and fully described interfaces. An overview of its architecture is shown in Figure 1.

The level of abstraction enforced by its standard interfaces and fully specified communication mechanisms allows the applications to be hardware-independent. The architecture choice also introduces the concept of AUTOSAR Runtime Environment (RTE), which caters to the transferability of functions and redundancy activation.

Virtual Functional Bus (VFB)

According to the AUTOSAR specification [2], "the Virtual Functional Bus (VFB) is the abstraction of the AUTOSAR software components interconnections to the entire vehicle."
The VFB can be thought of as a middleware layer technology that allows the communications between software components and between software components and the rest of the environment to be technology-independent. A schematic view of AUTOSAR components and services connected to the VFB is depicted in Figure 2.

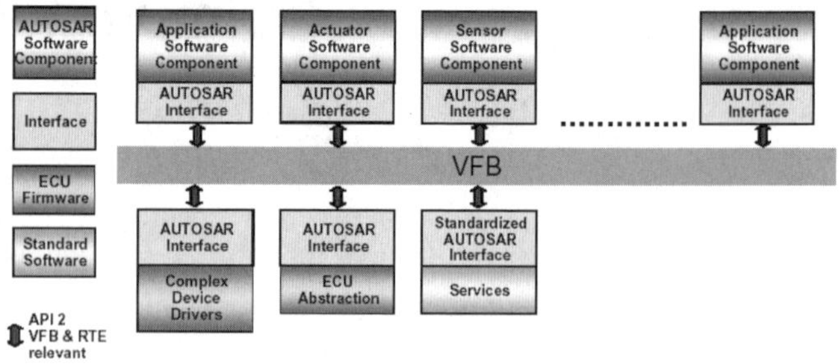

Figure 2 Representations of Atomic Software Components and AUTOSAR Services connected to the VFB [2]

In the above illustration, the "Complex Device Drivers", ECU Abstraction" and "Services" form what is called the "Basic Software".

The AUTOSAR RTE is the run-time implementation of the Virtual Functional Bus (VFB) on a specific ECU (Electronic Control Unit) [2] and provides the same interface and services to the Software Components attached to it for either inter-ECU (via CAN, LIN, Flexray or MOST) or intra-ECU communication. In other words, this makes the software components independent from the communication mechanisms and channels.

The RTE is a novel middleware layer technology that abstracts the Application Layer from all the implementation details of the basic software and hardware, enabling Application Layer software components to be transferable across the network.

AUTOSAR Software

The AUTOSAR Software is the layer that sits above the AUTOSAR Runtime Environment and is composed of AUTOSAR software components, which in turn are mapped on the ECU.

The AUTOSAR Software Component

A fundamental design concept of AUTOSAR is the separation between application and infrastructure. Consequently, the AUTOSAR software component here is designed to be independent from infrastructure and interacts with other components through well defined ports.
Figure 3 illustrates three AUTOSAR software components interconnected to each other.

Here, it is important to mention that an AUTOSAR software component is an "Atomic Software Component", i.e. it is designed to be deployed in only one ECU.

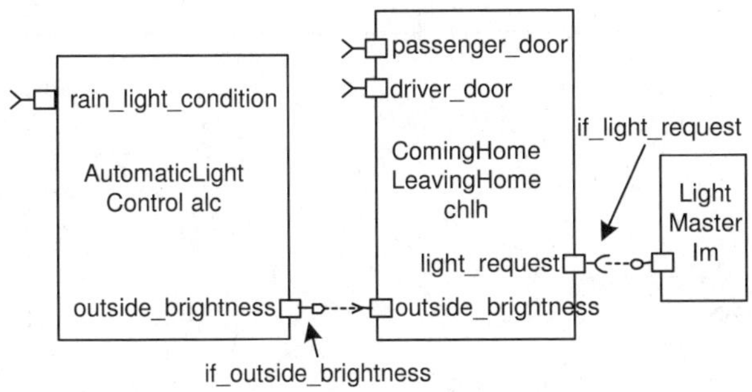

Figure 3 Example of AUTOSAR interconnected Software Components [2]

All interaction between the AUTOSAR software components is done via the AUTOSAR RTE, and the AUTOSAR interface assures their connectivity.

According to the specification, the AUTOSAR software component should be described in detail, as indeed should all AUTOSAR components. The description for the AUTOSAR software component should include:

- the operations and data elements that the software component provides and requires
- the requirements that a software component has on the infrastructure
- the resources needed by the software component
- information regarding the specific implementation of the software component

As shown in Figure 4, the specification recommends that the description of a software component in AUTOSAR should be done in three levels: Virtual Functional Bus Level, Run-time-Environment level and Implementation level.

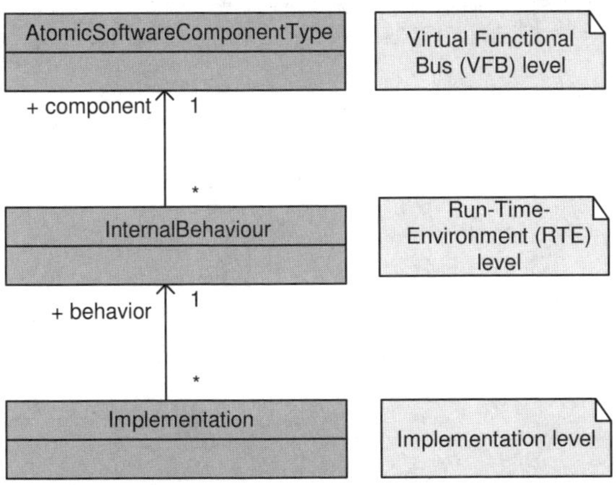

Figure 4 The Description of a software component is done on three levels [4]

AUTOSAR Basic Software

The AUTOSAR Basic Software is located below the AUTOSAR Runtime Environment. It contains standardized and ECU-specific components, and while it does not carry out any job itself, it provides standardized services to the AUTOSAR Software Components.

AUTOSAR METHODOLOGY

The AUTOSAR development process starts with formal descriptions of the interfaces of software and hardware components. Templates for the description of these interfaces conforming to the AUTOSAR standard are given, and the former are used as an input throughout the development process.

The common technical approach for the steps taken in developing the system is called the "AUTOSAR methodology".

According to the AUTOSAR specification:
"The AUTOSAR Methodology is neither a complete process description nor a business model and 'roles' and 'responsibilities' are not defined in this methodology. Furthermore it does not prescribe a precise order in which activities should be carried out. The methodology is a mere work-product flow: it defines the dependencies of activities on work-products."

AUTOSAR describes the methodology using the Software Process Engineering meta-model (SPEM). SPEM is a standard developed by the Object Management Group (OMG), which is designed to describe software development processes. SPEM includes the description of the appropriate graphical notations for a range of concepts such as Work Product, Activity, Guidance, Work-Flow Products, Dependency, etc.
Figure 5 provides an overview of the AUTOSAR methodology. It follows SPEM graphical notation to depict the design steps from the system configuration to the generation of an ECU executable.

AUTOSAR supports the formal description required in each step by requesting the use of an information exchange format and the use of templates. According to AUTOSAR: *"A Template is a structured collection of attributes that are required to formally describe AUTOSAR artifacts like software components or configurations of ECUs"* [5].

The templates in AUTOSAR are in the form of simplified UML class diagrams[1], and the resulting UML model is called the template model. Figure 6 shows the full AUTOSAR metamodel hierarchy.

The AUTOSAR methodology promotes an organic integration of tool support and strongly supports model-based design techniques.

---

[1] AUTOSAR uses an UML profile described in the AUTOSAR specification (in the Template UML Profile and Modelling Guide [6]).

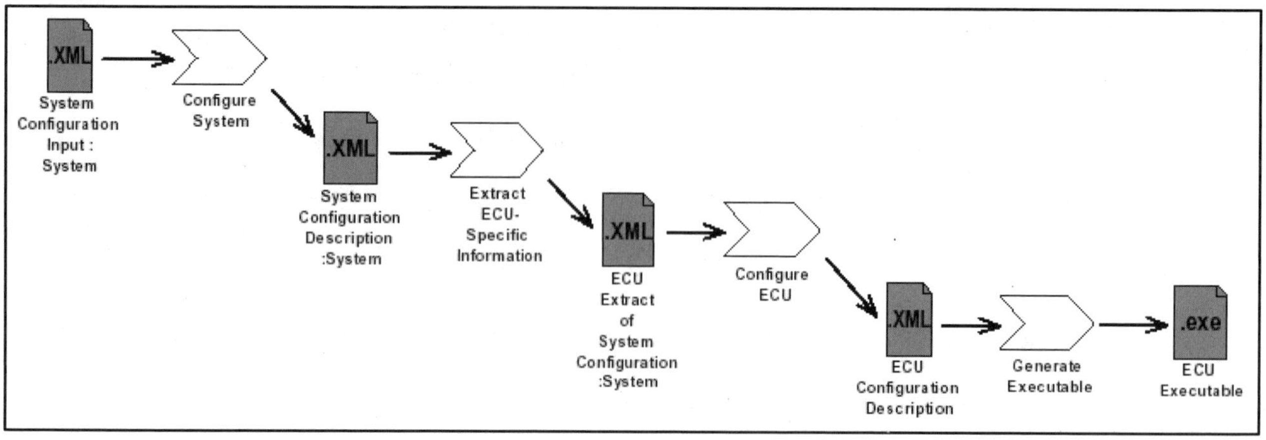

Figure 5 AUTOSAR Methodology Overview [2]

MAPPING OF AUTOSAR SOFTWARE COMPONENTS TO SIMULINK

Simulink is a model-based design environment that provides an interactive graphical environment and a customizable set of block libraries that allows users to accurately design, simulate, implement, and test dynamic systems.

Simulink is widely used in industry [7]. It allows the user to model and simulate a wide range of linear, nonlinear, continuous, discrete and hybrid dynamic systems. It has the capability to model just about anything that can be modeled mathematically.

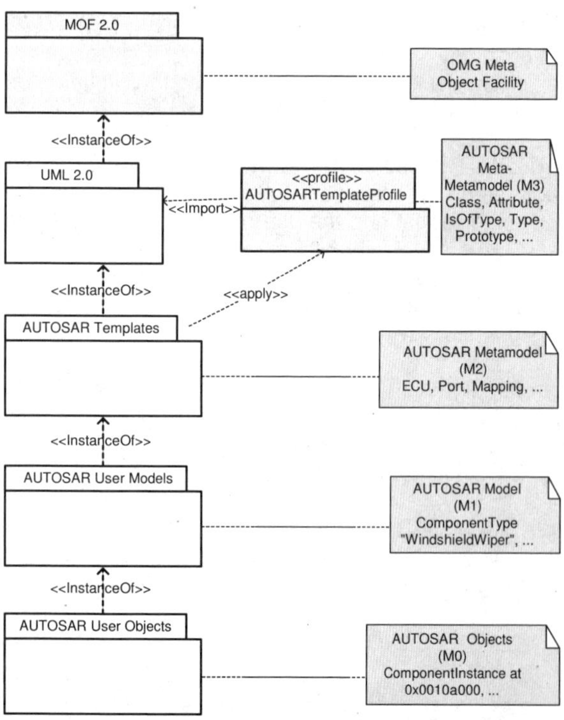

Figure 6 AUTOSAR Metamodel Hierarchy [6]

This section of the paper provides a review of the mapping of a few key AUTOSAR concepts to their Simulink counterparts, which should aid designers using Simulink to deliver AUTOSAR-compatible solutions.

<u>Atomic Software Component</u>

Atomic in the AUTOSAR context denotes a software component that has to be deployed in only one ECU, and it must not be confused with the concept of the atomic execution of Simulink subsystems. An AUTOSAR atomic software component can be represented in Simulink by a subsystem or a model.

The AUTOSAR specification gives the following canonical pattern for modeling atomic software components in Simulink (see Figure 7).

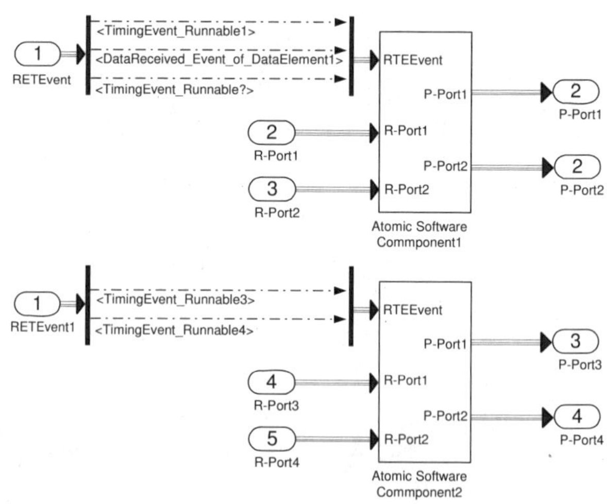

Figure 7 Canonical Pattern for Software Components [8]

Here it is important to highlight the fact that the first in-port in the Simulink block used to model an AUTOSAR atomic software component should be used to route RTE events (RTEEvents) to the software component's runnables.

AUTOSAR Ports

AUTOSAR uses specific ports requiring or providing data or a service from/to a server, named respectively Require-Ports (R-Ports) and Provide-Ports (P-Ports).
An AUTOSAR R-Port is modeled in Simulink by an in-port for sender/receiver communication, while the P-Port is modeled by an out-port for sender/receiver communication.

ComSpec

The communication specification (ComSpec) classes in AUTOSAR capture the information regarding the quality of data communication. *Figure 8* and *Figure 9* show a summary of how to capture information on the quality of communication in Simulink.

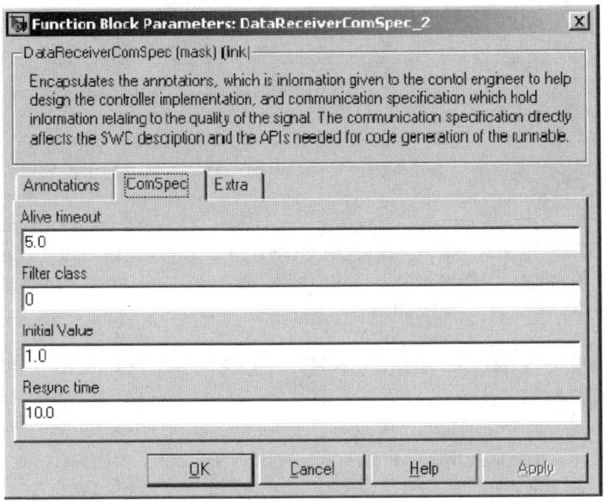

Figure 8 DataReceiverComSpec Parameters [8]

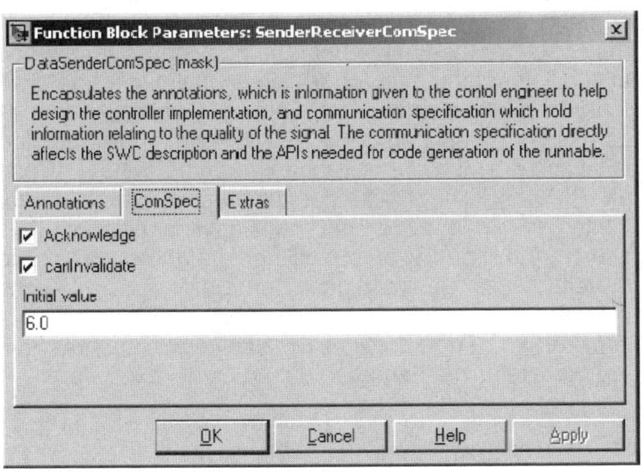

Figure 9 DataSenderComSpec Parameters [8]

Sender/Receiver Interface

A SenderReceiverInterface is an AUTOSAR port interface used for sender/receiver communication, and it is recommended that it be modeled in Simulink via a Simulink BusObject, as shown in Figure 10.

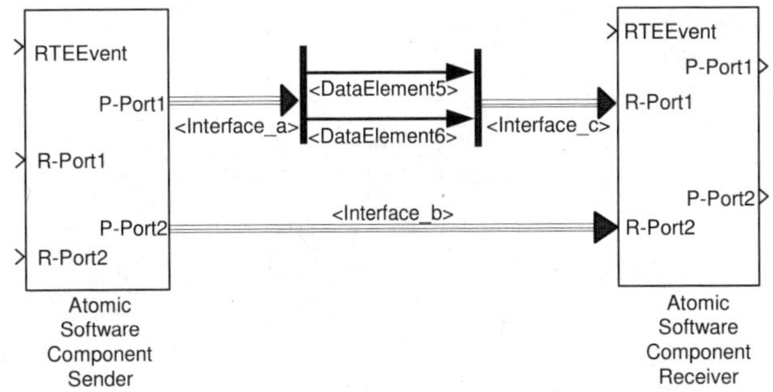

Figure 10 Respecting AUTOSAR's interface compatibility rules using a bus creator (not strictly needed) and a bus selector block [8]

Here it is important to emphasize that this interface only describes the structure of the data elements required or provided by these ports, and does not contain information about the quality of the communication (this information as described above is to be found in the ComSpec classes).

Client Server Interface

This interface is used for client/server communication. The AUTOSAR specification to date does not cover client/server communication among atomic software components, but it does tackle client/server communication between atomic software components (in the role of the client) and AUTOSAR services, as well as sensor actuator software components (as client) and the ECU abstraction. These ports can be modeled in Simulink as a masked s-function or a Stateflow chart.

Sender Receiver Annotation

SenderReceiverAnnotations are basically comments on the data elements in a sender/receiver port and are modeled as such in Simulink; hence they do not influence the code generation, but serve as information to help with the design of the system.

Sensor Actuator Software Components

The sensor and actuator software components offer real-world signals to the application software components, and they are the only components in that level of the AUTOSAR architecture that can access ports from the ECU abstraction below the RTE layer. They are modeled in Simulink as virtual subsystems that contain both "normal" ports and ECU abstraction ports.

Services

AUTOSAR services are functions provided by the RTE, and they can be modeled in Simulink as virtual subsystems.

Runnable

Runnables are the smallest code fragments inside an atomic software component that can be activated by the RTE using RTEEvents independently from the other parts (runnables) of the atomic software component. A runnable is modeled in Simulink as a function call subsystem.

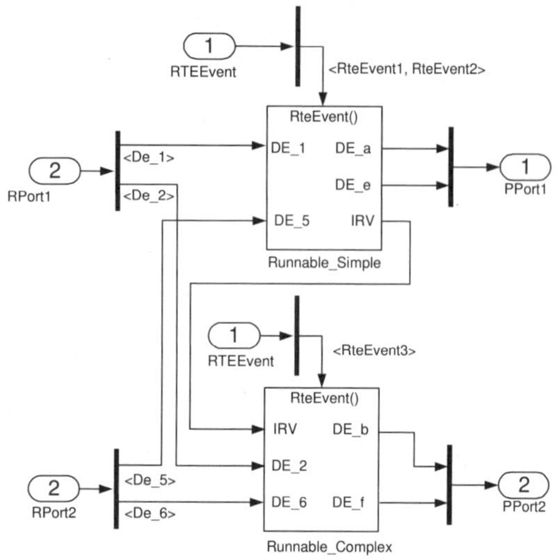

Figure 11 Canonical Pattern for Runnables. Runnable_Simple is activated by multiple RTEEvents [8].

RTEEvents

RTEEvents are used by the RTE to trigger the execution of runnables. In Simulink they are modeled as function calls.

Exclusive Areas

Exclusive areas are regions of code within which RTE blocks concurrent data access. In Simulink they are represented as atomic subsystems marked as an exclusive area. In the event when an entire runnable runs inside an exclusive area, the top-level runnable subsystem should be marked as an exclusive area in Simulink.

The Simulink representation of a runnable only containing parts that belong in an exclusive area is done via modeling nested subsystems (within the runnable) which are marked as exclusive areas.

Composition

Compositions are used in AUTOSAR to create higher abstraction levels. They encapsulate collaboration of components, and are represented in Simulink by virtual subsystems.

Datatypes

The primitive data types used by AUTOSAR are mapped in Simulink as shown in Table 2.

AUTOSAR also uses two types of composite datatypes, arrays and records. Arrays in AUTOSAR have zero indexing, and are represented in Simulink by wide signals with individual elements concatenated together using mux blocks and separated using demux or selector blocks. Records can be represented by bus objects or as Simulink StrucType objects.

AUTOSAR Type	*BSW Type*	*Simulink Datatype*
UInt4	uint8	uint8
SInt4	sint8	int8
UInt8	uint8	uint8
SInt8	sint8	int8
UInt16	uint16	uint16
SInt16	sint16	int16
UInt32	uint32	uint32
SInt32	sint32	int32
Float_with_NaN	float32	float
Float	float32	float
Double_with_NaN	float64	double
Double	float64	double
Boolean	boolean	boolean
Char8	uint8	uint8
Char16	uint16	uint16

Table 2 Autosar and Simulink's built in datatypes [8]

Characteristics

Characteristics are values that can be changed in an ECU, and they can be modeled by extending the Simulink.Parameter class to a new class: AUTOSAR.Characteristic.

APPLYING SIMULINK FOR AUTOSAR IN PRACTICE

A pre-existing Simulink system was redesigned according to the AUTOSAR methodology. The system in question controls an experimental engine management system for use in the automotive industry. The example in Figure 12 is a modification of the PID controller segment of the Simulink system. The modifications were made so that the operation of the PID controller could be tested without the need of an operational plant. The plant featured in the example is a rheostat. A voltage is placed across the rheostat and the desired output (the Setpoint) is selected by the user as the input to the system. When the PID controller is started it actuates an external motor controller, which moves the rheostat wiper position, thus altering the rheostat output voltage, i.e. the output of the system. The "Speed Signal Conditioning" block keeps the value of the output motor speed signal within a preset safe range. The "Position Limiting" block ensures that the rheostat is not damaged during model execution.

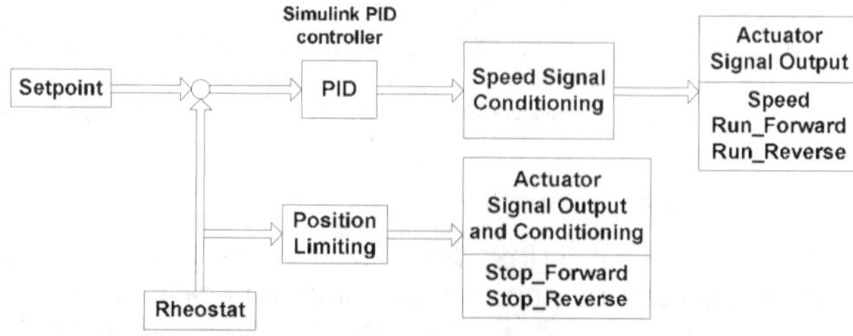

Figure 12 High level view of the PID test system

This System was modelled in Simulink according to the AUTOSAR methodology and the model in Figure 13 is the result.

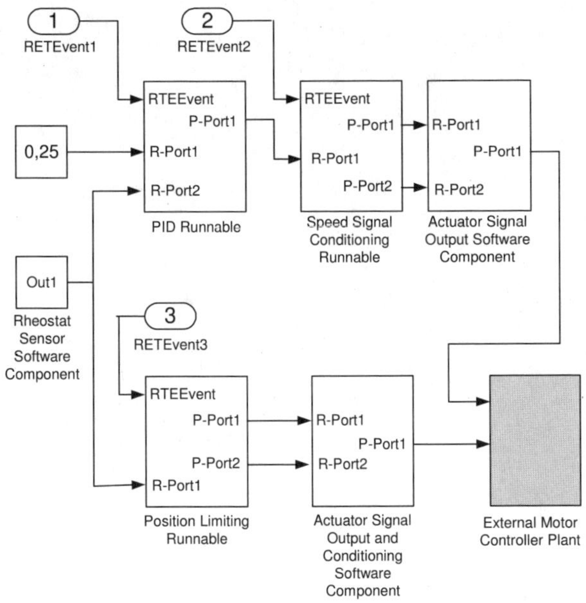

Figure 13 PID Test System in Simulink

This model takes the discrete blocks shown in Figure 12 and recreates them as AUTOSAR runnables in the form of Simulink function-call subsystems. All communication between the runnables takes place via the RTE. Each runnable is called as necessary and the final output of the system is routed to the External Motor Controller Plant.

The process of redesigning the Simulink model to conform to the AUTOSAR standard was found to be relatively straightforward once the AUTOSAR requirements were understood.

CONCLUSION

The emerging AUTOSAR standard presents a very interesting development for the automotive software field. It presents an innovative, layered architecture composed of modular components with standardized interfaces. Furthermore, AUTOSAR maximizes hardware independence for in-vehicle software.

The AUTOSAR methodology promotes a thorough integration of tool support and model-based design techniques.

A model-based design environment like Simulink is thoroughly supported by AUTOSAR, which describes in its specification the mapping of key AUTOSAR concepts into Simulink. This greatly helps system designers to model AUTOSAR conformant systems in Simulink.

ACKNOWLEDGMENTS

We wish to thank AUTOSAR for allowing the authors to reproduce illustrations from the AUTOSAR specification. Additionally the authors would like to acknowledge the contribution and support of: Lero – The Irish Software Engineering Research Centre; the John Holland Research Centre; the Circuits and Systems Research Centre. The authors wish to thank the SFI – Science Foundation Ireland for funding this research.

REFERENCES

1. Heinecke H., Bielefeld J., Schnelle, K., Maldener N., Fennel H., Weis O., Weber T., Ruh J., Lundh L., Sanden T., Heitkamper P., Rimkus R., Leflour J., Gilberg A., Virnich U., Voget S., Nishikawa K., Kajio K., Scharnhorst T., Kunkel B., 2006, "AUTOSAR – Current results and preparations for exploitation", Euroforum conference May 3-rd 2006, Stuttgart, Germany.

2. AUTOSAR Technical Overview, 2006, AUTOSAR Specification -Release 2.0, Retrieved on 20/05/2006 from www.autosar.org.

3. AUTOSAR Main Requirements, 2006, AUTOSAR Specification -Release 2.0, Retrieved on 20/05/2006 from www.autosar.org.

4. AUTOSAR Software Component Template, 2006, AUTOSAR Specification -Release 2.0, Retrieved on 20/05/2006 from www.autosar.org.

5. AUTOSAR Glossary, 2006, AUTOSAR Specification -Release 2.0, Retrieved on 20/05/2006 from www.autosar.org.

6. AUTOSAR Template UML Profile and Modelling Guide, 2006, AUTOSAR Specification -Release 2.0, Retrieved on 20/05/2006 from www.autosar.org.

7. Moretti, G., 2005, Design complexity requires system-level design, Technical Editor -- EDN, 14/09/2006, [Online], Available from; <http://www.edn.com/article/CA505068.html#TheevolutionofMatlabandSimulink> [10 March 2005].

8. Applying Simulink to AUTOSAR, 2006, AUTOSAR Specification – Release 2.0, Retrieved on 20/05/2006 from www.autosar.org

CONTACT

Anila Mjeda: **Anila.Mjeda@lero.ie**.

2005-01-0323

Wireless Multicasting for Remote Software Upload in Vehicles With Realistic Vehicle Movements

Radovan Miucic and Syed Masud Mahmud
Electrical and Computer Engineering Department, Wayne State University

ABSTRACT

Future vehicles will have many features that include, but are not limited to, drive-by-wire, telematics, pre-crash warning, highway guidance and traffic alert systems. From time to time the vehicles will need to have their software modules updated for various reasons, such as to introduce new features in vehicles, the need to change the navigation map, the need to fine tune various features of the vehicles, etc. A remote software update has a number of advantages, such as it does not require consumers to take their vehicles to the dealers, and the dealers do not need to spend time on vehicles on an individual basis. Thus, remote software updates can save consumers' valuable time, as well as cost savings for the vehicle manufacturers.

Since wireless links have limited bandwidth, uploading software in thousands of vehicles in a cost-effective and timely manner is a challenge. Another major issue related to the remote software update is the security of the update process. In another paper, we addressed the security issue of the update process. In this paper, we present a wireless multicasting technique for uploading software in vehicles. Since the servers that will be broadcasting the software are located in some permanent places, and the vehicles are located all over the country, the software upload process has to depend on an infrastructure such as the cellular infrastructure. We have developed simulation models to determine the performance of our proposed wireless multicasting technique for remote software uploads. We simulated hundreds of vehicles distributed around a city area. In the simulation model, we assumed realistic speeds for the vehicles depending upon where the vehicles were located. The vehicles transfer the software from a buffer to an electronic control unit (ECU) when their ignition is off. Our simulation results show that if the multicast technique is used instead of the unicast technique (one vehicle at a time), then the software can be updated in a very cost-effective manner. The paper will give a detailed description of our technique and provide numerous results of the simulations collected for various distributions of the systems and vehicles.

INTRODUCTION

Today, most of the electronic controller units (ECUs) have in-vehicle programming (IVP) capabilities. Some of the ECUs in the modern vehicle are IC (instrument cluster), ABS (antilock brake system), ECM (engine control module), PCM (power control module), BCM (body control module), HVAC, infotainment systems, radio, MP3 player, DVD, On Star, door module, seat module, airbag module, navigation module, etc.

Sometimes software needs to be updated for various reasons, such as: calibration update, a problem with the existing software in modules, a recall of the vehicle due to software error, a new implementation, or the addition of new features. Some component suppliers only have a limited time to develop their products, and sometimes products go into production with very little testing. Such components are at high risk of unacceptable behavior later on, and it is very useful to have a cost-effective reprogramming system in place. Nowadays, if there is a need for a software update, a customer usually goes to the dealer, and the technician reprograms the module by physically plugging a programmer into the connector that has access to the intervehicele bus or busses such as CAN, LIN, J1850, UBP, SCP, etc. The programmer then uploads software into the vehicle's modules. Technicians at a dealership upload new software into vehicles one vehicle at a time. If there is a vehicle recall due to software error, dealers would have to reprogram hundreds of thousands of vehicles. The process of uploading software into each vehicle is an inconvenience for both the dealers and the customers. The car manufacturers lose money and the customers lose confidence because of this process. For each module to be programmed, it will take time for setup and actual servicing, including taking the customer's time to make the appointment, physically bringing the vehicle to the dealer, and spending time while the vehicle is being serviced. In addition, it takes months to update the software in all the vehicles, and there is no guarantee that all customers will bring in their vehicles for service.

Our motivation is to bring down the cost of updating modules by broadcasting the software that will be updated in particular modules in vehicles. Cellular towers are currently located in cities, towns and near major roads where the most vehicles are located. Car manufacturers can jointly work with major cellular companies to have some channels reserved for their needs, or lease the channels when needed. Software can be updated in vehicles by using either a unicast or a multicast process. In a unicast process, the vehicles will receive software on an individual basis, but in a multicast process, all vehicles within the range of a tower will receive software in parallel. However, updating software using the multicast process will need significantly less bandwidth than that needed by the unicast process.

Security of the transferred software is an important aspect of multicast programming. A vehicle network must have a cost-effective security system. The desired level of security needs to have a good balance of cost and extensiveness [3]. We will mainly focus on the wireless update process and leave security issues for another paper. This paper presents simulation models for performing remote software updates in vehicles. The simulation results show that updating software using the multicast process is very cost-effective compared to using the unicast process.

RELATED WORK

Rooftop networks, proposed in [1], provide an alternative to wired networks. The rooftop network is not mobile. In this network, antennas are mounted on building roofs, and several can be installed in metropolitan areas. The antennas are placed in line-of-sight orientation to their neighbors. The routing algorithm for rooftop networks proposes self-configuration for hundreds of thousands of such nodes in a metropolitan area. However, the routing algorithm faces significant scalability and security challenges.

GeoMote [2] developed a routing algorithm for TinyOS (Operating System for Tiny Networked Sensors). Low-cost, densely placed networked sensors with limited available memory, power and processing resources are called "motes". Every mote must know its own location in order to participate in the network. Three types of motes: GeoRouters, GeoGateways and GeoHosts are used in the networks. GeoRouters run routing algorithms to decide how the messages are to be routed based on the geographical locations.

OnStar, Vetronix and Networkcar have remote diagnostics programs. If remote diagnostics programs prove to be successful, OEMs will be sure to invest more to exploit remote diagnostics [4].

SOFTWARE SIMULATION DESCRIPTION

Our software consists of the simulation of three major elements: a map, the towers and the vehicles. These elements interact with each other. The vehicle movement and the tower broadcast are represented on a map, as shown in Figure 1.

The map, shown in Figure 1, is an array representing city blocks. City blocks consist of empty spaces and roads. In our simulation model, a vehicle cannot exist in an empty space - it can only be on a road. Roads intersect with each other. Software simulation considers situations in which a vehicle can travel east or west, north or south, and north, west, south, and east at intersections (see Figure 2).

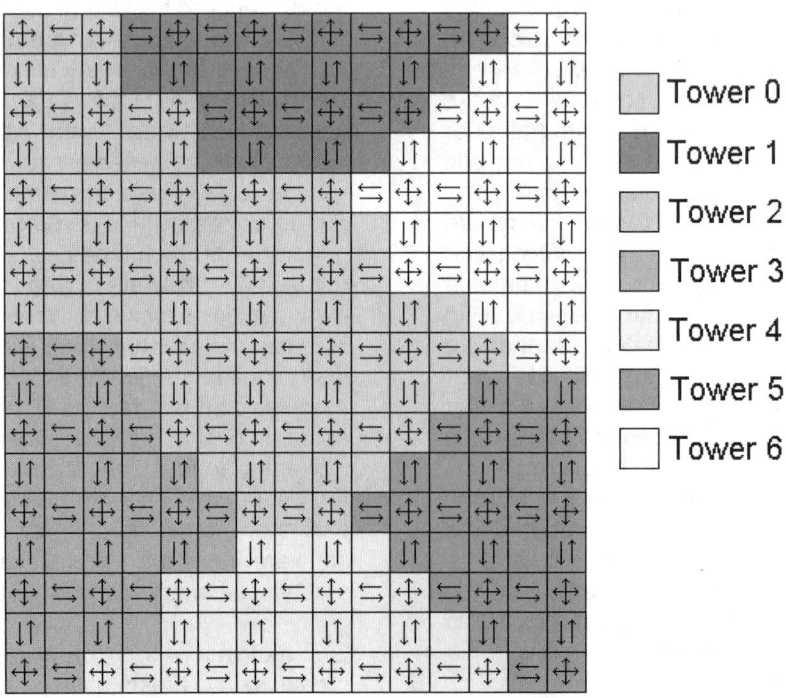

Figure 1: Map of the city blocks and towers' coverage areas

The towers are represented on the map. Each city block is under some tower coverage. Only the tower coverage of the roads is of interest to us. The towers broadcast software to their coverage area. For simplicity, we have assumed that there are no overlaps of the coverage areas of the towers. Assuming there is no overlap of tower coverage areas is reasonable, because a vehicle receiver can have a signal strength detector and the detector may be set to only accept the strongest signal.

Vehicles are simulated to be traveling on these roads. The vehicle position and direction is determined in the initialization phase of the simulation software. A vehicle may change direction when it reaches an intersection. When a vehicle enters an intersection, it randomly decides to change or not to change its current direction. For simplicity, if a vehicle reaches a boundary of the map, it reverses its direction. The vehicle receives software packets from the tower while it is moving. The vehicle may miss receiving a packet due to a weak signal and noise, or due to a change in the coverage area.

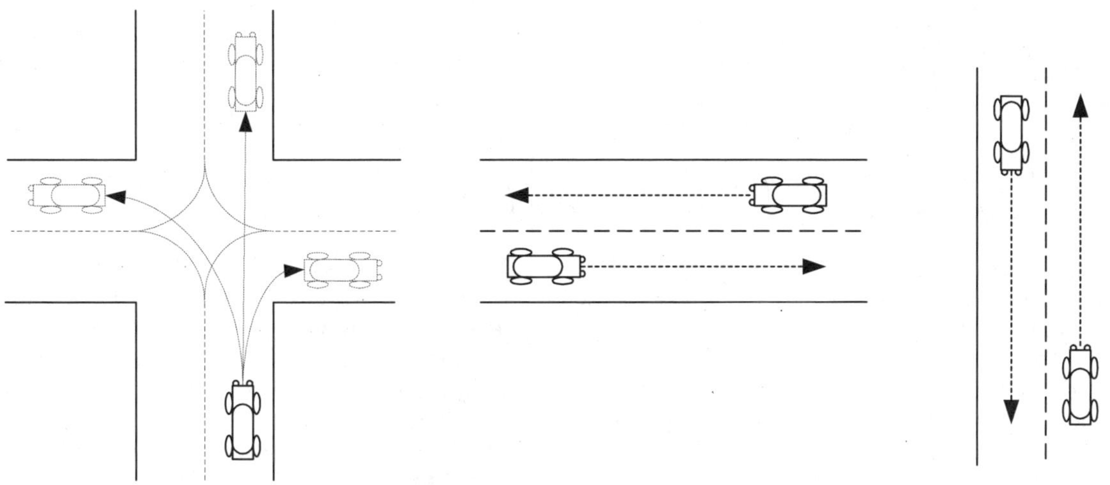

Figure 2: Possible vehicle movement in the simulation model

The original equipment manufacturer (OEM) or the supplier decides that a certain ECU needs an update. The OEM sends the software for a target ECU to the central server (CS). The CS uploads the software to the nearest tower, and the tower starts broadcasting the software to the vehicles within its coverage area. The tower also sends the software to its neighboring towers. The software must contain information about the vehicle model and year and about the ECU. The vehicle must recognize if the software that is being received is targeting one of its ECUs. If the software is targeting an ECU on the vehicle, the vehicle will buffer the received software. If the software is not targeting an ECU of the vehicle, the vehicle will ignore that software. The received software must contain version control information. The vehicle will compare the ECU's current software version with the received software version. The vehicle accepts received software only if the version of the broadcast software is newer than the version of the software currently available in the ECU. The strategy of matching the new software with the current software in the target ECU will be the topic of a different paper. In our simulation, we will only consider vehicles that have an ECU in need of an update.

Software Packets: The software is divided into smaller pieces of code, called packets. A tower sends packets sequentially, from the first packet to the last. Vehicles accept software packets that are being wirelessly sent from the tower. A vehicle may fail to receive a packet for various reasons, such as the presence of noise, transition from one tower to the next tower, etc. If a vehicle starts receiving a packet and does not receive the next packet for some time, or if it receives the last packet sent but some prior packets are missing, then it will start sending periodic "complain" messages indicating that the vehicle's target ECU has not been programmed. After a tower has sent all of the software packets it waits for some time to determine whether any vehicle sends a message indicating that the target ECU has not been programmed. We use the symbol VNP for any message that indicates that a vehicle has not been programmed, and the symbol WP to indicate the time during which the vehicle waits for the VNP message. A VNP message will identify what software is missing from a vehicle. If a tower receives a VNP message during the period WP, it starts transmitting the entire software all over again. If a vehicle exits and stays out of the coverage area after the WP period it will not be updated: the software will remain in the tower's buffer during the WP period. If a tower does not receive the VNP message, the tower flushes its buffer to make it free for other activities. If the tower receives a VNP message after the WP period, it will request the software from the central server, and the entire process of broadcasting the software is then repeated. Figure 3 shows the broadcasting timeline. The entire process includes the following steps, as shown in Figure 3:

1) The tower starts broadcasting the software.
2) The tower finishes broadcasting the software.
3) The tower waits in the WP state.
4) The tower receives a VNP message.
5) The tower starts broadcasting the software.
6) The tower waits in the WP state and does not receive any VNP message.
7) The tower deletes the software from its buffer.

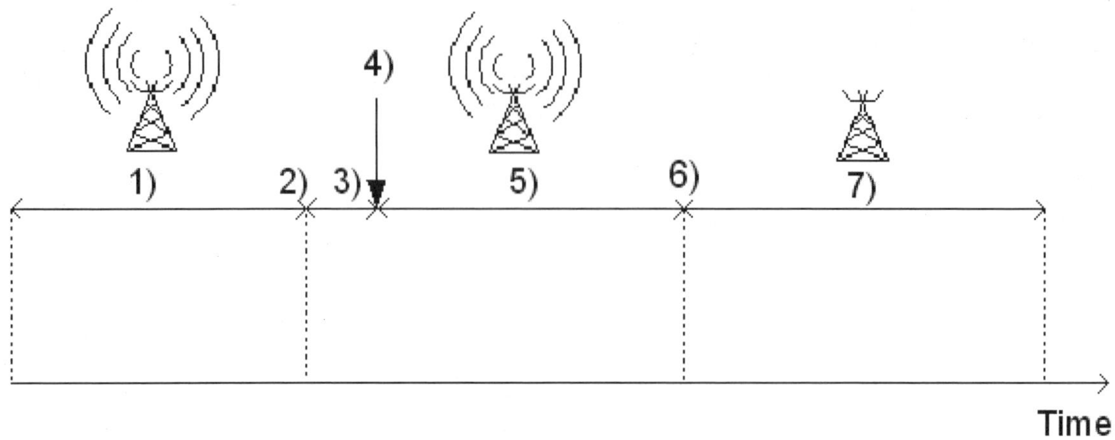

Figure 3 – Broadcasting timeline

There must be a dedicated device in the electrical architecture of the vehicle, perhaps a new ECU (WECU – Wireless ECU) which is capable of wireless communication. The vehicle will have a buffer large enough to store memory of the largest ECU in the vehicle's network architecture. The vehicle will receive the software via the WECU and save it in its buffer. The target ECU is reprogrammed from the buffer when it becomes convenient, i.e. safety critical ECUs may be updated when the vehicle stops and the ignition is off. Other ECUs may be updated on the fly. The WECU will determine if it is safe to update the target ECU. The designated ECU will check the battery condition and other target-specific conditions. Updating a vehicle without the customer's consent can pose problems. For example, the vehicle owner has memorized his/her favorite seat position. Their saved seat information will be lost during the software update, and the customer will notice the difference.

Simulation Process – Our software simulation executes in loops. Each loop takes the smallest time interval, here called time instance TI. In our simulation, the value of TI is 12.5 ms. The entire packet has been broken down in the simulation program into many small packets, and the size of each packet is 1KB (kilobytes). We assumed that a vehicle needs 8 time instances (TI) to receive a packet. In other words, the speed of the wireless communication is 10 KB/sec.

Broadcast Delay - The delay between a pair of neighboring towers is one hop. We consider one hop delay to be equal to one packet delay, or 8-TI delay. We assumed that tower T0 is the closest tower to the server. Since different towers are located at different hop distances away from Tower T0, different towers start broadcasting the software after a different length of delay, as shown in Figure 4. Tower T0, which is closest to the server, has no delay in broadcasting the software.

Signal Strength – The wireless signal is the strongest in the immediate vicinity of a tower. The signal strength of the broadcast in a city block depends on the distance from the city block to the broadcasting tower. We have defined four levels of signal strength. The city blocks closest to the tower have the strongest signal. The strongest signal is represented by using four fully colored bars, as shown in Figure 5. The city block that is farthest from the broadcasting tower has the weakest signal and it is represented with one fully colored bar, as shown in Figure 5. The vehicle in the city block with the strongest signal has the highest probability of receiving broadcasted packets. The vehicle in the city block with the weakest signal has the least probability of receiving broadcasted packets.

RESULTS

We ran our simulation with various input parameters. Figure 6 shows the outcome of the simulation. The cost, which is the number of times the towers had to rebroadcast the entire software, is shown on the Y-axis. The size of the software in packets is shown on the X-axis. The average cost to rebroadcast the software increases with the number of vehicles on the roads. As we mentioned earlier, packets may be lost due to low signal strength or due to movements of the vehicles from one tower region to another.

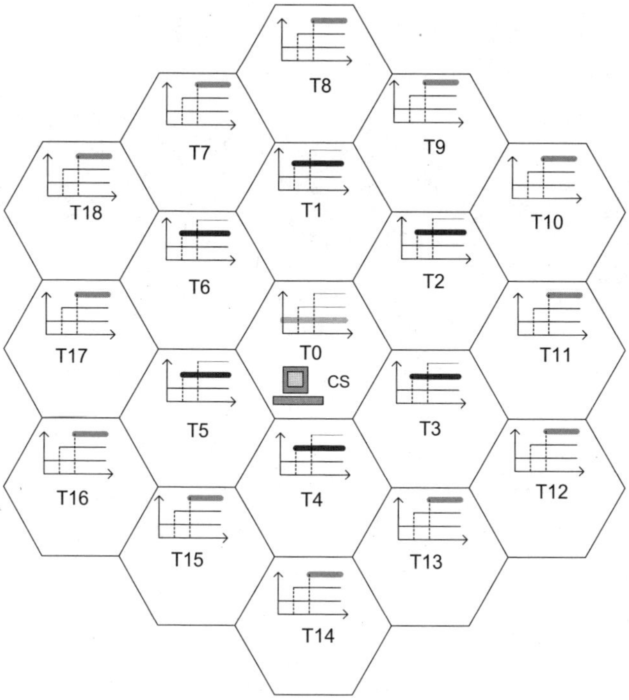

Figure 4 – Towers' broadcast delays.

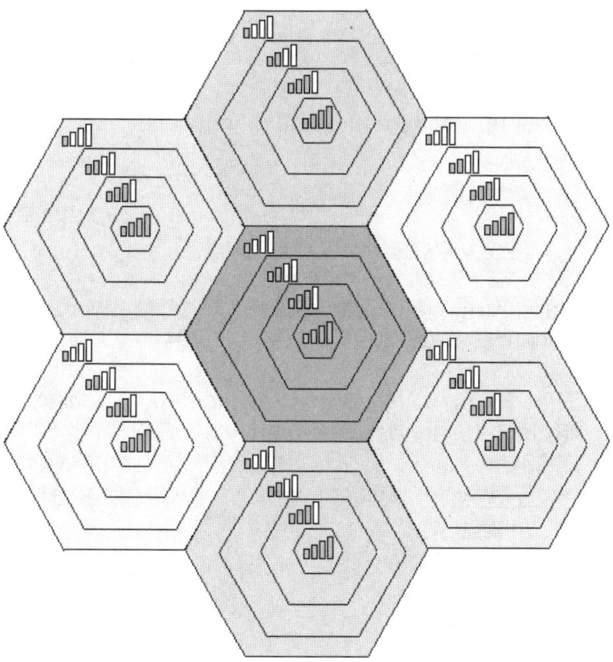

Figure 5 - Towers' signal strength

We assumed east-west and north-south roads connecting two intersections to be 800 meters long. Also, we assumed the length of the intersection to be 50 meters. Let's say that the bandwidth of the wireless link is 10 KB/sec. If a vehicle is moving at 100 km/hour it will travel 0.347 meter per time instance (12.5 ms). For simplicity, the simulation program updates the vehicle's position on the map after every 10 meters.
(Number of packets) x (number of instances per packet) x (time instance) = time for 1 software broadcast

For example, software containing 1500 packets will need 1500x 8 x 12.5 x 10^{-3} s = 150 sec to be uploaded in vehicles.

The signal strength at a vehicle depends on its distance from the nearest tower. In our simulation, a vehicle has to be in the coverage area during a software broadcast for 8 consecutive time instances in order for it to receive a complete packet. There is a possibility that the vehicle may receive corrupted data in any of the 8 time instances while a packet is being received, resulting in the loss of the packet. Figure 6 shows the results of the simulation runs for the following parameters.

- The probability of losing a packet is 10% in a region where the signal strength is the weakest (signal where only one bar is green, as shown in Figure 5)
- The probability of losing a packet is 5% in a region where the signal strength is nearly the weakest (signal where two bars are green, as shown in Figure 5)
- The probability of losing a packet is 2.5% in a region where the signal strength is nearly the strongest (signal where three bars are green, as shown in Figure 5)
- The probability of losing a packet is 0.01% in a region where the signal strength is the strongest (signal where all four bars are green, as shown in Figure 5)

Figure 6 is divided into two parts. The bottom part of Figure 6 shows the result for the case which assumes that the vehicles only lost packets because they were moving from one tower region to another. More specifically, this means that while a vehicle was receiving a packet it did not stay within the coverage of the tower from which it was receiving the packet for eight time instances (TI). For this case, the towers only broadcast the software a couple of times. The top part of Figure 6 shows the result for the case which took into consideration the vehicle movements and signal strengths. Figure 6 shows that the vehicles lost some packets mostly due to weak signals rather than due to vehicle movement. Thus, when signal strengths were taken into consideration, the towers had to broadcast the software significantly more times than when we were just considering vehicle movement. Figure 6 shows that the towers had to broadcast the software containing 1500 packets 18 times to load it into 500 vehicles. However, had the vehicles been uploaded one at a time instead of all 500 vehicles in parallel, then the towers would have been broadcasting the software 500 times. Thus, there is significant bandwidth saving when a group of vehicles is uploaded in parallel. This means that when compared to the unicast technique, a software upload using the multicast technique will result in significant cost savings.

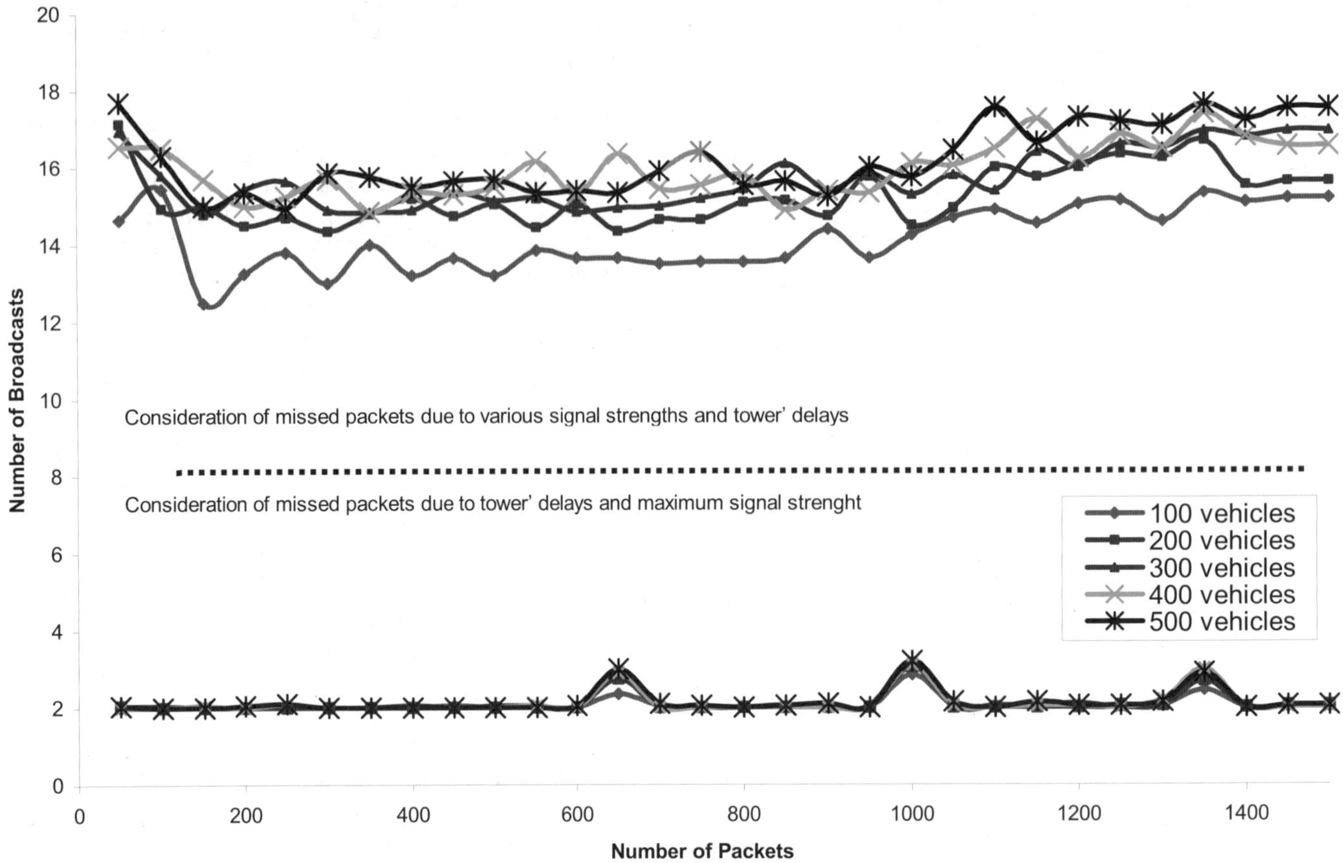

Figure 6 – Number of Broadcasts versus Number of Packets for various numbers of vehicles.

CONCLUSION

A study has been done to evaluate the effectiveness of software updates in vehicles using the multicast technique. We did a simulation assuming vehicles would move as predicted on city block maps. As the vehicles move from one city block to the next, they also move from one tower region to another tower region. According to the simulation results, updating software in vehicles using the multicast process is very cost-effective compared to that using the unicast process. Since the software can be updated using existing cell phone networks, no additional infrastructure is necessary for updating software in vehicles.

REFERENCES

1. Thanos Stathopoulos, John Heidemann, and Deborah Estrin. A Remote Code Update Mechanism for Wireless Sensor Networks. Technical Report CENS-TR-30, University of California, Los Angeles, Center for Embedded Networked Computing, November, 2003. http://www.isi.edu/~johnh/PAPERS/index.html

2. Peter Broadwell, Joseph Polastre, and Rachel Rubin, "GeoMote: Geographic Multicast for Networked Sensors." Class Project Paper 2001. 21 March 2004. Available: http://www.cs.berkeley.edu/~pbwell/

3. Mark Krage and Laci Jalics. "The Many Faces of Security," SAE, 2004-01-0236, 2004.

4. The Hansen Report on Automotive Electronics. "Remote Diagnostics— the Next OEM Frontier" dec. 2003/jan. 2004 Available: http://www.vetronix.com/pdf/press/vtx_2004-01-xx_hansen.pdf

CONTACT

Radovan Miucic received a B.S. degree in Electrical Engineering from Wayne State University, Detroit, in 2001 and his M.S. degree in Computer Engineering from Wayne State University, Detroit, in 2002. Currently he is working on his PhD degree, and as a software engineer in the automotive industry.

Email: radovanmiucic@hotmail.com

Syed Masud Mahmud, Ph.D.
Associate Professor
Department of Electrical and Computer Engineering
Wayne State University, Detroit, MI 48202
Phone: (313) 577-3855
Fax: (313) 577-1101
Email: smahmud@eng.wayne.edu

DEFINITIONS, ACRONYMS, ABBREVIATIONS

ECU – Electronic control unit.

CS – Central server. A computer repository for software to be broadcasted.

OEM – Original equipment manufacturer.

SFTE – Software for targeted ECU

VNP – The vehicle's targeted ECU is not programmed. A message from a vehicle to the tower indicating that some packets are missing in the vehicle's buffer.

TI –Time instance. This is the smallest time unit in the software simulation of loop time.

WP – Wait for VNP. The period of time the tower waits for a VNP message after a broadcast.

WECU – Wireless ECU.

2004-01-0678

Loading Flashware from External Interfaces Such as CD-ROM or W-LAN and Programming ECUs by an On-Board SW-Component

Cornelia Heinisch
STZ Softwaretechnik

Martin Simons
DaimlerChrysler

ABSTRACT

Electronic Control Units (ECUs) are typically programmed using external programming devices – frequently called Diagnostic Testers. We propose a system and software architecture that requires no Diagnostic Tester for ECU (re)programming. ECU (re)programming is instead managed by an on-board software component, the Flashware-Reprogramming-Controller. It can reside in any ECU that has sufficient memory and processing power as well as good connectivity to internal networks and external sources from which to receive the software to be installed. Appropriate choices could be modern telematic devices. A second co-located on-board software component – the Installation-Configuration-Controller – is used to supervise the installation of new software releases and to validate their integrity after installation. The proposed architecture can be used for software download into ECUs in development, end-of-line production and after sales. It is also suitable for software download over the air, which may be relevant for future provisioning scenarios. To accommodate these diverse use cases, flashable software, or flashware, may be loaded from any choice of transmission medium, e.g., a CD or a USB memory stick, or via any choice of transmission network, such as WLAN, GSM or GPRS. We illustrate the advantages of the new architecture using an OSGi-based prototype.

INTRODUCTION

A car without software would be impossible today, and the importance of software for modern vehicle functions will still grow in the coming years [1, 2]. Premium class vehicles already contain several dozens of MBytes of software and by 2010 this number may well reach 1 GByte. This software resides in dozens of interconnected embedded devices (electronic control units or ECUs) and implements vehicle functions ranging from hard real-time, highly safety-relevant vehicle control features to comfort and entertainment features. The dependencies between the distributed software parts and between software and hardware make it increasingly difficult to exchange only one individual hardware or software part. To avoid failures it is absolutely necessary to define valid *hardware* and *software configurations*, and to guarantee that only valid software configurations can be generated and loaded into the car. Furthermore, an automobile manufacturer has to support suitable hardware and software configurations for each *feature configuration*, which can be ordered within a production series.

The fact that a vehicle can be ordered in a lot of variants, and that most of these variants can be more easily implemented in software than in hardware, is the reason for the substitution of ROM by *flash memory* in more and more ECUs. The benefit is twofold: First, fewer hardware variants of an ECU need to be stocked in production and in after-sales, because the variants are generated by programming the hardware. This can be done in production as well as in after-sales. Secondly, software errors can be removed by reprogramming an ECU, so there is no longer the need to replace the ECU. Additionally, it is possible to update the functionality or to integrate new hardware-independent functionality over the life cycle of a car, provided the ECU has sufficient memory.

To profit from these advantages and to manage the significant complexities introduced by the need to provision millions of vehicles across the world with software, a vehicle manufacturer must solve two important challenges. First, the processes that govern the (re)programming of an ECU must be the same for all ECUs and for all situations, i.e., for development, production, and after sales. Second, the integrity of the vehicle after reprogramming must be assured. We propose a system and software architecture that helps to solve these challenges. We illustrate the architecture by means of a prototype. The key building blocks of this architecture are:

1. A *Flashware-Reprogramming-Controller* which implements the Diagnostic Tester functionality for (re)programming ECUs connected to in-vehicle sub-networks. This component can be deployed on an ECU itself or on an external device, depending on further design choices.
2. An *Installation-Configuration-Controller* which supervises the installation procedure of a new *software release* and cyclically validates the integrity of an installed software release.
3. A container construct for encapsulating *flashware modules*. ECU specific software together with auxiliary and administrative information is packed into a container; the container is transported to the vehicle where it is unpacked and the contained software is installed by the Flashware-Reprogramming-Controller.

The main part of this paper is organized as follows. After presenting the state of the art, the basic concepts of the new architecture are discussed. Next, a platform-independent model (PIM) [3] of the architecture is introduced. That means the system is decomposed into its parts, and the co-operation of these parts is shown without considering specific platforms and technologies which may be used for implementation. The mapping to the platform and technologies used is shown in the section "PROTOTYPE".

STATE OF THE ART

A software component – the so-called *flash loader* – is required in all ECUs with flash memory. The flash loader receives new ECU software over a sub-network of the vehicle and installs it in the flash memory of the ECU. Modern flash memories allow the separation of the memory into segments, which can be separately erased and written-to. We call a piece of software which fits into such a memory segment and which can be loaded and installed by the flash loader a *flashware module*. Accordingly, the flashware of an ECU consists of 1 to n flashware modules.

At present, an external (re)programming device (Diagnostic Tester) is connected to the diagnostic connector of the car and sends a flashware module to its destination ECU by using the transport protocol ISO 15765-2 [4] and the diagnostic protocol KWP2000 [5]. KWP2000 protocol options are used to specify the required additional (re)programming services. The conventional Diagnostic Tester is appropriately extended and implements these services. During (re)programming the Diagnostic Tester then coordinates its actions with those of an ECU's flash loader.

Figure 1 shows how an ECU located on a CAN sub-network is reprogrammed by an external (re)programming device. The Diagnostic Tester is connected to the diagnostic connector of the car, and the diagnostic connector is linked with a gateway ECU, which forwards messages from the Diagnostic Tester either to the CAN sub-network or to the MOST sub-network. In the first step, the ECU to be (re)programmed is placed into diagnostic mode by sending a specific KWP2000 message to the destination ECU. The ECU returns a KWP2000 response message to indicate whether or not the request has been executed successfully. The next step is to place the ECU into (re)programming mode. In this mode, the processor fetches instructions from a designated part of memory, e.g., a write-protected flash memory segment or ROM, containing a minimal software stack necessary to execute a full reprogramming session [9]. Before any KWP2000 service that manipulates the flash memory is executed in an ECU, the ECU typically authenticates the Diagnostic Tester, e.g., by executing a "Seed and Key algorithm" [5]. When the authentication has been successfully completed, a flashware module can be sent to the ECU. Depending on the security requirements or guidelines of the ECU supplier or the automotive manufacturer [6, 9], a *checksum* calculation and a signature check is executed optionally in the ECU to ensure that all the data have been correctly received and written to the flash memory, and that the downloaded flashware module was intended to run inside the destination ECU. After successful installation, the ECU is restarted in application mode, executing the new application.

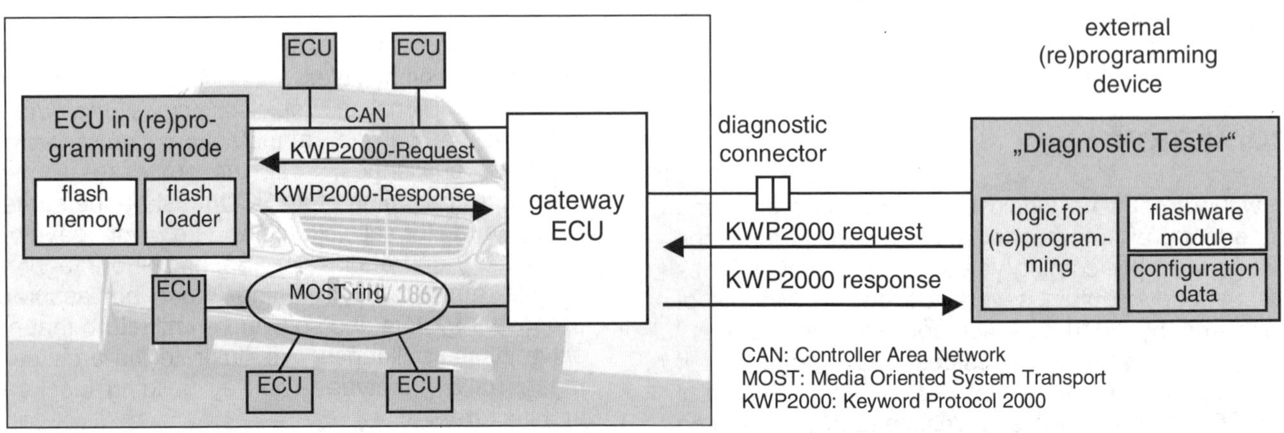

Figure 1: (Re)programming ECUs by an external (re)programming device

To be able to (re)program an ECU, the Diagnostic Tester needs the flashware modules – making up the new application software for the ECU – as well as configuration data (see Figure 1). Configuration data contains information about the flashware modules – for example, start addresses and lengths of the individual segments, and *checksums* of the flashware modules. If no standard flash loader is available for a specific ECU, it is necessary to provide additional configuration data describing the KWP2000 messages and their order required for (re)programming the ECU.

The problem of different flash loaders has already been recognized, and a standard flash loader is being specified within the HIS consortium [7, 8]. In this way, flash loaders will behave identically in the future. This is an important step towards reducing the complexity of flash (re)programming because information about ECU-specific (re)programming sequences and KWP2000 message formats are no longer required as part of the configuration data.

THE BASIC CONCEPTS OF THE ARCHITECTURE

This section presents details on the three basic building blocks of our proposed architecture. Each subsection covers one basic building block.

FLASHWARE REPROGRAMMING CONTROLLER

As already mentioned, today's ECUs are (re)programmed using a Diagnostic Tester. An advantage of this approach is, of course, that the Diagnostic Tester is available in most workshops for diagnostic purposes. In this way, the available infrastructure for diagnosis can be reused for ECU (re)programming. A further advantage is that an ECU can only be (re)programmed in the secure and controlled environment of a workshop. However, the Diagnostic Tester can only be used for one task at a time – either for diagnosis or for (re)programming. Depending on the amount of software to be installed, (re)programming ECUs may take anything between a few minutes to several hours. A diagnosis tester may therefore be blocked for a considerable amount of time. The strict requirement of Diagnostic Tester equipment (hard- and software) for ECU (re)programming is not only an advantage but also a limitation that can be particularly pronounced in countries where only a few dealer workshops exist. It also precludes (re)programming scenarios that can be fully automated and performed by the owner. A third disadvantage is that workshop engineers have to be trained to perform flash (re)programming with a Diagnostic Tester.

The first key idea then is how to factor the (re)programming functionality out of the Diagnostic Tester and to encapsulate it into a self-contained SW-component called Flashware-Reprogramming-Controller. This component may be deployed in an ECU of the car with sufficient memory and processing power and appropriate access to internal sub-networks and to external sources of flashware modules such as a CD ROM drive or wireless communication links such as GSM, GPRS or WLAN. This concept makes a broad range of technical possibilities for the download of software feasible. No Diagnostic Tester is required for reprogramming – despite the fact that the Flashware-Reprogramming-Controller may run in an external (re)programming device. Whether the Flashware-Reprogramming-Controller runs inside or outside the car in an external (re)programming device depends on the operational area. We distinguish the operational areas development, end-of-line production, and after-sales. The host ECU of the Flashware-Reprogramming-Controller may not be fully operational during the car's development. In this case, the Flashware-Reprogramming-Controller may be deployed on a laptop. This laptop would be connected to the ECUs to be (re)programmed via CAN or MOST. In end-of-line production there may be a similar problem, when the host ECU of the Flashware-Reprogramming-Controller is not programmed or mounted. Then it would be necessary to run the Flashware-Reprogramming-Controller outside the car in an external (re)programming device. In after-sales, the Flashware-Reprogramming-Controller will run on the host ECU inside the car. A typical candidate for a host ECU would be a telematics ECU, such as a head-unit. Our aim was to design a software download architecture that is flexible enough to accommodate all of these operational areas. Consequently, the Flashware-Reprogramming-Controller should be deployable on devices internal or external to the vehicle. Moreover, the Flashware-Reprogramming-Controller should be capable of accepting flashware modules from arbitrary sources as CDROM, or USB memory stick, or from networks such as W-LAN, GSM or GPRS (see Figure 2).

All flashware modules are typically stored on a central flashware server of the automotive manufacturer. The flashware modules that make up a new software release for a car are combined and can then be transferred via wireless means (e.g., GSM, GPRS, or UMTS) directly to the host devices of the Flashware-Reprogramming-Controller. Once a flashware module is downloaded, the Flashware-Reprogramming-Controller transfers the flashware module to the destination ECU and controls its correct installation. This "remote software update" scenario is under strict configuration control. The configuration control is located inside the car as well as in the infrastructure of the automotive manufacturer.

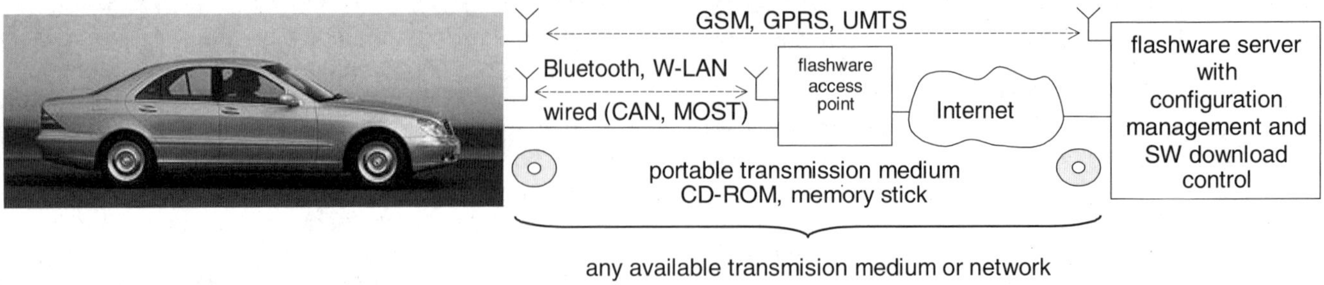

Figure 2: Loading flashware into a car using any available transmission medium or network

Another scenario is that the car is in a workshop and requires a new software release to be installed. This can be realized in different ways: First, the flashware modules for the new software release are transferred over the Internet to a PC in the workshop (the flashware access point in Figure 2). From there, the flashware modules are transferred either by a wired connection (e.g., CAN or MOST) or by a wireless connection (e.g., Bluetooth or WLAN) to the car. The Flashware-Reprogramming-Controller receives the flashware modules, transfers them via KWP2000 messages to the destination ECUs and instructing the ECUs flash loaders to install the new software in the flash memory. Secondly, the flashware modules reside on a CDROM or any other appropriate static storage medium. The Flashware-Reprogramming-Controller reads the flashware modules from the CDROM and again installs them in the destination ECUs. This scenario is shown in Figure 3.

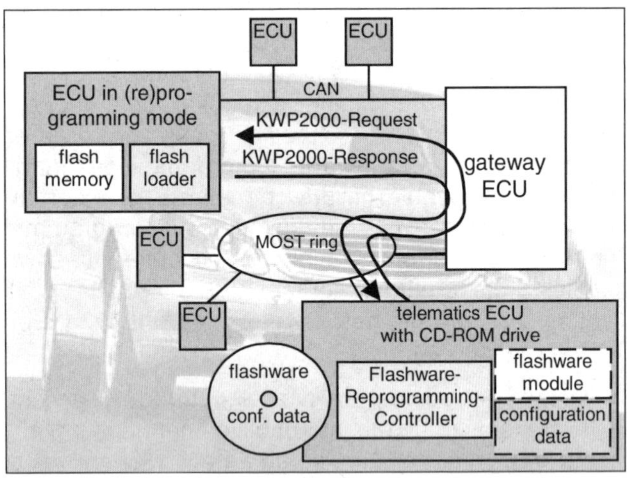

Figure 3: (Re)programming functionality as a SW-component in a telematics ECU

INSTALATION CONFIGURATION CONTROLLER

In addition to the Flashware-Reprogramming-Controller we propose a further component to be integrated into the car, which shall be responsible for supervising the installation of a new software release and for validating the installed software release. This is necessary, because otherwise an inconsistent software release might lead to an undesired behavior of a car. The proposed component – called Installation-Configuration-Controller – uses a hash-based algorithm and a simple logic to ensure that each installation will be complete and will be performed consistently. In the following, the hash-based algorithm is explained before the installation procedure of a new software release is discussed.

Hash-based algorithm

The objective here is to calculate a *hash value* for a software release with a one way hash function like SHA or MD5 [10]. A software release consists of a set of flashwares each in turn consisting of a number of flashware modules. For each of the flashware modules, a separate hash value is calculated using a one-way hash function. The hash value for a software release is calculated with a string of hash values that belong to the flashware modules of the software release. Remember that a hash value is not the same as a checksum. A simple checksum is calculated by summing up the bytes or words of the flashware and ignoring overflow. A hash value is calculated using a one-way hash function.

The hash value for a software release is calculated in the infrastructure and sent to the car to validate that all flashware modules of a software release have been installed and the software release is consistent. Consider the following example. Software release A has the modules M1, M2, M3, M4, M5, M6, and software release B has the modules M1, M3, M4, M5, M6 and M7. Software release A is being installed at the moment and software release B is to be installed later. The back-end calculates a hash value over the string of hash values from the modules M1, M3, M4, M5, M6 and M7. This hash value is sent to the Installation-Configuration-Controller in the car, together with the instruction to delete module M2 and the number of new modules which have to be installed – in this case just 1. After the installation of module M7 the hash value is calculated in the car via the string of hash values of all modules present. It is important that the order of the modules' hash values in the string be identical in the car and in the infrastructure to obtain the same result.

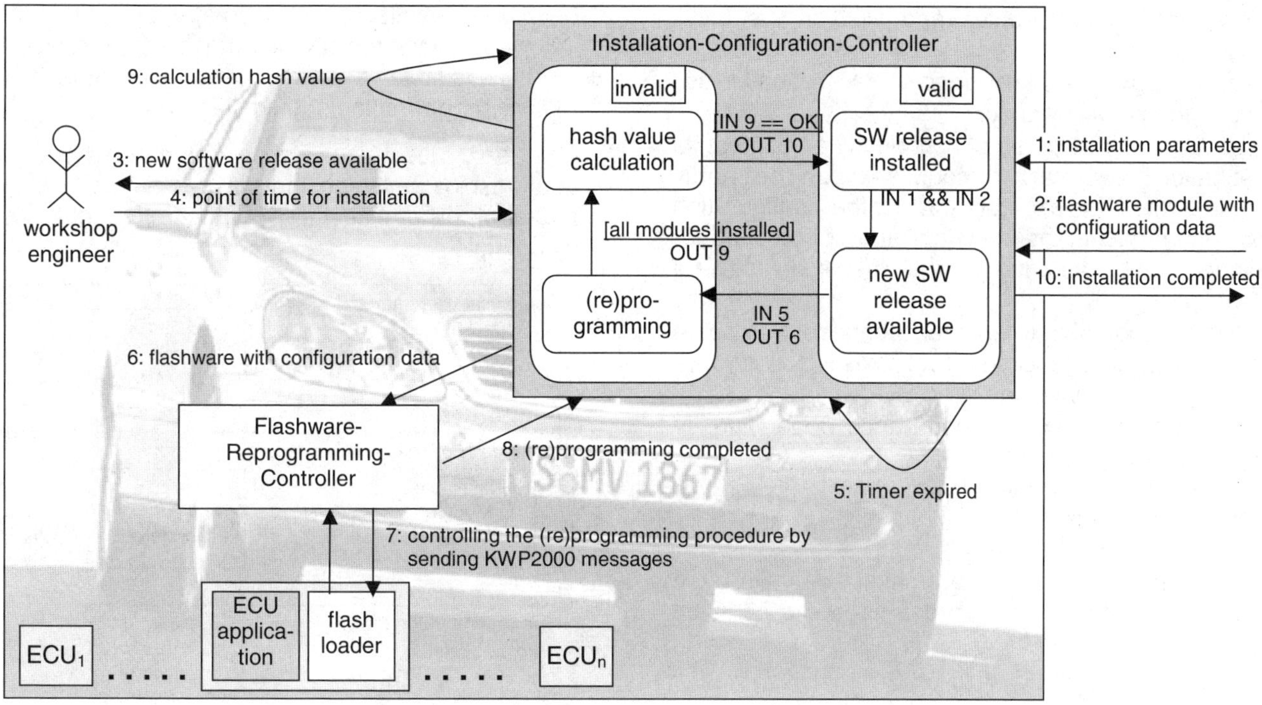

Figure 4: Installation-Configuration-Controller and Flashware-Reprogramming-Controller

To avoid sending the ordering from the infrastructure to the Installation-Configuration-Controller we use an ordering criteria, which is implicitly available. Each flashware module is identified by a unique number – the so-called part number. We define that the hash value of the module with the lowest part number has the first position in the hash value string and that the hash value of the module with the highest part number has the last position in the hash value string.

Collaboration to install a new software release

The installation procedure is discussed considering a state-based collaboration diagram shown in Figure 4. Before the installation of a new software release can be started, installation parameters for the new software release are sent to the Installation-Configuration-Controller (1). These parameters consist of a hash value for the software release to be installed, identification numbers of modules which have to be removed and the number of modules that have to be installed. In a second step the flashware modules and the corresponding configuration data are sent to the Installation-Configuration-Controller (2). When both messages (1 and 2) have been received, a transition to the "new SW-release available" state takes place. The workshop engineer of the car is notified that a new software release is available for installation, (3) and is asked to input the time when the installation should be started (4). A timer is set internally in the Installation-Configuration-Controller to the time when the installation should take place[1]. When the timer expires, and the car is in a state where (re)programming of ECUs is possible, a transition to the "(re)programming" state takes place (5) and the flashware module with the corresponding configuration data is sent to the Flashware-Reprogramming-Controller (6). From this point on the car contains an invalid software configuration until the installation is successfully completed. It is not possible to start the car while it has an invalid software configuration. The Flashware-Reprogramming-Controller sends the flashware module to the destination ECU and controls the (re)programming procedure by sending KWP2000 messages, which are executed by the flash loader in the destination ECU (7). When (re)programming of a flashware module has successfully been completed (8) either another flashware module is installed, or, when all flashware modules have been installed – in the scenario in Figure 4 only one new flashware module has to be installed – a hash value calculation takes place to test whether the installed flashware modules form a valid software release (9). If the hash value generated over all installed flashware modules in the car and the hash value provided in message 1 are identical, the installed software release is valid and a state transition to the state "SW-release installed" takes place. A message (10) is then sent to the infrastructure to indicate that the installation is finished.

FLASHWARE CONTAINER

If a new software release is installed, all flashware modules which are not included in the new release but which are still installed are deleted. Those flashware modules are installed which are not included in the old release but are required in the new release. Typically flashware modules of the old release are replaced by flashware modules of the new release. The new flashware modules to be installed will be encapsulated in containers. A container has the following characteristics:

- A container contains flashware module and corresponding configuration data

[1] The steps 3 and 4 are optional. In this case the installation immediately starts when the car is in a secure state.

- A container is constructed and filled in the infrastructure.
- A container will be transported to its destination via various media or networks.
- A container will be partly or completely emptied at its destination in a car. A container can be partly emptied when for example part of the configuration data will remain in the container and will be used for validating the integrity of the installed software release.
- A partly or completely emptied container will serve as a as a proxy to the real existing flashware module, which is installed in an ECU.
- A container can vary in appearance depending on the middleware used.
- A container will automatically be identified when it is loaded into the car.

So far the basic concepts of the architecture have been discussed. The next section presents some relevant architectural details.

ARCHITECTURE

This section describes structural elements of the architecture and specifies features of the architecture.

STRUCTURAL ELEMENTS

Some important elements of the architecture have just been identified: Flashware-Reprogramming-Controller, Installation-Configuration-Controller, and a container construct for each flashware module. In addition to these components, components for communication and the graphical user interface have to be added to the system design. The following components are required to (re)program ECUs without an external (re)programming device.

1. The Flashware-Reprogramming-Controller component – parses the configuration data and controls the download of flashware modules into ECUs.
2. The KWP2000 component – provides all KWP2000 services required for (re)programming ECUs.
3. Adapters to various transport protocols. We consider two adapters – a CAN-TP adapter component and a MOST-TP adapter component. These adapter components implement an interface for sending synchronous and asynchronous transport messages to ECUs connected to CAN or MOST sub-networks. Mapping from the ECU name to the transport protocol IDs is also provided inside this adapter.
4. Flashware-Module-Proxies, which implement the container functionality and represent an installed flashware module after a successful installation.
5. The Installation-Configuration-Controller component for controlling the installation procedure of a new software release and for validating whether an installed software release is valid.
6. The Installation-GUI component to notify the mechanic in a workshop that a new software release is available and to accept the time, when the (re)programming should start.

The next illustration shows the classes and the relationships between the classes as well as the layer model of the architecture. Each component is visualized by a single class.

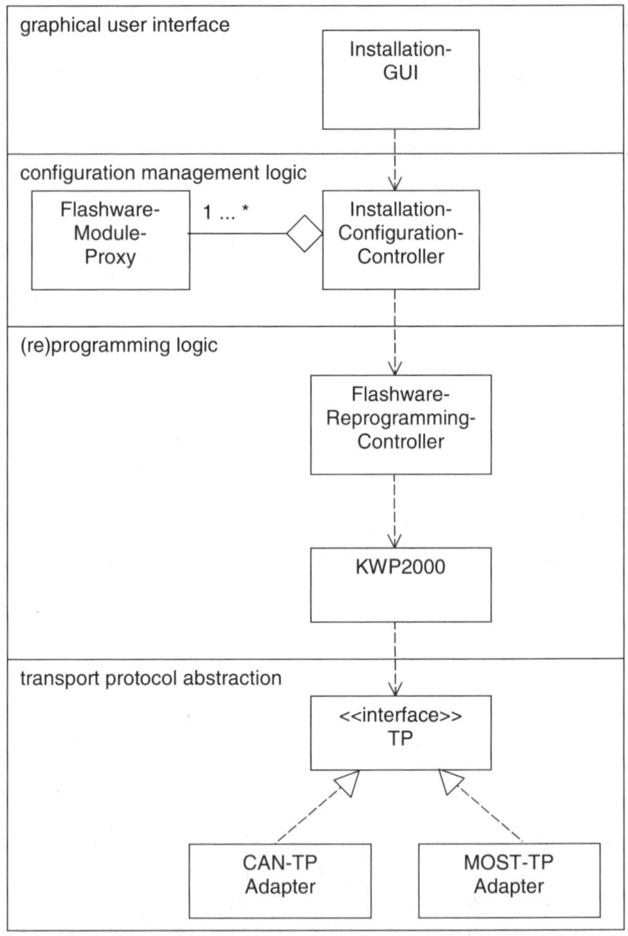

Figure 5 Class diagram in a layer model

The following relationships exist between the classes and interfaces of Figure 5:

- Dependency relationships:
  - Between the KWP2000 class and the interface TP (transport protocol). This dependency is required for sending synchronous and asynchronous KWP2000 messages over various sub-networks. Synchronous method calls are used for KWP2000 messages, which return a response code, and asynchronous message calls are used for sending messages which return no response code, like the Tester-Present messages.
  - Between the class Flashware-Reprogramming-Controller and the class KWP2000. This dependency is required for sending KWP2000 messages, which are defined in the (re)programming logic of the Flashware-Repro-

gramming-Controller, to the flash loader in the destination ECU.

- Between the class Installation-Configuration-Controller and the class Flashware-Reprogramming-Controller. The Installation-Configuration-Controller is responsible for supervising the installation of the flashware modules by using the functionality of the Flashware-Reprogramming-Controller.
- Between the Installation-GUI and the Installation-Configuration-Controller. The user interaction is processed by the Installation-GUI.

- Realization relationships between the TP-Adapter classes and the interface TP. The TP interface provides methods for sending synchronous and asynchronous messages. These methods are implemented by the TP-Adapter classes, and the adaptation to the protocols of the corresponding subnetworks is done in the adapter classes.
- Aggregation or part-of relationship between the Installation-Configuration-Controller and the Flashware-Module-Proxies. A valid configuration consists of 1 to n flashware modules, and each Flashware-Module-Proxy represents one already installed or one to be installed flashware module.

Additionally, some callback interfaces are required to indicate changes in a component to dependent components. We suggest callback interfaces between

- the Installation-Configuration-Controller and the Installation-GUI to notify the GUI when a new software release is available and when the installation is finished.
- the Flashware-Module-Proxies and the Installation-Configuration-Controller to indicate that the installation of a module is finished.
- the Flashware-Reprogramming-Controller and the Installation-Configuration-Controller to indicate the state of the installation and the end of the installation.

All of the components have an internal structure. In this paper we only show the structure of the component Flashware-Reprogramming-Controller (see Figure 6). We use two design patterns [17] in this component. First, the Facade-Pattern for providing a uniform component interface. Secondly, the Observer-Pattern for sending status information to the Installation-Configuration-Controller. The Facade is implemented in the class Flashware-Reprogramming-Facade. An object of this class either delegates incoming method calls to an object of type Flash-Sequence or of Configuration-Data-Parser.

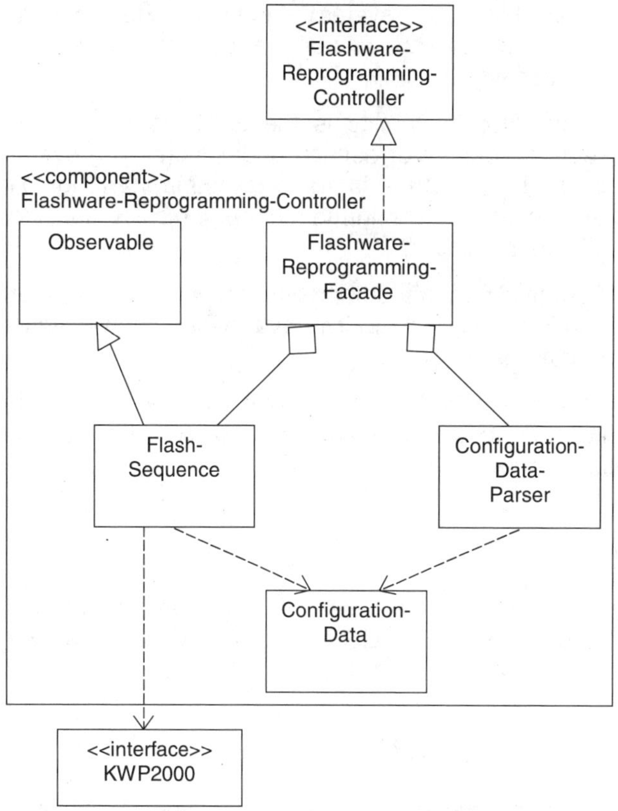

Figure 6 Decomposition of the Flashware-Reprogramming-Controller

The class Configuration-Data-Parser implements a parser to parse the configuration data of a flashware-module which is described in XML. The class Flash-Sequence implements the functionality for (re)programming individual ECUs. The Configuration-Data class holds only the configuration data, which is extracted from the XML documents by the Configuration-Data-Parser and is used in the Flash-Sequence class to parameterize the flash sequence.

FEATURES OF THE ARCHITECTURE

A prototype which implements the presented architecture should have the following features [16]:

1. Maintainability: Errors of a component should be removable, and the functionality should be changeable without affecting other components. An easily maintainable system should be designed according to the design criteria “high cohesion” and “low coupling”.
2. Availability: The services provided by the system should be available at any time. That means it should be possible to download and install new software releases anytime and anywhere.
3. Performance: Downloading and installing new software releases should be performed as fast as possible, because driving is not possible during a software update.

4. Extensibility: The system should be extensible with new functionality without affecting the existing functionality.
5. Scalability: Scalability is the ability to provide the required quality of service under increasing system load. This feature is especially important for the architecture of the infrastructure, which is not dealt with in this paper.
6. Security: Security comprises mechanisms to ensure confidentiality, integrity, availability, non-rejection and authenticity.

In the next section we will show the mapping of the architecture to our prototype and we will evaluate the features of the architecture.

PROTOTYPE

To evaluate the architecture we implemented a prototype based on OSGi (Open Service Gateway Initiative) technology [11-15].

SYSTEM ARCHITECTURE

The system architecture of the prototype is shown in Figure 7. Three subsystems can be observed: A vehicle ECU, a PC representing a powerful telematics ECU and a flashware server representing the infrastructure. Each sub-system is discussed in a corresponding subsection.

The vehicle ECU

The vehicle ECU integrates a standard flash loader as specified by the HIS consortium [8, 9]. The flashware for this special ECU consists of just one flashware module. For test purposes there are two different flashware modules available for this ECU, which represent two different ECU applications. In Figure 7, flashware module A is installed. As can also been seen, the flashware module consists of the ECU application and a standard communication stack with an operating system core that fits the ECU application. It would also be possible to separate the ECU application from the standard communication stack and the operating system and encapsulate each of them in a separate flashware module.

PC representing a telematics ECU

A PC represents our telematics ECU, which is used for building up a fast prototype and evaluating the architectural features. Basic communication protocols are integrated in the layer operating system and native modules. The next layers are a Java Virtual Machine and an OSGi Service Gateway. An OSGi Service Gateway is a platform which manages the life cycle of components – called bundles in OSGi – and provides some basic services to manage components. A bundle is a component which can be loaded into a Service Gateway, installed, started, stopped and uninstalled. A bundle can provide services to other bundles, and of course can use services which are provided by other bundles. All components, which have been identified in the section "ARCHITECTURE" are implemented in the form of a bundle.

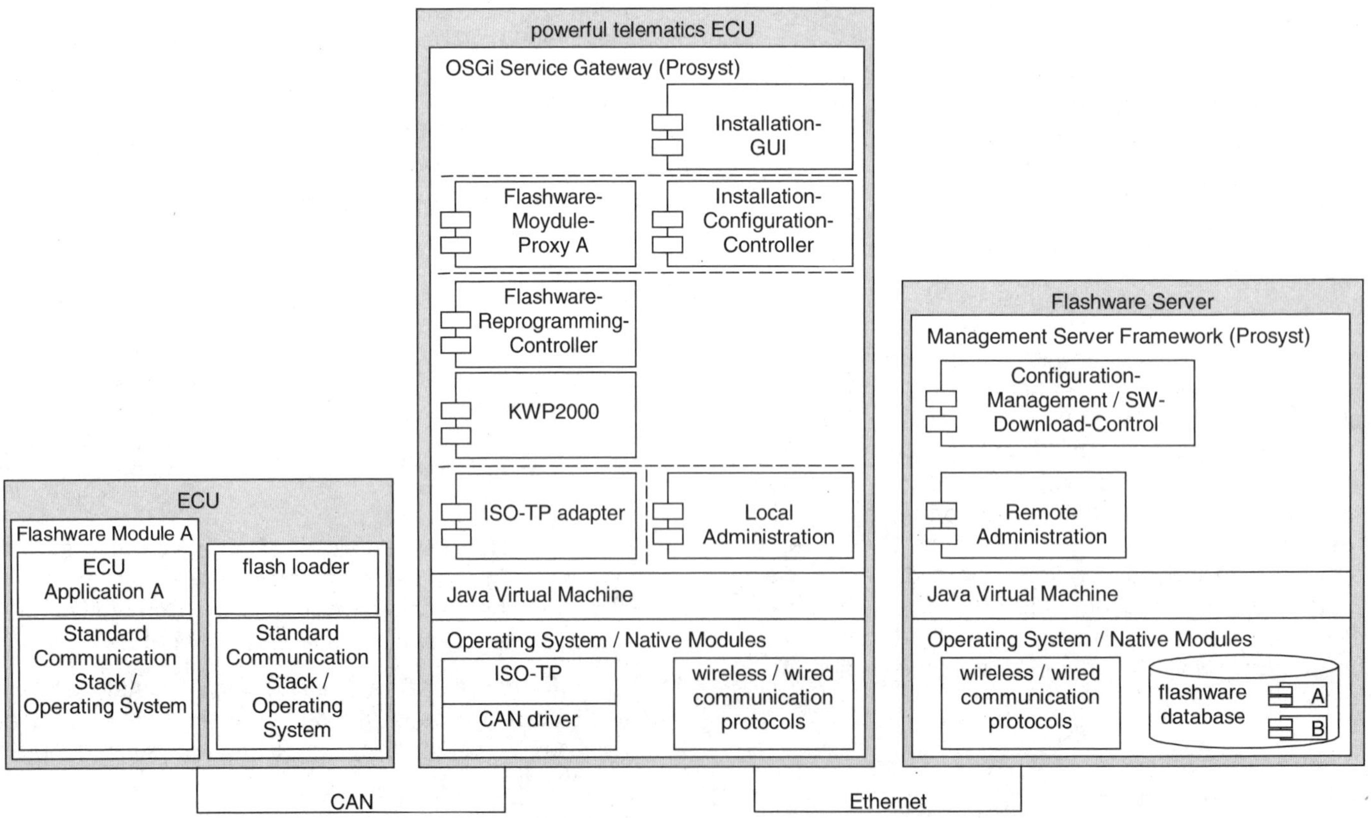

Figure 7 System architecture of the prototype

PC representing the infrastructure

In the infrastructure we use the Management Server Framework from PROSYST [18]. This framework enables remote management of OSGi Service Gateways and is extended by a component "Configuration-Management and SW-Download-Control". The flashware modules are encapsulated in bundles and are stored in a flashware database. The component Remote Administration and the corresponding component Local Administration are parts of the framework provided by the Service Gateway and the Management Server Framework.

EVALUATION OF THE ARCHITECTURAL FEATURES

In this section we will evaluate the architectural features of the prototype:

Maintainability

Each functionality is encapsulated in a bundle with well-defined interfaces. A bundle can be dynamically installed and uninstalled. As long as the interfaces which a bundle provides to other bundles remain the same, the bundle implementation can be changed without affecting other bundles. New functionality can either be added in separate bundles or by adding additional services to still existing bundles.

Availability

To provide the highest possible availability, the architecture supports the download of flashware containers by means of any available transmission medium or network. It does not matter whether the flashware encapsulating bundles are loaded from a CD or a USB memory stick, or whether the bundles are received via GSM, GPRS or WLAN. A concrete instantiation of the architecture therefore depends on the transmission media available as well as on the remote software update strategy of the car manufacturer (i.e., whether remote software updates are permitted or not).

Performance

New software releases should be downloaded and installed as fast as possible, because driving is not possible during a software update. The suggested architecture accelerates the installation procedure by:

- (re)programming only the difference between two software releases. The difference between two software releases is calculated in the back-end.
- separating the download procedure from the installation procedure. The installation procedure starts when a new flashware module is completely downloaded. This means the vehicle is still operational while a flashware module is downloaded.
- parallel (re)programming can be done within a sub-network until all of the available bandwidth is utilized. This is effective when processing the received flashware modules is the bottleneck and not transmitting them over the sub-networks. Parallel (re)programming can also be done over two distinct sub-networks at the same time.

Extensibility

ECUs connected to various sub-networks can be (re)programmed by integrating a TP adapter component for the specific sub-network.

The complete functionality (all bundles) for (re)programming can easily be completely exchanged by using the remote administration functionality and the life cycle management of the OSGi Service Gateway. In this way the system can be easily adapted to new functionality and is easily extensible.

The architecture can also be used in the development, end-of-line production and after-sales operational areas. In development and end-of-line production the OSGi-Service-Gateway runs outside the car instead of inside the car.

Security

Depending on the security strategy of the car manufacturer, each flashware module can be signed by a signature, which prevents manipulation of the flashware module and ensures that flashware modules are only installed on ECUs for which they were intended. This is not a special feature of this architecture – it depends on the implementation of the flash loader for each ECU.

The hash based algorithm ensures that the flashware modules installed in a car form a valid software release. A further security feature is the Installation-Configuration-Controller which supervises the installation procedure to ensure that only valid and complete software releases can be installed, and that a car cannot be started when no valid software release is available.

Furthermore the Installation-Configuration-Controller will cyclically test the integrity of an installed software release.

The Flashware-Reprogramming-Controller provides the functionality for (re)programming. This component can be located inside the car, but it can also be loaded into the car before a (re)programming session takes place. This can easily be done, because the Flashware-Reprogramming-Controller is implemented as a bundle that can be dynamically loaded, installed and uninstalled.

CONCLUSION

In this article we proposed an architecture for ECU (re)programming that can be used in development, end-of-line production, and after sales. The architecture is based on three basic concepts: First, encapsulate the (re)programming functionality in its own software component – the Flashware-Reprogramming-Controller. This makes ECU (re)programming independent from the Diagnostic Tester. Secondly, encapsulate the supervision of the installation procedure and the validation of the integrity of a software release in a second software component – the Installation-Configuration-Controller. Thirdly, encapsulate a flashware module in a container construct, which is used to transport a flashware module from the infrastructure to the vehicle. After installation, the emptied container serves as a proxy for the installed flashware module and is used for configuration control. The structural elements and the characteristic features of the architecture were discussed. Next we presented a prototype, which uses an OSGi Service Gateway as a platform. It has been shown that the suggested platform-independent architecture can easily be mapped to the OSGi Service Gateway technology used in the prototype. Each component has been implemented easily in a single bundle. A bundle also serves as a container to encapsulate a flashware module. The architectural features have also been evaluated considering the prototype. It has been shown that the suggested architecture is easy to maintain, has the potential for high availability, uses all possibilities to speed up the installation procedure without changing the existing ECUs or the flash loaders inside the ECUs, is easy extensible and integrates various security functions to meet the high security requirements for such a critical functionality.

ACKNOWLEDGEMENTS

We would like to thank our colleagues of Mercedes-Benz PKW Development and the Center for Diagnosis and Flash Technologies. Additionally the authors would like to thank Professor Dr. Wolfgang Rosenstiel of the University Tübingen and Prof. Dr. Joachim Goll of the University of Applied Science Esslingen.

REFERENCES

1. DaimlerChrysler Hightech Report, „Programme für mehr Intelligenz im Auto“, 1/2002.
2. A. Kifmann, „Die Softwarefalle“, Editorial Auto & Elektronik, Ausgabe 5/2002
3. P. Roßbach, “Model Driven Architecture – Grundlegende Konzepte und Einordnung der Model Driven Architecture (MDA)”, Java Magazin, ISSN: 1619-795X, 9/2003
4. ISO 15765: “Diagnostics on CAN – Part 2: Network layer services”
5. ISO 14230: „Road vehicles – Diagnostic systems – Keyword Protocol 2000 – Part 3: Application Layer“
6. T. Kühner, S. Kreuser, „Prozessicheres Flashen in der Entwicklung, der Produktion und der Außenorganisation bei DaimlerChrysler“, Software-Flashen im Kfz, Stuttgart, Jan. 2003
7. G. Wagner, H. Merkle, J. Bortolazzi, D. Marx, K. Lange, „Herstellerinitiative Software“, Automotive Electronics ATZ MTZ, March 2003
8. http://www.automotive-his.de/
9. M. Huber, T. Weber, T. Miehling, “Standard software for in-vehicle flash reprogramming”, “Elektronik im Kraftfahrzeug”, Sep. 2003
10. B. Schneier, “Applied Cryptography”, Second Edition, ISBN: 0-471-11709-9, 1996
11. H.-U. Michel, „Open Services Gateway Initiative (OSGi) – Standardisierung einer offenen Infotainment-Plattform“, Telematik im Kraftfahrzeug, VDI-Berichte 1728, 27 – 39, 2002
12. S. Schwarze, „Was sind Vorteile einer OSGi-Lösung für Hersteller und Service Provider?“, Embedded World Conference, Nürnberg, 2003
13. M. Wagner, „Hardware- und Softwarevoraussetzungen für OSGi in Embedded Systemen“, Embedded World Conference, Nürnberg, 2003
14. 14. K. Hackbarth, „Offene Plattformen für Infotainmentund Telematik-Systeme“, Embedded World Conference, Nürnberg, 2003
15. V. Fricke, „Embedded Java und OSGi – Neue Technologien im Fahrzeug der Zukunft“, Embedded World Conference, Nürnberg, 2003
16. A. Andresen, “Komponentenbasierte Softwareentwicklung mit MDA, UML und XML”, Hanser Verlag, ISBN: 3-446-22282-0, 2003
17. E. Gamma, “Design Patterns. Elements of Reusable Object-Oriented Software”, Addison-Wesley Professional, ISBN: 0201633612, 1997
18. http://www.prosyst.com, "mPower Remote Manager Data Sheets"

CONTACT

Cornelia Heinisch:
Cornelia.Heinisch@stz-softwaretechnik.de
Martin Simons:
Martin.Simons@daimlerchrysler.com

DEFINITIONS, ACRONYMS, ABBREVIATIONS

flash memory: The word flash memory is derived from "**flash** erasable programmable read-only **memory**" (FEPROM). It is a kind of non-volatile storage device similar to an EEPROM, but erasing can only be done for blocks or the entire chip.

flash loader: The flash loader is a small program in a protected memory area which is responsible for managing the flash memory (re)programming procedure on the ECU side. It is responsible for erasing the flash memory, receiving ECU software from a vehicle sub-network and installing the software in the flash memory, taking various security considerations into account.

feature configuration: All standard and optional equipment that is ordered for an individual car is called the feature configuration of a car. All valid combinations of standard and optional equipment build up the set of valid feature configurations for a production series.

hardware configuration: A hardware configuration is a valid set of ECUs which can be mounted in a car in order to implement a given *feature configuration*.

software configuration: A software configuration is a valid set of *flashware modules* and corresponding coding parameters, which can be programmed in the ECUs of a hardware configuration in order to realize a given feature configuration.

flashware: The software of an ECU which is written into the flash memory of an ECU is called flashware. A flashware consists of 1 to n *flashware modules*.

flashware module: Flash memories allow the separation of the memory into segments, which can be separately erased and rewritten with new data. A piece of software, which fits into such a memory segment and can be loaded and installed by the flash loader is called a flashware module.

software release: A software release is a valid *software configuration* which has been released.

checksum: A computed value, which depends on the contents of a block of data, and which is transmitted or stored along with the data in order to detect data corruption. A simple checksum is calculated by summing up the bytes or words of the *flashware*, ignoring overflow.

hash value: A hash value is calculated using a one-way hash function. A hash function is a function which takes a variable length input string and converts it to a fixed length output string called a hash value.

ECU = Electronic Control Unit

OSGi = Open Service Gateway Initiative

CAN = Controller Area Network

2001-01-0074

Hardware Independent Software Framework for In-Vehicle Information Systems

Hass Machlab, James C. Griffin Jr., Ron E. Stahlberg and Greg A. Dils
Diversified Software Industries, Inc.

ABSTRACT

New technologies are being incorporated into vehicles more rapidly then ever before. These products require a display to present information, and a reliable in-vehicle network to communicate. Speed to market is critical. In order to compete, manufacturers, suppliers and third-party developers must have a dynamic, robust testing and development environment for these products. Any integrated environment must facilitate easy creation and on-going support of devices that interface with in-vehicle networks and digital displays. Such devices will shape the future of transportation.

The In-Vehicle Information System (IVIS) framework allows vehicle manufacturers to integrate, test, and maintain on-board information systems. A new system is assembled from software and hardware components, interconnected using desktop graphical design tools, and tested in both simulated and bench environments.

INTRODUCTION

In today's market, as the product development cycle shortens, reuse, easy modification and addition of new software applications in the vehicle has become increasingly important. In addition, a shortage in software developers has made it more difficult and expensive to meet the demands required to create in-vehicle applications. In order to alleviate this problem, it is becoming more important to empower automotive designers and human factors engineers with tools that allow them to easily and quickly build in-vehicle applications that are production ready and do not require software development expertise. In addition, it is important that these applications are portable to different hardware and software platforms, reducing the cost for the automotive manufacturers as they integrate new technologies in the vehicle.

The IVIS development environment provides straightforward mechanisms for plugging applications into the IVIS framework. A visual development environment generates the user interface utilizing real-time graphics and corresponding user input devices such as buttons, knobs, and voice activated commands. In addition, the development environment, establishes each application's access to vehicle data such as speed, oil pressure, or engine RPM. User-specific application data such as navigation or communication device data is treated in the same fashion. The development environment provides code generation for every framework interface allowing rapid and error free application integration and development.

An easy-to-use system development tool kit, combined with a flexible software framework, provides fast and low-cost system development through the following capabilities:

- Streamlined performance for processor- and memory-constrained embedded systems
- A flexible framework with simple modifications for changes to communications, vehicle parametric data, devices, and graphical user interfaces
- An extensible framework for the addition of application software modules using vehicle data and devices.
- An interoperable framework with open standards for communication, operating system, device drivers, graphics hardware, and system definition tools
- A reliable framework with error reporting, error analysis, and tools for development, testing, and debugging
- Anti-aliased, real-time graphics for multi-colored LCD panel vehicle interfaces
- Platform independence for applications with plug and play devices and vehicle buses

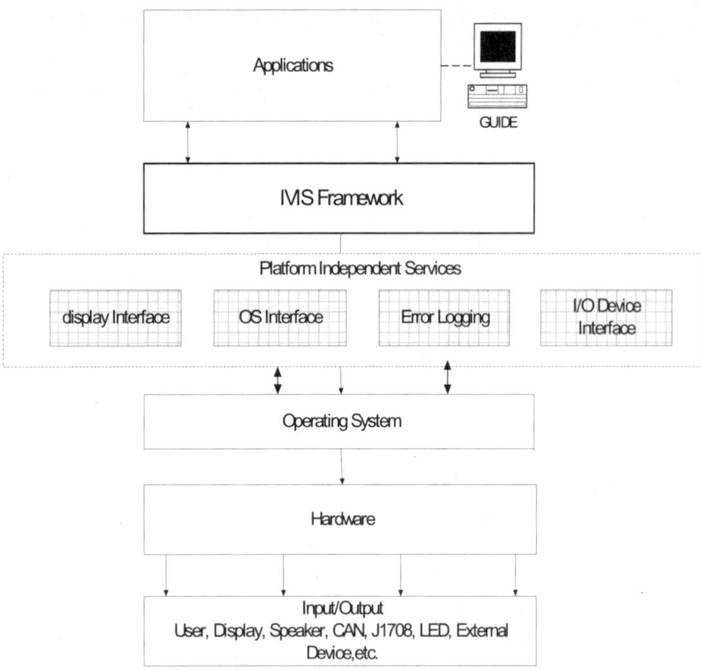

Figure 1: Top Level view of the In-Vehicle Information System.

PLATFORM INDEPENDENT SOFTWARE FRAMEWORK

Figure 1 shows the In-Vehicle Information System top-level architecture. An In-Vehicle Information System consists of a hardware platform with an existing operating system (OS) and, optionally, a Java Virtual Machine. The platform independence layer isolates applications and the framework from specific target hardware and OS configurations. This layer ensures portability by providing a consistent interface to operating system services, display devices, error logging and device communications. This consistent interface allows applications to be developed without any reliance on a specific hardware or operating system target. Concurrent execution is provided by the real-time operating system and is important to the reliable expansion of applications that share framework resources such as the CPU. Applications written for the IVIS framework need to conform to well-defined IVIS Application Programmer Interfaces (APIs), allowing input from the user, the vehicle network, or remote devices. The Graphical User Interface Development Environment (GUIDE) is a PC-based development tool that allows both technical and non-technical individuals to graphically create applications based on IVIS APIs. GUIDE serves to greatly reduce both the time and effort involved in creating in-vehicle applications by using a graphical component model to allow users to layout interfaces, incorporate artwork, specify behaviors and automatically generate executables utilizing the infrastructure provided by the IVIS Framework.

APPLICATION FRAMEWORK COMPONENTS

The IVIS application framework provides a set of dedicated components that provides services, facilitates integration of applications and provides a high quality graphical presentation layer.

THE DISPLAY MANAGER is a component that is responsible for controlling access to the system display. The Display Manager contains a registry of all Display Objects that wish to access the screen and will be responsible for ensuring that all rendering is done in a deterministic manner, based on the state of the system and the priorities assigned to competing objects.

THE GRAPHICS LIBRARY provides a high-performance rendering library for the display interface. It provides advanced features, such as real-time anti-aliasing and advanced color management in a small footprint, easy-to-use library. The graphics library provides standard geometric primitives, such as polygons, ellipses, lines and rectangles, combined with text and bitmaps. Also included are geometric transformations and clipping, all without any hardware dependencies or required floating point support.

THE DATA WAREHOUSE is a registry of all data sources within the system. Any part of the system needing access to common vehicle data can access it from this central location without needing to know where the data originated or how it was processed from its raw form. Applications wishing to provide data to the rest of the system can register as a Data Source in the Data Warehouse.

THE COMMUNICATIONS AND DEVICE MANAGERS are responsible for controlling the individual Communication and Device Modules in the system. Each module handles the parsing of input from a specific external device, such as a J1708 or CAN vehicle bus or a bank of hardware switches, and places its received data into the Data Warehouse. Modules also handle output from the system to external devices, including any protocol-specific information that must be included in output messages. The common interface allows new Modules to be seamlessly integrated into the system as additional protocols are developed.

THE DATA FILTER PACKAGE provides an interface for objects to use data that has been filtered from its original representation. Examples of filters include smoothing, unit conversion, clamping, and scaling. The filters are plug and play components for use with any input data stream. Filters can also be registered in the data warehouse.

THE ERROR LOGGING interface is available for use by any module. Error logs are created and written through this module. The module hides changes to underlying logging destinations such as flash EPROM or sending logs externally.

PLATFORM INDEPENDENCE Portability to different platforms is a key IVIS framework feature. The standard interfaces for display control, real-time operating system functions, and device drivers provide this portability. The modules supporting these interfaces are the only components that need to be ported to a new platform.

The Display interface hides changes in the display panel hardware. It presents a standard for use by the graphics routines. The display interface will initialize pixel geometry and configure the display interface hardware.

The real-time operating system (RTOS) interface hides changes to the underlying operating system through the presentation of standard services to modules. The RTOS services include thread management, concurrent resource access, interrupt vectoring, and management of process memory spaces.

Device Driver Interface Devices such as non-volatile memory, serial ports, parallel ports, and discrete I/O require standard interfaces. The interface performs initialization, configuration, read, and write operations. Mutual exclusion between read and write operations on a device can be enforced.

APPLICATION DEVELOPMENT

A key feature of the IVIS Framework is the ease with which applications can be developed that utilize the capabilities it provides. The open nature of the Framework provides for rapid application development by non-programmers, while still allowing the flexibility to greatly enhance the productivity of programmers wishing to build applications on an established infrastructure.

THE GRAPHICAL USER INTERFACE DEVELOPMENT ENVIRONMENT (GUIDE) is the gateway to the IVIS Framework for the Man-Machine Interface (MMI) designer. GUIDE is a Windows based visual development environment that generates code for plugging applications into the IVIS framework. It provides an easy-to-use, drag-and-drop WYSIWYG interface, minimizing the learning curve and facilitating rapid application development. It also supports the direct use of artwork generated by other graphics packages, allowing the continued use of existing graphics tools and enhancing collaboration with other designers. GUIDE uses the same portable graphics libraries as the framework, allowing the designer to exactly emulate the appearance that will be available on the target platform, including any color restrictions involved. Access to data values and conditions is through the use of intuitive pull-down menus, rather than vehicle and bus specific code, allowing applications to be developed independent of specific protocols. It is compatible with many popular C++ tools.

IVIS APPLICATIONS are traditionally created using the IVIS toolkit. In addition, IVIS applications may be created using any popular C++ tool, by utilizing the documented API for the desired framework components. By complying with the framework, a new application can be rapidly created without re-programming the underlying infrastructure, reducing development time and enhancing robustness. Wide ranges of vehicle applications are easily integrated, such as safety, cell phones, navigation, vehicle diagnostics and personal information management. The abstraction provided by the framework components also insures that individual applications can share data and yet be easily interchanged, without affecting other IVIS applications.

BENEFITS OF THE IVIS FRAMEWORK

The IVIS Framework provides a number of advantages for the development of multi-function embedded in-vehicle applications. These advantages touch all segments involved from the developer, through the vehicle OEM to the end-user.

TIME-TO-MARKET Integrated applications require less development time thanks to the full-featured IVIS Framework. IVIS provides developers with ready-to-use, high-quality embedded graphics and communications libraries. An intuitive, drag-and-drop graphical interface allows developers of all levels of technical sophistication to easily design content and specify system performance.

RELIABILITY The functionality provided by the IVIS Framework means that applications are built upon fully tested components, rather than newly developed code and infrastructure. For any new application, the majority of the code involved remains unchanged and previously tested. All the testing effort that goes into the Framework means that the reliability of any new application is greatly enhanced compared to any new development.

REDUCED HARDWARE REQUIREMENTS Using a standard protocol, one display is able to provide the graphics interface for a number of applications and replace the traditional one device, one display approach. This frees up space for additional instrumentation and provides a cleaner environment for the driver.

IMPROVED DRIVER PERFORMANCE With digital displays, a wide variety of information can be presented to the driver in one central location. The driver has only one place to look to receive all the information he needs at any time about vehicle performance. Further, with this advanced technology, display information can be prioritized in ways not possible with current instrument clusters, making the driver immediately aware of the most important information about the vehicle at any moment.

The ease with which content can be developed using the IVIS Framework means that specific driver customization of the operator interface is truly a reality. The content presented can be tailored to compensate for the driver's limitations or concerns, such as font size, color or type and quantity of information presented.

PLATFORM DIFFERENTIATION The user or manufacturer can also easily customize the appearance or functionality of any IVIS application, allowing unique products to be deployed on identical hardware. This capability allows the use of a standard hardware platform across different models, while maintaining the differentiation key to customer acceptance and recognition.

PLATFORM PORTABILITY With the IVIS Framework's well-documented API and cross-platform portability, target platforms can be selected that most closely match product requirements. The porting layer guarantees that as processors and display technologies evolve, the IVIS Framework grows too, allowing rapid deployment on the most up-to-date technology.

CONCLUSION

A platform independent In-Vehicle Information System (IVIS) development environment has been presented. IVIS is a powerful, flexible and scalable development environment for the automotive industry that allows the vehicle manufacturer to create custom branding across product lines while staying independent of the hardware platform. In addition, IVIS empowers the graphical designer or human factors engineer to independently develop entire systems, generate production quality code and readily execute them on the final embedded platform.

CONTACT:

Hass Machlab
Diversified Software Industries, Inc.
2475 Coral Court
Coralville, IA 52241
Phone: 319-545-5400
Fax: 319-545-5315
hmachlab@dsi-inc.net

James C.Griffin Jr.
Diversified Software Industries, Inc.
2475 Coral Court
Coralville, IA 52241
Phone: 319-545-5400
Fax: 319-545-5315
jim@dsi-inc.net

Ron E. Stahlberg
Diversified Software Industries, Inc.
2475 Coral Court
Coralville, IA 52241
Phone: 319-545-5400
Fax: 319-545-5315
ron@dsi-inc.net

Greg A. Dils
Diversified Software Industries, Inc.
2475 Coral Court
Coralville, IA 52241
Phone: 319-545-5400
Fax: 319-545-5315
gdils@dsi-inc.net

2002-01-2150

Software Development for Driver Information Systems – Problems, Processes, Solutions

Jens Ohler and Peter Roessger
CAA AG

ABSTRACT

The number of functionalities in vehicles is constantly rising. Audio systems, telephone, fleet management systems, and navigation are state of the development today. Telematic services, dynamic route guidance and concierge services are invented at the moment. Internet applications, mobile services, and others will come soon. To allow the in-vehicle use of these applications without a loss in safety, the systems have to fit drivers´ needs, expectations, and abilities as much as possible. Highly integrated software based solutions allow to fit functionalities and human machine interfaces to the driver. Results of this developmental process are driver information systems or CarPCs. With these systems the IT world and the vehicle world are tied together.

To allow a fast and direct development of the software, a straight and complete developmental process is essential. First steps of the development include task analysis, user studies, and identifying customer CI. The resulting concepts are used to simulate the DIS on PC. Stepping forward, hardware like cell phones or seats are connected to the simulation. PC based solutions are then integrated into seating bucks and prototype cars. An automatic code transfer then makes the final step to series production from the PC to the target processor.

To realize this developmental process, a software tool was evolved and introduced. This tool allows working on the complete process. Major focus was set on the code transfer from the PC to the target processor. This means, that the software, that simulated the driver information system on the PC, is used in the final system as well. Besides saving time and money this strategy allows fast and flexible changes and updates, even after the SOP.

INTRODUCTION

The number of functionalities in vehicles is constantly rising. Audio systems, telephone, fleet management systems, and navigation are state of the development today. Telematic services, dynamic route guidance and concierge services are invented at the moment. Internet applications, mobile services, and others will come soon. To allow the in-vehicle use of these applications without a loss in safety, the systems have to fit drivers´ needs, expectations, and abilities as much as possible. Highly integrated software based solutions allow to fit functionalities and human machine interfaces to the driver. Results of this developmental process are driver information systems or CarPCs. With these systems the IT world and the vehicle world are tied together.

To allow a fast and direct development of the software, a straight and complete developmental process is essential. First steps of the development include task analysis, user studies, and identifying customer CI. The resulting concepts are used to simulate the DIS on PC. Stepping forward, hardware like cell phones or seats are connected to the simulation. PC based solutions are then integrated into seating bucks and prototype cars. An automatic code transfer then makes the final step to series production from the PC to the target processor.

To realize this developmental process, a software tool was evolved and introduced. This tool allows working on the complete process. Major focus was set on the code transfer from the PC to the target processor. This means, that the software, that simulated the driver information system on the PC, is used in the final system as well. Besides saving time and money this strategy allows fast and flexible changes and updates, even after the SOP.

THE DEVELOPMENTAL PROCESS

INFLUENCES

The development of DIS is clearly influenced by different interests (Fig. 1). Major influence is, or at least should be, the user. People driving on the streets have limited capacities for using a DIS, main task is driving. Users have certain expectations, capabilities and needs while in the car. The functionality of a DIS has to fit these to

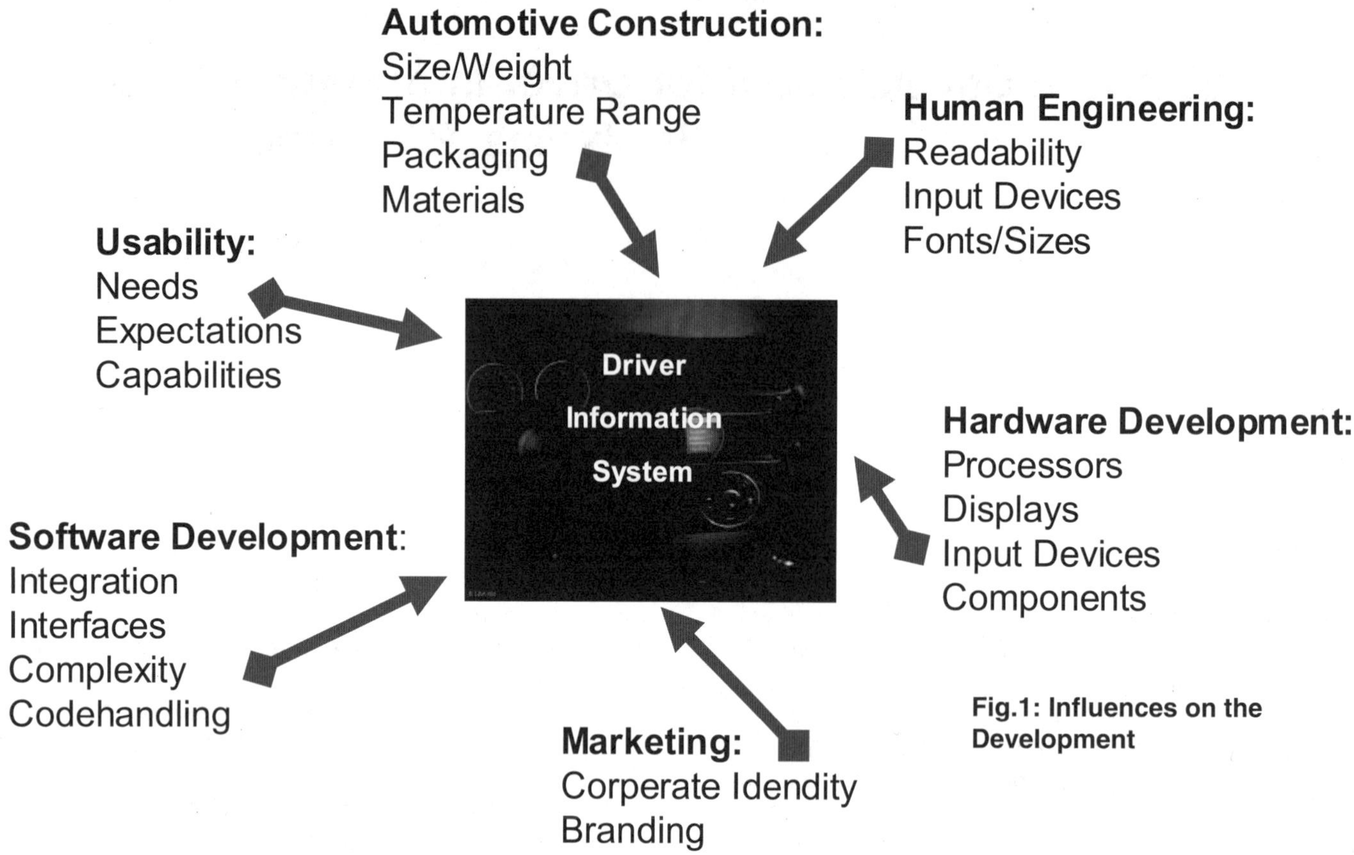

Fig.1: Influences on the Development

allow save driving. To compensate costs of the systems some kind of value has to be present, either on an economical or on an emotional level.

Interests of software developers are to produce code of a low complexity which is easy to handle. Other focuses lie on the integration of the software into the hardware and into the vehicle, the handling of interfaces, e.g. CAN Busses, MOST, or GSM. Hardware developers care about processors and other components, data storage, display configurations and the electrical behavior of input devices. The focuses of automotive construction are size, weight and packaging, materials and temperature ranges. Marketing prefers systems that support the corporate identity of a brand, or ever better help to improve the image of a brand or a model.

INTEGRATION

To allow fast and direct development of DIS interdisciplinary teams were installed. Besides software developers, graphic designer, human engineers,

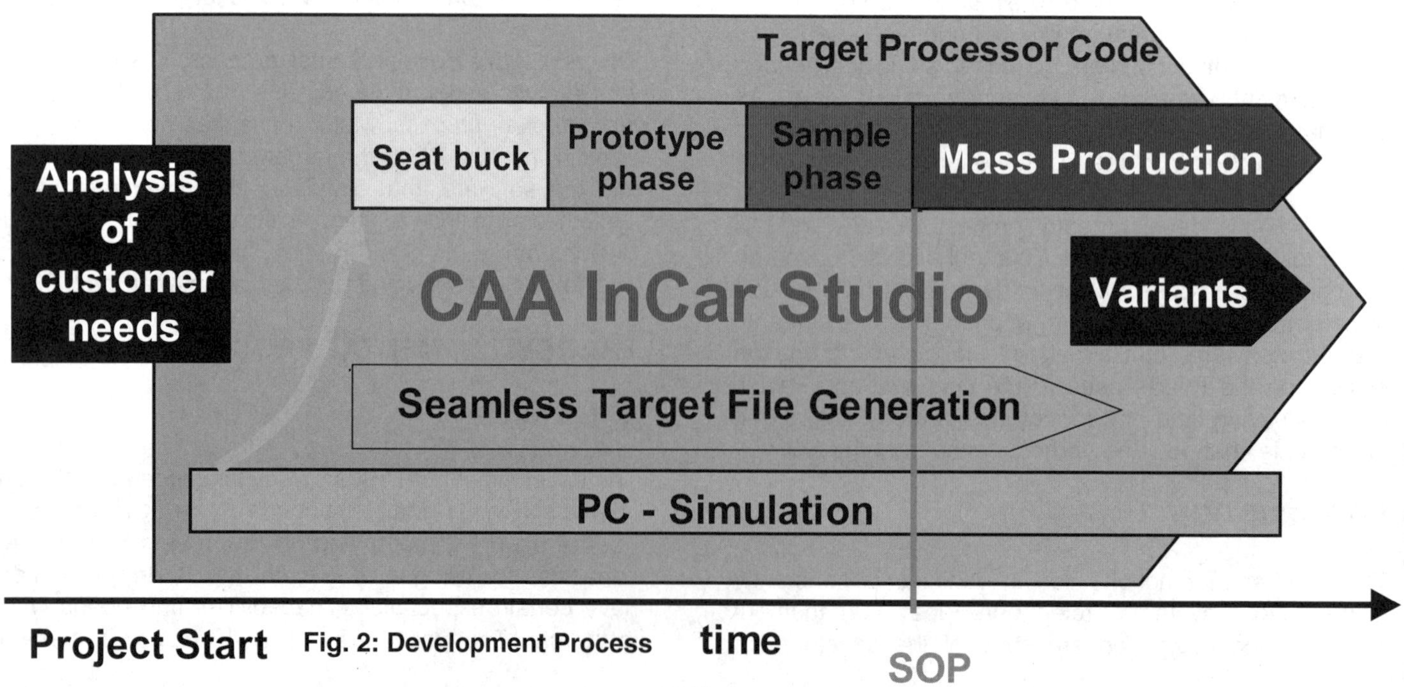

Fig. 2: Development Process

hardware and interface experts are included. Human engineers and marketing trigger the development. Their input adds the user's view. Market analysis, usability testing, construction of use cases and needs lead to a general concept of a system (Figure 1). Further on menu trees, interaction design(TM), graphical concepts and input procedures are fixed. Software development uses this information to start their process. Predefined functionalities and applications allow fast programming of a simulation. PC based simulations are used for usability check up before any hardware is produced. Hardware engineers in the teams care for the integration into the vehicle, both the electrical way and the physical.

HANDLING OF VARIANTS

DIS should fit to the mental models of their users perfectly. Different vehicle lines or models require different screen designs and input devices. So variants have to be handled. This includes the use of different languages, different screen designs, and different screen structures. But also menu-trees and interaction vary from country to country. Technology should be more or less the same for all market, dues to cost reduction. So the HMI-software should be independent from the functional structure of the system.

THE TOOL CHAIN

The tool chain consists of the InCar-Studio™ Editor, the so called GUI Builder, a XML Editor, a Target Builder, HMI Framework Technology, and several "ready to use" applications, the Application Toolkit. Results of the human engineering work are turned into graphic design, behavior and the use of communication interfaces (Figure 2). Graphic design work is then completed in the highly automated GUI Builder. Buttons, lists and control are predefined, so their use can easily be designed. To realize the interaction design with the XML-Editor XML-files are created, which describe the behavior of any of the elements. To develop communication functions for the interfaces provider routines are programmed, which also lead to XML-files. All three parts are connected in the CAA InCar-Studio™. The migration of the software in the Target Builder leads to target applications. The three different working areas are mirrored in three levels of the target application. The Representation Layer contents all graphics. The Service Layer controls the logic and different APIs, needed to connect different parts of the software. The Provider Layer controls the interfaces and the external communication of the system. Any automotive (seat, AC), IT (PDA, WAP Browser,) or telecommunications (GSM phone, GPRS phone) hard- or software may be included, either in real or as a simulated system. Some of these software components exist as "ready to use" applications.

The software requires a WIN2000 environment for the programming phase. The target file generator produces a HMI-software piece, which is independent from the operating system of the target hardware (which in most cases will be the DIS hardware one might find in a vehicle). Only small pieces of the software, such as the hardware management, or an OS_Kernel need a specific OS-adaptation. Ready to use versions for Win NT, WinCEfA, and QNX are available. The target file is then generated, meeting the requirements of the runtime environment.

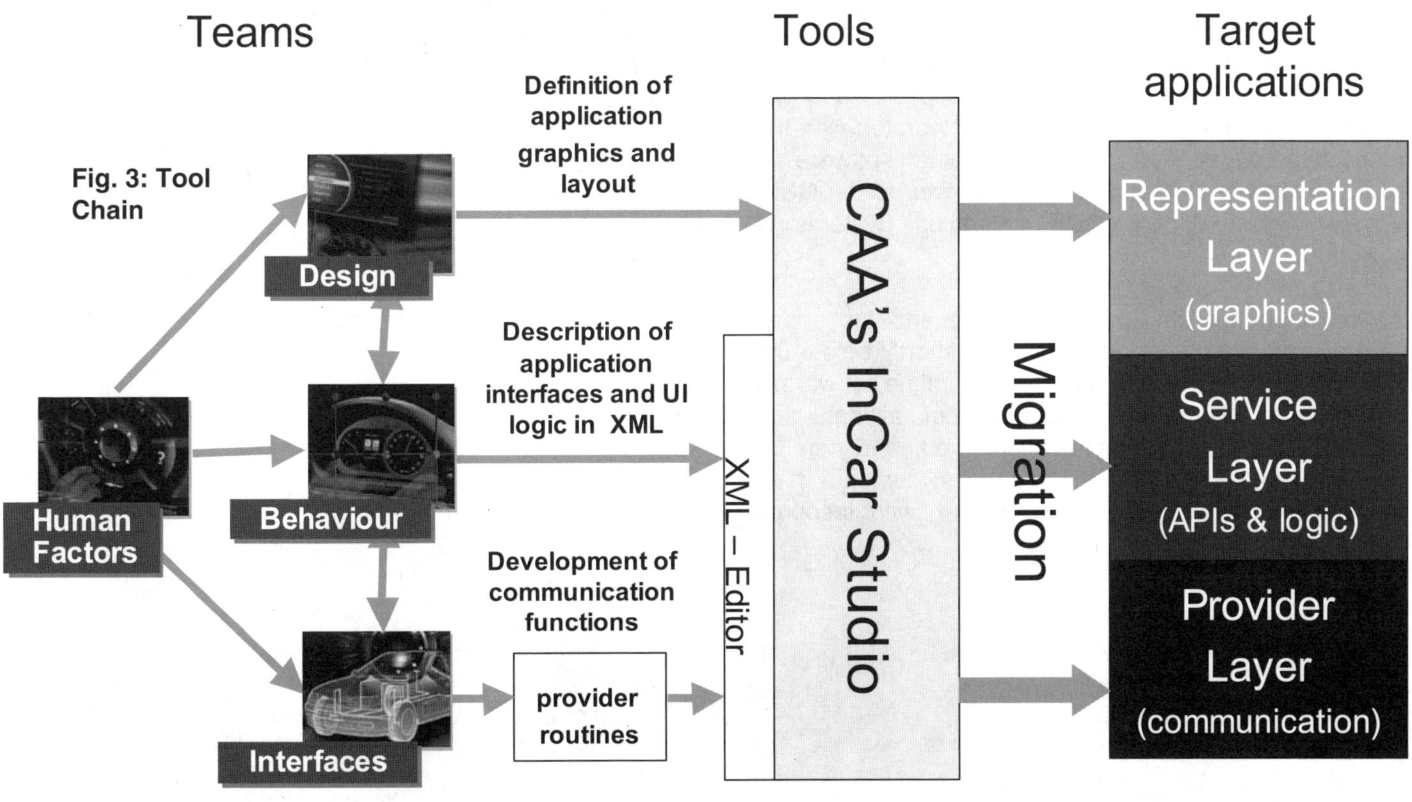

Fig. 3: Tool Chain

THE HMI-FRAMEWORK

The HMI-Framework consists of a graphical editor, an interaction editor, and a runtime software. The graphical editor, which allows logical structures and graphical objects to be created and processed, creates the user interface of the driver information system. While a portfolio of standard graphical objects are at the disposal of the User, additional objects can be produced and used at any time. Version-management is supported via a Style Sheet concept (versions for countries, devices, users and configurations).

The editor supports multiple users, so that several developers with licensed workstations can form a team to work in parallel on the same project.

Parallel to the graphical creation of a driver information system, it is necessary to establish a logical operational process. This is done in the interaction editor. This operational process is responsible for the structure of menus and submenus. The appropriate control logic is illustrated in XML, which permits the simple, real-time exchange of objects in order to alter or change the control concept.

The so-called application-interfaces provide the functional description for integrating applications into the system. Since these interface descriptions are likewise illustrated in XML, they are code-free and are directly readable by the runtime software. Savings in terms of hardware resources, as well as simplicity in the description, are therefore achieved.

Using the runtime editor, it is possible to combine the design and layout information, created using the graphical editor, with the interaction logic and defined application-interfaces, which are described in XML. These are then transferred onto and integrated with the respective target system. The runtime software is platform independent and series operation on the QNX, VxWorks, and Windows CE Operating Systems is guaranteed.

An exchange of the series hardware and the series Operating System is still possible until shortly before the SOP (start of production). As only the runtime software is co-ordinated with the Operating System, all data and relevant information remains unchanged, and can be used by both simulation and series systems. A high stability and robustness of the system, with resource optimisation, is therefore assured.

THE APPLICATION TOOLKIT

The elements of the Application Toolkit are pieces of software that allow the control of either external software components or hardware. They can be integrated into the main software and together with the rest migrated to the runtime environment. The applications usually do not include any functionality themselves, but they control the functions of a CD player or a navigation system. Other available applications include MP3-Player, radio, navigation, voice input, voice output, phone, email, WAP, or forced feedback input devices.

THE VISION

The tool chain links simulation, software development, and series production of driver-information-systems. In projects with major automotive OEMs and 1st Tiers the tool proofed its usability and usefulness. Development times went down by 10-70%, the creation of variants was even faster. By setting standards in the software development of DIS, communication between the different parties (OEM, 1st Tier, software developer, integrator) will be much easier. Reduction in time and cost will push the technology.

CONTACT

Dipl.-Ing Jens Ohler
Product Management
CAA AG
Raiffeisenstr. 34
70794 Filderstadt
Tel.: +49 711 907700
Fax.: +49 711 90770 199
e-Mail: j.ohler@caa.de
Web: www.caa.de

2000-01-1312

CPJazz – A Software Framework for Vehicle Systems Integration and Wireless Connectivity

M. Tim Jones
CellPort Labs Inc.

ABSTRACT

Integration of new technology into vehicles continues at a rapid pace. New technology includes not only deeply embedded devices for vehicle systems management but also operator interfaces such as navigation systems, voice-recognition/text-to-speech interfaces and integration of consumer electronic appliances such as the Personal Digital Assistant (PDA). Standardization efforts have attempted to bring these technologies together through common buses, but because these devices have different capabilities and requirements of their own this is most likely impossible. The CPJazz framework was designed to provide integration of disparate devices and protocols through a dynamic and scalable component-like architecture. In this paper the capabilities and services provided by CPJazz for vehicle-based software integrators will be discussed as well as the identification of key scenarios that demonstrate its contributions to the vehicle and wireless environment.

INTRODUCTION

A number of trends are occuring in the evolution of consumer and commercial vehicles. These include the integration of:

- Numerous Vehicular Networks,
- Consumer Electronic Subsystems, and
- Wireless Network (IP) Connectivity.

These trends create new challenges such as the need for resource sharing, interconnectity and security. CPJazz, an architecture for in-vehicle computing and integration, was designed to address these challenges.

CPJazz is a middleware layer designed to simplify the development of complex multi-protocol, multi-application communication systems. CPJazz builds services on a POSIX compliant operating system to provide a component-like model for application development. This paper discusses CPJazz and its applicability in development of networked vehicle systems.

CPJAZZ ARCHITECTURE

The CPJazz architecture is a message-passing framework that provides communication capabilities between software components in addition to a set of components that provide a specific set of services such as bus interfaces or device interfaces.

CPJazz provides a set of communication APIs that provide component connectivity. The APIs are layered providing two methods of communication. The first is known as the "Bus" API that provides message-based communication. The second is the "Stream" API that provides communication between two dedicated end-points.

Broadcast and multicast (group) communication is provided through the Bus API as well as the ability to identify services provided by components. Synchronization on services or the presence of components is also provided at the Bus layer.

As discussed, CPJazz provides the basic mechanisms for communication between components. Standard platform components provide the necessary functionality for vehicle and communications systems development.

ANATOMY OF A CPJAZZ COMPONENT – CPJazz components share a common structure: a native interface (the components native protocol), the CPJazz interface (implemented through the Bus or Stream API) and the internal processing element (performs the internal processing of information). Each component is an independent program, whose linkage to other components is provided through the CPJazz API.

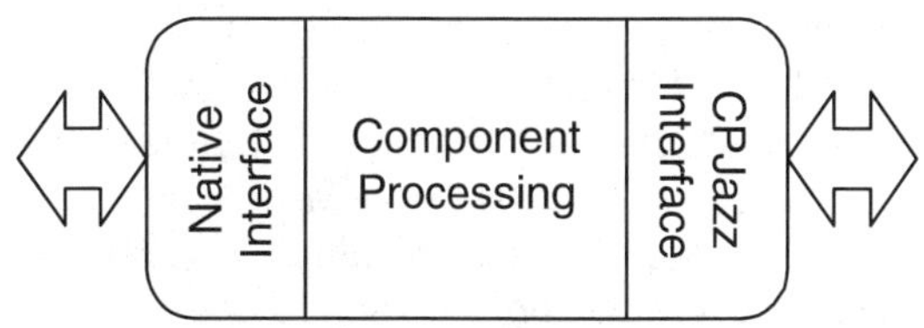

Figure 1. Basic Component Structure

Examples of CPJazz components include an IDB Protocol Manager (arbitrates between the ITS data bus and the CPJazz communication medium), a Text-to-Speech Device Manager (arbitrates between the CPJazz bus and the Text-to-Speech Codec) and an Internet Protocol Manager (arbitrates between IP and CPJazz). CPJazz treats all interfaces the same (such as IDB or IP links) so that communicating between them is simplified.

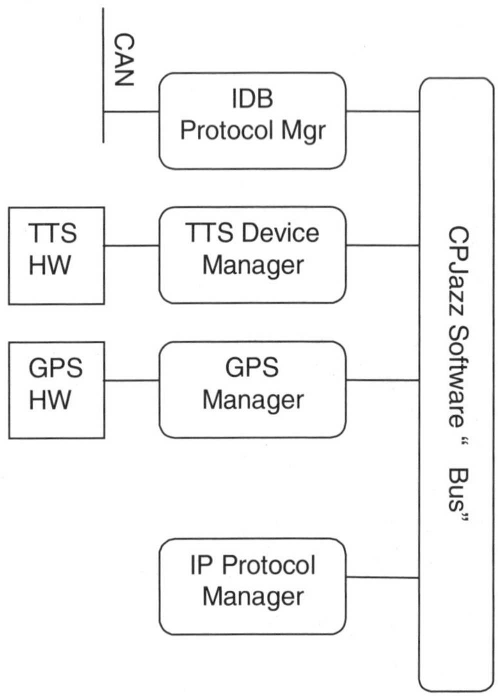

Figure 2. CPJazz architecture showing the software "bus" which provides the basic communication capabilities and a set of components that provide specific interface functionality.

CPJazz provides a number of communication capabilities while minimizing overhead. These capabilities include:

- Name-space management (static and dynamic names)
- Service identification and lookup
- Component synchronization

Every component in the system must have a name in order to communicate. Names can be statically defined (well-known services such as GPS) or dynamically assigned by the bus (such as client components that use services but do not export any services). Services can be identified to CPJazz using a simple text name that allows other components to find it using the service API. Finally, synchronization services are provided to permit components to wait for a particular component to be available before performing bus-related operations.

As shown in the diagrams, this structure is very conducive to protocol translation. Packets of information arrive through the native-side of the component and are translated into the CPJazz-based protocols on the software bus side of the component. Alternatively, information flowing from the CPJazz side of the component is translated into the native protocol of the particular component. This general structure simplifies the bridging and routing of information between disparate protocols and devices.

Using the facilities of the underlying POSIX operating system, the architecture is very dynamic supporting the registration and deregistration of components. This permits dynamic scaling and reconfiguration of CPJazz.

BRIDGING OVER CPJAZZ – The CPJazz architecture simplifies the routing of data from disparate protocols. For example, the GPS Manager component could be configured by an external device on the CAN bus to emit location data at some frequency. The GPS Manager component creates a thread that communicates with an associated CAN protocol thread. Location data flows from the GPS thread to the CAN thread through the bus API. The CAN thread, having knowledge of its private interface, emits the collected GPS data to the appropriate destination. Additionally, an external application could connect via wireless IP to the CPJazz host and request a specific IDB message. This results in the creation of an IP Protocol Manager thread that communicates to an IDB thread. The IDB driver is registered with the particular message of interest and data automatically routed from the IDB thread to the IP Protocol Manager thread when available through the bus API.

KEY ARCHITECTURAL ELEMENTS

A platform providing communication between individual components is in itself not novel. The key to the CPJazz architecture is a set of components that provide key functionality within the vehicle domain. This section discusses some of these components.

LINK MANAGEMENT AND DYNAMIC SELECTION – The wireless market is currently segmented and exists as different offerings based upon bandwidth, reliability and geographic availability. For these reasons, connectivity to a vehicle may utilize different links based upon its geographic location as well as the desired application constraints. These include cost, reliability and availability of the link.

Dynamic Link Selection solves this problem by intelligently selecting the most optimal link (given the available options) for the current desired constraints in a policy-based fashion. The CPJazz model utilizes a market-based model whereby Link Broker components (attached to each available link) bid on the right to enable their link based upon their constraints compared to the application desired constraints. The Dynamic Link Selection component broadcasts the bid defined by particular application(s) and then accepts bids back from the Link Broker components. The closest bid (based upon constraints represented by a bid vector) is chosen and the particular Link Broker notified to enable the link.

This model matches a market-based model for the sale of goods in which data represent goods, consumers represent applications and producers represent the available links. This approach has been used successfully in scheduling and resource allocation systems for many years with roots in Contract Net Systems. [1, 2]

The logistics of managing modems, overlaying network stacks and overall link maintenance is supplied by the Link Manager. The Link Manager provides the ability to script a modem to a particular mode (such as CDPD or CSC) and then overlay the appropriate link-layer protocol (such as SLIP or PPP). The Link Manager may also be driven by applications to force a particular link outside of the control of dynamic link selection.

MANAGED FLOWS – A common design pattern for data movement through a network is for the data to be altered in some desired way. In many cases, the modification of the data can be invisible to the producing component. Take for example the migration of data from an onboard computer to an external host over the Internet. It may be desirable for the data to be first encrypted (for security purposes) and then compressed (for bandwidth savings).

The Flow Manager was designed for this purpose to provide a transparent construction of a data flow between a producing component and an anticipated destination component such as a procotol manager.

Using the transparent and dynamic features of the CPJazz architecture, the flow manager can automatically create intermediary components that provide the necessary services on the data flow.

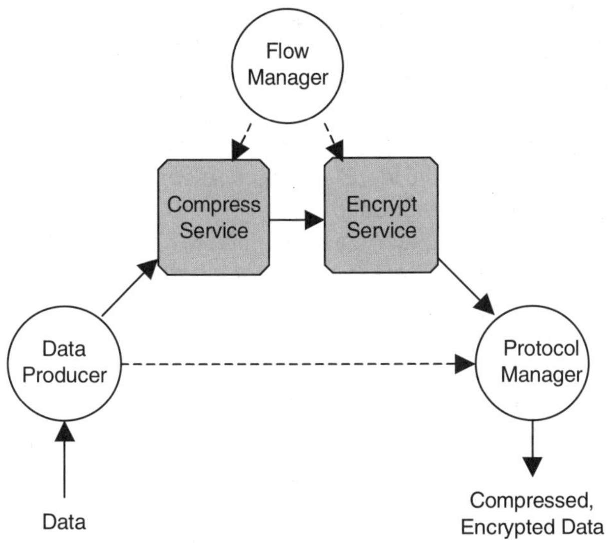

Figure 3. Flow Management Example illustrating the transparent generation of services to build into a flow between a data producer and consumer. The ability to install user-defined intermediary components is also permitted to further tailor the managed flow process.

SECURITY – Building a networked vehicle computer implies accessibility that in turn mandates validation for access. CPJazz provides features for both Internet access as well as disparate bus access and therefore the ability to grant or deny access is a strict requirement.

The CPJazz paradigm for external access is that any access, which is not expressly permitted, is prohibited. This paradigm requires that access be defined per interface in very specific terms. This can represent a large administration task for nodes but is necessary for both node and data protection.

CPJAZZ SOFTWARE CONSTRUCTION

CPJazz, being a component-like model, borrows heavily from the Component Based Design methodology. In this model, system construction leverages heavily from existing software components to provide desired functionality within the system. For example, a GPS Manager component provides GPS data in a standard bus API form that other components may interrogate. The requesting component therefore does not need to understand various GPS protocols, but instead the abstraction of the protocol provided by the GPS Manager component.

This model is desirable for many reasons. One advantage is containment of complexity. A system is built from a set of components (either pre-built or custom designed for the system's purpose). The system is therefore built from a number of simpler components that integrate to provide more complex behavior. The CBD model has been called "the industrialization of software development". [3] This lesson of moving from custom development to development based upon the assembly of prefabricated components was learned from the manufacturing industries long ago. The benefits and leverage of time-to-market and cost reduction are clear.

Fast prototyping is also simplified with the model. The ability to collect a number of pre-fabricated components that are used by a custom component for a data management or control task means that systems may be more quickly developed and verified.

Another advantage is the natural firewall to changes. A component does not need to know that another component was redesigned or that it now speaks to different hardware as long as its basic interfaces (via CPJazz) remain the same.

This component-like model provides another step towards large-scale reuse for software development which can lead to higher quality, higher reliability and lower development costs.

SAMPLE SCENARIOS

WIRELESS VEHICLE MONITORING – The ability to monitor vehicles for performance, tracking and/or operational characterization helps fleet-based businesses increase efficiency. The CPJazz architecture and supporting components provide the vehicular interfaces (such as OBD, GPS and others) as well as common interfaces to wireless links. With dynamic link selection, the ability to monitor remote vehicles also becomes more cost-efficient with the concept of policy-based wireless link selection. Providing vehicles with multiple links provides for distribution of data based upon criticality or cost. Therefore, non-critical data can be stored for distribution when a low-cost link (such as spread-spectrum or Bluetooth) is available or critical data can utilize a transient link such as a satellite phone or CSC modem.

VEHICULAR RESOURCE SHARING – As vehicles incorporate more technology (non-critical, such as navigation systems), the ability to share some of the common resources becomes attractive. For example, a GPS receiver is useful not only for an inboard navigation system but also as a time source. A Voice Recognition device is useful to any device that can benefit from voice commands such as a cellphone or entertainment radio. The CPJazz architecture provides the bridging glue in this application to tie the non-critical disparate subsystems together (regardless of physical bus used) so that cooperative use is possible. The bottom-line is subsystem reuse in vehicles that can represent significant cost reductions.

RESOURCE-CONSTRAINED EMBEDDED VEHICLE SYSTEMS – Embedded system developers commonly attempt to size the resources needed in a system in order to reduce the overall cost of the hardware components. These components include not only FLASH, EEPROM or RAM but also the performance rating of the processor. CPJazz supports these efforts through its dynamic abilities. Systems that include transient components (components that are enabled to perform a task, and are then removed from active execution) can benefit from CPJazz. For example, consider a vehicle that includes a docked cellphone (connected to a vehicle bus) that provides data services. A component operating on CPJazz could request, through the link manager, that the cellphone be enabled for use through a PPP link. The link manager would build the PPP-based network stack over the particular bus and make it available for the requesting component. Once the link was no longer needed, the link manager would tear the network stack down and remove it from active memory making the memory and processing capacity available for other component's use.

CONCLUSION

This paper discussed the CPJazz architecture and its applicability to embedded vehicle systems development. CPJazz is based upon a component model for software development where each component is an individual executable that provides a common API interface over the CPJazz communication framework. Key features of the architecture such as link selection and managed flows simplify the job of applications developers through transparent services. The dynamic nature of the architecture also supports systems with minimal resources.

REFERENCES

1. A. Goscinski, 'Distributed Operating Systems: The Logical Design', Addison-Wesley, 1992
2. R. G. Smith, 'The contract net protocol: High-level communication and control in a distributed problem solver', IEEE Transactions on Computers, 29(1980).
3. K. Short, 'Component Based Development and Object Modeling', Sterling Software, February 1997.

CONTACT

CellPort Labs Inc. currently employs Mr. Jones in Boulder, Co as the principal software engineer for the Mobile Networking Technologies group. He can be reached at mtj@cellport.com. CellPort Lab's URL is http://www.cellport.com

DEFINITIONS, ACRONYMS, ABBREVIATIONS

API: Application Programmers Interface
CDPD: Cellular Digital Packet Data
CSC: Circuit Switched Cellular
GPS: Global Positioning System
IP: Internet Protocol
NMEA: National Marine Electronics Association
OBD: OnBoard Diagnostic
PDA: Personal Digital Assistant
POSIX: Portable Operating System Interface
PPP: Point to Point Protocol
SLIP: Serial Link Interface Protocol
TTS: Text-To-Speech
VR: Voice Recognition

COMMUNICATIONS

2007-01-1714

Prevention of DoS Attacks on Inter-Vehicle Communications

Bryan Fleming, Jason Watson, Mark Pellerito and Huirong Fu[1]
Oakland University

ABSTRACT

Inter-vehicle communication (IVC) is the next step in developing a coordinated vehicular transportation system. With today's concerns of security in Internet communications, it is critical that the security in IVC be considered. With its many life-depending implications it is crucial that an IVC system be tolerant of both natural and man-made interference. The goal of our research was to explore solutions to address the issues of security of IVC in spite of its vulnerability to Denial-of-Service (DoS) attacks, in which an attacker systematically or selectively jams the signals exchanged by the vehicles. We present proposed solutions to DoS attacks on IVC, as well as introduce additional concepts and ideas that help address this important problem.

INTRODUCTION

Automobiles of the future will take advantage of Inter-Vehicular Communication (IVC) capabilities, in which vehicles will communicate with one another wirelessly. An IVC network is a type of mobile ad hoc network (MANET), commonly referred to as a vehicular ad hoc network (VANET), in which the nodes of the network are vehicles. There are numerous logistical issues involving the creation of efficient, robust IVC networks that are still being researched. The most critical of these is the issue of security. While security concerns exist with all types of networks, there are additional concerns with IVC networks, due to the safety-critical nature of the networks. Not only can attacks on IVC networks cripple the communication between vehicles, there is also the potential for injuries and death related to vehicle collisions.

This research aims to address the problem of Denial-of-Service (DoS) or Distributed Denial-of-Service (DDoS) attacks on IVC networks. The current body of literature regarding the creation of IVC networks includes some proposed solutions to DoS attacks on IVC. The goal of the research contained herein is to present these proposed solutions and to highlight the benefits and drawbacks of each. This research aims to propose new solutions, and/or enhance elements of existing solutions.

MOTIVATION

The following sections provide an overview of IVC, and discuss the security issues, including DoS attacks, that need to be addressed if the widespread use of IVC networks is to become a reality.

OVERVIEW OF IVC

IVC can be used to achieve a number of goals. One day, it may be possible for vehicles to drive themselves using a coordinated IVC system. More likely in the nearer future, however, will be the ability for vehicles to assist drivers either actively or passively to avoid collisions or other road hazards.

For an IVC implementation to be successful it must effectively reduce some combination of vehicle collision, accident rate or fatality rate. It must also do so reliably. It would be considered unacceptable for an IVC system to provide these benefits only some of the time, as the result could be lost lives. In response to this issue, various methods have been proposed to implement IVC.

Most proposed methods of IVC implementation involve some key elements. Figure 1 illustrates one such proposed architecture [2]. There are three types of nodes in the infrastructure: clusterheads (shown in red), gateway nodes (shown in green), and ordinary nodes (shown in yellow). Clusterheads "perform access control, coordinate access to the media, and provide guaranteed delivery of messages within the cluster" [2]. Gateway nodes fall within the range of two clusterheads, and together with the clusterheads, form a "virtual network backbone," along which "intercluster coordination and message routing" occurs [2]. All other nodes are ordinary nodes, which fall within the range of one clusterhead and communicate via the network backbone.

[1] This material is based upon work supported by the National Science Foundation under Grant No. 0542374. Any opinions, findings, and conclusions or recommendations expressed in this material are those of the authors and do not necessarily reflect the views of the National Science Foundation.

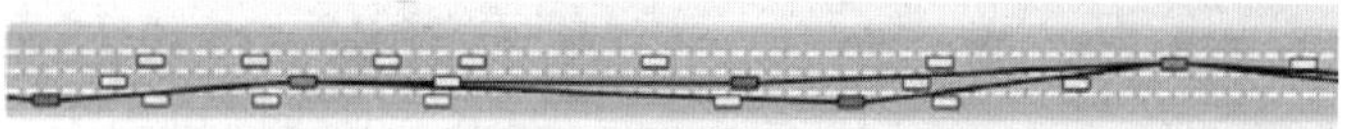

Figure 1: SecCar Virtual Network Infrastructure [2]

In addition, most proposed implementations include the concept of an "electronic license plate." The electronic license plate is essentially a digital identifier for a vehicle, much the VIN number and the physical license plate are identifiers for today's vehicles.

IVC SECURITY

Safety is a primary concern for automobile companies today, and the deployment of VANETs introduces potential threats for today's drivers. Now that the ideas of VANETs are in place, ways to protect the system and others are the next priority when developing this system. Many researchers have identified common threats that may occur if VANETs are deployed, including fabrication attacks, tampering attacks, hardware tampering, DoS attacks, and DDoS attacks. These threats to the system need to be identified so that the structure of the VANETs will minimize any threats of future misuse.

Disabling attacks are those in which "an attacker may attempt to disable the communication and storage abilities of an electronic license plate for a vehicle" [1]. Fabrication or impersonation attacks are those in which "an attacker may attempt to steal another vehicle's identity and apply it to his or her own vehicle" [1]. Hardware tampering attacks involve physical modification to the IVC communication hardware, in order to cause undesired behavior when in use.

DoS or DDoS attacks represent the single greatest risk to security in IVC mobile ad hoc networks. DoS attacks on IVC networks are similar in nature to DoS attacks on other mobile ad hoc networks. The major difference is that the occurrence of a DoS attack on an IVC network can result in dire, sometimes fatal, consequences. Due to its severe nature, the prevention of DoS attacks on IVC networks is the focus of this research. Table 1 provides a summary of the IVC security threats that have been identified herein.

IVC Security Issue	Description
Disabling attack	Disabling of communication and storage abilities
Fabrication attack	Impersonation of another vehicle
Hardware tampering	Physical modification of IVC hardware
DoS attack	Depletion of bandwidth typically caused by rapid transmission of network packets, resulting in loss of service to users
DDoS attack	Form of DoS attack in which multiple systems are used to disrupt service

Table 1: Attacks on IVC Networks

Consider the following scenario, involving a DoS attack on a vehicle platoon [2]. Suppose the lead car in the platoon is forced to brake hard due to another vehicle merging into the platoon's lane. The lead car transmits a signal to the vehicle behind it, notifying it that its brakes have been applying. This signal continues to propagate down the platoon. If, however, a DoS attack disrupts the communication between two of the vehicles in the platoon, a collision may occur. This scenario is illustrated in Figure 2.

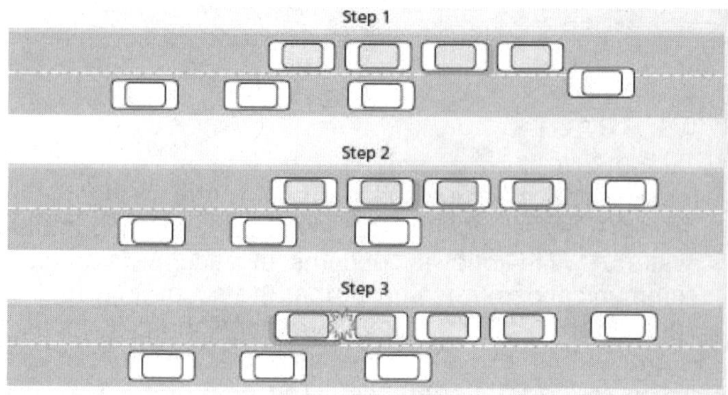

Figure 2: Attack on a Vehicle Platoon [2]

Another example involves the concept of "virtual mirrors" to detect potential collisions. A vehicle that wishes to change lanes may rely on nearby vehicles to report their positions, which are displayed to the driver on a "virtual mirror." If the communication between it and another vehicle is disrupted as a result of a DoS attack, the vehicle may not recognize the presence of a vehicle in the destination lane, and a collision may occur. This scenario is illustrated in Figure 3.

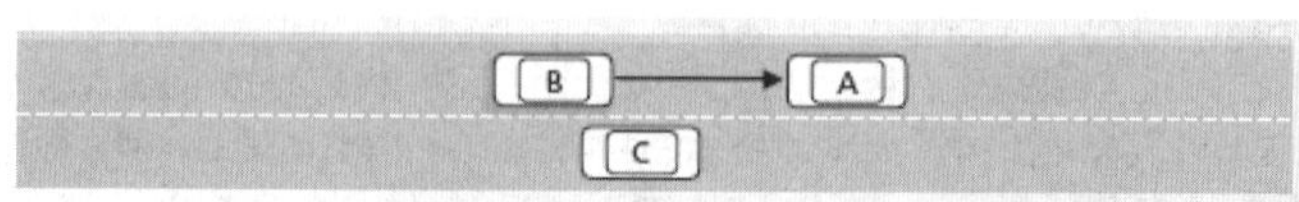

Figure 3: Attack on a Virtual Mirror [2]

RESEARCH MATERIAL

The following sections highlight current research and proposed solutions to the prevention of DoS attacks on IVC networks.

ATTACKS ON INTER-VEHICLE COMMUNICATION SYSTEMS

Aijaz et al. (2006) present the concepts of Threat Modeling and Attack Trees, which can be used to reduce the possible threats to a VANET system [3]. Threat modeling is a process that represents real world experiences as mathematical equations. This way of thinking can help with actual coding to stop potential threats before they happen or to advance existing models. Before the models can be developed for the threats, an attack tree must be made to help identify those threats. An attack tree provides a formal way of describing the security of systems, based on various attacks that may occur. An attack tree will describe the goals and sub goals for each threat, presented in a structured way [3]. This will help visualize what the threats are and how to proceed with solving the situation. Aijaz et al. (2006) also discuss applications a VANET would have in the real world, which include Car-to-Car Traffic Applications, Car-to-Infrastructure Applications, Car-to-Home Applications, and Routing-based Applications [3]. These four applications are the major parts of the VANET itself, and form the focus of the attack trees and threat modeling for VANETs. After an attack tree has been developed, threat modeling can be performed. Aijaz et al. (2006) present four typical attackers and what they can do to the applications [3]. The four attacks presented are self explanatory to most situations on this topic, but still need to be addressed as potential threats to the system. These typical or reusable attacks are done in a separate attack tree called a *reusable attack subtree,* which identifies attacks that will be used for all the attack trees, and minimizes redundancy [3].

SECURE COMMUNICATION ARCHITECTURE (SECCAR)

Blum and Eskandarian (2004) propose the Secure Communication Architecture (SecCar). The infrastructure for SecCar is described in the *OVERVIEW OF IVC* section above. SecCar provides the following security services [2]:

- An authentication service that "ensures that the architecture can discover malicious users' identities while preserving the privacy of all other users"
- A nonrepudiation service that "ensures that entities cannot later deny participating in a security attack"
- An access control service that "prevents unauthorized entities from accessing the system functions"
- An availability service that "manages DoS attacks to ensure that the system continues functioning even when under attack."
- A confidentiality service "for the SecCar control messages"

As stated above, the availability service is the SecCar solution to mitigation of DoS attacks. SecCar uses a combination of time-division multiplexing (TDM) and frequency hopping spread spectrum (FHSS) to aid in the prevention of DoS attacks. FHSS is a "spread-spectrum method of transmitting radio signals by rapidly switching a carrier among many frequency channels, using a pseudorandom sequence known to both transmitter and receiver" [4]. TDM is the "means by which multiple digital signals (or analogue signals carrying digital data) can be carried on a single transmission path by interleaving portions of each signal in time" [5]. Each node is assigned its own unique hopping sequence of frequency bands by which to transmit data. Time synchronization is achieved by using GPS receivers. In order to join an existing network, a node must send a request message to a clusterhead along with the node's certificate. The clusterhead verifies the validity of the signature, and ensures that the node has not been "blacklisted." If the node is permitted to join the network, the clusterhead assigns it a time slot and hopping sequence. This combination of TDM and FHSS helps to prevent DoS attacks, since a malicious node will first need to acquire a hopping sequence from a clusterhead. Malicious activity by the node can cause the node to be "blacklisted" in the future, preventing it from acquiring additional hopping sequences.

COLLABORATIVE REPUTATION MECHANISM (CORE)

Michiardi and Molva (2002) propose a Collaborative Reputation Mechanism (CORE) to enforce node cooperation in Mobile Ad hoc Networks [6]. CORE uses the concept of reputation to enforce cooperation among nodes and prevent DoS attacks. Using the reputation technique, each entity keeps track of other entities' collaboration. Reputation is computed based on data monitored by the local entity, as well as by data supplied by other nodes in the network. The reputation metric considers both subjective reputation and indirect reputation.

Subjective reputation is "calculated directly from a subject's observation" [6]. A subjective reputation "at time t by subject s_i on subject s_j" is determined by calculating a "weighted mean of the observations' rating factors, giving more relevance to past observations" [6]. The scale for subjective reputation ranges from -1 (negative impression) to +1 (positive impression).

Indirect reputation is derived from "information provided by other members of the community [or network]" [6]. An indirect reputation "at time t by subject s_i on subject s_j" is determined by calculating a "weighted mean of the observations' rating factors, giving more relevance to past observations" [6]. The indirect reputation must be a positive value. This prevents DoS attacks in which a malicious node broadcasts unwarranted negative reputation values for a particular node. Negative reputation can only by computed locally via the subjective reputation component.

Reputation affects the manner in which nodes communicate on the network. If a request is made by one node to another, and the request is not processed correctly, or is not processed in a timely or efficient manner, the reputation of the node will decrease. Likewise, if malicious activity is observed for a node, the reputation of the node will also decrease. Future requests by behaving nodes will not be routed through malicious nodes. Behaving nodes will ignore future requests by malicious nodes. This helps in the prevention of DoS attacks by nodes for which previous malicious activity has been detected. Attempted DoS attacks by nodes with a negative reputation will fail, since the messages from these nodes will be ignored.

INTRINSIC VALUE APPROACH

Elhajj, Fu, Padilla, and Aloi (2005) have proposed a system that could also be helpful in preventing a DoS attack [7]. Rather than using the traditional approach of utilizing encryption, keys, and unique identifiers, this approach, which will be called Vehicle Immediate Vicinity Awareness (VIVA), relies on authentication between vehicles based on their intrinsic values of velocity and position. By using transmission and reception times, VIVA allows the distance between vehicles to be computed and used to verify a vehicle's claimed position or speed. This solution can be used to assist in DoS prevention.

DISCUSSION / CONTRIBUTIONS

The following sections highlight the contributions to the field of IVC security provided by this research, concentrating on modifications to or combinations of the existing solutions presented in the previous sections.

PRIMARY CONTRIBUTIONS

The following sections discuss the contributions of this research aimed at addressing the problem of DoS attacks on IVC networks.

Combination of SecCar and CORE

The concepts presented in the SecCar and CORE research can be combined into a single, comprehension solution to the problem of DoS attacks on IVC networks. SecCar provides a fundamental protocol for communication between vehicles on an IVC network. That is, a combination of FHSS and TDM can be used to ensure that transmissions between nodes are valid and benign. What SecCar does not inherently provide, however, is a means by which to determine if a node should be allowed to join an IVC network. When a vehicle wants to join an existing network, it must first request a unique FHSS hopping sequence and TDM time slot from a clusterhead. The clusterhead must verify the validity of the node's certificate, as well as determine if the node has been "blacklisted." SecCar does not provide a means for blacklisting a node. The concepts presented in the CORE research are well suited to perform this task for the SecCar model. The CORE concept of reputation can be used to "blacklist" nodes on a SecCar IVC network. If the reputation of a node is poor, it will not be assigned an FHSS hopping sequence or TDM time slot, and will therefore not be allowed to join the network. The combination of these two approaches represents a viable solution to the prevention of DoS attacks on IVC networks.

SecCar and CDMA Technology

As previously stated, the SecCar communication protocol relies on TDM to manage multiple transmissions on the communication medium. GPS receivers are used to synchronize time between the vehicles on the network. There are obvious flaws to using GPS for time synchronization. First, the GPS hardware may be tampered with. Second, communication lag could exist in maintaining time synchronization between two nodes. Finally, attacks on GPS itself can be performed, resulting in a loss of synchronization between the vehicles.

As an alternative to using TDM, and therefore an alternative to the reliance on GPS receivers, is the use of Code Division Multiple Access (CDMA) technology, as is commonly used in cellular phone networks. Instead of using designated time slots to process multiple signals on a single channel, CDMA typically involves attaching a unique code to the transmitted data packet. The receiver can then use this code to determine the node from which the data packet was sent.

There is a tradeoff between using CDMA versus using TDM. With CDMA, the need for GPS receivers and time synchronization using GPS is eliminating. This reduces the number of hardware devices required, as well as eradicates the issues inherent to the use of GPS as previously discussed. The use of CDMA, however, introduces the possibility of code spoofing attacks, in which a node intentionally transmits data using an invalid or forged code. This can be used to perform malicious behavior while masking the true identity of the sender. More research and analysis is needed to determine which transmission-multiplexing scheme presents the greatest cost-benefit advantage for use in IVC networks.

Intrinsic Value Approach (IVA) to DoS Prevention

A possible way to attempt to prevent DoS attacks is by increasing the security behind the vehicle identification. While not necessarily a candidate for a primary means of message authentication in DoS prevention, the Intrinsic Value Approach (IVA) might very well be the necessary means for redundancy in an IVC system.

Behind this approach is a method of authenticating messages based on the position and velocity characteristics. Because there is no way to forge actual position and velocity, these characteristics can be used to verify the claimed position and velocity of a vehicle on a VANET. This is done using a third intrinsic value: time. Since the passage of time is considered relatively constant and can be resynchronized with GPS, time can be used to determine the actual distance between two vehicles by timing the communications between them.

The distance between vehicles cannot be forged since there is no way to send a response to a requesting vehicle faster than the speed of light. No vehicle could therefore transmit an illegitimately quick response to a location query. This check-response technique can be used to effectively filter out and ignore the responses of rogue vehicles whose VANET systems are attempting to produce a DoS attack.

ANCILLARY CONTRIBUTIONS

During the course of research, a number of potential implementations have presented themselves as possible avenues for future research and development. It seems that these might be strong augmentations to the implementations of IVC systems that could reduce risks of IVC affected by DoS, or could help to mitigate other IVC security risks.

Visual Cues

Instead of allowing a vehicle to completely control itself to avoid a collision, lights could be used to indicate appropriate actions to the driver. While this does reintroduce human response time, it also prevents a victim of a DoS attack from causing potentially greater damage or loss-of-life. The lights could be used to actively display whether an escape route is available to the left or right of a driver's vehicle, in order to indicate the possibility of swerving at any given moment. This could also be used to alert a driver to any sudden changes to road conditions, or changes to driver behavior further up the road, allowing for greater response time.

Video Monitoring

The addition of IVC technology into vehicles can be accompanied by additional mechanisms by which to alert the driver of nearby dangers. For example, the installation of visual devices that display nearby vehicles as a series of dots can be used to augment rearview mirrors and aid in the prevention of accidents. Audio cues could also be used to alert drivers of other vehicles. This technology may aid those who may have difficulty checking blind spots, or those that are not aware of other passing vehicles. While this device would not be used to prevent attacks on IVC security, it could be used as a supplemental system to the IVC networking capabilities once sufficient security measures are in place.

CONCLUSION

The current research regarding IVC and IVC security is in its developing stages. While no strong candidate has presented itself as a complete solution to all vulnerabilities surrounding IVC, a number of solutions would clearly be instrumental in IVC implementation. The SecCar solution provides an availability security service, which aims to prevent and diminish the effects of DoS attacks. CORE provides a mechanism to identify potential attackers through "blacklisting." IVA can be used to identify and authenticate a vehicle via intrinsic, non-traditional means. Through a combination of these technologies, a reasonable IVC prototype system could be built with significant prevention of DoS attacks. Visual cues and video monitoring techniques can also be implemented to augment IVC capabilities. Sufficient testing of such an implementation would likely reveal the direction that is most suitable for further development and research. With the collaborative efforts in IVC research, it is clear that successful IVC implementations may exist in the near future.

REFERENCES

1. Hubaux, Jean-Pierre, S. Capkun, and J. Luo, "The Security and Privacy of Smart Vehicles," IEEE Security and Privacy, May/June 2004, 49 – 55.
2. Blum, Jeremy and Azim Eskandarian, "The Threat of Intelligent Collisions," IT Pro, January/February 2004, 24 – 29.
3. Aijaz, Amer, Bernd Bochow, Florian Dotzer, Andreas Festag, Matthias Gerlach, Rainer Kroh, and Tim Leinmuller, "Attacks on Inter Vehicle Communication Systems – an Analysis," 3rd International Workshop on Intelligent Transportation (WIT 2006), March 14 – 15, 2006.
4. Wikimedia Foundation, Inc., "Frequency-hopping spread spectrum," Wikipedia, the free encyclopedia, http://en.wikipedia.org/wiki/Frequency-hopping_spread_spectrum, March 7, 2006.
5. Wikimedia Foundation, Inc., "Time-division multiplexing," Wikipedia, the free encyclopedia, http://en.wikipedia.org/wiki/Time-Division_Multiplexing, March 30, 2006.
6. Michiardi, Pietro and Refik Molva, "CORE: A Collaborative Reputation Mechanism to enforce node cooperation in Mobile Ad hoc Networks," Communication and Multimedia Security Conference 2002, September 26 – 27, 2002.
7. Elhajj, Imad H., Huirong Fu, Adrian Padilla, and Daniel Aloi, "Keyless Message Authentication by Verifying Position and Velocity for Inter-Vehicle Communication," 06AE-192, SAE International, 2005.

CONTACT

Huirong Fu, Ph.D.
Assistant Professor
Department of Computer Science and Engineering
Oakland University
Rochester, MI 48309

Phone: (248) 370-4456
Fax: (248) 370-4625
Email: fu@oakland.edu
URL: http://www.secs.oakland.edu/~fu/

2007-01-1709

Add-On Device Network for Passenger Cars

Holger Zeltwanger
CAN in Automation International Users' and Manufacturers' Group

ABSTRACT

Police cars, taxi/cabs, and other special-purpose passenger cars are equipped with add-on devices such as blue-light, special horns, taximeter, digital radio, etc. In the past, such equipment was connected via discrete I/O lines or proprietary interfaces, e.g. RS-232, RS-485, J1850, or CAN. The CAN in Automation (CiA) international users and manufacturers group has established a technical group specifying an open CAN-based network for such car add-on devices. The physical layer is based on ISO 11898-2 (CAN high-speed), and the CAN data link layer (ISO 11898-1) uses the base frame format (11-bit CAN identifier). The selected application layer is compliant to CANopen (EN 50325-4). In order to achieve easy system integration, the group is specifying an application profile describing the content of the transmitted messages.

INTRODUCTION

Special-purpose cars sales figures are low. In many cases, there are produced just a few hundreds of a specific kind – sometimes even less. Nevertheless, original equipment manufacturers (OEM) or value-added resellers (VAR) equip special-purpose cars with an increasing number of add-on devices. Those add-on devices provide more and more functions. The necessary communication between the add-on devices becomes more complex and demands the use of networks. Due to the fact that the add-on devices or aftermarket devices are developed and manufactured by different companies standardized communication shall be used to reduce system integration effort.

Several European add-on manufacturers and some OEMs (DaimlerChrysler, General Motors Europe, and the Volkswagen group) initiated the standardization of an open network for special-purpose car add-on devices. CiA, the international CAN users' and manufacturers' group, umbrellas and hosts this standardization activity.

The specification to be developed covers all seven layers of the ISO/OSI reference model. In addition, it also specifies the process data to be transmitted between the add-on devices and to the gateway to the in-vehicle networks (IVN). *Figure 1* shows the used reference model and the selected protocols.

Application profile	CiA 447
Application layer	EN 50325-4/CiA 301
Presentation layer	Not used
Session layer	Not used
Transport layer	EN 50325-4/CiA 301
Network layer	Not used
Data link layer	ISO 11898-1
Physical layer	ISO 11898-2/CiA 301

Figure 1 – Reference model and selected protocols

The selected physical layer uses so-called CAN high-speed transceiver chips compliant to ISO 11898-2. The transmission rate is specified as 125 kbit/s. The bit-timing follows the specification given in the CiA 301 (CANopen application layer). The valid range for the location of the sample point is between 75% and 90% of the nominal bit-time (8μs). The recommended location of the sample point is at 87,5% of the bit-time. It is recommended to use the 18-pin VDA interface connector (e.g. *micro quadlok system 0.64* from Tyco or equivalent connectors from other manufacturers) shown in *Figure 2.*

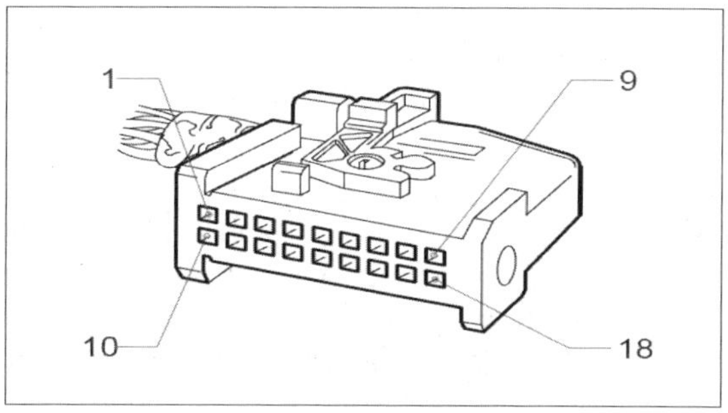

Figure 2 – 18-pin VDA connector

Table 1 – Pin assignment

Pin	Name	Description
1	KL31	Ground (0 V/max. 4 A)
2	PTT 1	Reserved for PTT
3	PTT 2	Reserved for PTT
4	MUTE	Reserved for audio mute
5		reserved
6		reserved
7	AUDIO_OUT	Reserved for audio receiver
8	CAN_L	CAN low line
9	MIC_SHIELD	Reserved for microphone shield/ground
10	KL15	Ignition
11	KL30	Power supply voltage (+12 V/max. 4 A)
12	KL58	Illumination
13		reserved
14		reserved
15		reserved
16	AUDIO_GND	Reserved for ground for audio signals
17	CAN_H	CAN high line
18	AUDIO_IN/MIC	Reserved for audio transmitter (e.g. microphone)

The network uses the base frame format as defined in ISO 11898-1 (CAN data link layer standard). The use of the 11-bit CAN identifiers is pre-defined by the selected application layer and application profile.

The selected CANopen application layer was originally designed for open systems. It was developed as European research project more than 10 years ago. After handing it over to CiA for further development and maintenance, it has been used in many application domains such as machine control systems, medical devices, rail vehicles, etc. CANopen defines several application layer services and protocols.

The CANopen application profile for special-purpose cars defines the content of the CAN messages exchanged between the special-purpose car add-on devices. This includes the process data, configuration parameter and diagnostic information mapped into the CAN messages. In order to achieve interoperability between the IVN gateway provided by the OEMs and the add-on devices manufactured by the suppliers, it is necessary to standardize especially the consumed and produced messages of the IVN gateway.

CANOPEN DEVICE MODEL

The most important elements of a CANopen device are the CAN communication interface including the CAN hardware and the application layer protocol stack, the process interface (inputs and outputs), and last but not least the CANopen object dictionary. The CANopen object dictionary comprises a list of parameters with a unique address (16-bit index and 8-bit sub-index). Using an application profile, the indices in the range 6000_h to $9FFF_h$ are shared by all devices.

CANopen supports two levels of device abstractions. Each physical CANopen device may comprise up to eight logical devices (*Figure 3*). The standardized profile area (CANopen dictionary index range 6000_h to $9FFF_h$) in the object dictionary is organized in eight blocks by 800_h indices. Each block may comprise several virtual devices. This approach allows running up to eight application profiles on the very same physical network. In addition, each CANopen device provides in its object dictionary a range of indices (2000_h to $5FFF_h$) for manufacturer-specific purposes.

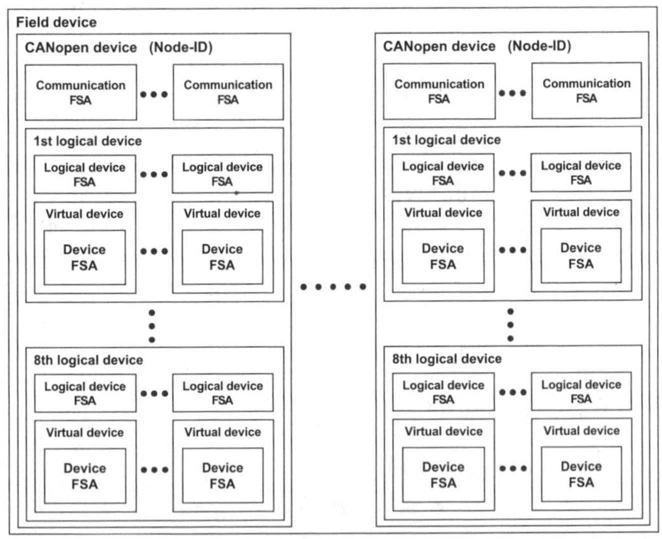

Figure 3 – CANopen device model

The IVN gateway implements basically the virtual gateway functional elements. Optionally it may provide discrete interfaces or other network interfaces. Additional virtual devices represent those functional elements, e.g. RS-232 connected blue-lights or taximeter linked via a proprietary CAN network. A typical multi-virtual device implementation is an IVN gateway virtual device plus one or more user interface virtual devices (e.g. car status, powertrain, body electronics, user interface, and GPS virtual devices). In this case, the keys and displays are physically connected to the in-vehicle networks and are represented by means of CANopen virtual devices implemented in the ECU (electronic control unit) with CANopen gateway functionality. Another example is the roof top controller: it may comprise the blue-light, the siren, the acoustic announcement, and the display virtual devices. In another implementation all virtual devices may be realized in separate CANopen devices.

In special-purpose car add-on devices, there will be mostly one logical device implemented. The logical device approach may be used for further extensions, if other CANopen applications are used (e.g. ambulance application profile connecting medical equipment).

CANOPEN APPLICATION LAYER

The CANopen application layer provides also transport layer functions, in particular the segmentation of information to be transmitted that is longer as 8 bytes. This necessary, if program download via CANopen is demanded, or if larger diagnostic information should be uploaded. The application layer is standardized in EN 50325-4 and CiA 301 (next version that will be submitted for international standardization in the next maintenance cycle). It specifies several communication services and protocols:

- *Process data object (PDO)* protocol: Single CAN message containing up to 8 byte process data. This is an unconfirmed service.
- *Service data object (SDO)* protocols: Two 8-byte CAN messages realizing the client/server communication between two CANopen devices. They may be transmitted multiply in order to upload or download segmented data using the same CAN identifier. This is a confirmed service. The SDO protocols use the index and sub-index as a multiplexor.
- *Emergency (EMCY)* protocol: Single 8-byte message containing defined error and diagnostic information. This is an unconfirmed service.
- *Network management (NMT)* protocol: Single 2-byte message transmitted by the CANopen manager device controlling the NMT state machines of the CANopen slave devices. Car add-on devices use the self-starting option. It is an unconfirmed service.
- *Heartbeat* protocol: Single 1-byte message containing the current NMT state. It is transmitted periodically with the heartbeat producer time. It is an unconfirmed service. The heartbeat consuming devices indicates missing heartbeat messages by events to the application.

These protocols and optional ones are implemented in the CANopen protocol stack software. Some CAN modules implement some functions (SDO protocol) in firmware. The IVN gateway device implements the CANopen manager functionality and is the SDO client for all other add-on devices.

PDO COMMUNICATION

Car add-on devices compliant to the CiA 447 application profile use pre-defined PDOs. All PDOs have pre-assigned CAN identifiers. PDOs are defined by means of pre-defined transmission types, event-timers, inhibit-timers.

Also the mapping of process data is pre-defined. The mapped process data is described in the PDO mapping parameter set. This parameter set contains pointer (index and sub-index) to the process data. These pre-definitions provide a high degree of off-the-shelf plug-and-play capability. The PDO communication parameter and the PDO mapping parameters are accessible by means of SDO services. The IVN gateway may check not only the presence of the car add-on devices but also the consistence of the PDO communication by reading the PDO parameter sets.

All devices compliant to CiA 447 are self-starting devices. This means, they transit automatically to the NMT operational state, in which they may receive and transmit PDOs. In all other NMT states, PDO communication is not allowed.

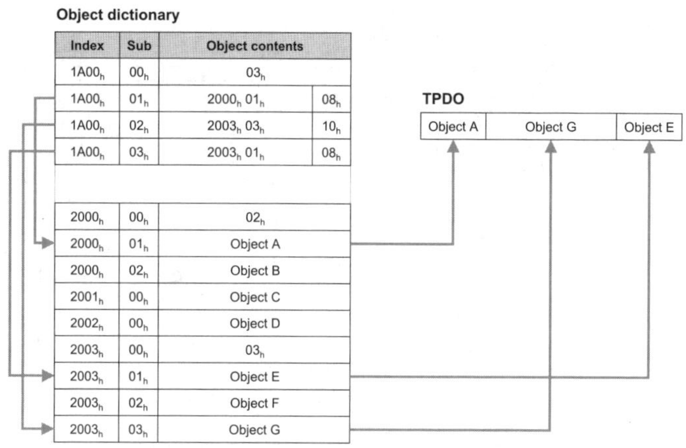

Figure 4 – TPDO mapping principle

In order to achieve a high level of off-the-shelf plug-and-play capability, the profile pre-defines most of the necessary PDOs. The IVN gateway provides for example several PDOs with pre-defined CAN-IDs. The PDOs are assigned to virtual devices as defined in CiA 447. The IVN gateway comprises in passenger cars from DaimlerChrysler and General Motors several virtual devices (e.g. car status, powertrain, body electronics, and optionally GPS). Each of these virtual devices supports several PDOs to be received and to be transmitted. The car status virtual device supports for example a TPDO that contains the *switch illumination level* object, a 1-byte parameter indicating the status of the illumination power supply (KL58) in percentage.

SDO COMMUNICATION

Each CANopen device provides an SDO server function, the so-called default SDO server. The CANopen manager device providing the NMT master function implements the corresponding SDO clients. This means, the CANopen manager is able to configure all CANopen devices in a network via SDO services. Besides these default SDOs, the CiA 447 specifies additional pre-configuring SDO channels. SDOs use two CAN messages: One for the client-to-server and the other for the server-to-client communication. The SDO protocol header includes the control byte and the 3-byte index plus sub-index. SDOs are made to access any entry of the device's object dictionary.

NMT COMMUNICATION

The CANopen manager provides the NMT master functionality. It uses the NMT message to control the NMT slave state machines. The 2-byte message contains the command specifier and the unique node-ID of the addressed CANopen device. The node-ID of 0 indicates a broadcast NMT command to be performed by all devices. The CANopen manager is located in the device that implements the car status virtual devices.

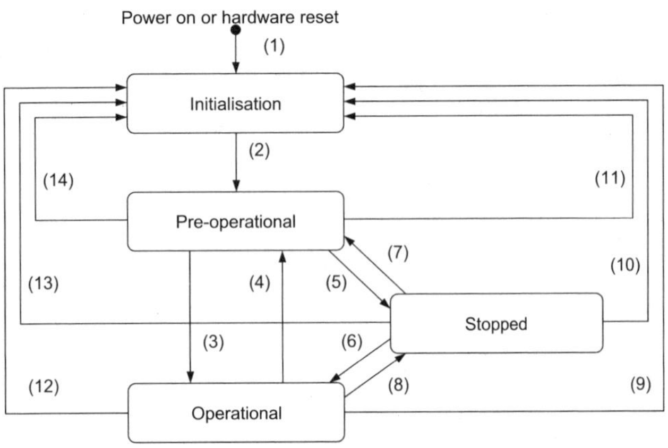

Figure 5 – NMT slave state machine

The device monitoring is performed by the heartbeat messages. Every device transmits periodically this message with a CAN-ID deriving from the node-ID. Every device may consume the heartbeat from every device. This means the device monitoring function is distributed.

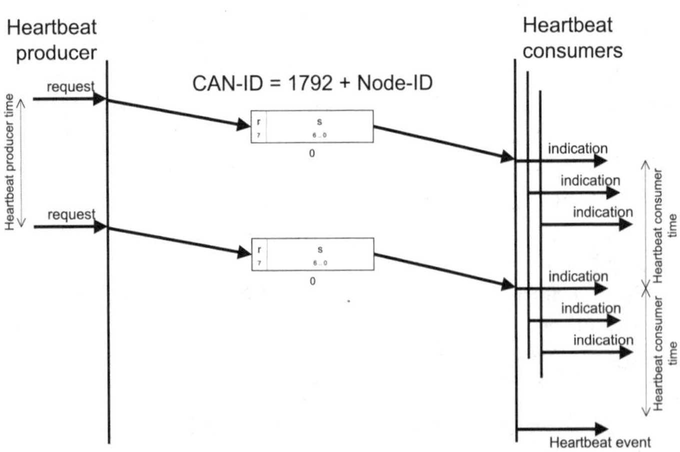

Figure 6 – Heartbeat protocol

EMCY COMMUNICATION

Emergency messages indicate problems and errors in the devices. They contain the 2-byte standardized emergency error code (EEC), the 1-byte error register (object 1001_h), the 2-byte internationally standardized diagnostic trouble code (DTC), and optionally the 3-byte pointer (index and sub-index), where additional diagnostic information is stored in the object dictionary. This additional information is accessible via the IVN gateway by means of SDO upload services.

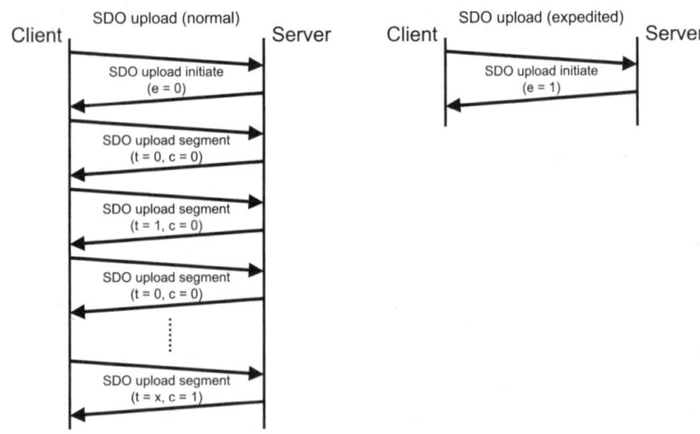

Figure 7 – SDO upload protocols used for reading diagnostic data

CANOPEN OBJECT DICTIONARY

The CANopen application profile defines all process data, configuration parameter, and diagnostic information. All these objects are listed in the CANopen object dictionary.

Each CANopen special-purpose car add-on device implements one or more virtual devices. Which virtual devices are implemented is indicated in the device type parameter (object 1000_h) and in the supported virtual devices parameter (object 6000_h). The virtual devices shall share the object dictionary index range 6000_h to $67FE_h$. A single virtual device shall not be distributed to several CANopen devices. Each virtual device implements different process and configuration parameter, some shall be supported (Mandatory) and some may be supported (Optional).

An example of the process data defined for is the *ignition switch state* object. It is of the data type Unsigned8 and uses three bits as shown in Table 2. It is provided by the car status virtual device and is consumed by several other virtual devices such as the blue-light, the taximeter, and the digital radio virtual devices.

Table 2 – Value definition for ignition switch state

Bit 2	Bit 1	Bit 0	Description
0	0	0	Ignition lock
0	0	1	Ignition off
0	1	0	Ignition accessory
1	0	0	Ignition on
1	0	1	Ignition start
1	1	1	Signal not available

NODE-ID ASSIGNMENT

CANopen requires a unique node-ID assignment in order to create the CAN-IDs for the default SDO server messages as well as for the heartbeat message. In the application profile for car add-on devices, the node claiming procedure is used. This procedure is using a similar mechanism as the CAN arbitration. Depending on the uniquely vendor-ID (assigned by CAN in Automation), the product code, the revision number, and the serial number each CANopen device sends CAN messages with a 0-byte data field. If the message is delayed by a higher prior message, the device stops claiming procedure. At the end of this first claiming, only one device is allowed to claim a node-ID. After the claiming, the second cycle of the claiming procedure starts. This is repeated until all devices have claimed a node-ID. It is possible to pre-assign node-IDs to dedicated devices such as the IVN gateway. Those node-IDs are excluded from the node-ID claiming procedure. The claiming procedure is patent protected. In order to avoid problems when install pre-assigned devices are integrated in an already configured network, all NMT slave devices waits in the initialization state until they have received a dedicated message from the CANopen manager device containing the vendor-ID and the serial number. If they do not match with the stored information, the device knows that it is not in the network where it was originally configured. It shall than stop initialization and sends a node-ID claiming procedure request. The CANopen manager than may start the node-ID claiming procedure by transmitting the node-ID claiming synchronization message.

CONCLUSION

The CANopen application profile for special-purpose passenger cars supports easy integration of standardized devices such as digital radio, blue lights, taximeter, etc. The standardized gateway to the in-vehicle networks forwards the diagnostic information in ISO format allowing the use of common tools to maintain the add-on devices. Nevertheless the proprietary devices not specified in the CANopen application profile can be integrated in the open network. The specification of the application profile is still in progress and will be released by end of this year.

REFERENCES

[1] CiA 301: CANopen application layer and communication profile (version 4.1), 2006, to be downloadable (www.can-cia.org)

[2] CiA 302 series: CANopen additional application layer functions, CiA internal publication

[3] CiA 447: CANopen application profile for car add-on devices, CiA internal publication

[4] Olaf Pfeiffer, etc, CAN and CANopen embedded networking, 2004

CONTACT

CAN in Automation (CiA)
international users and manufacturers group
Am Weichselgarten 26
D-91056 Erlangen (Germany)
Phone +49-9131-69086-0
Fax +49-9131-69086-79
headquarters@can-cia.org
www.can-cia.org

ACRONYMS

CAN (controller area network)
CAN-ID (CAN identifier)
DTC (diagnostic trouble code)
IVN (in-vehicle network)
PDO (process data object)
SDO (service data object)
NMT (network management)

2006-01-1493

Decentralized Secure Protocol for Inter-Vehicle Communication Networks

Nader Mazen Rabadi and Syed Masud Mahmud
Wayne State University

ABSTRACT

In this paper, we propose a secure protocol for inter-vehicle communication (IVC) networks without the use of centralized roadside infrastructure. Future vehicles may use wireless IVC networks to exchange safety-critical information among each other. IVC networks do not have a centralized control, and instead rely on vehicles to coordinate with each other to exchange information. Because of the open medium, security is a concern in IVC networks. Vehicles need a mechanism to authenticate the safety-critical information that will be exchanged in IVC networks. A trusted third party Certificate Authority (CA) can provide such a mechanism through public-key certificates. However, the disadvantage of using public-key certificates is that drivers can identify each other. The certificate will allow drivers to trace each other's movements and will raise a privacy concern. In this paper, we propose to use RSA public key algorithm and Digital Signature Algorithm (DSA) to solve the security and privacy concerns in IVC networks. The paper presents a detailed description of our protocol, and shows its performance analysis in terms of processing times.

INTRODUCTION

The development and deployment of intelligent transportation system (ITS) technologies will reduce the risk of traffic accidents, improve safety, and solve traffic problems [1][2]. ITS technologies will allow vehicles to exchange safety-critical information among each other via wireless inter-vehicle communication (IVC) networks. IVC networks will provide drivers with warnings and updated information on vehicles' conditions on the road, such as, velocity, acceleration, position, and heading. IVC networks have no roadside infrastructure and instead, vehicles coordinate with each other to exchange safety-critical information securely and without any corruption of its contents.

In order for vehicles to receive safety-critical information from other vehicles, a level of trust among vehicles is necessary for the operation of IVC networks. Therefore, vehicles may only receive safety-critical information from other vehicles that are participants in IVC networks. Participation can be a formal process that is controlled by authorities. Vehicles have to authenticate each other and verify that they are participants in IVC networks before exchanging safety-critical information. Besides vehicle authentication, IVC networks must provide mechanisms to guarantee that the contents of safety-critical information are authentic, unalterable, and not outdated. If the mechanisms are not provided, then the contents of safety-critical information can be forged, which may cause accidents and damages.

The challenges of vehicle and data authentication can be solved using cryptographic public-key algorithms, digital signatures, and public key infrastructure (PKI). Public-key algorithms provide users with two numbers, or keys, to exchange secure messages with other users. If one key is used for encryption, the other one can only be used for decryption, and vice versa. One of the keys is public and can be given to other users. The other key must be kept private and must not be revealed. Digital signature verifies the authenticity of a message. Digital signature uses hash functions in signing a message. Hash functions generate small fixed-sized message digest from the original one. Two messages cannot have the same digest when applying a hash function. After applying a hash function, the message digest is encrypted with the private key of the user. The encrypted digest is the signature of the owner of the message. Both, the encrypted digest and the original message are sent out to other users. To verify the signature, use the public key of the user who signed the message to recover the message digest. In addition, apply the same hash function to the original message to generate a message digest. If the two digest are equal, then the message is authentic.

PKI provides a level of trust between users of public keys. PKI is run by a trusted third party, the certificate authority (CA). The CA issues the public/private keys to users in a form of a certificate. The certificate contains information about the identity of the holder, the public key of the holder, the validity period, the certificate issuer name, and the encryption method used by the CA. The CA certifies the public key of the holder of the certificate by signing the certificate using digital signature techniques. X.509 [3] is an international standard that specifies the contents of a valid certificate.

The disadvantage of applying PKI to IVC networks is the privacy concern among drivers. When vehicles authenticate each other, they first have to exchange their certificates. Then, vehicles will obtain the public key of other vehicles from their certificates and use it to authenticate and exchange messages in a secure channel. Since a public key is a constant value and associates itself to its owner, then drivers will be able to trace each other's movements. Therefore, drivers will raise the privacy concern.

Several researchers have proposed solutions to protect the privacy of users of wireless networks [4]-[8]. The main idea is to change the value of the public key frequently. Hence, users of wireless networks will not be able to identify and trace each other's movements. This can be accomplished by establishing a secure wireless link with a roadside CA infrastructure. The CA will first authenticate the user that requests a change to its public key. If the CA cannot authenticate that user because a different CA issued the certificate, then CAs will communicate with each other to verify the authenticity of the user. Once the CA authenticate the user, then the CA will issue a new certificate with a new public key, and then transmit back to the user using the established secure wireless link.

In this paper, we propose a secure protocol for IVC networks without the use of roadside infrastructure. The protocol is based on the public-key RSA algorithm and the Digital Signature Algorithm (DSA). Our protocol solves the challenges of vehicle and data authentication while protecting the privacy of drivers.

BACKGROUND

In this section, we describe how RSA and DSA algorithms work. These two algorithms are the basis of our secure protocol in this paper.

RSA algorithm: It is a public key algorithm that provides a pair of keys: a public key and a private key. If one of the keys is used for encryption, the other can only be used for decryption, and vice versa. RSA is named after three inventors: R. Rivest, A. Shamir, and L. Adleman. To generate the two keys in RSA, choose two random large prime numbers p and q, and compute the product $n = p.q$. Then choose one of the keys, e, such that e and $(p-1)(q-1)$ are relatively prime. To compute the other key, d, use the extended Euclidean algorithm and find d:

$$d \equiv e^{-1} \bmod((p-1)(q-1)) \tag{1}$$

($a \equiv b \bmod n$ means that the integers (a,b) are congruent modulo *n* and their difference is divisible by *n*. In other words, The integers (a,b) have the same remainder when divided by *n*.)

The public keys are e and n, while the private key is d. The two primes p and q are no longer needed and must not be revealed. RSA gets its security from the difficulty of factoring the number n. If an attacker has one of the keys, e, and the number n, then to find the other key, d, the attacker has to factor the number n, which is difficult if n is very large (1024 bits). In this paper, we use RSA as a component for encrypting messages, decrypting messages, and generating the keys e and d.

DSA: It is an algorithm used only for digitally signing messages, and is not intended for encryption. The National Institute of Standards and Technology (NIST) proposed it for use in their Digital Signature Standard (DSS). The algorithm uses the following parameters:

- p a prime number of 1024-bit long.
- q a 160-bit prime factor of $p-1$.
- x a number less than q.
- $H(m)$ a one way hash function of message m.
- h a number less than $p-1$ such that $h^{(p-1)/q} \bmod p$ is greater than 1.

Then,

$$g \equiv h^{(p-1)/q} \bmod p \tag{2}$$

$$y \equiv g^{x} \bmod p \tag{3}$$

The public keys are p, q, g, and y. The private key is x. To sign a message, m, a user generates a random number k less than q. Then the user computes:

$$r \equiv (g^{k} \bmod p) \bmod q \tag{4}$$

$$s \equiv (k^{-1} \cdot (H(m) + x \cdot r)) \bmod q \tag{5}$$

The signature is (r,s). To verify the signature, compute the following:

$$w \equiv s^{-1} \bmod q \tag{6}$$

$$u_1 \equiv (H(m) \cdot w) \bmod q \tag{7}$$

$$u_2 \equiv (r \cdot w) \bmod q \tag{8}$$

$$v \equiv ((g^{u_1} \cdot g^{u_2}) \bmod p) \bmod q \tag{9}$$

If $v = r$, then the signature is verified. In this paper, we use DSA as a component for signing messages, verifying signatures, and generating the public keys g and y, as shown in Figure 1.

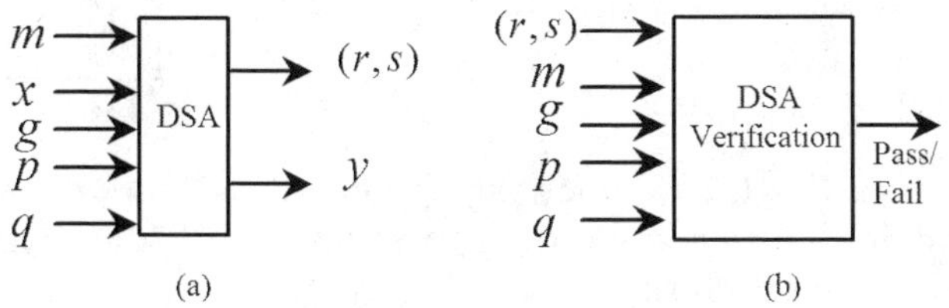

Figure 1. Components of (a) DSA algorithm (b) DSA verification algorithm.

DESCRIPTION OF OUR PROPOSED SECURE PROTOCOL WITH PRIVACY PROTECTION

In this section, we propose a secure protocol for use in IVC networks. We first describe how to use RSA and DSA algorithms to protect the privacy of drivers. Then we present in details our secure protocol that solves the challenges of vehicle and data authentication while protecting the privacy of drivers.

We use the following notations:

$V^i_{G_n}$	Vehicle $i \in group\ of\ vehicles\ G_n$
Pu_A	Public key of a group (Group A) of entities issued by a CA
Pv_A	Private key of a group (Group A) of entities issued by a CA
X_B	Private key of entity B issued by a CA
Cu_B	Public key of entity B issued by B
Cv_B	Private key of entity B issued by B
$Cert_A$	Certificate of a group (Group A) of entities issued by a CA
$Enc_k(M)$	Encryption of message *M* using key *k*
$Dec_k(M)$	Decryption of message *M* using key *k*

To protect the privacy of drivers, we propose to arrange vehicles into several groups. Vehicles in a group will share one pair of public/private keys, and hence will share one certificate. Each group has a pair of public/private keys that is different from other groups. When a driver applies for a certificate, the CA will determine the group that this driver belongs to and provide an associated pair of public/private keys to the driver. The public key will be included in the group certificate. By arranging vehicles in groups, it is difficult to trace an individual vehicle in a group using the group public key. Hence, the privacy of drivers can be protected. To generate a pair of group public/private keys, (Pu_{G_n}, Pv_{G_n}), the CA uses RSA algorithm and associates this pair to a group of vehicles, as shown in Figure 2.

However, malicious drivers can take advantage of this anonymity, use this pair of keys, and transmit inaccurate safety-critical information. Since it is difficult to trace an individual vehicle in a group, it is also difficult to trace malicious drivers. Therefore, to protect IVC networks from such malicious drivers, we propose that the CA generates a private key $X_{V^i_{G_n}}$ for each vehicle, as shown in Figure 2. The CA installs this private key inside a tamper-proof hardware in the vehicle. This private key must be kept secret and never be revealed to other vehicles. As a result, each vehicle will have a pair of group public/private keys and one private key. In addition, the CA maintains a database that relates the pair of group keys (Pu_{G_n}, Pv_{G_n}) and the private keys $X_{V^i_{G_n}}$ for each vehicle in a group. Therefore, by maintaining this database, the authorities can identify malicious drivers. The process of identifying malicious drivers by the authorities is described in the next section.

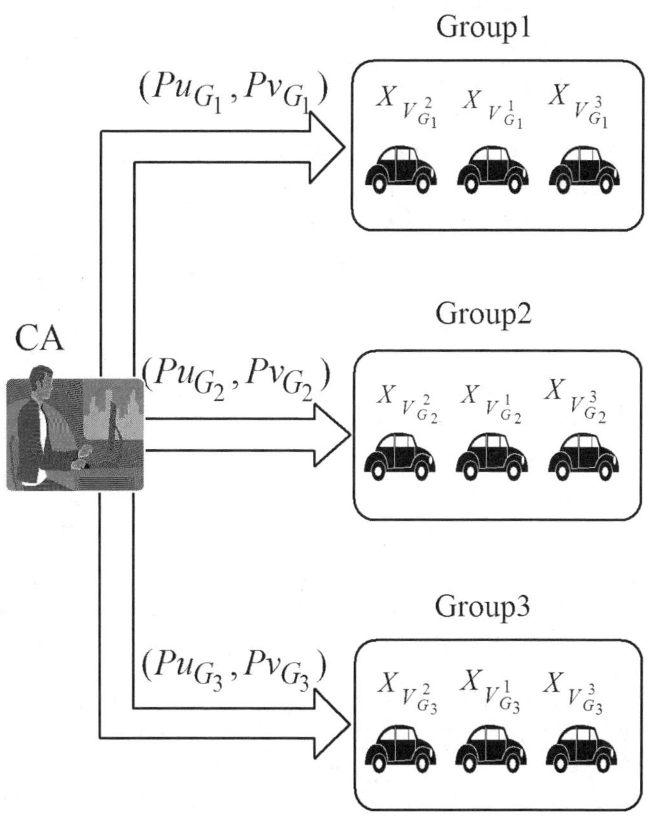

Figure 2. Distribution of group public keys and private keys by CA.

After obtaining the keys from the CA, a vehicle can now use DSA algorithm to generate its own public keys $(y_{V^i_{G_n}}, g_{V^i_{G_n}})$, according to equations (2) and (3), as shown below

$$y_{V^i_{G_n}} \equiv \left(g_{V^i_{G_n}} \right)^{X_{V^i_{G_n}}} \bmod Pu_{G_n} \qquad (10)$$

The public keys of vehicle $V^i_{G_n}$ are $(y_{V^i_{G_n}}, g_{V^i_{G_n}}, Pu_{G_n})$ and the private key of vehicle $V^i_{G_n}$ is $X_{V^i_{G_n}}$. Equation (10) allows vehicles to change their public keys $(y_{V^i_{G_n}}, g_{V^i_{G_n}})$ frequently while maintaining their group public Pu_{G_n} constant. Therefore, it is not necessary to acquire a new certificate with new keys from the CA. Hence, a centralized roadside infrastructure of CA is not required for our proposed protocol.

IDENTIFYING DRIVERS

The advantage of using DSA algorithm is that the private key of a vehicle and the group public key of the vehicle are included in the signature process, according to equation (10). The authorities, using DSA algorithm, may identify those vehicles that transmit inaccurate safety-critical information. We assume that the public keys $(y_{V^i_{G_n}}, g_{V^i_{G_n}}, Pu_{G_n})$ of a vehicle are transmitted with the safety-critical information. As shown in Figure 3-a, a message m contains the certificate of the transmitter, a pubic key g generated by equation (2), a public key y generated by equation (3), and a public key q. The transmitter must first sign the message m using DSA, and then include the signature (r,s) and m in the transmitted message. When a vehicle receives a message, we assume that the public keys of the transmitter will be stored in a tamper-proof hardware inside the receiving vehicle. In addition, we assume that the message m and its signature are also stored in the tamper-proof hardware. Therefore, by obtaining Pu_{G_n} from the certificate, the authorities can get, from the CA's database, the set of private keys $X_{V^i_{G_n}}$ that are associated with this group public key. As shown in Figure 3-b, the authorities apply DSA to m in order to identify a vehicle. The private key $X_{V^i_{G_n}}$ that gives the same signature stored in the tamper-proof hardware reveals the identity of the driver who transmitted inaccurate information.

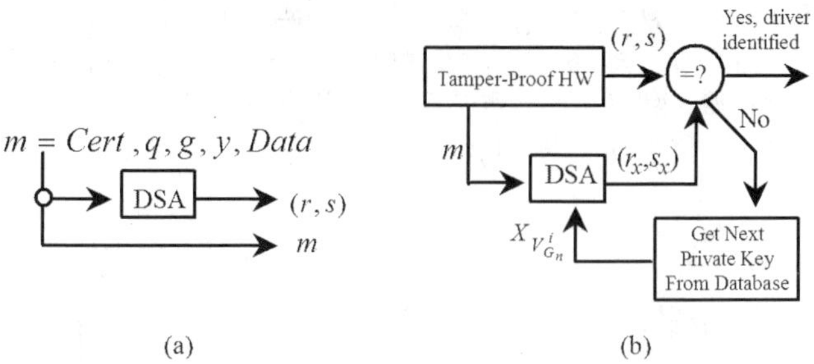

Figure 3. (a) A message and its signature are included in the transmission (b) Identifying malicious drivers.

SECURE COMMUNICATION PROTOCOL

Assume vehicle $V^1_{G_1}$ has a request to join IVC networks to transmit and receive safety-critical information. Also, assume there is vehicle $V^2_{G_2}$, which has already established a secure IVC network with other vehicles, responds to $V^1_{G_1}$ request. Figures 4 and 5 show the secure communication protocol with privacy protection.

Step 1: As shown in Figure 4, Vehicle $V^1_{G_1}$ uses RSA algorithm to generate its own public/private keys $(Cu_{V^1_{G_1}}, Cv_{V^1_{G_1}})$. These keys will be used in the handshake protocol to guarantee that messages received by Vehicle $V^1_{G_1}$ in the protocol can only be read by Vehicle $V^1_{G_1}$. If the group keys (Pu_{G_1}, Pv_{G_1}) are the only keys used in the protocol, then any vehicle that belongs to this group can interfere with the handshake protocol and read the messages.

Vehicle $V^1_{G_1}$ generates a message m_1 that contains the certificate $Cert_{G_1}$, the public keys $(Cu_{V^1_{G_1}}, g_{V^1_{G_1}}, y_{V^1_{G_1}}, q_{V^1_{G_1}})$, a random number a_1, and a request-to-join (REQ) field. The reason to include this random number is to ensure that the response from Step 2 is recent and not outdated. Vehicle $V^1_{G_1}$ expects from Vehicle $V^2_{G_2}$ to return this random number in Step 2. This random number has a predefined lifetime. If its lifetime expires before Step 2, then this random number is considered invalid and will not be recognized.

Then, Vehicle $V^1_{G_1}$ performs the following steps:

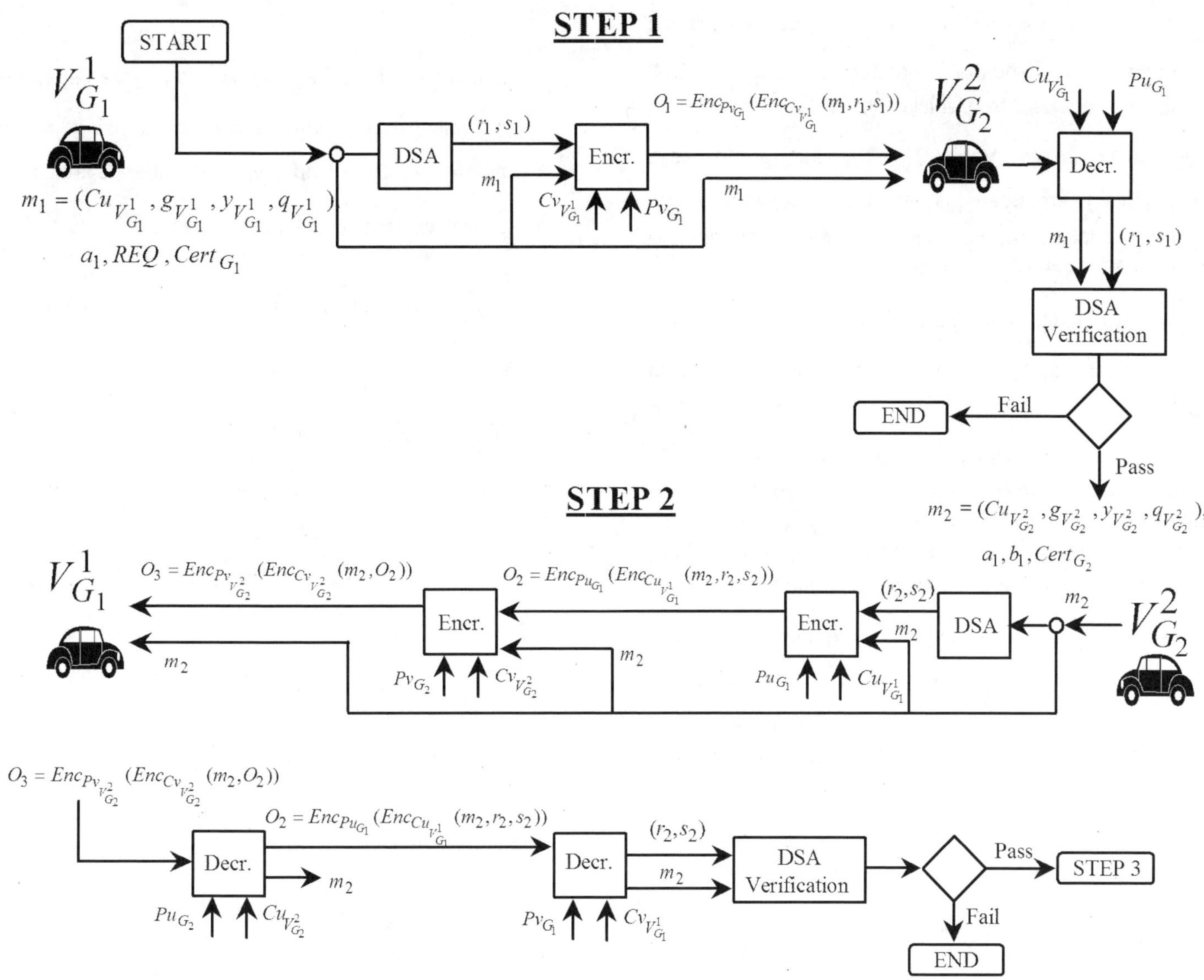

Figure 4. Security protocol with privacy protection: steps 1 and 2.

- Vehicle $V_{G_1}^1$ signs the message m_1 using DSA to generate the signature (r_1, s_1).

- Then, Vehicle $V_{G_1}^1$ encrypts m_1 and (r_1, s_1) using its private keys $Cv_{V_{G_1}^1}$ and Pv_{G_1}. The outcome of this encryption is

$$O_1 = Enc_{Pv_{G_1}}(Enc_{Cv_{V_{G_1}^1}}(m_1, r_1, s_1)) \tag{11}$$

Since only Vehicle $V_{G_1}^1$ knows its private keys, the fact that m_1 and (r_1, s_1) can be recovered using $V_{G_1}^1$'s public keys, $Cu_{V_{G_1}^1}$ and Pu_{G_1}, is an evidence that only $V_{G_1}^1$ has generated message O_1.

- Finally, Vehicle $V_{G_1}^1$ sends m_1 and O_1 to Vehicle $V_{G_2}^2$.

Vehicle $V_{G_2}^2$ receives m_1 and O_1 from Vehicle $V_{G_1}^1$ and decrypts O_1 using Vehicle $V_{G_1}^1$ public keys, $Cu_{V_{G_1}^1}$ and Pu_{G_1}. The outcome is the message m_1 and its signature (r_1, s_1). Vehicle $V_{G_2}^2$ verifies the signature using DSA verification algorithm. If the message is not authentic, then Vehicle $V_{G_2}^2$ will ignore the request from Vehicle

$V_{G_1}^1$. Otherwise, Vehicle $V_{G_2}^2$ uses RSA algorithm to generate its own keys $(Cu_{V_{G_2}^2}, Cv_{V_{G_2}^2})$. These keys will be used in the handshake protocol to guarantee that messages received by Vehicle $V_{G_2}^2$ in the protocol can only be read by Vehicle $V_{G_2}^2$. If the group keys (Pu_{G_2}, Pv_{G_2}) are used instead, then any vehicle that belongs to this group can interfere with the handshake protocol and read the messages.

Step 2: As shown in Figure 4, Vehicle $V_{G_2}^2$ generates a message m_2 that contains the certificate $Cert_{G_2}$, the public keys $(Cu_{V_{G_2}^2}, g_{V_{G_2}^2}, y_{V_{G_2}^2}, q_{V_{G_2}^2})$, the random number a_1, and a random number b_1. The reason to include b_1 is that the message in Step 1 may be recorded and replayed later by an eavesdropper for an attempt to gain access to the secure channel. Therefore, to verify that Vehicle $V_{G_1}^1$ is the one that initiated the request in Step 1, Vehicle $V_{G_2}^2$ generates the random number b_1. Vehicle $V_{G_2}^2$ expects form $V_{G_1}^1$ to return this random number in Step 3. This random number has a predefined lifetime. If its lifetime expires before Step 3, then this random number is considered invalid and will not be recognized.

Then, Vehicle $V_{G_2}^2$ performs the following steps:

- Vehicle $V_{G_2}^2$ signs the message m_2 using DSA to generate the signature (r_2, s_2).

- Then, Vehicle $V_{G_2}^2$ encrypts the message m_2 and the signature (r_2, s_2) with the public keys $Cu_{V_{G_1}^1}$ and Pu_{G_1} of Vehicle $V_{G_1}^1$. The outcome of this encryption is

$$O_2 = Enc_{Pu_{G_1}}(Enc_{Cu_{V_{G_1}^1}}(m_2, r_2, s_2)) \quad (12)$$

  The reason for this encryption is to guarantee that only Vehicle $V_{G_1}^1$ that belongs to Group G_1 will read it.

- Then, Vehicle $V_{G_2}^2$ encrypts message m_2 and O_2 using Vehicle $V_{G_2}^2$'s private keys $Cv_{V_{G_2}^2}$ and Pv_{G_2}. The outcome of this encryption is

$$O_3 = Enc_{Pv_{G_2}}(Enc_{Cv_{V_{G_2}^2}}(m_2, O_2)) \quad (13)$$

  Since only Vehicle $V_{G_2}^2$ knows its private keys, the fact that (m_2, O_2) can be recovered using $V_{G_2}^2$'s public keys, $Cu_{V_{G_2}^2}$ and Pu_{G_2}, is evidence that only $V_{G_2}^2$ has generated the message O_3.

- Finally, Vehicle $V_{G_2}^2$ sends m_2 and O_3 to Vehicle $V_{G_1}^1$.

Vehicle $V_{G_1}^1$ receives m_2 and O_3 from Vehicle $V_{G_2}^2$ and decrypts it using Vehicle $V_{G_2}^2$'s group public keys $Cu_{V_{G_2}^2}$ and Pu_{G_2}. The output of this decryption is (m_2, O_2). Then Vehicle $V_{G_1}^1$ decrypts the output using its own private keys $Cv_{V_{G_1}^1}$ and Pv_{G_1}. The output of the decryption process is the message m_2, and its signature (r_2, s_2). Since Vehicle $V_{G_1}^1$ receives its random number a_1 back, then the message O_3 is recent and not outdated. If the message is received after the lifetime of the random number has expired, then the response is outdated and may be due to a replay attack.

Vehicle $V_{G_1}^1$ will verify the signature using DSA verification algorithm. If the verification fails, then Vehicle $V_{G_1}^1$ will initiate a new request to join the IVC networks.

Step 3: As shown in Figure 5, If the authentication of Vehicle $V_{G_2}^2$ passes, then Vehicle $V_{G_1}^1$ generates a message m_3 that contains a random number a_2, and the random number b_1. The message in Step 2 may be recorded and replayed at a later time by an eavesdropper for an attempt to gain access to the secure channel. To verify that Vehicle $V_{G_2}^2$ is the one that sent m_2 and O_3 in Step 2, Vehicle $V_{G_1}^1$ generates the random number a_2. Vehicle $V_{G_1}^1$ expects form $V_{G_2}^2$ to return this random number in Step 4. This random number has a predefined lifetime. If its lifetime expires before Step 4, then this random number is considered invalid and will not be recognized.

Then, Vehicle $V_{G_1}^1$ performs the following steps:

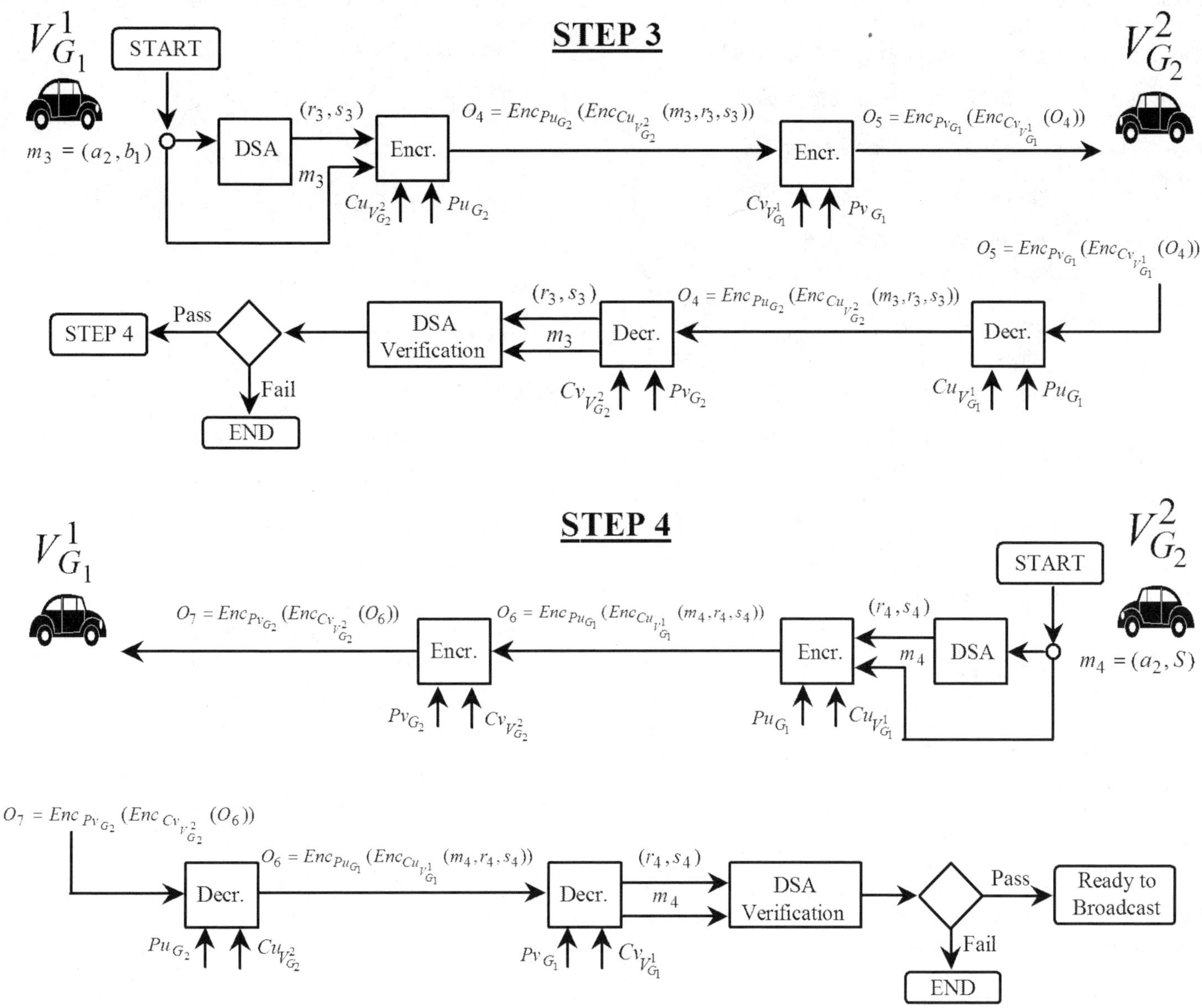

Figure 5. Security protocol with privacy protection: steps 3 and 4.

- Vehicle $V_{G_1}^1$ signs the message m_3 using DSA to generate the signature (r_3, s_3).

- Then, Vehicle $V_{G_1}^1$ encrypts the message m_3 and the signature (r_3, s_3) using the public keys $Cu_{V_{G_2}^2}$ and Pu_{G_2} of Vehicle $V_{G_2}^2$. The outcome of this encryption is

$$O_4 = Enc_{Pu_{G_2}}(Enc_{Cu_{V_{G_2}^2}}(m_3, r_3, s_3)) \tag{14}$$

The reason for this encryption is to guarantee that only Vehicle $V_{G_2}^2$ will read it.

- Then, Vehicle $V_{G_1}^1$ encrypts O_4 using Vehicle $V_{G_1}^1$'s private keys $Cv_{V_{G_1}^1}$ and Pv_{G_1}. The outcome of this encryption is

$$O_5 = Enc_{Pv_{G_1}}(Enc_{Cv_{V_{G_1}^1}}(O_4)) \tag{15}$$

- Finally, Vehicle $V_{G_1}^1$ sends O_5 to Vehicle $V_{G_2}^2$.

Vehicle $V_{G_2}^2$ receives O_5 from Vehicle $V_{G_1}^1$ and decrypts it using Vehicle $V_{G_1}^1$'s group public key $Cu_{V_{G_1}^1}$ and Pu_{G_1}. The output of this decryption is (O_4). Then Vehicle $V_{G_2}^2$ decrypts the output using its own private keys $Cv_{V_{G_2}^2}$ and Pv_{G_2}. The output of the decryption process is message m_3 and its signature (r_3, s_3). Since Vehicle $V_{G_2}^2$ receives its random number b_1 back, then the messages exchanged in Steps 1, 2, and 3 are fresh and are not due to a replay attack. If the message is received after the lifetime of the random number b_1 has expired, then the message is not fresh. As a result, the authentication process fails, and Vehicle $V_{G_2}^2$ will ignore any subsequent message from Vehicle $V_{G_1}^1$.

Otherwise, Vehicle $V_{G_2}^2$ will verify the signature using DSA verification algorithm. If the verification fails, then Vehicle $V_{G_2}^2$ will not respond to Vehicle $V_{G_1}^1$.

Step 4: As shown in Figure 5, If the authentication of Vehicle $V_{G_1}^1$ passes, then Vehicle $V_{G_2}^2$ generates a message m_4 that contains the random number a_2, and a symmetric key S. The symmetric key is used after the four authentication steps and when a vehicle is ready to broadcast safety-critical information to other vehicles. This symmetric key serves as part of message authentication during broadcast, as described in next section. Unlike RSA, one symmetric key is used to encrypt and decrypt messages.

Then, Vehicle $V_{G_2}^2$ performs the following steps:

- Vehicle $V_{G_2}^2$ signs the message m_4 using DSA to generate the signature (r_4, s_4).
- Then, Vehicle $V_{G_2}^2$ encrypts the message m_4 and the signature (r_4, s_4) with the public keys $Cu_{V_{G_1}^1}$ and Pu_{G_1} of Vehicle $V_{G_1}^1$. The outcome of this encryption is

$$O_6 = Enc_{Pu_{G_1}}(Enc_{Cu_{V_{G_1}^1}}(m_4, r_4, s_4)) \quad (16)$$

- Then, Vehicle $V_{G_2}^2$ encrypts message O_6 using Vehicle $V_{G_2}^2$'s private keys $Cv_{V_{G_2}^2}$ and Pv_{G_2}. The outcome of this encryption is

$$O_7 = Enc_{Pv_{G_2}}(Enc_{Cv_{V_{G_2}^2}}(O_6)) \quad (17)$$

- Finally, Vehicle $V_{G_2}^2$ sends O_7 to Vehicle $V_{G_1}^1$.

Vehicle $V_{G_1}^1$ receives O_7 from Vehicle $V_{G_2}^2$ and decrypts it using Vehicle $V_{G_2}^2$'s public keys $Cu_{V_{G_2}^2}$ and Pu_{G_2}. The outcome of this decryption is O_6. Then Vehicle $V_{G_1}^1$ decrypts the outcome using its own private keys $Cv_{V_{G_1}^1}$ and Pv_{G_1}. The output of the decryption process is the message m_4 and its signature (r_4, s_4). Since Vehicle $V_{G_1}^1$ receives its random number a_2 back, then the messages exchanged in previous steps are fresh and are not due to a replay attack. If the message is received after the lifetime of the random number a_2 has expired, then the message is not fresh. As a result, the authentication process fails, and Vehicle $V_{G_1}^1$ will initiate a new request to join the IVC network. Otherwise, Vehicle $V_{G_1}^1$ will verify the signature using DSA verification algorithm. If the verification fails, then Vehicle $V_{G_1}^1$ will initiate a new request to join the IVC networks.

Now Vehicle $V_{G_1}^1$ can use the symmetric key S to exchange safety-critical information over the secure IVC network.

BROADCASTING SAFETY-CRITICAL INFORMATION

Figure 6 shows the steps to broadcast message m_5 from vehicle $V_{G_1}^1$ to nearby vehicles using the symmetric key S. We assume that vehicles are equipped with a GPS device to achieve time accuracy and synchronization for message freshness. Vehicle $V_{G_1}^1$ signs the message using DSA and includes the signature (r_5, s_5) with the message. Message m_5 contains the certificate of $V_{G_1}^1$, the public keys $(Cu_{V_{G_1}^1}, g_{V_{G_1}^1}, y_{V_{G_1}^1}, q_{V_{G_1}^1})$, a *TimeStamp*, and the safety-critical information. Then, Vehicle $V_{G_1}^1$ encrypts the message and its digital signature with its private keys

$Cv_{V_{G_1}^1}$ and Pv_{G_1} to generate message m_6. Finally, Vehicle $V_{G_1}^1$ encrypts m_6 and m_5 using the symmetric key S. As shown in Figure 7, the receivers, who have the symmetric key S, decrypt the broadcast message using S to get m_5 and m_6. Then, the receivers decrypt m_6 using Vehicle $V_{G_1}^1$'s public keys $Cu_{V_{G_1}^1}$ and Pu_{G_1} to get the signature (r_5, s_5). Finally, the receivers run the DSA verification algorithm to authenticate message m_5. If the verification passes, then the receivers will accept message m_5 and act upon its contents.

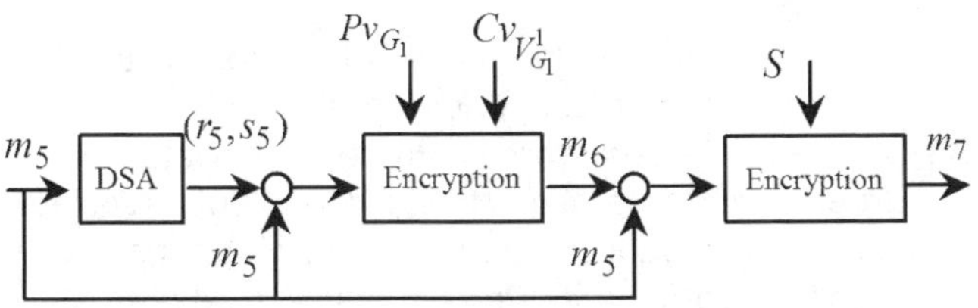

Figure 6. Broadcast safety-critical information using symmetric key.

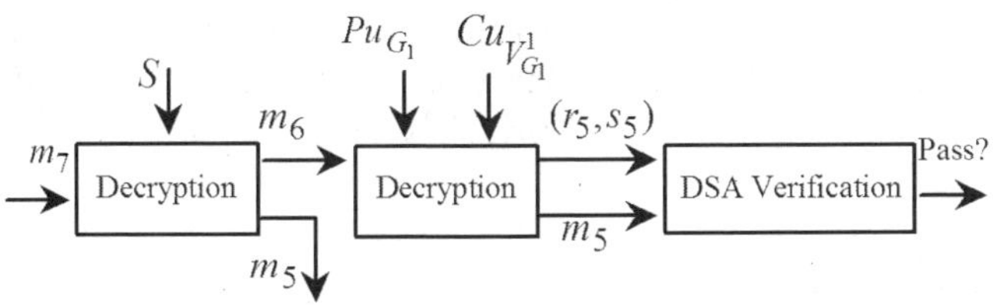

Figure 7. Receiving broadcasted safety-critical information.

IDENTIFYING MALICIOUS DRIVERS WHO BROADCAST INACCURATE INFORMATION

To identify drivers who broadcast inaccurate safety-critical information using the symmetric key S, we assume that the symmetric key and the encrypted broadcasted message are stored in a tamper-proof hardware inside the receivers. As shown in Figure 8, the authorities decrypt the message using the symmetric key S to get the original message m_5 and the encrypted message m_6. From message m_5, the authorities get the group public key Pu_{G_1} and obtain from CA's database the set of private keys that are associated with this public key. Then, the authorities use Pu_{G_1} to decrypt m_6 and to get the signature (r_5, s_5). Finally, the authorities run DSA on message m_5 using every private key. The private key that generates the same signature as (r_5, s_5) identifies the malicious driver.

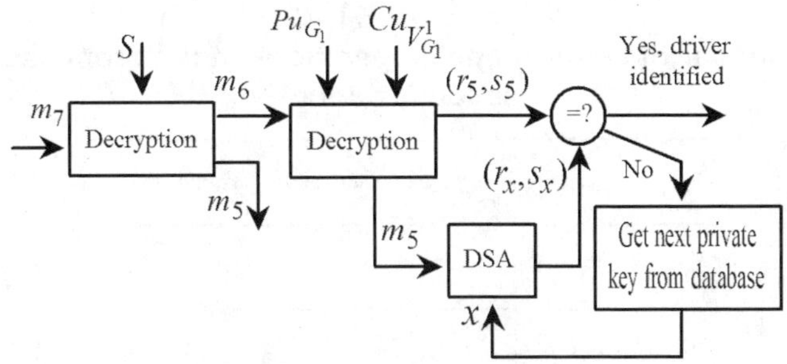

Figure 8. Identifying malicious driver who broadcasted intentional inaccurate information.

PERFORMANCE ANALYSIS

Table I shows the number of RSA, DSA, and symmetric cryptographic operations in our proposed protocol. In general, cryptographic algorithms take a significant amount of time if the algorithms are implemented in software. To speed up the processing time, current advancements in technologies provide hardware cryptographic coprocessors for use in securing financial applications, e-commerce and SSL (Secure Socket Layer) transactions. These cryptographic coprocessors can perform 800 to 4000 RSA operations per second and can perform symmetric key operations at a rate of 5 Mbps to 500 Mbps [9]-[12]. Other coprocessors can perform 1250 DSA signatures per second and 620 DSA signature verifications per second [12]. In our proposed protocol, we will assume that IVC networks will use a cryptographic coprocessor that performs 4000 RSA operations per second, 1250 DSA signatures per second, 620 DSA signature verifications per second, and 10 Mbps symmetric operations. Table II shows the estimated processing time for our proposed protocol.

CONCLUSION

In this paper, we presented a secure protocol for IVC networks. Our secure protocol protects the privacy of drivers during vehicle authentication and broadcast. We proposed to use a combination of RSA and DSA algorithms to achieve privacy protection and vehicle authentication. We proposed to have the vehicles arranged in groups. Each group owns a unique pair of group public/private keys. We also proposed that each vehicle owns its unique private key. The keys are distributed and maintained by a CA. Therefore, it is impossible for drivers to trace each other because vehicles use a shared public key. However, since a unique private key is used in our secure protocol, only the authorities can identify the drivers who transmit inaccurate information via IVC networks. Our proposed authentication protocol is a 4-step handshake protocol. We showed that by using current technologies in hardware cryptographic coprocessors, our protocol could be processed in 13.15 ms. Similarly, the broadcast of secure safety-critical information could be processed in 3.7 ms.

TABLE I
Number of cryptographic operations in the proposed secure protocol

Operation	Authentication	Broadcast
RSA Encryption	7	1
RSA Decryption	7	1
DSA Signature	4	1
DSA Signature Verification	4	1
Symmetric Key Encryption	0	1
Symmetric Key Decryption	0	1

TABLE II
Estimated processing time of the proposed secure protocol

Operation	Authentication (ms)	Broadcast (ms)
RSA Encryption	1.75	0.25
RSA Decryption	1.75	0.25
DSA Signature	3.2	0.8
DSA Signature Verification	6.45	1.6
Symmetric Key Encryption	0	0.4
Symmetric Key Decryption	0	0.4
Total	13.15	3.7

REFERENCES

1. http://www.its.dot.gov/
2. http://www.itsa.org/
3. ITU-T. Recommendation X.509, The Directory-Authentication Framework, 1993. International Telecommunication Union, Geneva, Switzerland.
4. S. Capkun, J.-P. Hubaux and M. Jakobsson, "Secure and privacy-preserving communication in hybrid ad hoc networks," EPFL I&C Technical Reports in Computer and Communication Sciences, 2004.
5. J. Zhu and J. Ma, "A new authentication scheme with anonymity for wireless environments," IEEE Transactions on Consumer Electronics, vol. 50, issue 1, pp. 231 – 235, Feb 2004.
6. N. Asokan, "Anonymity in a mobile computing environment," in Proc.of IEEE Workshop on Mobile Computing Systems and Applications, 8-9 Dec. 1994, pp. 200 – 204.
7. D. Samfat, R. Molva, "A method providing identity privacy to mobile users during authentication," in Proc. of IEEE Workshop on Mobile Computing Systems and Applications. 8-9 Dec. 1994, pp. 196 – 199.
8. B. Askwith, M. Merabti, Q. Shi, and K. Whiteley, "Achieving user privacy in mobile networks," in Proc. of IEEE 13th Annual Computer Security Applications Conference, 8-12 Dec. 1997, pp. 108 – 116.
9. Sun Crypto Accelerator 1000 Specifications, SUN MICROSYSTEMS, Inc., Palo Alto, CA, 2002. Available: http://www.sun.com/products/networking/sslaccel/suncryptoaccel1000/sun_crypto_100_ds.pdf
10. BCM5820 eCommerce Processor Data Sheet, Broadcom Corporation, Irvine, CA, 2002. Available: http://www.broadcom.com/products/Enterprise-Small-Office/Security-Processors/BCM5820
11. IBM 4758 Models 2 and 23 PCI Cryptographic Coprocessor Technical Specifications, IBM Corporation, Somers, NY, 2004. Available: http://www1.ibm.com/servers/eserver/zseries/library/specsheets/pdf/g2219091.pdf
12. SafeXcel-1841 Product Brief, SafeNet Inc., Belcamp, MD, 2005. Available: http://www.safenet-inc.com/Library/3/SafeXcel-1841_ProductBrief.pdf

CONTACT

Nader Mazen Rabadi
Graduate Student
Department of Electrical and Computer Engineering
Wayne State University, Detroit, MI 48202
Email: nrabadi@wayne.edu

Dr. Syed Masud Mahmud
Associate Professor
Department of Electrical and Computer Engineering
Wayne State University, Detroit, MI 48202
Phone: (313) 577-3855
Fax: (313) 577-1101
Email: smahmud@eng.wayne.edu

Many products, no wires

by **Terry Costlow**

The Bluetooth wireless protocol is helping consumers to bring their personal electronics along for the ride.

The explosion of portable digital entertainment technologies and the growing amount of time spent commuting are sparking major changes in automotive infotainment systems. Drivers and passengers want the ability to carry cell phones, MP3 players, and even DVDs into the vehicle, linking them in with a minimum of hassle.

Letting consumers bring these devices into their cars poses myriad challenges for both vendors and carmakers. Cars last a decade, but cell phones and other consumer products have short lifetimes, and there's always the possibility that a new technology could take hold in the same way that iPods and other MP3 players burst onto the scene. Providing connections for all of them is no easy task.

Then there is the nontrivial task of controlling these products while driving. Voice recognition is generally viewed as the best alternative, but it is proving difficult to deploy (see sidebar). Regardless of the challenges, consumers are demanding these links.

"Connectivity will have a dramatic impact on entertainment, providing much more linkage for portable products brought into the car, led by the cell phone and followed by iPods and other portable players," said Torsten Lehmann, Marketing Manager for **Philips Semiconductor**'s Car Entertainment Solutions.

Though many technologies are involved in this type of connectivity, two stand out. One is Bluetooth, a wireless standard that automatically links compatible products together. Its adoption is driven by a combination of consumer demand and government regulations. Bluetooth is especially relevant in states and countries that legislate hands-free calling in vehicles, letting drivers leave their cell phones turned on in their briefcase or purse and still use the phone hands-free.

Another key technology is voice recognition, which gives drivers a safe way to control their products without looking for buttons, dials, or displays. They are often considered to be symbiotic technologies.

"Voice and Bluetooth will be important additions for improving both the driver experience and safety," said Scott Saari, Senior Manager of Infotainment Electronics at **Visteon**.

The two are already being deployed by companies like **Chrysler**, which calls its Bluetooth link UConnect. "UConnect is activated with just one touch of a button," said Vance Peacock, Senior Manager of Vehicle Entertainment and Communications at the Chrysler Group. "The system then utilizes voice recognition technology to allow the customers hands to remain on the steering wheel."

The Bluetooth wireless standard helps connect consumer products to vehicle systems.

Now engineers are moving to provide improved connectivity and better speech recognition. They are also expanding the market. "We've seen a dramatic increase in adoption, it's not just in high-end cars any more," said Stephan Thaler, Director of Marketing for **National Semiconductor**'s Device Connectivity Division.

By 2010, **Frost & Sullivan** expects that 16.6% of cars sold in North America will be Bluetooth-enabled. In 2005, a scant 2.5% featured Bluetooth. Bluetooth's overall acceptance is also soaring, with expectations of nearly tripling from 2005 to 2009, when **In-Stat** says nearly 1 billion Bluetooth devices will ship.

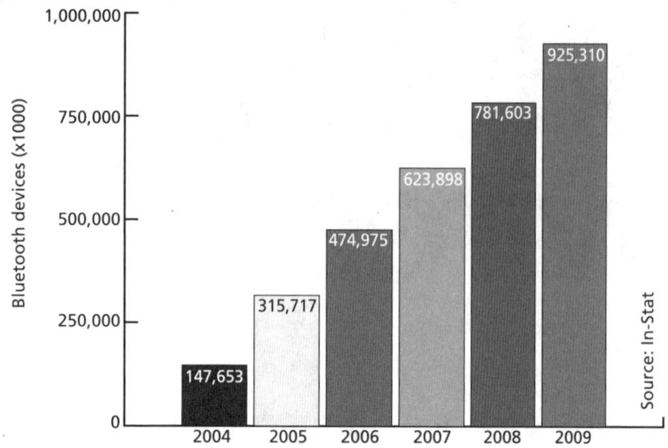

Worldwide shipments of Bluetooth-enabled devices are expected to soar.

Bluetooth works well for voice, but may not be best for music and other data.

Real-time operating systems help manage the many consumer products being connected to vehicle systems.

Bluetooth profiles are making it simpler to assure compatibility.

Beyond phones

Cell phones comprise the majority of Bluetooth applications, but there is a push to link MP3 players and other products to the car's stereo wirelessly. There is some disagreement on whether this will become a major trend, but many contend it will gain popularity.

"The first device is the mobile phone for the driving and talking hands-free experience. Shortly, we expect to see music transferred wirelessly from Bluetooth MP3 players to the car," said Mike Foley, Executive Director, **Bluetooth Special Interest Group** (SIG). "We've also seen some work in the area of connecting PDAs to car navigation systems for address information."

That is already beginning to occur in some high-end vehicles. "We're delivering an iPod interface to **Mercedes**, so you can plug the iPod in and control it through the steering wheel buttons and hear it over the car's speakers," said Bruce Clutton, CEO at **Peiker acustic**.

However, others wonder if wireless technologies are the best solution to this challenge. "Bluetooth is really good for voice, but for data, there are other wireless techniques like Wi-Fi," said Tarun Gupta, Product & Innovation Manager for **Siemens VDO**'s North American Infotainment Systems Division. "But it might be easier and faster to have a USB interface."

Others agree, noting that this PC-based interface is easier to integrate onto CPUs than Bluetooth. "I see more usage of USB than Bluetooth to communicate with portable equipment like MP3 players," Philips' Lehmann said. "From a chip point of view, it's more logical to embed USB on the processor."

He predicts that Bluetooth will remain a separate module, though these Bluetooth chips will go in the same box as the CPU. Others contend that using the USB interface may let consumers eliminate hardware, using memory sticks alone.

"Once you have a DSP chip, you can do things like streaming MP3s directly from a memory stick connected via USB," Thaler said. "You don't need an MP3 player."

Design teams are responding to the uncertainty by teaming up with companies that help them alter products quickly. For example, Peiker teamed up with real-time operating system (RTOS) maker **Green Hills Software**. "The RTOS lets us add features easily and do it with a small footprint," Clutton said.

Though there are questions surrounding the role of Bluetooth for products beyond phones and headsets, many observers predict that the specification will become a common technology for linking consumer products to vehicles.

"We feel confident that Bluetooth audio and video profiles will soon allow consumers to as easily integrate their portable media devices into the car as they can cell phones and PDAs today," said Mark Spain, Director of **Microsoft**'s Automotive Business Unit.

Profiles proliferate

The profiles are key to Bluetooth's success, since they attempt to eliminate problems by defining the aspects of the standard that should be used for headsets, handsets, and other product categories. The Bluetooth SIG has written a number of profiles that are widely used by consumer and automotive companies.

However, there have been some issues with these profiles, which still allow product designers to create incompatibilities. "The biggest barriers have been the profiles," said Brian O'Rourke, Senior Analyst at In-Stat. "They've made communication between devices problematic."

Talk to the car

Voice recognition continues to improve, helping drivers keep their hands on the wheel.

As Bluetooth makes it simpler to bring more consumer products into the vehicle, safely controlling the devices becomes more of an issue. There is fairly widespread agreement that voice recognition will become the human machine interface of choice, but there are plenty of questions about how this will evolve.

Many Bluetooth-enabled cell phones already have voice dialing. But in the noisy environment of a moving vehicle, it may not work well. "If you don't have a hands-free kit, the phone will probably have trouble understanding you because of the background noise," said Tom Houy, a Vice President at **CSR** plc.

Developers are already focusing on techniques for reducing the impact of vehicular noise. "We're working closely with people who provide echo cancellation and noise suppression to tune speech recognition for each car so recognition is as accurate as possible," said Andrew Poliak, Automotive Business Manager at **QNX Software Systems**.

Though ease of use is a key benefit of voice recognition, some observers note that there are other justifications for using it.

"Besides safety, the added benefit of using a speech-driven user interface is it allows automakers worldwide to offer in-car infotainment systems to drivers and passengers at much less cost than they can today because they do not require the use of expensive screens or touch input displays," said Mark Spain, Director of **Microsoft**'s Automotive Business Unit.

The technology will follow conventional market trends. "Voice recognition will be a part of any sophisticated hands-free car kit, and later it will migrate down to mid-level kits," said Stephan Thaler, Director of Marketing for **National Semiconductor**'s Device Connectivity Division.

Once it is in the car, it can be used to personalize the vehicle, setting radio stations and seat positions, for example. "Voice biometrics is a very effective way to determine who's driving the car," said Tom Freeman, Marketing Vice President at **Voice Box Technologies**.

While most companies focus on recognizing a few key commands, Voice Box has developed a system that understands conversational speech. One of the many aspects of responding to a complete sentence is speed. "We can process an utterance in about 1.2 times the speed of speech, which is fast enough to do a whole lot of processing before the person realizes there's any delay," Freeman said.

Terry Costlow

Tying various consumer products to the vehicle's sound system simplifies control.

That creates challenges for developers. "One of the biggest problems is the profiles," said Andrew Poliak, Automotive Business Manager at **QNX Software Systems**. "Not all headset makers do things the same way, so a lot of testing is required."

Another monkey wrench enters the mix when functions such as MP3 playback are added to phones after the profiles are completed. These new products may not be compatible unless software in cars can be upgraded when new profiles are ready. But most observers feel these are temporary issues that will be resolved.

The Bluetooth SIG is attempting to upgrade existing profiles and write more for different applications. An updated version of the hands-free profile, HFP 1.5, will be released next year. "This profile will allow access to the phone book of the phone by the car so that users won't have to record their information in two places [the phone and car]," Foley said.

Even without new profiles, vendors are resolving these issues. Product developers realize that incompatibilities will not help the market, so many are working together to eliminate problems. "It's much better than it was three or four years ago," Clutton said. "GSM (Global System for Mobile communications) phones are pretty consistent, but CDMA (Code Division Multiple Access) tends to be a bit difficult."

The continued improvements have resulted in a successful implementation for at least one carmaker. "Our customer call center has no reports of concerns with the UConnect feature," Peacock said.

Rock in the cradle

Observers note that there are regional differences in the way Bluetooth is being used. U.S. consumers seem to want to leave their phones or iPods in their purse or briefcase, while European drivers prefer to plug phones into the vehicle.

"Most European customers want a cradled phone, but that's not a sought-after commodity in North America. Europeans are very concerned about RF (radio frequency) radiation, so they need to have an external antenna," Clutton said.

"The advantage of a cradle is that it can charge the phone, but adding Bluetooth to this type of wired car has tremendous value," Thaler said. "When another driver brings in a different phone or you buy a new phone that won't fit, you can still connect to the vehicle using Bluetooth." ***aei***

2006-01-1330

Latency Analysis for Inter-Vehicle Communications

Chao Wang, Syed Masud Mahmud and Feng Lin
Wayne State University

ABSTRACT

The study done by the U.S. National Highway Traffic Safety Administration (NHTSA) shows that developing automotive collision warning and avoidance systems will be very effective in order to significantly reduce fatalities, injuries and associated costs. In order to develop an automotive collision warning and avoidance system, it will be necessary that the vehicles should be able to exchange (in real-time) their dynamic information such as speed, acceleration, direction, relative position, status of some devices like brake, steering wheel, gas pedal, etc. The only feasible way to exchange the vehicles' dynamic information will be through the use of wireless communication technology. However, the wireless link setup time and communication latencies should be under certain bounds so that the vehicles can appropriately react on time to avoid collisions. This paper will present results from an experimental setup that simulates inter-vehicle communications.

The experimental setup has been prepared using a number of CAN and Bluetooth modules. The communication system of each vehicle has been simulated using several CAN nodes and a wireless module. In addition, a number of stand-alone Bluetooth modules have been used in the experiment to increase the wireless communication traffic through the air. An event such as pressing the brake pedal or turning on the turn signals has been simulated using buttons. At the occurrence of an event, the simulated vehicle system automatically sends a message through its CAN bus, then it broadcasts the message via its wireless module. Other simulated vehicles receive the message via their wireless modules and then send the message via their CAN buses. Eventually the message triggers some actuators in the destination vehicles. The latencies have been measured from the time an event occurred and until the time some actions have been taken by the actuators of the destination vehicles.

The paper presents results on inter-vehicle communication latencies under various types of traffic conditions. Other researchers and engineers will get valuable information from this paper which will help them in designing wireless communication systems for the future vehicles.

INTRODUCTION

In this paper, we design a system, as shown in Figure 1, to simulate inter-vehicle communication system. Two vehicles, A and B, have CAN-wireless gateway connected to their in-vehicle CAN bus. The gateway on one vehicle converts its in-vehicle CAN message into wireless message and transmits it onto the air. The other vehicle then receives the wireless message and converts it into a CAN message. This way, these two vehicles communicate with each other.

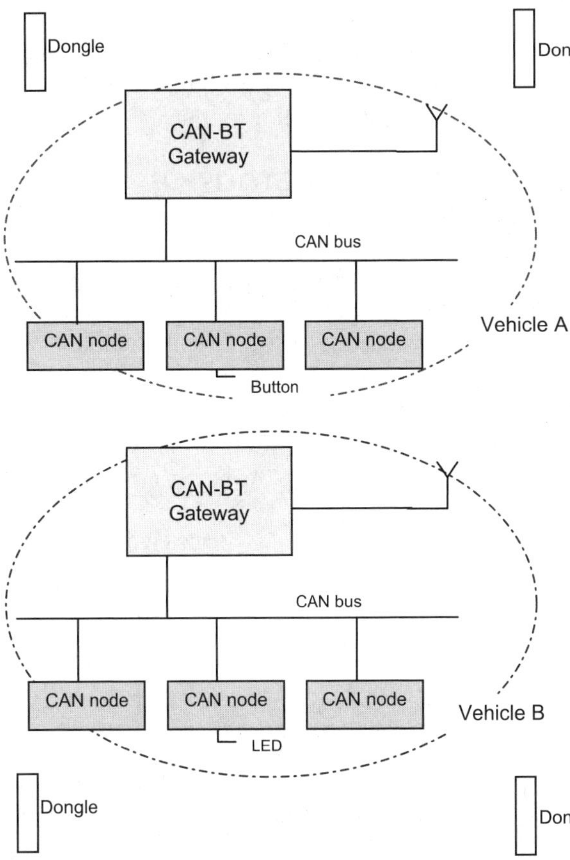

Figure 1. Functional block diagram of the system

We compared different wireless technologies and choose Bluetooth technology to build our inter-vehicle communication system. Our choice of Bluetooth technology was due to its ease of availability and low cost.

We review the current status on inter-vehicle communication research and we present how we build our own CAN-Bluetooth gateway and CAN nodes, in both aspects of hardware and firmware.

We test the latency from a button pressed on vehicle A to LED flashing on vehicle B. We explain the method we use to test the latency. Then we put the latency on different scenarios to discuss the feasibility of our proposal.

BLUETOOTH, WI-FI AND ZIGBEE

At first glance, Bluetooth, Wi-Fi and Zigbee are very similar. Actually they are designed for different purposes. Wi-Fi is made for wired LAN replacement and Zigbee is most suitable for control, monitor and automation, etc. [1]. Furthermore, inter-vehicle network is a typical ad-hoc network. In this sense, though Wi-Fi and Zigbee could be configured to work in ad-hoc fashion, Bluetooth technology offers automatic network configuration, authentication and service discovery without any fixed infrastructure to make the network establishment most convenient.

Meanwhile, the lack of the availability of affordable Wi-Fi module for CAN based systems is another reason for us to use Bluetooth to implement our proposal.

CURRENT STUDY ON BLUETOOTH INTER-VEHICLE COMMNUNICATION

There have been a few studies in Bluetooth inter-vehicle communication area. Sussex University [2] has built an in-vehicle network with Bluetooth. They calculated the time period in which two traveling vehicles can stay in Bluetooth signal range. We will put more focus on latency of message transmission in a CAN-Bluetooth hybrid network.

Although we notice there are some industry level CAN-Bluetooth gateway devices available in the market [3, 4], we decided to build our own CAN-Bluetooth gateway to reduce research cost and gain more control to the details.

CAN-BLUETOOTH HYBRID COMMNICATION SYSTEM

HARDWARE

Figure 2 shows hardware design for one vehicle. We choose Freescale 16-bit microcontroller MC9S12DP256 (thereafter S12) to implement CAN-Bluetooth gateway. We connect S12 to CAN bus through CAN transceiver MCP2551 from Microchip.

We use Bluetooth module EB505 [5] which has SCI port available to connect to S12. EB505 provides transparent transmission for data from SCI to Bluetooth, and in the reverse way, from Bluetooth to SCI when it is configured in data mode.

S12 can control EB505 by sending ASCII commands to its SCI port when EB505 works in command mode. S12 can switch EB505 between data mode and command mode by connecting S12's GPIO to EB505's mode signals.

To emulate CAN nodes in a vehicle, we use Microchip 8-bit microcontroller PIC18F2480 (thereafter PIC) which has on-chip CAN controller. Similarly, we connect PIC to CAN bus through CAN transceiver MPC2551. Meanwhile, we have buttons and LEDs connected to PIC to get input and output.

We have one CAN-Bluetooth gateway and three CAN nodes connected to the CAN bus to emulate each vehicle.

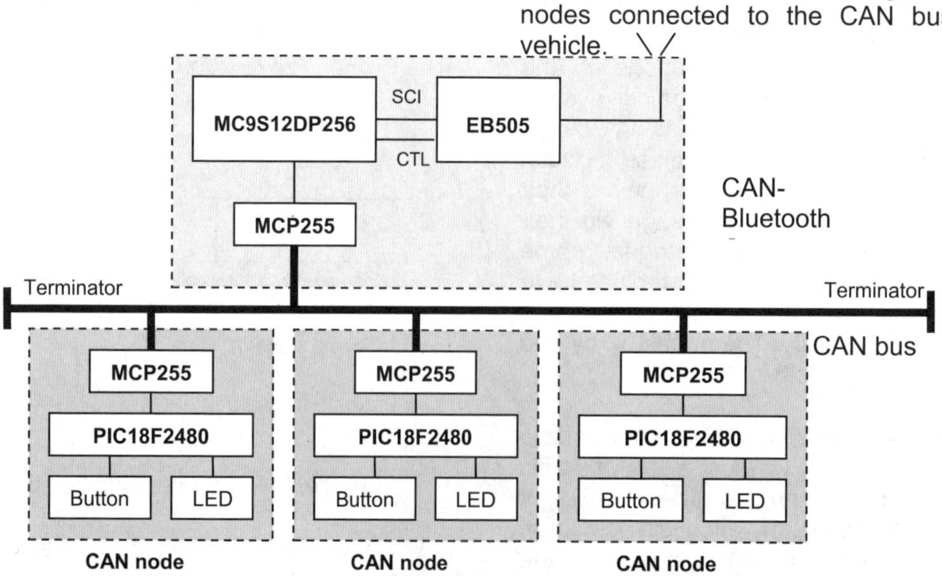

Figure 2. Inter-vehicle Communication System Hardware Design

We design the system with relatively low cost. The Bluetooth module we select costs about $70 for each. The total hardware cost for each emulated vehicle is around $130.

FIRMWARE

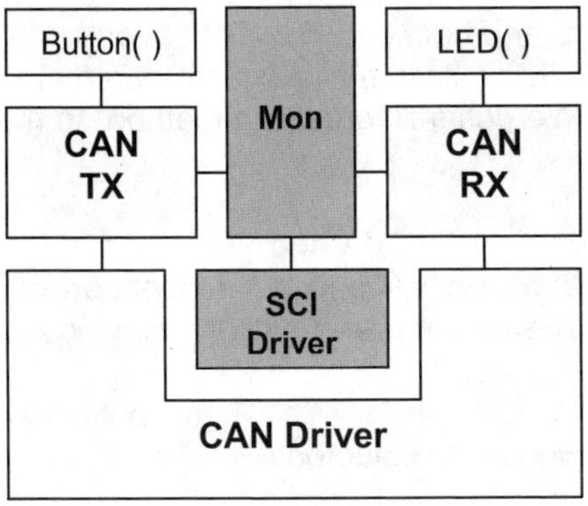

Figure 3. The firmware structure of a CAN node

Figure 3 shows the firmware structure of a CAN node running in a PIC. If the button status gets changed by a user, Module CAN TX sends a CAN message onto the CAN bus through the CAN driver. We design the CAN message format for our system like the one shown in Figure 4. The nodes use CAN message ID 0x200 - 0x2FF for in-vehicle communications. Nodes may leave source Vehicle ID ("source VID" in Figure 4) and/or destination Vehicle ID as 0xFF, while CAN-Bluetooth gateway will take care of these fields at the vehicle communication level.

All inter-vehicle message received by CAN nodes use CAN message ID 0x600 – 0x6FF. CAN RX module gets these messages and outputs to LEDs.

Monitor Module ("Mon" in Figure 3) monitors all inward and outward CAN traffic and put them out onto SCI port. We connect this port to PC's RS232 to monitor those CAN traffic with a RS232 terminal software. Our final test result is also processed and output by Monitor Module.

Figure 5 shows the firmware structure of CAN-Bluetooth gateway running in S12. The CAN RX gets a CAN message from the CAN bus and packages it into SCI message, as shown in Figure 6. First we put three bytes of 0x55 as preamble, then put appropriate source vehicle ID and destination vehicle ID in data bytes while leave other bytes as is. After the CAN RX transfers the SCI message to the SCI TX module, the SCI TX puts the SCI message to S12's SCI port and transmits it through Bluetooth module.

		0	1	2	3	4	5	6	7
XX	XX	XX	XX	XX	XX	XX	XX	XX	XX
msgID H	msgID L	source VID	source node ID	destin VID	destin node ID	data0	data1	data2	data3

Figure 4. CAN message Format

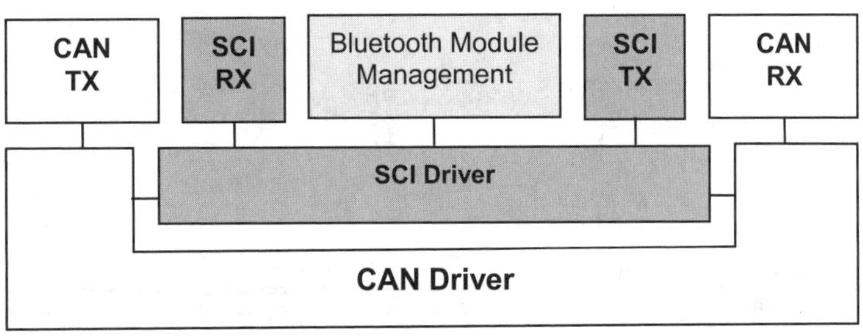

Figure 5. Firmware structure of CAN-Bluetooth Gateway

	0	1	2	3	4	5	6	7
55 55 55	XX	XX	XX	XX	XX	XX	XX	XX
preamble	source VID	source node ID	destin VID	destin node ID	data0	data1	data2	data3

Figure 6. SCI Message Format

Meanwhile, the SCI RX receives the SCI message from EB505, packages it into CAN message. We put appropriate CAN message ID (0x600 – 0x6FF) and transfer it to the CAN TX module. The CAN TX module is responsible for putting the CAN message onto the CAN bus.

We control EB505 Bluetooth module with Bluetooth Module Management Module. We control S12's behavior by sending ASCII commands through the SCI port.

In Bluetooth Module Management Module, we take the security mechanism provided by EB505 Bluetooth module. PIN code (passkey) is needed to establish a trusted relationship before two vehicles can communicate.

All theses modules of both CAN nodes and CAN-Bluetooth gateway are implemented with C and assembly in ISR (interrupt service routine) and task level. Message Flags and data buffers are set in ISR and processed in task level. We use a scheduler mechanism to dispatch tasks.

TEST METHOD

Now if we press button in one vehicle, we get LED flashing in another vehicle. The latency from button pressed to LED flashing is critical parameter for us to measure. We design "round-trip method" to measure the latency.

See the two vehicles, VA and VB shown in Figure 7. We press a button on VA and get response on VB's LED. The message transmission path is shown by red arrow:

VA: button→PIC→CAN bus→S12→EB505→Bluetooth→

VB: Bluetooth→EB505→S12→CAN bus→PIC→LED

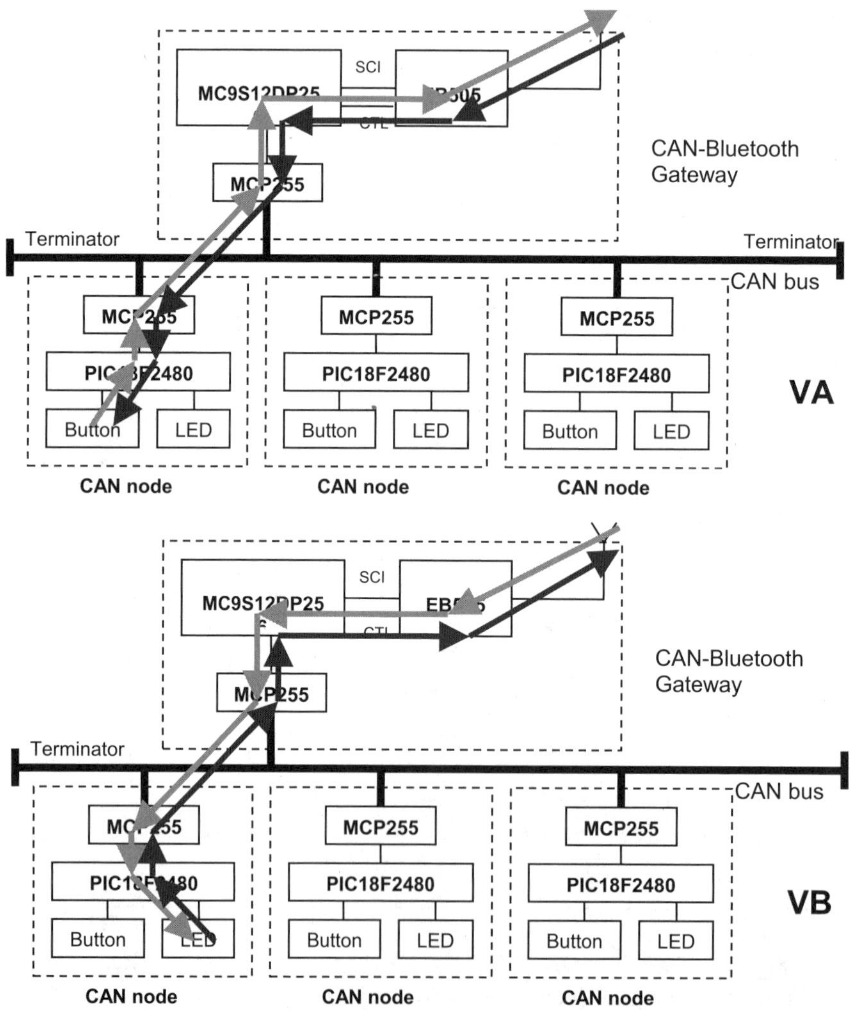

Figure 7. Communication between two vehicles

It is difficult to test latency from button pressed on VA to LED flashing on VB since we do not have common clock for VA and VB. But if VB bounces the message back to VA as shown by blue arrow in Figure 7, VA can test the latency of round-trip transmission (red arrow and blue arrow), then get the one-way latency by dividing the round-trip result by 2. The PIC's Mon Module (in Figure 3) is responsible for tracking the round-trip latency and output it to PC. Then we can process the result on PC with appropriate software.

RESULT AND DISCUSSION

We test the transmission latency on different CAN bus baud rate using the round-trip method we just mentioned. For each baud rate, we test for 4000 times and get the mean value. The results are shown in Table 1.

Then we plug four USB Bluetooth adapters ("dongles") on four computers and turn them on, we configure them send Bluetooth messages to each other periodically to make Bluetooth traffic busy. We did not find significant difference on our test result for latency.

Assuming VA and VB are heading to the same way on highway. VA is traveling at 100 mph and VB is traveling at 50 mph, then the speed difference is 50 mph. Let's take the lowest CAN Baud Rate result, one-way latency is 32.56 ms. In 32.56 ms, the two vehicles become 0.73 meter (2.40 feet) closer. Similar results are shown in Table 2.

Table 1. One-way Latency in different CAN Baud Rate

CAN Baud Rate (kbps)	125	250	500
One-way Latency (ms)	32.56	30.34	29.46

Table 2. Distance change between two vehicles during signal transmission

CAN Baud Rate (kbps)	125	250	500
One-way Latency (ms)	32.56	30.34	29.46
Distance change when speed difference is 25 mph (m)	0.37	0.34	0.33
Distance change when speed difference is 50 mph (m)	0.73	0.68	0.66
Distance change when speed difference is 100 mph (m)	1.46	1.36	1.32

Another factor we may consider is the SCI overhead between S12 and EB505. If we used a microcontroller with on-chip Bluetooth module, the SCI overhead would be spared from the latency. The SCI overhead includes the SCI transmission overhead and code overhead running in S12. We calculate the overhead and deduct it from the result:

Table 3. Distance change between two vehicles during signal transmission after deduction of SCI overhead

CAN Baud Rate (kbps)	125	250	500
One-way Latency (ms)	30.16	27.88	27.00
Distance change when speed difference is 25 mph (m)	0.34	0.31	0.30
Distance change when speed difference is 50 mph (m)	0.68	0.62	0.60
Distance change when speed difference is 100 mph (m)	1.36	1.24	1.20

CONCLUSION

From Table 2 and 3 we can find that this latency is acceptable for vehicles to take appropriate action to avoid collisions.

Furthermore, we notice that Bluetooth needs up to six seconds to discovery device and establish connection. Although some research [6] shows that we can make it faster with certain technology, the whole latency time would become not acceptable if we consider the connection set-up time.

Therefore, if we assume two vehicles have already set up connection, this message transmission latency is acceptable.

We did not test our system when more than two vehicles exist in one piconet due to the fact that the current version of EB505 has limited support on that. We expect that can be done in near future. Also, if we could shorten the Bluetooth connection set-up time further, that would be positive for our proposal.

REFERENCES

1. http://www.zigbee.org/en/resources/documents/2004_04_01_cdc_810_craig_slides.pdf
2. http://www.comms.scitech.susx.ac.uk/research/bluetooth.php
3. www.dcmtech.com/CAN-BT-GATEWAY.pdf

4. www.esd-electronics.com/german/manuals_pdf/ENGLISH/c.2065.21_CAN-bluetooth/Bluetooth_Hardware.pdf
5. http://www.a7eng.com/products/embeddedblue/articles/eb505-AHC-IN.htm
6. Ryan Woodings, Derek Joos, Trevor Clifton, Charles D. Knutson, "Rapid Heterogeneous Connection Establishment: Accelerating Bluetooth Inquiry Using IrDA"., Department of Computer Science, Brigham Young University

CONTACT

Chao Wang
Graduate Student
Department of Electrical and Computer Engineering
Wayne State University, Detroit, MI 48202
Phone: (313) 577-5506
Fax: (313) 577-1101
Email: chaowang99@gmail.com

Syed Masud Mahmud, Ph.D.
Associate Professor
Department of Electrical and Computer Engineering
Wayne State University
Detroit MI 48202
Phone: (313) 577-3855
Fax: (313) 577-1101
Email: smahmud@eng.wayne.edu

Feng Lin, Ph.D.
Professor
Department of Electrical and Computer Engineering
Wayne State University
Detroit MI 48202
Phone: (313) 577-3428
Fax: (313) 577-1101
Email: flin@ece.eng.wayne.edu

2005-01-1484

A Multi-hop Mobile Networking Test-bed for Telematics

Rahul Mangharam, Jacob J. Meyers, Ragunathan Rajkumar and Daniel D. Stancil
Department of Electrical & Computer Engineering
Carnegie Mellon University

Jayendra S. Parikh, Hariharan Krishnan and Christopher Kellum
General Motors Corporation

ABSTRACT

An onboard vehicle-to-vehicle multi-hop wireless networking system has been developed to test the real-world performance of telematics applications. The system targets emergency and safety messaging, traffic updates, audio/video streaming and commercial announcements. The test-bed includes a Differential GPS receiver, an IEEE 802.11a radio card modified to emulate the DSRC standard, a 1xRTT cellular-data connection, an onboard computer and audio-visual equipment. Vehicles exchange data directly or via intermediate vehicles using a multi-hop routing protocol. The focus of the test-bed is to (a) evaluate the feasibility of high-speed inter-vehicular networking, (b) characterize 5.8GHz signal propagation within a dynamic mobile ad hoc environment, and (c) develop routing protocols for highly mobile networks. The test-bed has been deployed across five vehicles and tested over 400 miles on the road.

INTRODUCTION

The commoditization of high-speed wireless interfaces and low-cost Global Positioning System (GPS) devices provides the opportunity to deploy a range of useful and practical inter-vehicular communication applications. A test-bed has been developed primarily to evaluate the feasibility of high-speed networking between vehicles for emergency and safety notification and to support multimedia telematics applications. The focus is to develop and deploy a multi-hop wireless routing platform to facilitate on-road testing. We observe significant divergence in the performance of multi-hop wireless routing protocols between simulation and implementation and therefore stress the importance of on-road testing. In addition, channel measurements and propagation analysis have been carried out to further understand the nature of the communication environment. This paper discusses the platform deployment process and shares our driving experiences. Based on the network performance analysis and insights from the test-bed, a vehicular networking architecture is being developed across multiple networking layers targeted specifically for inter-vehicular communication.

Consider the case when a vehicle accident on a freeway blocks two of the three available lanes. Most freeways rely on other drivers to notify the highway patrol, which in turn updates the freeway management system and messages are eventually broadcast on electronic signs along the highway. While the turnaround duration for accident notification may take considerable time, the traffic buildup is rapid and consequent blocking of emergency vehicles is still an unsolved and pressing problem.

Now consider the response when a subset of the vehicles has onboard inter-vehicular networking capability. From the accident site, alert messages are broadcasted and directed to all approaching vehicles. As the range of each wireless interface extends to less than a few hundred meters, it is essential to employ a multi-hop routing protocol to communicate 2-3 miles down the freeway. By using this mechanism to broadcast the event and its position information, approaching vehicles are notified of the hazard and possible congestion. As the broadcast message ripples through the traffic at high speed, approaching vehicles can use the next exit to plan a detour.

While traffic and alert notification systems such as OnStar [1] have been deployed, they are centrally managed entities. In the above example, we observe that the problem is local and requires action within the vicinity of the accident. Attempting a cellular call (used by OnStar) to each of the hundreds of vehicles in a particular region is not cost effective. Furthermore, the alert notifications are relevant only during the event lifetime and should be targeted specifically to approaching traffic.

In the following section, we discuss the range of vehicular applications and their unique networking challenges. We then describe the multi-hop mobile vehicular test-bed, our design decisions and driving experiences.

MULIT-HOP VEHICULAR NETWORKING

The primary goal of the multi-hop mobile test-bed is to provide insights towards the design of networking infrastructure necessary to support a range of inter-vehicular applications.

APPLICATION CATEGORIES

We focus on four application categories that encompass a broad range of possible services.

<u>Emergency and Safety Messaging</u>
Messages reporting vehicle accidents, sudden breaking, oil spills and other critical events need to be disseminated instantly and for the duration of the event's lifetime. As shown in Fig. 1, such messages are broadcast but within the scope of relevant vehicles approaching the event's position. Emergency messages are pertinent within the relative region of the event. This may be determined by restricting the message to be accepted and forwarded by only those nodes within a geographic region. In addition, navigation information such as vehicle direction and planned route may be leveraged. As the messages are critical, they must be delivered with the highest packet priority.

<u>Traffic and Congestion Updates</u>
These are semi-critical messages with updates on road conditions and congestion information. They may be delivered by fixed infrastructure-based transceivers or via mobile gateway vehicles equipped with both inter-vehicula wireless interfaces and cellular-data connections. Traffic and congestion updates are pertinent in the general scope of a region. A region may be described by a set of GPS coordinates. For example, a circular region may be described the GPS coordinate marking its center and the radius in meters. All vehicles within this region will accept and forward updates. Vehicles outside the designated region will drop any region-specific updates received. Updates will be delivered as broadcast packets.

<u>Multimedia Telematics Applications</u>
Feature-rich and interactive applications such as inter-vehicular voice communication, video streaming, file transfer and collaborative driving applications fall within the scope of telematics applications. Using such applications, users can form or join public and private groups of vehicles. For example, a group of friends driving on a day trip will be continuously informed of the position of their friends' cars and can maintain a voice and chat channel to communicate collectively to the group. Such applications may be scaled to the enterprise level for fleet management or connect all vehicles heading to a particular destination. Telematics applications require a robust network and transport layer where connections are reliable and may be suspended and resumed smoothly based on the connectivity between interested parties. Furthermore, as all vehicles are connected across one or more hops, it is essential that the routes selected satisfy minimum admission control requirements and are self-healing.

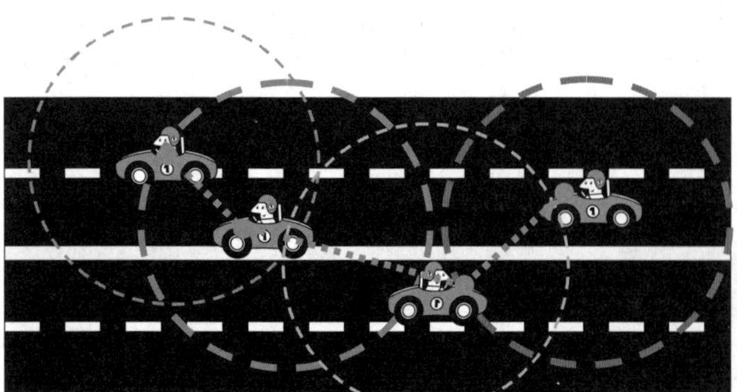

Figure 1. Vehicle-to-vehicle multi-hop networking showing each vehicle's wireless range

<u>Commercial Announcements</u>
Travelers may choose to subscribe to commercial announcements regarding parking lots with empty slots, regional boarding and lodging information and other travel-related advertisements. Such applications require a subscription service and also a lightweight acknowledgement scheme to estimate the size of the targeted population.

In order to analyze the performance of the above application categories, we evaluated an application from each category over our test-bed. The next section describes the test-bed design followed by the unique challenges vehicular networks pose over traditional topology-based ad hoc networks.

TEST-BED DESIGN AND DEPLOYMENT

TEST-BED HARDWARE

The multi-hop wireless vehicular networking test-bed developed at Carnegie Mellon University (Fig. 2) employs a Differential GPS (DGPS) receiver with a magnetically mounted antenna. An onboard computer with a modified mini-PCI IEEE 802.11a wireless [2] interface forms the main entity of the setup. The physical layer has been modified to emulate the Dedicated Short Range Communication (DSRC) [3] standard specifications with a

Figure 2. Portable multi-hop mobile test-bed with DGPS receiver and onboard computer

10MHz signal bandwidth and operates at a variable carrier frequency which includes the 5.85 – 5.925 GHz spectrum.

Vehicles communicate with each other via a magnetic-mounted wireless antenna. The range of the wireless link is approx. 300m for line-of-sight reception. To facilitate multimedia applications, the test-bed includes a voice headset and a camera. All devices are powered by the vehicle's DC power system via the cigarette lighter, utilizing DC-DC power converters as needed. The equipment fits neatly in a plastic molded case and is easy to carry and quick to set up.

TEST-BED SOFTWARE

All onboard computers run RedHat 9 Linux (kernel 2.4.18-3) as this provides a fertile platform for network protocol and application development. We primarily use three layers of software on the test-kit. The software is built from open source libraries and is available for free.

Mapping and Communication Software

In order to visualize the current position of the vehicle, we adapted the RoadMap tool [4] for our test-bed. We added runtime display capability for multiple vehicles so the movement of each vehicle can be tracked as we drive. We added communication capability so that each vehicle's onboard computer acts as a server and accepts connections from other vehicles. Each vehicle runs a User Datagram Protocol (UDP) client thread to connect to all other machines in the test-bed. As the connections are at the socket level, the application manages the end-to-end data exchange between the client and server. The underlying kernel-based networking software handles multi-hop routing along the set of links between the client and server. Using this client-server setup, each vehicle exchanges its GPS information (position, speed, direction, etc.) and its network information (packet sequence number, fragmentation, frame length, etc). We implemented our own packet headers for efficient exchange of position and network information. GPS coordinates are computed five times every second and have an accuracy of ≤ 2m. Consequently packets are exchanged five times every second.

All GPS and network information exchanged between vehicles is logged by each machine. This enables us to playback the route driven and visualize the vehicles on a vector-based rendering of the map traversed. The maps use TIGER/Line 2002 data files available for free from the U.S. Census Bureau [5]. In Figure 3, we observe the playback of a trip with five vehicles (top right) illustrating the vehicles connected, a panel to send emergency messages, a playback control (bottom left) to speedup or

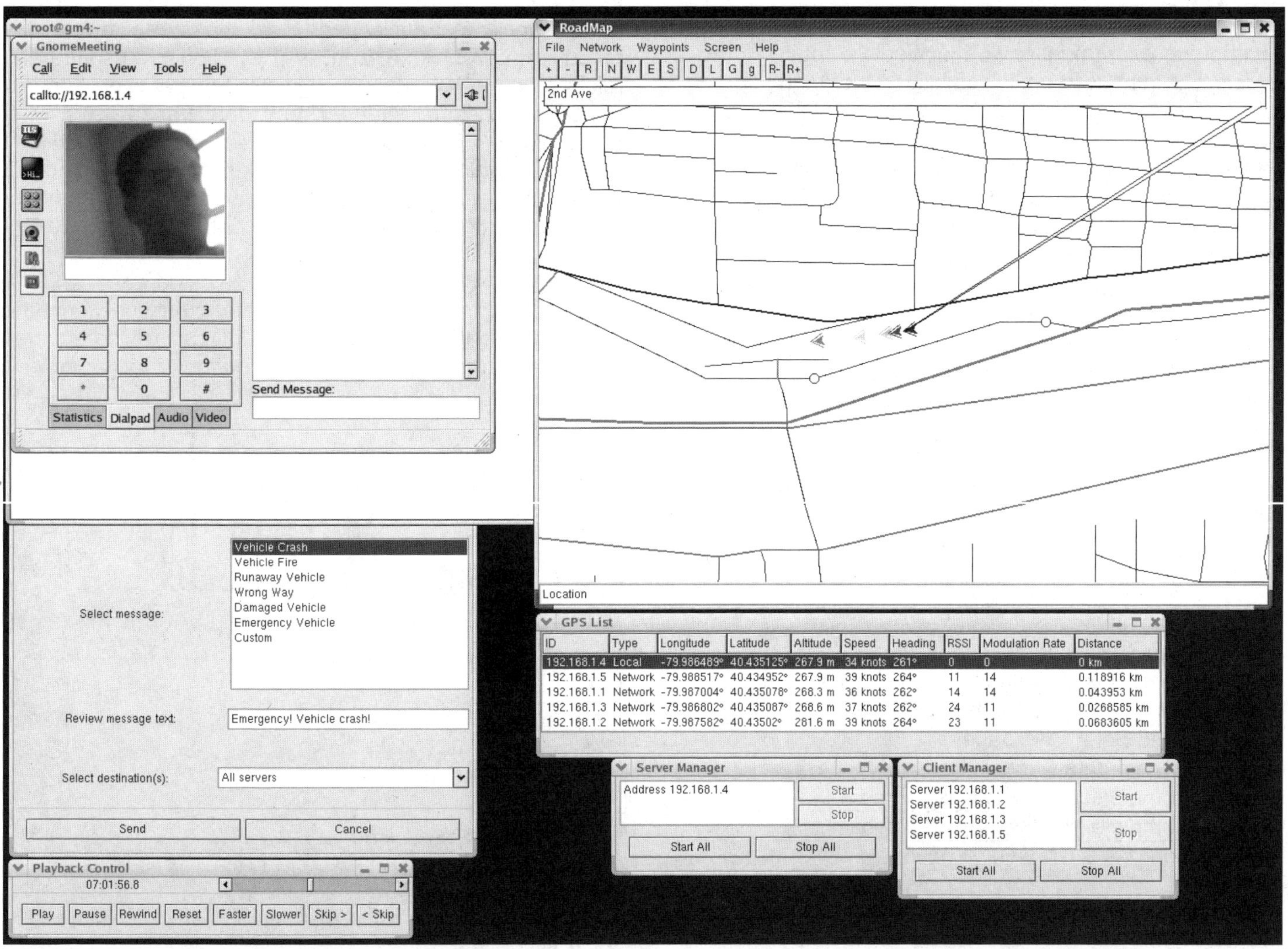

Figure 3. RoadGPS vehicle visualization with GPS tracking, network connectivity and audio/video/messaging communication tool. A playback control is provided for viewing logged trips.

slow down the playback, client and server connections and a multimedia application with voice and video (top left)

Table I lists the current functionality of our mapping and communication application – RoadGPS. All position and networking information within the multi-hop network on the road can also be channeled to the Internet via the 1xRTT cellular connection. This way, our team at the GM Technical Center in Warren, MI can monitor all of the vehicles and the data transmitted between them as they drive in Pittsburgh, PA or anywhere else with cellular network access. The ability to monitor the network in real-time assures that data is correctly being logged and allows real-time network performance and signal propagation analysis.

Multi-hop Networking Software

We tested several existing ad hoc routing protocols such as DSR [6] and AODV [7] kernel implementations. While the protocols provide connectivity across multiple hops, their performance in a highly mobile environment was unreliable. Most ad hoc routing protocols have been tested primarily through simulation or in small test-beds (< 10 nodes) with low mobility. In a highly mobile environment such as inter-vehicular communications where connectivity changes often, these protocols were unable to reconstruct routes fast enough.

To improve performance, we modified the routing protocol to select paths based on link stability rather than hop-count to dampen the rapid link oscillation when vehicles are in contact only briefly. Several conceptual changes are required to tailor multi-hop routing for vehicular networks and they are discussed in the following sections.

Multimedia Conferencing and Application Software

Audio and video streaming was carried out using conferencing software based on the H.323 standard libraries. The reception of the audio and video codec was clear but suffered from an extended delay when reconnecting temporarily broken links. New buffering implementations to address the frequent but brief link connection are necessary. In addition, a new session layer protocol that can suspend an open connection when the link is briefly disconnected and resume the flow upon subsequent connection would be very useful.

Table I

Functionality of RoadGPS Vehicular Networking Tool

1	Map & Display multiple vehicles
2	Communicate with multiple vehicles
3	Communicate over multiple hops
4	Send Safety Messages
5	Stream data & music files
6	Communicate using Cellular 1xRTT
7	Complete trip logging and playback
8	Analysis & Graphing functions

DRIVING EXPERIENCES & ANALYSIS

The multi-hop networking test-bed has been deployed across five vehicles provided by GM. The group of vehicles has been driven over 400 miles each. We chose four environments: urban (densely populated and crowded with several high-rise buildings such as downtown Pittsburgh), rural (flat with fairly open roads), highway (high speed driving along I-79) and city driving through Pittsburgh. In general we were able to maintain connectivity across all vehicles over 1.2km using multi-hop routing. This shows the basic usefulness of multi-hop networking as the range of each vehicle's wireless connection is limited to 300m under good conditions. The terrain of the city of Pittsburgh is quite hilly and offered us several non-line-of-sight opportunities where multi-hop routing proved to be very useful in maintaining connectivity.

We have developed a data analysis toolkit in MATLAB to analyze connectivity, signal-to-noise ratio, error rates, and data rates over different distances, speeds and link transmission rates. A comparison of logged packets transmitted from each local node with packets received by each of the other nodes in the network, combined with the GPS data from both nodes, allows a detailed statistical analysis of the network's connectivity performance with regard to dropped packets. The network connectivity performance for each node, as measured by packet reception, can be analyzed as a function of absolute and relative node speed, the distance between nodes, transmission signal strength, and data transmission rate. For example, Fig. 4 shows that the percentage of total sent packets which are dropped increases roughly exponentially as the distance between nodes increases for data transmitted at a data rate of 6MBPS, as one might expect.

The 5.8 GHz signal propagation characteristics within the dynamic mobile ad hoc environment can be determined

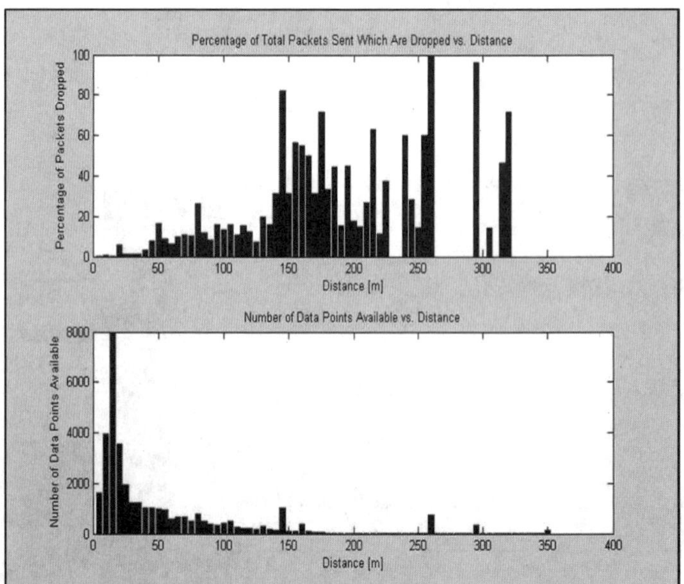

Figure 4. Percentage of total packets sent which are dropped vs. distance

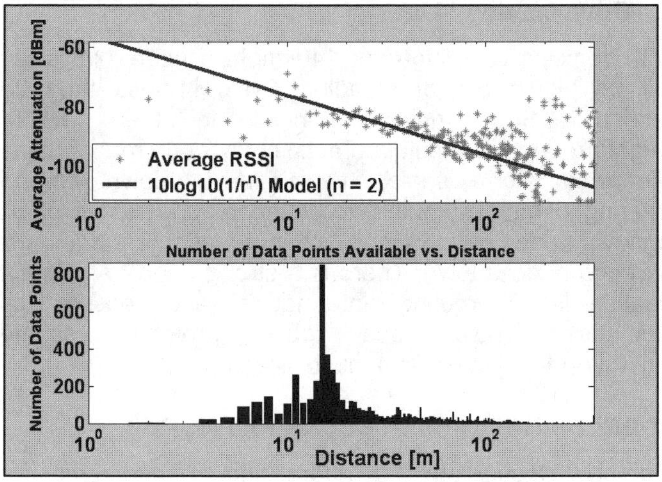

Figure 5. Total Average Measured Signal Attenuation and Free Space Propagation Model vs. Distance

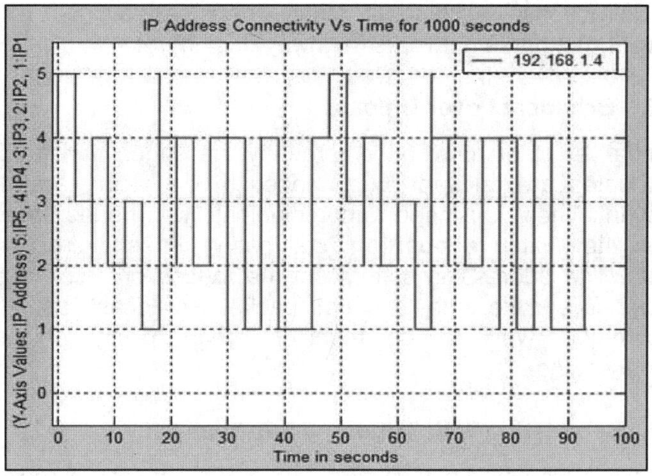

Figure 6. Graphical representation of a vehicle's routing table over time

using calibrated measurements of received and transmitted signal strengths in conjunction with the GPS data. The signal attenuation between each node can also be determined and modeled as a function of absolute and relative node speed, the distance between nodes, transmission signal strength, and data transmission rate. For example, the initial data shown in Fig. 5 suggests that signal attenuation can be roughly modeled using the free space propagation model

$$P_s \cong \frac{1}{r^n} + Offset$$

where r = distance between nodes, and n ≈ 2, as one might expect.

Fig. 6 provides a graphical representation of the routing table over time for source node with IP address 192.168.1.4 (referred to as IP4 here) attempting to communicate with destination node IP2 across one or more intermediate nodes. The y-axis plots the connectivity to nodes with IP addresses IP1, IP2, IP3 and IP5 with respect to IP4. A connection to IP4 is represented by a line passing through 4 on the y-axis. We observe that initially, IP4 is connected only to IP5 and sends the packet to IP5. IP5 forwards the packet to IP3 which in turn forwards it to IP2. This is the situation when the cars were parked in the order of their IP addresses and were in range of only their immediate neighbors. However, at a later time, we see considerable activity as cars overtake each other, or are separated by traffic lights or when direct connection is obstructed by passing large transportation carriers.

Our results are based on a modified implementation of AODV routing protocol. In the following section we outline several aspects where a new class of routing protocols needs to be developed to address the different aspects of vehicular networks.

UNIQUE CHALLENGES FOR VEHICULAR NETWORKS

Several designs for infrastructure-less "ad hoc" wireless networks have been proposed over the past decade [6]. They predominantly belong to the class of Topology-based protocols where a source node, *s*, requires a communication path with destination, *d*. As the range of the wireless interfaces is limited, the communication path will generally traverse multiple intermediate nodes, each of which relay messages. Such protocols assume every node is described by a logical (named) address (e.g IP address) and require a full search of the network to find the destination node. This search procedure (or link flooding) generally does not leverage any topological structure of the network and therefore floods the network with broadcast requests to find the destination node. Examples of such protocols are: Dynamic Source Routing (DSR), Ad hoc On-Demand Distance Vector Routing (AODV) and Optimized Link State Routing Protocol (OLSR) [6].

Are Topology-based Routing Protocols suitable for Vehicular Networks?

Several Topology-based ad hoc routing protocols have been shown to work for small and lightly mobile networks. We outline several factors in the routing protocol requirements for vehicular protocols that are not addressed by existing protocols as the challenges and applications addressed are largely different.

1. High Mobility

Ad hoc networking protocols have traditionally been simulated with average speeds less than 30kmph [6] and have shown to perform poorly under higher mobility conditions. In contrast, a vehicular network is by definition always mobile with automobiles moving in excess of 140kmph and reaching relative speeds over 300kmph. This **10x** difference of node speed requires rewriting the protocol to not be limited by (a) handshaking (e.g. route-request/route-reply), (b) formation of end-to-end connection oriented communication along fixed intermediate nodes (e.g. source routing), and (c) rebroadcasts of end-to-end route information (e.g. route-broken alerts). Furthermore, there is a need to test the correctness and performance of routing protocols through implementation rather than simulation. On-road implementation and testing bring about anomalies such as obstructions (buildings), highly dense networks (city driving), sparse networks (highway driving), etc.

2. Broadcast over Unicast

In a vehicular network, emergency messages and traffic updates are relevant to all nodes in the vicinity of the event. There is a need to communicate with nodes based on their **relative position**, destination, speed, direction, etc. The addressing scheme of the routing protocol must therefore take into account packet broadcast as the common way to communicate than using unicast messaging.

3. Geocasting with Topology Information:

As vehicle paths are constrained by the network of roads, connectivity and flooding will benefit from leveraging knowledge of the **traffic topology**. Most Topology-based protocols do not assume any known network structure and flood the entire network. This severely limits their scalability to less than 30 nodes. Furthermore, as messages have a geographic relevance, it is essential to use node position as a key network construct.

4. Intersection-Intersection Routing Vs. Vehicle-to-Vehicle Routing:

In order to exploit geographic information, several greedy location-aware routing protocols have been proposed. These however fall short when a road bends and the path to the destination is not as the crow flies. Greedy location-aware routing protocols attempt to reach an intermediate node only if it is geographically closer to the destination, and therefore the packet delivery rate is severely limited by their use of local information. On the other hand, using limited navigation information, packets can be routed from intersection-to-intersection rather than from vehicle-to-vehicle. This eliminates the need to keep track of the addresses of intermediate hops or to maintain a destination-based routing table. Topology-based protocols do not exploit any such information and are based solely on logical addressing. Using intersection-based routing, vehicles are used opportunistically if they lie along the region of interest. Furthermore, by fixing routing to static intermediate points, vehicles moving outside the area of interest will not adversely affect the path.

5. Message Lifetime:

Topology-based protocols aim to eliminate duplicate messaging and stop sending a message once an acknowledgement is received. In a vehicular network, if an incident occurs at a particular location, there is a constant need to update all vehicles approaching the incident site. It is therefore necessary to continue broadcasting the message to all new nodes until the incident lifetime has expired. Furthermore, as the network connectivity may be sparse, it is useful to hold the message until a new neighbor is detected. Topology-based protocols employ a "hot-potato" approach to routing where once a packet is forwarded it is forgotten. Message lifetime support is crucial to maintaining alert status and also increasing message delivery rate in sparsely connected networks.

6. Dirty Routing Tables:

With vehicles traveling over 140kmph, a node 1km away will be within 5m of standing traffic in less than 25 seconds. Such quick changes in the network neighborhood will result in drastic changes in routing table information. For example, a vehicle leaving downtown and entering a highway will corrupt the routing tables of all highway nodes in its vicinity with information of nodes just traveling in downtown. There is a strong need to maintain location-based routing information and ensure its freshness. Topology-based routing protocols assume routing updates occur at a much slower pace.

ADDRESSING FOR VEHICULAR NETWORKS

We now focus on the addressing requirements for vehicular networks. In addition to sending messages targeted to a particular vehicle, there are several instances where a message is targeted to a group of vehicles that meet a particular criterion such as current position within region of interest, speed, direction, etc. Three addressing schemes have been identified to support named, geographic and node property-based addressing. The following addressing schemes will be incrementally deployed in the test-bed.

A. Named/Assigned Addresses:
For unicast messaging and to identify vehicle-type groups, Assigned Addresses provide a single vehicle logical naming such as IP address, VIN, MAC address, etc. An example is: "Message for Buick FJF2323"

B. Geographic Addresses:
For messages focused on a particular geographic region, vehicles may choose to accept, forward or drop packets based on their geographic attribute.

1. **Absolute Geography**
   - **Direction:** "Message for - All neighbors driving east on I-90"
   - **Navigation:** "Message for - All cars headed for Exit 22"
   - **Region:** "Message for Downtown Pittsburgh"

2. **Relative Geography**
   - **Hop count:** "Message for - All cars within 6 hops radius"
   - **Speed:** "Message for - All cars moving within +/- 8mph of my speed"

C. Property-based Addresses:
For messages focused on an attribute of a vehicle:

1. **Connectivity:** "Message for any mobile gateway"
2. **Vehicle Type:** "Message for Trucks only, or GM vehicles only, or 2-wheelers
3. **Vehicle Dynamics:** e.g. Absolute Speed: "Message for vehicles moving at 40kmph +/-5kmph"

We observe that the vehicular network routing protocol will need to support all three addressing schemes and ensure their coexistence. Therefore, based on the application, an appropriate addressing scheme will utilize broadcast, multicast groups and unicast for a well-defined subset of vehicles.

CONCLUSION

We describe the design and deployment of an experimental multi-hop mobile test-bed for vehicular networks. The goal of the test-bed is to get insights into the vagaries of the wireless channel and routing protocols to deliver both mission-critical emergency messages and interactive telematics applications. Our current deployment includes a DGPS receiver, an onboard computer, a modified 802.11a radio card, a 1xRTT cellular-data connection and multimedia peripherals. Our experiences from driving the test-bed over 400 miles indicate that traditional applications and network infrastructure are usable. However, to meet the demands for a scalable and stable vehicular network both routing protocols and transport protocols need to be developed to address the dynamism of a highly mobile and lightly connected network of vehicles. We provide a list of technical requirements for the design of routing protocols and highlight the unique addressing capabilities necessary. As future work, we aim to develop and deploy the ideas presented in this paper.

ACKNOWLEDGMENTS

The authors would like to thank Daniel Weller and Suchit Mishra for their valuable inputs.

REFERENCES

1. OnStar Safety System. http://www.onstar.com
2. IEEE 802.11a, Part 11: High-speed Physical Layer in the 5 GHz Band, Supplement to IEEE 802.11 Standard, September 1999.
3. Dedicated Short Range Communications. http://www.leearmstrong.com/DSRC
4. Roadmap. http://sourceforge.net/projects/roadmap/
5. Census 2000 TIGER/Line Data. http://www.esri.com/data/download/census2000_tigerline/
6. J. Broch, et al. A performance comparison of multi-hop wireless ad hoc network routing protocols. In Proc. Mobicom, pages 85--97, 1998
7. Charles E. Perkins, Elizabeth M. Belding-Royer, and Samir Das. "Ad Hoc On Demand Distance Vector (AODV) Routing." IETF RFC 3561

2004-01-0283

Messaging and Telematics

Randy Carroll, Brett Hackleman and David Locke
International Business Machines Corporation, Inc.

ABSTRACT

With the introduction of increasingly sophisticated electronics in modern vehicles, it is easy to see how the functionality provided by these electronics is becoming richer and more complex. To provide this functionality, a telematics system relies on collaboration with off-vehicle computers. This creates the requirement for an efficient, reliable, and secure communications framework suitable for use over wireless networks. This paper will discuss how a modern messaging system combined with Java Message Service can be a strong base to build upon.

INTRODUCTION

The term "telematics" is used to describe a wide range of vehicle-related functions available to the complete spectrum of all interested parties. For the vehicle occupant, a telematics system can include safety, security, and infotainment applications. For the vehicle owner or fleet manager, the system can offer vehicle tracking and maintenance information. For the vehicle manufacturer, the system can provide vehicle prognostics and diagnostics, lowering future manufacturing and subsequent warranty costs.

This in-vehicle device increasingly relies on collaboration with off-vehicle computers to augment the capabilities and resources of in-vehicle devices. This drives the subsequent need for an efficient, reliable, and secure communications framework suitable for use over wireless networks.

In this paper we discuss the communication-related requirements for implementing several telematics scenarios. We discuss strategies for using a flexible messaging-based software architecture based on the Java™ Message Service (JMS), the value it brings, and the missing elements of such a system. Finally, we use IBM's WebSphere® MQ Everyplace (MQe) as an example of enhancing the robustness of a JMS telematics solution.

TELEMATICS DOMAIN BACKGROUND

A BRIEF SAMPLING OF USE CASES

We'll begin by presenting five typical telematics use cases with communication requirements. These are only a fraction of the possible telematics scenarios, and the specifics of each scenario are only illustrative, as they vary greatly from implementation to implementation. They are useful to consider so that we can extract the subsequent communications characteristics and requirements.

Vehicle Accident

First, what may be most important to the vehicle occupants is the emergency procedure the vehicle uses in the event of a crash. A typical example begins with the car detecting that a crash has occurred. This can be done by observing messages sent on the vehicle's communication bus, such as "airbag deployment". The next step is to query the vehicle systems for the various data that you may want to report. This probably includes the time, GPS location, VIN[1], and other data that the vehicle may be capable of sensing, such as crumple detection or spatial orientation so the severity of the crash may be determined. This data is collected into a data packet along with the reason code for the message and is sent to the call center[2] for processing. The call center commonly reacts by establishing a voice call with the vehicle and talking to the occupants to determine the severity of the emergency and the action to be taken.

Emergency Call

This is similar to the Vehicle Accident use case, except the trigger for the event is not the computer detecting an accident, but rather an occupant pushing a button, or speaking a command, to indicate an emergency condition. The use case flow from there would then be similar. The computer would send a message to the call center letting it know the condition and the current

[1] Vehicle Identification Number – a unique vehicle ID
[2] Call center – a generic term for the dedicated communication center that fields and acts on vehicle communications

vehicle data, to which the call center would respond by establishing a voice call with the occupants to determine the action to be taken.

Vehicle Theft

Upon realizing the vehicle is missing, the owner would notify the call center. After verification of the owner, the call center would send a message to the missing vehicle instructing it to enter "stolen vehicle" mode. In this mode, the vehicle would periodically send location and condition information messages back to the call center so that its status can be tracked. In the event that the engine is turned off, the vehicle would no longer restart. All these communications would be surreptitious so that the thief is unaware that the vehicle is being tracked.

Navigation Instructions from Off-Board System

Navigation can have a wide range of functionality and requisite hardware/software needs (such as large databases and expensive displays). One of the lower cost solutions is to supply the driver with turn-by-turn instructions that are calculated by an off-board computer system. To do this the driver would first specify the desired destination. This could be done with a predetermined set of locations (such as home, work, airport), but in general this can be a somewhat difficult user interface problem. The device would then send a message to the call center that contains the vehicle's current GPS location and the target destination. The call center (or provider) would respond with a message that contains the necessary instructions and route details. This would then be displayed (and/or spoken) to the driver and updated as the driver proceeds along the route.

Diagnostic Data Request

For OEMs and fleet owners it is important to collect various operating performance data from the vehicle. This can be useful in ensuring the vehicle is maintained in good condition and for planning preventive maintenance. It helps an owner establish a baseline for the expected life and usage of a vehicle that can be combined with data from other vehicles to determine overall expectations of similar vehicles for fleet management purposes.

The scenario would start with the call center sending a request to the vehicle for its diagnostic data. The vehicle would take its accumulated performance data and send it to the call center for analysis and storage. This shows how performance data would be "pulled" from the vehicle on demand.

This scenario could also be triggered when a vehicle experiences an operational difficulty and contacts the call center to report the problem and receive assistance to determine the problem. At this point, the call center would then issue a diagnostic data request to gather more specific information needed to isolate the problem.

COMMON THEMES

When we look at the 5 use cases, we begin to see some common communication requirements.

Bi-Directional

The system will need to be bi-directional; as communication needs to be initiated from both the vehicle (client) and from the call center (server). These flows could potentially be either open-ended, in that a message would be sent from one end with no acknowledgement required of the receiver (datagram), or the message could be closed-ended, in that some sort of acknowledgement would have to be received by the initiator of the message flow to signal function completion (request/reply).

Asynchronous

The system will need to be asynchronous, as we cannot assume that the message destination can be reached immediately by typical wireless communication. In fact this should be the design point norm as cellular coverage should be considered unreliable for myriad reasons even where coverage is typically good.

Assured Delivery

Most importantly, we want guaranteed delivery. For many messages we want to be certain that the data successfully reaches its destination intact. This is a critical design point. It must be a certainty that exactly one copy of the message did indeed arrive intact at its target. Combining this with the asynchronous requirement mentioned above implies that this delivery also needs to be accomplished in an asynchronous manner.

Security

Data security becomes important when transmitting data over public wireless networks. This is commonly dealt with by various encryption techniques. The importance, privacy, and value of the data will vary greatly from essentially minimal importance, such as the engine operating data, to vital importance such as passing credit information. The subsequent security processing therefore should be flexible enough to handle all situations.

Compression

Public wireless networks can provide fairly low bandwidth. A robust assortment of compression technologies can be used to raise the effective bandwidth.

Other General Aspects

It is also important that the messaging system not be tied to any single communication technology. Rather, it should be robust enough to allow for multiple communication technologies and should allow the various properties of each message to determine the appropriate communication path. These properties can include the priority of the message, the amount of data to pass, and the current qualities of service of the available communications paths.

Additionally, the solution must be small enough to work in an embedded device, be flexible enough to fit with current device and back-end needs, and grow easily with enhancements to both the device and back-end systems.

PROPERTIES OF A MESSAGING SYSTEM

The architecture of a telematics system consists of a series of layers. The primary purpose of these layers is to abstract a particular system function. This abstraction serves several purposes. Most important to the software developer is that it relieves the software author from the burden of the intricacies of the function. This simplifies the overall system complexities and allows the software author to focus on the desired application. Additionally, it allows the function supplier to focus on the integrity, improvement, and maintenance of the function over time.

A messaging system is an example of one such abstraction layer that can be a significant part of an overall communications solution. It can absorb the task of communicating the desired data from one collaborating computing system to another, making the communication task easy and transparent to the application author.

At a high level, the messaging system takes a block of data that an application needs to transmit, packages it with some flow information (creating a message object), and transmits it to the waiting target. The messaging system also accepts incoming messages and passes them on to the corresponding application handler.

In order to support asynchronous communication, persistent message queues are required. Any message that is not deliverable for any reason, such as poor or no wireless signal, can wait in a queue on some non-volatile storage device for a more opportune moment when it is finally delivered. In a telematics solution, queuing is required both in the vehicle and in the call center. This enables messages destined for the vehicle to be temporarily stored in the call center and likewise, messages destined for the call center can be temporarily stored in the vehicle. Most commercial messaging systems support a message queuing architecture.

Another important aspect of a robust messaging system is the scalability of the system. It is important that it work with clients with limited resources, such as the devices that would reside in a vehicle, but equally important, it must support the needs of the back-end system. The back-end system will need to handle large numbers of distributed clients, storing a plethora of pending messages and interacting with disparate and perhaps legacy systems.

One messaging system abstraction layer that is growing in popularity is the Java Message Service.

JAVA MESSAGE SERVICE

OVERVIEW

JMS is a Java-based unifier of the many existing proprietary messaging systems. It defines an API and messaging architecture that encompasses the functionality of the various messaging systems, such that the application code can be blissfully unaware of the particular messaging system being employed and can migrate from one system to another without code alteration. To do this, JMS only specifies the architecture and relevant API that the application would need in order to accomplish its desired messaging work. JMS does not define the underlying implementation; it only serves as a common veneer so applications are isolated from the specifics of any particular system.

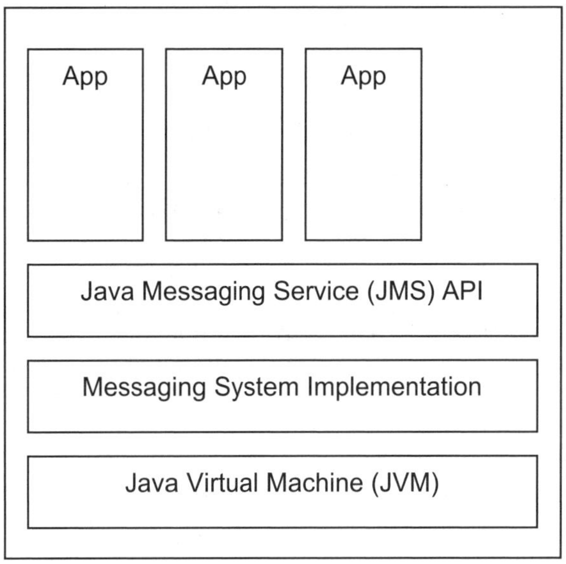

BASE CONCEPTS

The two primary types of systems are point-to-point and publish-and-subscribe. As the name implies, point-to-point is the type of message conversation that is between two and only two parties. Both parties typically have a prior knowledge of each other. Publish-and-subscribe on the other hand, is intended for messaging communications where the sources or publishers of information and the consumers or subscribers of information have no knowledge of each other.

Additionally, there may be a large indeterminate number of subscribers for any item of information. This is particularly useful in disseminating information to a large ad hoc list of interested parties.

Playing the role of messaging systems unifier, JMS provides three sets of API. One set of JMS API exists for each of the two types of messaging systems, point-to-point and publish-and-subscribe. Another more generic set of API was added in a later release, so that the application doesn't have to choose a specific type.

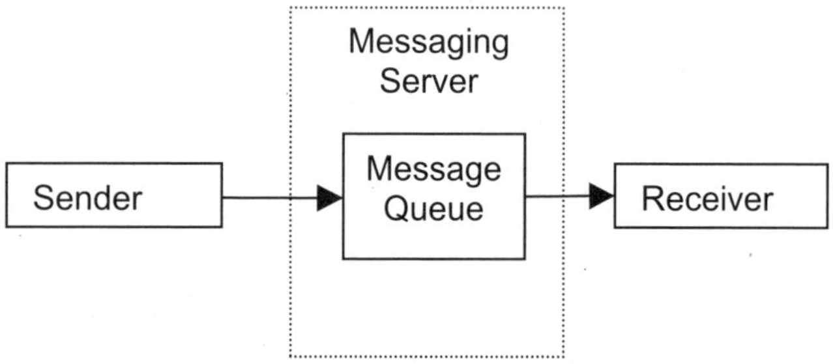

Point-to-Point Queue-based Messaging System

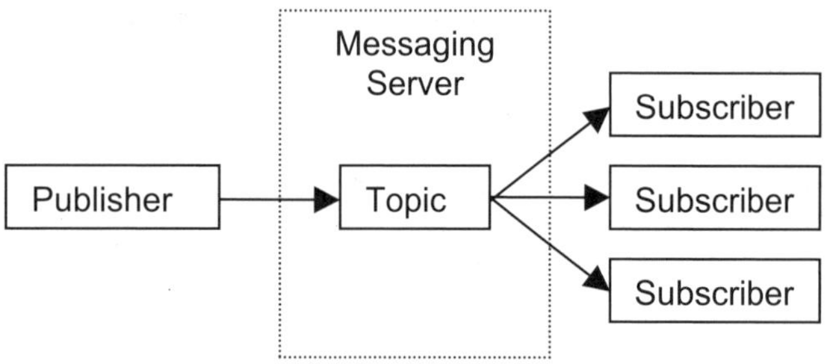

Publisher-Subscriber Based Messaging System

The point-to-point interface best suits the needs of the telematics scenarios we have presented and will be the interface we will use for the rest of the paper. However, it should be noted though that the publish-and-subscribe style would be very suitable for a set of possible information push scenarios such as current weather conditions, stock pricing information, traffic conditions, etc.

FUNDAMENTAL OBJECTS

Messages

As you might expect with a messaging system, the most important object in the system is the message itself. This object encapsulates the information for a particular domain task to be communicated to a collaborating application. In JMS, the message object comes in five different varieties, based on the fundamental data type on which you wish to operate. The following table shows the message types and their primary features.

TextMessage	The message body consists of a single Java String
BytesMessage	The message body consists of an array of bytes, the content of which is defined and interpreted by the application
MapMessage	The message body consists of a collection of key/value pairs where the value is any Java type and the key is a Java String
StreamMessage	The message body consists of a self defining collection of fundamental data types that are created and accessed in a sequential order
ObjectMessage	The message body consists of any single serializable[3] Java object

Queue

As with any messaging system that supports asynchronous messages, there must be a way to retain pending messages. In JMS these are called Queues, and they are responsible for persistently storing messages until they are successfully delivered.

The application code has a choice in how it operates on the pending messages. It can do so in a synchronous or asynchronous manner. In the synchronous manner, an application invokes the message receive protocol and is "blocked" until a message arrives. In the asynchronous manner, an application registers a listener[4]. This listener must implement the MessageListener interface that consists of a single method. This method is called whenever a message arrives where it can then be processed by the application. For our telematics purposes, where CPU availability may be critical for all manner of various tasks at all times, the asynchronous manner of operation is the one typically employed.

QueueConnectionFactory

This is the object that is utilized by the application to establish a connection for point-to-point communication. The QueueConnectionFactory encapsulates the implementation-specific connection parameters, as defined by the underlying messaging system.

[3] An object is considered to be serializable if it implements the Java Serializable interface.

[4] The Listener pattern is a Java-specific version of the Observer/Observable pattern, which is used for receiving notification of events.

QueueConnection

The connection object is the entity that encapsulates the state required to maintain an active communication channel with a target collaborator. If supported by the underlying messaging system, authentication and compression will be handled automatically when the connection is established.

QueueSession

The session object is created by the connection object and serves several purposes. It is the factory object for Receiver and Sender objects. It is utilized to create Queue objects. It provides the transaction capability used by the session's Receivers and Senders. It also manages the flow of messages and the delivery acknowledgement.

QueueSender

The QueueSender object is used by the application to send new messages to a target queue. This destination may be specified when the QueueSender object is created or when the QueueSender is ready to send the message.

QueueReceiver

The QueueReceiver object is used by the application to receive incoming messages from a particular Queue in an asynchronous manner. When a message flows into the system it is delivered to the currently registered QueueReceiver for processing.

JMS RELATIONSHIP TO UNDERLYING MESSAGING IMPLEMENTATION

JMS is an abstract, vendor-neutral way for an application to accomplish its messaging needs without having to worry about (or even be aware of) the specifics of the underlying messaging system. This therefore allows a JMS application to be portable across any JMS conforming implementation. It also allows the application writer to focus on constructing good JMS applications, and not the underlying message system setup and operation.

There are many JMS implementations on the market today, each of which may provide a subset or superset of the JMS functionality. Each implementation tends to be best suited for a particular domain, depending on the requirements and experience that drove its development.

JMS AND TELEMATICS

JMS provides a solid yet flexible architecture on which to base your application, but it leaves a sizeable portion of the telematics requirements unsatisfied. These requirements therefore fall to the underlying messaging system to be fulfilled. For illustrative purposes, we will use IBM's WebSphere MQ Everyplace (MQe) product to describe how the implementation supports and augments the JMS layer.

Bi-Directional

The JMS specification provides an API for sending messages bi-directionally and supports both the point-to-point and publish/subscribe messaging models. How the messages are moved between a sender and a receiver is specific to the underlying messaging layer. The MQe messaging layer supports both client to server and server to server communication styles, together with a variety of communication protocols enabling it to be used in a wide variety of network types and configurations.

Asynchronous

JMS and MQe support both synchronous and asynchronous message delivery. As previously discussed, asynchronous messaging is more suitable for the unreliable connectivity associated with wireless communications. To support this a variety of queue types are provided; queues for local storage of messages , store and forward queues to hold messages until they can be delivered and queues for other specialized purposes such as administration.

Assured Delivery

Most importantly, JMS provides an assured messaging delivery quality of service so that the application can be assured that one and only one copy of a message is delivered to the target destination. This JMS capability is fully supported by MQe. In fact, many financial institutions trust their transaction flow to the WebSphere MQ product family, including MQe.

Now that we've discussed how MQe supports the required JMS features, let's take a look at the features needed for our telematics scenarios that are beyond the scope of the JMS specification but provided by an MQe-based implementation.

Security

Any time data flows over an unsecured wireless network, security becomes an issue. The nature of a telematics device also means that the physical security cannot be assured, making local encryption of incoming and outgoing messages a requirement. MQe supports a number of encryption standards out of the box. These can be applied to an individual queue, between two queues, or on a message level, depending on the level of security desired. Standard support includes:

- Triple DES
- DES

- MARS
- RC4
- RC6
- XOR

Compression

Until high-bandwidth wireless connections become ubiquitous and cheap, telematics applications will need to conserve the bandwidth available to them. MQe addresses this by providing a number of compression options, and features an efficient wire protocol and automated recovery from communication link failures.

- LZW - The simplest form of the LZW algorithm uses a dictionary data structure in which various words, or data patterns, are stored in a hash table. This compressor is likely to be most effective where the data has a significant number of repeating words, or data patterns.

- Run Length Encoding (RLE) - the compressor routines compress or expand repeated bytes. Hence it is effective in compressing and decompressing data with many repeated bytes.

- GZIP - uses the same compression algorithm as the **gzip** command on UNIX. This searches for repeating patterns in the data and replaces subsequent occurrences of a pattern with a reference back to the first occurrence of the pattern.

Other General Aspects

The actual transmission of messages by the MQe system is performed by a range of transport classes that support common protocols such as HTTP, TCP/IP, and UDP. These transporters together with many aspects of MQe are controllable by Rule classes that allow the MQe system to be tailored to suit the needs of the application. Transmission rules enable easy optimization of an operation, such as when message transmission can be attempted. In order to provide optimal use of the network, a rule could be employed that allows high priority messages like an "accident occurred" message to flow on any network no matter what the bandwidth, quality or cost and lower priority messages such as a "diagnostics message" to only flow when a fast cheap network is available.

Cross Platform

It can be a nightmare for application providers to support the wide range of hardware platforms and operating systems used to build a telematics device across many vehicle models. However, by using a Java-based solution, the development, testing, and installation of telematics applications is greatly simplified. Since JMS and MQe are written in Java, this makes them portable across a wide range of telematics devices.

MQe is also compatible with the Open Services Gateway initiative (OSGi™) specification, so it can run unmodified on any OSGi client device.

Resource Constraints

The JMS specification is part of the Java 2 Enterprise Edition (J2EE) specifications that target back-end server systems (as opposed to the Java 2 Micro Edition (J2ME) specifications). This means that many JMS implementations have significant memory and processor requirements. However, MQe was designed from the ground up to run on a standard Java 2 Micro Edition runtime (J2ME) as well as IBM's WebSphere Custom Environment (WCE). This enables it to run on a wide range of embedded devices ranging from mobile phones to PDAs to large embedded devices. Therefore it has very low storage (ROM) and run-time (RAM) memory requirements required by a telematics device.

Flexibility

MQe was designed to address a wide range of domains, and as a result is very flexible. The entire MQe framework is built on a plug-in component model. This means that MQe can be configured with the exact features desired, leaving out any unnecessary services. This architecture also makes it possible to customize MQe. Need your own unique type of encryption? Just implement it using the correct interface and insert it into the MQe framework. This is also true for compression, queue message storage, and the wireless transport type.

Back-End Integration

MQe was designed to provide industrial-strength messaging for low-end devices. A client running JMS and MQe integrates smoothly with the full range of back-end WebSphere MQ products. These leading message-oriented middleware products were designed for reliability and can be distributed across almost any back-end system topology. They can be scaled to meet any number of client devices and servers.

Finally, the JMS specification is supported across the full spectrum of WebSphere MQ products, making it easy to learn a single API that will be provided on both the client device and back-end system.

CONCLUSION

The nature of the automotive environment makes implementing even relatively simple telematics scenarios complex, due to their communication requirements. Asynchronous messaging helps to manage this hostile environment by hiding the intermittent connectivity to the back-end systems.

The Java Message Service API defines a simple and elegant framework that simplifies development by isolating the software developer from the low-level communication details. It also allows the application provider to easily move between JMS implementations without being locked into a proprietary messaging API.

Finally, we have shown that is it up to the underlying messaging implementation (such as MQe) to fill the gaps between what JMS provides and the requirements of typical telematics functions. Together, JMS and MQe can be used to create a robust communication framework suitable for the automotive telematics environment.

REFERENCES

1. Java Message Service API (Sun Microsystems, Inc.) http://java.sun.com/products/jms/
2. WebSphere MQ Everyplace Home page http://www.ibm.com/software/integration/appconn/wmqe
3. WebSphere MQ Family home page http://www.ibm.com/software/mqseries/
4. Open Services Gateway initiative page http://www.osgi.org

CONTACT

Randy Carroll has a B.S. / M.S. in Computer Science from the University of Kentucky and an MBA from Wake Forest. He has spent 28 years roaming the spectrum of computing, but his heart remains in embedded systems. He now spends his time working on telematics-oriented projects.
(rwcarroll@us.ibm.com)

Brett Hackleman has a degree in Computer Engineering from North Carolina State University. He works with automotive suppliers building telematics solutions.
(bhackleman@us.ibm.com)

Dave Locke spent the last 20 years tinkering with various aspects of middleware, in particular working on the development of CICS and the WebSphere MQ family of products. His most recent focus has been on creating messaging middleware for resource-constrained runtimes.
(LOCKE@uk.ibm.com)

No hands with Bluetooth

A major effort is under way to implement the wireless specification in cars and cell phones to reduce driver distraction.

by Terry Costlow

Phone calls made and received in cars may soon sound larger than life, coming over multi-speaker sound systems normally used for the likes of Pavarotti or Jewel. There is a major effort to implement the Bluetooth wireless specification in cars and cell phones so drivers will not have to do anything to make or receive phone calls other than talk. Bluetooth appears to have significant momentum as a solution that lets various types of electronic gear such as phones, PDAs (personal digital assistants), and automotive systems communicate with any equipment that is compatible. The wireless link forms what is sometimes called a personal network, providing seamless communication between a person's equipment and environment.

Support is coming from many different fields. Chipmakers and cell-phone suppliers are racing to get a piece of what is potentially a huge market (see sidebar). **Microsoft** Corp. made Bluetooth a centerpiece when it rolled out Version 4.2 of its Windows Automotive operating system in April. The company's research showed that 85% of U.S. cell-phone owners use their phone in the car, as do 50% of PDA owners.

Unless some unexpected change in technology occurs, automotive vendors predict near ubiquity. "If Bluetooth remains the standard in telecommunications, there's a real possibility of having Bluetooth in every car by the end of the decade," said Bob Schumacher, General Director of Wireless Products and Mobile Multimedia at **Delphi**. The supplier designed a system that is going into production in the **Saab** 9-3. Using the model that is widely envisioned for Bluetooth phones, the driver can talk on the phone hands-free. The voice comes through the speakers, and the radio will mute when it senses a call. "You can keep your phone in your pocket; it just has to be turned on. It's sleek and seamless," Schumacher said.

The hands-free aspect is critical, since the issue of safety for drivers using cellular phones is not going away. Drivers in New York cannot legally drive while holding a cell phone, and 15 states are at various stages of debate on banning cell phones. In Europe, many countries allow only hands-free operation.

That need is being addressed by a trade group that is promoting Bluetooth; the **Bluetooth Special Interest Group** (SIG) is driving both its name-recognition efforts and Bluetooth's technological infrastructure. That infrastructure is centered on a base of standards-like profiles that will ensure compatibility in specific applications and markets such as printing and imaging.

The Bluetooth SIG made automotive one of its first targets. Committee members

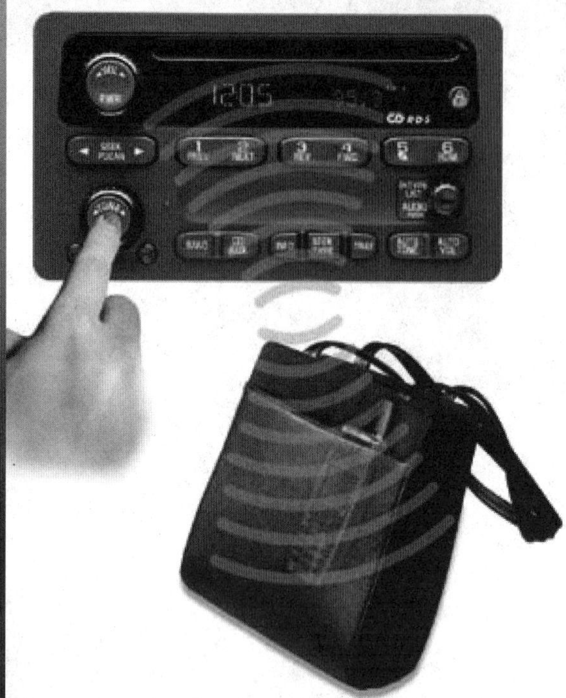

Companies such as Delphi are developing systems that allow Bluetooth phones tucked away in a briefcase or purse to use a car's radio for hands-free calls.

have already completed a hands-free profile that companies are beginning to deploy. Eager phone companies showed their support by adding the profile to products as soon as the hands-free spec was ready, even though only a handful of high-end cars can synch up with Bluetooth phones.

"Automotive is very important," said Mike McCamon, Executive Director of the Bluetooth SIG. He noted that success will be measured when hundreds of millions of devices use the technology, adding that "the two most obvious ways to get there are mobile phones and automobiles."

What remains to be seen is which profiles are picked up by the designers of phones and other portable electronic gear that might enter the vehicle, as well as how many profiles automakers include. Though much of the focus in vehicles is on hands-free operation, the Bluetooth SIG profile for headsets is now being implemented; however, this is not seen as the best way for carmakers to go.

"Some automakers will include both hands-free and headset profiles in the car," McCamon said. He added that over time, the automotive profile will gain acceptance, so the headset profile would no longer be needed.

Whatever form it might take in the future, cost is going to be a big factor that determines when carmakers adopt the technology and how rapidly auto buyers embrace it. At present, the economics are something of an obstacle. "Bluetooth nodes are still pretty expensive," said Paul Hansen of **Paul Hansen Associates** in Portsmouth, NH.

Bluetooth on the rise

If indeed automakers implement Bluetooth during the next few years as expected, they will be going along with a solid industry trend. If prognosticators are correct, Bluetooth designs now hitting the market will see solid success, making the wireless link a standard feature in many product categories.

The Zelos Group predicts that 90% of PDAs and 75% of mobile handsets will be Bluetooth-compatible by 2006. Phones will be the real driver for the technology, selling more than 153 million units in 2006 alone, according to Zelos. That is more than half the anticipated 258 million unit sales for that year. Chip sales are expected to soar dramatically. Allied Business Intelligence predicts that worldwide shipments of Bluetooth chipsets will grow

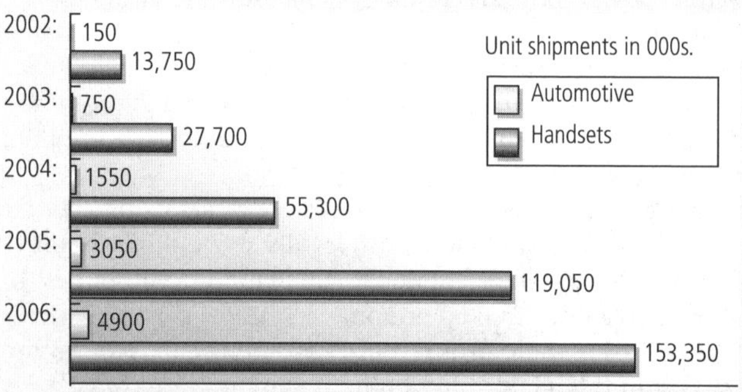

Source: Zelos Group

Fueled by sharp increases in Bluetooth-compatible phones, automakers are expected to quickly adopt the technology.

from 33.8 million last year to 1.1 billion by 2007.

In the automotive field, Zelos predicts that Bluetooth unit shipments in the U.S. and Europe will soar from a paltry 750,000 this year to 3 million in 2005 and 4.9 million in 2006. That means that by 2006, consumers will have purchased a total of 10.4 million Bluetooth-enabled cars. That cumulative figure will be almost evenly divided between Europe and the U.S., with fractionally more European vehicles offering the wireless technology.

Bluetooth's main benefit is simplicity. Bluetooth-compatible devices will automatically work together, so users can move from one environment to another without hooking up cables or configuring a machine.

Along with ease of use, there are other societal issues driving the marketplace. Money is a big one. Analysts say anywhere from 50 to 70% of cell phone calls are made from vehicles. If the focus on driver safety causes any reduction in that aspect of the business, cellular companies could see a noticeable decline in income.

"One thing that's really pushing Bluetooth forward is the public safety aspect. New York State banned mobile phones, and service providers will lose revenue if that happens elsewhere," said Penny Breyer, Senior Applications

Engineer at CSR.

Zelos analysts do not see any losses arising. Instead, they expect carrier service companies to see revenues from U.S. automotive users rise to $60.1 million in 2006, up from $3.8 million this year.

Terry Costlow

However, that is changing quickly as semiconductor geometries shrink and production volumes rise. Market analysts at the **Zelos Group** estimate the cost of adding Bluetooth capability to a device at around $4 to $8 today, a cost that is expected to drop by about 50% by 2005.

If and when they decide to implement Bluetooth, the specifics of implementing this new technology are a key question for automakers as well as for those who create the hardware and software. While automakers determine what they are going to do, most leave the details to their electronic suppliers. "It would not make any sense for us to invest in Bluetooth. The more detailed work is done by our suppliers," said Ben Baker, Product Engineering Director at **General Motors**.

For those designers, there are a number of technical issues and challenges. One is that automotive designers cannot simply integrate the ICs that are used in cell phones; they need to put much more focus on long-term reliability. "In autos, you're talking about seven to 10 years. In a phone, it's more like two years," said Ken Noblitt, North American Technical Business Development Director at **CSR**.

Other technical concerns go far beyond the Bluetooth specification. Some, such as voice recognition technology that is needed to facilitate true hands-free operations for tasks such as dialing, do not even come into close contact with the Bluetooth specification. But it is a concern for engineers who must supply a complete, easy-to-use system that can be used by any consumer under almost any circumstance, including rolled-down windows and extraneous conversations.

"One of the concerns will be voice recognition; that's a very difficult problem to solve," said Harry Asher, Product Strategy Manager at **Siemens VDO**'s Infotainment Solution Group. He noted that most consumers expect things in the vehicle to work all the time, having higher expectations than for products like a personal computer in the home. That should not be overly difficult to achieve, since there are "no major hurdles" expected to slow Bluetooth's implementation, Asher added. Many of the issues have been solved for higher frequencies than Bluetooth's 2.4-GHz range; however, designers still have to take care when they are laying out circuit boards.

"Bluetooth is a microwave radio, so designing the traces on a circuit board is not always trivial," said CSR's Noblitt. He added that engineers do not need to move to ceramics or other substrates, but rather can use conventional circuit board materials.

As in all markets, chipmakers are continuously adding more functionality to their ICs, making it simpler for engineers to complete a system. Today, many functions are within the main IC. "We have integrated many functions and we put a lot of passives on the chip, including RF components such as bandpass filters. You can basically connect the chip to an antenna with a crystal and some resistors," Noblitt said.

As these technical challenges are overcome and acceptance grows, users will not be satisfied linking only phones to their cars. Many predict that in the future, automakers will offer a number of profiles, addressing many types of portable consumer products. "There are MP3 players with Bluetooth, so you may be able to bring an MP3 player in and play it through the sound system," Bluetooth SIG's McCamon said.

He noted that manufacturers can implement any combination of Bluetooth profiles they choose, depending on their customer base. Implementations can be bare bones or multifaceted. "Someone buying a top-of-the-line **BMW** will have different expectations than someone buying a basic **Honda** Civic," McCamon said. He noted that profiles do not require a significant amount of memory space, so supporting multiple profiles will not be a huge burden.

Other automotive-related profiles are in the works, with no firm completion date at this time. One of them makes it simple to share data, letting users transfer business card information that is stored on a phone to a navigation system, using the stored data instead of forcing the user to type it in. Another profile addresses remote diagnostics, providing VIN numbers and other information when a vehicle is pulled into a repair bay. ***aei***

Mike McCamon of the Bluetooth Special Interest Group believes the automotive industry will be a key driver for the wireless technology.

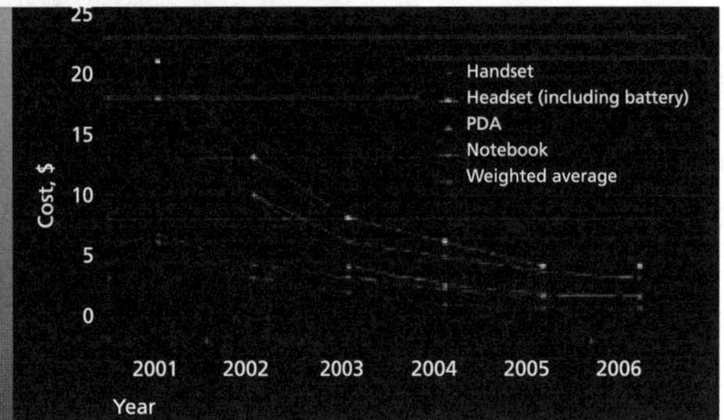

Automotive pricing will follow handset costs as they quickly decline.

With hands-free systems, drivers can make or receive calls without distractions, then pick up the phone and use it outside the vehicle.

2003-01-0132

A Study of a Telematics Communication Method Involving Switching Signals to Voice and Data Lines

Toru Takagi and Takuji Nakazawa
Nissan Motor Co., Ltd.

ABSTRACT

This paper proposes a new voice and data wireless communication method for telematics services. Data-voice (DV) modems have conventionally been used for simultaneous transmission of voice and data. With this method, however, one line is split between the data part and voice part. Lost data are retransmitted, but the voice signal is not resent because voice communication requires a real-time characteristic. The new voice and data wireless communication method proposed here switches voice to a voice line and data to a data line.

INTRODUCTION

Drivers can now obtain a variety of information in their vehicles, including traffic and weather reports, news and information about restaurants and other amenities, over their cellular phones from content servers on the Internet. Such in-vehicle information services have become possible through the advances achieved in cellular phone and Internet technologies [1].

Because it is difficult for drivers to operate information device switches while driving, they can request the information they desire by voice commands. Their voice requests are handled by a speech recognition server or a human operator at an information service center. While it is possible to equip a vehicle with a simple speech recognition device, it is difficult for such equipment to handle users' complicated requests because it can only accommodate simple voice commands owing to its limited voice dictionary. Consequently, drivers' complicated requests must be handled by a speech recognition system with an extensive voice dictionary or by a human operator who converts a request into a form that allows data searches. The desired information is then obtained from a content server in a data format and provided to the driver via data communication. In order to provide sophisticated telematics services therefore, a wireless communication system should be able to support both voice and data. Methods of transmitting both voice and data include a line-splitting system based on a data-voice (DV) modem, a voice/data switching system and a system that uses separate voice and data lines. In this study, a telematics system is proposed that employs a voice/data switching method. Tests were conducted to measure the time needed for switching between the voice and data modes, and an investigation was made of user waiting time assuming that the proposed system was applied to the provision of telematics services.

VOICE AND DATA TRANSMISSION METHODS

This section outlines the three methods of transmitting both voice and data, namely, the line-splitting system using a DV modem, the voice/data switching system and the system with separate lines for voice and data.

LINE-SPLITTING SYSTEM USING A DV MODEM

One method of transmitting voice and data is to use a DV modem to split the voice and data signals for simultaneous transmission over a single line as illustrated in Fig. 1 [2]. With this method, there is little user waiting time because data can be transmitted while the driver is talking. However, because this method divides the voice and data parts for transmission over a single data communication line, there are times when the voice signal may be partially lost. Loss of data tends to occur more frequently in wireless communication systems than in their wired line counterparts. A transmission system that uses a DV modem retransmits lost data, but a dropped voice signal is not resent because voice communication requires a real-time characteristic. When a vehicle is traveling in an area where the received signal level of cellular phones is weak, voice communication quality may deteriorate further owing to intermittent dropping of the voice signal.

VOICE/DATA SWITCHING SYSTEM

This system switches between voice and data lines when transmitting voice and data, instead of sending both signals simultaneously. The system configuration is shown in Fig. 2. Voice is sent from the car navigation unit via a cellular phone without passing through a modem. The system switches between voice and data communication, as it cannot accommodate both simultaneously. Speech quality is markedly improved over that obtained with a DV modem because there is less dropping of the voice signal and it is also possible to take advantage of the improved voice codec technology of wireless communication operators. The modem construction can also be simplified to achieve more compact in-vehicle devices. On the negative side, the switching between voice and data lines increases user waiting time.

SYSTEM WITH SEPARATE VOICE AND DATA LINES

While the two preceding methods transmit voice and data by means of a single cellular phone, the third method considered here uses separate cellular phones for voice and data. The system configuration is shown in Fig. 3. Voice is transmitted from the car navigation unit via a cellular phone without going through a modem. Data are sent through a general-purpose data communication modem and are transmitted via another cellular phone. Voice communication and data communication are available simultaneously because separate cellular phones are used for each signal. In order to receive information services with this method, the ID of the cellular phone for voice communication must be correlated in advance with that of the cellular phone for data communication at the information service center. Another drawback of this approach is that users must pay the basic monthly fee for two cellular phones. Third-generation cellular phones are capable of supporting voice communication while data communication is in progress. If that capability is utilized, there is no need for an information service center to correlate IDs because only one cellular phone is used, though there are separate lines for voice and data.

Table 1 summarizes the features of the foregoing methods of transmitting both voice and data. With the line-splitting method based on a DV modem, the information service center operator can obtain real-time vehicle information and the user profile while simultaneously listening to the driver's voice request. Because the operator can grasp the situation accurately and understand the driver's meaning efficiently, services can be provided that are fine-tuned to individual needs. On the other hand, speech quality may be poor. With the system of separate voice and data lines, users must have two wireless communication lines, which means the basic fees are double. The voice/data switching system is advantageous with respect to speech quality and cost, but user waiting time is a problem.

MEASUREMENT OF SWITCHING TIME OF COMMUNICATION SYSTEMS

Among the three methods of transmitting both voice and data, it was seen in the foregoing discussion that the voice/data switching system offers advantages for speech quality and cost, but user waiting time is a drawback. User waiting time in these systems is defined as the interval from the completion of voice communication to the presentation of the information on the in-vehicle monitor after establishing a data communication connection and downloading the relevant data. It is generally known that users are willing to wait 15 s on average. Accordingly, with the aim of determining the reliability and practicability of the voice/data switching system, measurements were made of the time needed for switching from the voice mode to the data mode, i.e., from the completion of voice communication to the establishment of a data communication connection. Both a circuit-switched service and a packet-switched service (i-mode service provided by NTT DoCoMo, Inc.) were used for the data mode, and evaluations were made of the switching time and incidence of trouble. The number of samples used was 182.

SWITCHING TIME TEST FROM VOICE TO PACKET-SWITCHED SERVICE

The test was conducted according to the procedure outlined in Fig. 4. After first disconnecting the active voice line, the i-mode service menu was accessed and the menu was displayed. The time from disconnecting the voice line to the display of the i-mode menu was measured. The transmission speed of the packet-switched service was 9.6 kbps.

The measured results are shown in the graph in Fig. 5. The mean connection time (μ) was 8.17 s, the standard deviation (σ) was 3.08 and the incidence of trouble (defined as connection time greater than $\mu + \sigma$ or a disconnection) was 15.93%.

SWITCHING TIME TEST FROM VOICE TO CIRCUIT-SWITCHED SERVICE

The test procedure is outlined in Fig. 6. As the first step, the active voice line was disconnected. A dial-up data communication connection was then established by accessing the Internet and a text-based homepage corresponding to the i-mode service menu was displayed. The time from disconnecting the voice line to the display of the text-based homepage was measured. The transmission speed of the circuit-switched service was 9.6 kbps.

The measured results are shown in the graph in Fig. 7. The mean connection time (μ) was 25.74 s, the standard deviation (σ) was 3.58 and the incidence of trouble (i.e., connection time greater than $\mu + \sigma$ or a disconnection) was 21.43%.

SUMMARY OF TEST RESULTS

The results of the two tests made the following points clear.

(1) The mean connection time with the circuit-switched service was approximately three times longer than that

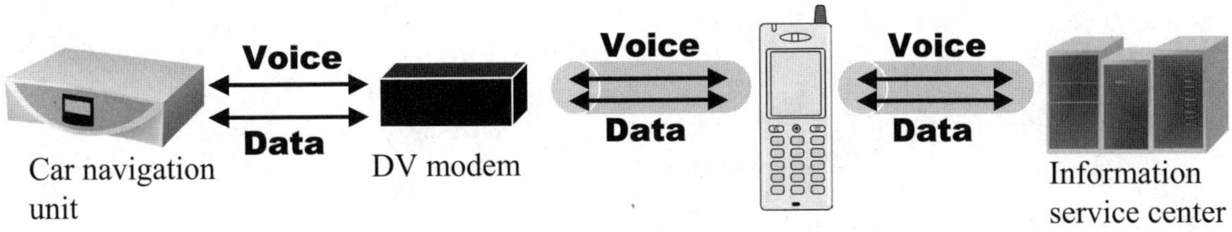

Fig. 1 Line-splitting System based on Data-Voice Modem

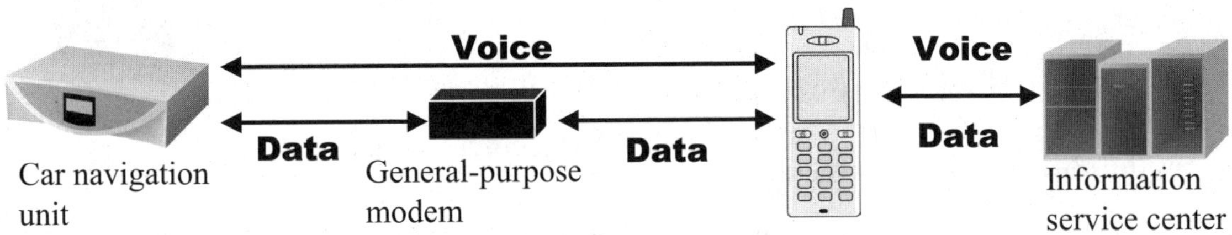

Fig. 2 Voice/Data Switching System

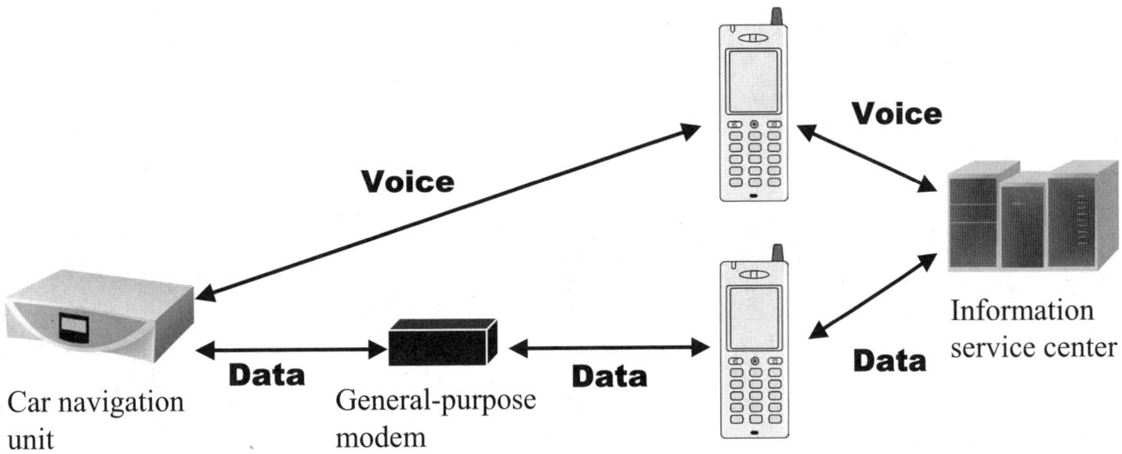

Fig. 3 System Using Separate Voice and Data Lines

Table.1 Features of Voice/Data Transmission Methods

	Data transmission speed (kbps)	Speech quality	Cost	User waiting time	Overall evaluation
DV modem based line-splitting system	9.6	Δ	Δ	○	Δ
Voice/data switching system	9.6	○	○	Not evaluated	○
System using separate voice and data lines	9.6	○	×	○	Δ

○ : Good, Δ : Fair, × : Poor

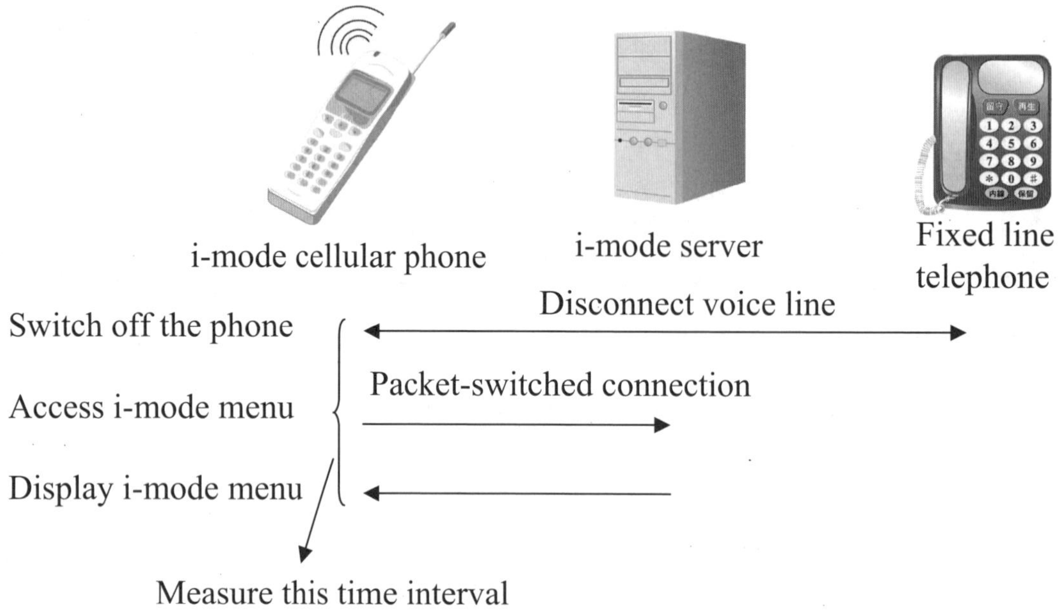

Fig.4 Test Procedure for Measuring Switching Time between Voice and Packet-switched service

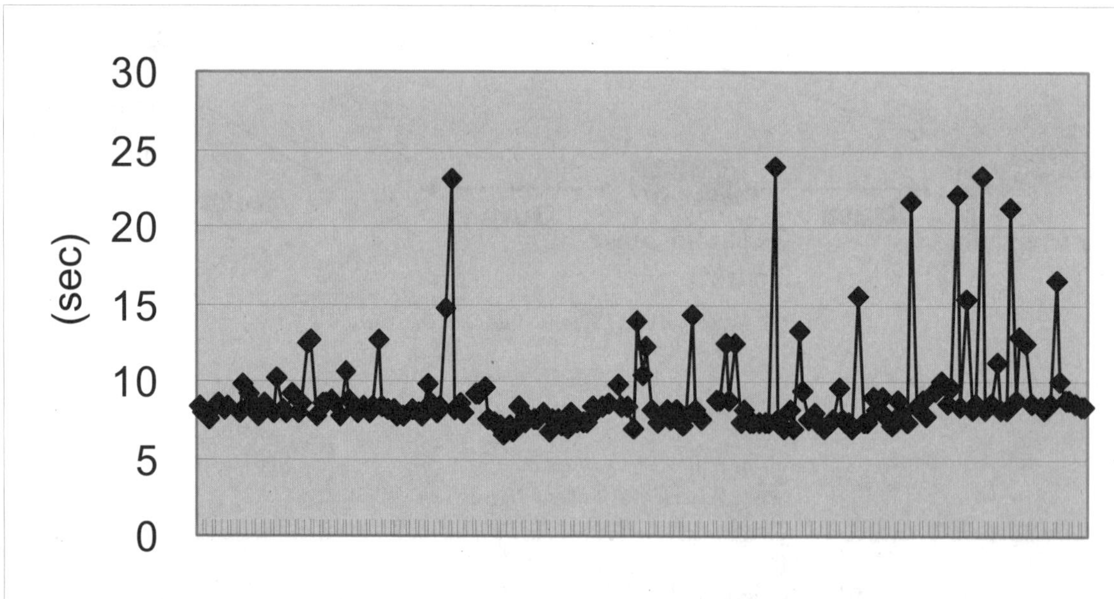

Fig.5 Measured Switching Time between Voice and Packet-switched service (sample number: 182)

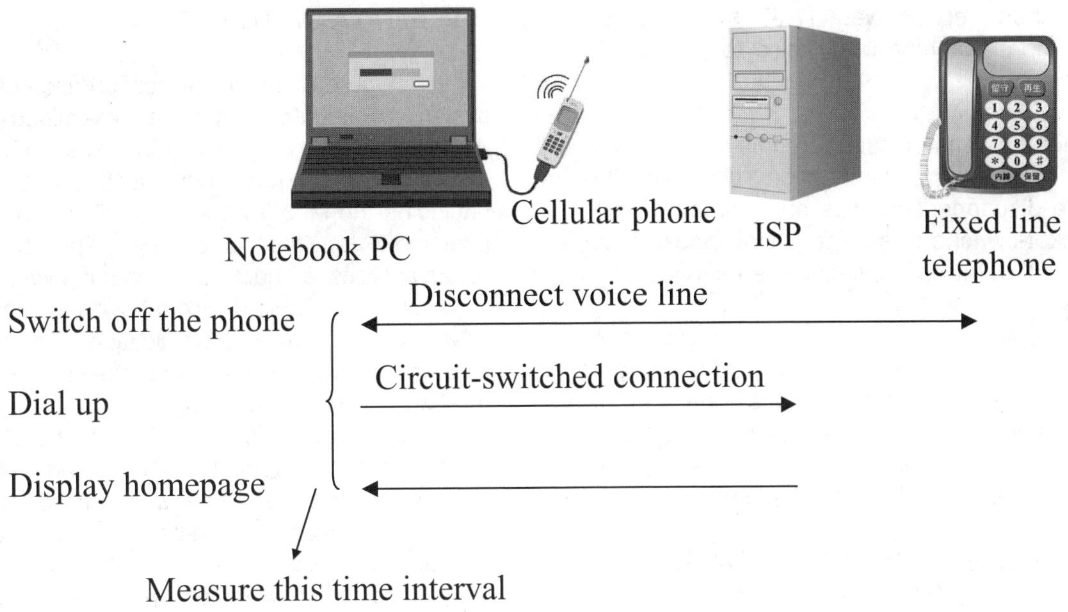

Fig. 6 Test Procedure for Measuring Switching Time between Voice and Circuit-switched Service

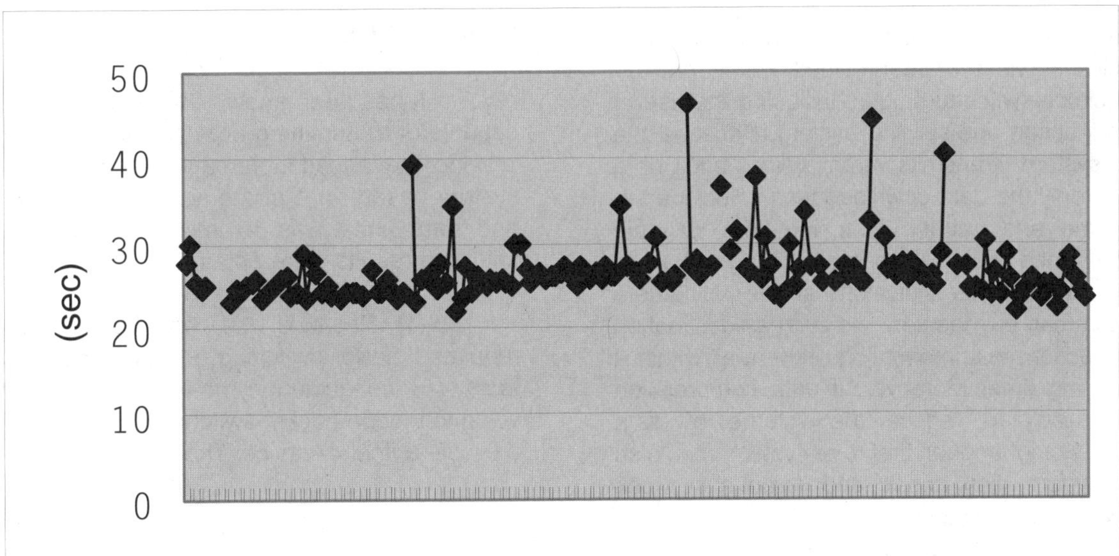

Fig. 7 Measured Switching Time between Voice and Circuit-switched Service (sample number: 182)

Table2 Measured Switching Time for Voice/Data Switching Systems

	Voice→data switching time (sec)	Standard deviation	Incidence of trouble
Packet-switched	8.17	3.08	15.93%
Circuit-switched	25.74	3.58	21.43%

of the packet-switched service. Switching from voice to the packet-switched service was 17.57 s shorter on average than when switching from voice to the circuit-switched service.

(2) The incidence of communication trouble, either in the form of abnormally long connection time or the occurrence of a disconnection, was approximately 16% with the packet-switched service as opposed to approximately 21% with the circuit-switched service.

These results indicate that the use of a packet-switched service, having a short switching time and a low incidence of trouble, as the data line of the voice/data switching system should make it possible to provide service with a user waiting time of less than the 15-second interval generally tolerated by users.

STUDY OF A TELEMATICS SYSTEM BASED ON VOICE/DATA SWITCHING

INVESTIGATION OF USER WAITING TIME IN TELEMATICS SERVICES

Table 3 shows a comparison of user waiting time when telematics services were provided in the packet-switched and circuit-switched modes, including the use of the DV modem-based line-splitting system. Because the DV modem system transmits both voice and data simultaneously, only the data download time is included in user waiting time and not the switching time for data communication. Since users are generally willing to wait 15 s on average, the results indicate that the voice/data switching system can provide services such as destination entry, call connection, text information and e-mail within a satisfactory waiting time. Moreover, if data compression technology is used to reduce the volume of data downloaded, it would appear that the system can also provide image information, music and karaoke services within a waiting time acceptable to users.

TELEMATICS SYSTEM CONFIGURATION BASED ON VOICE/DATA SWITCHING

Figure 8 shows the configuration of the telematics system configuration that was examined based on the principle of switching between voice and data lines. As shown in the figure, both a packet-switched service (including the i-mode) and a circuit-switched service were examined for the data line. The advantages and disadvantages of each data communication method are summarized in Table 4. Packet-switched service offers the advantage of lower communication costs because of the shorter user waiting time due to the shorter switching time. It has the disadvantages that the number of telecommunication operators is limited and also the types of cellular phone capable of outputting data to an in-vehicle information terminal are also limited. Unlike packet-switched service, circuit-switched service offers the advantages that there are no limitations on cellular phone types or telecommunication operators. On the other hand, it has the disadvantage that communication costs are higher because of the longer user waiting time due to the longer connection time.

CONCLUSION

It has been shown that a communication system capable of transmitting both voice and data is needed to provide advanced telematics services. A telematics system based on a strategy of switching between voice and data lines was examined in this study and the following results were obtained.

(1) Because the voice/data switching system requires time for switching between voice and data lines, tests were conducted to measure the switching time from voice to i-mode packet-switched service and from voice to a circuit-switched service. The results showed that for

Table 3 User Waiting Time in Telematics Services

(sec)

	DV	Packet -switched	Circuit -switched
Destination entry	0	8	25
Call connection	0	8	25
Text information	2	10	27
Image information	30	38	55
Music, karaoke	30	38	55
E-mail	0	10	30

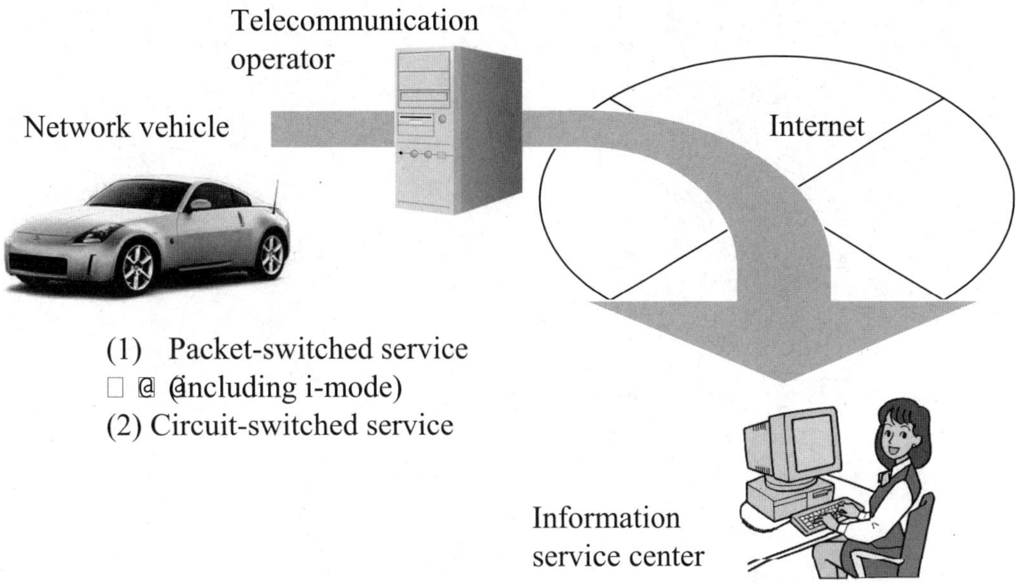

Fig. 8 Telematics System Configuration based on Voice/Data Switching

Table4 Advantages and Disadvantages of Different Communication Methods for Telematics System based on Voice/Data Switching

	Advantages	Disadvantages
Packet-switched service	• Shorter user waiting time •Lower incidence of communication trouble (16%) •Lower communication costs	•Usable cellular phones are limited •Limited number of telecom operators
Circuit-switched service	•No limitation on cellular phones •No limitation on telecom operators	• Longer user waiting time •Higher incidence of communication trouble (21%) •Higher communication costs

in-vehicle information services the switching time from voice to i-mode packet-switched service was only one-third of the time needed for switching from voice to the circuit-switched service.

(2) It was also found that the incidence of trouble during the switching operation was lower with packet-switched service (16%) than with the circuit-switched service (21%).

(3) User waiting time represents the sum of the switching time and download time. It is generally known that users are willing to wait 15 s on average. It was found that a system of switching between voice and packet-switched service could satisfactorily provide services such as destination entry, call connection, text information and e-mail within an acceptable waiting time.

(4) A telematics system configuration based on voice/data switching was examined, and the advantages and disadvantages of using packet-switched service or a circuit-switched service for the data line were made clear.

REFERENCES

1. N. Honda et al, "Information Services for Greater Driving Enjoyment", SAE Technical Paper 980614, Feb. 1998.
2. T. Futami et al, "Development of Practical HMI by Operator-attended Agent", Nissan Technical Review No. 49, 2001.

2002-01-0438

Development of Car Intranet Infrastructure

Rami Baroody and Nizar Al-Holou
University of Detroit Mercy

Salim Hariri
University of Arizona

ABSTRACT

The automobile currently has a number of processors to control different subsystems such as engine controller, transmission controller, ABS controller, lighting controller, entertainment controller, and airbag controller. These subsystems are connected as a single vehicle network. Different vehicle networks can run under different protocols such as CAN, VAN, SCP, DLC, ACP, and J1939. Controller Area Network (CAN) has become the standard for the automotive industry. However, CAN has limited speed to incorporate new applications, such as in-vehicle multimedia, entertainment, navigation, and computing. A new technology, Media Oriented Systems Transport (MOST), provides high bandwidth to accommodate such applications. Moreover, a trend exists to include other functionality, such as access to information in the car through wireless technology to provide Internet access that enables remote diagnostics, status update, roadside assistance, navigation, global positioning, infotainment, traffic monitoring, emergency, safety, and security service.

A system architecture approach to integrate CAN, MOST and wireless communication system into the car environment has been presented in this paper. Moreover, an open and universally accessible architecture of a Car Intranet infrastructure that includes three network technologies CAN, MOST, and Wireless communication has been proposed. This infrastructure can provide an entirely new type of service in addition to current services can be delivered to cars in an efficient and secure way through wireless data connectivity over the Internet.

INTRODUCTION

Electronics were introduced in automobiles with the advent of integrated circuits. The main application of electronics was found in the automotive engine's electrical system, with the next application of electronics found in the fuel ignition control, cruise control, ABS, and transmission control unit. Further, use of electronics was extended to the instrument panel, suspension control, air-conditioning system, and other body control systems.

With advances in (VLSI) and computers more electronics are being introduced in today's cars and trucks, providing many new features such as: navigation system, intelligent highway system support, automated collision avoidance system, etc [1]. Furthermore automotive electronics have been used to introduce other new features (e.g., accessing the internet, read newspaper, send e-email, search the net, listen to music, make phone calls, participate in video conferencing, and conduct remote diagnostics) with all services that are available to people through the Internet extended to the automobile [2].

As the application of automotive electronics increases to enhance exiting features and introduce new features in automobiles, the need for more electronic control units (ECU) becomes mandatory, fast communication links are needed [3]. As the number of node increase, associated costs also increase. To overcome this difficulty, multiplexing is used in automotive applications, with many signals transmitted over a single medium using a time-sharing basis. In multiplexing, a serial bus connects nodes inside a vehicle; allowing data transfer between sensors, actuators, switches, and processors over a common bus. A Controller Area Network (CAN) can be used as an embedded communication system for micro controllers, as well as an open communication system for intelligent devices. Also the extended version of CAN protocol (J1939) also can be used.

As electronics are used inside the car for multimedia applications, such as CD quality audio, surround sound, and high quality video, a high-speed network running protocols that satisfy the data rate requirements for those applications is needed. CAN have a limit speed, which is 1 Mbps [4], which is not sufficient for some Multimedia applications. A high-speed network, fiber-optic bus, known as Media Oriented Systems Transfer (MOST), is a high performance, low-cost multimedia network technology, created by the MOST Cooperation (Karlsruhe, Germany) that uses a 25-Mbit/second fiber-optic bus and is best suited for these applications.

While initial vehicle multiplex applications concentrated on single vehicle-wide networks running certain protocols, additional factors are causing a shift toward the use of multiple vehicle networks. Speed, application differences, costs, new emerging interconnection trends, and other influences are impacting the single network philosophy. The application of multiple vehicle networks is growing and methods for supporting this direction are required. Multiple vehicle networks may result in major changes in the meaning of vehicle diagnostics that may require the use of gateways. These changes may require modification of the original single network solutions to handle new requirements. From the industry perspective, a variety of vehicle network protocols exist, including CAN, MOST, VAN, LIN, etc. Each of these robust, powerful solutions represents a major technological investment in a single vehicle-wide network [5].

In this paper, an open, and universally accessible, architecture along with development of a car Intranet infrastructure that enables each vehicle to access and use Internet technologies for communication (voice, video), entertainment, monitoring traffic, emergencies, etc has been proposed. In Section II, classification of automotive communications, multiplexing protocols, CAN protocols and J1939 are presented. Section III, MOST is presented. In section IV the proposed System architecture and networks Gateways between CAN, MOST are presented. Finally, conclusions are discussed in section V.

CLASSIFICATION OF AUTOMOTIVE COMMUNICATION

The Society of Automotive Engineers (SAE) has defined three distinct protocol classifications, Class A, Class B, and Class C [6]. Class A is the first SAE classification and maintains the lowest data rate, a rate that peaks as high as 1Kbps and supports up to 100 nodes. Class A devices typically support convenience operations like actuators and "smart" sensors. The second SAE classification is Class B protocol. Class B supports data rates as high as 100Kbps and supports up to 50 nodes. Class B typically supports non-real time control and communications. Utilization of Class B can eliminate redundant sensors and other system elements by providing a means to transfer data between different nodes. Class C protocol is used for real time control applications with critical speed and accuracy and supports a data rate of up to 1Mbps.

MUTIPLEXING PROTOCOLS CONTROLLER AREA NETWORK (CAN)

Communication signals are transmitted and received by various network nodes according to a set of rules called protocols. Protocols set rules for coding, address structure, transmission sequence, error detection, and handling. The protocols also define the medium (copper wires or optical fiber), transmission speed, and electrical signal requirements. Protocols for automotive networking cover most of the Open System Interconnection (OSI) model [7]. In the harsh, noisy automotive environment, a multiplexing protocol should be optimized to meet technical and functional requirements of the application. Various network protocols have been developed for automotive multiplexing (e.g., controller area network (CAN), SAE J1939, vehicle area network (VAN), class2, etc.).

CONTROLLER AREA NETWORK (CAN)

CAN is an advanced serial bus system that efficiently supports distributed control systems. Robert Boost of GmbH, Germany initially developed CAN for the use in motor vehicles in the late 1980s. CAN is internationally standardized by the International Standardization Organization (ISO) and the Society of Automotive Engineers (SAE). The CAN protocol uses the Data Link Layer and the Physical Layer in the ISO - OSI model. CAN is most widely used in automotive and industrial market segments. Typical applications for CAN are motor vehicles, utility vehicles, and industrial automation. Other applications for CAN are trains, medical equipment, building automation, household appliances, and office automation. CAN is a protocol for short messages, with each transmission carrying 0 to 8 bytes of data, making it suitable for transmission of trigger signals and measurement values. CAN is a CSMA/AMP (Carrier Sense Multiple Access / Arbitration by Message Priority) type of protocol. The protocol is message oriented and each message has a specific priority according to which message gains access to the bus in case of simultaneous transmission. An ongoing transmission is never interrupted. Any node that wants to transmit a message waits until the bus is free and then starts to send the identifier of its message bit by bit. A zero is dominant over a one and a node loses the arbitration when it has written a one but reads a zero on the bus. As soon as a node has lost the arbitration, it stops transmitting but continues reading bus signals. When the bus is free again the CAN Controller automatically makes a new attempt to transmit its message. The CAN Controller chips complete this procedure, as well as error checking and retransmission of corrupted messages. The arbitration procedure requires that a limited number of identifiers (more than 500 million in Extended CAN) and that a specific identifier be sent only by one node. The only exception from this rule is when a message carries no data. As the amount of data that can be sent in one transmission is limited to eight bytes, the maximum latency time of the highest priority message can be calculated if the nodes are restricted to the use of the same message identifier, once transmitted, until a specified time has elapsed. Every CAN Controller in a network receives any message transmitted on the bus. Each node has to check whether a message is for him or not. Any CAN controller on the market offers some filtering capacity to reduce the processor capacity needed for this activity; with some more elaborate than others DO [8]. Figure 1 shows an example for CAN network within the car.

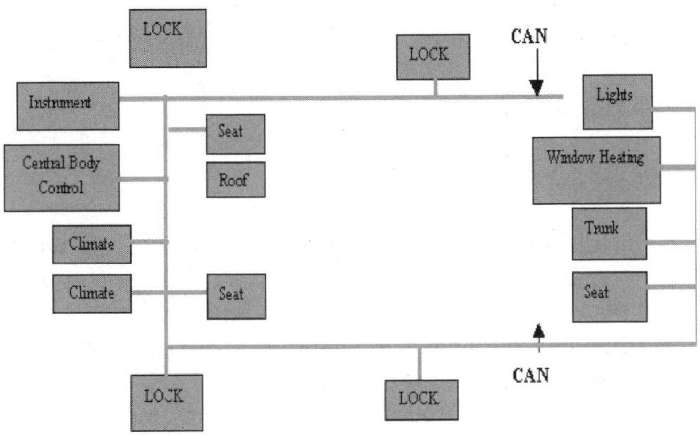

Figure 1 shows an example for CAN network within the car.

SAE J1939

CAN, introduced by Robert Boost, is a network protocol designed specially for in-vehicle networking [9]. The previous version of CAN version 1.2 has been successfully implemented in passenger cars, trains, and factory automation [3]. CAN protocol has been extended with a second message format called CAN V 2.0 [9]. The ASE has accepted this extended version of CAN protocol as the basis for in-vehicle networks in trucks and buses. The extended version protocol is called SAE J1939 [10].

J 1939 is a high speed, Class C type communications network designed to support real-time closed loop control functions between electronic control devices that may be physically distributed throughout the vehicle. SAE J1939 defines all relevant communication layers to support automotive multiplexing. Within J1939, a message is called the protocol data unit (PDU). There are two existing formats for the protocol data unit called PDU1 and PDU2. Format PDU1 includes source and destination address. Format PDU2 is used to send the data frames that are not destination specific.

MEDIA ORIENTED SYSTEMS TRANSFER (MOST)

Electronically controlled systems in automobiles are becoming increasingly dependent on rapid and reliable exchange of significant quantities of data. Within the communication and infotainment field, the secure transfer of high data volumes becomes more and more important. Apart from the data transfer for radio, CD players, telephone and navigation systems, the multi-channel usage of video data for TV-images, video games, DVD, voice-activated control for many functions, Internet accesses from the car, text-to-speech, and e-mail. These functions require a high bandwidth and reliability. These requirements can be met by the newly developed optical bus systems, which allow signal transfer via Plastic Optical Fiber (POF), combining advantages of a high bandwidth and insensitivity to electromagnetic interference with the weight-saving that can be compared to copper technology. This high-speed network, fiber-optic bus known as Media Oriented Systems Transfer (MOST), created by the MOST cooperation (Karlsruhe, Germany), uses a 25-Mbit/second fiber-optic bus is best-suited [11]. The topological structure of the MOST networks is a ring. Light signals are transported via POF from one connected apparatus to the next. In each apparatus, received light signals are transformed into electrical signals, which are then further processed by the MOST-processor. Generated signals are subsequently sent to an LED, which in turn converts this back into optical signals again. Figure 2 shows the MOST networks within the car.

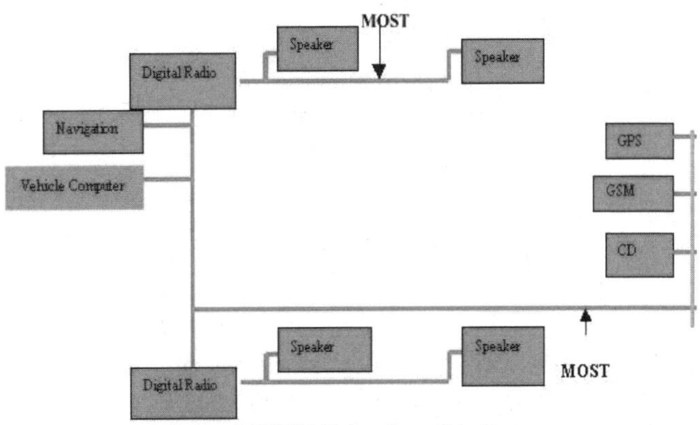

Figure 2 MOST Networks within the car

SYSTEM ARCHITECTURE

In automobiles, many subsystems need extensive interactions for information exchange. For example, an engine management system and transmission controller may work closely together for proper gear change. These kinds of interactions are becoming so numerous that the traditional view of vehicle electronics as independent sub-systems my not be adequate. The concept of local area network (LAN) has been introduced in automobiles to improve communications and interactions among different electronics systems. In applying a LAN to automotive electronics systems, an optimal protocol has been adopted for each system and each system may run different protocols that satisfy the data rate for their applications.

Multiple sub-networks are proposed in this section. Different groups of an electronics system may need different bus speeds. To accommodate this need, multiple buses can be introduced in automobiles, with these buses connected through Gateways. Figure 3 shows the proposed multiple networks scheme for automotive applications.

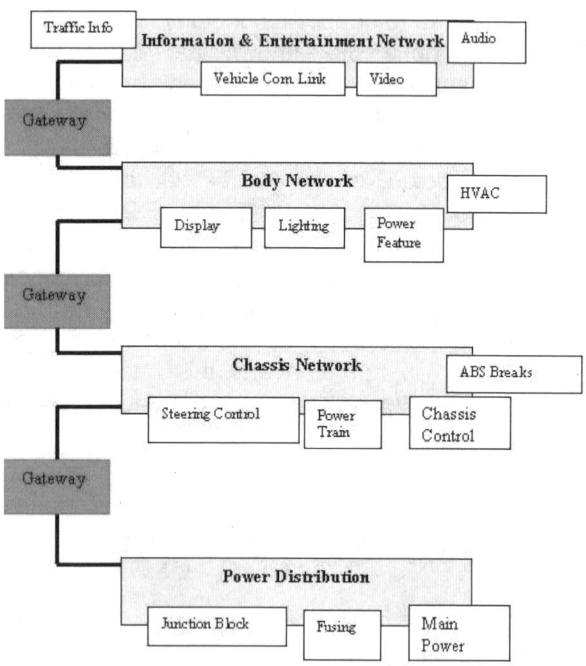

Figure 3. In-car network four Layers architecture

Each sub network consists of necessary electronics devices. Electronics devices within a sub network communicate with each through the local bus. For communications among various sub-networks, electronics devices can use Gateway. Because of the different requirement speed for applications running in these sub-networks, individual sub networks can contain individual protocols. In this scheme, no global bus has been used. This feature eliminates the bottleneck of global bus failure, and provides more reliability and bandwidth for multi-channel usage of video data for TV-images, video games, DVD; Voice activated control for many functions etc. Because the general trend today in vehicle development is to carry an increasing number of information and control messages via serial busses, we proposed system architecture inside the vehicle as we mentioned before in this section and as shown in Figure 3. For technical information and machine control, the CAN bus is dominating. For radio, CD player, telephone and navigation system, the multi-channel usage of video data for TV-images, video games, DVD, voice activated, control for many functions, Internet accesses, MOST Technology dominates. The proposed four basic sub-networks are:

- Information Network. Digital High Speed "Source Data" (MOST,)
- Body Network. Low / Medium Speed "Control Data" (J1939, CAN-B/C, LIN, etc. Multiplex).
- Chassis Network. Control of Critical Power train, Chassis & Safety Systems (CAN C)
- Power Distribution.

NETWORK GATEWAYS

Gateways between CAN, MOST

The Gateway between CAN and MOST provides connectivity from an automotive control bus (such as CAN or J1939) to MOST and is the emerging networking standard for in-vehicle multimedia and entertainment. The basic function of a data gateway is data translation and data routing. Figure 4 shows the network Gateway between Controller Area Network and Media Oriented Systems Transport. The Gateway functions are:

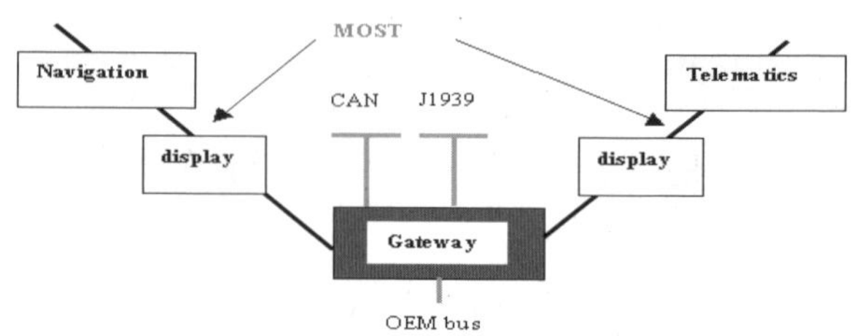

Figure 4 networks Gateway

Connecting two of the same or two different networks. Data from one or more input messages feeds in one or many output messages. The Gateway has the ability to connect networks with different baud rates and can provide a firewall for security of data between networks.

MOBILE IP

To provide access from automobiles to the Internet we consider the wireless communication aspect and the idea of Mobile Internet Protocol (IP), first, at the Home LAN (home, office), and then during travel time (foreign LAN). Standardization efforts have been made in this area already in the Internet community (e.g., the Mobile IP along with the IPv6)[2]. In summary, Mobile IP assigns temporary IP addresses to visiting hosts and directs Internet packets addressed to them at home locations to be forwarded to the point of attachment when a mobile IP (Car) moves from one sub-net to another. Figure 5 shows a mobile vehicle with services available on the Internet.

Networking can be carried out using a wireless technology, with satellite one of the most attractive technologies in USA for connectivity between the Internets from the road

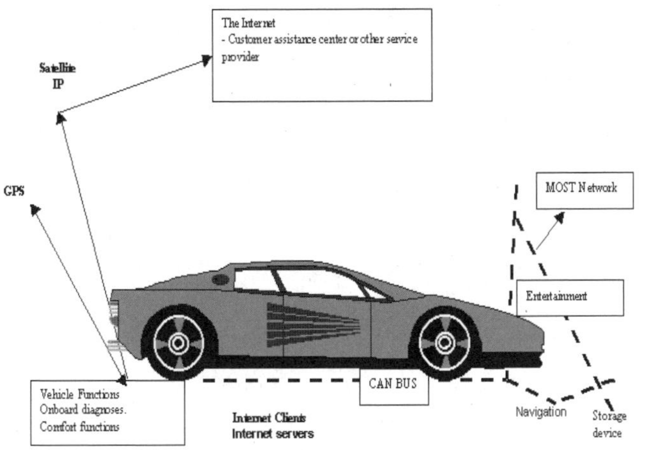

Figure 5 shows a mobile vehicle with services available on the Internet

CONCLUSION

As people continue to demand additional functions and features in their automobiles and technology continue to expand to meet these demands, developing the appropriate networks and connectivity protocols has become a priority for the automotive companies. Engineers and computer specialists need to work collaboratively to produce the types of systems and networks that will allow automobiles to be able to perform these functions at a reasonable cost and with good reliability.

REFERENCES

1. Ronal K.Jurgen, " The electronic Motorist," IEEE Spectrum, March 1995, pp.37-48.
2. Aktar Jameel, Axel Fuchs, and Matthlas Stuempfle " Internet multimedia on Wheels: Connecting Car to Cyberspace. " IEEE 1998, pp 637-642.
3. Tom Denton, "Automobiles electrical and electronics systems," 1995,SAE International, Warrendale, PA.
4. http://www.microcontroller.com/Learn Embedded/CAN1 sie/CAN1 files/frame.htm
5. Bruce D. Emaus " Aspects and Issues of Multiple Vehicle Networks. SAE 1995.
6. Friedrick H.Phail and David arnet, "In-Vehicle Networking-Serial Communication requirements and directions, SAE paper 8603901998.
7. http://www.nsi.fr/can2.html
8. http://www.kvaser.se/can/index.htm
9. Bosch, "CAN specification, ver2.0, Robert Bosch GmbH, Stuttgart 1991.
10. http://www.kvaser.se/can/hlps/index.htm
11. http://www.oasis.com/technology/technology.htm
12. Video and audio applications in Vehicles Enabled by Networked systems IEEE 1999.
13. Akihiro Tanaka, Masachika kamiya and kazunori Sakai " Gateway Application for Automotive Network System" "BEAN" SAE 1999.

CONTACT

Rami Baroody

Rbaroody@ecs.syr.edu

Professor: Nizar Alholou

Alholoun@udmercy.edu

2002-01-0264

The Application of Middleware to In-Vehicle Applications

Hasina M. Abdu and David H. Yoon
University of Michigan-Dearborn

ABSTRACT

With the increasing presence of the Internet in today's applications, ranging from legacy enterprise systems to handheld devices and home appliances, there is an increasing need for a generic middleware that can enable the interoperability between heterogeneous systems. In the specific case of in-vehicle networks, a generic middleware would enable the vehicle/driver to interact with a diversity of applications, including legacy enterprise systems, other embedded systems and wireless ad-hoc and ubiquitous applications. This paper is the result of an initial investigation into the requirements for such a middleware, and possible directions to be taken for its implementation.

INTRODUCTION

Recent advances in technology and the emergence of Internet-based applications have resulted in a distributed application environment that differs from the typical enterprise application scenario. Formerly independent applications must interact to access and share functions and data stored in heterogeneous database [13]. Collaborations with other enterprises, mergers, acquisitions, and the Internet further diversify this scenario. A variety of performance issues must also be considered: a fluctuating and unpredictable number of users, the need to satisfy increasingly demanding Quality of Service (QoS) requirements, and the need for interoperability between existing legacy applications and new web-based applications. To make the situation more complicated recent trends such as nomadic mobility, ubiquitous and ad-hoc computing, telematics and real-time applications impose an additional set of constraints on existing systems.

Middleware solutions such as CORBA [28], DCOM [31] and Java RMI, despite providing a framework to design and implement distributed applications, do not support the ever increasing set of requirements imposed by existing technology. In addition, these solutions are not interoperable, i.e., an application developed in a CORBA framework cannot communicate with an application under DCOM or Java RMI, unless a specialized bridge or gateway is used. What is needed is a generic middleware approach that is robust, flexible and scalable enough to support the rapidly changing trends in technology, without losing the interoperability with existing legacy applications. This *new-generation* middleware should enable the design, implementation and integration of heterogeneous applications, ranging from legacy enterprise systems to embedded in-vehicle applications. In addition, a varying set of QoS requirements specified by users and applications should also be satisfied.

This paper discusses the role of the *new-generation* middleware in enabling open and distributed in-vehicle applications. The following issues, along with possible solutions, are discussed:

- Need to satisfy QoS (fault-tolerance, real-time, etc.)
- Support for wireless communication with remote systems.
- Support for a programming model that enables the design and implementation of in-vehicle applications and integration with external applications.
- Need for efficient management of in-vehicle systems and applications

The rest of this paper is organized as follows. The next section justifies the application of middleware to in-vehicle applications, focusing on their main requirements. The *Related Work* section describes related work in applying existing middleware to in-vehicle applications, as well as approaches that focus on achieving interoperability between heterogeneous application frameworks. The *Proposed Approach* outlines the main issues that are being investigated by the authors and possible approaches to be taken. A summary of this initial investigation and future directions for this research are presented in the *Summary* section.

IN-VEHICLE APPLICATIONS: MOTIVATION AND REQUIREMENTS

One of the motivations for a framework for open in-vehicle applications is to efficiently communicate with external applications via the Internet. This would enable applications such as remote traffic control or remote fault detection and monitoring of the sensors in a car. Figure 1 illustrates an example in which the car driver can obtain information on traffic ahead of him/her through a wireless connection to the Internet. In Figure 2, sensors in the back of the car can detect objects when parking or backing-up. This information can be transmitted to the engine or break, slowing down or stopping the car if necessary. Remote management of in-vehicle networks is another application, as illustrated in Figure 3: management stations located at remote dealers can monitor and locate faults in different parts of the network, without being restricted to a given location, e.g., mechanic or dealer. The challenge does not lie on

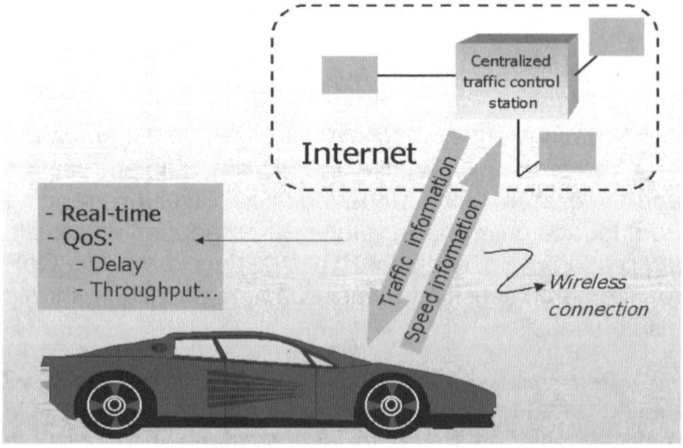

Figure 1 - Traffic control application

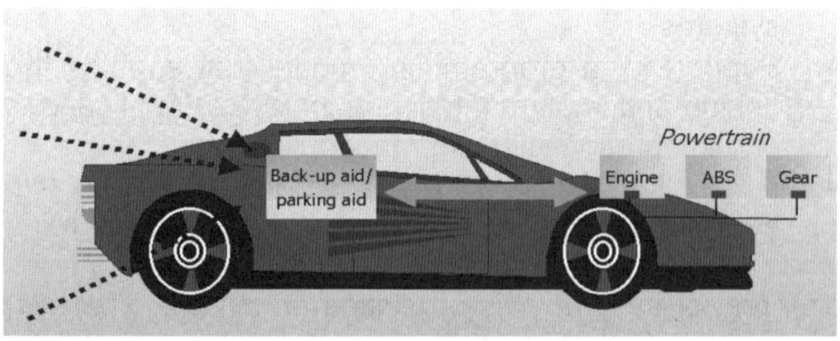

Figure 2 - Parking aid application

the applications themselves (in fact, some car manufacturers have implemented part of these applications), but in creating a framework that supports the modeling, implementation and deployment of a variety of applications. This framework will be the *middle tier* between the in-vehicle network and external applications, thus referred to as middleware. A generic middleware serves as a software bus connecting different application components, as illustrated in Figure 4. The main advantage of middleware approach over custom designed applications is that the former can free software designers from developing custom communication layers between processes. In addition, a middleware can provide a generic and structured approach to:

- Intranet/Internet connectivity
- Fault detection, isolation and recovery
- Satisfy Quality of Service (QoS) requirements, such as fault-tolerance and real-time constraints.
- Enable access to services under different framework/architecture/implementation

A properly designed solution offers additional benefits [24]: *composability*: large systems can be built in an incremental manner by integrating a set of well-specified and tested subsystems; *extensibility*: existing systems are open to incremental modification and extensible without some predefined upper limit; and *maintainability*: it is possible to implement well-defined error-containment regions and to achieve fault tolerance by replicating nodes.

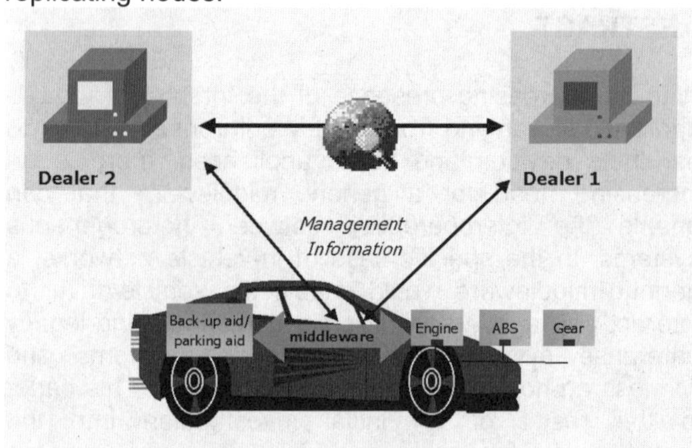

Figure 3 - Sample management scenario

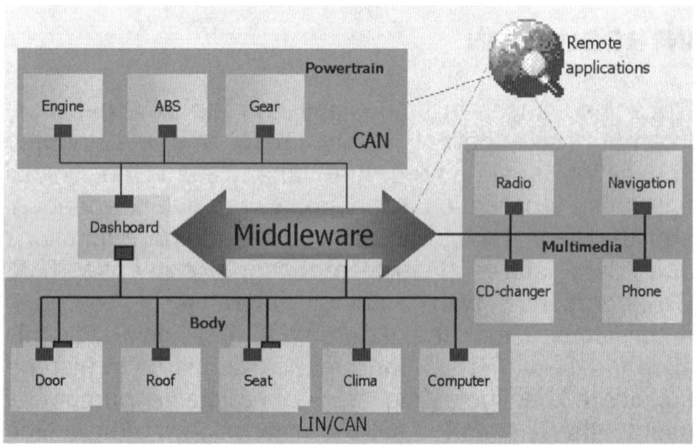

Figure 4 - A middleware for in-vehicle networks

The described functionality of a generic middleware cannot be achieved without software support. Due to the stringent conditions of real-time embedded systems, what is known as the embedded software crisis, open distributed frameworks cannot be employed as easily as in enterprise systems. In other words, middleware solutions such as OMG's CORBA, Microsoft's DCOM and Sun's Java RMI, cannot be directly integrated into embedded systems due the following:

- Most of these technologies assume a point-to-point, connection-oriented, transport protocol, whereas embedded systems are based on group communication.

- As opposed to enterprise systems, embedded systems have reduced resource footprint.
- Real-time embedded systems require predictable behavior, which is not supported by existing middleware solutions.

Another drawback of utilizing existing middleware solutions is that they are not interoperable, i.e., an application under a CORBA framework cannot communicate with an application under Java RMI or DCOM framework, unless specific bridges/gateways are deployed.

There have been attempts to tailor CORBA to CAN (Controller Area Network) systems used in cars. In addition, OMG has recently released a new version of CORBA for real-time systems [30], *Real-time CORBA*, which also supports the specification of QoS requirements. However, the suitability of CORBA to the restricted world of in-vehicle applications remains questionable, especially with the advent of more recent XML-based approaches that focus on interoperability and connectivity, and that consume fewer resources. Related work that address these issues are discussed in detail in the next section

RELATED WORK

We divide related work into two main groups: those that focus on tailoring existing middleware such as CORBA to embedded systems, and those that focus on creating new solutions that enable interoperability with heterogeneous applications.

TAILORING CORBA - Distributed object computing has been a promising approach to support the implementation of complex distributed applications. At the heart of contemporary distributed object computing models are *Object Request Brokers* (ORBs), which facilitate communication between local and remote objects. ORBs eliminate many tedious, error-prone, and non-portable aspects of creating and managing distributed applications. One of the widely used ORB models is the Common Object Request Broker Architecture (CORBA) [28], which is standardized by the Object Management Group (OMG).

Since 1991, CORBA has been the *de-facto* middleware used in building distributed enterprise applications. Language, platform and location independence enables the communication between objects implemented in different languages, running on different platforms and on different hosts in a transparent manner. To access a service offered by a remote server, a client only has to make a local method invocation and the ORB will take care of locating the server, transferring parameters and returning results. If client and server are located in different platforms, the ORB will also take care of any required conversions.

The interoperability between ORBs from different vendors is possible through the *General Inter-ORB Protocol* (GIOP). A specific example of GIOP is the *Internet Inter-ORB Protocol* (IIOP), that includes a mapping to TCP/IP.

CORBA's language independence is achieved through the *Interface Definition Language* (IDL). An IDL file contains the specification of attributes and operations that can be invoked by a client on a given server. The specification also includes exception values, type definitions, constants and operation signatures. The IDL compiler generates *client stubs* and *server skeletons* based on the specified information. Stubs and skeletons serve as the "glue" connecting remote application processes, and can be generated in various languages, including C, C++, Ada, Smalltalk and Java. Figure 5 illustrates the main components of a CORBA framework.

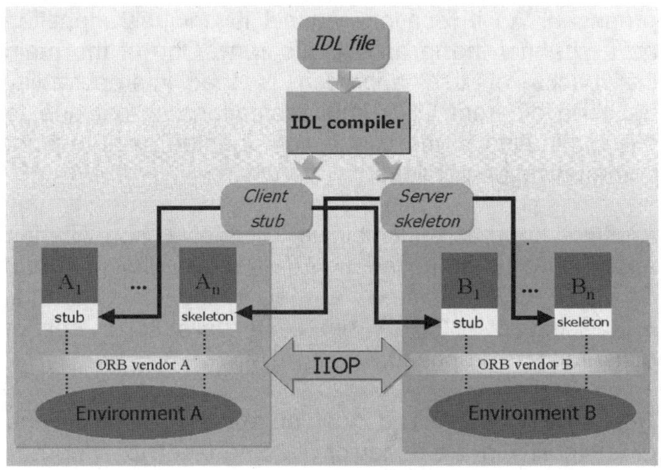

Figure 5 - Stubs, Skeletons, ORB, IDL and IIOP

CORBA was developed for enterprise systems that do not have the resource-constrained environment of embedded systems. In addition, group communication and real-time requirements need to be addressed. Some of the work that addresses these points are briefly described below.

<u>Group Communication</u> - CORBA is based on the connection-oriented transport model and an object reference denotes only a single CORBA object, thus resulting in a point-to-point communication. Embedded systems such as CAN offer a consistent broadcast mechanism in a straightforward manner via a serial broadcast medium and non-destructive priority-based bus arbitration. It also supports the producer/consumer model of data transmission, which is often referred to as the publisher/subscriber communication model [25]. In this context, a producer of a message is totally unaware of its consumers and simply broadcasts messages over the bus without specifying their destinations. Consider, for example, stopping a set of motors. When issuing a stop command, it is not of interest to address a specific motor, rather it must be ensured that all relevant motors

receive the command. Similarly, when reacting to a stop command, it is not of interest which controller has issued that command. On a more abstract level, a sensor object triggered by the progression of time or the occurrence of an event spontaneously generates the respective information and distributed it to the system. It can thus be considered as a producer. There have been different approaches towards including group communication and publisher/subscriber support to CORBA. In [24], a CAN-based transport protocol is designed to support group communication. This protocol makes use of the CAN identifier structure to implement a subject-based addressing scheme, which supports the anonymous publisher/subscriber communication model. [24] also proposed an abstraction scheme called *invocation channel*, which denotes a virtual communication channel connecting a group of communication ports and a group of receivers. A *conjoiner* object, responsible for group management, dynamic channel binding and address translation, is also proposed. An invocation channel is uniquely identified as a channel tag in an IDL program. One of the main drawbacks of this approach is that interoperability between different ORB implementations is lost due to the elimination of the connection-oriented point-to-point communication services.

Another approach, combining broadcast and filtering approaches, is proposed in [22]. In [7] an *Object Group Service* (OGS) aimed at facilitating the parallel processing of CORBA operation calls to a set of consumers is proposed.

Real-time support. The goal of real-time is achieving predictability in the behavior of some external attributes of a system, such as response time to inputs [10]. Obtaining this predictability (or ``end-to-end predictability" of the system) requires that all the components in the system behave predictably. Thus, if CORBA is to be used in real-time systems, its behavior must be predictable. Making the CORBA component of a real-time system predictable means making the time of operations invoked on CORBA objects predictable.

There have been different approaches towards achieving predictability in CORBA and other frameworks [16,20]. In [21], a framework for invoking real-time objects on a CAN bus is proposed. The first byte of the arbitration field in a CAN message is used to define three levels of priority that can be assigned to any message: *hard*, *soft* and *no* real-time constraint. The deadline or scheduling of a message is done based on this priority value.

In [22] the use of asynchronous operations, as opposed to the synchronous request-response nature of CORBA and JAVA RMI is proposed. The motivation being the fact that synchronous operations result in blocking the caller until a response is obtained from the receiver, thus not resulting in a ``predictable" behavior. An asynchronous or event-driven paradigm would not block the sender and would contribute in maintaining an end-to-end predictability.

In [23] an API for real-time Distributed Object Programming is proposed, which enables deadline imposition for arrival of results from an invoked object method, time-triggered actions and non-blocking invocation of object methods.

An extended IDL enabling the specification of timing constraints in a CORBA program, as well as ``fast-track messages" used for time critical real-time traffic, are proposed in [19]. The ``fast-track messages" can bypass layers of software and be sent to guarantee predictability.

Finally, we have OMG/s *Real-time* CORBA [30], with the goal of synchronizing the ORB operations with those of the underlying Real-time Operating system's environment in order to make operations predictable.

Reduced Resource Footprint - With the goal of reducing the resource footprint of CORBA, OMG has launched *Minimum* CORBA [29], primarily intended for embedded systems. The approach was to exclude dynamic aspects of standard CORBA, that are not required for embedded systems, e.g., the Dynamic Invocation Interface and the Interface Repository that supports it.

In [24], a resource-conscious customization of CORBA is proposed for CAN-based embedded systems, by reducing the size of data representation and by customizing GIOP with simplified message types and reduced headers.

FOCUS ON INTEROPERABILITY - The main drawback of existing middleware solutions is the lack of interoperability. For example, an application under a CORBA framework cannot communicate with an application under COM/DCOM, unless a specialized bridge or gateway is used. The lack of interoperability between existing middleware solutions is a challenge in achieving truly open distributed frameworks. This section outlines some of the work that has been done to address this problem.

One of the most recent approaches towards integrating existing applications over the Internet is the Simple Object Access Protocol or SOAP [11]. SOAP is a relatively new development born to meet the needs of developers who found DCOM and CORBA difficult to deploy in a world of the Internet and firewall requirements. SOAP is intended for ease of use and greater platform independence. Although DCOM and IIOP offer a broad range of services (albeit a bit complex) some developers consider that in 80 to 90 percent of potential applications they would gladly trade some features for a simpler technology that "guarantees the greatest interoperability in conjunction with simplicity" [11]. SOAP was developed to meet those needs.

In simplistic terms, SOAP is an open protocol specification that defines a method for using Remote Procedure Calls (RPC) with HTTP as the underlying protocol and XML as the data serialization format. The simplicity is introduced in that XML is the wire protocol, using its text-based format for data encoding. Every method call is translated into XML at run-time. To guarantee uniformity, the SOAP protocol requires adherence to a generic XML vocabulary. The data is parsed at the server side SOAP gateway. Information is encapsulated in an HTTP request in the form of a POST packet and then sent to a server. The calling browser utilizes a small number of HTTP headers that signal the target that a SOAP service is being transported by the HTTP packet. The text-based information makes developer comprehension and troubleshooting much easier. SOAP focuses on the familiarity of HTTP and XML systems to programmers and developers. Some of the main concerns/drawbacks with this approach are:

- Overhead - there is a high overhead associated with parsing ASCII requests. In addition, exchanging
- XML data can be a great toll on the limited bandwidth available in applications running in embedded/real-time systems.
- Simplicity - SOAP cannot perform the same variety of services DCOM or IIOP can perform. Instead, this component technology is evolving in response to immediate development needs in the current marketplace.
- Quality of Service and other requirements- it is not clear whether SOAP can support the specification of QoS or real-time constraints.

Others approaches towards interoperability include:

- XOIP (XML Object Interface Protocol)[26] – describes a way in which heterogeneous networked embedded systems can interface to a variety of distributed object architectures using XML.
- Generalized dispatch mechanism [17] – a flexible notion of dispatching is used to integrate objects belonging to different models, systems, and paradigms.
- OMG's Interworking Architecture [27] – specifies support for two-way communication between CORBA objects and COM objects. The goal is that objects from one object model should be able to be viewed as if they existed in the other object model. For example, a client working in a CORBA model should be able to view a COM object as if it were a CORBA object. Likewise, a client working in a COM object model should be able to view a CORBA object as if it were a COM object.
- Wireless applications for automobile applications [35] – the possibility of using Bluetooth with CAN systems for automobile applications is explored. However, the question is whether Bluetooth can offer the end-to-end predictability required for CAN systems.

SUMMARY – This section summarized two types of work: tailoring CORBA to support embedded real-time systems; and achieving interoperability between heterogeneous systems. The CORBA based solutions, despite attempting to address the needs of embedded systems such as in-vehicle networks, have the following drawbacks:

- They are not interoperable with other systems. For example, the management scenario illustrated in Figure 3 cannot be implemented if the management applications at the dealers are not running under a CORBA framework.
- The *Real-time* and *Minimum* CORBA versions, the only standard solutions, are still in early stages of deployment. Unless thoroughly tested with in-vehicle applications, it remains unclear if the complexity and overhead of CORBA is adequate for the resource-constrained environment of in-vehicle networks such as, for example, CAN applications.

The XML-based solutions and other approaches to interoperability, despite addressing the interoperability issue, present the following issues:

- QoS – The current XML-based approaches do not support the specification and enforcement of QoS requirements. In the case of in-vehicle applications, requirements include, for example, the specification of real-time constraints.
- Network bandwidth - The XML approach may be an overhead for the limited bandwidth available in in-vehicle networks as well as in wireless connections to external applications, such as the scenario illustrated in Figure 1.
- Programming model – as opposed to CORBA, SOAP and other XML based approaches do not provide a programming model to create distributed applications; being restricted to existing applications.

PROPOSED APPROACH

Unlike related work that propose a framework for in-vehicle applications based on tailoring CORBA to CAN systems, we investigate the use of an XML-based middleware to achieve interoperability between in-vehicle applications, legacy enterprise systems, other embedded systems and wireless applications such as ad-hoc and ubiquitous systems. We also investigate methods to include the specification and enforcement of QoS requirements, a programming model that will enable the design and implementation of new distributed applications and a framework for efficient management of in-vehicle networks and applications (Figure 6). The next sections will outline the main points being investigated in this work.

XML AND QOS – Future in-vehicle applications will consist of a combination of embedded systems, wireless and multimedia applications. For example, the future automobile may enable the passengers to view videos or join video conferencing through a wireless connection from an embedded browser. Despite the shortage of the underlying resources, such as network bandwidth, automobile drivers and passengers hope to receive consistent, predictable, timely and reliable services. Their hope can only be realized with the efficient specification and provision of Quality of Service (QoS). The term "QoS" involves [15] the specification and provision of *predictability*, *continuity* and *accessibility.* [15] defines *predictability* as the ability to maintain the contracted QoS and have minimum probability of QoS violations during the resource fluctuation period. *Continuity* is defined as the ability to degrade gracefully and adjust resource allocation distributions dynamically to tolerate transient resource scarcity. *Accessibility* is the ability to access the server from a wide range of devices, including PCs, workstations, cellphones, and PDAs.

A wealth of research work has been done to support the QoS specification for different types of applications. Recent approaches include solutions for setup and enforcement of QoS in middleware systems [8], [14], [15], [34]. An XML based QoS specification for multimedia applications is proposed in [15]. Figure 7 illustrates two examples of specifying QoS parameters for two in-vehicle applications: remote traffic control and remote video transmission. Delay (or response time), throughput and jitter are examples of QoS parameters.

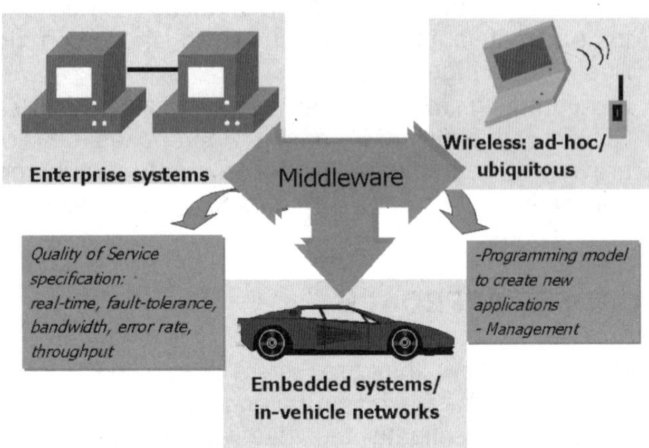

Figure 6 - Proposed framework

Our approach should include the following:

- A QoS enforcer that can detect illegal QoS specifications made by users.
- A QoS specification tool that facilitates the specification task, by relieving user from dealing with low-level system and resource information. This may involve the specification of *levels* of QoS, which can later be mapped to numbers, based on specific system parameters and low-level resource information.

```
<App name = "Remote traffic control">
    <QoS>
        <Delay> 10 </Delay>
        <Throughput> 230 </Throughput>
    </QoS>
</App>
```

```
<App name = "Remote Video TX">
    <QoS>
        <Delay> 10 </Delay>
        <Jitter> 30 </Jitter>
    </QoS>
</App>
```

Figure 7 - Using XML to specify QoS

DEALING WITH LIMITED NETWORK BANDWIDTH – One of the main drawbacks of using XML for in-vehicle networks is the overhead that it can have on network bandwidth. In-vehicle networks and embedded systems in general have serious bandwidth constraints. These constraints are also present when communicating with remote applications through a wireless connection.

We propose the use of a compressed format of XML, such as the Wireless Markup Language (WML) used by the Wireless Application Protocol (WAP). WML is a tag-based browsing language with screen management, data input and hyperlink capabilities. It is based on XML and inherits technology from HTML. It was designed to satisfy the resource constraints of wireless devices: small memory, limited CPU, small screen and limited input mode. These constraints are similar to the constraints found in embedded systems. WML's compressed and reduced format results in reduced network traffic and better caching. The use of WML can also be linked to the use of embedded browsers for in-vehicle applications.

The use of WML presents the same obstacle as XML: the need to specify and enforce QoS. We are currently looking into extending WML to support QoS specification and enforcement, based on the same requirements described in the previous section.

PROGRAMMING MODEL – Related work in interoperability with XML focus on communication between existing applications, but do not address the need of creating new applications.

Existing middleware frameworks are *process-oriented* methods based on a client server programming model, e.g., CORBA, COM, DCE [32], resulting in synchronous communication and tightly coupled systems. They are also based on point-to-point communication, instead of the publisher/subscriber interaction found in embedded systems.

XML, on the other hand, is a *data-centric* method for getting disparate systems to interoperate. Unlike, a client-server model, XML is message oriented, and promotes building loosely coupled systems.

The challenge in creating a programming model for a generic middleware is to give the user the choice of a programming model based on the application in question. For example, embedded systems are based on publisher/subscriber message oriented interaction, whereas many legacy enterprise applications are based on a client-server model. The proposed middleware should, therefore, support both communication paradigms. In this context, the authors are looking into the following question: how can XML be used to design and implement new applications under either communication paradigms?

MANAGEMENT OF IN-VEHICLE APPLICATIONS – Management consists of monitoring, analyzing and controlling the behavior of network components, to ensure that they behave as expected or specified by users. In this context, the proposed middleware should support two levels of management: internal management and remote management.

Remote management was illustrated in Figure 3: fault/failure of sensors and/or controllers in an in-vehicle network is detected at remotely located sites, without restricting the user to a given location, e.g., mechanic or dealer. This involves a wireless communication to a remote system, as well as satisfying QoS requirements such as the maximum delay time in obtaining a diagnostic or in locating a fault. Another issue to be considered is the choice of which remote location to connect to. This will depend on where the car is located, the type of diagnostic, the resource to be managed, and the requested QoS. The middleware should be equipped to locate the dealers or remote sites based on these requirements. We are currently examining previous work in management optimization ([1], [2], [3], [4], [5], [6]) to model this problem and include such specification in the XML/WML schema. For example, in addition to the desired QoS, an XML specification can include the type of diagnostics or resource being managed.

Internal management, on the other hand, involves management from within the in-vehicle network. In the particular case of CAN in cars, network management is implemented by CAN application layers ([9],[12], [18],[33]) following a master-slave configuration. The master node polls the slaves for a given set of information. If the information indicates a problem, the corresponding alert message is given to the user. Complex analysis or control functions that change the state of a component as a result of analyzing the monitored information are not implemented. In addition, most of the existing approaches are based on a master-slave format, being a centralized approach. We propose a distributed management approach, where one or more managers monitor, analyze and execute control functions on the different parts of the network. The number of managers and how their functions are distributed will depend on the network in question, the desired QoS and other requirements. Figure 8 illustrates a distributed management scenario.

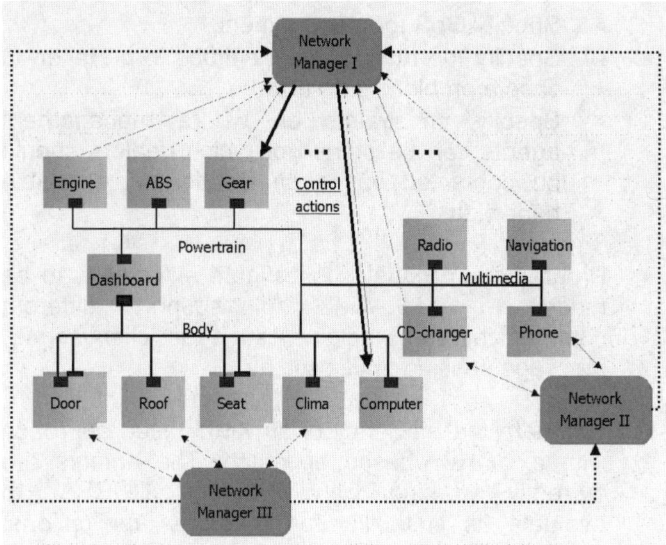

Figure 8 - Distributed management example

As in the case of remote management, the data to be collected, the analysis to be done and actions to be taken can be included in the XML/WML specification.

SUMMARY

This paper introduced the need for a generic middleware and its use in in-vehicle applications, enabling the seamless communication within the vehicle and with remotely located heterogeneous applications. Due to the stringent nature of embedded systems, there are many requirements to be satisfied. In addition, existing middleware frameworks cannot be easily adapted to the constrained world of in-vehicle networks.

We examined existing work on tailoring CORBA to CAN systems, as well as XML based approaches. We proposed the implementation of an XML based middleware that supports QoS specification and enforcement, satisfies resource constraints, supports multiple programming models and enables efficient management of in-vehicle network and applications. To achieve this goal, the following are the steps to be taken:

- Investigate the use of a compressed form of XML, such as WML, to address the problem of limited resources in embedded systems as well as wireless connections.

- Investigate existing work in QoS specification and enforcement, such as [15], to implement a framework for efficient specification, enforcement and execution of generic QoS specifications.

- Examine the author's previous work in modeling efficient management configurations based on a set of requirements. This will enable the user to:

    - Chose which resource to be managed
    - Specify QoS for management
    - Specify the management actions to be taken in case a problem is detected
    - Specify constraints on where management agents can be started or which dealers should be contacted based on location, or available bandwidth.

- Programming model – investigate extensions to be made to XML/WML to support different communication paradigms, such as client/server, message passing, multicast, etc.

- Compare the efficiency of an XML-based approach with a CORBA-based approach. The authors are currently working with *Real-time* CORBA, to evaluate its suitability for in-vehicle applications. The following will be examined:

    - How easily can QoS requirements be specified?
    - How is group communication implemented?
    - Is the overhead, if any, justifiable?

    Both approaches will be compared in terms of:

    - Resource consumption
    - Scalability
    - Interoperability
    - Flexibility
    - Complexity and ease of use

REFERENCES

[1] Abdu H., Lutfiyya H., Bauer M., *"Investigating Monitoring Configurations*", Proceedings of ACM Symposium on Applied Computing, Pennsylvania, pp 366-373, 1995

[2] Abdu H., Lutfiyya H., Bauer M., *"A Model for Adaptive Monitoring Configurations",* Proceedings of the 6th IFIP/IEEE International Symposium on Integrated Network Management, pp 371-384

[3] Abdu H., Lutfiyya H., Bauer M., *"Modeling Management Requirements in Distributed Systems",* Submitted to the Journal of Parallel and Distributed Computing, 2000

[4] Abdu H., Lutfiyya H., Bauer M., "*Towards Efficient Management of Distributed Systems,"* Submitted to the Journal of Computer Networks

[5] Abdu H., Lutfiyya H., Bauer M., "*A Model for Efficient Configuration of Management Agents in Distributed Systems,"* Submitted to the Elsevier Journal of Performance Evaluation

[6] Abdu H., Lutfiyya H., Bauer M.*, "Towards Efficient Resource Management in Distributed Systems",* Proceedings of the IEEE International Parallel and Distributed Processing Symposium (IPDPS) 2001-April, 2001 - San Francisco

[7] Axel M. A., "*Design and Implementation of a CORBA-based Object Group Service Supporting Different Data Dispatching Strategies",* http://citeseer.nj.nec.com/335099.html

[8] Becker C., Geihs K., *"Generic QoS Support for CORBA",* Proceedings of the International Symposium of Computers and Communication (ISCC 2000), IEEE CS Press, Los Alamitos, Calif., pp. 60-65, 2000

[9] CAN in Automation (CiA), *"CAN Application Layer for Industrial Applications",* DS 201-201 Version 1.1, 1996

[10] Currey J., *"Real-time CORBA Theory and Practice*: *A Standards-based Approach of Distributed Real-time Systems"*, Embedded Systems Conference – San Jose, 2000

[11] DevelopMentor, IBM, Lotus Development Corporation, Microsoft, UserLand Software, "*SOAP: Simple Object Access Protocol*", http://www.w3.org/TR/SOAP

[12] Etschberger I. K., *"CAN-based Higher Layer protocols and profiles"*, http://www.ixxat.de/english/knowhow/artikel/hlp.shtml

[13] Geihs K., *"Middleware Challenges Ahead"*, IEEE Computer, Vol 34:6, pp 24-31, 2001

[14] Gill C. D., Levine D., Schmidt D. C., *"Towards Real-time Adaptive QoS Management in Middleware for Embedded Computing Systems"*, Fourth Annual Workshop on High Performance Embedded Computing, MIT Lincoln Laboratory, 2000, http://www.ll.mit.edu/HPEC/

[15] Gu X., Nahrtedt K., Yuan W. Wichadakul D. Xu D., "*An XML-based Quality of Service Enabling Language for the Web*", Journal of Visual Language and Computing, special issue on multimedia languages for the Web. Dec. 2001

[16] Hong S., *"Coping with Embedded Software Crisis using Real-time Operating Systems and Embedded Middleware",* Invited for presentation at IEEE Asian Pacific ASIC (AP-ASIC) Conference, Korea, 2000

[17] Hurwitz B. *et al.*, "*Generalizing Dispatching in a Distributed Object System"*, ECOOP'94, pp. 450 ff, http://www.ifs.uni-linz.ac.at/~ecoop/cd/papers/0821/08210450.pdf

[18] J1939 Committee Draft, *"SAE: Recommended Practice for a Serial Control and Communication Vehicle Network", 1996*

[19] Jeon G., Kim T. H., Hong S., *"Seamless Integration of Real-time Communications into CAN-CORBA with Extended IDL and Fast-Track Messages",* Proceedings of IFAC Workshop on Distributed Computer Control Systems (DCCS), Australia , 2000

[20] Jeon G., Kim T. H., Hong S., Kim S., *"A Fault Tolerance Extension to the Embedded CORBA for the CAN Bus Systems"*, Lecture Notes in Computer Sciences, 2000

[21] Kaiser J., Livani M., *"Invocation of real-time objects in a CAN bus-system",* IEEE International Symposium on Object-oriented Real-time Distributed computing, 1998, http://citeseer.nj.nec.com/kaiser98invocation.html

[22] Kaiser J., Mock M., *"Implementing the Real-time Publisher/Subscriber Model on the Controller Area Network (CAN)"*, Proceedings of the 2nd Int. Symp. On Object-Oriented Real-time distributed Computing (ISORC99), France, 1999, http://www.infomatik.uni-ulm.de/rs/core/isorc99.ps

[23] Kim K. H., *"APIs for Real-time Distributed Object Programming"*, IEEE Computer, pp 72-80, 2000

[24] Kim K., Jeon G., Hong S., Kim S., Kim T., *"Resource-conscious Customization of CORBA for CAN-based Distributed Embedded Systems*", In the Proceedings of 2000 IEEE International Symposium on Object-Oriented Real-time Distributed Computing , Newport Beach, pp 34-41, 2000

[25] Kim H., Jeon G., Hong S., Kim T. H., Kim S., *"Integrating Subscription-based and Connection-oriented Communications into the Embedded CORBA for CAN Bus"*, Proceedings of 2000 IEEE Real-time Technology and Applications Symposium Washington DC, 2000

[26] Nielsen M. K., Jorgensen A. B., *"XOIP – XML Object Interface Protocol",* Center for Object Technology, COT/3-34, 2000

[27] Object Management Group (OMG), "*Interworking Architecture"*, CORBA V2.3, 1999

[28] Object Management Group (OMG), *"The Common Object Request Broker: Architecture and Specification Revision 2.4"*, OMG Technical Document formal/00-11-07, 2000

[29] Object Management Group (OMG), *"Minimum CORBA"*, OMG Document formal/00-10-59, 2000

[30] Object Management Group (OMG), *"Real-time CORBA",* OMG Document formal/00-10-60 edition, 2000

[31] Platt D.S., *"Understanding COM+"*, Microsoft Press, Redmond, Wash., 1999

[32] Rosenberry W., Kenney D., Fisher G., *"Understanding DCE"*, O'Reilly & Associates, Sebastopol., Calif., 1992

[33] Schofield M., "*An Introduction to CAN – The serial data communication bus"*, http://www-ife.tu-graz.ac.at/Local/Tech/Can-Bus/schofield.htm

[34] Vanegas R. *et al.*, *"QuO's Runtime Support for Quality of Service in Distributed Objects"*, Proceedings of IFIP International Conference in Distributed System Platforms and Open Distributed Processing, Springer-Verlag, New York, pp. 207-223, 1998

[35] Wunderlich H., Schwab M., "*The Potential of Bluetooth in Automotive Applications",* Embedded Systems Conference – San Jose, 2000

2001-01-0069

A Case Study in Remote Connectivity to Automotive Communication Networks

Glen Courtright
Science Applications International Corporation

Mark Zachos
Dearborn Group, Inc.

Louis Y. Tsui
University of Michigan-Dearborn

ABSTRACT

This paper describes a case study led by Science Applications International Corporation (SAIC) of Dayton, OH USA and Dearborn Group Inc. to prove the feasibility of employing Telematics technologies to the vehicle test and measurement industry.

Many test functions can be automated through the use of secure wireless technologies. For example, vehicle data can be dynamically monitored on the vehicle and data meeting pre-determined criteria could be downloaded via the wireless communications center. Additionally, central, real-time wireless monitoring of vehicle fleets provides the vehicle fleet manager with the ability to manage multiple tests simultaneously, thus improving efficiencies and potentially reducing manpower costs and compressing test schedules.

GPS enabled wireless systems also provide the vehicle engineer with insight of how test vehicles are driven, their location (whether the vehicles are staying within the prescribed test area), and what the effects are of altitude and terrain conditions on performance.

I. CASE STUDY - INTRODUCTION

Science Applications International Corporation (SAIC) and Dearborn Group Inc. have collaborated on the development and fielding of a Telematics solution for the vehicle test and measurement industry. The solution was designed and built to offer worldwide, Telematics enabled asset management, consumer test data correlation, and consumer wireless data services, regardless of wireless communication protocols.

Within the past year, the SAIC-led consortia has proven the feasibility of reliable, secure vehicle data acquisition via terrestrial wireless data networks and wireless local-area-networks. The SAIC consortia solution consists of:

- In-vehicle data acquisition hardware;
- Integrated Telematics Application;
- Telematics network operations center.

Once the in-vehicle hardware is plugged into a vehicle's diagnostic connector, vehicle data and global positioning data are compressed and encrypted into packets via commercial wireless networks and/or wireless LAN to the SAIC Telematics Network Operations Center in Dayton, OH USA. In Dayton, the data is analyzed, archived, and disseminated to the vehicle design teams. Additionally, test engineers are on-line to verify vehicle test operations and to remotely configure field test operations.

A. IN-VEHICLE HARDWARE

The in-vehicle hardware consists three separate components to form a wireless enabled vehicle data acquisition tool. The parts are: DG's Gryphon tool, SAIC's Telematics application, and a commercially available wireless communications middleware.

GRYPHON

The Gryphon hardware is a stand-alone platform running a Linux operating system with an Ethernet connection (1). The main features are:

- Interchangeable modules that support multiple vehicle networks, such as SAE J1850, SAE J1939, ISO 9141-2, Keyword Protocol 2000, and CAN.

- Modules that support multiple analog and digital I/O channels.

- PCMCIA slots, any off-the-shelf hardware can be supported.

Beyeler and Pheanis (2) describe an architecture for the framework for remote vehicle access. The architecture we have implemented this framework as illustrated in figure 1.

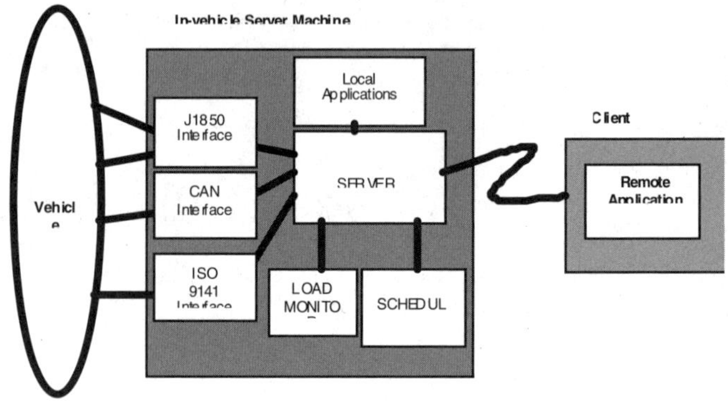

Figure: 1 Gryphon Functional Diagram

SERVER

This main program communicates with the client application program over TCP/IP. The server provides functions for the application to transmit and receive messages to and from the vehicle network. There are various types of communication frames between the server and the clients, including:

- Server;
- Scheduler;
- Load Monitor;
- J1850, ISO 9141, CAN Interfaces;
- Local/Remote Applications.

SCHEDULER

This program unit schedules the sending of messages to the vehicle. The user can specify a list of messages to be sent to different channels. For each message, the user specifies the message itself, where the message is to be sent, how long the scheduler waits before it sends the first message, how many times the message is to be sent, and the time between two consecutive transmissions. Since the messages are treated as data by the scheduler, the client can send any proprietary messages as long as the interface module can decipher them. When used with the reception of event notification, powerful applications can be derived.

LOAD MONITOR

This program unit collects data on the vehicle network. It calculates the average bus load, peak bus load, current bus load and historic load on the channel specified.

J1850, ISO 9141, CAN INTERFACES

This program unit implements the vehicle network protocol, sends and receives messages to/from the vehicle network.

LOCAL/REMOTE APPLICATIONS

These programs reside outside the server. For example, a flight recorder application would collect the data from the vehicle to be downloaded and analyzed later.

B. INTEGRATED TELEMATICS APPLICATION

SAIC integrated a Telematics capability with the Gryphon to remotely control and configure the Gryphon via terrestrial wireless.

SAIC developed an application to remotely collect and store data acquired through the hardware. The application polls the vehicle to retrieve GM Class-II or Ford SCP messages at periodic intervals and monitors the vehicle data busses for exceptions (i.e., diagnostic trouble codes). During the pilot program SAIC remotely monitored vehicle functions.

The Telematics application provides two-way data communication between the vehicle and the Network Operations Center. To illustrate this function, the user remotely activates the vehicle's horn, lights, door locks, and reconfigured the data acquisition sample rate.

Additionally, an application was developed to provide store and forward capability. In cases where data is collected in areas outside the wireless coverage, the data is stored in memory while continuing collection. When the vehicle enters areas of wireless service, the stored data is transmitted to the SAIC Network Operations Center. System tests were conducted where data was collected for 48 hours and stored in flash memory until wireless coverage was achieved. For longer durations, additional memory can be installed.[1]

SAIC installed and tested the Telematics solution on a 2000 Ford Windstar and a 2000 General Motors Jimmy. Vehicles were acquired from local rental car agencies; therefore permanent, invasive installations were prohibited. Access to the vehicle data bus was achieved by connecting to the OBD-II connector via an ALDL connector. Magnetic mount wireless and GPS antennas were installed to support communications and location determination. Figure 2 illustrates the antenna installation on the 2000 General Motors Jimmy.

Figure 2: Communications and GPS Antenna Installation

BellSouth Intelligent Wireless Network

The BellSouth Intelligent Wireless Network was chosen for the terrestrial communications carrier for the pilot project (3). The two-way wireless data service, combining its core network's Mobitex® technology with the ability to connect with other complementary networks and offer multiple host connectivity options to provide the most advanced and robust wireless data communications service available today. Mobitex® provides a sustained data throughput of 8 kbits/sec.

Mobitex technology is an international standard for wireless data communications with networks operating in 22 countries. It is a packet-switched radio technology that provides for a single integrated network that is cellular in design with distributed intelligence. The core network has an open systems architecture that is non-proprietary and supports IP-based mobile data applications. There are currently more than 1,900 base stations deployed nationwide and plans to increase that number to 2,500 by the year 2001.

OTHER SERVICES

Many test and measurement operations require vast amounts of data, many cases making terrestrial wireless transmission of data uneconomical. Also, in rural test

[1] Memory requirements are based upon data frame size, sample rate, and test duration.

areas, where no network coverage is available data can be stored on local storage until the test vehicle returns to a central test center. In the pilot system an IEEE-802.11 wireless LAN modem was incorporated in the Telematics solution. With IEEE 802.11 it is possible to achieve transmission rates up to 11 Mbits/sec.

C. SAIC TELEMATICS NETWORK OPERATIONS CENTER

SAIC conducted a pilot project in the Summer of 2000 to determine the feasibility of a wireless interface to consumer vehicles to transmit integrated voice and data and provide integrated support services through an IP-based distributed contact center environment. Technical issues addressed in the pilot included:

- Demonstration of the feasibility of reliably sending and receiving vehicle instrumentation via a commercial wireless data solution;
- Demonstration of how voice and data may be integrated and transmitted to/from a vehicle via a contact center;
- Demonstration of how automated solutions (e.g., speech recognition, IVR) may be implemented to solve specific customer problems such as remote door locking and unlocking, remote data acquisition configuration;
- Viability of voice over IP (VoIP) to interface with a multi-media contact center providing customer support via the Public Services Telephony Network (PSTN);
- Viability of voice over IP (VoIP) to interface with a multi-media contact center providing customer support via the Internet;
- Demonstration of VoIP capability to support a distributed contact center;
- Investigation of cost savings that may be associated with IP technology over a traditional telephony infrastructure.

The goal of the initial effort was to integrate these systems into a 100% IP-based solution. The pilot project demonstrated and delivered wireless voice and data services, remote diagnostics, remote vehicle horn and light activation, and web-based vehicle tracking using IP-based solutions.

II. CASE STUDY RESULTS

In May 2000 an end-to-end Telematics solution was developed for test and measurement and fleet management applications. The following paragraphs explain the current customer derived capabilities.

Vehicle Polling

Applications were developed to retrieve vehicle location and display upon a Geographic Information System (GIS). The GIS is developed in Java and can be web enabled or be part of an integrated Telematics Service Center.

Unauthorized Movement

An electronic geographic fence was developed and demonstrated to monitor unauthorized vehicle movement. The system interacts with the in-vehicle hardware. When a vehicle is detected outside of its established operational area, an email and/or wireless paging message is automatically placed to the vehicle driver and/or fleet manager.

Automatic Mileage Monitor

Two separate systems were developed to collect mileage information via on-board diagnostics ports on Ford and GM vehicles. The data is read from the bus at user-defined intervals, translate the data into human readable format, and store the data into an Oracle 8i database for manipulation and display.

Route Navigation

MapInfo's routing package (based upon NavTech and ESRI data) was integrated into the Network Operations Center. Each application is tailored for specific geographic regions. Regional traffic sources could be integrated for each fleet operation. However, traffic conditions have not integrated at this point.

Text Messaging

The capability for sending in-vehicle hardware configuration commands (vehicle polling intervals, dynamic information requests, vehicle commands) and driver messaging has been incorporated into the Network Operations Center.

Remote Vehicle Functions: Door Unlock, Horn Activation, Light Flash

Necessary security functions, customer verification functions, and service scheduling functions are built-in. Each of these functions has been developed in Java and has been integrated into a customer contact center architecture augmented by Interactive Voice Response (IVR).

Remote Diagnostics

The data center application supports remote requests for DTCs on Ford and GM vehicles. Additionally, the data center supports DTC exception reporting initiated by the in-vehicle hardware

Vehicle Performance Statistics / Monitoring

The system can retrieve and interpret any message available on the vehicle data bus with Ford and GM vehicles. It can remotely configure the in-vehicle hardware to respond on a periodic basis or dynamically request data from a vehicle. Collected data is presented in graphs, charts, or ASCII data for post-test analysis.

III. CONCLUSION

It was proven that commercial wireless data solutions are ready to support the automotive test and measurement industry. A combination of terrestrial wireless and wireless LAN systems are required to support the full range of data acquisition requirements.

It is imperative that a robust wireless middleware solution is key to providing reliable and secure communications to mobile clients. Wireless data solutions must incorporate security and encryption to extend the corporate enterprise to the wireless domain. The AirBoss™ wireless data solution supports these requirements.

Many test functions can be automated through the use of secure wireless technologies. For example, vehicle data can be dynamically monitored on the vehicle and data meeting pre-determined criteria could be downloaded via the wireless communications center. Additionally, central, real-time wireless monitoring of vehicle fleets provides the vehicle fleet manager with the ability to manage multiple tests simultaneously, thus improving efficiencies and potentially reducing manpower costs and compressing test schedules.

GPS enabled wireless systems also provide the vehicle engineer with insight of how test vehicles are driven, what's their location (are the vehicles staying within the prescribed test area), and what are the effects of altitude and terrain conditions on performance.

Wireless data acquisition enables remote, real-time data acquisition and reconfiguration of in-vehicle test equipment. Historically, vehicle data recorders were installed in vehicles and deployed for long periods of time. With reliable wireless systems, critical data can be acquired in real-time at any desired location. Importantly, instrumentation equipment can be isolated and corrected as failures occur, instead of waiting until the test is completed.

This application is also well-suited for vehicle maintenance facilities (i.e., vehicle dealerships, fleet operators, and vehicle manufacturers, and component manufacturers).

ACKNOWLEDGMENTS

We'd like to thank all the engineers and visionaries for making this solution a reality. Science Applications International Corporation (SAIC) for defining the concept and integrating the technology and Dearborn Group for their assistance in development and integration of the in-vehicle data acquisition system.

REFERENCES

1. "Gryphon User's Manual," 1998, Dearborn Group Inc.
2. Bruce Beyeler, Pheanis D. "Communication Framework for Remote Vehicle Access," 2000, SAE International
3. "BellSouth Wireless Data Overview." 2000, BellSouth Wireless Data LP.

2000-01-0814

Evolving Telematics Systems and Standards

D. Rogers and S. Wallace
Motorola Australia Software Centre

J. Emrich, S. Chaput and R. Noens
Motorola Telematics Communications Group

ABSTRACT

A Telematics System is an end-to-end system that delivers personal communications, safety and security, entertainment and information services to a vehicle with a location specific context. Typical service examples include Emergency Call, Roadside Assistance, Fleet Management, Yellow Pages and Real-time Vehicle Diagnostics.

Telematics has wide ranging benefits for a number of different industry participants. For a telecommunications operator, Telematics may provide the necessary paradigm shift to grow the wireless data market whilst leveraging existing infrastructure. For vehicle manufacturers, it offers the opportunity to obtain an ongoing revenue stream while enhancing both standard and after-market product lines. For regulators, there is a progression towards intelligent transportation systems and their associated benefits of pollution reduction, reduced transit times, and reduced road fatalities. For emergency (including paramedic, police and fire brigades), there is improved locating information and response times. Finally, for consumers there should be an effective service price reduction via economies of scope, and the less quantifiable benefits associated with access to safety and security services.

Motorola, in partnership with telecommunications carriers and vehicle manufacturers has been an active participant in the development of Telematics systems such as OnStar™, Integrated Mayday™, TeleAid™ and Rescue™, and in the development of wireless protocols such as MEMS and ACP. However, with an increase in the technical capability of vehicle-based processors, communications networks, and display devices, there is an opportunity to progress from these older proprietary systems to open evolving systems and standards. This progression would then contribute to ensuring sustained market growth, building upon the increasing market acceptance and visibility for Telematics products.

This paper summarizes the research and development undertaken by the Telematics Communications Group of Motorola in the area of Telematics systems and standards. The paper compares and contrasts a number of existing standards (ACP, MEMS, WAP-T and GATS) in terms of their capability to support a suite of services, and their evolution toward an open standard. In addition, the paper discusses the development of a simulation and prototype framework to allow an investigation of the various protocol options and provide performance comparisons. The paper then concludes with a series of recommendations for further research and development.

INTRODUCTION

A Telematics system is an end-to-end system that delivers personal communications, safety and security, entertainment and information services to a vehicle in a location specific context. To realize this system for a consumer requires cooperation between vehicle manufacturers, telecommunications equipment manufacturers and carriers, content providers, and industry regulators.

The benefits to telecommunications operators from Telematics include an opportunity to realize the long-predicted growth of the wireless data market. In addition, they offer an after-market or standard product development opportunity for vehicular manufacturers.

To regulators, Telematics applications offer a progression towards the goal of intelligent transportation systems, the perceived benefits of which are outlined in studies such as [3,4] and include predictions of:

- 15% higher survival rate via emergency call facilities
- 50% reduction in road fatalities
- 25% reduction in freight and fleet operations costs
- 25% reduction in public transport delays
- 50% reduction in urban pollution

Benefits to consumers derive from both economies of scope through service combination, and the currently less quantifiable benefits of access to positioning information, and safety and security services.

As an interesting aside, a recent survey at the 1999 GSM World Congress reported in [5] that 34.3% of respondents considered vehicle tracking and security services to grow the fastest in the next two years. This was followed by location information, 21%, traffic jam alerts, 18.1%, navigation aids, 14.3%, emergency call 6.7%, and roadside assistance 5.7%.

Key enablers to the acceptance of Telematics, also reported in [5], for GSM subscribers included reliable traffic and location information and GSM/GPS linkage, both at 27.3%; voice controlled user interfaces by 17%, and new cars fitted with standard GSM adapter or terminal equipment, 14.8%.

However, GSM is only one of a number of potential bearer services for Telematics. Others, including analog AMPS, NMT and TACS, as well as other second-generation digital standards such as PDC, IS-95, IS54/IS-136, may also be used for Telematics services. Finally, newly licensed third-generation operators of UMTS or cdma2000 may consider Telematics as a value proposition for churning customers from incumbent operators.

With Telematics services new to the market place, it will be important that open standards are developed to avoid market fragmentation. A case study of GSM shows the importance of open, flexible and evolving standards in terms of market stimulation, inter-working and innovation, and Telematics should adopt this philosophy on a global basis, or minimally on a regional basis. Typically, the larger the region in which a standard applies and is accepted, the greater the potential market base that exists, and hence the greater the potential for economies of scale and social benefit.

Later sections of this paper explore the basic issues of Telematics standards, and discuss prior work undertaken by the Telematics Communications Group of Motorola in the area of Telematic Systems. The final section of the paper then concludes with some recommendations for further work and issues for further consideration. However, because cooperation between participants in different industries, and different industry and government segments has been identified as crucial to developing a workable Telematics solution, the following section discusses the formation of Telematics industry forums and highlights some of the key issues for them to resolve.

INDUSTRY CONSORTIA

The growth of the market for Telematics systems can be considered as uncertain for a number of reasons. One reason given is the large entrenched customer base for personal communications products. The increasing capability of those products also poses a barrier to market acceptance, however they suffer battery power and weight limitations that are far more restrictive than for vehicle devices.

This then associates with a second reason, the need for cross-industry relationships, and the complexities that this introduces. Product branding is an example of a complex issue in this environment and either co-branding, or the development of new brands with an associated market acceptance time are strategies to address this.

Tegaron is perhaps an example of a new brand and this is a consortium between T-Mobil, the German cellular carrier, and Debis from the Daimler-Benz group.

The Telematics Suppliers Consortium (TSC) is an another example of a cross-industry forum. The Telematics Suppliers Consortium includes the Automobile Association of the UK, Alpine, Hewlett Packard, Shell, Siemens, Motorola, Microsoft, Mannesmann VDO, NavTech, InfoMove.com and ATX technologies among others listed at [1].

The Global Automotive Telematics Standards (GATS) Forum [2], a part of ERTICO, comprises AB Volvo, Audi AG, BMW AG, Ericsson, Motorola, Nokia, and Rohde and Schwarz GmbH among others and actively contributes to the standards process.

The reader should notice both vehicle manufacturers, telecommunications manufacturers and carriers, and content suppliers among those listed for the TSC and GATS Forum.

However in addition to the need for cross-industry consortia, the issue of standards remains. This is a complex issue and is likely to remain an issue that requires development work within, and increased cooperation between, various existing standards bodies and participants in the process.

TELEMATICS STANDARDS ORGANIZATIONS

Internationally work is progressing on standards relevant to transportation Telematics by both the International Standards Organization (ISO) and the International Electro-technical Commission (IEC). These organizations are part of the United Nations and voting rights are ascribed to country representatives. However each major region also has its own standards organizations and industry forums and as [6] discusses the standards process irrespective of a region should reflect openness and a balanced (or consensus-based) view of the participants. The inclusion of intellectual property rights agreements and consideration of cycle-time reduction (or time-to-market) are other crucial factors as [7] highlights; as is a market-driven rather than technology push approach as [8] explains.

In Europe the European Committee for Standardization (CEN), European Committee for Electro-technical Standardization (CENELEC), and the European Telecommunications Standards Institute (ETSI) are important and relevant standards bodies. And of note, CEN, Technical Committee 278, and ISO Technical Committee 204 have been specifically setup to address standardization issues for transportation Telematics [9,10].

In Australasia (Asia, Australia, and the Pacific), the diversity of cultures and interests has so far precluded a regional standards organization. However responsibility in Australia would fall with the Australia Communications Authority and Standards Australia, among others. In Japan, the Ministry of Posts and Telecommunications and in Singapore the Ministry of Communications and Information Technology are important standards organizations.

In the US, the standards environment is very different to Europe with many standards of a voluntary rather than mandatory nature. In addition to ANSI (American National Standards Organization) and the Federal Communications Commission (FCC) many combined industry, government and public forums can contribute to the standards process. Examples of participants include, the Telecommunications Industry Association (TIA), and Committee T1 both in the areas of network-side standards. The Society for Automotive Engineers (SAE) that focuses primarily on vehicular standards such as IDB, the Intelligent Transportation Systems Databus Standard; and Intelligent Transportation Systems America (ITSA), an active participant in the development of end-to-end standards.

Whilst this paper cannot discuss the work of Motorola in detail, it provides an overview of selected prior research and development in the area of Telematics Systems.

TELEMATIC SYSTEM MODEL

An example architecture model of a Telematics system developed by Motorola comprises four simple entities as shown in figure 1. The Consumer (representing both the driver and/or passengers), the Vehicle that contains a Telematics Control Unit (TCU), and connects across an air-interface to a Server and Call Centre System, and Content Sources. Content Sources represent access to external Call Centres (or Response Centres) and Information databases or the Internet.

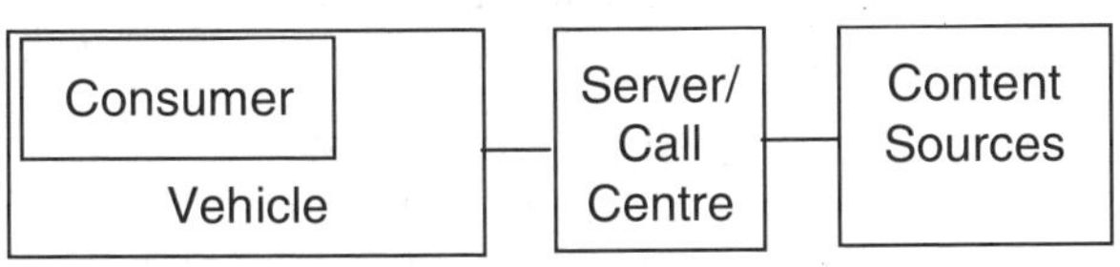

Figure 1. Example Telematics System Architecture

The Vehicle Subsystem (VS) can also be further decomposed into in-vehicle devices as shown in the example in figure 2. The Telematics Display Interface (TDI) or Vehicle End User Interface (VEUI) represents the audio-visual display and input devices (such as buttons and sliders) in the vehicle. The Vehicle Subsystem Controller contains the majority of intelligence to ensure services interact correctly and to control other elements of the example architecture. The OEM Gateway connects to internal vehicle components such as engine management systems, or crash and theft sensors, and door locking mechanisms. The Positioning Subsystem nominally connects to a Global Positioning System, but may also include gyroscope functionality. A Black Box Subsystem may be included to store critical information that can be retrieved in the event of an accident and the Wireless Gateway Subsystem provides communications to the network-side. Together the VSC, OEMG, WGS and PS may also contain the functionality of the Telematics Control Unit (TCU), another term commonly used by Motorola.

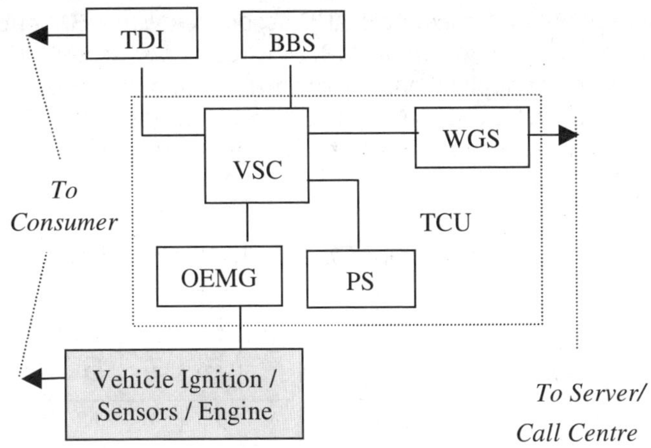

Figure 2. Vehicle Subsystem Decomposition[1]

However it is the protocols across some of these interfaces that are currently proprietary that will require open standardization. Protocols across the air-interface, to content sources, and between in-vehicle components are key examples.

End-to-end protocols are also important, and Motorola's previous expertise in this area has included the development of MEMS (Motorola Emergency Messaging System) and ACP (Applications Communications Protocol) for example. End-to-end is used here in the context of protocols that communicate over both cellular and land line connections, nominally between the Vehicle Subsystem (VS), and Content Sources (CS) of figure 1.

Table 1 below contrasts MEMS and ACP against the newly developing end-to-end protocols of GATS and WAP-T and the protocol for GPRS. Strictly speaking GPRS is a bearer and hence in a different category to the others. However, as an interesting aside, [11] reports that the development of GPRS, a derivative of the cellular communications standard GSM, was driven by Telematics applications. GPRS is a packet-based or connectionless communications protocol that provides higher data rates, up to 114 kb/s, and faster access times (of less than 2 seconds) compared to GSM; and perhaps more importantly GSM's Short Message Service (SMS), upon which ACP is based. In addition, GPRS offers flexible addressing schemes for single-cast, multicast (group

[1] This diagram represents one of several functional views of the vehicle subsystem. The diagram does not represent a physical implementation.

addressing), broadcast, and geographical routing; another enhancement over SMS.

WAP-T, the Telematics derivative of the Wireless Application Protocol is yet a newer development and aims to provide the benefits of WAP such as bearer independence, a standard mechanism to connect to the Internet, and standard content type definitions in a Telematics environment.

As an aside, where an end-to-end protocol is not bearer independent, for example ACP associates with GSM and MEMS associates with AMPS, this can often restrict the services or applications available with that protocol. Table 2 contrasts MEMS, ACP, GPRS, GATS, and WAP-T in relation to selected Telematics services provided to consumers.

Table 1. Protocol comparison against functionality

Criterion/Protocol	ACP	MEMS	WAP-T	GPRS	GATS
Bearer independence	N	N	Y	N	N
Built in security	N	Y	Y	Y	Y
Compatibility with IP	N	N	Y	Y	N
Connection and connection-less oriented	Y	N	Y	N	N
Transaction Oriented	Y	N	Y	Y	Y
Efficient bandwidth use	Y	Y	Y	Y	N
Multiple vendors	N	N	Y	Y	N
Radios with protocol stack resident	N	N	Y	Y	Y
End to end security	N	N	Y	Y	Y
Central location for client information	N	N	Y	---	N
Reuse with new bearers	Y	N	Y	N	N
Supports future applications	Y	N	Y	Y	N
Supports external devices	Y	N	Y	Y	N
Supports multiple wireless technologies	Y	N	Y	Y	N
Supports third party applications	N	N	Y	Y	N
Wireless community acceptance	N	N	Y	Y	N
Wireless technology bearer selection	N	N	Y	N	N
Anonymous Access	N	N	Y	Y	N

Table 2. Services provided by selected protocols

Service/Protocol	ACP	MEMS	WAP-T	GPRS	GATS
Automatic Emergency Call	Y	Y	Y	Y	Y
Manual Emergency Call	Y	Y	Y	Y	Y
Roadside Assistance	Y	Y	Y	Y	Y
Concierge	Y	Y	Y	Y	Y
Locate and Track Vehicle	Y	Y	Y	Y	Y
Points of Interest	Y	Y	Y	Y	Y
Centralized Route Guidance	Y	N	Y	Y	Y
Software Updates/Downloads	N	N	Y	Y	N
Floating Car Data	N	N	Y	Y	Y
E-Commerce	N	N	Y	Y	N
Email	N	N	Y	Y	N
Internet	N	N	Y	Y	N
Multimedia (28kb/s to 64 kb/s)	N	N	Y	Y	N
Remote Vehicle Control	N	Y	Y	Y	N
OEM Diagnostics	N	N	Y	Y	N
Traffic Information	N	N	Y	Y	Y
Weather	Y	Y	Y	Y	N

The evaluation criteria of Table 1, above, were chosen based on the authors' experience with Telematics applications in the wireless environment. Whilst this paper cannot discuss each of the listed criterion in detail, selected criteria have been discussed below; many of which are crucial depending upon the type of wireless environment, and the nature of the services provided.

i. A minimal connection setup time, for example, is important when the size of transmitted messages is small. In a low bit-rate bursty environment, a transaction-based or connection-less design may be more suitable for some types of applications or services that transmit small-sized messages.

ii. The selection of an end-to-end protocol that is widely accepted is also an important criterion because it helps the migration path of Telematics products and it reduces their subsequent time to market. Widespread acceptance also helps products to migrate to newer bearers when they become available. One of the problems the authors' have encountered is that a bearer is defined, but not provided consistently enough for products to rely on it for critical applications[2]. Wireless bearer selection, or bearer independence, are possible techniques to overcome this limitation.

iii. Multiple vendor supply is also an indication of widespread acceptance and this can aid in reducing the end cost of a product to a consumer via the economic benefits of competition. Support for third party applications and external devices also helps to gain market acceptance as the product can then be tailored to meet specific needs.

iv. Finally, because the location of the vehicle (and hence the consumer) is known in a Telematics system, security, encryption, and privacy should be key criteria in any evaluation process. This guards against eavesdropping, fraud, and the misuse of location information, and is reflected by the line items of end-to-end security and anonymous access, for example, in Table 1.

However, in the comparison and standardization of various protocols, both across the air, and within the vehicle and in the development of a logical service description, it is important to develop a simulation framework that provides a method of comparing various options and quantifying any limitations. In the following section, an example of this type of development work by Motorola has been reported.

TELEMATICS SYSTEM MODELS

Some of the previous work within Motorola has concentrated on end-to-end protocols and exploring the interaction of prioritized services for the example architecture shown in figures 1 and 2. This framework was developed using the Telelogic Tau™ SDL design tool interfacing with a Telematics GUI front-end and live content source backends, and it allows the exploration of a larger number of issues in addition to protocol performance.

However, an important aspect in the development of any standard is ensuring that the design decisions and tradeoffs made have a solid engineering and commercial foundation behind them. The Telematics groups of Motorola have been active in this regard via the development of technical models and financial models, the latter of which are not discussed.

The example technical model discussed here adopted the approach of modeling the system architecture using the CCITT[3] Recommendation Z.100 Specification and Description Language (SDL) [12,13]. The ITU Recommendation Q.65 [14] for telecommunications system engineering was also followed to produce a stage 2 functional model.

For the interested reader, ITU Recommendation Q.65 describes a three-stage process. Stage 1 (Service Aspects) produces a prose description of a service, a static description of the service using attributes, and a graphical dynamic description of the service.

Stage 2 (Functional Network Aspects) then derives a functional model, information flow diagrams[4], SDL diagrams for functional entities, and a list of functional entity actions. These functional entities are then allocated to physical locations. The final stage of the process, Stage 3 (Network Implementation Aspects), produces a detailed design of both the protocols and message formats used, and the switching and service nodes.

In summary, the developers of the model considered the use of SDL and an associated CASE tool, Telelogic Tau 3.3, to be beneficial to the modeling approach because of:

1. a flow chart design style,
2. the inclusion of modular building blocks for encapsulation,
3. strict and defined syntax, semantics, and scope rules,
4. auto-generated C++ code,
5. the ability to interface external applications with the model, and
6. the ability to layer, abstract, or hide different levels of complexity as necessary.

The last point (6) is important for the understanding of both the architecture of the model and any message sequence charts produced via simulation. Point (5) is also important as it allowed the software model to be converted piece-meal to a prototype system.

This then allowed the Integrated Telematics Services Model [15] to be distributed into network side and vehicle side models that communicated via a TCP/IP link. Connections were also established via Internet links from Motorola Australia to an SQL database in Motorola India that supplied Stock information for that service.

Similarly the vehicle side of the model interfaced with the Motorola Oncore™ Global Positioning System (GPS) unit [16]. This provided information that could be used as part of an emergency call, roadside assistance, or navigation service and it highlighted some limitations of the CASE tool used; limitations that were subsequently corrected by Telelogic.

The example message sequence chart in figure 3 shows how this type of model can be used to examine various

[2] This may make the bearer a suitable choice for less critical applications, but not for those such as Emergency Call where life may be threatened.

[3] CCITT was later renamed ITU-T a subgroup of the International Telecommunications Union, an organization of the United Nations for global telecommunications standards issues and frequency assignments.

[4] These are equivalent to Message Sequence Charts or Sequence Diagrams.

protocols via the message flows. This figure shows the messages used to start the vehicle, request the service, initialize the communications link, request content, and then return this to the vehicle end user for display before closing the communications link.

The reader should note however that not only must a protocol perform for an individual service, but also perform for the interaction of services should a higher-priority service be invoked. That is, if an emergency or roadside assistance call occurs whilst a stock service is active, the emergency call or roadside assistance call must proceed until completion before the stock service is potentially resumed at an appropriate point.

Tracing through more detailed Message Sequence Charts allows a Test Engineer to verify that the interaction of prioritized services is consistent with any specifications for the system.

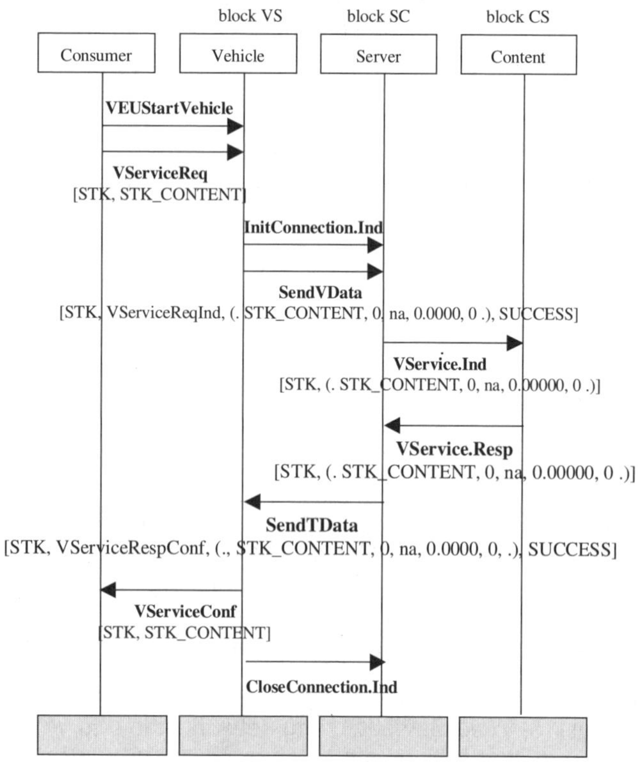

Figure 3. Example Message Sequence Chart

The measurement of delays with the real-time simulation option of the CASE tool also provides an indication of call set-up times and highlights any bottlenecks in the performance of a protocol. Hence this provides an important framework for developers to examine, compare, and optimize the operation of various proposed Telematics standards.

In the following section of this paper the authors discuss another extension to the model and hence prototype, the inclusion of a vehicle side Graphical User Interface (GUI).

HUMAN FACTORS

Message Sequence Charts provide a convenient tool for Engineers to verify the logical operation of a protocol or service and to measure their performance using common attributes. However, any performance requirements included in a standard need to be understood in terms of human interaction. By interfacing a graphical user interface with the example model, the developers were able to explore how information should be presented to a user in the vehicle. For the prototype developed, the Interactive Integrated Telematics Services Model (IITSM) [17], the Vehicle End User Interface GUI was a menu-driven text-based display as shown by figure 4.

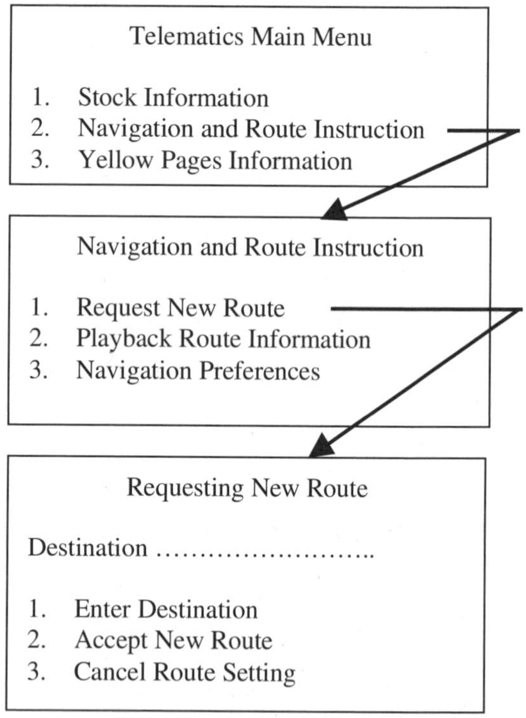

Figure 4. Vehicle End User Interface- Example Menus

Replacing this text-based display with alternatives, for example a display with graphical functionality for navigation and route instruction, or more restricted capabilities such as LED displays, allows the VEUI to be emulated for various platform or market segment options.

This then provides a convenient and cost-effective framework for initial utilization, human-computer interaction (HCI), or ergonomics studies. Whilst these studies have not been conducted by the authors of this paper another group within Motorola is investigating human factors with regard to Telematics systems.

Text-to-speech conversion capabilities have also been included with the prototype developed and this can be extended further to explore voice recognition (or speech-to-text) options as a method of improving the safety of the system in the context of a vehicle. That is, minimizing the time required by the driver to take their eyes off the road to use the system.

In further work, this type of prototype can be used to rapidly examine the operation of proposed Telematics protocols or standards. The results of which can then be fed into the standards process for discussion as appropriate. In addition it can be used within Motorola to explore various product options as a method of market differentiation.

CONCLUSION

In conclusion, this paper has explored a variety of issues in relation to Telematics systems and standards.

The need for open, flexible, and evolving standards is a key recommendation of this paper. Another key recommendation is that the standards process be market focussed, but built upon a thorough and solid technical understanding. The paper discussed an example of one of several approaches used by Motorola to gain this understanding, additionally, highlighting the use of CASE tools to simplify the development process.

Applications for this framework such as the evaluation of current standards were discussed, and a comparison provided of a variety of current Telematics protocols. In addition the use of the framework for human computer interaction, or utilization studies was highlighted. This type of framework may therefore be used as a method of actively contributing to the Telematics standardization debate, an important debate given the relationships between standards and market growth or fragmentation.

The relationship of market growth and standards was highlighted in the paper by reference to GSM, and barriers to this growth such as the complexity of industry relationships have been discussed. This then led the paper to overview various new cross-industry forums for Telematics and to acknowledge their important contributions in the standardization process.

The introduction of the paper also provided a discussion on the benefits that Telematics systems provide to various participants and stakeholders. However, as already emphasized, open, flexible and evolving standards and systems will be the key to market growth.

ACKNOWLEDGMENTS

Whilst this paper only lists five authors, the authors acknowledge that there have been a number of other people within the Motorola organization who have contributed to the developments reported here and provided editorial comments upon the paper. Their assistance and contributions are both acknowledged and have been appreciated.

Dr Rogers also thanks Mr John Leske of the Centre for Telecommunications and Information Netwoking, previously ETSI PT12 Secretariat on GPRS, for information provided on the GPRS standard.

REFERENCES

1. "Telematics Suppliers Consortium", available at http://www.telematics-suppliers.org/supp.htm accessed 15 July 1999, [6 pages].
2. "Members", available at http://gatsforum.com/members/members.htm accessed 18 August 1999, [2 pages]
3. "European Telematics: Advancing the Information Society", Telematics Applications Programme, Conference Proceedings, Barcelona Spain, 4-7 February, 1998, [105 pages].
4. "Telematics Application Program (1994-1998)", European Commission DGXIII, available at http://wise.felk.cvut.cz/Mirror/globals/ecinfo/frameworks/4th/telematics/WorkProgramme.html, [167 pages].
5. "Calling all cars", Hibberd M., Mobile Communications International, April 1999, pp.42-44
6. "A U.S. Perspective on Standards Development", Reilly A.K., IEEE Communications Magazine, January 1994, pp.30-36.
7. "Global Standards", Peterson G.H., Dvorak C.A., IEEE Communications Magazine, January 1994, pp.68-70.
8. "Shaping Future Telecommunications: The Challenge of Global Stabdardization", Irmer T., IEEE Communications Magazine, January 1994, pp.20-28.
9. "Standardisation", ERTICO, available at http://www.ertico.com/what_is/standcon.htm [1 page]
10. "TT Standards News", Issues 1,2,3, and 4 available at http://www.ertico.com/what_is/standcon.htm
11. "Traffic Management Improvement by Integrating Modern Communication Systems", Schulz W., IEEE Communications Magazine, October 1996, pp.56-60.
12. "SDL: Formal Object-oriented Language for Communicating Systems", Ellsberger J., Hogrefe D., Sarma A., Prentice Hall, London, 1997.
13. "CCITT Recommendation Z.100: Specification and Description Language SDL", Blue Book, Volume X.1-X.5, 1988, ITU General Secretariat Sales Section, Places des Nations, CH-1211 Geneva 20.
14. "ITU-T Recommendation Q.65", International Telecommunications Union, 1993.
15. "Integrated Telematics Services Model: AN Overview of the Model and SDL Design Process", Rogers D., Motorola Software Engineering Symposium SES'99, Fort Lauderdale, Florida USA, June 21-24, 1999, [8 pages].
16. "Oncore GPS User's Guide", Motorola, 1997.
17. "Interactive Integrated Telematics Services Model", Rogers D., Merchant R., Sivadas M., Rasiah A., Motorola Simulation and Modeling Symposium SMS'99, Fort Lauderdale Florida USA, June 21-24, 1999, [8 pages].

CONTACT

Dr Derek Rogers,
Motorola Australia Software Centre, 2 Second Avenue, Technology Park – The Levels, Adelaide, South Australia, Australia, 5095.

Mr Steve Chaput,
Motorola Telematics Communications Group, 4100 Commercial Drive, Northbrook, Chicago, Illinois, 60062.

GLOSSARY

Acronym	Definition
ACP	Applications Communication Protocol
AMPS	Advanced Mobile Phone System
ANSI	American National Standards Institute
BBS	Black Box Subsystem
CASE	Computer Aided Software Environment
CCITT	Consultative Committee of International Telegraphy and Telephony
CEN	European Committee for Standardization
CENELEC	European Committee for Electro-technical Standardization
CS	Content Source(s)
ETSI	European Telecommunications Standards Institute
FCC	Federal Communications Commission
GATS	Global Automotive Telematics Standard
GPRS	Generalized Packet Radio Service
GPS	Global Positioning System
GSM	Global System for Mobile Communications
GUI	Graphical User Interface
HCI	Human Computer Interaction
IDB	Intelligent Transportation Systems Databus
IEC	International Electro-technical Commission
IITSM	Interactive Integrated Telematics Services Model
ISO	International Standards Organization
IS-XX	Interim Standard number XX
ITSA	Intelligent Transportation Systems America
ITU	International Telecommunications Union
LED	Light Emitting Diode
MEMS	Motorola Emergency Messaging System
NMT	Nordic Mobile Telephone System
OEM	Original Equipment Manufacturer
OEMG	OEM Gateway
PDC	Personal Digital Cellular
PS	Positioning Subsystem
SAE	Society of Automotive Engineers
SDL	Specification and Description Language
SMS	Short Message Service
SQL	Structured Query Language
TACS	Total Access Communications System
TCP/IP	Transmission Control Protocol / Internet Protocol
TIA	Telecommunications Industry Association
TIGS	Telematics Internet Gateway Subsystem *(Server / Call Centre)*
UMTS	Universal Mobile Telecommunications System
VEUI	Vehicle End User Interface
VS	Vehicle Subsystem
VSC	Vehicle Subsystem Controller
WAP	Wireless Application Protocol
WAP-T	Telematics Derivative of WAP
WGS	Wireless Gateway Subsystem

2000-01-0812

A Distributed Java Architecture for Telematics Services

Parvathy Bhaskaran and Mark Clayton
Motorola Inc

ABSTRACT

This paper describes a robust, secure Java-based Telematics platform that enables the rapid development and deployment of distributed infotainment and safety service applications. Such a distributed architecture allows the Telematics client in the vehicle to offload data- and compute-intensive operations to the server, while executing location-sensitive and vehicle-centric services onboard. Further, by careful segmentation of the client and server modules, multiple tiers of the client product can be designed and rapidly assembled, ranging from inexpensive, thin clients to costlier, self-contained ones. By basing it on Java, we harness and empower a large development community, while reaping all the benefits of Java.

INTRODUCTION

The automobile space is one of the few remaining untapped frontiers of the information revolution. Currently, there is no standard architecture that allows safety, information and entertainment services to be delivered to the automobile. Most systems today limit themselves to simple emergency services that involve intervention by a human operator. More elaborate ones like navigation are autonomous; they are contained in the car and do not lend themselves to deliver timely information like traffic updates, road detours, etc.

In the following sections we describe and examine the proposed distributed Java Telematics platform in terms of its key enabling components, both on the client and the server. These components would be available as Java API classes and interfaces that applications would be built upon.

WHY JAVA

THE LANGUAGE – The Java language offers true portability across hardware platforms and different operating systems. Once an infotainment application or service is developed on this Java platform, it can be seamlessly made available on a multitude of client hardware with the availability of a standard Java VM and APIs as the only constraint. The ability to upgrade hardware without changing code results in huge cost savings in the development and time-to-market areas.

An extensive set of libraries currently available (security, UI, networking, database), and new ones being developed just for Telematics, provide a rich foundation for rapid application development. These libraries are common across vendors, ensuring that precious development costs are not locked into a proprietary platform. For example, the recently announced kJava, for small embedded devices, ran on several devices at its introduction including the Motorola Pagewriter and the 3Com PalmV.

The inherent strengths of the Java language are additional pluses. Its strong typing, enforcement of object oriented data protection, memory management are some examples of built-in protection against common programming errors. In addition, the security provided by the byte-code verifier, an intrinsic part of the VM, helps ensure that questionable applications are avoided.

THE TOOLS – Multi-vendor support and strong competition has resulted in a proliferation of tools, many of them free, and a rich programming and development environment. The breadth of the available tool-sets is impressive and includes pre-compilers as well as selective and JIT compilers. Apart from the standard Java Development Kit, complete development environments are available from many vendors. These include advanced scripting languages (which later generate standard Java), debuggers, applet libraries and front-ends to most commercial databases.

The Java VM area is also very vibrant. Currently, several JVMs are available from different vendors. While some of these are not officially certified as 100% Java by Sun, standard Java programs run interchangeably on most of them. More importantly, this competition has driven forward improvements in the JVM in terms of performance and features, and engendered more favorable licensing terms.

THE DIVERSITY – Java has gone beyond Web applications and garnered wide acceptance in diverse industries including telephony (JavaPhone [4], JTAPI [5]), smartcards (JavaCard [9]), speech and audio/video entertainment (JSAPI/JSML [7], Java Media Framework [6], JavaTV [8]). Java is used in a wide variety of devices (phones, pagers, set top boxes, printers, remote controls, hand-held computers) including the concept car at JavaOne in 1999. While the latter may not be the how Java ultimately exists in the automobile, the diversity of Java makes a compelling case for its use.

Until recently, due to the processing requirements of multi-media programs and the performance constraints of Java, most multi-media APIs were available only in native form. But with availability of more powerful and specialized hardware coupled with improvements in Java performance, many voice recognition (VR) and text-to-speech (TTS) systems are now standardizing on Java as are audio and video software.

To ensure a rich and extensible framework for developing infotainment services in the automobile, many of the device classes (phones, pagers, streaming audio/video, smartcards) mentioned earlier need to be supported. Unless the current internal automobile architectures can standardize on a single internal operating system like Linux or WinCE, it is prudent to harness the necessary diversity through Java.

THE COMMUNITY – A Java based development framework, in addition to the other factors listed above, may be used to harness a large and enthusiastic development community that can rapidly offer a large and diverse portfolio of application services for the automotive space. Conventions like JavaOne (the largest programming convention in the world) and active internet newsgroups facilitate communication in the Java community. The Sun Developer Connection [1] program, a comprehensive set of resources and information tailored to meet the needs of Sun's Java developer community, boasts more than a million members, making it the fastest growing and second largest developer community in the industry (IBM [3] and HP [2] have their own Java developer groups). In addition, the Java Community Process [11] empowers the creation of open standards with input from diverse industry and academic sources, through draft reviews as well as expert, working and discussion groups.

While it may appear that multiple developers groups (Sun, HP, IBM, etc) fragment the community and pull it in different directions, the actual reality is that the community pressures from customers tasting the benefits of standardization and platform independence is forcing more convergence: IBM and HP are now working on aligning more closely with 100% Java efforts.

JAVA TELMATICS APIS

In addition to the general purpose Java libraries available today, the following telematics specific ones are needed to provide a complete and rich environment for developing distributed telmatics applications for the vehicle:

- Location Services API
- Abstract UI
- Profile Manager
- Network Interface Manager
- Service Discovery/Lookup
- Application Management
- Data Synchronization

These APIs are explained in more detail in the following sections.

CLIENT SERVER ARCHITECTURE

Figure 1 shows a distributed telematics architecture, where the mobile client (vehicle) uses a wireless link (typically cellular) to communicate with a remote server to access services. It also uses a wireless link (IR, Bluetooth [14]) to communicate with "accommodated" devices such as a PDA or laptop, as well as local proximity servers like a kiosk at a dealership.

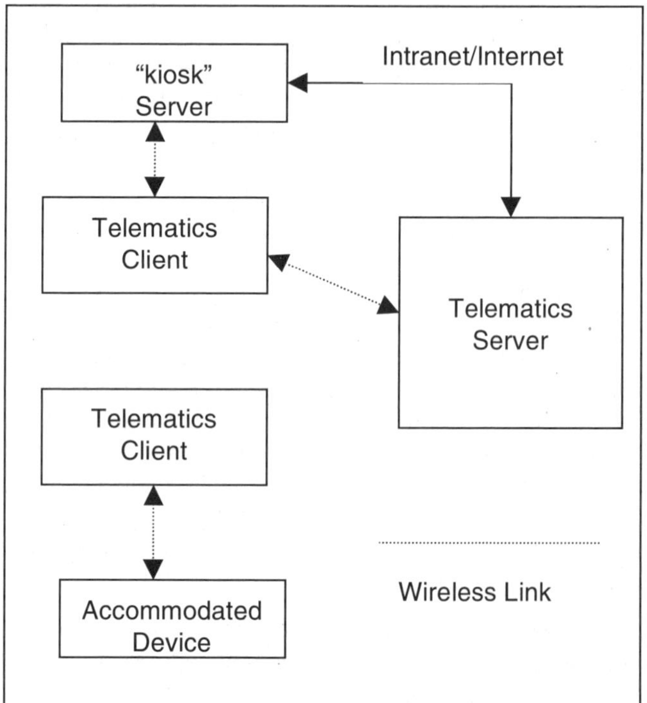

Figure 1: Distributed Telematics Architecture

Most automotive applications today are autonomous, i.e., the are fully contained in the vehicle and do not need a communication link to a remote server to provide services. While this is definitely an advantage in areas where there is no wireless coverage, a distributed architecture overcomes several limitations of an autonomous architecture:

- Provides support for time-sensitive services, e.g., traffic, stock, weather, sports updates.

- Provides up-to-date location services, e.g., navigation that takes into account current detours and road closures, point-of-interest (POI) information that includes news restaurants, shops, parking garages, theatres, etc.
- Offloads computing to a common server to reduce the cost of the client computing platform.
- Upgrades and configures both device and user profiles remotely.
- Allows user to set preferences from the comfort of a desktop.

TIERED CLIENTS – One of the main advantages of the proposed client-server architecture is that by the careful segmentation of the client and server modules of an application, multiple tiers of the client product can be designed and rapidly assembled. These can range from inexpensive, thin clients where the bulk of the work is done on the server to costlier, self-contained clients that are not dependent on a server and the associated communication channels.

In order to rapidly assemble tiered client products, an application should be designed in a modular form and segmented based on the planned tiers. For example, a navigation service that guides drivers from their current position to a desired destination is planned to be offered in three tiers: the low-end has minimal computing resources and no display, the mid-level has a two-line text display while the high-end has a nice multi-media display. To be used across all these products, one way to segment the navigation application is as follows:

- A module to extract the current location of the vehicle from an on-board position device such as GPS.
- A module to verbally interact with the user to determine the desired destination.
- A module to do the actual route calculation.
- Multiple modules to speak out the directions, display the directions as simple text or rich media (glyphs, sound cues overlaid on actual map data).

For the low-end product, just the first module that determined the current location would run on the client. The remaining modules would run on the server, which would interact with the user through server-based speech interaction. If the client supported VR and TTS on board, then the second and the final (spoken directions) modules could also be moved to the client.

In all cases, the compute intensive route calculation module would run on the server and only the final route would be sent back to the client in the desired form. For the mid-level product a simpler display module would be used than for the high-end product. If the high-end product had sufficient computing power and memory, even the route calculation module and associated map data could be resident on the client to eliminate any loss of service while roaming in an area with no wireless coverage. The low-end and mid-level products would, unfortunately, have no such backup measures.

SECURE APPLICATION MANAGEMENT – An important component of the framework is the Application Manager that remotely controls the installation, removal and update of service applications on the client, as well as the management of critical resources during their execution. It is foreseen that in order to provide a wide range of services, applications from multiple vendors may be required to assemble a comprehensive service portfolio. Rigorous testing by trusted third-party developers and equally stiff subsequent acceptance testing will not be sufficient. More safeguards need to be in place to ensure that all these varied applications can play in the same sandbox together harmoniously

On the server, approved applications are preprocessed prior to loading. Bytecode verification, selective compilation for performance, attachment of digital signatures and encryption are some of the operations done before a profile is generated for the application. In addition, run-time characteristics of the application are also specified. These include required attributes such as anticipated resource (CPU, memory, threads) usage and dependencies on other services, as well as optional ones such as desired operating conditions for optimal execution. On the client, an application will adhere to this profile in order for it to be recognized by the client Application Manager and be allowed to load and run.

Under the aegis of such an Application Manager, the client device can be open enough to allow well-behaved third-party applications to execute in its controlled environment. This allows new and enhanced services to be made rapidly available to users from multiple sources in the industry. The Application Manager component is planned to be Open Services Gateway interface (OSGi) [10] compliant when the OSGi specifications are finalized and become available.

SECURITY – The mechanisms provided by Java 2 security [12] form the basis for this framework's security. These features include authentication, authorization, non-repudiation, containment, privacy and audit trails using a layer of appropriate policy modules on the client and the server. Functional areas where security is critical include:

- Interfaces to eCommerce modules
- Facilities for setting up Virtual Private Networks (VPNs). This is required in order to support productivity services such as email, applications that require access to enterprise data, etc.
- Gated access to sensitive vehicle information, location and diagnostic data through the Vehicle Information Gateway. For example, a trivia game application should be restricted from accessing any vehicle information by its profile specification.

- Resource monitoring to prevent unintended as well as malicious monopoly by run-away threads.

PROFILE/CONFIGURATION MANAGEMENT – An important attribute of the proposed framework is the ability for the extensive configuration of the final product:

- A service application on the client may have its own personality based on user profiles and preferences residing on the server. For example, one user of a navigation application may want elaborate turn-by-turn route guidance, while another user (maybe on the same car), would prefer all the directions to be displayed at once and minimal sound cues when a new maneuver is coming up.
- User profiles are also valuable in transporting the preferences of a user between vehicles.
- Client device profiles are maintained on the server so that content may be appropriately shaped for the device before transmittal. For example, if the client device just supports a simple two-line display, based on its profile the server can send a more compact route containing just text descriptions and not download associated map data.
- Client device profiles may also be used by the Application Manager to update the device with appropriate Java modules when a user adds or deletes a new service, upgrades the equipment in the car, etc.

To support these features, a secure Web interface would be available to provision these configuration profiles.

SERVICE DISCOVERY & LOOKUP – The mobile nature of the proposed framework requires a mechanism (possibly an existing one, like Sun's Jini or SLP) that detects the availability of new services and secures access to them. This would involve:

- Detection of devices (telephones, PDAs) brought into the automobile and access to associated services (address book, calendar, etc).
- Detection of "kiosk" servers (available at a dealership or home) that provide short-range, high bandwidth services. These could be Bluetooth (or similarly) enabled devices.

This facility would provide the client with a simple lookup service so that the user could select from the available list of services.

MOBILE NETWORK INTERFACE MANAGEMENT – To facilitate rapid development of service applications for the automobile, it is important to transparently handle the complexities of the underlying mobile communication. A simple API abstracts the underlying wireless interfaces and takes into account quality of service and security issues. The Mobile Network Interface Manager deals with:

- High bandwidth, short-range interfaces like Bluetooth, 802.11, IRDA.
- Low bandwidth, long-range cellular interfaces (circuit switched CDMA, AMPS, GSM).
- High bandwidth, long-range interfaces like satellite channels and, as they become available, 3G, GPRS.

Session Management – One challenge faced by this component is the management of a mobile session across a geographically distributed server network. For example, during a download/upload operation between the vehicle and the server, the wireless communication link may go down for several reasons:

- Urban canyons or cell boundary crossings may cause the call to be dropped.
- User drives outside the coverage perimeter.
- User or system (based on user preferences) deliberately shuts down the link if it becomes more expensive, e.g., when roaming.

When a session is suspended, the system keeps track of the session so that it can be resumed smoothly when the conditions are favorable again. In order to do this, after securing each session, its state is maintained with hand-offs between different types of sessions and between session suspensions and resumptions.

DATA SYNCHRONIZATION – The system will provide the framework for multi-point data synchronization. This would allow synchronization of PIM data between a user's phones, PDA or similar device.

Another important need that this framework would address is that of enterprise data synchronization. For example, fleet personnel or travelling salesmen would be able to synchronize their local data securely with the enterprise servers from the vehicle instead of waiting to reach a wired LAN access point.

TELEMATICS CLIENT

The telematics client architecture shown in Figure 2 shows the client Java framework on which the infotainment applications execute. The Java Native Interface (JNI) provides access to platform dependent native code from the pure Java applications. In the real world, there are always modules (communication stacks, device drivers and other compute intensive elements) that must be written in native platform code to meet performance requirements.

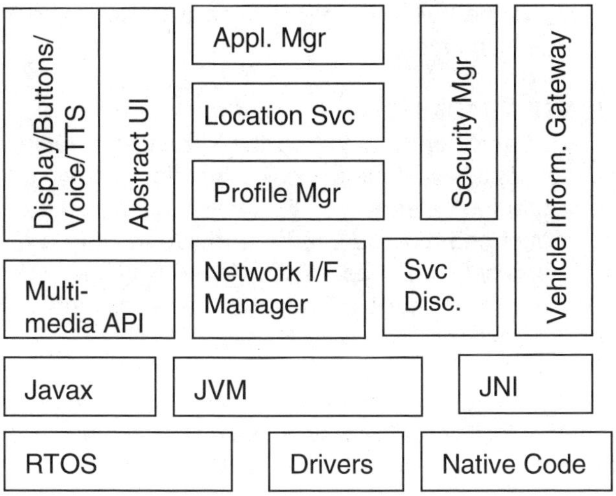

Figure 2: Telematics Client Architecture

EASE OF CUSTOMIZATION: ABSTRACT UI – While this framework enables rapid development of new telematics services, an important consideration is the ability for an OEM to easily customize the client product's look-and-feel to adhere to their branding requirements. Thus, the proposed framework provides the Abstract User Interface (AUI) on the client to allow application developers to design user interactions while sheltering them from the actual look-and-feel, which will be under the control of the OEM designers. The AUI consists of a set of widgets and a Dialog Controller to support multi-modal I/O.

The AUI also allows the same application to run on a broad range of client devices, since the mapping of the AUI widgets to the physical I/O elements is done on the client during execution. For example, a selection widget may be physically implemented using a touch-screen display, tactile buttons on the steering wheel or through spoken commands depending on the capability of the widgets on the client device. Thus using the AUI, the core application and its user interaction is shielded from rewrites required to achieve an OEM's look -and-feel.

MULTIMEDIA FRAMEWORK – A large number of the services available on this platform will require multimedia. The Multimedia Framework component is slated to deliver the required support. It will incorporate the Java Media Framework, which provides support for capturing, storing, and broadcasting time-sensitive/streaming media, using custom codecs, and manipulating media data before rendering it. In addition, it will provide the following extensions:

- A Tuner API to control a digital audio from multiple applications.
- A Content Management API to control broadcast filtering and trickle-in, background pre-loading of content.

VEHICLE INFORMATION GATEWAY – In the case of the automobile, for obvious safety and security reasons, a highly secure line needs to be drawn between facilities that support infotainment services and those that provide access to vehicle safety, information and control. The Vehicle Information Gateway (VIG) component provides this gatekeeper function and allows secure access to vehicle information, such as engine data, vehicle body and climate controls, through a firewall.

Such a Java abstraction also hides the variances in the internal buses and control units between different manufacturers (and even models) from the application service developers. For example, a safety application that runs on Motorola's MobileGT [15] platform using the VIG API could access similar information transparently from the underlying vehicle control systems on another manufacturer's platform if the latter also provided the standard VIG API.

Java 2 security is used to restrict access to this API from unauthorized applications.

NATIVE CODE SUPPORT – This framework will allow for simultaneous execution of stand-alone, non-interactive C or other native applications on the client. These would typically be daemons or monitors. Further, JNI support tools would be available to provide access to underlying native code libraries.

TELEMATICS SERVER

CONTENT MANAGEMENT – One of the more complex functions provided by the telematics server is that of content management. To take proper advantage of the distributed architecture, the system should provide timely and up-to-date content for the various applications to serve to the client:

- Map data with updates to reflect newest roads and latest road closures and detours
- Point-of-interest databases with updates to list the newest items (restaurants, shops, parking garages, etc) and delete obsolete ones.
- More frequent data feeds like stock/weather/news updates that constitute more transient data.

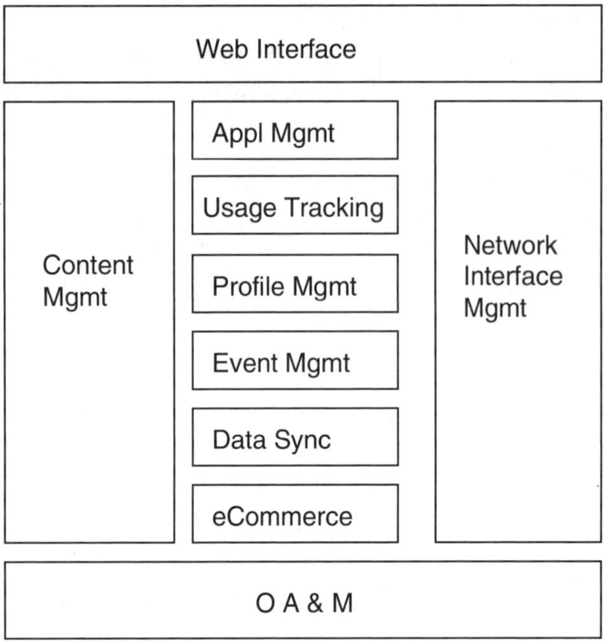

Figure 3: Telematics Server Architecture

Content Rendering – The framework provides facilities for Content Rendering based on any or a combination of the following:

- Content type
- User preferences
- Application configuration
- Client device characteristics

This is another enabling component that allows the same service application to be executed for multiple client devices. For example, weather reports generated by a service application as XML [13], can be shaped as a voice report for voice-enabled devices like phones. On the other hand, if the client device can support sophisticated graphics and an inexpensive, high-speed wireless channel is available, the information could be delivered superimposed on color satellite images.

Another example of controlled content rendering is email. The user may prefer to see messages displayed if the client has a display unit or the entire interaction could be in audio.

EVENT MANAGEMENT – The proposed framework will support an elegant Event Management system to allow users to receive notification when events subscribed to occur. This component will allow service applications to define event categories (traffic alerts, weather conditions, entertainment, sports or sales events). The list of event categories a user is subscribed to is maintained as part of the user profile.

E-COMMERCE SUPPORT – The framework provides a secure environment for conducting wireless eCommerce, which will be built on top of standard COTS systems for internet eCommerce.

USAGE TRACKING – An important enabler component of this framework resides on the server and tracks subscriber and application usage profiles under various demographic categories. This information is a valuable byproduct and may be used to provide input to a myriad of data-mining activities. A significant use of this information is to drive directed advertising, sales and promotional activities.

OA & M – Operational, Administrative and Maintenance (OA&M) facilities will be available on the Telematics servers for:

- Network availability at a 5Nines level.
- Billing
- Mail server
- Directory services
- General system administration

CONCLUSION

This flexible yet powerful distributed Java framework can play a central role in storming one of the last remaining bastions left untouched by the current information revolution. It harnesses the large and growing Java development community and enables them to rapidly design, build and securely deploy infotainment services and bring pervasive computing to the automotive space.

REFERENCES

1. Sun Java, http://java.sun.com
2. HP Java, http://www.chai.com
3. IBM Java, http://www.ibm.com/developer/java/
4. JavaPhone, http://java.sun.com/products/javaphone/
5. JTAPI, http://java.sun.com/products/jtapi/
6. Java Media Framework, http://java.sun.com/products/java-media/jmf/index.html
7. JSAPI, http://java.sun.com/products/java-media/speech/
8. JavaTV, http://java.sun.com/products/javatv/overview.html
9. Javacard, http://java.sun.com/products/javacard/htmldoc/overview-summary.html
10. OSGi: http://www.osgi.org
11. Sun Java Community Process, http://java.sun.com/aboutJava/communityprocess/
12. Java 2 Security, http://java.sun.com/products/jdk/1.2/docs/guide/security/

13. XML, http:// www.xml.com/
14. Bluetooth, http://www.bluetooth.org/
15. MobileGT Telematics Platform, http://www.mot-sps.com/automotive/mobilegt/index.html

DEFINITIONS, ACRONYMS, ABBREVIATIONS

5Nines:: A Motorola initiative to ensure 99.999% system availability.
Applets: : Java code that is downloaded and run locally inside a Web browser that may even interface with back-end servers.
COTS: : Commercial-Off-The-Shelf.
Infotainment: : A service that has both informational and entertainment value to a subscriber.
JVM: : Java Virtual Machine.
OEM: : Original Equipment Manufacturer.
OSGi: : Open Services Gateway interface.
PDA: : Personal Digital Assistant.
PIM: : Personal Information Management. Typically refers to address book, calendar and to-do data managed by PDA devices.
SLP: : Service Location Protocol, an IETF draft standard.
Telematics: : Delivery of mobile or location aware infotainment services.
VM: : Virtual Machine.

2000-01-0152

Design of Intelligent Body Networks

Ralf Hadeler and Hans-Jörg Mathony
Robert Bosch Corp.

ABSTRACT

With additional new or more intelligent functions emerging in the vehicle, engineers are facing new challenges in the design of the Automotive Electric/Electronic System. New ECUs, actuators and sensors have to be provided with information, energy and control signals. In order to limit the weight of the wiring harness and to guarantee the electrical supply of the components an improved design and architecture of the body network is required.

Communication is being handled by several bus systems which are connected via gateways. Sensors and actuators are getting smarter. The existing 12V electrical supply system will be supplemented or replaced by a 42V network. Several new functions (e.g. extended systems diagnostics) will be added without additional actuators but just by additional software, requiring more computing power in the vehicle.

All this will require a systems approach for the body networks resulting in an improved functionality and reliability keeping the costs and complexity of the system limited.

INTRODUCTION

Body electronics offer a variety of well-known and new functions:

- basic functions: external and internal lighting, windshield washing and wiping, signalling
- comfort functions: seat, mirror and steering wheel adjustment, power window control, sunroof adjustment
- vehicle security functions: central door locking, keyless entry, immobilizer, anti-theft system
- heating and climate control systems
- driver information systems: user interface, instrument cluster, navigation, communication, multimedia.

The Intelligent Body Network – as we understand it – provides the sensors and actuators of the vehicle body electronics with the required **intelligence** to utilize them in an optimum way, plus the infrastructure: **communication** and **power supply**.

Today several trends are changing the world of body electronics:

- System and module approach: the vehicle is subdivided into systems and modules, reducing the complexity for development and manufacturing.
- Distributed Intelligence: additional functions will not necessarily result in additional ECUs, intelligence will be distributed.
- Networking: more and more systems and components are communicating via several networks.
- Innovative power distribution: the power distribution system is getting more sophisticated, a new voltage level (42V) is going to be introduced.

1 SYSTEM APPROACH

The challenge in vehicle E/E design has shifted from optimizing individual components like ECUs, sensors, actuators, mechanical or electrical elements to the optimization of complete systems within the vehicle. Examples are: signal and power distribution system, vehicle security system (immobilizer, keyless entry/go, anti-theft control) and cockpit electronic system (instrument cluster, driving access, driver information system, HVAC, etc.). The base technology of these systems is multiplexing: the electronic control units (ECUs) distributed across the car body are interconnected by means of a bus system. The objective is to minimize the number of wires, connectors and contacts, so even for the cars´ base equipment multiplexing can be introduced without additional costs. This is achieved by placing ECUs in those sections of a car, where electronics are required, e.g. dashboard, door, seat, roof and rear. Within a section sensors, actuators and switches are connected to the nearest electronic control unit, irrespective of the unit´s function. The systems are characterized by the following features:

- Multiple functions are integrated into a single ECU. In order to amortize the electronics´ costs multiple functions are integrated in a single ECU. Examples are functions like external and internal lighting, hazard warning control, front and rear wiper control, central door locking among others.

- Functions are distributed across multiple ECUs; for example the function “central door (un)locking via remote control” is typically realized by cooperation of the ECU in which the remote control receiver is integrated and the door electronic units integrating the lock function.
- Electrical distribution systems junction boxes are replaced by more expensive smart power distribution units (PDUs) including electronic functions and a bus interface. Additionally the distribution system is modularized by several PDUs into clusters. Each of these units add costs, but the cost reduction in the wiring harness and the easier handling of the system compensate these additional cost for the whole power distribution system.
- Smart sensors and actuators are naturally more expensive than simple ones, but they offer advantages in function (self-diagnostics, control), wiring and system availability, as several ECUs can utilize the same components. Actuators will include a power device, communication and maybe even intelligence. The smart actuator is reacting to the request of his „master ECU“ given by e.g. serial communication and is controlling his inner control circuit independently. Functions like current limitation etc. can be handled by the actuator itself. The intelligence may be incorporated directly into the actuator or in the connector. With less control outputs on the ECUs the system becomes more flexible. An addition of a smart component is much easier than an addition of a simple component as less additional connectors, terminals etc are required. Just the software in the „master ECU“ has to be adapted (control algorithm, CAN messages).
- Subsystems with sub-busses etc (e.g. doors, seats, cockpit) may include rather expensive ECUs and components, but reduce the complexity of the complete system and offer advantages in packaging.
- ECUs with rather high computing power will handle different tasks. The number of these multifunctional ECUs will be different in different cars. They will include software for „their“ sensors and actuators as well as software with no dedicated component like gateway, diagnostics, personal profiling, power management etc. Thus additional functions can be added just by adding software.

There is a common denominator of all these features and examples: not an individual component is optimized (costs, packaging...), but a whole system. The optimized system may consist of non-optimum components.

Putting all these characteristics together, the most likely E/E architecture of the future is a hierarchical system, as shown in Figure 1.

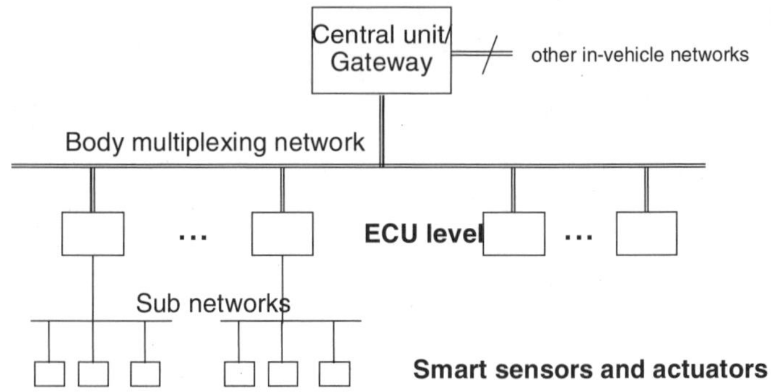

Figure 1. Hierarchical electronics architecture

Dependent on the vehicle type, packaging, equipment and the OEMs philosophy the functions are implemented in different ECUs and integrated in a vehicle- or OEM-specific electronic architecture. This poses a major challenge to the suppliers requiring a lot of flexibility. They have to develop their software in a way that it can be transferred between different ECUs at a rather late state of a project. Even during the lifetime of a product major changes may occur caused by added features in the vehicle. And a full system supplier has to be able to include software developed and tested by another supplier or the OEM. This results in the following requirements:

- Clear decoupling of ECU hardware and software by means of a layered software architecture. The OSEK/VDX open architecture – comprising real-time operating system, communication protocols (intra-ECU and inter-ECU) and network management – is the fundamental basis for future ECUs software architecture and is the prerequisite for the introduction of software techniques and tools that support portability, reuse, software sharing and code generation. Figure 2 shows as an example a typical future ECU software architecture, including OSEK/VDX and additional hardware encapsulation software components like I/O, flash programming and diagnosis drivers.
- The functions and thus the software have to be structured in a modular way with very easy interfaces allowing easy reuse in different configurations. For this purpose Bosch has developed the CARTRONIC® approach. CARTRONIC® is an ordering concept for all vehicle control systems. The concept comprises modular expandable functions, safety and electronics architectures. Fundamental architectural structuring and modeling rules are established in order to organize networked systems independently of a special hardware topology from a functional point of view. The rules define components, their permitted interactions and patterns for recurring tasks independent from a special function. This means that the

rules and patterns are a "common language" for engineers to analyze functions in the entire vehicle from the same view. CARTRONIC® is providing a consistent methodology to handle the challenges that arise by increasing system interconnections starting from the abstract level of function analysis [1, 3].

- Tools have to be available to enable software design independent of the hardware architecture. A step in this direction is the TITUS approach which was developed in a joint project of DaimlerChrysler and IBM [5]. TITUS uses the client/server model for the structuring of distributed applications. The TITUS architecture defines an application software framework with 6 different types of components which communicate with each other by use of well-defined interfaces and protocols. During the SW design phase ECU implementation aspects are not taken into account; the application software can be developed without knowledge of the target hardware configuration. The implementation phase is supported by code generators which generate the application (control) and the communication software based on the OSEK/VDX system software infrastructure. The TITUS approach makes a simple and tool-supported integration of software components possible. The software architecture is the basis to design software components which can be reused for different vehicle model lines.

2 NETWORKING

Most new vehicles nowadays offer at least one bus system for ECU communication and diagnostics.

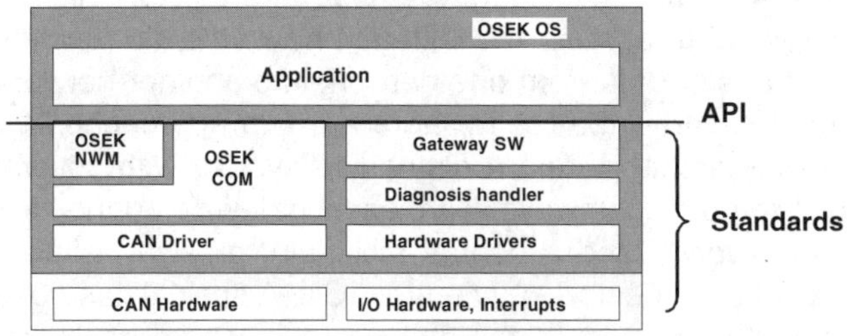

Figure 2. Structure of future ECU architecture

2.1 IN VEHICLE NETWORKS – The requirements with respect to data transfer rate, protocol mechanism, reliability, fault tolerance and costs are dependent of their applications and have lead to the development and introduction of different network types (see Table 1). Network technology is further pushed by standards like CAN and OSEK/VDX [Kie98]. With OSEK/VDX, protocols and services in the areas of network communication, network management and ECU operating system have been specified and will be used from 2000 on in production cars by several European car manufacturers. The use of the OSEK/VDX standards simplifies significantly the development of network-based distributed applications and the integration of ECUs and software coming from different suppliers.

In future cars the communication across network limits will increase. Functions like HMI, user profile, power supply management, tele-diagnosis, etc. will require integrating all ECUs in a global vehicle network. This global network is the interconnection of the different vehicle networks by means of special gateways.

Table 1. Characteristics of in-vehicle networks

Network	Interconnection of	Data transfer rate	Network features	Data transfer mechanism	Example
Powertrain network	Engine Man., ABS, TCS, VDC, Transm., Suspen., ACC, etc.	Typ. 500 Kbit/s	Multi-master bus, twisted pair line	Asynch., mess. priority based bus access, cyclic and event driven transfer	CAN High Speed
Body network	Door ECU, Seat ECU, Instrum. cluster, Climate control, Keyless go, etc.	< 125 Kbit/s	Multi-master bus, twisted pair line, fault-tolerant physical layer	Asynch., mess. priority based bus access, cyclic and event driven transfer	CAN Low Speed (Europe) J1850 (US)
Multi-media network	Navigation, Video, Audio receiver, Audio amplifierHMI panels, DisplaysCDC, Mobile phone	5 – 100 Mbit/s	Plastic optical fiber, Ring topology	Synchr. transfer of audio and video data, Asynch. transfer of control data	D2B optical MOST (Media Oriented Systems Transport) MML (Mobile Media Link)
X-by-wire network	x-by-wire ECUs, e.g. brakes, steering	1 Mbit/s, 2 Mbit/s	Fault tolerant physical layer, 2 wires	Time-triggered (TDMA), Static mess. scheduling, Global time	TTP/C

2.2 GATEWAYS – A gateway node is an ECU which is connected to at least two different networks. Its function is to transfer data from one network into another network and vice versa. Basically, there are two approaches for gateway architectures: a distributed system with several point-to-point gateways with each gateway connecting two networks, and a central multipoint gateway with all networks connected to a central ECU. A special case of a distributed gateway is the gateway bus, where each network is connected via a gateway node to the gateway bus, so that information can be exchanged between all networks via the gateway bus.

Distributed gateway – In a distributed gateway system several gateway nodes are implemented to achieve a global network. Typically the gateways are no standalone ECUs but integrated with other functions in a multifunctional ECU. To enable data exchange between each pair of N networks at least N-1 gateways are required. To have a minium distance of 1 between all N networks, N*(N-1)/2 gateways are necessary. In this case each network is directly connected with each other network by means of a gateway.

Central gateway – In a central gateway a single ECU integrates the gateway function. The microprocessor of the central gateway has access to several networks and is responsible for exchanging data across the different networks. Compared to the solution discussed above the central gateway realizes a minimum distance inter-network communication with the minium amount of hardware.

Gateway bus – The gateway bus solution is a special case of a distributed gateway system. Each network has access to the gateway bus via its own gateway node. In case of N networks, N nodes with a gateway function are required. The distance between two arbitrary networks is always 2.

Besides the general solutions described above, there are a lot of specific hybrid solutions which result from partitioning a set of networks into different clusters where each cluster is interconnected according to one of the described architectures.

Comparison – The central gateway has clear advantages in terms of system costs and latency time. However, in case of a gateway failure the corresponding networks are isolated. Fault-tolerance could be achieved by redundancy in form of additional gateway units or a central gateway with a multi-processor architecture.

The gateway bus is a very flexible solution, if new networks or messages are to be added; however it is a costly solution as an additional bus is required.

The distributed gateway system is feasible for a small number of networks. In case of a single gateway failure only a single network is isolated.

For more details see [6].

2.3 SUB-NETWORKS – Driven by semiconductor technology there is a continuous trend to integrate electronics into sensors, actuators and switch panels. The communication interface of smart sensors and actuators is rather simple compared to multiplexing networks like CAN. In most cases a low-cost SCI or UART-based master-slave communication scheme is used. The communication line is typically a single wire, the signal levels correspond to the 12V ISO 9141 physical interface (k-line), data transfer rate is 9.6 Kbit/s. Examples of such sub-busses are described in [7] and [8]. Application areas for sub-networks are for example:

Area	Sensors, actuators
Cockpit	Switch panels, steering wheel column stalk, radio satellite, air conditioning motors, displays, etc.
Door	Switch panel, lock, window lift motor, mirror (see Fig. 3)
Seat	Seat adjustment motors, switch panel
Roof	Sensors, roof adjustment motor, interior lighting control
Others	Alternator, headlamps, headlamps adjustment, smart wiper etc.

Currently there are activities driven by Motorola and european car manufacturers to establish a international standard for in-vehicle sub-networks. For more details, see [4].

Sub-networks will be connected to the entire vehicle network by means of gateways, which are integrated in the ECUs of the multiplexing bus, so that the resulting network is a hierarchical system (see Figures 1, 3). In a hierarchical electronics architecture, the smart sensor/ actuator level components provide clearly defined functions and services which can be accessed by the higher levels in order to implement ECU- and cross-network functions.

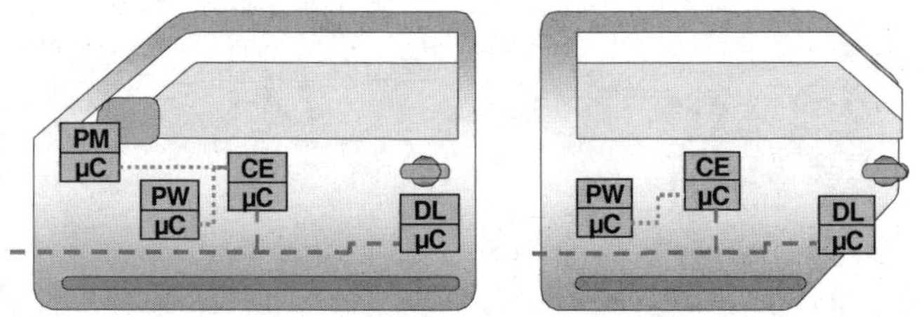

Advantages:

- Reduction of wiring harness and simple assembly
- Use of identical components
- Reduction of HW variants
- Higher reliability and lower costs because of mechatronics
- Easy integration of further functions

- - - CAN-Bus
.... Sub-network

PM: Power Mirror
PW: Power Window
CE: Control Elements
DL: Door Latch

Figure 3. Sub-network within the door (example)

3. POWER DISTRIBUTION SYSTEM

With more and more functions being requested in upper class vehicles the power demand is increasing rapidly. Additionally efforts to reduce fuel consumption and emissions lead to the tendency of replacing direct drives by electronically controlled drives. This increases the demand of electrical power while reducing the demand of „mechanical power“ – thus fuel. As the conventional 12V power supply system is hardly able to provide the required currents, the industry is discussing the introduction of a 42V PowerNet.

3.1 INTRODUCTION SCENARIO – Potential high power electric consumers include:

- Front window defroster
- Auxiliary electric heating
- Electromagnetic valve control
- Electric power steering
- Electromechanical brakes
- Electromechanical suspension control
- Heated catalyst
- Integrated starter/alternator
- Rear window defroster
- Electric pumps (ABS, cooling, water..)
- Electric motors (power seats...).

The introduction scenario of 42V will be different for each vehicle manufacturer. Main motivations are:

- Some loads require a higher voltage level (e.g. front window defroster).
- The current 12V (14V) system cannot supply the power requested by new loads (e.g. heated catalyst) anymore.
- Wiring harness or power dissipation are reduced.
- The redundant 12V/42V power supply is used for safety critical systems (e.g. electric steering/braking/ locking)
- The integrated starter/alternator is utilized as auxiliary drive to reduce emissions and fuel consumption.

With a great number of 12V loads already introduced in today's vehicle, a complete conversion to a pure 42V car is not likely. So a dual voltage power supply will be the common architecture for the next several years. The major additional costs (DC/DC converter) and the additional failure modes (shortcut between 14V and 42V) will in the long run drive automotive manufacturers and suppliers to a complete conversion to 42V. The new 42V PowerNet will then display 42V as the only common voltage level with some locally available lower voltages (12V, 5V..).

3.2 POWER DISTRIBUTION ECU – Back bone of the Power Distribution System are the wiring harness and the smart junction boxes or Power Distribution Units (PDU). The PDUs as the active part protect, switch and control the electric consumers and provide communication. Additionally they divide the E/E-system into smaller clusters reducing complexity of the system and the handling of the wiring harness (s. figure 4).

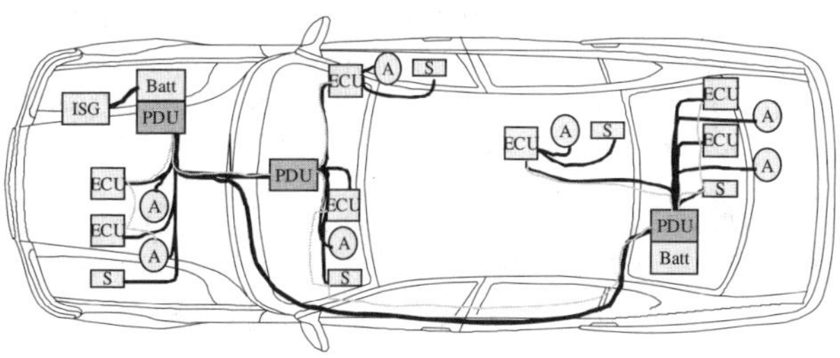

Figure 4: Clusters created by different PDUs

The transition from junction boxes to PDUs offers the chance to add intelligence to the Power Distribution System:

- improved diagnostics, including system diagnostics
- fail safe functions, keep alive functions
- personal profiling
- load management and management of the quiescient current.

Improved systems diagnostics will only partly be incorporated into the PDUs as they require a lot of computing power. But by diagnosing their subsystem and providing "meta-information" the PDUs ease the task of a central body computer responsible for system diagnostics and the proper communication with driver and garage. With improved on-board-diagnostics the PDUs identify defect actuators and sensors, and drive the system into a safe state or replace the defect function by a similar feature without adding cost to the original actuators. So a defect low beam lamp function may be replaced by pulse width modulating the high beam lamp; and with a detected failure of the lamp switch all lights may be turned on guaranteeing a safe vehicle.

Personal profiles allow to adapt comfort functions to the individual driver or passenger of the vehicle. The stored characteristics of the users are transferred to the respective actuators which are set to the predefined status.

Load management and management of the quiescient current shall prevent discharge of the battery and allow reduction of battery and alternator by taking better advantage of their abilities.

3.3 DUAL VOLTAGE SYSTEM ARCHITECTURE – Up to now no standard architecture for a dual voltage network has been established. Some alternatives are:

- 42V alternator, DC/DC converter
- Alternator with dual voltage output
- 42V alternator, 12V alternator.

Most alternatives include a 36V as well as a 12V battery. Instead of a starter battery a "supercap" may be used as well. The approach with a DC/DC converter may incorporate several DC/DC converters to generate local distribution networks. The other approaches may include a (small) DC/DC converter as well for improved flexibility and jump starting.

Power generation by 42V alternator and DC/DC converter may be the best solution for a system with low power demand on 12V. If with the introduction of 42V only a small number of loads is on 42V and the majority stays on 12V, the DC/DC converter has to provide lots of power, creating a rather costly solution. In this case the introduction of two different alternators becomes an attractive solution.

The power distribution system is divided into several clusters by the addition of several PDUs. A very attractive solution appears to be the combination of PDU and DC/DC converter. The combination of a central PDU/Converter offers advantages in costs and failure handling, while the combination of local PDUs with DC/DC converters allows the reduction of the wiring harness and a very easy system approach (s. figure 5).

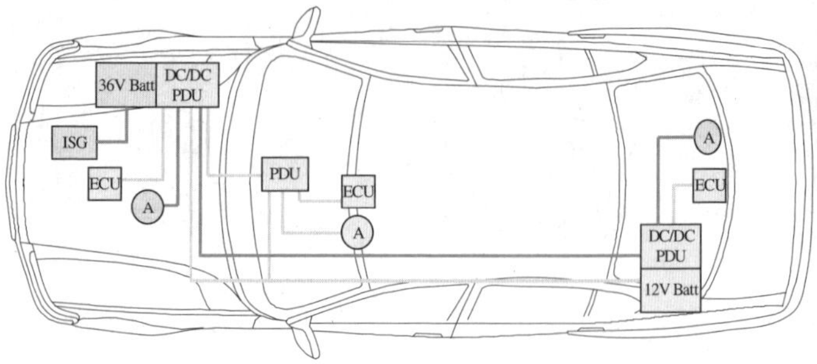

Figure 5: Dual voltage architecture with combined PDU/Converter

3.4 FAILURE HANDLING – A new technical problem will be the potential shortcut between the 14V and the 42V voltage levels. Shortcuts are an issue in every electrical network, but the automotive dual voltage network displays a special problem. Whenever a shortcut between 42V and a 14V device switched by a MOS switch occurs, not only this 14V device, but the whole 14V network is connected to the 42V level. This is due to the unavoidable reverse diode of MOS switch S1 (s. figure 6).

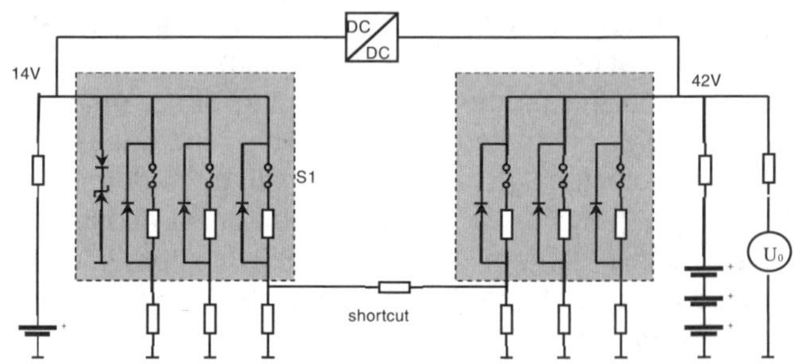

Figure 6: Shortcut between 14V and 42V

The most effective way to protect the 14V loads is detecting the "driving" 42V load and turning it off as soon as possible. In order to switch off the source of the short cut current unprotected 42V lines have to be avoided. In a very common architecture (see figure 7) the powerlines between starter/alternator, battery, DC/DC converters and PDUs can only be protected by switching off the smart battery post disabling the whole vehicle.

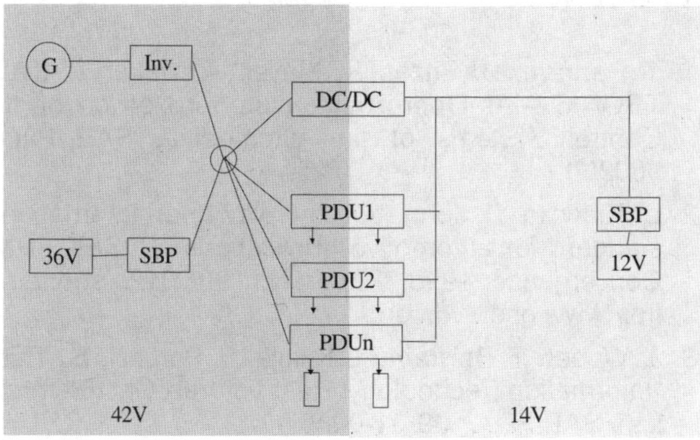

Figure 7: common architecture

To reduce the possibility of this major fault, some general rules should be applied:

- combine DC/DC converter and one PDU to a "Master-PDU/converter"
- mount Master-PDU close to battery
- mount battery close to starter/alternator.

Additionally

- protect all "satellite-PDUs" by the Master-PDU
- protect all 42V loads in PDUs
- minimize unprotected 42V lines
- avoid neighboring 14V and 42V lines.

To reduce the effect of the shortcut to the 14V loads, basically two different methods are possible. The first alternative avoids switches with a reverse diode, separating the shortcut from the 14V net. The 14V net is saved, but major problems may appear detecting the fault and the driving 42V switch, as the additional current through the 14V device may be small compared to the standard current through the 42V source.

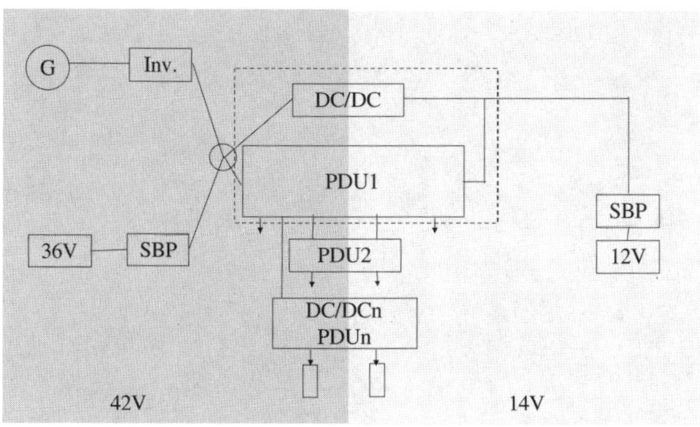

Figure 8: Proposed architecture

The second alternative is installing a "sacrificial device" on the 14V level. This device has to accept the whole current from the short cut reducing the overvoltage in the system and protecting the 14V loads until the short cut is detected. It has to stand currents close to 1000A and to limit the system voltage to a level of approximately 24V, still allowing the 14V and the 42V components to work. With this high current the source on the 42V level can easily be detected and turned off.

Different sacrificial devices are currently under investigation.

Both strategies turn off the minimum number of components or subsystems in case of a failure and protect all but one 14V device. Proper architectures, devices and strategies have to ensure the detection is fast and no device is destroyed by the current through short cut and other devices.

3.5 TECHNOLOGY – With the introduction of 42V using semiconductors is getting more (cost) attractive. Relays (with fuses) may be replaced by solid state relays, and fuses may be replaced by solid state relays or polyswitches. Tables 2 and 3 show some advantages, disadvantages and features of the different alternatives.

Table 2. Comparison of solid state and mechanical relays

Solid State Relays	Mechanical Relays
Current sensing, diagnostics	-
PWM control possible	-
-	Complete blocking, no reverse current
-	Different control and load circuits
Reliable	Robust (against overload)
Low control power	No quiescient current
Advantages in ECU construction	Easy servicing
Cheaper with small currents	Cheaper with high currents

Table 3. Comparison of fuses, solid state relays and polyswitches

Fuses	Solid State Relays	Polyswitches
-	Additional functionality	-
-	Self healing	Self healing
Low power dissipation	Medium power dissipation	High power dissipation
-	Quiescient current required, Load management possible	-
High currents	Medium currents	Low currents
Low costs	High costs	Medium costs

It is expected that most relays (especially for low power devices) will be replaced by semiconductors, while fuses will still be prominently displayed in PDUs. Small loads may be protected by polyswitches while solid state relays will only be used for fusing in special cases.

CONCLUSION

In an effort to enhance the vehicles' comfort, safety and efficiency the electronics are getting more and more complex: huge software modules, a large number of ECUs, and different voltage levels are the flip side of the continuous evolution of the automobile.

A consequent systems approach is introduced in order to control the complexity of body electronics. Intelligent Body Networks organize the intelligence, communication and power supply in a novel way and open the door for more innovation and customer satisfaction.

REFERENCES

1. T. Bertram, R. Bitzer, R. Mayer, A. Volkart, " CARTRONIC – An Open Architecture for Networking the Control Systems of an Automobile", SAE Paper 980200
2. U. Kiencke, D. John, "On the way to an international standard for automotive applications – OSEK/VDX", Convergence 1998, Paper No. 98C012, see also: ftp://www.osek-vdx.org/
3. J. Weber, T. Bertram, T. Kytölä, F. Peruzzi, S. Thiel, "Information Technology Restructures Car Electronics", SAE Paper 99-01-0485
4. H.Chr. v. d. Wense, W. Specks, A. Krüger, "Anforderungen und Implementierungen von Sub-Bussen in hierarchischen Automobilnetzwerken", Conference "Embedded Intelligence 99", Nürnberg
5. P. Lanches, J. Eisenmann, et. al. "Client/Server Architecture – Managing New technologies for Automotive Embedded systems – A Joint Project of Daimler-Benz & IBM", Convergence 98, Paper No. 98C014
6. H.-J. Mathony, J. Maier, "Trends in Vehicle Body Electronics", International Symposium "ATA-EL 99", Como, Paper 99A1009
7. G. Bierbaum, "Multiplex bus system for sensors and actuators in automotive A/C systems", Conference "Elektronik im Kraftfahrzeug", Baden-Baden 1998, VDI Berichte 1415, 315-324
8. J.W. Specks, A. Rajnak, "Die skalierbare Netzwerkarchitektur des Volvo S80 mit Echtzeit-Betriebssystem und Mechatronikbausteinen", Conference "Elektronik im Kraftfahrzeug", Baden-Baden 1998, VDI Berichte 1415, 597-613

VOICE RECOGNITION, SPEECH SYNTHESIS

2005-01-3973

Using SIL/PSIL to Estimate Speech Intelligibility in Vehicles

Helcio Onusic
Instituto de Física – Universidade de São Paulo

Edgar L. Baptista
Marcelo M. Hage
DaimlerChrysler do Brasil

ABSTRACT

The paper looks for the degree of linear correlation of some acoustic parameters concerning Speech Intelligibility in vehicles. The Articulation Index (AI) was originally a criterion to characterize the influence of parasite noise on the Intelligibility of a conversation in the design of speech communication systems. Introduced in the automobile acoustics, it is more and more commonly used by vehicles manufacturers to estimate the middle and high frequency content of spectra noise inside various types of vehicles driven under several running conditions. The correlation with Speech Intelligibility, measured through subjective measurements is well known. Presently we have more sophisticated parameters like STI, RASTI, SII... directed mainly to architectural acoustics and sometimes used in vehicle acoustics. They require specific hardwares and softwares and are more complicated to deal with and often are called machine measures of Speech Intelligibility. On the other side, a simplified way to estimate Speech Intelligibility was proposed by Beranek in the fifties, introducing Speech Interference Level (SIL). Later a new version named Preferred Speech Interference Level (PSIL) was developed. They are calculated using measurements of sound pressure levels in octave bands above 500 Hz. This work, as a pioneer application, uses a set of passenger cars and a set of commercial vehicles to study the correlation of these parameters regarding internal noise. Besides the usual definitions, we propose new approaches for these alternative parameters, SIL and PSIL, introducing some frequency weightings similar to those existing in the calculation of AI in third octave bands. We apply to the experimental data a least-squares curve fitting by straight lines. The results observed through graphics show the degree of linear correlation for the separated sets and also for all the data jointed together. For some parameters we obtain a high degree of linear correlation in such way we expect simplifications and facilities in the estimation of Speech Intelligibility inside vehicles. We use propagation of errors in the mathematical expressions regarding the acoustic parameters to discuss the establishment of a ranking using a specific category of vehicles. We can see that using sound pressure levels in octave bands from 1kHz to 4kHz we are able to have SIL as an alternative picture of Speech Intelligibility, and due to this simplicity we also recommmend them for quality control.

INTRODUCTION

We use today a lot of acoustic parameters trying to quantify/qualify the acoustic sensations and attributes concerning the internal noise of automotive vehicles(1,2,3)*. In this paper we deal with the evaluation of the Speech Intelligibility in vehicles.

This is an important attribute to characterize their acoustic behaviour. For this purpose we consider Articulation Index (AI), Speech Interference Level (SIL) and PSIL (Preferred Speech Interference Level) as parameters associated to speech communication. Although we can say they are different in concept, they are obtained, for instance, through the use of the measurements of the same sound pressure levels with some boundary conditions, frequency decompositions and distinct weightings.

As they come from the same data which are manipulated in different ways, it is interesting to know how they are correlated. It means to investigate the degree of correlation we can obtain when we compare one to another. In our case we are looking for the correlation between AI and SIL/PSIL. A high linear correlation allows the use of SIL/PSIL, in a pioneer application, as an alternative to evaluate Speech Intelligibility in vehicles, with the advantage of their simplicity.

The work has the following steps:

- we choose a set of passenger cars and a set of commercial vehicles;
- we measure the internal sound pressure levels versus velocity according to ISO 5128;
- we choose some specific velocities, from 40 km/h to 100 km/h;

---

* Number in parentheses designate references at the end of paper.

- we calculate the acoustic parameters we are interested. In our case the parameters are: AI, SIL and PSIL;

- in addition we apply to SIL and PSIL some weightings similar to those existing in the calculation of AI, with the purpose of improving the behaviour of SIL and PSIL. It means to define new acoustic parameters we named SIL_w and $PSIL_w$;

- for each set of passenger cars and commercial vehicles we apply a least-squares fit to a straight line to each pair of the acoustic parameters[4,5];

- we apply a least-squares fit to both data sets jointed together;

- we use propagation of errors in the mathematical expressions which define the acoustic parameters, to discuss the establishment of a ranking using a specific category of vehicles in a common running condition;

- the results are discussed taking into consideration the degree of correlation, the behaviour of each pair and the vehicle families.

AI – ARTICULATION INDEX[6,7]

The Articulation Index (AI) was originally a criterion to characterize the influence of parasite noise on the Intelligibility of a conversation in the desing of speech comunication systems. Introduced in the automobile acoustics it is more and more commonly used by vehicle manufacturers to estimate the middle and high frequency content of spectra noise inside various types of vehicles driven under several running conditions.

The concept of Articulation Index (AI) was introduced by Fletcher in studies at Bell Telephone Laboratories. Some advanced concepts were developed by French and Steinberg in the same company. In 1947, Beranek[8] published a paper regarding a method to calculate the ability of a communication system to transmit Speech Intelligibility in the presence of noise. In his experiments, three main results are important:

- extending the frequency range of a communication system below 200 Hz or above 6000 Hz contributes nothing to the Intelligibility of Speech;

- twenty frequency bands were determined with equal contribution to AI, or 5 per cent contribution each;

- total dynamic range of speech is about 30 decibels in any one band.

Only in 1962, Kryter[9] published a paper with the purpose of prescribing procedures for computing AI, proposing some new modifications and variations for AI, and providing functions relating AI to Speech Intelligibility scores.

In 1969, ANSI – American National Standard Institute, published a complete standard for general use, providing several ways to calculate AI, including octave band method and one-third-octave band method. Unfortunately, it is a complicated standard, and very difficult to understand and apply.

In the seventies, Interkeller AG, following the work of Beranek, derived a simple calculation procedure with the help of a table,using one-third-octave spectra, oriented to the automotive industry[10]. Several European car makers began to use the AI to summarize the position and shape of an one-third interior noise spectrum in the medium and high frequency range. In Brazil, the first AI presentation to the technical society was in the Third South American Quality Control Seminary[11] in 1984. In 1993, ABNT (Technical Standards Brazilian Association) published a pioneer Brazilian standard in the world context, regarding AI calculations elaborated by the Vehicle Acoustic Commission[12], including some curves relating AI to Speech Intelligibility.

According to the table adapted by Interkeller based on Beranek's article, we elaborated a summarized expression based on an idealized speech region as represented in Fig. 1, and written below:

$$AI = \sum_{f} \left[L_u(f) - L(f) \right] \frac{P(f)}{30}$$

where

$200Hz \leq f \leq 6000Hz$ in one-third-octave bands

$L_u(f) \rightarrow$ upper boundary level of speech range

$L_\ell(f) \rightarrow$ lower boundary level of speech range

$P(f) \rightarrow$ frequency weigthing adaptation

$L(f) \rightarrow$ noise spectrum

The sum is made with two conditions:

- for $L(f) \leq L_\ell(f)$ maximum contribution is P(f)

- for $L(f) \geq L_u(f)$ contribution is null

The data corresponding to $L_u(f)$, and $L_\ell(f)$ can be found in the mentioned Brazilian standard.

The frequency weighting adaptation can be seen in Fig. 2.

RELATION OF AI TO SPEECH INTELLIGIBILITY

It is common to misunderstand the meaning of AI. AI is a parameter calculated from physical measurements. Intelligibility is a psychologic parameter evaluated by speech perception tests administrated to a given group of talkers and listeners. These subjective measurements as mentioned before use sets of phonetically balanced monosyllabic words, sentences or words; getting in this way a score meaning a percentage of syllabes, words or sentences understood correctly. AI may be converted to estimate Speech Intelligibility scores by use of non-linear curves of the types showing Fig. 3. It is specially noted that the Intelligibility scores, in percent correct, depend highly on the constraints placed upon the message being communicated.

Intelligibility depends on various factors as follows: vocal effort, distance, background noise, amplification, reverberation, language, ...

SPEECH INTELLIGIBILITY TEST METHODS[13]

Other parameters were developed for the purpose of estimating Speech Intelligibility. Unfortunately they are more complicated and require specific hardwares and softwares. They are in the class of machine measures of Speech Intelligibility. They were introduced in the market mainly for applications in architectural acoustics. An overview of some methods can be observed in Table I.

SPEECH INTERFERENCE LEVEL (SIL)/PREFERRED SPEECH INTERFERENCE LEVEL (PSIL)[14,15,16]

In the fifties Beranek proposed a simplified parameter, named SIL – Speech Interference Level to estimate the Speech Intelligibility. Later, another parameter PSIL – Preferred Speech Interference Level was introduced in the market. They use sound pressure levels in octave bands above 500 Hz.

The general definition applies an arithmetic average to the sound pressure levels in dB depending on the parameter considered. So we can write:

$$\text{Parameter} = \frac{\sum_{i}^{n} L_i}{n}\ \text{dB}$$

where $L_i \equiv$ sound pressured level (dB) from octave bands.

In this way, we have used:

$$\text{PSIL} = \frac{L_{500} + L_{1K} + L_{2K}}{3}$$

$$\text{SIL 1} = \frac{L_{500} + L_{1K} + L_{2K} + L_{4K}}{4}$$

$$\text{SIL 2} = \frac{L_{1K} + L_{2K} + L_{4K}}{3}$$

Besides, trying to improve the behaviour of the parameters we defined new versions using some kind of weghtings similar to those existing in the calculation of AI. The final result for them is as follows:

$$\text{PSIL}_w = 0.2052L_{500} + 0.3261L_{1K} + 0.4690L_{2K}$$

$$\text{SIL1}_w = 0.1530L_{500} + 0.2431L_{1K} + 0.3497L_{2K} + 0.2513L_{4K}$$

$$\text{SIL2}_w = 0.2880L_{1K} + 0.4142L_{2K} + 0.2977L_{4K}$$

In the above results we used the general expression

$$\text{Parameter} = \frac{\sum_{i}^{n} \alpha_i L_i}{\sum \alpha_i}$$

where α_i are the weigthings as we have mentioned before, similar to those existing in AI calculation.

We applied our definitions in a set of passsenger cars and in a set of commercial vehicles. All the parameters were calculated, including AI. We crossed the results, using a least-squares fit to a straight line to see the linear correlation between these parameters and AI, for each set of vehicles and for both sets jointed together.

RESULTS

We show the results in two different ways: separated data sets, using passengers cars and commercial vehicles and putting all the data together to see the behaviour of the parameters.

A – Separated Sets

A summary of the results showing the linear correlation coefficients can be observed in Table II. Some examples of the least-squares fit to straight lines with the best results are demonstrated in Figs. 4 to 7. We see how strong is the linear correlation of SIL2 and SIL2_w with AI.

B – Jointed Sets

A summary of the results can be observed in Table III. The graphics in Figs. 8 and 9 illustrate some results.

ESTABLISHING A RANKING

It is interesting to use the acoustic parameters AI and SIL2 to establish a ranking regarding vehicles, since they showed the best performance concerning linear correlation. As an example we consider the set of passenger cars in the running condition of 80 km/h. See Table IV. In this Table we show also the overall noise in sones, only for characterization purposes and additional information.

PROPAGATION OF ERRORS[17,18]

- To help in the analysis of the linear correlation and in the attempt to understand the ranking we use propagation of errors in the mathematical expressions of the parameters as well in the data reduction through the least-squares fit to a straight line.

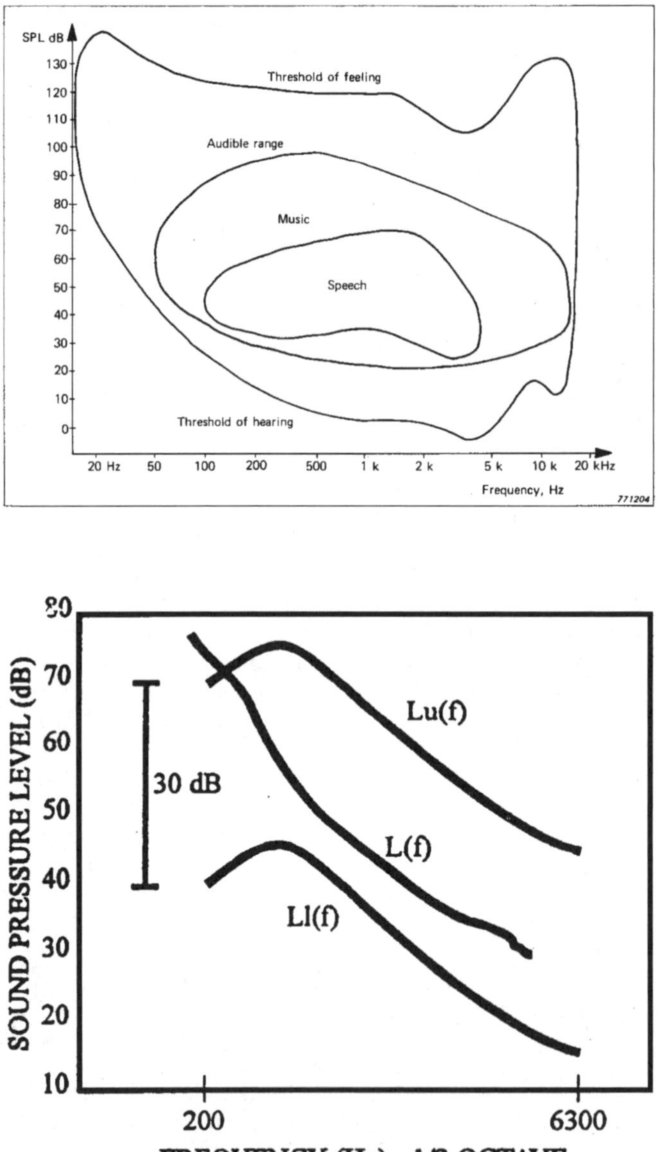

Fig. 1. Articulation Index definition and Speech Region Position.

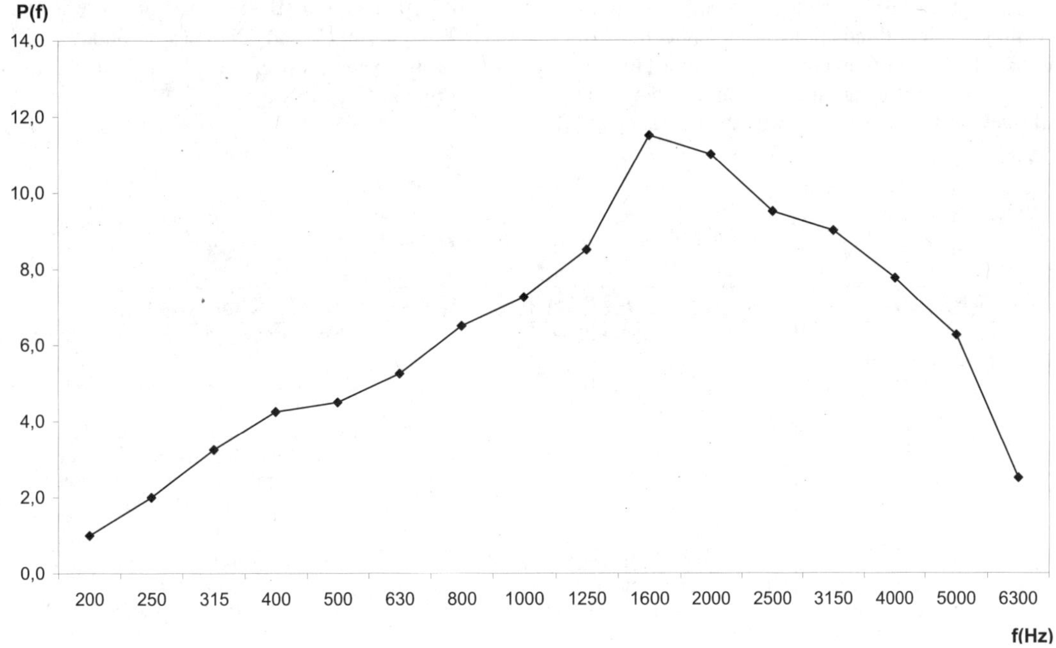

Fig. 2. Frequency weighting adaptation for AI.

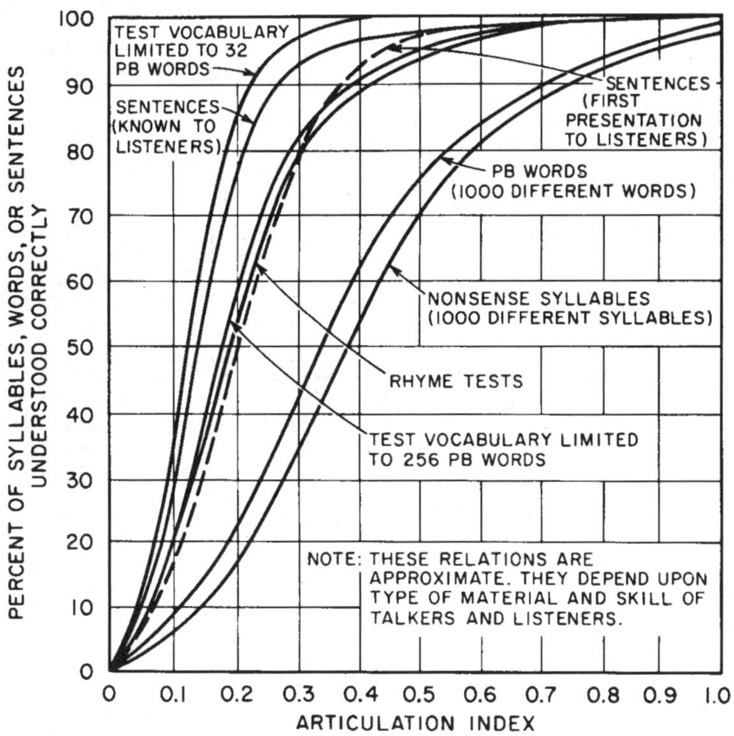

Fig. 3. Relation of AI and various measures of Speech Intelligibility.

- We consider instrumental uncertainties and deviations coming from statistical fluctuations in the collections of finite numbers of measurements. According to our experience the overall uncertainty is dominated by the statistical fluctuations. In this way we assume a standard deviation of 1.0 dB for sound pressure levels with 200 Hz $\leq$ f < 500 Hz and 0.5 dB for f$\geq$ 500 Hz.
- Applying the propagation of errors in the mathematical formula of AI we have

Table I. "Speech Intellligibility test methods"

Method	Standard Ref. in IEC 60849	Comments
STI – Speech Transmission Index	IEC 60268-16 The objective rating of speech intelligibility by speech transmission index, 1988	This is an objective, instrument-based method. Requires hardware and software for measurement and solution. Available in a computer-based olution, as a feature of some multifunction audio analysis equipment, and as a handheld meter.
RASTI – Rapid Acoustics Speech Transmission Index	IEC 60268-16 The objective rating of speech intelligibility by speech transmission index, 1998	This is an objective, instrument-based method. Reduced STI method. Available in a handheld format.
PB – Phonetically Balanced Word Scores	ISO/TR 4870 Acoustics – The construction and calibration of speech intelligibility tests, 1991	This is an objective, subject-based method. ANSI S3.2 Method for measuring the intelligibility of speech over communication systems, 1989, is a better reference for evaluations using the English language. Notification Appliances Chapter permits ANSI S3.2 use, although ISO/TR 4870 is also permitted.
MRT – Modified Rhyme Test	No reference given	This is an objective, subject-based method. No standard listed. ANSI S3.5 notes that the method has the same limits as given in ISO/TR 4870 (PB). Good reference is ANSI S3.2 Method for measuring the intelligibility of speech over communication systems, 1989.
AI – Articulation Index	ANSI S 3.5, Methods for the calculation of the articulation index, 1969 ANSI S 3.5, Methods for the calculation of the speech intelligibility index (SII), 1997	This is an objective, instrument-based method. The 1969 version is referenced. This has been updated to the 1997 edition. Requires hardware and software for measurement and solution.
%AL_{cons} – Articulation Loss of Consonants	Peutz, V.M.A., "Articulation loss of consonants as a criteria for speech transmission in a room," *J. Aud. Eng. Soc.* 19, 12, December 1971	This is an objective, instrument-based method or an objective, subject-based method. Available in a computer-based solution.

Table II. Summary – Linear Correlation Coefficient.

	Correlation Coefficient	
	Passenger Cars	**Commercial Vehicles**
AI × PSIL	0.72	0.78
AI × SIL1	0.72	0.79
AI × SIL2	0.96	0.96
AI × $PSIL_w$	0.75	0.86
AI × $SIL1_w$	0.75	0.87
AI × $SIL2_w$	0.97	0.96

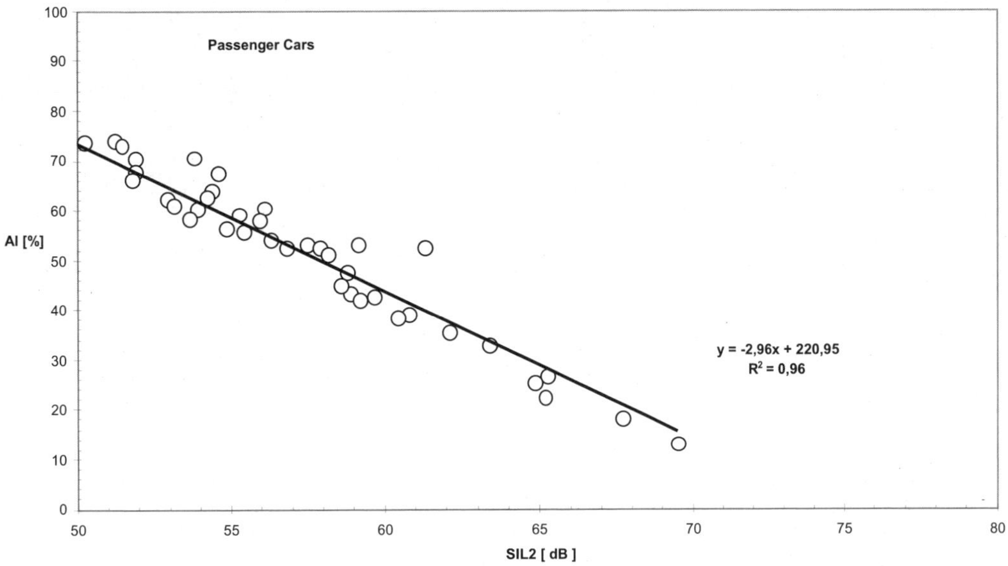

Fig. 4. AI versus SIL2 passenger cars.

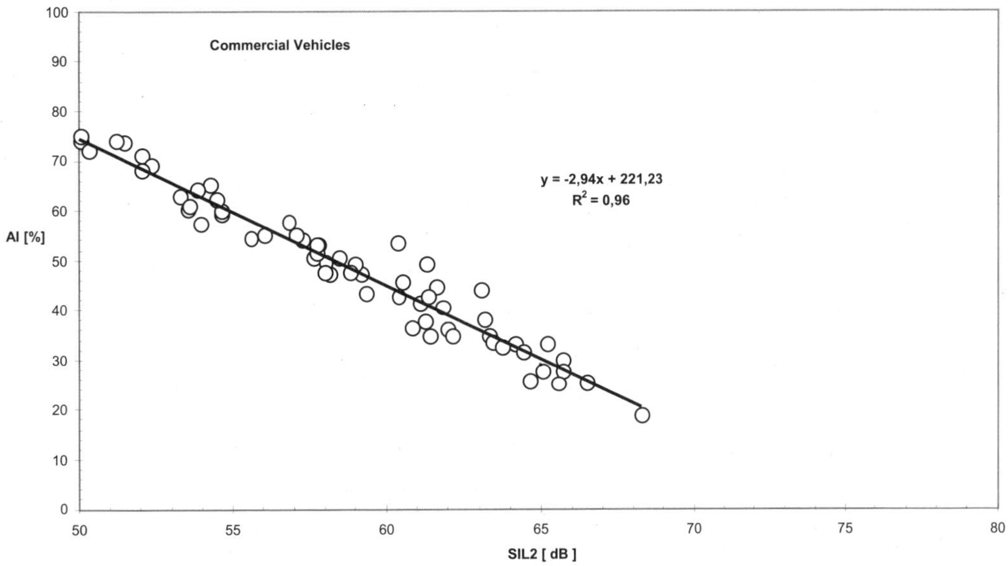

Fig. 5. AI versus SIL2 – commercial vehicles.

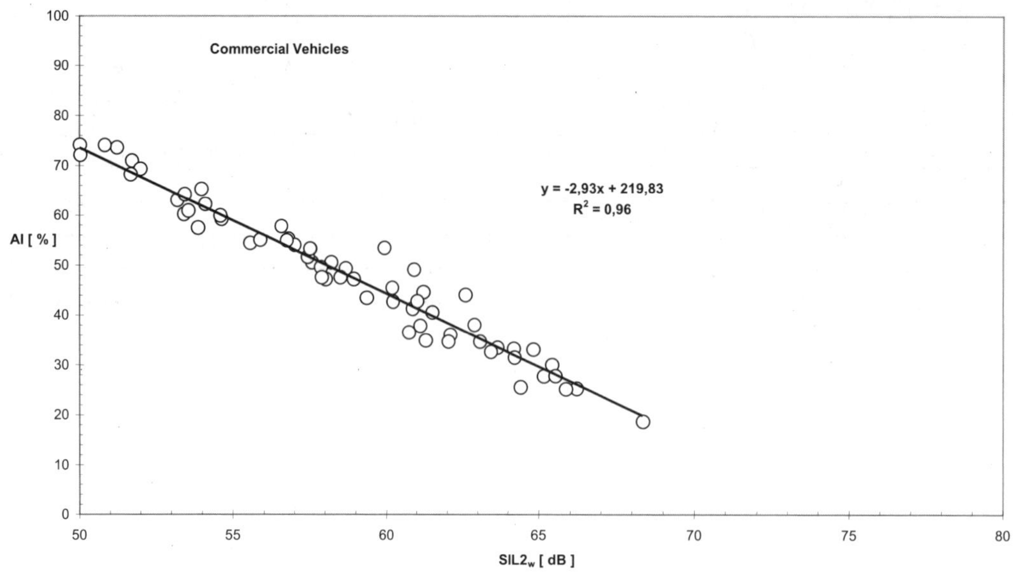

Fig. 6. AI versus $SIL2_w$ – commercial vehicles.

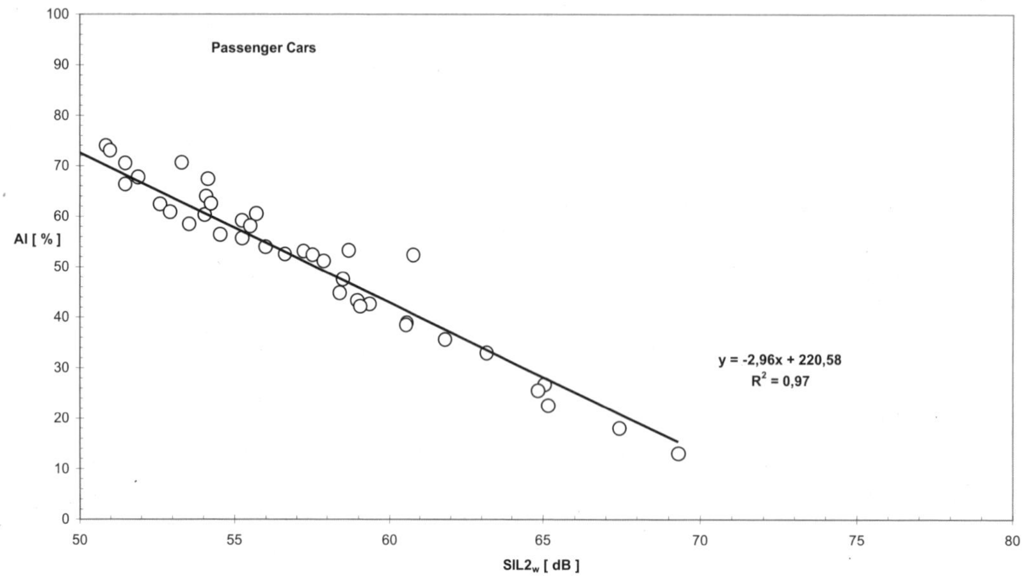

Fig. 7. AI versus $SIL2_w$ – passengers cars.

Table III. Summary – Jointed Sets.

	Correlation Coefficient
AI × PSIL	0.68
AI × SIL1	0.69
AI × SIL2	0.96

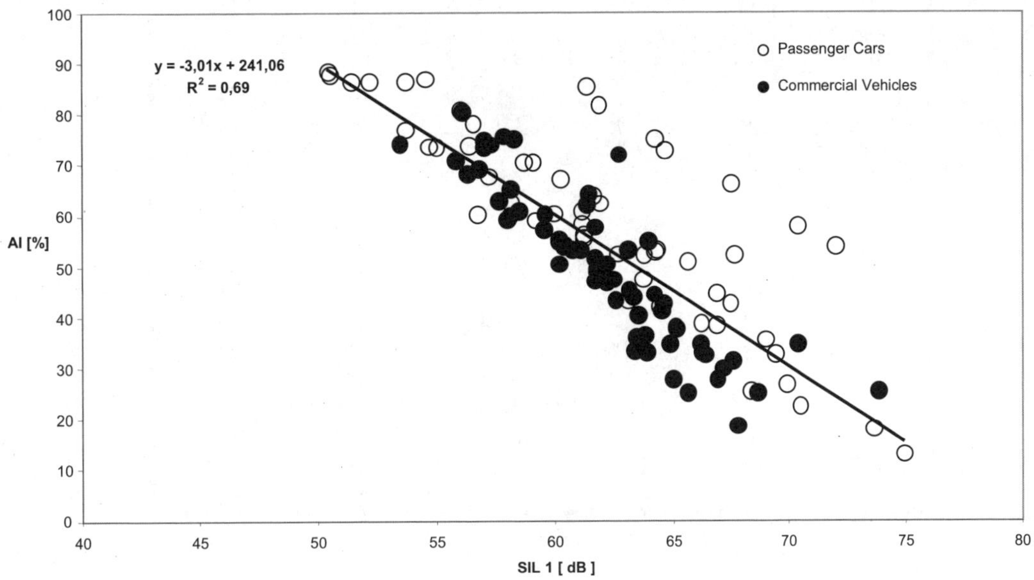

Fig. 8. AI versus SIL1.

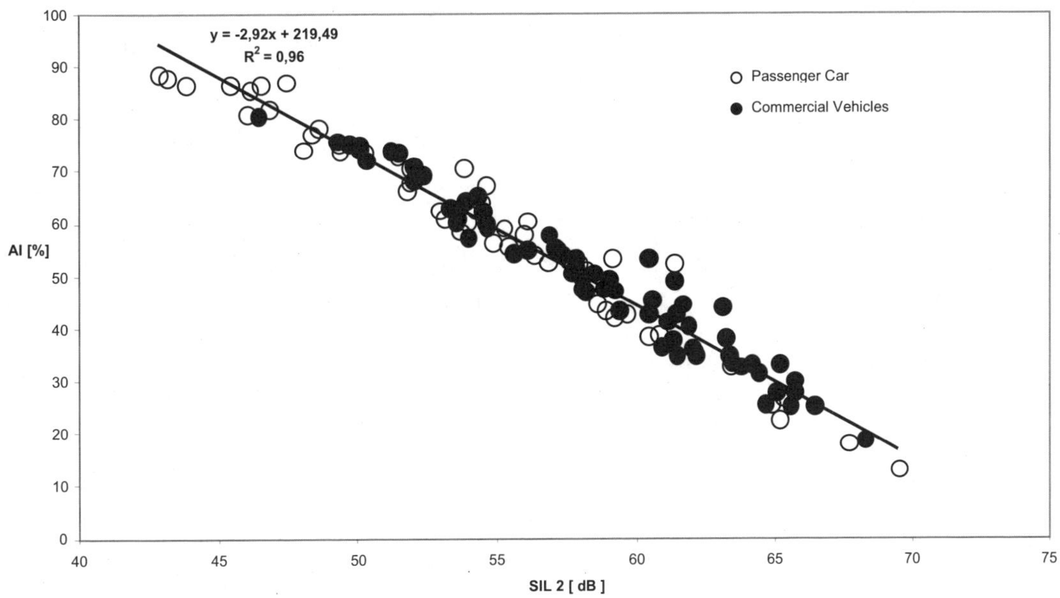

Fig. 9. AI versus SIL2.

Table IV. Ranking – Passenger Cars – 80 km/h

AI (%)	VEH	VEH	SIL2 (dB)	VEH	SONES
62.6	1	4	53.7	1	25.1
60.5	2	1	54.2	3	26.6
59.2	3	3	55.2	4	31.2
58.5	4	5	55.9	6	31.8
58.1	5	2	56.1	7	32.3
54.0	6	6	56.3	8	33.1
53.3	7	9	58.2	2	35.1
52.4	8	10	58.6	5	36.0
51.2	9	7	59.1	13	36.9
44.8	10	12	59.2	11	38.5
42.7	11	11	59.6	15	42.0
42.2	12	13	60.4	14	42.4
38.5	13	8	61.3	10	43.0
35.7	14	14	62.1	12	43.5
25.5	15	15	64.9	9	50.3
22.6	16	16	65.2	17	55.4
18.1	17	17	67.7	16	61.7
13.1	18	18	69.5	18	64.0

$$\sigma^2_{AI} = \sum_f \left(\frac{\delta AI}{\delta L(f)}\right)^2 \sigma^2_{L(f)}$$

$$\sigma^2_{AI} = \sum_f \left(\frac{P(f)}{30}\right)^2 \sigma^2_{L(f)}$$

$$\sigma^2_{AI} = \left[\frac{P(200)}{30}\right]^2 \sigma^2_{L(200)} + \left[\frac{P(250)}{30}\right]^2 \sigma^2_{L(250)} + \dots +$$

- The calculation produces $\sigma_{AI} \approx 0.5\%$.
- Applying the propagation of errors in the mathematical formula of SIL2 we get

$$\sigma^2_{SIL2} = \sum_f \left(\frac{\delta SIL2}{\delta L_{(f)}}\right)^2 \sigma^2_{L(f)}$$

$$\sigma^2_{SIL2} = \left(\frac{1}{3}\right)^2 \sigma^2_{L(1K)} + \left(\frac{1}{3}\right)^2 \sigma^2_{L(2K)} + \left(\frac{1}{3}\right)^2 \sigma^2_{L(4K)}$$

- The calculation produces $\sigma_{SIL2} \approx 0.3$ dB.

- In addition, we apply to our ranking of Table IV a least squares fit to a straight line, but now we consider the standard deviation in the straight line parameters. We get

$$(AI) = a + b\,(SIL2)$$

or

$$(AI) = 239.00 - 3.25\,(SIL2)$$

with

$$\sigma_a = 8.50,\quad \sigma_b = 0.14$$

and linear correlation coefficient ≈ 0.97.

- Considering the standard deviations σ_a (σ_b is very small) we can see in Fig. 10 a fluctuation range in the least-squares fit to a straight line of our example.
- It means we are speaking about bands or strips, where we have as average a straight line!

DISCUSSION AND CONCLUSIONS

According to the results we obtained, we can make some remarks and conclusions:

- SIL2 and $SIL2_w$ presented a strong linear correlation (≈ 0.96) with AI.

- As they showed similar results we can use SIL2(1kHz, 2kHz, 4kHz) for our purposes. It means we do not need weightings in the sound pressure levels.

- Even when we jointed all the data together (passenger cars + commercial vehicles) the behaviour of SIL2 continued to be excellent regarding its linear correlation with AI. It is independent concerning the vehicle type!
- In this way, SIL2 can be an alternative to estimate Speech Intelligibility, with the advantage of its simplicity.

- If we take the equation of Fig. 9

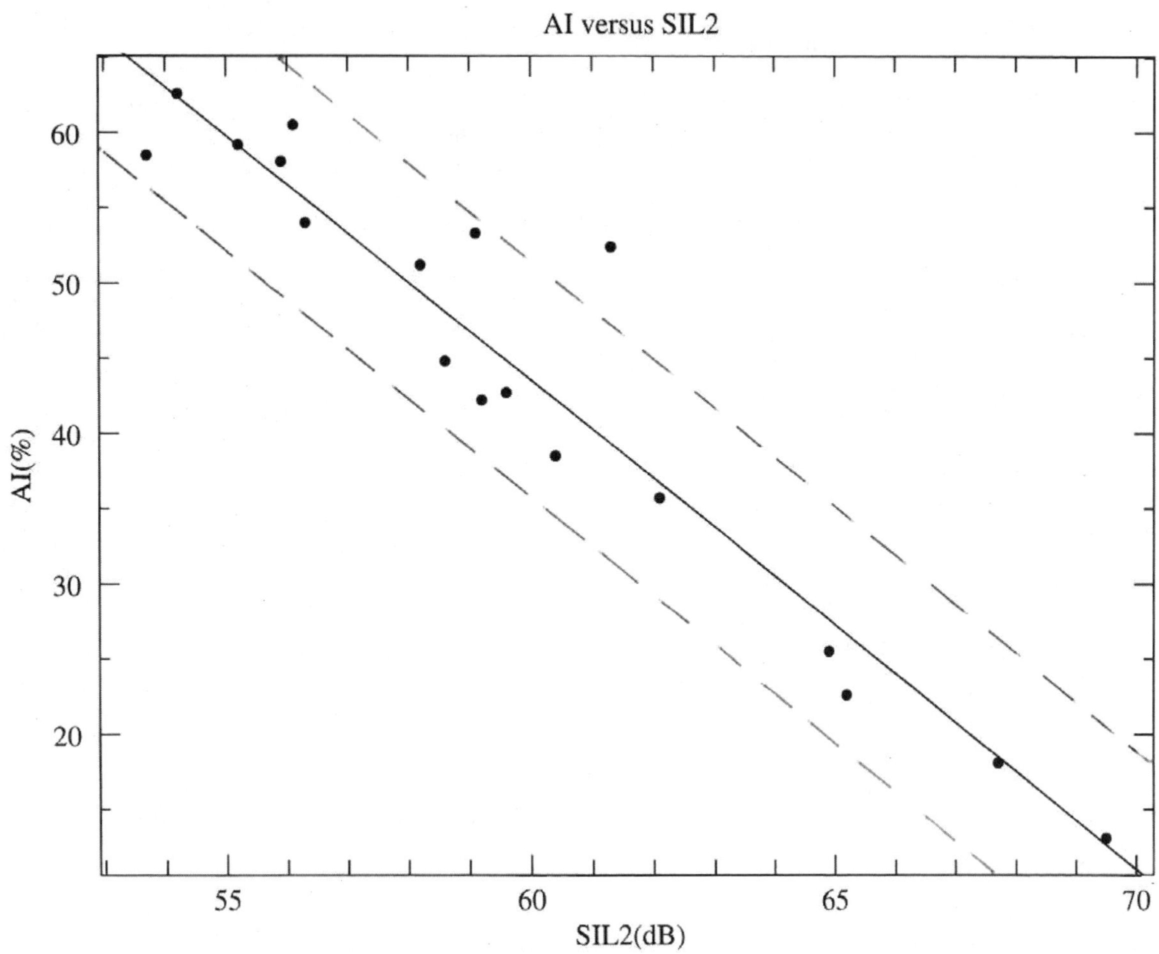

Fig. 10. Curve fitting incorporating standard deviations.

AI = -2.92 (SIL2) + 219.49

We get the following correlations:

AI (%)	SIL2 (dB)
20	68
30	65
40	61.5
50	58
60	54.5

- As we have seen the correlation of AI with Intelligibility is not so trivial. See Fig. 3. It depends on the kind of measurement we choose and a lot of factors. As a guide, based on empirical measurements and subjective evaluations, with some flexibility we have[14,19,20],

	AI	Communication
	< 0.30	unsatisfactory
between	0.30 and 0.45	marginal, but sometimes acceptable
between	0.45 and 0.65	good
above	0.65	very good/excellent

- According to the above results the recommendation for SIL2 would be lower than ≈ 60 dB for a good communication.
- Due to its simplicity, SIL2 can be used also as a parameter for quality control in vehicle acoustics, according to the correspondences of the above items.
- If we go deeper and try to establish a ranking, like Table IV, we see we have some divergences between AI and SIL2, although they have a high linear correlation. The behaviour between other acoustic parameters is similar[21,22].
- We can have a better understanding of this ranking, if we consider the standard deviations, in our propagation of errors.
- Using in our case ± 0.5% for AI and ± 0.3 dB for SIL2 we can see that the results for some specific vehicles are equivalent, if we look only the values. We must have in mind that 0.3 dB is lower than the average JND (just noticeable difference)[23,24], usually ≥ 1.0 dB.
- In addition, when we used the data from Table IV, regarding passenger cars at 80 km/h, and applied a least squares fit to a straight line, taking into consideration the standard deviations due to the curve fitting, we got Fig. 10.
- We see now that the curve fitting can be imagined as a band/strip accommodating the data where the straight line is an average line. This approach helps to explain the divergencies between AI and SIL2.
- According to the considerations we wrote above we conclude that we can use AI or SIL2 to characterize Speech Intelligibility in vehicles, because they showed similar results. But it is always mandatory to perform subjective evaluations to complement the objective measurements.

REFERENCES

1. H. Onusic and M.M. Hage – Parameters used for Acoustic Qualification/quantification of Automotive Vehicles – Int. J. Vehicle Design, vol. 37, n.° 1, pp 81-98 – 2005 – England.

2. H. Onusic and M.M. Hage - Interior Noise of Automotive Vehicles: A Proposition for Objective Characterization - SAE paper 921457 – November 1992.

3. H. Onusic, E.L. Baptista and M.M. Hage – Considerations Regarding the use of Loudness (Mark VI) and Perceived Magnitude (Mark VII) in Vehicle Acoustics – Ingénieurs de l'Automobile – n.° 755 – September 2002 – Editions VB – pp 26-36 – France.

4. H. Onusic, E.L. Baptista and M.M. Hage – Noise Inside Motor Vehicles: Acoustic Parameters Correlation – SAE paper 2003-01-3532 – November 2003.

5. H. Onusic et al. – Correlation and Evaluation of Passby and Stationary Noises – Proceedings 2000 FISITA World Automotive Congress – paper F2000H196 – June 2000 – Seoul – Korea.

6. H. Onusic, M.M. Hage and E.L. Baptista – Articulation Index (AI): Concepts and Applications – SAE paper 2000-01-3150 – October 2000.

7. H. Onusic, E.L. Baptista and M.M. Hage – Speech Intelligibility in Vehicles; Articulation Index Revisited – Proceedings SIBRAV 2005 – Brazilian Symposium of Vehicle Acoustics – June 2005.

8. L.L. Beranek – The Design of Speech Communication Systems – Proc. I.R.E., V. 35, pp 880-890 – September 1947.

9. K.D. Kryter – Methods for Calculation and Use of the Articulation Index – J. Acoust. Soc. Amer., V 34, n.° 11, pp 1689-1697 – November 1962.

10. R.H. Van Ligten – Interkeller S.A. – Zurich – private communication – May 1982.

11. H. Onusic et al. - Caracterização do Ruído Interno de Veículos - Anais do III Seminário Sul-Americano de

Controle de Qualidade – Novembro 1984 – Revista ABCQ - pp. 100-106.

12. Associação Brasileira de Normas Técnicas – ABNT – NBR 12969 – Cálculo do Índice de Articulação em Veículos Rodoviários Automotores – Julho 1993.

13. NEMA – Setting Standards for Excellence, Speech Intelligibility, 2002.

14. Handbook of Noise Assessment – Edited by D.N. May – Van Nostrand Reinhold – 1978.

15. Noise Reduction – Edited by L.L. Beranek – McGraw Hill – 1960.

16. Acoustics and Psychoacoustics – D.M. Howard and J. Angus – Focal Press – 2001.

17. Data Reduction and Error Analysis for the Physical Sciences – P.;R. Bevington – McGraw Hill – 1969.

18. H. Onusic and D. Mandic – Propagation of Errors in Chromaticity Coefficients (x,y) obtained from Spectroradiometric Curves: Tristimulus Covariances Included – Int. J. Veh. Design, V 10, n.° 1, pp 88-98 – 1989 – England.

19. M. Lower – Communications and Speech Intelligibility – ISVR Consulting – University of Southampton – UK – 2004.

20. A. Marah – Speech Intelligibillity – The Fridge – The University fo Western Australia – 1999.

21. R.H. Van Ligten - An Attempt at Comprehensive Presentation of Automobile Acoustic Questions – Unikeller Conference – 1977 – pp 02-20 – Switzerland.

22. H. Onusic, E.L. Baptista and M.M. Hage – Neither dB(A) nor Loudness: Beyond them? – SAE paper 2001-01-3971 – November 2001.

23. J. Baronese and L.G. Gibian – Experimental Determination of the Smallest Perceivable Changes in Octave Bands of Automobile Interior Noise-SAE paper 850980.

24. Acoustic Noise Measurements – J.R. Hassal and K. Zaneri – Bruel & Kjaer publication –1980.

2003-01-0127

Study of Driver Distraction Due to Voice Interaction

Noritoshi Yoshitsugu, Yonosuke Miki, Toshiyuki Ito and Mitsuhiro Matsunaga
Nissan Motor Co., LTD

ABSTRACT

A new telematics service has been launched by Nissan in the Japanese market that combines text-to-speech (TTS) technology with the communication function of a cellular phone. With this service, drivers operate their in-vehicle information system by simple voice commands, download news and the latest information from a portal site to the system via a cellular phone, and have the information read to them by the TTS synthesizer, thereby obtaining the desired information without relying on their visual processes. This paper describes the tests that were carried out in the course of developing the system to determine its potential influence on drivers' mental distraction. Tests were conducted with a driving simulator and an actual vehicle, with participation by twenty subjects, including five women. Both the driving simulator and actual vehicle were equipped with steering wheel buttons and an instrument panel LED that illuminated at random intervals during the driving tests. The subjects were instructed to follow a preceding vehicle and to press the steering wheel button when the LED illuminated. In addition, they were also given a simultaneous information device task such as listening to a prerecorded radio broadcast or news read aloud by the TTS synthesizer, viewing the navigation display or talking on a cellular phone. Their response time to the illumination of the LED was measured under these conditions. Vehicle data were also recorded to determine the amount of lateral lane displacement and change in the headway distance that occurred at the time the information device tasks were performed. The indexes were then compared for the different information device tasks assigned. The results obtained for all of the indexes showed that the mental distraction level when listening to a TTS reading of information was comparable to that of listening to the car radio.

INTRODUCTION

Text-to-speech (TTS) technology that uses speech recognition capability to convert text information into synthesized speech has made rapid progress in recent years. This progress has made it possible to develop in-vehicle systems that use a TTS synthesizer to read aloud to drivers whenever desired the latest news, e-mail and other text data downloaded from an external network via a cellular phone. At Nissan, we have developed a system that supports the provision of such services in Japan. Although new information device with TTS synthesizer might be expected to decrease the visual distraction when driver operate the information device, there is a possibility that the listening of information of high interest to a user might cause a delay in judgment due to mental distraction, which might affect the person's driving behavior. There are methods for quantifying distraction caused by visual information such as navigation map screens. One such method is the occlusion technique based on the glance time for operating equipment control switches. However, there are no effective indexes at present for evaluating mental distraction induced by spoken information. Consequently, there is a need to investigate the effect of equipment usage on driver behavior by using some method other than driver observation, such as vehicle control performance or indexes derived from a model of driver recognition and judgment when operating a vehicle.

EXPERIMENTAL DESIGN

BASIC CONCEPT OF EXPERIMENT

When in the process of driving, drivers are constantly repeating a cycle of:- information acquisition by their sensory receptors recognition/judgment and execution of driving actions in the process of operating a vehicle. Acquisition of visual information is particularly important while driving. Obstruction of a driver's field of view can easily result in a change in vehicle behavior, increased anxiety or other undesirable effects. For that reason, in evaluating the operability of navigation systems and other devices for presenting visual information to drivers while driving, a generally used technique is to quantify the length of time a driver glances away from the road ahead (i.e., visual distraction time), which can be measured relatively easily (1)(2). With in-vehicle services that combine speech recognition and TTS technology, on the other hand, it is presumed that listening to spoken information may affect driver behavior, but it is difficult to quantify that effect based on external observations such as eye movement analysis. Therefore, the indexes used in this study for evaluating mental distraction were determined on the basis of a driver recognition/judgment model while driving. The task of listening to a TTS reading was evaluated for each index in comparison with various other information device tasks given to the subjects, such as listening to a radio broadcast, talking on a cellular phone and viewing a navigation display, in order to examine the effect on mental distraction.

EVALUATION INDEXES (EXPERIMENTAL MEASURES)

A general model of driver recognition/judgment while driving is shown in Fig. 1. This model assumes that the driver's total processing capacity is allocated between that needed for driving, including confirmation of the external traffic environment, and that needed for operating in-vehicle devices and entering/receiving information. As indicated in condition (a) in the figure, even in situations with a high driving workload, such as when traveling in congested traffic or on a winding road, the driver has some spare processing capacity provided that the workload involved in operating in-vehicle devices or entering/receiving information is low. In contrast, under condition (c) where the operation of in-vehicle devices or the entering/receiving of information requires greater processing capacity, judgmental delay or error can occur due to the lack of any spare capacity. As a result, that can have the effect of influencing vehicle control or the mental workload perceived by the driver.

Therefore, it is thought that the mental workload required for voice-activated operations or listening to a TTS reading can be evaluated by measuring indexes such as vehicle control or the driver's spare capacity. The following items were used in the tests as the evaluation indexes of vehicle control performance, spare capacity and the overall mental workload.

Vehicle control performance

This was measured by the standard deviation of the amount of change in the headway distance to the preceding vehicle and the standard deviation of the host vehicle's lateral lane displacement.

Spare capacity (forward-view monitoring performance while driving)

This was measured by the secondary task response time for pressing a steering wheel button when an LED mounted directly in front of the subject was illuminated while the person was operating an in-vehicle device or listening to/reading information.

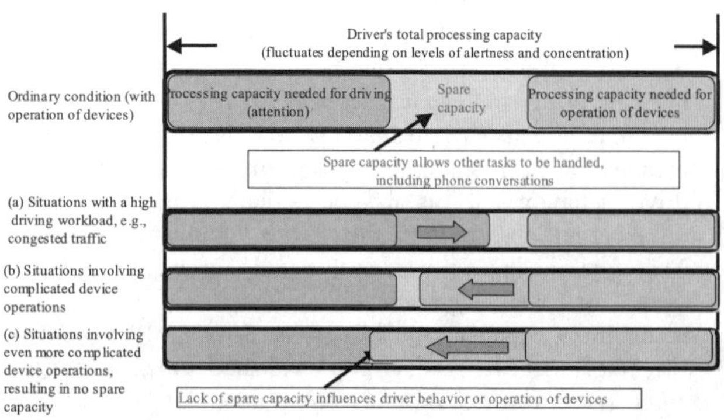

Fig. 1. Model of Driver Recognition and Judgment

Subjective evaluation of mental workload

This was measured by the Adaptive Weighted Work Load (AWWL) calculated from the National Aeronautics and Space Administration Task Load Index (NASA-TLX) scores (3).

METHODOLOGY

Tests were conducted on a driving simulator and the results obtained were then validated by conducting driving tests on a proving ground course with an actual vehicle.

Experimental conditions

Table 1 shows the experimental conditions designed for this study on the assumption that drivers generally operate in-vehicle information devices under a stable speed condition when following a preceding vehicle.

Table 1. Experimental Conditions

	Driving simulator tests	Actual vehicle tests
No. of test subjects	20 (15 men; 5 women)	6 (all men)
Age	25-40	25-42
Test course	Simulation of expressway driving	Oval proving ground course
Driving conditions	• Following a preceding vehicle at 100 km/h • Maintaining a constant headway distance of about 40 m • Presence of other vehicles	• Following a preceding vehicle at 60 km/h • Maintaining a constant headway distance of about 40 m • Presence of other vehicles

Tasks

Each subject was asked to perform two tasks simultaneously while operating either the driving simulator or the actual vehicle. As explained below, one task involved the operation of an in-vehicle information device and the other was a secondary task.

Information Device Tasks

Spoken information may be presented in a variety of forms. For instance, it may consist of long sentences, as in the case of e-mail, where the listener tries to grasp the overall meaning of the message. Alternatively, it may involve listening to information that can be partly anticipated such as weather reports. In view of these diverse forms, various listening tasks were designed for these tests as outlined in Table 2. In addition, entry of the destination in the navigation system, which involves a more complicated operating procedure, was also given as an operational task in order to make a comparison between auditory and visual tasks. The task of listening to a TTS reading also involved giving voice commands, i.e., the TTS reading began after a subject uttered the command three times. The subjects performed all of the tasks in the driving simulator tests, but from the standpoint of safety, they did not perform the telephone and complicated navigation system tasks while driving the actual vehicle.

Table 2. Information Device Tasks

Task	Device	Task Time	Task details
Listening to the radio	Radio	35-46 sec.	Subject listens to a recording of a news played through the speakers. (no operation involved)
Listening to TTS reading	--	28 sec.	Subject presses the voice switch on the steering wheel, gives voice commands to call up information and listens to a synthesized reading of e-mails about meeting places or listens to news.
Reading text information	Navigation system display	1-2 sec.	Subject reads text information consisting of 20 kanji characters shown on a display at the top of the center instrument cluster.
Entering destination	Navigation system	20-30 sec.	Subject enters the destination by inputting a 10-digit phone number using a joystick.
Receiving a call	Cellular phone	5-8 sec.	When the cellular phone rings, subject picks it up from the passenger's seat, puts it to the ear and confirms the sound.
Making a call	Cellular phone	5-8 sec.	Subject picks up the cellular phone from the passenger's seat and calls the third number registered in the memory.
Answering a question	Cellular phone	60 sec.	Subject answers a simple question. Example: "Did you eat breakfast?" "Yes"
No task (control condition)	--	60 sec.	No operational task

Secondary task

The LED mounted at the top of the instrument panel was illuminated for one second at random intervals of 5-10 seconds while the subjects were performing the information device tasks. The subjects were instructed to push a button mounted on the right side of the steering wheel as soon as they noticed that the LED was illuminated.

The configuration of the experimental setup is shown in Fig. 2. and Fig.3.

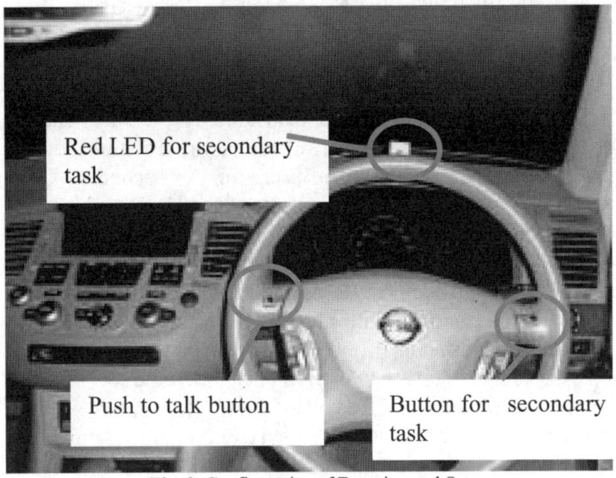

Fig. 2. Configuration of Experimental Setup

Fig3.Driving simulator

EXPERIMENTAL PROCEDURE

The tests were conducted according to the following procedure.

1. The subjects practiced the tasks outlined in Table 2 before the test began. They practiced to the extent that they were able to complete each task without making a mistake.
2. After practicing for about one minute to familiarize themselves with the operation of the driving simulator or the actual vehicle, the subjects then performed only the above-mentioned secondary task under a no-task condition (= control condition) and measurements were made for the evaluation indexes.
3. The subjects were asked to perform the secondary task simultaneously with the information device tasks in Table 2. They were informed in advance about the content of the radio broadcast and the TTS reading so that they would be able to follow the spoken information well.
4. The tests were repeated again under the control condition and the evaluation indexes were measured.

At the completion of each information device task, the subjects momentarily stopped the driving simulator or the vehicle and filled out a NASA-TLX form.

RESULTS

Figures 4-7 show the results measured for the evaluation indexes when the subjects performed the information device tasks. Similar tendencies were seen for the secondary task response times, lateral lane displacement and subjective mental workload ratings (NASA-TLX scores). Even when the subjects had listened to TTS reading, which combined the entry of a voice command, or listened to radio, their response times with respect to each evaluation index did not show any statistically significant differences when compared with the corresponding results for listening to the radio or for the control condition. On the other hand, for entry of the destination in the navigation system, requiring manual operations and visual concentration on the display screen significant differences ($P<0.05$) were seen compared with the control condition.

The standard deviation of the headway distance (Fig. 5), however, showed a different tendency from those seen for the other evaluation indexes. Only the task of entering the destination showed a significant difference ($P<0.05$) compared with the other tasks. Moreover, a comparison of the response times in the driving simulator and in the actual vehicle (Fig. 4) showed that there were no statistically significant differences between the control condition, listening to the radio and listening to TTS reading.

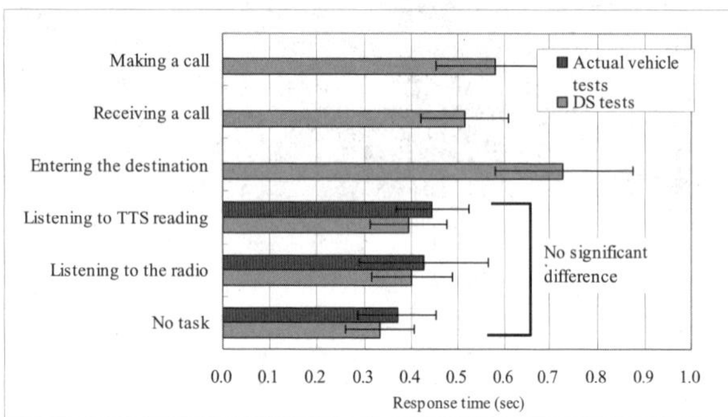

Fig. 4. Secondary task Response Time

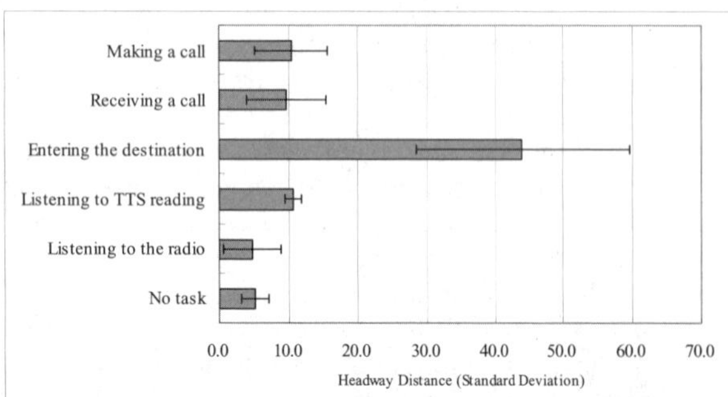

Fig. 5. Comparison of Variation in Headway Distance (Standard Deviation)

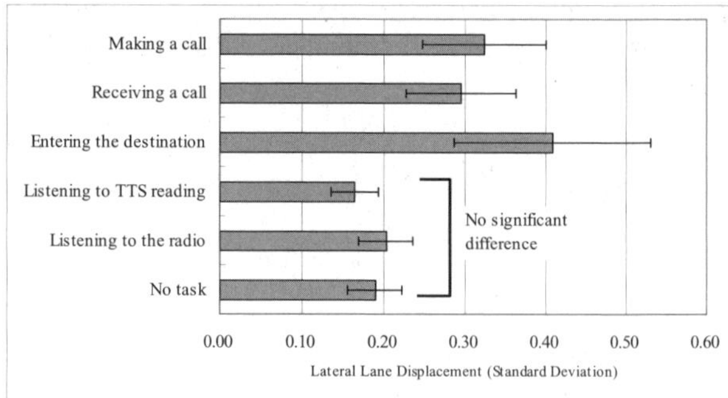

Fig. 6. Comparison of Lateral Lane Displacement (Standard Deviation)

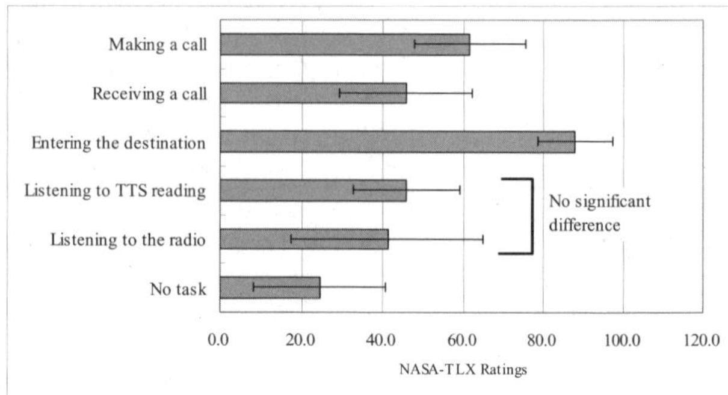

Fig. 7. Subjective Evaluation of Mental Workload

DISCUSSION

EFFECT ON DRIVER BEHAVIOR OF TTS-BASED PROVISION OF INFORMATION

For the task of listening to a TTS reading, which involved entering a voice command, the secondary task response time and lateral lane displacement did not show any significant difference compared with the results for listening to a radio. This suggests that the use of TTS technology to change the acquisition of text information to an auditory task would not have such a large influence on actual driving operations in situations where users are following a preceding vehicle, although the act of listening itself may increase the perceived mental workload. Even in the case of e-mail and other content in which users are highly interested, it is considered that the level of mental distraction would be comparable to that for listening to the car radio.

EVALUATION INDEX OF VOICE ACTIVATION

The result of headway distance displayed a different tendency from the other indexes. It showed that there were virtually no differences among the different tasks except entering destination task. This is thought to be attributable to the fact that the subjects paid the greatest attention to maintaining enough headway distance to avoid a rear-end collision with the vehicle in front when they performed the various information device tasks. However, entering the destination in the navigation system required visual concentration on the screen when inputting numbers and manual operations, making it difficult to maintain a constant headway distance. In fact, the average headway distance for the other tasks was 35-50 m, whereas it was 73 m for entry of the destination in the navigation system. This substantially longer distance would seem to indicate that the subjects unconsciously reduced their driving speed when performing this complicated task. Accordingly, it would be difficult to make a detailed comparison of the differences among the tasks with respect to the amount of change in the headway distance.

The correlation of the secondary task response time and lateral lane displacement, which displayed similar tendencies as noted earlier, with the NASA-TLX scores is shown in Figs. 8 and 9, respectively. The results indicate that both of these indexes correlated closely with the NASA-TLX ratings. Especially the reaction time was highly correlated to the NASA-TLX scores. This result shows that the response time can be an effective evaluation index.

However, if a test course involves winding roads, this button location could influence steering behavior itself, or if primary tasks are complicated, there is also a possibility that asking a subject to operate a button at the same time some other switch is operated could cause confusion, resulting in operational error.

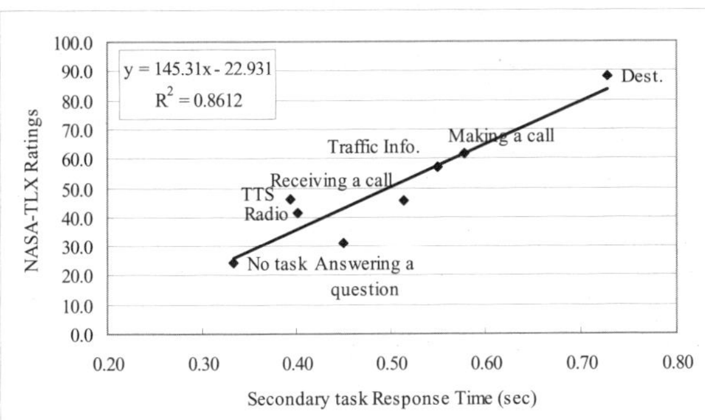

Fig. 8. Correlation Between Secondary task Response Time and NASA-TLX Ratings

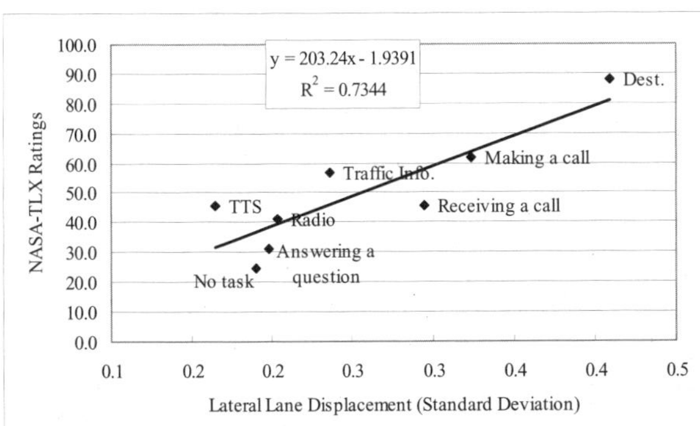

Fig. 9. Correlation Between Lateral Lane Displacement and NASA-TLX Ratings

Accordingly, if the primary task is complicated, it is thought that lateral lane displacement can be an effective index for evaluating the driver's mental workload for tasks, because this index does not require any additional task and easy to measure if a driving simulator is used.

CONCLUSION

The following results were obtained in this study based on a comparison of the driving test data and the various types of quantitative data obtained from the subjects.

1. In a driving situation like that of following the vehicle ahead, the use of TTS technology to transform text information acquisition into a listening task should not have an appreciable effect on driving behavior even in the case of information involving relatively long sentences. The mental workload involved in listening to spoken information is estimated to be similar to that of listening to the car radio.
2. Among the evaluation indexes used in this study, the host vehicle's lateral lane displacement and the secondary task response time were found to be effective in estimating the mental workload involved in listening to spoken information and in operating equipment by voice commands. Lateral lane displacement in particular is thought to be highly useful because it is easy to measure with a driving simulator and does not require test subjects to perform any particular task.

With respect to lateral lane displacement, the steering entropy method have also been established for quantifying perturbations in steering smoothness caused by external factors aside from driving tasks (4)(5). The potential application of this technique and other methods will be considered in our ongoing research into methods for quantifying drivers' mental workload.

REFERENCES

1. Kimura, K et. al. (1999). In-Vehicle Navigation System Operability while Driving. Proceeding of 6th World Congress on ITS.
2. Niiya, K. (2000). ISO/TC 22/SC 13/WG 8N289 Trial Evaluation Results on Navigation Operation using Occlusion Technique. Discussion Paper on ISO/TC22/SC13/WG8 Visual Distraction TF.
3. Miyake, S. Kumashiro, M. (1993). Subjective mental workload assessment technique – An introduction to NASA – TLX and SWAT and a proposal of simple scoring method -. The Japanese Journal of Ergonomics Vol. 29, No. 6
4. E.R. Boer and A. Liu (Eds.) (1997). Cambridge Basic Research 1997 Annual Report. CBR TR 97-7, Cambridge Basic Research, Cambridge Massachusetts.
5. Development of a Steering Entropy Method for Evaluating Driving Workload. Proceeding of 1999 JSAE Annual Congress.

2001-01-3839

The Mobile Productivity Center: Starting the Portable, Voice Enabled Future of Mobile Information and Productivity

Ronald K. Reger
Delphi Delco Electronics Systems

Joel C. Nunes
Delphi Automotive Systems do Brasil Ltda.

ABSTRACT

The use of portable information devices is rapidly becoming commonplace. Millions of cellular phones and personal digital assistants (PDAs) are sold each year and users are becoming dependent upon them for information storage and retrieval, and for increasing connectivity and productivity. However, the use of such devices while driving motor vehicles can be distracting due to the required visual and tactile interface. For example, to read one's schedule or other information in a PDA requires navigating to the information via a stylus or jog dial, and then reading a small screen of text. Similarly, most cellular phones require numerous touch inputs to place a call or retrieve a phone number stored in the device.

Delphi's Mobile Productivity Center (MPC) addresses these concerns by providing a single button activation and a speaker-independent voice interface. The MPC enables motor vehicle drivers to be productive while keeping their hands on the wheel and eyes on the road. The user interface scenarios are described, as is the electrical and software architecture. Also mentioned are future generations of the MPC that will support wireless delivery of user-specified content controlled by a voice interface.

BACKGROUND/INTRODUCTION

Portable consumer electronic devices that provide wireless voice and data communications are being sold and used extensively throughout modern society. The recent evolution of these devices has really been an accelerated revolution of portable connectivity. The revolution started with "car phones," typically a large phone in a carrying case that utilized power from the accessory jack of the vehicle. These early car phones were primarily used for business and professional purposes as the equipment and service were both expensive and bulky. The early service provided voice calls over analog technology.

The next devices were smaller and thus more portable. The "car phone" became the "cellular phone," offering small hand-held communication devices that are easily carried by individuals. Also, digital voice technology started to emerge, but with a variety of different digital protocol technologies. In North America two main digital voice technologies emerged, Time Division Multiple Access (TDMA) and Code Division Multiple Access (CDMA). These two standards competed for customers who had a variety of service provider options. Infrastructure continued to be built and subscription service fees dropped. Because of lower service fees and the practical benefit of mobile connectivity, subscriber numbers increased dramatically. The revolution continued rapidly with other technologies, including GSM and PCS, with even more options for customers.

Today it is commonplace for individuals to have cellular phones for personal use as well as business use. Moreover, these cell phones continue to be capable of more digital features and functions including paging, short message service, web connectivity, and other wireless data services.

In the same time as cellular technology was emerging, another revolution was taking place. This was the use of small hand-held computing devices used primarily for storage of personal and professional information. These devices typically are held in one's hand and have a screen for text and simple graphics display. Input and output of information is accomplished via a serial connection to a personal computer or through handwriting recognition and/or key press inputs on the device itself. These devices store thousands of contact names, addresses, and phone numbers as well as provide a simple way to manage appointments, memos, to-do lists, and e-mail. Millions of these devices have been sold to individuals for personal and business use.

THE VEHICLE OPPORTUNITY

As users become comfortable with their wireless phones and PIM products they also become reliant upon them to stay productive and connected while away from the office and home. This reliance leads to an increased frequency and duration of use, and this use occurs at a high percentage of time in motor vehicles. Unfortunately, the user interface to these devices was not designed for interactive use while piloting a moving vehicle in traffic. These devices require looking at a small screen, entering several button presses, and/or navigating menus with a jog dial or stylus. In all respects these interfaces interfere with the primary task of steering a motor vehicle while keeping attention focused on pedestrians and traffic.

The Delphi Automotive Systems Mobile Productivity Center (MPC) solves the problem of interacting with these devices while driving because the MPC voice enables the Palm V and the cellular phone. The components of the MPC are shown in Figure 1.

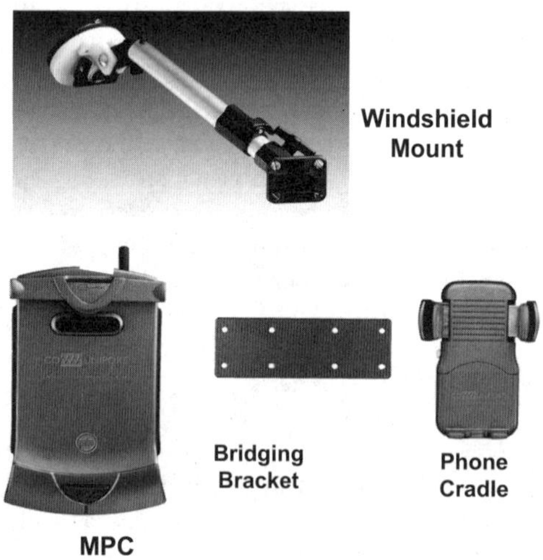

Figure 1 . Components

The Palm V/Vx docking station contains a computing platform for running the voice recognition and text-to-speech software and for managing serial communications with the Palm and phone. Also within the enclosure is a low-power FM transmitter for audio output, and this transmitter is tunable across the FM band. In the top of the dock is housed a directional microphone that is aimed in the direction of the user's voice. This helps to increase command recognition performance by blocking out extraneous noise coming from other angles within the vehicle. The phone is held securely in an adjustable mechanical cradle, and the cradle and dock are secured to a bridging bracket that rigidly holds them in place. Serial and voice communications are provided between the MPC dock and the phone via a cable. Charging for the phone is also provided in this cable. The entire assembly is then snapped to a quick-disconnect fixture on the end of an adjustable mounting arm that adheres to the windshield with a strong suction cup. The arm rests on top of the vehicle's dash, providing easy reach and access to the MPC button.

The MPC provides a voice interface to your Palm V or Palm Vx hand-held computer and cellular phone. Voice recognition software is utilized to recognize requests for information from your Palm, and text-to-speech software reads the data back to the user. The recognition engine provides for continuous speech recognition so that numbers and phrases can be spoken without pauses between utterances. Audio output is provided by the FM transmitter to the vehicle FM receiver, or through an earphone, or through a cassette adapter used in conjunction with the vehicle's cassette player. A plug that is inserted into the 12-volt accessory jack provides power to the unit. The entire unit is self-contained and is therefore portable from vehicle to vehicle. The mechanization is shown in Figure 2.

The MPC is simple and easy to use. The user voice-navigates through a simple menu tree to retrieve information from data bases in the Palm, or to voice-dial the dial the phone by speaking the phone number as a string of digits. One button is pressed to start the MPC's recognition software, the MPC responds with an audible "ready," and the user then talks to the MPC to command it to do a variety of things. The MPC menu tree is shown in Figure 3.

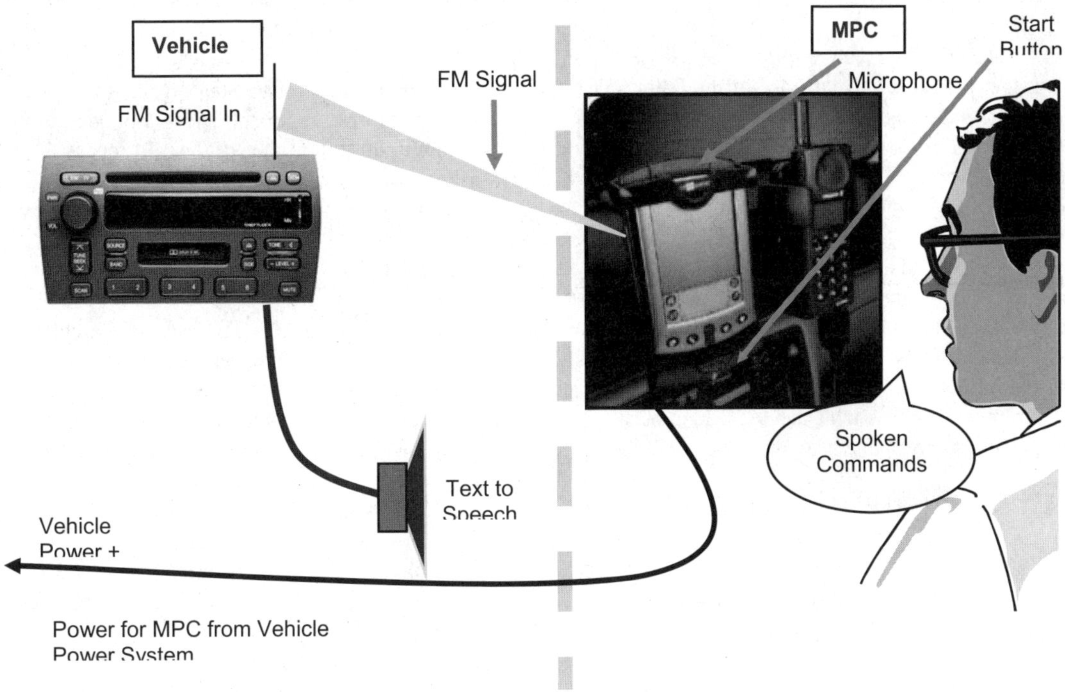

Figure 2 . Mechanization

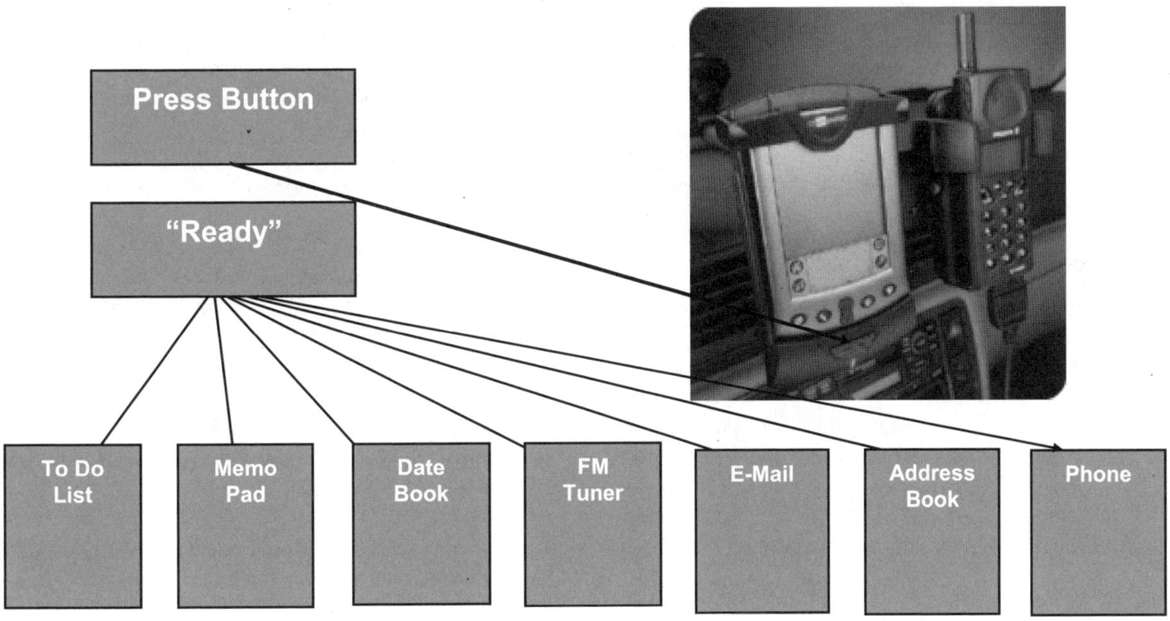

Figure 3 . Menu Tree

The respective menu features allow the user to do a variety of productive functions as described below:

TO DO LIST - This feature allows the user to listen to entries in the "To Do List" database of the Palm V/Vx. One can also move through the entries by speaking "go to first, go to last, next, or previous." When finished with the interaction with the "To Do List" then one can return to the top of the menu by saying, "Main Menu."

MEMO PAD - This Palm database can be voice navigated much like the "To Do List" but with one difference. Memo Pad entries contain text below the title line, so the MPC allows the user to voice navigate title lines until the proper one is selected, then the user speaks the "read" command which tells the MPC to process the content of that entry through text-to-speech.

DATE BOOK -This feature allows the user to speak any date, such as, "November 9th," or to say such commands as "tomorrow, yesterday, Saturday, or next Friday." Once into the specific day, the MPC reads back the first appointment and waits for the next verbal command from the user. At this point the user can say, "next, previous, go to first, go to last, or repeat" to navigate through a specific day's appointments. The "Main Menu" command returns the user to the "Ready" response from the MPC.

FM TUNER - One method of audio output from the MPC is through a tunable FM transmitter within the MPC. The FM Tuner menu allows the user to change broadcast frequencies by simply stating a new frequency, such as "ninety-seven point five." The MPC then tunes the internal FM transmitter to broadcast on 97.5 and reminds the user to tune the receiver to 97.5.

E-MAIL - The MPC reads e-mail through text-to-speech, and allows voice navigation through e-mail subjects/authors prior to reading the body of the memo. This is similar to the memo pad function of the MPC. The MPC allows the user to voice navigate subjects/authors by speaking the familiar commands, "next, previous, go to first, go to last, etc." Then, once the chosen title/author is located the command, "read" starts the MPC processing the body of the message through text-to-speech.

ADDRESS BOOK - This feature is very useful for the mobile professional wishing to place cellular phone calls to clients and associates whose numbers are in the address book. Upon initialization, the MPC creates a phonetic representation of every name in the address book and stores these in memory. When names are spoken, for example, "John Smith," then MPC matches the spoken name with the one stored in memory and asks the user to verify that a correct match has taken place. Then the MPC extracts the information associated with that name and reads it back to the user. The user can also command the MPC to place the person's phone number into the phone and dial that number. This can all be done hands-free with only voice interaction, and the user can select which phone to dial, such as home, work, or mobile. Therefore, a user can call anyone in the address book without looking at a cellular phone or PDA!

PHONE - The state-of-the-art voice recognition system allows the user to speak a phone number naturally without pause, and the MPC will process the information, ask the user for verification, and place the call. This is very useful for numbers that are memorized by the user.

TECHNOLOGY

HARDWARE - The hardware architecture consists of a 120 MHz microprocessor to handle the voice recognition and text-to-speech software, as well as serial communications with the Palm and the phone. A DSP is used for acoustic echo cancellation and handling voice responses. Application software is resident on flash memory, and SDRAM is used for storing phonetic representations of the address book names as well as other dynamically changing information. A low power FM transmitter is on board and it is tunable across the FM band in 100 KHz increments. A directional microphone focuses on the main user as the spoken command sound source, and all the pieces are bracketed together for easy installation in any vehicle. Power is provided through the 12-volt accessory jack of the vehicle, and a PIC processor monitors input voltage to infer vehicle battery strength. If the input voltage drops below a certain level the PIC turns off all MPC functions to save the vehicle battery. Optional audio output paths include a cassette adapter and/or an earphone, both of which plug into the audio output jack of the MPC, and are volume-adjustable with a small potentiometer dial on the unit.

SOFTWARE - The MPC software consists of proprietary code developed for specific applications, as well as the Lernaut and Hauspie ASR 1600 and TTS 3000 speech engines. Additional software packages run on the Palm to facilitate serial communications with the MPC and to set the FM frequency of the transmitter. A CD-ROM is included with each MPC for loading the Palm-side code on the user's PDA. The unit has a field upgrade port for future software upgrades.

SYSTEM - The system was designed to accommodate nearly all vehicles. The only requirement is for the vehicle to have a 12 accessory plug for powering the unit and a windshield for mounting the unit. As previously mentioned, the mounting arm suctions to the windshield and rests on the top of the dash. A universal joint on the end of the arm allows the user to position the MPC in the proper orientation toward the driver. This maximizes the benefit of the directional microphone and provides easy access to the start button. The MPC works with both the Palm V and Vx, and the 1228d and R280 Ericsson cellular phones.

CONCLUSION

Delphi Automotive Systems' MPC pro has solved the problem of interacting with a cell phone and PDA while driving. It provides easy, voice-interactive continuous use and allows the user to be productive while keeping their eyes on the road and hands on the wheel. Delphi Automotive Systems is working on next generation MPCs which will provide wireless data and location based services for added convenience, features, and increased productivity of the user.

AUTHOR BIOGRAPH

Ronald K. Reger, Technical Manager, Mobile Productivity Center
Delphi Delco Electronics Systems
1800 E. Lincoln Rd., M/C E 103
Kokomo, IN 46904
Ph: 765-451-9102
Fax: 765-451-8852
E-mail: ron.k.reger@delphiauto.com

Mr. Reger holds BS and MS degrees in Physics, and has worked at Delphi Delco Electronics Systems for 21 years. He has held a variety of positions in all aspects of engineering, including wafer fab engineering, advanced engineering, and project management. He holds 2 patents and is the author/co-author of numerous technical papers.

2001-01-1530

The Influence of In-Vehicle Noise on Speech Recognition for Automotive Voice-Activated Control Systems

Dave G. Fish
MIRA

ABSTRACT

Voice activation provides a safe and convenient method of controlling vehicle systems such as in-car entertainment, telecommunications, and climate control. In the fullness of time it is likely that there will be a high demand across all vehicle classes for such systems for a wide range of vehicle control functions. One of the challenges facing their development and introduction into vehicles is that of the in-vehicle noise environment. This paper investigates the influence of in-vehicle noise on speech recognition performance for an automotive voice-activated system over a range of vehicle classes and typical vehicle operating conditions. The investigation was carried out in a controlled laboratory environment using pre-recorded speech and in-vehicle noise recordings. Analysis of the experimental data showed significant system performance sensitivity and well defined, consistent, performance thresholds to the overall level of noise and spectral balance components typically found in the automotive environment. Significant differences in speech recognition performance between the male and female voice were also found. With this information it has been possible to identify both the vehicle classes and operating conditions that are likely to create the most challenging environments for acceptable speech recognition performance. This provides a useful reference for further research and development of both voice-activated speech recognition (VSR) system software and hardware design, and identification of in-vehicle noise targets for future vehicles.

INTRODUCTION

Speech recognition systems are modules that deal with speech input, in this case from the vehicle driver, to deliver a command to in-vehicle control systems. A correct interpretation of the acoustic waveform is critical to successful control of these in-vehicle systems. There are a number of recogniser systems available, based upon various methods of speech modelling using paradigms such as Hidden Markov Modelling. Most approaches distinguish two phases: a training phase and an exploitation phase. In general, these systems utilise a limited contextual vocabulary to reduce complexity and errors in the speech recognition process. However, accurate speech recognition even for the smallest set of vocabulary will be compromised where the signal (speech) levels are low compared to the in-vehicle background noise. As VSR systems are introduced into a wider range of vehicles, the demands upon them will become greater both in terms of their breadth of functionality and also in their ability to accurately interpret spoken driver commands. The level and character of noise environments that such systems have to operate in is diverse. Road, wind and engine noise sources combine to generate a complex noise signal over which a person's voice is superimposed and interpreted.

There are a number of standards and recognised practices used in the analysis of VSR systems (1,2). The application of these standards is implicit in the experimental work described here and is only described, where necessary, for clarity. The application of standardised material and methods allows future analysis of such systems to be compared directly with these results.

This paper describes an experiment conducted at MIRA towards defining speech recognition performance thresholds to in-vehicle noise for a typical in-vehicle VSR system. Through the identification of the in-vehicle noise parameters that compromise VSR for both male and female speakers, it should be possible to identify the primary parameters that cause significant breakdown in VSR performance in vehicles.

THE EXPERIMENT

EXPERIMENTAL METHOD – A voice-activated speech recognition buck was used for these experiments. This had a number of functions including the commonly used remote phone-dial function: this function was chosen for the purposes of the experiment. Following activation of the VSR through a spoken "phone dial" prompt, up to ten digits were then spoken to the VRS in two groups of five. The VRS confirmed the digits upon completion, both verbally and through a digital display.

A vocabulary of ten digits (0 to 9) from pre-recorded reference speech were used for this purpose; taken from the Noisex-92 studies (2): these are available in the public domain. Through editing, the speech files were arranged as twenty separate electronically stored waveforms, each containing a string of ten spoken digits in the order 1 to 9, and 0 (zero). Ten of these files were individually generated from a male speaker and ten from a female speaker. A gap of approximately 3 seconds was placed between each spoken digit to reduce inter-digit pre- and post-masking conflicts for the VSR system.

In-vehicle noise was recorded for a range of vehicle classes, operating speeds (including operation at idle), road surfaces and traffic conditions that would normally be encountered on the public highway within the United Kingdom. Thirty-eight vehicle noise recordings were used in total. Each of the noise signals was approximately one minute in length.

A workstation and signal processing software were used for calibrating, filtering, presenting and analysing the different signals. A block diagram of the experimental set up is shown in figure1. Reproduction of both speech and vehicle noise were reproduced through a loudspeaker adjacent to the VSR system. The speaker was located at the driver's head position relative a typical in-vehicle VSR system microphone location. Following calibration of the complete system, digital filters were applied to the in-vehicle noise signals ensuring correct signal amplitudes and spectral balance at the VSR system microphone. The speech signals were calibrated separately using a procedure described in reference 2. The output from the VSR system for each file was recorded and compared against the actual spoken numeric string. These comparisons formed the basis of the analysis described below.

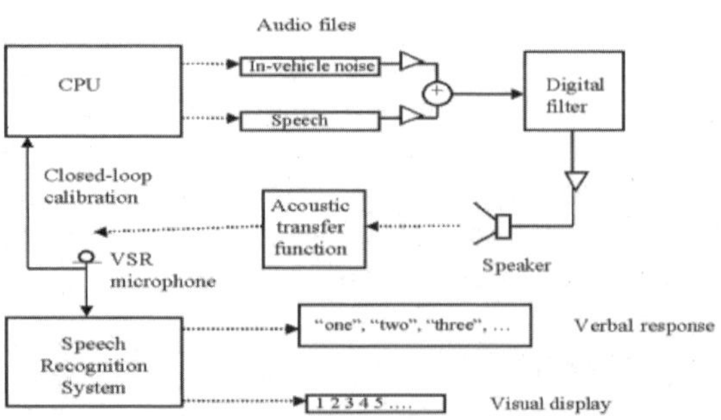

Figure 1. Experimental Method and Process

The VSR system response was recorded and analysed for all speech files against each recorded vehicle noise. Initial analysis of the experimental data included the calculation of metrics for the in-vehicle noise and analysis of VSR performance.

<u>In-vehicle noise</u> – Metrics that defined the overall quantity of noise and the spectral balance were calculated for each vehicle. These included dBA, Zwicker Loudness, Intelligibility, SIL, PSIL etc. for the overall levels, and Spectrum Balance (3) and Sharpness for the definition of high-to-low frequency ratio. These were subsequently used for correlation with the VSR system performance described below. Calculations for these metrics were made over the entire time history for each vehicle recording.

<u>VSR system performance analysis</u>

VSR accuracy is primarily defined by the number of actual correct responses against the maximum number of possible correct responses. In this case, since there were ten digits and ten files for the male and female respectively then there are 100 possible correct responses for each. In addition, the incorrect responses are classified according to the following regime:

- Deletions – the VSR system does not provide any response to a given input
- Insertions – an additional digit is identified by the VSR system where no input was made
- Substitution – a given input to the VSR system is identified as a different (incorrect) digit

Deletions, insertions and substitutions need to be accounted for if the full picture of VSR system accuracy is to be determined: there is the potential for greater error in the system response than is indicated by the number of correct responses alone. In this case the accuracy of the VSR system was defined as:

VSR System Accuracy

= Number of correct responses minus total number of deletions, insertions and substitutions

For cases where there are no insertions It can be seen that the score awarded can range from +100 to –100.

EXPERMENTAL RESULTS

Pearson Correlation Coefficients of the speech recognition accuracy against a number of the vehicle noise metrics is shown in table 1. The VSR system performance for both the male and female voices show a high level of correlation with Intelligibility as compared to other metrics, including Zwicker Loudness and dBA; two of the most commonly used in-vehicle noise metrics. There is also significant correlation of spectral balance components (Tonality and Spectrum Balance) with the accuracy of the VSR system response.

Intelligibility is a method devised by Beranek (4) to evaluate speech disruption from background noise in a variety of environments, including vehicles. It seems logical that this human-to-human speech interference metric would also work well for human-to-VSR system performance definition. Intelligibility is calculated from non-linear weighting of the 1/3-octave band levels between 160 Hz and 6300 Hz.

Metric	Accuracy (female)	Accuracy (male)
Zwicker Loudness	**-0.57**	**-0.65**
dB(lin)	**-0.44**	**-0.52**
dBA	**-0.52**	**-0.61**
dB (Speech)	**-0.66**	**-0.73**
PSIL	**-0.71**	**-0.78**
SIL	**-0.77**	**-0.82**
Intelligibiltiy	**0.89**	**0.90**
Kurtosis	**-0.13**	**-0.20**
Sharpness	**-0.75**	**-0.71**
Tonality	**0.31**	**0.34**
Spectrum Balance	**0.74**	**0.71**
High Frequency Factor	**0.73**	**0.68**

Table 1: Pearson Correlation Coefficients for VSR System Accuracy Versus In-vehicle Noise Metrics

Figure 2a and 2b show the relationship between Intelligibility and VSR system accuracy for both the female and male voice reproduction across the range of in-vehicle background noises. In general, it can be seen that high levels of intelligibility correspond to high levels of performance in the VSR system accuracy. Two other observations can also be made:

- The VSR accuracy levels are generally poorer for the respective male speech than female speech.
- The variance in VSR system accuracy at high levels of Intelligibility is greater for the male speech than the female.

The mean VSR system score for the female speech was recorded as 74.7 as compared to 62.3 for the male speech. Statistical analysis showed this difference to be significant at the 95% confidence interval.

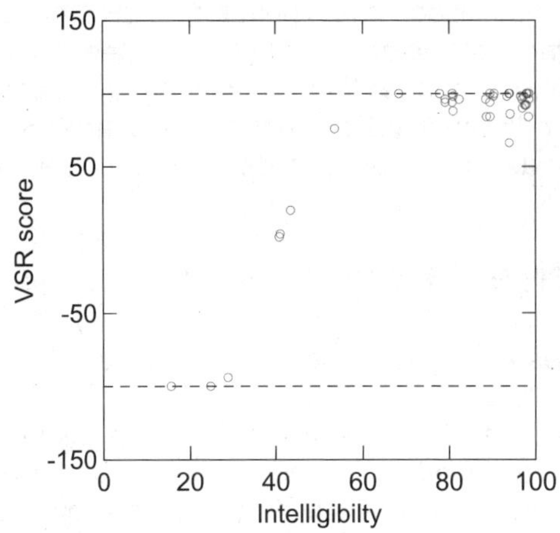

Figure 2a. VSR Accuracy for Female Speech for a Range of In-vehicle Intelligibility Levels

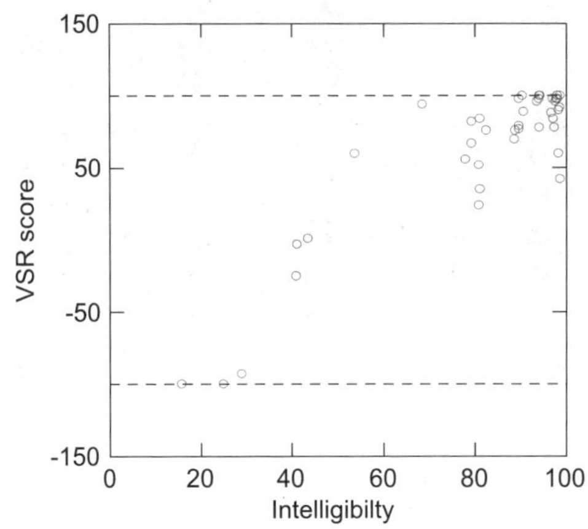

Figure 2b. VSR Accuracy for Male Speech for a Range of In-vehicle Intelligibility Levels

Given the high degree of (statistically significant) correlation for VSR accuracy with Intelligibility, it is possible to predict with a certain degree of confidence the VSR performance for a given vehicle condition. This cannot be an absolute prediction since there are variables such as speech pitch and speech level that vary from person-to-person and with driver workload that are not accounted for within this experiment. However, within these constraints and with a knowledge of particular in-vehicle noise levels, it is now possible to identify vehicle classes and vehicle operating conditions for which this type of VSR system is likely to be compromised in its function.

EXPERIMENTAL ANALYSIS

Having identified the primary VSR performance-controlling parameter, the in-vehicle speech intelligibility levels, further analysis was conducted to understand and identify additional VSR performance characteristics and variation as a result of gender-related pitch frequencies.

SPEECH PITCH ANALYSIS

Examples of wavelet analysis for the female and male spoken digits, used in this experiment, are shown in figures 3a and 3b respectively. These highlight the pitch variation between male and female voice for the given digits and that there is significant information in the male voice at lower frequencies. Given large lower frequency level variations between vehicle classes, operating conditions and road surfaces (3), it is likely that there are greater levels of masking for the male voice in certain conditions for the same level of speech, than for the female voice.

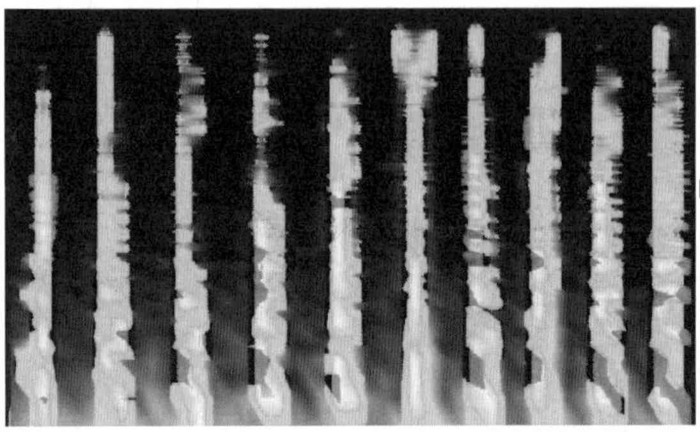

Figure 3a. Wavelet Transform of Female Speech

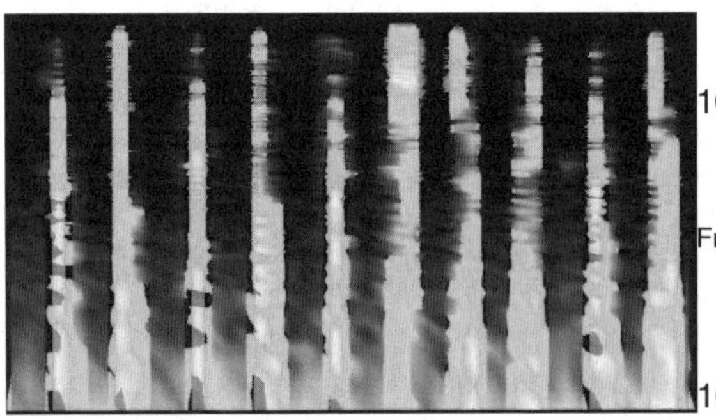

Figure 3b. Wavelet Transform of Male Speech

CORRELATION

Factor analysis of the in-vehicle noise metrics revealed significant independent (orthogonal) variation in the metrics associated with low-high frequency balance as compared to bands associated with the mid-frequency (200 to 1kHz) level metrics. This is consistent with findings in previous studies (3). Spectral balance metrics include Spectrum Balance (SB) and Sharpness. Figure 4 shows the orthogonal relationship, in two dimensions, for the in-vehicle noise data set used in this experiment.

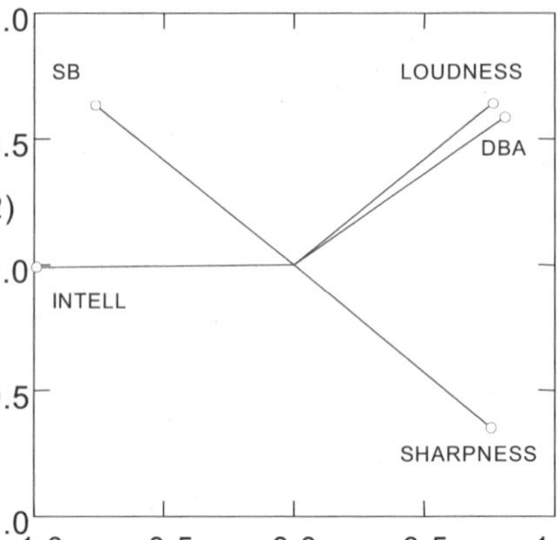

Figure 4. Data Reduction of In-vehicle Noise Metrics Using Factor Analysis

Linear regression of the VSR scores with combined metrics yields improved levels of correlation for both male speech and female speech recognition. For example a Pearson Correlation Coefficient of 0.95 was achieved for a linear combination of Intelligibility and Spectrum Balance as compared to 0.90 for Intelligibility alone. Based upon these two factors, predictions of the VSR system performance can be calculated (figures 5a and 5b) for the female and male speech respectively. A greater sensivity to spectral balance components can be seen for the male speech indicating that pitch frequency influences in the VSR system performance and that this cannot be accounted for by the overall level of noise alone. It must be noted here that due to the sample sizes this variation in sensitivity cannot be stated with a high level of confidence: further, extensive, investigations are required.

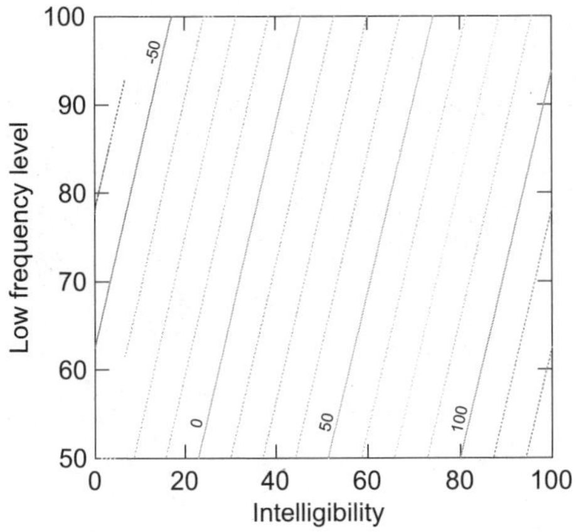

Figure 5a. Predicted VSR System Accuracy Score from Combining Level and Spectral Balance Noise Components for the Female Speech

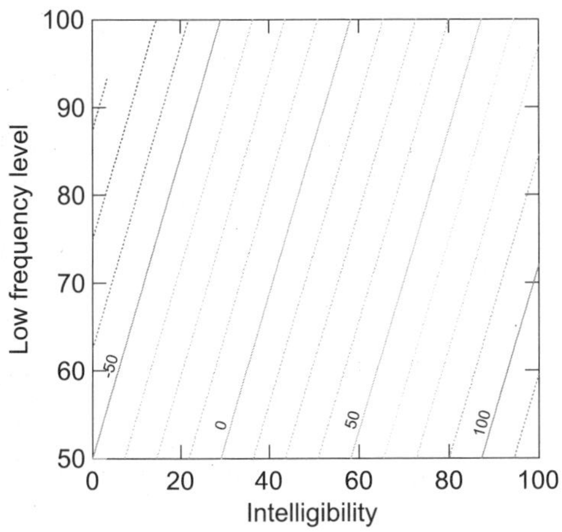

Figure 5b. Predicted VSR System Accuracy Score from Combining Level and Spectral Balance Noise Components for the Male Speech

*Low frequency level: Mean of the unweighted 32, 63, and 125 Hz 1/3-octave bands

CONCLUSION

VSR system performance is strongly influenced by the speech band intelligibility levels normally present in vehicles. For the current range of saloon vehicles, it can be determined that during certain operating conditions and on particular road surfaces these systems are potentially heavily compromised and unable to perform satisfactorily. The VSR system performance was generally poorer for male speech as compared to female speech for the same level of vehicle noise. There was significant variation the level and spectra balance of the in-vehicle noise data set for these experiments. It was found that accounting for both of these factors improved the correlation of in-vehicle noise metrics with VSR system performance and also accounted for VSR system performance variation between female and male speakers.

ACKNOWLEDGMENTS

I would like to acknowledge the support of the following:

- Lewis Mowatt, of Jaguar Cars, for the loan of a Voice-activated Speech Recognition System and the provision of some of the in-vehicle noise recordings.

- Brian Mellor, of 20/20 Speech, for technical support and provision of speech signals.

- Nyoka Hatch for her hard work and diligence in conducting the experiment.

REFERENCES

1. D. Gibbon, R. Moore, R. Winski. Handbook of Standards and Resources for Spoken Language Systems. ISBN 3-11-015366-1
2. A. Varga, H.J.M. Steeneken, M. Tomlinson. The Noisex-92 Study on the Effect of Additive Noise on Automatic Speech Recognition. NATO Research Study Group (RSG.10) laboratories (in liaison with the ESPRIT SAM project laboratories).
3. D.G.Fish, Application of the Composite Rating of Preference to Road and Wind Noise. SAE NVH Conference. Traverse City 1997.
4. L.L.Beranek. Criteria for Noise and Vibration in Communities, Buildings and Vehicles In Noise and Vibration Control. Revised edition, McGraw-Hill Inc. 1988.

DEFINITIONS, ACRONYMS, ABBREVIATIONS

Spectrum Balance: Mean of the unweighted 32, 63, and 125 Hz 1/3-octave bands minus Speech Interference Levels.

2000-01-3286

Improving In-Vehicle Voice Recognition Systems: Basis for Enhancing the Telematics Experience

Rogerio Vollet
General Motors do Brasil Ltda.

ABSTRACT

Although voice recognition is not essential for telematics application, it is certainly one of the most attractive features for the customer who buys it. The appealing is such that may determine the whole system success in the market and, therefore, deserves our attention. This paper discusses the voice recognition task and ways to improve it in the vehicle hostile environment. In order to create a robust system, artificial neural networks are being used in combination to the appropriate signal processing, which includes temporal alignment and spectral transformation for MFCCs features extraction. The problems related to in-vehicle application are described and feasible solutions are suggested. A proposed architecture is then designed considering all foreseen complications, taking advantage of sensors already available in other vehicle systems, ensuring the performance optimization at minimum cost increase.

INTRODUCTION

Customers are silently demanding improvements in the interaction between the driver/passengers and the vehicle, and this claim is even more evident in telematics systems. A voice recognition system is the first natural step for making it easier and more pleasant for them, and it is needless to say that the recognition performance is crucial for achieving such objective. Nevertheless, safety is certainly improved because of the reduced distraction while driving and, sometimes, it is also taken as the main reason for improving it. Anyway, nobody can deny the enjoyable experience of driving a voice-commanded vehicle and that is the main motivation of this work.

Voice recognition is herein considered as both: speaker and speech recognition. The first can be used to recognize, for instance, who said a *good morning* greeting to the system and answer it mentioning the speaker's name. This could be accomplished by using artificial neural networks for learning the voice differences among all users while they are effectively using the system. When the speaker is recognized by an answer like *good morning George*, it will make him feel special, increasing the customer value for sure. The second one is the heart of the system, where voice commands are identified and processed. Here it is very important to have a robust recognition, even on severe conditions like a raining day, to avoid bothering the customer by asking him to repeat the last command or by a misinterpretation.

This paper is structured as follows. Firstly the voice signal production is described and a features extraction process is presented for creating the most appropriate representation of the voice signal for speaker and speech classification tasks, which are conceptually discussed next. Secondly, artificial neural networks are introduced with an explanation about their capabilities on learning and generalization, and some key networks suitable for this work are explained. Thereafter, in-vehicle specific environmental conditions are stressed and suggestions to suppress them are supported. The paper ends by proposing an architecture to minimize the problems and increase the overall recognition rate of the system.

THE VOICE SIGNAL

Independently of its application (speaker or speech recognition systems), voice recognition requires first the proper representation of the voice signal. In order to define the best one, we have first to understand the human vocal organ complex schematically illustrated in Figure 1.

It consists of the lungs, trachea, larynx, pharynx, and nasal and oral cavities, where the portion from larynx to nasal and oral cavities is referred as the vocal tract.

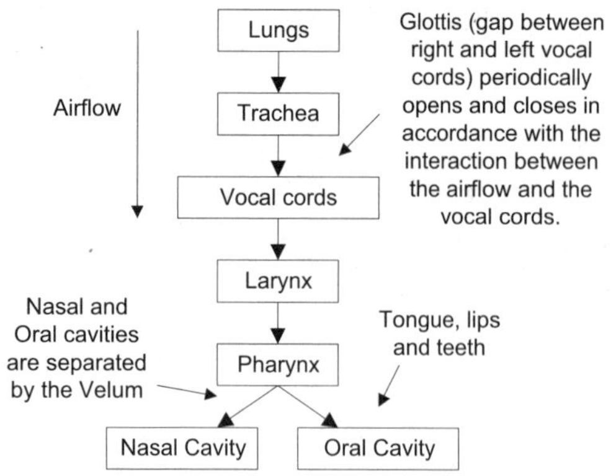

Figure 1: Human vocal organ complex

While speaking, the airflow coming from lungs and passing through the trachea is periodically interrupted by opening and closing the glottis (gap between right and left vocal cords). This periodical interruption works like an impulse generator for the vibration frequency produced by the vocal cords. This impulsed vibration is then molded by the vocal tract, which is changed by moving muscles, including tongue and lips, producing the final utterance. This process is illustrated in Figure 2 by an equivalent model [1].

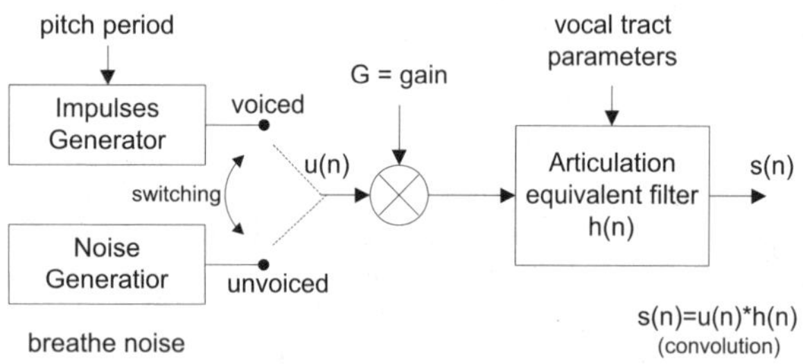

Figure 2: Linear separable equivalent model of the speech production mechanism

We have voiced and unvoiced segments, where the first occurs when the person is speaking, and the other when breathing (breathe noise only). The vibration frequency of the vocal cords in voiced segments is called fundamental or pitch frequency F_0, and is represented by the impulses generator in Figure 2. It ranges from 50 to 800 Hz for a person speaking normally and carries the prosodic information of the locution. The Articulation Equivalent Filter represents the vocal tract, whose resonance frequencies are named as formant frequencies. The first two formants define well certain acoustic events and vocals, and the others define speaker's characteristics due to their dependency on the details of the vocal tract, which is unique for each person. The typical ranges for the first 3 formants are: F_1 from 200 to 900 Hz, F_2 from 550 to 2700 Hz and F_3 from 1100 to 2950 Hz.

As illustrated in this model, the voice signal is the convolution between the pitch contour curve and the vocal tract transfer function, and carries the speech information as well as speaker specific characteristics (mainly defined by high order formant frequencies). Therefore, if we can extract features that represent well these characteristics, we can design speech and speaker recognition systems.

FEATURES EXTRACTION – Given a spoken word or sentence, the features extraction can be done in several ways. As Cepstrum and Mel-Frequency Cepstrum coefficients have proved better performance [2], they have been chosen for this work. The process for getting these coefficients is showed in Figure 3 and you will find below a brief description of these steps and the rational behind each one of them.

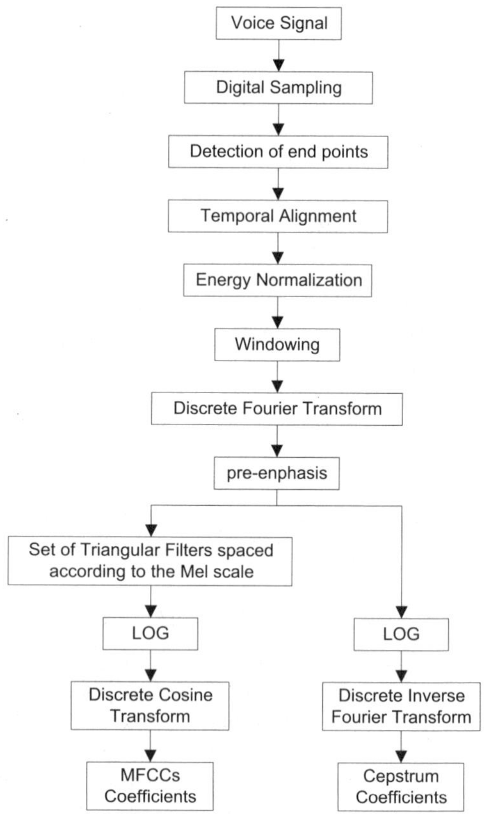

Figure 3: MFCCs and Cepstrum coefficients extraction

Digital Sampling – Analog systems are susceptible to noise interferences, usually are not accurate and are obviously improper for the use in control units like the one to be designed for the voice-controlled vehicle. Therefore, the first step is to sample the voice signal and convert it to digital, obtaining a series $x[n]$, with $n=0, 2, \ldots, N-1$, which is the discrete-time representation of the voice signal.

Detection of end points – The ambient sound is continuously received in a microphone and the voice signal of interest can start at any time. It makes necessary to determine the start and end points of the voice signal input. It can be done either by Energy Analysis of the input signal (low energy indicates a silence area) or by zero-crossing detection (high zero-crossing rate indicates a silence area).

Temporal Alignment – Every person can say the same command in different speeds and the system has to be able to compare it to the target pattern stored internally. For this reason it is necessary to perform the temporal alignment between the input command and the stored command pattern in order to explore the voice signal property of being time-invariant in short-time-spectral analysis.

Dynamic Time Warping (DTW) described in [1] is the most accurate temporal alignment process. DTW process nonlinearly expands or contracts the time axis to match the same phoneme positions between the input speech and reference templates. The optimal function to align them is defined by calculating the minimum spectral distance over the mapping function. This same distance is also used to define which target pattern is the closest to the input pattern (as we have several target patterns, this temporal alignment must be done in relation to the most similar one to the input). Although it represents the best temporal alignment, DTW is not usually used on real time applications because of the huge computational effort required.

A good alternative is the Linear Time Warping (LTW) that presents very good results [3] with reduced computational timing. LTW process measures the total length of the locution, compares it to the total length of the target voice commands stored and then linearly contract or expand the input signal to match the size of the stored pattern to optimize the comparison in short-time analysis. For discrete-time analysis it is done by defining a fixed number of samples and using interpolation (or extrapolation) for converting the data.

Energy Normalization – The voice command loudness cannot be controlled, so we need to have a normalization of the input to ensure that they will produce coefficients within the same range of the coefficients of the target pattern stored. This normalization limits the range of these parameters, which are going to be used as input for a neural network, improving then the generalization as will be explained later.

Windowing – voice signal has the property of being time-invariant in short time analysis. Therefore, we split the voiced segment in several small segments (dozens of milliseconds, each) before to extract features from it. The idea behind is that, as we are going to produce coefficients for each segment to be compared to the coefficients of the stored pattern, it is important to compare segments that theoretically carry the same information (either from the speech or from the speaker) and this is achieved only with short time spectral analysis of the voice signal after the proper temporal alignment. In order to avoid frequency leakage due to the abrupt transitions in windows boundaries (it generates high frequency components that are not part of the voice signal – Figure 4), the window has to gradually decay to zero in the boundaries [4]. Several windows could be used and the Hamming window produces good results. It is illustrated in Figure 5 and is defined by equation 1.

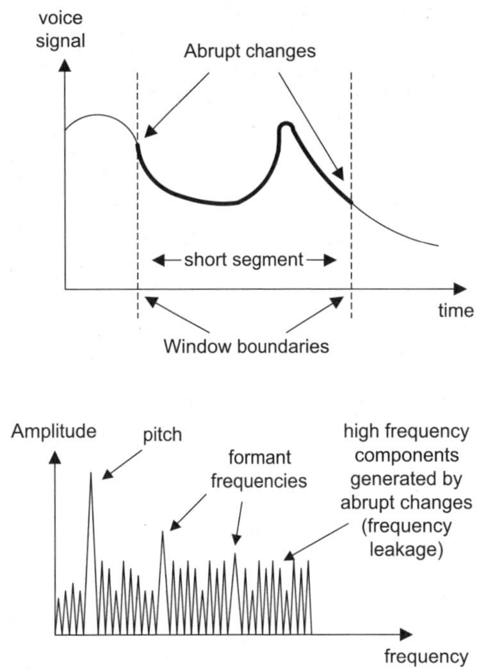

Figure 4: Abrupt changes in window boundaries generating high frequency components

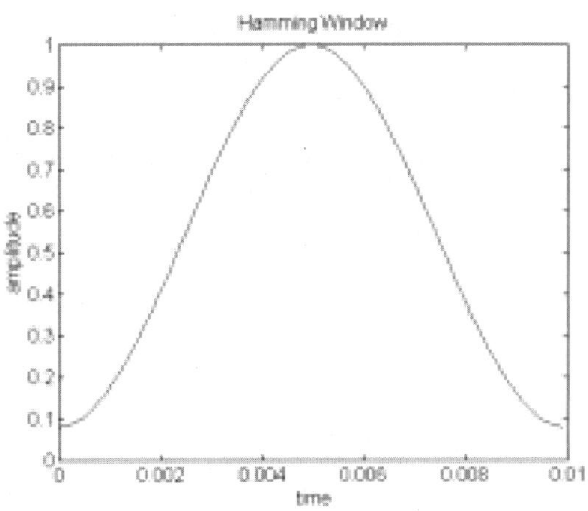

Figure 5: Hamming Window

$$W(n) = 0.54 - 0.46 \cdot \cos\left(\frac{2 \cdot \pi \cdot n}{N-1}\right) \tag{1}$$

Where n is the component number and N is the total amount of components in the window (amount of samples of the voice signal).

Note that by eliminating abrupt transitions in windows boundaries we are also loosing information comprehended in these areas. In order to avoid this problem, windows have to be superposed to ensure complete coverage of the voice signal information.

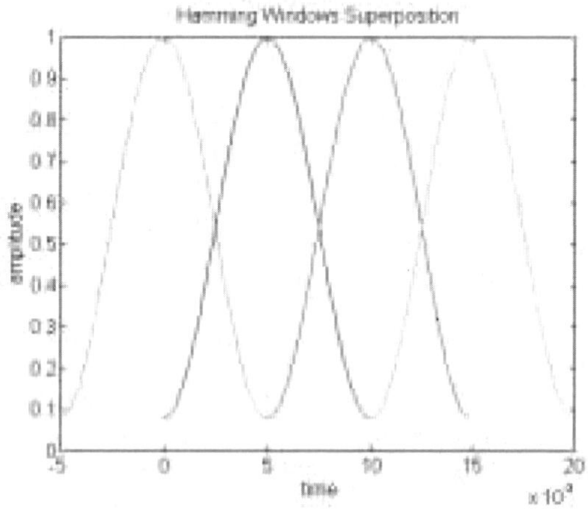

Figure 6: Hamming Windows Superposition

The best approach is showed in Figure 6, where the center of a Hamming Window is right over the boundary of the previous window [5].

Discrete Fourier Transform – Transforms the data from time to frequency domain [4]. This transformation turns the convolution-in-time in a multiplication in frequency.

$$s(t) = u(t) * h(t) \quad \Rightarrow \quad S(w) = U(w) \cdot H(w) \tag{2}$$

Equation 3 is the Discrete Fourier Transform (DFT) for the sampled signal $x[n]$, $n = 0, 1, 2, \ldots, N-1$, and equation 7 is the Inverse Discrete Fourier Transform (IDFT).

$$X[k] = \sum_{n=0}^{N-1} x[n] \cdot e^{-j \cdot 2 \cdot \pi \cdot k \cdot n / N}, \quad k = 0, 1, \ldots, N-1 \tag{3}$$

To minimize computational efforts, only the amplitude spectrum is used (real portion of the DFT).

Pre-emphasis – The voice energy is concentrated on lower frequencies with an attenuation of 20dB/decade [5]. The pre-emphasis compensate this effect using a first order FIR (Finite Impulse Response) filter.

$$H_{pre}(z) = 1 - \alpha_{pre} \cdot z^{-1} \tag{4}$$

After sampling it becomes:

$$y(n) = x(n) - \alpha \cdot x(n-1), \tag{5}$$

Where $x(n)$ is the sampled signal, $y(n)$ is the signal after pre-emphasis and α ranges from 0.9 to 1, and 0.9375 is normally used with good results.

LOG – From the model used for generating the voice signal (Figure 2), the problem of analyzing the voice signal in short time segments, can be understood as a problem of separating the components of the convolution between the excitation function and the vocal tract resonance frequencies (Homomorphic deconvolution [4]). The DFT turned the convolution in a multiplication of the frequency response of these components, and the logarithm turns this multiplication in an addition of components as showed in equation 6.

$$Log(S) = Log(U \cdot H) = Log(U) + Log(H) \tag{6}$$

Discrete Inverse Fourier Transform – Transforms the data from frequency to time domain, but due to the LOG operation the components are no longer convoluted. The Discrete-time Inverse Fourier Transform (IDFT) is the one showed in equation 7 and as the result we have the called cepstrum coefficients [4].

$$c[n] = \frac{1}{N} \cdot \sum_{k=0}^{N-1} X[k] \cdot e^{j \cdot 2 \cdot \pi \cdot k \cdot n / N}, \quad n = 0, 1, \ldots, N-1 \tag{7}$$

These coefficients are a good representation of the voice signal and can be used to form features vectors to be used in a classifier like a neural network.

Mel-spaced Triangular Filters – A study about parameters used in voice recognition systems done in [6] shows that all representations that simulates the human hearing system achieves better results. The use of filters spaced according to the Mel scale is one way of doing it (the band-pass of the filters are shorter for low frequencies and bigger for higher frequencies, simulating the human perception).

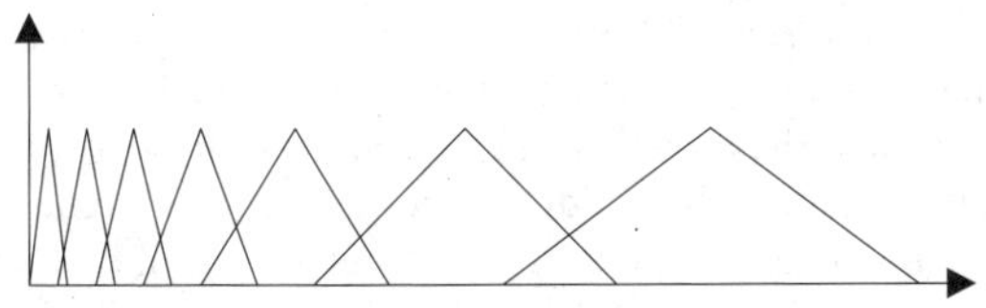

Figure 7: Mel-spaced Triangular Filters

$$f_{Mel} = 2595 \cdot \log_{10}\left(1 + f_{Hz}/700\right) \quad (8)$$

The number of filters is freely determined by the designer and usually varies from 20 to 30 filters for each short-time segment. The energy in dB from these filters is then used as new data for the Discrete Cosine Transform.

Discrete Cosine Transform – [2] shows that recognition systems using Artificial Neural Networks have better performance when Mel-cepstrais parameters are used, specially those generated by Discrete Cosine Transform (DCT). This comes from the DCT property of sorting the coefficients by descending variance. This ensures that the parameters that carry more information are always used once we have a limited number of coefficients. The DCT coefficients are calculated by equation 9 and are named as Mel-Frequency Cepstrum Coefficients (MFCCs) due to the process illustrated in Figure 3. The number of coefficients used to represent the voice signal usually varies from 8 to 16, depending on the complexity of the classification and available computational resources of the system.

$$C[i] = \sum_{k=1}^{N} X[k] \cdot \cos\left[i \cdot \left(k - \frac{1}{2}\right) \cdot \frac{\pi}{N}\right], \quad (9)$$

Where $i=1,2,...,M$, and M is the number of coefficients and $X[k]$ is the energy (dB) of the kth filter. N is the amount of filters used. As C_0 represents the window total energy it is not used to compose the features vectors for the classifier.

Cepstrum and Mel-cepstrum coefficients are currently the best representation of voice signals. They are perfect for determining the fundamental frequency of voiced segment, or to determine the voice signal presence or not. The vocal tract transfer function (corresponding to the contour of the frequency spectrum) can be obtained by removing the fast components of the above transformations. One way of obtaining this transfer function is to calculate the DFT of the obtained cepstrum. The peaks analysis of this function is a good way of estimating the pitch as well as the formant frequencies.

FEATURES VECTORS – After above calculations, each window (or segment) has a set of MFCCs or Cepstrum coefficients that are the best representation of voice signal comprehended in that window. The voice signal is divided in W superposed windows and there are C coefficients for each window, thus the feature vector has $W \cdot C$ coefficients (or parameters) to be used as the input for the classifier.

GENERAL CONSIDERATIONS ABOUT SPEAKER AND SPEECH RECOGNITION SYSTEMS

SPEAKER RECOGNITION – Speaker Recognition can be divided according to the task being performed: speaker identification or speaker verification. In speaker verification the input voice features vectors are compared to a single stored pattern only, and the answer is YES (the input voice is from the same speaker whose features were learned) or NO. In speaker identification, a set of features vectors are considered, each one representing a specific speaker, and the input is compared to all of them searching the closest one (eventually none of them is close enough to the input and the answer from the recognition system is that the input voice has not been recognized).

The speaker recognition is also classified according to the input text. It can be text-dependent or text-independent. For the first one the speaker has to say a specific statement or word, and for the second one it is not needed [7] [8].

In text-dependent system, a special care should be taken while selecting the reference word or statement for the classification. This is necessary because, as already explained, speaker individual characteristics are found in high-order formant frequencies (vocal tract resonance frequencies). To emphasize these frequencies it is important to select nasal sounds, which not only use the oral cavity but also the nasal cavity, what is the most complete use of the vocal tract. The efficiency of this is evident in the work performed in [9] where 93% to 97% of correct identifications were reached for a small population of speakers (10 to 30).

The in-vehicle voice recognition system can be understood as text-depended because we have only specific commands that can be used as input to the system; and is certainly a speaker identification system because we will probably have more than one user. Regarding the selection of a word or statement for speaker identification, the sentence *good morning* is appropriate because of the nasal consonants *"m"* and *"n"*. These considerations shall be used when designing the system.

SPEECH RECOGNITION – Speech recognition task can be classified in isolated word/sentences or continuous speech recognition; and in speaker-dependant or speaker-independent systems.

Thankfully the voice commands in a telematics system are usually words or short sentences. This avoids several complications on segmenting the input voice signal and difficulties on identifying and selecting words that could produce good features for being used for speech classification. However, it is certainly a speaker-independent speech recognition system because any person can buy the vehicle, and the system has to accept commands from anybody (unless it is blocked by special command from the vehicle owner, what would be possible by the jointly use of the speaker and the speech recognition systems).

The speaker-independent and isolated word/sentence recognition characteristics shall be also considered for designing the whole system.

ARTIFICIAL NEURAL NETWORKS

Artificial Neural Networks (ANNs) are parallel distributed processing systems composed of simple processing units massively interconnected. They can store knowledge and generalize it for processing new inputs [10]. ANNs are based and motivated by the current knowledge about biological neural networks.

The main advantages of using ANNs are:

a. The generalization capacity that ensures reasonable answers for inputs that have never been seen during training. Hence, it is ideal for the application on voice recognition systems, because the network will produce proper outputs even not knowing the speaker and the way they will utter the commands.

b. The learning capability, which makes possible the solution of very complex systems (hard of being mathematically modeled) without the need of any previous knowledge about it. This is valid for classification problems or functions approximation (like a noise filter).

NEURONS – Neurons (or Perceptrons) in ANNs try to simulate the behavior of biological neurons (Figure 8).

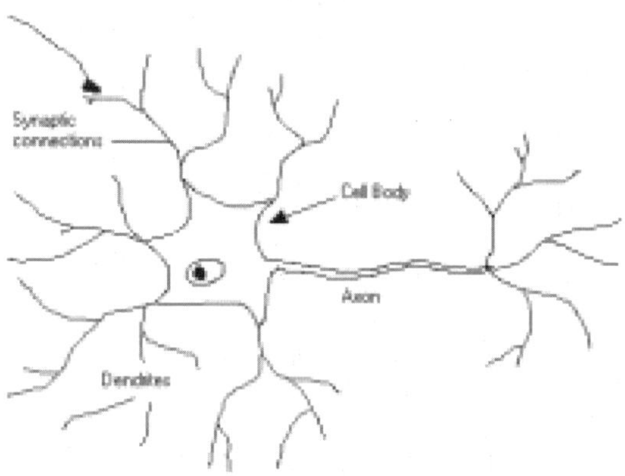

Figure 8: Schematic drawing of a biological neuron.

They receive excitatory and inhibitory inputs from other neurons' axons through synaptic connections with their dendrites, which are electrical-chemical reactions changing the polarization of the neuron membrane. When this polarization exceeds a certain threshold level, the neuron discharge it by an electrical pulse sent through its axon, which will serve as input for other synaptic connections.

Based on the explanation above, the neuron can be modeled as showed in Figure 9 with the non-linear activation function *f(x)* example showed in Figure 10.

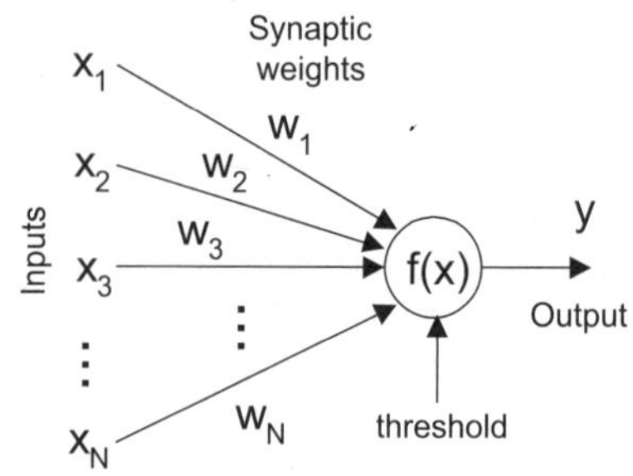

Figure 9: Nonlinear model of a neuron

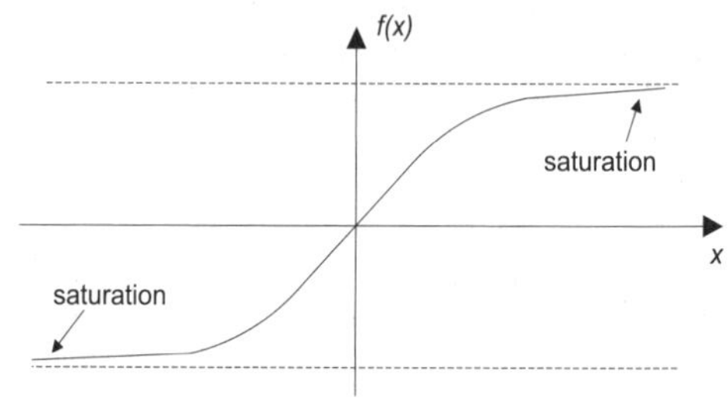

Figure 10: Example of activation function

This simple model is already capable of selecting two classes: firing for Class A and not firing for Class B, for instance. This can be accomplished by adjusting the weights through training (to be explained later for the multi-layer perceptrons) which changes the decision boundary. Figure 11 shows this evolution when there are only two inputs and, in this case, the decision region is a simple line.

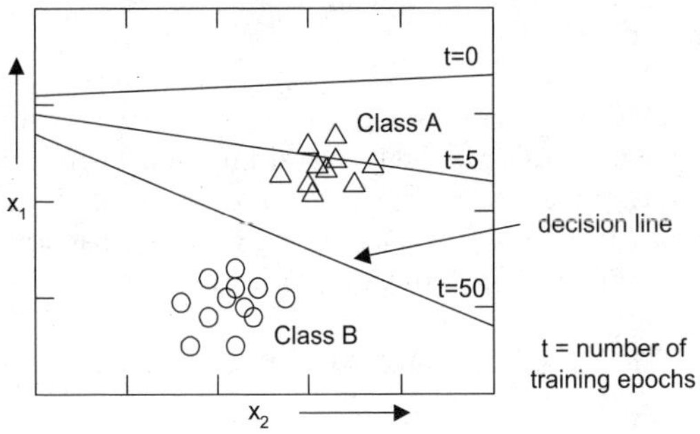

Figure 11: Decision regions of a single neuron (perceptron)

Note that if we have three inputs the decision boundary is a plane, and if we have four or more inputs a multi-dimensional plane called hyper-plane does the decision.

MULTI-LAYER PERCEPTRON (MLP) – By arranging neurons in several layers, decision regions can be more complex. It happens because the decision hyper-plane of each neuron is combined and classified by hyper-planes of the neurons in the following layers. [11] studied the effect of the number of layers and showed that 3-layers is enough for creating disjoint and arbitrary decision regions. A 3-layer MLP is illustrated in Figure 12.

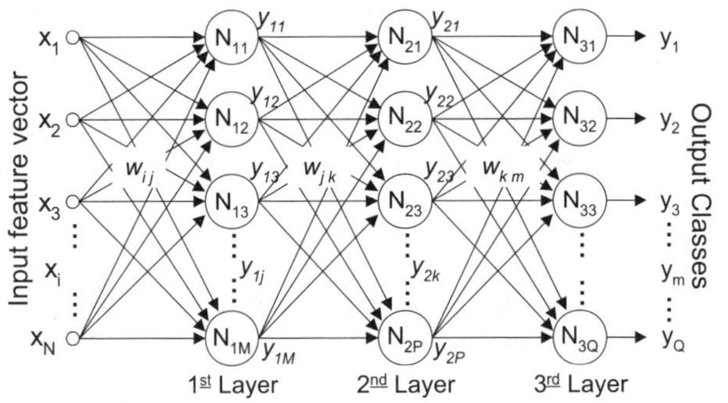

Figure 12: 3-layers MLP.

The training algorithm of the MLP is called *error-backpropagation* and basically changes connection weights using the generalized delta rule for minimizing the quadratic error of the output.

MLP Training Algorithm:

1. Define small random values for the weights w_{ij} , w_{ik} and w_{km}, as well as for the decision thresholds θ_j , θ_k, θ_m , for $i = 1, 2, ..., N$; $j = 1, 2, ..., M$; $k = 1, 2, ..., P$; and $m = 1, 2, ..., Q$.

2. Choose an appropriate activation function. For instance:

$$f(x) = \frac{2}{\pi}\arctan(x), \tag{10}$$

$$\text{With } f'(x) = \frac{2}{\pi}\cdot\frac{1}{1+x^2}, \tag{11}$$

3. Define the training stop condition, which can be a maximum number of iterations or a maximum error allowed.

4. For each training pair input/output, steps from 5 to 11 shall be executed:

Feed-Forward:

5. Calculate the output from the neurons of the first layer:

$$input\_y_{1j} = \sum_{i=1}^{N} w_{ij}\cdot x_i - \theta_j \text{ , and} \tag{12}$$

$$y_{1j} = f(input\_y_{1j}), \text{ for } j = 1, 2, ..., M. \tag{13}$$

6. Calculate the output from the neurons of the second layer:

$$input\_y_{2k} = \sum_{j=1}^{M} w_{jk}\cdot y_{1j} - \theta_k \text{ , and} \tag{14}$$

$$y_{2k} = f(input\_y_{2k}), \text{ for } k = 1, 2, ..., P. \tag{15}$$

7. Calculate the output from the neurons of the third (last) layer:

$$input\_y_m = \sum_{k=1}^{P} w_{km}\cdot y_{2k} - \theta_m \text{ , and} \tag{16}$$

$$y_m = f(input\_y_m), \text{ for } m = 1, 2, ..., Q. \tag{17}$$

Error-Backpropagation:

8. Calculate the error information of the last layer:

$$\delta_m = (d_m - y_m)\cdot f'(input\_y_m), \text{ for } m = 1,2,...,Q. \tag{18}$$

9. Calculate the error information for the second layer:

$$input\_\delta_k = \sum_{m=1}^{Q} \delta_m \cdot w_{km} \text{, and} \quad (19)$$

$$\delta_k = (input\_\delta_k) \cdot f'(input\_y_{2k}) \text{, for } k = 1,2,...,P. \quad (20)$$

10. Calculate the error information for the first layer:

$$input\_\delta_j = \sum_{k=1}^{P} \delta_k \cdot w_{jk} \text{, and} \quad (21)$$

$$\delta_j = (input\_\delta_j) \cdot f'(input\_y_{1j}) \text{, for } j = 1,2,...,M. \quad (22)$$

11. Update the weights and the decision thresholds:

$$w_{km} = w_{km} + \eta \cdot \delta_m \cdot y_{2k} \text{,} \quad (23)$$
for $k = 1,2,...,P$ and $m = 1, 2, ..., Q$.

$$w_{jk} = w_{jk} + \eta \cdot \delta_k \cdot y_{1j} \text{,} \quad (24)$$
for $j = 1,2,...,M$ and $k = 1, 2, ..., P$.

$$w_{ij} = w_{ij} + \eta \cdot \delta_j \cdot x_i \text{,} \quad (25)$$
for $i = 1,2,...,N$ and $j = 1, 2, ..., M$.

$$\theta_m = \theta_m + \eta \cdot \delta_m \text{, for } m = 1, 2, ..., Q. \quad (26)$$

$$\theta_k = \theta_k + \eta \cdot \delta_k \text{, for } k = 1, 2, ..., P. \quad (27)$$

$$\theta_j = \theta_j + \eta \cdot \delta_j \text{, for } j = 1, 2, ..., M. \quad (28)$$

12. Verify the training stop condition and get back for step 2 in case it has not been reached yet.

The process described above creates clusters (groups that represent the same pattern) defined by the output neurons, where each cluster (or output neuron) represents one speaker or one of the voice commands, for instance. During the training process above, several patterns have to be presented for the same speaker or the same voice command (to be used in step 4) to better explore the network generalization capacity.

It is important to mention that concluded the training of the MLP, all weights are frozen and additional patterns cannot be learned; and the MLP structure is fixed a priori when defining the number of layers and the number of neurons per layer.

ADAPTIVE RESONANCE THEORY (ART) – This network is very useful because has the ability to learn new patterns after the training process is complete. The MLP presented above has its structure fixed before training and all weights fixed after training, that is, it does not have any plasticity.

ART neural network dynamically changes its structure and the connection weights to learn new patterns belonging to current clusters, or even creates new clusters (adding neurons to the output layer) when the input pattern is too much different from those already learned.

The network basic structure is showed in Figure 13.

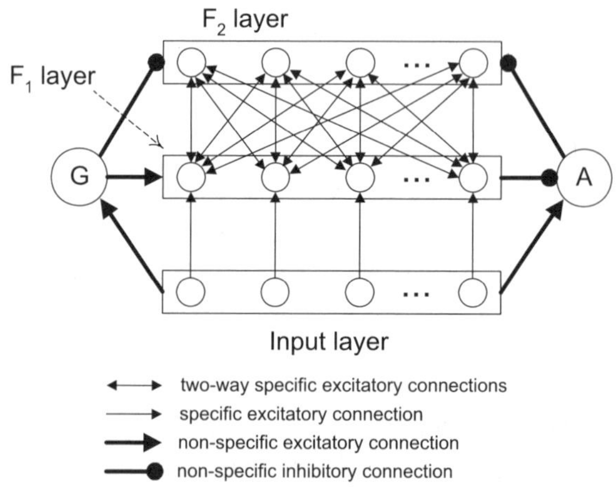

Figure 13: ART Neural Network basic structure

The input layer receives the features vectors. F_1 layer distribute the input layer data to F_2 layer when the gateway G is active. F_2 layer is the output layer and selects a winner neuron by competition. Every neuron in this last layer has a self-excitatory connection to itself and inhibitory connections to all other neurons (not showed in Figure 13 to keep the drawing uncluttered). This connection structure promotes the competition between these neurons by gradually deactivating some of them (those with smaller outputs). The winner is the neuron with the highest output.

G is the gain node and *A* is the reset/activation control node. Their function will be understood by the explanation of whole the network functionality following below.

The network has specific connections between neurons and non-specific connections that act over the complete layer at once. The only non-specific connection that is individually presented to every neuron is the inhibitory one from the node *A* (the reason for that will be found in the algorithm). Connections ended by an arrow are excitatory and those ended by a circle are inhibitory.

<u>ART Functionality and Algorithm</u> – The algorithm will be first described for the binary ART network for general understanding. When we have continuous input

data, the algorithm needs some changes described in [12]. The ART algorithm works as follows:

1. Set all connection weights between F_1 and F_2 layers to 1 (in both directions). During the clustering process, these connections can be converted to 0 but they never become 1 again. This ensures that the network will be stable (avoid modifications that could make it loose the knowledge already acquired).

2. Present an input pattern and enable all neurons in F_2 layer by setting to zero the output from control node A (this is called a reset). This node A has individual connections to every neuron in F_2 layer and this will allow us to inhibit specific neurons later on.

3. Enable all neurons in F_1 layer by setting to 1 the output from the gateway G. This allows the F_1 layer to send the input pattern to the F_2 layer.

4. Define a winning neuron in F_2 layer by competition. The winner will be the neuron that is enabled and has the bottom-up connection weights (from F_1 layer to F_2 layer) most similar to the input pattern, giving the highest output.

5. Verify the network resonance by comparing the top-down connection weights of the winning neuron to the input pattern. If they are close enough, moves to step 8, otherwise disables this specific neuron and moves to step 6.

6. Check if all neurons in F_2 layer are disabled. If there are still neurons enabled, restart from step 4.

7. If all neurons in F_2 layer were disabled, the following actions can be taken:

    a. Add a neuron in F_2 layer to represent the new pattern and train it in step 8. Here a warning can be sent also to inform the system about the added neuron (new user in a speaker recognition system, for instance).

    b. Increase the network tolerance (in order to have the resonance in step 5 for one of the F_2 neurons) and restart from step 2.

    c. Send a warning saying that the input pattern does not belong to any of the clusters available and restart from step 2.

8. Update the connections between F_1 layer and F_2 layer according to the input pattern. For the binary network, it is done by setting to zero the connections weights that are different from the respective input.

9. Inform client system that the active neuron in the output layer (F_2 layer) is the class that represents the input pattern (indicates who is speaking in a speaker recognition system, for instance).

10. Restart from step 2.

The mathematical formulation of this algorithm for both cases (binary and continuous-valued inputs) can be found in [13] and will not be repeated here. For the purpose of this work it is important to understand the network functionality as it was done by the above generic algorithm description.

An important consideration about the ART network is that the algorithm is executed while training or using (testing) the network, hence existing classes can be improved and new classes can be learned anytime.

THE VEHICLE ENVIRONMENT

For the development of a speaker or speech recognition system, the ideal condition would be to have only the voice signal for processing and classification, but the vehicle environment is passive of several interferences, as listed below:

1. Rain noise inside the vehicle that depends not only on the rainfall, but also on the vehicle speed, body characteristics and trim level.

2. Suspension noise that depends on the vehicle design and on the road condition, as well as on the vehicle speed, body characteristics and trim level again.

3. Vehicle noise when accelerating and braking on all possible different speeds (mainly engine and wind noise).

4. Vehicle sound system audio output that may be a music, a song or voice signals from advertisements, news programs or mobile phone conversations.

5. People conversation inside the vehicle that does not represent voice commands to the system.

6. Electrical interference from other vehicles in the voice acquisition circuit.

7. Spurious noise

8. Combinations of all above.

The list of problems above is obviously impossible of being mathematically modeled (due to its complexity) and is the main motivation for the use of self-learning systems like neural networks proposed in this work.

ARCHITECTURE PROPOSAL AND DISCUSSION

In-vehicle voice recognition systems usually make the mistake of considering the microphone as the only input to the system. This makes the system vulnerable to all interferences mentioned in the previous section. Probably the main reason for this simplification lies on the complexity of modeling these interferences but, even though, there are sensors in the vehicle that supply information about them or, at least, parameters that somehow control their behavior.

The rain noise, for example, depends on the rainfall, which is indirectly measured by the rain sensor available for controlling the windshield wiper speed. It depends also on the vehicle speed signal already available for instruments and displays, and on the body and trim characteristics that are fixed and can be calibrated if the system allows it.

In the same way, suspension noise depends on the vehicle speed and other vehicle characteristics that can be calibrated. This is somehow linked to the vehicle noise when accelerating and braking, and these two conditions can be parameterized by the acceleration sensor used for the engine control unit and the braking switch used for the stop lights, respectively. An additional parameter is certainly the engine rotation speed, which is already measured by a sensor for the engine control unit also.

Vehicle sound system interference is certainly the easiest one because we have the audio output available, but others like general conversations inside the vehicle, electrical interferences and spurious noises do not have any controlling parameter.

From the above considerations it is clear that, besides the microphone, several other sensors available in a regular vehicle could be used as parameters for the voice recognition system. It is true though that we cannot build an algebraic expression that shows the relationship between them and the microphone input received, so we need to develop a system capable of learning it and artificial neural networks (ANNs) are the only feasible solution. Such system architecture is illustrated in Figure 14.

The first step is to digitize the microphone input to prevent additional electrical interferences in the rest of the data processing. The digitized signal has not only voice commands, but also all audible noises convoluted to it.

The audio system output is the only one that is very well defined and, therefore, can be easily removed. Although the audio system outputs to speakers is known, it cannot be directly subtracted from the microphone input because it still depends on speakers' response curves, on the vehicle acoustics and on the microphone response curve. These three characteristics together can be named as the Vehicle Transfer Function for the audio system output. This function can be estimated by doing a frequency sweep (for a flat audio curve) for every speaker individually, and measuring the audio curve received by the microphone. Note that it has to be done individually for each speaker because the user may change the balance and fader control settings, and the system has to be prepared for it. Having the information about the transfer function for every speaker, a digital filter can be designed to convert the dynamic audio system output into the equivalent audio received by the microphone (including delays). This filter has the audio system output for each speaker and the fader/balance control settings as its inputs, and provides as output the equivalent audio received in the microphone to be removed from the input signal.

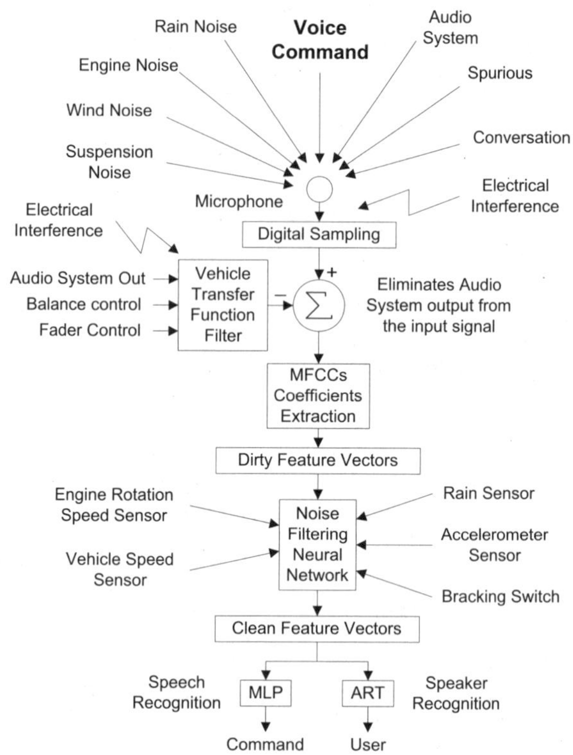

Figure 14: In-vehicle voice recognition system architecture

Removed the audio system interference, the proper representation of the input signal is done by extracting MFCCs (Mel-Frequency Cepstrum Coefficients). This will generate dirty features vectors because they still have components from noise inputs that were convoluted to the voice command. To filter them out, we need to use a neural network to learn the noise information and how it is affected by the input parameters: engine speed, vehicle speed, rainfall, and acceleration or braking status. This network is a modified MLP (Multi-Layer Perceptron) with 4 layers and additional inputs from the above parameters to first and second layers, as showed in Figure 15.

The number of neurons in the first and last layer has to be equal to the size of the feature vectors. All other layers may have different number of neurons. Although 3 layers would solve the problem reasonably, 4 layers are suggested because of the filter complexity. The additional layer will define a more accurate approximation of the noise filter transfer function by gradually reducing the features observation field of the layers. These modifications also allow us to use the first two layers to input the vehicle parameters, increasing the amount of information for neurons decisions (this shall not be done for the above layers to ease the network approximation of the noise filter response). However, additional layers charge the system with additional computation efforts. The compromise between them shall be defined during the development (the neural network is implemented by software).

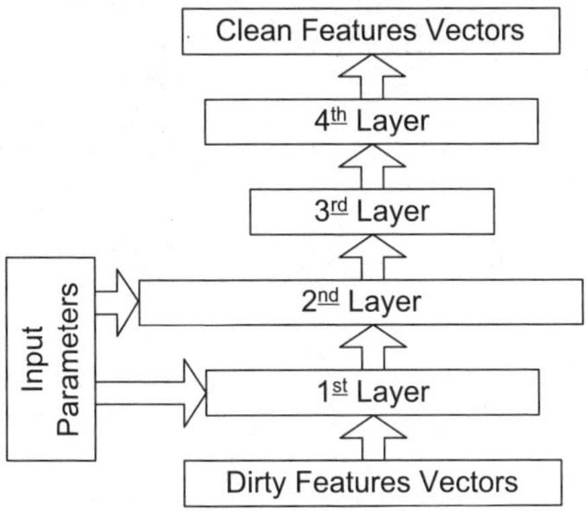

Figure 15: Noise Filtering Neural Network

In order to teach this network for noise filtering, we have first to record the noise input through the microphone and collect all parameters data in all possible vehicle conditions of use. Secondly, we have to create a database with all possible voice commands in a silent (perfect) condition. Next, the clean voice commands have to be mixed to the noise information recorded to create dirty feature vectors, which will serve as inputs for the network training. The target outputs for training are clean feature vectors produced from clean voice commands of the database. Both are repeatedly presented to the network until it learns to filter the noise out from the voice commands MFCCs using the MLP training algorithm.

The noise filtering neural network described above was the first step for creating a robust system, which is even improved by the use of neural networks for classifying the voice commands and identifying the speaker.

The classification and identification of the voice commands is also performed by a MLP. This network suits well the application because it has proved excellent performance in classification [14], and there is a fixed number of commands, eliminating the need of plasticity. The MLP is trained having the MFCCs from clean voice commands as input (clean features vectors) and the target outputs are the commands that they represent. Thus, the output layer has the number o neurons equal to the number of possible commands of the system, and every neuron informs if the input features vectors represent its target command by firing (high neuron output) or not (low neuron output).

Although it has not been mentioned before, the voice commands have to be defined as short as possible to reduce the features vectors size and, as consequence, the number of neurons in the networks that is related to the number of calculations performed. Besides that, shorter the commands are, better will be the performance of the LTW for temporal alignment, and it may help us on defining a single standard duration for all commands. It is important because in short time analysis we need to compare commands of same duration to match the information content of every windowed segment (see temporal alignment), and, having a single standard duration for all, we can perform a single temporal alignment for any voice command input in order match this standard duration. (If we had different durations for stored commands, there would be necessary as many temporal alignments as the number of existing durations to allow their proper comparison to the input).

The speaker identification network cannot have a fixed structure because the number of users is unknown and the vehicle may also have several owners during its life. Therefore, an ART neural network shall be used because of its plasticity. This network does not have a fixed number of output neurons, and can add neurons to represent new speakers without forgetting those that have been already learned. No training is required and only the first step of the algorithm presented has to be executed (start-up only). The learning will occur during the use of the system, and whenever the input voice does not match any of the learned classes (or speakers), the system has to send a warning (mentioned in step 7.a of the algorithm) to inform the system control unit to get into a *speaker input mode*. In this mode, the system asks the user to say his name in order to store it in the system memory for future use answering a *good morning* greeting, for instance, as mentioned in the introduction. The best way of storing the user's name is to ask him to spell it and recognize every letter through the same MLP used for speech recognition (eventually a specific MLP may be designed for this operation). Obviously a different duration shall be considered for the LTW temporal alignment and the MLP has to be trained for recognizing single letters also besides input commands (depending of the amount of commands it is even recommended the use a separated MLP network only for this function). Stored the spelling of the name, the system should ask for a confirmation saying the user's name using a synthesizer. After confirmation the system gets back to normal operation and will be able to answer future *good morning* greetings mentioning the user's name and, every time the same user is identified again, the network will improve its connection weights to better recognize him.

The capability of identifying the system user brings unlimited opportunities. The vehicle now can associate the user identity to vehicle preference settings, like the preferred temperature level for the air conditioning, seat comfort position, sport or conventional powertrain transmission, among others.

Although it is not showed in Figure 14, a control unit is required to execute the recognized commands and a synthesizer is necessary to speak with the user. A set of recorded sentences could be used also, but it would limit the system by obligating it to record the user's name with the user's own voice. This is certainly a bad idea because when answering the *good morning* greeting, we can have a male voice saying *good morning* and a female voice saying *Laura* (user's name), what is simply unacceptable.

CONCLUSION

This paper proposes an intelligent architecture for solving the in-vehicle voice recognition problem using artificial neural networks, with the following commended characteristics:

- Accurately removes the vehicle audio system interference through a digital filter designed according to the vehicle transfer function for every speaker.

- Uses up-to-date voice signals representations composed of Mel-Frequency Cepstrum Coefficients organized in features vectors.

- One of the system modules is capable of learning interference complex functions from several noise sources and parameterizes the solution internally to a noise-filtering network, improving the whole system robustness. The parameterization uses only sensors already available in other vehicle systems, minimizing total cost.

- A Multi-Layer Perceptron neural network performs the speech recognition task, and its proved generalization and classification power on adverse conditions is explored.

- An adaptive neural network ART2, which has the ability to continuously learn while the system is effectively being used, performs the speaker identification. This makes possible the recognition of an unlimited number of users and gives to system designers the opportunity to interact with every user adjusting vehicle settings to match users preferences right after his voice is recognized.

Although the main motivation of this work was the use on telemetics systems, the proposed architecture shall not be limited to it. This architecture can be used as the heart of several other systems, actuating as the human-machine communication interface, even out of the vehicle environment once the concept is valid for use on any hostile environment.

REFERENCES

[1] Furui, S. *Digital Speech Processing, Synthesis, and Recognition.* New York, Publisher: Marcel Dekker Inc.,1989, ISBN:0-8247-7965-7.

[2] Runstein, F.; Violaro, F.; Nunes, H.F. "Uso de diferentes parâmetros de entrada em um sistema de reconhecimento de fala baseado em redes neurais". *In: Simpósio Brasileiro de Telecomunicações, 13º*, Águas de Lindóia, 1995. *Anais.* Campinas, Unicamp, 1995, p. 155-160.

[3] Linford, P. W.; Tattersall, G. D. "Non-linear time normalization of utterances for speech recognition using MLP's". *Proceedings of the Institute of Acoustics, Speech and Signal Processing*, v. 33, n. 3, p. 587-594, June 1985.

[4] Oppenheim, A. V.; Schafer, R. W. *Discrete-Time Signal Processing.* Prentice Hall, Englewood Cliffs, New Jersey 1989. ISBN 0-13-216292-X.

[5] Timoszczuk, A. P. *Reconhecimento Automático do Locutor com Redes Neurais Artificiais do Tipo Radia Basis Function (RBF) e Minimal Temporal Information (MTI).* Dissertação de mestrado, Escola Politécnica da USP, São Paulo, 1998.

[6] Picone, J. W. "Signal modeling techniques in speech recognition". *Proceedings of the IEEE*, v.81, n.9, p.1215-1247, September 1993.

[7] Atal, B.S. "Automatic recognition of speakers from their voices". *Proceedings of IEEE*, v. 64, n. 4, p. 460-475, Apr. 1976.

[8] Corsi, P. "Speaker recognition: a survey". *In: PROCEEDINGS OF THE NATO ADVANCED STUDY INSTITUTE*, Bonas, 1982, Automatic Speech Analysis and Recognition, Dordrecht, D. Reidel Publishing Company, 1982. p. 277-308.

[9] Glenn, J. W.; Kleiner, N. "Speaker identification based on nasal phonation". *The Journal of the Acoustic Society of America*, v. 43, n. 4, p. 368-372, 1968.

[10] Hertz, J.; Krogh, A. Palmer, R. G. *Introduction to the Theory of Neural Computation.* Addison-Wesley Publishing Company, California, 1991, ISBN: 0-201-50395-6.

[11] Lippman, R. P. "An Introduction to Computing with Neural Nets". *IEEE ASSP Magazine*, April 1987, p.4-21.

[12] Carpenter, G. A.; Grossberg, S. "ART2: Self-organization of Stable Category Recognition Codes for Analog Input Patterns". *Applied Optics*, 26:4919-4930. Reprinted in Anderson, Pellionisz, & Rosenfeld, 1990, p.151-162.

[13] Fausett, L. *Fundamentals of Neural Networks – Architectures, Algorithms and Applications*. Prentice-Hall, New Jersey, 1994, ISBN: 0-13-042250-9.

[14] McCulloch, N.; Ainsworth, W. A.; Linggard, R. "Multi-layer perceptrons applied to speech technology", *Br Telecom Technology Journal*, v. 6, n. 2, April 1988.

Rogerio Vollet received the B.S. Degree in Electronics from Escola de Engenharia Mauá in 1994 and, since then he is working at General Motors Brasil Ltda as project engineer for vehicle electrical and electronic components. He joined the Man-Machine Communication Group at University of São Paulo in 1997, where he is currently studying toward the Master Science Degree in Electronic Systems. His research focuses on movements recognition using neural networks.

General Motors do Brasil Ltda.
Tech Center – Electrical, Electronics & HVAC Engineering
Avenida Goiás, 2769 – São Caetano do Sul – SP – Brazil
Zip Code: 09501-970 – P.O.Box 197
Phone: +55 11 4234 8723 Fax: +55 11 4234 6333
e-mail: rogerio.vollet@gm.com

2000-01-0820

Human Machine Interfaces Supported by Voice Recognition

Peter Scholz and Ulrich Weinmann
BMW AG, Germany

ABSTRACT

This report describes different new concepts and methodologies of how to integrate voice activation into a multi-modal automotive environment. Beside the physical recognizer additional features are discussed to improve the overall recognition rate and the user satisfaction of a voice controlled system. This integrated system provides the basis for a natural language interface and becomes the main distinctive feature for future automotive applications.

INTRODUCTION

In recent years significant theoretical and practical advances have been made for voice recognition. Relatively little effort has been devoted to the integration of this technology into a multi-modal environment.

Standard home/office speech programs can not be applied directly to automotive applications. The use of such systems in cars require not only specific adaptation to environmental conditions (e.g. noise), but also to the human interface. So, for example, the voice interaction has to be strongly supported by the visual and audio feedback, always matched to different driving situations, which leads to different dialogue structures in the car.

The quality of a voice control system usually is being determined by the recognition rate. The proposed concept shows that, beside microphone placement, noise cancellation and adapted DSP algorithms, a specific dialogue structure can also improve the *subjective* recognition rate for the user.

Today integrated automotive recognition systems are able to control virtually any function in the car. However this contradicts the goal to reduce complexity for the user. Recognition algorithms are not only able to identify command control features in noisy environments, but also to handle larger libraries of words for applications like navigation input or even dictation systems. Therefore a careful selection of suitable applications controlled by voice is necessary.

Additionally, different forms of psychological influences of using voice interaction have to be addressed. Many customers are not familiar with this new form of man machine interaction and feel uncomfortable using it. For that reason voice control can not be offered in the car without additional training for the user. The advantages of oral interaction have to be accompanied by corresponding audio/visual support functions in order to guide the user to the technology.

STATE OF THE ART

In recent years, systems for voice recognition found application in many areas and now ease the daily life of many people in standard office software packages. However, not only computer scientists investigated this interesting new feature. In the automobile industry engineers discovered the use of voice recognition in order to establish virtual co-drivers who listen to the driver's commands. Of course, if systems for voice recognition are applied to vehicles, this cannot be transferred one by one, but a number of side conditions and restrictions have to be kept in mind. A brief overview of the state of the art of current in-car voice recognition systems follows.

OVERVIEW – Current voice recognition systems combine safety and convenience issues in order to operate several functions in the automotive interior [1]. Such features are, for instance, telephone access or radio climate and CD control. There still is a number of further features that are pre-designated to be operated by voice (Figure 1).

The success story of voice recognition systems started with speaker-dependent systems in the mid 90s. Here, the system had to be taught for every user anew. A couple of years later the speaker-independent input of command words was enabled. Most systems use a speaker independent approach to avoid the training process for the user. However speaker independence results typically in a lower recognition rate and less flexibility in comparison to speaker dependent systems. Today modern systems can be controlled by coherent phrases. A rather challenging step is the development of natural speech, which avoids any adaptation of the user to the system

Speaker independent systems require large sets of training samples and therefore large storage space for each language. Currently major languages like GB- and US-English, German, French and Italian are supported. For the next couple of years the fast implementation of additional languages will be a major distinctive feature.

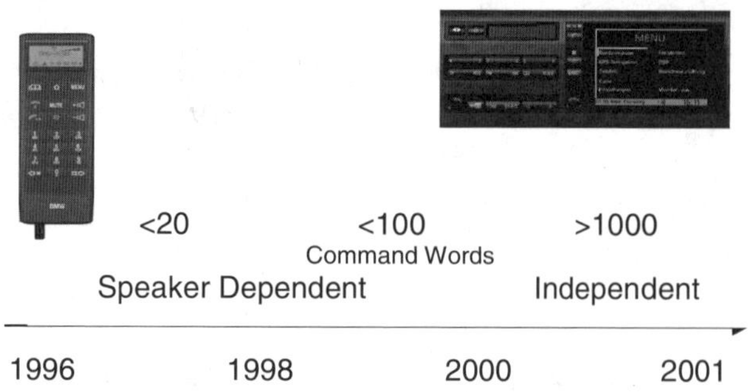

Figure 1: Development Steps for Voice Recognition

Voice recognition is not only an interesting marketing idea but indeed required by the automotive community. A human machine interface (HMI) that supports voice recognition does not only increase safety and convenience but is – at least to some extent – even required by law: hands-free speaking systems are mandatory in many European countries like Switzerland, Great Britain, or Portugal, for instance. Other countries such as Germany will soon follow.

SYSTEM INTEGRATION – The first implementations of voice recognition systems were directly connected to a specific application. The growing number of control functions require integrated systems with direct access to each application. This can only be reached by information busses, which transport the control and content information throughout the car (see Figure 2).

The development will also lead away from single DSP based voice units towards software based activation systems running on all purpose processors. This progress allows flexible implementations that also allow simple updates during an automotive life cycle.

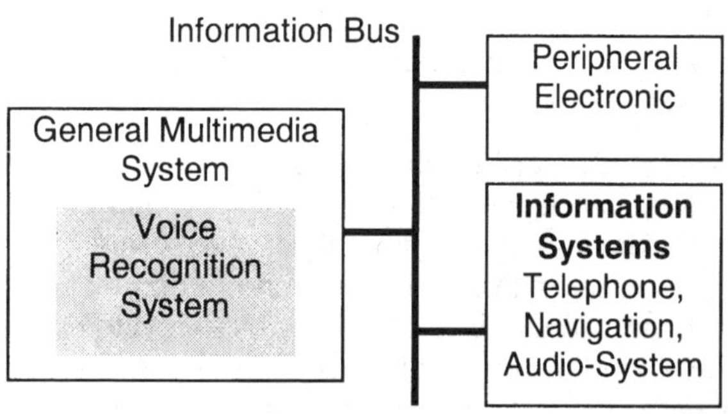

Figure 2: System Integration

NATURAL LANGUAGE VS. COMMAND CONTROL – Existing automotive voice activation systems use a command control structure for recognition. Here the user only speaks a specific word or phrase which will be matched to a stored signal. This approach results in a relatively high recognition rate, but lacks flexibility for the user.

Natural language recognition allows a user to speak in a "conversational tone". The recognizer can essentially spot the key words that make up a dialog. With natural language recognition, the user can say "I'd like to call John please", "John please," or "call John" and the system will branch to the address book and telephone application.

However, a natural language interface demands substantially more memory and therefore higher costs for implementation. Today stand alone automotive recognition systems can not offer the necessary memory and computing power due to cost restraints. This restriction will be resolved by the integration of multimedia application into a central computing unit.

THE MULTI-MODAL-APPROACH

A general overview of the multi-modal approach is described in Figure 3. The implementation consists of given variables by the user and automotive environment. The dialogue structure for voice recognition is adapted to the application controlled by voice, to the driving scenario and to special user adaptations. As a result a *subjective* recognition rate for the user can be determined. Following these influence factors are described.

ENVIRONMENTAL NOISE

The variables, which are optimized in state of the art voice activation systems, are environmental noise and the corresponding cancellation techniques. Noise cancellation algorithms should not only be used for improving the recognition rate, but also to improve the hands-free mode of a telephone conversation. In this case the microphone does not directly provide the input signal for the telephone, but the signal is filtered by the voice recognition system. Especially systems that transfer the audio signals digitally on a bus system are determined to implement this feature.

Furthermore, the placement of the microphone(s) influences very strongly the recognition rate [3]. Microphone arrays are even able to trace directly the source of the signal and give a better basis for noise suppression. Technologically, these systems perform very well, but they are rarely used due to additional costs and package problems in the car.

APPLICATIONS

The main issue for voice recognition is the selection of functions to be controlled by voice. Early systems used the telephone as a "killer" application because of safety reasons. In the next step several comfort functions were integrated in the systems like radio, in-car computer or peripheral function (Figure 1).

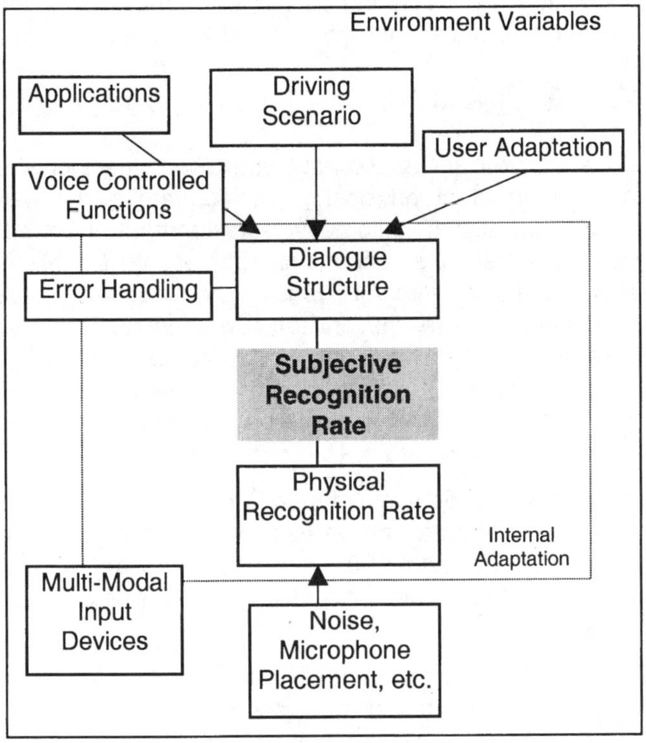

Figure 3: Automotive Environment for Voice Recognition

Several studies with user observations showed different degrees of acceptance for voice applications. For continuous functions, like window control, voice control is very difficult to apply. A free and defined *analog* control of the window is only possible with a manual input device. Though the voice control of the *binary* functions "open" or "close" are accepted by the user.

The next big step will be the development of larger libraries for recognition systems, especially for the implementation of navigation functions. Concerning the HMI the input of the destination into a navigation system is very difficult without a keyboard. Voice recognition gives an excellent opportunity to resolve this problem. However, the large amount of data (for Germany more than 80k Cities) can not be handled at once. Special selection techniques like area input can reduce the amount of data.

For voice recognition the overall functions inside a car can be divided into three groups: driving / safety related, comfort functions and office applications.

In terms of *safety* related functions it is very difficult to find corresponding functions that can be used for voice recognition. Especially if the recognition rate is far below 100% these functions are not applicable for voice recognition. Possible functions in this area would be speed or distance control settings.

The biggest and strongest field for voice application is the area of *comfort*. Here several function can be adopted to the voice recognition functionality. Beside telephone, navigation or in-car computer also the climate and air conditioning can be controlled.

In recent years, more and more *office* applications were added or even integrated into the car environment. Voice recognition plays a significant role in the acceptance of these functions. Especially the integration of text-to-speech and dictation functions ease the usability of standard office applications. Still the complexity of the applications and the corresponding distraction of the driver require additional adaptation for the in-car use.

DRIVING SCENARIOS

One important factor for the future is the adaptation of voice recognition to different driving scenarios. This means that different menu and dialogue structures will be used depending on environmental influences.

In order to define the scenarios, different user studies were performed and the interaction car-user was observed. As a result three main scenarios could be extracted:

- Highway,
- City and County road and
- Parking/Traffic Jam

To measure the environmental influences, the recognition rates for different driving scenarios were measured. Table 1 shows a subjective observation of three users averaged over three on the market available recognition systems for cars. The applications used for the evaluation are telephone control, board computer functions and basic navigation commands (e.g. map scaling, no destination input). As expected the recognition rate decreases with a rising noise level.

Table 1. RECOGNITION RATES AT DIFFERENT SCENARIOS

Scenario	Recognition Rate (%)	
	Sedan	Convertible
Highway (av. 50 mph)	92	83
Highway (av. 80 mph)	83	70
City	89	90
City - heavy traffic	82	79
Parking (calm environment)	96	96

Driving on a *highway* requires the highest attention of the driver. Therefore, voice recognition only can be used in a very restricted way. At higher speeds a reduced dialogue structure will be used without complex feedback from the car.

The scenario *city* and country roads with lower speed allows additional dialog structures and interaction with the car. The communication channel is mainly from the car to the user.

In the *no driving* scenario the attention of the driver can be focused to the HMI and dialogue. Correspondingly all possible interactions can be allowed. Here the whole variety of possible applications can be applied.

Table 2. DRIVING SCENARIOS AND APPLICATIONS

Command/Control	Highway (50 mph)	City	Parking/ Traffic Jam
Telephone	X	X	X
Bord Computer		X	X
Navigation		X	X
Internet (Browser)			X
Reading Email – Text-to-Speech Applications		X	X
Office Applications			X

The results of Table 2 are based on the distraction level, which is measured by the time the driver can not keep the eyes on the road. For driving on a highway this time level was reduced to zero. Therefore only application could be handled without visual interaction. During the scenario "city" the time was set to maximal 1 s disturbance. For parking no restriction was given.

All scenarios can be determined during driving by information of the navigation system in combination with the speed information. The voice control system processes this information and determines the corresponding dialogue structure.

USER ADAPTATION

As shown environmental parameters to adapt the recognition system can be defined and measured. Even more important is the adaptation of a human interface to the users needs. To reach the goal of a natural interface first the specific behavior of the user has to be investigated. There are already several studies available about recognizing the driving behavior resulting in a defined adaptation of the engine and suspension.

As a first step, the BMW voice recognition system uses a dialogue structure that can adapt to the confidence level of the user with the system. For example, the command "dial number" leads to a dialogue with a detailed feedback structure (e.g. options are explained). As soon as the user feels familiar with the interface, the reduced command "dial" only uses a basic dialogue, which is necessary to perform the function.

In the next step, this "manual" adaptation will be enhanced by an automatic adjustment. Here the behavior of the user for voice recognition has to be stored, studied and evaluated to adapt the dialogue structure. This can be reached by observing the input behavior [2], the reaction to errors and the general use of input devices.

ERROR HANDLING

At the moment recognition systems concentrate on the improvement of the physical recognition rate itself. It was shown that in an automotive environment it is not possible to reach a recognition rate of 100%. This is caused by many factors influencing the recognition rates like speaker's voice, the environmental noise in the car (passengers speaking) or microphone placement. Therefore, a high recognition rate can not be achieved and additional methods have to be evaluated to improve the "soft" recognition rate.

The soft recognition rate depends on the sense of the user how accurate the system works. Even with a recognition rate below 90% the user can get a higher perception of the system if an adopted handling of errors is being used.

The goal is to lead the user to the desired function, even though the system did not recognize the command exactly. In the first step the system should never reject a command by the user saying „function not available" or "repeat the command". This would lead to a negative emotion of the user. If a command was not understood correctly the user should be given some options of commands, which are close to the input. This closeness is being calculated with a differential factor to the word spoken by the user. Further, if the input did not lead to a exact command additional questions can resolve the problem.

Overall it is important to see that a driver should not be overloaded with questions and answers. Therefore, a very restrictive subset should be used, especially depending on different driving situations (see section Driving Scenarios).

INCORPORATION WITH OTHER IN- / OUTPUT DEVICES

Before the introduction of voice activation all applications were controlled by buttons, knobs or other physical interaction devices. Today voice recognition does not reach 100% recognition rate, is not available in all languages and can not handle very complex human machine interactions. Consequently voice control can only be a redundant device to existing interaction structures and has to incorporate with this environment.

ACTIVATION – The activation of the voice input function technically can be implemented in two ways. The "*word-spotting*" approach listens to every word spoken by the user and compares the signal to a stored keyword. This keyword actually activates the recognizer. The "*push-to-talk*" approach starts the recognition by pressing a button (e.g. placed on the steering wheel).

Internal studies have shown that the "push-to-talk" method shows several advantages to the "word-spotting" approach with possible miss-activations due to the recognition rate. By pressing a button, physiologically the user prepares himself subconsciously for voice activation. This concentration is especially important for an accurate and clear voice and results in a significant higher recognition rate. Using the "word-spotting" the user follows a conversational tone that reduced the understandability.

HELP FUNCTION – The rising complexity of voice control demands - except for a clear structure dialogue - additional support functions. Especially during the training phase the user has to be lead towards the use of this new technology. Beside an audio response the input can be supported by a visual feedback. After activation ("push-to-talk") the board-monitor system can not only display the functions supported by a manual input, but also emphasize the application interface in a specific state of the dialogue. The navigation control for example can display the address book or possible city/street lists depending on the users needs.

CONTROL OF SOFT BUTTONS – By combining standard buttons with voice activation a further reduction of input devices can be reached. So-called "Soft-Buttons" are able to control different functions and applications. The definition of the active application is controlled by voice. For example, with one regular up/ down button function like windows, sun roof or even the in-car computer display can be invoked.

FUTURE WORK

In the future the human machine interface will be the main distinctive feature between automobiles. Similar technology developments will be reached by all manufactures or are available by suppliers. As a result only the HMI will provide an unique appearance in an automobile. The HMI can represent a special style of car, a special adaptation to the clientele of the car or how the manufacturer would like to see the car positioned in the market. Beside exterior or interior design the soft factor will be an important influence factor for future cars.

CONCLUSION

It was shown that beside the technology for voice recognition especially in automotive applications additional factors have to be addressed. First the dialogue structure has to be adapted to specific needs of the applications. Depending on the complexity of the application a driving scenario specific adaptation of the human machine interface can be developed. These configurations lead to a subjective higher recognition rate for the user. Integrated error handling in the dialogue support this development.

ACKNOWLEDGMENTS

The authors would like to thank the BMW i-car team for their ideas and support.

REFERENCES

1. Yeshwant K. Muthusamy, Rajeev Agarwal, Yifan Gong, Vishu R. Viswanathan, "Speech-Enabled Information Retrieval in the Automobile Environment"; ICASSP ´99, Phoenix, 1999.
2. Herman J.M. Steeneken, John H.L. Hansen, "Speech Under Stress Conditions: Overview Of The Effect On Speech Production and On System Performance", ICASSP ´99, Phoenix, 1999.
3. Robert Frodl, "New Generation of Active Microphones for Hands-free Communications and Voice Recognition", SAE ´99, Detroit, 1999.

DISPLAYS

2007-01-1105

An Efficient Visual Forward Collision Warning Display for Vehicles

Henrik Lind
Volvo Car Corporation

ABSTRACT

The aim of the present study was to investigate how quickly and efficiently distracted drivers react to four different visual warning displays intended for a Forward Collision Warning system for vehicles. The displays are the Collision Warning Head Up Display (CWHUD), the Steering Wheel Warning Display, The High Head Down Display (HHDD), and the Cluster display. The study was performed in a simulator.

Warnings were randomly presented to drivers when they were visually distracted away from the road by a traffic sign discrimination task. Brake reaction times to the different warnings were recorded. From the results of performance tests and preference ratings, the CWHUD, provided the best performance in terms of 200 ms lower reaction time and low amount of missed warnings. The average brake reaction times were significantly faster for the CWHUD warnings. There were no significant differences in reaction times among the other three warnings. One CWHUD warning was missed during the experiment, whereas 17 High Head Down Display, HHDD, warnings were missed. The CWHUD was rated first among the user preferences. The second, third and fourth choices were HHDD, Cluster Display, and Steering Wheel Warning Displays. It is concluded from the results of this study that the CWHUD was the best of the four FCW visual displays tested in the study.

The high performance and high subjective driver preference is contributed to the location color and brightness of the CWHUD providing the driver with an intuitive understanding of a forward braking vehicle.

INTRODUCTION

The present study investigates the performance of different Forward Collision Warning (FCW) displays in a driving simulator. FCW systems provide alerts to assist drivers in avoiding or mitigating rear-end crashes. A warning must provide a fast and appropriate response from drivers in critical close to impact situations. The design of the warning displays for FCW is very important for safety because a poorly designed display may reduce its effectiveness.

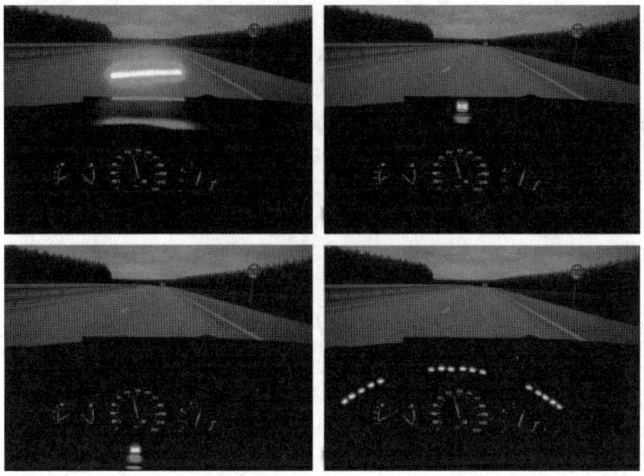

Figure 1 ***Warning displays in study***

It has been demonstrated that visual warnings are an essential component of the single stage FCW[1] however there is much uncertainty about how and where this warning should appear. Conspicuity is an important issue in the design of warning displays. Cole and Hughes[2] discuss issues relating to visibility or target conspicuity while driving. Conspicuity is "...the property that leads to a target object having a high probability of being seen within a very short time" [2]. They summarize the following factors that determine conspicuity: eccentricity from line of sight, contrast between target and background, complexity of background, co lour and the boldness of information on the target. For maximum conspicuity, a FCW visual warning display should be near to a driver's line of sight, have high contrast against a uniform background, and be bright and colorful. Unfortunately it is not that simple, particularly for the line of sight issue.

Guidelines recommend that visual warnings be placed within 15 degrees of the driver's normal sight line. The vast majority of driver's visual attention is on the forward road scene (roughly 85-90%[3]). The visual warning should be easily visible when the driver is looking forward. More than 75% of the drivers are non-attentive to the road-way before a frontal collision according to the 100 cars naturalistic driving study[7]. If they were looking at the forward road scene, they would be able to see and avoid a hazardous situation. Therefore an FCW system should be seen as an intelligent "Anti-distraction system" and must provide the property of directing the sight of a distracted driver to the forward road scene.

Where do drivers look when they are distracted (i.e., not looking at the road)? They could be checking their mirrors, looking ahead but not attending, interacting with an information system (e.g., radio), or perhaps talking with a passenger. According to field research by Lansdown[3] on drivers in the U.K., the mean percentage of time spent looking to the different regions of the visual scene were: 4.6 % rear-view mirror, 2.8 % right region, 1.3 % left region and 3.9 % instrument panel & centre stack. It is important that when drivers are looking in these four areas, and not looking at the road, the FCW display must also be visible. Meanwhile, the display should still be central to the forward view because the warning must direct the driver's attention to the hazard. A disadvantage of highly conspicuous visual displays is that they can capture attention rather than direct the eye to a hazard ahead.

WARNING DISPLAY CHARACTERISTICS

Two new warning display concepts, the Collision Warning Head Up Display, CWHUD, (figure 2) and the Steering Wheel Display (figure 5), with the aim to provide visibility, attention and intuitiveness.

A selection of two different visual warning displays was made from literature and from market available systems. These were the High Head Down Display, HHDD (figure 3) and the Cluster Display (figure 4).

Table 1 to 4 lists the characteristics of the warning displays.

A flashing red warning was selected to allow for a good peripheral recognition of the activation.

Each warning lasted 1.2 second and flashed at a rate of 4 times per second. The on flash lasted 0.15 seconds with 0.1 seconds between flashes. The table below describes how the displays differed. Figure 1 shows pictures of how the four different warnings appeared to the driver.

COLLISION WARNING HEAD UP DISPLAY, CWHUD

Figure 2 ***Collision Warning Head Up Display***

Position:	Top of instrument panel reflected in lower part of windscreen
Appearance:	Red light
Intensity measured from eye position:	1000 mcd
Size:	14.5 x 0,5 cm
Light source:	23 round clear red high intensity LED's of 1000mcd each. High intensity is required since only roughly 10% of the visual intensity is reaching the eye through the reflection in windshield.

Table 1 ***Collision Warning Head Up Display characteristics***

HIGH HEAD DOWN DISPLAY, HHDD

Figure 3 ***High Head Down Display***

Position:	Direct view display on top of instrument panel.
Appearance:	Telltale & warning in text (*CAMP symbol*)
Intensity measured from eye position:	80 + 80 mcd covered with icon frame
Size:	2.0 x 1.0 cm
Light source:	2 red back-lighters composed of 16 LEDs

Table 2 ***High Head Down Display characteristics***

CLUSTER DISPLAY

Figure 4 ***Cluster Display***

Position:	Direct view, In instrument cluster
Appearance:	Telltale & warning in text (*CAMP symbol*)
Intensity measured from eye position:	80 mcd - covered with icon frame
Size:	1.5 x 0.7 cm
Light source:	1 red back-lighter composed of 8 LEDs

Table 3 **Cluster display characteristics**

STEERING WHEEL DISPLAY

Figure 5 *Steering Wheel Display*

Position:	Direct view, Top centre of steering wheel rim
Appearance:	Lights
Intensity measured from eye position:	80 mcd
Size:	26 cm x 0.2 cm
Light source:	16 square LEDs grouped as 5, 6 and 5.

Table 4 ***Steering Wheel Display characteristics***

METHOD

Sixteen experienced drivers aged 24 to 60 years (mean age = 37 years) participated in the study. Nine were female and seven were male.

The study was run in a stationary base driving simulator to be able to measure the performance in a controlled environment. Participants were given a five-minute practice drive to become familiar with the driving simulator. The test drive lasted for approximately 15 minutes on a motorway. Participants were instructed to drive as they normally would, but to maintain the speed limit (110 km/h). A forward vehicle was cruising at fixed distance to the ego vehicle approximating about 1.5 second's headway. There was other traffic, but nothing that interfered with the driver's speed.

During the test drive, participants were presented with random targets in four different locations. The targets are provided in the following pictures taken from the driver position. Figure 6a shows a target in the Centre stack display. Figure 6b shows the target in the far left of the projected road scene approximating the left mirror position. Figure 6c shows the image in the far right approximating the right mirror position and finally figure 6d shows the image in high centre approximating the inner rear view mirror position. The targets were five different road signs that appeared in one of the locations every four seconds on average. Drivers were asked to respond, with a button press, to the appearance of one of five target options (the deer sign). Target detection was rewarded with points. Approximately 12 responses per target position were recorded amongst about 225 total signals.

Figure 6a *Centre stack position*

Figure 6b *Left mirror position*

Figure 6c *Right Mirror position*

Figure 6d ***Rear view mirror position***

The number and frequency of targets were selected to create a realistic amount of visual distraction. FCW warning events were distributed where the visual warning display would light up and the drivers were instructed to press the brake as fast as possible. A warning could only occur 0.5 seconds after a target sign was displayed so the driver would be looking at the sign when the warning light appeared. The drivers were warned every 30 seconds on average with a minimum spacing of at least 15 seconds between signals. The drivers brake reaction times to the FCW warnings were timed. Approximately 8 responses per warning type were recorded.

All of the reaction time data for both the warnings and targets were recorded in a computer log file. The reaction time data for each participant were summarized and transcribed into Statistica where they could be further analyzed.

RESULTS

Repeated measure ANOVAs were conducted on the reaction times to the four warning lights. There were significant differences between the warning lights for the mean [$F(3, 45) = 10.8$, $p < 0.0001$], median [$F(3, 45) = 11.4$, $p < 0.0001$] and maximum [$F(3, 45) = 4.28$, $p < 0.01$] reaction times. Post-hoc comparisons using Tukey's HSD indicated, for these measures, that the reaction times were significantly faster for the CWHUD than the other three warning displays, figure 7. This difference was nearly 200 ms for the mean brake reaction times.

The standardized effect between the CWHUD and Cluster warnings was 0.87, which constitutes a large difference. No significant differences were found among the other warning lights and there were no gender differences in reaction time.

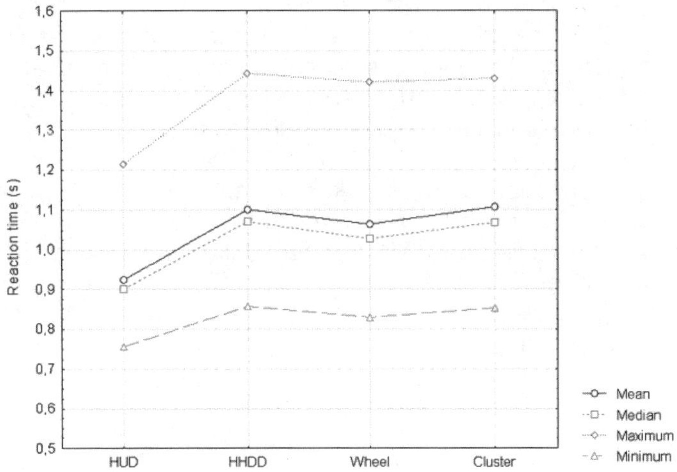

Figure 7 ***Reaction time to warning***

Regarding the number of participants who missed a warning, only one driver missed a HUD warning, 6 drivers missed a Steering Wheel warning, 5 missed a HHDD warning and 11 missed Cluster warnings. Some people missed more than one warning. The number of missed warnings per display distributed as an average per driver is shown in figure 8. The total number of missed warnings was as follows: 1 CWHUD, 6 HHDD, 12 SW and 17 Cluster warnings. Paired comparisons with the Wilcoxon matched pairs test indicated that this difference was statistically significant between the CWHUD and other warnings ($a = 0.05$).

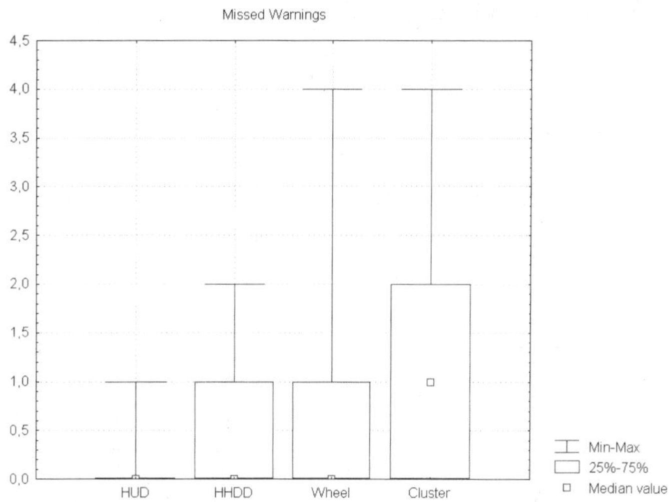

Figure 8 ***Missed warnings per warning display***

Repeated measure ANOVAs were conducted on the average reaction times to the four target positions. There were significant differences between the four locations [$F(3, 39) = 27.0$, $p < 0.0001$; note two participants were excluded from this analysis because they missed all the targets that appeared on the centre stack monitor]. Post-hoc comparisons using Tukey's HSD indicated that the reaction times were significantly faster for the middle screen targets than the other 3 locations. Also the right screen targets had significantly faster responses than the left screen position.

The participants were asked to rank the four warning lights according to their preference at the end of their drive, see figure 9. Most preferred the CWHUD warning light overall followed closely by the Steering wheel. The HHDD was third choice and Cluster warning was the least preferred option.

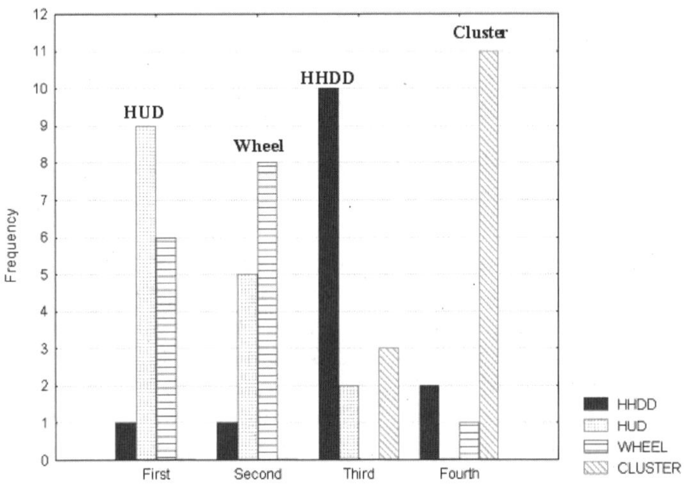

Figure 9 ***Ranking of visual warning display***

SOURCES OF ERROR

Before concluding with some recommendations, some limitations of this study should be discussed. One limitation was that the warnings were given during 'normal' driving rather than collision scenarios (e.g., sudden braking vehicle ahead). This may have surprised drivers because they had no indication of when the warning would appear. An opposing problem was the test drivers were expecting the warning throughout the drive, so they may have responded faster than they would have in a real collision-warning situation. On the balance of these factors, it is believed that this study obtained a reasonably accurate measure of the speed to which distracted drivers react to collision warning displays since the results are comparable to the CAMP study results[1] of 1,18 seconds 85 percentile reaction time for a combined HHDD and audible warning. The aim of the study was to make an interface comparison and not to define the reaction time. For this purpose the method is believed to be fully valid.

The simulator setup with lower environmental brightness than a real world scenario may improve the performance. However the relationship in brake reaction time between warning displays may still be similar.

The driver foot position before warning was not recorded in the study. However since all drivers experienced the same warnings the distribution of error for different drivers foot position should be evenly spread over the warning displays.

Another limitation of this study was that, because the four warnings were unique, no conclusions regarding the ideal design for a FCW can be made. For example, little can be said about the general effectiveness of LED's versus telltales, or high versus low warnings. The study can only say what is best among a limited selection of visual warning types rather than what is the best possible visual warning for FCW.

CONCLUSION

From the results of the performance tests and preference ratings, the CWHUD display was in the study found to be the best for the FCW. The average brake reaction times were significantly faster for the CWHUD warnings (approximately 200 ms). The same result was found for the median, minimum and maximum reaction times. There were no significant differences in reaction times among the other three warnings. The CWHUD also performed best related to low amount of missed warnings. Only one CWHUD warning was missed during the experiment, whereas 17 of the total number of instrument Cluster warnings were missed by the drivers. Also, the CWHUD rated first among the user preferences. The second, third and fourth choices were Steering wheel, HHDD, and Cluster.

The cluster position had the worst performance and preferences ratings. Also, it was the only warning display that was not within 15 degrees of the driver's normal site line which is a NHTSA recommendation[4].

The explanation for the performance of the CWHUD is the greater size and brightness combined with the similarity and the position of a red brake light that together provide driver with an intuitive understanding of the situation.

Not considered in this study was the problem of driver annoyance. Frequent false alarms or nuisance warnings may cause the drivers to become irritated and this risk of irritation increases when the warnings are intrusive. Further studies preferably in realistic on road driving conditions on should be done to ensure that an efficient FCW visual display is not too annoying under normal realistic operating conditions which include false and nuisance alarms. A system utilizing an intrusive type of Collision Warning Display is expected to demand less nuisance warnings and a very low amount of false warnings than a low intrusive Collision Warning system.

The use of complementary warning modalities can not be ruled out as efficient means of warning. I.e. less intrusive visual warning signals like the HHDD, Steering Wheel Display and Cluster Display used together with an audible warning can not be ruled out as an efficient collision warning.

Low sunlight may in real life reduce the visibility of the warning as well as if the CWHUD warning is outside the peripheral vision of the driver. It is therefore recommended to combine the CWHUD with a complementary warning modality.

Internal studies on the CWHUD have been performed in more realistic FCW scenarios both in simulator and on road. These studies show that the proposed CWHUD visual warning device is efficient and intuitive in collision scenarios.

To conclude the results shows that the Collision Warning Head Up Display, CWHUD, provided the best performance in a distracted driver situation based on a low amount of missed warnings, low reaction time and high driver preference out of the four FCW visual displays tested.

ACKNOWLEDGEMENT

The author likes to acknowledge the excellent study layout, execution and analysis to Peter Burns and the execution of the study to Maria Tevell.

REFERENCES

1. Kiefer, R., LeBlanc, D., Palmer, M., Salinger, J., Deering, R., & Shulman, M. (1999). CAMP Report: *Development and validation of functional definitions and evaluation procedures for collision warning/ avoidance systems.* (DOT HS 808 964). Washington, DC: NHTSA.
2. Cole, B. L., & Hughes, P. K. (1988). *Driver's don't search: they just notice.* In D. Brogan (Ed.), Visual Search, (pp. 407-417). Durham, U.K.: Taylor & Francis.
3. Lansdown, T.C. (1996) *Visual Demand and the Introduction of Advanced Driver Information Systems into Road Vehicles*, Doctoral Thesis, Loughborough University, Leicestershire.
4. Lerner, N.D., Kotwal, B.M., Lyons, R.D., & Gardner-Bonneau, D.J. (1996). *Preliminary Human Factors Guidelines for Crash Avoidance Devices* (DOT HS 808 342). Washington, DC: NHTSA.
5. Wang, J. S., Knipling, R. R., & Goodman, M. J. (1996). *The role of driver inattention in crashes*; new statistics from the 1995 Crashworthiness Data System. Proceedings of 40th Annual meeting of the Association for the Advancement of Automotive Medicine, Vancouver (October, 1996).
6. Wickens, C.D. (1992). *Engineering Psychology and Human Performance.* London: Harper-Collins.
7. Dingus et. al (2006). *The 100 car naturalistic driving study, Phase 2 - Results of the 100-Car Field experiment* (DOT HS 810 593). Washington, DC: NHTSA.

CONTACT

Henrik Lind, Technical Expert
Volvo Car Corporation
Safety Electronics
Dep. 94354 PV4A2
SE-405 31 Gothenburg
SWEDEN
Tel: +46 (31) 595361
E-mail: hlind1@volvocars.com

2006-01-0951

Driver Information Utilizing Flat Panel Display

Vyacheslav Birman and Pavel Birman
Siemens VDO

ABSTRACT

The size of an average instrument cluster is much larger than what is actually required to present information on vehicle conditions. There exists an opportunity to present all of that information on a PDA size (3.1" – 3.8") color display. The use of color in different areas of informational gauges, such as temperature or fuel levels, provides another way of presenting the driver with information, while also visually enhancing the appearance of the display.

INTRODUCTION

Spatial resolution of the retina of a human eye varies significantly within different portions of the retina [1]. Fovea, a portion of the retina, has much higher spatial resolution than other portions. Color resolution, however remains constant over different portions of the retina. When a red or yellow telltale turns ON, a driver keeping his/her eyes on the road can see something red or yellow on the cluster, but cannot see the shape of the telltale without looking at the cluster.

In order to read information from the cluster, a driver has to do the following:

1. move his/her eyes from the road to the cluster
2. adapt his/her eye to a distance of about 0.5m
3. scan the cluster (if a driver wants to read all information on the cluster).

It is not very easy to measure the time that each of these acts takes, but the last one is not negligible. It seems obvious that a smaller cluster requires a shorter time to scan it. When looking at the cluster, a driver does not scan the entire area. In most cases, he/she just looks at the area of the cluster containing the required information. For example, to get the speed, a driver looks only at the speedometer near the pointer and then looks back to the road. It is a characteristic of human vision to scan just an area of interest. A driver only looks at the portion of the gauge located near the pointer and not the entire gauge. This can be interpreted as a reason to display the significant portion of a scale instead of the entire scale.

Telltales on a cluster use two channels of information: geometry and color. Gauges use 1.5 or 1 (one) channel. For example, tachometer and temperature gauge usually have red zones. In those cases, color is used to present information, whereas other gauges use geometry alone to present information. Color as an information carrier can be used wider than just existence of red zones.

It seems reasonable to develop a cluster of a much smaller size utilizing color as an information carrier for gauges as well as telltales. This would decrease the "eyes off the road" time, provide two channels of information to the driver and improve cluster appearance.

RESULTS

Using a common font size, the complete range of information on vehicle conditions including speedometer, tachometer, gas level, temperature, odometer, telltales, as well as information on radio station, calling phone number and directions can be presented on a common PDA size display (3.1"-3.8"). Luminance of common transflective PDA displays is close to automotive requirements.

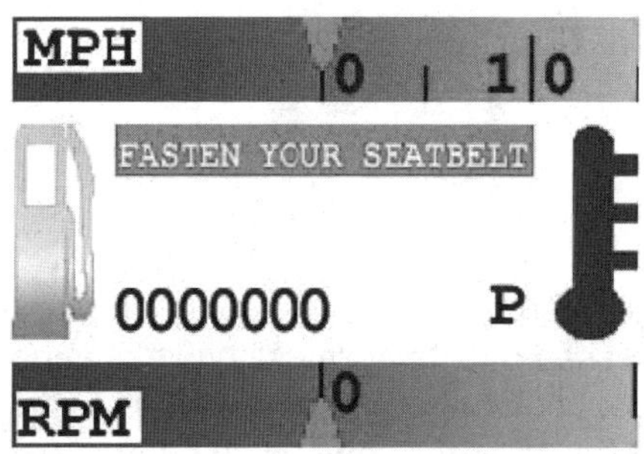

Fig.1.

Fig. 1 shows examples of the appearance of such a display at starting condition. Empty space in the center portion can be used to display telltales such as "airbag".

A full gas tank can be presented by continuous change from red to green, as well as by green color only. To signify that the engine is cold, particularly when starting the car, the entire temperature gauge is shown as blue. After the engine temperature changes the display only shows a portion of the scale with color indicating appropriate temperature as shown in Fig. 2. At this point, both color and geometry carry information on engine temperature.

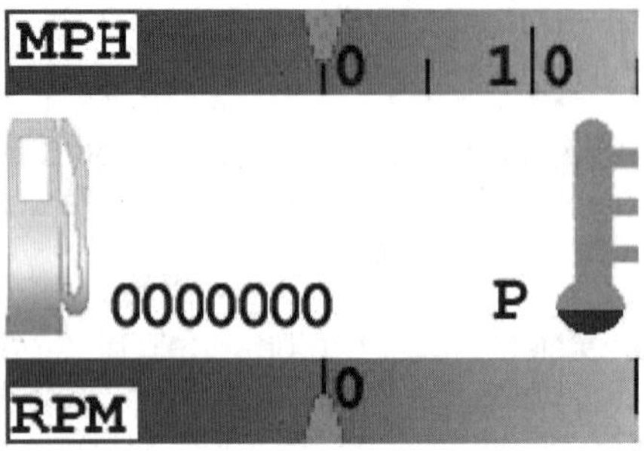

Fig. 2.

The appearance of the display during driving conditions is shown in Fig. 3. This is a normal condition for a vehicle. Consequently, the dominant color is green. Note that the area required for presenting information on gear position is 5-7 times smaller than in a regular cluster. Displaying a part of the speedometer and tachometer scale saves room, while keeping a common font size for numbers.

Spatial resolution of a normal human eye at a distance of 0.5m is about 3 lines per millimeter. Resolution of a VGA display is 9 lines per millimeter. Consequently, all the lines have a smooth appearance and different fonts can be used.

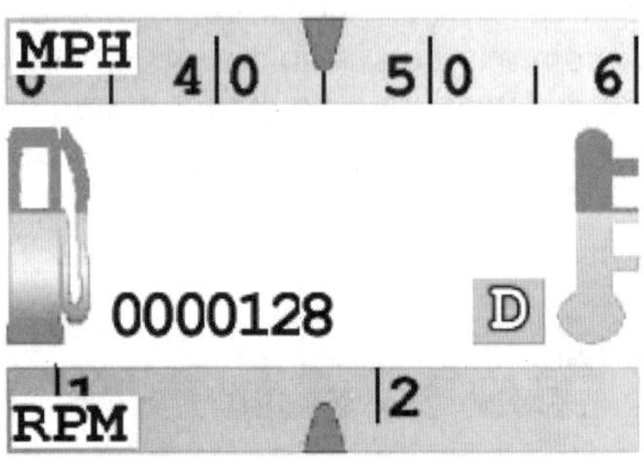

Fig. 3.

In this case, both values of fuel and temperature levels are expressed qualitatively using two channels of information: color and geometry. When expressing values in this manner, there is no need to use numbers to show fuel level and temperature value. Information is presented to a driver with about the same precision as it would be in a regular cluster.

Part of the display can be used for presenting information on phone calls [Fig. 4.] or radio, [Fig. 5] as well as for any other messages. The amount of space required for the turn signals is half that required in a regular cluster, because the space on the display is shared between both left and right turn signals.

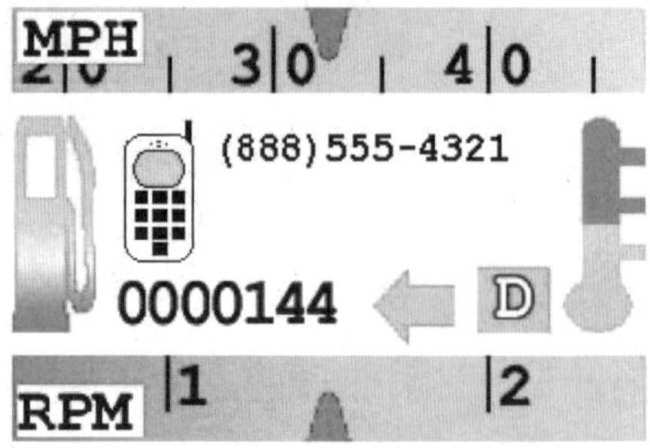

Fig. 4.

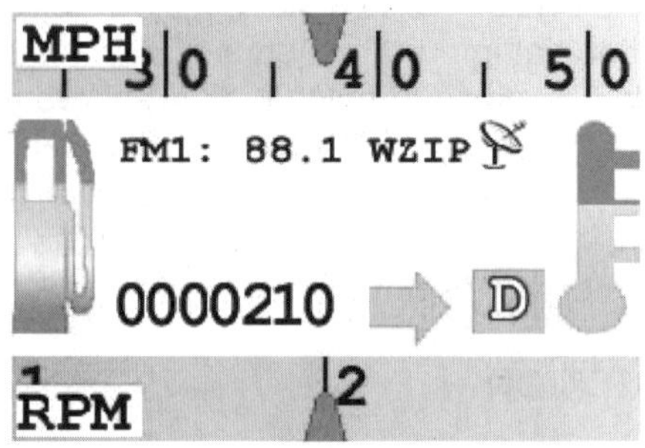

Fig. 5.

The remaining space can be utilized for presenting navigation information, as shown in Fig. 6. After the entire area of the display is filled, a question of room for telltales appears. Before answering that question, there is reason to raise other questions. Does a driver need radio and phone information at the same time? Is there a disadvantage to presenting only one piece of information at a time? The answer is most likely no, because a driver only needs information that is important at the time. For example, if there is phone and radio information in two separate locations on a cluster then when the phone rings, the driver will not look at the radio, as well as would not listen to it during the phone conversation. Thus, placing both phone and radio information in one shared location not only saves space, but can also decreases the "eyes off the road" time and consequently increases safety or at least comfort of the driver.

There is also one other question with regard to sharing display space. Is it a big loss for a driver to lose radio or phone information if a telltale such as "check engine soon" replaces it? The answer is probably no, because such a telltale requires immediate response, while the radio or phone does not. Telltales that are not critical can share the same space used for turn signals. This is only a disadvantage when the vehicle is making a turn. The disadvantage, however, is negligible, because it is very unlikely for a driver to look at the cluster during a turn. Cruise control can also be shown as a line on the speedometer instead of using up space as a telltale.

One of the advantages of using a flat panel display as a cluster is that the cruise control, for example, can be shown as a symbol, a line on speedometer scale, a point on the same scale, a ring with central line or as a rectangle with central line. This decision can be made by the vehicle's owner rather than the manufacturer. Other reconfigurable options, such as moving scales with numbers can be used for presenting information on fuel and temperature levels instead of predefined settings.

Fig. 6.

Fig. 7 shows unrealistic, extreme conditions of a vehicle. The dominant color in this case is red. It shows an empty gas tank, boiling coolant temperature, reverse gear, high speed and RPM. All other possible problems can be expressed in the empty white area of the display.

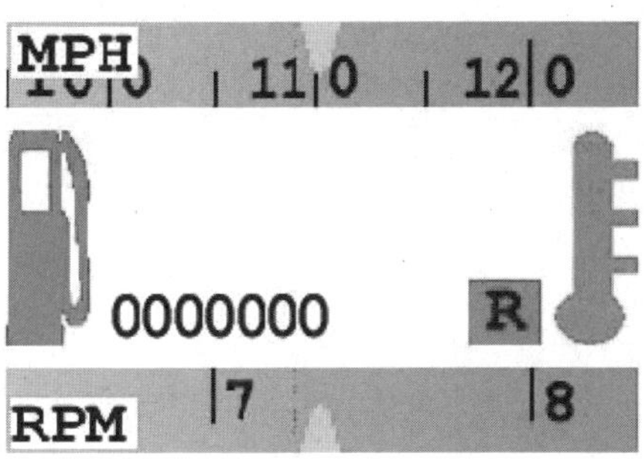

Fig. 7.

"Green borders" for gas level, temperature, battery voltage and oil pressure depend on vehicle design. "Green borders" for RPM depend on vehicle conditions (temperature, oil pressure, etc). "Green borders" for velocity are undefined. If the vehicle is connected to Global Positioning System (GPS) and GPS has information on speed limits in the location of the vehicle, the only information that a driver needs from the cluster, in most cases, is that the vehicle is in "Green condition". This information can be received while the driver's eyes are on the road.

In addition to extra cost, the idea of keeping information on speed limit in GPS has significant advantages. Speed limit signs on U.S. roads do not change with weather conditions, but road conditions do. A safe speed under dry conditions is much different than when there is ice, rain or snow present. Visibility depends not only on weather, but also on the time of day. A safe speed under dry conditions at night time is lower than at day time. Certain speed limit adjustments can be set once and used in the future. For example, data on sunrise and sunset can be set in advance, thus letting the GPS make speed limit adjustments automatically. Other conditions, which cannot be predicted such as bad weather or traffic jams, have to be set manually. Updated information would be continuously sent to the cluster, which would display appropriate speed limits.

3 LED's, green, yellow and red with a very simple and inexpensive optical system placed near the windshield can give the driver qualitative information on vehicle conditions. These LED's can be placed in any other location convenient for the driver. Continuous green "means don't look at the cluster." Blinking green means "nothing is wrong but look at the cluster" (phone calls, etc). Yellow means "something is not good" (low battery, gas, a little over speed limit, etc). Red means "immediate attention required." Existence of this qualitative information would drastically decrease the "eyes off the road" time. Moreover, most of the vehicles equipped with HUD are also equipped with regular clusters, which mean that "eyes off the road" time for drivers of these vehicles is not zero.

CONCLUSION

- Color can be used as an information carrier.
- PDA size display (3.5"-3.8") is sufficient to present all cluster information to a driver.
- Color scales are visually appealing.
- Time needed for a driver to receive qualitative information can be significantly decreased.
- A driver can choose from several options of fonts, hues, shapes and screen location of scales, but not predetermined symbols, such as phone, etc.
- Display area sharing between elements that do not have to appear simultaneously enables a significant decrease of the display size and consequently price.

REFERENCES

1. Levi, Leo, *Applied optics; a guide to optical system design*, Wiley (1980), New York

2005-01-0425

Alliance Principle 1.4: Visual Downangle Criteria for Navigation and Telematics Displays in Vehicles

Richard A. Young, Jeffrey R. Dixon and W. Weston Meyer
General Motors Corp.

ABSTRACT

The Alliance of Automotive Manufacturers (Alliance) has produced a document in which Principle 1.4 gives criteria and methods for calculating downvision angles to navigation and telematics displays in vehicles. This paper describes the details of the criteria and methods for determining compliance. Visual displays placed high in the vehicle instrument panel help drivers to use their peripheral vision to monitor the roadway for major developments, even during brief glances to the display. The Alliance has developed two criteria to define the maximum allowable downward viewing angle for displayed information in North American vehicles. One criterion is for use in two-dimensional Computer Aided Design (CAD) analyses, and one is for use in three-dimensional CAD analyses. Alliance Principle 1.4 is consistent with known driver performance research data, and known facts about the peripheral sensitivity of the human visual system.

INTRODUCTION

Alliance Principle 1.4 reads:

1.4 Visual displays that carry information relevant to the driving task and visually-intensive information should be positioned as close as practicable [1] to the driver's forward line of sight.

For a driver to be in full control of the vehicle and aware of the dynamic roadway there is a broad consensus that, apart from brief glances at mirrors or instrumentation, the driver's gaze should be directed towards the roadway. Visual displays positioned close to the normal line of sight reduce the total eyes-off-the-road time relative to those that are positioned further away. Such positioning also maximizes the possibility for a driver to use peripheral vision to monitor the roadway for major developments while principally looking at the display.

A manufacturer may use either Criterion 1.4A or Criterion 1.4B below to define the allowable downward viewing angle to displayed information. One is for use in two-dimensional Computer-Aided Design (CAD) analyses, and one is for use in three-dimensional CAD analyses. Both of these criteria have been derived from research that underlies a JAMA guideline on downward viewing angle. As a result, these criteria are based on a reference point called the Japanese eye point. In order to apply these practices in North America in a way that is consistent with Japanese criteria, it is necessary to establish a corresponding point in terms of North American practice. In this Principle, therefore, the term 'eye point' is the SAE equivalent of the JIS (Japanese Industrial Standard) eye point [2], which is the SAE J941 [3] 2D eyellipse side view intersection of XX and ZZ locator (datum) lines. This corresponding point is located 8.4 mm up and 22.9 mm rearward of the mid-eye centroid of the SAE eyellipse [3].

CRITERION 1.4A (2D CAD ANALYSIS)

If head-down, the display shall be mounted in a position where the 2D downward viewing angle is less than or equal to 30 degrees at the geometric center of display.

Since the eye point height from the ground differs greatly between passenger cars and large trucks, the relationship between eye point height and the perceptible distance was calculated with a compensation equation given below in Eq. 1 in relation to the eye point height from the ground.

When the height of the eye point above the ground is 1700 mm or more, the display shall be mounted in the position at which the downward viewing angle shall be less than the value obtained from Eq. 1 [4]:

$$\text{Angle (degrees)} = 0.01303 \times (\text{eye point height from the ground (mm)}) + 15.07 \quad (1)$$

Although no lateral viewing angle provision is specified, current research has validated this Principle only for display locations up to 40 degrees laterally from the driver. The intent of this Principle is to apply to visually intensive displays located in the instrument panel center stack.

CRITERION 1.4A VERIFICATION METHOD

This method represents an angular measurement done in two dimensions at the centerline of the display. It duplicates what is in the JAMA Guidelines [5].

This procedure is to be applied within a computer-aided design or modeling tool (or some equivalent measurement method). It is also intended to be applied when the seat is in its design nominal position, and the display is located at its design-intent position. This recognizes that some variations around these design nominal positions may occur at the time of vehicle build or assembly, but need not be individually measured.

If head-down, the display shall be mounted in a position where the downward viewing angle is less than 30 degrees. The downward viewing angle should be set between two lines that project on the vehicle's *Y* plane. The first line projected on the *Y* plane should be drawn from the Japanese eye point – or, in North America, from the corresponding point 8.4 mm up and 22.9 mm rearward of the mid-eye centroid of the SAE eyellipse – parallel to the *X*-axis. The second line should be drawn from the center of the display monitor to the same eye point (8.4 mm up and 22.9 mm rearward of the mid-eye centroid of the SAE eyellipse (or corresponding point in the Japanese practice). It should be noted that the term *center of the display monitor* corresponded to the bottom of the display information in the empirical study upon which this criterion is based.

CRITERION 1.4B (3D CAD ANALYSIS)

If information subject to this Principle is displayed at a head-down location, the displayed information must be located at or above the criterion downward viewing angle [6] at the geometric center of the active display area as determined by the following procedure [7]. Note that the "active display area" excludes unused display surface and hard switches. Fig. 1 [8, adapted from their Fig. 1] shows the three-dimensional reference system that will be used to describe the method.

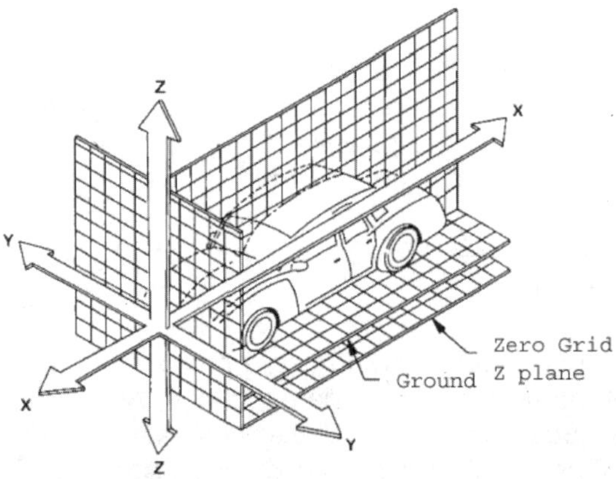

Fig. 1 Three-dimensional reference system (redrawn from SAE J1100).

The maximum allowable 3D downward viewing angle (*3D downangle)* for a particular vehicle is set in a manner consistent with the JAMA data [9], [10] that formed the basis for the 2D downward viewing Criterion 1.4A. In particular, the maximum allowable 3D downward viewing angle is given by the dimensions of the CAD model in [9], their Fig. 3, which they used to express the main findings of their study in 3D terms. The maximum 3D downangle is likewise set to be dependent upon the height of the eye point above ground, again as per [9], their Eq. 5. *Ground* is here defined as in terms of *curb weight* as per SAE J1100 [8], Section 3.2.1 [11], and will be referred to as *SAE curb ground* or *curb ground* in the rest of this paper.

Fig. 2 shows an *Eye Box* that illustrates the symbols and variables used in describing the 3D downangle procedure.

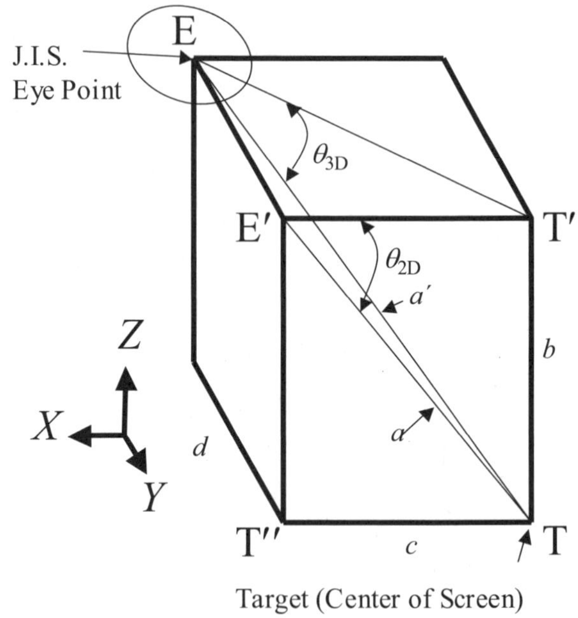

Fig. 2. Definition of axes and symbols for box encompassing the eye and the display. The drawing defines an *eye box* formed by eye point E (upper left corner of eye box), and target point T on the display (lower right corner of eye box). The *X*, *Y*, *Z* axes are vehicle coordinates as per Fig. 1. The view is from the right side of the vehicle towards the driver. The near plane E'T'TT" is the right face of the eye box, typically at or near the centerline of a vehicle.

Key: ***X*, *Y*, *Z*** = vehicle coordinates in front-rear (*X*), side-side (*Y*), and up-down (*Z*) directions; **E** = J.I.S. Eye Point; **E′** = projected E Point; **T** = Target point on display screen; **T′**, **T″** = projections of T point; ***b*** = downward distance (ΔZ) from eye to target; ***c*** = forward distance (ΔX) from eye to target; ***d*** = cross-car distance (ΔY) from eye to target; ***a′*** = length of 3D ray from eye point E to target point T = sqrt(a^2 + d^2); ***a*** = length of eye-to-target ray *a′* in projected (side) view = the distance E′T from eye to target when both points are projected onto the same side plane = sqrt(b^2 + c^2); $\boldsymbol{\theta_{2D}}$ = 2D downward viewing angle E′T′T = atan(b/c); $\boldsymbol{\theta_{3D}}$ = 3D downward viewing angle ET′T = asin(b/a').

Maximum Allowable 3D Downward Viewing Angle:

The method to derive the appropriate maximum allowable 3D downward viewing angle for a specific vehicle is described below.

a) *Measure the height Z_{ground} of the J.I.S. eye point from the SAE curb ground [11] for the vehicle.* In North America, this would be the distance from the mid-eye centroid of the SAE eyellipse [3], [12] to the SAE curb ground for that vehicle, plus 8.4 mm to convert to JIS eye coordinates.

b) *Substitute the greater of Z_{ground} or 1146 into the right side of Eq. 1, and calculate the angle.* The calculated angle is the maximum allowable 2D downward viewing angle for that particular eye height, here termed θ_{2Dmax}. It is measured from the JIS eye point to the display point in side view. That is, the JIS eye point and target point are projected to the same side plane, and then the angle between the two points is the maximum 2D downangle (see θ_{2D} angle E'T'T in Fig. 2). Unlike Principle 1.4A, the maximum 2D downangle limit is variable for vehicles with eye-to-ground heights less than 1700 mm as well as greater than 1700mm, following Eq. 1 and results from [9], [10]. θ_{2Dmax} is used here solely as an intermediate step in calculating the maximum allowable 3D downward viewing angle as per step (c). (Note: θ_{2Dmax} is a different angle than the criterion 2D angle described in Principle 1.4A and is not intended to be used as a substitute for the 2D angle method in section 1.4A.)

c) *Convert this 2D angle solution (θ_{2Dmax}) to a 3D angle (θ_{3Dmax}).* The 2D angle is the downangle in terms of the side view, but the 3D angle is the true downangle to the display from the driver-centered point of view, measured from the driver's seated position. That is, the 3D downangle is measured in the rotated vertical plane in which lie both the JIS eye point and the display point. (It can loosely be thought of as associated with the downangle formed as if the driver rotated his head [13] and then looks down, to direct the center of gaze to the display point.) θ_{3Dmax} is the maximum allowable 3D downward viewing angle for a given vehicle with a certain eye height above ground, as given by Eq. 2.

$$\theta_{3Dmax} = \arctan[\tan(\theta_{2Dmax} * \pi/180)/\mathrm{sqrt}\,(1+ d_{00}^2/c_{00}^2)] \quad (2)$$

Note that c_{00} and d_{00} in Eq. 2 are the specific vehicle dimensions from the JAMA CAD model [9] summarizing the empirical data, and *not* the values for the new test vehicle under investigation. The value of c_{00} is the forward distance from the eye point to the vertical plane (*Y-Z* plane, see Fig. 1) containing the display point, and d_{00} is the cross-car distance between the eye-point and the vertical plane (*X-Z* plane, see Fig. 1) at the centerline of the vehicle, for the JAMA CAD model [9], [14]. Yoshitsugu [15] gives these values as c_{00} = 550 mm, d_{00} = 370 mm. Substituting, Eqs. 1 and 2 may be combined and simplified into Eq. 3. This method ensures that the more general equations for the 3D downangle derived here always contain the JAMA model [9] and empirical data as a special case.

$$\theta_{3Dmax} = 57.2958 \times \arctan[0.829722 \tan(0.263021 + 0.000227416 \max(1146, Z_{ground}))] \quad (3)$$

Fig. 3 shows that the maximum allowable 3D angle goes from 25.6 degrees at an eye height above ground of 1146 mm to 35.93 degrees at an eye height of 2000 mm.

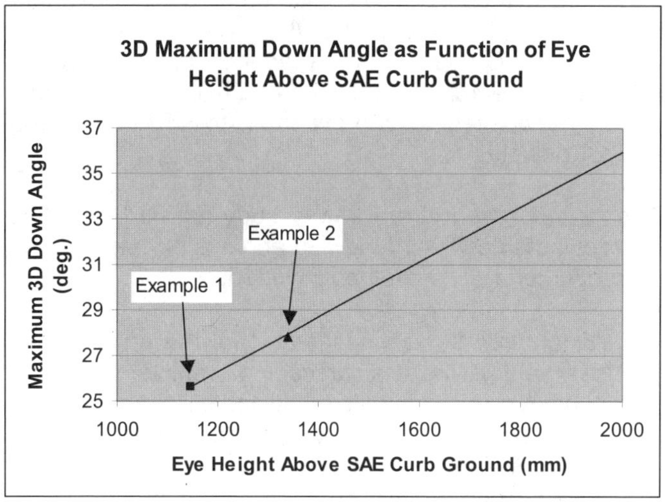

Fig. 3. Maximum 3D downangle as a function of eye height above ground for Principle 1.4B. The points labeled Example 1 and Example 2 are discussed in the Appendix.

In short, this method guarantees that the calculations for a new vehicle 3D maximum downangle encompass the empirically based CAD model and equations as given in [9]. That is, the model [9] has now been generalized to allow for a true 3D downangle, which more closely approximates the actual downangle of the driver's visual system when observing the display.

Examples are given in the Appendix.

Justification:

A driver will be better able to monitor the roadway and the driving environment if the display location is kept as close as practicable to the driver's forward view. A display that is located too low in the vehicle may divert the driver's attention from the roadway and may cause a dangerous situation. Several studies on driver inattention or distraction have shown that rear-end type crashes are a predominant scenario [16], [17], [18].

This Principle is based on the JAMA Guideline [5] concerning the monitor location of image display devices, and test results on which these Guidelines are based [9], [10]. These provisions were adopted when the JAMA Guidelines were revised in February 2000.

The JAMA study [9], [10] determined the lower limit of a display's downward viewing angle at which drivers focused on the display are still able to perceive they are closing on a preceding vehicle within the distance needed to avoid a rear-end collision. It should be noted that, to date, this study appears to be the only one published which has addressed downward viewing angle in terms of the driver's ability to perceive a lead vehicle at the time that a glance to an in-vehicle display is occurring. As such, it has formed the basis for criteria 1.4A and 1.4B above. However, it would be desirable to have a more substantial body of research on which to base these criteria and it is an area that deserves further research in the future so that these criteria and verification procedures can be refined. In the future, as additional research is conducted and becomes available, it can be applied to improve and solidify the criteria under Principle 1.4.

The method used in the JAMA study [9], [10] to define an allowable downward viewing angle is pertinent to the current criteria. This method included:

- Visual target: The visual target for the driver of the test vehicle was a preceding vehicle that was stopped on road with its brake lights illuminated.
- Visual task: Test subjects were instructed to watch for a preceding vehicle by means of peripheral vision while looking intently at single-digit numbers (7 mm in height).
- Evaluation index: The distance at which test subjects became aware of presence of the preceding vehicle by means of peripheral vision measured and defined as perceptible distance was the evaluation index for this task.

Calculation of Lower Limit of Display:

Based on the experimental results [9], [10] the relationship between (1) the distance at which drivers can perceive they are closing on a preceding vehicle while gazing at the monitor and (2) the downward viewing angle of the monitor, can be approximated with Eq. 4 [9] for a passenger car (eye point height from the ground of 1146 mm).

$$y = -1.151\ x + 85.250\ \text{(average value)} \quad (4)$$

A rear-end collision may be avoided if the following vehicle begins to brake by the time it reaches a point where the preceding vehicle started to brake. Consequently, the required headway must include braking response time of the driver of the following vehicle.

A conservative estimate of approximately 2 second headway may be considered desirable, as it includes delayed reactions and variation among drivers when braking suddenly to avoid an unexpected vehicle ahead in city driving [19]. From this headway time, at 60 km/h drivers should be able to detect a preceding vehicle at a distance of 33 meters.

This relationship is shown in Fig. 4.

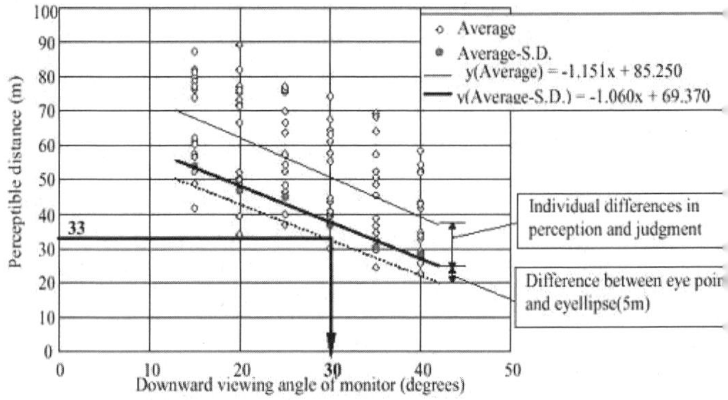

Fig. 4. Relationship between downward viewing angle of display and perceptible distance (from [9]).

In order to account for individual differences in perception, judgment and vision, it was decided to subtract the average standard deviation (S.D.) of the perceptible distance from the average value. From the data in Fig. 4, the relationship between the average S.D. of the distance for perceiving a preceding vehicle and the downward viewing angle of the monitor can be approximated with Eq. 5:

$$y = -1.060\ x + 69.370\ \text{(average -S.D.)} \quad (5)$$

The difference in the monitor's downward viewing angle in terms of the eye point and the normal eyellipse is approximately 5 degrees, which corresponds to a difference of approximately 5 meters in the distance for perceiving a preceding vehicle (see Fig. 4). In order to account for difference in eye point positions, a margin of 5 meters should be provided for the perceptible distance.

From Fig. 4, at a perceptible distance of 33 meters in city driving, the intersection of the difference between eye point and ellipse data occurs at approximately a 30° downward viewing angle. Taking the above considerations into account, the lower limit of the downward viewing angle of the screen in a passenger car was found to be approximately 30°. This observation formed the basis for Criterion 1.4A.

The JAMA study [8], [9] also examined perceptible distance to a lead vehicle at various eye height locations (1146 mm, 1393 mm, 1737 mm, and 2388 mm). The results revealed that as drivers' eye height above ground increases, the further they could see down the road.

Essentially, the line of sight to the lead vehicle at elevated eye heights declines slightly from horizontal. The angular distance between a lead vehicle and the display decreases the higher the driver is above the ground. This means that a lead vehicle can be detected with display placements at larger downward viewing angles. The authors [8], [9] provided the regression equation specified under Criterion 1B above, as the description of allowable downward viewing angle as a function of eye height. In addition to varying eye height above ground, the JAMA study [8], [9] also examined display locations at various horizontal angles from centerline of driver (in seated position). These results suggest that an angle measured in three dimensions (from driver seated position) is appropriate as lateral displacement of the display increases (within the range studied) [22]. Together, the results from both of these additional research manipulations provided the basis for Criterion 1.4A (in which downward viewing angle is determined as a function of eye point height) and Verification Procedure 1.4B (with is measured in three dimensions from the driver seated position to the display location).

Comparison of 2D and 3D Methods

Criterion 1.4B accounts for the actual downward viewing angle of the driver's vision system when viewing the display. Drivers typically move their head and/or their eyes to a display to bring the fovea or area of highest acuity vision onto the display. The ability of the driver to detect and respond to vehicles or objects on the road ahead when glancing downward is determined by the limits of the human peripheral visual system, more so by the up-down visual dimension rather than the left-right one, as shown in the [9], [10] data, and is well known from human visual periphery studies [20]. These limits are more closely associated with the actual downward angle in the vertical dimension of the driver's eyes, not the 2D side angle in vehicle coordinates. Therefore, the 3D angle as shown is a better approximation to the driver's actual downward visual angle than the 2D angle measured in the side view, from a human vision standpoint. On this basis, the 2D downangle method in 1.4A is overly strict for cross-car distances greater than the intersection point of the two curves and overly lenient for cross-car distances smaller than that intersection point (see Appendix Fig. A1). The 2D downangle method leads to a constant horizontal constraint line on the instrument panel (see Appendix Fig. A1). At greater cross-car distances, this fixed distance down leads to smaller and smaller true visual angles the further the displacement is away from the driver, just due to basic geometry. Likewise, the 2D method may be overly lenient if the cross-car location of the display were to be moved closer and closer to the driver (for example, at or near the instrument cluster). Nonetheless, the 2D method is simple to understand and implement, can be based on grid coordinates without the need for a ground plane definition, and it encourages higher and more optimal display placement at a typical display location in the center stack.

CRITERION 1.4B VERIFICATION (FOR USE WITH 3D CRITERION ANGLES):

This verification procedure is appropriate for use with Criterion 1.4B (and represents an angular measurement done in three dimensions from eye point height at the driver's seated position). It is also appropriate when the height and width of a vehicle might differ from those for which the simpler 2D criterion and measurement were developed.

This procedure is to be applied within a computer-aided design or modeling tool (or some equivalent measurement method). It is also intended to be applied when the seat is in its design nominal position, and the display is located at its design-intent position. This recognizes that some variations around these design nominal positions may occur at the time of vehicle build or assembly, but need not be individually measured.

Three alternate methods are given for Section 1.4B, all of which produce an equivalent answer. In all three methods for 1.4B, it is perhaps easiest to first translate and then rotate the world coordinate system (WCS) to align with the SAE curb ground plane. The original grid coordinate system (as in Fig. 1) must not be used, or it violates the assumptions of Criterion 1.4B.

Method 1 – CAD Measurement

1. Ensure that both the driver's seat and the display to be analyzed are placed at their respective nominal design positions in the three-dimensional CAD representation (or equivalent).
2. Locate the driver eyellipse according to SAE J941-Rev. June 1997 [3] eyellipse.
3. Determine the location of the centroid of the combined eyellipse (mid-eye centroid), and then find the point corresponding to the Japanese eye point, 8.4 mm up and 22.9 mm back for the SAE eyellipse.
4. Determine the location of the display point, defined as in the first paragraph of Section 1.4B.
5. Determine the 3D downward viewing angle. This can be done by going through steps a, b, and c, below or by using some simple CAD methods noted after step c.
   a. Construct a line representing the driver's line-of-sight to the display point. This can be done by drawing a line between the eye point (located in step 3, above) and the display point (located in step 4, above). This represents the line-of-sight to the displayed information. (See line ET in Fig. 2).
   b. Construct a line in the horizontal plane of the driver's eye point, to a point in that plane directly above the display point (line ET′ in Fig. 2). The angle that lies between these two lines (the line of sight to a point in the horizontal viewing plane directly above the display point and the line of sight to the display point) represents the actual downward viewing angle to the display point.

c. Measure (or calculate) the size of the 3D downward viewing angle using the formula θ_{3D} = asin (b/a') (see Fig. 2), where:

   a' = Distance from eye point to display point along the line of sight ET to the display.

   b = Vertical distance from the eye point down to the horizontal plane encompassing the display point (line T'T in Fig. 2).

If this angle is equal to or less than the maximum allowable downward viewing angle computed for Criteria 1.4B, then the display location meets the criterion.

<u>Method 2 – Swept Line Method</u>

Another way to implement this verification method in a Computer Aided Design (CAD) system is to create a swept line. Construct a single line that has a fixed angle down from the horizontal plane containing the eye point – that is, a fixed angle down from the driver's forward line of sight to the roadway. The down angle to the forward line of sight should be set at a value of θ_{3Dmax} – the maximum allowable 3D downward viewing angle (as determined from Criteria 1.4B). Once anchored and positioned this way, the line can be swept laterally, such that it makes a constant downangle with the horizontal plane containing the eye point. This swept line will trace an intersection path on the dashboard representing the lower limit for the display point. This trace is the 3D constraint line. If the displayed information lies above the intersection of the display and this constraint line, it is considered to meet the 1.4B downward viewing angle requirement.

The swept line also creates a cone [21]. The cone that is generated by the swept line is illustrated in Figs. 5-7. Fig. 5 is a perspective view, Fig. 6 is a side view, and Fig. 7 is a rear view. The apex of the cone is at the eye point E. If the criterion display point were inside the boundary of the cone shown, the component placement would *not* meet criterion 1.4B. Because it is outside the boundary of the cone (see Fig. 7), it meets criterion 1.4B [22]. The intersection of the cone with the vertical *YZ* plane containing the display point traces a hyperbola, which is the line shown in Appendix Fig. A1, labeled "1.4B 3D constraint line."

Fig. 5. Perspective view of cone as swept by a line drawn from the eye point at a fixed downangle from the horizontal plane containing the eye point, with coordinate system aligned with SAE curb ground. The eye point is at the apex of the cone. The smaller shaded object is the instrument panel. The rear portion of the cone is cut away so the interior can be seen. If the display point is outside the boundary of the cone, it meets criterion 1.4B.

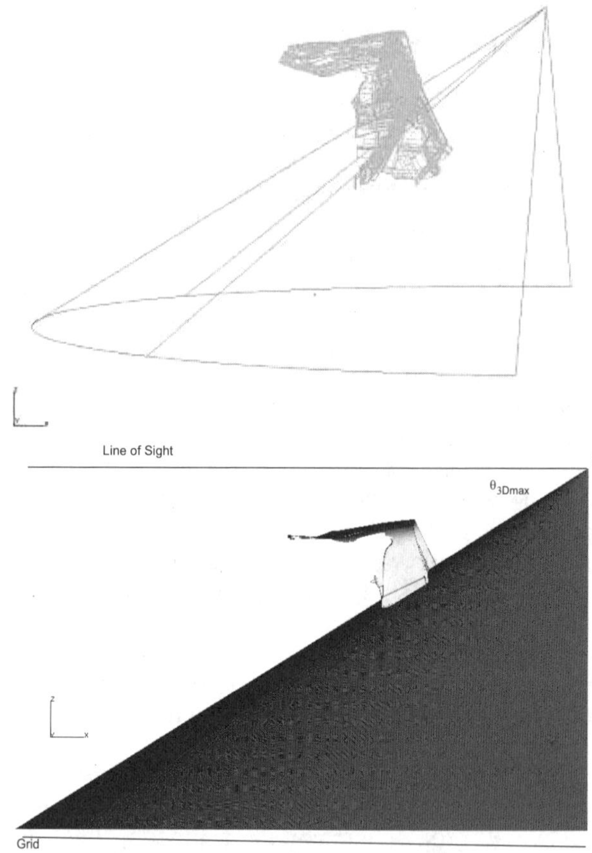

Fig. 6. Side view of object in Fig. 5 (coordinate system aligned with SAE curb ground). Top view is wire-frame and bottom is solid. Consider a horizontal extending to the left from the eye point E at the upper right as the line of sight. The angle between that and a lower line is fixed at θ_{3Dmax}. This line then sweeps out the cone shown. Note that the grid coordinate line (bottom of image) is at a slight tilt with respect to the SAE curb ground coordinates in this case. If incorrectly measured on the grid coordinate system, the rear of the vehicle might have been lowered relative to the front, incorrectly decreasing the measured 3D downangle.

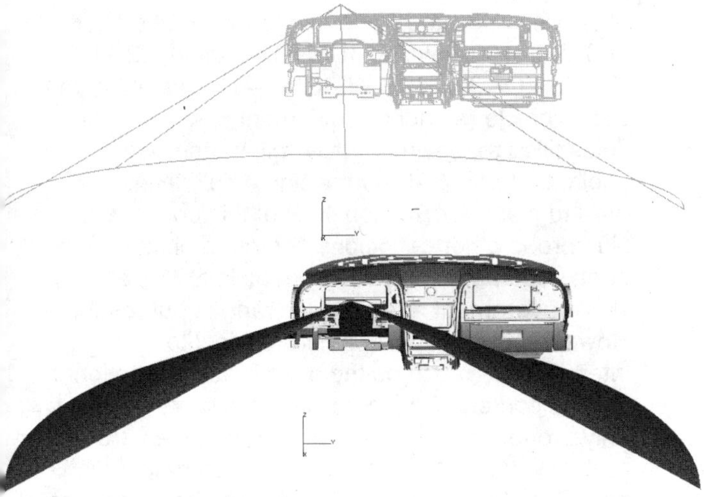

Fig. 7. Rear view of same cone and instrument panel as in Figs. 5 and 6. The top picture is a wire-frame view. The bottom picture is a solid view, with the rear portion of the cone cut away so the interior can be seen.

Method 3 – Two-Point Math-Based Method

A final way to implement method 1.4B is to ask a CAD operator to determine the *X,Y,Z* values of two points: the mid-eye eyellipse centroid, and the display point. (Note: the *X* and *Z* values need to be determined with respect to the SAE curb ground plane [11], not the grid coordinate system of the vehicle as in Fig. 1.) Then the formulas given below can be easily placed for example in an Excel spreadsheet to calculate the maximum allowable 3D angle, and the actual 3D angle.

Let $X_{display}$, $Y_{display}$, $Z_{display}$ be the coordinates of the display. Let X_{eyeSAE}, Y_{eyeSAE}, and Z_{eyeSAE} be the SAE eye coordinates. Then calculate the JIS eye point as per Eqs. 6:

$$X_{eyeJIS} = X_{eyeSAE} + 22.9 \text{ (rearward)}$$

$$Y_{eyeJIS} = Y_{eyeSAE}$$

$$Z_{eyeJIS} = Z_{eyeSAE} + 8.4 \text{ (upward)} \qquad (6)$$

Then calculate:

Forward distance from eye point to display point (ΔX or c) = X_{eyeJIS} - $X_{display}$

Cross-car distance from eye point to display point (ΔY or d) = Y_{eyeJIS} - $Y_{display}$

Actual height distance from eye point to display (ΔZ or b) = Z_{eyeJIS} - $Z_{display}$

Length of eye-to-target ray in true (i.e. 3D) view (a') = SQRT(b^2+c^2+d^2) (7)

Finally calculate:

Maximum 2D downangle for this eye height = θ_{2Dmax} = 0.01303* Z_{eyeJIS} + 15.07

Maximum 3D downangle for eye height =57.29*ATAN(TAN(θ_{2Dmax}*0.017)/SQRT(1+d_{00}^2/ c_{00}^2))

Actual 3D downangle = DEGREES(ASIN(b/a')) (8)

Note that c_{00} must be fixed at 550 mm, and d_{00} at 370 mm, based on the JAMA CAD model of the experimental results (see section "Maximum Allowable 3D Downward Viewing Angle").

Examples:

Good: Visual display positioned high on the instrument panel towards the driver's side of the central console, but not being obstructed by the steering wheel or obstructing the forward vision.

Bad: Display positioned too low in the console area towards the front passenger's side or within a glove compartment.

DISCUSSION AND CONCLUSION

Two methods of downangle calculation are shown which both are consistent with known data on the ability of drivers to detect and respond to a vehicle brake light in a vehicle in front of them. At this point in time, either method of downvision calculation can be a useful tool to assess vehicles for compliance with Principle 1.4

Additional studies are recommended to further test and validate the Alliance Principle 1.4 criteria and model. These methods also be further refined and explored to determine sensitivity to both vertical and horizontal vision. Further mathematical modeling work can potentially unify the 2D and 3D criteria into a single downangle metric. The objective would be to merge the motion and luminance contrast sensitivity contour plots of the human visual system as a function of retinal eccentricity, into a common mathematical model with the geometry of the driver, roadway scene, display, and vehicle interior.

In conclusion, downvision metrics are presented with verification procedures to ensure that visual displays that carry information relevant to the driving task and visually-intensive information shall be positioned such that a driver's peripheral vision can still monitor the roadway for visual changes when the driver briefly glances at a display.

ACKNOWLEDGMENTS

The authors would like to acknowledge help and support from the Alliance members who contributed time and effort to this endeavor, but especially: Linda Angell, General Motors Corporation; Don Mission, Daimler-Chrysler Corporation; and Gary Rupp, Ford Motor Corporation. This paper is dedicated to the memory of our esteemed colleague and dear friend W. Weston Meyer, 12/1/21 - 11/24/04.

REFERENCES AND NOTES

[1] Practicability is introduced to allow a reasonable trade-off between closeness to the driver's normal line of sight and other issues of allocation of devices to a limited instrument panel space.

[2] JIS Eye Point is defined by JIS D0021 and JIS D1702.

[3] SAE J941, Society of Automotive Engineers Surface Vehicle Recommended Practice, "Motor vehicle drivers' eye locations," Rev. June 1997.

[4] The coefficient of the eye height from ground is set at 0.01303 to be consistent with the JAMA published guidelines [5], although 0.013 is used in Eq. 5 in [9] Yoshitsugu et al. (2000). This difference does not materially affect the calculations.

[5] JAMA "Guideline for in-vehicle display systems," version 2.1, February 22, 2000, http://www.umich.edu/~driving/guidelines/JAMA_Guidelines_(Draft).pdf.

[6] Although no lateral viewing angle provision is specified here, [9] validated this principle only for display locations up to 40 degrees laterally from the driver.

[7] Alternatively, the display may be mounted in a position where the downward viewing angle is less than or equal to the criterion viewing angle at the geometric center of display.

[8] SAE J1100 "Motor vehicle dimensions," July 2002 revision.

[9] N. Yoshitsugu, T. Ito, and T. Asoh, "JAMA's safety guideline on in-vehicle display systems (The study of monitor location of in-vehicle displays)," ITS World Congress, Turin, Italy, 2000, http://202.53.41.14/itslibrary/CONFERENCES/ITS_WORLD_CONGRESS_7th_Turin_ITALY/3548.pdf.

[10] T. Asoh, K. Kimura, and T. Ito, "JAMA's study on the location of in-vehicle displays," SAE Paper 2001-01-C010, 2000.

[11] In Section 1.4B, coordinate dimensions are specified as per SAE J1100 Revised JUL2002 [8]: "Unless otherwise specified, all dimensions are measured normal to the three-dimensional reference system (see SAE J182), except ground-related dimensions, which are defined normal to ground. All dimensions are taken with the vehicle at curb weight unless otherwise specified." The term *curb weight* is defined in SAE J1100 Revised JUL2002 section 3.2.1: "CURB LOAD, CURB WEIGHT—The weight of the base vehicle (standard equipment only), with all fluids filled to maximum (fuel, oil, transmission, coolant, etc.)." SAE curb weight shall define the ground plane for Section 1.4B of this document. Numerous other definitions of ground planes have been used both internally by vehicle OEMs and by U.S. government agencies for various purposes. However, other definitions are subject to interpretation, such as the specification of optional vehicle content. SAE curb weight is currently the only ground plane on which vehicle values are routinely publicly reported by vehicle companies selling in North America. Finally, the tire size tends to be smallest in the base vehicle, leading to a lower eye height and stricter section 1.4B criterion compared to larger tire sizes (see main body section "Maximum Allowable 3D Viewing Angle"). It is to be noted that the zero-grid Z plane (see main body Fig. 1) must not be used as the ground plane for Section 1.4B, because it is an arbitrary grid not directly related to true ground.

[12] SAE J941, Society of Automotive Engineers Surface Vehicle Recommended Practice, "Motor vehicle drivers' eye locations," Rev. Sept. 2002.

[13] Technically the current method is equivalent to rotating the eye, not the head.

[14] The centerline of the vehicle and the centerline of the display coincide in the JAMA model [9], [10].

[15] Personal communication.

[16] D. L. Hendricks, J. C. Fell, and M. Freedman, "The relative frequency of unsafe driving acts in serious traffic crashes," Prepared for U.S. Department of Transportation, National Highway Traffic Safety Administration, Traffic Safety Programs, Office of Research and Traffic Records, Under Contract No. DTNH22-94-C-05020, 2001.

[17] J. C. Stutts, D. W. Reinfurt, L. Staplin and E. A. Rodgman, "The role of driver distraction in traffic crashes, phase I final project report," University of North Carolina Highway Safety Research Center Chapel Hill, NC. Prepared for AAA Foundation for Traffic Safety,1440 New York Avenue, NW, Suite 201, Washington, DC, 2001.

[18] J. Wang, R. R. Knipling and M. J. Goodman, "The role of driver inattention in crashes; New statistics from the 1995 crashworthiness data system," 1996.

[19] P. L. Olson and M. Sivak, "Perception-response time to unexpected roadway hazards," *Human Factors*, vol. 28, pp. 91-96, 1986.

[20] L. M. Forbes (1970) "Geometric Vision Requirements in the Driving Task," SAE #700395, Automobile Safety, 1970 - Conference Compendium. International Automobile Safety Conference (Detroit and Brussels), Society of Automotive Engineers, series P-30, Conference held

May 13-15, 1970, Detroit, MI; June 8-11, 1970, Brussels, Belgium.

[21] Note: This cone should not be confused with the *cone of vision* or the *effective* or *inductive* field of vision as referred to by [9], their Fig. 3.

[22] Although no lateral viewing angle provision is specified, current research has validated this principle only for display locations up to 40 degrees laterally from the driver.

[23] The θ_{2Dmax0} value can be easily calculated in the JAMA CAD model [9] because the center point of the display was at the center line of the vehicle – that is, the display was centered on the center stack in the middle of the vehicle, midway in cross-vehicle distance between the driver and the passenger.

[24] Note that the 2D angle shown here is calculated in ground coordinates, but it is often necessary in practice to calculate it in *grid* or vehicle coordinates (main body Fig. 1) early in vehicle design, when no ground plane may be defined.

[25] The general constraint solution for a curved or sloping instrument panel is more complicated than for the planar assumption, but can be established via a direct CAD model measurement if desired.

CONTACT

richard.a.young@gm.com

ADDITIONAL SOURCES

1. Japanese Industrial Standards, "Eye range of drivers for automobiles," JIS D 0021, 2000, http://www.webstore.jsa.or.jp/webstore/Top/indexEn.jsp (In Japanese). See also "Road vehicles – Visibility – Method for establishment of eyellipses for drivers eye location," ISO 4513:2003, Available from http://webstore.ansi.org/.
2. Japanese Industrial Standards, "Road vehicles – Test method for the direct driver's field of view," JIS D 1702:1996, 1996, http://www.webstore.jsa.or.jp/webstore/Top/indexEn.jsp. (In English).
3. K. Morita, M. Sekine, J. Mashiko and T. Okada, "Safety of in-vehicle displays of automobiles – effect of mounting position differences," in *Vision in Vehicles*, vol. 10, North Holland: Elsevier Science, 2003.

DEFINITIONS, ACRONYMS, ABBREVIATIONS

2D: Two-dimensional space

3D: Three-dimensional space

Alliance: Alliance of Automobile Manufacturers

CAD: Computer-Aided Design

JAMA: Japanese Automobile Manufacturers Association

JIS: Japanese Industrial Standard

SAE: Society of Automotive Engineers

APPENDIX

EXAMPLE 1: JAMA CAD MODEL CAR

For the eye height Z_{ground} of 1146 mm used in the JAMA CAD model [9], the θ_{2Dmax0} value via Eq. 2 is exactly 30 degrees (the identical 30-degree 2D downangle limit value as per Criterion 1.4A) [23]. The maximum permissible 3D downangle θ_{3Dmax0} for [9], their Fig. 3, for the eye height of 1146 mm is then 25.6 degrees via Eq. 2 or Eq. 3 (see point labeled "Example 1" in Fig. 3).

Table A1 gives parameters of the driver-car model that match to the forward event braking data [9]. The 3D downangle limit is 25.6 degrees for the particular car used in study [9] with the parameters given, when the display is at the maximum 2D downangle of 30 degrees.

Parameter Description	Symbol	JIS Eye	Units
J.I.S. eye point height from SAE curb ground	Z_0	1146.00	mm
Maximum 2D downward viewing angle for this eye height	θ_{2Dmax0}	30.00	deg
Maximum 3D downward viewing angle for this eye height	θ_{3Dmax0}	25.60	deg
Forward distance from eye centroid to display point (ΔX)	c_0	550.00	mm
Cross-car distance from eye point to display point (ΔY)	d_0	370.00	mm
Height distance from eye point to display point (ΔZ)	b_0	317.54	mm
Length of eye-to-target ray in projected (i.e. side) view	a_0	635.09	mm
Length of eye-to-target ray in true (i.e. 3D) view	a'_0	735.01	mm
2D downward viewing angle (curb ground)	θ_{2D0}	30.00	deg
3D downward viewing angle (curb ground)	θ_{3D0}	25.60	deg

Table A1. Parameters for the CAD model that matches the empirical driver performance braking data to forward events[9]. The maximum 2D downward viewing angle is 30 degrees, which the display location just meets. The corresponding maximum 3D downward viewing angle is 25.6 degrees (for SAE curb ground), which the display location also just meets.

Fig. A1 illustrates a more general 3D solution that includes the CAD model [9] as a special case. For illustrative purposes, it is easiest to reference the driver coordinate system to an eye point located at (0, 0, 0). The 2D downward viewing angle of the display point (marked T in Fig. A1) is at the 2D maximum of 30 degrees. The horizontal 2D constraint line in Fig. A1 shows that the 2D angle stays fixed at 30 degrees (317.54 mm below the eye point in side view) as a function of cross-car distance. The curved line in Fig. A1 labeled "1.4B 3D constraint line" gives the permissible maximum permissible downward distances for the 1.4B criterion for that vehicle as a function of cross-car distance. The 3D downward viewing angle is fixed at 25.6 degrees for that curved line.

The 3D constraint line in Fig. A1 is equivalent to assuming a line is positioned with one end at the eye point, and the other at the instrument panel. The line is then swept from the centerline of the driver (that is, from d = 0 mm), to some position to the right of the centerline of the vehicle (say d = 800 mm). The intersection of the line with the vertical YZ plane in which the display point lies is the 3D constraint line in Fig. A1. The length of the line (or ray) from the eye point to the display point is given by Eq. A1.

$$a' = \mathrm{sqrt}(a_0^2 + d^2) \qquad \text{(A1)}$$

The downward physical limit b_{sweep} is where the swept line intersects the vertical YZ plane in which the display point lies. This sweep is a hyperbola, given by Eq. A2.

$$b_{sweep} = a' \sin(\theta_{3Dmax0} * \pi/180) \qquad \text{(A2)}$$

This swept line in fact traces out a cone in 3D. Let **C** denote a right circular cone with apex at the eye point, central axis vertical, and central (or apex) angle equal to $(180 - 2 * \theta_{3Dmax})$ in degrees. (Note: the central angle of a cone is the angle across the full diameter of the cone, not just its radius.) Then every longitudinal (or rectilinear) element of **C**'s surface is a line of sight deflecting downward from the horizontal plane by the angle θ_{3Dmax}. Moreover, the surface of **C** is the locus of all such lines of sight. It does not take a great deal of geometric intuition to see the validity of this construction. Clearly, every longitudinal element of a right circular cone's surface makes a fixed angle with the central axis, that angle being one-half the apex angle – in the case of **C**, this half-angle is $(90 - \theta_{3Dmax})$. If the central axis is vertical, the angle with respect to the horizontal is θ_{3Dmax}.

This swept line or cone method is further described and illustrated in the verification "Method 2 – Swept Line Method" for Principle 1.4B, and main body Figs. 5-7. Without benefit of analysis, we know that the intersection of **C**'s surface with a vertical plane must be a hyperbola. (In the study of conic sections, a cone extends to infinity in both directions from the apex, so that a plane parallel to its axis will intersect the cone's surface in two disconnected branches, necessitating that the intersection be hyperbolic. In our case, we are interested only in that half of the cone that lies below the apex, and only in the lower branch of the hyperbola.) The volume inside the cone represents the locations in which the display point should *not* be placed.

The 2D angle constraint line (assuming SAE curb ground) is the dashed line in Fig. A1, given by the constant height $b = a' \sin(30 * \pi/180)$.

Fig. A1 shows that when the display point is closer to the driver than the intersection of the two constraint lines, the 3D constraint line is higher (i.e., stricter) than the 2D constraint line given by Section 1.4A (assuming SAE curb ground for both), whereas the opposite is true for display positions to the right of the intersection point. Hence the 3D method in Section 1.4B is neither stricter nor more permissive than the 2D method in Section 1.4A; it depends upon the cross-car distance of the display (see also main body section "Comparison of 2D and 3D Methods").

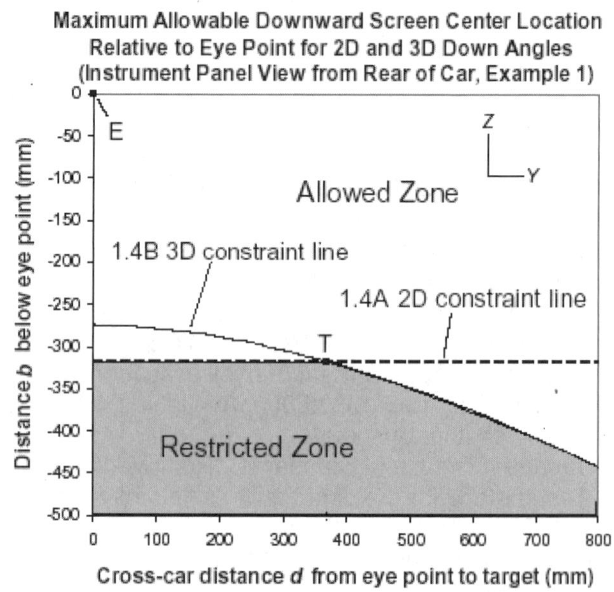

Fig. A1. The graph depicts a view from the rear of the vehicle towards the instrument panel. The graph describes a vertical YZ plane containing the display point T in Example 1, which is based on the car CAD model [9]. The dashed horizontal line shows the 2D design constraint line above which the display point T must be placed, for different cross-car positions d (X-axis). The solid curved line is the 3D design constraint line, above which the display point must be placed to meet criterion 1.4B. As long as the display point T is at or above either the 2D or 3D constraint line, it meets criterion 1.4. In this case, the target point T meets both 1.4A and 1.4B criteria. Point T in this CAD model [9] example is at the exact intersection of the 2D and 3D constraint lines.

Obviously, other vehicles will have different sizes than in the JAMA data and model [9], [10]. Principle 1.4B generalizes the 2D Principle 1.4A to three dimensions, with a true ground line, and ensures that common 3D downangle methods are used for vehicles of different sizes, while ensuring that the JAMA empirical model [9] is always included as a special case.

EXAMPLE 2: CRITERION 1.4B SOLUTION FOR A NEW VEHICLE DESIGN

Assume a new vehicle has eye height from SAE curb ground of $Z_{ground1}$. Let the X, Y, Z distances between the eye point and the display point in the new vehicle be c_1, d_1, and b_1 respectively. That is, assume forward distance c_1, cross-car distance d_1, and height offset b_1 between the eye point and the display point. By substituting the actual eye height $Z_{ground1}$ in Eq. 1, the maximum allowable 2D downward viewing angle θ_{2Dmax1} for the new vehicle may be calculated. (Note that θ_{2Dmax1} is just an intermediate 2D angle used for calculating the 3D angle, and is not the same 2D angle criterion as in section 1.4A.) The maximum 3D downangle θ_{3Dmax1} permitted for this new vehicle design is then derived from main body Eq. 2 or Eq. 3.

To determine if the new vehicle meets the 3D downangle criterion from Section 1.4B, calculate the corresponding length of the line from the eye point to the display point in side view, given by a_1 = sqrt $(b_1^2 + c_1^2)$. Then the distance a_1' from the eye point to the display point along the line of sight to the display is given by a_1' = sqrt$(a_1^2 + d_1^2)$. The 3D downangle for this vehicle is then asin(b_1/a_1'), which can be compared with the limit θ_{3Dmax1}.

To illustrate, Table A2 shows a vehicle with its SAE eyellipse centroid coordinates, as well as its JIS eye coordinates and display coordinates measured according to the SAE curb ground plane [11].

Dimen. Descrip.	Dim.	SAE Eyellipse Centroid	JIS Eye Point	Display Point	Units
Distance behind the front of vehicle	X	3011.31	3034.21	2506	mm
Side distance from car centerline	Y	-370.00	-370.00	12	mm
Height above SAE curb ground	Z	1327.28	1335.68	969	mm

Table A2. Eye centroid and display position for car Example 2, measured from SAE curb ground.

Fig. A2 shows a side view graph of the point locations in Table A2 along with a CAD model representation of the human mannequin commonly used in automotive applications. Fig. A3 shows the rear view of the same data. Neither view shows the true 3D downangle, which can only be seen in an oblique view.

Table A3 shows the 2D and 3D angle calculations for the Example 2 vehicle, based on the JIS eye point and display point in Table A2, assuming SAE ground coordinates [24]. The display point T is at a 3D downangle value of 29.36 degrees and must be moved up on the instrument panel such that a vertical height increase of at least 1.52 degrees (22.46 mm) occurs, in order to meet the 3D downangle limit of 27.64 degrees. Note that the dashboard is usually curved and tilted rather than a vertical plane, so the offset height increase required to meet the criterion should only be viewed as approximation to the actual distance that the display needs to be moved up on the dashboard itself. The final position of the display on the dashboard should be again validated against the criterion after the display is moved upwards in the CAD model.

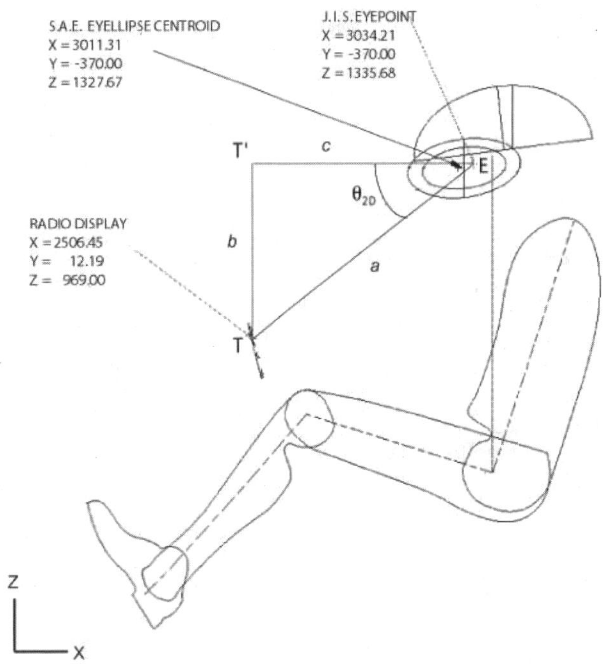

Fig. A2. Example 2, Side view. J.I.S. Eye Point E and display point T, projected into the side view XZ plane. θ_{2D} is the two-dimensional downward viewing angle in curb ground coordinates.

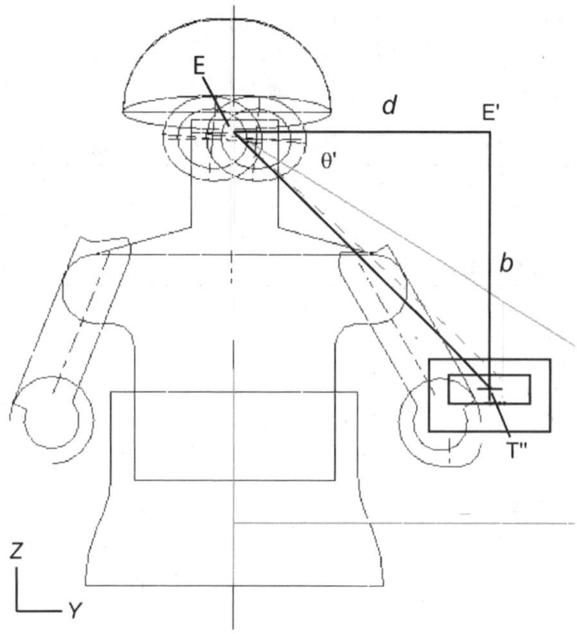

Fig. A3. Rear view. J.I.S. eye point E, projected eye point E′ and display point T″ for car example 2, projected into the *YZ* plane. The angle θ formed from triangle EE′T″ as shown is atan(b/d) = 43.84 degrees. Only the view in the oblique plane formed by ET′T (see for example main body Fig. 2) will directly show the correct 3D downangle of 29.36 deg.

Parameter Description	Symbol	JIS Eye	Units
J.I.S. eye point height from SAE curb ground	Z_1	1335.77	mm
Maximum 2D downward viewing angle for this eye height	θ_{2Dmax1}	32.48	deg
Maximum 3D downward viewing angle for this eye height	θ_{3Dmax1}	27.84	deg
Forward distance from eye centroid to display point (ΔX)	c_1	528.21	mm
Cross-car distance from eye point to display point (ΔY)	d_1	-382.00	mm
Height distance from eye point to display point (ΔZ)	b_1	366.77	mm
Length of eye-to-target ray in projected (i.e. side) view	a_1	643.06	mm
Length of eye-to-target ray in true (i.e. 3D) view	a'_1	747.96	mm
2D downward viewing angle (curb ground)	θ_{2D1}	34.77	deg
3D downward viewing angle (curb ground)	θ_{3D1}	29.36	deg

Table A3. 3D downangle calculations for car in Example 2 based on J.I.S. eye point.

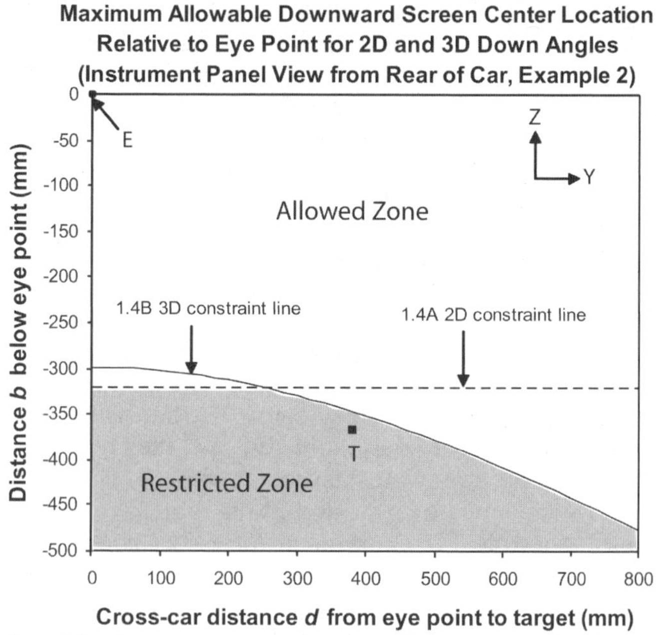

Fig. A4. Instrument panel zones for Example 2. The horizontal dashed line is the 30-degree downangle 2D constraint line (30° constant downangle). The curved solid line is the 3D constraint line based on a constant downangle from the driver's viewpoint in SAE curb ground. The J.I.S. eye point is E and the actual display point location is T. The display needs to be raised vertically at least 1.52 degrees (22.46 mm) to meet the 3D downangle criterion of 27.84 degrees for this vehicle, and even further to meet the 2D downangle criterion.

It would again be useful for design and vehicle architecture purposes to evaluate the downward viewing limit for the vehicle not just for one particular display location, but for an extended constraint line on the instrument panel above which the display point should be placed. This constraint line allows determination of how high the display must go for all side-to-side positions along the instrument panel [25]. By treating the cross-vehicle distance d as a variable, a 3D downangle constraint line b_{sweep} on the instrument panel as a function of d is then given by substituting a_1 into Eq. A1 for a_0, and θ_{3Dmax1} for θ_{3Dmax1} in Eq. A2. The intersection of a plane and a swept line at a constant downangle from the horizontal, traces a hyperbola (see main body section "Method 2 – Swept Line Method").

Fig. A4 illustrates this constraint line method for the car parameters in Example 2. It can be easily seen that the target point T in Fig. A4 is in the restricted zone for both the 1.4A and 1.4B downangle criteria. Fig. A4 and the data in Table A3 indicate that the display must be raised at least 22 mm vertically to meet the 3D criterion of Principle 1.4B.

2004-01-2587

Caution and Warning in the Cockpit Dashboard

T. Bagian, J. Lindner and E. Gardetto
U.S. Environmental Protection Agency

J. Gordon
Gordon Darby Inc.

ABSTRACT

Today's motor vehicles are approaching the complexity of aircraft and spacecraft, but have a slightly different set of variables for the human operator; the driver. Gravitational forces rarely vary significantly for the vehicle driver; the ability to alter the trajectory usually exists; and refueling opportunities are seldom mission-limiting. Yet the driver is performing in an abnormal, dynamic environment with uncontrolled events and potential life-threatening outcomes just like the aviator or astronaut. Defining and managing 'acceptable risk' in the high performance environments of space and aviation continues to challenge today's engineers and human factors researchers. In the automotive industry, engineers have traditionally approached this challenge by insuring the vehicle design is robust enough to accommodate the full range of potential operators. Automotive visionaries strive to analyze the task of driving and provide appropriate operator feedback, including insight on the vehicle's health, without ever knowing the performance capacity of a specific end-user. Thus today's complex automobiles have primarily incorporated rudimentary caution and warning systems founded on the paradigm of drivers calling upon expert technicians for help in diagnosis and repair; usually bringing the vehicle in for service. As the general public becomes more familiar with advisory systems signaling a range of response criticality [such as message lights on cell phones, clothes dryers buzzing while tumbling, computer windows letting you know a virus scan is occurring], what strategies would be most promising for providing the driver with more insight? What have we learned from other complex, dynamic operator environments that would appropriately transfer to this setting and help the driver evaluate urgency as well as options? **This paper will discuss the need for and potential future of such human-system messaging strategies in the On-Board Diagnostic system of today's motor vehicles.**

INTRODUCTION

This paper discusses the human factors issues associated with insuring the continued effectiveness of On-Board Diagnostics [OBD] in controlling pollution from the U.S. light duty fleet of automotive vehicles. Of specific interest is the dashboard illumination of the 'check engine' light to the driver. The intended action is that the driver voluntarily seeks diagnostic attention which may result in car repair, thus avoiding excess air pollution. In areas with specified air quality problems drivers may be required to obtain needed repairs that extinguish the dashboard light prior to annual vehicle registration. The required involvement of the driver in such a pollution control strategy hinges on providing information that the driver will understand and be motivated to act upon. This paper will discuss and compare the involvement of pilots in cockpit-annunciated system maintenance requirements with the evolving role of drivers in dashboard-annunciated system maintenance requirements. The intent is to identify essential operational elements, and elicit discussion of potential human-machine system design strategies to describe those essential elements, for effective vehicle On-Board Diagnostic systems in the future fleet.

BACKGROUND

Society has come to realize that along with the benefits of using technology comes a need for the human operator to be able to effectively and productively interact with the technology. Wheels make the job easier, but you'd better have brakes and a good idea of when to start applying them. Much work has been done to learn how to **best partner humans with technology;** to 'human factor' the design and operation of the person-technology. One has only to look at the most challenging marriages of humans and technologies, such as in high-performance aviation or spacecraft operations, to appreciate the body of knowledge that has advanced the use of technology in everyday life.

To successfully partner humans with technology the behavior and performance of both the human and the technology need to be understood. Researchers in human behavior have identified requirements for the human to successfully survive, be it on the caveman's hunting expedition or the pilot's reconnaissance sortie. Humans need to be able to **perceive; to evaluate; and to act** to continue to thrive [1]. Limiting the ability to perform these key tasks limits the success of the human. An appropriately camouflaged predator can overcome a human by challenging this ability to perceive: a cat in the jungle, a snake on the trail, or a radar-defeating aircraft. If the human isn't able to appropriately evaluate the information he or she perceives, success can also be compromised: is there enough space between cars to parallel park, is the anthill housing fire ants, is the stove burner turned off, is that pain a simple headache or something more serious? Finally, even if appropriate perception and evaluation occur, if no appropriate actions are or can be taken the abilities to perceive and evaluate are moot: trapped in a burning building you may perceive the flames and heat, evaluate the extreme danger of the situation, yet be unable to escape.

The classic areas of human factors research have provided **standards for the design** of displays and controls taking into account the capabilities and limitations of the human operator and these needs to perceive, evaluate, and act. Range of eyepoint and visual acuity of the population of operators drives the size of font, lighting/contrast requirements, etc. to insure the human can perceive needed information for the task; be it maintaining heading and altitude or staying in the lane at the right speed. Conventions are established to help the human effectively evaluate the conditions, such as using colors and sounds to suggest criticality: amber warns, red alarms. Control design is based on human physiology and psychology, with data from the user population on reaction time, anthropometry [reach, hand/finger size, eyepoint], and biomechanics [force to activate, etc.] to make sure the human can perform the needed task; to act. Human factors experts have produced a number of important reference documents, and disciplines traditionally associated with complex operations, such as nuclear reactor control and medical operations, are increasingly aware of the critical nature of **including the human's ability in task design** as the human is an essential component of the overall system [2,3].

Key assumptions in human factors analyses, however, define the value and utility of the research. They include the ability to **establish the range of performance characteristics for potential human operators** – be they reach, size, vision, or alertness. Aircraft design engineers historically minimize this variable by selecting operators who met very stringent physical and mental criteria, including a rigorous training and proficiency requirement; and by imposing crew rest requirements for operations. Automotive design engineers historically encounter a much broader range of operator, with a much less stringent requirement that proficiency or even alertness be demonstrated prior to operation: a sixteen-year old that can pass a minimal driver test and eye exam. The inability to 'know the user' can severely limit the successful design of a complex operation. The human factors discipline has responded by entertaining the concept of a dynamic operator: be it through selectable computer-assisted functions or display and control characteristics specified by the pilot; or selectable computer-stored seat and pedal positions specified by the driver.

Another key human factors assumption is that the **potential task can be clearly defined**, and a set of performance requirements established. Aircraft design engineers and automotive design engineers alike are thoroughly trained to put trust in the system that generates such requirements, with formalized quality assurance, safety, and reliability oversight elements based on extensive testing and inspection. The inability to foresee all potential tasks that the human-machine team could ever attempt can severely limit the successful design of a complex operation. Again, the human factors discipline recognized the concept of dynamic tasking, and 'autopilot' and 'cruise control' operations are examples of design solutions incorporating the reality that many operating situations don't constantly require intense vigilance and rapid operator assessment/input. The driving or flying task can be thought as dynamic in this regard, and the operator has the ability to select a level of participation that best matches the task demand. The adage that 'form follows function' captures the importance engineers place in understanding the function, or task, of interest. For Caution and Warning, and Maintenance tasks, the tasks or required functions are by nature often ill-defined. Lights and sounds help the operator perceive a condition needing attention, and often contribute to evaluating and acting. Matching the information the operator receives, to the ability to utilize the information and perform the task, is the job of the human factors engineer.

THE ON-BOARD DIAGNOSTIC CHALLENGE

This paper provides a specific example of a situation ripe for just such human factors attention. Vehicle **on-board diagnostics [OBD] were regulated into existence in 1993** to be included into the design of all 1996 and newer light-duty cars and trucks [up to 8,500 pounds gross vehicle weight] sold in America. These systems are to illuminate the Malfunction Indication Light [MIL], an amber 'check engine' light, to the operator when the diagnostics confirm the potential exists for excess vehicle emissions - which can be a vital tool for controlling air pollution. Scan tools which plug into the vehicle computer system and 'read' the diagnostic trouble codes can be used by technicians or interested vehicle operators to identify the vehicle component in need of attention. The light is extinguished upon successful component repair.

Since that time, it could be argued that a greater percentage of the population of operators [drivers] is familiar with and interested in understanding computer diagnostics. People own personal computers and install tax programs, games, and virus scanning software; people query bank accounts and credit card companies via the internet and the telephone. In general, a larger part of the operator population is no longer satisfied to merely know that something needs attention; they want the power, or information, to make a judgement about attending to a situation. Perhaps operators have an increased 'capability' that didn't exist a decade or two ago; an ability to perceive an indicator, like an illuminated cell phone message light, and **participate to a greater extent in the evaluation** of the underlying information. Therefore it could be argued that the **user population might be changing** from the original performance range captured in vehicle design configurations. Newly-introduced services such as OnStar which provide the driver with diagnostic and operations assistance [like a good co-pilot or control tower] provide an interesting experiment; perhaps a significant part of the operator population is interested in incorporating this dimension of information into the driving task.

The **task might also be changing**. Part of the driving, and flying, task is to ensure proper maintenance. As a final element to well-documented activities performed by aircraft maintenance crews, pilots have standardized pre-briefs and pre-flight check-outs prior to declaring themselves 'ready' for operations. The physical maintenance of the aircraft is rarely a task performed by the pilot. The role of the aircraft operator is to react as trained to indications that the system is in need of attention; the action is to continue to monitor, return to base, or eject per the procedures. Aircraft caution and warning systems are fairly standard, and a pilot could likely strap in to almost any contemporary aircraft and understand the diagnostic information and required responses. In contrast, automotive vehicle owners traditionally do very little to ensure vehicle readiness. Many if not most opt to wait until they can perceive something as functioning incorrectly and then evaluate the relative benefit of restoring the component to normal configuration. In years gone by, this entailed popping the hood and checking the components yourself. Today's more complex vehicles have computerized diagnostic systems to aid in maintenance; but unlike the pilot, a driver 'buckling up' in different cars may not enjoy a standardized display of information. Likewise, without a pit crew, the driver must seek out scan tools and technical information to fully understand and trust the diagnosis for needed repair. This **ability to act** has for the most part been relegated to service technicians due to the increasing complexity of computerized vehicles. But the **decision to act** is left to the operator, and his or her judgement that the vehicle is driveable – unless, of course, the local air quality mandates the vehicle pass an inspection test.

DISCUSSION

As noted by human factors researchers tasked with designing navigation aids for drivers, "Some of what is known from human/computer interaction research can be applied to drivers' interactions with automotive systems; however, driving is a complex combination of tasks that may be executed in potentially dangerous situations. In this sense, automotive human factors shares much with avionic human factors (Marshak, Kuperman, Ramsey and Wilson, 1987; Roscoe, 1980). However, the automobile user is quite different from the specially selected, highly trained population of pilots. So, it is generally necessary to develop laboratory and simulator research, along with field studies, to better understand driving with advanced displays, as well as cognitively complex tasks such as way finding (Wetherell, 1979; Zwahlen and DeBald, 1986; Streeter, Vitello, and Wonsiewicz, 1985). A primary reason for this research requirement is that many differences among individual drivers and many different driving situations exist, making modeling and generalization difficult (Noy, 1990; Avolio, Kroeck, and Panek, 1985; Pauzie, Marin Lamellet, and Trauchessec, 1989)." [4]

The introduction of automotive navigation aids has thus recognized the need for specific, focused research to identify and test design solutions, rather than relying on 'lessons-learned' in aviation. While this may also be the case for communicating the need for automotive system maintenance, some insight might be gained from re-examining the aviation analog.

Aircraft human factors engineers have improved human-system performance by identifying and **controlling key design variables**. The range of human performance is controlled through operator/pilot selection/retention requirements and proficiency measures. The range of vehicle performance is controlled by including maintenance as a required, formalized pre-requisite for aircraft operations. The human-machine task is also somewhat controlled since in order for a pilot to legally operate an aircraft, he or she must be able to demonstrate an appropriate interpretation of system status; including caution and warning information.

A human factors analysis of today's OBD situation would result in the identification of a few key elements which currently influence the design of a robust, effective operational system. The current **design is intended to serve the technician** in identifying specific problems and providing effective maintenance; and **also is intended to serve the driver**, with change-in-status information being displayed to the driver via the 'check engine' light. Most drivers can perceive a situation exists via the MIL; but then the ability to evaluate is limited, and the need to act is conditional.

In states with air quality problems drivers are **required to act** and maintain the vehicle through a formal state inspection program; otherwise, America's drivers **choose to understand and respond** to diagnostic information displayed on the dashboard. Drivers are currently limited to a **few options for evaluating** the meaning of the light. They can bring the vehicle to a service technician; access a scan tool from an auto supply to read the information and then find the meanings on a website; or utilize OnStar or some such service that provides the driver with specific trouble codes, their meanings, and recommended actions. The presentation of all diagnostic information is represented through a common cautionary element, the Malfunction Indication Light [MIL], rather than allowing real-time access to underlying diagnostic trouble codes. The triggering of the dashboard light can be due to anticipated or potential excess emissions as well as actual, measurable excess emissions. So what does 'Check Engine' mean to today's driver?

Once the meaning of the message is measured, how can the effectiveness of this diagnostic information be managed or improved? If indeed there have been changes from the original design assumptions about drivers or the maintenance tasks associated with driving since the inception of On-Board Diagnostics, perhaps one near-term engineering option is to **provide some of the increased flexibility** that has been welcomed in other venues. Motor vehicle owners now can stand in line OR mail OR fax OR email OR phone for annual license plate renewal tags. This example demonstrates one successful system redesign strategy, created as a reaction to changes from the original design assumptions. **Today's driver** has increased capability to utilize remote communications; and **today's task** of vehicle registration can now be done without having to be in town – a 'plus' for those drivers interested in alternatives to the traditional annual visit to the Secretary of State office. This could serve as one model worthy of examination for accessing and acting upon OBD information.

Perhaps the message can be better tailored to reflect the need for local air quality control, for example in urban areas, similar to the situational priority of communications for air traffic control in congested aircraft areas. It seems that matching the information associated with the 'check engine' light to any potential increased capability of the user population could argue for allowing operator insight to the underlying diagnostic trouble codes that set the light. Yet we see a large and relatively uncontrolled range of operators. Would using the Malfunction Indicator Light as a 'master alarm' to advise the driver that there has been a detection of an out-of-normal condition be one option that allowed more insight into the maintenance task, for those who chose to use it? Electing to email or otherwise remotely connect to expert technician advisors could be another option, similar to the Mission Control or air traffic control function, that could offer more flexibility than the current need to bring the car in for service. Developing the capability for a second level of warning, one that communicates a measurable risk is now at hand, could also help advise the driver on the relative priority required.

The current light allows the driver to perceive, but not evaluate the situation; then suggests he or she act. Perhaps providing 'more options' for each driver to choose from, similar to the new options for annual vehicle registration, would help achieve the end goal of well-maintained vehicles.

GETTING FROM HERE TO THERE: SUGGESTED RESEARCH

How will the operator population change? The utility and effectiveness of the current message, which basically indicates to the driver that something needs attention, could be measured against other strategies for providing a clear message: which is, there's a risk to continuing operations without attending to maintenance tasks. Perhaps allowing some level of insight about the nature of needed maintenance would better match the increased capability and interest of the operator, and thus reinforce the value and accuracy of the light. Whether this would result in more choice to act, to respond and get the needed repair, could also be measured and compared to likelihood of choosing to act based on the current MIL, which merely signals the need for attention.

How will the task change? Today's driving task often includes a number of subtasks, such as eating, talking, navigating, and entertaining. If the task could be anticipated to eventually include a 'pre-flight check-out', where the operator is monitoring system health to a finer endpoint than sheer driveability, the OBD system could be key in establishing this confidence in vehicle performance. However, examining a potential change in task could be a challenge. The measurement is only as precise as the tool. The success of services such as OnStar, as well as pilot programs where drivers voluntarily seek confirmation of 'all systems go', prior to accepting a rental car for example, could provide first insights.

How well and when does the current strategy work? As simple as this sounds, unless a measure can be made of how well the design of the interface impacts the overall task performance, improvements can not be effectively considered. In the controlled research environment, a given pilot can perform a given task such as approach and landing runs with different cockpit displays and caution and warning systems; and the optimal cockpit lay-out can be defined based on measurable optimal performance. To translate what is learned in those controlled conditions to the real-world requires a thorough understanding of all the variables, and how they differ from lab conditions. But the primary factor in designing the interface is making sure the operator has information that can be effectively used to successfully perform the task.

For the task of automotive maintenance, how much more information than 'check engine' does today's driver need – especially if the driver is unlikely to personally perform the needed repairs? Subtle but critical underlying performance factors include the trust the driver or pilot has in the accuracy of displayed information; and in the value of responding to the information. In the situation of a driver with a 'check engine' light, there may not be a way most drivers could assure themselves that the indicated repair was truly needed for the sustained performance of their vehicle; or that the repair improved the condition. There also may not be inherent trust that 'someone' isn't requiring profitable vehicle repair for other than environmental reasons. This contrasts with the highly-trained aviator's ability to cross-check and confirm accuracy of displayed information, and the confidence a pilot has that indicated maintenance activities are for his or her benefit, and for the benefit of the aircraft.

CONCLUSIONS

The specific conclusion is that **re-examining and confirming the design** of the On-Board Diagnostic MIL-illumination strategy is an important element to ensure sustained, successful human-system automotive maintenance operations; and signaling the driver is effective as long as the variables assumed in the original design remain relatively constant. It behooves an interested human factors engineer to recheck that **original assumptions still hold**, and that there is no new information that could improve the likelihood of operator success. No more vivid examples can be found than those associated with space operations or high performance aviation; when accidents occur, often information is found after the fact that could have been utilized to prevent the adverse outcome. Yet how does one design a complex operation which formally seeks out and incorporates system updates as knowledge about the changing human operator, or the changing task, is discovered? Suggestions include periodically and formally considering and studying the changing capability of the operator; the changing task being performed; and methods to best measure 'real-world' performance.

The more general conclusion is that 'human factoring' our ability to improve the design of ongoing operations is perhaps the greatest challenge the human factors community faces. Individual disciplines have internal strategies. Aviation and medical 'close call' reporting systems tend to identify aspects of operations that can be made more robust, thus improving overall system performance. Bringing that kind of attention to the much more familiar and generalized tasks of society, be they driving or teaching or banking, will require new strategies for thinking of 'second order' design and performance requirements; dynamic or changing operators performing dynamic or changing tasks. It may be much easier to outline the research questions for human performance of a Mars mission, than to imagine the research questions for the next generation of drivers. The evolving design and utilization of dashboard caution and warning systems could be a ripe testbed for examining our discipline's ability to successfully perceive and evaluate the phenomenon of dynamic or changing performance requirements; and an area that could benefit from timely attention.

ACKNOWLEDGMENTS

TB wants to thank NASA for decades of fun imagining what it takes to evolve to the next level of human-machine operations; from Apollo getting there and back, to Shuttle re-using, to Station self-sustaining, to Exploration self-directing. Also thanks to the three co-authors who have lived through similar technical evolutions with the creation and implementation of the first automotive OBD systems; and who have personally experienced the challenges of these pioneering efforts to include the individual driver in the control of vehicle emissions.

REFERENCES

[1] S. Kaplan and R. Kaplan (Eds.). (1978) Humanscape: Environments for people. Belmont, CA: Duxbury. (Republished by Ann Arbor, MI: Ulrich's, 1982.)

[2] R. DeHart and J. Davis (Eds.). (2002) Fundamentals of Aerospace Medicine. Philadelphia, PA: Lippincott Williams & Wilkins

[3] NASA Man-Systems Integration Standards. NASA-STD-3000, Rev B

[4] D.L. Clarke, M.E. McCauley, T.J. Sharkey, T.A. Dingus, J.D. Lee . Development of Human Factors Guidelines for Advanced Traveler Information Systems [ATIS] and Commercial Vehicle Operations [CVO]: Task D. Comparable Systems Analysis. www.fhwa.dot.gov/tfhrc/safety/pubs/95197/index.html.

2004-01-0270

A Practical, C Programming Architecture for Developing Graphics for In-Vehicle Displays

Michael T. Juran
Altia, Inc

ABSTRACT

This paper presents a practical, C programming architecture for developing graphics and graphical user interface (GUI) software for in-vehicle displays such as those found in automotive telematics, shipboard engine control panels and airplane glass cockpits. This paper will compare C graphics to several other methodologies for writing in-vehicle display software. It will also discuss techniques for mixing C graphics with application code written in object oriented languages such as C++ and Java.

INTRODUCTION

Improvements in display technology have produced an explosion of uses for graphics displays in vehicles. Figure 1 illustrates a few potential uses in the automobile cockpit – from the center stack and instrument cluster to rear seat entertainment systems and heads up displays.

Figure 1: *Example of in-vehicle graphics displays.*

Unfortunately, display hardware technology has outpaced software technology and there are currently no established, predictable methods for developing graphics software for vehicles. Consequently, it takes an exorbitant amount of time to design, test and deploy graphics software. Worse yet, a change in the underlying hardware or real-time operating system (RTOS) could require a complete rewrite of the graphics code.

Other industries, such as consumer electronics, information technology, and telecom offer solutions for building GUIs quickly, but these are rarely appropriate for the tight cost, size, performance, reliability and safety constraints found in land, sea and air vehicles.

Thus, there exists a need to alleviate today's graphics development bottleneck for vehicles. This paper explores the issues surrounding embedded systems graphics development and offers some potential solutions.

THE HISTORY OF THE EMBEDDED GUI

In the early days of microprocessor control, embedded systems were faceless. The computer under the hood did its thing and the user never knew about it. If a user needed status or information, he looked at the mechanical gauges. If a user needed to provide input, he would turn knobs, press buttons and step on the gas pedal. Everyone was happy and this arrangement worked for decades.

As solid state LED display technology became available and cost effective, someone got the bright idea of hooking up a simple 7 segment numeric display to a 4-bit microprocessor. Figure 2 is a sample of such a display. With an I/O port and a few well written assembly language commands, the digital odometer was conceived. It didn't take much memory or computer power, yet it was far more reliable than its mechanical counterpart.

Later, embedded processors got a little more powerful and programmers had a few more bytes to spend on graphics. The first pixilated, multipurpose displays became available and programmers built reusable graphics libraries using the C programming language.

In the meantime, desktop computing power has gone through the roof. At the turn of the millennium, 32 bit processors became the norm. Memory hit the gigabyte mark. High-speed graphics boards became standard. A single desktop OS dominated. Graphics programming in this environment was "no holds barred." In the context of graphics development, desktop computers became virtually limitless.

***Figure 2:** A first generation embedded display.*

Embedded systems, however, have not experienced this exponential growth. To be sure, they are endowed with more memory and power than their early predecessors, but the market tendency is to keep these systems as small, lightweight and inexpensive as possible. In addition, processor longevity, reliability and low power consumption are far more important than cutting edge speed and memory size[1]. Consequently, the speed and capability gap between the desktop PC and embedded systems has widened significantly. As a result, the tools and techniques needed to build embedded systems must be quite different.

JAVA and C++ are currently the standard programming languages for desktop, workstation and server applications. These computers have ample power and resources to support the large object oriented graphics widget sets and Java virtual machines. On the embedded system, however, C programming still rules the roost.

Unfortunately, the expectation for GUIs in the embedded world is driven by what people see on their desktops, where there exists more memory and computer power. This disparity has created a problem because, on the low end, displays may have gotten cheap enough to provide lots of pixels, but there still isn't the memory and processor power for massive graphics code. How do we create sophisticated GUIs within the embedded systems limitations? To answer this, we need to first explore the way people build embedded GUIs today.

CURRENT METHODS AND TOOLS

Today there still exist a wide range of embedded systems. The methods used to program such systems range widely as well – from very simple, bare-bones techniques to using toolkits and libraries. Murphy offers an excellent book on this subject.[2] This paper simply introduce a few basic techniques.

BARE-BONES EMBEDDED GUI PROGRAMMING

When programmers have an extremely small amount of computer memory with which to work, the approach to graphics is often attacked from the bottom up. It usually starts with a frame buffer that stores graphics as individual pixels. When the programmer needs to change something on the display, such as an icon or piece of text, he determines which individual pixels needs to be turned off and on, and writes the appropriate data to the frame buffer. Specialized hardware and driver software then refreshes the display at regular intervals.

This method, of course, can be accomplished using any programming language from assembly to Java but is most typically done in C because efficient access to the hardware is crucial.

THE GRAPHICS LIBRARY (GL)

After most programmers have built at least one "bare-bones" system, they discover that it is useful to create routines that do typical tasks like draw lines, circles and text. Instead of writing directly to the frame buffer and setting individual pixels, they simply call these routines with the appropriate parameters and let the routine fill in the frame buffer. These collections of reusable graphics routines are called Graphics Libraries, GLs or drawing libraries.

Many programmers build their own GLs. There are also a myriad of commercially available GLs. GLs tend to be specific to the target operating system ("OS") because the way each OS draws to the screen or fills its frame buffer is different. For example, the GL for MS Windows is Win32. For Unix it is Xlib. OpenGL is a GL ported to multiple operating systems. And there are many more. Like bare-bones programming, GLs can be accessed via C or object oriented languages such as C++ and Java. For efficiency's sake, GLs themselves are almost always written in C.

WIDGETS AND TOOLKITS

GLs usually focus on basic primitive drawing routines for objects such as circles, polygons, lines or text. Of course, many of today's GUIs require more sophisticated objects (widgets) such as menus, buttons and windows. It is possible to build these objects from the basic primitives and many programmers still successfully achieve this on their own. However, like GLs, there are numerous commercially available widget sets and toolkits that are built on top of GLs. For example, Motif is built on Xlib. MS Foundation classes are built on Win32. Widgets and toolkits can be object oriented (Swing, AWT, SWT, Qt, and Interviews) or they can simply be C based (Motif).

JAVA

This section will explore the confusion surrounding the relationship between Java and graphics development.

A significant distinction between Java and other languages is that it is interpreted and thus requires a target specific interpreter – Java Virtual Machine ("JVM") – for each target computer or embedded system. It is often thought that Java magically draws graphics without the need for target specific GLs, widget toolkits, frame buffers or drivers. Somehow the JVM simply handles this and there is no need to port the graphics to different targets. This is not the case. Java is a programming language like C++, C# and C. There are widget sets that are specific to Java. SWT, Swing, and AWT are examples. These Java widgets plug into GLs just like any other.

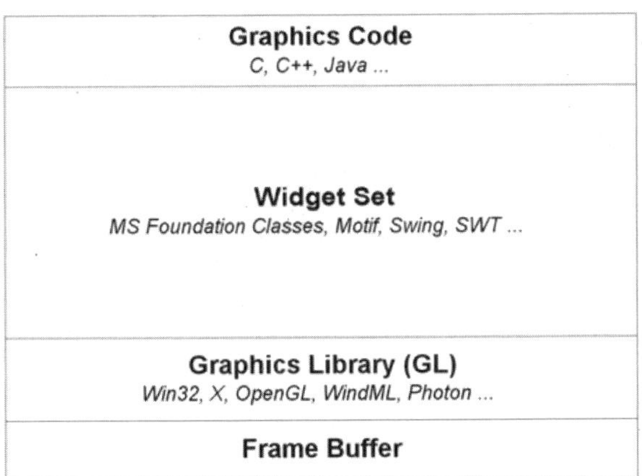

Figure 3: *Graphics layers from the bottom up.*

On the desktop, this transformation may seem magical because most desktops can afford the addition of a JVM and multiple GLs. Therefore it is transparent to the programmer. In the embedded world, the extra resources needed to run Java rarely reside naturally on the system. An explicit decision must be made to include it, which leads to significant concern over JVM and OS compatibility. Memory size and performance are also a major concern when including a JVM in an embedded system.

Figure 3 illustrates a bottom-up view of the tools and libraries embedded programmers use today.

COMPARISON OF CURRENT METHODS

With a basic understanding of some of the options, the embedded programmer is faced with the question: "What is the graphics strategy for my next project?" As is so often the case, the answer is: "It depends." It depends on (1) available memory, (2) the processor power, and (3) the company's future product strategy. Williamson explores this question in "Choosing the Right Graphics Development Approach"[3]. This section will explore the strengths and weaknesses of each approach.

Bare-bones programming strengths are (1) small code size, (2) high performance, and (3) minimum requirements for additional target software and hardware layers. Disadvantages include the facts that it can be (1) very time consuming to code, (2) difficult to change, and (3) often impossible to build sophisticated GUIs.

GLs have the advantage of separating the programmer from the hardware and providing a large percentage of the graphics and drawing functionality needed. GLs improve programmer productivity while providing a degree of portability. The disadvantages of GLs are that they increase the memory requirements and are often not full-featured enough for very sophisticated GUIs such as in-car navigation systems or complex control screens.

Widgets and toolkits have the advantage of providing very sophisticated graphics objects with less programming effort. Their disadvantages are that they add significant code size – on the order of megabytes – and require much more computing power. In addition, many embedded systems require custom, unique widgets that are specific only to that product – such as an artificial horizon, speedometer or animated graphic of battlefield status. Widgets only provide standard desktop GUI objects such as menus or buttons. Programming custom widgets can be time-consuming. Finally, widgets typically are delivered in binary form, which means they cannot be changed and bugs cannot be fixed.

Java's strengths include ease of use, the advantages of object-oriented programming, and portability, even on the fly. Java's disadvantages are its large code size, slow performance and requirement of a virtual machine.

Figure 4 lists the types of libraries and toolkits and approximate sizes that might be used depending on the programming technique chosen. As shown on Figure 4, there is a much higher price to pay the more a programmer takes advantage of higher productivity solutions.

Component	Memory
Java Virtual Machine	**1 MB**
Java Widget Set (AWT, Swing, SWT, etc.)	**2 MB**
C++ Widget Set	**1.5 MB**
C Widget Set (Motif)	**1 MB**
Graphics Library (GL)	**50 KB**

Figure 4: *Approximate memory requirements for components you might use to develop you graphics application.*

A PRACTICAL C GRAPHICS ARCHITECTURE

Knowing the strengths and weaknesses, it is safe to say that no single approach fits all. Therefore, this paper focuses on a mixture of approaches that could satisfy the widest variety of applications.

In a nutshell, this approach suggests developing all of the graphics using the C programming language and a generic, portable, GL interface. The proposed architecture also allows for the possibility of developing application, logic, and control code in languages other than C.

This architecture is chosen because it is the lowest risk and highest performance. That is, it is guaranteed to run on any target. It does not require a lot of memory, a 32-bit processor, or a virtual machine. Equally important, it has the best chance of being ported if the target needs to change because of last minute system specification changes. The C architecture allows for some breathing room. It doesn't eat up every last bit of processor power or memory, leaving room for application code or last minute changes and bug fixes.

Finally, the proposed approach also does not require a high level toolkit or widget set – although it does not preclude it and those could be added later if necessary.

THE ARCHITECTURE

To develop this architecture, it is first useful to address the weaknesses of the C programming approach. This offers an opportunity to create an architecture that minimizes these weaknesses. The primary disadvantage of using C is its relatively long development time. That is, the time needed to write the initial code and to make changes.

Some ideas that can be implemented to minimize C coding inefficiency include the following:

1. Critical to minimizing the amount of C code needed is the choice of a GL. The GL should have ample functionality, but be capable of scaling down if not every function is needed. (Note: Make sure you have the rights to modify the source for this GL. This will allow you to make changes and tradeoffs necessary for code reduction.)

2. Provide the ability for other applications to draw on the display. Many applications, such as mapping software, already have drawing capability and routines. There is no need to reinvent the wheel. Design graphics libraries so these off-the-shelf applications can draw directly into the frame buffer. This way, items like map drawing routines won't have to be built from scratch.

3. Build the graphics code to allow import of graphics generated from other tools. These tools will greatly improve graphics development efficiency. (Image editing tools that produce bitmaps are a good example.)

4. When possible, use graphics code generators – as long as they output portable C code and you have access and rights to the generated C source code.

5. Create your own graphics routines, libraries and modules and use them from project to project. This will improve C programming productivity and reliability.

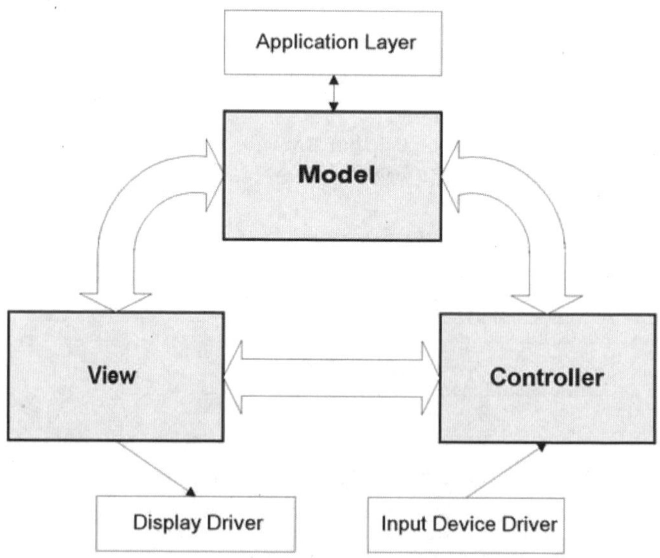

Figure 5: *Classic Model-View-Controller architecture.*

6. Build functions and graphics structures that make sense for the current application. Don't try to make them too general or plan too far ahead for future projects. If functions get too general at the early stages, code size will grow too large. As you move onto the next project, you can continue to generalize your graphics libraries and interfaces to suit your needs.

7. When the schedule gets tight, simplify the GUI and eliminate snazzy graphics. This may even have the positive side effect of creating a more usable GUI.

In general, improving C coding efficiency requires that you reuse existing code, add layers as needed, and code other parts of the application in structures and languages appropriate to the application domain. To achieve this, the architecture must distinctly separate the graphics code from the logic, control, algorithmic, and application code. This idea is, of course, not new. The Smalltalk folks have been using this separation principle since the 80's. Figure 5 illustrates the classic model-view-controller architecture proposed by Smalltalk.

Figure 6 is a detailed view of the recommended C based architecture. Critical to this architecture's success is a sufficient event API that adequately handles the communication between the application code and the graphics. This API is the key to programming flexibility and the ability to add off-the-shelf program modules as needed. It is also important to separate the physical display driver and input driver from the rest of the code. This enables the portability needed as hardware and OS requirements change.

Separating the graphics from the behavior makes intuitive sense. Graphics and behavior are very distinct problems that require different technologies and solutions to solve them. For example, there are software development tools that are very good at designing application behavior, but not good at creating graphics code. Likewise, there are good graphics development tools that don't do a good job describing logic and algorithms. If graphics are intertwined with behavior, it

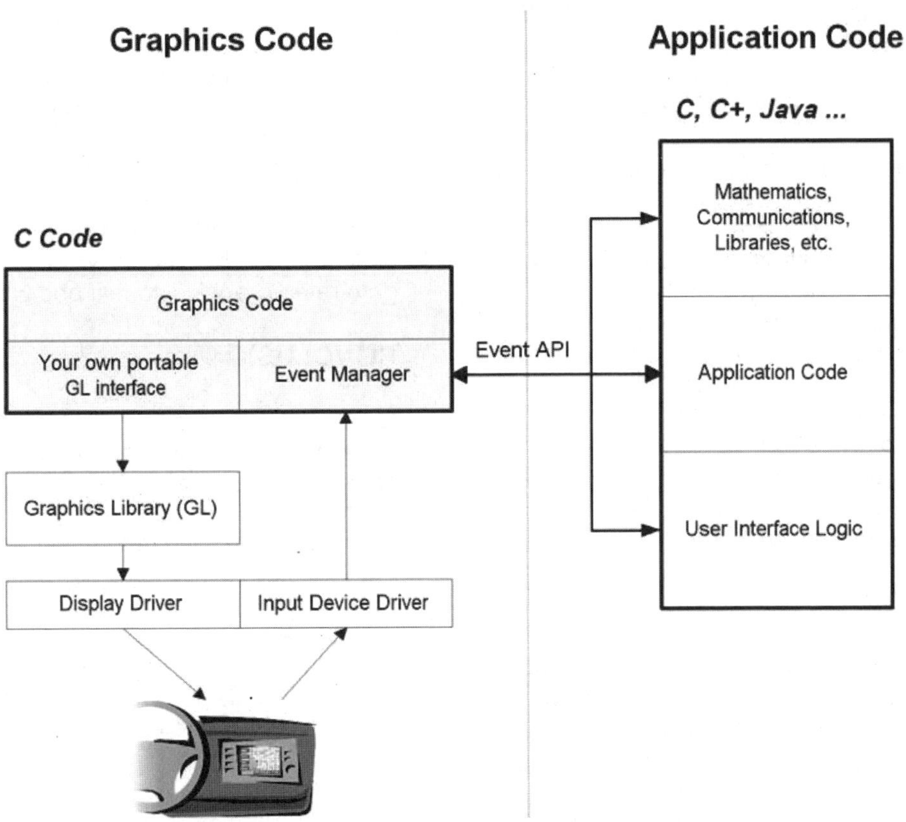

Figure 6: *Architecture that separates your graphics code from application code. This allows you to take advantage of C's small size and portability while still using other programming methodologies and languages that may be more appropriate for your application.*

becomes impossible to choose best in class tools to do the job.

Finally, building graphics applications is very different than behavior. Graphics and GUIs have a very clean transition from the what-you-see-is-what-you-get ("WYSIWYG") representation devised by the graphics designers, artists and human factors engineers. Application code, on the other hand, starts from a more abstract form (flow charts, UML diagrams, and statecharts) and must be converted to explicit lines of code.

The tools and languages used to accomplish these distinct tasks can, and should, be very different. For example, C is a perfectly fine language to capture pixels from an artist's drawing and render them on an embedded system display screen. It's a very straightforward translation. However, building complex communications, engine control, body control and navigation system user interface logic requires languages with more structure and methodology – such as that found in UML based languages like Java and C++. The architecture proposed in this paper will allow the programmer to save processing power and memory for the complex application code. The architecture judiciously uses the austerity of C for the basic graphics grunt work.

MIXING C GRAPHICS WITH C++ AND JAVA

In many cases, memory and processing power will be sufficient only to allow use of C code throughout the entire application. However, there are times when a programmer may be able to introduce some C++ or Java code into the system. There might be libraries or subsystems that will be much more efficiently programmed in C++ or Java. For that reason there may be a need to make C API calls from C++ or Java. Making C calls from C++ is pretty straightforward and there is no need to discuss that here. Making C calls from Java is not too difficult either, but it requires calls through the Java native interface ("JNI"). Pont provides some useful tips on how to achieve this.[4]

FUTURE DIRECTION

To be sure, memory and processing power within embedded systems will, on average, increase. However, there will always be low-end systems because of the ever-present drive to produce smaller and cheaper devices. For this reason, the industry will never be relieved of the need to handcraft software and squeeze it into tight spaces.

However, some relief may be available from tools targeted at this problem. Code generators are an area to consider for this purpose.

CODE GENERATORS

Code generators automatically turn high-level descriptions and views of a design into lines of programming code. Code generation is a relatively new technology that promises to significantly raise the productivity of programmers. Of course, these tools are not without risks and overhead – just as early compilers were met with skepticism from a generation of grizzled assembly programmers. However, modern tool vendors claim that code generators produce error-free code that exactly matches the specifications and is more compact than handwritten code[5]. While the jury is still out, early results show promise.

For purposes of this paper, a distinction must be drawn between graphics code generation and application code generation. Application code generators typically take some abstract view of a system – flowcharts, UML diagrams, statecharts, etc. – and turn it into lines of compilable code. Graphics code generators are a bit more straightforward, taking the exact 2D graphical representations of GUIs from a host development system and turning them into code that renders the exact same graphical representation on the target display. This "translation" is less prone to errors or misinterpretation of the designer's intent.

Because of the direct one-to-one translation, graphics code generators may be more viable in the short term – provided they can generate efficient C code that comfortably fits into the target memory space. You may or may not be able to use a code generator for your system today, but if the system has been architected as described in this paper, you'll be ready to drop in the generated graphics code if and when you're ready.

CONCLUSION

Given the stringent, unique requirements of in-vehicle software, this paper concludes that a C programming based architecture is the most practical and efficient method of building embedded displays. New methodologies and languages are emerging, but they are still not appropriate for most embedded systems. The C based architecture is efficient, reliable and portable across multiple projects and it can be used on both low and high-end hardware. This portability provides significant reuse within an organization, raising reliability and reducing development time.

REFERENCES

1. Turley, Jim. "Motoring with Microprocessors," Embedded Systems Programming, September 2003, p. 43.
2. Murphy, Niall. *Front Panel, Designing Software for the Embedded User Interface,* Emeryville, CA: Publishers Group West. ISBN:0-87930-528-2

3. Williamson, Jason and Henry, Hannah. “Choosing the Right Graphics Development Approach,” *Embedded Developers Journal*, June 2001, p.19.
4. Pont, Mick. “Calling C Library Routines From Java,” Dr. Dobb’s Journal, July 2003, p. 28.
5. Webb, Warren. “Virtual Programmers Build Embedded Code,” *EDN,* February 21, 2002, p. 32.

CONTACT

Mr. Juran began developing embedded systems hardware and software in 1985. He holds BS and MS degrees in Electrical Engineering from Carnegie Mellon University. After graduating, he joined Bell Labs to develop microprocessors, single board computers and microprocessor emulators. In 1989, Mr. Juran joined Hewlett Packard as an embedded software engineer. In 1992, he co-founded Altia, Inc.

Email: mikej@altia.com Web: www.altia.com

2002-01-1039

Instrument Cluster Design Options Using Electroluminescent Lighting

Lincoln D. McFerren, Claude L. Barker and Rodney T. Eckersley
Durel Corp.

ABSTRACT

Electroluminescent (EL) backlighting has enticed the automobile industry for many years with its thin, uniform lighting characteristics. This paper will illustrate the history and material science of EL lighting. The benefits and design parameters of EL as a backlighting source for instrument clusters will be discussed. Comparisons of EL versus incandescent bulbs, LED's, and CCFL are shown. Design criteria and options will be reviewed including luminance, color, electrical characteristics, assembly methods, inverter choices, and interconnect solutions.

INTRODUCTION

Designing an instrument cluster with EL lighting offers unique opportunities for automotive product designers. Imagine a light source that generates little heat, is less than 0.5 mm thick, does not require light pipes or compensation, creates uniform lighting and does not burn out. EL lighting technology and manufacturing have advanced tremendously in the last ten years. EL lamps are used today in many silhouette instrument clusters and are now positioned to become the backlighting of choice for both traditional and silhouette designs.

ELECTROLUMINESCENCE AND EL LAMP FUNDAMENTALS

How do EL lamps work? An EL lamp is electrically similar to a capacitor—it consists of a dielectric layer and a light-emitting phosphor layer between two conductive surfaces. The dielectric layer is an insulator and allows the lamp to withstand high voltages without shorting between the conductive surfaces. EL lamps illuminate when powered with alternating current (AC power). As voltage is applied to the conductive surfaces, an electric field is generated across the phosphor and dielectric layers. The electric field excites the phosphor electrons, moving some from the valence band into the higher energy orbit of the conductive band. Eventually, these electrons release energy as they fall from the high-energy state towards the ground state with intermediate stops at doping levels.

The base material used for many EL lamps is polyester (polyethylene terephthalate or PET) as shown in Figure 1. A front electrode is created by sputtering a conductive indium tin oxide (ITO) layer onto one side of the polyester. The phosphor, dielectric, and rear electrode layers are screen-printed over the ITO side of the polyester. The result is a thin, flat, light source.

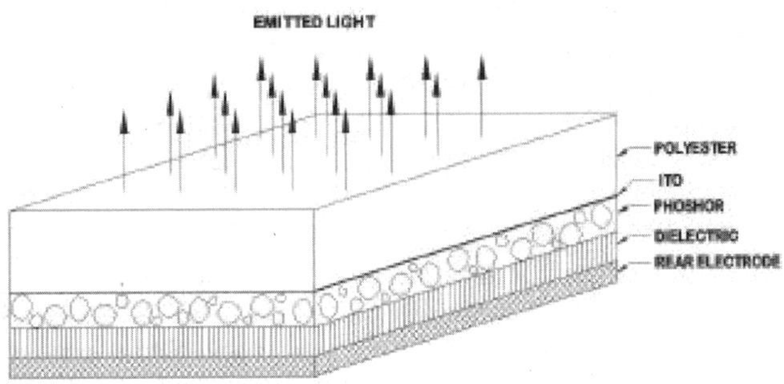

Figure 1: Cross-section of EL Lamp
Approximate thickness is 0.25 mm; layer thickness not to scale

ELECTROLUMINESCENCE HISTORY – Luminescence from polycrystalline material was discovered by H.J. Round in 1907 and O.V. Losev in 1923. Several years later in June, 1936, Professor Georges Destriau, a French physicist at The University of Paris, was studying the scintillation of phosphors using alpha rays. He observed that a photoluminescent phosphor, zinc sulfide, emitted light when an electric field was applied. He was the first to publish experimental evidence proving that phosphor powder dispersed into an insulator and sandwiched between two electrode plates emitted light when a high AC voltage was applied.

Another solid-state lamp technology was developed during the same period called single-crystal electro-luminescence. Single-crystal electroluminescence is commonly known today as a light emitting diode (LED). The first patent application for a light emitting diode lamp was filed in 1939 by Bay and Szigeti.

Serious study of electroluminescence by scientists and engineers did not resume until the late 1940's because of the distraction of war. By then, electroluminescent phosphor powders offered a cheap, readily available alternative to LED semiconductors for making solid-state lamps. By the 1960's, an AC-powered EL structure was developed into a functional, yet commercially weak, lamp product. The basic structure still serves as a standard today. However, the next twenty years generated improvements that provided wide-scale appeal to automakers.

Applications in the mid-1980's used EL lamps made with fluoropolymer binders, which required a moisture protective packaging film to encapsulate the entire device. This device was later called a macro-encapsulated EL lamp. Although still more successful than its predecessors, the primary problem was that it dimmed very quickly. The time to half luminance was typically less than 1,000 hours. In addition, the lamp was susceptible to moisture incursion to the phosphor particles, which would degenerate and become inoperable over time.

A breakthrough invention in the late 1980's made possible the practical use of EL devices in automotive applications. The discovery consisted of a glass-like coating around each individual phosphor particle. EL lamps made with coated phosphor no longer required thick packaging to protect from moisture. The invention also allowed for segmented and selectively lit areas, as well as internal holes in the EL film.

PHOSPHOR CRYSTAL MATERIAL SCIENCE – The most common phosphor powder is zinc sulfide. A theoretically ideal zinc sulfide crystal is defect-free. In reality, crystals always have defects that determine their actual properties. Zinc sulfide is a cubic crystal with defects such as dislocations that form localized regions of hexagonal crystal structure. The most common defects in zinc sulfide are point defects: lattice vacancies, substitutions, and interstitials.

Zinc sulfide (ZnS) is a wide-gap semiconductor with a band gap of 3.7 eV between the valence band and the conduction band. A chlorine (Cl) atom has seven valence electrons and sulfur (S) has only six. Therefore, when a chlorine atom replaces a sulfur atom it donates one excess electron. The donor energy is about 0.25 eV below the conduction band. A monovalent copper atom has one valence electron while zinc has two. Therefore, a copper atom replacing a zinc atom is an acceptor. It has energy of about one eV above the valence band.

When EL phosphors are made, both copper (Cu) and chlorine (Cl) are thermally diffused into the zinc sulfide at a very high temperature. When a copper and chlorine atom come together during this process, the chlorine donor spends its excess electron into the lower copper acceptor level. Both are now electrically charged—the chlorine is positive and the copper is negative. These atoms are electrostatically attracted and form CuCl molecules that dissolve into the zinc sulfide crystal lattice.

Powder electroluminescent phosphors are made with slightly more copper than what is soluble in the zinc sulfide. While some of the copper combines with the chlorine, the rest of the copper forms copper sulfide, mainly Cu_xS. After various manufacturing steps, the Cu_xS that has precipitated to the surface remains only at the dislocations. In the presence of an alternating electric field, the Cu_xS glows at a relatively low field strength. As the field strength increases, the glowing region increases in luminance and size. The orientation of these Cu_xS segregations is fixed and dependent on defect orientation.

A simplified depiction of the electron transitions involved in excitation and luminescence of ZnS:Cu,Cl is shown in Figure 2. The shaded lower portion is the valence band, the top horizontal line indicates the start of the conduction band, and the space between these features represents the band gap. The electron transitions are labeled as follows: transition I is Excitation, II is Trapping, III is De-trapping, IV is Recombination (green transmission), and V is Recombination (blue transmission).

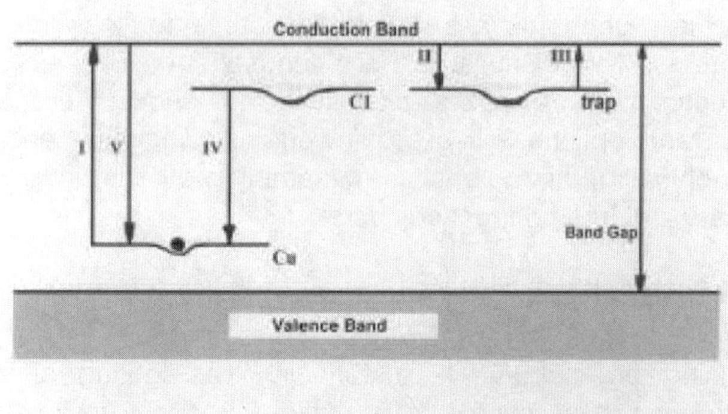

Figure 2: Electron transitions in ZnS:Cu,Cl

Transition I, Excitation, illustrates the lifting of an electron out of a Cu-level into the conduction band. This electron is free to move about in the conduction band until it has a chance to fall into an empty level, or trap, below the conduction band. After some time delay depending on the trap energy and the temperature, the electron is thermally moved back into the conduction band and can recombine with the Cu-level and emit light through either transition IV or transition V. The effect of the time delay caused by trapping is an emission, called "afterglow", which occurs after the excitation has stopped. Transition IV, responsible for the transmission band of ZnS:Cu,Cl, is believed to be within the CuCl molecule. Transition V, the blue emission, is less certain. The involved defect may contain something else, like a sulfur or zinc vacancy.

Under a sustained electric field and with increases in temperature, the intensities of the light emissions will decrease over time while the phosphors are being electrically stressed. This slow deterioration is thought to be caused by ionic migration. Improvements in delaying this effect have led to phosphors and EL lamp devices that have luminance and lifetime characteristics that are suitable for a variety of automotive applications and the harsh environments they must survive.

BRIEF HISTORY OF AUTOMOTIVE EL LIGHTING

EL technology has been used in automobiles for more than forty years. To demonstrate the evolution of EL lighting, the history will be divided into three periods: 1) the novelty period of EL, 2) the exploration period of EL, and 3) the practical period of EL.

NOVELTY PERIOD – In the early 60's, engineers made efforts to develop and prove out EL devices for use in automotive applications. Fascination on the part of designers and the desire for an improved lighting system led to the use of EL lamps in Chrysler and Dodge vehicle dash displays. The device structures used glass as the binder for the phosphor filler, a thick metal plate for the rear electrode, and welded metal leads as interconnects. Although functional, they were dim and heavy, and interconnect reliability was poor.

Figure 3: 1960 Chrysler New Yorker EL Dashboard "Panelescent Lighting - radiates a uniform, glare-free glow"

EXPLORATION PERIOD – The exploring 80's led designers to improvements in durability, brightness, manufacturing processes, and design flexibility of EL devices. Examples of the applications in this period are the '86-'88 Riviera coach lamps, PRNDL, interior switches and CRT Switches. The Ford keyless-entry module was one of the first large volume programs to introduce the new microencapsulated EL, virtually eliminating field failures due to moisture incursion. The Ford LUX radio backlight took advantage of the segmented, selective lighting benefit of EL, where the backlighting of the button graphics would switch between tape/CD and radio modes.

Figure 4: A 2001 MY Instrument Cluster and EL lamp

PRACTICAL PERIOD – Having established itself as a worthy lighting option for use in automotive applications, EL entered the practical use era of the 90's and beyond. OEMs continued to choose EL lighting for use in high volume components such as the Chrysler 300M/LHS instrument cluster, the Ford Taurus/Sable radio/HVAC module, and the Chrysler large and midsize car platform PRNDLs. Designers and engineers are now more informed and skilled with the design, performance, and cost advantages of EL lighting.

BENEFITS OF EL LIGHTING

EL lighting provides a variety of benefits for backlighting automotive instrument clusters. These benefits include:

- Uniform lighting (luminance and color)
- Durable, long-lasting, and rugged
- Thin, flexible, and lightweight
- Variety of shapes and sizes
- Low power consumption
- Low heat generation
- Simple to design

Current lighting technology for automotive instrument clusters is limited to a select group of light sources. This group includes EL lighting, incandescent bulbs, LED's, and cold-cathode fluorescent lamps (CCFL). EL lamps are frequently superior to these sources, especially when evaluating instrument clusters as a system. Table 1 illustrates a relative comparison of these lighting technologies.

Characteristic	EL	Bulb	LED	CCFL
Light / Color Uniformity	♦♦♦♦	♦	♦	♦♦♦
Light Intensity	♦♦♦	♦♦♦♦	♦♦♦♦	♦♦♦♦
Color Choices	♦♦♦	♦	♦♦	♦♦
Power Use	♦♦♦♦	♦	♦♦♦♦	♦♦
Heat Generated	♦♦♦♦	♦	♦♦♦	♦♦♦
Durability	♦♦♦	♦♦	♦♦♦	♦♦♦
Part Cost	♦♦	♦♦♦♦	♦♦♦	♦
Development Time	♦♦♦	♦♦	♦♦	♦♦
OEM Comfort Level	♦♦♦	♦♦♦♦	♦♦♦	♦♦

Table 1: Relative Comparison of Lighting Technologies Poor-♦, Fair-♦♦, Good-♦♦♦, Excellent-♦♦♦♦

LIGHTING – EL lamps are well known for their unique uniform lighting in a flat flexible piece of film. Luminance and color are evenly distributed across the surface of the lamp. This provides a clean, consistent, uniform display regardless of size or configuration. Other technologies are point sources of light (bulbs or LED's) or are manufactured in various tube shapes (CCFL), requiring additional light pipes and lighting compensation in the graphics.

Color Choices – EL phosphor is traditionally made from zinc sulfide micro-crystals that contain dopents of copper or manganese. These particles emit certain base colors such as green, blue-green, blue, and orange. Small shifts in the phosphor color can be achieved by changing the drive frequency. A larger variety of colors can be created by blending combinations of phosphors before screen-printing. Selective areas of a lamp can also be printed with different phosphors, creating a multi-color lamp.

ELECTRICAL – EL lamps require AC voltage to emit light. Inverters are used to convert the DC voltage in automotive electrical systems to an AC voltage. Traditionally the waveform is an approximate sine wave with a shape that depends on the type of inverter. Typical voltage and frequency for an automotive EL lamp is 60-150 Vrms, 300-500 Hz.

EL lamps are very efficient in converting electricity to light. Typical lamp input current is 0.03-0.16 mA/cm^2 lit area and depends on the lamp construction, phosphor, and drive conditions. The current draw of a lamp and inverter system is approximately 1-2 mA/cm^2 lit area.

PERFORMANCE – EL construction and phosphor advancements in the last 10 years have improved EL performance dramatically. Improvements to phosphors and phosphor coatings technology led to the acceptance of EL backlighting in the 90's. Current automotive-grade EL lamps surpass OEM interior environmental requirements. Typical environmental tests include:

- Storage Temperature (-40 to 100 °C)
- Operating Temperature (-40 to 85 °C)
- Thermal Shock cycling (-40 to 85 °C)
- Temp. / Humidity cycling (-40 to 85 °C, 40-95% RH)
- High Temperature / High Humidity (65 °C, 95% RH)
- Temperature / Vibration
- Mechanical Shock
- Spill Test (Cola, Coffee, Water, Cleansers, etc.)

Lifetime / Durability – Since an EL lamp is essentially a solid-state lighting device, it is not prone to failure by vibration or repetitive on/off cycling. EL lamps are also very flexible, so they can be used in applications that require flexing, such as radio cassette doors and switches.

EL lamps exhibit a decay curve similar to LED's and incandescent bulbs. However, EL and LED's do not burn out. They can operate for more than 20,000 hours, surpassing the equivalent expected life of a vehicle. There are three main factors that influence the life of the EL lamp: 1) the phosphor, 2) the drive frequency, and 3) the drive voltage. Figure 5 shows some sample ambient life curves.

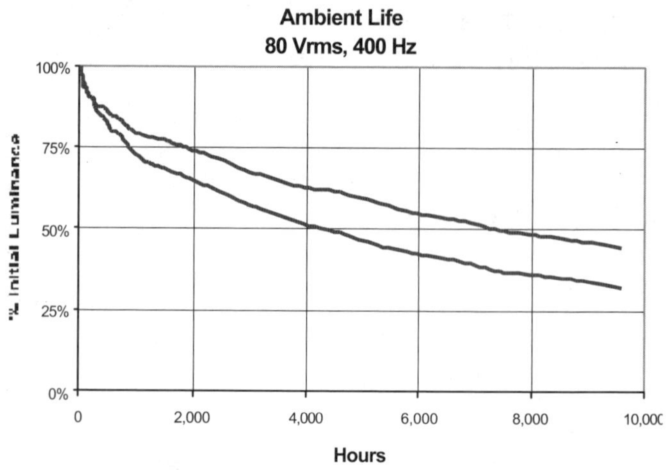

Figure 5: Typical Range of EL Life Curves
100% Duty Cycle, Ambient Conditions (22.5°C, 45% RH)

EL CLUSTER DESIGN

An automotive instrument cluster is an ideal application for EL backlighting. The benefits of EL technology provide excellent value for designers and engineers as a general illumination source of high information content displays. EL lamps can be easily designed into an existing cluster with minimum impact on component interfaces and tooling. However, in order to maximize the benefits of the compact size of EL lamps, an EL instrument cluster should be designed early in the vehicle program.

CLUSTER DESIGN OPTIONS – Analog instrument clusters commonly use one of two popular lighting design themes. One is negative lighting, also called traditional or standard, where the numbers and tick marks illuminate at night, against a dark background. Usually these clusters use white numbers on a black dial face (see Fig. 6). The other design is positive lighting, also called silhouette, where the numbers and tick marks are visible as a dark silhouette against an illuminated background. Usually these designs use black numbers on a white or gray dial face (see Fig. 7). Combinations of these designs are also possible, with dark graphics on a white background during the day, and illuminated graphics on a dark background at night.

EL lamps are designed for selective lighting for instrument clusters, so that only the areas that require light are illuminated. This keeps costs low by not wasting phosphor and other materials in areas they are not needed. Lighting only those areas that actually need to be lit also helps reduce the power requirements and minimizes the transformer inverter size.

Figure 6: Standard (Negative) Cluster Graphics
White graphics become blue-green at night

Figure 7: Silhouette (Positive) Cluster Graphics
White background becomes blue-green at night

A positive cluster requires a larger lit area than a negative cluster since the entire background of the dial face is illuminated. In some cases, it may be beneficial to use a positive cluster lamp for platforms offering both positive and negative lighting. The common lamp design may cost slightly more, but it benefits from larger part volumes and reduced assembly complexity.

LIGHTING OPTIONS – The uniform lighting of EL lamps provides design options that other lighting technologies cannot provide without additional costly components. Even with light pipes and graphic compensation layers, luminance and color of other lighting technologies are often non-uniform across the surface of the cluster. Positive lighting designs with a large lit area are typically only feasible with EL or more expensive CCFL lighting. Even standard negative lighting designs can require costly sorting for certain LED colors. With EL lighting, the designer chooses exactly where the light should be, without having to block or mask light leaks in unwanted areas.

Uniformity – EL lamps provide a uniform light source across the entire length of the instrument cluster. Luminance variation across the part surface is less than 10% of the average part. This contrasts starkly with incandescent bulbs, LED's, and CCFL lamps. They are local sources of light that must be distributed across the cluster display. Usually this is achieved with a plastic light pipe and additional compensation layers in the printed graphics. These layers let more or less light through in certain areas to compensate for the bright and dim spots of the light pipe. Achieving the correct light distribution is a 'black art', often requiring multiple design iterations and software modeling to predict lighting patterns. EL lamps do not require these light distribution and compensation components.

Luminance – Lamp luminance is dependent on several variables of the EL system: the lamp construction, inverter design, voltage and frequency drive conditions, and phosphor color. Typical luminance values range from 3-35 cd/m^2. Lower values are generally not discernable and higher values are too bright for the driver in nighttime applications.

Determining the appropriate luminance of an EL lamp is often a case of working backwards from the cluster assembly design. The starting point is the OEM standard for luminance to the driver. Based on this value, the graphics and EL lamp are configured as a matched pair to provide the correct luminance. The ratio of light transmitted through the graphic layers is called the transmissivity and is expressed as a percentage. This value depends on the color and desired appearance. With known values for the transmissivity and assembly luminance, we can easily determine the EL luminance. For example, a cluster designed for 6 cd/m^2 to the viewer, with a 30% transmissive overlay, will require 20 cd/m^2 from the EL lamp.

Color – A variety of colors is used in instrument cluster backlighting. Each OEM has a group of colors used for each vehicle platforms or brands. These colors are used to specify all the interior lighting components, regardless of the lighting technology. Common interior lighting colors are blue-green, green, yellow-green, white, blue, and orange-red. Determining the required EL lamp color is similar to luminance, requiring coordinated development with the graphics.

Phosphor – In addition to the base phosphor colors, blended phosphor inks can be made with a combination of phosphors. Numerous color blends are possible with different combinations of two or more phosphors. For example, white appearing light can be created by blending a combination of blue-green and orange phosphor. White EL is increasingly popular because it enables a wide range of colors through the graphics. See Figure 8 and Table 2 for typical EL lamp colors.

Filters – Filters and dyes offer another method for color variety. Filters printed on the top surface of the lamp are commonly referred to as overprints. They shift, or 'cascade', the color wavelength of the emitted light. The wavelength can only be shifted to a higher wavelength (lower frequency). For example, a pink overprint on a blue-green EL lamp will cascade some of the light to the red region of the color spectrum. The emitted light will appear white.

Another option for shifting color is an underprint, which uses a dye in the phosphor ink (printed under the polyester surface). The dye performs just as an overprint, cascading the emitted light wavelength to a different color. The lamp's reflective appearance looks the same as an overprint lamp, and common underprints are pink or orange in color when turned off.

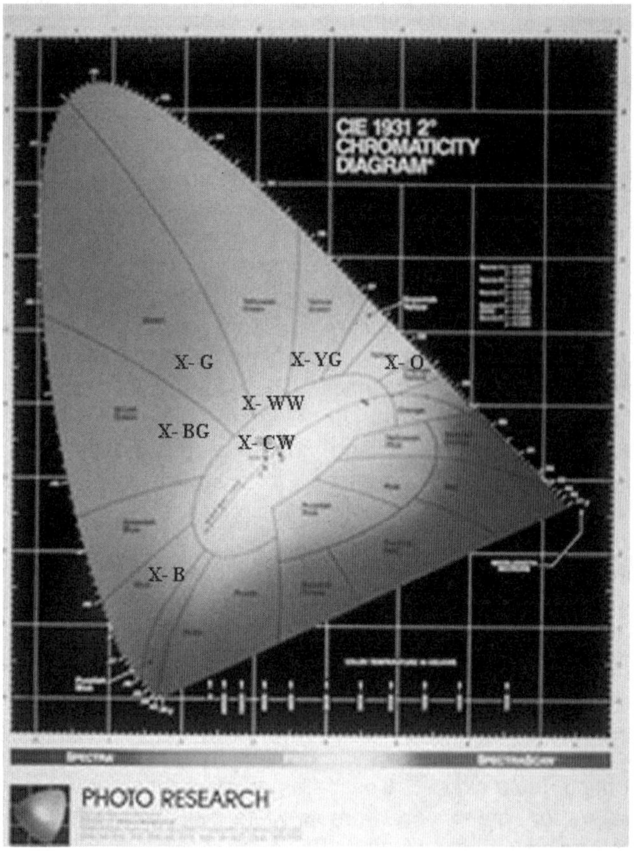

Figure 8: 1931 C.I.E. Chromaticity Diagram

	1931 CIE		1976 CIE	
Color	x	y	u'	v'
Blue (B)	0.16	0.21	0.123	0.361
Blue-green (BG)	0.17	0.35	0.098	0.456
Green (G)	0.18	0.45	0.088	0.501
Cool White (CW)	0.27	0.34	0.165	0.468
Warm White (WW)	0.30	0.39	0.169	0.496
Yellow-green (YG)	0.34	0.45	0.179	0.525
Orange (O)	0.54	0.45	0.297	0.553

Table 2: Typical EL Lamp Colors

Color Selection Considerations – Each color technique must be evaluated based on the customer requirements. Phosphor life and efficiency vary with color, so a blended lamp will not be as bright as its brightest constituent. For example, blue-green phosphor is brighter than orange phosphor, so a blue-green EL lamp is brighter and will last longer than a blended-white lamp made with a mix of blue-green and orange phosphor.

The appearance of a pink overprint or underprint may be visible through the graphics and must be considered. It is usually hidden by denser ink in the graphics overlay or applique, which lowers the transmissivity. In addition, overprints add a layer to the lamp, which adds cost.

ELECTRICAL CHARACTERISTICS – The electrical drive conditions of an EL lamp are the AC voltage and frequency required to power the lamp. The choice of drive conditions is determined from a variety of design parameters including the required light intensity to the viewer, transmissivity of the graphic overlay, EL lamp construction, and phosphor color. Increasing voltage and frequency will increase luminance, but also reduce the life of EL. A balance of electrical drive conditions, lighting design, and performance requirements will achieve a successful EL lamp design.

Drive Voltage – The drive voltage for an EL lamp is typically in the 60-150 Vrms range. Luminance is proportional to input voltage. Changing the voltage of the lamp will not affect the color, which makes voltage ideal for brightness control. Increasing the voltage accelerates phosphor degradation, which shortens the life of the lamp.

Drive Frequency – The drive frequency for an EL lamp is typically in the 200-500 Hz range. Frequency changes will impact both luminance and color. Increasing the frequency will increase the luminance and shift the color toward the blue side of the color spectrum. Frequency has a direct effect on the life of EL since higher frequencies reduce the life. Because the frequency also affects color, it is typically fixed in automotive applications.

Power Consumption – Instrument clusters designed with EL lighting for general illumination use less power than incandescent bulbs or LEDs. This reduced power consumption leads to higher fuel economy and lighter wiring harnesses. A typical EL instrument cluster lamp has a lit area of 200 cm^2 and will draw up to 200 mA for general illumination lighting. A similar cluster using incandescent bulbs uses 1,600 mA. Most of the additional power is wasted in the form of heat generation.

Compensation for Extended Life – Most automotive EL applications use transformer-based inverters. These inverters generate a load-based output. As an EL lamp degrades, the capacitive load decreases and the inverter 'compensates' with an increasing voltage. This increase in output voltage results in a flatter life curve for the EL lamp. The lamp luminance decays at a slower rate than it would on a constant voltage power supply, thereby extending the THL an additional 500-1,000 hours. Additional options include open loop and closed-loop control systems. The EL drive circuitry can be designed to increase the voltage over time, compensating for the predictable luminance decay characteristics of EL lamps.

PHYSICAL CONFIGURATION – The thin, flexible nature of EL is an important feature. If an instrument cluster is designed with EL from the beginning, the cluster can be thinner and lighter. It will require fewer components and less printed circuit board space. By reducing the size of the cluster, more room is available in the instrument panel for additional electronics such as body computer functions, heads-up displays, GPS systems, and telematic systems.

Dimensional Shape – The outline of the lamp can be complex, with odd shapes and multiple features such as holes and slots. Since the EL lamp is essentially a thin piece of polyester, it can bend and flex to fit various curves or levels to achieve a multi-dimensional appearance. To maintain the structural integrity of the conductive layers, the recommended minimum bend radius is 6 mm.

EL lamps are typically printed on a rectangular panel. The panels are printed in a batch process, so each panel carries a certain labor and material cost with it. Other printing methods include roll-to-roll processing. Fitting the largest number of parts across the panel or roll is the key to keeping costs low. This arrangement is called 'nesting'. The design of the lamp is crucial to the nesting pattern. See Figure 9 for an example of an instrument cluster in a six-cavity nesting pattern. Even if a lamp design requires only a small area to be lit, an inefficient part shape can lead to a low nesting density and therefore higher costs. Early program involvement can help keep the nesting density as high as possible while the part design is still flexible.

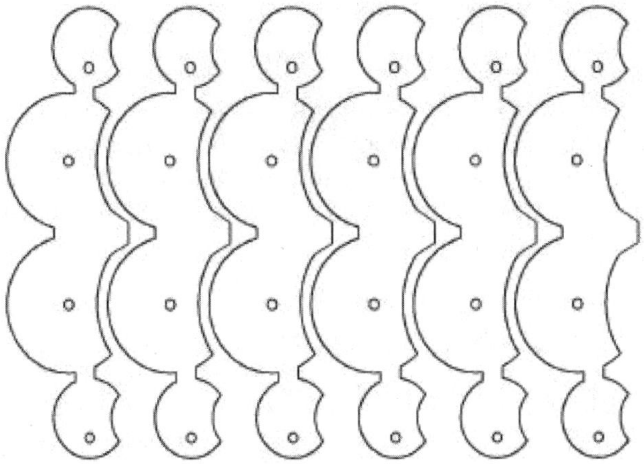

Figure 9: Typical Instrument Cluster Nesting Pattern

Reduced Size – When EL is used for general illumination the need for a light pipe is eliminated. When incandescent bulbs are not used, the wall height of the plastic housing can be reduced because it doesn't need to dissipate the heat from the bulbs. Therefore, a much lighter and thinner housing can be used for the cluster. If stepper motors are used for the pointers, and if LED's are used for the warning lamps instead of incandescent bulbs, additional thickness is removed from the housing. Typical instrument clusters designed for EL can be 1-2 cm thinner than their incandescent counterparts.

Reduced Part Complexity – In addition to the elimination of the light pipe noted above, the graphic overlay is also simplified. Light compensation layers are normally used in the graphics to achieve uniform lighting. Since EL provides uniform lighting, these layers are eliminated from the graphics. Also noted previously, 6-8 bulbs or LED's are replaced with one piece of EL. In many positive cluster designs the pointers are not lit, eliminating the need for bulbs or LED's and the optics inside the pointer.

Reduced PC Board Space – When an EL lamp is used for general illumination in an instrument cluster, valuable PC board space is saved. A typical incandescent bulb takes up 4.5 cm^2 of board area, while an LED uses 0.5 cm^2. With 6-8 bulbs or LED's in a typical cluster, the board space savings can be 3-4 cm^2 for LED's and 27-36 cm^2 for bulbs. The additional space can be used to add other electronic systems onto the PCB, such as body controllers.

Components – No major changes are required to other components used in an instrument cluster. Holes are placed in the EL to allow pointers to pass through. Additional holes can be used for pointer stops but are not required, since many manufacturers attach the pointer stops directly to the graphics overlay. The EL lamp profile is also designed to fit around telltale warning lamps, tunnels, and VF or LCD displays.

Locations of intense heat sources must be reviewed when designing EL instrument clusters. Local heat sources may cause portions of the EL lamp to dim faster than others, resulting in uneven lighting over time. Common heat sources include light bulbs, heat sinks, and some LED's. Shielding the heat from the EL, or avoiding it all together, are the best options

ASSEMBLY OPTIONS – The EL lamp is essentially a piece of film that is 0.25 mm thick and sandwiched between a backplate and a graphic overlay. The backplate, also called a subdial, is similar to a light pipe. However, since light is not transmitted through the back of the lamp, the subdial can be made from inexpensive black ABS plastic rather than optical grade polycarbonate. Alignment holes or slots are commonly used for locating the EL and graphics into position.

Another option is to screen the graphics directly onto the EL panel, thus eliminating a separate graphic overlay. In theory, this seems like an ideal method to reduce the number of parts and the assembly time. However, an EL lamp panel is a more expensive substrate than a typical sheet of polycarbonate. The graphic printing yield must be very low to make this option economically viable.

Once the EL and graphics are assembled, a bezel and lens assembly is snapped or screwed on top of the cluster and holds the perimeter of the graphics in place. There are several options available for retaining the EL lamp into an instrument cluster:

- Adhesive
- Ultrasonic welding
- Press fit
- Orbital forming

COST / TIME – Cost savings are realized with EL lighting when product development and service are considered. While difficult to quantify into a part price savings, the benefits are significant across the entire program cycle.

Reduced Development Work – Since part complexity is significantly reduced with an EL cluster, design changes are simpler and can be implemented faster. EL tooling is comprised of screen-printing artwork and a matched metal die to cut the part from the panel. This tooling is cheaper and can be changed faster than expensive plastic mold tools for the light pipe and frame. Additionally, prototypes can be laser cut, water jet cut, or digital knife cut, virtually eliminating tooling costs during the development stage of a program. This design flexibility reduces development time and costs, and provides the opportunity for last minute changes.

Reduced Warranty – Bulbs do not need to be replaced as a warranty item because EL lamps do not have filaments to break or burn out. Warranty repairs are virtually eliminated with EL lighting, and the customer does not have to put up with a partially dark display due to a burned out bulb.

INVERTERS

In order for the EL lamp to work you must power it with alternating current (Vac). Since the automobile voltage source is Vdc, an inverter is needed to transform the DC to AC voltage. The inverter required for an EL lamp can be placed in variety of locations on the PC board, providing design flexibility for the electrical circuit layout. There are two primary inverters that are commonly used in EL applications today, the transformer-based inverter and the integrated circuit (IC) driver (see Figure 10).

Figure 10: Transformer Inverter and IC Drivers

TRANSFORMER-BASED INVERTERS – These are the most popular inverters today for instrument clusters due to the large lit area required to backlight an instrument cluster. In addition to the transformer, several additional components are used to tune the circuit to the application, including one or two electrolytic capacitors. These components are sold as a self-contained inverter module, or the components can be placed directly on an available printed circuit board (PCB).

INTEGRATED CIRCUIT (IC) DRIVERS – IC drivers were released to market in 1994. They provide designers a useful alternative to transformer-based inverters. Tuning of the circuit to optimize application performance is achieved by selecting the appropriate off-chip components, such as an inductor, resistors, and capacitors. IC drivers were developed initially for the timepiece and wireless communications markets with 3-6 Vdc electrical systems. New automotive IC drivers are under development to use 12-42 Vdc inputs and PWM signals for dimming control. In addition to the lower cost, the benefits of designing with an IC driver is the increase in available PCB space and the opportunity to place all components with surface mount devices (SMD).

INTERFACE / CONNECTOR OPTIONS

The instrument cluster designer has a variety of options to select from to connect the EL lamp to the inverter or PCB. These are some of the current methods for automotive applications:

CRIMPED WIRE HARNESS – The wires from a wire harness or inverter are crimped through the polyester EL lamp usually by a semiautomated or fully automated crimp machine. The other end of the wire harness may contain a connector that plugs into a header connector on the PCB or inserts into the inverter. This method is proven and adequate for most applications. The relative cost adder is about 3-10% of the price of the lamp. A wire harness requires three connections: 1) the crimp contact to the EL lamp, 2) the contact to the wire harness connector, and 3) the header connector on the PCB.

CRIMPED CONNECTOR – This connection usually requires the EL designer to create a short tail with the polyester and then crimp a connector directly to the tail. This method is cheaper than wire crimps but still may add 2-5% to the lamp price and possibly more if the tail design reduces the EL lamp nesting density.

PRESSURE-FIT CONNECTION – This method of connecting the EL lamp with a snap-on or pressure-fit connector has been used for years in commercial EL applications but sparingly in the automotive market. There is usually no additional cost to the EL lamp for this connection method since simple contact pads are all that are required. Extensive environmental testing including vibration testing should be performed with the entire module to ensure a good connection is achieved.

CONCLUSION

The future of EL as a backlighting source is very positive. Reduced costs and superb uniform lighting characteristics have positioned EL for extensive use in instrument clusters. Designers can leverage the benefits of EL instrument cluster lighting in new and unique ways. For example, a cluster with one EL lamp can use a variety of applique designs for trim level or brand differentiation.

EL lamp designs free up valuable instrument cluster PCB space. This becomes more important as PCB densities increase and more content is added into the instrument cluster. Automotive use of EL for general illumination backlighting is well past the early adoptive stage, and engineers are now designing EL into high-volume clusters with both silhouette and standard graphics. With continued development of brighter EL lamps, daytime-visible or telltale lighting could be the next cluster application.

ACKNOWLEDGMENTS

1. Figure 4: Instrument Cluster designed by N.S. International, LTD.
2. Figure 8: 1931 C.I.E. Chromaticity Diagram. Courtesy of Photo Research.

REFERENCES

1. C.I. Zovko, T.C. Nerz, White polymer thick film electroluminescent lamps and their applications for backlighting liquid crystal displays in portable electronic devices, Displays December 20 (1999).
2. A.G. Fisher, Electroluminescent lines in ZnS powder particles. I. Embedding media and basic observations, Journal of the Electrochemical Society November (1962).
3. A.G. Fisher, Electroluminescent lines in ZnS powder particles. II. Models and comparison and experience, Journal of the Electrochemical Society July (1963).
4. R.T. Eckersley, Analysis of emission spectra deconvoluted into color centers for modern AC powder thick film electroluminescent lamps, Society for Information Display, Seattle, April 1993. Arizona State University M.S. Thesis, August (1993).

CONTACT

The authors can be contacted via email or telephone. Comments or questions are encouraged.

- Lincoln McFerren – lmcferren@durel.com, 480-917-6246.
- Claude Barker – cbarker@durel.com, 480-917-6275.
- Rodney Eckersley – reckersley@durel.com, 480-917-6210.

ADDITIONAL SOURCES

1. Uruo Kobayashi, Osamu Miayata, and Takahiro Saida, SAE paper 890280, Development of Thin Structure Cluster with EL Backlighting.

DEFINITIONS, ACRONYMS, ABBREVIATIONS

Brightness: A subjective attribute of light to which humans assign a label between very dim and very bright (brilliant). The human eye's sensitivity decreases with increasing luminance, so brightness is not the same as luminance. See Luminance below.

CCFL: Cold-cathode fluorescent – One mode of backlighting currently used in instrument cluster design.

Compensation: There are two definitions for compensation depending on the context of the sentence:

1) Light compensation (Graphic Applique/Overlay): The extra passes of ink required on the back side of the applique to remove the hot spots of light generated by traditional LED and incandescent lighting,
2) Electrical Compensation (Inverter Design): The increase in the drive conditions that are either designed in or manually defined to increase the life of the EL lamp.

Dielectric: A material used as an electrical insulator or in which an electric field can be sustained with a minimum dissipation of power.

EL: Electroluminescent – A surface-area light source employing the principle of electroluminescence; consists of a suitable phosphor placed between sheet electrodes, one of which is essentially transparent, with an alternating current applied between the electrodes.

fL: Footlambert – a unit of luminance (photometric brightness) equal to the uniform luminance of a perfectly diffusing surface emitting or reflecting light at the rate of 1 lumen per square foot; equal to approximately 3.42625 nits or candelas per square meter (cd/m^2).

ITO: Indium Tin Oxide – A conductive coating that is sputtered onto one side of the base polyester material, and serves as the front transparent electrode for the EL lamp.

LED: Light Emitting Diode - A semiconductor device used as a backlighting source for instrument clusters.

Light Pipe: A solid transparent plastic rod or sheet that transmits or distributes light.

Luminance: The luminous intensity per unit area projected in a given direction. Measured in candela per square meter (equal to 1 nit) or foot lambert (fL). Luminance is an objective measure, whereas brightness is a subjective evaluation made by the observer.

Nesting Pattern: The arrangement of parts on a screen-printed panel. The number of parts per panel is also called the nesting density.

PET: Polyester or Polyethylene terephthalate material; used as the base material for many EL lamps.

PRNDL: Gearshift indicator. Usually mounted on the floor console and in the instrument cluster.

PWM: Pulse Width Modulation – A square wave signal set at a constant voltage and frequency. Modulation of the square wave provides a range of 'effective' voltage, used to dim interior lighting.

RH: Relative Humidity.

Silhouette Cluster: A positive image instrument cluster graphics. Usually the background is white with dark letters.

Standard Cluster: A negative image instrument cluster graphics. Usually the background is black with white letters.

Time to half luminance (THL): The amount of time for a lamp to reach one half the initial brightness. Also called time to half brightness (THB).

Transmissivity: The ratio of transmitted light through an applique to the total transmitted light of the light source. Usually expressed as a percentage.

Valence Band: The highest electronic energy band in a semiconductor or insulator that can be filled with electrons.

Vac (rms): AC Voltage, root-mean-squared. The effective voltage of the input into the EL lamp.

Vdc: Direct Voltage – a voltage that forces electrons to move in the same direction continuously, thereby producing a direct current. Also known as direct current voltage.

2002-01-0978

A Mercury-Free CFL Backlight for Car-Navigation Display

Hidehiko Noguchi, Ryuji Tsuchiya, Hidetoshi Yano and Hirozumi Nakamura
Harison Toshiba Lighting Corp.

ABSTRACT

A mercury-free backlight in which Xe-type small diameter CFLs are installed, has been developed. We have evaluated the 7 inch-size backlight. Luminance of the backlight is 6,000cd/m^2 at 6.5W. And this backlight has stable light output, rapid light output response and wide dimming capability over the wide temperature range. Therefore, it is suitable for a car-navigation display.

INTRODUCTION

Mercury-type cold cathode fluorescent lamps (Hg-CFLs) are widely used as light sources of LCD backlighting for car-navigations. These applications require a stable light output over the wide temperature range. But, the light intensity of Hg-CFL depends on the mercury vapor pressure (i.e. lamp temperature), and is obviously insufficient at low ambient temperature. Furthermore, use of mercury is not recommended for environmental protection in recent years. In order to solve these problems, kinds of mercury-free lamps have been investigated [1][2]. But these lamps have not been widely accepted by the LCD industry because of its restriction against mechanical dimension.

We have developed a small diameter mercury-free cold cathode fluorescent lamp which uses VUV radiation from xenon (Xe-CFL)[3]. It is easy to replace from Hg-CFLs because of its dimensional similarity to Hg-CFLs. In this paper, we will report a mercury-free backlight in which these Xe-CFLs are installed.

LAMP STRUCTURE

As far as the backlighting for a car navigation is concerned, a compact dimension and a stable light output over the wide temperature range from –40℃ to 85℃, are required. We investigated the suitable structure of a Xe-CFL for this application.

Fig.1 shows the structure of a Xe-CFL in our approach. Outer diameter of the glass tube is ϕ 2.4mm. R, G, B tri-phosphor is coated on the inner wall of the glass tube. The mixture of xenon and neon (Xe:Ne=70:30) is enclosed in the glass tube. Electrodes consist of one inner electrode and one outer electrode. The inner electrode is the same structure as one for a conventional Hg-CFL. The outer electrode is made of a thin metal wire. It is coiled around the glass tube and is fixed by the transparent shrinking tube.

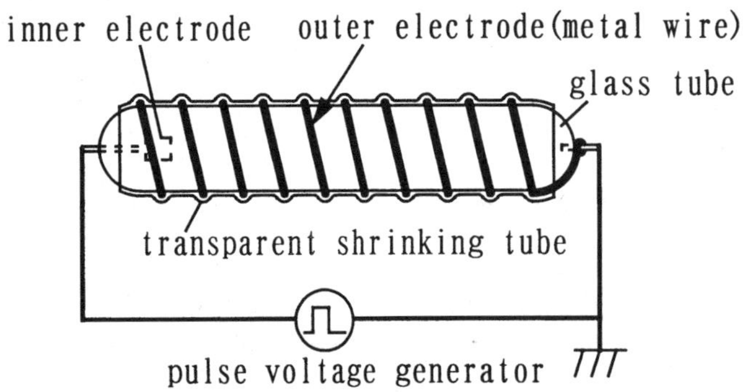

Fig.1 Structure of a Xe-CFL

OPERATING CONDITION

In case of rare gas discharge lamp like the Xe-CFL, a discharge has a general tendency that the positive column is easy to be contracted. Once the positive column is contracted, the light output becomes unstable and low. To keep away from the contracted positive column, it is necessary for the lamp to be driven by pulse-mode operation and the operating frequency (i.e. suspended term between the discharges) must be optimized.

Fig.2 shows a typical example of operating condition. Rectangular-mode voltage is applied between inner electrode and outer electrode, and the pulse-mode current flows.

The hatched region in Fig.3 represents operating frequency margin in which stable light output is established. When the operating frequency is over 28kHz, the positive column is contracted because the suspended term between the discharges is too short. As a result, the light output becomes unstable. On the other hand, when the operating frequency is under 28kHz, the positive column is diffused because of the long suspended term between the discharges. In this case, the light output becomes stable. It has better operated at 20~25kHz.

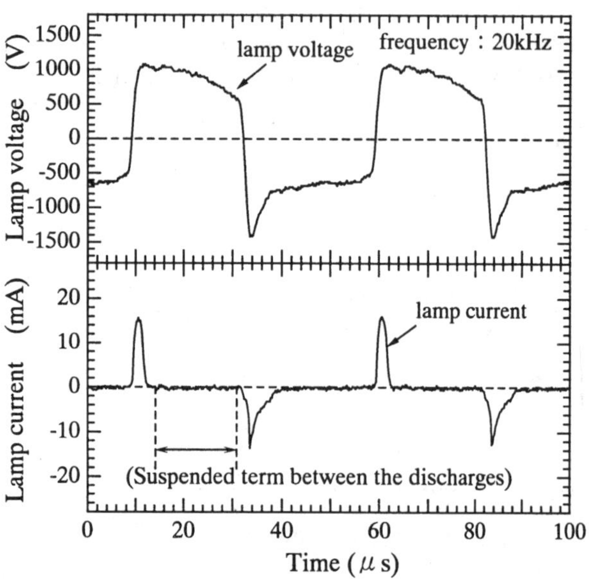

Fig.2 Example of operating waveform

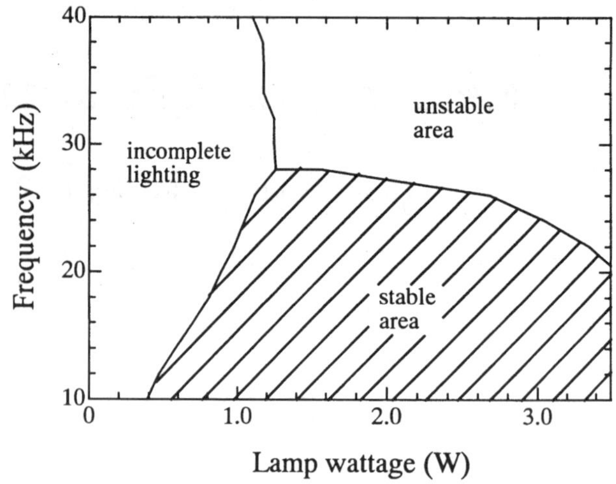

Fig.3 Operating frequency margins in which stable light output are established.

STRUCTURE OF THE MERCURY-FREE BACKLIGHT

At the present time, luminous efficiency of the Xe-CFL is about 60% as much as that of a Hg-CFL. So, the mercury-free backlight needs twice as many CFLs as the conventional Hg-CFL backlight. Fig.4 shows the newly developed mercury-free backlight with Xe-CFLs. The dimension of the backlight is wide 7 inch. Two lamps are arranged at both side edges of a light guide plate. Total four lamps are installed. The light emitting surface is equipped with a prism sheet and a diffuser sheet. The thickness of backlight is 10mm.

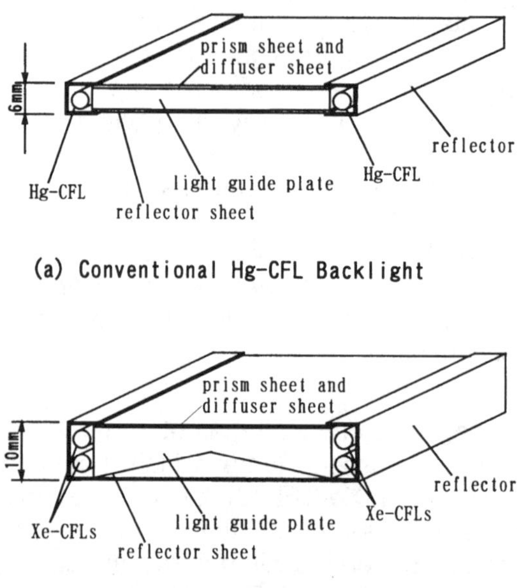

Fig.4 Structure of the backlight

LUMINANCE CHARACTERISTICS OF THE BACKLIGHT

The luminance of the mercury-free backlight as a function of the total lamp wattage is indicated in Fig.5. The luminance increases according to the lamp wattage. When the total lamp wattage is 6.5W, the luminance is 6000cd/m^2. It is enough luminance for car-navigation display.

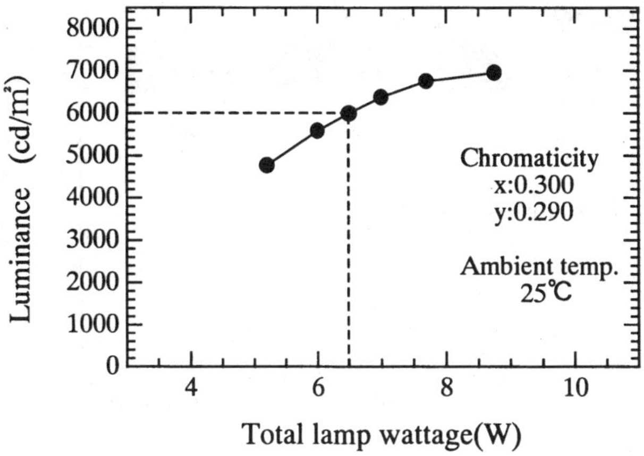

Fig.5 Relation between total lamp wattage and backlight luminance

Relation between the ambient temperature and the luminance is indicated in Fig.6. The mercury-free backlight has more stable luminance characteristics than the conventional Hg-CFL backlight in the wide temperature range from –40℃ to 85℃.In case of mercury-free backlight, the luminance becomes the highest at ambient temperature of –40℃. And it becomes slightly smaller as the ambient temperature becomes higher. This is because VUV radiation in the discharge space becomes fainter as the temperature of xenon gas becomes higher. But the deviation of the luminance in the ambient temperature from –40℃ to 85℃, is within ±15% of the luminance at 25℃.

Compared to this, the luminance of the conventional Hg-CFL backlight varies widely according to the ambient temperature. When the ambient temperature is –40℃, the luminance of the conventional Hg-CFL backlight even with a heating system is about 80% as much as that at 25℃. If the backlight did not have the heating system, the luminance at –40℃ would be less than 40% as much as that at 25℃.

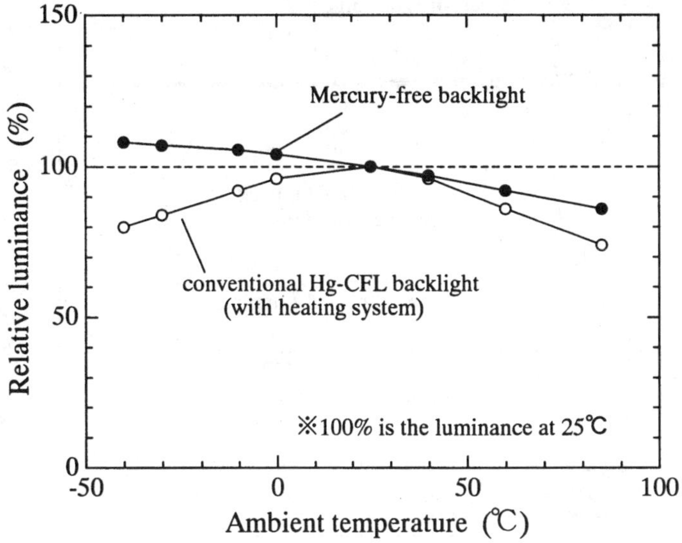

Fig.6 Relation between ambient temperature and luminance

Light output rise up characteristic of the backlight is indicated in Fig.7 (a)(b). The light output of mercury-free backlight rises up more rapidly than that of conventional Hg-CFL backlight. When the ambient temperature is 25℃, light output of a mercury-free backlight reaches to over 100% of stable luminance at 25℃ within 1 second(Fig.7(a)). On the other hand, the conventional Hg-CFL backlight with heating system takes about 40 seconds to reach the 100%. The difference becomes more remarkable when the ambient temperature is low. When the ambient temperature is –40℃, light output of mercury-free backlight also reaches to over 100% within 1 second(Fig.7(b)). But the conventional Hg-CFL backlight takes more than 120 seconds to reach the 80% of the luminance at 25℃.

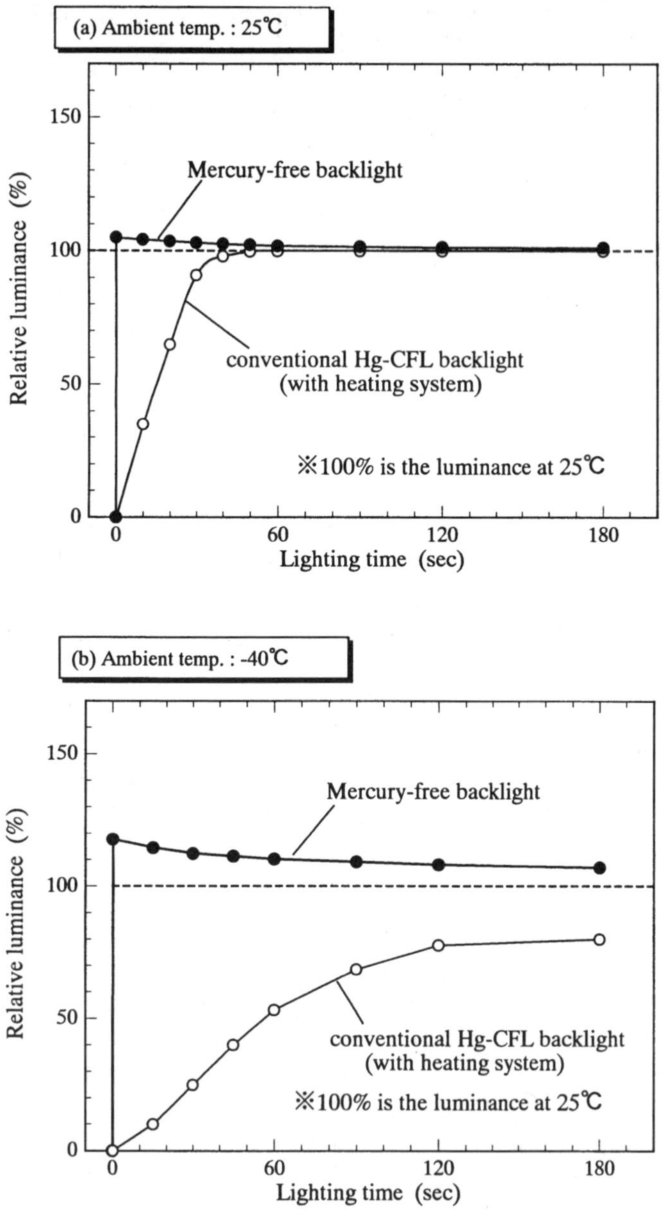

Fig.7 Light output rise up characteristic

DIMMING CHARACTERISTICS OF THE BACKLIGHT

Our newly developed mercury-free backlight has wide dimming capability. Relation between the duty ratio of the dimming signal and the luminance is indicated in Fig. 8. Operating frequency is 20kHz, and dimming frequency is 100Hz.

Output voltage waveform is controlled to keep the same waveform every cycle. And duty ratio can be performed every 0.5% from 100% to 0.5%. As a result, the backlight has stable light output characteristic without flickering in the wide dimming control range from 100% to 1%.

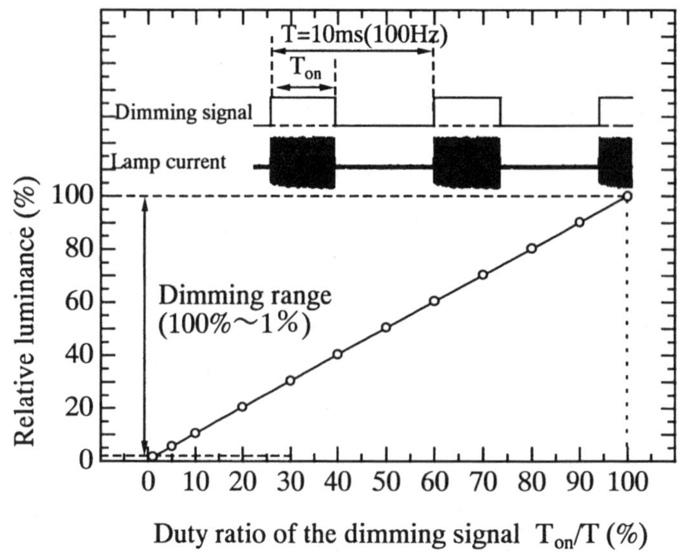

Fig.8 Relation between the duty ratio of the dimming signal and relative luminance

LIFE CHARACTERISTIC OF THE BACKLIGHT

The life characteristic of our newly developed mercury-free backlight is indicated in Fig. 8. The luminance decreases gradually according to the lighting time. After 10000 hours operation, the luminance of the backlight maintains 60% of its initial luminance. The chromaticity also changes slightly according to the lighting time. After 10000 hours operation, the chromaticity of backlight is shifted about ⊿ x=0.035, ⊿ y=0.035 from its initial chromaticity. These life characteristics of the mercury-free backlight can stand comparison with those of the conventional Hg-CFL backlight.

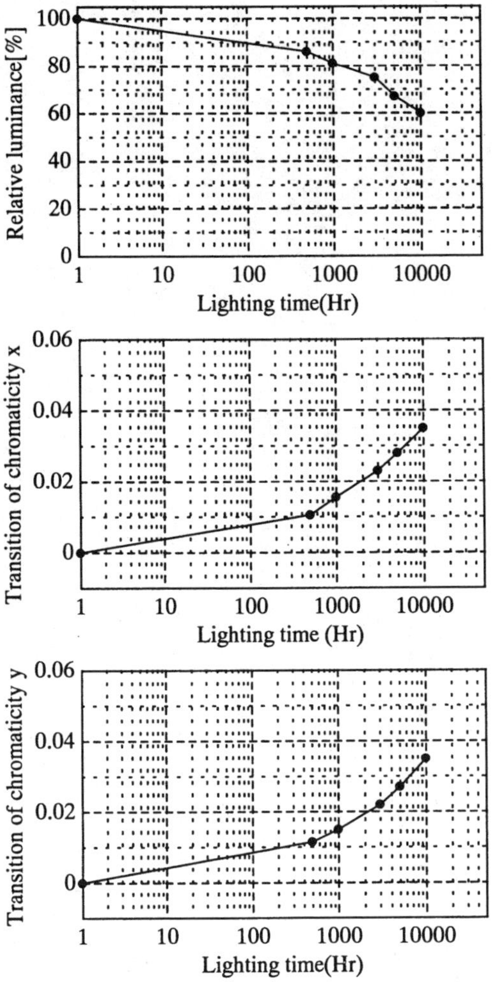

Fig.9 Life characteristic of the backlight

CONCLUSION

The characteristics of our newly developed mercury-free backlight are summarized in Table 1. Backlight dimension is wide 7 inch and thickness is 10mm. This backlight has a comparable luminance with conventional backlight with Hg-CFLs, better light output response, and wide dimming capability over the wide temperature range. Therefore, it could be a suitable candidate for a car-navigation display.

Table1 Characteristics of the mercury-free backlight.

Item	Characteristic
Backlight size	wide 7 inch
Thickness	10mm
Amount of lamps	4 lamps
Total lamp wattage	6.5W
Luminance	6,000cd/m²
Luminance uniformity	75%
Chromaticity	x:0.300 y:0.290
Dimming capability	from 100% to 1%
Life time	Min 10000hrs
Transition of chromaticity after 10000 hours	$\Delta x \leqq 0.04$ $\Delta y \leqq 0.04$

REFERENCES

[1] M. Ilmer, et al. : "Hg-free Flat Panel Source PLANON a Promising Candidate for Future LCD Backlights", SID '00 Digest, pp. 931-933, (2000)

[2] S. Mikoshiba : "Xe Discharge Backlights for LCDs", SID '01 Digest, pp. 286-289, (2001)

[3] H. Noghchi, et al. : "A Mercury-free Cold Cathode Fluorescent Lamp for LCD Backlighting", SID '00 Digest, pp. 935-937,(2000)

2002-01-0123

OLED- Automotive Application Strengths

Russ Johnston
Pioneer Automotive Electronics

ABSTRACT

Organic EL (OEL) has the potential to contribute significantly to our automotive lifestyles in the near future. Some of the advantages of OEL are:

- Great visibility and high contrast
- Rich expressions of gray scale
- Fast response time
- Low power consumption

For these characteristics, OEL is superior to existing displays. On the other hand, OEL display technology has needed further development to be suitable for automotive application's. Most notably, high temperature display life and color variation are key the improvements needed. When these problems are solved, OEL will make a significant contribution towards improving display visibility and information recognition. Furthermore, new advances in OEL technology will provide flexible/formable displays that can be applied to a contoured surface and Full Color OEL.

INTRODUCTION

THE TECHNOLOGY

Organic Electro Luminescent displays contain self-luminous pixels that convert electrical energy into light thus, Electroluminescence. Properties of certain organic materials emit light when an electrical current passes though them. In basic form OEL displays consist of a layer of luminescent material sandwiched between tow electrodes. When the current is passed between two electrodes, light is emitted, and the color depends upon the particular compound of the material used. To see the light that is being emitted one electrode must be transparent so as not to be seen.

THE NEED

The past few years have provided an unprecedented amount of new data delivering technology to be integrated into the mobile environment. North American in particular, has experienced the emergence of Telematics, Navigation and Digital Satellite Radio (SDAR) to name a few. All of which demands the in-car environment.

A key factor for driver information equipment is how thoroughly the information is presented to the driver. This means a good visible display bears a very important role in giving us a H.M.I.(Human machine Interface). Pioneer has been researching and developing Organic EL as a good display technology solution for 10 years.

MARKET SIZE

Currently, LCD is the most popular display device, and has reached a commodity status. It is used in numerous applications such as electric appliances, digital clocks, computer games, and so on because of its usefulness and low cost. There are also a number of automotive applications for LCD, such as Navigation systems, car radios and instrument panels.

Figure 1 below shows the sales growth of LCD displays, in US Dollars, from small clock applications to TFT-LCD for personal computers. As you can see, LCD sales are steadily increasing and are huge at $7.9Billion.

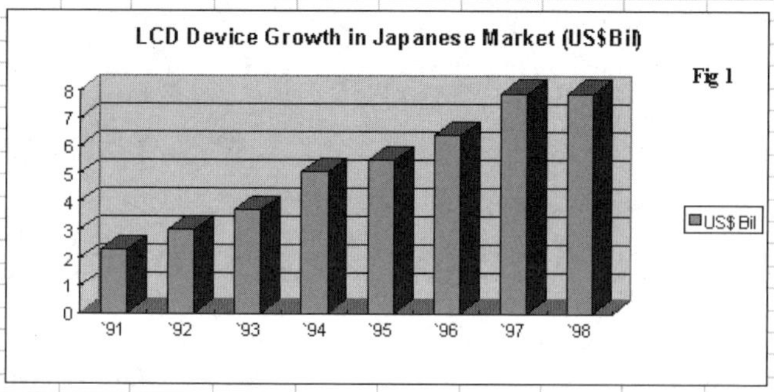

Year		`91	`92	`93	`94	`95	`96	`97	`98
Value	US$ Bil	2.3	3.0	3.7	5.1	5.5	6.4	7.9	7.9
%			130%	123%	138%	108%	116%	123%	100%

However, the highly popular LCD has its faults, such as:

- Narrow viewing angles
- Difficulty reading- The color balance changes when viewed from the side.
- Slow response.
- As it is widely known, an LCD's response time slows down in low temperatures to the point they cannot be read.
- LCD's need back lighting
- Thick construction- because LCD's aren't self-illuminated devices and require a back light.
- High power consumption due to the back-light.

OEL technology will enable a new generation of display devices such as digital cameras, mobile phones, PDA's and mobile electronics. These devices will offer clearer images crisper video as well as thinner designs than similar products with LCDs.

Stanford Resources, Inc. a leading market research firm that focuses on the global display electronics industry projects the worldwide market for OEL displays will grow to $1.6 billion in 2007, or 63% a year over that period. Stanford Resources also forecasts the automobile display market growing to $145 million in 2007.

IN-CAR DISPLAY TREND

Pioneer recognizes that much of the LCD market will be replaced by OEL, but not all. As stated earlier, many advanced intelligent electronic devices are expected to appear in automobiles. There are two ways in which to transmit the information to the driver. One way is to transmit information by voice; the other way is to use a highly visible display. Obviously, there are distinctive differences between the two. One involves the driver moving his eyes off the road and the other does not.

When the use of navigation systems expand, and watching movies and playing computer games in the car are more popular, the instrument panel will be merged together with entertainment equipment. As a result of this movement, rich expression grayscale display devices will be appreciated.

ORGANIC EL OUTLINE

HISTORY

In 1987, Kodak published a technical paper about high efficiency Organic EL. That publication triggered the present OEL research and development. Some key reasons were:

1) OEL is a self-illuminating and a high brightness display.

2) OEL has fast response times.

Pioneer found that OEL compensates for LCD's weaknesses and started R&D activities in 1988. Today, Pioneer is the first and only mass production manufacturer of Organic EL.

In the appendices, please see Figure 3 showing the milestones for Pioneer's OEL development.

CONSTRUCTION

Figure 2 explains the construction of a Pioneer dot matrix organic EL display. Light is emitted at the junction of the anode and the cathode, which are at right angles to each other. Organic materials and electrode layers are applied by vacuum deposition on a glass substrate that is pre-processed with an ITO transparent electrode. The assembly is encapsulated to a metal back-plate, sealing the organic materials and electrodes completely. Encapsulation allows the OEL display to maintain stable luminescence by protecting it against environmental damage.

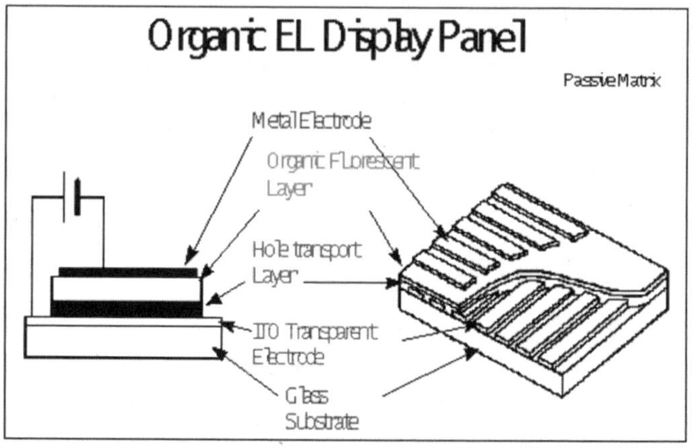

Encapsulation

As mentioned above, keeping the organic material and electrodes stable is very important for OEL panels. Penetration of humidity shortens the life of an OEL display. Therefore, the organic material and electrodes are sealed by a metal plate and an adhesive to protect against moisture. The photograph in figure 3 shows a dark spot caused by a non-lighted area created by moisture.

Figure 3

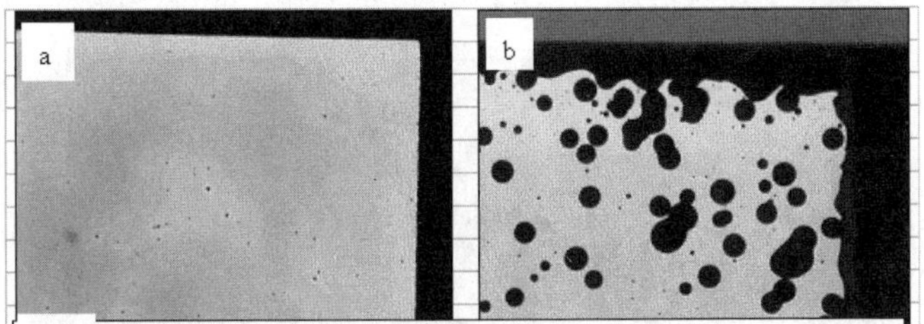

Photographs of dark spots after storage tests at 85°C for 500 hours using a drying material (a), and not using a drying material (b).

IMPROVING CONTRAST

An Organic EL self-emitting display has high contrast in dark rooms. Contrast between lighted areas and non-lighted areas are infinite. Since LCD's cannot control the light coming from the back light, the contrast for LCD's are much lower than the that of OEL. This means poor direct visibility for LCD's.

Another self-emitting display, VFD has high contrast in dark rooms as well, but when VFD is placed under sunlight, then contrast drops down drastically. All segments, whether lighted or not can be seen, so as a result, no one can read the display. In order to avoid this problem, dark filters are used over the front of the VFD panel. This sacrifices brightness in order to get better visibility.

OEL has the advantage of having high contrast in a dark room, but in order to keep high contrast in bright environments, reflection from the cathode electrode needs to be reduced. Pioneer has improved OEL contrast in bright environments by utilizing a circular polarizing film located on the front of the glass panel. As a result, light reflected from the cathode electrode, which acts like a mirror, is reduced. This drastically improves contrast.

ADVANTAGES AND DISADVANTAGES

This section will point our advantages of Organic EL display technology.

Figure 4 **Characteristics of OEL- Advantages**
Features:
1) High brightness
2) Wide viewing angles
3) Low voltage operation
4) Superior gray tones
5) Fast response
6) Wide operating temperature range
Improvement Issues:
1) Extend lifetime in high temperature operation.
2) Develop large panel displays.
3) Develop additional colors and color variations.
4) Develop high density patterning technology

ADVANTAGES

OEL is a self-emitting type display with a high brightness level and wide viewing angles. It also has a fast response.

<u>High brightness level and wide viewing angles.</u>

Self-emitting type displays, such as OEL, have wide viewing angles and do not need a back light. In recent years, LCD displays have improved significantly, but viewing from slanted angles is still a problem. Text is difficult to read , and the color balance changes.

Organic EL achieves a contrast ratio up to 100:1 at 500 Lux. brightness by utilizing a circular polarizing filter.

<u>Low voltage operation</u>

The device is driven by 9VDC and 5VDC. It doesn't require AC input or DC high voltage like other devices. It has extremely high luminance efficiency.

<u>Superior expressions of gray scale</u>

The brightness characteristic curve in figure 5 below shows OEL's good linearity.

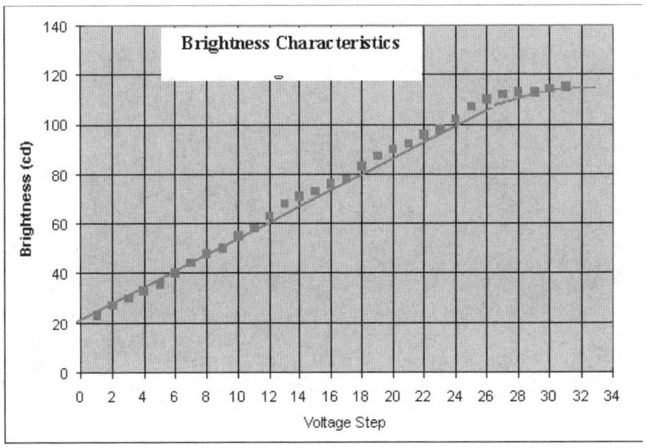

Figure 5

High speed switching

There are no flickering and after-images thanks to the OEL's fast response. This also gives us a very sharp image.

The response time comparisons of each device are as follows:

- OEL: 2μSec
- LCD: a few 10μSec.
- VFD :10μSec

OEL's switching speed is 5 times more than that of VFD's. Also, an LCD work just like a shutter, switching on and off. Therefore the response times for LCD's are slower than OEL.

THE FUTURE:

Flexible Film OEL

One of the key atributes of Organic EL technology is the process in the way it emits light. Unlike traditional liquid crystal displays that require bulky back-lighting, Organic El is self emitting when a current is passed through it, thus allowing for thinner screens.

As mentioned earlier in this paper, the Organic materials and electrode layers are applied by vacuum deposition on a glass substrate. In search of wider versatility of the thinner OEL display module, Pioneer looked to replacing the glass substrate with a flexible material. To do this Pioneer looked to our background in polymer and functional film technologies of optical disc.

In R&D labs, Pioneer has developed first trial samples of thin film OEL displays. These displays used super high-grade optical plastic films to lay organic materials and electrode layers upon. The result, ultra-thin, light weight, easy to bend/flexible, robust displays.

The result of Pioneer's efforts have produced two types of trial samples, thin film segment type and full dot type. Figure 6 and Figure 7 shows a monochrome segment display only 0.2mm thick and weighing less than 1 gram.

Figure 6

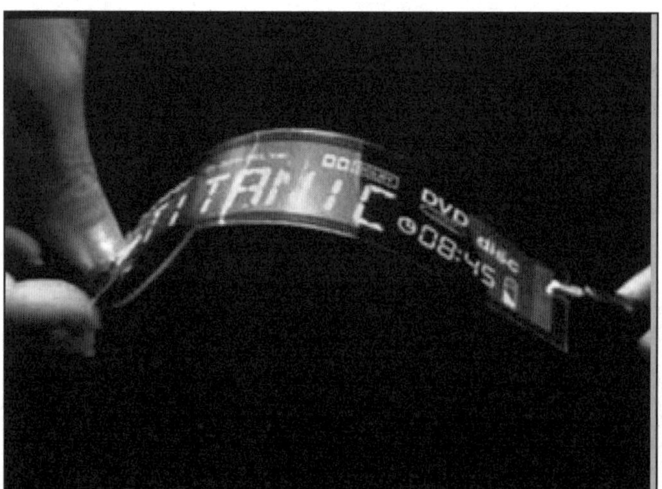

Figure 7

Figure 8 and figure 9 shows a monochrome full dot display only weighing 1 gram and is 0.2mm thick.

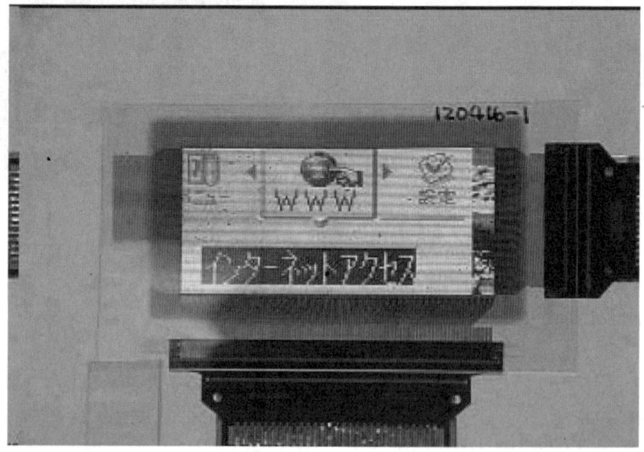

Figure 8

Figure 9

The development of thin film applications will lead to need and unique in-vehicle designs. These new designs will provide easier to read displays but also applications that may lead to a less distractive man to machine interface.

CONCLUSION

Drivers are assured of driving safely and comfortably in a highly sophisticated information society. This will be achieved with a superior human-machine interface system. Pioneer is developing Organic EL displays with the idea that this is becoming a reality.

CONTACT

Author: Russ Jonston
Pioneer Automotive Sales, Inc.
22630 Haggerty Rd.
Farmington Hills, MI 48167
248-449-6799

DEFINITIONS, ACRONYMS, ABBREVIATIONS

OEL: Organic Electro-luminescent (EL)
LCD: Liquid Crystal Display
VFD: Vacuum Florescent Display

APPENDIX

OEL Development Milestones Fig 3

1987 Eastman Kodak publishes paper on high efficency OEL

1988 Pioneer Corporate R&D starts OEL research

1989 Pioneer discovers high efficiency dopant - Patented

1993 Long life OEL device is developed

1995 Kodak - Pioneer establish licensing agreement

1995 Pioneer presents 256x64 dot matrix display at Japan Electronics Show - Industry 1st

Tohoku Pioneer establishes a small size assembly line and starts production

1997 Green mono chrome 256x64 dot matrix display mass production starts in Pioneer's Yonezawa factory.

1997 Pioneer starts sales of FM text information receiver with OEL display.

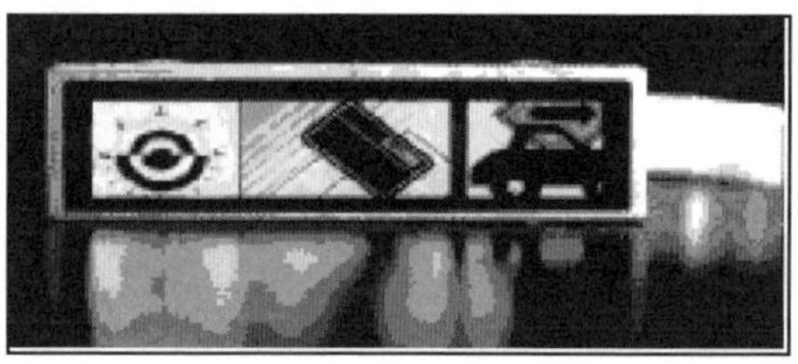

1998 Fullcolor 5.2" QVGA OEL display prototype is presented at SID conference. Industry 1st

Tohoku Pioneer is awarded SID Display of the Year 98 Gold.

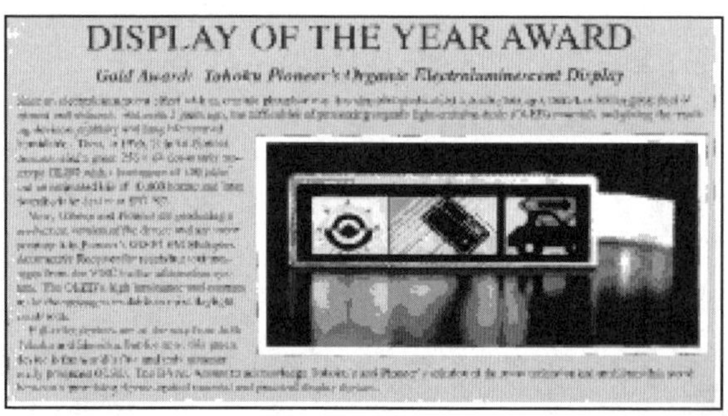
DISPLAY OF THE YEAR AWARD

Gold Award: Tohoku Pioneer's Organic Electroluminescent Display

1999 Pioneer presents `99 spring model car radios featuring 4 color OEL display at WCES - Las Vegas.

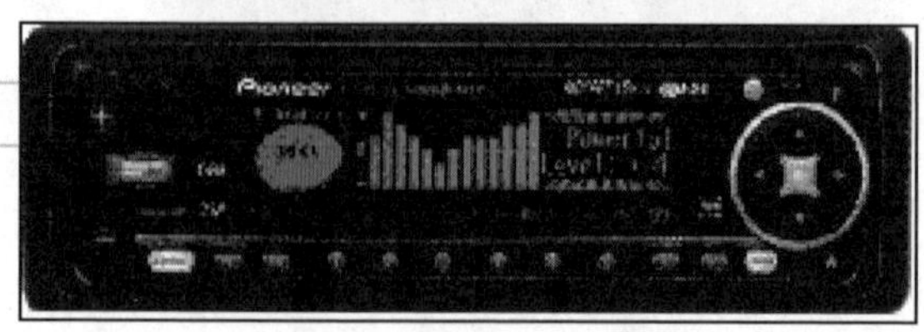

RADIO SYSTEMS

2007-01-1731

Automotive FM Diversity Systems, Part I: Propagation Channel Modeling and Multipath Review

Raed S. Shatara and Jeffrey J. Marrah
Delphi Corporation, Delphi Electronics & Safety

ABSTRACT

This paper represents Part I of a three part series on automotive FM diversity systems. Part I focuses on a review of multipath fading. Part II (2007-01-1732) deals with analog diversity systems which have been developed to combat the effects of this fading in an FM broadcast and Part III (2007-01-1734) discusses new digital implementations of FM diversity systems that have been implemented in DSP algorithms.

This paper reviews propagation channel modeling and multipath. Three cases are studied: Additive white Gaussian noise channel, the Rician channel and the Rayleigh channel. It is further noted that the Rician and Rayleigh channels can be either flat or frequency selective based on the values of the time delays in the reflected signal paths. When the delays are relatively short the channel acts like a wide filter and the fading acts on all spectral components of the signal equally. When the time delays are long the channel acts like a narrow band filter resulting in frequency selective fading.

INTRODUCTION

In an ideal wireless communication channel link, the mobile antenna receives the transmitter signal without any distortions or signal alterations. In a realistic communication link however, nature makes it much more difficult to receive radio frequency (RF) signals. The channel adds noise and superimposes an amplitude and phase response caused by the filtering effects of the multitude of paths the signal can take in traveling between the transmitter and receiver. For the case of mobile reception the channel is constantly changing and Doppler shifts are present due to the relative velocity of the receiver and the transmitter.

Multipath distortion is caused when two or more signal rays converge upon a receiving antenna at significantly differing times. The mobile antenna acts like a summer; it adds direct and reflected signals. This "misalignment" of several delayed replicas of the direct signal causes distortion in the recovered audio.

In an urban environment the RF signals experience changes in amplitude and phase due to short delay multipath. This results in broadband signal fades of 40dB or more as the vehicle moves. Normal highway speeds of passenger vehicles result in signal fluctuation rates in the range of 100 to 1000Hz [1]. Long delay multipath (or frequency selective multipath) is found in environments where reflectors are greater than 6 to 8 kilometers away. This can occur in cities with larger buildings as well as mountainous regions. In general, long and short delay multipath coexist creating frequency selective and broadband fading simultaneously.

CHANNEL MODELING

The channel between the transmit and the receive antennas can be modeled as a linear filter with additive noise. Within the general channel the signal can take many paths while propagating from transmitter to receiver. One path is an un-interrupted line-of-sight ray. Other paths result from reflections off a multitude of structures such as buildings, bridges, mountains, etc. Scattering results in signal loss while the path length provides the delay relative to the line-of-sight (LOS) path. Fig. 1 shows the filter topology used for modeling the channel. The gain/attenuation blocks model the path loss and the delay sections model the various path lengths relative to the line-of-sight path length. The LOS path is modeled without delay since all other delays are referenced to it.

As with any filter, the characteristics such as center frequency, bandwidth and gain are all a function of the filter parameter values for a given topology. It should be noted that the parameters of the channel filter are, in general, time varying due to the relative motion of the transmitter and receiver. Obstructions and objects reflect, scatter and shadow the signal. The relative motion changes the path loss, the delay times and the angle of arrival of the signal upon the receiving antenna. The loss terms A_{LOS} and B_k and the delay terms τ_i

must therefore be time varying to accurately model the channel.

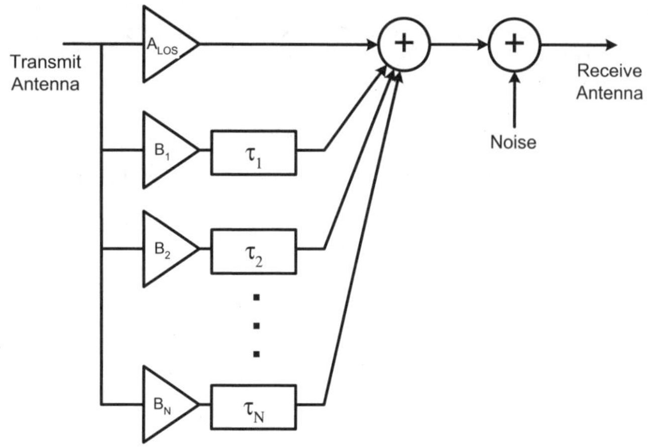

Fig. 1 General Linear Channel Model

Mathematically the received signal is represented in Equation (1) in complex baseband domain

$$\bar{s}(t) = A_{LOS} \cdot e^{j(\phi(t)+\varphi_0)} + \sum_{k=1}^{N} B_k \cdot e^{j(\phi(t-\tau_k)+\varphi_k)} \qquad (1)$$

where

A_{LOS} = Amplitude of line-of-sight (LOS) component

B_k = Amplitude of the delayed component

τ = Time delay [μsec]

$\phi(t)$ = Modulating FM signal

φ = Uniformily distributed phase $[-\pi, \pi]$

The propagation channel for mobile reception can be classified into two general categories. The first is fading over long distances traveled, which is referred in the literature as large-scale fading [8]. In large scale fading the primary channel impairments are free space path loss and shadowing. The second category is fading over short distances, which is referred to as small-scale fading. In small scale fading the channel impairments are primarily due to reflections and scattering from objects. If the channel provides a line-of-sight path then the small-scale fading is said to be Rician because the variations of the voltage envelope of the carrier have statistics that are characterized by the Rice probability density function (PDF). If no LOS path exists then the variations of the voltage envelope of the carrier have statistics that are characterized by the Rayleigh PDF.

It should be noted here that the terms **large-scale** and **small-scale** fading refer to effects that happen over large and small distances respectfully. The reader should not assume that large-scale means large signal fluctuations and small-scale means small signal fluctuations. In fact, in many cases the opposite is true. In a Rayleigh fading situation where there is no line-of-sight path and the reflectors are all relatively close together so that the various path length differences are short relative to the wavelength of the carrier, the signal fades can be very dramatic; on the order of 40dB over distances of a few meters (for FM). Large-scale fading on the other hand generally refers to situations where distances traveled are in kilometers such as driving away from a city or driving behind a mountain. In general large-scale fading and small-scale fading occur simultaneously.

Fig. 2 shows the effects of large-scale fading due to path loss and shadowing. The trace labeled small-scale fading shows the effects of fades that happen over short distances. Note that there is still large-scale fading present in the small-scale fading trace.

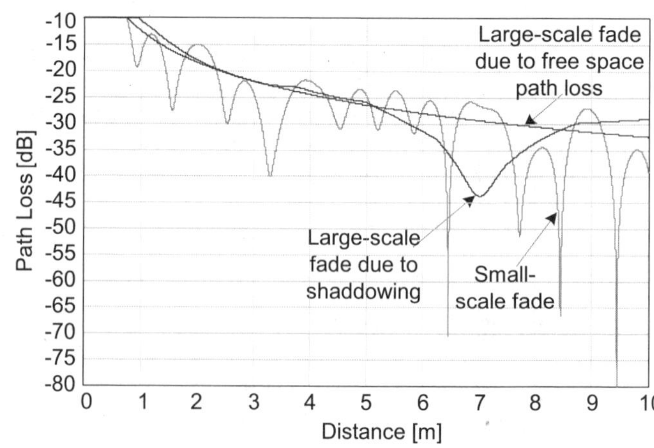

Fig. 2 Plot of carrier signal amplitude envelope voltage as a function of distance traveled. Large-scale fading due to path loss and shadowing is evident. Small-scale fading is shown superimposed on the large-scale fading.

The general channel model of Fig. 1 can be sub-divided into three of the most typical channel characteristics used to create simulations and bench tests for receiver evaluations.

1. **Additive White Gaussian Noise (AWGN) Channel** or sometimes referred to as a specular channel. In this case there are no reflected waves, only the direct line-of-sight signal. Thus $A_{LOS} = 1$, All $B_k = 0$.

2. **Rician Channel** where there is a mixture of direct line-of-sight and reflected signals. Thus

A_{LOS} and B_k's are non-zero. The depth of the signal fade is dependent on the ratio of A_{LOS}/B_k.

3. **Rayleigh Channel** where the line-of-sight signal is blocked leaving only a multitude of reflected signals. Here $A_{LOS}=0$ and B_k's are non-zero.

Cases 2 and 3 above can be further subdivided based on the values of the delay terms of the model. For the case where the delays are relatively short, on the order of $3\mu\sec$ or less than the channel is said to exhibit flat fading because the resulting channel filter has a bandwidth (referred to as coherence bandwidth) that is wider than the signal bandwidth. Thus the signal spectral components are all acted upon equally resulting in amplitude fluctuations that affect all signal frequencies the same. Fig. 3 shows a typical situation commonly referred to as an "urban canyon" where signal reflections are all relatively short.

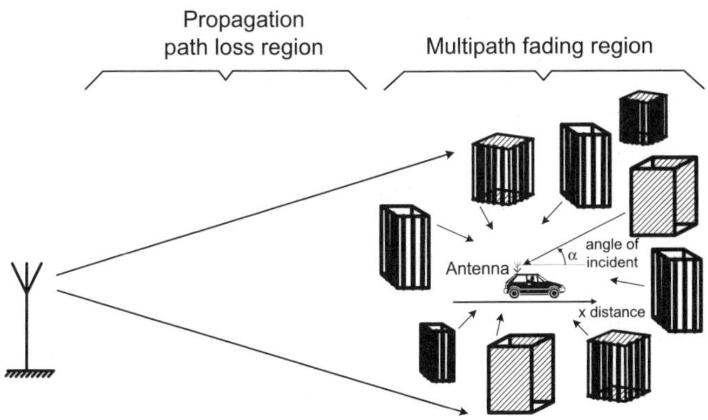

Fig. 3 Typical mobile receiver urban environment.

In an FM broadcast environment flat fading results in dynamically varying signal strengths, which manifests as dynamically varying carrier-to-noise ratio (CNR) into the receiver demodulator. The end user hears audio signal-to-noise ratio (SNR) fluctuations that sound like "spits and pops."

When delay spreads are larger than $3\mu\sec$ the channel filter bandwidth starts becoming narrow relative to the signal bandwidth resulting in frequency selective fading. Fig. 4 shows a picture of a Rayleigh channel with frequency selective fading in Cincinnati, Ohio. The direct paths travel across the river to Kentucky and come back with different delays. The estimated delays are around $20\mu\sec$. The end user hears harmonically distorted audio.

Fig. 4 A picture of Columbia Pkwy in Cincinnati, OH showing a Rayleigh channel with frequency selective fading. This channel has a LOS signal that is comparable in amplitude to the reflected signals because it is blocked from the hill. The reflected signals have large time delays since they must travel across the Ohio River and back before reaching the receive antenna.

Each condition has its own characteristics that will be discussed next.

CASE 1: ADDITIVE WHITE GAUSSIAN NOISE CHANNEL

An AWGN channel is the ideal channel where the signal propagates through free space without atmospheric losses, and no obstacles cause scattering, diffusion or reflection of the signal. The channel is merely a direct path that contains a gain term A_{LOS} which represents the free space path loss of the signal as it propagates through the channel. Equation (2) is the power at the receiving antenna as a function of the transmit power and antenna gain terms.

$$P_r = \frac{P_t G_t G_r \lambda_o^2}{(4\pi d)^2} \tag{2}$$

where

P_r = received power

P_t = transmitted power

G_t = transmitter antenna gain

G_r = receiver antenna gain

$$\lambda_o = \text{wavelength} = \frac{c}{f} = \frac{\text{speed of light}}{\text{frequency}} \quad [\text{meters}]$$

$d = \text{distance}$ [meters]

The following collection of terms is called the free space path loss between isotropic antennas (set antenna gains to 1) [8,9],

$$PL(dB) = 10\log\left(\frac{P_t}{P_r}\right) = -10\log\left(\frac{\lambda_o}{4\pi d}\right)^2 \qquad (3)$$

The model contains an additive white Gaussian noise source which represents the noise induced on the signal at the receiving antenna by man-made sources such as automotive ignition systems, digital circuits, electrical power lines, fluorescent and neon lights, etc. These noise sources contribute to the receive antenna noise temperature. The noise figure (NF) of the receiver input stages also contributes to this overall noise. This channel acts upon the signal in a way that degrades the CNR of the received signal but does not affect the signal's bandwidth. To model large scale fading effects, the A_{LOS} term is varied in a log-normal distribution with its mean changing in proportion to $1/d^2$ to model path loss, where d represents the distance between the transmitting and receiving antennas.

For purposes of receiver design this channel model can be used to provide a static CNR so that parameters such as sensitivity and minimum detectable signal can be simulated and/or measured on the bench.

CASE 2: RICIAN CHANNEL

Flat Fading Rician Channel

As mentioned above, flat fading occurs when the channel filter delay terms are relatively short causing the channel bandwidth to be larger than the signal bandwidth. To be a Rician channel the LOS signal amplitude dominates the reflected signals.

Typical Rician fading is shown in Fig. 5 where the simulation was conducted over a distance $x = 110 \cdot \lambda_o$ with 30 incoming waves that have random angles of incident, amplitudes and phase. The simulated drive in the x direction is shown for 60 meters (wavelength $\lambda_o = 3\text{m}$ for the FM band). The LOS path was set to $A_{LOS} = 0.5$. Voltage amplitude fades of <10dB are evident. These fades are relatively minor due to the dominant LOS path in the channel.

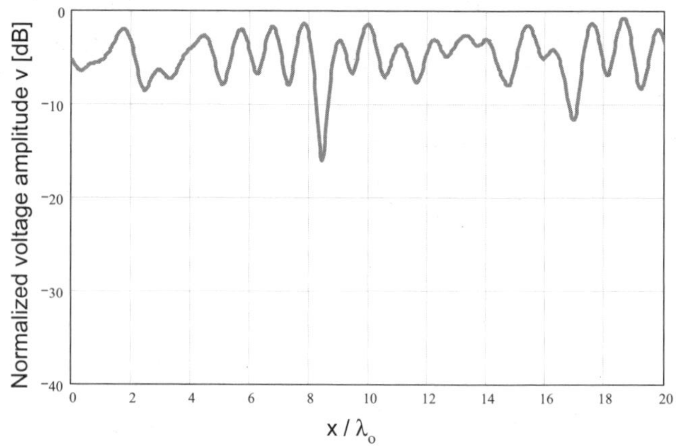

Fig. 5 Simulation snapshot of voltage envelope amplitude with LOS component; less fades are evident.

The histogram and resulting probability density of the multipath condition simulated above is shown in Fig 6. Here it is clear the data fits the Rician probability density function (PDF). The Rician PDF is defined as

$$p(v) = \frac{v}{\sigma^2} e^{-\frac{(v^2 + A_{LOS}^2)}{2\sigma^2}} I_0\left(\frac{v \cdot A_{LOS}}{\sigma^2}\right) \qquad (4)$$

where the expected value of v is

$$E\{v\} = \sqrt{\frac{\pi}{2}} \cdot \sigma \cdot \left[(1+r) \cdot I_0\left(\frac{r}{2}\right) + r \cdot I_1\left(\frac{r}{2}\right)\right] \cdot e^{\left(\frac{r}{2}\right)} \qquad (5)$$

where,

$$r = \frac{A_{LOS}^2}{\sigma^2}$$

$I_n = n_{th}$ order modified Bessel function $(I_0(0) = 1)$

and σ is the standard deviation of the population.

A more general distribution that characterizes the amplitude fading is called Nakagami or m-distribution. Its PDF is defined as

$$p(v) = \frac{2}{\Gamma(m)} \cdot \left(\frac{m}{\Omega}\right)^m \cdot v^{2m-1} \cdot e^{\left(-\frac{mv^2}{\Omega}\right)} \qquad (6)$$

where

$$\Omega = E(v^2), \quad m = \frac{\Omega^2}{E\{(v^2 - \Omega)^2\}}, \quad m \geq \frac{1}{2}$$

and $\Gamma(\bullet)$ is the Gamma function, and "m" is called the fading figure. When $m = 1$, Nakagami distribution reduces to Rayleigh and $m = 1/2$ corresponds to one-sided Gaussian PDF. "m" values of $1/2 \leq m < 1$ represent deeper fades than Rayleigh. Those $m \geq 1$ correspond to less fades than Rayleigh due to the line-of-sight component, which resembles Rice distribution.

The Rician parameter K is defined as

$$K = \frac{\text{Power in the dominant path}}{\text{Power in the scattered paths}} = \frac{A_{LOS}^2}{2 \cdot \sigma^2} \tag{7}$$

When $K = 0$, it yields Rayleigh fading as in (12), whereas if K is infinite the mobile channel is Gaussian. Rice and Nakagami are both considered general distributions that model mobile channel fading with their K and m factors, respectively. When $K = 0$ and $m = 1$ they both yield Rayleigh fading. As K increases to infinity and m is large they both yield Gaussian which represents a dominant component in the mobile channel.

It is evident that both Rice and Nakagami fit the Gaussian shaped data of the voltage amplitude for $K = 10.5$ and $m = 5.3$, respectively. We can observe that the mean of the distribution is centered on the LOS component which is the case for both Rice and Nakagami.

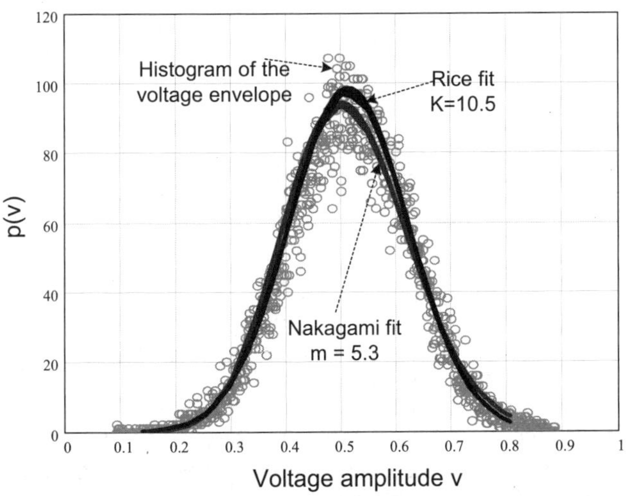

Fig. 6 Rice and Nakagami PDFs of the voltage amplitude.

Frequency Selective Rician Channel

In mountainous environments, strong reflections are present with long time delays ($\tau > 3\mu\,\text{sec}$). In this situation it becomes challenging for the FM receiver to demodulate the information accurately. Due to the frequency modulation imposed on the carrier, the reflected signal will not arrive at the receiving antenna at the same frequency as the carrier. For clarity we will model just one reflected signal. Equation 1 simplifies to the following

$$\begin{aligned} \bar{s}(t) &= A_{LOS} \cdot e^{j(\phi(t) + \varphi_0)} \\ &\quad + B_1 \cdot e^{j(\phi(t - \tau_1) + \varphi_1)} \end{aligned} \tag{8}$$

Fig. 7 shows vector representations of the direct and reflected signals along with the resultant vector due to the summing action at the receive antenna. Since the reflected signal arrives at the receiving antenna at a different frequency the reflected signal vector is rotating around the direct signal vector. The dashed line in Fig. 7 indicates the trajectory of the resultant signal's vector. It must be kept in mind that an FM demodulator only sees the resultant vector and as long as the receiver is in limiting it is only sensitive to the change in phase of the resultant vector not its amplitude. Recall that,

$$\text{Frequency} = \frac{d\phi(t)}{dt} \tag{9}$$

Therefore as the resultant vector sweeps past the origin, its change in phase becomes very large. The closer the relative amplitudes of the direct and reflected signal, the larger the phase change as the resultant signal trajectory sweeps even closer to the origin. This accounts for the spikes seen in the recovered audio in Fig. 8.

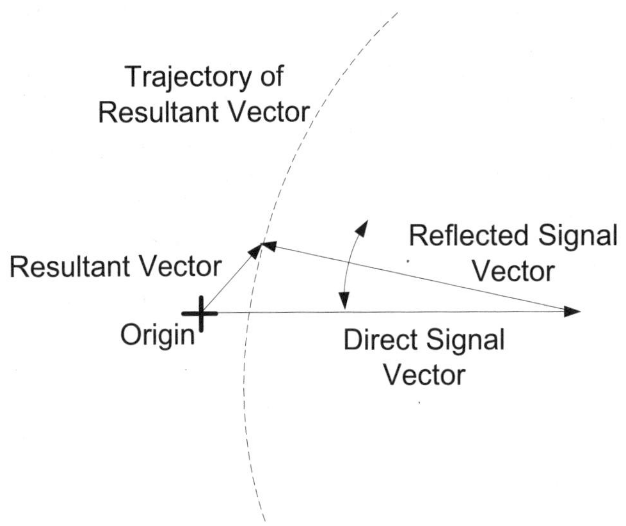

Fig. 7 Vector diagram of a direct signal and a single reflected signal which arrives at the receiving antenna at a different frequency than the direct. The dashed line shows the trajectory of the resultant vector which sweeps past the origin creating spikes in the FM demodulator output.

The recovered audio shown in Fig. 8 is the output of a FM demodulator resulting from a long delay multipath situation. The carrier is FM modulated with a 1kHz tone at 75kHz deviation. The reflected signal (B_1) has an amplitude of 0.9 and the direct signal (A_{LOS}) has an amplitude of 1. The time delay (τ_1) of the reflected signal is $30\mu\,sec$. The distortion resulting from this multipath condition was calculated to be 12% [3,4].

Since the frequency shift of the reflected signal is due to the modulation imposed on the carrier it is clear that as the modulation frequency increases the number of spikes will increase since the reflected signal will be rotating faster resulting in more sweeps past the origin. This is why high modulation frequencies in FM are more susceptible to long delay multipath (frequency selective fading) than lower modulation frequencies. Higher pitch instruments such as flutes, cymbals and higher notes from pianos as well as "s" sounds in speech are all victims of frequency selective fading caused by long delay multipath.

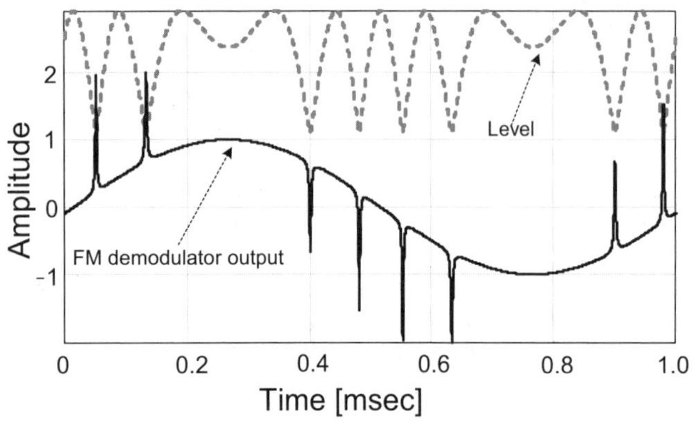

Fig. 8 Distorted demodulated FM signal due to long time delay of the reflected signal.

Fig. 8 represents a specific set of multipath conditions, namely an amplitude ratio between the direct and reflected signals of 0.9 and a reflected signal delay of $30\mu\,sec$. To gain a better understanding of a wider range of conditions the same analysis was repeated for amplitude ratios ranging from 1 ± 1 and delays ranging from $0\text{ to }100\mu\,sec$. The results are shown in Fig. 9. Note that as the amplitudes of the direct and reflected signals become equal and as the delay times increase the audio distortion of the FM demodulator output approaches 30%.

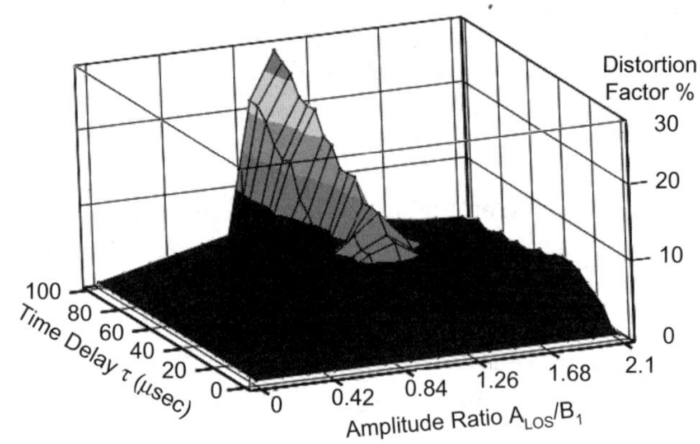

Fig. 9 Audio distortion as a function of the amplitude radio of the LOS and a single reflected signal and the time delay difference between the LOS and reflected signals.

CASE 3: RAYLEIGH CHANNEL

Flat Fading Rayleigh Channel

For the case where there is no LOS signal ($A_{LOS} = 0$), and the carrier is unmodulated ($\phi(t) = 0$), and the vehicle is moving in the x-direction as shown in Fig. 3, Equation (1) reduces to the following when multiplied by the antenna effective length ($v = \bar{s}(t) \cdot l_{eff}$)

$$v = \left(\sum_{k=1}^{NW} B_k \cdot e^{j\varphi_k} \right) \tag{10}$$

where

$$B_k = b_k e^{j\frac{2\pi}{\lambda_o} x \cos(\alpha_k)} \tag{11}$$

and b_k is Gaussian distributed random amplitude and α_k is the angle of incidence uniformly distributed between 0 and 2π. Equation (10) represents the sum of scattered waves in the city (urban areas) and the envelope (magnitude) of it can be modeled by the Rayleigh fading distribution function.

Typical Rayleigh fading is shown Fig. 10 where the simulation was conducted over a distance $x = 110 \cdot \lambda_o$ with 30 incoming waves that each have a random angle of incidence, amplitude and phase. The simulated drive in the x-distance direction is shown for 60 meters (wavelength $\lambda_o = 3m$ for FM). The voltage amplitude fades of 30dB or more are evident. The histogram for the simulated data is shown in Fig 11, which shows that it fits the Rayleigh PDF. The Rayleigh PDF is defined as

$$p(v) = \frac{v}{\sigma^2} e^{-\frac{v^2}{2\sigma^2}} \qquad (12)$$

where the expected value of v is

$$E\{v\} = \sqrt{\frac{\pi}{2}} \cdot \sigma \qquad (13)$$

and the mean square is

$$E\{v^2\} = 2 \cdot \sigma^2 \qquad (14)$$

where σ is the standard deviation of the population.

The Doppler frequency shift f_D for each scattered wave is defined as

$$f_D = \frac{v}{\lambda_o} \cos(\alpha) = f_m \cos(\alpha) \qquad (15)$$

where v is the speed of the mobile in meters per second (m/s). The maximum Doppler shift $\pm f_m$ is defined at 0 degrees angle of incidence. The theoretical maximum Doppler shift in an FM environment is about 9.3Hz for a vehicle traveling 100km/hr given that the wavelength λ_o is 3 meters at 100MHz. In a realistic environment, it is possible to obtain $\pm 2 \cdot f_m$ Doppler shift due to signal reflections off vehicles traveling in the opposite direction. Due to the relatively slow traveling speed and long wavelength in the FM environment, the Doppler shift for a single FM receiver is insignificant. It becomes significant when we design FM diversity systems such as the phase aligning system that is mentioned in the second part of this three parts series.

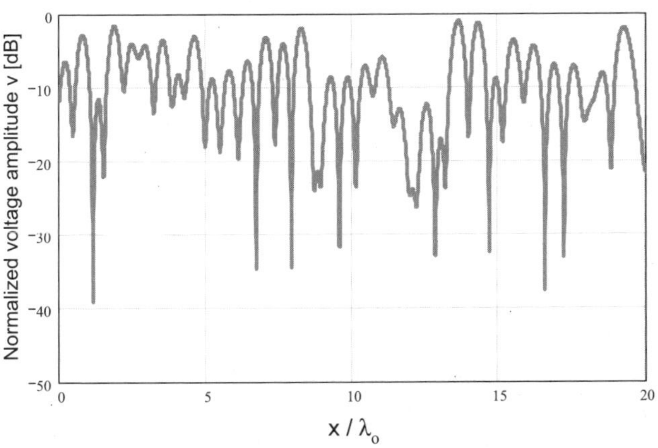

Fig. 10 A typical Rayleigh fading field in mobile environment.

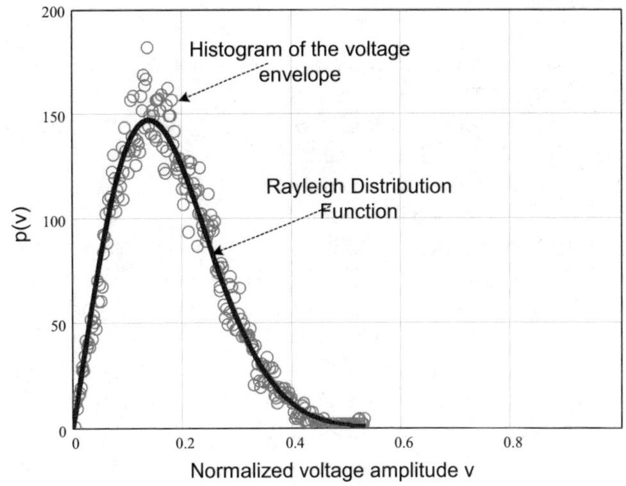

Fig. 11 Rayleigh PDF of the voltage amplitude.

Appendix A shows that the Rayleigh and Rice distributions are special cases of a more general distribution called Chi-Square χ^2 which is used extensively in communication theory.

ACKNOWLEDGMENTS

The authors would like to extend their gratitude to Steve Alverson, Delphi Corporation, Electronics & Safety systems, for help with editing this text.

REFERENCES

[1] C. William Jakes, "Microwave Mobile communications", IEEE Press, Reissued edition 1994 (original edition 1974)

[2] D. G. Brennan, "Linear Diversity Combining Techniques", Proceedings of the IRE, Vol. 47, pp.1075-1102, June 1959.

[3] E. Manner, "Stoerungen und Ihre Beseitigung durch Mehrantennendiversity beim Frequenzmodulierten Funkempfang im Auto", Doctor Thesis, University of the Bundeswehr Munich, 1985.

[4] R. Leopold, "Mobile Rundfunkempfangstechnik", Habilitationsschrift zur Erteilung der Lehrbefugnis in der Fakultaet fuer Elektrotechnik der Universitaet der Bundeswehr Muenchen, February 1995.

[5] R. S. Shatara, "Combined Switched and Phase Aligned Multi-Antenna Diversity System for Signal-Error-Reduction in Mobile Receiving Systems", Ph.D. thesis, University of Bundeswehr, Munich Germany, January 2003.

[6] J. G. Proakis, "Digital Communications", McGraw-Hill, Third Edition, 1995.

[7] R. S. Shatara, "Combined Switched and Phase Aligned Multi-Antenna Diversity System for Signal-Error-Reduction in Mobile Receiving Systems", Ph.D. thesis, University of Bundeswehr, Munich Germany, January 2003.

[8] Sklar, B. " Digital Communications, Fundamentals and Applications", Prentice Hall PTR, Second Edition, 2001.

[9] Rappaport. T. S., "Wireless Communications", Prentice Hall PTR, Second Edition, 2002.

CONTACT

Dr. Raed Shatara began his career at Delphi in 1992 after receiving a BSEE from Western Michigan University. He received the M.S. EE degree from Purdue University, IN, 1998. Raed received the Delphi fellowship in 1999 to pursue a Ph.D. EE from the Bundeswehr University Munich, Germany, which he completed in January 2003. He initially worked on the Phase Aligning System (PAS) and FM receivers. Currently, he is working on advanced diversity systems and next generation receivers. His research interests are in mobile communications, RF receiver design, receiver diversity and signal processing. He has one patent and recently filed for 5 new inventions for his work on diversity systems. He is currently in the RF Design Group at the Electronics and Safety division of Delphi Corporation. (Raed.s.shatara@delphi.com)

Jeff Marrah is a Principal Technical Fellow at Delphi Electronics and Safety in Kokomo, Indiana. He began his career at Delphi in 1981 after receiving a BSEE from Michigan Technological University. He received a MSEE from Purdue University in 1985. Jeff's initial programs were hybrid electronic spark control and mass airflow sensors. He then spent six years as a BiCMOS mixed signal IC design engineer working on radio IC's. In 1991 he became the manager of the RF Technologies Development Group responsible for all tuner chipset and applications development for Delphi AM / FM radios, Satellite Digital Audio Receivers and 2-way satellite modems. He has nineteen patents, one trade secret and one defensive publication for his work in the radio field and was inducted into the Delphi Innovation Hall of Fame in 1998. (Jeffrey.j.marrah@delphi.com)

APPENDIX A :

Chi-Square Distribution

Let $Y=\sum_{i=1}^{N} X_i^2$, where X_i (i = 1,2,3...N) are statistically independent Gaussian random variables with means μ_i and variances σ_i. The non-central Chi-Square PDF with n-degrees of freedom is given by [6]

$$p_Y(y)=\frac{1}{2\sigma^2}\cdot\left(\frac{y}{s^2}\right)^{(n-2)/4}\cdot e^{-(s^2+y)/2\sigma^2}\cdot I_{(n/2)-1}\left(\sqrt{y}\cdot\frac{s}{\sigma^2}\right),\quad y\geq 0 \qquad \ldots\text{(A1)}$$

where

$$s^2=\sum_{i=1}^{N}\mu_i^2 \qquad \text{(A2)}$$

and $I_k(x)$ is the k-th order modified Bessel function of the first kind, which is given by

$$I_k(x)=\sum_{j=0}^{\infty}\frac{(x/2)^{k+2j}}{j!\,\Gamma(k+j+1)},\quad x\geq 0 \qquad \text{(A3)}$$

The Γ function is defined as

$$\Gamma(p)=\int_0^{\infty} t^{p-1}\cdot e^{-t}\cdot dt \quad \text{if } p>0$$
$$\Gamma(p)=(p-1)! \qquad \text{if } p>0 \text{ integer} \qquad \text{(A4)}$$
$$\Gamma\left(\frac{1}{2}\right)=\sqrt{\pi}, \qquad \Gamma\left(\frac{3}{2}\right)=\frac{\sqrt{\pi}}{2}$$

If $v^2=Y=X_1^2+X_2^2$, $n=2$, and $s^2=\mu_1^2+\mu_2^2=A_{LOS}^2$ then the Rician PDF of v (Eq. 4) is obtained with a simple change of variable.

Similarly, when X_i (i = 1,2,3...N) are statistically independent Gaussian random variables with zero means and variances σ_i. The central Chi-Square PDF with n-degrees of freedom is given by [6]

$$p_Y(y)=\frac{1}{\sigma^n\cdot 2^{n/2}\cdot\Gamma(n/2)}\cdot y^{(n/2)-1}\cdot e^{-y/2\sigma^2},\quad y\geq 0 \qquad \text{(A5)}$$

If $v^2=Y=X_1^2+X_2^2$ and $n=2$, then the Rayleigh PDF of v (Eq. 12) is obtained with a simple change of variable.

DEFINITIONS, ACRONYMS, ABBREVIATIONS

AWGN: Additive White Gaussian Noise Channel
LOS: Line-of-sight
NLOS: No line-of-sight
PDF: Probability density function
CDF: Cumulative density function
RF: Radio Frequency
IF: Intermediate Frequency
E{.}: Expected value operator (mean value)

2007-01-1732

Automotive FM Diversity Systems, Part II: Analog Systems

Raed S. Shatara and Jeffrey J. Marrah
Delphi Corporation, Delphi Electronics & Safety

ABSTRACT

This paper represents Part II of a three part series on automotive FM diversity systems. Part I (2007-01-1731) focuses on a review of propagation channel modeling and multipath fading. Part II deals with analog diversity systems which have been developed to combat the effects of this fading in an FM broadcast signal. Part III (2007-01-1734) discusses new FM diversity system designs that have been implemented in digital signal processors (DSP's).

Analog automotive diversity systems have been in production for more than 20 years. The main purpose of a diversity system is to reduce the degraded reception performance caused by multipath propagation, mainly, the flat (amplitude) fading of the carrier. This is often accomplished by the use of two or more uncorrelated receiving antennas. This paper investigates the performance of analog implementations of Phase Aligning Systems (PAS) and Switched Antenna diversity systems in flat fading conditions and frequency selective multipath (long-delay) situation.

INTRODUCTION

The primary purpose of a diversity system is to reduce degraded reception performance caused by multipath propagation. This is often accomplished by the use of two or more uncorrelated FM receiving antennas. Diversity reception in mobile communication systems has been reported in past literature to reduce distortion due to fading. The following three systems were compared by [1]: (i) selection diversity (SD), (ii) equal gain combiner (EGC), (iii) maximal ratio combiners (MRC). Systems (ii) and (iii) outperformed system (i), but they require multiple receiver sections and tend to be more expensive to implement in analog circuitry. Systems (ii) and (iii) attempt to optimize certain characteristics of the received signal in order to minimize the number of fades while maximizing the desired signal. System (i) uses only one antenna for reception at any instant in time. The other antennas do not contribute to the demodulated signal. Systems (ii) and (iii) utilize the signal from both antennas through a variety of combining techniques. When scaling the system to more than 2 antennas the switched diversity system gains a cost advantage over the phased aligning system.

LINEAR DIVERSITY SYSTEMS REVIEW

The systems, which were mentioned in the introductory section, were compared in M independent Rayleigh distributed branches with signal-to-noise ratio of Γ in each branch. The average SNR for each system is given by [1]

$$\overline{SNR}_{SD} = \Gamma \cdot \sum_{k=1}^{M} \frac{1}{k} \qquad (1)$$

$$\overline{SNR}_{MRC} = M \cdot \Gamma \qquad (2)$$

$$\overline{SNR}_{EGC} = \Gamma \cdot \left[1 + (M-1) \cdot \frac{\pi}{4}\right] \qquad (3)$$

Fig. 1 shows the average SNR diversity improvement for SD, MRC, and EGC over one branch. It is interesting to observe that MRC and EGC have significant performance improvement in SNR over SD when $M \geq 3$.

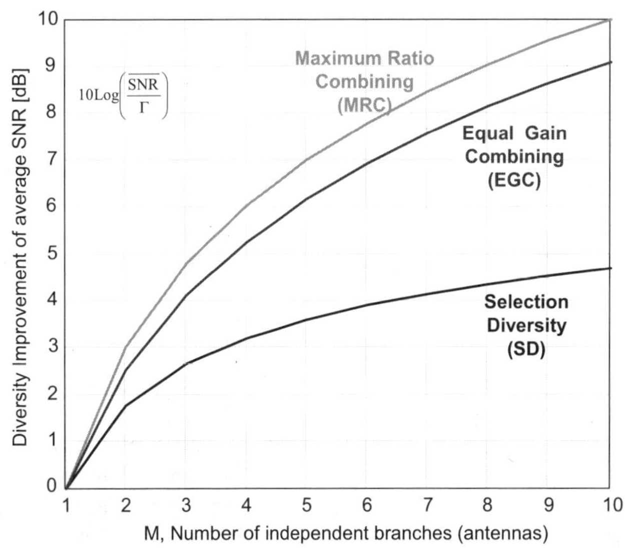

Fig. 1: Average SNR diversity improvement over one branch.

PHASE ALIGNING DIVERSITY SYSTEM

SYSTEM DESCRIPTION

Fig. 2 illustrates the PAS packaging in an automobile. By properly combining the inputs from an array of multiple printed on glass antennas, the resulting performance can meet or exceed that of a mast antenna. The phase aligning diversity system is shown in Fig. 3. The basic idea of the system is to align both antenna signals in-phase at the RF section of the receiver [2-3]. This approach applies to multiple numbers of antennas but for simplicity a two-antenna system is described here. The first step to phase alignment is to determine the amount of phase correction that must be applied. To accomplish this, one of the two antenna signals is Amplitude Modulated (AM) with a reference signal (dither tone), then it is added to the signal of the other antenna. When the two antenna signals are not in-phase, the AM will produce Phase Modulation (PM) at the sum. The AM-to-PM conversion that takes place at the summing node is illustrated in Fig. 4. The resulting PM is detected by the FM receiver thus producing a signal at the FM detector output that is equal in frequency to the AM modulating tone but whose amplitude and phase are proportional to the phase difference between to the two antenna signals. This technique provides a means of detecting the phase difference between the two signals after summation thus enabling this diversity technique to be added to the antenna system of an existing receiver with very minimal change to the receiver itself. Once the phase difference between the two antenna signals is known a phase shift network in one of the antenna signal paths can be adjusted to correct the phase difference. This is a closed-loop system that continuously corrects incoming phase differences between the two antenna signals.

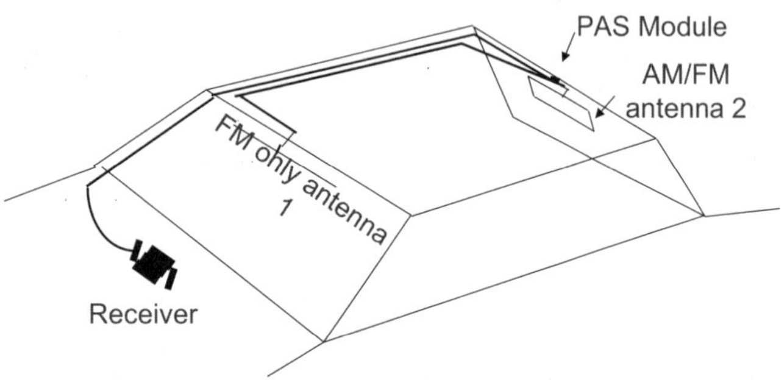

Fig. 2 PAS packaging in Vehicle.

The PAS can be implemented with existing single receivers. It is also important to note that the antennas must be placed far apart (at least half wavelength) to insure proper spatial diversity performance. While omni-directional gain patterns of each antenna will optimize PAS system performance, this system can also compensate for poor antenna patterns inherent in printed on glass antennas.

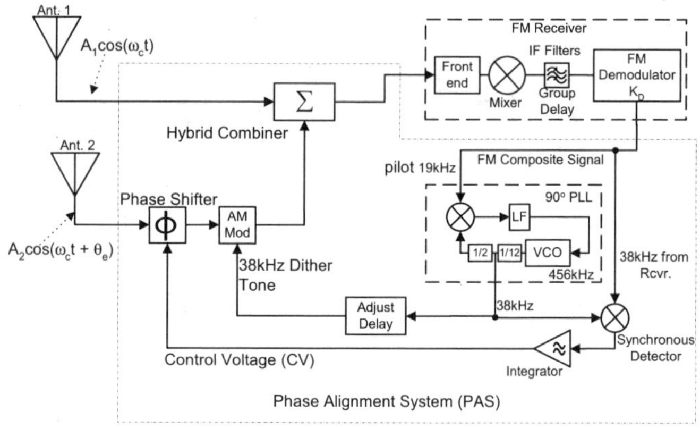

Fig. 3 Block diagram of phased aligning diversity system.

Fig. 4 shows the sum of the signal vectors of $\overline{y}_1$ and $\overline{y}_2$ where $\overline{y}_2$ is AM modulated. When $\overline{y}_2$ leads $\overline{y}_1$ as in Fig. 2a the phase change in the sum is in-phase with the AM modulating signal. When $\overline{y}_2$ lags $\overline{y}_1$ as in Fig. 2b, the phase change in the sum has the opposite polarity to the AM modulating signal. The final case is shown in Fig. 3c where the two vectors are in-phase, therefore the AM modulation does not create phase modulation in the sum of the two vectors.

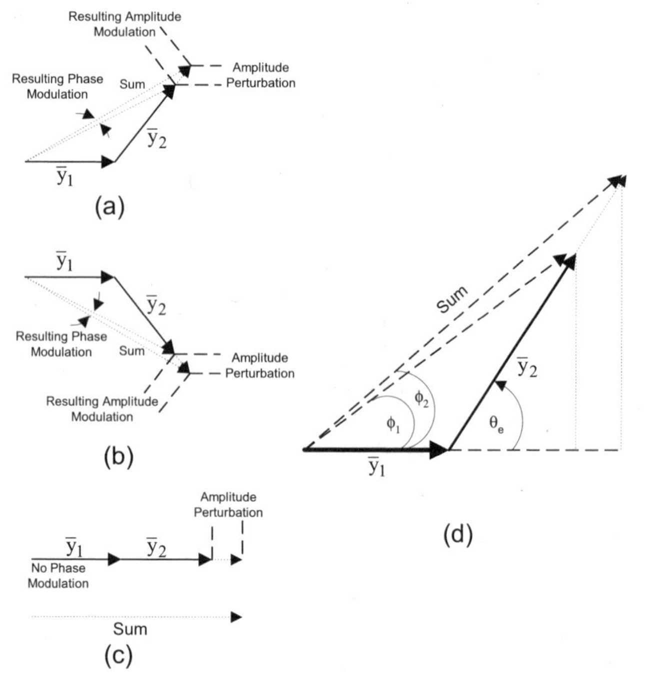

Fig. 4 Vector diagram of the direct signals $\overline{y}_1$ and $\overline{y}_2$ as seen by each antenna and the resulting sum. (a) $\overline{y}_2$ leads $\overline{y}_1$, (b) $\overline{y}_2$ lags $\overline{y}_1$, (c) $\overline{y}_2$ and $\overline{y}_1$ are in phase. Note the amplitude modulation $\overline{y}_2$ creating phase modulation in the sum vector when the two antenna signals are not co-phased (d) Vectors geometry analysis [2].

The placement of the dither tone is important because it must not introduce any distortion or audible products to the FM receiver. It was determined by [3] that the placement must be in quadrature to the L-R baseband modulation, via a PLL to the pilot tone. Fig. 5 shows the dither tone of 38kHz placement in the FM baseband spectrum.

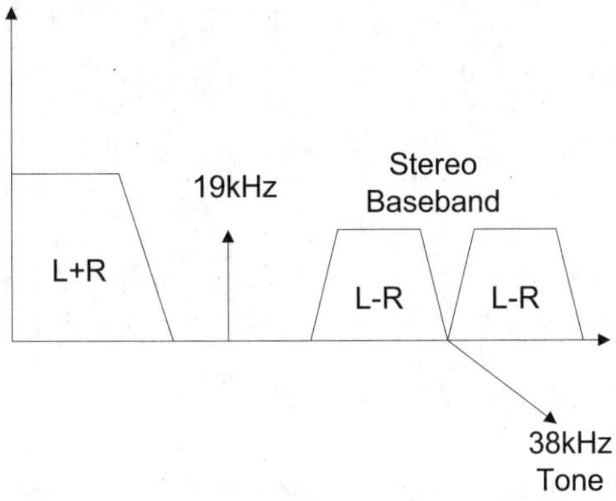

Fig. 5 Placement of the dither tone.

The resulting phase modulation $\delta = \phi_2 - \phi_1$ from the sum of the two antenna signals as a function of the error angle θ_e (of Fig. 4(d)) is shown is shown in Fig. 6.

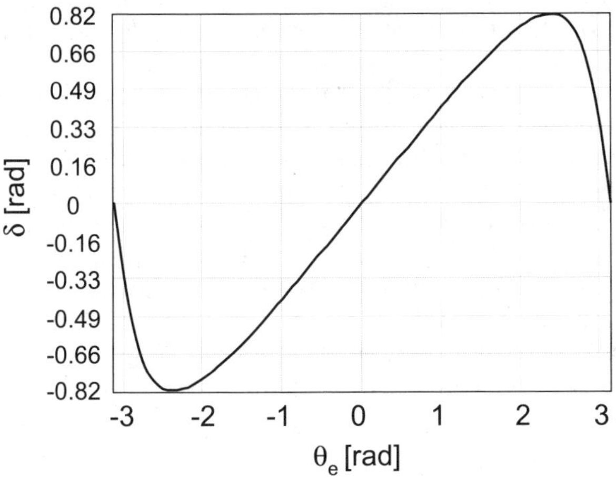

Fig. 6 Resulting phase modulation (PM).

MATHEMATICAL MODEL OF PAS

Assume the reception of an ummodulated carrier to simplify the mathematical analysis of the system. We define the signal received by Ant. 1 as

$$\bar{y}_1 = A_1 \cos(\omega_c t) \quad (1)$$

and the signal received by Ant. 2 after the AM modulation block in Fig. 2 is defined as

$$\bar{y}_2 = A_2 \cos(\omega_c t + \theta_e) \cdot (1 + m\cos(\omega_r t)) \quad (2)$$

where A_1 and A_2 are the peak signal amplitudes in the two branches, ω_c is the carrier frequency, θ_e is the error angle between the two signal vectors, $m = \frac{A_r}{A_2}$ is the AM modulation index, A_r is the AM modulation amplitude, and ω_r is the dither tone frequency which is generated by the PAS system. The resulting signal after the summing block is given by

$$\bar{y}_1 + \bar{y}_2 = A_3 \cos(\omega_c t + \phi_3) \quad (3)$$

where the total amplitude is

$$A_3 = \sqrt{A_1^2 + A_2^2(1 + m\cos(\omega_r t))^2 + 2A_1A_2(1 + m\cos(\omega_r t))\cos\theta_e} \quad (4)$$

and the resulting phase is

$$\phi_3 = \arctan\left(\frac{\frac{A_2}{A_1}(1 + m\cos(\omega_r t))\sin\theta_e}{1 + (\frac{A_2}{A_1})(1 + m\cos(\omega_r t))\cos\theta_e}\right) \quad (5)$$

The output of an ideal FM demodulator is

$$D_{FM}(t) = \frac{1}{2\pi} \cdot K_D \cdot \frac{\partial \phi_3}{\partial t} \quad (6)$$

where K_D is the FM demodulator constant in V/kHz and

$$\frac{\partial \phi_3}{\partial t} = \frac{-\left(\frac{A_2}{A_1}\right) \cdot m \cdot \omega_r}{R(t)} \sin(\omega_r t)\sin(\theta_e) \quad (7)$$

where

$$R(t) = 1 + 2\frac{A_2}{A_1}(1 + m\cos(\omega_r t))\cos(\theta_e) + \left(\frac{A_2}{A_1}\right)^2 (1 + m\cos(\omega_r t))^2 \quad (8)$$

Substituting (7) into (6) yields

$$D_{FM}(t) = \frac{-1}{2\pi} \cdot K_D \cdot \frac{\left(\frac{A_2}{A_1}\right) \cdot m \cdot \omega_r}{R(t)} \sin(\omega_r t)\sin(\theta_e) \quad (9)$$

The output of the FM demodulator shows clearly that the amplitude is proportional to the sine of the error angle θ_e. Thus the FM detector output can be used as the control signal to reduce the phase difference between the two antenna signals as described previously by adjusting the phase control voltage until the detector output, at the dither frequency, goes to zero at which point the phase is aligned.

PAS PERFORMANCE UNDER MULTIPATH

The phase aligning system employs feedback to continuously correct for phase changes in the incoming signals. The control loop accomplishes this by always trying to null the phase modulation resulting from the constant AM modulation. This feedback loop has a bandwidth that is sufficient to track out slow varying fades in the signal but narrow enough to limit noise. Closed loop bandwidths of 20Hz are typical. This means this system will be able to respond in flat fading multipath conditions where the signal fades are relatively slow but will not be able to respond to the quick, frequency selective fades that result from long delay reflections (i.e. τ >3μsec) [2]. A snapshot simulation of PAS performance, using the VisSim (registered trademark) software package, in flat fading environment is shown in Fig. 7. Fig. 6(a) shows Ant1, Ant2, and PAS signals amplitudes. It is evident that the PAS output has higher amplitude than both Ant1 and Ant2 signals. The demodulated output is shown in Fig. 7(b) for each antenna signal. The PAS performs well in this kind of environment.

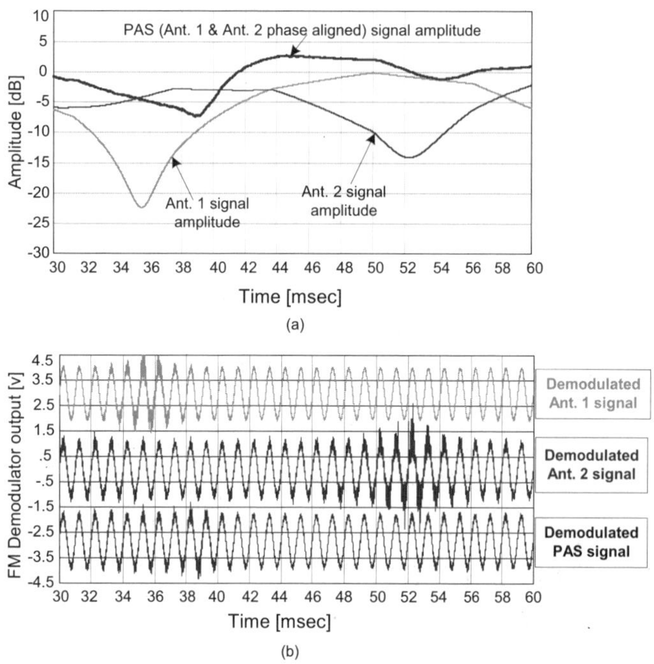

Fig. 7 Example of PAS performance in flat fading environment. (a) Ant. 1, Ant. 2 and PAS signal amplitudes, (b) Demodulated output for each antenna signal and PAS signal. A DC offset was applied to each signal so they could be individually identified.

On the other hand, when a strong reflection of the desired signal is present with long time delay, the PAS does not improve the situation because of its slow response as mentioned above [2]. This is shown clearly in Fig. 8 where the demodulated output of PAS is also distorted due to the sum of desired signal (amplitude is 1) and reflected signal (amplitude is 0.9 with 20usec delay relative to the desired signal).

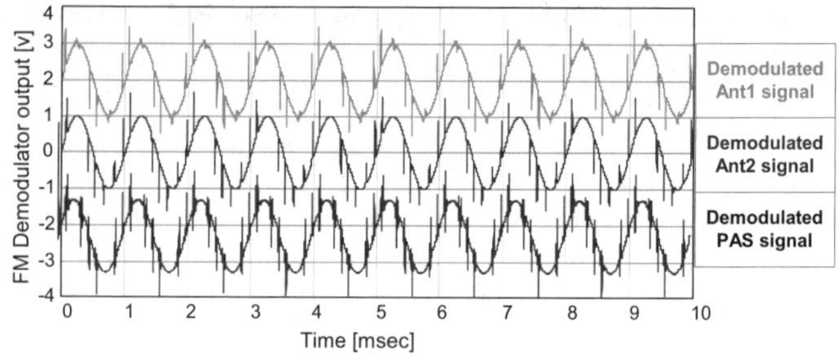

Fig. 8 PAS output (bottom trace) with a direct ray with amplitude of 1 and a strong reflection with 20uSec delay and amplitude of 0.9. The antennas are omni directional with gain of 1 and spaced half-wavelength apart at 100Mhz (1.5 meters).

The advantages of PAS are summarized next. First, It works with only a single receiver and can be implemented at the RF level as a single separate unit. Second, it performs well in flat fading environments where it tracks slowly varying fades.

The disadvantages of PAS are summarized next. First, it has a high noise figure due to the signal loss in the phase shifter when implemented in the RF section. One solution is to implement the system inside the receiver after the tuner in the Intermediate Frequency (IF) section as shown in Fig. 9. Here extra gain can be provided to compensate for the loss in the phase shifter without affecting the noise figure of the whole system. This requires a second RF front end however. The second disadvantage is that the system cannot eliminate the frequency selective multipath fading as explained earlier. The solution for this situation is an advanced dual tuner digital system implemented in a digital signal processor (DSP). It is described in the third paper of this three part series.

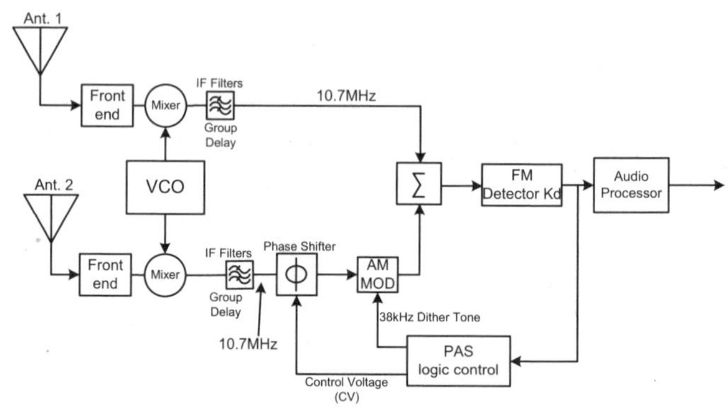

Fig. 9 PAS implementation in the IF (10.7MHz) section in an FM receiver.

SWITCHED ANTENNA DIVERSITY SYSTEM

SYSTEM DESCRIPTION

The correlation between the erroneous audio pulses and the RF amplitude minima is an excellent and fast indication for distortion as shown in Fig. 10 [4]. The Switching Antenna System (SAS) recognizes the above-mentioned correlation and is called a Fast Distortion Detector (FDD). The input to the FDD uses both the FM demodulator audio output and the carrier envelope amplitude voltage as shown in Fig. 11. The signals go through non-linear circuits so that the erroneous pulses and amplitude minima are differentiated and sharpened. The AND logic circuit indicates the presence of the erroneous pulse in the frequency deviation and amplitude minima in the RF carrier. When this occurs, the binary logic quickly switches to a different antenna (typically 30μsec) searching for an antenna with less distortion. The SAS provides good performance in multipath environments when implemented with 4 independent antennas. The SAS is cost effective diversity solution when more than 2 antennas are desired. It uses only one antenna for reception at any instant in time, while the other antennas do not contribute to the demodulated signal. The system has been implemented with a single receiver and up to four antennas.

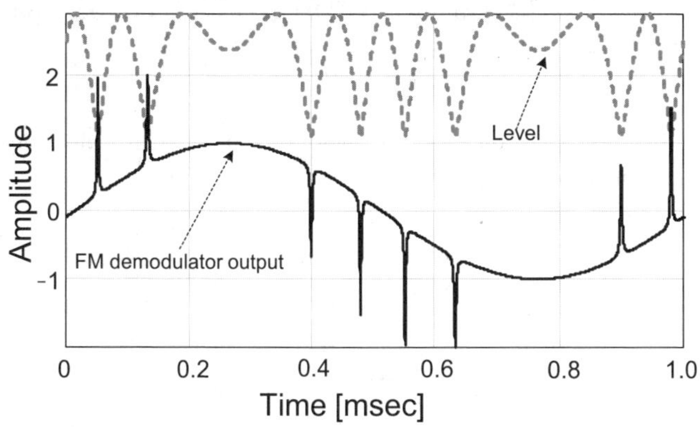

Fig. 10 FM demodulator and Level outputs in frequency selective multipath.

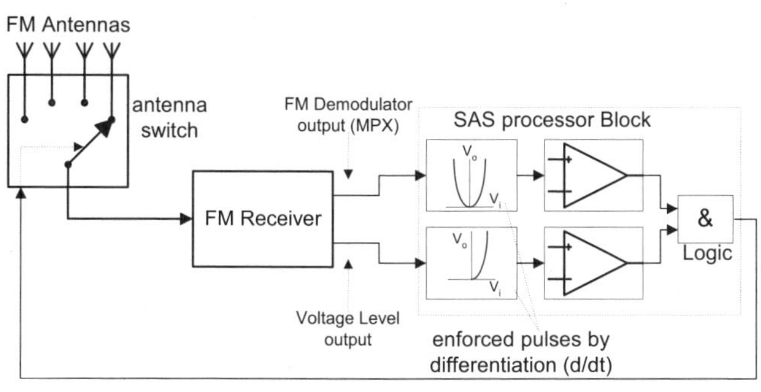

Fig. 11 Switched antenna diversity system [4].

Mathematical Model of SAS

Consider the Rayleigh probability density function

$$p(v) = \frac{2v}{\overline{v^2}} e^{-\frac{v^2}{\overline{v^2}}} \tag{10}$$

where $\overline{v^2} = E\{v^2\}$ is the mean-square of the received voltage. The probability that the received voltage v is less or equal than a V_{min} (threshold voltage) is

$$q = P(v \le V_{min}) = 1 - e^{-\frac{V_{min}^2}{\overline{v^2}}} \tag{11}$$

and the probability that the received voltage v is above V_{min} is

$$P(v > V_{min}) = e^{-\frac{V_{min}^2}{\overline{v^2}}} = 1 - q \tag{12}$$

A simulation example of the resultant voltage envelope v_{SAS} for a two-antenna switched diversity system is shown in Fig. 12. V_{min} was set to –10dB in the simulation. Ant.1 V_1 and Ant.2 V_2 signal amplitudes are Rayleigh distributed and indistinguishable.

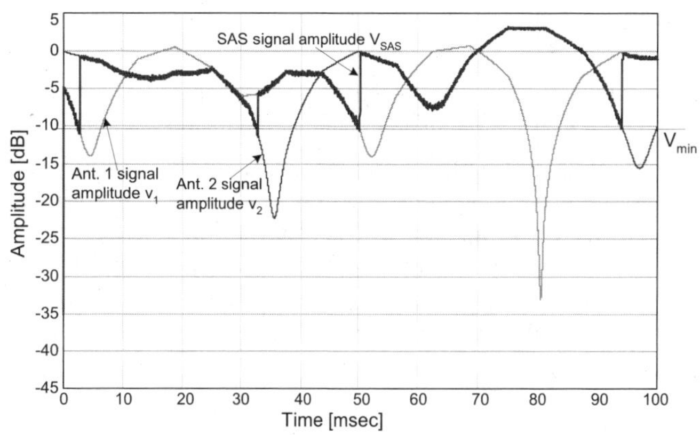

Fig. 12 Resultant envelope v_{SAS} of two-antenna switched diversity system.

The distribution of v_{SAS} for any arbitrary level B is given by [8-9]

$$P(v_{SAS} \le B) = \begin{cases} P_v(B) - q + q \cdot P_v(B) & B > V_{min} \\ q \cdot P_v(B) & B \le V_{min} \end{cases} \tag{13}$$

where

$$P_v(B) = 1 - e^{\frac{-B^2}{\overline{v^2}}} \tag{14}$$

The distribution of v_{SAS} for several V_{min} values is shown in Fig. 13. The ideal distribution of two-antenna selection diversity is also plotted for comparison. It can be realized that the switched diversity has V_{min} break points. Above V_{min}, the distribution merges quickly with a single Rayleigh branch. Below V_{min}, the distributions follow the Rayleigh slope with V_{min} delta displacement.

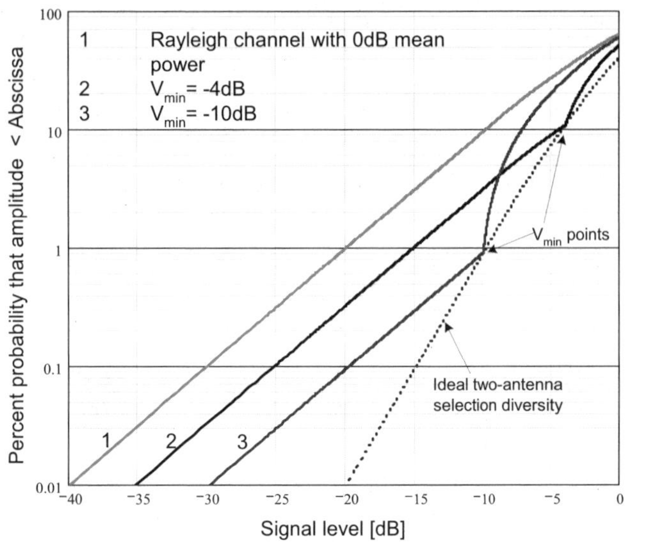

Fig. 13 Cumulative Distribution Function of two-antenna switched diversity.

SAS PERFORMANCE UNDER MULTIPATH

A simulation example snapshot using VisSim (registered trademark) of the switched diversity performance in Rayleigh field is shown in Fig. 14(a). Fig. 14(b) shows the demodulated output which clearly shows the signal improvement over a single antenna. The point at which the system will switch to another antenna, V_{min}, is set to –10dB.

In a frequency selective multipath situation, switched diversity outperforms PAS due to its ability to reduce the spikes (due to multiapth) in the demodulated output. A simulation example is shown in Fig. 15 where the exact signal conditions for the PAS of Fig. 8 were used. Fig. 15 shows the output of SAS which clearly shows the reduction of the spikes that were caused by multipath. The simulation was done with no filter in the signal path, i.e. no delay. When implementing a SAS, a minimum delay should be used to obtain close to optimum results. Reference [8] shows a degradation of the distribution function of V_{SAS} with fixed delay.

A disadvantage of the system is in weak signal conditions where the repetition rate of switching increases to a point where the switching itself causes audio disturbances. It can be improved with a good impulse noise blanker to mask the audible switching noise in the receiver. This requires synchronization between the SAS and receiver units. The next generation of SAS addresses these issues and provides significant improvement over the old system. The reader can also refer to [4-9] for more detailed information on the SAS.

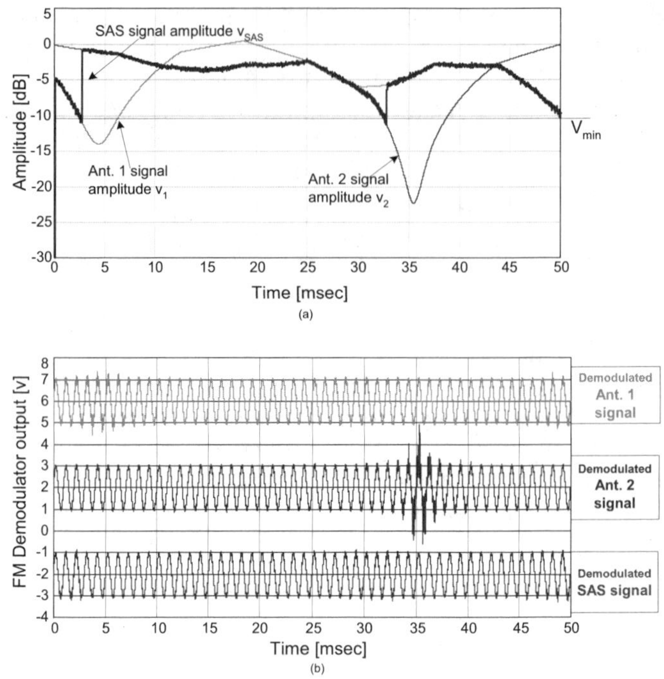

Fig. 14 A simulation example snapshot of the Switched diversity system output with V_{min} = -10dB.

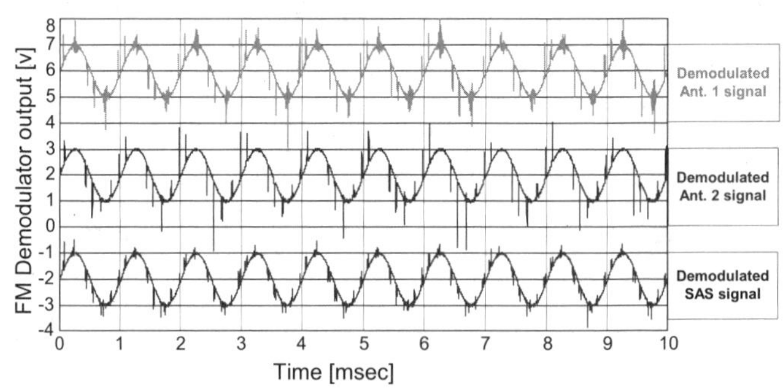

Fig. 15 SAS output (bottom trace) with a direct ray with amplitude of 1 and a strong reflection with 20uSec delay and amplitude of 0.9. The antennas are omni directional with gain of 1 and spaced half-wavelength apart at 100Mhz (1.5 meters).

CONCLUSION

PAS and SAS are existing analog FM diversity systems. The SAS is a cost effective solution when more than 2 antennas are desired. It requires a single receiver and an external switching unit. The PAS is also a cost effective solution when two antennas are available. It will provide acceptable performance in most signal conditions except frequency selective multipath. It can be implemented in the RF section with an external unit and a single receiver. It also can be implemented inside the receiver unit in the IF section but this requires two RF front ends.

ACKNOWLEDGMENTS

The authors would like to extend their gratitude to Steve Alverson, Delphi Corporation, Electronics & Safety systems, for help with editing this text.

REFERENCES

[1] D. G. Brennan, "Linear Diversity Combining Techniques", Proceedings of the IRE, Vol. 47, pp.1075-1102, June 1959.

[2] R. S. Shatara, "Combined Switched and Phase Aligned Multi-Antenna Diversity System for Signal-Error-Reduction in Mobile Receiving Systems", Ph.D. thesis, University of Bundeswehr, Munich Germany, January 2003.

[3] Kock, B. and Kennedy, R.,"Diversity receiver for FM stereo utilizing a pilot tone multiple for phase alignment of received signals",} Delphi Delco Electronics, U.S. Patent No. 5,517,686, 1996

[4] Lindenmeier H. K., Manner E. J., University of the Bundeswehr Munich, Germany; Sessink F., Philips Car Audio Development in Eindhoven/Holland, "FM Antenna Diversity Experiments in Philips Car Radios in Theory and Practice", Society of Automotive Engineers, Inc. 1986 Nr. 850021.H.

[5] R. Leopold, "Mobile Rundfunkempfangstechnik", Habilitationsschrift zur Erteilung der Lehrbefugnis in der Fakultaet fuer Elektrotechnik der Universitaet der Bundeswehr Muenchen, February 1995.

[6] H. K. Lindenmeier, E. J. Manner, University of the Bundeswehr Munich, Germany; F. Sessink, Philips Car Audio Development in Eindhoven/Holland, "FM Antenna Diversity Experiments in Philips Car Radios in Theory and Practice", Society of Automotive Engineers, Inc. 1986 Nr. 850021.

[7] W. E. Shortall, "A Switched Diversity Receiving System for Mobile Radio", IEEE Trans. on Communications, Vol. Com 21 No. 11, 1973.

[8] C. William Jakes, "Microwave Mobile communications", IEEE Press, Reissued edition 1994 (original edition 1974)

[9] Lee W. C. Y., "Mobile Communication Engineering", McGraw-Hill, Second Edition 1998.

CONTACT

Dr. Raed Shatara began his career at Delphi in 1992 after receiving a BSEE from Western Michigan University. He received the M.S. EE degree from Purdue University, IN, 1998. Raed received the Delphi fellowship in 1999 to pursue a Ph.D. EE from the Bundeswehr University Munich, Germany, which he completed in January 2003. He initially worked on the Phase Aligning System (PAS) and FM receivers. Currently, he is working on advanced diversity systems and next generation receivers. His research interests are in mobile communications, RF receiver design, receiver diversity and signal processing. He has one patent and recently filed for 5 new inventions for his work on diversity systems. He is currently in the RF Design Group at the Electronics and Safety division of Delphi Corporation. (Raed.s.shatara@delphi.com)

Jeff Marrah is a Principal Technical Fellow at Delphi Electronics and Safety in Kokomo, Indiana. He began his career at Delphi in 1981 after receiving a BSEE from Michigan Technological University. He received a MSEE from Purdue University in 1985. Jeff's initial programs were hybrid electronic spark control and mass airflow sensors. He then spent six years as a BiCMOS mixed signal IC design engineer working on radio IC's. In 1991 he became the manager of the RF Technologies Development Group responsible for all tuner chipset and applications development for Delphi AM / FM radios, Satellite Digital Audio Receivers and 2-way satellite modems. He has nineteen patents, one trade secret and one defensive publication for his work in the radio field and was inducted into the Delphi Innovation Hall of Fame in 1998. (Jeffrey.j.marrah@delphi.com)

DEFINITIONS, ACRONYMS, ABBREVIATIONS

MRC: Maximal Ratio Combiner
EGC: Equal Gain Combiner
SD: Selection Diversity
PAS: Phase Aligning System
SAS: Switched Antenna System
DSP: Digital Signal Processor
RF: Radio Frequency
IF: Intermediate Frequency
PLL: Phase locked loop
AM: Amplitude modulation
FM: Frequency modulation
PM: Phase modulation
m: AM index [%]
L+R: Left audio channel plus right audio channel
VCO: Voltage controlled oscillator
E{.}: Expected value operator (mean value)

2007-01-1734

Automotive FM Diversity Systems, Part III: Digital Systems

Raed S. Shatara, Mathew A. Boytim and Jeffrey J. Marrah
Delphi Corporation, Delphi Electronics & Safety

ABSTRACT

This paper represents Part III of a three part series on automotive FM diversity systems. Part I (2007-01-1731) focuses on a review of propagation channel modeling and multipath fading. Part II (2007-01-1732) deals with analog diversity systems which have been developed to combat the effects of this fading in an FM broadcast signal and Part III discusses new digital implementations of FM diversity systems that have been designed in DSP algorithms.

This paper investigates the performance of digital implementations of the Constant Modulus Algorithm (CMA) and switched diversity for two-antenna system in frequency selective multipath (long-delay) fading. It compares their performances to the analog Phase Aligning System (PAS) under the same signal conditions.

INTRODUCTION

In part II of the three part series we discussed the analog systems implementations and performance in different multipath situations. We analyzed the Phase Aligning System (PAS) performance under multipath conditions. The PAS was designed to combat flat fading but it suffers in frequency selective multipath. This paper describes the implementation of the Constant Modulus Algorithm (CMA) for a two-antenna FM system and a two-antenna single tuner switched diversity system. Both systems performances were compared to PAS in the presence of frequency selective multipath fading.

DUAL TUNER CONSTANT MODULUS ALGORITHM

Combining (controlled summation) signals from multiple antennas offers the advantage that directionality of the antenna system can be achieved and interferers (multipath rays) can potentially be suppressed by creating a null in the antenna pattern in the direction of the multipath interferer.
For narrowband modulation, antenna combining is accomplished by adjusting the amplitudes and phases of the individual antenna signals prior to summation. The gain and phase applied to each antenna signal are equivalent to complex weighting in the complex baseband model and are referred to as simply the antenna or combining 'weights'. The weights are continuously adapted (adjusted) to optimize certain reception performance metrics.
The method of determining the combining weights varies with the application, but the case of mobile reception of broadcast FM is particularly challenging because the combining must be adapted as the vehicle moves. The adaptation is 'blind' (no cooperation from the transmitter), and the signal is analog (signal imperfections are difficult to mask). A characteristic of FM modulation is that the modulated waveform has constant modulus (amplitude) as shown in Fig. 1, which provides prior knowledge about the transmitted signal [1-2].

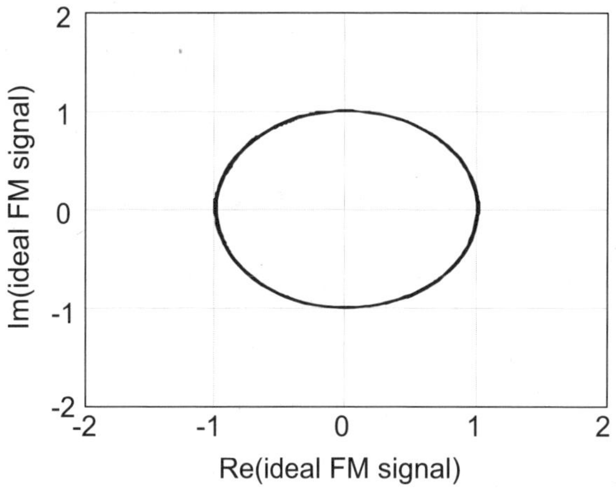

Fig. 1 Ideal FM complex baseband signal.

However, in a multipath reception environment, the received signal no longer possesses this constant modulus property because of flat or frequency selective fading. Thus the complex baseband signal trajectory is no longer a circle but a complicated spiral pattern as shown in Fig. 2. This provides information about the reception environment that can be used to determine the combining weights. The CMA is an efficient algorithm that allows adaptation of the diversity system parameters based on amplitude variation of known constant amplitude signals. For the two-antenna case with a direct and single delayed reflection, which is under consideration here, it is always possible to position a null in the direction of the multipath interferer.

Note that for an incident plane wave, only the phase of the received signal will differ between the two antennas and hence combining weights can always be found such that the signals cancel in the combined output. However, while this solution does in fact satisfy the constant modulus constraint, it does not guarantee that the CMA algorithm will adapt to this solution and, in general, the CMA solution is not unique. For example, the null could be placed in the direction of the direct path instead of the reflected path and still satisfy the CMA constraint.

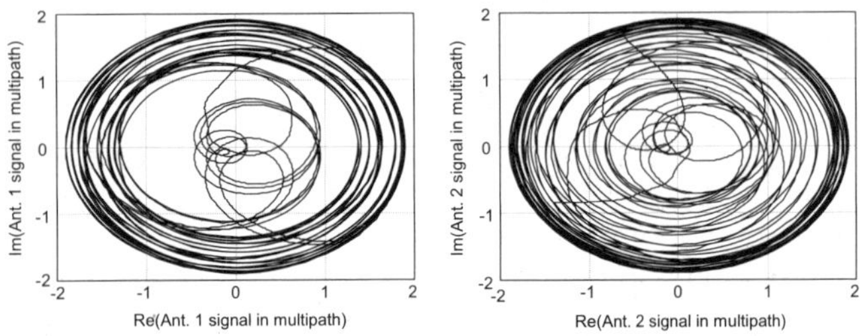

Fig. 2 FM Complex baseband signal in multipath.

Fig. 3 shows a two antenna combining system with the CMA update block implemented in a Digital Signal Processor (DSP). The system requires two front ends.

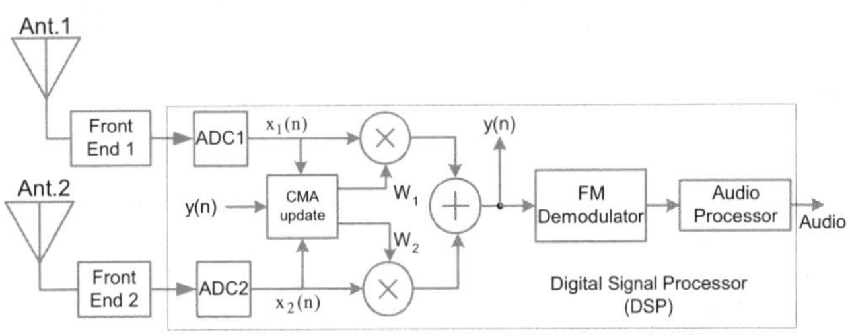

Fig. 3 Two-antenna CMA combining system.

The objective of CMA is to determine the antenna combining weights that minimize the cost function $J_{CMA_{p,q}}$, which is defined as [1 -2]

$$J_{CMA_{p,q}} = E\left\{\left||y(n)|^p - R^p\right|^q\right\} \tag{1}$$

where R is the desired modulus (called the Godard radius) and p and q are arbitrary positive integers that define a class of CMA algorithms. The output $y(n)$ is given by

$$y(n) = \mathbf{W}^{\mathbf{H}}\,\mathbf{x(n)} \tag{2}$$

where $\mathbf{W}^{\mathbf{H}}$ is the Hermitian (conjugate transpose) weight vector and $\mathbf{x(n)}$ is the input vector. The choice of (p,q) is somewhat arbitrary and particular choice of (p,q) yields a specific CMA cost function called CMA (p,q). (p,q) are usually chosen for computational convenience with (2,2) and (1,2) being popular choices. CMA (2,2) was chosen for simplicity and it is easy to implement in a digital signal processor. In addition, assume the Godard radius R = 1.

The CMA cost function can be minimized with the Stochastic Gradient Descent (SGD) technique using the gradient operator ∇ as follows

$$\begin{aligned}\nabla J_{CMA_{2,2}}(\mathbf{W}) &= 2E\left\{(|y(n)|^2 - 1)\right\}\nabla|y(n)|^2 \\ &= 4E\left\{(|y(n)|^2 - 1)\right\} y(n)^*\,\mathbf{x(n)}\end{aligned} \tag{3}$$

By replacing the stochastic gradient with the 'instantaneous' gradient (dropping the E[.] operator) an efficient least mean square (LMS) like algorithm suitable for real-time implementation is obtained. Therefore, the weight update equation becomes

$$\begin{aligned}\mathbf{W(n+1)} &= \mathbf{W(n)} - \mu\nabla J_{CMA_{2,2}}(\mathbf{W}) \\ &= \mathbf{W(n)} - \mu\,\mathbf{x(n)}\cdot\varepsilon(n)\cdot y(n)^*\end{aligned} \tag{4}$$

where $\varepsilon(n) = (|y(n)|^2 - 1)$ and μ is the adaptation step size which affects speed, quality, and stability of convergence.

Because the CMA cost function is phase invariant, any 'rotation' of a solution yields another solution, which is equally as good, and hence the CMA solution is inherently non-unique. The particular solution to which the algorithm converges will depend on the initial value of the weights and will tend toward the 'nearest' solution. While this ambiguity could be resolved by further constraining the solution, this degree of freedom tends to improve the transient behavior by allowing convergence to a solution that is nearest the current state (minimum time solution). The CMA solution restores the constant modulus (CM) property of the signal as shown in Fig. 4. It shows the restored CM of the signals of Fig. 2.

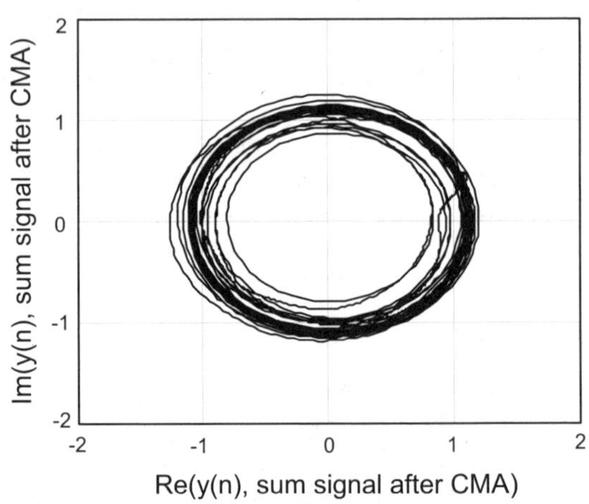

Fig. 4 Output y(n) of CMA.

SINGLE TUNER TWO-ANTENNA SWITCHED DIVERSITY SYSTEM

The basic block diagram of the switched diversity system is shown in Fig. 5, which requires one front end only. This implementation is more economical than the dual tuner CMA system. The switched diversity algorithm block shown in Fig. 5 uses both the FM demodulator and the carrier envelope amplitude voltage level outputs. The correlation between the erroneous pulses (or spikes) of the FM demodulator output and the amplitude minima of the level that occurs in a frequency selective multipath situation is an excellent indication of a distortion event. The switched diversity algorithm block recognizes the above-mentioned correlation and reacts fast to select a new antenna as shown by the dotted lines to the antenna switches.

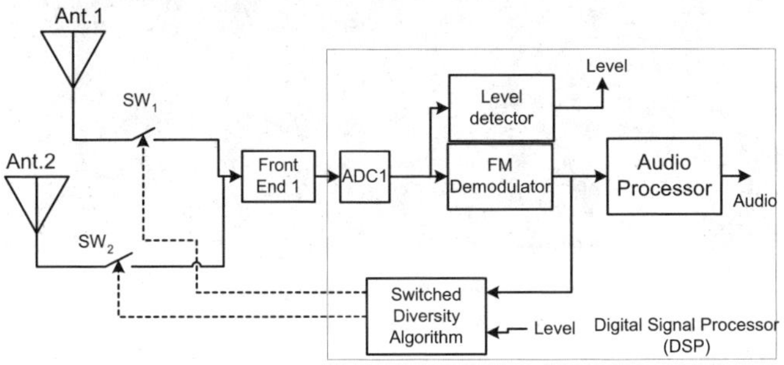

Fig. 5 Single tuner two-antenna switched diversity system.

SIMULATED RESULTS

All simulations were done using the baseband model in Appendix B with $A_1 = A_2 = 1$, $B_1 = B_2 = 0.9$, $\theta_d = 16^\circ$, $\theta_i = 42^\circ$, modulating frequency =1kHz, frequency deviation =75kHz, and time delay τ in μsec. Fig. 6 shows an initial simulation of the FM demodulator output for each diversity system and each demodulated single antenna output (single receiver). A time delay of $20\mu\,\mathrm{sec}$ is applied. The distortion factor was calculated after a 15kHz low-pass filter as shown in Appendix B.

The distortion factor of demodulated Ant. 1 signal is 2.7% and Ant. 2 signal is 2.9% (single receiver).

The switched diversity demodulated output distortion factor is 1.25% and it exhibits lower distortion than a single antenna in this situation due to some avoidance of multipath. Some of the spikes that are shown in the switched diversity output are due to the switching noise. Blanking the pulses or spikes (by means of sample & hold) that the switched diversity produces can reduce the evident distortion factor to less than 1.0%.

The phase aligning system (PAS) has a distortion factor of 1.8%, which is less than a single antenna but could be higher in some situations. This is expected because the system control loop is slow and cannot co-phase the two antenna signals in a frequency selective multipath fading. Therefore, it will add the antenna signals with some arbitrary phase set by the phase shifter and it will not improve the distortion factor dramatically when the time delay is greater than 3μsec.

The demodulator output of the dual tuner CMA has a distortion factor of 0.16%. This is significantly lower distortion than the other systems due to the cancellation of the interference (reflection). All of the other systems try to avoid distortion but do not have the means of solving the root cause of the distortion, which is the strong signal reflection. The CMA dual tuner can put a null in the direction of the reflection or the null can be placed in the direction of the direct path and still satisfy the CMA constraint. Either way, we obtain a dramatically reduced distortion factor as the simulation shows.

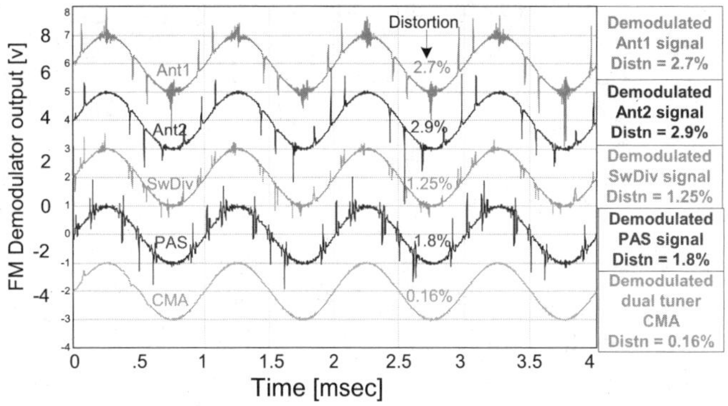

Fig. 6 Simulated FM demodulator output signal of Ant. 1, Ant. 2, SwDiv, PAS, and dual tuner CMA.

MEASURED RESULTS

The above-mentioned systems' performances in multipath were compared in the laboratory with the hardware setup that is shown in Fig. 7. It includes an RF generator, mulltipath generator, 2 antenna dummies, the diversity system under test (DSUT), and a digital scope. The RF generator feeds the multipath generator with the desired RF signal. The multipath generator splits the RF signal into two paths, a direct path and delayed path. The direct path is applied to a main attenuator which feeds a three-way RF splitter. Each output of the direct signal splitter is added to the each output of the delayed signals after they go through attenuators and phase shifters. Two of the delayed signals are applied to an attenuator and phase shifter before they are combined with direct signals. The main delayed signal is only applied to an attenuator before it is combined with the direct signal so that the system provides a reference signal at channel 1 output. The delay block can provide 5, 10, 20, 40, or 80μsec. The attenuators provide attenuation from 0 to 12.7dB in 0.1dB steps.

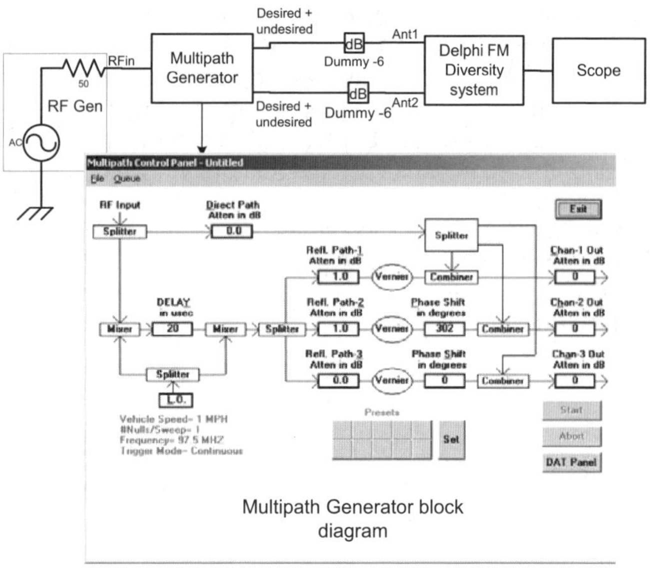

Fig. 7 Laboratory hardware test setup.

Each diversity system was tested with the same signal conditions as in the simulated results section. Fig. 8 shows the results of the FM demodulator output for each system. The digital FM demodulator output signal of Ant.1, Ant. 2, Switched diversity, and dual tuner CMA is from a 9-bit DAC within the DSP IC. The PAS has an analog FM demodulator. For the digital system, the spikes in the output are limited by the filtering in the DSP DAC.

Single receiver distortion measurement of Ant. 1 and Ant. 2 signals are similar to the simulation of 2.7% and 2.9%, respectively. This correlates very well the simulation results.

The switched diversity system actually reduces the distortion slightly to 1.6% as shown in Fig. 8 which is a good correlation with the simulation results. It does not avoid the distortion spikes completely due to some inherent delay in the implementation of the system as expected. Nevertheless, it is an improvement over a single antenna performance.

The PAS measures a distortion factor of 1.7% in this case. It could measure significantly higher distortion values especially at higher modulating frequencies. This is expected because the system control loop is slow and cannot co-phase the two antenna signals in a frequency selective multipath situation.

The distortion factor of the dual tuner CMA system measures 0.4%. This correlates with the simulation and is shown clearly in Fig. 8. The dual tuner CMA reduces the distortion factor significantly as expected because it places a null in the direction of the delayed signal (reflection).

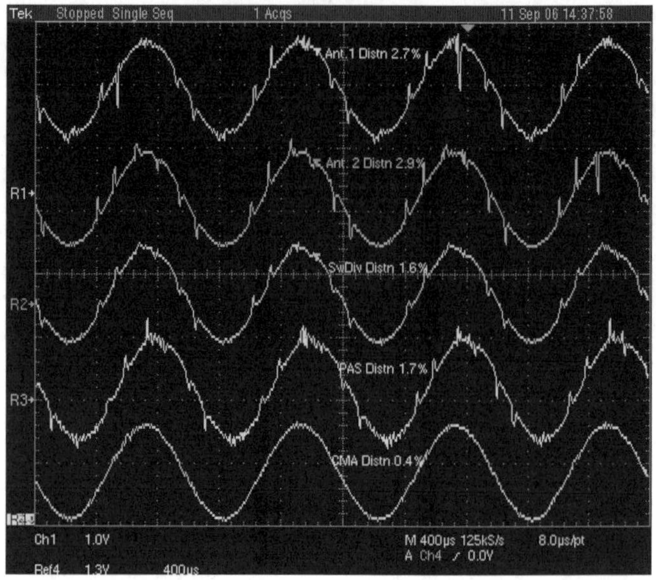

Fig. 8: Measured FM demodulator output signal of Ant.1, Ant.2, switched diversity, PAS, and dual tuner CMA.

CONCLUSION

Two digital FM diversity systems were implemented in DSP's, the dual tuner CMA and switched diversity system. Each system was simulated with the VisSim communication system modeling program. The DSP algorithms were implemented in hardware and the performance was measured in the lab. The measurements correlate well with the simulation. The dual tuner CMA outperforms the other systems in multipath environment.

ACKNOWLEDGMENTS

The authors would like to extend their gratitude to Jim Arnett, Delphi Corporation, Electronics & Safety systems, for implementing the multipath generator, and to Steve Alverson, also of Delphi, for help with editing this text.

REFERENCES

[1] D. M. Godard, "Self-recovering equalization and carrier tracking in two-dimensional data communications systems", IEEE Transaction on Communications, vol. COM-28, Nov. 1980.

[2] J. R. Treichler and B. G. Agee, " A new approach to multipath correction of constant modulus signals", IEEE Trans. Acoust., speech, Signal Processing, vol ASSP-31, pp. 459-472, Apr. 1983.

[3] S. Haykin, "An Introduction to Analog and Digital Communications", Wiley 1989.

[4] R. S. Shatara, "Combined Switched and Phase Aligned Multi-Antenna Diversity System for Signal-Error-Reduction in Mobile Receiving Systems", Ph.D. thesis, University of Bundeswehr, Munich Germany, January 2003.

CONTACT

Dr. Raed Shatara began his career at Delphi in 1992 after receiving a BSEE from Western Michigan University. He received the M.S. EE degree from Purdue University, IN, 1998. Raed received the Delphi fellowship in 1999 to pursue a Ph.D. EE from the Bundeswehr University Munich, Germany, which he completed in January 2003. He initially worked on the Phase Aligning System (PAS) and FM receivers. Currently, he is working on advanced diversity systems and next generation receivers. His research interests are in mobile communications, RF receiver design, receiver diversity and signal processing. He has one patent and recently filed for 5 new inventions for his work on diversity systems. He is currently in the RF Design Group at the Electronics and Safety division of Delphi Corporation. (Raed.s.shatara@delphi.com)

Matt Boytim is a Technical Fellow at Delphi Electronics and Safety in Kokomo, Indiana. He hired into Delphi in 1984 after receiving a BSEE from the University of Pittsburgh. He received a MSEE from Purdue University in 1988 and attended Carnegie Mellon University as a General Motors Fellow in 1989. Matt initially investigated algorithms, hardware, software, architectures, data converters, and ASIC's for digital audio processing applications. He later developed algorithms for DSP based active noise cancellation systems for vehicular applications. In the mid 90's he developed a high speed fiber optic data network for vehicle infotainment applications. Since then Matt has developed DSP algorithms and architectures for digital and digitized radio applications. Most recently he has developed DSP algorithms for car radio applications. (Matt.a.boytim@delphi.com)

Jeff Marrah is a Principal Technical Fellow at Delphi Electronics and Safety in Kokomo, Indiana. He began his career at Delphi in 1981 after receiving a BSEE from Michigan Technological University. He received a MSEE from Purdue University in 1985. Jeff's initial programs were hybrid electronic spark control and mass airflow sensors. He then spent six years as a BiCMOS mixed signal IC design engineer working on radio IC's. In 1991 he became the manager of the RF Technologies Development Group responsible for all tuner chipset and applications development for Delphi AM / FM radios, Satellite Digital Audio Receivers and 2-way satellite modems. He has nineteen patents, one trade secret and one defensive publication for his work in the radio field and was inducted into the Delphi Innovation Hall of Fame in 1998. (Jeffrey.j.marrah@delphi.com)

APPENDIX A

Switching Noise of a two-Antenna Switched Diversity System

The disadvantage of the switched diversity system is the switching noise pulses that it produces due to abrupt phase changes when it switches between the two antennas. To illustrate this point, consider the simple switched diversity system shown in Figure I. This system has access to both antenna levels at the same time and it selects the antenna that has the higher level at each sample. Mathematically the signal level of each antenna can be calculated by taking the absolute value of the sum of the direct and reflected signals. Appendix B shows the signal definitions in Figure I.

The resulting spikes that are present in the FM demodulator output as seen in Fig. 5 (Ant1 or Ant2 signal) are due to long delay multipath. They occur at minimum level transitions. On the other hand, the spikes that are produced due the abrupt phase jumps when switching between antennas are shown in Figure II. It is evident that switched diversity avoids the multipath spikes but it introduces its own switching transient noise. Figure II illustrates the transition between antennas 1 and 2 as the levels fluctuate. The spikes are evident in the demodulated 1kHz tone (75kHz deviation, $A_1 = A_2 = 1, B_1 = B_2 = 0.9, \tau = 30\mu\,\text{sec}$). The spikes caused by switching can be blanked by means of a sample & hold to improve the audio distortion. In most switched diversity systems in production for mobile automotive applications the antenna switching circuitry is located outside the receiver near the antennas.

To minimize wire harness cost and weight the switching logic signal is not passed to the tuner in the receiver. Thus to adequately "blank" the impulses generated by the switched diversity system an "impulse noise blanker" circuit within the receiver must provide it's own means of detecting the incoming impulse noise and then provide a sample and hold which is designed to provide the correct hold time that is synchronized such that the blank window completely covers the duration of the impulse. This is not a trivial task which generates it's own set of challenges. This sample & hold topic is outside the scope of this work.

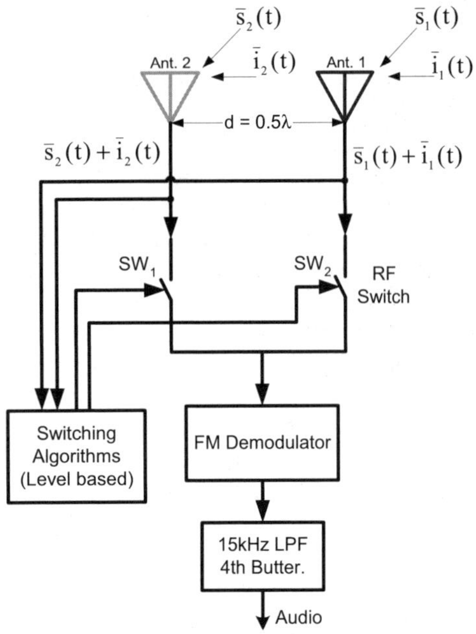

Figure I: Level dependent switched diversity system.

The signal level of antenna 1 L_{Ant1} is given by

$$L_{Ant1} = \left|\bar{s}_1(t) + \bar{i}_1(t)\right| = \sqrt{A_1^2 + B_1^2 + 2A_1B_1\cos(\phi(t) - \phi(t-\tau))} \tag{A1}$$

Similarly, the signal level of antenna 2 L_{Ant2} is given by

$$L_{Ant2} = \left|\bar{s}_2(t) + \bar{i}_2(t)\right| = \sqrt{A_2^2 + B_2^2 + 2A_2B_2\cos(\phi(t) - \phi(t-\tau) + (\psi_d - \psi_i))} \tag{A2}$$

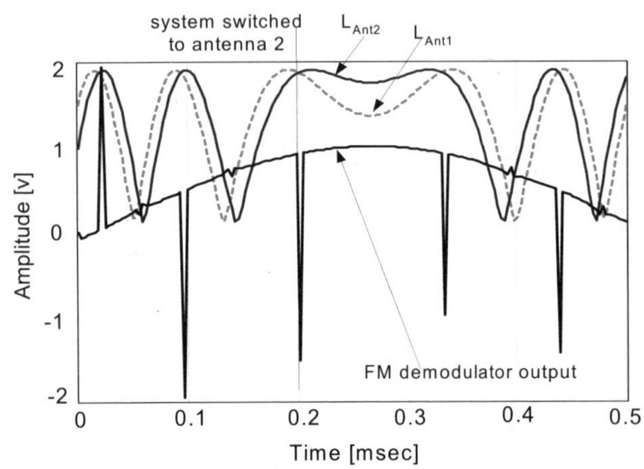

Figure II: Switching spikes caused by abrupt changes in RF phase and amplitude between the two antennas.

APPENDIX B

Two-ray Multipath Model

The block diagram of the mathematical model that is used to predict a two-antenna FM diversity system performance in multipath is shown in Figure III.

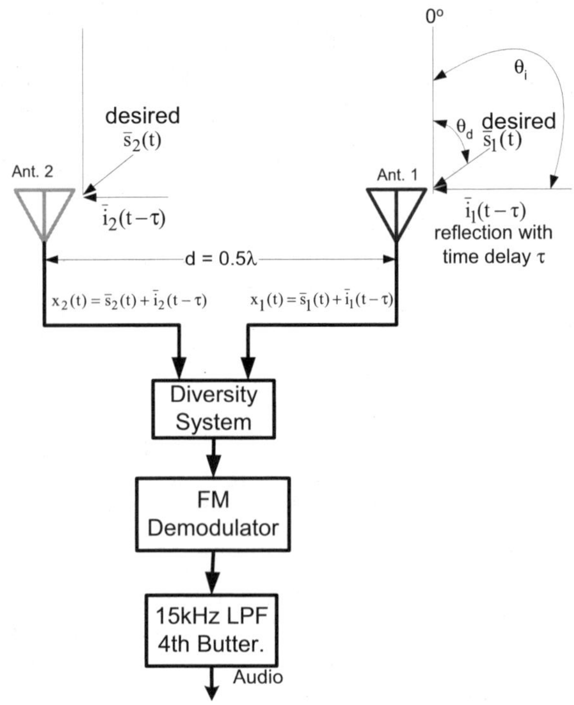

Figure III: Simulation Block Diagram

The antennas are spaced one-half wavelength apart at the carrier frequency f_c (100MHz for FM). The sum of the signals (desired signal and reflected signal) received by antenna 1 of Figure III represented as complex baseband is defined as

$$x_1(t) = \bar{s}_1(t) + \bar{i}_1(t-\tau) = A_1 e^{j\phi(t)} + B_1 e^{j\phi(t-\tau)} \tag{B1}$$

where $\tau = \text{Time delay [sec]}$ and

$\phi(t) =$ Modulating or message signal

$A_1, B_1 =$ Amplitudes

When $\bar{s}_1(t)$ impinges on the two antennas with an angle θ_d with respect to the normal axis, antenna 2 experiences phase shift with respect to antenna 1. The signal that has this extra phase shift ψ_d is represented by

$$\bar{s}_2(t) = A_2 e^{j(\phi(t) + \psi_d)} \tag{B2}$$

where

$$\psi_d = \left(\frac{2\pi \cdot d}{\lambda_o}\right)\sin\theta_d = \pi\sin\theta_d \tag{B3}$$

Similarly, the reflected signal experiences a similar phase shift ψ_i as it impinges on the antennas with angle

θ_i. The reflected signal $\bar{i}_2(t-\tau)$ received by the second antenna is given by

$$\bar{i}_2(t-\tau) = B_2 e^{j(\phi(t-\tau)+\psi_i)} \qquad \text{(B4)}$$

where

$$\psi_i = \left(\frac{2\pi \cdot d}{\lambda_o}\right)\sin\theta_i = \pi \sin\theta_i \qquad \text{(B5)}$$

The diversity system would be simulated with the signal conditions as in Figure III with an ideal FM demodulator. The distortion is calculated at the output of the 4th order 15kHz low pass filter.

This model assumes that the antennas have a gain of 1 and they are omni directional. It is possible to expand the model to include gain measurement of the antennas as a function of the azimuth angle. Reference [4] shows detailed method to include actual antenna measurement with the simulation.

DEFINITIONS, ACRONYMS, ABBREVIATIONS

CMA: Constant modulus algorithm
PAS: Phase Aligning System
SAS: Switched Antenna System
DSP: Digital Signal Processor
AM: Amplitude modulation
FM: Frequency modulation
PM: Phase modulation
ADC: Analog to digital converter
DAC: Digital to analog converter
SGD: Stochastic gradient descent
LMS: Least mean square
E{.}: Expected value operator (mean value)

2005-01-0569

Rapid Spherical Near-Field Antenna Measurements for Vehicle Applications

Janalee A. Graham
General Motors

Per O. Iversen
Satimo USA

ABSTRACT

As more wireless services such as satellite radio (SDARS), navigation systems, OnStar, and mobile telephones are installed on GM vehicles, there is a need to make quick and accurate vehicle antenna pattern measurements. The interaction between vehicle and antenna must be included to ensure accurate vehicle antenna measurements. This implies that the size of the effective antenna should include both the antenna and vehicle interaction dimensions. For the frequency range of 500 MHz to 6 GHz, one solution is to use a spherical near-field system. The Satimo rapid probe array technology was selected to develop a vehicle antenna test system (ATS), which minimizes test time and maintains data accuracy. The ATS was designed to operate inside of an existing GM electromagnetic compatibility (EMC) anechoic chamber equipped with a nine-meter turntable. It includes a fully autonomous transport and deployment system allowing the ATS hardware to be removed and the chamber returned to its EMC configuration. This paper presents the ATS design, summary of the verification test results, and a modal analysis showing vehicle to antenna interaction.

INTRODUCTION

Vehicle antenna pattern measurements have been performed for over 20 years at the General Motors Milford Proving Ground (MPG). Initially, the measurements were limited to AM and FM frequencies. In 1995, GM constructed an outdoor antenna range (MPG Range), which has the capability of testing 530 kHz to 3 GHz using a 5.5 m turntable covered by a radome. In 2000, the need to test in the SDARS band arose as XM satellite radios were installed on GM vehicles (12/01). Initial testing at the MPG Range showed that significant improvements were needed to use this facility for XM testing. In the interim, vehicle testing was done at Motorola's Schaumburg, IL facility [1].

To determine what type of facility GM needed, the effective dimension of an antenna on a vehicle, D, had to be determined. Once D was known, the far field separation equation, $2 \cdot D^2/\lambda$, could be used. This issue was discussed with the National Institute of Standards and Technology (NIST) during a videoconference (January of 2002). The group concluded that since the vehicle/antenna interaction is unknown, it should be assumed that D is the length of the vehicle. Based on this assumption, NIST recommended that GM obtain a spherical near-field measurement system.

GM submitted an order to purchase a Satimo spherical near-field system in April 2003. The Satimo ATS is housed in one of four newly constructed GM EMC anechoic chambers. The external dimensions of each of these hybrid chambers are: 19.9m (W) x 28.9m (L) x 9.14m (H) and include a 9m turntable. The ATS was completed and awarded XM certification the first quarter of 2004.

Figure 1. Photograph showing a vehicle installed in GM's ATS. *(Photograph courtesy of GM Milford Proving Ground)*

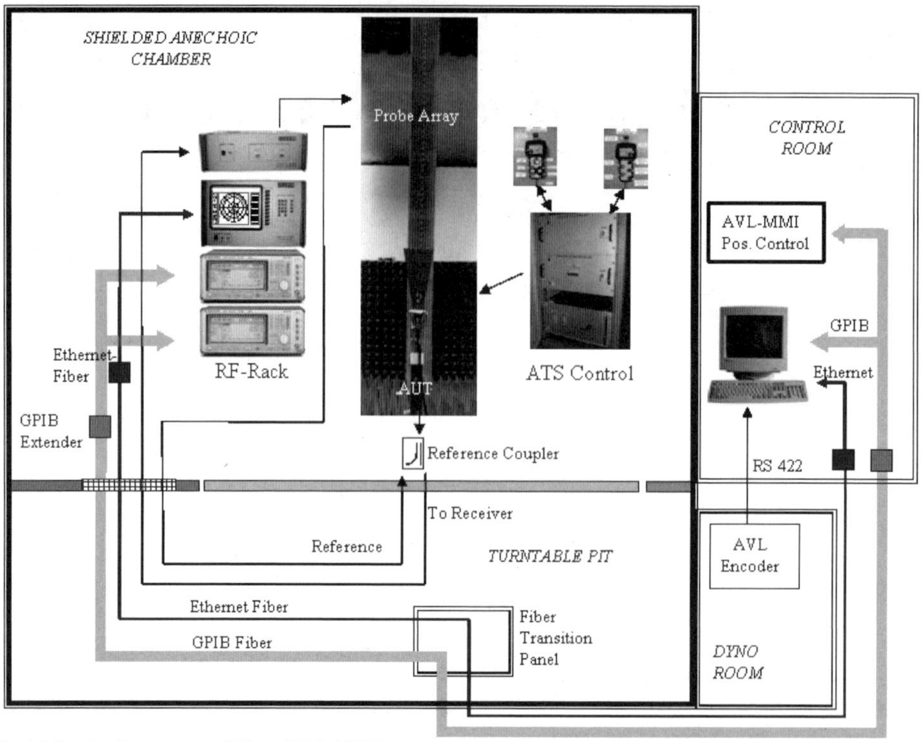

Figure 2. Simplified block diagram of the GM ATS

SYSTEM DESCRIPTION

A simplified block diagram of the ATS system is shown in Figure 2. The measurement system is based on Satimo's Stargate technology [2]. The system allows for near "real-time" measurement of the amplitude and phase at each probe location without the need for an expensive high frequency multiplexing network. Important system design goals were:

1. Maximize the re-use of the existing facilities at GM.
2. Minimize any degradation of the EMC chamber performance and avoid re-certification (e.g. normalized site attenuation) by having a completely removable measurement system.
3. Minimize time required to switch between EMC and ATS configurations.

The key system components and design challenges are described in the following paragraphs.

ANECHOIC CHAMBER

The main issue regarding the existing equipment was related to the performance of the anechoic chamber at microwave frequencies. The walls are covered with microwave absorbing materials designed for EMC applications. Additional EMC absorber was added to the wall opposite to the ATS to further reduce reflections. The EMC absorber has -28 dB normal incidence reflectivity at 6 GHz, whereas typical microwave absorber has greater than – 40 dB reflectivity. To eliminate the main specular reflections caused by reflections from the two closest walls, several movable microwave absorbing panels were also installed.

TURNTABLE

The existing 9m turntable had limited positioning control accuracy and only allowed for +/-190 degree of rotation. However, there was direct access to a high accuracy absolute position encoder. With the absence of an accurate positioning control system that could command the turntable to a precise position, it was necessary to do "on-the-fly" measurements.

A traditional mechanical "gantry arm" system as used by Motorola [1], with the same angular resolution, would require 100 turns of the turntable. Such a system would require at least three hours to complete a test instead of the five minutes achieved by the ATS.

The key components of the system are described in the following paragraphs.

PROBE ARRAY

The probe array is a segment of a circular arch with an internal radius of six meters. The key elements of the probe array are 103 dual-polarized measurement probes that are located at 1 degree spacing along the arch. The probes operate from 400 MHz to 6 GHz. The signals, from each probe, are collected via a passive power-combining network. The probes and the supporting RF and control electronics are embedded in a conformal multilayer absorbing material such that only the tips of the probes protrude.

PROBE ARRAY CONTROLLER

The Probe Array Controller (PAC) is the management unit of the probe array. It contains the IF receiver and an industrial PC with several dedicated interface cards. The PAC has a similar appearance and user interface to that of a network analyzer. The PAC displays the amplitude and phase of the vector field measured at each one of the probes, in real-time. All typical network analyzer display features are available. In automatic measurement mode, the PAC is fully controlled from the Data Acquisition and Control PC.

CONTROL AND PROCESSING SOFTWARE

All functions of the antenna measurement system are controlled via a PC and a software package called SAT_ENV. The software is written such that all functions can be either controlled via "point and click" menus or from the built in command shell. Complicated measurement campaigns, including post-processing, can be run automatically using macro commands or via Java scripts. A complete set of data visualization tools is included in the software.

DATA ACQUISITION SEQUENCE

The system collects near-field data through the following sequence:

1. Move azimuth turntable to +/- 185 degrees (whichever the turntable is closest to at the start of measurement)
2. Start the azimuth turntable in slow rotation mode (about 1.2 deg/sec)
3. Monitor the position encoder and for each one-degree in azimuth, trigger a scan of the probe array for each frequency, sequentially.

The total time required to read the encoder, set frequency, and sweep the 103 dual-polarized probes, including software overhead, is approximately 150 ms. The system is able to measure five frequencies in one rotation of the turntable.

SYSTEM VALIDATION AND SPECIFICATIONS

The ATS went through an extensive verification plan to ensure that all the requirements of the purchase agreement were met. Sections of the verification plan, prepared with inputs from References [3,4,5], are listed below. In addition, an uncertainty error budget was created.

CHAMBER MODIFICATION VERIFICATION

This section contained information on chamber scattering performance, minimum AUT height, vehicle ramp impact, and absorber layout verification.

ATS PERFORMANCE VERIFICATION

The key ATS performance requirements included frequency range, minimum sphere dimensions, peak gain, radiation pattern error, azimuth and elevation angle sampling, dynamic range, cross polarization isolation, third harmonic distortion, axial ratio, phase, antenna efficiency, field uniformity, and test time requirements. The maximum AUT dimensions are shown in Table 1.

Frequency (MHz)	500	800	2300	6000
X, Y AUT size (m)	8	9	4	1.6
* Z dimension is 1.0 – 3.0 m above the turntable				

Table 1. X and Y Maximum AUT Dimensions

Peak Gain Accuracy is specified to be:

500 MHz – 800 MHz maximum error of 1.1 dB
800 MHz – 6 GHz maximum error of 1.0 dB

Radiation Pattern Error (as normalized to 0 dB) is shown in Table 2.

Relative Pattern Level (dB) where $D_n = \lvert D(\theta,\phi)/D_{max} \rvert$	Measurement Uncertainty at 95% Confidence (dB)
0.0 to –5.0	$< \pm 0.25$
-5.0 to –30.0	$< \pm 0.1 \times (-D_n)$

Table 2. Radiation Pattern Error

ATS TRANSPORTATION VERIFICATION

This section discussed how to verify the transportation system requirements. Key requirements included; moving the arch from test position to stow position in under one hour, determining arch position accuracy, demonstrating all safety features were operational, and returning the chamber to its EMC configuration in under three hours.

TEST VEHICLE POSITIONING VERIFICATION

This section described verification of turntable functions, X, Y, and Z wobble for the turntable, and vehicle placement.

ATS FIELD UNIFORMITY VERIFICATION

This section covered field uniformity using various receive antennas placed throughout the test volume. Antennas were placed at the center and at the edges of minimum sphere, one to three meters above the turntable. Total variation was not allowed to exceed the ATS performance requirements.

ATS UNCERTAINTY BUDGET ANALYSIS

A detailed uncertainty budget was developed for the entire system [4]. The magnitude of each error for both peak gain and side lobe gain were measured and documented as part of the system verification process. The major categories contributing to the uncertainty budget are:

- RF measurement system
- ATS positioning system
- Near-field probes
- Environmental effects
- Reference antennas
- Measurement procedure

An example of an uncertainty budget for the case of a 2.3 GHz monopole antenna on a one-meter ground plane is shown in Table 3. This uncertainty budget refers to radiation pattern accuracy at 10 dB below peak pattern level and in the angular range of 20° to 90° above horizon.

CALIBRATION AND VERIFICATION RESULTS

A full account of all the tests performed under the verification plan is beyond the scope of this paper, but two of the main items are described below.

QUIET ZONE TESTS

One of the key tests was the evaluation of the performance of the existing anechoic chamber. The chamber was assessed by probing the quiet zone using a monopole over a 1m circular ground plane, as shown in Figure 3.

Figure 3. Photograph of a high precision Satimo monopole mounted on a light weight 1.0m diameter circular ground plane as used during the verification tests

The monopole was offset from the center of the turntable at various distances and measurements were taken for a full rotation of the azimuth turntable. The monopole sampled the field over a circular trajectory centered on the turntable. A monopole, which has a symmetrical pattern in the azimuth plane, should generate a constant field as a function of azimuth, except for path loss variations.

Radiation Pattern Uncertainty Budget
Monopole 2338MHz – Errors at 10dB from peak

	Uncertainty	(dB)	Method
1	Probe Gain	0.000	Estimated
2	Probe Polarization	0.004	Estimated
3	Relative Probe Pattern	0.100	Estimated
4	Probe Compensation Effects	0.000	Estimated
5	Probe Alignment	0.002	Measured
6	AUT Alignment	0.000	Estimated
7	Insertion Loss	0.000	Measured
8	Impedance Mismatch	0.000	Measured Analysis
9	Aliasing	0.000	Estimated
10	Solid Angle Truncation	0.250	Estimated Analysis
11	θ,ϕ Position Errors	0.120	Measured
12	r- Position Errors	0.147	Measured
13	Probe-AUT multiple reflections	0.000	Estimated
14	Non-Linearity of Receiver	0.100	Measured
15	I-Q Channel Imbalance	0.050	Measured
16	Cable Flexing	0.100	Measured
17	Drift	0.050	Measured
18	Leakage and Crosstalk	0.050	Measured
19	Room Scattering	0.228	Measured
20	Noise	0.080	Measured
21	Probe Array Amplitude Uniformity	0.056	Measured
22	Probe Array Phase Uniformity	0.053	Measured
	TOTAL UNCERTAINTY	0.448	(RSS)
	Coverage Factor (@ 95% Confidence)	2	
	EXPANDED UNCERTAINTY	**0.9**	**dB**

Table 3. Example of a radiation pattern uncertainty budget for a 2.3 GHz monopole antenna on a 1m ground plane.

Any perturbations in the field can be attributed to imperfections in the chamber design. Figure 4 shows the chamber performance at 20° above the horizon, where the peak reflections are approximately ±0.5dB. In summary, the maximum reflections are approximately ±1dB and occur at the horizon. The reflections decrease for higher elevation angles.

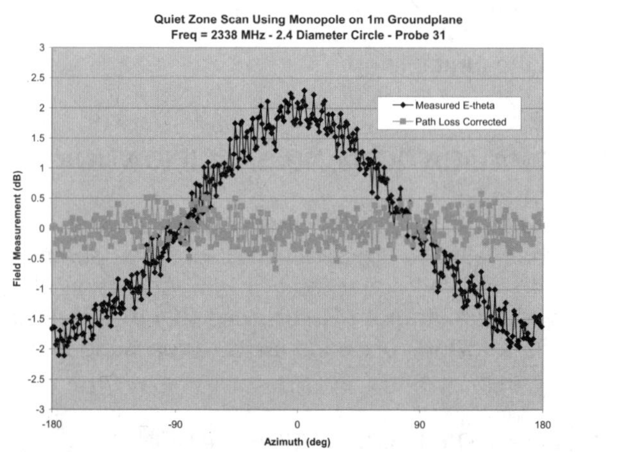

Figure 4. 20° above horizon quiet zone scan in the SDARS frequency band showing raw data and path loss compensated data.

PROBE ARRAY CALIBRATION

The probe array was calibrated following Satimo's standard procedure. An extended boom with counterweights and dedicated positioning hardware was manufactured to accommodate the larger radius of this system compared to standard Stargate systems. A picture of the calibration setup is shown in Figure 5. The center of rotation for elevation is aligned using various lasers to within 1-2mm of the center of the arch. Probe position and calibration hardware are aligned to within 0.05° to guarantee low cross-polarization and to ensure that the horn is pointing directly towards the probe under calibration. For each probe and at fine frequency intervals, four complex calibration coefficients are determined to ensure equal amplitude and phase response as well as polarization alignment and cross-polar isolation. An example of the measured probe uniformity, after calibration, is shown in Figure 6.

Figure 5. Probe array calibration setup consists of a precision positioning system, a 3m boom, and a linearly polarized antenna.

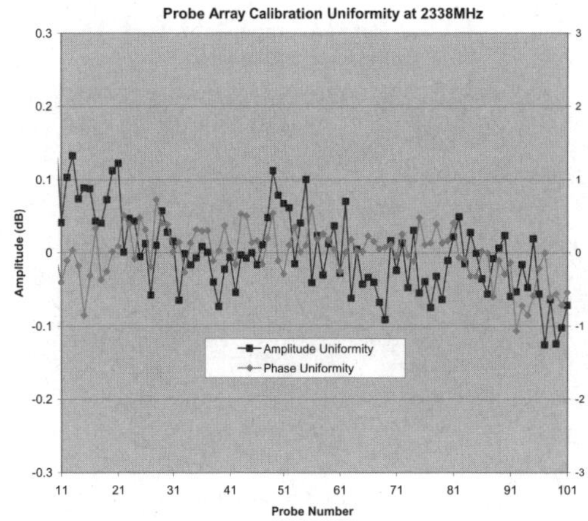

FIGURE 6. Measured amplitude and phase uniformity after probe array calibration.

INTER-LABORATORY COMPARISONS.

Monopole antennas (see Figure 3) were tested at the Satimo Stargate-64 facility and later at GM. A comparison plot of the monopole elevation pattern is shown in Figure 7. Excellent agreement between the two facilities is obtained over the full hemisphere. The results compare well, even below horizon.

Another set of inter-laboratory comparisons were made with Motorola's facility in Schaumburg, IL. Reference XM antennas were tested in both facilities and performance parameters were compared. Figure 8 shows the comparison between azimuth averaged gain for various elevation angles. The results compare to within 0.6 dB.

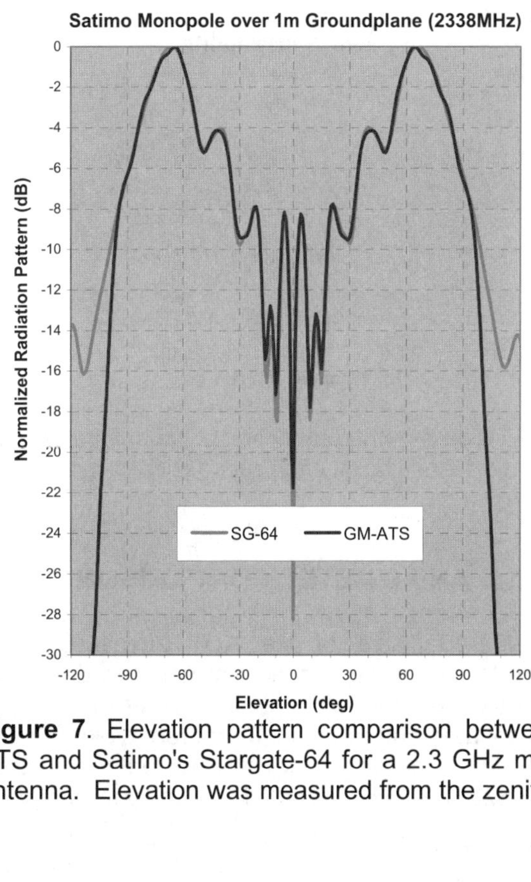

Figure 7. Elevation pattern comparison between GM-ATS and Satimo's Stargate-64 for a 2.3 GHz monopole antenna. Elevation was measured from the zenith.

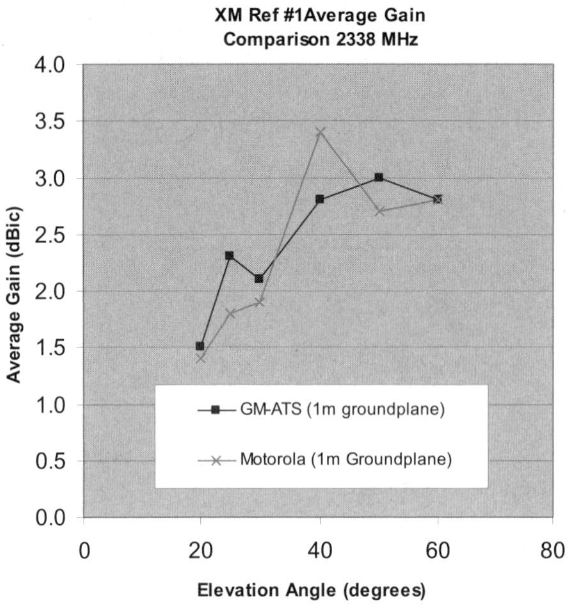

Figure 8: Correlation between results obtained at the GM-ATS with those obtained at Motorola's facility in Schaumburg, IL. Elevation was measured from the horizon

SYSTEM REPEATABILITY

The complete system has been removed and installed, on a monthly basis, since the initial installation. The same standard gain horn has been measured each time after installation. The un-calibrated peak gain measurements have been repeatable to within a few tenths of a dB, as shown in Figure 9.

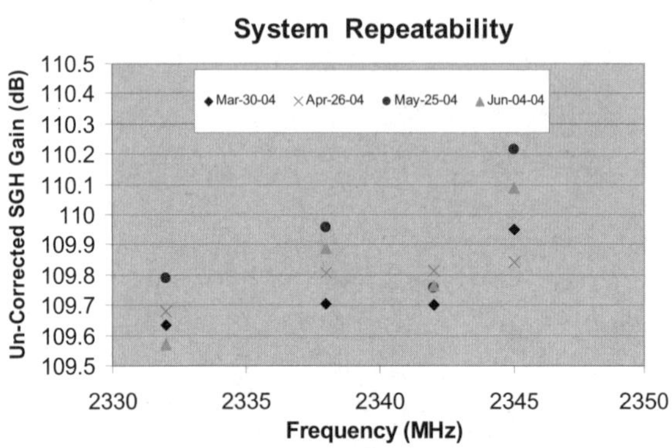

Figure 9. Three month comparison of un-calibrated gain of a standard gain horn after successive removal and installation.

FAR-FIELD AND 9 METER COMPARISON

As the effective size of the AUT increases, it is necessary to use more spherical modes to adequately describe the true far-field antenna pattern. SDARS antennas located on the center of the roof typically have low coupling to the vehicle. For such antennas, their effective size can be assumed to be one meter in diameter or less. The modal distribution for a SDARS antenna located centerline rear on the roof of a large passenger sedan is shown in Figure 10. It demonstrates how a "small" AUT has a low number of modes with high energy content.

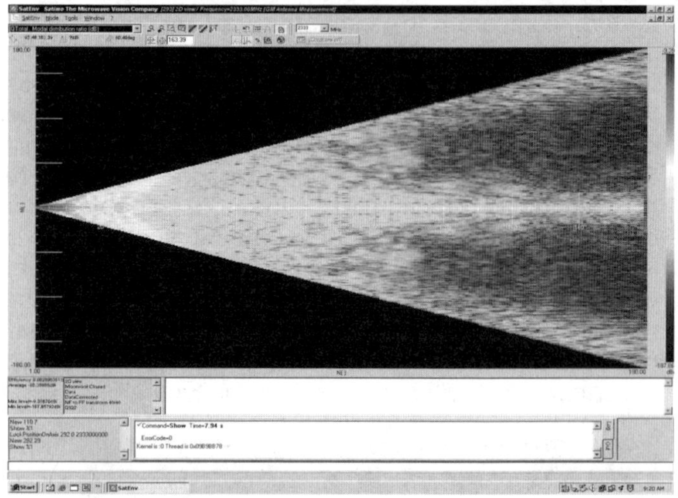

Figure 10. Modal distribution for SDARS antenna located on roof of passenger sedan at 2332 MHz (N = 40, M = 40).

The corresponding azimuth data is shown in Figure 11.

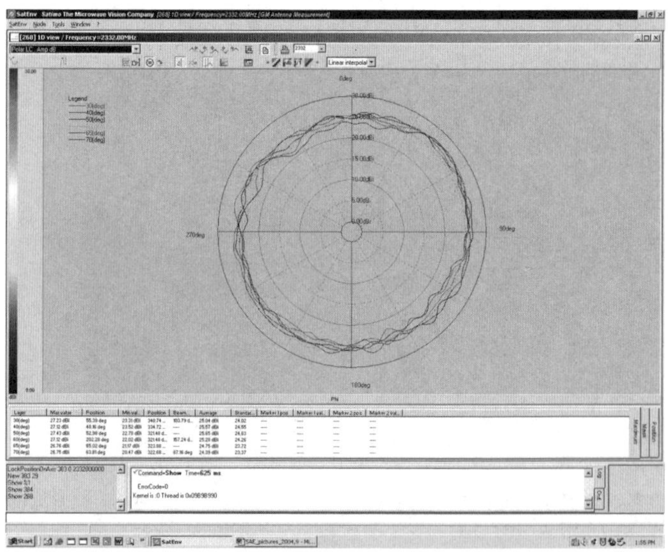

Figure 11. Satellite azimuth plot for SDARS antenna located on roof of passenger sedan at 2332 MHz.

However, once a SDARS antenna is located on the rear decklid of a vehicle, the number of spherical modes needed greatly increases due to the strong coupling between the SDARS antenna and the vehicle. The effective AUT size can approach the size of the vehicle. Shown in Figure 12 is the modal distribution for a "large" AUT requiring more modes (compared to Figure 10).

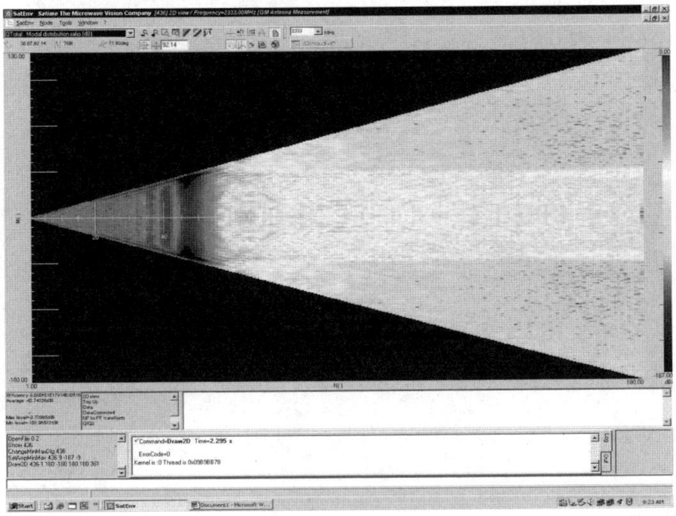

Figure 12. Modal distribution for SDAR antenna located on the rear decklid of a passenger vehicle at 2332.5 MHz (N =70, M = 70) with top up.

The corresponding terrestrial azimuth data is shown in Figure 13.

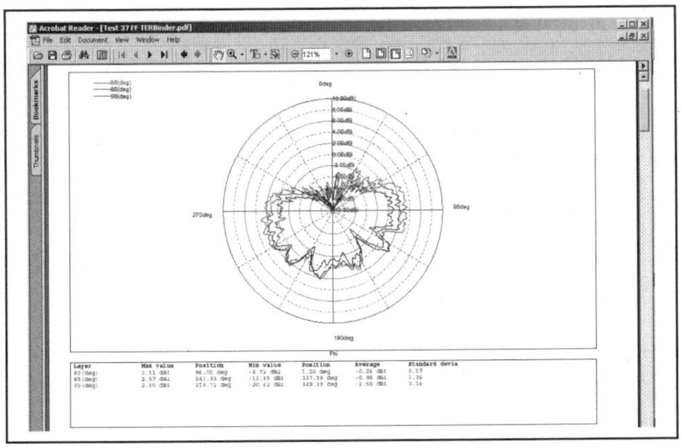

Figure 13. Terrestrial far-field azimuth data. Elevation was measured from the zenith.

Satimo is currently working on developing back transformation software, which will allow the near-field data to be transformed to a nine meter separation distance between the transmitting antenna and the received antenna (vehicle). Nine meter separation was chosen to simulate typical far-field gantry systems. Once this software is available, nine meter gain data will be generated and compared to the original far-field data. It is doubtful that the difference seen between far-field and 9m for one vehicle configuration will translate to all vehicle configurations. More vehicles will need to be analyzed prior to making any generalizations on the differences between far-field measurements and 9m measurements.

DATA ANALYSIS AND DISPLAY

In addition to modal distribution information, the system has antenna efficiency measurements capability, 3D plots of the radiation pattern, and elevation cuts. Figures 14 and 15 show the far-field radiation data for a SDARS antenna installed on the rear decklid of a vehicle at 2332.5 MHz. Due to the positioning of the antenna on the rear of the vehicle, a significant portion of the front of the vehicle is shadowed causing a large null in the pattern.

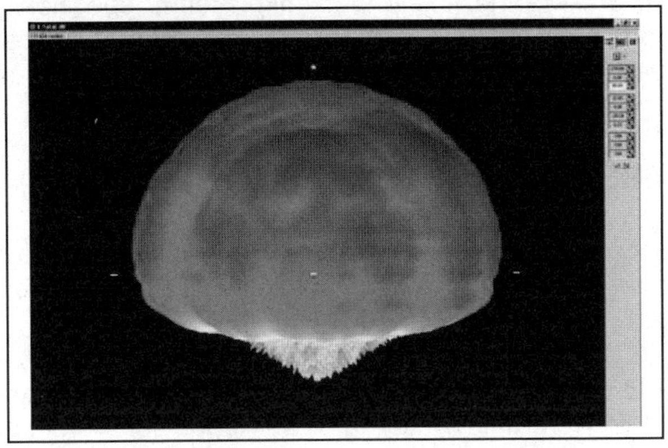

Figure 14. 3D far-field gain plot of a passive SDARS antenna mounted on the rear decklid of a vehicle as seen looking towards the front of the vehicle.

Example of an elevation cut (phi = 0) is shown in Figure 15.

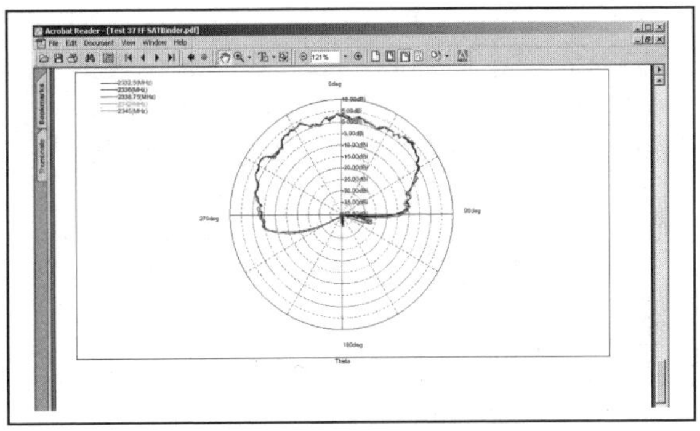

Figure 15. Multi-frequency far-field elevation cuts of a SDARS antenna mounted on the rear decklid of a vehicle. The front of the vehicle points to the right (90°).

CONCLUSION

By utilizing Satimo's rapid probe array technology and incorporating it into a vehicle-sized arch, a system has been created that can quickly and accurately measure vehicle antenna patterns. Due to the portability of the ATS, an existing anechoic chamber can be used as both an antenna test facility and an EMC facility. An extensive validation plan was completed to ensure the accuracy of the ATS data. A correlation study was done between Motorola and GM, again, to ensure ATS data accuracy. Correlation between the two sites was typically within 1.0 dB. The GM ATS also provides insight to the effective size of antennas integrated onto vehicles.

ACKNOWLEDGEMENTS

The authors wish to acknowledge Louis Nagy, of Delphi Research Labs, the General Motors team specifically, Donald Hibbard, Doug Martin, Gary Meloeny, and Scott Yencer, Ed Porrett, of Motorola, Mike Francis, of NIST, Robert Johnk, of NIST, Ron Wittmann, of NIST, Craig Wadin, of XM, and finally the Satimo team, specifically Philippe Garreau, Arnaud Gandois, John Estrada, Jacques Lesang, Fabrice Subirada, and Francesca Mioc.

REFERENCES

[1] A.R. Howland et al, "Novel Spherical Near-Field Antenna Measurement Techniques Advance State-of-the –Art", AMTA, October 2001.

[2] P.O. Iversen, Ph. Garreau, et al, "Real Time Spherical Near-field Antenna Test Range for Personal Communications Applications", AMTA, October 1999.

[3] E. Joy, "Near-Field Range Qualification Methodology," IEEE Transactions on Antennas and Propagation, Vol. 36, No. 6, June 1988.

[4] M. Francis, R. Wittmann, "NIST Spherical Near-Field Class for GM", September 2003.

[5] A. Newell, "Error Analysis Techniques for Planar Near-Field Measurements," IEEE Transactions on Antennas and Propagation, Vol. 36, No. 6, June 1988.

CONTACT

Janalee A. Graham
Milford Proving Ground
M/C 483-340-111
3300 General Motors Road
Milford, MI 48380-3726
e-mail: Janalee.a.graham@gm.com

Per O. Iversen
Satimo USA
2105 Barrett Park Dr. Suite 104
Kennesaw, GA 30144
e-mail: piversen@satimo.com

DEFINITIONS, ACRONYMS, ABBREVIATIONS

none

2004-01-1748

Digital Audio for FM Hybrid HD Radio

Brian W. Kroeger
iBiquity Digital Corporation

ABSTRACT

The audio qualities of the digital and analog signals are characterized and compared for the HD Radio In-Band On-Channel (IBOC) Hybrid FM broadcast system. The Hybrid HD Radio modes of transmission carry the original (host) analog signals simultaneously with a digital signal conveying the same audio program, but with superior sound quality. The digital signal is transmitted at a lower level than the analog signal in a carefully designed modulation scheme that minimizes corruption and maximizes compatibility with the host analog audio. Audio quality characteristics, such as SNR for an analog signal, are compared to audio characteristics for a digital audio codec.

INTRODUCTION

HD Radio is a medium for providing digital-quality audio, superior to existing analog broadcasting formats. The advantages of digital transmission for audio include better signal quality with virtually no noise, and wider dynamic range than with existing FM and AM radio. The goal of FM HD Radio is to provide robust, virtual-CD quality stereo audio along with a capacity for a data channel. New high-quality stereo codec algorithms, such as HDC, can provide virtual-CD stereo quality at rates below 96 kbps. IBOC HD Radio systems require no new spectral allocations because each digital signal is simultaneously transmitted within the spectral mask of an existing analog signal allocation.

IBOC HD Radio is designed, through power level and spectral occupancy, to be transparent to the analog radio listener. Therefore it promotes economy of spectrum while enabling broadcasters to offer digital quality audio to their present base of listeners.

A brief overview of the HD Radio's FM Hybrid system appears in the next section. Additional information on compatibility of the IBOC analog and digital signals in the FM Hybrid system can be found in [1]. Some additional details on the modulation, interleaving, and forward error correction (FEC) coding methods are presented in [2]. A brief description and some characteristics of the digital audio codec used in this system is also provided. This High Definition Codec (HDC), and is tailored for outstanding state-of-the-art audio performance in the HD Radio system. The primary purpose of this paper is to analyze and compare the audio performance and coverage for an analog FM host and its digital signals. The performance is compared in various reception conditions, including the relatively benign Additive White Gaussian Noise (AWGN) channel, dynamic Rayleigh fading, and interference. The analog and digital audio qualities are compared and show that the digital audio quality is generally superior to the analog audio quality in most reception conditions.

OVERVIEW OF HD RADIO FM HYBRID SYSTEM

Figure 1 is a representation of the frequency allocations of the signal components for the Hybrid FM HD Radio signal. The hybrid format includes the conventional FM stereo analog host signal having a power spectral density positioned in the central frequency band. The digital signal is transmitted using Orthogonal Frequency Division Multiplex (OFDM) modulation at a level 20 dB below the analog FM signal. The OFDM signal consists of 191 subcarriers in each of the lower and upper sidebands of the signal. These subcarriers span the frequencies from approximately 129 to 198 kHz from center frequency. All of the subcarriers are transmitted at a power level that falls within the United States Federal Communications Commission channel mask; however, a more restrictive mask is being considered to reduce interference in the FM band.

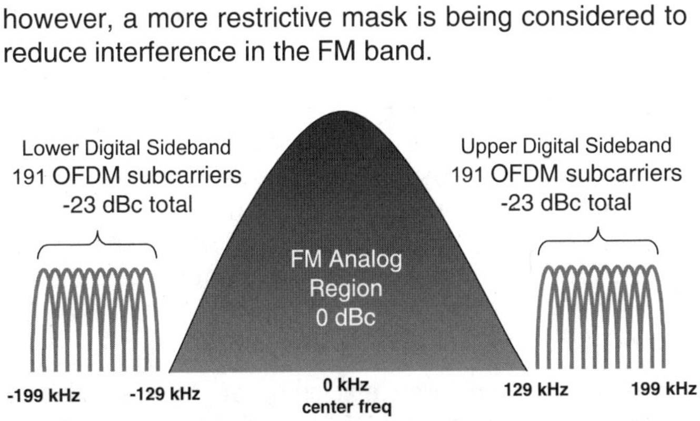

Figure 1. HD Radio FM Hybrid signal spectrum.

The OFDM subcarriers on each sideband carry about 96 kbps of information after FEC decoding. This placement allows any one sideband to be completely corrupted while the other sideband carries the information. The placement of digital subcarriers at ± 15 kHz about 114 kHz is avoided in the baseline system, in order to reduce the noise introduced into inadequately filtered receivers. However the broadcaster will have the option to utilize this portion of the spectrum to provide additional datacasting capacity. This option is attractive if the broadcaster avoids stereo operation of the FM analog host signal.

In the presence of adjacent channel interference, the outer OFDM subcarriers are most vulnerable to corruption, and the interference on the upper and lower sidebands is independent. The coding and interleaving are specially tailored to deal with such nonuniform interference and fading that the communication of information is robust. A new Complementary Puncture Pattern Convolutional (CPPC) FEC technique was designed to maximize performance in this system [2].

The system replicates all the digital audio information on each digital sideband (upper or lower) of the FM carrier. The baseline Hybrid FM system employs a code rate of 2/5 with both digital sidebands combined. However, each sideband can also be detected and decoded independently with an FEC coding gain achieved by a rate 4/5 convolutional code. Further error detection capability is provided with an 8-bit CRC on each audio or data field for digital error concealment or analog blend purposes. The dual sideband redundancy permits operation on one sideband while the other is completely corrupted. However, usually both sides are combined to provide additional signal power and coding gain. Special techniques can also be employed to demodulate and separate strong first adjacent interferers, such that "recovered" digital sidebands can be successfully combined to tolerate large first adjacent interferers.

OFDM MODULATION - OFDM modulation has proven to be very effective in channels experiencing multipath fading and nonuniform interference. OFDM differs from conventional single carrier modulation techniques, because the digitally modulated symbols are grouped in parallel vectors for transmission over multiple subcarriers instead of being serially transmitted over a single carrier. The OFDM technique uses a set of overlapping, orthogonally-spaced narrowband subcarriers to transport the same symbols as a wideband serial stream of single carrier modulation, as depicted in Figure 2. Each modulated subcarrier usually carries a small number of bits. For example, one bit per BPSK symbol, 2 bits per QPSK symbol, 3 bits per 8PSK symbol, and 4 to 8 bits per QAM symbol.

Although the spectral efficiency of Nyquist filtered symbols is similar for OFDM versus single carrier modulation, the spectral compactness of OFDM is efficiently and practically achieved through a windowed FFT technique, versus Nyquist FIR filtering of the serial symbol stream. The bit error rate (BER) performance of OFDM versus single carrier modulation is identical when corrupted only by AWGN. However, the performance in a mobile multipath channel with nonuniform interference across the signal bandwidth favors OFDM. A guard time is used to space the OFDM symbols such that multiple reflections of the signal arriving at different times don't interfere with each other. This guard time consumes a small fraction of the throughput for OFDM, but the same guard time is impractical for single carrier modulation since it would consume a much larger fraction of the throughput.

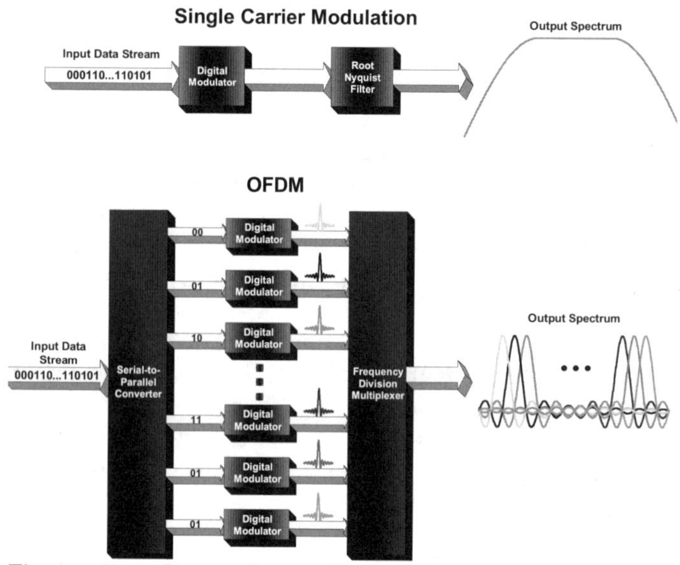

Figure 2. Comparison of single carrier modulation versus OFDM.

Practical digital radio transmission systems employ FEC techniques to repair digital errors that occur over the transmission channel. These techniques add redundancy to the information stream in such a way that the receiver can identify and correct a number of errors as they are received. This FEC coding combined with OFDM modulation (Coded OFDM, or COFDM) is a powerful combination, effective against the interference which corrupts a portion of the channel bandwidth. In these nonuniform interference cases (similar to frequency selective fading), the corrupted subcarriers can be erased instead of allowing the corrupted symbols to contaminate the decoding process. The FEC coding is designed to correctly decode the signal under these interference conditions by suppressing or erasing the contribution from the corrupted subcarriers. A single carrier system in this scenario would likely be unsalvageable since all of the symbols would be contaminated.

Furthermore, receiver equalization of a single carrier modulation is required in frequency selective channels, although the equalization results in noise enhancement. In contrast, it is reasonable to assume that the channel is flat over each individual subcarrier of an OFDM signal; therefore equalization is not required. OFDM offers very robust digital signal reception in the presence of fading and interference within the coverage area, where the existing analog signal experiences the effects of noise and fades.

TIME DIVERSITY & BLEND-TO-ANALOG - Time diversity is imposed on the transmission between the analog and digital signal to improve coverage. This time diversity ensures that a brief channel outage does not corrupt the same audio portion in both the analog and digital signals. A blend-to-analog technique is used to fill gaps in the digital coverage when outages do occur. An example of the benefit of time diversity is illustrated in Figure 3.

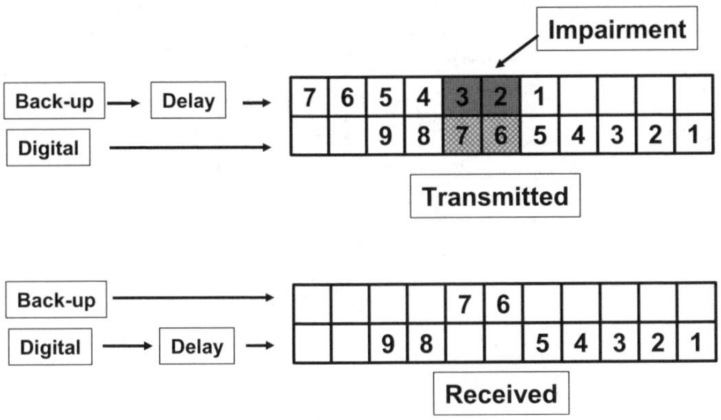

Figure 3. Time diversity example uses the analog signal as a Back-up "gap filler".

PERCEPTUAL AUDIO CODING AND HDC CHARACTERISTICS

The High Definition Codec is used to encode digital audio in the HD Radio system [5]. HDC incorporates several techniques to maximize audio quality at lower bit rates, such as filterbank optimization to encode transients within a signal (e.g., sharp attacks in castanets, triangles, drums, etc.). Distortion of attacks is a particularly noticeable artifact at lower bit rates. In HDC, a signal-adaptive switched filterbank, which switches between two Modified Discrete Cosine Transforms (MDCT), is employed for analysis and synthesis. This practice allows for higher frequency resolution and transient control. Sophisticated bit allocation and quantization strategies which rely upon non-uniform quantization, analysis-by-synthesis, and entropy coding are also introduced to allow reduced bit rates and improved quality.

Perhaps the single most important technique is the use of Spectral Band Replication (SBR). SBR is a new method for highly efficient coding of high frequencies that can be used with most any audio codec. By efficient encoding of the high frequency information the underlying perceptual codec is only responsible for accurately reproducing the lower frequencies. This results in the significant reduction of noticeable artifacts, especially at the lower bit rates.

An important feature of HDC is that it has been optimized for use in digital audio broadcast systems. It incorporates powerful error concealment techniques for mitigating the effects of channel errors. It also offers the ability to split the bit stream into a core bitstream (which is independently decodable), and an enhanced bitstream, providing the optimal audio quality for the prevailing channel conditions and/or interference scenarios.

In the compression of audio material, human perception plays a key role. This is evidenced by the fact that source coding, a method used very successfully in speech signal compression, does not work nearly as well for music. Recent U.S. and international audio standards work (HDTV, DAB, MPEG-1, MPEG-2, CCIR) have therefore centered on a class of audio compression algorithms known as *perceptual coders*. Rather than minimizing analytic measures of distortion, such as Signal-to-Noise Ratio (SNR), perceptual coders attempt to minimize perceived distortion. Implicit in this approach is the idea that the signal fidelity perceived by humans is a better quality measure than the signal fidelity computed by traditional distortion measures. Perceptual coders define *compact disc quality* to mean *perceptually indistinguishable from compact disc audio.* HDC employs source coding techniques to remove signal redundancy and perceptual coding techniques to remove signal irrelevancy.

HDC is employing a novel technology known as Spectral Band Replication (SBR). The basic principle of SBR relies on the fact that, although the higher one or two octaves are psychoacoustically less relevant, they still require a significant part of the overall bit consumption when coded with a perceptual codec. SBR is an efficient method to code the high frequency part of the spectrum by extracting guiding information of the originals high frequency characteristic. Only the low frequency part is coded by the perceptual coder. In the decoder the high frequency part is recreated though guided transposition methods from the low frequency portion, thereby matching the original frequency response. The amount of SBR guiding information required for transmission is much less throughput when compared to conventional perceptual coding. A dramatic further efficiency increase can be therefore be achieved while maintaining the original sound characteristic. Combined, these methods yield a high compression ratio, while ensuring maximal quality in the decoded signal. The result is a high quality, high compression rate coding algorithm for audio signals.

HDC STRUCTURE - Figure 4 shows a more detailed block diagram of the HDC algorithm, and illustrates the flow of data between the algorithmic blocks. There are 7 basic parts:

Downsampler – A high quality FIR-based 2:1 downsampler feeds the perceptual audio coder. Since SBR processes the original high frequency content, the perceptual coder needs only to code the low frequency portion and can thus operate at a lower rate. This improves the efficiency of the analysis filterbank.

Analysis Filterbank - The MDCT filterbank converts the time domain audio signal to short-term or long-term frequency domain representation, depending on the characteristics of the input signal.

Perceptual Model - The perceptual model takes the output of the filterbank and calculates a frequency domain threshold of masking. The threshold of masking is a frequency dependent calculation of the maximum noise that can be added to the source audio material without perceptibly altering the source

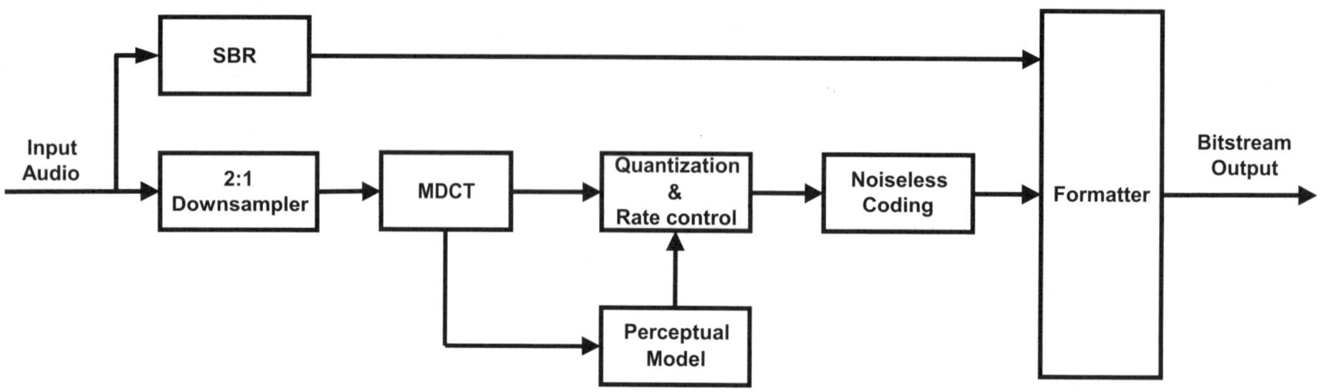

Figure 4. Block functional diagram of the HDC algorithm.

SBR - SBR uses transposition to reconstruct the higher frequencies at the decoder, instead of transmitting them as spectral data. To ensure an accurate reconstruction, some guidance information, such as the spectral envelope and noise floor level, is transmitted in the encoded bitstream at a very low data rate.

Quantization & Rate Control - Noise is inherently added to the signal in the process of quantizing the filter bank outputs. As mentioned above, the perceptual threshold is expressed as a noise level for each filterbank frequency. Quantizers are adjusted such that the perceptual thresholds are met or exceeded in a perceptually gentle fashion. While it is always possible to meet the perceptual threshold in an unlimited rate coder, coding at high compression ratios requires both over coding (adding less noise to the signal than the perceptual threshold requires) and under-coding (adding more noise to the signal than the perceptual threshold requires). HDC's noise allocation algorithm allows for time buffering and the smoothing of local peaks and troughs in the bitrate demand. In addition, the HDC encoder allows the bit-rate to be dynamically scaled to allow greater throughput of ancillary data being transmitted with the encoded audio.

Stereo Encoding - HDC employs the well-known Mid/Side (M/S) stereo coding technique (also known as "sum/difference coding"). The M/S stereo coding strategies can be selectively applied to different frequency regions. By using M/S stereo and L/R (independent) coding as appropriate, it is possible to achieve a significant saving in bit rate. However, at very low bit-rates it is not possible to use the aforementioned techniques without creating audible artifacts. Therefore; the novel parametric stereo coding technique is often used. Parametric stereo works by performing an analysis of the stereophonic signal at the encoder and encodes, at a very low bit rate, a parametric description of the spatial properties of the original signal along with a compressed monophonic signal down mixed from the original stereophonic signal. At the decoder the stereophonic signal is reconstructed based on the decompressed monophonic bitstream and the parametric description of the stereo image.

Noiseless Compression - Many of the quantized frequency coefficients produced by the quantization module are zero; the remainder of the coefficients have a non-uniform distribution. Information theoretic methods such as Huffman or delta coding in frequency or in time are employed to provide a compact representation of the quantized coefficients.

Bitstream Formatter - This module forms the bitstream, and encodes the entire set of information for transmission. A *multistream* CODEC is required (for some modes of operation) in the iBiquity HD Radio system to provide robustness of coverage and fast tuning times. A multistream CODEC segregates the encoded audio content into separate bitstreams. The "more important" encoded bits are placed in a *core* bitstream, such that it is independently decodable, albeit at reduced audio quality. The remaining bits are placed in an *enhanced* bitstream. The enhanced bitstream is not required to be independently decodable.

The HDC codec is a variable bit-rate process in which each input audio frame corresponds to a variable length output encoded packet. However, the HD Radio system is a constant-capacity channel. Therefore, a rate control mechanism must be used. This rate control mechanism is one of the main functions of the HDC transport. The HDC transport is also responsible for framing the encoded audio packets into protocol data units (PDUs) by adding additional protocol information. The additional protocol information is used for error detection and correction as well as synchronization. Furthermore, the HDC transport manages the unused bandwidth by making it available to data applications such as program associated data (PAD).

The HD Radio FM Hybrid system operates at a 96 kbps rate, offering virtual CD quality. The audio signal dynamic range is 90 dB, with 90 dB of stereo separation. The frequency response is 0-20 kHz, with THD of less than 0.04%. The HDC codec can also operate at lower rates, down to about 12 kbps. Near-CD quality can be achieved at rates as low as 64 kbps. This allows the broadcaster to utilize the extra capacity for other digital services.

PERFORMANCE OF FM HYBRID HD RADIO

In this section the performance of the analog and digital signals of the FM Hybrid HD Radio system is characterized and compared. The audio performance for the analog signal is characterized in terms of postdetection audio SNR. The digital audio quality is affected by the audio frame error rate, although it can be estimated by the probability of bit error, or Bit Error Rate (BER). The effects of AWGN on these signals are first analyzed to assess relative performance in reception conditions that are generally free of multiple signal reflections (multipath). This is when the receiver in a well-sited stationary location (home receiver), or in a vehicle in an open area where line-of-site or good Fresnel-zone [3] reception dominates. The effects of multipath fading channels (i.e., Rayleigh fading) are also analyzed and compared in a dynamic channel, such as a moving vehicle without a strong direct signal path to the receiver. Interference from cochannel and adjacent channel interference also affects signal quality. It is shown that the digital signal has a significant advantage under most of these conditions, and requires significantly lower power than the analog FM signal for good audio signal quality and coverage.

FM ANALOG PERFORMANCE IN AWGN - The performance of an FM broadcast signal in noise has been previously characterized in the literature using a quasi-static approximation method (e.g., [4]), and a brief summary is presented here. For high predetection SNR (e.g., > 13 dB), the performance of FM as a function of its predetection SNR in AWGN is

$$\left(\frac{S}{N}\right)_D = 3\cdot D^2\cdot\frac{M^2}{2}\cdot\frac{140}{15}\cdot\left(\frac{S}{N}\right)_T \quad \text{; (equation 1)}$$

where $\left(\frac{S}{N}\right)_D$ is the postdetection SNR over a 15 kHz bandwidth, and $\left(\frac{S}{N}\right)_T$ is the predetection SNR is normalized to a transmission bandwidth of 140 kHz for this example. The actual predetection bandwidth is usually considered to be approximately 210 kHz, according to Carson's rule. Equation 1 employs a 140/15 factor since the usual form of equation 1 normalizes the noise bandwidth to 15 kHz for direct comparison to linear modulation in the audio postdetection bandwidth [4]. However, the 140 kHz noise bandwidth normalization allows for later convenient comparison to the digital signal. *D* is the deviation ratio of the maximum (100%) deviation f_d to the maximum audio signal bandwidth *W*, and *M* is the ratio of the peak modulation deviation of a sinewave input relative to 100% modulation. The factor $M^2/2$ can be interpreted as the ratio of the audio input signal power to the peak deviation power. This power ratio is a function of the audio processing prior to modulation and is usually set between -10 to -15 dB for typical audio programs. The power ratio $M^2/2$ for a sinewave with 100% modulation is 0.5 (or -3 dB), while this ratio for a sinewave with 30% modulation is 0.045 (or -13.5 dB), which is within the typical range and will be used for further analyses.

Consider first the performance of monophonic FM without de-emphasis. The deviation ratio for a 15 kHz audio signal with a maximum deviation of 75 kHz is *D*=5. The postdetection SNR gain with 30% modulation according to equation 1 is then 31.5, or about 15 dB. However, this gain is evaluated assuming the predetection SNR is in a 140 kHz bandwidth, instead of the 15 kHz signal bandwidth, accounting for about 9.7 dB of the gain using this normalization.

A de-emphasis filter at the receiver, with a corresponding pre-emphasis at the transmitter, is used to improve the SNR. The quasi-static approximation method reveals that the noise power spectrum at the audio output of the FM detector is parabolic and is proportional to the square of the frequency from center. It is therefore desirable to attenuate the increased noise at higher frequencies using a de-emphasis filter. Of course, an inverse pre-emphasis filter is used at the transmitter such that the resulting audio signal gain is flat over 15 kHz. A typical de-emphasis filter has a frequency transfer function of a 1-pole RC filter with a 3 dB breakpoint frequency at 2.1 kHz. Its magnitude-squared characteristic *P(f)* expressed as a function of frequency (in kHz) is

$$P(f)=\frac{1}{1+\left(\frac{f}{2.1}\right)^2}$$

Then the de-emphasis gain is simply the reduction ratio of the de-emphasized noise expressed in dB as

$$G_{de-emph,mono}=10\cdot\log\left(\frac{\int_0^{15} f^2\cdot df}{\int_0^{15} f^2\cdot P(f)\cdot df}\right)=13.3\,\text{dB}.$$

This de-emphasis gain is really an upper bound because it assumes that the peak deviation of the pre-emphasized audio signal is not significantly increased. This is somewhat reasonable since typical audio signals have lower signal power at higher frequencies. Then the overall SNR gain of an audio signal (sinewave) with 30% modulation is about 28 dB.

FM broadcast stereo multiplex transmission incurs a penalty due to the increased input signal bandwidth, W=53 kHz. Furthermore, the pre-emphasis/de-emphasis advantage of monophonic FM is decreased for FM stereo. This is because the postdetection noise is predominately contributed by the 38 kHz stereo subcarrier signal (L-R) between 23 and 38 kHz, and the pre-emphasis characteristic is no longer matched to the resulting noise spectrum of the stereo subcarrier signal. Although the performance of stereo FM without de-emphasis can also be approximated using equation 1, an alternate approach of noise integration yields results that allow evaluation of the de-emphasis gain for FM stereo. In the stereo case, the noise power from 0 to 15 kHz and from 23 to 53 kHz is integrated relative to the original monophonic signal without pre-emphasis. The effects of both stereo and pre-emphasis on the SNR gain relative to FM mono with no pre-emphasis can be expressed as

$$G_{de-emph,stereo} = 10\cdot\log\left(\frac{\int_0^{15} f^2\cdot df}{\int_0^{15} f^2\cdot P(f)\cdot df + \int_{23}^{53} f^2\cdot P(f-38)\cdot df}\right) = -9\,\text{dB}.$$

Therefore the overall SNR gain for FM stereo with 30% modulation and de-emphasis is 15 dB (mono without de-emphasis) minus 9 dB, or about 6 dB.

The SNR penalty for converting from FM mono to stereo transmission is then about 22 dB; however, receivers typically employ a blend-to-mono function when the stereo SNR is below a predetermined value (e.g., 40 dB). Therefore, the stereo signal can benefit in conditions where the SNR is sufficiently high, and the stereo subcarrier signal (L-R) is suppressed to improve postdetection SNR under weaker signal conditions. However, the SNR gain resulting from monophonic demodulation of the transmitted stereo signal is not quite as high as that from a monophonic FM transmission. The postdetection SNR of this monophonic signal from a stereo broadcast is closer to 22 dB, but still about 16 dB better than the stereo signal.

The FM performance of mono and stereo FM signals with pre-emphasis is plotted in Figure 5. These plots show the postdetection (audio output) SNR over a 15 kHz audio bandwidth as a function of predetection SNR in a 140 kHz AWGN bandwidth.

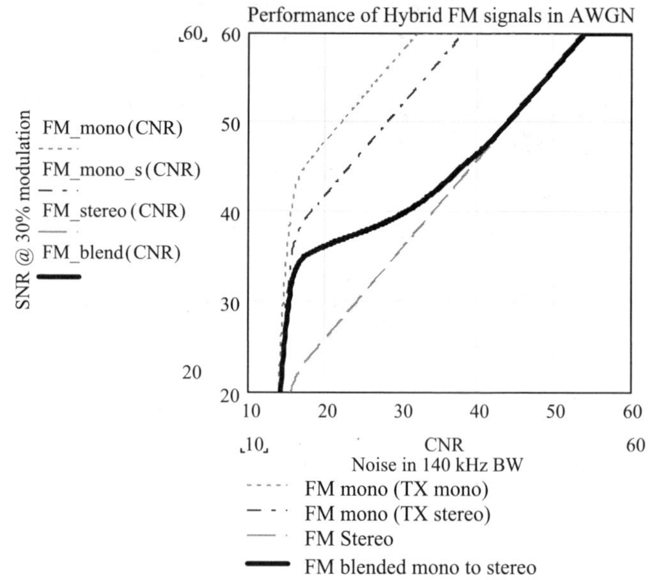

Figure 5. FM postdetection SNR performance as a function of predetection SNR.

DIGITAL PERFORMANCE IN AWGN - The digital FM Hybrid HD Radio signal is transmitted in the sidebands extending from about 129 kHz to 199 kHz on either side of the FM center frequency. The effective noise bandwidth of the digital signal is approximately 140 kHz. After subtracting the overhead for FEC and digital transport framing, the resulting audio throughput rate is 96 kbps. The digital BER performance of HD Radio FM Hybrid signal (mode MP1) is plotted in Figure 6.

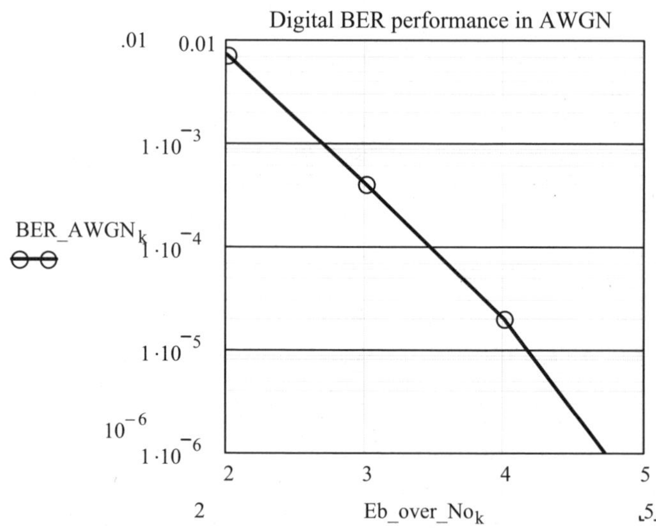

Figure 6. Digital BER performance in AWGN.

In AWGN, the required predetection SNR digital threshold in a 140 kHz bandwidth is approximately 3 dB (equivalently, Eb/No=4.5 dB after FEC). This SNR results in a BER of 10^{-5}, corresponding to an audio frame error rate of about 0.1%, which yields virtually no noticeable artifacts after error concealment by the HDC codec. Since this digital signal is transmitted 20 dB below the FM analog power, its digital threshold can be adjusted to 23 dB on the FM predetection SNR axis.

Although the digital threshold is about 10 dB higher than the analog FM threshold, virtually perfect digital reception is achieved above the threshold.

ANALOG VS. DIGITAL PERFORMANCE IN AWGN - The performance of FM analog and digital is compared in AWGN. Figure 8 shows the effective postdetection audio SNR for both the digital and analog signals for a range of predetection SNRs. Although the digital threshold is 3 dB, the FM HD Radio system places the total digital signal power 20 dB below the host FM analog power to avoid interference issues. Therefore, the plot shows the digital performance threshold at 23 dB for direct comparison with FM performance. Furthermore, the SNR for a digital audio signal is not an appropriate metric, so a subjective value of 70 dB postdetection SNR is used for direct comparison with the analog FM audio signal. This is a realistic value that can be justified through subjective MOS comparison of the audio signals. Figure 7 clearly shows that the digital signal offers superior audio quality above 25 dB predetection SNR.

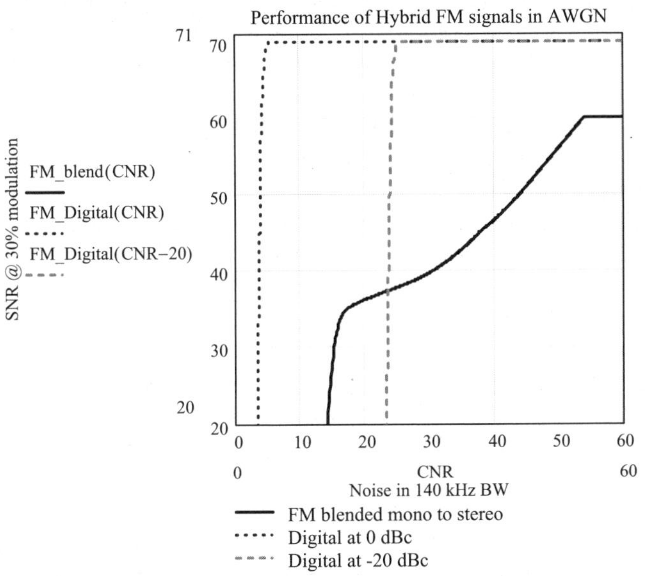

Figure 7. Comparison of digital and analog performance in AWGN.

The HD Radio system employs a blend-to-analog feature that outputs the demodulated FM audio when the digital signal is corrupted, such that the audio quality of the result is at least as good as the analog signal in these cases. Time diversity between the digital and analog signal also mitigates outages such that the digital and analog outages are decorrelated over several seconds.

EFFECTS OF MULTIPATH FADING - Propagation of signals in the FM band is often affected by multipath fading. This phenomenon is a result of signal paths reflected from objects such as buildings and geographic features. In many cases, there is no line-of-site propagation path from the transmission antenna to the receiver, and the receiver relies solely on reflected scatterers. The Rayleigh fading model is commonly used to characterize these fading effects. One characteristic of Rayleigh fading is that the signal power varies as multiple rays of the signal add and cancel. For a receiver in a moving vehicle, the fading is dynamic over the maximum fading bandwidth f_m, which is equal to the product of the carrier frequency and the vehicle speed, divided by the speed of light. The fading bandwidth is roughly 10 Hz at highway speeds (67 mph), and a few Hz in typical urban environments. The probability density function (PDF) of a Rayleigh-fading signal having an average power ^{2} and an instantaneous envelope r is

$$p(r) = \frac{r}{\sigma^2} \cdot \exp\left(-\frac{r^2}{2 \cdot \sigma^2}\right) \; ; \text{ for } r \geq 0$$

The probability (or fractional time) of the faded signal having an envelope r less than a specified value R is

$$\text{Prob}(r < R) = 1 - \exp\left(-\frac{R^2}{2 \cdot \sigma^2}\right) \; ;$$

$$\text{or Prob}(r < R) \cong \frac{R^2}{2 \cdot \sigma^2} \; ; \text{ for } R < 1$$

or most conveniently,

$$\text{Prob}(\sigma_{inst} < \rho \cdot \sigma_{rms}) =$$

$$\text{Prob}(\sigma_{inst}^2 < \rho^2 \cdot \sigma_{avg}^2) \cong \rho^2 \; ; \text{ for } \rho << 1$$

For example, a Rayleigh-fading signal experiences a reduction of power from the long-term average by a factor of ^{2} for approximately the fraction ^{2} (assuming <<1) of the overall time. Figure 8 shows a plot of a Raleigh fading signal normalized to an average predetection signal power of 0 dB.

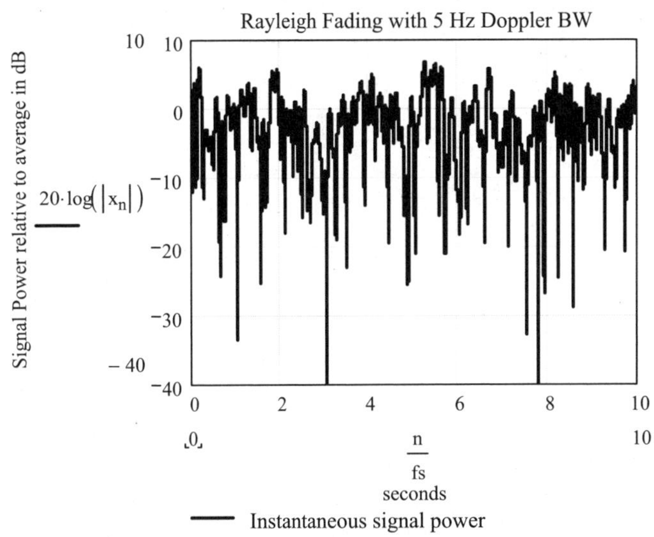

Figure 8. Example of Rayleigh fading signal with 5 Hz Doppler bandwidth.

The primary concern of fading on the signal is when the signal is faded below the threshold predetection SNR, whether analog FM or digital. For example, a Rayleigh fading signal with an average power of 10 dB above threshold power falls below this threshold for about 10%

of the time. Similarly, a faded signal with an average power of 20 dB above threshold falls below this threshold for about 1% of the time. This property is illustrated in the plot of Figure 9.

The fading rate [2], or the frequency of signal fades below a specified level for a Rayleigh fading signal is

$$N = \sqrt{2 \cdot \pi} \cdot f_m \cdot \rho \cdot e^{-\rho^2},$$
$$N \cong 2.5 \cdot f_m \cdot \rho; \quad \text{for } \rho << 1$$

The average fade duration below a particular value is computed as the fade probability divided by the fade rate at a particular power factor ^{2} below average power [2]. An expression for the fade duration using the previous approximations yields

$$\tau = \frac{\exp(\rho^2) - 1}{\rho \cdot f_m \cdot \sqrt{2 \cdot \pi}} \cong \frac{\rho}{2.5 \cdot f_m}$$

For example, a vehicle with a 5 Hz Doppler bandwidth (about 33 mph) experiences fades of 20 dB below average power at about one per second with 10 milliseconds duration, or 40 dB fades about 10 seconds apart with 1 millisecond duration on average. Figure 9 shows the Rayleigh fading characteristics for a signal with a Doppler bandwidth of 5 Hz.

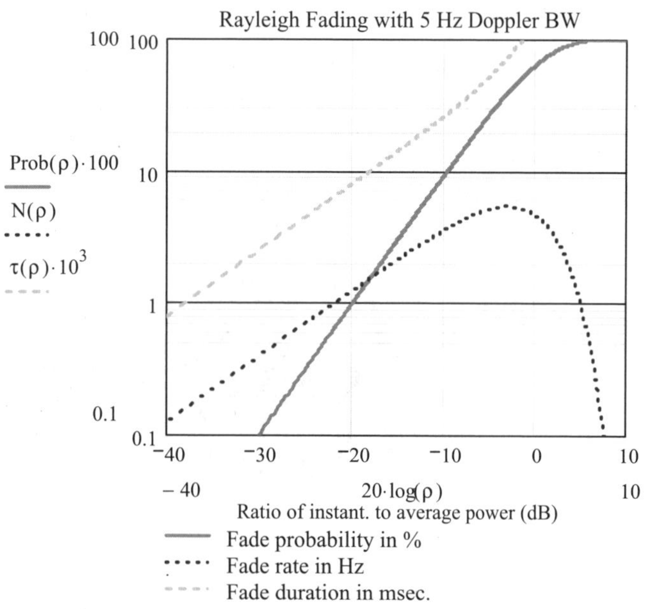

Figure 9. Fade probability, fade rate, and fade duration for 5 Hz Doppler BW.

Effects of Rayleigh fading on the FM analog signal - The primary concern of fading on the FM signal is when the signal is faded below the FM threshold predetection SNR. This fading below the FM threshold is often characterized as "clicks" in the audio output. This threshold was previously defined to be about 13 dB predetection SNR in a 140 kHz noise bandwidth.

Frequency selective fading also has an impact on the FM signal when the signal multipath reflections are from more distant objects (e.g., mountains in the distance). The signal distortion due to selective fading occurs even when the predetection SNR is high.

Although it is clear that multipath fading has a very significant impact on FM signal quality in terms of average SNR, the perceived audio quality of the resulting audio is difficult to characterize. For example, a Rayleigh faded FM signal with an average power 20 dB above threshold will experience the clicks for 1% of the time, possibly resulting in an average audio SNR of 20 dB due to the clicks. Even if the receiver mutes during the clicks, the average SNR measured by subtracting the ideal and received signals is still 20 dB. However, the degradation perceived by the listener may not seem quite that severe. A Rayleigh fading margin of at least 20 dB over FM threshold to avoid the audio clicks seem reasonable.

Effects of Rayleigh fading on the digital signal - The impact of Rayleigh fading on the digital signal is much less than for analog. The use of multipath-resistant OFDM modulation in conjunction with FEC techniques and interleaving over time and frequency makes the digital signal less vulnerable to the effects of Rayleigh and frequency-selective fading. An FEC coding rate of 2/5 and interleaving over more than 1 second ensures that the loss of code bits due to fades below digital threshold have a significantly lower effect on the digital audio information. For example, a 20 dB margin above the digital threshold of 3 dB (Eb/No=4.5 dB) predetection SNR results in about 1% of the bits lost in fades. The FEC and interleaving is designed to tolerate a loss of greater than 50% of the bits in some interference scenarios when one digital sideband is lost due to interference. It is reasonable to recover a virtually perfect decoded signal (audio frame error rate of 0.1% at 10^{-5} BER) with a randomly chosen 20% of the pre-FEC code bits lost to fades. The predetection SNR at this error rate is 6.5 dB (Eb/No=8 dB), which corresponds to a fade margin of about 3.5 dB over the AWGN digital threshold. The digital BER performance vs. Eb/No in fading (frequency selective, Rayleigh 4-ray model) with a Doppler bandwidth of 5 Hz (34 mph) is plotted in Figure 10.

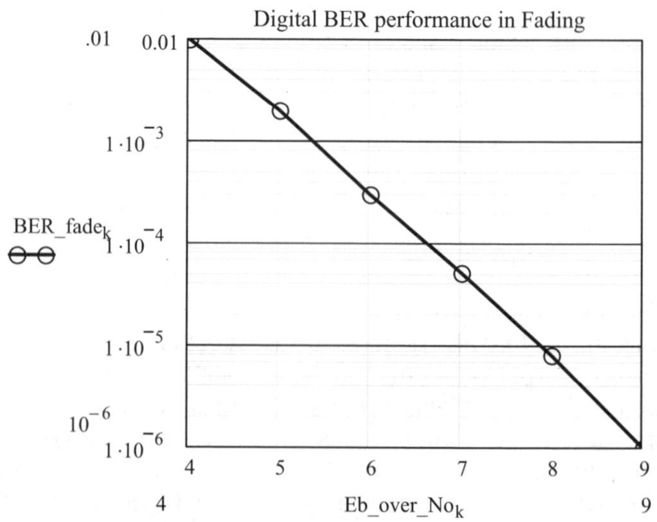

Figure 10. Digital BER performance in Rayleigh fading with 5 Hz Doppler BW.

Analog vs. digital performance in Rayleigh fading - The performance of FM analog and digital is compared in a Rayleigh fading channel. Figure 12 shows the effective postdetection audio SNR for both the digital and analog signals for a range of predetection SNRs. The thresholds for both the FM analog and digital signals have been adjusted by 20 dB and 3.5 dB, respectively, to account for the fading margins previously discussed.

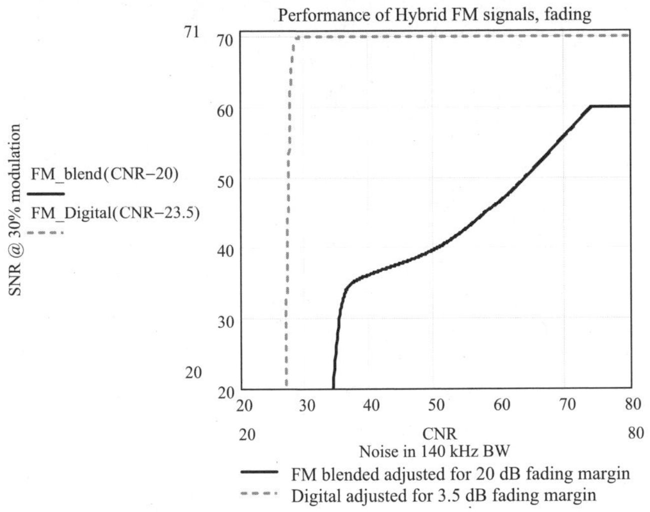

Figure 11. Performance of FM Hybrid analog and digital signals in Rayleigh fading.

The plots clearly show the superior performance of the digital signal over the full range of predetection SNR. Although both analog and digital signals experience some loss compared to the AWGN channel, the increased relative digital performance is due to the minimal effects of Rayleigh fading on the digital signal.

OVERALL PERFORMANCE COMPARISONS - The performance of the digital and analog FM signals was compared in AWGN and Rayleigh fading channels. In AWGN only, the digital signal offers superior performance when the predetection SNR is above 25 dB in a 140 kHz noise bandwidth. The analog signal offers extended monophonic coverage down to about 13 dB predetection SNR. The blend-to-analog feature takes advantage of the best audio signal available in this case. The AWGN performance is also applicable to channels where shadowing reduces the received signal power, but no multipath is present.

The Rayleigh fading channel is an extreme case of fading where no line-of-site signal is available from the transmitter antenna, and the received signal is a combination of multiple reflected paths. The digital performance is clearly superior in these conditions. Although the performance in real channel conditions without significant interference is somewhere between these two extremes, the digital signal appears to perform better in most of these conditions.

Interference from cochannel and first-adjacent signals must also be considered to assess performance. When the cochannel interferer is the only source of noise, the interference power to the digital is 20 dB lower than the analog interference because of the lower digital sideband interference power (-20 dB). For this case, the digital signal has a 10 dB lower threshold than the analog. Furthermore the analog is not fully blended to stereo until 30 dB above the digital threshold as evidenced in Figure 5. Cochannel interference is usually not an issue for analog FM reception due to the FCC protection ratios; it is even less of a concern for the digital signal.

First adjacent interfering signals have a greater affect on the digital than the analog component, due to the spectral placement of the digital sidebands. Analog FM receivers with good selectivity are tolerant to first adjacent interference since the degradation is generally masked by the noise in coverage regions where the interference is significant. The FM HD Radio receiver employs a First-Adjacent Cancellation (FAC) technique to mitigate the interference to the digital sidebands, although some corruption still occurs. The plot of Figure 12 shows the digital BER performance with a first adjacent interferer at -6 dB desired-to-undesired D/U ratio, with and without Rayleigh fading. In AWGN a first adjacent interferer at -6 dBc (the protection ratio relative to the signal of interest) degrades digital coverage by about 2.5 dB. This interference degrades performance in Rayleigh fading by about 5 dB relative to the Rayleigh fading performance without the interferer. These degradation values are characterized at 10^{-5} BER, where the digital audio is virtually perfect. The degradation relative to AWGN performance is less than 9 dB for all of these interference and fading scenarios. The performance loss is reduced for lower quality digital audio at a higher BER, which can still exceed the analog audio quality.

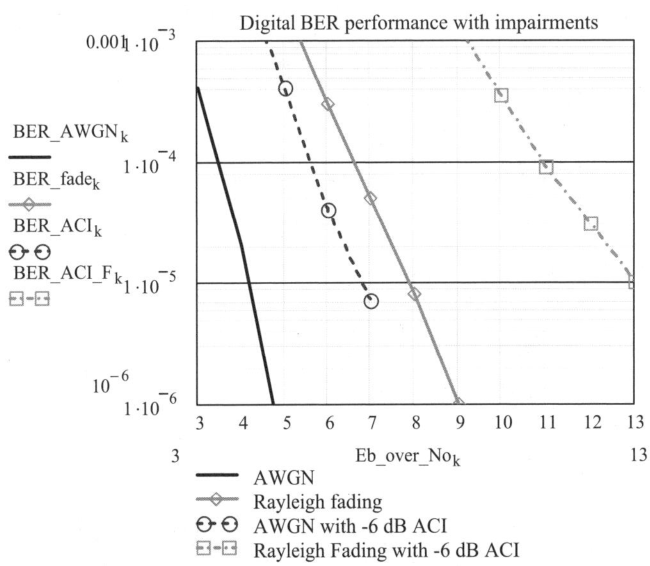

Figure 12. Digital performance with and without -6 dB first adjacent interferer in AWGN and fading.

CONCLUSIONS

A brief overview of the FM Hybrid HD Radio signal was presented. The performance of the FM analog host signal was compared to that of the digital sidebands. The performance comparisons included the postdetection audio signal for FM analog and digital in the presence of both noise and fading. Some interference scenarios were also considered. In summary, the digital audio quality was shown to be superior to analog audio quality under most reception conditions. Under conditions when the digital signal is lost, the analog signal, when available, is used as a backup to ensure that the audio quality is generally better than the original analog signal.

ACKNOWLEDGEMENT

The author expresses his thanks to Paul Peyla of iBiquity Digital Corporation for his thorough review and helpful suggestions in the writing of this paper.

REFERENCES

1. B. Kroeger & P. Peyla, "Compatibility of FM Hybrid IBOC System for Digital Audio Broadcasting," IEEE Trans. Broadcasting, Vol. 43, No. 4, pp. 421-430, December, 1997.
2. B. Kroeger & D. Cammarata, "Robust Modem and Coding Techniques for FM Hybrid IBOC DAB," IEEE Trans. Broadcasting, Vol 43, No. 4, pp. 412-420, December, 1997.
3. T. Rappaport, *Wireless Communications Principles and Practice*, pgs. 89 & 185, IEEE Press, NY, 1996.
4. A. Bruce Carlson, *Communications Systems: An Introduction to Signals and Noise in Electrical Communication*, pg. 262, McGraw-Hill, NY, 1968.
5. Annex A: HDC Encoder/Decoder Characteristics (Normative), Rev. A, iBiquity Digital Corp., November 20, 2003.

CONTACT

The author, Dr. Brian Kroeger, is Chief Scientist for iBiquity Digital Corporation headquartered in Columbia, Maryland.

Email: kroeger@ibiquity.com.

Website: www.ibiquity.com.

2002-01-0822

Hidden Antennas for the Foresight Vehicle

Richard Langley, Richard Breden, Didier Viratelle and Lazaros Economou
University of Kent

ABSTRACT

This paper describes the research and development of innovative multiband antenna modules to replace multiple individual antennas on vehicles. The antenna modules were designed for mounting beneath plastic panels on the car where they would be completely out of sight and hence secure, leaving the aerodynamics and styling of the vehicle unimpaired. This project was the first step to further integration of other antennas into the modules as new services become economical for inclusion into vehicle telematics systems. Printed fractal and spiral antennas, suitable for broadcast signal reception, together with two antennas designed for mobile vehicle telematics applications are described. The latter are based on PIFA and hybrid geometries offering low profile and wide bandwidth operation at 900 MHz and 1800 MHz, with a VSWR of better than 1.7.

INTRODUCTION

Four different antennas are presented in this paper covering broadcast reception frequencies and dual-band telephone antennas. These designs address problems encountered when integrating antennas into vehicles so that they remain hidden while performing to a high standard. To keep costs down the antenna constructions are simple. One class of multiband antenna to replace the monopole for broadcast applications is the printed fractal antenna [1-3]. Fractals are widely known mathematically and are in effect structures with self-similar shapes. Two types of fractal antenna, the Koch fractal patterns and the Sierpinski Gasket, were investigated giving possibilities for reducing the size of printed antennas while offering multiband operation. The printed triangle antenna is described as a viable alternative with more control over the operating bands. Designed to operate over the AM/FM and DAB bands we have evaluated their performance in cars. The next section describes advances made on telephone antennas, presenting two dual band designs with a low profile. The first is a wide bandwidth PIFA antenna [4,5] while the second is hybrid antenna based an antenna by Delavaud [6], both being designed to fit under plastic panels on a vehicle. Where possible measurements are presented for antennas mounted on vehicles.

PRINTED ANTENNAS

FRACTAL ANTENNAS - Photograph 1 compares three antennas: a simple 40cm standard roof mount monopole at the bottom of the picture, together with third and fourth order Koch fractal curves. Each of these antennas resonate at the same frequency and from Photograph 1 it can be seen that there is considerable scope for reducing the size of the antenna when a fractal geometry is used.

The fractal antennas have the same overall wire length. The number of fractal resonances increases with order and the ratio between the frequencies changes. The band ratio between resonances can be varied, particularly for the higher fractal orders, by changing the individual segmented lengths. 3rd and 4th order fractal resonant ratios can be varied typically from 1.8 to 2.5 giving significant flexibility. Figure 2 shows the return loss for the 1st, 3rd and 4th order fractals and an equivalent monopole antenna. The fundamental resonance reduces in frequency as the order of the curve increases, falling from 300 MHz for the monopole to 175MHz for the 4th order fractal. The lowest mode current distribution over the 4th order fractal is also shown in Figure 1 where it behaves as a monopole.

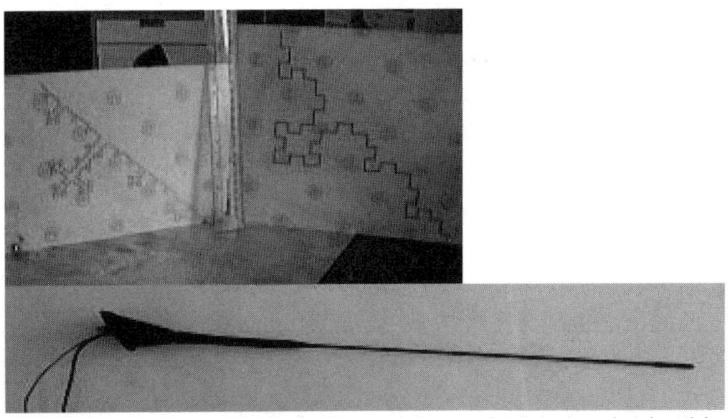

Photograph 1 Koch fractal antennas with a standard whip antenna

The current distribution at the fundamental resonant frequency is also shown in Figure 1. This is essentially like a monopole excitation.

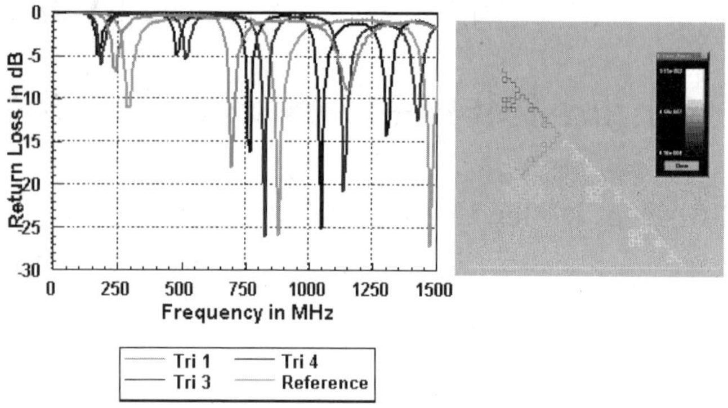

Figure 1 Return loss for Koch fractals and a reference monopole with current distribution over 4th order Koch fractal

Radiation patterns were measured at the first four resonant bands for the 4th order fractal and these will be presented at the conference. Vertical polarisation gain for the fractal is about 2 dB lower than the monopole but the polar patterns were virtually identical. Horizontal polarisation patterns have nulls but the gain is 10 dB higher than a vertical monopole making the antenna ideal for mixed polarisation broadcast reception such as FM broadcasts. There are no significant overmoding problems at the higher frequencies making these antennas useful across the multiple bands.

TRIANGLE PRINTED ANTENNA - The general antenna geometry for this printed triangular spiral is shown in Figure 2 where the structure is essentially equilateral. The stub at the side is tuned for the high DAB band at 1470MHz. Changing the aspect ratio and size of the antenna while keeping the frequency bands constant allows the antenna to be reconfigured to fit a designated area or to change the ratio of vertical to horizontal polarisation which is useful for broadcast systems. For example in DAB broadcasts the polarisation is vertical whereas for analogue FM radio mixed polarisation is often used.

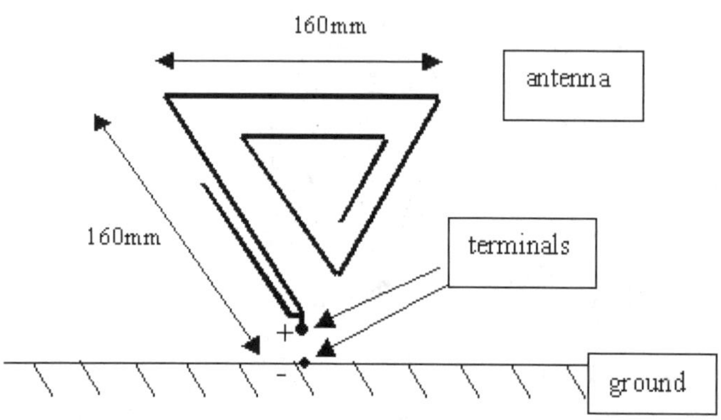

Figure 2 Geometry of triangle antenna

This design was tested on the glass windscreen of a car near the right hand corner to determine its performance with respect to a tuned mast antenna mounted vertically on the roof of a car. The car had infrared reflective glass on all but the front window. In Figure 3 the measured return loss is plotted over the FM band and DAB band III which includes the matching circuit. At L-band the DAB return loss was better than –17dB across the band, from 1450-1490MHz. Simulation indicates that the antenna radiates as a quarter wave monopole at the FM band and a half wave monopole at the lower DAB band (225MHz). At 1470MHz the stub is now excited as expected. The radiation patterns were measured on the vehicle and are plotted in Figure 4. The arrow depicts the forward direction of the car. Radiation patterns from the reference are nominally omnidirectional around the car. At the FM band the patterns were similar for the triangle and monopole antennas giving acceptable all round coverage. The performance of the DAB antenna at band III, Figure 4a, was better than the reference due to the signal amplification apart from a hole near 30 degrees due to the A pillar. At the higher DAB band at 1470MHz the radiation pattern is severely attenuated in all directions other than forward, Figure 4b. This was largely due to an infrared reflective coating on the windows which attenuates and scatters radio waves at all frequencies but particularly above 1GHz.

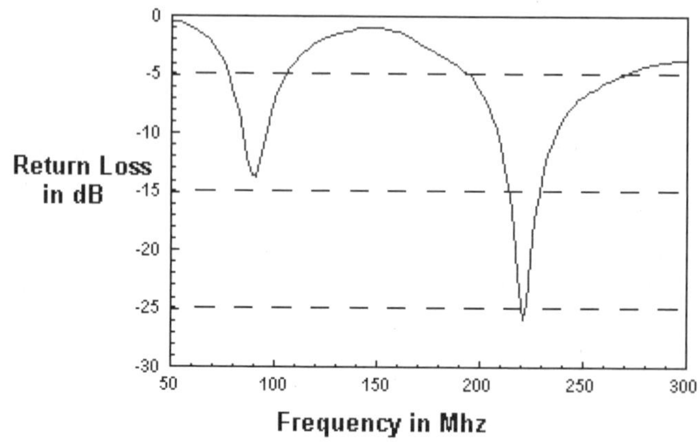

Figure 3 Measured return loss

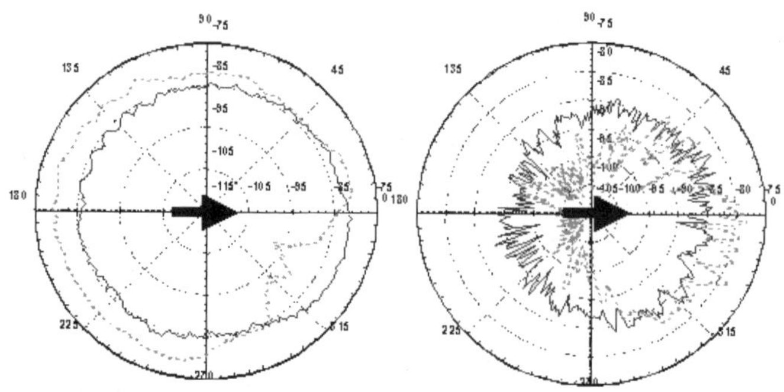

Figure 4 Radiation patterns at two DAB bands compared to reference monopole antenna
(a) 225MHz (b) 1470MHz

DUAL-BAND TELEPHONE ANTENNAS

Two telephone antennas suitable for mounting on vehicles are described. They possess a good impedance match across the bands, 7% at 925 MHz (890-960MHz) and 10% at 1800 MHz (1710-1880MHz). In each case the antennas are fed by a single coaxial feed and provide full azimuth coverage round the vehicle.

DUAL BAND PIFA TELEPHONE ANTENNA - Figure 5 shows the geometry of a PIFA antenna designed to operate at the 900 and 1800 MHz telephone bands. The conductors have been cut away to provide a dual resonant frequency response with wide bandwidths [5]. This antenna was mounted in the bumper of a car in various different positions and tested. The aim was to give equal radiation performance around the car and examine the blocking effects due to the bodywork. The current distribution plots show that at 900 MHz the outer parts of the structure are responsible for the radiation. At the higher band the inner section is excited. Figure 6 compares the measured and computed return loss for this antenna. There is good agreement at the upper band but it is less so at the lower band. Nevertheless a good bandwidth is measured at each band with a vswr < 1.6.

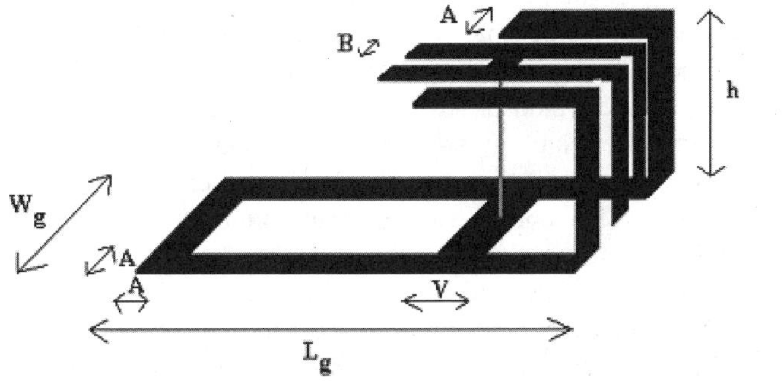

Figure 5 View of the dual band antenna
L_g = 124 mm, L_{p1} = 82.5 mm, L_{p2} = 83.5 mm
W_g = W_p = 30 mm, h = 15 mm.

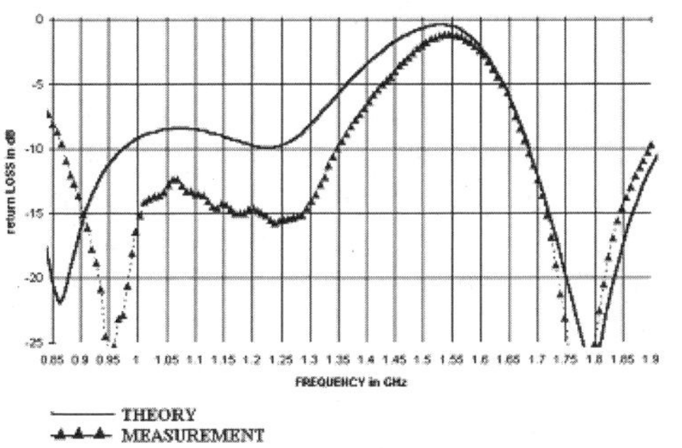

Figure 6 Return loss: measurement and simulation

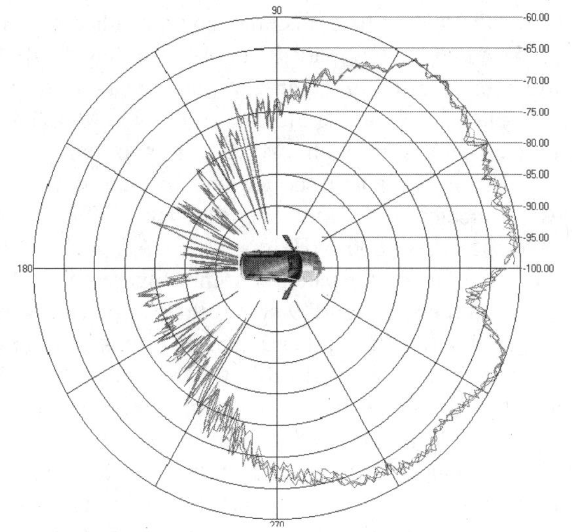

Figure 7 Radiation pattern for antenna

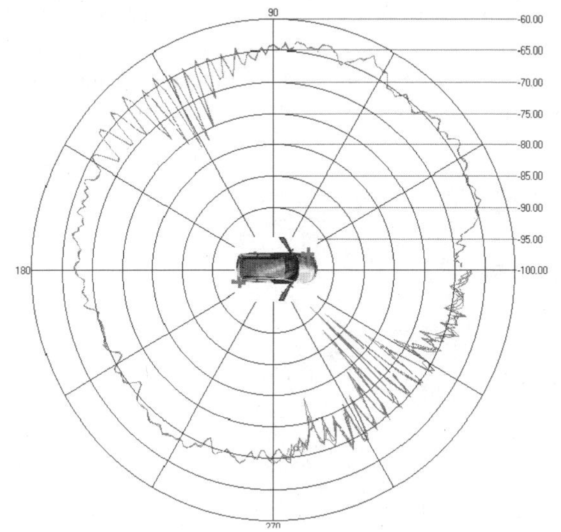

Figure 8 : Antennas installed diagonally on the two bumper corners

The vertically polarised radiation pattern measurements are shown for the 900 MHz band in Figures 7 & 8, with the antenna installed vertically on the car. The red crosses on the car drawing gives the position of the antenna/s. The PIFA antennas were mounted with the side L_g vertical to give vertical polarisation. The antenna alone gives monopole like radiation patterns in this orientation and hence an omnidirectional azimuth coverage.

In Figure 7 with the antenna placed in the centre the forward visiblity is good but the car body blocks the rear directed radiation. Similar blocking is found in other positions. Therefore two antenna were used, the best coverage being obtained when the antennas were placed on opposite corners of the bumpers front and rear as shown in Figure 8. Here we observe that there is good all-round coverage with ripple where the two radiation patterns overlap. At the higher frequency band similar results were measured although the ripple increased.

HYBRID ANTENNA - The antenna shown in Photograph 2 is a design based on the top loaded monopole principle [6], the upper plate being shorted to the ground plane by a pair of pins strategically placed to tune the antenna to the 900 MHz band. A second pair passes through two 6 mm x 6 mm square clearance holes on the patch surface and extends beyond it. The holes are located at 5.5 mm from the centre. This second pair provide the DCS-1800 MHz operation. All pins are 1.2 mm in diameter. The upper patch is 56mm square and is low profile, just 15mm high. Figure 9 shows the computed current distribution at the 1800 MHz band. The two pins protruding above the upper plate are responsible for the radiation at this band, see Figure 9, while the shorting pins together with the feed are responsible for the radiation at the lower band. The DCS-1800 band can be fine-tuned by adjusting the length of the corresponding pins. The GSM band remains unaffected from any change in the pin length. The maximum return loss for the GSM band is –26 dB at 0.925 GHz and for the DCS is –27 dB at 1.785 GHz. The corresponding bandwidths are 90 MHz and 170 MHz respectively. Figure10 shows typical azimuth radiation pattern measured for the antenna placed under the rear screen at the top. It is compared with a roof mounted monopole. The radiation to the rear of the car is slightly enhanced while that at the front is reduced when compared to the monopole as in Figure10.

Photograph 2 Dual band 900/1800 MHz antenna

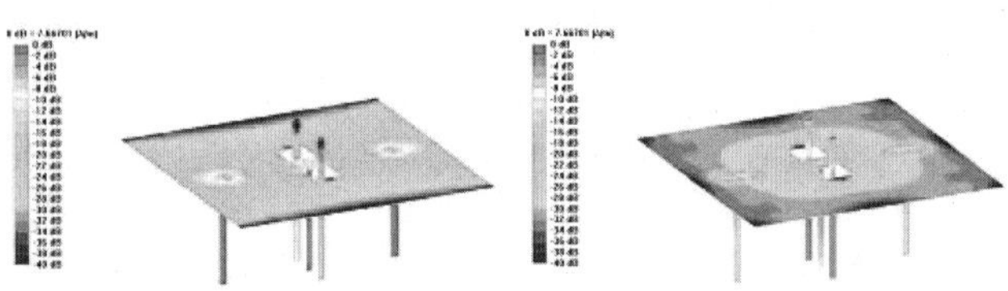

Figure 9 Computed current distributions

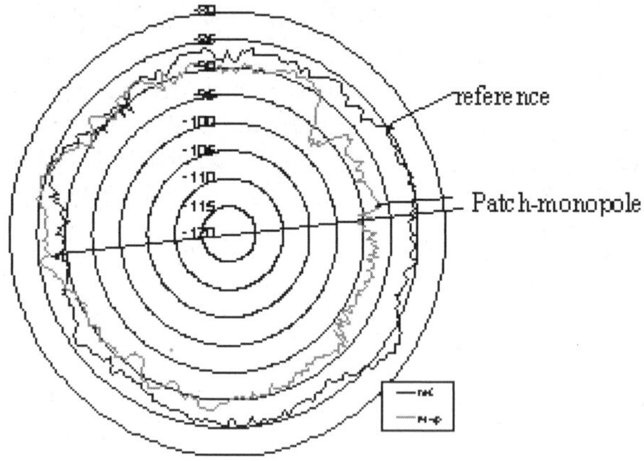

Figure 10 Polar Azimuth Radiation Pattern -antenna at top of rear screen

CONCLUSIONS

The paper has presented results for two multiband printed antennas which can be placed on glass or under plastic panels on a car providing reception at AM, FM, and both DAB bands. The antenna geometries are flexible so that other band spacings, polarisation responses or positions on the car can be accommodated. The radiation patterns are nearly omni-directional at the lower frequency bands although the car bodywork may block part of the radiation pattern particularly at higher frequencies. At 1.5GHz the reflective infrared coating on the windows has a very significant attenuation and scattering effect and, given that in future most cars will be so equipped, this presents a challenge for antenna engineers to overcome. The antennas are clear alternatives to other emerging printed designs.

A wide bandwidth dual band PIFA antenna has been presented. Using two antennas on a bumper allround coverage can be obtained. A hybrid telephone antenna is described which gives omni-directional radiation patterns in azimuth while providing wide bandwidths at two frequency bands, 900 and 1800 MHz. The antenna is low profile and designed to be roof mounted or hidden under a plastic panel.

ACKNOWLEDGEMENTS

The authors thank the UK Engineering & Physical Sciences Research Council, Department of Trade & Industry, Harada Industries Europe, Nissan Europe and Rover Group for supporting this project under the Innovative Manufacturing Initiative, part of the Foresight Vehicle Programme in the UK.

REFERENCES

1. Puente, C., Romeu, R.. and Benitez, F.:'Small but long Koch fractal monopole', *Electron. Letts.*, 1998, vol 34 (7), pp. 9-10
2. Puente, C., Romeu, J., Pous, R., Garcia, X. and Benitez, F.: 'Fractal multiband antenna based on the Sierpinski gasket', *Electron. Letts.*, 1996, vol 32 (1), pp. 1-2
3. Breden, R. and Langley, R.J.: 'Printed fractal antennas', *IEE Conf. on Ant. & Prop.*, 1999, pp.1-4

4. Dong Liu, Z. and Hall, P. S.: ' Dual-Frequency Planar Inverted-F Antenna ', *IEEE Transactions on Antennas and Propagation,*.1997, **45**, (10), pp. 1451-1457
5. Viratelle, D. and Langley, R.J.: 'Dual-band printed antenna for mobile telephone applications', IEE Proc. Microwaves, Antennas and Propagation, Vol.147 (6) , October 2000, pp.381-384
6. Delavaud, Ch., Leveque, Ph. and Jecko, B.: 'Small-sized low-profile antenna to replace monopole antennas', *Electron.Lett.*, 1998, **34**, (8), pp. 716-717

CONTACT

Professor Richard Langley
Electronic Engineering Dept
University of Kent
Canterbury
Kent CT2 7NT
UK

Email r.j.langley@ukc.ac.uk

2001-01-1328

XM Satellite Radio Technology Fundamentals

Stellios J. Patsiokas
XM Satellite Radio Inc.

ABSTRACT

In October of 1997, the Federal Communications Commission (FCC) granted two national satellite radio licenses. The FCC allocated 25 MHz of the electromagnetic spectrum (2.3 GHz frequency band) for satellite digital broadcasting to two companies: 12.5 MHz to XM Satellite Radio and 12.5 MHz to Sirius Satellite Radio. This paper is an overview of the XM Satellite Radio technology. Four major components of the overall Network are described: a) The ground segment; b) The space segment; c) The terrestrial repeater segment and the d) The technology segment. Mobile antenna design challenges are also being addressed and optimum antenna configurations are presented.

INTRODUCTION

The car and home radio world has not experienced an innovation in 45 years, not since the advent of FM radio. In the mean time we have seen the "digitization" of almost all of the major wireless technologies as well as wide adoption by consumers of Cable and Satellite television. XM Satellite Radio is part of this "digital revolution" and it will start broadcasting up to 100 channels of music and talk to car, home and portable radios beginning the second quarter of 2001.

There are two commercially available digital audio broadcasting (DAB) technologies today: a) Worldspace and b) Eureka 147. The Worldspace technology utilizes geostationary satellites (AFRIstar over Africa and ASIAstar over Asia) to broadcast digital audio content to mainly stationary radios. It implements a QPSK/TDM signalling format as well as Forward Error Correction (FEC) techniques. Eureka 147 is the European standard for Digital Audio broadcasting. It utilizes terrestrial base stations to broadcast digital audio and data to mobile and stationary radios. The technology expands Radio Frequency coverage by offering Single Frequency Network (SFN) configurations and implementing Orthogonal Frequency Division Multiplexing (OFDM) modulation to mitigate the vagaries of Raleigh fading.

XM's Technology incorporates key technologies from both of these proven systems by way of enhancements that have resulted from lessons learned. Specifically, XM's infrastructure consists of a ground segment (studios and uplink station), two geostationary satellites (XM Rock and XM Roll) and terrestrial repeaters, primarily in Urban Centers to reinforce satellite coverage. The Uplink frequencies are at X-band (7 GHz) with the downlinks operating at the licensed S-band (2.3 GHz) spectrum. Figure 1 is a simplified diagram of XM's infrastructure.

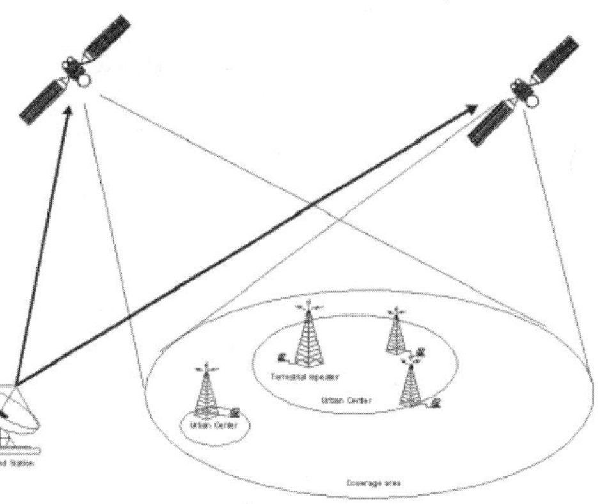

Figure 1. XM Infrastructure

The same Digital content is transmitted to both satellites through the uplinks. The X-band Uplink carriers undergo a frequency translation at the satellites to S-band and are re-transmitted to the radio receivers on earth. Radio frequency carriers from one of the satellites are also received by the terrestrial repeaters and the content is "repeated" at a different (Terrestrial) S-band carrier to the same radios. At any given time the mobile radios are "looking" for the same content from three sources: 1) XM Rock: 2) XM Roll and 3) terrestrial repeaters.

WAVEFORM FUNDAMENTALS

The Over-the-Air radio frequency protocol of the XM System is referred to as the XM "Waveform". The waveform is constructed of the RF signals transmitted from XM's two geostationary satellites and from the terrestrial repeater network. These RF signals, which are contained within the XM Band centered at 2337.5 MHz, contain identical program content. This provides three independent signal paths for the XM receiver to recover the audio programming error free.

Figure 2 represents the frequency plan for the XM system. The overall spectrum is divided into six Radio frequency carriers. There are four carriers allocated to the satellites and two carriers allocated to the terrestrial repeaters.

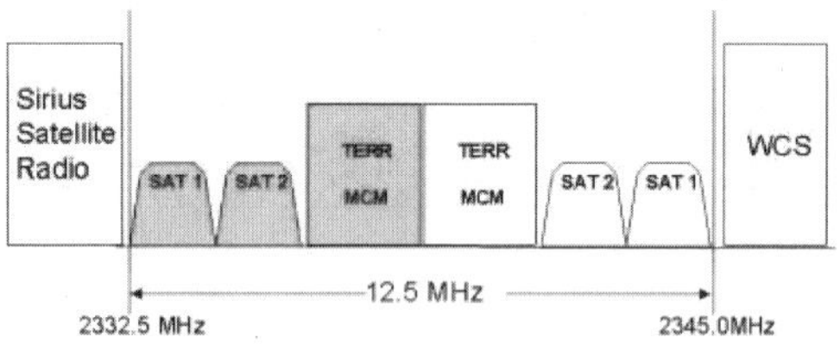

Figure 2. Frequency Plan

The satellite signals are broadcast using QPSK modulation. Data received from the two satellite signals are buffered and combined in the receiver so that a short signal outage, such as driving under a bridge, does not cause an interruption to the music.

The terrestrial signal is broadcast using Multi-Carrier Modulation (similar to OFDM). This transmission technique has a proven track record in DAB Systems currently in operation in both Europe and Canada. Receivers in the XM System simultaneously receive the satellite and terrestrial transmissions and continuously output the best available signal. Soft handovers between the satellite signals and terrestrial signals are totally transparent to the listener.

The XM digital format is based upon a 432 mS Master Frame and is shown in Figure 3. Each frame is subdivided into 8 kilobit per second sub channels, which may be dynamically grouped to form higher bit rate Payload Channels. The Payload Channel provides the necessary bandwidth to transport a high-quality digital audio signal to the listener. When the listener changes channels, the XM receiver simply extracts a different Payload Channel from the Master Frame.

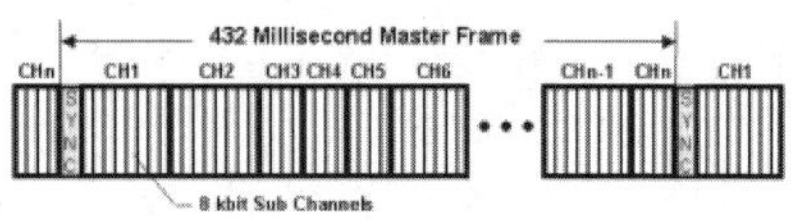

Figure 3. XM Wave Form Master Frame

Each receiver in the XM System has a unique identifier. The XM Waveform provides the capability of individually addressing each receiver Over-the-Air to enable or disable services. This capability is extendable to custom applications, such as individual data services or group data services.

GROUND, SPACE, REPEATER AND TECHNOLOGY SEGMENTS

There are four major segments associated with the XM System: 1) The ground segment; 2) The Space Segment; 3) The Repeater Segment and 4) The Technology Segment. These are depicted in Figure 4.

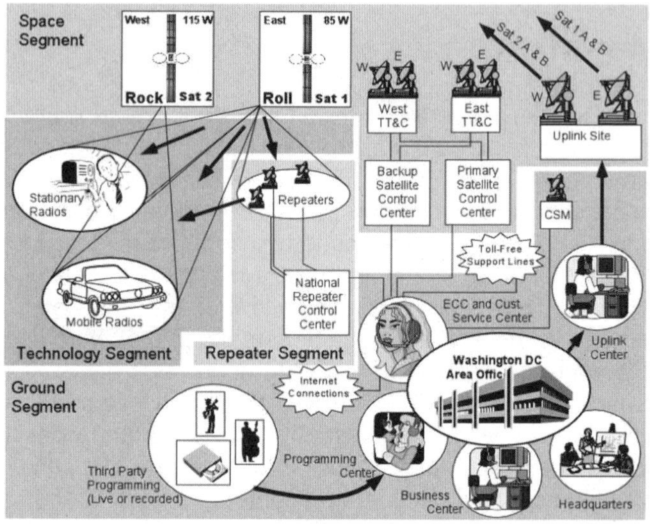

Figure 4. XM Service Segments

The Ground Segment produces and/or acquires content for the service. It also monitors the quality of the service, provides customer support, customer billing and manages the day-to-day financial and business systems. Another important function of the ground segment is the management of the conditional access system. Most of these functions are shown in Figure 5.

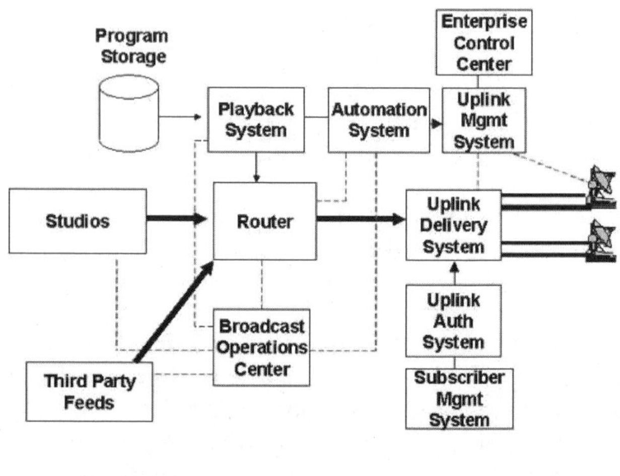

Figure 5. Ground Segment Functionality

The Space segment is comprised of the two satellites with a ground spare, redundant satellite control centers and redundant Telemetry and Control facilities, as well as the Uplink site. XM utilizes two Hughes HS-702 satellites, the most powerful satellites built for commercial use. The major attributes of the HS-702 are given in Figure 6.

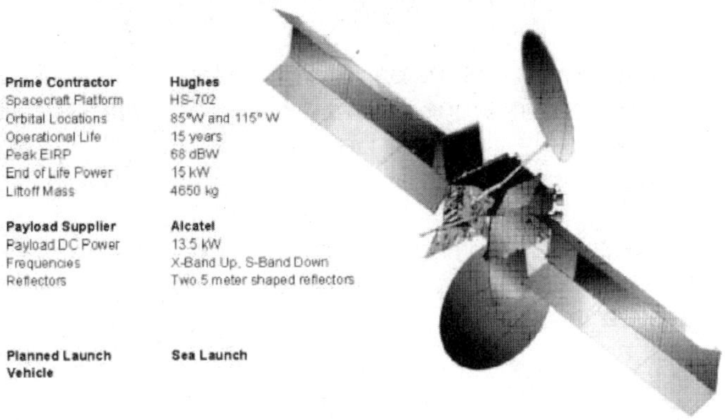

Figure 6. HS-702 Satellite Characteristics

Both geostationary satellites provide coverage for the entire Continental United States (CONUS) but their Effective Isotropically Radiated Power (EIRP) is weighted toward lower elevation angles and higher population densities. This "focusing" of the energy to areas where the population density is high is shown in Figure 7

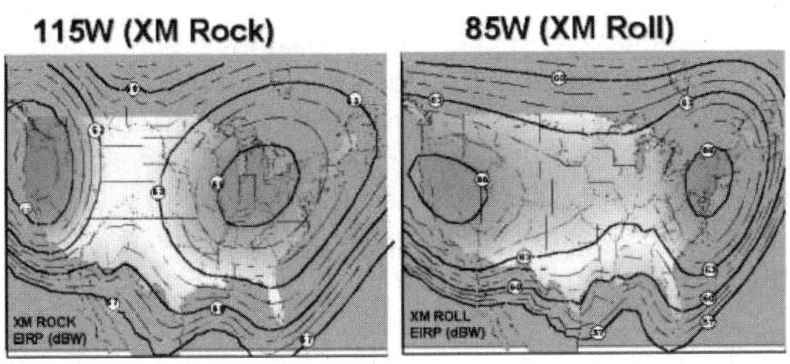

Figure 7. Satellite Coverage Contours

The signal strength contours reflect satellite EIRP. Furthermore, the service reliability based on the composite signal availability from both satellites is provided in Figure 8. The percentage contours in this figure represent signal availability above the minimum signal required for error free reception by the receivers on the ground.

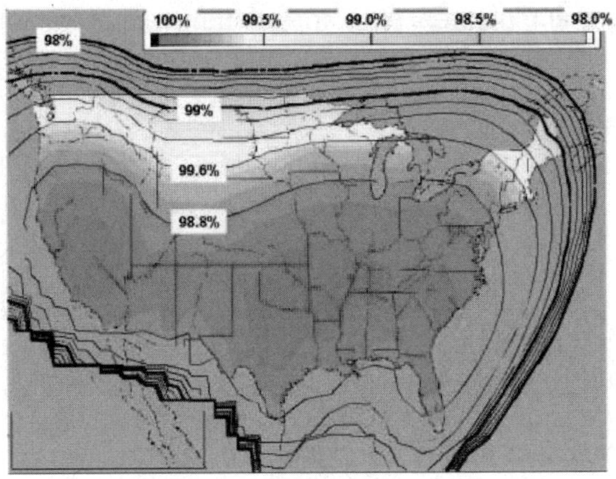

Figure 8. Signal Availability

The repeater segment consists of approximately 1500 repeaters and a Network Management System for the entire Terrestrial Network. Typical repeater radiated power is 2 kilowatts. The repeaters are employed mostly in downtown areas where tall buildings completely "block" the satellites. They receive signals from one of the satellites, and re-transmit them after demodulation to baseband and re-modulation in a format more suitable for the urban multipath environment (Multicarrier Modulation).

The Technology Segment is responsible for all aspects of the Waveform, the development of custom Integrated circuits and the definition of hardware architectures for the radio receivers. Figure 9 is a simplified diagram of an XM radio. There are two main blocks consisting of a) Hardware Reference Platform and b) the Manufacturer Platform.

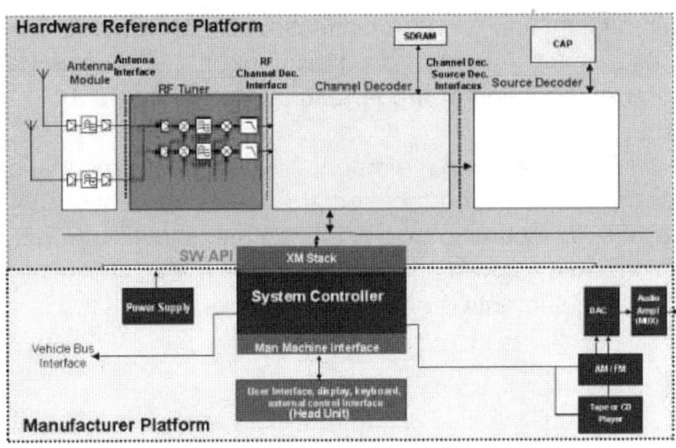

Figure 9. XM Radio Block Diagram

The Hardware Reference Platform includes an antenna module, an RF tuner, a channel decoder IC with external memory and a source decoder IC connected to a conditional Access Processor. The channel decoder and the source decoder are the only two custom chips in the first generation XM radios. The Hardware Reference platform also provides a software API (XM Stack) interfacing the manufacturer platform with the rest of the radio.

The manufacturer platform includes a power supply module, a system controller and peripheral circuitry for AM/FM reception as well as cassette or CD player.

The system controller communicates with the head unit in the dashboard via the vehicle bus wiring harness interface.

The XM tuner is a two-arm, double conversion receiver for simultaneous reception of both terrestrial and satellite signals. Major functions of the channel decoder are analog to digital conversion of the two second Intermediate frequency signals; b) Demultiplexing of the TDM satellite and terrestrial signals and c) Combining of the satellite and terrestrial signals. Major functions of the source decoder IC are a) Demultiplexing of all payload channels; b) Audio/Speech decoding; c) Data decoding.

Finally the XM antenna module utilizes two passive elements, one for satellite reception and the other for terrestrial, as well as active low noise amplifiers to overcome 10 dB of coaxial cable loss. Unlike other wireless technologies (e.g., PCS) where the antenna design of the subscriber unit is almost an afterthought the XM antenna particularly for mobile application is one of the most important elements of the radio design. It is required to receive signals of both circular and linear polarization. The antenna placement on the vehicle is critical, as it must be positioned for clear line of sight to the satellites independent of the direction the car is headed. This normally requires an antenna positioned at or above the roof of the car.

The terrestrial antenna element is linearly polarized, aligned with the polarization of the terrestrial base stations. It has an omnidirectional pattern with the primary lobe focused on the horizon. This provides optimum reception of the terrestrial signal.

The satellite antenna element has circular polarization with the primary lobe focused at an elevation angle of 45 degrees to optimize reception of the satellite signals. Typical antenna radiation patterns for both satellite and terrestrial elements are shown in Figure 10.

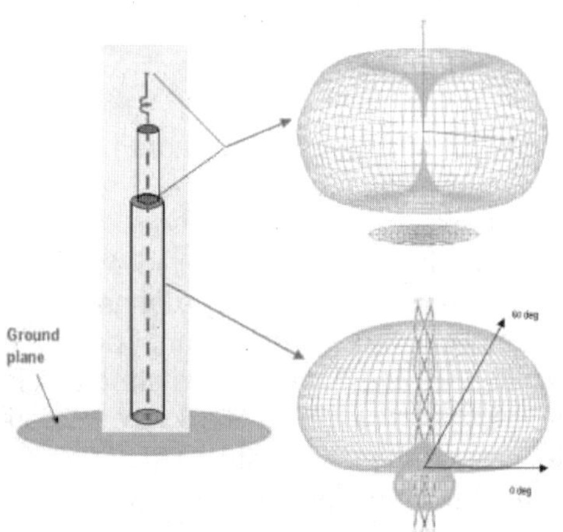

Figure 10. XM Antenna Radiation Patterns

The dual antenna structure maximizes overall signal reliability and provides excellent quality of service.

CONCLUSION

XM Technology is a second-generation Digital Audio Broadcasting technology with lessons learned from both Worldspace and Eureka 147.

A nation wide repeater network offers blanket Radio Frequency Coverage in Urban Centers, where satellite coverage is marginal, in a Single Frequency Network configuration.

Large-scale integration of the first generation receiver (only two custom chips) contributes to low cost receiver design.

The combination of three signal redundancy, low noise figure tuner and dual element active antenna module provides for seamless reception of signals and excellent digital audio quality for both car and home radios

ACKNOWLEGMENTS

The author wishes to express his gratitude to Jack Wormington, Paul Marko, Craig Wadin, Richard Michalski, Diane Strait and Dr. Argy Petros for their assistance toward the completion of this paper.

CONTACT

Dr. Patsiokas is Senior Vice President, Technology, for XM Satellite Radio, Inc. since October, 1998. Previously, Dr. Patsiokas was with Motorola, Inc., where he served in Engineering and Executive Management capacities for nineteen years. Dr. Patsiokas has served in a variety of consumer electronics design and development roles and holds 24 United States patents.

Dr. Patsiokas' email; stell.patsiokas@xmradio.com

2001-01-0011

S-C.A.R.E.S. Satellite Car Audio Reception Evaluation System

Andreas Fuchs and Sven Conrad
RecepTec l.l.c.

ABSTRACT

During 2001, vehicle owners will subscribe to new services provided by Sirius Satellite Radio, Inc. and XM Radio, Inc., who offer coast to coast, digital quality radio programming via satellite. Vehicles will be equipped with a unique reception system (receiver and antenna), initially dealer installed or purchased in the retail aftermarket, but shortly available as original equipment from vehicle manufacturers.

The introduction and application of this new technology in a relatively short timeframe poses special challenges to service providers, vehicle manufacturers and system suppliers in terms of measuring, evaluating and validating the quality of broadcasts and the performance of system components under various critical conditions. This paper presents an innovative method for simultaneously recording satellite reception characteristics under those conditions and for evaluating reception quality in a repeatable and documented manner

SATELLITE RADIO

XM Radio, Inc. and Sirius Satellite Radio, Inc. have launched satellites, supported by a network of terrestrial repeaters, each providing up to 100 stations of digital quality radio programming nationwide.

The two companies employ differing approaches in configuring their satellite and repeater networks.

XM employs two geostationary satellites at a distance of 43,000 kilometers from the earth's center and is reliant on a planned network of approximately 1,500 terrestrial repeaters strategically located across the country. The satellites, named "Rock" and "Roll", produced by Hughes Space & Communication Inc., are spaced 30 degrees apart at 85 degrees and 115 degrees west longitude. Their angle of elevation varies with location, from approximately 20 degrees in the northern to approximately 60 degrees in the southern part of the US.

Sirius relies on an unrestricted view to two of its three satellites which are in elliptical orbit at a distance from the earth's center varying during orbit from approximately 30,800 to 53,500 kilometers. In an elliptical orbit, the elevation angle of any one of the three satellites will be above 57 degrees at any point in the US. Sirius satellites were produced by Loral Space Systems Inc. with an effective radiated power of approximately 60 dBW, and are supported by approximately 150 terrestrial repeaters located in major cities.

RECEPTION CONDITIONS

The quality of reception of satellite broadcasts, whether directly from the satellite itself or from a terrestrial repeater, is impacted by some conditions, which are inherent to S-band frequencies. In addition, there are several important measures or characteristics affecting reception quality, which are unique to satellite broadcasts. The most significant of these conditions and characteristics are:

- Obstructions
- Weather conditions
- Geographic location
- Position of satellites
- Position of terrestrial repeaters
- Location and direction of vehicle

OBSTRUCTIONS

Buildings, trees, tunnels, overpasses and indeed large trucks can potentially obstruct the view to the satellite/repeater or degrade the signal quality due to reflections. This can result in a total loss of signal or some degree of multipath effects.

XM and Sirius will both transmit left hand circular polarized (LHC) signals in the frequency range of 2.320 to 2.345 GHz. Since satellite signals change polarization from LHC to RHC when reflected off a non-absorbent surface, signals transmitted by the satellite are almost immune to multipath effects. Both providers also use COFDM modulation for their terrestrial signals in order to reduce the effects of multipath

WEATHER CONDITIONS

Satellite radio signals are affected by weather conditions. Heavy rain and snow, as well as thick clouds, increase the path loss between the transmitting and receiving antenna. The effects on S-band frequencies (2.320-2.345 GHZ) are nevertheless minor in comparison to Ku-band frequencies used for direct satellite television

GEOGRAPHIC LOCATION AND TIME

Sirius and XM have configured their satellite/repeater networks to provide national coverage. However, the signal strength across the United States varies with location and in the case of Sirius (non-geostationary orbit) also over time.

POSITION OF SATELLITES

The direction and elevation of the satellite is important to correlate obstructions to the received signal. Since the elevation and direction of the satellites (Sirius) changes over time, effects of obstructions blocking the signal may vary.

POSITION OF TERRESTRIAL REPEATERS

The coverage area of a terrestrial repeater is limited by spherical surface of the earth in conjunction with the height of the transmitter. The direction and distance is important to correlate signal strength and multipath effects to environmental conditions.

The terrestrial broadcast of one service provider (XM or Sirius) may interfere with the satellite signal of the other.

LOCATION AND DIRECTION OF VEHICLE

An antenna mounted on a vehicle may not provide omni directional reception at all elevation angles. The satellite and terrestrial signal may be degraded depending on the location, direction and slope of the vehicle.

S-C.A.R.E.S^{SM}

Satellite radio reception is a new and untested technology in North America. At the time of writing, the broadcasting infrastructure is not fully in place and operational and the reception system itself (receiver and antenna combination) is not fully developed and supplied. Nevertheless, service providers, vehicle manufacturers and numerous system component suppliers have been challenged to introduce and validate this technology in a variety of combinations (vehicle/receiver/antenna) within a relatively short period. This validation process requires a complete understanding of the conditions and characteristics outlined above.

Existing software packages (used in GPS applications) are capable of monitoring the carrier to noise ratio (C/N) or signal strength of several satellites but do not have the capability of recording signals strength or C/N in time domain. Although useful, this information is not comprehensive enough to describe a reception situation in detail. In addition, an operator must manually create a record of the measurements and provide detailed documentation of test locations, times, weather conditions as well as obstructions (buildings, trees, bridges). This process is very time consuming and the accuracy of the results is dependant on the operator. Results acquired in this way are frequently questioned and the test areas are often revisited to verify the results.

S-C.A.R.E.S^{SM} is a computerized system of recording, measuring and evaluating reception quality of Sirius or XM signals received by a receiver / antenna combination in various locations (fringe, urban etc) and under various reception conditions (weather, tunnels etc).

S-C.A.R.E.S^{SM} has been developed to collect objective, independent data and to accurately record test locations and reception conditions. By creating a "virtual test ride", S-C.A.R.E.S^{SM} enables all interested parties to see and hear recorded data, repeatedly if necessary, and to participate in the evaluation process.

An S-C.A.R.E.S^{SM} system combines readily available hardware with specially written recording and evaluation software

a) System Hardware

system hardware currently comprises:

- 900 MHz computer with removable hard drive
- GPS receiver and antenna
- Spectrum analyzer (satellite)
- Spectrum analyzer (terrestrial)
- Digital camcorder with wide-angle lens

The system mechanization shown in Fig.1 describes the hardware configuration required to evaluate one satellite radio receiver and one antenna incorporating terrestrial and satellite antenna elements. This configuration can be expanded to evaluate up to four receivers with either four alternative antennas or a single antenna connected to all receivers via a signal splitter.

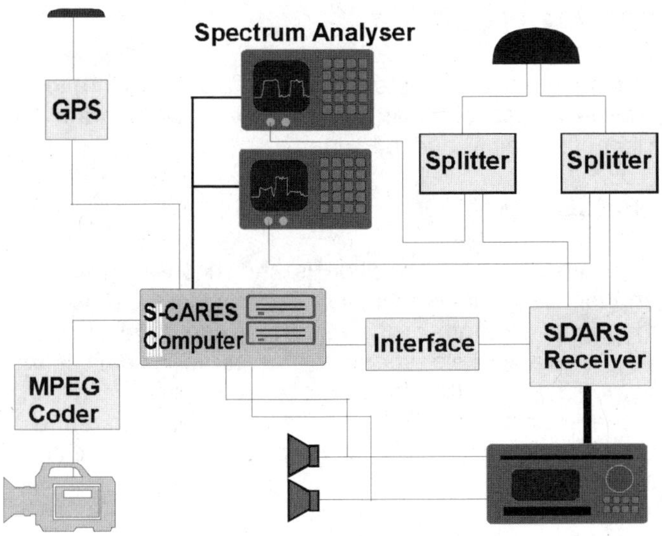

Fig.1 S-C.A.R.E.S^{SM} System Mechanization

COMPUTER

A commercially available 900 MHz computer is used to record data to a removable hard drive. This makes it possible to transfer data to another computer for evaluation while the recording computer remains installed in the test vehicle. The audio signal reproduced by the receiver is recorded either from the unbalanced audio line outputs or directly at the speaker outputs. The S-CARES^{SM} computer uses a multi channel audio card (Aardwark Aark 20/20) to record audio signals of up to four receivers. The audio signal is not used to determine reception quality and is stored in a compressed format (MPEG 1 Layer 3) in order to reduce disk space usage.

When production receivers become available, the recording method of bit error rate will be finalized. However current receivers are capable of providing this information through an external bus interface connected to the RS 232 interface. It is possible to monitor and record certain receiver specific data, which helps to accelerate the development process.

GPS RECEIVER

GPS receivers and electronic mapping software are readily available. A Magellan receiver, with dead reckoning, is particularly helpful in situations where the GPS signals are blocked by buildings or other obstructions. A magnet mount GPS antenna (patch antenna with 27 dB LNA gain) is installed on the roof of the vehicle in order to provide maximum antenna performance. The S-CARES^{SM} computer is connected to the GPS receiver via RS 232 and receives global positioning information in NMEA format. Currently used with the S-CARES^{SM} system are two different GPS receivers.(Garmin and Magellan) The update rate for both types is one data set per second.

SPECTRUM ANALYZER

In order to analyze the cause of degradation in signal quality, a spectrum analyzer is used to distinguish if the received RF signal is affected by interference from other signal sources or the signal strength is degraded due to blockage or multipath.

Due to the importance of this information, two spectrum analyzers are used to monitor the terrestrial and satellite signal. The spectrum analyzers (Agillent EXXXX) are connected to the S-CARES^{SM} computer via GPIB (IEEE-488). The computer acquires and records frequency sweeps of 101 data points with a rate of 10 sweeps per second. The analyzer settings (center frequency, frequency span, video band width, resolution band width, frequency points) are predetermined and saved internally to the analyzer. The software recalls these settings but directly controls the reference line as well as input attenuation in order to prevent the analyzer from overloading in strong signal areas

VIDEO CAMCORDER

Weather conditions affect the satellite link budget and must therefore be documented. (It is possible to receive weather information via the Internet, but this was ruled out due to the risk of interference from the transmitting cellular phone) The use of a digital video camcorder with a wide angle lens was considered the most practical alternative to record weather conditions and a complete image of the surrounding area.

A Sony Digital Camcorder is positioned inside the vehicle (facing forward) in a location where an unobstructed view of the surrounding area is possible. The video signal is recorded to the hard drive in MPEG 1 with a typical rate of 512 KBit per second. This is achieved by an external compressing video grabber interface(Dazzle DVC, Pinnacle MP10).

b) Software

S-C.A.R.E.S^{SM} software has two program sections - record and playback.

When recording, the video image and vehicle position is not displayed in order to provide 100% of the available I/O and processor performance to the recording itself. A health status is displayed in the corresponding window to inform the operator that the recording is in progress.

The recording software consists of independent threads for all streams used for recording (Fig.2).

To correlate the data streams during playback it is necessary to store synchronization information in all data streams during recording. Video, Audio and GPS provide internally generated timing information. By adding timestamps to the spectrum analyzer stream, this information can be used for synchronization.

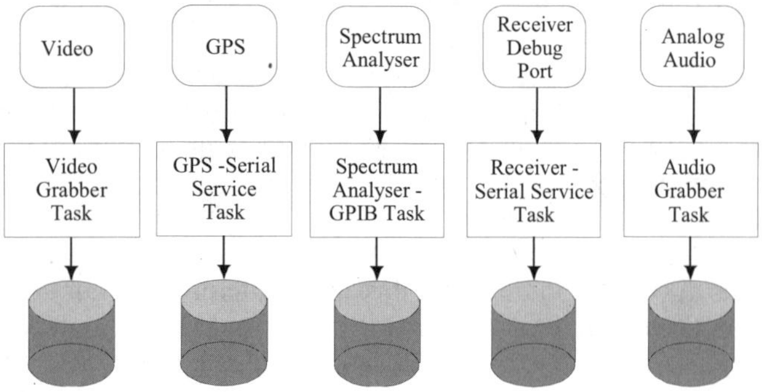

Fig 2. S-CARES^{SM} tasks

EXCEPTION RECORDING

In record mode it is possible to make a continuous recording of data for the duration of the test ride. Alternatively, in order to conserve disk space, and in order to present only meaningful data (requiring interpretation or reaction), the program may be set to identify and record only those instances when reception quality falls outside of selected acceptable parameters thresholds (bit error rate or signal to noise ratio).

The playback window (Fig. 3) recreates a virtual ride trip and displays the various data streams, recorded during the test ride, to show the critical reception conditions required for the validation process.

VIDEO IMAGE

The viewer is able to participate in the test ride on screen and witness the progress of the test vehicle, the road conditions, the weather conditions, any obstructions etc. and at the same time observe and hear how these conditions affect reception quality.

SATELLITE POSITION

Satellite position relative to the vehicle is calculated and displayed using orbital information in conjunction with the GPS time (UTC), vehicle location and direction. The elevation angle and direction of the satellite is displayed relative to the vehicle heading in graphical (polar diagram 15 degrees per division) and text form. This information is helpful to correlate degradation in signal quality to obstructions recorded by the camera.

(The use of an inclinometer was considered in order to calculate the elevation angle to the satellites relative to the incline of the vehicle. Since the value of this information was unclear and drive testing would help clarify the importance, it was decided to disregard the incline and to calculate the elevation angle using the vehicle position only.)

REPEATER POSITION

The proximity of repeaters (distance and direction) to the vehicle is also displayed graphically (polar diagram 100 kilometer radius) and in text form.

VEHICLE LOCATION

The current vehicle position is shown on a street map and the test route is marked with two colors representing the signal strength of the terrestrial and satellite signal. The available field strength of satellite signals is not homogeneous throughout the US and terrestrial repeaters provide only localized coverage. Therefore, it is desirable to provide geographical documentation of the test location.

FREQUENCY SPECTRUMS

The frequency spectrum of the satellite and terrestrial antenna is displayed as it was recorded during the test ride. By observing the video image and the satellite position, it is possible to correlate signal degradations caused by obstructions or other environmental conditions.

The detailed display of signal strength over the frequency band enables the evaluator to identify interference. Radio frequency interference (RFI) caused by electronic devices or by an adjacent frequency sources (XM or Sirius transmitter) have distinguishing characteristics and can easily identified.

SIGNAL TO NOISE / BIT ERROR RATE / AUDIO SIGNAL SPECTROGRAM

This section of the window can be configured to display, in time domain, up to four cartesian diagrams of the signal to noise ratio of each satellite and terrestrial signal, or the bit error rate, or a spectrogram of the audio signal.

Digital systems reproduce equal quality audio even if the quality of the received RF signal is degraded. When the receiver is tuned to a specific channel, it is not possible to make any meaningful measurements of an audio signal from an uncontrolled audio source (music or talk).

It is useful to record the audio signal for later evaluation but it does not replicate a true image of the RF signal quality.

Bit error rate is a receiver internal indicator for the ability to demodulate the digital signal received. It can be correlated to the signal quality received by the antenna. The spectrum analyzer data in conjunction with bit error rate and analog audio provide a comprehensive picture of reception quality.

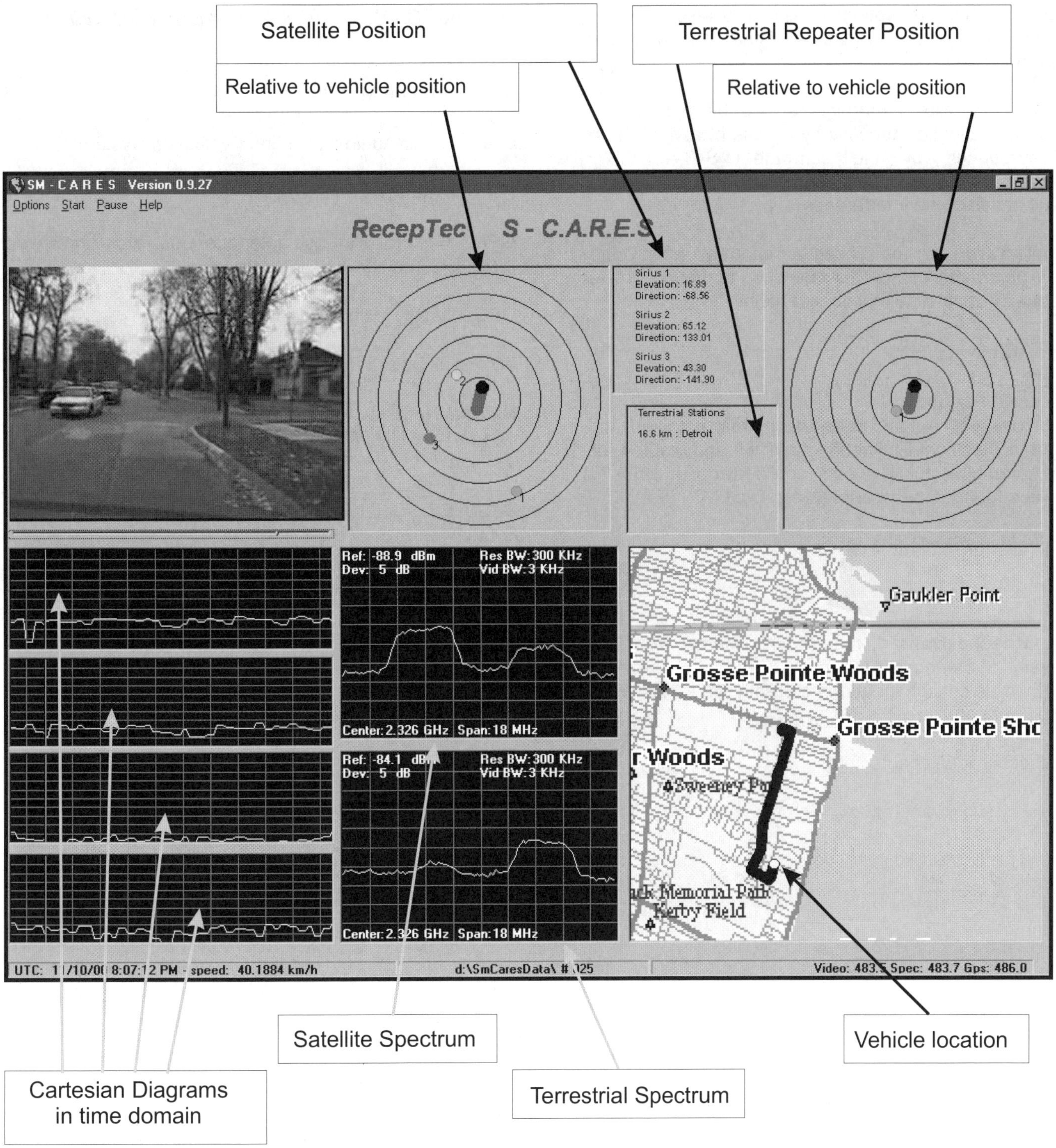

Fig. 3 S-CARES Playback screen

SEARCH AND FIND

S-C.A.R.E.S[SM] playback software is able to find critical segments of the recorded data by using a scrolling function (synchronized to the video recording) to recover a recorded sequence which best illustrates a point. Alternatively, by setting a specific threshold (e.g. bit error rate or a signal to noise ratio), the program will search for and find those occurrences which meet the selected criteria. These findings may be exported in table format (e.g. to Excel.) and presented in hard copy.

CONCLUSION

S-C.A.R.E.S[SM] is currently used by Sirius Satellite Radio, Inc. and has proved itself as a useful tool during the initial phase, verifying the signal conditions within the network in critical reception areas. It is also used for analyzing and verifying the antenna and receiver performance.

S-C.A.R.E.S^{SM} allows management to be part of the testing and validation process by means of a virtual ride trip reproduced by the computer. S-C.A.R.E.S^{SM} documents signal conditions and points in most cases to the root cause of the interference.

The integration of the essential information on one screen generates comprehensive documentation of the functionality of satellite mobile reception.

CONTACT

Andreas D. Fuchs
Vice President, Advanced Development obtained his Degree in Electrical Engineering in 1989 and worked for Fuba Automotive for 10 years until leaving in 1999 to become a founder member of RecepTec LLC.

E-mail: afuchs@receptec.net

Sven Grosche Conrad, received his Master from the University of Hannover, Germany in 1995. He worked since then as consultant and is currently senior software development engineer for RecepTec LLC.

E-mail: sconrad@receptec.net

DEFINITIONS, ACRONYMS, ABBREVIATIONS

AM: Amplitude Modulation

CARES: Car Audio Reception Evaluation System

FM: Frequency modulation

GPIB: General Purpose Interface Bus, also known as IEEE 488 and HP-IB

GPS: Global Positioning System

I/O: Input/Output (Interface)

NMEA: National Marine Electronics Association, here referred to NMEA 0183 ASCII Interface Specification, Version 2.0

S-CARES: Satellite Car Audio Reception Evaluation System

UTC: Coordinated Universal Time

2001-01-0006

Peripheral SDAR Interoperability

Robert Hjelmeland and Chris Ols
Delphi Automotive Systems, Delco Electronics

ABSTRACT

Radio broadcasting has entered the digital era, where services are delivered from the studio to the listener entirely in the digital domain. The Satellite Digital Audio Receiver Systems (SDARS) being developed provides the means to receive high-quality digital radio services. The SDARS receiver will be a peripheral component to the existing audio system in the vehicle for the first generation. Subsequent generations of the product will examine the opportunity for up-integrating the SDARS receiver into the modules of existing entertainment system. This paper will outline a set of common operating characteristics that may be used in peripheral SDAR applications. If adhered to, this will allow the XM Satellite Radio service and Sirius Satellite Radio service to co-habitat on the same audio system or be interchangeable at a receiver module level. Many of the points discussed in this paper are not specific to or under the control of the SDARs service providers. Some items require compliance with existing vehicle practices while others are new to the automotive environment.

INTRODUCTION

There are two SDAR service providers: Sirius Satellite Radio and XM Satellite Radio. Each service provider will be capable of producing commercial free entertainment for vehicular applications by early 2001 for a small monthly fee (~10/month).

Sirius Satellite Radio uses three Space Systems / Loral satellites in a inclined elliptical orbit constellation. The satellites are backed up by a terrestrial repeater system consisting of ~100 sights in 56 markets.

In contrast, XM uses two of the most powerful communications satellites known (Hughs HS702, with communication payloads by Acatel) in a geo-stationary configuration. Any gaps in the coverage are addressed by the planned 1,500 terrestrial repeaters.

XM and Sirius have agreed that certain aspects of the receivers shall be similar, if not the same. This will allow each service provider to be implemented in a vehicle with little or no impact to the OEM.

The SDAR service providers are working to define the technology for internal interoperability (a single receiver that can comprehend both services). The goal of this paper is to discuss peripheral interoperable applications. A peripheral SDAR receiver, for the purpose of this paper, is defined as a component of an audio system that can be added to an existing audio system for the purpose of receiving XM Satellite Radio or Sirius Satellite Radio programming.

Peripheral interoperability for SDARS can be addressed in three categories: Hardware, Software, and Human Factors. Hardware issues will cover aspects of SDARS such as connectors and audio interface features. Software will cover aspects of SDARS such as reporting common quality indicators. Human Factors will examine the similarities and differences of how the receivers are manipulated in various 'typical' applications.

HARDWARE

The obvious starting point for commonality between XM Satellite Radio and Sirius Satellite Radio is in the interface hardware. The hardware issue can be narrowed down to: RF Connectors, Body Connectors, Labels, Displays, Line Level Audio and Antenna configurations.

RF CONNECTOR

There will be two RF connectors for each SDAR receiver, in the first generation. One connector will be used for the satellite signal, the other for the terrestrial signal. Since the connectors are used in automotive applications, they must be colored and keyed in such a fashion as to ensure proper connections in "blind" mating situations.

The FAKRA standard for SMB type connectors has been adopted. This standard calls for impedance of 50Ω, Shielding value of 40dB/1GHz minimum, contact resistance of 40mΩ, 25 mating cycles minimum.

The Terrestrial connection shall be BLACK (A keying). The Satellite connection shall be CURRY in color (K keying). A XM only application may typically use GREEN (key E) for Terrestrial and BORDEAUX VIOLET for the satellite path. A SIRIUS only application may typically use Natural (key B) for Terrestrial and BLUE (Code C) for Satellite. The Z key <u>should not</u> be used for production as it can be mated to any other connector. The following diagram illustrates the connector color & keying combinations.

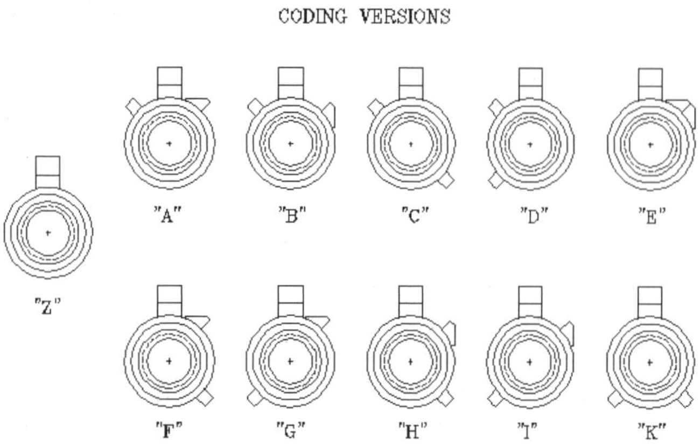

CODING	COLOR	
A	BLACK	
B	NATURAL	
C	BLUE	
D	BORDEAUX VIOLET	
E	GREEN	
F	BROWN	
G	GREY	
H	VIOLET	
I	BEIGE	
K	CURRY	
Z	WATERBLUE	

BODY CONNECTOR

The "Body Connector" may contain power, ground, line level audio out and vehicle/HMI communications. The specific connector signal assignment (e.g. pin 1 is Battery) will vary from vehicle to vehicle. However, the USCAR standard has been adopted for SDARS use.

LABELING

Labeling is important on SDAR applications due to the requirement to track Electronic Serial Numbers (ESN's). The ESN is an alpha-numeric code which allows the service providers to track individual units.

The details of the label design are left to the discreation of the hardware manufacturer, however the label should contain the following information at a minimum: ESN, Service Provider "Marks", hardware manufacturers "Mark". The label should be printed using a 10pt font.

DISPLAY'S

The patrons visual experience with SDAR will revolve directly around the HMI (Human Machine Interface) display. As such, the service providers have established a common set of minimum requirements for the display.

The display shall have a minimum of one line of 8 character text. The character set provided to the display shall be consistent with 7 bit US-ASCII characters (ISO-8859-1, Latin 1). The display may be Liquid Crystal (LCD), Vacuum Florescent (VF) or whatever is deemed appropriate to remain in harmony with other displays in the system.

Additional display interoperability issues are outlined in the HMI section of this report. (e.g. what type of information is displayed)

AUDIO

Several scenarios may be used to convert the satellite and terrestrial signals into audio. The specific scenario is dependent on the audio system. Optical Data bus / Digital audio, Line level audio, audio signals that can directly drive speakers are all being currently developed.

In addition, some applications are converting the SDAR service to be compatible with FM transmissions. This would allow the SDAR receiver to be connected to a typical radio.

The audio experience of the patron will be heavily impacted by software driven issues. Decisions about muting, handling digital "artifacts" that result from error rate correction, and switching strategies become more crucial when the installer or end user is exposed to both services (XM or Sirius) through the same audio system. Due to the detail associated with these topics, their discussion is reserved for a later paper.

ANTENNA

The antenna can be argued as the single most critical component of the SDAR system. From the OEM point of view it is highly desirable to have an antenna that could be placed on a vehicle and be compatible with both SDAR service providers.

Although several antenna vendors have elements of an antenna, few have a truly interoperable antenna solution at the time of writing. The major stumbling block has revolved around the active circuitry that is unique to each service providers allocated RF spectrum.

To address this issue, it is recommended that the DC power for the XM antenna be supplied to the active circuitry by via the Terrestrial coax. For a Sirius application, the DC power for the antenna can be supplied to the active circuitry via the Satellite coax.

This scheme has the advantage that a single antenna can be placed on the vehicle, the remote SDAR unit would essentially "configure" the antenna for the correct application. In addition, this scenario would allow for both remote receivers to share the same antenna in the same application.

The next issue revolving around the antenna sub-system is the selection and length of coaxial cable. It is recommended that the coax be RG315 or similar with a total length not to exceed 10 feet, loss for each connector should be factored into the coax length calculations.

SOFTWARE

For the purposes of this paper, the topic of software is limited to the software that is running on the system controller (i.e. this report will not examine the nuances of the software in either service providers DSP or ASIC's).

The majority of software developed for the system controller will be unique for the vehicle application. (e.g. power moding, vehicle communications) However, there are some common behavioral elements that are applicable to all SDAR receivers.

RECEPTION QUALITY INDICATORS

The major reception quality indicator is BER (Bit Error Rate). For SDAR applications, BER indicates how many symbols have been altered as a result of the various error correction algorithms within the signal processing chain. BER should be made available to the service tool that is used by the OEM's trouble-shooter. Some applications have considered making the BER available to the patron through the HMI's display. In these cases the BER is initiated following a unique button press sequence.

POWER MODING

In a vehicle application, the use of vehicle power – whether supplied by the charging system or battery – can be a great concern to the OEM. Each vehicle platform may set out unique requirements for power moding the SDAR receiver during various ignition conditions.

HUMAN Machine Interface

Human Machine Interface (HMI) can be viewed as a combination of hardware and software issues that directly impact the patrons' SDAR experience.

The HMI may take several forms for any given audio system. The Radio Head Unit (RHU) may serve as the HMI for manipulating SDARS. In other applications the RHU may be augmented by a dedicated HMI remotely located.

This section will describe a common set of performance expectations for SDAR receivers HMI.

ENTERING SDARS MODE

SDARS mode on a typical radio head unit (RHU) may be entered by cycling the "band" button AM→FM1→FM2→SDARS. If SIRIUS and XM cohabitant on the same audio system, the OEM shall provide direction as to which service appears after FM2 in the band selection sequence.

If the audio system includes a remote HMI (Human Machine Interface), but relies on the RHU for audio amplification, SDARS mode may be entered by using the AUXILARY audio mode on the RHU. The HMI will then illuminate and SDARS will be acknowledged as the active audio source.

MANUAL TUNING

Manual tuning (tuning without the aid of classification) will have a common set of characteristics.

Initial offerings from both SDAR providers will be limited to 100 channels of programming. As the market demand changes, or on special occasions (game of the week), the actual number of channels available to the patron may increase or decrease from 100. No matter the channel count, the tuning operation shall wrap from the highest available channel to the lowest (and from the lowest to the highest).

With 100 or more channels of programming it may take an unacceptably long time to increment or decrement through the entire service offers. Some systems will address this issue by the use of a numeric entry system, others will elect to a 'quick step' approach.

The 'quick step' manual tuning would be entered by the patron holding the manual increment/decrement button for a calibratable time, the SDAR receiver would then mute audio, and begin incrementing / decrementing through the service offerings at a calibratable rate. The time to enter the 'quick step' and the rate at which they dwell on a channel shall be calibratable to match or the other audio sources in the audio system.

SEEKING BY CLASSIFICATION

SEEK in a typical AM/FM receiver was a function that would test the band for stations that meet criteria of signal strength. Since all the channels provided in an SDARS application are of the same signal strength the SEEK function has been redefined to SEEK by CLASSIFICATION.

Classification is a term associated with the programming format available on the subscribed channel. For example: Country, Rock, Classical, Jazz etc. Sometimes this is referred to as PTY (Program Type), Genre, or Category.

While the audio system has SDARS selected as the active audio source, the patron may enter SEEK mode by pressing the same button on the RHU as they would to enter AM/FM Seek. The audio may mute, while the display refreshes to show the available classifications. The patron may navigate through the available classifications by manipulating the tune button/knob. Once a desired classification has been selected, the patron may manipulate the Seek button. The receiver would then increment or decrement to the next available channel with the matching Classification.

Unlike FM RDS the SDAR programming classifications are dynamic in nature. That is to say that from time to time the service providers may elect to modify their classification schemes, therefor the HMI must be capable of adapting. Both service providers ASIC's have the capability of reporting to a system controller if a change is required and the nature of the change.

SCAN FUNCTIONS

SDARS may implement a SCAN function similar to AM/FM. Once this mode is entered, the receiver shall dwell on channel for a calibratable time and then automatically increment / decrement to the next channel, regardless of that channels classification.

PRESETS AND RECALLS

Each SDAR receiver shall retain at least 24 channels. This memory may be parsed for multiple drivers, multiple modes and multiple buttons.

For example, one vehicle application may have up to three drivers identified through personalization, with 6 preset buttons, and two SDAR modes (SDAR1, SDAR2) for a total of 36 total memory locations. Another application may have 4 drivers, 6 buttons and one SDAR mode for 24 memory locations.

Setting and recalling channel memories shall be done in accordance with other AM/FM memory functions found in the existing entertainment system.

ANNOUNCEMENT MESSAGES

Announcement Messages are a collection of standardized text displays that appear for a given condition that may result in the patron being inconvenienced in some fashion.

No RF Signal

No RF Signal is a condition that may result from a prolonged period of time in an area that is not covered by the satellite or terrestrial signals (tunnels for example).

Display Size	Display Reading
8 Character	No Signl
10 Character	No Signal
16 Character	No Signal

Weak RF Signal

Weak RF signals may be the result of foliage, other RF sources that generate 'noise' (microwave ovens), or objects blocking the interfering with the antenna's performance.

Display Size	Display Reading
8 Character	Signal
10 Character	Wk Signal
16 Character	Weak Signal

Unauthorized Subscription

Unauthorized Subscription is a condition where the SDAR mode has been entered but the service provider has not enabled the service (typically a result of the patron not being in the subscription data base), or the channel selected is not available at to this patron at this time.

Due to the length of the information required displays shall be required to cycle through several pages of text. Each line in the table will be displayed for 2 seconds +/- 250mS. Once all lines have been displayed the cycle shall be repeated from the beginning. In the event that an XM Satellite Radio and Sirius Satellite Radio receiver cohabitant in the same audio system, the OEM shall state a preference for which is displayed first.

Display Size	Display Reading
8 Character (Sirius Only)	SUBSCRIB 1-888- 539-SIRI
8 Character (XM Only)	SUBSCRIB 1-888- xxx-xxxx
10 Character (Sirius Only)	SUBSCRIBE 1-888- 539-SIRI
10 Character (XM Only)	SUBSCRIBE 1-888- xxx-xxxx
16 Character (Sirius Only)	SUBSCRIBE 1-888-539-SIRI 1-888-539-7474
16 Character (XM Only)	SUBSCRIBE 1-888- xxx-xxxx

NOTE: XM subscription number was not available at the time of writing.

Service Update

Service Update is the phrase associated with the occasional modification by the service provider to the programming line up.

Display Size	Display Reading
8 character	Updating
10 character	Updating
16 character	Service Updating

Antenna Fault

In the unlikely event that the antenna becomes damaged or disconnected, the patron will be notified.

Display Size	Display Reading
8 character	Antenna?
10 character	Chk Antena
16 character	Check Antenna

Channel not in Service

If a patron were to set a preset to a channel that was removed by the service provider from the channel line up the following message would occur for 2 seconds, while the audio was muted, the receiver would then default to channel 1.

Display Size	Display Reading
8 character	Removed
10 character	Removed
16 character	Removed

CONCLUSION

This paper has outlined a set of common elements for peripheral SDAR applications. Communization between XM and Sirius will allow the OEM's a degree of flexibility to meet the demands of the market place. Communization will also lead to fewer permutations of the SDAR product, thereby leading to a common SDAR experience for the patron.

ACKNOWLEDGMENTS

The authors would like to gratefully acknowledge the participation of Sirius Satellite Radio and XM Satellite Radio.

REFERENCES

1. Performance Standard for Automotive Electrical Connector Standard, Rev 2 12/9/99, SAE/USCAR
2. Road vehicles –Radio-frequency (MVRF) interface – Dimensions and electrical requirements, AK 22/5 Nr. 08/00. (FAKRA Spec).

DEFINITIONS, ACRONYMS, ABBREVIATIONS

SDARS: Satellite Digital Audio Receiver Systems

Patron: the person or persons who purchase the SDAR services from either XM Satellite Radio or Sirius Satellite Radio.

HMI: Human Machine Interface. The HMI varies from vehicle to vehicle, but is essentially the device that the patron uses to access the SDAR service. Physically, the HMI may take the form of a Radio Head Unit (RHU) or a separate display/controller.

ESN: Electronics Serial Number, alphanumeric representation of the individual SDAR unit.

ASIC: Application Specific Integrated Circuit

OEM: Original Equipment Manufacturer

Blind Mating: a situation where the receiver is not visible to the person attempting to connect the antenna or body harness.

Classification: the term associated with the programming format available on the subscribed channel. For example: Country, Rock, Classical. Sometimes this is referred to as PTY (Program Type), Genre, or Category.

2001-01-0002

A Noise Cancellation for FM Broadcast Receiver Using DSP Techniques

Masayuki Tsuji, Kenichi Taura, Masahiro Tsujishita and Masayuki Ishida
Imaging Systems Lab, Mitsubishi Electric Corp.

Eiji Asano
Sanda Works, Mitsubishi Electric Corp.

ABSTRACT

This paper describes the development of a VHF/FM broadcast receiver and its noise cancellation system, which uses digital signal processing techniques. The developed method provides an improved receiver performance, and enables it to be integrated into general digital signal processing systems.

INTRODUCTION

We have developed a new VHF/FM broadcast receiver that performs FM demodulation, stereo decoding and noise reduction functions by using digital signal processing. This paper describes mainly a newly developed noise cancellation process, and follows our paper on FM demodulation and stereo decoding at ICCE2000 [1].

For pulse noise, we adopted procedures that remove noise pulses and interpolate an audio signal waveform when a noise is detected. Since this noise cancellation process operates independently on each audio signal channel, it enables avoidance of the secondary noise generation that is inevitable with conventional systems.

For multi-path noise, a stereo reception control (SRC) process was adopted. Moreover, we adopted procedures to cut off the noise spikes that appear at periods of the stereo sub-carrier on the stereo composite signal. Since this noise cancellation process cuts off noise spikes due to multi-path noise in stereo composite signals, it enables the hard noise occurring in heavy multi-path situations to be reduced.

RECEIVER STRUCTURE

Figure 1 shows a block diagram of the FM broadcast receiver. A double conversion system is adopted for analog signal processing in order to make a 608kHz IF (intermediate frequency) signal suitable for input to the FM demodulator. An anti-alias analog filter is placed before the AD converter to suppress the higher harmonic component of the IF signal. The pulse noise cancellation process is placed after the stereo decoder in order to operate on each audio signal. The multi-path noise cancellation process is placed before the stereo decoder in order to operate on stereo composite signals.

FM DEMODULATION

The demodulator is composed of a basic quadrature demodulator for its simple structure, an AM cancellation process and an arcsine compensation process. To fulfill the conditions of quadrature demodulation, we selected the sampling frequency of 2.432MHz and the FM carrier frequency of 608kHz.

It is understood that the following two problems are implied in the quadrature type demodulator.

1. The demodulated output is directly proportional to the square of the input amplitude. This means that any fluctuation of the input amplitude would cause amplitude fluctuation of the demodulated signal.
2. To be precise demodulation characteristic is of the sine function shape. The non-linear demodulation characteristics cause distortion in the demodulated sound signal, especially when the modulation index is large.

An AM cancellation process was adopted for the former, and an arcsine compensation process for the latter.

STEREO DECODER

The stereo decoder is based on a process that is similar to the switching system that has been used on conventional analog LSI in general. In this type of stereo decoder, it is essential to ensure that the sampling timing accurately coincides with the peak point of the sub-carrier in order to achieve an accurate stereo decoding and obtain good channel separation. For this purpose, we have incorporated a phase-locked loop operation to the pilot signal to generate accurate timing which synchronize with the pilot signal.

In conventional systems, the sampling frequency of the AD converter is usually controlled in order to synchronize it with the pilot signal of the stereo decoder. However, such a system is not suitable for general purpose digital signal processing, because of the necessity of special analog components, e.g. a voltage controlled crystal oscillator (VCXO), and the high cost of the product.

In our method, the sample timing is controlled by using an interpolation-decimation filtering technique applied to the FM demodulated sound signal.

NOISE CANCELER

It is almost mandatory to fit car-use receivers with noise reduction systems. The two main causes of system noise generation in car-use FM receivers are the impulsive electromagnetic noise caused by the engine ignition system, electric motors, switches etc. and the multi-path noise caused by the multiple propagation paths of radio waves and interference due to the phase differences between the signals.

CONVENTIONAL METHOD – In conventional system, the pulse noise canceler adopts procedures that detect the noise on a composite stereo signal and interpolates the detected period with an immediate signal level by level-holding. Secondary noise generation is inevitable in the conventional method, which operates on a composite stereo signal because of the sub-carrier loss during the noise cancellation operation.

When an audio signal containing a frequency component close to 10kHz is over-modulated, distortion based on the fricative sound is generated. This is one of the side effects that the noise cancellation operates by mistaking the higher harmonic component of the fricative sound. In noise detection, the cut-off frequency of the HPF is selected containing the fricative sound of nearly 10kHz. Since the threshold level for noise detection is based on the HPF output, it is raised by the fricative sound and the sensitivity of the noise detection drops as a result. However, this method also operates similarly on a stereo sub-channel signal (L-R) and the sensitivity of noise detection is reduced for a stereo sound containing a large L-R signal.

An SRC process is adopted to reduce the multi-path noise. But there are cases in which reduction effects are inadequate to deal with a heavy multi-path situation, in which the amplitude of the direct radio wave is near to the indirect one.

PULSE NOISE CANCELER – In our system a pulse noise canceler that detects the noise on a composite stereo signal was adopted, this removes the noise and interpolates the audio signal waveform when the noise has been detected. It enables any secondary noise generation to be avoided, and improves the performance of the pulse noise cancellation.

We also adopted a newly developed method that solves the above-mentioned adverse influence on the noise detection. For the noise correction, we adopted a newly developed method that selects a correction method that adapts to the frequency component of each audio signal.

Pulse noise detection – Figure 2 shows a block diagram of the noise detection division. In noise detection, we selected a cut-off frequency of 60kHz on the HPF, and adopted a procedure that detects a fricative sound close to 10kHz in the stereo main-channel signal (L+R) independently. So that in our system, the sensitivity of noise detection isn't affected with a stereo sub-channel signal (L-R). Details of each of the components are as follows.

- The calculation of a ground noise has been performed by smoothing the high frequency band component that is extracted by HPF from a stereo composite signal, and used it as the main component of the threshold for noise detection.
- In the situation where a pulse noise is generated intensively, it isn't suitable to correct all noise pulses faithfully, because such a procedure imposes an unpleasant influence on the primary noise. We adopted a procedure that controls the ratio of the detected period within suitable value limits so as to correct any high amplitude noise selectively.
- The threshold level for detecting the pulse noise is based on the calculation of the grand noise, the level of the fricative sound and the ratio of the detected period. The results of detecting the pulse noise are obtained by comparison of the threshold level with the high frequency band component from the HPF.

Pulse noise correction – Figure 3 shows a block diagram of the noise correction division. The noise correction process operates independently on each of the audio signal channels and the main-channel, and adopts a correction method selectively according to the audio signal level and frequency. Details of the correction process are as follows.

- Figure 4 shows the effect of correcting the pulse noise independently on each of the audio signal channels. As an extreme case, the L-channel of the sine wave and the R-channel of none, (a) is a case that the conventional process operates on a composite stereo signal according to level-holding. (b) is the proposed system, the secondary isn't generated in this case noise correction.

- Figure 5 shows the computer simulation results for the distortion, by changing the correcting method, generating the pulse noise of 100 microsecond width, 10 millisecond cycle. The distortion is in low order, a 3rd-order polynomial interpolation, a linear interpolation, a level-holding on a lower frequency area. Figure 6 shows a case in which the audio signal level is as low as the ground noise. Figure 6a shows a correction by a 3rd polynomial interpolation. Figure 6b shows a correction by a linear interpolation. In the worst case, a 3rd-order polynomial interpolation generates a correction noise with a higher level than a ground noise. So we adopted a linear interpolation that the distortion is advantageous in cases in which the audio signal level is so low.
- In Figure 5, there is very little difference in the distortion between the correction methods in the higher frequency areas. Figure 7 shows the correction waveform on an audio signal that contains a high frequency component. It is expected that a linear interpolation brings a large error for correction, and an interpolation with a low frequency component of an audio signal by level-holding cannot make an exact correction but doesn't bring a large error for correction. So we adopted a level-holding on an audio signal that contains a high frequency component. Figure 8 shows an audio signal waveform and the selecting signal of correction method.

Performance – Figure 9 shows an example of an audio signal waveform when the pulse noise canceler operates. Figure 9a shows a correction result by the conventional analog process, Figure 9b shows one corrected by our system. Secondary noise generation is inevitable in the conventional analog process, but it is avoidable in our system.

MULTI-PATH NOISE CANCELER – The first waveform (a) in Figure 10 shows a typical episode of multi-path noise in a stereo composite signal. The second waveform (b) shows an enlargement of one multi-path noise interval. Multi-path noise comprises a series of spikes (spike noise), occurring at intervals equal to the FM composite sub-carrier period. We adopted a procedure that cuts off each of the spikes of a stereo composite signal and reduces any heavy multi-path noise, that isn't reduced sufficiently by the SRC.

Figure 11 shows the block diagram of the newly developed multi-path noise canceler. It detects spike noise of minimum width on a stereo composite signal and corrects each of the spikes selectively at a suitable width in a receiving condition, that is actually a radio signal level and a modulation level.

Multi-path noise detection – At the noise detection division in Figure 11, the HPF detects the edge of multi-path noise spikes at the first step, and the calculation of the ground noise has been performed by smoothing the HPF output at the second step. Figure 12 shows the detection waveform of the multi-path noise, the HPF output in (a), the ground noise in (b), the limited ground noise, that is the threshold level for detection in (c), the results of detection in (d). The threshold decision unit limits the level of the ground noise to a suitable level on a radio signal level, because the level of the ground noise rises under the influence of the multi-path noise and the radio signal level. The results of the detection of the multi-path noise are obtained by comparing them with the threshold level and the HPF output.

Multi-path noise correction – Figure 13 shows the waveform of the process that the multi-path noise correction operates, the stereo composite signal containing the multi-path noise spikes in (a), the HPF output in (b), the gate-pulse for correcting in (c), the stereo composite signal after correction in (d). The detected pulse signal of the HPF output has minimum width and is extended selectively to a suitable width on the modulation level by the gate-pulse unit.

Correction is performed by level-holding on the stereo composite signal, with a low frequency component that is obtained by smoothing on a stereo composite signal. Because a stereo composite signal before multi-path noise spikes is not a little distorted by multi-path noise, a low frequency component is used in anticipation of a small correction error.

The correction width is suitable for a close to minimum width on the higher modulation level signal, because of the adverse influence causing of a partial loss of the stereo composite signal. But at the lower modulation signal level, the correction width can be extended as a result of minimal influence. In our system, the multi-path noise canceler selectively adopts correcting width between about 5 and 25 microsecond, monitoring the radio signal level and the modulation level.

Performance – Figure 14 shows an example of a stereo composite signal waveform operated by the multi-path noise canceler. Figure 15 shows an example of an audio signal waveform operated by the multi-path noise canceler. Figures 14a and 15a show the correction results by the conventional analog process, Figures 14b and 15b show the correction results by our system. In our system, multi-path noise spikes are cut off on the stereo composite signal and the multi-path noise is reduced in the audio signal.

EXPERIMENT RESULTS

The trial receiver has been experimentally made , that is based on our system algorithm, it uses DSP and FPGA. DSP constitutes the greater part of our system, which contains adaptive processes. Table 1 shows the results of the experiment. The trial receiver was mounted in an passenger car, which was made field tests on our test course, that contains a heavy multi-path situation in

Kansai-area in Japan, in order to evaluate the performance of the noise canceler. Table 1 shows results of a subjective evaluation by eight researchers, comparing the experimental receiver with a standard FM analog radio (placing it in the 3rd grade of 5 grades). The performance of the noise canceler of our system was highly rated (between 3.5 to 4.5).

CONCLUSION

The proposed system can provide an advanced noise reduction process for pulse and multi-path noise, and we confirmed the effects of cancellation in the trial receiver as an experiment. The multi-path noise cancellation process that cuts off the multi-path noise spikes, is especially effective for a heavy multi-path situation.

REFERENCES

1. K.Taura, et al. "A New Approach to VHF/FM Broadcast Receiver Using Digital Signal Processing Techniques", ICCE2000 digest of technical papers

CONTACT

Masayuki Tsuji, Researcher, Imaging Systems Lab., Mitsubishi Electric Corp.
1 Zusho Baba Nagaokakyo City Kyoto 617-8550, Japan
Phone: +81-75-958-3257 Fax: +81-75-958-3703
e-mail:tj@img.kyo.melco.co.jp

Table 1 Results of Estimation

	Standard FM analog radio(reference)	Trial product (Proposed system)
Pulse noise (miller motor)	3	4.5
Pulse noise (igunition)	3	4.5
Multi-path noise (middle radio signal level)	3	4
Multi-path noise (low radio signal level)	3	4
weak radio signal level	3	3.5

evaluation : 5 (superior) ← 3 (middle) → 1 (inferior)

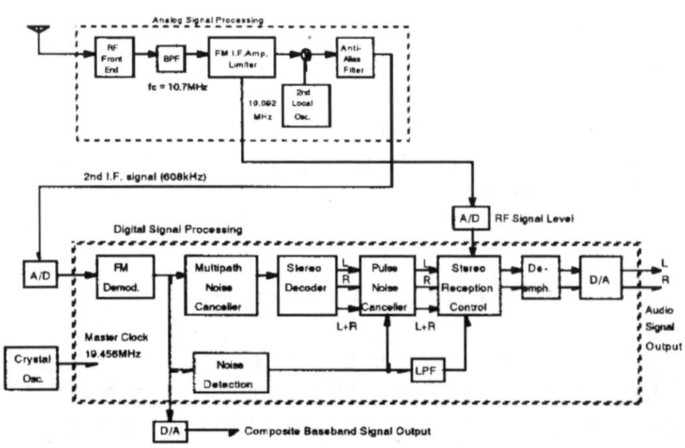

Figure 1 FM Receiver Signal Processing Block Diagram

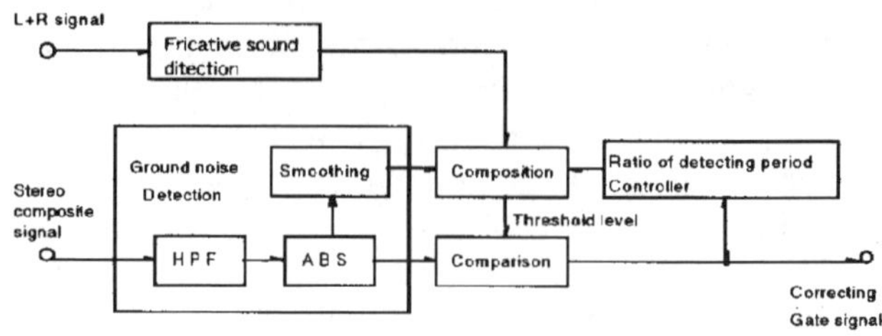

Figure 2 Block Diagram of The Pulse Noise Detection Division

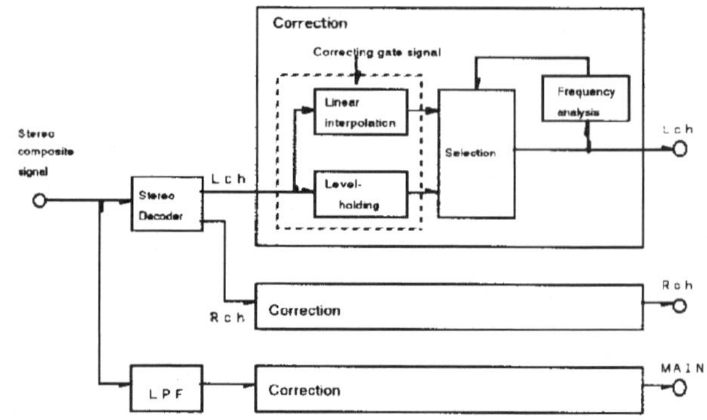

Figure 3 Block Diagram of The Pulse Noise Correction Division

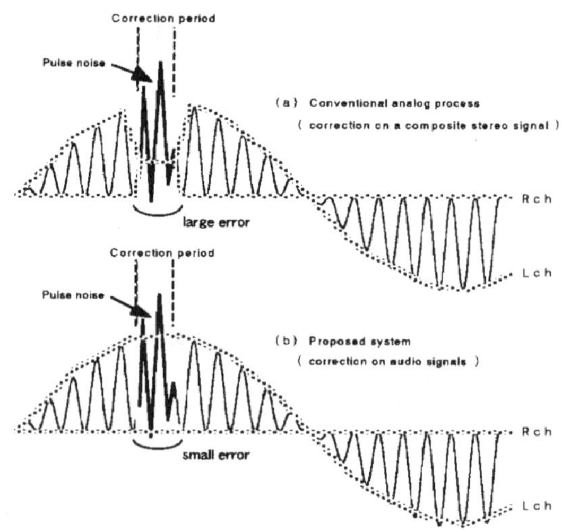

Figure 4 Waveform diagram illustrating the pulse noise correction

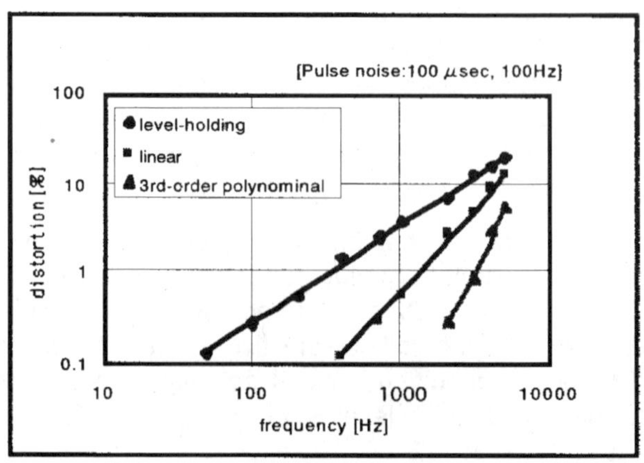

Figure 5 Distortion by changing the correcti on method

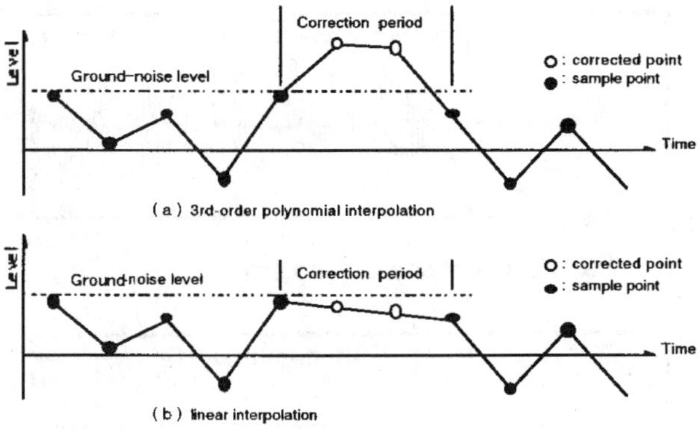

Figure 6 Waveform diagram illustrating the pulse noise correction, in a low audio level case

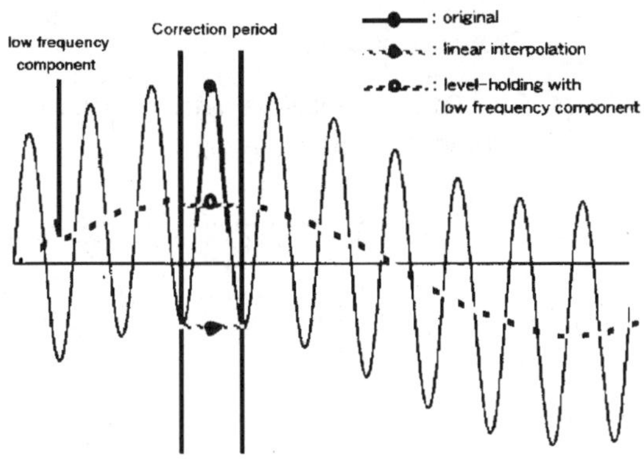

Figure 7 Waveform diagram illustrating the pulse noise correction, in a case of an audio signal containing a high frequencies

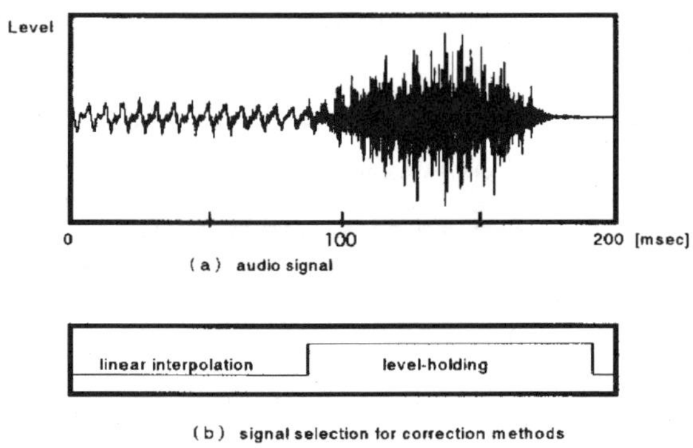

Figure 8 Waveform diagram selection of correction methods

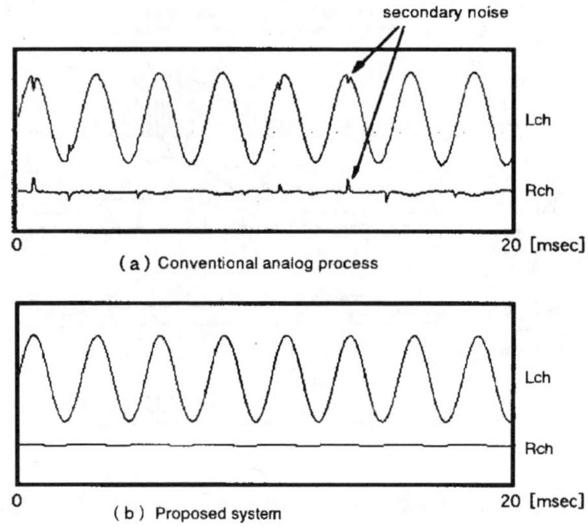

Figure 9 Results of the pulse noise correction (after de-emphasis)

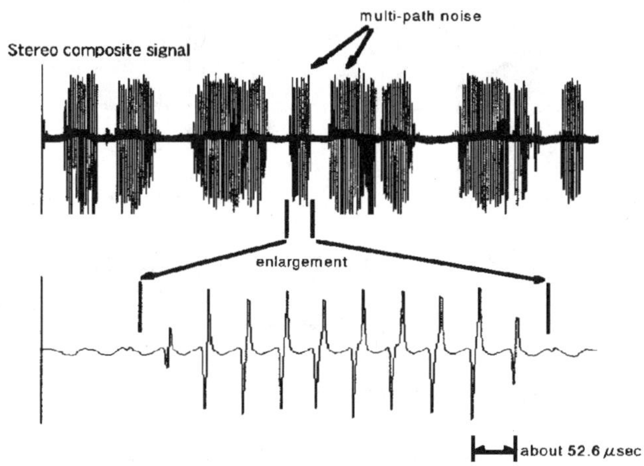

Figure 10 Illustrates a typical multi-path noise waveform

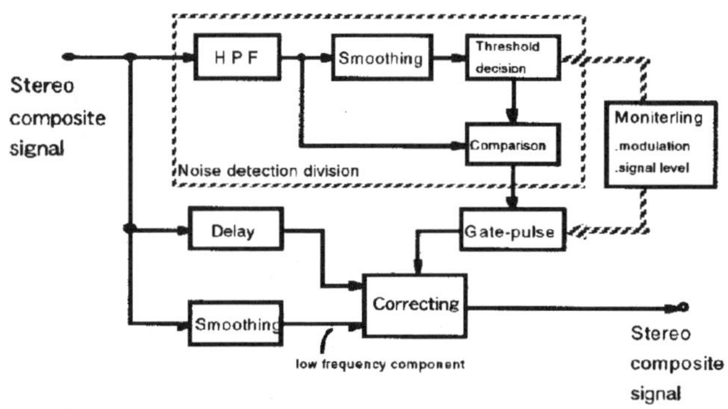

Figure 11 Block Diagram of The Multi-path Noise Canceller

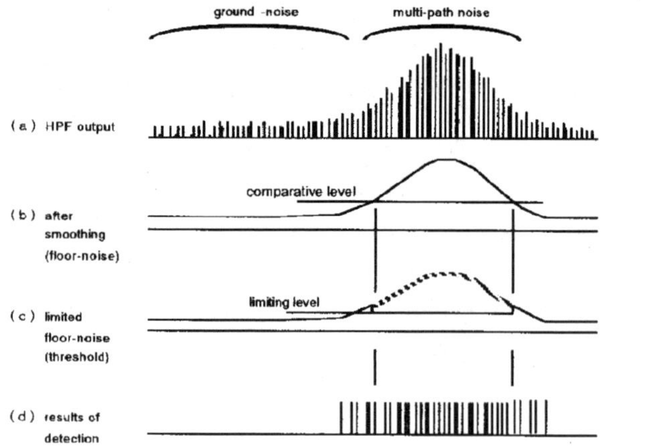

Figure 12 Waveform diagram illustrating the multi-path noise detection

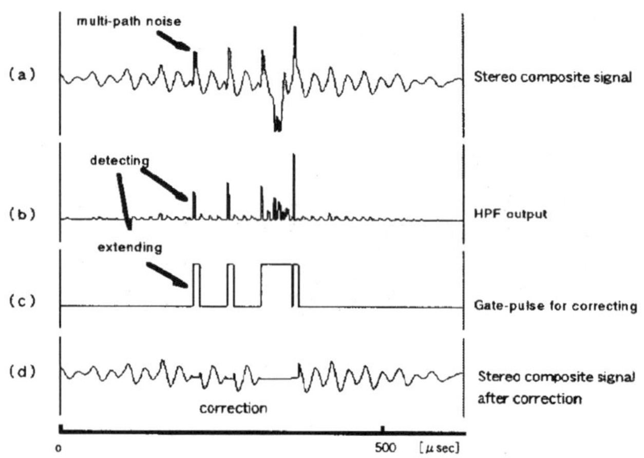

Figure 13 Waveform of the multi-path correcti on process

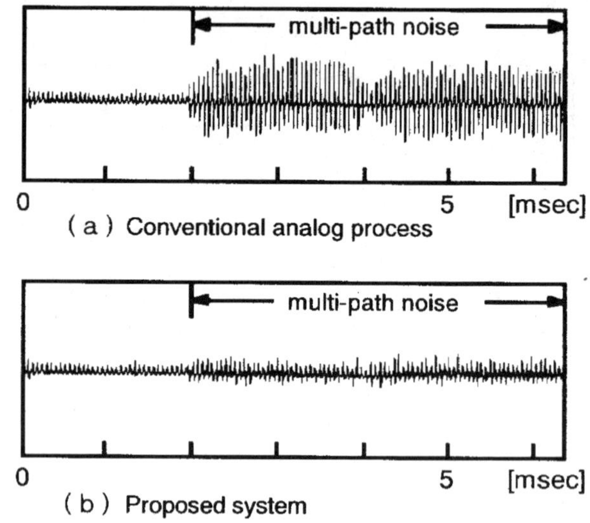

Figure 14 Results of the multi-path noise correction (a stereo composite signal)

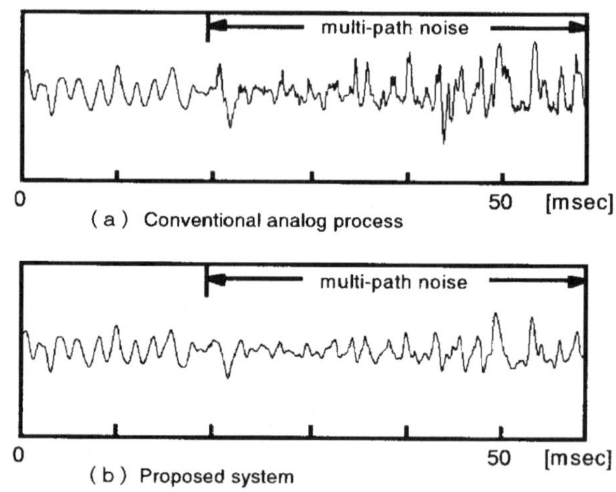

Figure 15 Results of the multi-path noise correction (an audio signal)

2000-01-3194

The RDS (Radio Data System) as a Transmission Way of Information for Automotive Vehicles

Alexandre de Almeida Guimarães
General Motors do Brasil Ltda.

ABSTRACT

Real-time information, standardized and interacting with radio broadcasting listeners during the time they spend driving their cars, could be extremely interesting and useful whether it offers public concerned information and make feasible the complete application of the system (hardware and software) it is based on. The RDS (Radio Data System) standard, which modulation characteristic is based on the concept its data signals are carried on a subcarrier which is added to the stereo multiplex signal at the stereo encoder, make feasible this benefits with extremely low cost, for the listener and even for the broadcaster.

Being applied in Europe for more than 15 years, the RDS offers features that improve the operation of the receiver and take advantage of the architecture available in some vehicles through remote actuation of many parts of the car. All this features has been superficially used in Brazil, due to the lack of information to the broadcasters and even the existence of a standard focused on Brazilian requirements.

KEYWORDS

RDS, Radio Data System, Teletext Systems, Radio Frequency Modulation – Standards, FM Broadcasting.

INTRODUCTION [1]

Through adjustable options available in the radio's headunit (receiver), the listener is able to have customized the style of music and programs he want to listen to at the same time he can enable or not the receiving of traffic messages and emergency warnings that would happen during his journey. Those messages and warnings would give opportunity to the driver to decide which way could be better and which one could not be, avoiding awful situations – really common in many Brazilian cities.

Besides that, RDS has a technical characteristic that makes possible the interaction of the drive and his/her vehicle remotely. Just contacting a call center, the drive could request a specific action, that will be addressed to the RDS modulator, added to the normal FM signal, transmitted and received by the car (by the receiver or by a special device installed in the car), that will perform the related action.

While it has been applied to Europe and USA since the 90's, in Brazil its application was just started for few broadcasters that have been used some of the main features of the system. The standard requires transmission infrastructure extremely simple and cheap, besides a reception structure really simple, cheap and already available at the Brazilian market.

Through this paper, I am going to demonstrate the system's possibilities to the Brazilian reality, explaining the available feature already in use in other countries and some potential characteristics that would be fully developed to support Brazilian requirements. The application of those features or services could be seen as a way to improve information availability to the Brazilian fleet; passenger cars or commercial vehicles.

WHAT RDS IS

The Radio Data System [2] was developed by the European Broadcasting Union (EBU) member countries and is a standard that provides advanced radio tuning and program information from the broadcaster to the listener through a subcarrier signal applied to VHF / FM sound.

During the transmission [3], the subcarrier frequency is locked to the third harmonic of the 19 kHz pilot-tone, what means a 57 kHz subcarrier. The figure #1 below shows the FM spectrum with the RDS signal incorporated.

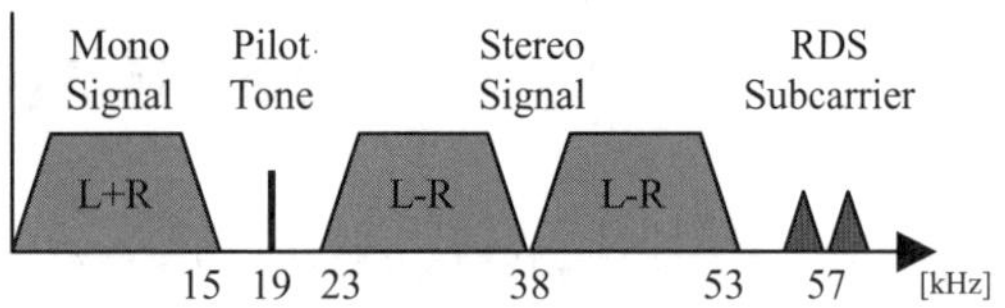

Figure #1: FM Signal Spectrum with RDS incorporated.

As the tolerance of the pilot-tone is +/-2 Hz, for the RDS subcarrier we have +/-6 Hz. About the phase angle, its tolerance is +/-10%, measured at the modulation input to the FM transmitter. Also, according to the European Specification, the deviation range of the FM carrier due to the unmodulated subcarrier is from +/-1 kHz to +/-7,5 kHz and the recommended value is +/-2 kHz.

The basic data-rate of the system is 1187,5 bits/s +/-0,125 bit/s and this streamline is divided in blocks of 26 bits each. The largest element in the RDS structure is a group of 104 bits, what means 4 blocks of 26 bits. All blocks are comprised of a 16-bit information word and a 10-bit checkword. This checkword has capabilities to detect all single and double bit errors in a block, to detect any single error burst spanning 10 bits or less and to detect about 99,8% of bursts spanning 11 bits and about 99,9% of all longer bursts.

There are 16 group types, from "0" to "15" split in two classes "A" and "B". These groups were divided according to their application and version. We have a group for basic tuning, one for clock-time and date, one for traffic messages, one for open data applications and so on.

Our proposal is not to explain each technical issue of RDS, what would be better understood directly from the specification (CENELEC - EN 50067). We would like to provide you just a basic overview about what RDS is from a technical standpoint and emphasize this paper on potential applications that are already available and under analyzes.

Reading all this information and conditions to have the RDS signal, you may ask what is happening today? How the signal is being transmitted and received in the real life? That is a good question and really easy to be answered. All infrastructure required for the transmission is a RDS encoder - a small module connected to a conventional FM modulator and operated by a Personnel Computer. From this computer, all parameters can be changed friendly any time. About the infrastructure required to receive the signal? You need a receiver equipped with an internal RDS microprocessor. All these equipment, RDS encoder and receiver with RDS microprocessor are already available for a price extremely reduced.

But how could you know if an equipment, specially a receiver, was developed to decode the RDS signal? There are 2 kinds of logo, standardized by the European and the American RDS Unions, that represents the system and should be printed on the face of the headunit you imagine is ready to treat RDS signals. The figures below show the available logos. The first one represents the equipment that has the most common features while the second one represents the receivers that are equipped with the Enhanced Other Network (EON) feature.

Figure #2: Basic RDS Logo.

R·D·S
RADIO DATA SYSTEM

Figure #3: RDS EON Logo.

R D S
E O N

RDS AVAILABLE FEATURES [2]

Let's go directly to the point – The Features! There are two sets of features, the primary and the secondary. The primary features are contained in all groups, while secondary features are transmitted only if you are using the feature. Following I would like to explain the main features available in the system:

PI (Program Identification): Code that identifies the Broadcaster. Each Radio Station, here named as Broadcaster, has a specific number that identifies itself, for example in Brazil, the PI of some Broadcaster would be "B000". In other words, the Broadcasters would be known by their PI numbers instead of their FM Frequencies.

PS (Program Service Name): To display the name of the broadcaster instead of the FM frequency. If the Broadcaster has programmed this feature, once tuned its frequency, the programmed name will be shown on the receiver display instead of the FM frequency.

AF (Alternate Frequency): To tune automatically to the best Broadcaster considering same "PI" in the region. Suppose you are driving your car through the State and you have tuned a specific Radio Station. As you are going opposite from the Radio Station, its signal becomes weak and the reception bad. With the AF selected, the receiver is always looking for other Radio Station with the same PI and with the strongest signal in the same area. If it is found, the receiver automatically switches the tuner to the best signal detected. It is transparent to the listener that still seeing the name of the broadcaster instead of the FM frequency (due to PS feature).

TP (Traffic Program): To identify Broadcasters that offer traffic bulletins and enables or not the receiver to automatically receive Traffic Announcements (see next feature).

TA (Traffic Announcements): To identify that an announcement is being transmitted. The receiver will detect that and stop any playback, returning to FM tuner mode. If the receiver is turned off, it will be turned on and the announcement will be shown. An announcement is a voice message that is played on the vehicle's loudspeakers and informs the driver a specific condition of any part of the city (an accident for example). Known what is happening in that area, the driver is able to change his/her prior route and avoid some potential traffic jam.

TMC (Traffic Message Channel): Is intended to provide traffic messages relevant to the driver's journey. A list of streets and a list of potential problems (flood, traffic jam, etc) is available in the receiver's memory. When some traffic department detects that something wrong is happening, the related street and problem numbers are transmitted. If your receiver was set up to that street, your display is going to flash the name of the street and what is going on there. As we have for TA, the driver can choose which way to drive through after informed about the problem.

PTY (Program Type): To designate which kind of program is being transmitted. The driver can select which one is desired to the receiver stops during a band scan. A list of 31 types of programs is available with kinds of music, kinds of programs, etc. The Broadcaster transmits with the music, for example, its type (rock, jazz, country, etc). The driver set the receiver up to detect just that kind of music and during a scan, the tuner will just stop scanning when the type of the music transmitted matches with that set up in the receiver.

PTYN (Program Type Name): To display the name of the program being transmitted instead of the frequency.

M/S (Music / Speech Switch Code): To identify when music or speech is being transmitted. This feature intends to optimize, automatically, all audio noise present in each kind of transmission.

CT (Clock Time and Date): To show on the receiver's display the clock Time and the date. This feature, depending on the car's receiver, can update time and calendar of the receiver remotely.

RT (Radio Text): Able to transmit messages with 64 characters of ASCII text. It works properly with home-receivers that have bigger displays.

DGPS (Differential Global Positioning System): As the spatial position of each Broadcaster is known, the Radio Station, that receives the GPS satellites signals, calculates the error inserted into the satellites information and transmits that to the receiver installed in the car. With this value, the receiver is able to calculate the deviation in a real-time approach and perform all correction required for example, for navigation.

EON (Enhanced Other Network): This function allows data to be shared among affiliated broadcasters. Besides PS, PI and PTY, Traffic Announcements on affiliated network can be tuned automatically through EON and it is not dependent of each station you are, once it, the broadcaster, is part of a network.

ODA (Open Data Application): There are available groups within the specification to make feasible new implementation using RDS. Actually we can find, around Europe mainly, some applications that applies their information to a specific group from ODA group.

REMOTE ACTUATION ON CARS VIA RDS [1]

Suppose you have parked your car outside a shopping center. After 3 hours of shopping, you decide to leave the place and go through the parking lot with no idea where your car is stopped. It would be strange and I think never happened to you but did to me! Now, imagine a service, like a call center to contact. You can inform your personnel password and request to the operator to activate your car's horn or turn on the headlamps to help you localize the car. The operator would be able even to unlock your car's doors and/or start your engine remotely, depending just your desires. Wouldn't be great?! It is possible via RDS.

As we saw on the last section, RDS has a lot of features and groups of functions. One of them is the ODA (Open Data Application), an open group that supports services like that mentioned above. We can assign an ID for each receiver (or a small box assembled with an internal RDS microprocessor and some I/O ports) and just that receiver (or box) will be able to perform the required function as soon a message is transmitted by the call center.

Suppose now your car parked in front of your house, Sunday afternoon and nobody walking outside on the street. All of a sudden you perceive that your car is being stolen. You decide to stay calm and wait for the action of the thief. He unlocks your car, turn it on and leave in front of your eyes. Hopefully you were not there, thus, imagine you have installed that small box, with a RDS microprocessor and some outputs connected, for example, to your car's ECM (Engine Control Module). You dial to the call center and warn it about the theft. Again, the operator, knowing your car's Id, transmits an information that is going to be received by all cars with RDS capability but just your car, that has that specific Id, will respond and the action is to shut the engine off. With a properly algorithm, your car's engine would be stopped and recovered easier than in a normal police investigation.

Your question would be what should be done to achieve some of the examples given, up to now? Some of the available car's architectures are distributed while some of them are centralized and with no Central Body Controller. Each infrastructure should be analyzed carefully and mainly the I/O port and the firmware of the receiver or box should be designed to fit that specific function for that specific architecture.

Some enterprises are already marketing accessories based on RDS, specially alarms with capability to control remotely some parts of the car, as mentioned above.

RDS AROUND THE WORLD

Before explain what is going on around the World about RDS, let's give some background information to clarify when and how it started. I am going to provide you some milestone related to the whole World, including Brazil:

1974	Pre-development of RDS started
1980	First Field Test at Switzerland
1984	Ford starts RDS Car Radio design
1987	1st RDS Receiver shown at Berlin
1990	RDS European Standard EN 50067 is issued by CENELEC
1992	RBDS Standard completed in USA
1993	RDS Portable Radios become available and the RDS Forum is created
1994	Cidade Radio station starts RDS (PS) in Brazil
1998	RDS European Standard EN 50067 is revised by CENELEC
2000	**Standardization studies start in Brazil**

Table #1: RDS Milestones.

For your reference, in 1998, 90% of the European FM Stations were broadcasting some RDS feature while 10% of the American FM Stations were using this system. In South Africa, 70% of the FM Stations were applying RDS in 1995 [4]. As you can see, this system is much more popular in Europe than in USA (that applies the RBDS – Radio Broadcast Data System, a variant of the European Standard with some differences mainly market driven). In Europe, 60% of all receivers sold are equipped with RDS capability. Besides those regions, Asia and Australia were analyzing the applications of RDS in 1990 and should be using the system nowadays.

In Brazil, up to April 2000, no more than 10 FM Stations were broadcasting information through RDS while at least 3 Cars' Manufactures were marketing their vehicle with receivers RDS compatible [5]. Mr. Scott Wright [2] has mentioned that "the true success of any information service is that the more dynamic and relevant the information is, more interesting it is for the listener". That is what should be considered when specifying an information system.

Other concern may rise is about the DAB – Digital Audio Broadcasting and its compatibility with RDS infrastructure. "Digital radio will only expand upon the feature of RDS. Digital radio will be compatible with RDS, so your equipment will not become outdated or incompatible". Digital Radio Broadcasting is one of the technological trends of broadcasting information under analyzes around the World.

STANDARDZATION IN BRAZIL [1]

As mentioned, some Brazilian FM Stations are using RDS to broadcast information but with no reference of what and how each feature should be set up. They are not working based on a standard or a regulatory description, but they still trying to provide information to the listener.

In a quick brainstorming, we can easily understand that apply this system to Brazilian region would be pretty interesting. I will try to summarize in some bulletins, the reasons why to have the system standardized in Brazil:

1) The RDS was already tested and is working in Europe and USA for more than 15 years;

2) Almost every major manufactures make RDS receivers;

3) Usage of RDS modulator by FM Radio Stations is increasing in Brazil;

4) Misuse of RDS may cause either problems for on board electronic equipment (displays, receivers, etc) or dangerous situations for driver;

5) Opportunities for an user-friendly interaction with vehicle sound system;

6) Take advantage of traffic available information to reduce Brazilian traffic constraints and avoid emergency situations (flood, mountain fog, accidents, traffic jam, etc);

7) A good opportunity for: Cars' and Radios' Manufactures, FM Radio Stations, Government and Related Departments and specially for the Consumers (direct or not !!!).

Looking forward to having a standard that reflects the Brazilian requirements, an Electronic Commission was placed by the AEA (Brazilian Association of Automotive Engineering). This commission has representatives from many segments related to the RDS. Cars', Radios' and RDS Encoders' Manufactures, FM Stations and the ABERT (Brazilian Association of Broadcasters), and the ANATEL (National Association of Telecommunication) have joined the group and are working to provide, as soon as possible, a standard to cover the Brazilian requirements. This commission was created last April and is engaged to understand how the European standard works and what should be done to adequate that to Brazil.

CONCLUSIONS

As we could see, the RDS is a well-studied protocol that improves FM Radio tuning and is opened enough to have incorporated any application where data transmission is required. One concern must be analyzed when working with new application based on RDS is the low transmission rate available, what is about 1200 bits/s. That would be a bottle neck for some application which requires high transmission rate. Any way, solutions like that applied to the TMC feature, where a list of information is stored in the receiver's memory and just some bits is transmitted by the Broadcaster and decoded by the RDS microprocessors works properly.

A point we should keep in mind is that the RDS transmission is becoming very popular in Brazil and no standard is being considered. That can cause awful and dangerous situations for the consumers. The initiative to create a Brazilian standard, specially based on the European one that has 15 years of experience, should be faced as a clever decision and should has our support from a technical and a consumer point of view.

ABOUT THE AUTHOR

Alexandre de Almeida Guimarães works at GM do Brasil since 1993. Started working with Industrial Automation what performed for about 4 (four) years. Was moved to the Product Engineering Administration where worked for about 2 (two) years with budget analyses and is actually working as a Product Engineer being responsible for Infotainment and Data Bus based Systems for passenger cars. Was graduated Electrical Engineer in the Pontifícia Universidade Católica de São Paulo and is studying Master in Science in the Polytechnic School of Universidade de São Paulo. The theme is based on CAN Bus (Controller Area Network) standard and its application to on-board electronics for vehicles.

REFERENCES

[1] Guimarães, Alexandre A.; 1st Meeting for RDS Standardization in Brazil – Presentation to AEA; April 2000.

[2] Wright, Scott; The Broadcaster's guide to RDS; Focal Press; 1997.

[3] CENELEC; EN 50067: Specification of the radio data system (RDS) for VHF/FM sound broadcasting in the frequency range from 87,5 to 108,0 MHz; April 1998.

[4] www.rdsforum.com; RDS Forum – Site with RDS General Information; May 2000.

[5] Audi Magazine; On Line Section; October 1999.

2000-01-0071

Cellular Radio Car Antenna Array for Smart Antenna Transmission and Diversity Reception

H. Lindenmeier, L. Reiter and J. Hopf
University of the Bundeswehr Munich

R. Kronberger
Fuba Automotive

ABSTRACT

The application of smart or intelligent antennas at base stations of cellular radio systems has been proven to be a successful way to enhance the performance and the channel capacity of personal communication systems. In contrast to those technically highly developed base station antennas, the appearance and the functional principle of car antennas with omnidirectional pattern has been almost the same during the last few years. This paper presents a new type of mobile phone car antenna, which is implemented as a phased array of multiple short antennas with optimum omnidirectional pattern. In addition, it will allow adaptive beam steering as well. Optimum reception can be achieved by using the same set of antennas in diversity mode. In spite of the comparatively low technical effort and the small dimensions this highly effective antenna configuration opens the possibility for smart antenna application in vehicles as well.

1 INTRODUCTION

Research activities in mobile communications have been focused on the topic of smart antennas in the past few years to enhance the performance of cellular mobile radio systems. In this context, the term smart antenna implies the application of sophisticated methods at cellular radio base stations, i. e. diversity reception, direction-finding and tracking with adaptive antennas and digital signal processing.

There are well known diversity techniques for reception that are used to improve the signal quality at the base station. Usually the received signal from the mobile station is highly influenced by multipath fading. Using any of the following diversity techniques, polarization diversity, pattern diversity or maximum ratio combining, increases the carrier to interference ratio (CIR) and reduces the bit error rate (BER) of digital radio signals [1].

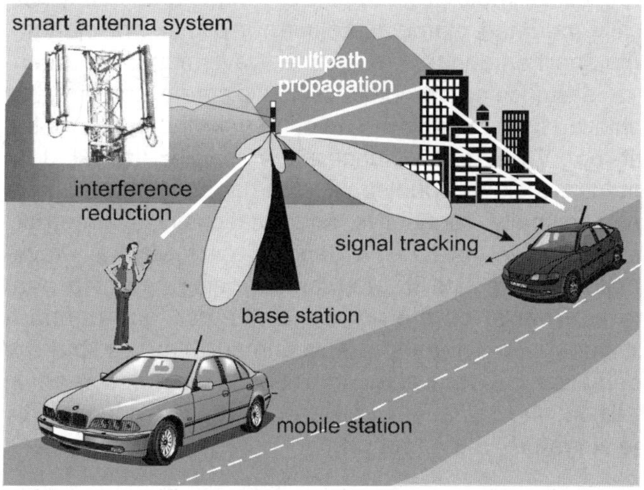

Figure 1. Cellular radio scenario with smart antenna principle

The use of adaptive beamforming techniques in combination with direction finding and signal tracking will increase the channel capacity significantly compared to single antenna base station systems. As a result, mobile users which are located at spatially different angular positions related to the base station can operate in TDMA-systems (time domain multiple access, i. e. GSM or PCS) on the same frequency or in the same timeslot. Investigations have shown that a replacement of approximately 50% of standard base stations with intelligent antennas would almost double the number of free available radio channels [2], which seems to be the most attractive solution to overcome capacity limits due to the nowadays rapidly increasing number of mobile users. As a result, the use of directive high gain antennas will reduce the required transmission power at base and mobile stations. In addition co-channel and adjacent channel interferences will be reduced.

New communication services for mobile multi media include rapid data transfer and mobile internet access. These services require enhanced spectral efficiency that can be achieved by means of intelligent antennas. Therefore, smart antenna systems at base stations are being already included in the system planning for future generation of mobile communication systems (i.e. UMTS).

Unfortunately, due to the high technical effort which is still required for the realization of smart antennas, i.e. huge array antennas, multiple RF-front ends and very powerful signal processors etc., the study of smart antennas has been restricted so far to base stations only.

2 MOBILE PHONE CAR ANTENNAS

The appearance and the functional principle of car antennas has not been changed significantly in past years (fig. 2). Optimum communication performance between the base station and the mobile station with nowadays car antennas requires omnidirectional radiation pattern in the azimuth plane. Thus for vertical polarization that is used with cellular radio systems, the antennas are usually vertically mounted elements of quarter or half wavelength. With short antennas, i. e. quarter-wave monopole antennas, a sufficiently omnidirectional diagram can only be achieved by mounting the antenna near the center of the car-roof. Due to the functional principle, this kind of antenna is highly coupled with the car body and requires an electrically conductive and rotationally symmetrical ground plane, with an extension over several wavelengths. In practice, roof antennas being mounted near the roof rim or on the backlite of the car tend to find a rotational-non-symmetric environment caused by the conductive car body at the transition to the rear screen. In addition, the radiation properties are often changed by the curvature of the roof [3].

In order to avoid the coupling with the car body it is state of the art with ordinary phone antennas to add a half-wave vertical antenna element above a short antenna element. Thus an inappropriate long antenna being mounted on the backlite or on the fender, often causes vibrations, windnoise and problems at car washers.

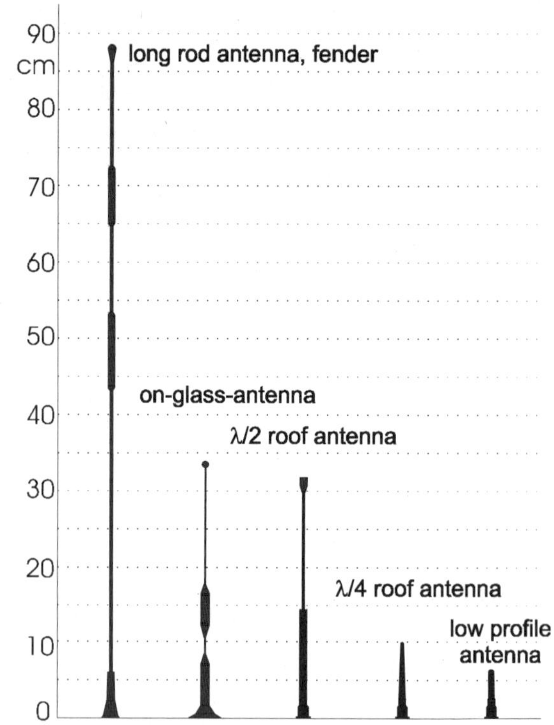

Figure 2. Cellular radio car antennas (GSM900 / AMPS)

3 CAR ANTENNA PATTERN SYNTHESIS

A new design principle for car antennas, based on multi element phased array technique, allows the flexibility to change the antenna pattern. Using several short antenna elements as array, which are in interaction with the car body, a desired omnidirectional or directive radiation pattern in the azimuth plane can be achieved. Therefore highly efficient low profile antennas with vertical dimensions less than a quarter wavelength can be implemented.

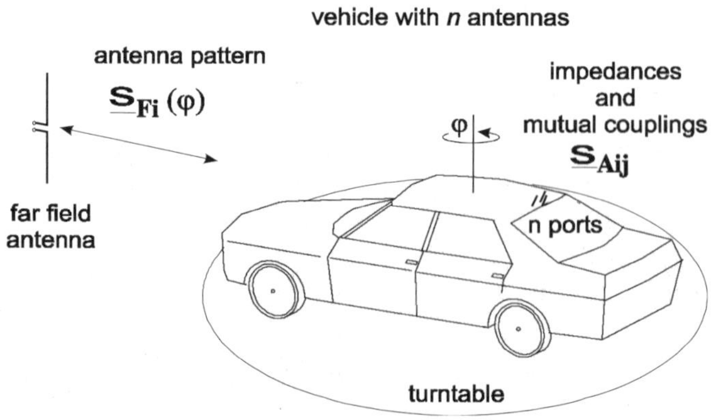

Figure 3. Car antenna measurement principle

For array antenna pattern synthesis on cars a combined method of highly accurate measurements and mathematical optimization has been developed [3]. By measuring the azimuth pattern $s_{Fi}(\varphi)$ of each antenna element in its position on the car and in combination with measurements of the impedance s_{Aii} and the mutual coupling s_{Aij}, a complete equation system, expressed by scattering parameters, can be formed (eqn. (1), resp. eqn. (2) in vector form).

$$\begin{pmatrix} \underline{b}_1 \\ \vdots \\ \underline{b}_n \\ \underline{b}_F \end{pmatrix} = \begin{pmatrix} \underline{s}_{A11} & \cdots & \underline{s}_{A1n} & \underline{s}_{F1}(\varphi) \\ \vdots & \ddots & \vdots & \vdots \\ \underline{s}_{A1n} & \cdots & \underline{s}_{Ann} & \underline{s}_{Fn}(\varphi) \\ \underline{s}_{F1}(\varphi) & \cdots & \underline{s}_{Fn}(\varphi) & \underline{s}_{FA} \end{pmatrix} \begin{pmatrix} \underline{a}_1 \\ \vdots \\ \underline{a}_n \\ \underline{a}_F \end{pmatrix} \tag{1}$$

$$\begin{pmatrix} \underline{\mathbf{B}} \\ \underline{\mathbf{B}}_F \end{pmatrix} = \begin{pmatrix} \underline{\mathbf{S}}_A & \underline{\mathbf{S}}_F \\ \underline{\mathbf{S}}_F^T & \underline{\mathbf{S}}_{FA} \end{pmatrix} \begin{pmatrix} \underline{\mathbf{A}} \\ \underline{\mathbf{A}}_F \end{pmatrix} \tag{2}$$

$$G(\varphi) = \frac{\left|\underline{\mathbf{S}}_F^T \underline{\mathbf{A}}\right|^2}{\left|\underline{\mathbf{A}}\right|^2 - \left|\underline{\mathbf{S}}_A \underline{\mathbf{A}}\right|^2} \tag{3}$$

In fig. 3 the measuring principle that is used for pattern optimization is shown. The car is placed on a low profile turn table and the radiation pattern of the individual antennas are measured in steps of the azimuth angle φ for a full turn.

In fig. 4 the block diagram shows the mathematical structure of the complete array antenna which includes the port of the far field test antenna and the feeding network. The design for optimization of the antenna pattern requires the optimization of the parameters of the feeding network being connected to the ports of the antenna array, which provides the required amplitude and phase distribution of the different antenna elements on the car for a desired radiation pattern. Thus by variation of the port waves $\underline{\boldsymbol{A}}$, the antenna gain function $G(\varphi)$ of the array can be influenced in an appropriate way (eqn. 3). Using variation calculus techniques, the optimum set of waves $\underline{\boldsymbol{A}}$ for a desired pattern has to be found.

3.1 OMNIDIRECTIONAL CAR ANTENNA – Optimum communication performance between the base station and the mobile user in a vehicle demands a car antenna with omnidirectional radiation. Therefore it is important that with a given transmitter power, the far field radiation density exceeds a minimum required value with phone antennas for all directions of the car. As a result, with a given distribution of antenna elements on the car body, the design criterion for the array antenna must achieve maximum far field radiation density at this horizontal direction where minimum radiation occurs. In fig. 5 a low profile cellular radio antenna, consisting of 3 short antenna elements being mounted on the backlite of the car is shown, which has been developed with the above described method [4].

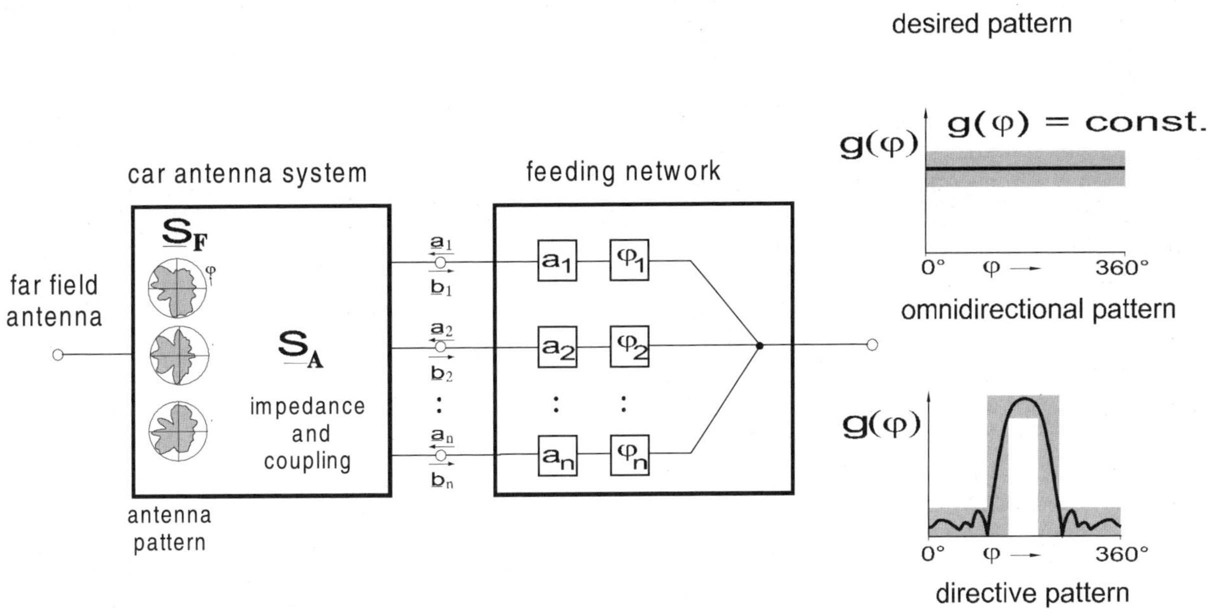

Figure 4. Pattern synthesis with cellular radio car antennas

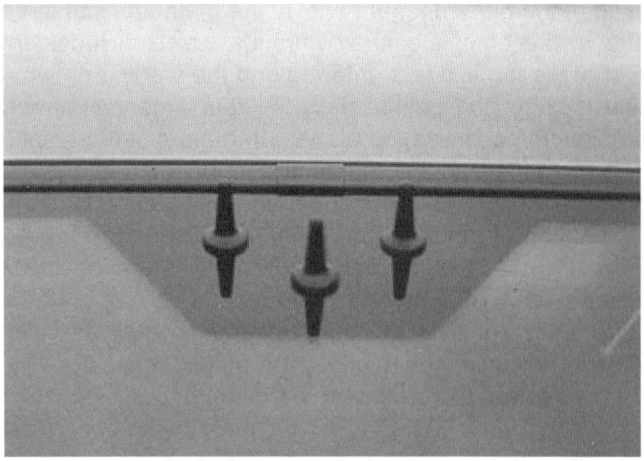

Figure 5. 3-element antenna on the backlite with optimized omnidirectional pattern

With respect to stylistic requirements of car producers an improvement of radiation pattern may also be achieved when using only two elements instead of three. Applying the same optimization method this leads to an array antenna, longitudinally positioned on the car very close to the roof rim, either on the backlite or on the roof itself (fig. 6 and fig. 7). Minimum element length with respect to radiation efficiency of the antenna is approximately 40 - 50 mm, as well as spacing distance of the elements, but depending on the individual type of car. To cover the entire bandwidth (i. e. 824 MHz to 960 MHz for AMPS and GSM) the antenna elements are optimized with additionally integrated inductances being realized in low cost printed circuit technique. In fig. 6 the element height and spacing distance is 45 mm. To protect antenna elements from water, snow or dirt the arrangement is covered with a special housing, being made of RF-suitable material for the desired frequency range. Additionally an active GPS antenna is mounted between the elements (see fig. 7). Fig. 8 shows the improvement of radiation pattern that has been achieved with this type of antenna arrangement. The radiation pattern of the array antenna can be regarded as almost omnidirectional in the azimuth plane with a ripple of about 6 dB. In addition, fig. 8 shows the advantage of the phased array antenna radiation pattern over the radiation pattern of a monopole antenna with the same length and at the same location. Especially the shading towards front direction of the car ($\varphi = 0°$), mainly caused by the curvature of the roof and significant sidelobes have almost been compensated by this technique. The mean antenna gain in the azimuthal plane is only 1.5 dB less than that of a monopole at roof center. In practice, these antennas performed as well as a long rod antenna mounted on the backlite.

Figure 6. 2-element pattern optimized antenna GSM900

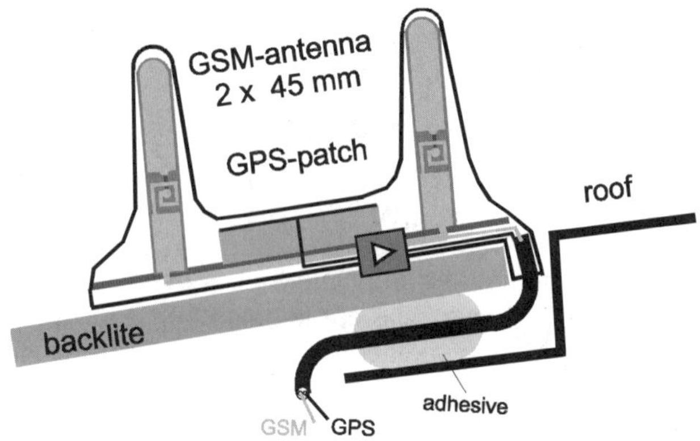

Figure 7. 2-element antenna with integrated active GPS antenna

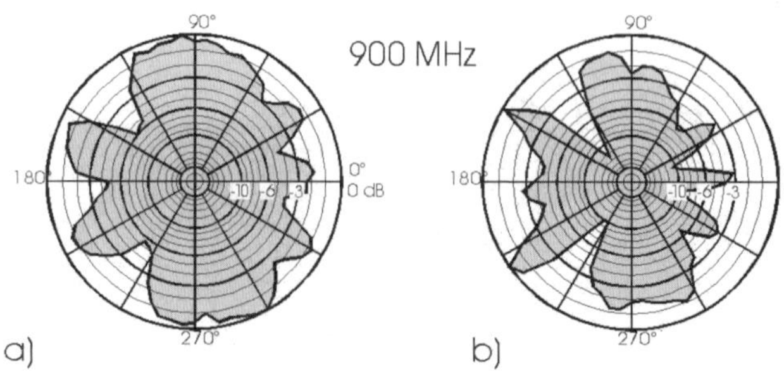

Figure 8. Radiation pattern of a) optimized 2-element antenna b) monopole antenna at roof rim

3.2 ANTENNA WITH DIRECTIVE PATTERN – Based upon the above developed multi-element omnidirectional antennas, further research has been concentrated on the question whether those car array antennas could basically be used as directive antennas and whether the quality of the antenna pattern is sufficient for adaptive beamforming applications. This would give the opportunity for the application of smart antennas at mobile stations (vehicles) as well.

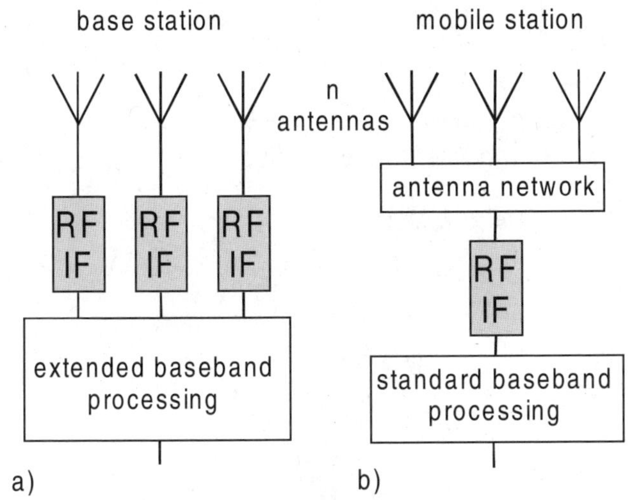

Figure 9. Smart antenna principles a) beamforming with digital signal processing techniques b) beamforming with antenna network

Adaptive beamforming and signal tracking at the base station is usually realized with digital signal processing techniques in the baseband of the cellular phone system. With n antennas of the array this requires also n times complete RX/TX front ends for signal conversion into the baseband. Digital signal processing algorithms with individual digital weight factors for each path allows beam forming for the individual tracking and signal optimization of mobile stations (fig. 9a)

At the mobile station the technical effort has to be reduced to a minimum effort. Therefore, it is preferred to use conventional antenna techniques for beam steering and tracking (see fig. 9b and fig. 4). Variable phase shifters in each path between the antenna elements and the common power splitter/combiner will create the required phase distribution of the antenna currents for the desired pattern. Thus, only one RX/TX front-end unit, as available in the mobile phone set, and the feeding network are required. Additional amplitude adjustment of the antenna signals, as required for optimum omnidirectional pattern, is avoided because the required variable digital step attenuators would reduce the antenna efficiency.

The main goal for pattern optimization is the realization of an adjustable directive main beam, which covers the complete azimuth plane at least in steps of 45 degree. Maximum reduction of undesired sidelobes and optimum front to back-ratio of the antenna have been included in the optimization process as well.

With this simple antenna configuration consisting of only three short elements at the rear roof rim, astonishing results have been achieved, which are shown in fig. 10. The half power beam width in the azimuth plane approximately varies between 60° – 90°. In most cases the front/back–ratio and sidelobe supression is better than 10 dB. The typical antenna gain towards the main beam direction is approximately 4-5 dB higher than the average gain of a single monopole antenna at the roof center. Merely towards the front direction of the car, the resulting antenna pattern is slightly out of the desired specifications. Further improvements can be achieved with an optimized positioning of the antenna elements or with 4-element antenna configurations.

In fig. 11 the basic principle of an adaptive car antenna system is shown. For beam forming and signal tracking additional information of RF-signal strength, signal quality and bit error rate from the baseband processor of the mobile phone set are required. By means of an additional processor and signal-finding and -tracking algorithms, the phase settings for the beamforming network have to be determined. This processor also controls impedance matching of the antenna network.

With an internal link to the GPS navigational system in the car, the exact position of the vehicle is known. Thus, with data exchange with the base station, the direction vector between the car and the base station can be calculated, which could support and stabilize the tracking and beamfinding algorithms of the system. This would also support the smart antenna system of the base station.

4 DIVERSITY CAR ANTENNA FOR CELLULAR RADIO

Antenna diversity techniques have also been implemented successfully at base stations of cellular radio systems in the last few years to improve the reception quality of the incoming signal from the mobile station, which is influenced and disturbed by multipath propagation in the transfer channel. For space or polarization diversity, decorrelated antennas are required. With digital modulation, as used for modern cellular phone systems, diversity techniques will reduce the bit error rate of the signal and increase data transfer rates and channel capacity. Due to the technical effort, diversity techniques have mainly been installed at base stations, but latest trends already show the application of diversity reception in mobile phone handheld terminals [5].

Thus investigations have been made to realize cellular radio diversity reception in vehicles as well. Multiple element antenna configurations, as shown in section 3, seem to be an ideal basis for this. Using the omnidirectional or directive antenna pattern for transmitting from the mobile station to the base station the reception quality of the transmitted base station signal can also be improved with scanning diversity techniques by using the same set of antennas. In spite of the fact that the antenna elements are packed closely together (i.e. less then $\lambda/8$ at 900 MHz), the radiation pattern of the individual elements are extremely different and therefore such antenna configurations are well suited for scanning diversity in the reception mode [6].

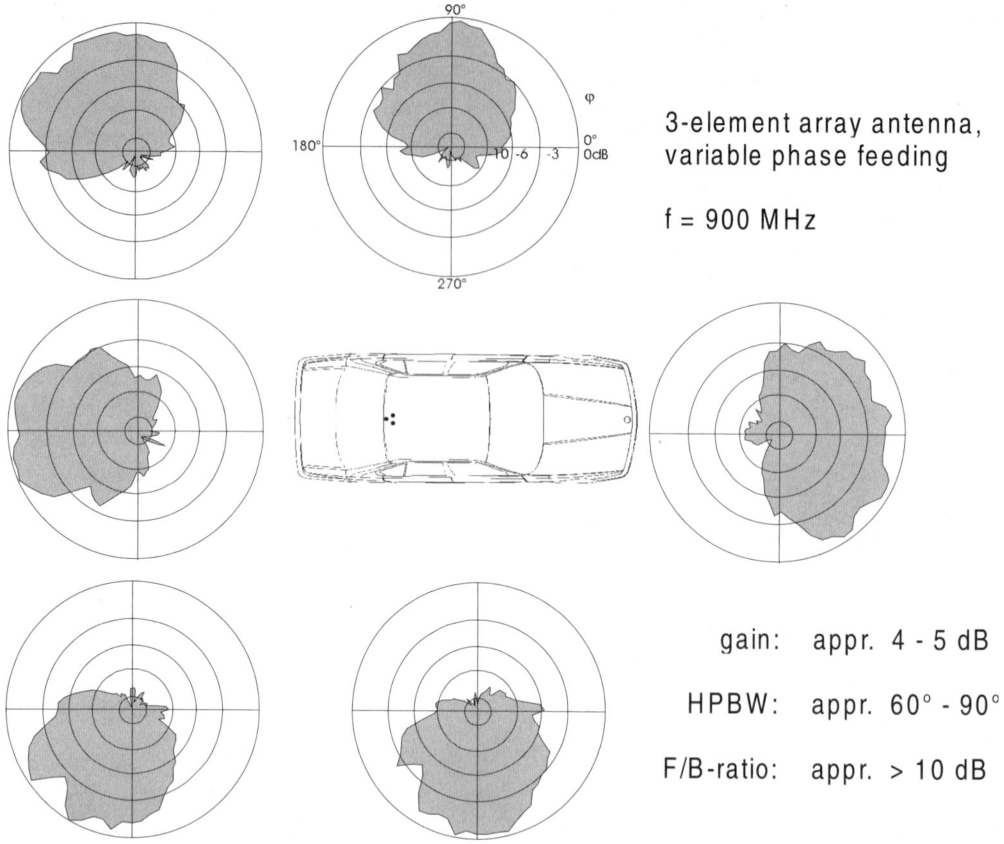

Figure 10. Calculated antenna pattern of a 3-element antenna on the car

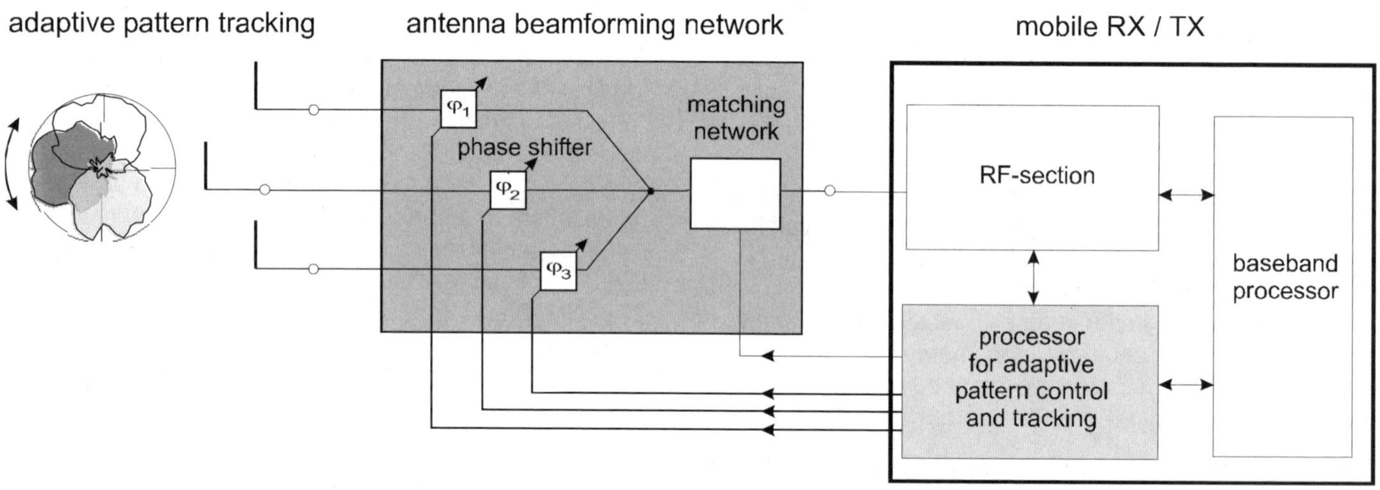

Figure 11. Adaptive beamforming and signal tracking with car antennas for cellular radio

To prove this statement almost the same method as for the evaluation of the diversity effectiveness of FM and TV diversity systems has been used [7]. For the simulation of the system, a set of waves with randomly chosen amplitudes and phases are defined. For simulation of Rayleigh distributed fields (standard situation with mobile reception), the sources are equi-angle distributed over the azimuth, for simulation of Rice distributed fields the sources are chosen with a concentration at a certain region of the azimuth. The car is driven virtually through the resulting field of the superimposed waves and, in consequence, the output signals at the antenna ports can be evaluated. By a second set of waves with independently chosen values for amplitude and phase, a second field is generated which relates to the distortions which in practice result from multipath propagation with large delay, adjacent channel or equal channel interference.

The criterion is based upon the improvement factor i_f of the signal quality obtained with the diversity system under test in comparison with the signal quality obtained with only one single antenna on the car. With p representing the likelihood of a signal level not exceeding a certain threshold during the drive, the signal quality q in dB is defined as:

$$q = 20 \log (1/p) \tag{4}$$

In a theoretical optimum case of all N antennas on the car being decorrelated and each antenna performing equal likelihood of distortions which results in an equal signal quality q_s, the likelihood of distortions in the diversity mode is reduced to $p_d = p_s^N$. Thus the optimum available factor i_f of improvement in dB is defined as:

$$i_f = q_d - q_s = (N\text{-}1)\ q_s \qquad (5)$$

The method for evaluating the improvement factor i_f of the antenna system under test is based upon the same antenna measurements which are required for the pattern synthesis.

In fig. 12 the signal qualities of different antenna combinations of a 3 element GSM antenna are calculated. On the left side the signal quality of each single element is displayed, which is approximately 13 dB. With any of two antenna-combinations in diversity mode the signal quality would already improve to approximately 25 dB. The signal quality reaches 35 dB, when using a diversity system with all three antennas. Thus the improvement factor i_f of this system is 22 dB, which is very close to the theoretical optimum case of 24 dB of totally decorrelated antennas (refer eqn. 5). Further simulations and comparisons of single antenna reception versus diversity reception, which also consider the digital modulation of the cellular radio signal (GMSK) and specific system parameters, have confirmed the advantage of diversity reception in vehicles [8].

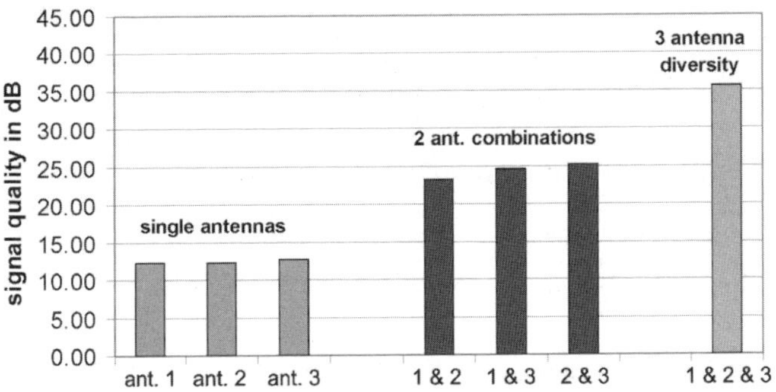

Figure 12. Signal quality with different antenna combinations of a 3-elemet antenna

5 SMART ANTENNA SYSTEM FOR CARS

In fig. 13 a general future principle of a smart antenna system for vehicles is shown. Therein all major aspects of antenna control, as described in the previous sections, are considered. First time link between the mobile and base station in the cellular network requires an omnidirectional antenna pattern. To improve the uplink performance, adaptive beamforming and signal tracking will be used for transmission. For better reception quality highly efficient diversity techniques are applied. Similar to the beamforming process, the complete antenna system will be controlled by an additional processor, which evaluates the baseband signal in the mobile phone car terminal.

6 CONCLUSION

Such a highly effective but very small and comparatively low cost array antenna system on a car, as presented in this paper, generally opens the technical possibility of a future implementation of smart antenna techniques to mobile users as well. This would further improve the performance of cellular radio systems.

7 REFERENCES

1. W. C. Jakes: Microwave Mobile Communications. Wiley & Sons, New York, 1974.
2. R. Bormann, M. Frerich: System Performance of Base Stations with Adaptive Antennas in a GSM 900 Network. Proc. ITG-Diskussionssitzung Systeme mit intelligenten Antennen, Stuttgart, 1999.
3. Kronberger, Lindenmeier, Reiter, Hopf: Design Method for Array Antennas on Cars with Electrically Short Elements under Incorporation of the Radiation Properties of the Car Body. IEEE-APS International Symposium, Montreal, 1997.
4. Lindenmeier, Hopf, Reiter, Kronberger, Leinwetter: Low Profile Cellular Radio Antenna Combined with a Highly Effective Low Cost FM-Antenna- Diversity System on the Backlite. International SAE Conference, Detroit, Feb. 1996.
5. K. Ogawa, T. Matsuyoshi, K. Monma: An Analysis of the Performance of a Handset Diversity Antenna Influenced by Head, Hand and Shoulder Effects at 900 MHz. IEEE-APS International Symposium, Orlando, 1999.
6. Reiter, Lindenmeier, Hopf, Kronberger. Antenna-Diversity Techniques in Cars for FM-Radio, TV and Cellular Phone. 29th European Microwave Conference, Munich, Oct. 1999.
7. Lindenmeier, Hopf, Reiter, Leinwetter: Diversity-Effectiven-ess and Programmable Device for Self-Testing of Operating Functions in Complex OEM-AM/FM/TV-Car-Antenna Systems. International SAE Conference, Detroit Feb. 1998.
8. A. Hammerschmitt, A. Hutter, C. Drewes: Comparison of single antenna, selection combining and optimum combining reception at the vehicle. Vehicular Technology Conference, Amsterdam, 1999.

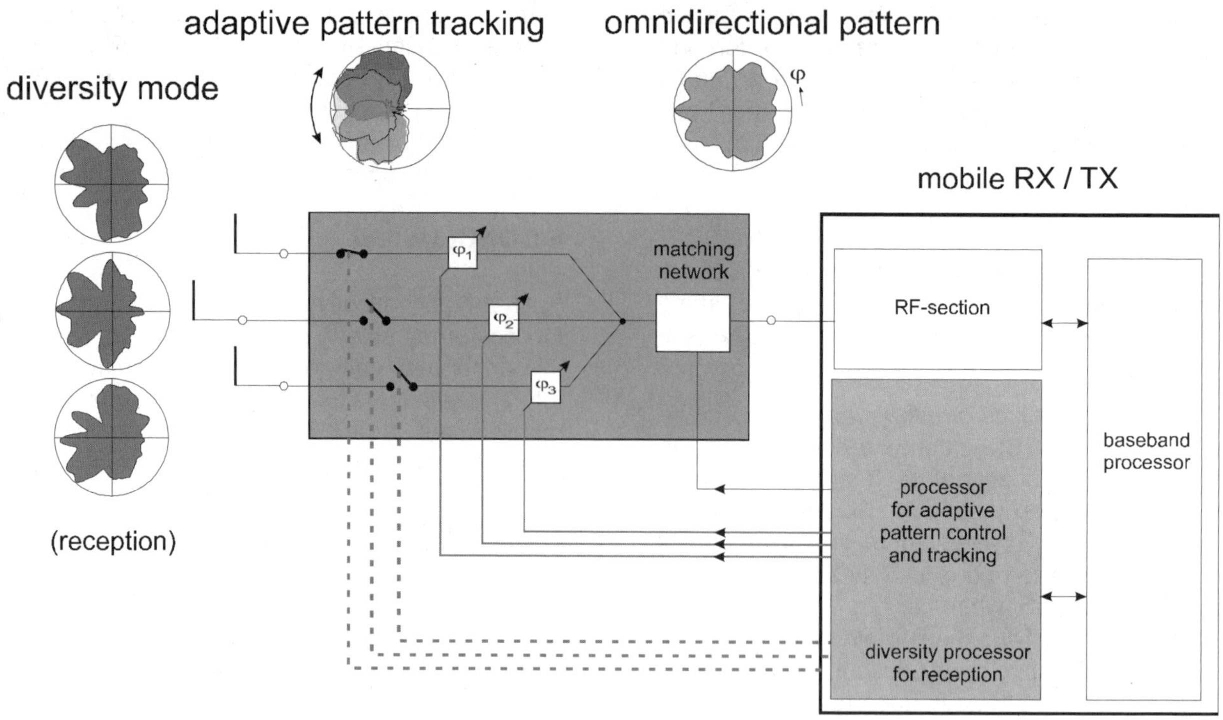

Figure 13. Smart cellular radio car antenna system with diversity reception and adaptive beamforming for transmission

2000-01-0069

DSP-Based Radio with IF Processing

J. William Whikehart
Visteon Automotive Systems

ABSTRACT

Digital Signal Processing (DSP) is applicable to many types of wireless products and systems, and automotive AM/FM receivers are no exception. Processing intermediate-frequency (IF) radio signals in DSP is the logical extension of baseband and audio DSP already commonplace, and is enabled by current analog-to-digital (A/D) technology and digital logic densities. This paper describes the functionality and development of a DSP integrated circuit providing complete IF, baseband, and audio processing for automotive receivers.

INTRODUCTION

The signal processing path of a radio receiver consists of radio frequency (RF), IF, baseband, and audio circuitry. DSP implementation of the latter three parts of this path for automotive AM/FM receivers is made practical by current A/D and IC process technologies and by ever increasing digital logic densities. The signal path benefits from DSP's programmability and its capabilities for exact and repeatable operation, complex functionality, and high integration.

The purpose of IF processing in a receiver is to isolate (along with a tuning mechanism) the desired channel, and then demodulate that channel to produce a baseband signal. Isolation is provided by filtering, and in a DSP receiver, this filtering can easily be made programmable and adaptable. Programmability allows a key receiver attribute, channel selectivity, to be controlled by digital filter coefficients, so that selectivity requirements can be tailored for any market or any OEM customer with no hardware change. Furthermore, by automatically changing the coefficients in response to reception conditions, such as the presence strong interfering channels, the receiver can provide the best overall fidelity.

Another way DSP IF processing can improve reception is by the reduction of noise and interference that falls in the IF bandwidth and therefore cannot be removed just by IF filtering. Complex DSP algorithms can be used to reduce noise, such as ignition noise and multipath spits, and interference, such as co-channel and strong adjacent channel signals. These algorithms also have parametric controls that may be customized. In fact, the use of DSP in IF, baseband, and audio processing means that many aspects of receiver functionality and performance can be determined by parameters controlling the DSP, thus allowing the receiver designer not only to tailor the design to his or her needs but also to decide which of these parameters might be made user-controllable features.

MADRE DSP IF IC

Visteon has co-developed with Philips Semiconductors a DSP IC, called MADRE (Monolithic Advanced Digital Radio Engine), that contains IF, baseband, and audio processing for AM/FM automotive receivers. It is a mixed-signal IC that inputs standard AM and FM IF signals and outputs four channels of line audio for the vehicle's satellite speakers, and it has been designed into Visteon radios. The remainder of this paper will describe the functionality and structure of the IC, the critical design areas in its development, and bench and field test results.

FUNCTIONALITY – The AM/FM IF, baseband, and audio functions of the MADRE IC are listed below, including those for tape and CD. All functions in the table except the actual IF digitization can be customized for particular OEM's and markets using coefficients that are downloaded from the receiver's microcontroller.

- AM
  - Digitization of analog IF input at 450 kHz
  - Adaptive IF filter, including adjacent channel interference detection and mitigation, and wideband AM
  - Narrowband AGC
  - CQUAM demodulator
  - Stereo pilot detection
  - Co-channel detection and mitigation
  - Stereo matrix with automatic blend control
  - Audio high-cut and adaptive noise reduction
- FM
  - Digitization of analog IF input at 10.7 MHz
  - Adaptive IF filter, including adjacent channel interference detection and mitigation
  - Limiter and demodulator

    - Noise blanker
    - MPX stereo decoder
    - Stereo pilot detection
    - Multipath detection and mitigation
    - Stereo matrix with automatic blend control
    - Audio high-cut and adaptive noise reduction
    - RDS demodulator and decoder
- CD and Tape
    - CD compression
    - Tape Dolby B
    - Tape blank skip and music search
- All
    - Parametric equalization
    - Volume, tone, balance, fade

An important feature of MADRE is its ability to simultaneously process one signal from an IF source (AM or FM) and one from an audio source (tape or CD) simultaneously, or to simultaneously process tape and CD audio. Re-configuration of DSP resources on the IC for different modes makes this possible.

DESCRIPTION – The MADRE IC consists of hardwired and programmable DSP as well as analog blocks. It is implemented in 0.5-micron CMOS technology. Between the on-board IF A/D and audio digital-to-analog (D/A) converters are about 550 Mega Operations Per Second (MOPS) of digital signal processing power. A MOP is a single operation, like a multiply or an add.

Hardwired DSP is fixed logic circuitry that performs DSP functions with reconfigurability determined by downloadable parameters, and is appropriate for functions that are not expected to change in structure over the life of an IC. Programmable DSP is performed on DSP cores running code, and MADRE has two – one for IF and one for audio processing. There is a total of about 70 MOPS in the cores. The cores are reconfigurable both by changing their code and by downloading parameters.

The various analog and digital blocks of the MADRE IC are described in the following sub-sections. A block diagram of the IC in the receiver system is shown in Figure 1.

IF Analog-to-Digital Converter – The IF A/D directly digitizes either the 10.7 MHz FM or the 450 kHz AM IF signal from the Tuner, which is similar to typical automotive Tuners except that the AM and FM demodulators and some IF filtering have been removed, these functions now being performed in DSP. In fact, the DSP sets the narrowband IF selectivity characteristics for the receiver.

IF digitization occurs at about 40 MHz, and timing of the rest of the IC is based on this rate. The IF A/D must be treated as a linear element of the signal path, since final IF selectivity and demodulation occurs in the DSP. If FM limiting were performed prior to the A/D, which would allow simple digitization using a comparator, severe intermodulation distortion would occur between the multiple channels that could be present due to the wider Tuner selectivity.

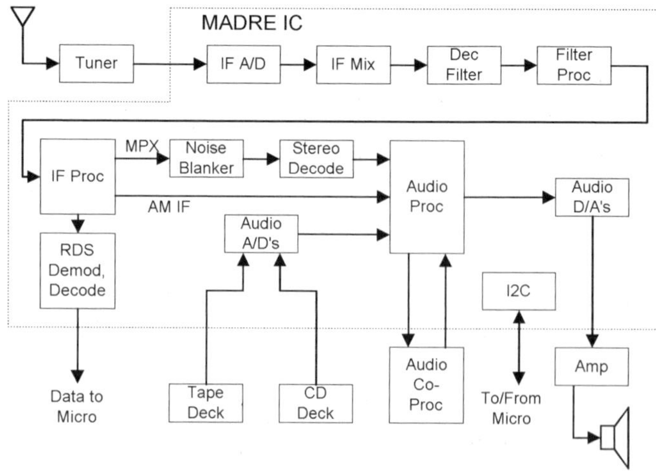

Figure 1. MADRE-Based DSP Radio Block Diagram

A dither signal is added to the IF A/D's input to de-correlate quantization error from the signal and thus make the error appear as noise rather than distortion. This is especially important for low IF input levels to the A/D. The dither is generated digitally and spectrally shaped to avoid adding noise in the AM and FM IF bandwidths. A D/A converts the dither signal to analog for adding to the IF input.

Hardwired IF DSP Blocks – Three hardwired IF DSP blocks follow the IF A/D in series, the first being the IF Mixer. This block mixes the real 10.7 MHz or 450 kHz IF down to about 0 Hz, producing a complex output containing real and imaginary components. Cosine and sine injections are generated within the block, with each multiplying the real IF input to generate the two output components. The IF Decimation Filter, which uses a Cascade-Integrator-Comb (CIC) structure [1], reduces the sample rate of the complex IF signal, and removes the unneeded second IF image from the original real IF signal. The filter also provides some rejection of strong interfering channels.

After decimation, the complex AM or FM IF signal is passed through the Filter Processor block, which executes the main DSP IF filter for FM or performs an additional sample rate decimation filter for AM. The coefficients of the Filter Processor, which uses an FIR structure, are downloadable, and in FM can be changed very quickly to adapt the IF bandwidth to varying reception conditions. The IF Mixer, Decimation Filter, and Filter Processor are implemented in hardwired DSP because their basic functions do not change.

IF Processor and Audio Processor Cores – Two programmable DSP cores are used for IF and audio processing. The IF Processor is fed by the Filter Processor complex output. In FM, it provides the limiting function and the demodulator, producing the MPX signal. When the mode is AM, the IF Processor performs the final narrowband IF filter and narrowband AGC. As in FM, the IF bandwidth adapts to reception conditions. The MPX signal is fed through the Noise Blanker to the Stereo Decoder (these are hardwired DSP blocks) to generate the audio sum (left+right) and difference (left-right) signals, and to extract the 19 kHz pilot. In the second programmable core, called the Audio Processor, the AM IF signal from the IF Processor is stereo demodulated based on the C-QUAM standard to produce sum and difference audio for AM mode.

Either the FM or AM sum and difference signals are processed in the Audio Processor to produce the AM/FM left and right audio signals. The processing starts with the de-matrix (to produce left and right), blend (to control the amount of stereo separation), AM/FM de-emphasis, high-cut, and adaptive noise reduction. High-cut is used to control the audio bandwidth in response to various signal level and quality measurables calculated on the IC. Blend is also determined by these measurables.

Tape, CD, and Audio Processing in the Audio Processor – In tape mode, the analog tape input to the IC is digitized and then followed by processing to perform Dolby B decoding, blank skip, and music search, all on the Audio Processor. Analog CD or CDDJ audio is also digitized and then optionally compressed to reduce its dynamic range to suit the vehicle environment. Actually, MADRE's dual-playback capability allows any two of the tape, CD, and CDDJ sources to be digitized and processed at the same time. Dual-playback also allows processing of the AM or FM signal simultaneously with tape or CD/CDDJ processing, thus allowing, for example, the driver to listen to FM while rear-seat passengers listen to CD on headphones.

Most of the remaining functionality in the Audio Processor operates on any one or two of the left/right sources (AM/FM, tape, CD, and CDDJ). The first of these functions is parametric audio equalization. The frequency path from the speakers to the listener's ears is affected by the shapes and textures of the vehicle interior, as well as by speaker placement. This problem is reduced by MADRE's three bands of independent equalization for each of the four audio channels (left front, right front, left rear, and right rear). Since the equalization is determined by DSP coefficients, it can easily be tailored to any vehicle interior, either at the radio or vehicle plant. The left and right audio signals can also be sent off-chip to a co-processor to produce the four audio channels with even more bands of equalization. The four channels are then brought back into the IC for the remainder of the audio processing. The external processing is also used for speaker delays to help center the sound image, concert hall effects, and subwoofer and center speaker outputs. After equalization, the standard volume, tone, loudness, balance, and fade functions are performed. During dual-playback, the front and rear balance and tone controls are independent. The final audio signals after processing are converted to analog in the four on-chip D/A converters.

Other MADRE Blocks – The FM MPX signal is fed to the RDS Demodulator and Decoder blocks. Either the raw RDS data stream from the demodulator or the decoded data can be read by the receiver's microcontroller. There are hardwired blocks for the decimation and interpolation filters for the over-sampled audio A/D's and D/A's. A standard I^2C interface block allows the receiver microcontroller to download various control words and parameters to MADRE, and it provides MADRE status information back to the microcontroller.

Development Responsibilities – The MADRE IC was co-developed by Visteon and Philips Semiconductors, with Visteon designing all the IF hardwired DSP algorithms and logic, the IF Processor core, and all the DSP algorithms and code residing in both cores. Visteon also specified the performance of the IF A/D and the audio A/D's and D/A's, which Philips provided.

CRITICAL DEVELOPMENT TASKS FOR DSP IF PROCESSING – The development of the MADRE IC with DSP IF processing required work in four critical areas – system analysis, simulation, integration, and bench and field test. These areas will be discussed in the following sections.

System Analysis – System analysis is a key task for any receiver design, and must take into consideration many factors. The system is defined as the signal path from the antenna input to stereo audio output, and therefore consists of the AM/FM Tuner, the IF A/D, and the digital signal processing that ultimately produces stereo audio.

The MADRE receiver system analysis was performed by Visteon and started with determining a set of radio-level performance requirements, for both on the bench and in the field. Of particular importance for the DSP IF design was sensitivity, strong-signal noise and distortion, and interference rejection, because these determine the IF A/D requirements as well as some Tuner requirements. Another design requirement was that the Tuner and IF A/D had to be realizable and practical. Typical front-end Tuner noise levels were assumed, and reasonable Tuner gain and selectivity were targeted. An 8-bit IF A/D was selected based on availability from Philips and a good probability that it could be integrated on the mixed-signal IC. Integration of the IF A/D was important for parts-count reduction and for avoiding EMI that could result from running the high-speed A/D outputs on the circuit board. Another input to the system analysis was an understanding of the characteristics of the AM and FM demodulators, in terms of output signal-to-noise (SNR) ratio versus input carrier-to-noise (CNR) ratio. This was accomplished by analysis and simulation, taking into account standard de-emphasis.

A factor that affected the whole system was the IF A/D sample rate, which was chosen to be around 40 MHz. This rate is much higher than the AM and FM IF channel bandwidths (about 10 kHz and 200 kHz), and thus provides "processing gain", meaning that the IF A/D quantization noise floors in the narrow bandwidths are much lower than would have been obtained with a lower sample rate. The IF sample rate was also selected such that an audio sample rate in the area of 40 kHz would result using a reasonable sample-rate decimation structure. Furthermore, the complexity of generating the cosine and sine injections in the IF Mixer block was determined by the IF sample rate.

All A/D's have distortion, and the distortion mechanisms, or modes, of MADRE's IF A/D were carefully identified and analyzed. This part of the system analysis required consideration of the radio-level interference-rejection requirements, spurious content in the IF Mixer injections, and the possible aliasing of IF A/D distortion products. Thus, the IF A/D sample rate was also a factor for distortion analysis, since it determined at what frequencies aliases would fall. About 25 distortion modes were identified for each of the AM and FM paths, and particular distortion products that could fall in-band for each mode were found using a custom search program. Analysis was then performed on each in-band product to determine its effects on performance and to specify its maximum level. For example, up to about 35th-order harmonics of the 10.7 MHz IF input were found that could alias into the desired FM passband, and this was actually observed on the bench.

The particular Tuner requirements resulting from the system analysis were minimum gain, automatic gain control (AGC) range, and selectivity, as well as validation of the Tuner front-end noise floor assumption. For the IF A/D, AM and FM narrowband noise floor requirements and maximum distortion levels associated with certain distortion modes were established.

Simulation – Another key development task for Visteon was simulation of the MADRE design at various levels – radio system, block, and code. The system level simulation included the Tuner and covered about 70 AM and FM reception scenarios, including weak-signal, strong-signal, and interference. This simulation required about 300 hours of workstation CPU time. Block level simulation validated the performance to bit-level accuracy, and code simulation was performed for all of the functions residing in the two cores.

Integration – A third important design effort was the integration of the various analog, hardwired DSP, and DSP cores into one IC. Visteon and Philips worked closely together on this, considering IC floor planning, pin-out, power and ground placement, and clock distribution.

Bench and Field Testing – After the first prototype MADRE IC's were fabricated, extensive bench and field testing at Visteon began. Bench testing verified the functionality and performance of the analog and DSP blocks, and field-testing was performed on various North American and European test routes. Of particular importance was the field-testing of the adaptive DSP IF filters to make sure the adaptation algorithms maximized fidelity under all reception conditions while not producing undesired audible artifacts.

RESULTS – An important feature of MADRE is the adaptive DSP IF bandwidth. In both AM and FM, the IF is narrowed automatically when the signal is weak or an adjacent channel is detected, and widened when these conditions cease. Bench testing in FM has shown significant improvement in adjacent and alternate channel rejection, as seen in Table 1.

Table 1. Bench FM Adjacent and Alternate Channel Interference Rejection Results

Market	Interferer	Interferer to Desired Channel Ratio, dB	Typical Analog Radio SNR, dB	MADRE Radio SNR, dB
North America	Adjacent	26	30	65
		70	<0	30
	Alternate	72	30	30 to 35
Europe	Adjacent	8	30	>70
		40	<0	65
	Alternate	66	30	50

Interference rejection improvement has been verified in the field also. Table 2 shows how reception is improved over a typical analog radio for various distances from the adjacent channel's broadcast tower. In this test, the test vehicle is driven away from the tower broadcasting the desired channel and towards the tower broadcasting the interfering adjacent channel. At a certain point along the route, the audio fidelity will start to fall due to the interference. At a point closer to the interfering tower, the audio signal becomes unlistenable. These two events and the miles from the interfering tower are shown in the table. The towers were about 60 miles apart at equal power levels. The improvement in reception range using MADRE's DSP IF processing is evident.

Table 2. FM Adjacent Channel Rejection Field Results

Listening Event	Miles from interfering tower when event occurs, typical analog radio	Miles from interfering tower when event occurs, MADRE radio
Fidelity begins to deteriorate.	15	7.5
Signal becomes unlistenable.	8	2.5

Field testing on the AM adaptive IF has also shown good results. When a wideband AM signal is received and no adjacent is present, the bandwidth widens to about 7.5 kHz at audio, giving fidelity that approaches FM. When an adjacent is detected, the bandwidth automatically narrows to the typical 3 kHz.

CONCLUSION

The MADRE IC was developed to provide integrated IF, baseband, and audio DSP for automotive AM/FM receivers. Functions were implemented in hardwired and programmable DSP, and extensive system analysis, simulation, and bench and field testing were performed. Development of the MADRE IC was completed on schedule for use in MY2000 Visteon radios, meeting all functional, performance, and cost targets. The result was a leading edge DSP technology solution for medium- and high-level AM/FM automotive radios that provides a very high degree of functional integration and flexibility for OEM and aftermarket customization.

ACKNOWLEDGMENTS

The author wishes to acknowledge the hard work and dedication of the MADRE design team in successfully developing such a complex IC. This team consisted of the Visteon DSP Development Group, designers at Ford Microelectronics Inc., and designers from Philips Semiconductors.

REFERENCES

1. E. B. Hogenauer, "An Economical Class of Digital Filters for Decimation and Interpolation," *IEEE Transactions on Acoustics, Speech, and Signal Processing*, vol. ASSP-29, No. 2, pp. 155-162, April 1981.

CONTACT

J. William Whikehart
Technical Specialist – Digital Signal Processing
Visteon Automotive Systems
Danou Technical Center
16630 Southfield Road
Allen Park, MI 48101
Phone and fax: (313) 390-4057
E-mail: bwhikeha@visteon.com

DEFINITIONS, ACRONYMS, ABBREVIATIONS

Adjacent Channel: The channel next to the desired channel on the tuning "dial".
Alternate Channel: The channel two channels away from the desired channel on the tuning "dial".

APPENDIX

"Dolby B" is a trademark of Dolby Laboratories Licensing Corporation.

PART IV
DRIVER ASSISTANCE SYSTEMS

2007-01-1736

Flexible Low Cost Lane Departure Warning System

M. Fornero, D. Lingenfelter, S. Litkouhi, K. Oster and R. Ong
University of Michigan

ABSTRACT

Many highway accidents are caused by distracted drivers and those suffering from drowsy driver syndrome. A driver alert indicating a lane departure could thwart such accidents, saving lives and making our roads safer.

Products called Lane Departure Warning Systems (LDWS) have been developed to alert drivers of a lane departure. However, due to their high cost, lane departure warning systems are available only on luxury vehicles, barring their benefits from the majority of drivers. With Field Programmable Gate Arrays (FPGA) becoming more powerful and more affordable, a LDWS implementation utilizing hardware rather than software to conduct image processing eliminates the need for a costly high-power microprocessor, and could bring LDWS to a broader user base.

This paper will discuss an FPGA based approach to LDWS. The proof-of-concept system is based on a Xilinx FPGA, taking its image data from an off-the-shelf NTSC camera. This implementation leverages the massively parallel nature of the FPGA to produce a high performance system that could be developed into a low-cost commercial LDWS.

The proof-of-concept system detected lane departures with a detection accuracy of 74%. With the low cost of FPGA-based designs, lane departure warning systems could become profitable on more automobile models, thus increasing their availability.

INTRODUCTION

Motor vehicle accidents due to drowsy drivers pose a serious problem. The National Highway Traffic Safety Administration (NHTSA) estimates that about 56,000 crashes each year are caused by driver fatigue. Driver fatigue accidents are generally the result of an unintended lane departure, which ultimately leads to roadway departure or collision with another vehicle. A device that warns a driver of an impending lane departure has the potential to save lives.

Lane departure warning systems are already commercially available. However, these systems are not widely available due to their high per unit cost. When available, consumers can pay upwards of two thousand dollars for an LDW option. This high price keeps the technology away from those who would benefit from it. A less expensive implementation would mean wider availability and more lives saved.

Current LDWS implementations that rely on microprocessors to process image data perform well, but costly hardware reduces their practicality. In order to implement a low-cost hardware design, algorithms used in proven lane departure warning systems must be modified to run in hardware rather than software. This study investigates the implementation of a set of such algorithms on an FPGA.

In order to investigate the feasibility of an FPGA-based LDWS, a prototype system was designed using an FPGA development board. The system was tested on an actual vehicle on a standard interstate highway in order to evaluate system performance.

The system was calibrated and tested in sunny conditions. Once an FPGA-based system is designed, previously proven logic to accommodate for varying conditions could be integrated.

PROJECT GOALS

This study aimed to create a system that would perform timely and reliable lane departure detection. To be considered timely, the system should respond before the vehicle leaves the lane. The system should detect 100% of lane departures while producing zero false warnings.

SYSTEM DESCRIPTION

ALGORITHM OVERVIEW

The lane departure system is composed of the following processes:

1) Grayscale images are read in from the camera

2) The images pass through an edge detection filter and are stored into memory.

3) A line drawing algorithm implemented in software accesses each image, determines the 10 brightest lines and passes their information to the three-feature [3] lane detection logic.

4) The three-feature lane detection logic chooses the best line and determines if the vehicle is out of lane.

5) If the vehicle is out of lane, the alarm is activated.

FPGA DESIGN

FPGA Overview

The system was implemented on a Xilinx Virtex-II Pro FPGA. The Virtex-II Pro provided an ideal prototyping platform with two embedded PowerPC processors and 30,816 logic cells, giving us far more processing power than was needed.

The algorithm is implemented in two separate parts: a hardware portion, designed in Verilog HDL, and a software portion, designed in C. The hardware portion, using the FPGA fabric, is connected to the PowerPC processor via the On-chip Peripheral Bus, allowing the software to directly access hardware registers. The hardware processes the raw video stream, extracts the luminance data, applies an edge detection filter, compares it to a threshold, and stores the binary result into memory. The software then reads and processes the data.

Video Stream

The system obtains image data through an NTSC camera connected to a VDEC1 daughter board from Digilent Inc. The daughter board itself simply served as a carrier for the ADV7183B Video Decoder chip, allowing us to simply plug the camera into the system.

Data Flow

The hardware portion of the algorithm was designed as a pipeline, allowing each all new bytes of data to be processed in serial as they arrive. Data enters the pipeline as a raw NTSC video stream, in YCrCb format. Next, the luminance data is extracted and the timing signals are detected, and the passed on down the pipeline. The luminance data is passed through an edge detection filter and compared against a software configurable threshold. If the result of the comparison is within the software selectable region of interest (of the image), it is stored in memory.

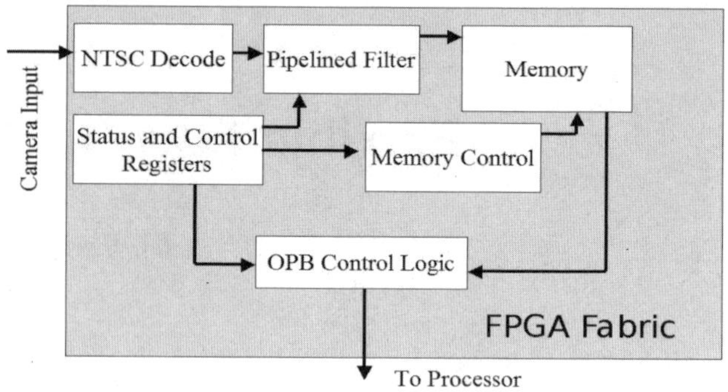

Figure 1: FPGA Data Flow

NTSC Decoding

The first stage of the pipeline decodes the raw NTSC video stream, extracting both the timing and luminance data. The timing data comes in the form of a timing reference signal, which can denote horizontal blanking, vertical blanking, or the end of a field of data. From these signals, the end of each line and the end of each field of data can be determined, which are used by later stages of the pipeline. As the data is in YCrCb format, only every other byte of data is actually processed by the later stages of the pipeline.

Edge Detection Filter

The edge detection filter is comprised of a 32 byte shift register, as well as shift registers for the timing and pixel position data. The FIR filter used is composed entirely of adds and subtracts, eliminating the need for any multipliers. The filter module also compares the output of the FIR filter to a threshold value and passes the binary result (1 or 0) to the next stage of the pipeline

Memory

The results of the edge detection filter and thresholding are placed into memory for those pixels within the image's region of interest. The memory itself consists of two banks so that software can read while hardware is processing another frame. The memory also contains a locking feature, preventing the hardware from processing a frame until software is ready. This allows software to process an entire image before any change is made to the memory being read.

Software Control

In addition to containing memory accessible to the processor, the hardware module also contains memory mapped control and status registers, allowing for software control over the threshold, top of the region of interest, and the bottom of the region of interest. These parameters can be changed dynamically, allowing for such features as dynamic thresholding, and recalibration of the region of interest In response to camera movement.

Edge Detection

As the image is read it is converted to grayscale and processed through an edge detection filter. In our case the goal is more specific: we sought not simply to accentuate the edges in the image, but to accentuate the lane markings themselves. After filtering, each value in the image is compared to a threshold, so the final output is a binary image.

Advantages of FPGA Image Processing

By performing the entire image processing in the FPGA fabric the overall system throughput is drastically increased, as the pipeline is able to process each pixel as it is received from the A/D converter. This differs from a microprocessor-based image processing system, where the processor must read each pixel or group of pixels from memory, process it, and then store the results, one at a time.

Creating a Different Method of Edge Detection

After experimenting with different types of edge detection filters, we started to make our own FIR 1-D edge detection filter. This was motivated by the following three principles:

1) Lane markers are primarily composed of vertical edges.

2) The filter should be fast enough to leave most of the time and computing resources for other routines in the algorithm such as line drawing.

3) The filter should take full advantage of all of the information in a lane marker, meaning it should recognize both edges as well as the stretch of white in the middle.

The result was a 1-D horizontal FIR lane detection filter. In order to calculate the output for a single pixel, it looks 16 pixels before it and 15 pixels after it. This length allows the filter to span an entire lane marker, capturing both edges and the span of white in the middle. The filter buffer is composed entirely of 1's and -1's, so no multiplies are required in implementation. The filter coefficients are graphed below.

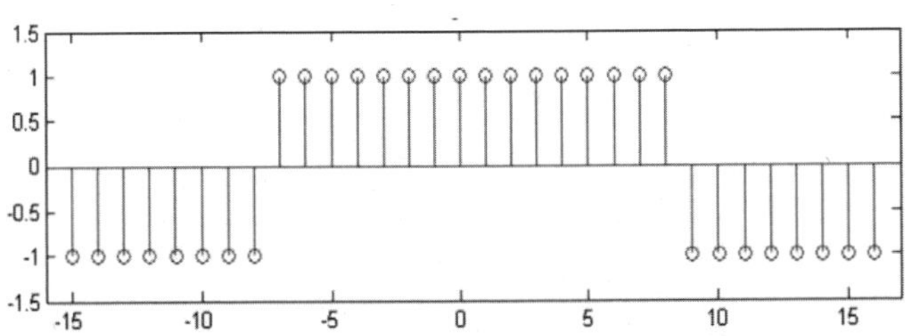

Figure 2: 1D FIR Edge Detection Filter

The large size of this filter makes it less vulnerable to small noisy edges such as dirt and pavement cracks. The figure below is an eroded road shoulder filtered for lane detection using the bank in Figure 2.

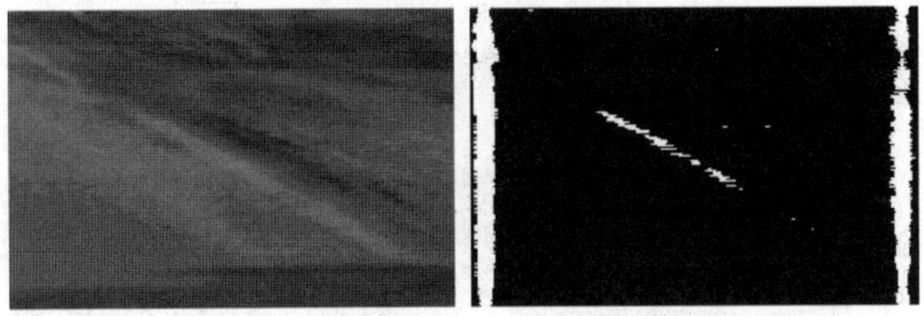

Figure 3: 1D Correlation Lane Detection

Note that in the figure above the lines on the left and right are merely edge effects that are simply thrown out.

We determined that the 1D filter outperformed the considered alternatives by comparing the peak filter outputs produced by various image features. On average, the ratio of the lane marker peak to the next highest noise peak was 20:1. Using another popular edge detection filter, the Sobel filter [4-6], this same ratio was only 5:1 on average.

Since the filter operates independently on each horizontal line, it does not matter if the odd and even lines of the image are available at different times. This is helpful because the camera signal is in NTSC format, which delivers interleaved image data.

In summary, this filter offers the following advantages:

1) Fast

2) Easy to use on an NTSC signal

3) Rejects high frequency, short duration noise such as cracks, tar sealant and dirt

4) Highest gain occurs over lane markers

One inherent disadvantage of this filter is that it detects a large number of edge pixels in the horizontal direction, which in certain situations may cause the line drawing algorithm to draw lines of widely varying angles through the same lane marker.

Threshold Tradeoffs

Choosing an appropriate threshold is very important in the edge detection filter. The ideal threshold is high enough to reject noise and low and enough to capture lane markers.

Our system was originally designed with a manually chosen threshold. However, the problem is that different lighting conditions require different thresholds for the system to function. If the lighting conditions are too dark or light, then the edge data is weakened. If the threshold remains at a level that was suitable for good lighting conditions, then when the lighting conditions become poor the system will fail to detect anything. The figure below shows the effects of choosing different thresholds.

Figure 4: The Effects of Threshold Selection

LINE EXTRACTION

The line extraction algorithm is based on the Hough transform. There are many ways to alter the Hough transform to tailor it to our specific need of detecting lane lines on an image of a road. First, the limited possible locations of lane boundaries allow the algorithm to only evaluate the Hough transform with line endpoints along a single horizontal path in the image. It is also not necessary to test all possible angles from 0 to 180 degrees because lane lines only appear at certain angles in the image. The tailored Hough transform was used to sum the edge pixels along many candidate lines to determine the most likely lane boundaries.

It was found experimentally that the most effective range of angles to scan is 20 to 48 degrees. These angles are measured from the positive horizontal direction to the line as it points toward the bottom of the image. It is also important to note that the slopes of the lane markers will be negative on the left side of the image and positive on the right. If this is exploited, the algorithm can test lines with angles from 20 to 48 degrees on one side, and the opposite of those angles on the other side. The resolution of line angles is also a tunable parameter. The system initially used steps of two degrees but later moved to steps of four degrees to improve execution time. There was negligible performance loss after decreasing the angle resolution.

Bresenham Line Drawing Algorithm

The most computationally intensive portion of the lane detection algorithm is drawing candidate lines and summing the edge pixels along those lines. It was crucial to find a fast algorithm to implement the line drawing without using multiplication, division, or lookup tables. The Bresenham line drawing algorithm [2] proved to best meet our requirements for evaluating the simplified Hough transform.

Finding the Best Line Candidates

Software implementation of the Hough transform requires a nested loop structure to loop across all possible horizontal pixels and then all possible angles of lines passing through those pixels. In this case, the computational complexity increases exponentially as the size of the image increases. The ten lines passing through the most edge pixels are stored and processed.

The figure below shows an example of the lines drawn by the modified Hough Transform.

Figure 5: Illustration of lines tested

LANE SELECTION

Introduction

The line drawing algorithm provides ten possible lanes for each region of interest. The two regions of interest are indicated by the two rectangles. The Three Feature Algorithm chooses the most likely lane boundary from these candidates.

Figure 6: Image with 10 possible lanes in each region of interest

Three-Feature Based Automatic Lane Detection Algorithm (TFALDA) [3]

Initially, the lane selection was based on the Three-Feature Based Automatic Lane Detection Algorithm (TFALDA)[i]. TFALDA selects the most probable lane in each region of interest. It claims to be simple, robust, and efficient, making it suitable for real-time processing in cluttered road environments without a priori knowledge on them.

The data that was tested and cited in TFALDA encompassed only limited conditions. We calibrated the variables in the algorithm and made several improvements to finally come up with a system that was able to perform well in the tested conditions.

TFALDA determines distance using three features: position, angle and intensity. The distance formula is given by:

$$D_i = K_p |P_i - P_{n-1}| + K_a |A_i - A_{n-1}| + K_I (I_{n-1} - I_i)$$

For each region of interest, D_i is the distance between the ith possible lane to the selected lane selected in the previous frame. K_p, K_a and K_i are the coefficients or weights applied to position, angle and intensity respectively. P_i is the position of the x-coordinate for the ith possible lane at the top of the region of interest. A_i is the angle that the ith possible lane makes with the horizontal. I_i is the intensity of the ith possible lane determined by the summation of binary values along the lane line. P_{n-1}, A_{n-1}, and I_{n-1} represent the position, angle and intensity values of the lane which was chosen in the previous frame.

TFALDA selects lanes based on the assumption that lane markings cannot exhibit abrupt discontinuity. Since our system operates at 30 frames per second (fps), there should not be a significant difference between the lanes of the previous frame and those of the present frame. For each region of interest, the most probable lane for the current frame is the lane with the shortest distance to that of the previous frame.

TFALDA sets initial conditions to standard handpicked values chosen to represent a typical, reasonable pair of lane markings. The TFALDA structure naturally compares current lanes to a previous lane. When the system first turns on or returns from an alarm state, the previous lane markings are initialized to these initial conditions. Given some time, TFALDA will be able to select the correct lanes. Since the system will be running at 30fps, the system will quickly begin to select lane markers. This eliminates the need for additional logic to handle situations where prior lane marking information is not available. However, an absence of pervious data forces the algorithm to choose the brightest lane marker irrespective of its position and angle, which in many scenarios will perpetuate poor data causing the system to stumble.

Improvements to TFALDA and calibration of variables

We made several improvements to TFALDA and calibrated the variables before the system was able to detect the correct lanes. Without the improvements, the algorithm only worked in specific conditions and relied more heavily on the continual presence of strong lane markings.

The first improvement was to add a distance threshold. If the shortest distance is greater than the distance threshold, the algorithm selects the lane on the previous frame. The reason for selecting the lane on the previous frame is because lane markings cannot exhibit abrupt discontinuity. If the shortest distance is greater than the threshold distance, it means that the line detected is likely to be a poor selection. The lane on the previous frame would be a better candidate than the lane on the current frame.

The second improvement that we made was to add a counter for each region of interest. As the algorithm continues to select the previous lane marker, the probability of an accurate choice decreases. On the 15th frame, the algorithm is forced to choose one of the 10 new lane candidates. This improvement ensures that we the algorithm will not select the previous line indefinitely after drifting significantly.

The third improvement was to introduce suitable initial conditions for the previous frame. The initial conditions refer to the three features of the lanes for the previous frame. Suitable initial conditions are beneficial because they provide a reasonable starting reference for the algorithm and discourage rash lane selections that tend to occur while changing lanes. We determined the initial conditions by obtaining the three features on a car that is centered on a road with clear lane markings. We then verified in simulation that the initial conditions helped the system recognize new lane markings after lane departure occurred.

The next step was to calibrate all the variables. The variables include the coefficients for the three features, the counters, and the distance threshold. Calibration proved to be difficult and time consuming because the system is non-linear and optimizing one variable changed the performance of other variables. This was accomplished by stepping frame by frame through many different segments of test data and tweaking the system until it exhibited good, reliable behavior in all of the test cases.

The system performed well after all the improvements were made. Figure 7 shows the simulation results after the improvements have been made. The second subplot shows that the improved system selected the correct lanes. Note that in order to truly judge the performance of the system it was necessary to observe whole movie segments.

Detecting lane departure

With good performance in lane detection, the next step was to detect lane departure. In order to determine lane departure, we required the positions of the wheels and the position of the lanes at the bottom of the region of interest. We were able to determine the tire positions in the image because the camera was mounted in a fixed position in the car. Determining lane positions at the bottom of the region of interest was slightly more complicated. As shown in Figure 4, the line drawing algorithm provides lane positions at the top of the region of interest (x1, y1) and not at the bottom (x0, y0). We interpolated the x-position from x1 to x0 to obtain the lane position at the bottom of the region of interest.

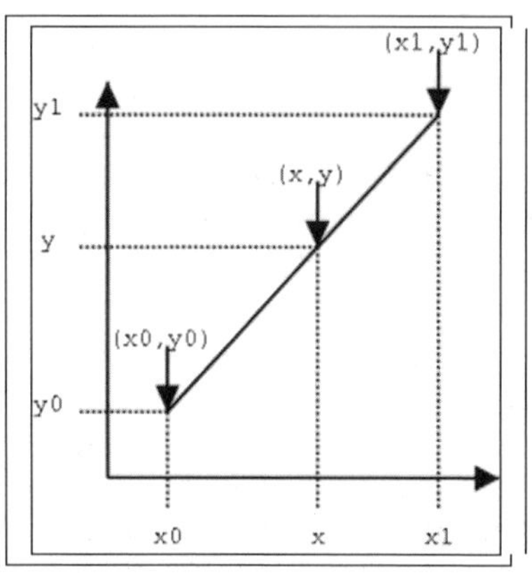

Figure 7: Illustration of lane positions at the top of the region of interest (x1, y1) and at the bottom (x0, y0)

If either tire crosses the lane for three frames, the alarm will be set and the system will stop functioning for 80 frames. 80 frames at 30fps correspond to 2.67 seconds, which is a suitable time to complete a lane departure. This is based on the assumption that the driver will either complete the lane change or return to within lane boundaries once the alarm is set. The alarm will be set again if the lane departure is not completed within 2.67 seconds. The tire has to cross the lane for three consecutive frames before the alarm is set in order to reduce the rate of false detection.

Figure 8 and Figure 9 show the simulation results before and after the alarm is set respectively. We tested the system in various road conditions with MATLAB and obtained a 100% detection rate for lane departure with no false alarms in each test case.

Figure 8: Frame just before alarm is set when the vehicle is out of the detected lanes

Figure 9: Frame when the alarm is set and a lane departure is detected

VEHICLE SETUP

The system was tested with a camera mounted in a 2000 Mazda 626. The camera, an NTSC security camera made by Swann, was mounted to a bracket made of 1 1/2" aluminum angle and was attached to the windshield using rearview mirror glue. *Note: a polarizer was added later to eliminate glare.*

The camera was mounted as high up on the windshield as possible and as close to the center of the windshield as possible in order to maximize the camera's field of view directly in front of the car and to give a symmetrical field of view. Mounting the camera just to the right of the rearview mirror allowed for minimum driver distraction, in fact making the camera nearly invisible to the driver and does not compromise the use of the rearview mirror.

Once the camera was mounted, it was adjusted so that the image was level and centered and the field of view in front of the car was such that the bottom of the image was just above the end of the hood of the car. This was achieved by centering the car on a straight line and viewing the camera output either on a TV or on a laptop via an NTSC capture device. Level and centered was determined by drawing a straight line down the center of the viewing screen.

Once the camera was positioned, the car was positioned just to the right and just to he left of the line in order to determine the position of the edge of the car in the image.

Unfortunately, due to the positioning of the camera in the windshield, there were some problems with glare, so a polarizer was added in order to eliminate this glare. Additionally, because of reflection off of the windshield and the polarizer, the camera's night-vision feature of the camera renders the system useless at night because the infrared LEDs reflect and blind the camera. Future implementations should move both the camera and the LEDs in order to minimize glare and allow the night-vision feature to become an asset rather then a problem.

Since the camera and FPGA both use power supplies that are designed for 120V AC power, a power inverter was used to power the setup. This type of setup would not be well suited for a commercial application, but a system running on 12V DC is feasible for a future prototype.

PROTOTYPE TESTING

The prototype system was tested on 19 miles of interstate highway using the described configuration. The statistics were gathered by analyzing a video recording from inside the vehicle. The weather conditions were sunny with a significant amount of traffic. The system was judged to be correct when the alarm sounded and the vehicle was within thirty centimeters of a lane boundary. Analysis of the video showed 45 correct warnings and 16 false warnings, yielding a detection accuracy of 74%. However, data collected on the same stretch of road during development yielded 96% accuracy when lighting conditions did not saturate the camera and the filter threshold was appropriate for the lighting conditions.

While testing the prototype, video was gathered in the same time period and simulated for comparison. These simulations revealed that brightness offsets and camera saturation reduced the image quality and were the most likely causes for false warnings. This meant that the filter threshold needed to be calibrated whenever lighting conditions changed due to factors such as time of day, direction of travel, or cloud cover.

An additional but less significant source of error came from other vehicles. The wheels and rims of cars produced noise signatures with a weak resemblance to short lane markers. In special scenarios like that shown in Figure 10, if these noise signatures are combined with weak lane markers for a sufficiently long period of time, lane tracking may be lost. Proper tuning of the feature coefficients reduces the likelihood of this event.

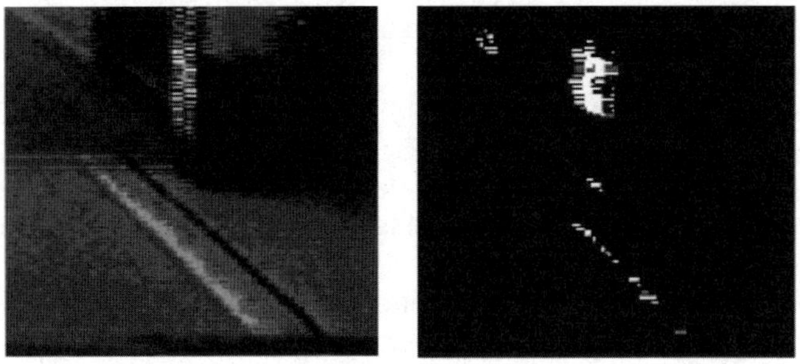

Figure 10: Undesired noise signatures caused by a tire and rim

FUTURE IMPROVEMENTS AND EXTENSIONS

ALGORITHM MOVEMENTS

The first revision of this system consists of both a hardware and software component, as mentioned above. However, this does not truly utilize the parallel processing capabilities of the FPGA to its fullest extent. The slowest portion of the algorithm is the drawing of lines through the filter output due to both the latency associated with memory accesses and the sheer volume of memory accesses required. The nature of the Bresenham line drawing algorithm, in that it sums over a discrete set of pixels based upon the start and end points of a line, make it an ideal candidate for implementation on an FPGA.

The massively parallel capabilities of FPGAs would allow all of the lines to be "drawn" simultaneously as the image was processed in the pipeline, replacing the large memory access delays (on the order of 20ms) with a minutely small pipeline delay (with a 24Mhz A/D clock, a three stage pipeline delay would be approximately 125ns).

While a memory accesses would still be needed to read the results from the accumulators, the number would be drastically reduced.

Platform Changes

While the system was developed on for the Virtex-II Pro, using such a system in production vehicles would not be financially feasible, due to the high cost of the FPGA. However, were the implementation to be modified as described above, such a system would be an ideal candidate for a lower end FPGA, such as the Cyclone II from Altera. These FPGAs are available at low costs ($171 for a Cyclone II 50K FPGA, which would be capable of holding the line drawing algorithm), and could be combined with a soft processor (such as Altera's NIOS II) to implement the entire algorithm. It would also be possible to eliminate the software component entirely, and port the entire algorithm to the FPGA.

Camera Considerations

The camera happened to have night vision, which in our situation is completely useless and actually degrades the system performance at night. Additionally, the camera was not well suited to direct sunlight applications as the image became saturated causing the edge detection filter to miss lane markers. At the time we purchased the camera our utmost priorities were to begin work as soon as possible and to ultimately make a proof of concept. This camera served us to these means, but choosing a better camera would certainly improve the system.

Cost Reduction

Based on the above algorithm and equipment modifications, the cost breakdown of the parts is as follows:

Digikey price list (12/05/2006)	
Altera CYCLONE II 50K FPGA	$171
CMOS Image Sensor	$15
MCM Electronics (12/05/2006)	
12MM Camera Lens	$20

Assuming additional overhead for power supply circuitry, and analog filtering, the systems could likely be built for under $300. Given that the prices above are based on single units, a discount could likely be had for mass production.

According to the Federal Motor Carrier Safety Administration, current aftermarket LDW systems retail for $1,000-$2,000 for an individual unit [1]. Even at a 100% profit margin on manufacturing cost, our FPGA-based implementation should be capable of selling for less than half the price of its competing systems.

Parameter Optimization

In our three feature lane detection algorithm, there are a vast amount of tunable parameters. While building our system, most of these parameters were chosen by observation and intuition. This process was very time consuming and difficult because the system was highly nonlinear and interdependent. If this system was to be used in production, a large scale computer optimization would help choose certain system parameters (for example, K_p , K_i , K_a , and the minimum distance threshold).

In [3], a computer was used to determine the optimal values for K_p, K_i, K_a. In order to perform a simulation like this, it would be necessary to go through each frame in simulation and indicate the correct lane locations manually. After this has been done, the computer can determine autonomously if each decision created by a certain set of parameters was correct or in error. Using this measure, the computer can try many sets of coefficients and repeat the same routine. This process will yield the optimal parameters.

The overall performance of the system is highly tunable. This gives the system great potential and flexibility that when met with sufficient time and resources will prove to be highly advantageous.

Dynamic Thresholding

As mentioned earlier, threshold selection in the edge detection filter has a heavy impact on its performance. As lighting conditions change due to the time of day or weather, the edge information may become stronger or weaker. If the threshold becomes too high, little or no edge pixels will be detected, and the system will be blind. If the threshold becomes too low, far too many edge pixels will be detected and the system will be prone to error.

Instead of manually adjusting this threshold before each drive, it will be necessary to add intelligence to the system so that it will automatically adjust the threshold to maintain reliable performance. This would be accomplished with the following logic:

> After each frame is filtered, count the amount of 1's present in the image.
>
> -If there were too many 1's, increase the threshold by some set amount
>
> -If there were too few 1's, decrease the threshold by some set amount

This will allow the system to adjust to different lighting conditions, making it very robust.

This was successfully implemented in simulation, but due to time constraints was not added into the working project. With a relatively small time investment this could be added into the system. The result would be an adaptive, highly robust lane departure system.

CONCLUSION

An FPGA-based lane departure warning system was developed. The study demonstrated that current proven algorithms in LDWS technology could be implemented in an FPGA environment. The system was prototyped and tested during daylight conditions on a standard interstate highway, accurately detecting 74% of all lane departures. With the improvements mentioned for hardware, algorithm and algorithm parameters, a feasible production system could be produced at a substantially lower parts cost than current systems on the market, which would increase profitability of such systems and widen their availability.

ACKNOWLEDGMENTS

Special thanks goes to Professor Kurt Metzger and Matthew Smith of the University of Michigan for providing assistance, equipment, and lab space for this project.

REFERENCES

1. Commercial Motor Vehicle Safety and Security Systems Technology. Retrieved December 5, 2006, from http://www.fmcsa.dot.gov/facts-research/systems-technology/product-guides/lane-departure.htm
2. J.E. Bresenham, R.A. Earnshaw, and M.L.V. Pitteway, Fundamental algorithms for computer graphics, NATO ASI series. Series F, Computer and systems sciences. no. 17.
3. Young Uk Yim, and Se-Young Oh, "Three-Feature Based Automatic Lane Detection Algorithm (TFALDA) for Autonomous Driving," in IEEE Transactions on Intelligent Transportation Systems, Vol. 4, No. 4, December 2003, pp. 219–225.
4. Bin Ran, and Henry Xianghong Liu, "Development of A Vision-Based Real Time Lane Detection and Tracking System for Intelligent Vehicles". Retrieved December 9, 2006, from http://www.fmcsa.dot.gov/facts-research/systems-technology/product-guides/lane-departure.htm
5. Seung Gweon Jeong, Chang Sup Kim, Dong Youp Lee, Sung Ki Ha, Dong Hwai Lee, Man Hyung Lee, and Hashimoto, H, "Real-time lane detection for autonomous vehicle"
Industrial Electronics, 2001. Proceedings. ISIE 2001. IEEE International Symposium on Volume 3, 12-16 June 2001 Page(s):1466 - 1471 vol.3
6. Takahashi, A, Ninomiya, Y, Ohta, and M, Tange, K, "A robust lane detection using real-time voting processor" in Intelligent Transportation Systems, 1999. Proceedings. 1999 IEEE/IEEJ/JSAI International Conference on 5-8 Oct. 1999 Page(s):577 - 580

2007-01-1318

Keeping the Driver in the Loop While Using Assistance Systems

Christoph Mayser and Joachim Steinle
BMW Group, Driver Assistance and Active Safety Systems

ABSTRACT

Driver Assistance Systems (DAS) like e.g. distance control systems are more and more evolving in a variety of cars, and the goal is mainly to support the driver in his driving task in order to improve convenience.

The strategic approach to DAS at BMW is outlined and resulting system functions are explained. The paper shows the specific design and implementation of systems that interact with the vehicle dynamics on the same level as the driver. Special emphasis is given to their interaction with the driver. Therefore the Human Machine Interaction is one of the focus points within the development process. BMW ensures the mode awareness of the driver by presenting the relevant information in optimized displays within the vehicle.

INTRODUCTION

Driver Assistance Systems (DAS) is a widely used term and therefore needs some clarification with respect to the topics of this paper. The driving task can generally be partitioned in 3 layers or tasks:

- navigation
- guidance
- stabilization

The navigation task deals with route planning in order to reach a certain target position: Which roads have to be taken, where to go at intersections, how to avoid traffic jams, etc. Driver Information Systems (DIS) like navigation systems or TMC (traffic message channel) support the planning task in this level (figure 1).

The stabilization task deals with keeping a vehicle in a dynamic region where it behaves nice and linear. Whenever the vehicle behavior becomes non-linear, i.e. generally in situations with excessive wheel spin that result in under- or over-steer conditions, blocked wheels during hard braking or the opposite during maximum acceleration, the driver has to counteract until the vehicle comes back in a linear region where it responds on driver input in a predictive way. Many active safety systems have been developed to support the driver in situations where he is usually overstrained, starting with Anti-Lock Braking Systems, Traction Control Systems and most recently Vehicle Stability Control Systems with wheel individual brake pressure control and / or steering control (like BMW's Active Front Steering) for controlling a vehicle's yaw rate. These chassis management systems (figure 1) definitely help improving Active Safety, but are not discussed in this paper.

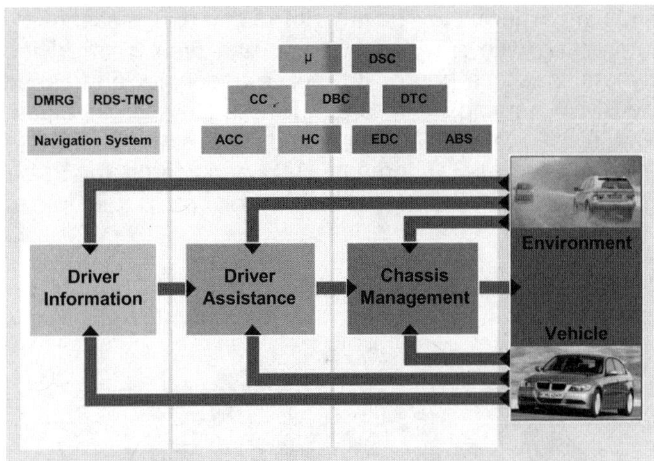

Figure 1: Classification of technical systems to the 3 layers of the driving task (Abbreviations: ABS: Anti Blocking System, EDC: Electronic Damping Control, ASC: Anti Skid Control, DSC: Dynamic Stability Control, DBC: Dynamic Brake Control, HC: Heading Control, μ: Friction Detection, CC: Cruise Control, ACC: Active Cruise Control, RDS-TMC: Radio Data System – Traffic Message Channel, DMRG: Dual Mode Route Guidance

The level in between navigation and stabilization is the vehicle guidance task, where the basic task is to maintain a desired speed or a desired distance to the car in front and to keep the vehicle in a correct position within the driving lane. Lane change or overtaking maneuvers are also tasks that belong to this level. So vehicle guidance means to properly control a car with respect to the road and to other traffic in order to avoid accidents. This is generally known as "driving a car" by operating the steering wheel, the accelerator and the brakes. With the introduction of systems like Cruise Control (CC) the notion "Driver Assistance Systems (DAS)" was established [1]. These types of systems do not aim at automating the driving task. At the driver's request, Cruise Control performs actions according to the rules of the driver in order to maintain a constant speed. The next step was distance control, available in BMW cars since 2000 starting in the 7-series as Active Cruise Control (ACC). This was the first system that required information of the surrounding traffic situation in order to perform the control task. ACC relies on information about the driving situation coming from environmental sensors like e.g. radars and will be the focus of this paper. This system interacts with the driver in the vehicle guidance level and therefore the driver has to be informed about the relevant system states.

STRATEGIC ASPECTS

DAS are often seen as systems that "unburden" the driver from his driving task. The implicit idea behind this is that driving is a complex task and a driver will be happy if a system supports him and he does not have to do it alone.

However, for most drivers driving a car is generally a situation where they have a lot of joy and pleasure by interacting with a responsive car and feeling its driving dynamics. This "joy of driving" is especially addressed by BMW naming their cars "Ultimate Driving Machines" and is one of the highest rated values within BMW's strategic targets. Therefore DAS engineered for BMW cars have to make sure that they support the joy of driving.

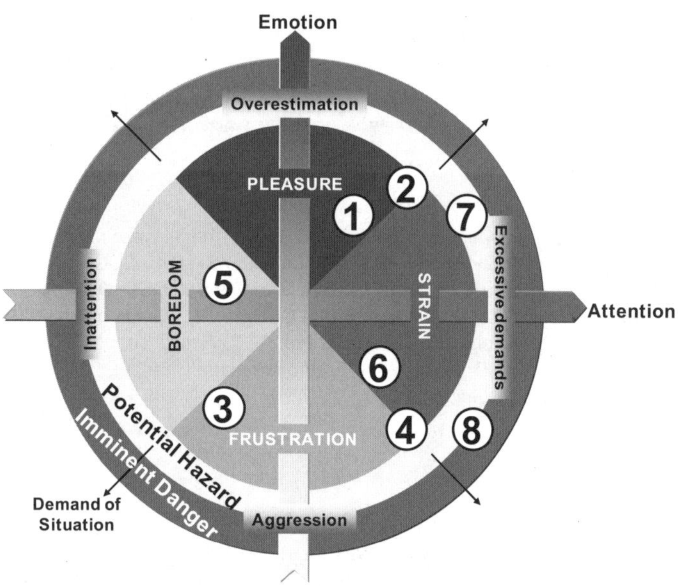

Figure 2: Driver oriented motivation

But, driving a car also involves situations with very little driving pleasure, e.g. driving in congested traffic, in complex traffic situations or driving in rain or fog. A driver oriented approach to clustering traffic situations is shown in Figure 2. The vertical axis shows the emotional feelings between joy and frustration, the horizontal axis shows the cognitive workload varying from tension / stress to relief / boredom. Normal driving situations are placed within these four circle segments (numbers refer to Figure 2), e.g.:

1. Winding country road, empty, dry, sunny: Lots of joy, some (positive) workload.
2. Race track: Also lots of joy, but also very high (positive) stress.
3. Stop and Go traffic with little dynamic: lots of frustration, little workload.
4. Aggressive, congested traffic with high dynamics: frustration coupled with high (negative) workload.
5. Driving on a long straight highway with little traffic and speed limit: Boring and very little emotional aspects.
6. Parallel parking in a crowded street: a complex task that can be frustrating if it has to be done in several tries.

The segments are surrounded by 2 circles, the inner circle named "potential hazard", the outer "imminent danger". From every driving situation there is a possible transition via "hazard" to "danger", when the situational demands can no longer be met by the driver. Following this line joy can turn into overestimation of capabilities, frustration can turn into aggression, tension into excessive demands and relief into inattentiveness. Examples for such situations are:

7. Winding country road at night in the rain.
8. Underestimating the deceleration of a car in front in dense traffic.

In the hazard stage there is still a possibility that the driver can avoid an accident by a quick corrective action like braking and / or steering. In the danger zone the accident is unavoidable by the driver; the goal in this situation is to mitigate the crash as much as possible.

Looking at this driver oriented approach, the strategic goals for the design of DAS and Active Safety Systems define as follows:

1. Increase the joy of driving
2. Avoid negative emotions
3. Preserve a safety margin

The first goal is reached by a sensible combination of systems in order to give the driver information needed for a perfect drive that he cannot sense directly. A navigation system e.g. shows him how the road will continue after the next bend, a night vision system improves the performance of his eyes, and a friction coefficient sensor – if it would be already available – could show him the limits of driving dynamics before the driver actually reaches them. The driving task itself is completely done by the driver, but his capability of sensing and evaluating his environment is supported and augmented.

The second goal is reached by the possibility for the driver to delegate parts of the vehicle guidance task in unpleasant driving situations to a DAS such as ACC. He does not need to be supported, as the driver is always able to do the driving himself, but he can delegate a part of the driving task to an assistant if he wants to. The driving task is then partially or completely taken over by a DAS as long as the driver wants it. But the driver is still responsible for his car and can override or switch off the DAS at any time. The dynamics of the DAS must therefore match the driver's expectations as close as possible so that the driver is satisfied with the completion of the driving task that he has delegated to the DAS, e.g. an ACC in dense traffic must have appropriate following dynamics and must be able to handle lane change and curve situations.

The third goal is reached with a combination of classic wheel slip control systems as described in the introduction and Active Safety Systems with environmental sensors that give the driver appropriate warnings when he reaches the hazard zone. The warnings can be optical, audible, haptic or kinaesthetic. They must be carefully designed in order to keep the false alarm rate low at the one hand and to animate the driver to a certain action in time at the other hand. In a second stage these systems may precondition or modify the braking effort of the driver. In a final stage autonomous emergency braking systems could come into effect, but development for these systems is still ongoing.

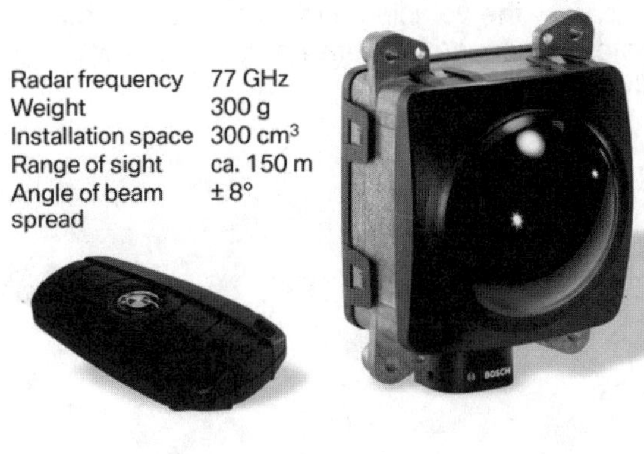

Figure 3: Radar sensor

THE BMW ACTIVE CRUISE CONTROL

ACC extends the ordinary Cruise Control by radar sensor based follow control. Without intervention from the driver, the distance from a slower, preceding vehicle and thus a lower vehicle speed can be controlled.

TECHNOLOGY

The technology of the BMW ACC system has been described in [2]. The basic component of the ACC system is a radar sensor which guarantees the object detection required for follow control. The physical layout of this sensor is shown in figure 3. In all BMW cars where ACC is available, i.e. the 3-, 5-, 6- and 7-series, the second generation radar sensor is the core element of the ACC system. It has reduced dimensions and even higher performance than the sensor used in the 1st generation ACC (see [3]).

The radar sensor scans the preceding area up to a range of approximately 150m with four overlapping radar beams. At ±8°, the effective angular aperture is now twice as large compared to the sensor used at 1st generation ACC.

Unlike many other ACC systems where the radar sensor is covered by fascia material, the BMW ACC radar sensor is integrated into the front end beneath the front bumper without an additional cover (figure 4). This position meets the requirements of object detection, package, installation and adjustment. Furthermore it provides maximum effect for an ambient temperature controlled sensor lens heating, which proved its worth already in the 1st generation ACC systems, by preventing wet snow and slush from settling on the sensor. The ACC function has increased system availability and is therefore retained in almost any weather condition.

Figure 4: Mounting position of the radar sensor

The signals reflected by preceding vehicles are used to constantly calculate distance, relative speed and lateral position of the lead vehicle. The standard DSC system's yaw rate sensor information is used to determine the vehicles most likely path. This lane prediction is the prerequisite for the comparison with position data of preceding vehicles and thus enabling a timely and correct response to objects in the vehicle's lane both on straight sections and in bends. Figure 5 shows an object configuration in a typical curve situation in which only one of the two cars – the vehicle on the left lane – is relevant for the system, because only this car is located within the most likely path.

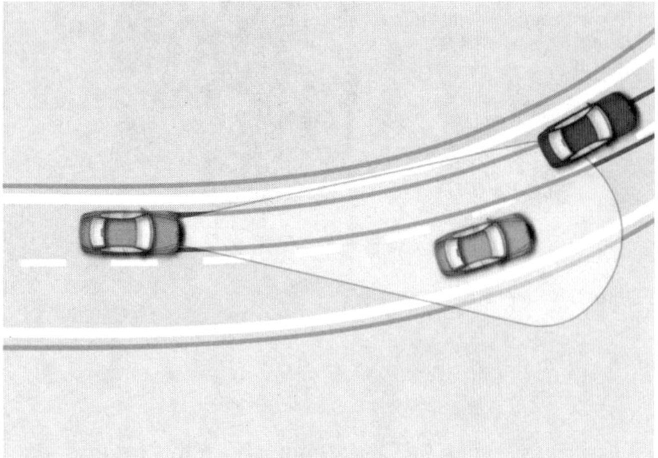

Figure 5: Typical object configuration in a curve situation: only one of the two cars is located within the most likely path and therefore relevant for the system

The ACC system's application range is between 20 mph and 110 mph. In this corridor, the vehicle can accelerate, depending on the current speed, up to a maximum of 1.2 m/s² and decelerate by an absolute maximum of 2.5 m/s². This layout covers the majority of speed changes which occur in traffic. The ACC function is thus particular beneficial on highways and major country roads.

ACTIVE CRUISE CONTROL WITH STOP AND GO FUNCTION

Most ACC systems on the market become deactivated when the preceding vehicle decelerates to speeds lower than 20 mph. But this behavior does not meet the expectations of the driver. Especially in situations with stop and go traffic the driver might want to delegate this boring part of the vehicle guidance task to an assistance system.

In order to further extend the possible situations of usage in this scenario, BMW is working on an ACC system that decelerates the vehicle down to a complete stop and holds it at rest, until the driver restarts the vehicle again. The basics of such a system are described in [4]. One of the challenges of "Active Cruise Control with Stop and Go Function" is the sensorial coverage of the complete vehicle width, as at lower speeds bicycles or pedestrians may appear in front of the car and must reliably be detected in order to have a predictable system behavior. BMW is examining additional 24GHz short range radar sensors along with the 77 GHz long range radar for this purpose. In combination, these sensors will cover the relevant area in front of the vehicle and also cover large parts of the adjacent lanes, which is necessary for early object detection during lane change situations with typical short following distances occurring at low speeds. Figure 6 shows a typical traffic scene with the necessary sensor coverage.

Another challenge is the braking down to a complete standstill. This requires both high dynamic performance and high control quality of the braking system with minimal noise generation. This is necessary as the absolute deceleration values in normal traffic become larger at low speeds. Moreover, following distances become smaller in these situations so that in terms of absolute distances only very small controller errors are tolerable. The braking system must operate silently, as overall noise in a car is reduced drastically at low speeds: no more tire noise is present and the engine in premium cars is mostly inaudible at cruising situations.

With an ACC system covering speeds down to complete standstill, the driver will be able to delegate the task of longitudinal vehicle control completely to ACC with Stop and Go function. Thus the driver can avoid negative emotions and frustration especially in stop and go traffic situations. He can preserve his mental and physical powers for the time when traffic clears up or he gets to his favourite open stretch of winding country road.

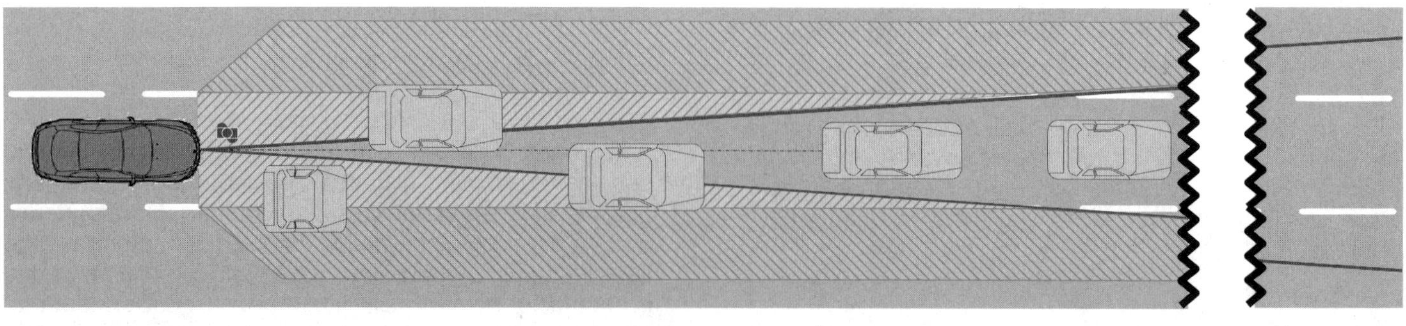

Figure 6: typical traffic scene and necessary sensor coverage at lower speeds

FUNCTIONS AND BENEFITS FOR THE DRIVER

As agile handling is one of the great virtues of BMW cars, a lot of effort was put into the ACC function's dynamic design without restricting driving or control comfort. Traveling in platoons at varying speeds is made more harmonious and smooth by minimizing the systems delay time which is resulting in immediate and crisp responses to acceleration changes. The number of interventions by the driver is thus reduced as the system behavior meets nearly all dynamic requirements in normal traffic.

If the driver accelerates to a speed significantly higher than his set speed and then releases the accelerator pedal without another car in the range of the radar sensor e.g. after a typical overtaking situation, the ACC system does not decelerate the car by using the brakes as it would do when the driver actively reduces set speed via the input control elements. Instead, ACC will let the car coast down to set speed (using the brakes only slightly when going downhill) in order to minimize fuel consumption and also trying to meet the driver's expectations in this situation.

ACC controlled cornering is limited to a certain level of comfortable lateral acceleration. Object loss, which is possible in tight corners, does not lead to autonomous vehicle acceleration. As a result of this, longitudinal dynamics is leveled out, further supporting harmonious system behavior.

In contrast to cornering control, dynamics are increased when the probability is high that the driver is starting an overtaking maneuver. This is detected when the driver operates the left turn indicator and when the set speed is significantly higher than the actual speed. The car accelerates and the following distance to the preceding vehicle is temporarily reduced. Furthermore the path prediction is subjected to a parallel translation to the left. When the driver then starts to move to the next lane, the combination of these measurements has the effect that the old "target car" is lost early and no longer limiting the vehicles acceleration. A possible new "target car" on the adjacent lane is also picked up earlier for controlling a new following distance, or, when the lane is free, the vehicle quickly accelerates to the desired set speed. If the driver cannot overtake for any reason, the reduced following distance is gradually augmented back to the original value after an appropriate time.

In cars with a navigation system BMW has established a link between the navigation data base and the ACC system, giving the ACC system more knowledge about the current driving situation. The basis for that is structural information, classification of bends and additional road data such as type of road or number of lanes. This data influences both the control dynamics and the recognition of traffic objects. Object recognition is affected in a way that ACC has a broad sensor recording area on single-lane roads in order to track the target vehicle in changing bends ("S-curves") and a narrow recognition field on multiple lane highways in order to minimize disturbances from cars in adjacent lanes.

With the navigation data ACC can comply with the increased dynamic demand on highways and reduce the dynamics on twisting sections of the road. The availability of navigation data therefore allows for a more dynamic application of the system behavior which better suits the expectations of the typical BMW driver on straight roads and on multiple-lane highways. The knowledge from the navigation data base about twisting sections of the road lying ahead is used to reduce the system dynamics to a level suitable to the actual type of road and the current curvature as depicted in figure 7. Consequently, the result is not some kind of automatic speed reduction to a supposedly safer or more comfortable speed in curves; instead, the overall dynamic behavior of ACC is adjusted while leaving its basic function otherwise unchanged.

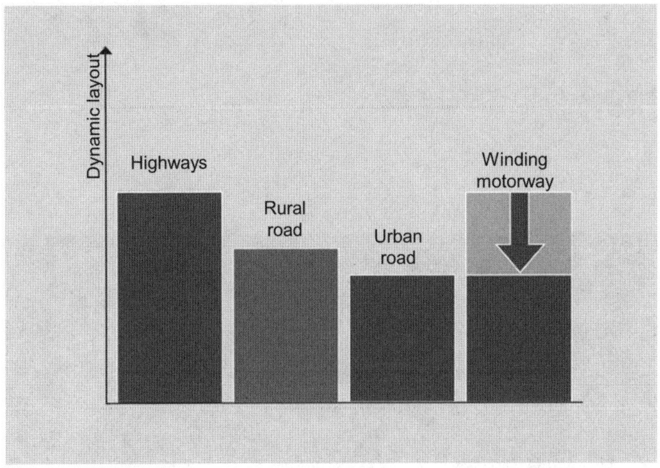

Figure 7: Dynamic layout based on navigation data: dynamic adapted to road type, especially reduction of dynamic at winding motorways

MAN MACHINE INTERFACE

ACC is controlled via a control lever at the steering column (figure 8). Starting at a vehicle speed of 20 mph the driver can accept the current driving speed as the set speed by pulling or pushing the control lever. He can then change the set speed within a range from 20 mph to 110 mph using increments or decrements of 1 mph or 5 mph. An additional rotary rocker switch on the lever allows the driver to vary the desired following distance. By operating the rocker switch the driver can select one of four different distance levels, corresponding to different time intervals up to a maximum of 2.5 seconds. The selected time gap is then controlled in accordance with the preceding vehicle. To deactivate the system the driver can either shift the control lever upwards or downwards, or he can just use the brake pedal. As long as the previously selected speed is still memorized the driver can reactivate the system with the Resume button at the control lever.

In the instrument cluster the selected speed is displayed permanently with an illuminated ring display around the speedometer. Other relevant information is shown in the "ACC display" between the tubes or in the information display which is used to present temporarily information to the driver (figure 9).

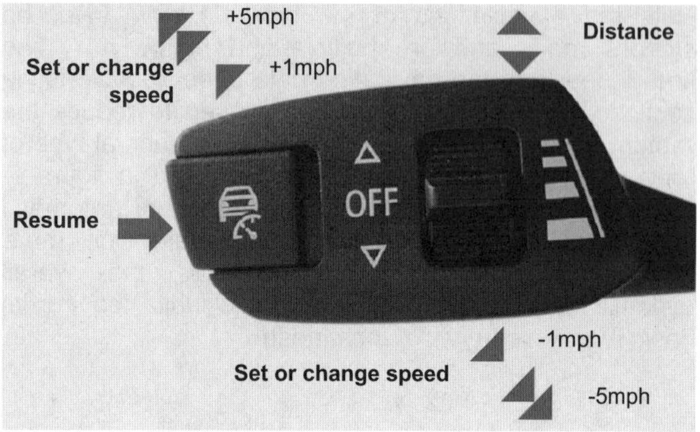

Figure 8: ACC Control Lever

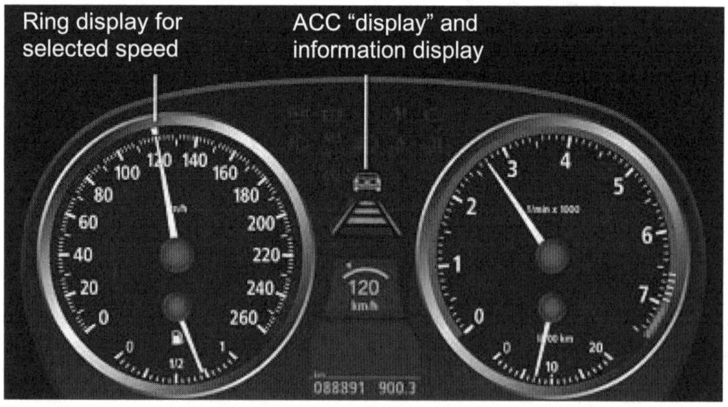

Figure 9: Instrument Cluster with ring display, ACC display and information display

DRIVER – VEHICLE RELATIONSHIP

Using a driver assistance system the driver delegates a part of the vehicle guidance task to the system. At the driver's request, Active Cruise Control performs actions according to the rules of the driver. Instead of the task of maintaining a suitable speed and a safe following distance the driver has the task of monitoring the correct functioning of the assistance system. This monitoring effort should be less than the effort to perform the driving task itself. The driver can intervene at any given time and still has full responsibility for the driving task. To reduce the driver's workload, the characteristic of an assistance system has to follow the mental model of the driver [5]. Thus, the possibilities of turning the system on and off as well as a high transparency of the different system states and limitations are important features. Furthermore, the driver's interface to the assistance system should be easy to understand [6].

The relationship between the driver, the system and the driving task is shown in figure 10. By setting the desired speed and choosing a comfortable following distance, the driver delegates this part of the vehicle guidance task to ACC with Stop and Go function. The system is now performing all necessary actions to fulfill that order and is displaying the relevant information to the driver. With the displayed information the driver can monitor the system and determine the expected system reaction to different situations. Using the system the driver is still performing other parts of the guidance task like keeping the vehicle in a suitable position within the current lane and is still responsible for "driving the car". At any given time the driver is able to regain complete control over the vehicle by switching off the system.

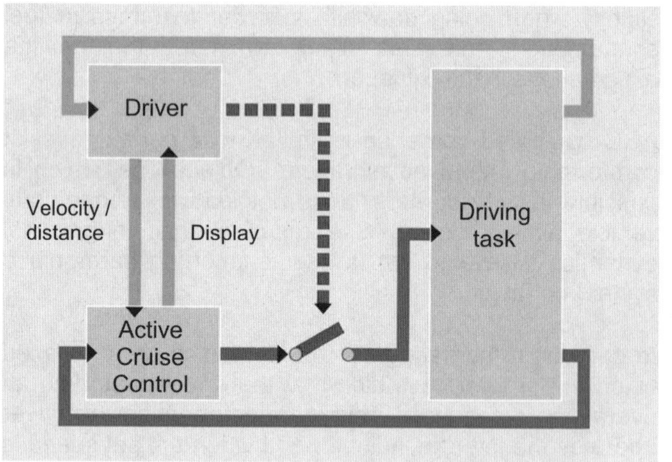

Figure 10: Driver – Vehicle relationship

INFORMATION IN THE INSTRUMENT CLUSTER

After activating the system with the control lever the selected speed is shown permanently in the ring display around the speedometer (figure 9). As long as the ACC system is active the ring display is illuminated in green. Because of the form as well as the position of this display, it is very easy for the driver to compare the desired speed with the actual driven speed.

At the same time the system is activated it shows the selected time gap symbolized by orange horizontal bars in the ACC display. Only one bar in the perspective scene stands for the shortest possible distance, three bars as shown in figure 9 are symbolizing the third step of the system controlled time gap. The bars are bordered by two orange sidelines which are creating a much better impression of the perspective scene.

Is there a relevant object in front of the vehicle the system is adapting the speed to a safe following distance. A yellow vehicle symbol is displayed in the ACC display just above the horizontal bars symbolizing the selected time gap. In this situation the ACC system is reducing the set speed because of the preceding vehicle cruising with a lower speed. The driver has three elements indicating that ACC is behaving correctly:

- A green mark at the ring display
- A yellow vehicle symbol in the ACC display
- Horizontal bars and two sidelines in the ACC display

If the preceding vehicle left the predicted path of the ACC vehicle, e.g. after a lane change to the right lane, ACC is accelerating to the previously selected set speed again. The yellow vehicle symbol is not displayed in the instrument cluster anymore. With the perspective scene in the ACC display the driver is able to compare the system state with the actual situation in front of his own vehicle. This intuitive depiction allows the driver to decide if it is necessary to turn of the system.

The driver can intervene at any given time and overrule the system. By pressing the accelerator pedal he can drive higher speeds as the active system would do. In situations like this, ACC would not react to preceding vehicles, since the driver is overruling. In the ACC display the horizontal bars are not shown to symbolize the driver that the safe following distance is not maintained by the system. As soon as the driver moves his foot away from the accelerator pedal, the system takes over and slows down to the previously selected speed or an appropriate speed in terms of a safe following distance. And, of course the horizontal bars for the selected time gap are displayed again.

Is the driver deactivating the system e.g. by using the brake pedal the selected speed is memorized. Even if the system is not controlling the velocity anymore, it displays the memorized speed by illuminating the mark at the ring display in orange. In this "standby mode" the sidelines are still displayed, but the horizontal bars are not shown. The driver can reactivate the system by pushing the resume button on the control lever. Along with the reactivation the mark in the ring display changes its color to green and the horizontal bars are shown again. Furthermore the set speed is temporarily shown as a digital number with a speedometer symbol on top in the information display, which is located just underneath the ACC display in the instrument cluster (see figure 9). In the standby mode the driver can shut of the system by shifting the control lever upwards or downwards. Doing that the memorized set speed is deleted and all displays related to ACC – the ring display and the ACC display – are turned of.

In congested traffic ACC can slow down the vehicle to a stop. After a complete stop ACC with Stop and Go function is not accelerating anymore and therefore it is changing the colour of the ring display from green to orange. The system is still monitoring the preceding vehicle and informing the driver as soon this vehicle starts moving again. An animation of the horizontal bars symbolizing the following distance is used; each bar is illuminated for approximately 0.3 seconds, beginning with the lowest horizontal bar. Now the driver can reactivate the system by pressing the resume button at the control lever or by tapping at the accelerator pedal. After this "go trigger" the system is active again; it accelerates comfortable to the set speed obeying a safe following distance and the displays are indicating a normal following situation.

The Human Machine Interface of ACC as described above is based on the concept to present the relevant information to the driver, but to omit information about system states which is not necessary to monitor the correct system behavior. No feedback is given to the driver if the system dynamics is changed e.g. due to the road type; in these situations the ACC system behaves closer to the expectation of the driver and therefore no additional information is needed.

The activation of the ACC system is not possible in certain situations, e.g. when the driver turned of the stability control system or in the moment he is braking. An attempt to activate the system in these situations fails; the system is showing three dashes with the speedometer symbol on top temporarily in the information display as feedback to the driver.

There are traffic situations where ACC reaches its limits and is not able to keep a safe following distance to the preceding vehicle. To alert the driver the vehicle symbol starts blinking in red. At the same time an acoustic warning is given to make sure the driver is taking over control again.

Is the ACC system deactivated because of a temporarily occurring sensor problem or an internal failure a standard error message is informing the driver. This message is containing a symbol in the information display of the instrument cluster and additional information in the central information display of the vehicle.

INFORMATION IN THE HEAD-UP DISPLAY

With the Head-Up Display (HUD) available in BMW 5- and 6 series cars the ACC display becomes even easier to perceive. The BMW HUD is a colored display that projects information directly in the field of view of the driver, with a focus point at approximately the end of the hood. The information presented in the HUD can thus be seen without taking the eyes off the road which is a great safety benefit. The ACC display is shown in the right part of the HUD and basically matches the display in the instrument cluster. However, the set speed is included in the display and is shown digitally with an additional speedometer symbol (figure 10).

Figure 10: HUD in Follow Mode

Figure 11: HUD in Free Flow Mode

At the left part of the Head-Up display the current speed is also shown digitally. When driving in free flow mode at the set speed the driver would have two digital numbers with the same value. To avoid this situation the selected speed of the ACC system changes to a symbol in the HUD when set speed is reached (figure 11).

CONCLUSION

The HUD in combination with ACC as well as the displays within the instrument cluster and the easy to use operation lever account for an optimal interface to the driver. All relevant system states are displayed using a combination of just a few symbols and in addition to that there is always a kinesthetic feedback of the system. The driver can predict the system reaction very quickly by reading the displays. Together with clear and reproducible system characteristics he can respond intuitively to unexpected driving situations, if necessary.

But even a predictable system behavior and an easy to understand concept for the man machine interaction does not release the driver from the obligation to drive the car. He is delegating only a part of the driving task and therefore still responsible for the complete vehicle guidance task.

REFERENCES

1. G. Reichart, R. Haller, K. Naab. (1995). "Towards future driver assistance systems". *Automotive Technology International*. pp. 25 – 29
2. J. Steinle, T. Toelge, S. Thissen, A. Pfeiffer, M. Brandstäter. (2005). „Kultivierte Dynamik – Geschwindigkeitsregelung im neuen BMW 3er", *ATZ/MTZ extra*. Vieweg Verlag. Wiesbaden. pp 122-131, Mai 2005.
3. W. Prestl, T. Sauer, J. Steinle, O. Tschernoster. (2000). The BMW Active Cruise Control ACC. SAE 2000-01-0344, SAE World Congress 2000, Detroit, Michigan.
4. E. P. Venhovens, K. Naab, B. Adiprasito. (2000). Stop and Go Cruise Control. Seoul. FISITA World Automotive Congress 2000.
5. D. A. Norman. (1983). "Some Observations on Mental Models". D. Gentner & A. L. Stevens (Eds.): *Mental Models*. pp. 7 – 14. Lawrence Erlbaum Associates Hillsdale, New Jersey. pp. 7 – 14.
6. R. Haller. (2000). „Wie erreicht man bei Fahrerassistenz, dass der Fahrer Herr der Situation bleibt?". H. Bubb (Ed.): *Ergonomie und Verkehrssicherheit*. Herbert Utz Verlag, München. pp. 64a – 64h

2007-01-1109

Fuzzy Information Fusion Based on Genetic Algorithm for Vehicle Navigation System

Yang Yi and Gu Zhengqi
State Key Laboratory of Advanced Design and Manufacture for Vehicle Body, Hunan University

ABSTRACT

In this paper, it is established the numerical model of federal Kalman filtering based on vehicle GPS/DR integrated location system. In order to resolve the shortcoming of the traditional federal Kalman filtering, a new method is presented in which the fuzzy logic system is combined with the traditional Kalman technology. This method can modify the statistical characteristic of noises on real time. It can not only modify the local filter but also bring forward a bran-new information fusion arithmetic which is applied to central filter. A fuzzy logic system is built to obtain different weights of the all states estimate values that are based on the actual circumstance and fuse these values. The acquisition of control rules and membership function of fuzzy controller usually rely to a great extent on empirical and heuristic knowledge. In this paper, genetic algorithm is used to optimize fuzzy logic controller and obtain the optimal or sub-optimal control rules. The result of simulation and road test indicates that it is useful with high effectiveness and practical.

INTRODUCTION

Vehicle navigation system has become a popular subject for automotive industry in recent years. The main purpose of a navigation system is to determine an appropriate position on a road segment represented in the database. This position is representative of the vehicle's position and is displayed as information to the driver. Therefore, how to get accurate vehicle positioning is important for the good performance of automotive navigation and route guidance systems.

Most of the navigation methods found in literature use the Kalman filter approach to integrate GPS with DR sensor. There are three major Kalman filter design options, centralized Kalman filtering (CKF), decentralized Kalman filtering (DKF), and federated Kalman filtering (FKF) [1][2]. In all these approaches exact knowledge about the sensed environment and sensors is required. However, in real applications, only certain information is known about the sensed environment and sensors are rarely perfect. Therefore, the Kalman filter must be capable of adaptation to changes in the sensed environment and to deal with imperfect sensors.

For resolving these problems, in this paper, a fuzzy logic adaptive controller(FLAC) is used to adjust the noise strengths in the local filter's internal model, and prevent the Kalman filter from divergence. Another FLAC is monitoring and assessing the performance of each local filter, and assigns a degree of confidence to each filter output. Finally, a defuzzification scheme obtains the fused state-vector estimate based on the confidence values. Because of navigation system complexity and the uncertain surroundings, there can't build veracious fuzzy system through human experience. The genetic algorithm is used to optimize fuzzy membership function and obtain the optimal or sub-optimal control rules. The results of simulation demonstrate the feasibility and effectiveness of the method.

MAIN SECTION

MODEL OF GPS/DR SYSTEM

The GPS receiver is local sensor 1 and the gyro and odometer of the DR system is local sensor 2. Local filter 1 and local filter 2 is the extended Kalman filter. The reference coordinate system is an East-North-up coordinate system. The frame of the federated Kalman filter is shown in Figure 1.

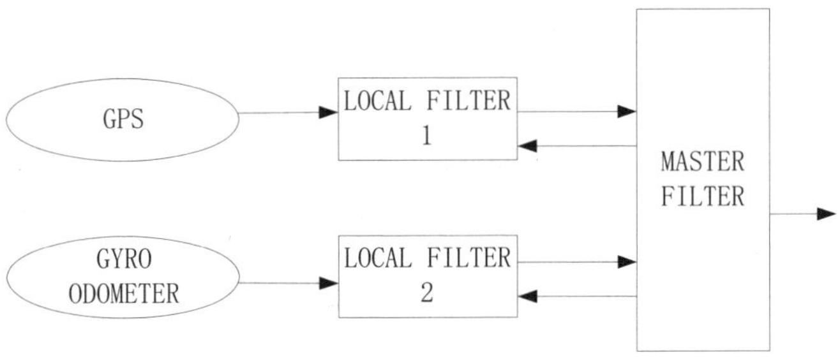

Figure 1 The federated Kalman filter of GPS/DR

The sate vector can be written as

$$X = [e \;\; v_e \;\; a_e \;\; n \;\; v_n \;\; a_n]^{\mathrm{T}}$$

Where, $(e \;\; v_e \;\; a_e)$, $(n \;\; v_n \;\; a_n)$ is the position, velocity and acceleration of the easting and northing of the vehicle, respectively. The discrete state model is presented as

$$X_{k+1} = \Phi_{k+1,k} X_k + W_k \tag{1}$$

$$\Phi_{k+1,k} = \begin{bmatrix} \Phi_e & 0 \\ 0 & \Phi_n \end{bmatrix} \quad \Phi_e = \Phi_n = \begin{bmatrix} 1 & T & T^2/2 \\ 0 & 1 & T \\ 0 & 0 & 1 \end{bmatrix}$$

Where W_k is the random error state vector.

The state vector of GPS local filter is:

$$X_1 = X$$

And the state equation is the same as the whole state model. The measurement model is presented as

$$Z_1 = \mathbf{H}_1 X_1 + V_1 \tag{2}$$

Where Z_1 is the measurement vector, V_1 is the measurement noise vector, $\mathbf{H}_1$ is the observation vector

$$\mathbf{H}_1 = \begin{bmatrix} 1 & 0 & 0 & 0 & 0 & 0 \\ 0 & 1 & 0 & 0 & 0 & 0 \end{bmatrix}$$

$$Z_1 = [e \quad n]^{\mathrm{T}}$$

The state vector of DR local filter is:

$$X_2 = X$$

And the state equation is the same as the whole state model. However the observation equation of DR is nonlinear. The variable of the gyro can be written as

$$\theta = \tan(\frac{v_e}{v_n}) + \varepsilon_1 \tag{3}$$

Where ε_1 is the gyro drift error. The variable of the odometer is

$$s = T\sqrt{v_e^2 + v_n^2} + \varepsilon_2 \tag{4}$$

Where ε_2 is the odometer error. The measurement model is present as

$$Z_2 = \mathbf{H}_2 X_2 + V_2 = h(x,t) + V_2 \tag{5}$$

$$h(x,t) = \begin{bmatrix} \theta \\ s \end{bmatrix} = \begin{bmatrix} \tan(\frac{v_e}{v_n}) \\ T\sqrt{v_e^2 + v_n^2} \end{bmatrix} \tag{6}$$

Where V_2 is the measurement noise vector.

Its discrete form can be written as[5]

$$Z_{2(k)} \approx \mathbf{H}_{2(k)} \hat{x}_{(k,k-1)} + V_{2(k)} \tag{7}$$

Where

$$\mathbf{H}_{2(k)} = \begin{bmatrix} 0 & h_{12} & 0 & 0 & h_{15} & 0 \\ 0 & h_{22} & 0 & 0 & h_{25} & 0 \end{bmatrix}$$

$$h_{12} = \frac{v_n}{(v_e^{\ 2} + v_n^{\ 2})} \qquad h_{15} = \frac{-v_e}{(v_e^{\ 2} + v_n^{\ 2})}$$

$$h_{22} = \frac{Tv_e}{\sqrt{(v_e^{\ 2} + v_n^{\ 2})}} \qquad h_{25} = \frac{Tv_n}{\sqrt{(v_e^{\ 2} + v_n^{\ 2})}}$$

The optimal estimation and the information fusion method of the whole state are presented using the following filtering equations[6]:

$$\mathbf{P}_{(k)}^{-1} \hat{X}_{(k)} = \mathbf{P}_{1(k)}^{-1} \hat{X}_{1(k)} + \mathbf{P}_{2(k)}^{-1} \hat{X}_{2(k)} \tag{8}$$

$$\beta_1 + \beta_2 = 1$$

$$\mathbf{P}_{1(k)}^{-1} = \beta_1 \mathbf{P}_{(k)}^{-1}, \qquad \mathbf{P}_{2(k)}^{-1} = \beta_2 \mathbf{P}_{(k)}^{-1} \tag{9}$$

$$\mathbf{Q}_{1(k)}^{-1} = \beta_1 \mathbf{Q}_{(k)}^{-1}, \qquad \mathbf{Q}_{2(k)}^{-1} = \beta_2 \mathbf{Q}_{(k)}^{-1}$$

Where $\mathbf{P}_{(k)}$ and $\mathbf{Q}_{(k)}$ are the covariance matrix, β_1 and β_2 are the fusion coefficients.

FUZZY LOGIC ADAPTIVE KALMAN FILTERING

FLAC of Local filter

The local Kalman gain can be computed as:

$$\mathbf{K}_k = \mathbf{P}_{k,k-1} \mathbf{H}_k^T \left(\mathbf{H}_k \mathbf{P}_{k,k-1} \mathbf{H}_k^{\mathrm{T}} + \mathbf{R}_k \right)^{-1}. \tag{10}$$

The updated estimation in the states can be computed as;

$$\hat{X}_k = \hat{X}_{k,k-1} + \mathbf{K}_k [Z_k - \mathbf{H}_k \hat{X}_{k,k-1}] \tag{11}$$

Computing the a priori covariance matrix gives:

$$\mathbf{P}_{k,k-1} = \Phi_{k,k-1} \mathbf{P}_{k-1} \Phi^{\mathrm{T}}{}_{k,k-1} + \mathbf{Q}_k \tag{12}$$

Computing the posterior covariance matrix gives:

$$\mathbf{P}_k = (\mathbf{I} - \mathbf{K}_k \mathbf{H}_k)\mathbf{P}_{k,k-1} \tag{13}$$

The term $\boldsymbol{Z}_k - \mathbf{H}_k \hat{\boldsymbol{X}}_{k,k-1} = \boldsymbol{r}$ is called residual or innovation vector. It reflects the degree to which the model fits the data. It is assumed that both the process noise and the measure noise are zero mean white sequences, with known covariance $\mathbf{Q}$ and $\mathbf{R}$ in the Kalman filter. To compute simply, $\mathbf{Q}$ is regarded as a constant. In general, $\mathbf{Q}$ and $\mathbf{R}$ are changing in different situations. If the Kalman filter is based on a completely and perfectly tuned model, the residuals should be a zero-mean white noise process. If the residuals are not white noise, this indicates the poor design, and filter does not perform optimally. A good way to verify whether the filter needs tuning is to monitor the residuals. In fact, the residuals are the differences between actual measurements and measurement predictions based on the filter's internal model, if the residuals would not be zero mean and the covariance of residuals became larger, the filter will divergence[3] .The indicate the filter is poor to process plant.

The covariance of the residual is used to decide the degree of divergence. The value of covariance relates to $\mathbf{R}$, the equation for covariance of the residual is:

$$\boldsymbol{P}_r = \mathbf{H}_k \mathbf{P}_{k,k-1} \mathbf{H}_k^T + \mathbf{R}_k \tag{14}$$

$\boldsymbol{P}_r$ is residual $\boldsymbol{r}$ theoretical covariance, the actual covariance $\boldsymbol{C}_r$ of $\boldsymbol{r}$ is approximately through averaging inside a moving estimation window of size $\boldsymbol{M}$.

$$\boldsymbol{C}_r = \frac{1}{\boldsymbol{M}} \sum_{i=k-M+1}^{k} \boldsymbol{r}_i \boldsymbol{r}_i^{\mathrm{T}} \tag{15}$$

This means that only the last $\boldsymbol{M}$ samples of $\boldsymbol{r}$ are used to estimate its covariance. The window size is chosen empirically to give some statistical smoothing, if it is found that the actual value of the covariance of $\boldsymbol{r}$ has a discrepancy with its theoretical value, then a FLAC derives adjustments from $\mathbf{R}_k$ based on the adjustments to correct this mismatch as well as possible. A new variable called the Degree of Matching is defined as:

$$\boldsymbol{DoM}_k = \boldsymbol{P}_{rk} - \boldsymbol{C}_{rk} \tag{16}$$

$\mathbf{R}_k$ can be computed as:

$$\mathbf{R}_k = \mathbf{R}_{k-1} + \Delta \mathbf{R}_k \tag{17}$$

An increment in $\mathbf{R}_k$ will increment $\boldsymbol{P}_r$ and vice versa. This mean that $\mathbf{R}_k$ can be used to vary $\boldsymbol{P}_r$, in accordance with the value of $\boldsymbol{DoM}_k$, in order to reduce the discrepancies between $\boldsymbol{P}_r$ and $\mathbf{R}_k$. Following the general rules of adaptation, the FIS can be implemented considering three fuzzy sets for $\boldsymbol{DoM}_k$: N=Negative, ZE=Zero and P=Positive; and three fuzzy sets for output $\Delta\mathbf{R}_k$: D=Decrease, M=Maintain and I=Increase. These membership functions are shown in Figure 2.

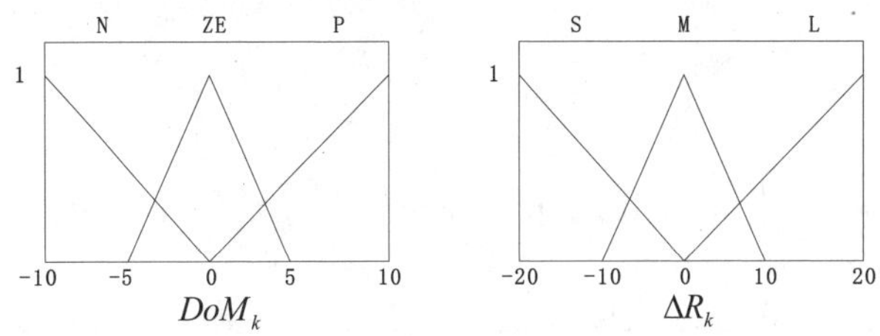

Figure 2 Membership function for $\boldsymbol{DoM}_k$ and $\Delta\mathbf{R}_k$

Three fuzzy rules are included in FIS rule base:

1. if $\boldsymbol{DoM}_k$ =P, then $\Delta\mathbf{R}_k$ =D;

2. if $\boldsymbol{DoM}_k$ =ZE, then $\Delta\mathbf{R}_k$ =M;

3. if $\boldsymbol{DoM}_k$ =N, then $\Delta\mathbf{R}_k$ =I;

The centre of area (COA) defuzzification method is taken. The frame of FLAC is shown in Figure 3.

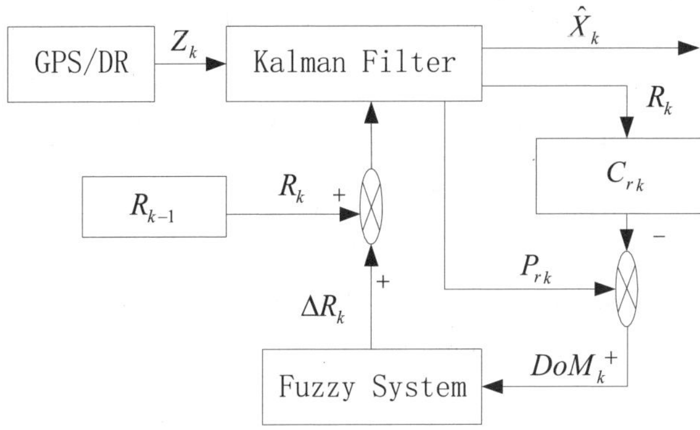

Figure 3 The fuzzy logic adaptive controller of GPS/DR

FLAC of master filter

The value of $\boldsymbol{\beta}_i$ decide the local filter $\boldsymbol{i}$ occupies the proportion to the output of the master filter. When the value of $\boldsymbol{\beta}_i$ is close to 1, the performance of the federated Kalman filter is close to the local filter $\boldsymbol{i}$. According to the characteristic, we can adjust the value of $\boldsymbol{\beta}_i$ automatically to realize the information fusion adaptively[7][8].

The FLAC of master filter is implemented using two inputs: the current values of $|\boldsymbol{DoM}_k|$ and $\boldsymbol{R}_k$, and one output, the degree of confidence denoted as $\boldsymbol{c}_k$. The membership functions for $|\boldsymbol{DoM}_k|$ and $\mathbf{R}_k$ are shown in Figure 4.

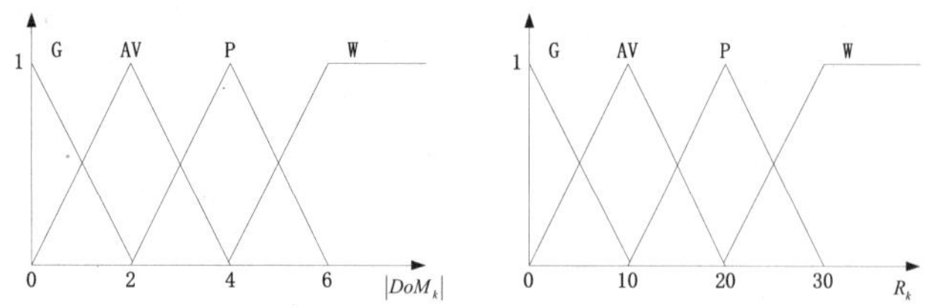

Figure 4 Membership function for $|\boldsymbol{DoM}_k|$ and $\mathbf{R}_k$

There the fuzzy labels mean: G=good, AV=average, P=poor and W=worse. The fuzzy rules are based on two simple heuristic considerations. First, if the value of $|\boldsymbol{DoM}_k|$ is near to zero and the value of $\mathbf{R}_k$ is near to zero, then it means the filter is working almost perfectly[4]: thus the degree of confidence assigned by the FLAC is near the maximum, 1. Second, if one or both of these values increases far from zero, it means that the filter performance is degrading; thus the degree of confidence assigned by the FLAC is decreased in accordance, up to the minimum 0. Thus, using the compositional rule of inference sum-prod and the centre of area defuzzification method, the FLA assigns a degree of confidence to the state-estimates made by the local filter. To each local filter, we can obtain the estimate matrix of each sample point according to membership function for $|\boldsymbol{DoM}_k|$ and $\mathbf{R}_k$.

$$\boldsymbol{u}_k = \begin{bmatrix} s_{D1} & s_{D2} & s_{D3} & s_{D4} \\ s_{R1} & s_{R2} & s_{R3} & s_{R4} \end{bmatrix} \tag{18}$$

Suppose the important coefficient of $|\boldsymbol{DoM}_k|$ and $\mathbf{R}_k$ is 0.5, the estimate result of local filter is:

$$\boldsymbol{B} = \begin{bmatrix} \frac{s_{D1}+s_{R1}}{2} & \frac{s_{D2}+s_{R2}}{2} & \frac{s_{D3}+s_{R3}}{2} & \frac{s_{D4}+s_{R4}}{2} \end{bmatrix}$$

The defuzzification method is rate parameter estimate method. The reliability of filter result is:

$$c_k = \boldsymbol{B} \bullet \boldsymbol{C} \tag{19}$$

$$\boldsymbol{C} = [1 \quad 0.75 \quad 0.5 \quad 0.01]^{\mathrm{T}} \tag{20}$$

$$\beta_1 = \frac{c_{k1}}{c_{k1}+c_{k2}} \tag{21}$$

$$\beta_2 = \frac{c_{k2}}{c_{k1}+c_{k2}} \tag{22}$$

When result of local filter is average or poor, the FLAC of local filter will adjust the measurement noise covariance $\mathbf{R}$. When the result is worse, the sample result is invalidation and eliminated. The digital approximation method is applied to keep the continuity of filter. The fuzzy federated Kalman filter is shown in Fig.5.

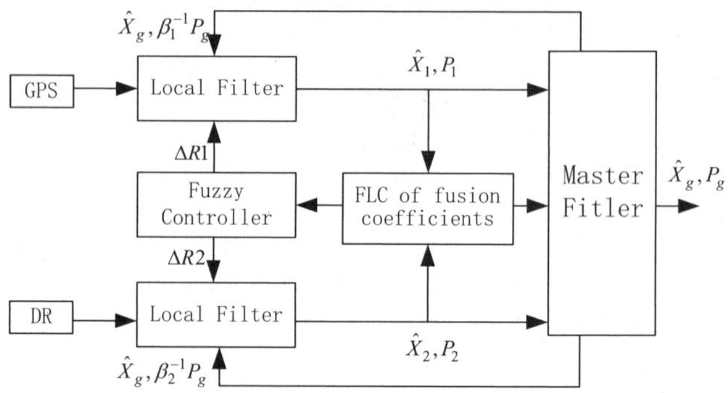

Figure 5 Fuzzy federated Kalman filter

OPTIMAL FUZZY MEMBERSHIP FUNCTIONS

In above section, the selection of fuzzy membership function is generally a subjective decision. A change in the membership functions may alter the performance of the fuzzy logic controller significantly. In practise, we found the performance of the fuzzy logic controller, which membership function is made subjectively, is not reliable. The error of the fusion data will become large in some area. The method to optimize fuzzy membership function is necessary for keep the fuzzy logic-based adaptive FKF good performance.

Obtaining an optimal set of fuzzy membership functions is not an easy task. It requires time, experience, and skills of the operator for the tedious fuzzy tuning exercise. In principle, there is no general rule or method for the fuzzy logic setup, although an heuristic and iterative procedure for altering the membership functions to improve performance has been proposed, although this is not optimal[9][10]. Here we introduce genetic algorithm to optimize fuzzy membership function and produce more optimal system behavior.

The genetic algorithm is a powerful search and optimization algorithm. In the genetic algorithm a candidate for solution is called a chromosome. It is a list of genes which assume a finite number of values. A population consists of a finite number of chromosomes. The genetic algorithm evaluates a population and generates a new one iteratively, with each successive population referred to as a generation. Given an initial population $\boldsymbol{G}(0)$, the GA generates a new generation $\boldsymbol{G}(t+1)$ based on the previous generation $\boldsymbol{G}(t)$ as follows:

1) set t to 0;

2) Generate an initial population $\boldsymbol{G}(t)$;

3) Evaluate $G(t)$;

4) If a termination condition is met, go to step 8;

5) Generate new generation $G(t+1)$ from $G(t)$;

6) Evaluate $G(t+1)$;

7) Go to step 4;

8) Stop.

The membership function for each fuzzy subset can be derived from a base function whose parameters may be adjusted to fit any specific membership function. This base function is defined as

$$f(x,a_i,b_i,r_i)=\begin{cases} 0, & x \le a_i \\ \dfrac{x-a_i}{b_i-a_i}, & a_i < x \le b_i \\ \dfrac{x-r_i}{b_i-r_i}, & b_i < x \le r_i \\ 0, & r_i < x \end{cases} \tag{23}$$

Where a_i, b_i and r_i are parameters.

Now, for each fuzzy subset i, we set up the following equations:

$$a_i = (a_i + \delta_i) - \eta_i \tag{24}$$

$$b_i = (b_i + \delta_i) \tag{25}$$

$$r_i = (r_i + \delta_i) + \eta_i \tag{26}$$

Where δ_i and η_i are adjustment coefficients. The coefficient δ_i makes the ith membership function shift to the right or to the left without changing its shape, whereas the coefficient η_i makes the ith membership function for ith fuzzy subset shrink or expand.

In this section, we use the GA to find the optimal values of δ_i and η_i for the fuzzy membership function of the FLAC for local filter and master filter. For the first and last fuzzy membership function, we set $f(x)=1$ if $x \le b_i$ and $f(x)=1$ if $x \ge b_i$. The coefficients δ_i and η_i are any real numbers taken from the range listed in Table. 1. Since there are eight element and three fuzzy membership functions for the local filter, four fuzzy membership functions for the master filter, the length of each chromosome is 112.

FLAC		δ_i and η_i range	
GPS local filter	north	[-3,3]	[-5,5]
	east	[-3,3]	[-5,5]
DR local filter	displacement	[-0.2,0.2]	[-0.01,0.01]
	angle	[-0.02,0.02]	[-0.001,0.001]
fusion coefficients for GPS	north	[-1,1]	[-5,5]
	east	[-1,1]	[-5,5]
fusion coefficients for DR	displacement	[-0.1,0.1]	[-0.01,0.01]
	angle	[-0.02,0.02]	[-0.001,0.001]

Table 1 Range of δ_i and η_i

The GA is composed of three operations: reproduction, crossover and mutation. Reproduction is a process in which individual strings are copied according to their fitness function. Copying strings according to their fitness values means that strings with higher value have a higher probability of contributing one or more offspring in the next generation. The implementation of reproduction is done by stochastic tournament mode. The scale of tournament is 2. After reproduction, crossover may proceed in two steps: First, members of the newly reproduced strings in the mating pool are mated at random; second, each pair undergoes crossing over. For example, consider string B_1, B_2, we get the result of crossover:

$$\begin{cases} B_1^{t+1} = aB_2^t + (1-a)B_1^t, \\ B_2^{t+1} = aB_1^t + (1-a)B_2^t \end{cases} \tag{27}$$

Where a is the crossover coefficient.

Mutation is the occasional alteration of some gene values in a chromosome. Every gene in each chromosome is a candidate for mutation, and its selection is determined by the mutation probability. The mutation probability is kept usually at a low value to avoid losing a large number of good chromosomes. The current value of the selected gene is then replaced by a random number choose from the range.

In the genetic algorithm an evaluation function which rates each chromosome relative to the others in the current population is necessary. Here the evaluation function is set as follows

$$fitness = f_1[J_1]f_2[J_2] \tag{28}$$

$$f_i[J_i] = \frac{J_{i\max} - J_i}{J_{i\max} - J_{i\min}}, \qquad i = 1,2$$

Where $J_{1\max}$, $J_{2\max}$ is the reference maximum of the error value of longitude direction, latitude direction. $J_{1\min}$, $J_{2\min}$ is the reference minimum of the error value of longitude direction, latitude direction.

SIMULATION AND EXPERIMENTAL RESULTS

To test the effectiveness of the genetic-based fuzzy federated Kalman filter model, field tests using combined GPS/DR were run through Changsha city. The 1000 test data from different street is taken as the input of FKF, use the GA to find the fuzzy membership function for FLAC. After optimal, some experiments on a closed road were taken to observe the performance of FKF provided by the human expert and the GA. Initial conditions and value are given below:

$$\sigma_\theta = 0.05rad \quad \sigma_s = 0.2m \qquad \mathbf{R}_{dr} = diag(\sigma_\theta^2, \sigma_s^2)$$
$$\sigma_e = \sigma_n = 5m/s^2 \qquad \mathbf{R}_{gps} = diag(\sigma_e^2, \sigma_n^2)$$

$$\mathbf{P}_k(0) = [2*5^2 \;\; 2*3^2 \;\; 2*3^2 \;\; 2*5^2 \;\; 2*3^2 \;\; 2*5^2]$$

The parameters for the genetic algorithm are set as follows:

Population size : 50,

Generation number: 100,

Crossover probability: 0.9,

Mutation probability : 0.1.

$$J_{1\max} = J_{2\max} = 5, J_{1\min} = J_{2\min} = 0$$

The fuzzy membership functions after optimal using the GA for north direction of GPS local filter and fusion coefficient are those given in Fig. 6. In Fig. 7, curve 1 is the true vehicle running path, curve 2 is the result of conventional federated Kalman filter, curve 3 is the result of using the fuzzy federated Kalman filter designed by human expert and curve 4 is the result of the fuzzy federated Kalman filter with membership function by genetic algorithm. A part of the result of field test is shown in Fig. 8. The triangle is the track of FKF without optimal. The point is the track of FKF after optimal.

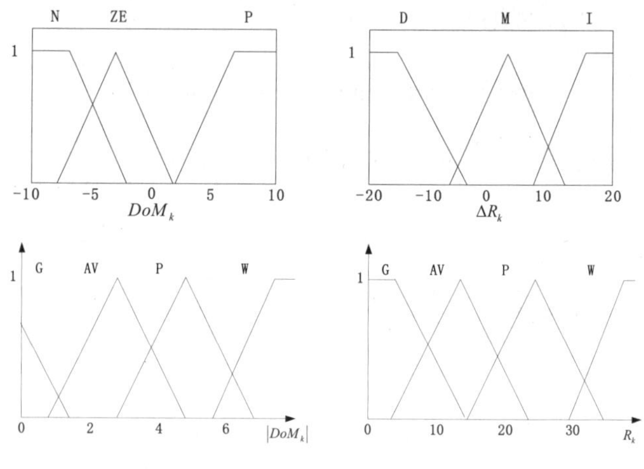

Figure 6 Fuzzy membership function after optimal

In Figure 9, east position errors are shown. The solid lines are the corrected errors of conventional federated Kalman filter, the dashed lines are the corrected errors of fuzzy federated Kalman filter, and the dash-doted lines are the corrected errors of the fuzzy federated Kalman filter with optimal membership function. In Figure 10, north position errors are shown. In comparison, the fuzzy federated Kalman filter significantly reduced the corrected position errors in the GPS/DR integration system. The east position error is improved about 1.18 metre (mean value), the north position error is improved about 0.86 metre. This simulation indicates that the fuzzy federated Kalman filter is valid to reduce errors of estimation. From the Figure 9-10, we also can see the effectiveness of the optimal fuzzy membership function by genetic algorithm. After optimize, the east position error decreased about 0.28 metre (mean value), the north position error decreased about 0.16 metre. Figure 11 shows the main elements in the measurement noise covariance matrix $\mathbf{R}_{GPS}$ obtained with the GA.

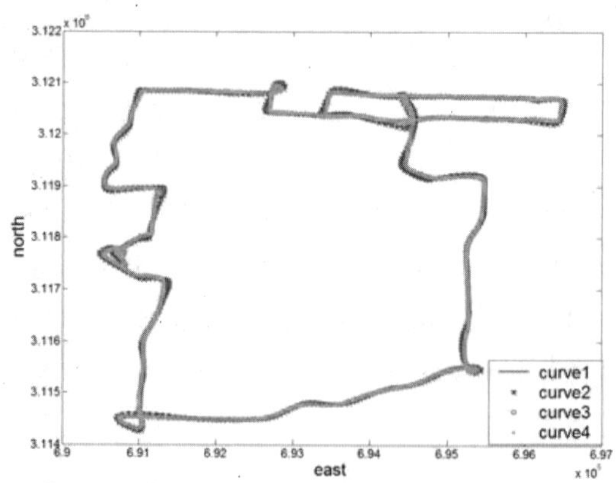

Figure 7 Result of field test

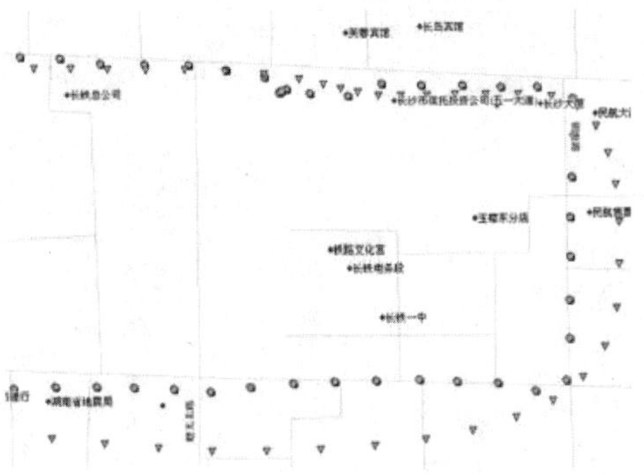

Figure 8 Part of the field test result

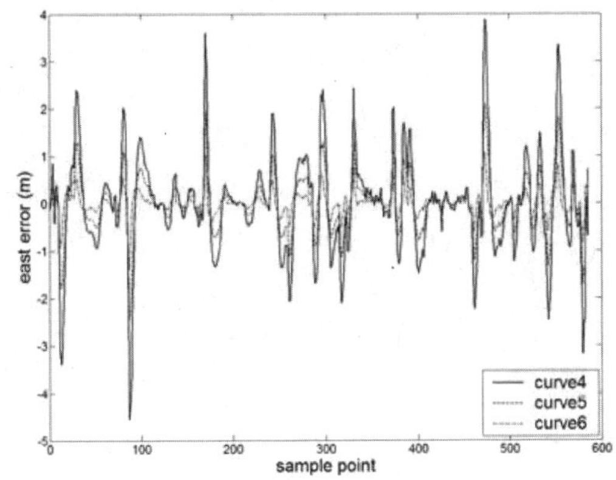

Figure 9 Error of east direction

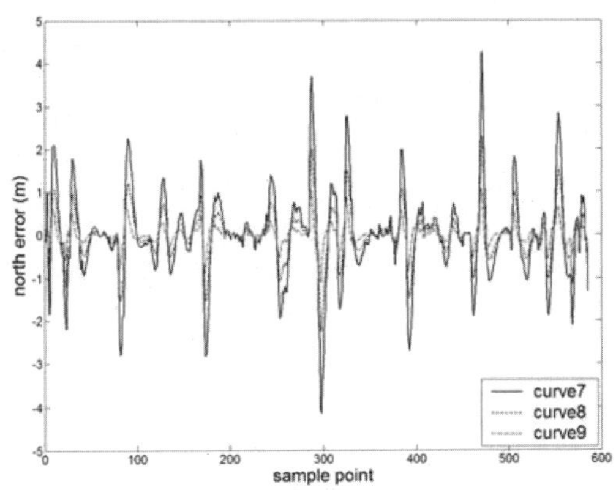

Figure 10 Error of north direction

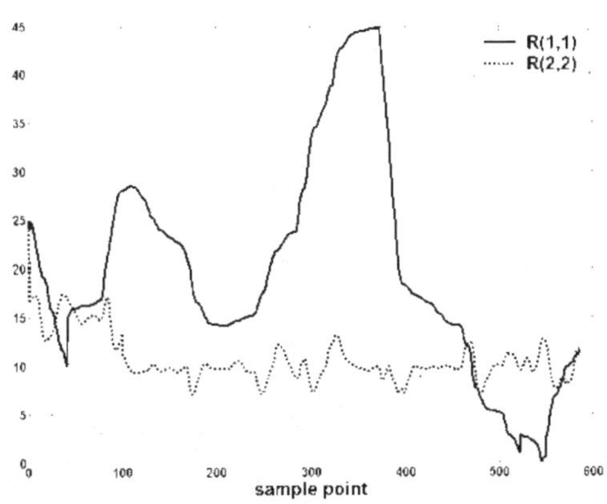

Figure 11 Elements in the main diagonal of R_{GPS}

CONCLUSION

In this paper, federated Kalman filtering and fuzzy logic techniques have been presented. This approach exploits the advantages that both approaches have the optimality of the Kalman filter and the capability of fuzzy systems to deal with imprecise information using "common sense" fuzzy rules. The FLAC of local filter requires smaller number of states for the same accuracy and therefore, it would need less computational effort. Alternatively, the same number of states would allow for more accurate navigation. This method prevents filter divergence and relaxes the priori assumption about the initial value of $\mathbf{R}$. The FLAC of master filter adjust the information fusion coefficient of local filter according to the situation of filter. In order to keep the filter good performance, genetic algorithm is introduced to adjust membership functions of fuzzy controller. Experiments using actual road test have shown that the approach is effective in solving the location problem and that the method can be used in vehicle navigation system.

REFERENCES

1. Ren Da, George Dedes. 'Nonlinear Smoothing of Dead Reckoning Data With GPS Measurements', Proceedings of ION GPS-95, California, pp. 1285—1294. 1995
2. SAN-TONG ZHANG. 'Land Vehicle Location Orientation Navigation System and Multi-sensor Integration', PH.D. dissertation (in Chinese), Beijing Institute of Technology, 1998.
3. Escamilla-Ambrosio, P.J, and Mort, N. 'Multi-sensor data fusion architecture based on adaptive Kalman filters and fuzzy logic performance assessment', Information Fusion, Proceedings of the 2002 First International IEEE Symposium, Vol.1 July 8-11 10-12, 2002, pp.1542-1549
4. Escamilla-Ambrosio, P.J, and Mort, N. 'A hybrid Kalman filter-fuzzy logic architecture for multi-sensor data fusion', Intelligent Control, Proceedings of the 2001 IEEE International Symposium, Sept 5-7, 2001, pp.364-369.
5. G B GREEN, P D MASSATT, and N W RHODUS. The GPS 21 Primary Satellite Constellation, Navigation, 1989,36(1): 9-24
6. M. S. GREWAL, A. P. ANDREW. Kalman Filtering: Theory and Practice. Englewood Cliffs, NJ: Prentice-Hall, 1993.
7. Carlson,H.A. 'Federated Filter for Fault-Tolerant Integrated Navigation Systems', IEEE PLANS, Position Location and Navigation Symposium, Nov 29-Dec 2, 1998, pp. 110-119.
8. Carlson,H.A. 'Information-Sharing Approach to Federated Kalman Filtering'. IEEE Proceedings of the National Aerospace and Electronics Conference, 1998, pp.1581.
9. D.Park, A.Kandel, and G.Langholz. 'Genetic-based New Fuzzy Reasoning Models with Application to Fuzzy Control',

IEEE Trans. On Systems, Man, and Cybernetics, 24(1): 39-47,1994.
10. L.X.Wang and J.M.Mendel. "Generating Fuzzy Rules by Learning from Example," IEEE Trans. On Systems, Man, and Cybernetics, Vol. 22, No.6, pp. 1414-1427, 1992.

CONTACT

Yang Yi: PHD student, State Key Laboratory of Advanced Design and Manufacture for Vehicle Body, Hunan University, China

E-mail: yangyi66mail@163.com

Tel: 86-0731-8821148

Gu Zhengqi: Professor, State Key Laboratory of Advanced Design and Manufacture for Vehicle Body, Hunan University, China

E-mail: guzhengqi63@126.com

Tel: 86-0731-8821458

2007-01-1108

Adaptive and Reconfigurable Data Fusion Architectures in Vehicle Positioning Navigation Systems

Guopei Liu and Denis Gingras
Université de Sherbrooke

ABSTRACT

In positioning navigation systems, at any time, any of the sensors can break down or stop sending information, temporarily or permanently. To ensure a practical solution for use in guidance and navigation systems, faulty sensors must be detected and isolated such that their erroneous data will not corrupt the global position estimates. It is well known that Kalman filter is usually being used for data fusion applications. An interesting novel alternative is to use it for fault detection architecture as well. This paper describes the research conducted to evaluate the potential of combining fault detection and data fusion into a single architecture to make a robust positioning navigation system.

INTRODUCTION

Either from a user's point of view or a designer's perspective, all automotive navigation systems should be fully reliable and prevent faults or failures. In all but the most trivial cases the existence of a fault may lead to situations with safety, health, environmental, financial or legal implications. Although good design practice tries to minimize the occurrence of faults and failures, it is recognized that such events do occur. In such cases, faulty sensors must be detected and the system must be able to reconfigure itself so as to overcome the deficiency caused by the fault. In brief, a navigation system must be robust and adaptive.

As mentioned previously, faults can cause the loss of the overall performance of a system, which may present hazards to personnel or lead to unacceptable economic loss. In order to minimize the impact, fault detection schemes must be developed. Actually, several fruitful research efforts in the field of fault detection and filter based adaptive architectures, combining fault detection and data fusion, have been proposed to improve the reliability and adaptability of various control systems [7, 8, 9]. However, little has been published in the area of automotive navigation systems.

FAULT DETECTION ARCHITECTURE

A fault is usually defined as an undesired change in system estimated parameters that degrade partial or overall performance. Fault detection is a binary decision making process. Either the system is functioning properly, or there is a fault present.

Generally speaking, fault detection consists of two processes: *residual generation* and *decision making*, as shown in Figure 1 [4].

Residual Generation

Residuals are defined as the resulting differences between analytically redundant quantities in the system model. These are similar to innovations generated by a Kalman filter, which are the differences between the measured and estimated outputs. Under normal conditions, residuals are small or zero mean; while the occurrence of a fault causes the residuals to go to non-zero or unusually large values.

Decision Making

The decision making process, which acts as an arbitrator, involves assessing the residuals and identifying when and where any abnormalities occur. This is done through threshold testing both static and dynamic residual behaviors, and various statistical tests, where the thresholds are typically based on signal/residual variance.

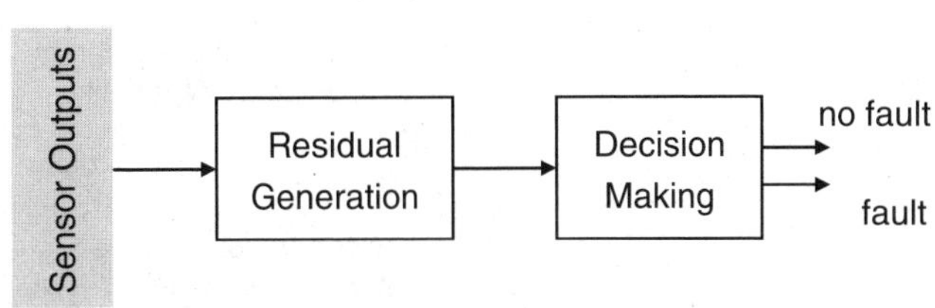

Figure 1. Fault Detection Architecture

FAULT DETECTION TECHNIQUES

The methods of fault detection and diagnosis may be classified into two major groups: hardware redundancy and analytical redundancy [10], which is shown in Figure 2.

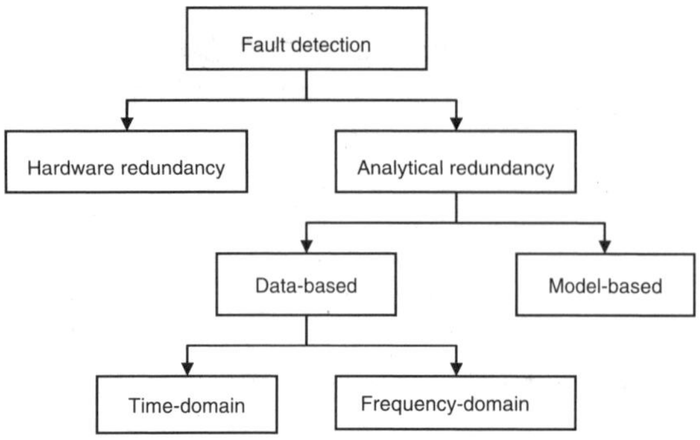

Figure 2. Fault Detection Tehcniques Taxonomy

Fault detection in dynamic systems is traditionally achieved through the use of hardware redundancy. But the major problems encountered are the extra cost and software requirements and, furthermore, the additional space required to accommodate the equipment. To overcome these issues, analytical redundancy has been developed to eliminate some or all of the redundant hardware. There are two generic ways to approach the analytical fault detection issue: the model-based approach and the data-based approach.

SENSOR FAULTY MODELS

To be useful, systems must interact with their environment. To achieve this objective, in positioning navigation system, various sensors are used. Generally speaking, a sensor is a device that responds to or detects a physical quantity and transmits the resulting signal to a controller. Position sensors can be designed to detect various parameters (coordinate, distance, direction, or angular velocity) of the position of vehicular mechanical systems. The detail relationship between the position and sensors is shown in Table 1.

Table 1. Relationship of Vehicle Position and Sensor Outputs

Sensor	Output	Relation to position
GPS	Rover position	Directly output position coordinates
IMU	Accelerations and angular rate	Outputs can be integrated by an INS to obtain the vehicle position
Odometer	Distance or increment of distance	Position coordinates are determined by dead reckoning from the distance and direction relative to a known location
Inclinometer	Inclination	
Magnetic compass	Azimuth	

So far, although the precision and reliability of sensors are improved significantly with the development of the technology, various sensor faults driven by different situations do exist. In the following, several faulty scenarios of sensors are investigated and discussed.

GLOBAL POSITIONING SYSTEM (GPS) FAULTY MODEL

A low-cost GPS receiver can output the vehicle position and driving speed. However, the measurement is likely to be corrupted by time-correlated noise and the GPS signal is susceptible to jamming. However, the position and velocity measurements do not drift over long periods of time.

A GPS faulty model can be based on four particular parts: typical error budget, environmental interferences, signal loss, and hardware malfunction.

Typical Error Budget

The main error sources in GPS are listed in Table 2. These errors can be divided into two categories [1]: common and non-common. Common errors are approximately the same for receivers operating within a limited geographic region. Non-common errors are unique to each receiver and depend on the receiver type and multipath mitigation technique being used (if any). The point of this classification is that DGPS can effectively remove the common errors.

Table 2. GPS Error Sources and their Approximate Deviation [2]

Source	Standard deviation (m)
Common	
Ionosphere	7.0
Clock and ephemeris	3.6
Troposphere	0.7
Non-common	
Receiver noise	0.1~0.7
Multipath	0.1~5.0

Environmental Interferences

GPS satellite signals, as with any other radio signals, are subject to some form of interference and jamming. It is known that GPS satellite currently transmit position information in the 1,500-MHz frequency band with a typical accuracy under 100 meters to anyone in the world who has a simple receiver costing as little as $100. Any electronic systems generating radio signals in this frequency band, main lobe or side lobe, will tend to be a source of inference to the GPS receiver. With the popularization of personal radio and Wi-Fi devices, electromagnetic interferences, intentional or unintentional, are more and more serious. As an example, the proliferation of ultra-wideband (UWB) devices intended to be mass-marketed to the public could cause harmful interference to GPS.

Signal loss

GPS is a line-of-sight sensor, and therefore GPS measurements are subject to signal outages. If it cannot "see" four satellites, then it will not produce the expected output. This case is called signal loss. It may include the following scenarios:

- Urban environments with all buildings (the so-called urban canyons).
- Inside parking structures.
- In a long tunnel without any relay station.
- Under heavy foliage.
- Under bridges.

Hardware Malfunction

A GPS receiver hardware malfunction can be caused by any abnormality of its components, such as antenna, amplifier, reference oscillator, frequency synthesizer, wire disconnection, and power lost, resulting to no output, or provide an unstable or incorrect signal.

Normally, the probability of the hardware malfunction of the GPS receiver is very low, so it is not taken into account in this simulation.

Sum up all above, the GPS faulty model can be described as in Figure 3.

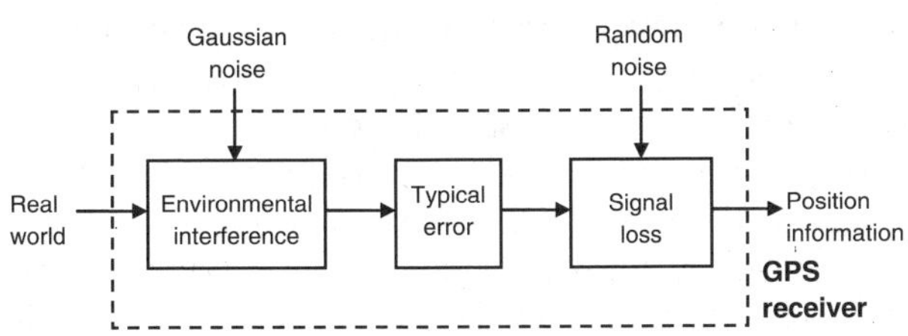

Figure 3. GPS Faulty Model

INERTIAL MEASUREMENT UNIT (IMU) FAULTY MODEL

A low-cost IMU can output the vehicle accelerations and angular rate which can then be integrated by an Inertial Navigation System (INS) to obtain the vehicle position, velocity, and attitude. The advantage of an INS is low sensitivity to high-frequency noise and external conditions. But the measurement error of INS will accumulate if it is not calibrated on-line. The scenarios driving the IMU to a faulty state are discussed in the following:

IMU Error Sources and Faulty Scenarios

1. Bias due to bearing torques (for momentum wheel types), drive excitation feedthrough, electronics offsets and environmental temperature fluctuations. Intuitively, bias is any nonzero sensor output when the input is zero.
2. Scale factor error, often resulting from aging or manufacturing tolerances.
3. Alignment errors: Most stand-alone IMU implementations include an initial transient period for alignment of the gimbals (for gimbaled systems) or attitude direction cosines (for strapdown systems) with respect to the navigation axes. Errors remaining at the end of this period are the alignment errors. These include tilts and azimuth reference errors. Tilt errors introduce acceleration errors through the miscalculation of gravitational acceleration, and these propagate primarily as Schuler oscillations plus a non-zero-mean position error approximately equal to the tilt error in radians times the radius from the earth center. Initial azimuth errors primarily rotate the system trajectory about the starting point, but there are secondary effects due to Coriolis accelerations and excitation of Schuler oscillations.
4. Cross coupling error (non-linearity).
5. Quantization error, which is inherent in all digitized systems.
6. Fault due to one or multiple of the moving parts wear out or jam, or gimbals lock.

IMU Faulty Model Diagram

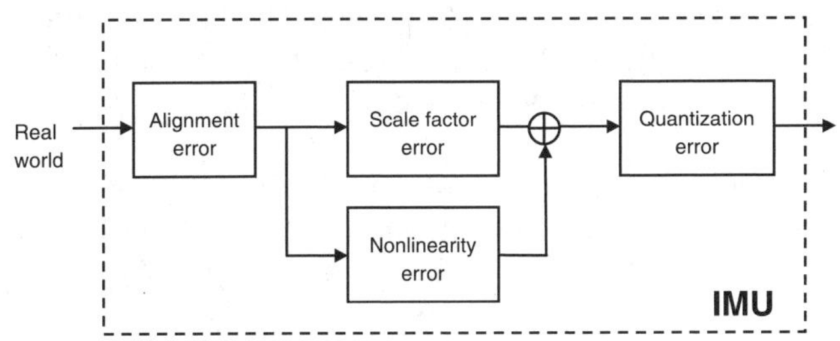

Figure 4. IMU Faulty Model

ODOMETER FAULTY MODEL

An odometer is one of the most common devices used for tracking and relative positioning of vehicles. In the transmission-based odometer, the distance to be determined is based on the number of counts for the wheel and calibration constants which are proportional to the radius of the tire. Thus any potential trends that change the radius and the number of counts can drive the odometer to a faulty output.

Tire radius change

The major sources of tire radius variation are listed in the following reference [5]:

1. Tire radius tends to increase as vehicle velocity increases because of increasing centrifugal force on the tire.
2. Tire radius tends to increase as air pressure within the tire increases due to increase tire temperature or other factors.
3. Tire radius tends to increase as tread is worn off during the lifetime of the tire.

Road Situation

These kinds of error sources depend on the road situation, including:

- Running over objects on the road, slips or skids involving one or more wheels when the vehicle accelerates or decelerates too rapidly or travels on a snowy, icy, or wet road.
- In sharp turns, the contact point between each wheel and the road can change, so that the actual distance between the left and right wheels will be different from the one used to derive the heading.

Gears Tooth Lost

An odometer can operate by counting the pass of teeth or tabs of the ferrous wheel mounted on the rotating shaft of the vehicle. If one or more teeth are lost, then the value will abate n/t, where n is the number of the lost teeth, t is the total teeth of the wheel. In the real situation, the occurrences of losing three or more teeth are so puny that they can be omitted.

In brief, the wear out of the tire, the pressure of the tire, the velocity of the vehicle, the slippage of the tire, and the gear teeth lost will contribute to the odometer fault.

INCLINOMETER FAULTY MODEL

The error sources of the inclinometer may consist of:

1. Error caused by thermal expansion or temperature changes. A normally distribution band-limited white noise is used to demonstrate the thermal noise.
2. Drift, calibration error or quantization error due to analog to digital converter resolution.
3. Electromagnetic interference (the major component of the inclinometer faulty model). It can be a uniform or a Gaussian distribution, or a combination of both. The variance and amplitude depend on the traveling environment.
4. Power lost or hardware malfunction: A permanent fault, but since it is only in a very low possibility, it is omitted in this simulation.

MAGNETIC COMPASS FAULTY MODEL (FLUXGATE COMPASS)

A magnetic compass is an inexpensive absolute direction sensor. The main drawback with this device is that the quantity measured, i.e. the intensity and direction of the magnetic field, can be distorted in the presence of metals and other electrical or magnetic fields, such as power lines, transformers and cars' powertrain system.

Our simulated compass operations include the following error sources:

1. Hilly road error [6]: When the vehicle is traveling over a hilly road, the compass plan will not be parallel to the plane of the Earth surface. The compass measures only the projection of the vector components. This is a short-term magnetic anomaly.
2. Random noise error [6]: a) In the situation of traveling nearby power lines, big trucks, steel structures (such as freeway underpasses and tunnels), reinforced concrete buildings, or bridges (short-term magnetic anomalies); b) In an environment of electrical or magnetic noise, or magnetization of the vehicle body (long-term magnetic anomalies).
3. Calibration error: Misalignment of the compass with respect to the vehicle frame simply results in a constant error. This type of error can also be attributed to an inaccurate estimation of the current declination.
4. Permanent fault: power lost or interface cable disconnected (very low possibility, they are being omitted in the simulation).

ADAPTIVE DATA FUSION ARCHITECTURE

In positioning navigation systems, high precision and reliability with low cost are always pursued. Actually, for road navigation, the benefits of the information obtained by the fusion process make it possible to use multiple less powerful, lower cost sensors to achieve as good a performance as those much more expensive ones. Kalman filter and its derivatives, the most popular data fusion methods, have been used extensively in autonomous or assisted navigation system for several years. But almost all of these applications are based on the assumption that all sensed data are complete and reliable. If one or more sensors are faulty, then the fusion filters will tend to choke. In order to ensure a reliable positioning estimate in the case of faulty sensors, an adaptive approach is proposed as in Figure 5.

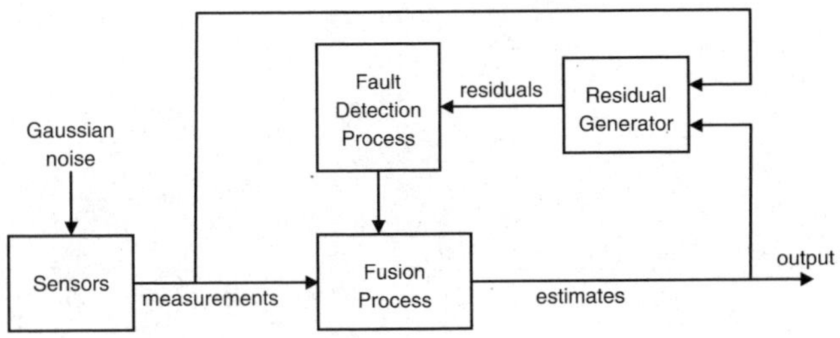

Figure 5. Adaptive Sensor Fusion System

As most of the navigation systems, the objective of the above system is to make the position estimate of the vehicle as accurate and reliable as possible. Sensors (GPS, IMU, odometer, inclinometer and compass) data which are used to compute the position and attitude of the vehicle, often involve sources of uncertainties. Meanwhile, a state space model can be constructed from the vehicle dynamic to perform the function of sensor fusion. Both their outputs (measurements and estimates) can be combined together through a particular function so as to generate a residual signal. Passing this signal through a detection process, a decision is made: either the system is running properly, or there is a fault occurring, which leads to the fusion process rerunning to optimize the position estimates.

From the diagram above, we can see how a residual signal generator and a fault detector are embedded into the conventional data fusion architecture. A Kalman filter approach is used, since it is simpler and more effective to attain the residual signal via state estimation. The key idea is to reconstruct the outputs of the process with the aid of Kalman filter and to use the estimation error, or some particular statistical functions of them to assess the residual signal. Then the faultiness can be detected by considering the residual properties against some threshold. If any information from the sensors is detected to be faulty (residual properties go over a given threshold), then the corresponding measurements are discarded. In that case, the position estimate needs to be re-updated. The detailed flow chart is shown in Figure 6. Note that the shaded blocks are part of the fault detection process.

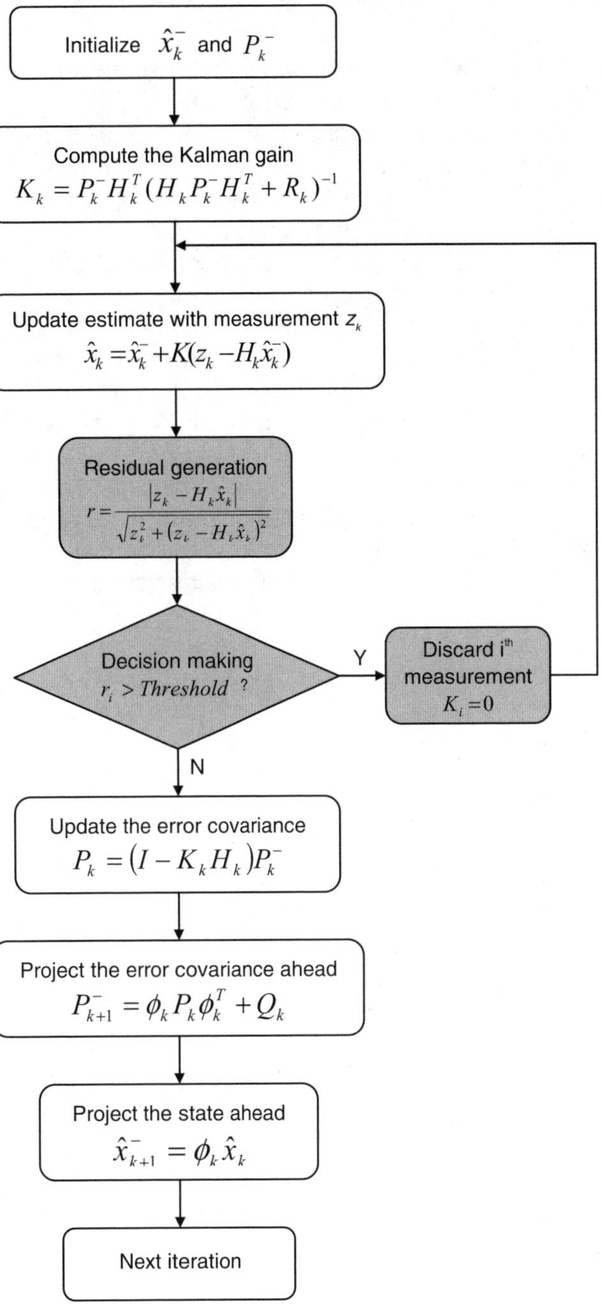

Figure 6. Adaptive Sensor Fusion Architecture Flow Chart

PERFORMANCE ANALYSIS

As mentioned previously, all position sensors have the risk of fault or failure. However, in the practical road driving environment, GPS signal loss, due to line-of-sight, is the most common and frequent event of sensor fault. So in this section, the cases of with and without GPS signal loss, will be considered respectively.

First, suppose there is no GPS signal loss. So, as described in the section of Sensor Faulty Models, uncertainties of the imperfect sensors would be including:

- GPS: environmental interference and typical error source.
- IMU: alignment error, scale factor error, nonlinearity error, and quantization error.
- Odometer: tire radius change, wheel slippage, and gears tooth loss.
- Inclinometer: environmental noise, drift, and electromagnetic interference.
- Magnetic compass: environmental noise, hilly road error, and calibration error.

In order to see the benefit, data with uncertainties from different sensors are fused using a conventional Kalman filter (Figure 6 without shaded blocks) and with the proposed embedded fault detection (FD) module respectively (Figure 6 with shaded blocks). The results (trajectory estimates in shaded bold gray line) are printed out comparing with the real trajectory (fine black full line) in Figure 7, and the statistics of their errors are shown in Table 3.

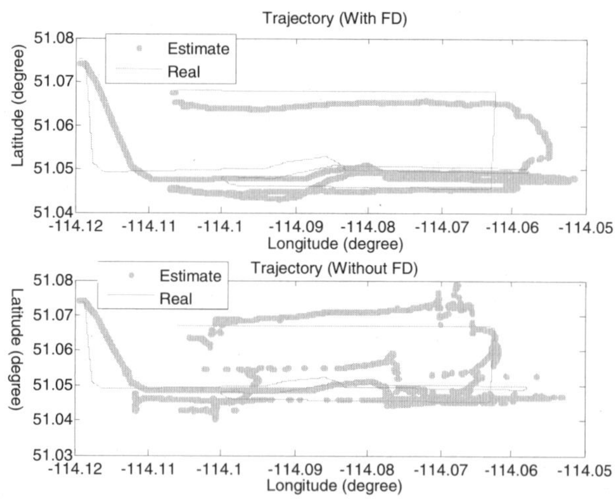

Figure 7. Estimated Trajectory of Proposed Architecture (no GPS signal loss)

Table 3. Statistics of Position Errors (no signal loss)

Position	SNR (dB)	Mean (m)			Variance(m^2)		
		Conventional	Adaptive	Gain (%)	Conventional	Adaptive	Gain (%)
Latitude	11.613	34.470	-49.193	243	$1.428*10^5$	$1.270*10^4$	91
Longitude	12.874	-42.881	122.850	386	$1.725*10^5$	$7.777*10^4$	54
Altitude	-9.813	93.736	114.159	-22	652.783	315.600	51

$$SNR = -10 \times \log \frac{\sum_{i=1}^{n} S_i^2}{\sum_{i=1}^{n} N_i^2}$$

$$Gain = \frac{V_{convention} - V_{adaptive}}{V_{convention}}$$

S_i and N_i are defined as the values of signal and noise at i^{th} sampling time.

Table 3 shows that there is at least 50% gain (91%, 54%, 51%) in error variance for the use of adaptive solution comparing to the conventional Kalman filter one.

Now suppose that all uncertainties described before are present at any time and also including a GPS signal loss. Similarly, the trajectories of this case are printed out in Figure 8 and error statistics are listed in Table 4.

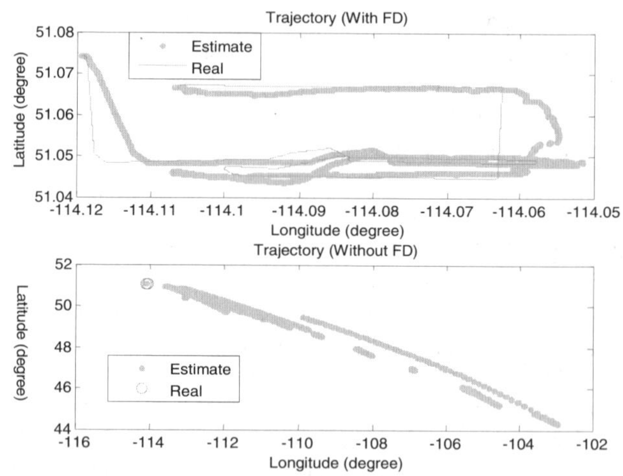

Figure 8. Estimated Trajectory of Proposed Architecture (with signal loss)

Note that the ranges of coordinate for the trajectories (With and Without FD) are not the same. The loss of GPS signal has a huge impact and makes the real trajectory just look like a point in the figure without fault detection.

Table 4. Statistics of Position Errors

Position	SNR (dB)	Mean(m)			Variance(m^2)		
		Conventional	Adaptive	Gain (%)	Conventional	Adaptive	Gain (%)
Latitude	-41.644	$-1.265*10^5$	-47.176	99	$2.214*10^{10}$	$1.217*10^4$	99
Longitude	-41.187	$1.624*10^5$	119.183	99	$2.586*10^{10}$	$7.480*10^4$	99
Altitude	-7.079	86.714	115.538	-33	427.985	328.102	23

Figure 8 shows that in the case of a GPS signal loss, conventional Kalman filter will choke: up to 126km error in latitude! While with the proposed adaptive solution, the error is only 47 meters. As to the error variances, the value of the gain is almost close to 100%.

CONCLUSION

A standard Kalman filter is usually being used for data fusion so as to provide better position estimates while using several poor sensors. The occurrences of sensor faults, which tend to degrade or paralyze the navigation solution, are simply not acceptable. In order to minimize the unexpected impact, many fruitful research efforts in the field of FDI have been made. Actually, by computing the differences between the estimates and the measurements, a residual can be generated and the sensor fault can be detected by a decision making process based on the residual statistical properties. In this paper, fault detection and data fusion are combined into a single Kalman architecture to construct a fault tolerance, robust and adaptable vehicle positioning system. Tests results show that the proposed Kalman filter based state estimation scheme ensures that the position estimate is always optimal and brings significant benefit to the data fusion system comparing with the conventional fusion architecture, as illustrated in particular for the frequent GPS signal loss case.

ACKNOWLEDGMENTS

The author would like to thank the Canadian NCE AUTO21 for funding this research project, and Mathieu St-Pierre for his fruitful work on the simulator.

REFERENCES

1. Jay Farrell and Matthew Barth. The Global Positioning System and Inertial Navigation. McGraw-Hill, 1999.
2. Jon Kronander. *Robust Automotive Positioning: Integration of GPS and Relative Motion Sensors.* December 2004
3. Masafumi Hashimoto, Hiroyuki Kawashima, Takashi Nakagami, and Fuminori Oba. *Sensor Fault detection and Identification in Dead-Reckoning System of Mobile Robot: Interacting Multiple Model Approach.* Proceedings of the 2001 IEEE/RSJ International Conference on Intelligent Robot and Systems, Mani, Hawaii, USA, Oct. 29 – Nov. 03, 2001.
4. *S.M. Magrabi and P.W. Gibbens. Decentralized Fault Detection and Diagnosis in Navigation Systems for Unmanned Aerial Vehicles.* IEEE Position Location and Navigation Symposium, *San Diego, 2000.*
5. Thomas W.Lezniak, Richard W.Lewis, and Robert A.Mcmillen. *A Dead Reckoning/Map Correlation System for Automatic Vehicle Tracking.* IEEE Transactions on Vehicular Technology, Vol. VT-26, No.1 February 1977
6. Yilin Zhao. (1997). *Vehicle Location and Navigation Systems.* Norwood, Artech House, 345 p.
7. R. Patton, P. Frank and R. Clarck. *Fault Diagnosis in Dynamic System: Theory and Applications*, Prentice Hall, 1989
8. A. D. Pouliezos and G.S. Stavrakakis, *Real Time Fault Monitoring of Industrial Processes.* Kluwer Academic Publishers, 1994
9. R. Isermann. *Fault-Diagnosis Systems: An Introduction From Fault Detection To Fault Tolerance.* Springer Verlag, 2005
10. Christopher Tubb, Edin Omerdic. *Fault Detection and Handling.* IMPROVES technical report FD 001(n). 8th October 2001.

CONTACT

Guopei Liu
guopei.liu@yahoo.com

Denis Gingras
denis.gingras@usherbrooke.ca

2007-01-1107

A Navigation Assistance Agent: Mobile LBS Web Service

Dengyue Li, Shengrui Wang and Wentao Cai
University of Sherbrooke

Zhen Mei
Manifold Data Mining, Inc.

ABSTRACT

Searching the Location-Based Service (LBS) on the Internet, such as Yellow Pages, has the advantage to have the most updated information, for free (at least for the moment). Due to a number of limitations, mobile users still encounter many troubles when they use wireless device to perform online LBS searching. Providing a convenient access to the online LBS information for those wireless users is a challenging problem and also a business opportunity. In this paper, we focus on building intelligent agents to provide online LBS via wireless Internet accessing. Such an agent, based on address identification, can analyze the content of certain Web pages (ex. Yellow Pages) to search desired LBS information. We propose an ontology-based conceptual information retrieval approach combined with tree structure matching and the nearest neighbor methods to perform this task. A prototype, RouteInfo Mobile LBS for automobile drivers, has been developed to perform LBS searching, mapping and route finding.

INTRODUCTION

Location-Based Service (LBS) information is an important component of navigation assistance systems, for which up-to-date online information is a valuable data source. On a conventional desktop, one can find easily local businesses and services through online search engine such as YellowPages [1], Canada411 [2] or Yahoo [3]. For example, using gasoline station as the keyword, one can find 67 results in downtown Toronto from YellowPages. If a driver could have easy access to the information on the road, he or she can then determine where to fill the tank either by driving distance, driving time, gas price or familiarity with the neighborhood.

Many handheld wireless devices such as cell phones and PDAs already have the ability to access the Internet. The WAP Forum was founded in 1997 to unify mobile access technologies. The WAP Forum, now numbering more than 400 members, has contributed to the adoption of Wireless Application Protocol (WAP) and Wireless Markup Language (WML) as de facto standards. WAP is a suite of specifications (including WML) that is based on variations of modern, open Web standards. Wireless specifications are designed for mobile devices. WML is loosely based on HTML, however WML is an XML-based language, which means that WML documents must follow stricter rules than HTML documents. However, there are a number of limitations to portable devices—such as memory, screen size and connection speed. The wireless devices perform online LBS information searching not as easily as to perform the email accessing, because they have more difficulties in inputting information and navigating numerous Web pages. It is, of course, also very expensive to do so because of the high price per unit of data transferred.

In this paper, we are interested in techniques for building smart agents that help automate the searching of online LBS information. Such an agent can analyze Web pages to extract the LBS information by identifying valid address. The advantage of a postal address is in its tree structure, from root to top: province, municipality, street and street number. The address structure can be represented by the ontology of a set of concepts. For example, "205-501 Alliance Ave, Toronto, ON M2K 1J4" is extracted into conceptual segments: <ON: Province>, <Toronto: Municipality>, <Alliance Ave: Street>, <501: Street number>, <205: Unit>, <M6N 2J1: Postal code>. By comparing with standard address structures, a possible address can be identified successfully. We propose an ontology-based conceptual information retrieval method to perform address extracting from unstructured texts. This approach overcomes many of difficulties encountered by keywords matching approaches.

To further enhance our approach as a valid alternative to traditional approach to LBS information delivery (ex. by on-board DVD), we make recourse to the technology of Web Service. Web Services enable applications that aggregate and interact with information and resources from distributed servers on the Internet. A Web method can be published as a remote public class via Web services. Client applications can easily invoke a Web Service via Internet protocols. Using TerraService [5], any Internet developer can directly access the TerraServer[6] database which stores aerial, satellite and topographic images of the earth. Based on this principle, if we construct a LBS online searching as a distributed object, we can relieve significantly the wireless Internet communication and still provide an efficient access to online LBS.

A prototype, named RouteInfo Mobile LBS has been developed to integrate address extracting, address geo-coding, mapping and route finding. In Section 2 we review the related work and technologies. We propose in Section 3 a new procedure for address extraction. Section 4 presents the framework of the RouteInfo Mobile LBS. In Section 5 we discuss on-road tests. Finally, we summarize in Section 6 the achievements and future works.

2 RELATED WORKS AND TECHNOLOGIES

Modern information retrieval (IR) [10] and information extraction (IE) approaches can help in collecting LBS information online. Based on an understanding of text, the information extraction (IE) application need to overcome that the extraction rules have to be adapted for specified domain, and rules self-learning is required. WHISK [11] has to operate in conjunction with a syntactic analyzer and a semantic tagger to learn extraction rules for unstructured text. Recent research on content-bases information retrieval (IR) focuses on conceptual analysis of unstructured texts on the Web. In such conceptual information retrieval systems, researchers tend to utilize the domain ontology as a conceptual structure to accomplish concept extraction by combining human knowledge and computing techniques. Mapping the words onto a set of predefined concepts (knowledge) is one efficient way to discover a text's underlying meanings. As an example, using conceptual graphs for representing the text content, it could discover detailed patterns [12].

A Navigation Assistance Agent: Online Access to LBS [13], which is the previous research in our group, is a good approach for retrieving online location-based information in real time. It employs ontology-based conceptual information retrieval combined with graph matching to perform address identification from Web pages. Using graph matching and graph similarity to extract the address structure is a remarkable attempt. There are still some problems on how to estimate the noises and figure out the range of an address from unstructured texts. For example, two joined addresses, "20 Portland Blvd Sherbrooke Quebec 100 King Street Cockville Quebec", will be regarded as one address segment. In order to build our mobile LBS Web Service, we make use of an information search technology developed in our group and Web service development technologies.

Here are a few Web Service related concepts that have played important roles in our prototype development. Simple Object Access Protocol (SOAP) [7] is the communication protocol that Web Service uses to expose its public functionality. Web Service Definition Language (WSDL) [8] describes the Web Service interfaces to allow a user to build a client application to talk to them. Web Services are registered in Universal Discovery Description and Integration (UDDI) [9], so that potential developers can find them easily.

- SOAP headers and documents describe the data types of parameters, returned data structures, and exceptions. SOAP is an ideal technology to solve interconnection between different component platforms, for it provides an extensible framing mechanism for XML messages. Using XML to describe and pack access protocols, it makes remote access protocol of all kinds of component platforms transfer message by identical standard message.
- WSDL describes the Web Service interfaces, based on XML. It is used to describe service content, service result and message used to bind service and communication protocol. It helps users to understand how the service looks like, what operations the service provides, and what information is exchanged during a call.
- UDDI is an industrial standard basing on information register of distributed Web Services. The UDDI directory provides service supply information, contacts, links and the WSDL file that describes the service technical details. UDDI makes it possible for developers to issue and find Web Services.

3 OUR PROPOSAL

Address extraction is the core feature of our online LBS information searching. We propose an ontology-based conceptual information retrieval approach combined with tree structure matching and the nearest neighbor methods to identify possible address in a Web page.

Extracting address information from unstructured texts is done in following steps.

Step 1: Address Tree Discovering: Using a pre-defined domain ontology, each address concept will be discovered from the plain text of Web pages. The address concepts will be assembled their tree representations.
Step 2: Address Evaluation: The order of concepts and noise are then used to evaluate these address candidates.
Step 3: Address Validation: The real address information is validated from possible address candidates by address Geo-coding.

3.1 PRE-DEFINED ADDRESS CONCEPT

According to the address structure in Figure 1 below, we define eight types of concepts in an address domain: <Province>, <Municipality>, <Street Number>, <Street Name>, <Street Type>, <Direction>, <Unit>, <Postal Code>. We use detailed digital street map data,

CanMap® Streetfiles from DMTI Spatial [14], to generate the pre-defined address concept set. In order to maintain the size of concept dataset, we do not regard detailed street number as a pre-defined concept. For instance, using detailed street data in Table 2, we create the address concepts in Table 1. We also create pre-defined concept based on the logogram of the address. Some of concepts may be defined with two or more types. For example, <Sherbrooke: Municipality> and <Sherbrooke: Street Name>, <Avenue: Street Name> and <Avenue: Street Type>.

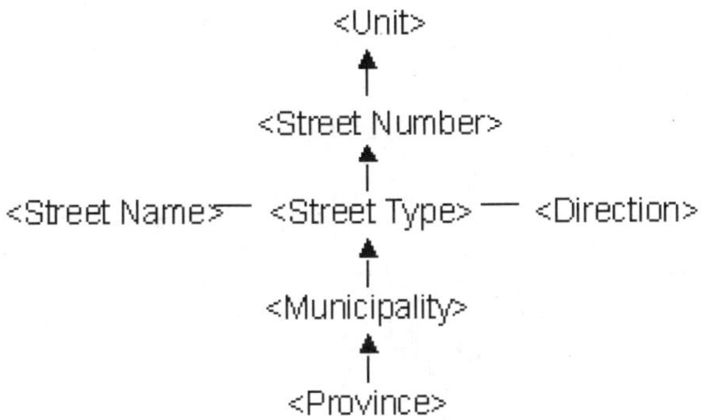

Figure 1: Address Tree Structure

CONCEPT	TYPE
ALMORE	Street Name
JOEL SWIRSKY	Street Name
W. R. ALLEN	Street Name
DE QUINCY	Street Name
WESTGATE	Street Name
SHEPPARD	Street Name
AVENUE	Street Name
AVE	Street Type
BLVD	Street Type
RD	Street Type
W	Direction
TORONTO	Municipality
ON	Province

Table 1: Pre-defined Concept

FROMLEFT	TOLEFT	FROMRIGHT	TORIGHT	STREETNAME	SUFTYPE	SUFDIR	LEFT MUN	RIGHT MUN	LEFT PRV	RIGHT PRV
141	159	144	160	ALMORE	AVE		TORONTO	TORONTO	ON	ON
1	15	2	16	JOEL SWIRSKY	BLVD		TORONTO	TORONTO	ON	ON
0	0	0	0	W. R. ALLEN	RD		TORONTO	TORONTO	ON	ON
19	21	6	22	DE QUINCY	BLVD		TORONTO	TORONTO	ON	ON
26	44	29	45	WESTGATE	BLVD		TORONTO	TORONTO	ON	ON
261	281	252	298	SHEPPARD	AVE	W	TORONTO	TORONTO	ON	ON
2140	2140	2125	2146	AVENUE	RD		TORONTO	TORONTO	ON	ON

Table 2: Detailed Street Data

3.2 ADDRESS TREE DISCOVERING

We define a common tree structure for a detailed address, which includes, from top to bottom: street number, street, municipality and province. Street could include street name, type and direction. In fact, not all address elements have to be included, such as <Direction>, <Unit> and etc.

The discoverer of address tree splits unstructured plain text into a series of segments. Each segment will be recognized as one or more concepts by searching pre-defined concepts, For example, the segment, "Ontario", will be cloned to two concepts: <Ontario: Province> and <Ontario: Street Name>. In addition, it automatically clones numeric segment into two concept: <Street Number> and <Unit>. Unknown segment will be regarded as a noise, and all neighboring noise will be merged into one union. The discoverer thus forms the address concept sequence. For example, the address, “1202 Kingston AVE Ottawa ON”, is splitted into the address segments in Figure 2, and then transferred to the address concept sequence in Figure 3.

Figure 2: Address Segments

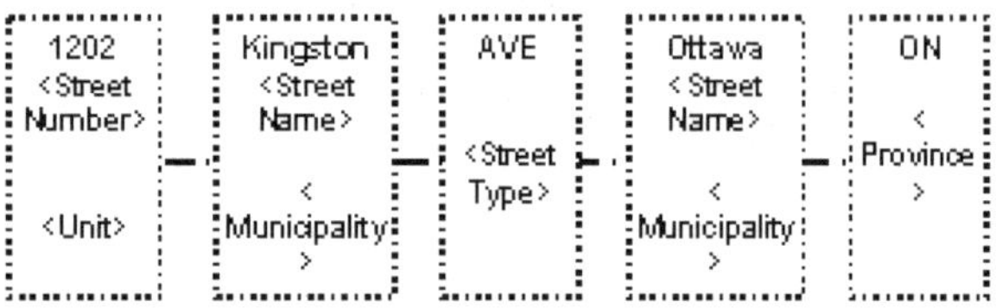

Figure 3: Address Concept Sequence

The discoverer then assembles the possible tree candidates from the address concept sequence. Cloned concepts, from the same segment, cannot be assembled to the same tree candidate. The discoverer could assemble the number of tree candidates based on cloned concepts. If a tree candidate has any node conflicted with the same type of concept, the discoverer will clear the candidate. For example, the address concept sequence in Figure 3 is assembled to eight tree candidates in Figure 4-1 … 4-8, but the conflicting trees, Figure 4-5, 4-6, 4-7 and 4-8 are all deleted. Therefore, Figure 4-1, 4-2, 4-3 and 4-4 will be delivered to the evaluation step.

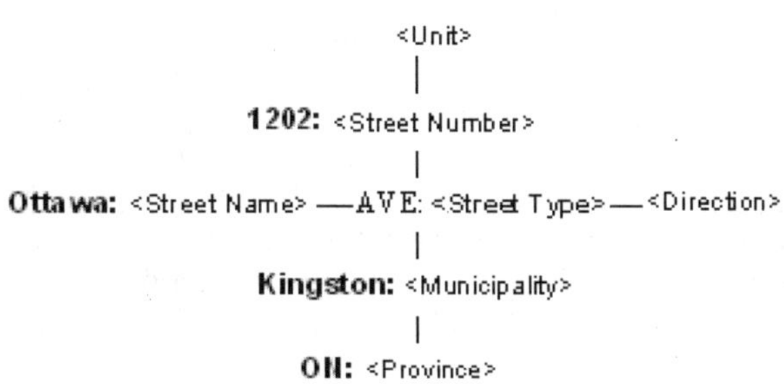

Figure 4-1: Address Tree Candidates

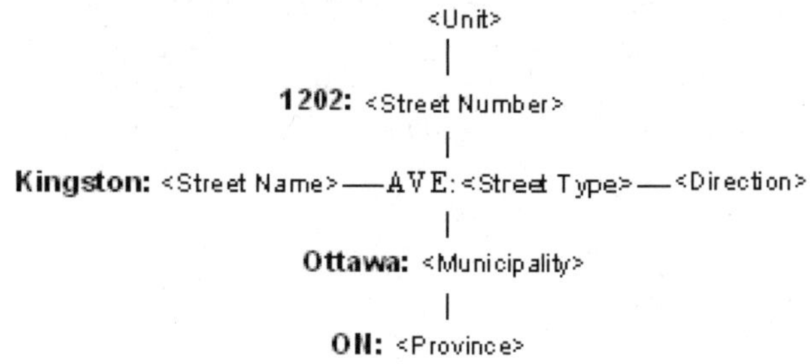

Figure 4-2: Address Tree Candidates

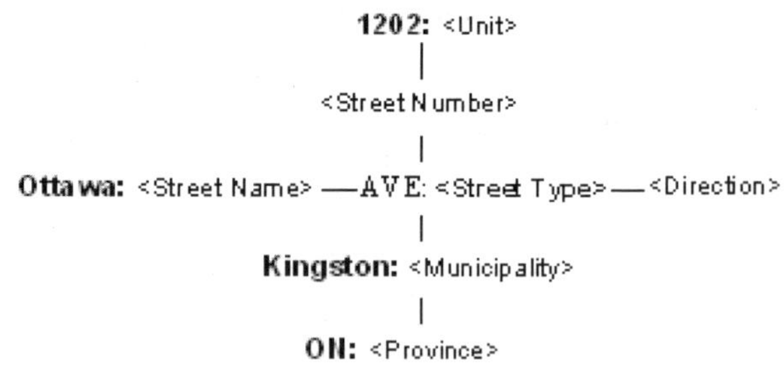

Figure 4-3: Address Tree Candidates

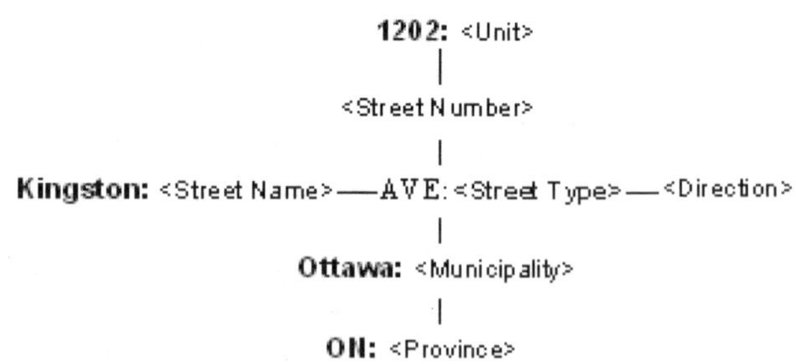

Figure 4-4: Address Tree Candidates

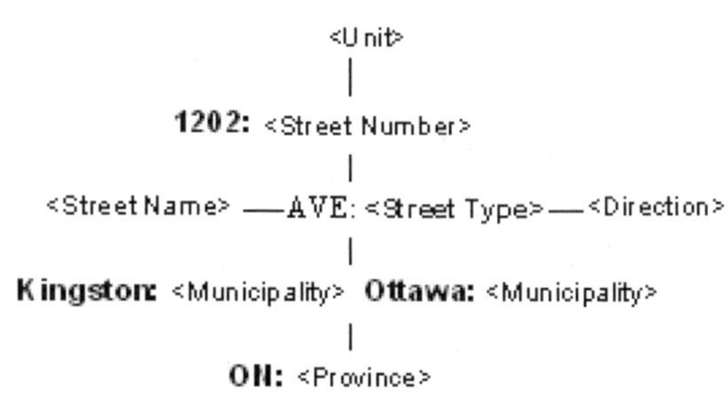

Figure 4-5: Address Tree Candidates

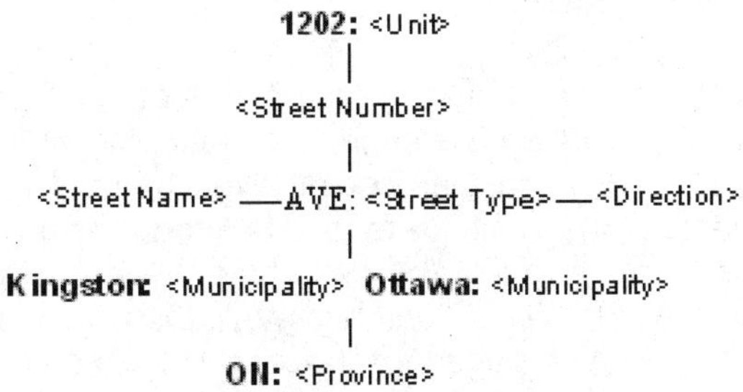

Figure 4-6: Address Tree Candidates

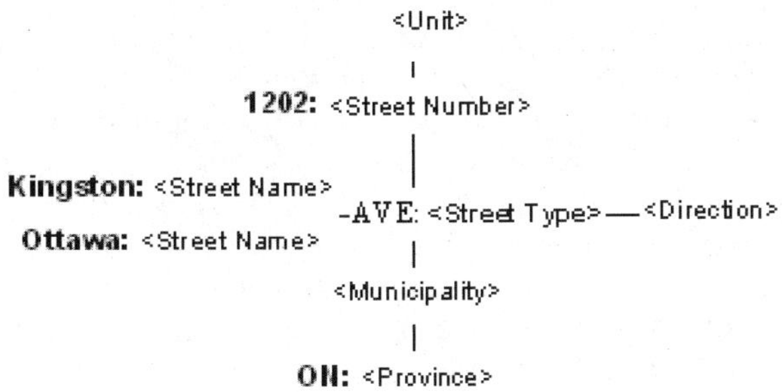

Figure 4-7: Address Tree Candidates

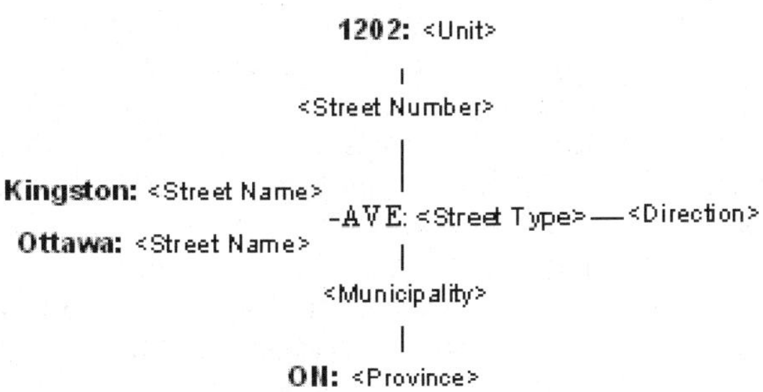

Figure 4-8: Address Tree Candidates

3.3 ADDRESS EVALUATION

Although the candidate has the acceptable address structure, we still have to review their address concept sequence to verify the concept order and noises. We make use of two methods to evaluate an address candidate: Nearest Neighbor and Confident Index.

In the nearest neighbor evaluation, the concept order is examined by neighboring concept type in the address concept sequence based on the recognizable address format. The noise is ignored, and only address concept is examined. <Street Name>, <Street Type> and <Direction> will be all regarded as the type: <Street> at same time, because there are different formats in writing order. For example, "Bloor St W" is in an order of <Street Name>, <Street Type> and <Direction>; "Boul Queen N" is in an order of <Street Type>, <Street Name> and <Direction>; "West Shawnigan Lake RD" is in an order of <Direction>, <Street Name>, <Street Type>. Five nearest neighbor rules proposed for our system are listed blow. The address candidate, whose concept is conflicted with the nearest neighbor rules, will be regarded as an untrusting candidate and will be abandoned.

Rule 1: The neighbors of <Street Number> are two options which is <Street> only, or <Unit> and <Street>.
Rule 2: <Street Name>, <Street Type> and <Direction> are a chain of neighbors which is not interrupted by any other concept.
Rule 3: The neighbors of <Street> are two options which is <Street Number> and <Municipality>, or <Street Number> and <Unit>.
Rule 4: The neighbors of <Municipality> are two options which is <Street> and <Province>, or <Unit> and <Province>.
Rule 5: The nearest neighbor of <Province> is the <Municipality>.

For example, evaluating the address candidate Figure 4-1 which is assembled from the address concept sequence in Figure 5, the neighbor of <1022: Street Number> is the <Kingston: Municipality>, which is a conflict by Rule 1; the neighbors of <Kingston: Municipality> are the <1202: Street Number> and <AVE: Street Type>, which is a conflict by Rule 4; the neighbors of <Ottawa: Street Name> are the <AVE: Street Type> and <ON: Province>, which is a conflict by Rule 3; the nearest neighbor of <ON: Province> is the <Ottawa: Street Name>, which is a conflict by Rule 5.

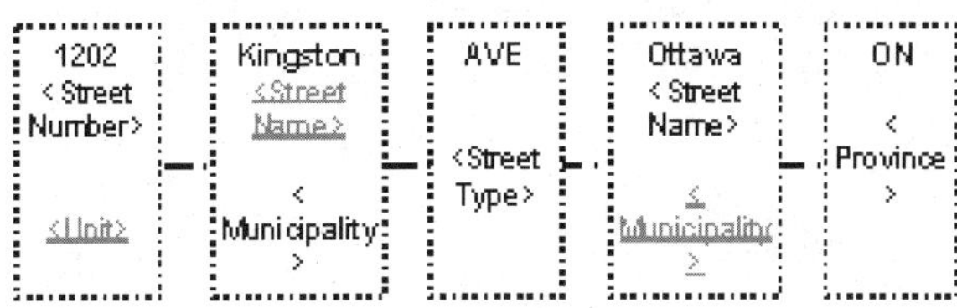

Figure 5: Address Concept Sequence

In the confident index evaluation, we have to estimate the possibility of an address candidate contained the noise, because data is mostly not noise-free, and noise is varying with different sources. The portion of concept segments in the sequence of the candidate shows how much the confidential level of the address is. Let N_{concept} be the number of concept segments and N be the number of concept or noise segment. The Confident Index is defined as

$$C = \frac{\sum N_{\text{concept}}}{\sum N}$$

The Confident Index C can lie from 0 to 1. C = 1 means that there is no noise included. The higher confident index is requested, the less noise is expected.

3.4 ADDRESS VALIDATING

The possible address candidates have to be validated as real address information. Postal code can be used to verify the reality of an address. Using postal code reverse searching from Canada Post [15], we can verify the street and municipality. In order to be coupled with mapping and other GIS application later, we choose location Geo-coding as the address validation. First, we standardize each address element. For example, <Street Type: Avenue> will be transferred to <Street Type: AVE>, and <Direction: West> will be transferred to <Direction: W>. Then we will assign the latitude-longitude coordinate to a real address by searching TIGER-format GIS database. However, we cannot regard an address as a wrong or unreal address if it is failed to Geo-coding.

4 FRAMEWORK OF THE ROUTEINFO MOBILE LBS

The service-oriented RouteInfo Mobile LBS system in Figure 6 is composed of two parts: service provider and client consumers. LBS Web Service provides online services for searching and mapping LBS information. RouteInfo Windows Client is a rich client application for Windows users, and RouteInfo Mobile Web Client is a thin client application for portable device users.

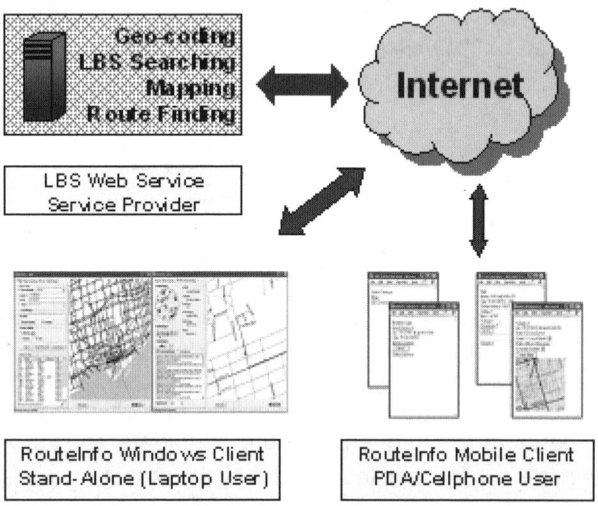

Figure 6: RouteInfo Mobile LBS

4.1 LBS WEB SERVICE

LBS Web Service publishes four Web methods: location Geo-coding, online LBS searching, mapping and route finding. The location Geo-coding Web method assigns or reverses the latitude-longitude coordinate to an address. The online LBS searching Web method is responsible for LBS searching by extracting postal address from Web pages via batches of links and URLs. The mapping Web method provides the street map for the Geo-coded address. The route finding Web method provides an efficient route planning strategy to guide the driver from the start point to the end goal.

The location Geo-coding Web method assigns a latitude-longitude coordinate to the address and reverses a latitude-longitude coordinated location to the nearest address. It is much easier to input a location information that user can use any format, such as 501 Alliance Ave Toronto ON M6N 2J1, or 46.787878, -79.98989 which is provided by the Global Positioning System (GPS) device. Search engines would respond with more specific results by searching the postal code location M6N 2J1 rather than the city of Toronto.

The online LBS searching Web method is responsible for extracting LBS information by address identification from Web pages. First, it intelligently selects the prior online searching engine from search engine YellowPages, 411.ca and etc. Then it automatically generates batches of URLs to download Web pages from prior search engine based on searching keywords and location. It would change prior searching engine if searching engine does not find related results. Next, it uses an ontology-based conceptual information retrieval approach combined with tree structure matching and the nearest neighbor methods to identify possible address in each Web page. Finally, it validates possible address candidates by location Geo-coding.

The mapping Web method provides the street map for the Geo-coded address. It uses digital street map from DMTI Spatial to view detailed location. Mapping feature is very helpful for those who are lost their ways or who are looking for the unfamiliar location.

The route finding [16] Web method provides an efficient route planning strategy to guide the driver from the start point to the end goal.

4.2 ROUTEINFO WINDOWS CLIENT

RouteInfo Windows Client uses a GPS device to position the location of the mobile user, consumes LBS Web Service and wireless Internet access to implement mobile LBS searching. The client can easily specify the searching location by a latitude-longitude coordinate, an address or region, and input keywords to automate the searching LBS information online. It also automatically displays available LBS locations on the street map, provides the route planning and route tracking.

4.3 ROUTEINFO MOBILE WEB CLIENT

RouteInfo Mobile Web Client is a Web server designed for WAP-enabled portable device, such as Cell phones, PDAs, etc. The Web client consumes LBS Web Service to search online LBS information.

5 ON-ROAD TESTS

We use Microsoft Internet Information Services 5 (IIS) as WWW Web Server and run LBS Web Service on Windows Server 2003. We run RouteInfo Windows Client on Windows XP Professional as the LBS client user, and choose Dell Axim X51 as the GPS receiver and BlackBerry 7130e as the wireless Internet connection in Figure 7.

Figure 7: On-Road Test

On-road test in Toronto, Ontario: We started RouteInfo Windows Client in the vehicle. First, we used the GPS receiver to automatically locate our position, Elkhorn Dr North York ON. We inputted gasoline station to search online LBS information. Found more than 20 stations round our location, we selected the nearest station as our destination, 3351 Bayview Ave North York ON. Finally, we planned the nearest route and tracked detailed route to the gasoline station.

On-road test in Vancouver, British Columbia: We started RouteInfo Windows Client in the vehicle after we were lost on our way to the Sheraton hotel in Vancouver. First, we used the GPS receiver to find our current location, Oak St Vancouver BC. Then, we searched the Sheraton hotel online and found the location, 1088 Burrard St Vancouver BC. Finally, we planned an easy route from current position and arrived at the hotel by route tracking.

Based on the on-road tests, drivers can perform online LBS searching easily without complex input procedures. Client application can greatly retrench the wireless Internet accessing by using LBS Web Service, which responds by the LBS list only.

6 ACHIEVEMENTS AND FUTURE WORK

Algorithms have been developed for conceptual information retrieval through postal address extraction. A service-oriented system has being developed to publish LBS Web service that can also be invoked by any other Internet developers. Distributed computing can relieve the burden of handheld devices. In order to discover the LBS information at the updated or new addresses, we could update the address geo-coding validation by the postal code validation. Furthermore, address concept self-learning is also required to enhance the system.

ACKNOWLEDGEMENT

This work is part of Auto21 project – "Integrated Vehicle Navigation and Communication Systems Development", supported by Canadian Network Centers of Excellence on Automobiles of 21st century (NCE Auto21) [17] and by our partner Manifold Data Mining Inc [18].

REFERENCES

1. YellowPages, http://www.yollowpages.ca.
2. Canada411, http://www.411.ca.
3. Yahoo, http://www.yahoo.com.
4. WAP, http://www.wapforum.org.
5. T. Barclay, J. Gray, E. Dtand, S. Ekblad and J. Richter, TerraService.Net: An Introduction to Web Services.
6. TerraServer, http://terraserver.net.
7. D. Box, D. Ehnebuske, G. Kakivaya, A. Layman, N. Mendelsohn, H. Nielsen, S. Thatte, and D. Winer, Simple Object Access Protocol (SOAP) 1.1, available from http://www.w3.org/TR/2000/NOTE-SOAP-20000508/, 2000.
8. E. Christensen, F. Curbera, G. Meredith, and S. Weerawarana, Web Services Description Language (WSDL) 1.2, available from http://www.w3.org/TR/2002/WD-wsdl12-20020709/, 2002.
9. UDDI Version 3.0 Published Specification, available from http://uddi.org/pubs/uddi_v3.htm, July 2002.
10. C. J. Van Rijsbergen, Information Retrieval (2nd edition), Butterworth-Heinemann, Newton, MA, 1979.
11. S. Soderland, Learning Information Extraction Rules for Semi-structured and Free Text, Machine Learning, vol. Numbers 1-3, February 1999.
12. M. Montes-y-Gómez, A. Gelbukh and A. López-López, Text Mining at Detail Level using Conceptual Graphs, Lecture Notes in Computer Science 2393, Spinger Berlin 2002
13. W. Cai and S. Wang, A Navigation Assistance Agent: Online Access to LBS, in SAE transactions vol. 114:77, pages 549-557, 2005
14. DMTI Spatial, http://www.dmtispatial.com
15. Canada Post, http://www.canadapost.ca.
16. W. Cai, S. Wang, Q. Jiang and J. Li, A Practical Implementation of Route Finding, in Proceedings of the 4th International Symposium on Mobile Mapping Technology, March 2004.
17. NCE Auto21, http://www.auto21.ca.
18. Manifold Data Mining Inc, http://www.manifolddatamining.com.

CONTACT

Dengyue Li is pursuing a master's degree in computer science at the Department of Computer Science of the University of Sherbrooke, Quebec, Canada. He has been involved in the Auto 21 – Theme FII research project since 2005. He has been a software architect and developer in Manifold Data Mining Inc, at Toronto, Ontario, Canada since 2002. His interests focus on information retrieval, information extraction, data mining and GIS. His email address is Dengyue.Li@Usherbrooke.ca.

Dr. Shengrui Wang is a full professor at the Department of Computer Science, University of Sherbrooke, Quebec, Canada. His research interests include pattern recognition, data mining, image processing, databases, geographical information systems and navigation systems. He is the co-leader of the project FII-02 (Integrated Vehicle Navigation and Communication Systems Development) in Theme F of NCE AUTU 21. His main research focus in this project is development of new techniques for building online access to location-based services and for updating geospatial information systems for navigation. His email address is Shengrui.Wang@Usherbrooke.ca.

Dr. Zhen Mei is the Principal of Manifold Data Mining Inc. He received the Ph.D. in Mathematics from Philipps-University of Marburg, Germany. He leads a team on modeling consumer behavior for business and marketing applications. He specializes in data fusion of demographic, expenditure and behavior databases. He has extensive experience in data mining, particularly in customer profile, segmentation and targeting for retail, packaged goods, food, financial and telecommunication industries. His email address is zhen@manifolddatamining.com.

Wentao Cai received the master's degree in computer science at the Department of Computer Science of the University of Sherbrooke, Quebec, Canada. He had been involved in the Auto 21 – Theme FII research project for 4 years. From 1999 to 2001, he was a software architect and developer in the navigation assistance industry in China. His interests focus on information retrieval, information extraction, data mining and GIS. His email address is Wentao.Cai@Usherbrooke.ca.

2007-01-1106

Standardised Interface Between Advanced Driver Assistance Systems and Digital Maps for Safer, Smarter and Cleaner Transport

Vincent Blervaque
ERTICO

Klaus Mezger
DaimlerChrysler

Leo Beuk
Siemens VDO

Jan Loewenau
BMW Group Research and Technology

ABSTRACT

Digital maps have large potential to enhance or enable Advanced Driver Assistance Systems (ADAS) by extending driver horizon and therefore to contribute to safer, smarter and cleaner road transport. As a predictive sensor called ADAS Horizon, in-vehicle digital maps are an important source of information providing look-ahead capability for ADAS applications and providing further information for on-board sensors to enhance environment perception.

This paper reports on results from the European Commission project MAPS&ADAS, part of PReVENT Integrated Project, dedicated to the development, test and validation of a standardized interface (ADAS Interface) between ADAS applications and ADAS map data sources for accessing map data regarding vehicle position.

INTRODUCTION

MAPS&ADAS (start February 2004, duration 3 years) is a sub-project of the Integrated Project (IP) Preventive Safety (PReVENT), funded by the European Commission. The MAPS&ADAS subproject seeks to develop and validate both appropriate methods for the collection and maintenance of safety content to be integrated into safety-enhanced in-vehicle digital maps and related changes of the standardized exchange format (GDF) to be used in ADAS and Navigation Applications, as well as a standard interface from navigation systems or general positioning and map systems towards ADAS that make use of map data for track preview purposes.

The MAPS&ADAS Consortium is composed of leading partners: ERTICO (project coordinator), BMW, DaimlerChrysler, Ford, Volvo Tech, Blaupunkt, Navigon, Siemens VDO, Navteq, Tele Atlas, Lower Saxony, Transver and Hanover University [1].

The ADASIS Forum acting as the MAPS&ADAS User Forum is a self-funded industry initiative launched in 2002 and coordinated by ERTICO, aiming at supporting and promoting the development and the implementation of a standardized interface between ADAS applications and digital map content. The ADASIS Forum is composed of 30 Members from vehicle manufacturers, ADAS suppliers, navigation system suppliers and map providers [2].

MAIN SECTION

THE ADAS HORIZON CONCEPT

The development of ADAS and, more generally, of in-vehicle ITS applications which support the driver in driving safely, comfortably and economically, are of major importance to the automotive industry. Typical examples of ADAS Applications are Adaptive Cruise Control (ACC) or Adaptive Front Lighting System (AFS) [3] & [4]. ADAS currently perform their function on the basis of information generated by sensors observing the vehicle's environment. There is a significant potential for the use of a digital map and the vehicle's position to predict the road geometry and to track related attributes ahead of the vehicle. ADAS Applications can benefit from this potential, and new functionality may likely be enabled [5]. Thanks to the ADAS Horizon concept composed of enhanced digital maps (ADAS maps) and an interface to access to map data sources (ADAS Interface), ADAS Applications could use map data for recognizing road infrastructure conditions at the vehicle's current position, and for a preview along the track ahead (see Figure 1).

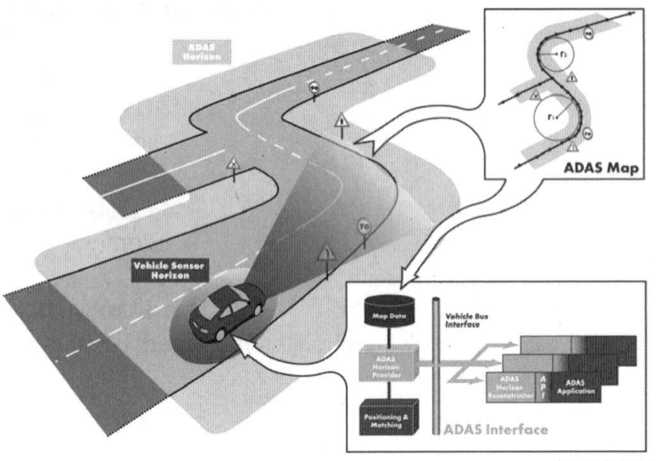

Figure 1 - ADAS Horizon concept developed in MAPS&ADAS

Digital maps can act both as a primary sensor and as a secondary sensor for ADAS applications. When used as a primary sensor, the map supplies the most important information, and may even be the application's sole source of information. When data from the map is used as a secondary sensor, other sensors supply more important information to the system and the map information is merely used to validate other sensor data or make the primary sensor work more efficiently. Tables 1 and 2 give an overview of ADAS applications that would be enabled or enhanced by accessing to map data.

Map-based ADAS (primary sensor)
Speed Limit Assistance: Informs the driver of the legal speed limit and/or warns the driver when he/she exceeds the speed limit.
Curve Warning: Warns the driver when the speed exceeds the safe speed for the curve ahead.
Predictive Powertrain Control: Informs of upcoming slopes, allowing the driver to shift gear and thereby avoid an inefficient speed reduction.
Intersection Assistance: Informs the driver of the characteristics of the intersection (right of way situation, traffic lights) and which lanes to choose in order to cross it safely.
"Hotspot" Warning: Informs the driver about a potentially hazardous location ahead.
Dynamic Pass Prediction: Informs the driver when it is not safe to overtake based on road geometry and driving dynamics

Table 1 – Map-based ADAS applications

Map-supported ADAS (secondary sensor)
Advanced front-lighting system: Directs the front light beam to the upcoming turn of the road and adapts the beam's width and reach based on the car's speed and the lay out of the road.
Adaptive cruise control: Adapts the speed to the cars or road ahead. Normally only works at higher speeds.
Stop & Go: Adapts the cars speed and course to the speed of the cars ahead. Stop & Go typically works at lower speeds.
Lane keeping assistance: Informs the driver when the vehicle risks leaving the current lane unintentionally.
Lane Change Assistance: Informs the driver when it is safe/unsafe to change lanes.
Collision avoidance: Adapts the cars speed and direction of travel in order to avoid a collision.

Table 2 – Map-supported ADAS applications

FUNCTIONAL ARCHITECTURE OF THE ADAS INTERFACE

Map data access for most ADAS-Applications normally use only a small map extract around the current vehicle position. This ADAS-specific map extract is called the ADAS Horizon. Figure 2 shows the overall functional architecture of the ADAS Interface and how the ADAS Horizon Provider (AHP) is the entity responsible for the interactions with and transmissions to the ADAS Applications [6]. The positioning module provides a map-matched position to both the navigation and the AHP. Using this position, the AHP extracts the necessary information from the navigation map and aggregates it into the ADAS Horizon which is sent to the application side

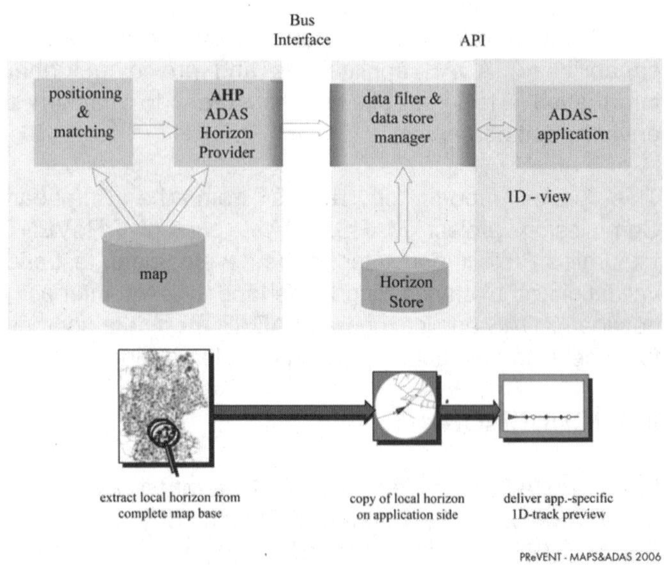

Figure 2 – Functional architecture of the ADAS Interface

The map preview extracted by the AHP is accessible by all map-supported ADAS applications through the vehicle bus interface. Incremental changes transmitted by the AHP are stored on application side by the ADAS Horizon Reconstructor (AHR) to build the 1D-track preview delivered to the ADAS application by means of an API.

FUNCTIONAL STRUCTURE ON APPLICATION SIDE OF THE ADAS INTERFACE

The ADAS Interface specification defines the content and organization of a data stream which is sent by the AHP to all ADAS Applications [6]. In a simple (near future) set-up with only one ADAS Application, this data stream may be dedicated; that means it only contains a configuration for data relevant to that application. In an advanced far future stage, several ADAS Applications may be listeners to the same data stream (e.g., transmitted via CAN bus or FlexRay). In this set-up, every ADAS Application filters out the data it needs from this stream and stores it locally. If the AHP knows the individual needs of all listening ADAS Applications, it can adapt the stream accordingly.

The data stream from AHP to ADAS Applications consists of:

- Horizon map elements: parts of the road network with attributes together with additional content
- Vehicle position information together with driving dynamics
- Metadata

For the internal architecture of the receiving side, passing the data stream to the ADAS-Application, see the figure 3.

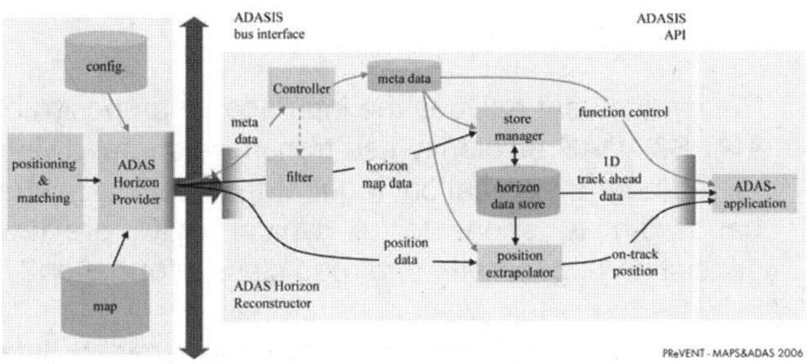

Figure 3: Architecture layout on application side of the ADAS Interface

The ADAS Application will receive the data-stream and handle it in the following way:

- In the multi-application environment the Horizon map elements are first filtered: only the road parts and attributes that are needed by the ADAS Application are passed. For a single application scenario, this filtering is probably not necessary as according the configuration as only required data is transmitted. Then the Horizon data store manager will store the filtered Horizon map elements in the Horizon map data store, assuming there is free storage space available. If there is no space, it will try to remove old elements that are no longer needed because the vehicle has advanced beyond them. For this, a mechanism to manage the available storage space is to be implemented.
- From this data store the relevant part for the Application can be reconstructed - the left hand block of the application is called ADAS Horizon Reconstructor for this reason. The AHR passes the relevant data to the application, generally in the convenient 1D-format for track preview functions, confined to its application-specific contents. The selection of the application contents should be performed to a maximum on the bus controller side (using e.g., message identifiers) and to a minimum by software mechanisms discarding non-relevant message parts in the application itself.
- Besides the basic geometry there is information that is continuous with respect to the along track distance (e.g. curvature) which can be modeled as profile along the track.
- The vehicle position, speed, heading, etc. is stored inside the AHR module of the application as the last known position, together with a time stamp. If the accuracy of the 'last known position' is sufficient for the ADAS Application, it can use it directly for look-ahead calculations. If the application needs more accurate data, information about the delay of the transmission of the position information is provided by using time stamp or age information. Based on the last transmitted position and its time stamp, the position extrapolator may compute an extrapolated vehicle position with higher accuracy at any time, independent from the rate it is transmitted from the AHP. For the extrapolation it is also required that there is some basic prediction of the most probable path in order to provide preview across junctions.

Metadata is handled by the controller. Depending on the type of Metadata, it is passed actively to the respective module to influence functionality, or it is stored in a Metadata store for access by the modules.

ADAS INTERFACE IMPLEMENTATION

Several components and systems have been developed and implemented within MAPS&ADAS to enable test and validation activities [7].

- An ADAS Horizon Provider is a system that generates an ADAS Horizon and distributes it on a bus. Four AHP systems have been developed, two dedicated by Navteq and Navigon and two navigation based systems by Siemens VDO and Blaupunkt.
- An ADAS Client is receiving the ADAS Horizon from the bus. It includes an AHR that reconstructs the received ADAS Horizon, and makes its content available to the application via an API.

- The ADAS Interface has been implemented in a sample ADAS application: Active Cruise Control. The implementation in the BMW ACC is based on an existing ACC, using the reference implementation of the AHR.

- A reference implementation of the AHR was developed for testing ADAS Horizon Providers systems and as the basis for the implementation of the ADAS Horizon in an ADAS client.

- The Test Container is a separate system that can measure the impact of the protocol on the CAN bus for assessment.

In a typical in-vehicle controller environment, storage space is limited, and fixed data entity sizes and limited quantities to avoid buffer overflow on the receiver side are required. The memory available on the receiving side is usually restricted to 1 – 10 kByte.

These tight constraints have to be taken into account when implementing the ADAS Horizon Provider and Reconstructor in a series car and the MAPS&ADAS protocol is designed to do so.

ADAS INTERFACE TESTING

The test container provided by DaimlerChrysler was intended for testing and evaluating the mutual influence of the original data traffic present on a vehicle CAN bus and the ADAS Horizon data stream injected onto this bus [8]. Mutual influence means how the characteristics of latency and transmission error statistics of one data stream are influenced by the presence of the other.

For these tests, the typical background CAN traffic of a vehicle that might use map supported ADAS function must be recorded and later replayed on a CAN bus injecting a corresponding data stream for transmission of horizon data using the ADAS Interface. The reason why this must be done off-line in a 'sand-box' environment is, that it is not possible to introduce extra data on the CAN of a series vehicle under normal operating conditions (i.e. driving on public roads) without incurring danger of vehicle malfunction and safety risks.

Consequently, the tests involving real vehicle CAN data streams were performed by the four OEMs (BMW, DaimlerChrysler, Ford, Volvo). On the other side, the four supplier companies (Blaupunkt, Navigon, Navteq, Siemens VDO) helped by producing the ADAS Interface data streams within the different vehicle CAN environments.

Of course it is interesting for each OEM how an implementation of the ADAS Interface performs on his vehicles and how it does influence the existing CAN traffic. For this reason, the main test task for all the OEMs was to evaluate the OEM specific properties of a possible interface usage on the own cars. Also, the OEMs were entitled to provide the background CAN traffic files for general testing, as they are able to produce relevant real life CAN traffic examples.

There are a number of factors that influence the behavior of the MAPS&ADAS transmission within an existing background CAN traffic. These factors on one hand originate from the background traffic, into which the MAPS&ADAS transmission is to be injected. On the other hand, they are influenced by the properties of the injected transmission itself.

ADAS INTERFACE VALIDATION

As one of the major the objectives of MAPS&ADAS, the definition and the development of an interface between in-vehicle map data sources and assistance systems is of pure technical nature, the technical validation of the interface properties is the most important issue of the validation task [9].

However, there are properties, which obviously do not need to be examined, as they are known to be uncritical from state-of-the-art. On the other hand there are interface properties whose outcome is unsure at the moment of its definition, but which may be very important for success or failure of a market introduction of such an interface.

Consequently, the technical validation performed within MAPS&ADAS is focused on these most critical or most important issues:

- Bandwidth usage: Does the interface as proposed by MAPS&ADAS efficiently use transmission bandwidth for standard application requirements? E. g., what bandwidth is spent for a typical ACC preview, consisting of geometry and road class information?

- Error properties and consistency of transmitted data: Is the interface transmission and interpretation error level sufficiently low? What level of Integrity (error recognition rate) can be reached?

- Timing Issues: How long does it take for the horizon and positioning data to be transmitted? How 'old' is the image presented to the application?

- Position and distance-to-object accuracy: How does the timing influence the knowledge and accuracy of the proper vehicle position and its relation to the event points of the preview?

- Interoperability: Is it assured that different horizon provider software solutions, based on different navigation systems and map databases deliver a horizon data stream fully compatible to the interface specification?

TEST AND VALIDATION RESULTS

Test drives have been performed on different vehicles in different environments and the resulting data streams been mixed off-line while varying several transmission parameters [8]. Of special interest were error and latency behavior of the MAPS&ADAS data stream itself and also its influence on the background traffic which is already present on that bus for normal vehicle control purposes. The whole variety of performed tests, even the most challenging set ups have shown the following validation results:

- Transmission latency time: The transmission latency of the ADAS Horizon CAN frames was incremented by the other (background) traffic. In general the added latency was less than 1 ms.
- Latency of position information: The latency on the CAN bus of the position messages was for all test cases less than 1 ms.
- Influence on position accuracy: In one millisecond the vehicle can travel at most 7 cm (for maximum speed of 250 km/h), which is negligible compared to the accuracy of the vehicle position.

The mixed traffic tests of the different OEMs showed some properties common to all performed tests. As a first observation it can be stated that the background traffic characteristics are invariant with respect to the environment scenario in which the test was performed (urban, rural, highway). However, this fact is not astonishing, since the bus on which the tests were performed is typically the most demanding CAN-bus segment of the vehicle which has to be traversed for reaching some ADAS destination controller. This segment normally transmits vital vehicle function information, which typically happens in a synchronous, periodic manner. Asynchronous, event- driven communication are untypical cases on the investigated CAN segments. Consequently, the total CAN background traffic load as well as the distribution of traffic over the used CAN-Ids have been observed as being practically independent from the driving situation in relation to the urban-, rural- or highway-environment.

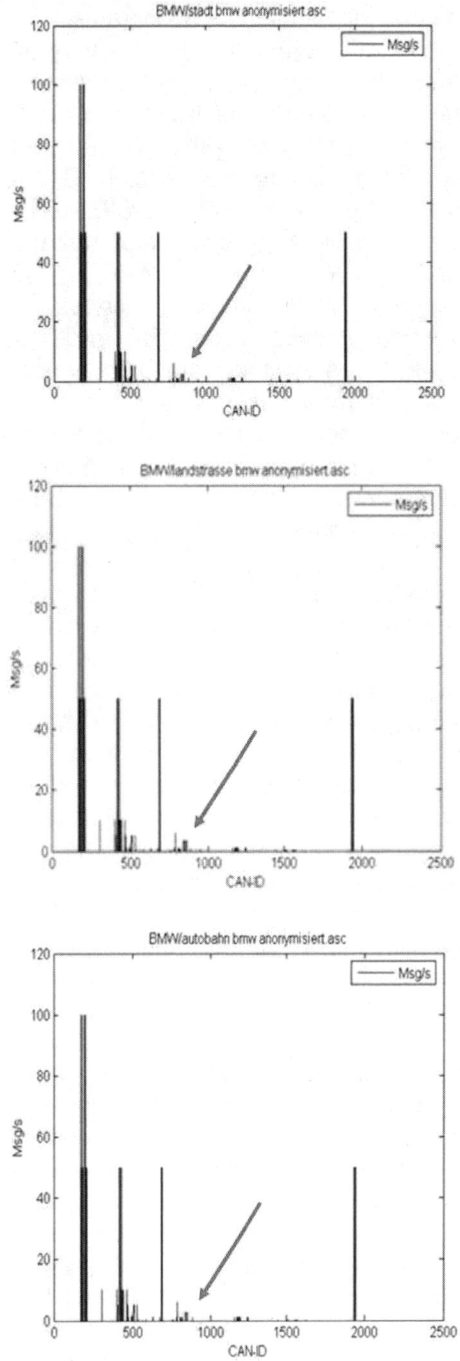

Figure 4 – Three different driving environments (from top urban, rural and highway)

As examples, examine the figures above, stating the CAN-Id usage histograms for the BMW-Tests in the three different driving environments – it can be clearly seen that the spectra for the three situations are practically undistinguishable. Figure 4 shows CAN-Id Usage histograms of Powertrain-CAN Background traffic for BMW 545i test-vehicle as recorded in the three different environments (the red lines are showing the CAN frames of the MAPS&ADAS transmission protocol). The CAN-Id usage histograms for the DC-Tests in the three different driving environments can also be clearly seen that the spectra for the three situations are also undistinguishable.

Of course, the CAN-usage histograms for the background traffic of different vehicles are very different from each other – for comparison, see the figures for DC and BMW and the histogram spectra of the Ford Galaxy and Volvo truck (see Ref. [8]). Observation of independency also applies for the absolute CAN usage percentages. The CAN traffic for the Ford Galaxy shows nearly constant behaviour at low usage rates around 13.3%. While the Volvo truck having an average bandwidth usage of 32.3% shows some variation of background traffic intensity from 28 to 34% with occasional peaks even reaching even 38% (especially experienced on the rural track). These are caused by some apparently asynchronous communication in the 3 highest priority CAN Ids – the other part of the histogram of in total 40 different CAN-Ids is essentially independent from the driving environment (see Ref. [8]).

Different from the background traffic characteristics, the density of the horizon transmission data stream is slightly dependent on the environment, since surrounding road network layout and driving speed influence the amount of transmittable horizon content. On the other hand, also the update rate by which the horizon content has to be exchanged is essentially directed by the vehicle speed. Consequently, this is also reflected in the histograms and total transmission figures of the CAN-traffic as produced by the MAPS&ADAS horizon provider modules.

So for typical CAN networks, the latency time, position information and position accuracy is not affected by the speed of the network.

- Influence on existing CAN traffic: The CAN traffic caused by the ADAS Horizon transmission will delay the existing CAN traffic. The measured delay strongly depends on the mix of priorities of the background traffic. For CAN messages with a higher priority than the ADAS Specific CAN Protocol (ASCP) messages, the delay was not significant, it is typically less then the transmission time of one CAN frame. For CAN frames with a lower priority, the measured delay was at most 0.53 ms. Note that this observation is only valid for one CAN segment. Care must be taken, when the data stream is to pass from one CAN segment to another via a gateway. It is a general challenge to in-vehicle network design to have a proper priority oriented design of the gateway. So with a proper priority scheme and gateway design the impact of the ADAS Horizon traffic on the existing network traffic can be minimized.

- ADAS Horizon Integrity: The ASCP messages generated by the 4 implementations of the AHP were received and analyzed by the reference implementation of the AHR. This analysis includes detection of warnings and errors. The number of warnings and errors decreased during the testing, until at the end the AHP's had minimal errors. So by introducing the error checking in the AHR and resolving the errors in the AHP's the integrity of the transmitted data was significantly improved. At the end of the testing all AHP's had the same interpretation of the data model, the protocol and operation principles.

- Component Interoperability: The output of all AHP's was interpreted and visualized by the visualizer of the reference implementation. With a visual inspection the result was compared to the data that had been intended for transmission on the source side. For all AHP's the shape of the roads transmitted was almost identical to the shape in the background map of the visualizer. Slight differences were found, which were caused by the fact that the AHP map and the background map of the visualizer were from different sources.

At interoperability workshop all AHP's were combined with different AHR implementations, all based on the reference implementation. For all combinations no problems were found that would have impact on the specification. So for all features tested the AHP's were interoperable with the reference implementation of the AHR. Figures 5 and 6 show examples of ADAS Horizon visualization.

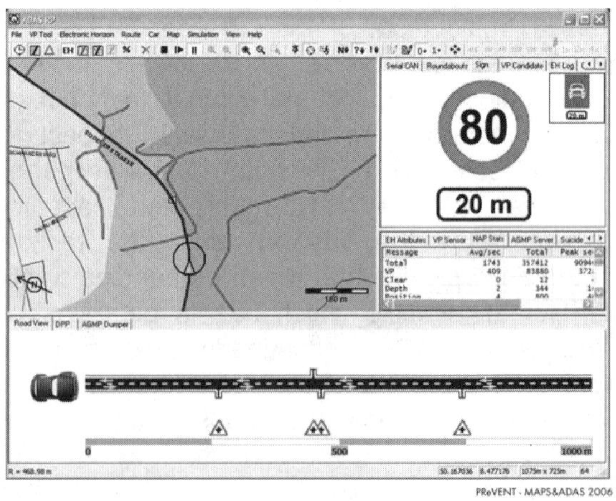

Figure 5: Example of ADAS Horizon visualization from NAVTEQ

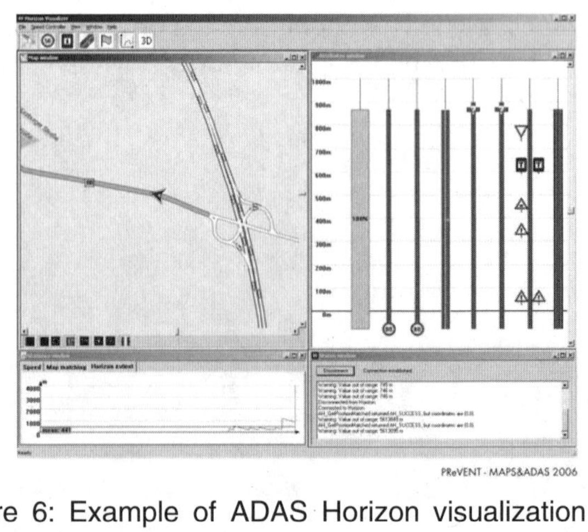

Figure 6: Example of ADAS Horizon visualization from NAVIGON

During validation no major barriers were found for further development and implementation of the ADAS Interface:

- The impact on the CAN bus traffic can be minimized
- The transmission delay on the CAN bus of ADAS Horizon messages is negligible with a proper design
- The interface has been implemented by different project partners and when connecting different modules interoperability could be shown.
- The reference implementation proved to be a valuable tool for testing AHP implementations

Transmission properties of MAPS&ADAS (transport) protocol are comparable to the BMW dedicated protocol implemented in the series map-supported ACC with respect to:

- Bandwidth usage figures
- Latency times
- Influence on background traffic

Further feedback from BMW series development is given by

- Multiplexing mechanisms used in the MAPS&ADAS protocol are not allowed in BMW network design.
- Network design issues from the series point of view.
- BMW has experienced the need for a two-way communication (already running in the series ACC), especially for error recovery.
- Define a 'static' version of the ADAS protocol to support strict CAN network policy, in close cooperation with series development.

Although developed completely independent from MAPS&ADAS, the BMW proprietary interface has similar characteristics and properties. In addition it is necessary to run long-time tests to fulfill the requirements of the series development (especially in light of effort and resources needed for test and analysis of bus systems). Further important issues need to be addressed from BMW point of view with regards to series implementation. These issues are detailed in Ref. [9]. Close cooperation with series departments is required to fulfill series constraints with respect to the share of car components (e.g., CAN bus...), quality policy, test environment and performances issues.

STANDARDIZATION

First approaches of map-supported ADAS entering the market will probably use the vehicle's navigation system as the map data source for this preview. The advantages of using the navigation system are that it already has a stored record of the map data, and it already performs the tasks of vehicle positioning and map matching. These functions can readily be used also for the ADAS preview. However, each navigation system stores map data in a system-specific format, and uses its own version of vehicle positioning and map matching. Moreover, when tailored to single ADAS Applications, the variety of different map interfaces may expand even more – not only due to different data sources, but also due to application-specific differences. By standardizing access to the map data, irrespective of the data provider and physical storage format, and by standardizing the way that position and track ahead information is presented to the applications, ADAS software can focus on performing its main task without having to deal with the complexities of map representation.

The absence of a common standardized interface offering map access to ADAS Applications has already been perceived in the industry community and has led to the foundation of an industry forum where ideas and requirements regarding such an interface have been deeply discussed. The extensive discussions and work already performed by the members of this group, known as ADASIS Forum [2], served as the basis for the MAPS&ADAS subproject part of the PReVENT Integrated Project [1]. Requirements and concept proposals discussed there among automotive OEMs, suppliers and map providers have already reached a certain maturity, stating the importance and close to market position for the MAP&ADAS subproject goals: To develop, test and validate a standardized interface able to serve a spectrum of different ADAS-Applications with map preview data.

NEXT STEPS – NECESSARY EFFORTS BEFORE MARKET INTRODUCTION

The feasibility assessment of an interface between ADAS and map data sources has technical, technological, economical and business aspects. As part of its major objectives MAPS&ADAS has addressed the technical and technological aspects and has achieved a major step by assessing the technical feasibility and the interoperability of such standardized interface. Next step that is out of the scope of MAPS&ADAS deals with the necessary efforts to integrate prototype implementation into series environment to enable market introduction. This phase requires close cooperation with series department to fulfill series development constraints with respect to the share of car components (e.g., CAN bus...), quality policy, test environment, performances... and is not anymore at the pre-competitive stage.

Due to the fact that BMW already has a map supported ACC system on the market, using a proprietary interface, MAPS&ADAS consortium decided to take advantage on this situation to work with the map supported ACC series application. It gave the opportunity to the consortium to explore in advance potential issues and needed cooperation with series department to enable successful series implementation and it contributed to clearly identify next steps towards market introduction.

Further steps are needed for implementation in a series environment considering the objectives of MAPS&ADAS with regards to the ADAS Interface to develop, test and validate an applicable standard. Discussions initiated with BMW series departments and research department of other OEMs and suppliers within MAPS&ADAS and the ADASIS forum showed the necessity to cooperate closely with series development (network and application) to assess the feasibility of the proposed mechanism. This cooperation has been intensified in the ADASIS Forum as an exploitation of the MAPS&ADAS results.

Beside this a major milestone was achieved at the end of 2005, with the MAPS&ADAS activities presenting and demonstrating the first results to the ADASIS Forum Members on 15 December 2005 at Honda in Offenbach. With 35 participants representing 24 Members, this successful event shows the increasing interest of the leading European automotive industry in the ADAS Horizon concept, and the benefit of using digital maps as a predictive sensor to enable or enhance ADAS applications.

In April 2006, BMW Group Research and Technology unveiled a new map-based ADAS application called Dynamic Pass Prediction [10]. Based on the driving dynamics and navigation map data, the application indicates road sections that are not safe for overtaking. .

Figure 7: BMW map-based Dynamic Pass Prediction application

CONCLUSIONS

The very encouraging results achieved within MAPS&ADAS assess the technical feasibility of a standardized interface between ADAS applications and digital map data and therefore confirm the potential of digital map for safer, smarter and cleaner road transport by enhancing or enabling innovative ADAS applications. As a predictive sensor called ADAS Horizon, in-vehicle digital maps are an important and valuable source of information providing look-ahead capability for ADAS applications and providing further information for on-board sensors to enhance environment perception.

These expected benefits of the ADAS Horizon concept are reflected by the increasing interest and support from the automotive industry. Since 2002 major industry stakeholders have been joining the ADASIS Forum to promote and support implementation and near future market introduction by means of standardization. The main direct impact of a standardized interface will be on the economic side – this impact may be roughly estimated in terms of economy on development efforts.

ACKNOWLEDGEMENTS

The authors kindly thank the European Commission and the ADASIS Forum Members for supporting MAPS&ADAS project activities.

REFERENCES

[1] PReVENT IP: http://www.prevent-ip.org

MAPS&ADAS: http://www.prevent-ip.org/maps_adas

[2] ADASIS Forum: http://www.ertico.com/adasis

[3] J.P. Loewenau, J. H. Bernasch, J. Rieker, P.J. Ph. Venhovens, J. Huber, Huhn and F.M. Reich, Adaptive Light Control - A New Light Concept Controlled by Vehicle Dynamics and Navigation, SAE 980007, Detroit, USA 1998

[4] J.P. Loewenau, P.J. Ph. Venhovens and J. H. Bernasch, Adaptive Light Control Controlled by Vehicle Dynamics and Navigation, 1998 SAE Transactions, Detroit, USA 1999

[5] P.J. Ph. Venhovens, J. H. Bernasch, J.P. Loewenau, H.G. Rieker, M. Schraut, The Application of Advanced Vehicle Navigation in BMW Driver Assistance Systems, SAE 1999-01-0490, Detroit, USA 1999

[6] K. Mezger (Editor) D12.32 Interface Requirements, Functional Architecture and Data Model, MAPS&ADAS project, Deliverable D12.32 revised version, Brussels, 2005

[7] L. Beuk (Editor) D12.72.1 Implementation Report, MAPS&ADAS project, Deliverable D12.72.1, Brussels, 2005

[8] J. Loewenau (Editor) D12.81 Interface Test Results, MAPS&ADAS project, Deliverable D12.81, Brussels, 2006

[9] J. Loewenau (Editor) D12.92.1 Interface Validation Results, MAPS&ADAS project, Deliverable D12.92.1, Brussels, 2006

[10] J.P. Löwenau, K. Gresser, D. Wisselmann, W. Richter, S. Durekovic, D. Rabel, Dynamic Pass Prediction – A New Driver Assistance System for Superior and Safe Overtaking, 10th International Forum on Advanced Microsystems for Automotive Applications (AMAA), April 2006, Berlin, Germany

CONTACT

Graduated in Computer Engineering at the University of Compiegne (France) in 1990, Vincent Blervaque has an experience of 5 years in software development and 11 years in project management, especially in the field of R&D and implementation of new technologies (visual simulation, ITS). Since 1999, he has been involved in the management and the co-ordination of EC projects focused on ITS (railways, public transport and road transport applications) and joined ERTICO in 2001 as Project and Development Manager. He is the co-ordinator of the ADASIS Forum and the MAPS&ADAS subproject (Safety-enhanced digital maps and standard interface to ADAS) within PReVENT Integrated Project (EC DG INFSO).He is also in charge of SpeedAlert activities (in-vehicle speed limit information and warning system).

v.blervaque@mail.ertico.com

DEFINITIONS, ACRONYMS, ABBREVIATIONS

ADAS: Advanced Driver Assistance Systems

AHP: ADAS Horizon Provider

AHR: ADAS Horizon Reconstructor

ASCP: ADAS Specific CAN Protocol

2007-01-1104

Object Detection and Tracking using an Optical Time-of-Flight Range Camera Module for Vehicle Safety and Driver Assist Applications

Steve Hsu and Abbas Rafii
Canesta, Inc.

David Hirvonen
Elucideye, Inc.

ABSTRACT

This paper describes a high frame rate focal-plane-array range camera module, based on optical time-of-flight measurement, along with machine vision algorithms that take advantage of the real-time 3D information. The utility of such technology is demonstrated in an advanced backup safety system. This system detects obstacles lying on the ground as well as tracks moving objects. Using dual detection criteria, the system outperforms existing backup proximity sensors. Based on 3D imagery collected from a rear-viewing camera configuration, we evaluate the detection and tracking accuracy for varying object sizes and ranges. Operational experience shows that our time-of-flight range camera can be a cost-effective and reliable component of intelligent automotive safety and driver assist systems.

INTRODUCTION

Growing government legislation, increasing liability concerns, and the inevitable consumer desire for improved safety and convenience make the introduction of intelligent safety and driver assistance features a high priority for automakers. Systems that detect lane departure or predict impending contact with people or objects–to the side, rear, or front of the vehicle–can help avoid accidents by warning drivers or initiating automatic braking/steering countermeasures. In case of an unavoidable collision, safety systems can reduce occupant injury by adjusting seat belts, seats, windows, and airbags, or mitigate pedestrian injury by deploying an exterior airbag or hood release. A driver monitor can warn of drowsy or DUI conditions, while an unattended pet/child detector may forestall hyperthermia in a parked vehicle or unintended vehicle motion. Adaptive cruise control and automatic parking can reduce the driver workload, and gestural human interfaces allow the driver to operate accessories while keeping eyes on the road and hands near the wheel.

Minivans, pickups, and SUVs represent a growing fraction of cars on the American road. Such vehicles create a large blind spot behind the vehicle, as much as 21m behind the rear end [5]. Consequently, a rapid increase in the rate of injuries and deaths due to backover accidents has been documented. Even some sedans are poor, the worst having a 17m blind spot.

Affordable rear-view cameras and proximity sensors are now widely available as OEM or aftermarket equipment. Such devices can assist the driver in parking as well as avoiding pedestrian contact, but the performance of existing systems leaves much to be desired. The effective range of proximity sensors is 2m at best [3], because the simple detection technology would produce too many nuisance alarms if extended out further. However, for a high degree of safety at a backup speed of 10 km/h, at least 5m detection range is required [5].

All these examples of safety and driver assistance features require sensing and analyzing the dynamic 3D environment inside or outside the car. Information from imaging sensors may help to achieve a high level of sensitivity to the phenomena of interest without false alarms. Machine vision applications based on conventional 2D imaging sensors, however, suffer from fundamental limitations. In order to extract objects from the background and determine their 3D position/velocity, such systems rely on cues from the appearance of the road and targets. The appearance of objects in a 2D image varies greatly, depending on illumination conditions, shading, surface materials, and object orientation. These variations in the image complicate the task of software that must interpret the scene. On the other hand, the 3D shape of objects is invariant to those confounding effects. But stereo-vision based 3D recovery is computationally complex, and fails on unpatterned surfaces. The range error of such devices grows rapidly with distance. Therefore, measurement of scene shape using direct range sensing modalities can vastly simplify or improve the performance of vision-based applications.

In particular, we have developed an advanced focal-plane-array range camera module using time-of-flight distance measurement, suitable for automotive applications. This paper begins by detailing the principles of operation of our range camera and the relative merits of this technology over other types of sensors. We present the machine vision algorithms employed by an advanced backup safety system using dual detection criteria, sensing object surfaces different from ground level as well as tracking moving objects. The performance of this system has been characterized in a test configuration similar to a vehicular installation. We report the detection rate and track accuracy for objects of varying sizes and locations.

RANGE SENSOR TECHNOLOGY

Our prototype backup safety system pairs a commercial off-the-shelf RGB camera with our time-of-flight range camera. The range camera module contains a light source constructed from a bank of infrared laser diodes, a lens system for the detector chip, a detector chip with 176×132 phase-sensitive pixels fabricated on standard CMOS process, and an embedded CPU for control and sensor data formatting. The video stream from the RGB camera and the range camera data stream are input to a conventional PC, where software can perform range estimation and then backup hazard detection.

Our experimental camera has the specifications shown in Table 1. The total IR power is relatively high because it illuminates an area much wider than necessary to be effective for backup safety. In a production version, of course, the fields of view of the cameras and light source, as well as the resolutions of the cameras and light source power, would be tailored to the desired detection area suggested in Figure 2.

Range Camera	
Imager size (HxV)	8.8mm x 6.6mm (2/3 inch optical format)
Total picture elements	176 x 132
Effective field of view	110° x 97°
Modulation frequencies	48.88 and 36.66 MHz
IR light source	Laser array providing up to 25W (peak) of eye-safe (Class 1) IR light at 808nm
Measurement range	20cm–10m
Frame rate	Up to 30 fps for full image size
Ambient light conditions	0–100 Klux, indoors and outdoors
RGB Camera	
Imager size (HxV)	5.0mm x 3.8mm (1/3 inch optical format)
Total picture elements	742 x 554
Effective field of view	114° x 100°
Frame rate	30 fps
Dynamic range	102 dB

Table 1. Specifications for prototype backup safety sensor.

PRINCIPLES OF OPERATION

An optical time-of-flight range measurement device determines distance by measuring the time delay ΔT between emission and detection of light that travels at speed *c* from the light source, reflects off a surface in the scene, and returns to the detector. In particular, the light source in our system [4] is switched on and off with 50% duty cycle at a modulation frequency *f* on the order of 40 MHz or higher. The camera sensor is designed to efficiently operate at high modulation frequencies to produce more accurate range measurements. The entire scene is flood-lit with the same modulated light, but each pixel in the detector array receives a signal with a different delay corresponding to the varying depths of points in the field of view.

Each pixel in the detector array produces a voltage related to its time delay. Within every pixel is a pair of charge accumulating gates, called A and B, which are alternately enabled in-phase and out-of-phase with the light source. We use an implementation of a method that is called quantum efficiency modulation (QEM). The gates are reset to 0 at the start of each frame and integrate over the frame exposure time S, typically 1 to 24ms. As the time delay varies, the amount of integrated charge in gates A and B will vary (Figure 1).

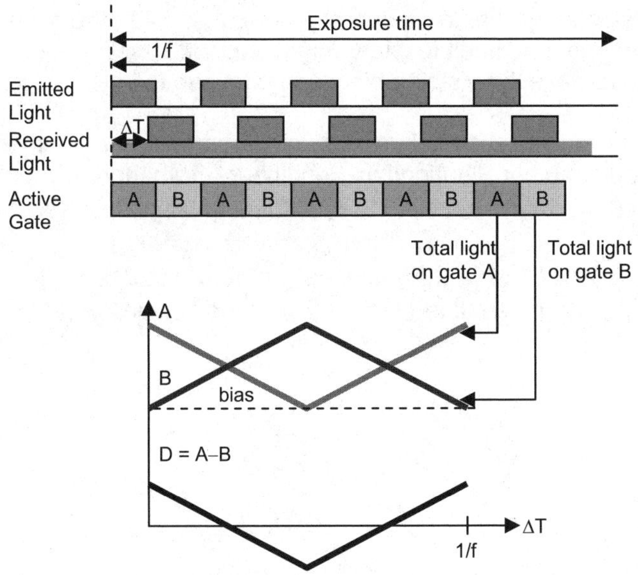

Figure 1. Principle of operation of the range detector pixel. As the time delay ΔT varies, so does the output differential signal D.

Even in the absence of modulated light, the charge in A and B would be biased from 0 due to dark current and ambient scene illumination. The offset is independent of the received phase, and the two pixels are enabled for the same amount of time, so the biases could be canceled by measuring only the differential signal D=A–B. The latter signal is digitized by an ADC and read by the embedded CPU.

While ambient illumination does not theoretically affect the D signal, it could potentially cause the gates A and B to saturate. To prevent this effect, the pixel periodically performs a Common Mode Reset (CMR) that discharges the A and B gates, leaving the differential signal unchanged. Typically, CMRs are performed thousands of times per second. Gate saturation could also potentially occur if the signal caused by modulated light is strong. To prevent that effect, the pixel performs a dump process that prevents the saturation of the differential signal. These measures to avoid saturation are among the key innovations in our pixel design that give our range camera a high dynamic range and resilience to high ambient illumination conditions, as required by automotive applications.

The ΔT value cannot be recovered from one measurement of D alone, since delays ΔT and 1/f-ΔT both yield the same D, and also D is scaled by received light power. Accordingly, measurements of D are repeated with four different detector clock phases, 0°, 90°, 180°, and 270°, from which ΔT can be deduced from the relative magnitudes of the D values. The four measurements can be acquired at the same pixel in four adjacent frames, or at the same frame in four adjacent pixels. The former case assumes the scene depth varies slowly over time, while the latter case assumes the scene depth varies slowly over space.

When the scene contains distances exceeding the unambiguous range c/2f, delays exceeding the signal period 1/f are aliased, i.e. indistinguishable from delays differing by a multiple of 1/f. Accordingly, another set of D measurements is taken at a second frequency f'. Time delay can then be uniquely determined since, in general, only one value of ΔT can be consistent with both sets of D measurements. This multi-frequency dealiasing approach enables the range camera to sense long distances despite high modulation frequencies, which are desirable from the standpoint of reducing noise.

In an ideal system with co-located point light source and sensor, with non-distorting optics of known focal length, and perfect square wave signals, it would be possible to convert ΔT directly to radial distance r and then to X,Y,Z coordinates in space by simple geometry. In practice, however, r=cΔT /2 does not hold exactly, due to pixel-to-pixel variations in gate timing, imperfect square wave signals, and use of a distributed light source. Moreover, a real lens distorts the field of view. Accordingly, a per-pixel calibration function may be used to map from measured ΔT value to Z. This calibration function may be determined empirically or analytically. In addition, a calibration function can be used to map from each pixel (row,column) to a 3D direction ray (X/Z,Y/Z,1). That function is obtained by imaging a grid pattern of known dimensions. Scaling that vector by the measured Z yields the desired 3D coordinates. Therefore, the final output of the range camera module is a collection of data points with accurate X,Y,Z position information in an absolute sense (e.g. real-world centimeters w.r.t. the camera), not just relative.

Automotive applications may jointly exploit the range camera data with the RGB camera image, to improve the performance of machine vision algorithms and to better visualize the 3D scene. For this purpose, it is useful to relate the direction rays of the pixels in the RGB camera to the 3D coordinate system of the depth camera. This is accomplished by calibrating the RGB camera lens and the relative 3D pose between the two cameras.

ALTERNATIVE 3D TECHNOLOGIES

Microwave radar, ultrasonic, and scanning lidar sensors are proposed for some automotive applications. Practical radar and ultrasonic sensors have crude angular resolution. 1D scanning lidar provides no resolution transverse to the scan direction; hence, the vehicle must move in order to form a 2D range image necessary for object detection and tracking. 2D scanning lidar provides good angular resolution, but the temporal sampling rate at any given scene point is usually low.

Backup sensors available on the market are based on ultrasonic or microwave sensing. Ultrasonic models tend to be adversely affected by atmospheric conditions. Such sensors must be mounted in several points around the back of the car, creating wiring, cost and maintenance issues. Microwave models tend to be less sensitive in detecting objects and require relative motion between the object and vehicle [1]. Above all, none of the proximity sensors are effective beyond a 2m range, which is sufficient for parking aids but not for pedestrian safety [3].

Focal-plane-array range cameras have been developed by several organizations, with various spatial resolution and frame rate capabilities. However, range cameras using short pulse modulation require high peak power lasers, with issues of slow rise time, eye safety, and high cost. Detector pixel designs utilizing charge transfer to alternately fill A and B accumulators need to be fabricated using special semiconductor processes that remain low volume and relatively expensive. Ambient light suppression by background subtraction approaches increases response time, adds noise, and requires large charge accumulators. Waveform sampling techniques for phase detection require a high complexity pixel design. In contrast, our range camera design combines 50% duty cycle laser or LED light sources, QEM, CMR, and multi-frequency and multi-phase modulation frequencies to optimize system performance and cost for automotive applications.

EXTERIOR HAZARD DETECTION AND TRACKING

BACKUP SAFETY SYSTEM REQUIREMENTS

A backup sensor system should detect stationary as well as moving objects (including pedestrians), whether the vehicle is stationary or moving. The alerting strategy is shown in Figure 2. Objects on the roadway should be detected in the path of the reversing vehicle, but the ground itself should not be detected as a false alarm. Objects that are outside the immediate vehicle path but are moving towards the path should be detected, but not objects moving away from danger. The system should measure the speed and distance of all objects in order to emit audible and visual alerts that are appropriate to the criticality level of the hazard. Nuisance detections must be minimized so that drivers will not turn off the system or ignore its warnings.

The detection zone should be large enough to prevent common accident scenarios. Analysis of sensor, driver, and braking latencies predicts that when a vehicle is reversing at 10 km/h, hazards must be detected no later than 5m away in order to consistently stop in time [5]. The vehicle path width should be 3m, as wide as a parking stall.

Visual alerts should be superimposed on a full-color live video display of the scene behind the vehicle, so that the driver can verify the existence and nature of any detected obstacle vs. a false alarm. Audible alerts without a rear-view display could be dangerously misleading, because when the scene contains both an object (e.g. another car) visible to the driver's unassisted vision as well as a hidden object (e.g. a child), the driver hearing the audible alert might suppose that the only obstacle is the visible object and continue to back up [3].

The sensor should be functional regardless of weather and ambient illumination conditions, from darkness of night to bright sunshine to oncoming headlights.

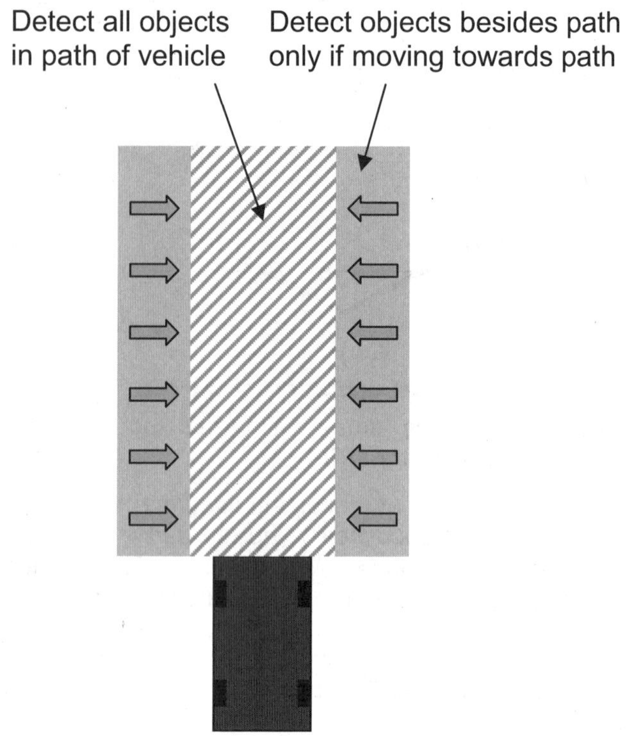

Figure 2. Alerting strategy for objects within vs. outside the path of the reversing vehicle.

ADVANCED BACKUP SENSING WITH DUAL DETECTION CRITERIA

In order to achieve a high rate of hazard detection with few false alarms, our backup system combines two detection criteria: depth and motion. The depth criterion measures the height and slope of scene points with respect to the ground. The motion criterion measures the speed of a moving point. For objects in the immediate path of the reversing vehicle, the driver is alerted whenever the depth criterion is satisfied. However, to minimize false alarms, the driver should be alerted about objects outside the immediate path of the vehicle only if both the depth and motion criteria are satisfied and the object is moving towards a dangerous situation.

OFF-GROUND OBJECT DETECTION ALGORITHM

Sensing and modeling depth information are the keys to reliably discriminating between objects and the ground itself. The system estimates a model for the road surface and then analyzes deviations from that model as potential hazards. In this manner, the system is acutely sensitive to objects low to the ground, even if the roadway slants or the vehicle attitude changes due to loading or bumps on the ground. In contrast, standard radar or ultrasound backup sensors cannot be tuned to detect low objects without constantly being triggered by signal returns from the ground itself.

To fit a planar road surface model, the robust estimation method RANSAC [2] is applied to the collection of XYZ data points from the range sensor. RANSAC will find the plane that fits most of the data, which should be the ground plane as long as the fraction of non-ground data points is small. To increase reliability, the collection of data points used for estimation is restricted to the subset of points lying near the prior ground plane estimate and inside a region of interest mask. The prior estimate is based on the known geometry of the camera mounted on the vehicle. Once the ground plane has been modeled, data points whose height above ground exceeds a threshold are identified.

In the next step, a local surface normal is estimated from the depth image, and data points with normals significantly different from vertical are also detected. This improves the sensitivity of the system to small objects so low to the ground that they would be missed by height thresholding alone.

Combining the height and slope tests yields a collection of XYZ data points deemed to arise from surfaces other than the roadway itself. The coordinates are projected into a top-down view coordinate system (x,z) where z is the rearward distance along the ground from the back of the vehicle and x is the distance in the perpendicular direction (Figure 5). The data points are accumulated into a histogram in the (x,z) space, weighted by radial distance from the camera so that bin counts will be proportional to fronto-parallel surface area. Peaks in the ground plane projection histogram are found using the mean shift method to define distinct object hypotheses. Each such peak consists of the set of histogram bins that share the same local maxima in the histogram. All range image pixels contributing to the same histogram peak are given an identical unique label, thereby segmenting the range image into non-overlapping object regions. Finally, regions above a threshold size are candidate hazards.

MOVING OBJECT TRACKING ALGORITHM

An outdoor scene is a juxtaposition of multiple off-ground objects, including stationary, moving erratically (e.g. trees in the wind), and moving consistently. Any automotive safety system that predicts collisions in a complex environment needs to isolate and track objects in order to confidently discern potential hazards. To this end, the system estimates a scene model comprised of the host vehicle state as well as the state of all substantial objects within the sensor field of view. Whereas the former is typically available via internal kinematic sensor readouts, the latter should be estimated from range camera measurements. In this application we define a general purpose object state model that consists of: 3D object size (3D bounding region), 3D position, and the 2D velocity and acceleration (both constrained to a planar road model). When used in conjunction with the host vehicle state, this 10D state vector provides a means of predicting collisions with obstacles in the scene.

Estimation of the complete 10D object state vectors proceeds in two steps: (1) at each frame, the segmented range map of off-ground objects is parsed into a set of distinct but unlabeled observation vectors consisting of 3D bounding region and position; and (2) a Kalman Filter tracking framework is applied to the sequence of observation vectors to provide a least squares recursive estimate of each object's complete state vector, including the second order motion model components.

The observation vectors are estimated from the previously segmented range image. A set of XYZ points is extracted from the sensor data for each unique object region, and object boundaries are delimited from the upper and lower deciles of the 1D distribution along each coordinate axis. The object boundaries provide the position and size components of the observation vector. In practice, this approach is an improvement to a simple minimum bounding region, and it provides a degree of tolerance to noise and aliasing effects in the range image.

The Kalman Filter is an efficient framework for providing recursive least squares state estimates in linear dynamical systems. Implementation of this framework requires both the specification of a motion model to govern the kinematics of the tracked objects, and a means of associating observations with existing tracks. For the former, we employ a second order motion model [7] to deal with the relatively unconstrained and sometimes erratic motion of vehicles, pedestrians, pets, etc. For the latter, we employ a greedy and mutually exclusive matching scheme, where the best matching observation-to-track assignment is determined iteratively until all tracks are paired with observations. If no suitable observation is found for a given track, the track is propagated by the Kalman Filter state prediction until such a time that it receives a observation update, or it is terminated because it has relied on prediction for too long. The match score is determined by the detection measurement residual (i.e., the difference between the predicted and observed data vector) weighted by the Kalman Filter's measurement prediction covariance. Potential matches are limited by a validation gate which places a threshold on this match score.

Finally, in the backup sensing application, hazard interpretation logic will raise alarms when a tracked object outside the immediate path of the vehicle is moving in the direction of a collision.

USER INTERFACE

A prototype user interface has been developed (Figure 3). Objects detected as potential obstacles are outlined on the live RGB video scene, with color based on distance. Object distances are also superimposed. Audible alarms are emitted when obstacles are present, with different sounds depending on the distance of the closest object.

Figure 3. Prototype user interface for backup safety system.

EVALUATION

DATA COLLECTION METHOD

Tests have been conducted to characterize the static and dynamic system performance. The static test maps out regions of detectability for objects of various sizes. The dynamic test verifies the detection and tracking of a subject at different locations.

The camera system is tripod mounted, angled down 40 degrees, at 1.6m above ground, as if it were located at the top rear of a minivan. The defined test area is a 6m wide × 8m long outdoor area, lit by skylight but shaded from direct sunlight (Figure 4). The floor tiles define a 2D grid of static test points spaced 60cm apart, starting from directly below the camera (Figure 5). Dynamic test object paths cross the test area laterally at 1.2, 2.4, and 3.7m rearward distances from the camera and longitudinally at 1.2m side distance.

The static test objects are 20cm diameter white painted cardboard cylinders of heights 30 and 60cm, the latter representing the shoulder height of a 2-year-old child [6]. As the leading edge of a cylinder is successively placed at each grid point in the right half of the test area, the presence of a steady object detection by the system, as well as the reported rearward distance, are noted.

The dynamic test subject is a 1.7m tall adult. As the person walks at a normal pace, about 1.3m/s, the depth and RGB sensor data streams are recorded. Subsequently, the recorded data stream is processed by the tracking algorithm and then the presence of a track and reported velocity are noted at each frame. The RGB stream is also reviewed by the experimenter to estimate the ground truth subject location at each frame and nominal average speed.

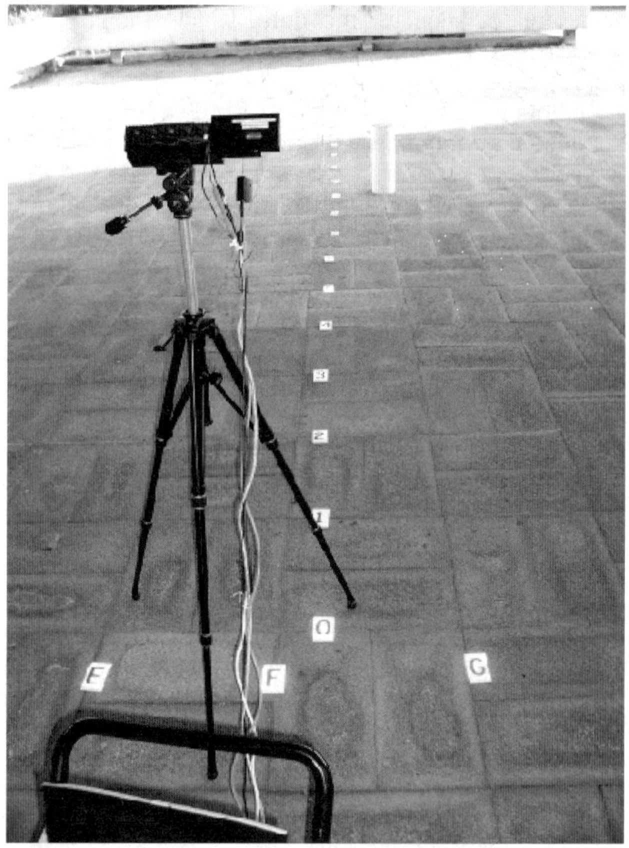

Figure 4. Range camera at outdoor test site.

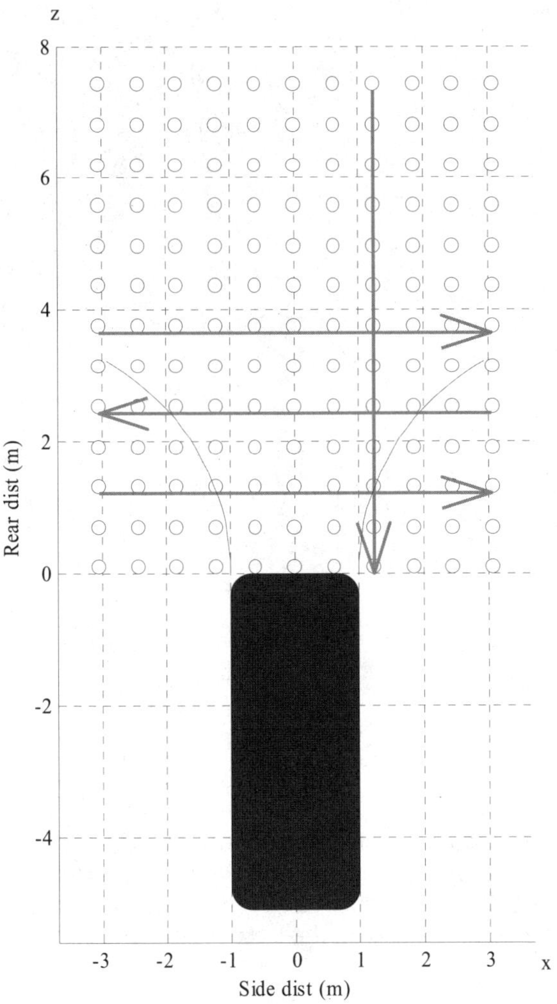

Figure 5. Test grid on (x,z) coordinate system. Static test objects are located at the circles, while the dynamic test object moves along the arrows. The machine vision algorithms detect objects without regard to the nominal vehicle footprint and trajectory, depicted solely for purposes of illustration.

OBJECT DETECTION TEST RESULTS

The floor regions in which the two test objects can be detected using depth criteria alone are shown in Figure 6 and Figure 7. Numbers in each square indicate the error in cm of the reported rearward distance. Only grid points on the right half are sampled, but performance on both halves should be identical by symmetry of the system.

The 30cm tall cylinder can be detected up to 3.7m rearward distance from the camera. Few commercial backup sensors can detect such small objects at any distance, because they must be adjusted to avoid false alarms from the ground itself. The range camera can readily discriminate between the ground and objects lying above it. The 60cm tall cylinder can be detected up to 5.5m rearward distance.

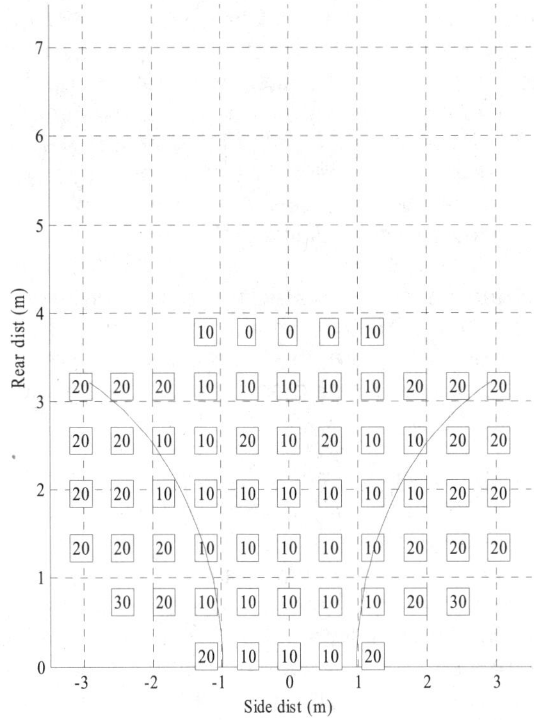

Figure 6. Detectability region for 30cm object. Numbers in each square indicate the error in cm of the reported rearward distance.

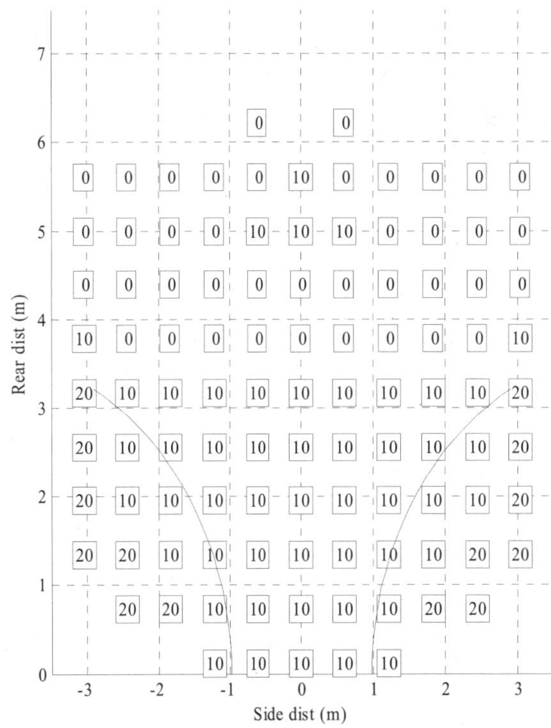

Figure 7. Detectability region for 60cm object. Numbers in each square indicate the error in cm of the reported rearward distance.

Notably, the sensor is not blind to objects at zero rearward distance, which is critical because pedestrians or objects could be located right up the rear bumper. The objects are detected without failure up to 1.2m away from the centerline of the test area. Although some objects beyond 1.2m side distance are sometimes missed, they are not in the path of the straight reversing vehicle and hence hazard interpretation logic would suppress alerts for those objects, anyway, unless they are moving towards the vehicle path.

The reported distances are accurate compared to true distances, typically only 10cm in error and at worst only 30cm in error. Therefore, the backup safety system can present appropriate warning sounds and displays to the driver.

DYNAMIC TEST RESULTS

The trajectory points at which the moving subject can be detected and tracked using both depth and motion criteria are shown in Figure 8. The subject is reliably tracked 100% of the time when it lies within the test area. Numbers in each square indicate the error in cm/s of the estimated speed. The reported speeds are always within –60%/+80% of the nominal average speed; therefore, the sign of the reported speed is never wrong, enabling successful hazard interpretation using the direction of motion. The apparent variance of reported speed is plausible since human motion is nonuniform and the true speed is not precisely known.

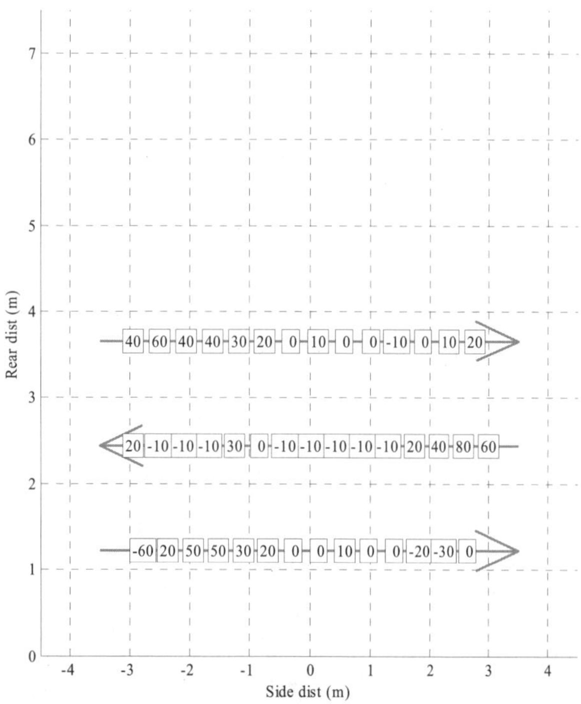

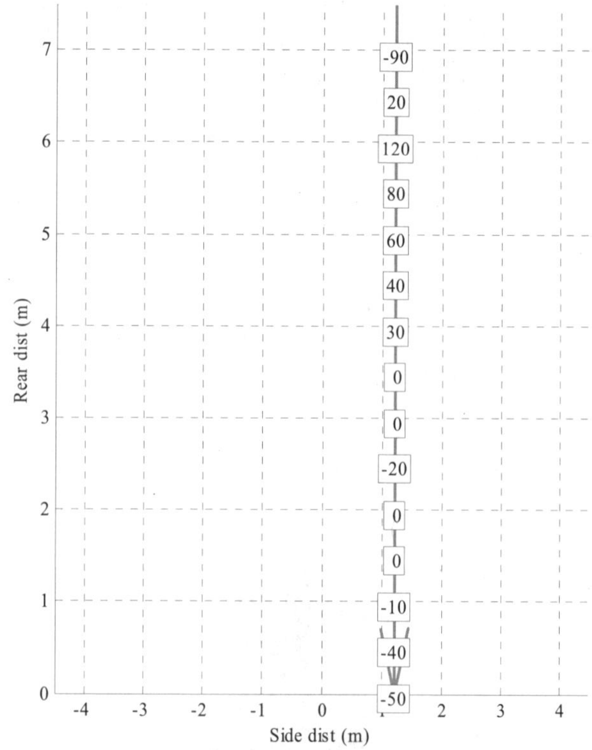

Figure 8. Detectability region of moving subject along specified dynamic test paths. Squares are true subject locations at each frame and numbers in each square indicate the error in cm/s of the reported speed.

CONCLUSION

In this paper, we have presented details of an optical time-of-flight range camera module and machine vision algorithms as configured for an advanced backup safety application. Key technologies in the camera's light source and detector are designed to optimize performance and hardware cost. The computational requirements of the range image formation, depth-based object detection, and motion tracking algorithm are compatible with real-time implementation on commodity microprocessors. No complex high-level image analysis is required for object segmentation and recognition because the time-of-flight range camera directly provides 3D measurements of the environment.

By virtue of dual detection criteria –depth and motion– the system is capable of detecting all hazards in a large region of interest with a low rate of false alarms. Depth information reliably discriminates between objects and the roadway itself, while motion information discriminates between clutter and potential hazards in the periphery of the vehicle path. The effective range of this prototype is 5.5m for a child-sized object, a significant improvement over commercial proximity devices. Further tests to validate the system will include static and dynamic objects while the camera is operating on a moving vehicle.

Additional safety and driver assistance applications, with sensors inside or outside the vehicle, are actively being pursued for our range camera and 3D image analysis technology.

ACKNOWLEDGMENTS

Cheng-feng Sze was instrumental in calibrating the camera and conducting the static and dynamic tests.

REFERENCES

1. "Backup Systems," *Consumer Reports,* 69(10):19–20, Oct. 2004.
2. M.A. Fischler, R.C. Bolles, "Random Sample Consensus: A Paradigm for Model Fitting with Applications to Image Analysis and Automated Cartography," *Commun. ACM,* 24:381—395, June 1981.
3. V. Glazduri, "An Investigation of the Potential Safety Benefits of Vehicle Backup Proximity Sensors", in *Proc. Int'l. Tech. Conf. Enhanced Safety Vehicles*, 2005.
4. S. Hsu, S. Acharya, A. Rafii, R. New, "Performance of a Time-of-Flight Range Camera for Intelligent Vehicle Safety Applications," in *Proc. Adv. Microsystems for Automotive Applications*, Berlin, 205–219, Apr. 2006.
5. M. Paine, A. Macbeth, M. Henderson, "The Danger to Young Pedestrians from Reversing Motor Vehicles," in *Proc. Int'l. Tech Conf. Enhanced Safety Vehicles*, 2003.
6. M. Paine, M. Henderson, "Devices to Assist in Reducing the Risk to Young Pedestrians from Reversing Motor Vehicles," Technical Specification 149, Roads and Traffic Authority, New South Wales, Australia, Oct. 2005.
7. R. Singer, "Estimating Optimal Tracking Filter Performance for Manned Maneuvering Targets," *IEEE Trans. Aerospace and Electronic Systems,* 6(4):473–483, July 1970.

CONTACT

shsu@canesta.com

2007-01-1103

Ultrasonic Sensor Modeling for Automatic Parallel Parking Systems in Passenger Cars

Pär Degerman, Jochen Pohl and Magnus Sethson
Linköping University

ABSTRACT

The performance of a parking system is dependent on many factors. One is the placement of the sensors. In this paper a system which uses ultrasonic ranging sensors is considered. The mounting of a ultrasonic sensor on a passenger vehicle is restricted by, among other factors, design, assembly process, enclosure cost and reliability. All of which must be considered when choosing optimal mounting locations.

The basis of this work includes a ray-trace based simulation environment which is used to capture the physical properties of sound traveling through air. The simulation environment together with sensor models, is used to evaluate the effect of different mounting positions on the accuracy of the detection of the parking space. The Hough transform is used here, as well as in the real system, in order to extract the confining lines of the parking space from the sensor measurements. The strength of these lines are then used to compare different sensor mounting locations.

The created simulation environment differs from other work in this area since it tries to capture the *physical* properties of the sound waves as opposed to the geometric-only approach. The emitted sound pulse is divided into a large number of rays, each with sound properties tied to them. These rays are then traced through a model of the parking space environment, reflections are calculated and finally the summarized echo into the listening sensor is calculated.

The simulation is implemented in 3D Studio MAX which make it relatively easy to create various realistic parking scenarios. An important factor for choosing 3D Studio MAX as the basis of the simulation environment was that it allowed for a new way of modeling ultrasonics using ray-tracing, and at the same time – using the same ray-tracing technology – excellent visualization capabilities.

Figure 1: Visualization generated from the simulation environment during simulation of a parking maneuver.

BACKGROUND

As described in [7] an automatic parking system has been developed by the Division of Mechanical Engineering, division of Fluid and Mechanical Engineering systems, at Linköping university in cooperation with Volvo Car Corporation. The system developed uses ultrasonic range sensing to estimate the position and size of a parking space in which it can park.

The placement of the sensors on the body of the car is crucial for the performance of the system. The sensors must be able to correctly identify all obstacles to prevent parking related damage and accidents. The sensor placement is further restricted to the design and materials of the body of the car.

To be able to evaluate different sensor mounting locations in terms of the performance of the final system, a simulation environment had to be developed. The presented simulation is based on physical properties of sound traversing through air and is implemented in 3D Studio MAX. The chosen environment has the added ben-

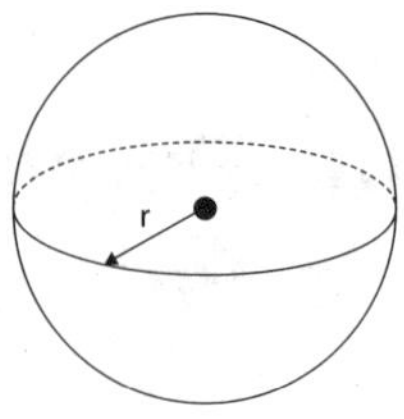

Figure 2: Expansion of a three-dimensional wave.

efit of "free" visualizations, as seen in Figure 1.

THEORETICAL OVERVIEW

The basis of the simulation model that was developed is the *physical* properties of sound traveling through air and reflecting on various surfaces. This section will try to give a brief overview of theses properties.

THE PHYSICS OF SOUND

The definition of a wave, according to [1], is a disturbance within some medium. This disturbance propagates with a medium dependent velocity, is often periodic, and transfers energy from its source to its destination.

There are two basic types of waves, transverse and longitudinal, which are distinguished by the direction of the wave oscillation relative to the direction of the wave propagation. In a transverse wave, each point in the medium moves in a sinusoidal pattern perpendicularly to the direction of the wave, as it propagates through the medium. In a longitudinal wave however, the motion of each point in the medium is in the same direction as the wave propagation.

The power of the an acoustic field is often expressed in terms of intensity. The definition of acoustic intensity is the rate of flow of acoustical energy through a unit area around the point of interest. This imaginary area is always oriented perpendicularly to the direction of wave motion. The intensity is expressed in watts per square meter (Wm^{-2}) and can be written as

$$I = \frac{p_0 u_0}{2} = \frac{u_0^2 \rho c}{2} = \frac{p_0^2}{2\rho c} \tag{1}$$

where p_0 is the acoustic pressure amplitude, and u_0 is the particle velocity amplitude [2].

Many kinds of sound sources produce diverging spherical waves in which the acoustical energy spreads over an increasingly larger area as the sound travels away from the source. This means that the sound intensity, as well as the acoustic pressure amplitude will decrease over distance. For a spherical point source, the acoustic intensity will decrease with the square of the distance from the source as

$$I = \frac{W}{4\pi r^2} \tag{2}$$

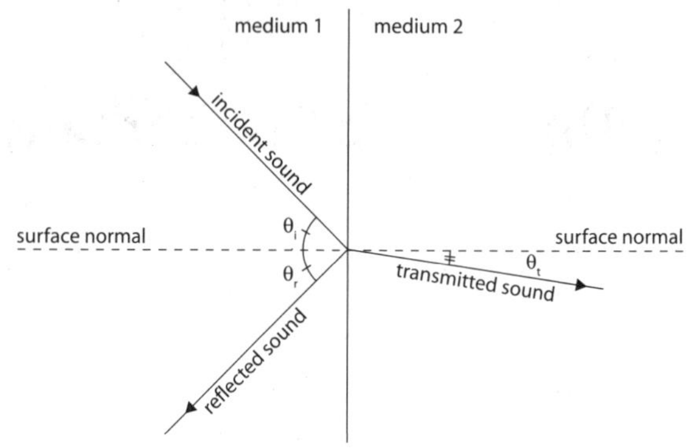

Figure 3: The reflection and refraction of a sound wave incident on a material boundary between medium 1 and medium 2 (Reproduced from [1])

due to the increasing area of the sphere, where W is the acoustic power of the source and r is the radius to the point of interest, [5]. See Figure 2.

When a sound wave traveling in medium 1 encounters a boundary of medium 2, some of the sound is reflected from the boundary back into medium 1, and some is transmitted into medium 2, according to [1] (see figure 3). How this occurs is dependent on the nature of the two medias. Within the scope of this work the case when medium 1 is a gas (air) and medium 2 is a solid (the obstacle we are trying to detect) is the relevant case, and it will be described in the following paragraphs.

According to [1], sound waves are reflected from a surface with the reflection angle equal to the incident angle of the wave, with respect to the surface normal as

$$\theta_r = \theta_i \tag{3}$$

The amount of sound reflected from the surface is dependent of the properties of the two medias [6]. The sound power reflection coefficient, α_r, describes the ratio of sound energy that is reflected to medium 1. If the reflection occurs at the surface of a solid, α_r can be calculated as

$$\alpha_r = \frac{I_r}{I_i} = \frac{\mathbf{z}_n - \rho_1 c_1}{\mathbf{z}_n + \rho_1 c_1} \tag{4}$$

where $\mathbf{z}_n$ is the normal specific acoustic impedance of medium 2 (the solid) [6]. If the solid body is stiff enough not to behave as a membrane and start vibrating when the sound hits the surface, $\mathbf{z}_n$ can be substituted with the characteristic impedance $\rho_2 c_2$ of the solid.

ULTRASONICS RANGE SENSING

An ultrasonic range measurement sensor is a SONAR[1] system, which measures distance by transmitting a sound pulse and listening for the returning echo. By measuring the time from the transmission of the sound pulse until the echo returns, the distance to the object which produced the echo can be calculated if the speed of sound is known

[1] Sound Navigation and Ranging

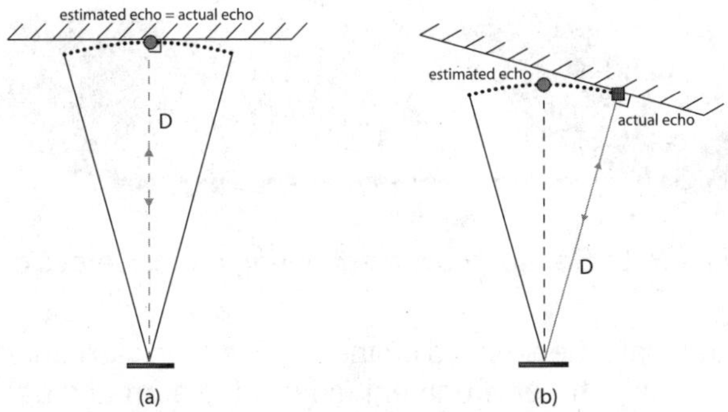

Figure 4: Estimation of sensor echo using a method where the estimated echo is placed perpendicularly in front of the sensor.

in the medium. The time between transmitting and receiving the sound is called the time of flight, or TOF, and the distance to an object is calculated as

$$D = \frac{TOF \cdot c}{2} \tag{5}$$

where c is the speed of sound. The reason for dividing the distance with two, is because the sound travels from the sensor to the object and back again, double the measured distance.

Ultrasonic range measurement gives a very accurate reading of the distance from the sensor to an object. One of the most significant drawbacks of ultrasonic range measurement is that, since the sound diverges in a conical beam from the sensor, the measured distance can lie anywhere on a spherical segment defined by the sensors beam angle and the distance to the echo, as in figure 4. There is no way of deciding exactly from where on this segment the echo actually comes.

The sensor will always measure the distance to the closest object perpendicular to a wavefront in the beam pattern, compare figure 4 (a) and (b). Since the exact position of an echo is not known, an estimation has to be made, and there are some different methods for this that are practiced in different applications. The most straight forward solution is to place the position of the echo perpendicularly in front of the sensor. This method produces an error of estimation as soon as the echo does not come from a wavefront directly in front of the sensor, at $\theta = 0$ in the beam, as in figure 4 (a). As soon as the echo comes from a wavefront at $\theta \neq 0$ in the beam, there will be an error of estimation, as in figure 4 (b).

An ultrasonic sensor emitting a pulse can be seen as a cylindrical piston source where the emitted intensity (or pressure amplitude) varies with the polar angle of the beam. This variation is described in the beam pattern, see Figure 5.

The beam pattern will depend on several characteristics of the sensor. Mainly the radius of the sensor and the emitted frequency. For a constant operating frequency, the beam angle of the sensor will be inversely proportional

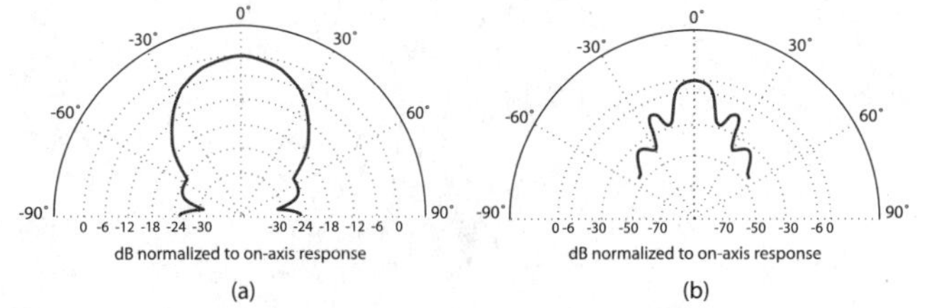

Figure 5: Beam patterns for two different sensors with (a) $a = 6.5\ mm,\ f = 40\ kHz$ and (b) $a = 20\ mm,\ f = 50\ kHz$ is shown.

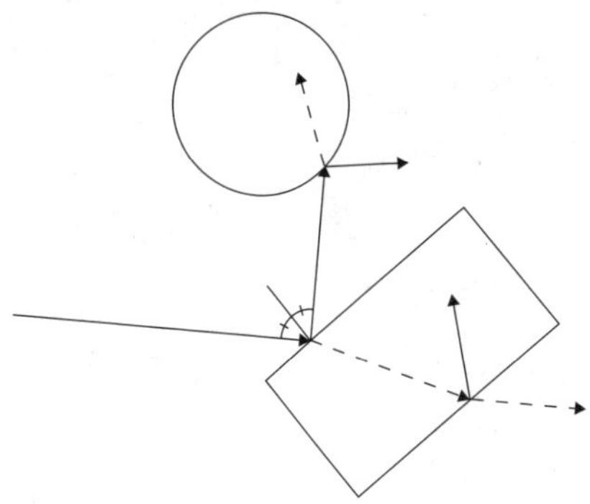

Figure 6: Ray tracing for a ray with both multiple reflections and transmissions. Reflection rays are illustrated as solid lines, and transmission rays as dashed lines.

to the sensor radius [6]. In figure 5 beam patterns for two different sensors with different diameters and operating frequencies is shown.

RAY TRACING

Ray Tracing is a method of creating photo realistic rendered images. It emulates phenomenas as lighting and shadowing, reflection and refraction among others. The basis of ray tracing is to follow rays through a 3D scene and calculating every reflection along its path [3]. The rays can be followed either from the position of the viewer to their source, or by following them from the source to the viewer. The first method is most commonly used since it requires less computations due to the fact that a lot of rays can be eliminated.

Using the rules described in the previous section, Equation 3, reflection can be calculated as the rays travel through the scene and collides with the objects [8]. Transparency is modeled using transmission rays which is passed into the object, the angle of the transmitted rays is dependent on the refraction index of the material. Figure 6 illustrates the reflection and refraction of a ray.

SIMULATION OF ULTRASONICS

When an object is measured using ultrasonic ranging, the end result is highly dependent on the geometry of the object. It is therefore important to be able to create a realistic model of not only the sensors but also the environment. The propagation, in terms of transmission through air and

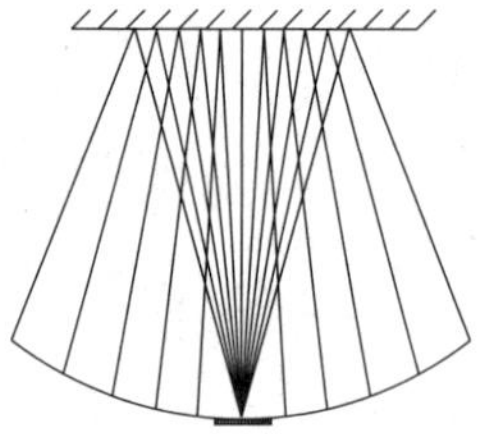

Figure 7: The sound pulse seen as rays.

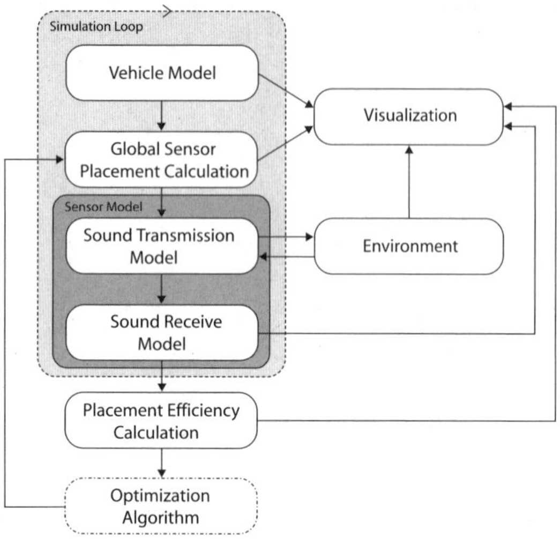

Figure 8: Simulation model overview with the simulation loop marked.

reflection on obstacles, of the sound pulse through the environment is the key element to modeling ultrasonics.

The different 3D modeling software packages that are available each meet that criteria if we can view the sound pulse as rays and using the ray tracing technology incorporated in the software. If each emitted pulse is divided into a large number of rays and spread as in Figure 7, the result should be a realistic model of the ultrasonic ranging. The complete model requires accurate models of the emitting, the transmission and the receiving of the sound pulses.

SIMULATION OVERVIEW

The chosen 3D modeling package is 3D Studio MAX since it contains the programming language MAX Script which makes it easy to implement control loops and an intuitive user interface all in one package. The main drawback of the created simulation is that the computing power required is extremely high. The computation time is dependent on the resolution of the rays. A high resolution requires that each sound pulse is divided into more rays which increases the number of calculations required.

The implemented simulation environment consist of several parts. The main simulation loop, top part in Figure 8, consist of the ultrasonic simulation. After a simulation is completed the result is evaluated using an efficiency algorithm which is based on the hough transform presented in [4]. The optimization can, using this efficiency calculation relocate the sensors on the car and then start another simulation. The environment models the surrounding obstacles, consisting of cars and the curb and the visualization of the scene comes "free" with 3D Studio MAX.

Figure 9: Sensor movement during a receive cycle.

TRANSMIT AND RECEIVE MODEL

The emitted sound pulse is divided into a number of distinct rays as can be seen in Figure 7. Each ray is associated with an intensity measure coming from the beam pattern (see Figure 5) and radiates in a spherical cone from the sensor. The friction against air is neglected so the intensity of *each* ray is constant as it propagates. Also reflection losses are neglected.

As the sensor starts listening for the returned echo the key factor is the accumulated returned intensity. A ray that passes through the sensor is considered to be "heard" by the sensor and the intensity of that ray is added.

Since the sensor in this case is mounted on a *moving* vehicle some care has to be taken when calculating if a ray passes through the sensor. To solve this problem a technique where the starting point (the location of the sensor when the pulse was emitted) and the ending point (the location when a maximum TOF has elapsed) of the sensor is determined. After that a rectangle is drawn between these points, see Figure 9. Any ray passing through this area is considered to be heard by the sensor. This is a simplification and will not produce large errors since the sensor movement during the transmit-receive cycle is small.

ENVIRONMENT MODEL

The environment model of a parking scenario must provide an accurate model of the surfaces of the other parked cars and the curb. The resolution of the parked cars is a significant factor of the computing time for a simulation run. The level of detail must be high enough to provide accurate measurements and at the same time low enough to keep computing power down. Figure 10 shows car models with different polygon counts.

The shape of the vehicles is also an important factor, a large SUV results in a completely different result than a small compact.

Figure 11 shows the two types of cars chosen for the simulation and sensor placement calculation. A larger station wagon in (a) and a smaller sedan vehicle in (b). Both cars have in the vicinity of 1000 polygons. This gives a good

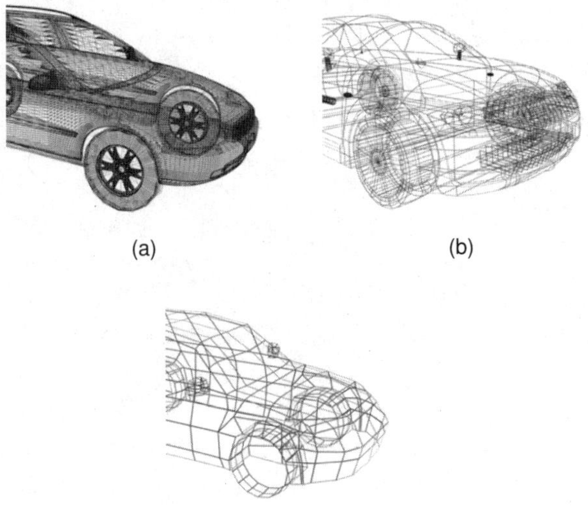

(a) (b)

(c)

Figure 10: Car models with about (a) 300 000 polygons, (b) 150 000 polygons and (c) 1 000 polygons

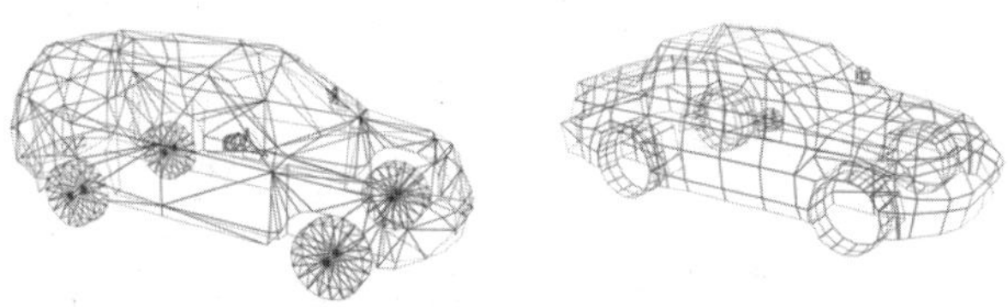

(a) (b)

Figure 11: Low polygon car surface models used in simulation in form of (a) a larger station wagon and (b) a smaller sedan.

enough surface approximation for ultrasonic modeling and at the same time keeps simulation time at an acceptable level.

The rest of the surrounding, the curb and the road, is modeled as a box with height 0.1 m and a plane respectively. It would be interesting to create a more realistic, rough model of the road surface since road roughness is the source for a high number of spuriouses when measuring with ultrasonics. This would, however, lead to extremely long calculation times. The algorithm presented in [4] is however proved to be robust against such spuriouses so it can be argued that they are not such an important factor.

MODEL VALIDATION

The validation was conducted using an ultrasonic sensor (SensComp Smart Sensor 600) attached to a angular servo (consisting of a motor, a gearbox and an encoder). The measurements where collected using a dSPACE system. Figure 12 shows the experimental setup.

The most interesting results are viewed Figures 13 through 16, plots that show both the good and the bad behavior of the model. It is observed that the real sensor almost every time gets more hits on its right side, which

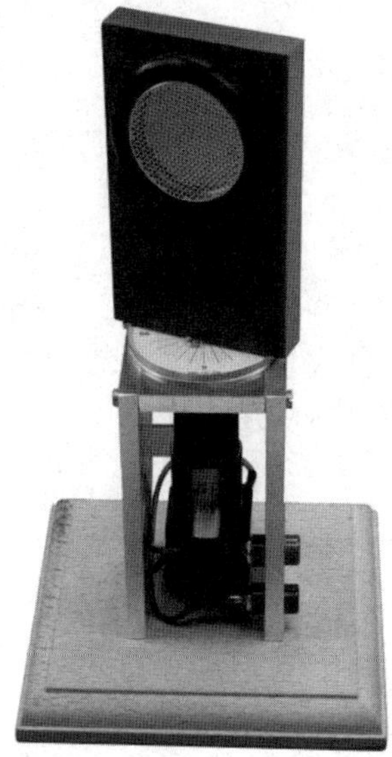

Figure 12: Ultrasonic sensor mounted on angle servo with a resolution of 0.5 degrees. With this angle servo connected to the real time system dSPACE accurate measurements can be made.

means that this particular sensor don't have a perfect symmetric beam pattern. The beam pattern varies between different sensors, probably because of differences in the membrane.

In Figure 13 the object is a plane wall (800 mm wide). At 1 m, it is seen how the simulation agrees well with the real measurements. Both the major and secondary lobes looks the same in simulation as in real measurements.

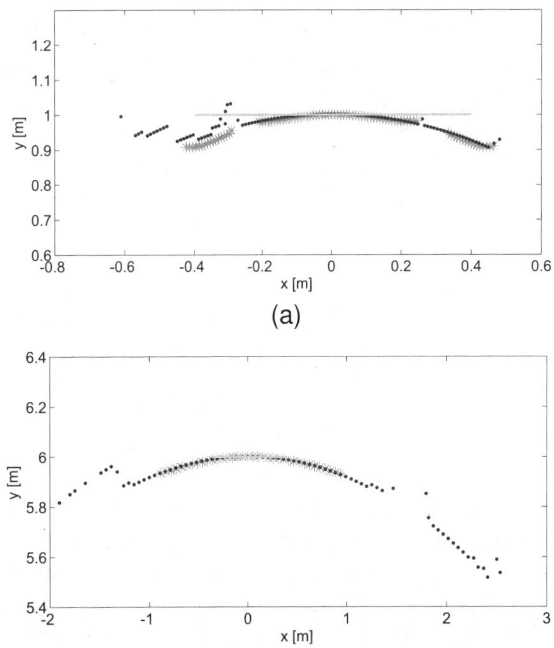

(a)

(b)

Figure 13: Real (dots) and simulated (asterisks) measurements on a 800 mm wide wall at (a) 1 m and (b) 6 m.

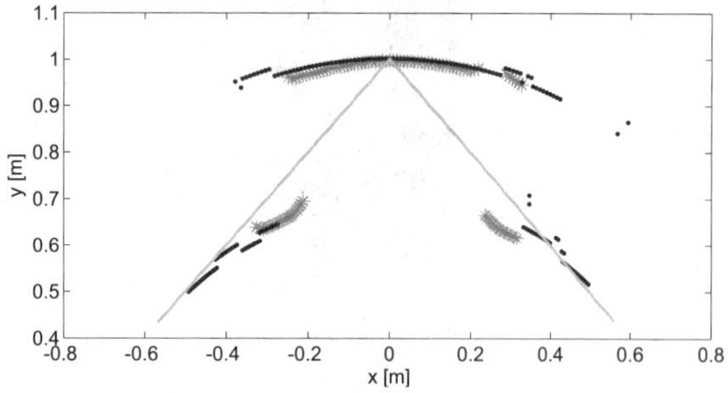

(a)

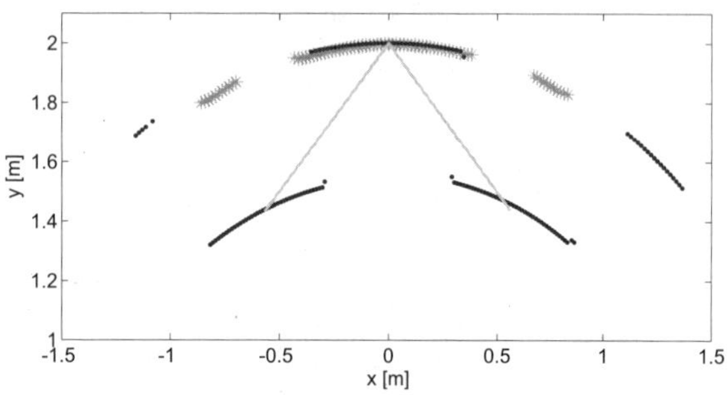

(b)

Figure 14: Real (dots) and simulated (asterisks) measurements on a inside corner with 800 mm sides at (a) 1 m and (b) 2 m.

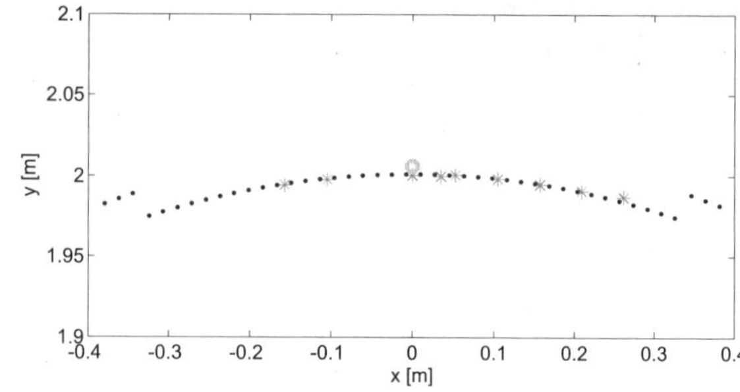

(a)

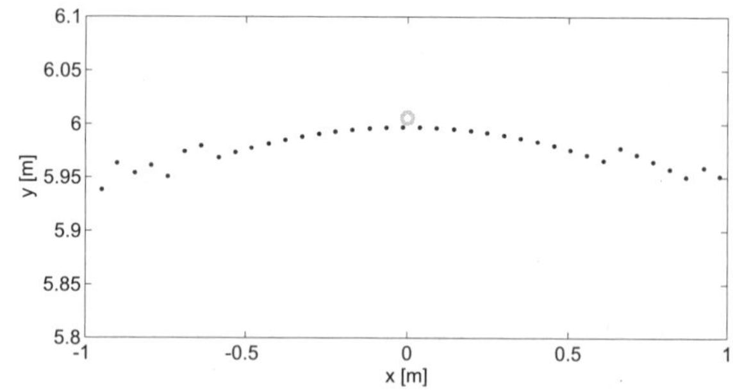

(b)

Figure 15: Real (dots) and simulated (asterisks) measurements on a cylinder with 12 mm in diameter at (a) 2 m and (b) 6 m.

Also at 6 m, where only the major lobe is seen, the results agrees. It should be noticed that the model don't have echoes for as wide angles as the real measurement.

In Figure 14 some interesting effects can be seen. In the experimental measurements, echoes occur as direct reflections from the side of the walls creating the inside corner. In the simulations however, the planes have no thickness and therefore no echoes can be detected. The double reflections coming from inside the corner is the same though.

In Figure 15 a small cylinder (12 mm in diameter) shows if the model can cope with smaller object. In these plots the weakness of the model can be seen. It doesn't get as many echoes as the experiments. There are almost no echoes at 2 m and none at all with at 6 m.

With the sensor sweeping almost 360 degrees in a smaller room (1.6 by 1.6 m) the results plotted in Figure16, is obtained. Simulations produce almost the same results as the real measurements. Echoes that occur at the middle of some walls are there because the walls where built up by two planes in the real measurements, which resulted in a small bump that the sensor registered. In reality echoes also occur at a longer distance (down to the right in the figure), because the sound have been reflected more than two times as in the model.

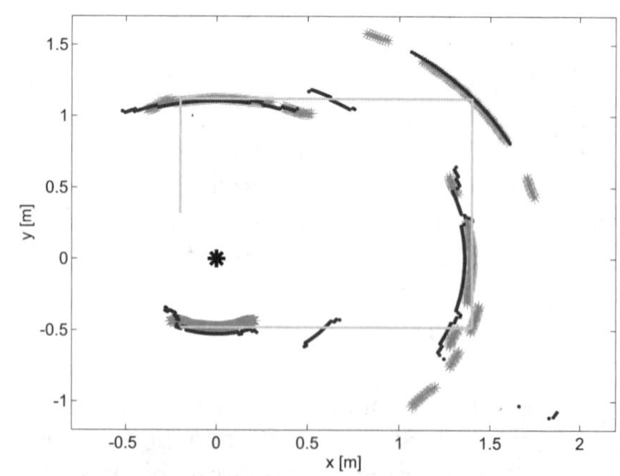

Figure 16: Real (dots) and simulated (asterisks) measurements in a small room ($1.6x1.6$ m). The large asterisk represent the sensor position.

CONCLUSIONS

The result of this work is a simulation environment created in 3D Studio MAX which can accurately model the physics of ultrasonic ranging in parking system applications. The model have been validated against experimental results using a real sensor and real objects.

Furthermore, initial studies in the placement of the sensors used in a parking system have been conducted. The results show that the simulation environment can correctly produce to evaluate different mounting locations of the sensor. The computing time is however extremely high so initial guesses must be relevant to get fast convergence in the optimization.

Furthermore the work has shown that 3D Studio MAX along with other 3D modeling packages can be used to model ultrasonics in a new way.

CONTACT

For additional information,
Pär Degerman
`parde@ikp.liu.se`
Department of Mechanical Engineering
Linköping University
SE-581 83 Linköping
SWEDEN

REFERENCES

[1] Richard E. Berg and David G. Stork. *The Physics of Sound, 2nd ed.* Prentice-Hall, 2 edition, 1995. ISBN 0-13-183047-3.

[2] Jack Blitz. *Ultrasonics: Methods and Applications.* Butterworth & Co Ltd, 1971. ISBN 0 408 70212 5.

[3] Samuel R. Buss. *3-D Computer Graphics.* University of California, 2003. ISBN 0-521-82103-7.

[4] Pär Degerman, Jochen Pohl, and Magnus Sethson. Hough transform for parking space estimation using long range ultrasonic sensors. *SAE Technical Papers*, 2006-01-0810, April 2006.

[5] Tor Kihlman. *Grundläggnade teknisk akustik.* CTH: Göteborg, 1982.

[6] Lawrence E. Kinsler and Austin R. Frey. *Fundamentals of Acoustics, 2nd ed.* John Wiley & Sons Inc, 2 edition, 1967.

[7] Jochen Pohl, Magnus Sethson, Pär Degerman, and Jonas Larsson. A semi-automated parallel parking system for passenger cars. *Proceedings of the Institution of Mechanical Engineers: Journal of Automobile Engineering - Part D*, 2006.

[8] Krister Samuelsson. *Raytracing.* Linköping University, 1987. LITH-ISY-EX 0805.

2006-01-1294

OptiVeo: A Vision-Based Platform for Driving Assistance

Patrice Reilhac, Julien Rebut, Joël Lelevé and Benoist Fleury
Valeo - Driving Assistance Domain

ABSTRACT

Most of the Driving Assistance functions require sensors that are looking ahead of the vehicle. Among these sensors, cameras, already providing Lane Departure Warning and Night Vision, will play a major role. Since it won't be possible to multiply the number of sensors located behind the windscreen, it is then crucial to perform with cameras as many detections as possible. We describe in this paper some algorithmic methods for performing camera based tunnel and fog detection.

INTRODUCTION

Pioneered by Lane Departure Warning and Night Vision Systems for front vehicle applications and by Park Assist Systems at the rear, embedded video cameras promise to play a major role in new Driving Assistance applications in the next decade.

Watching front, side and rear scenes, extracting information as diverse as pedestrian location or fog density, cameras address all types of Driving Assistance applications: night vision, obstacle detection, environment detection, parking assistance, automatic windscreen wiping and finally lighting related applications.

The potential functionalities of such sensors can be gathered into four main topics (Fig.1):

- Infrastructure Detection
- Night Vision
- Obstacle Detection
- Lighting and Wiping Automation

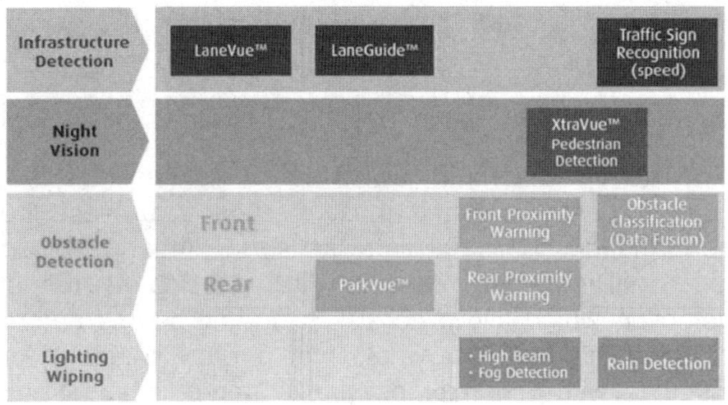

Figure 1 – Vision-based Application roadmap

Most of these vision-based applications are studied at Valeo within the framework of the OptiVeo™ project.

Valeo is currently providing IR-based RLT - for Rain, Light and Tunnel - sensors. These sensors, located behind the upper part of the windscreen, provide ambient light measurement and Tunnel Detection for Low beam automation and secondarily Rain detection for Wipers automation. On the other hand, Valeo is also producing front cameras, also located in the vicinity of the interior mirror, for Lane Departure Warning (Fig.2).

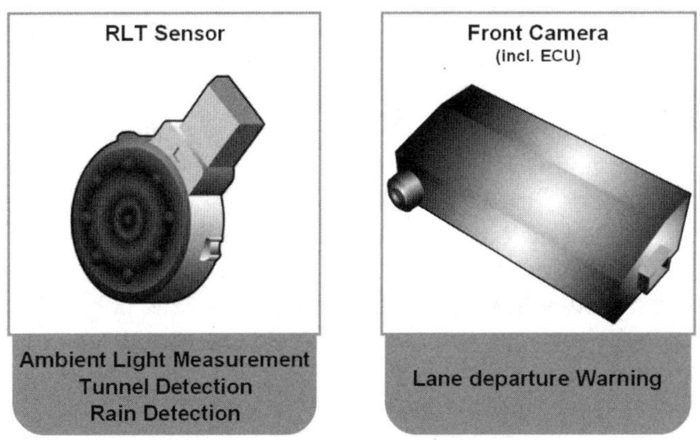

Figure 2 – Available systems

It is then obvious that it would be of a great benefit to integrate Low Beam and High Beam automation into this camera and to even extend its functionality to Fog detection and Rain detection (Fig.3).

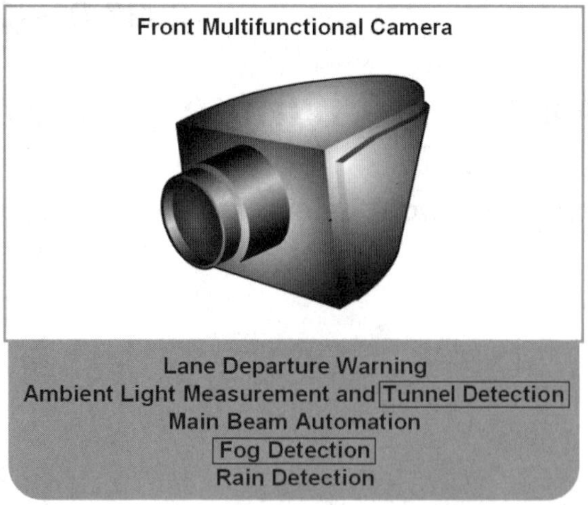

Figure 3 – Front multifunctional camera

Considering automatic switching of lighting devices, camera based systems must reproduce at least the performances of existing sensors. Among these functionalities, one can list the anticipated tunnel detection which allows to switch on low beams before entering into tunnels, what is of a great interest, for instance, with Xenon lamps whose ramp-up is about one second (Fig.4).

Figure 4 – Tunnel detection

We will describe in a first part how to perform Tunnel detection with a camera based system.

Among lighting lamps, the fog lamps have still no system for automatic activation. But to perform such automation, one needs to build a system able to detect the occurrence of fog (Fog.5) whatever is the ambient light condition. Moreover, in the case where such a system is able to evaluate the visibility distance, one can easily imagine how this information would be useful for other applications.

Figure 5 – Fog detection

Anticipating the decrease of visibility distance would allow to warn the driver, what would certainly reduce the number of accidents by fog condition; knowing that they represent 1% of the total number of accidents but are twice more fatal.

One can also point out that different algorithms using a same video signal would take benefit of working in collaboration. Indeed, the visibility distance evaluation would give to the other algorithms a good assessment of the relevance of the video information. In the case of a deep fog, the visibility distance would fall down and objects detection algorithm or infrastructure detection could warn the driver that they are no more active.

We will describe in a second part how to perform a Fog Detection and a Visibility Distance Measurement by using a video sensor at daylight and at night

TUNNEL DETECTION

For optimum lighting at the entrance to a dimly-lit tunnel or on bright days, it is appropriate to switch on dipped headlights in anticipation. However, the system as described above, does not provide for such anticipation, and specific processing therefore needs to be implemented.

At a speed of 130 km/h and assuming a 1-second response time for switching on Xenon headlamps, a tunnel must be detected at least 36 m before the vehicle enters.

Detection of the tunnel involves tracking the dark areas in the image [1]. In fact, a tunnel is a dark area of the image (low grey level ~0) featuring a roughly rectangular shape. Also, as the vehicle approaches the tunnel, the area of the corresponding dark zone is strictly increasing. After a sufficiently large number of appearances, it is then possible to establish the presence of a tunnel.

The image of a road scene includes zones of low interest (Fig6). In fact the bottom third of the image represents the road and the top third represents the sky. The area of interest is therefore defined as the central third of the image.

Figure 6 - Zone of interest

The dark areas are then extracted by segmentation. To do this we use thresholding with hysteresis which provides better results than simple thresholding for a slightly longer computing time. The dark areas in such case are correctly closed and located.

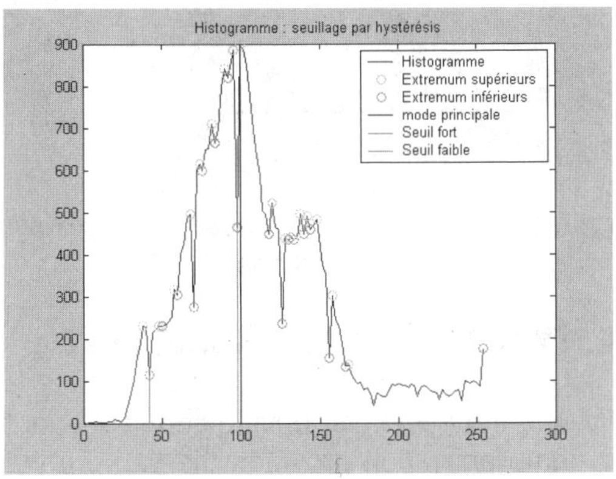

Histogram

High threshold

Low threshold

Thresholding with hysteresis

Figure 7 – Picture Thresholding

As stated previously, the area of the tunnel increases as the vehicle approaches it. To check this expanding area, the dark zones must be tracked with respect to time from one image to the next.

Space and time tracking enables the displacement of the dark source to be monitored from one image to the next. To do this, it is essential to be able to apply time correlation between the objects detected in the image at t=2 with those detected in the image at t=1 and so on. This correlation may be achieved for example by minimising the Euclidean distance. In such case, if R_i represents the regions detected in image 1 and R_j represents the regions detected in image 2, we can establish a matrix of distances:

$$
\begin{array}{cc}
 & R_j \\
R_i & \begin{array}{cccc} d_{11} & d_{12} & \dots & d_{1n} \\ d_{21} & d_{22} & \dots & d_{2n} \\ \dots & \dots & \dots & \dots \\ d_{m1} & d_{m2} & \dots & d_{mn} \end{array}
\end{array}
$$

where $d_{11} = \sqrt{(x_{R1} - x_{R2})^2 + (y_{R1} - y_{R2})^2}$

This matrix of distances enables allocation of a source R_j to the source R_i which will minimise the distance d_{ij} (Fig.8).

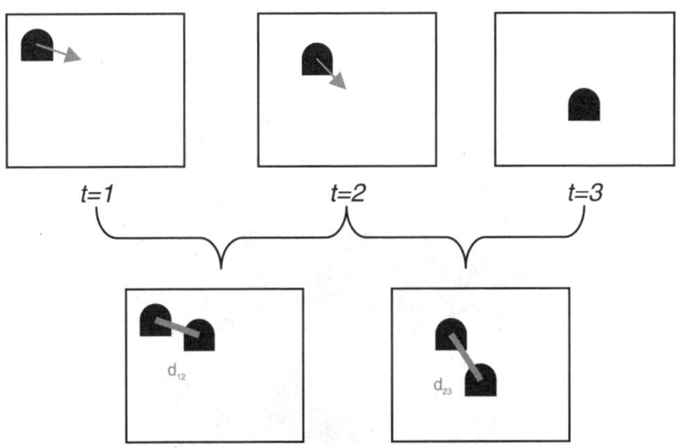

Figure 8 – Frame to frame object distance

Thus, the space and time tracking enables the elaboration of a history of the appearance of objects. According to the acquisition frequency and from a certain number of appearances, an object becomes a potential tunnel. To confirm the presence of a tunnel, it is simply required to confirm that its area is indeed increasing (Fig.9).

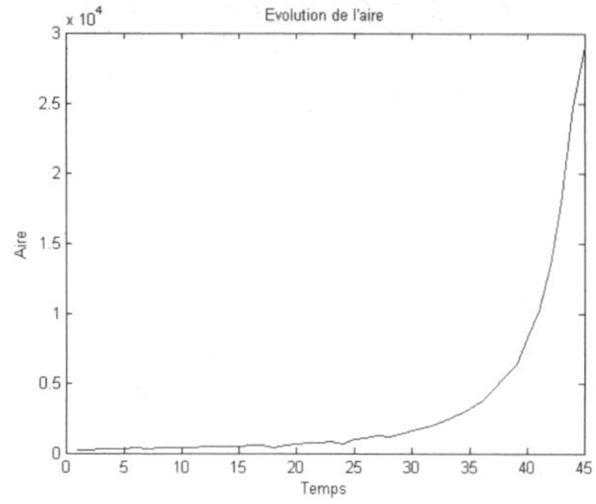

Figure 9 - Dark area (tunnel) growth.

The figure below (Fig.10) shows some results. In a straight line, a tunnel is detected at a distance of more than 150 m.

Figure 10 – Tunnel detection (snapshots)

As we have seen, the shutter speed is controlled automatically by the camera according to the ambient lighting. This integration time can then be used to confirm the presence of a tunnel, to detect the presence of a tunnel if it has failed to be detected by image processing (operation similar to a single photodiode) but especially it can be used to switch off the headlamps at the tunnel exit. The headlamps need to be extinguished about 15 seconds after leaving the tunnel. As is shown in the next figure (Fig.11), the integration time is very short in daylight conditions and increases significantly when the vehicle is in a tunnel.

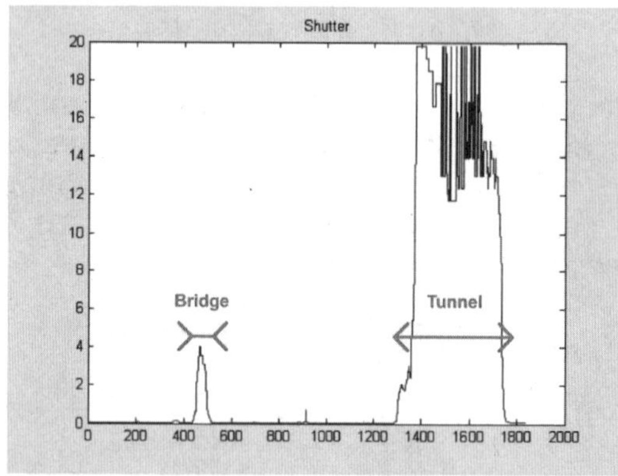

Figure11 - Integration time according to driving conditions

VISIBILITY DISTANCE MEASUREMENT

By optimising the lighting to driving conditions, automatic front fog lamp activation provides the same advantages for drivers as any other automatic front light activation. Rear fog lamps automatic activation would also provide outstanding advantages since this would anticipate the decreasing visibility distance and warn following drivers in time. Furthermore, it would, as well, turn off the fog lamps as soon as they are not required, preventing them from dazzling drivers behind.

Unfortunately, the influence of the fog on the recorded video is not the same at daytime and at night. Therefore, we need to consider dedicated algorithm for these two driving situations.

FOG DETECTION AT DAYLIGHT

The light beams passing through fog are diffused in all directions by the water droplets, thus reducing visibility. When the driver looks at the road, the objects contained within his field of view transmit or reflect light energy which penetrates the eye and illuminates the retina. This distribution of light is then analysed by the brain in terms of spatial frequencies. The following analogy can therefore be put forward : fog can be considered as an optical filter which modifies the visual signal by attenuating the frequency contrast. It is therefore possible to characterise the fog by a frequency contrast operator.

To do this, we begin by searching for the homogeneous zones of the image [1],[2]. In fact, a standard road scene generally contains two homogeneous zones, corresponding to the sky and the road. In fog, these zones tend to disappear to form a single region which is also homogeneous. To identify these homogeneous zones, we construct the correlation matrices.

In the example below (Fig.12), the homogeneous zones are the sky and the road.

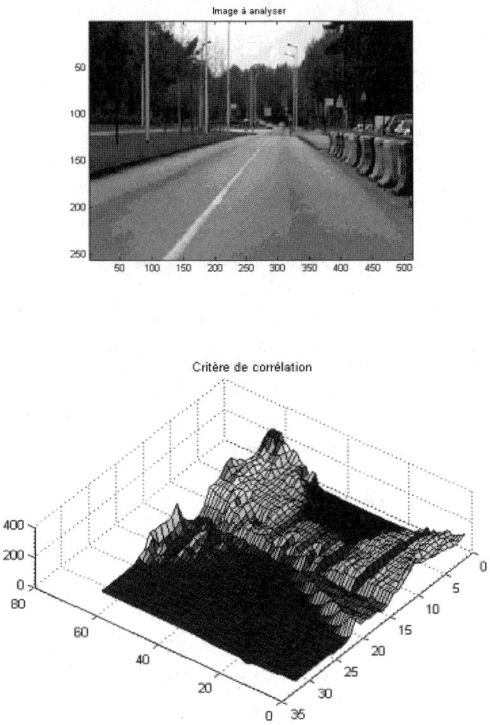

Figure 12 – Homogeneous zones

From this we can deduce (Fig.13) the correlation image of the homogeneous zones.

Figure 13 – Correlation image

Calculation of the parameters for these textured regions enables the detection of the presence or otherwise of fog. If this first stage confirms the presence of fog, the visibility range is then estimated by analysing the point of inflection of a vertical profile of the image passing through the centre of gravity of the homogeneous region (Fig.14).

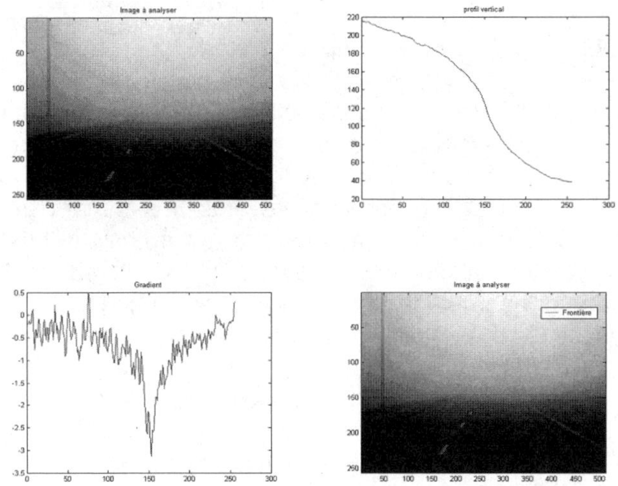

Figure 14 – Visibility distance evaluation

Below are some examples (Fig.15) of fog detection and visibility range measurement.

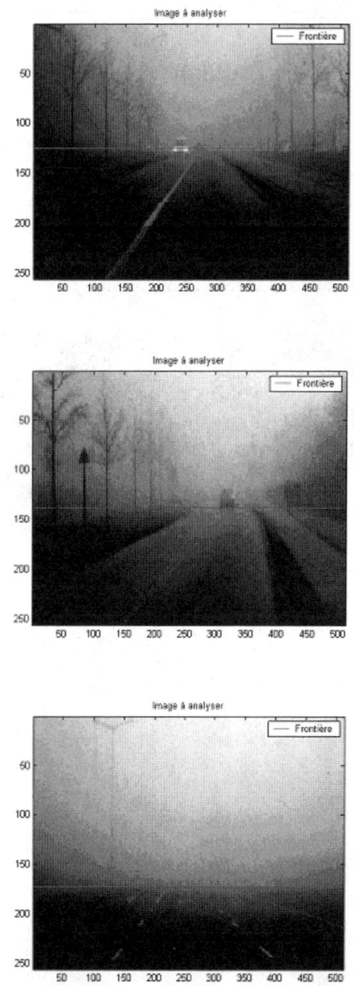

Figure 15 – Visibility distance evaluation (snapshots)

As soon as fog is detected and the visibility range falls below a predefined threshold, the fog lamps can be automatically activated.

FOG DETECTION AT NIGHT

At night, the former fog detection algorithm is no more applicable because of a lack of visibility of the scene. Indeed, the road is only lit by the car headlamps but the backlighting of fog droplets prevents the camera from recording in a proper way the road texture. We will then analyze the halation generated, being considered that its shape or geometrical characteristics are linked to the fog density i.e. the visibility distance.

To do so, the algorithm runs the following steps:

1) Shape extraction of the halation by thresholding the recording.

2) Thanks to tangential method, determination of the ellipse which is mostly corresponding to the halation. Evaluation of the ellipse parameters: 'a', 'b' and centre location.

3) Visibility distance evaluation deduced from the position of the point of inflection of a vertical profile of the image passing through the highest point of the ellipse.

On the two examples here bellow (with and without fog), one sees the contour extractions of the thresholding, the approximated ellipses and the point clouds of 'a' and 'b' values (Fig.16):

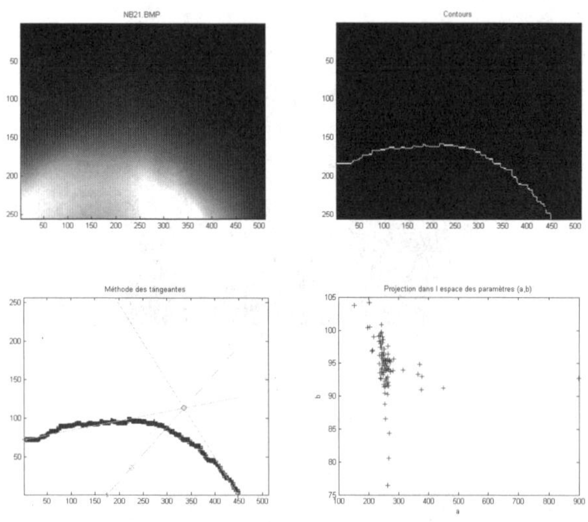

With fog

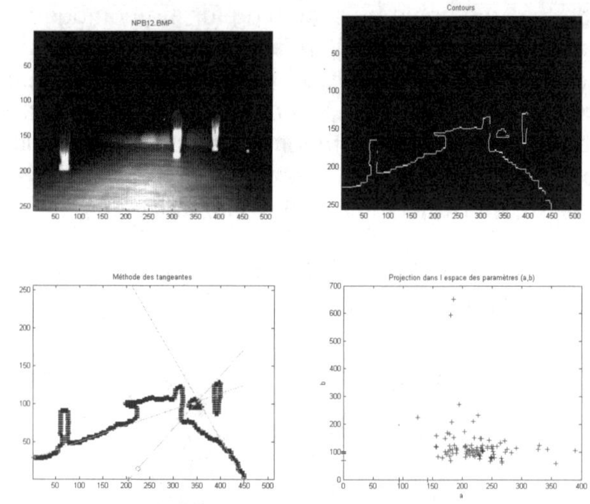

Without fog

Figure 16 – Visibility distance evaluation at night

We see that, despite scale differences, the two point clouds are significantly different. This would allow a rough estimation of the visibility distance. As said previously, we then improve the accuracy of the evaluation by locating point of inflection of a vertical profile of the image passing through the highest point of the ellipse.

On the other hand, we can see on the second example (without fog) that the ellipse calculation eliminates the distortions due to obstacles – such as pedestrians – in the field of view. Nevertheless, the spread of 'a' and 'b' values determines the quality of the measurement and gives the algorithm the possibility to reject wrong images.

This evaluation of visibility distance has to comply with:

- the different patterns of beams the future AFS regulation (Adaptive Front Lighting System) will allow (town lighting, motorway lighting).
- the combination of fog lamps with low-beam.
- the low-beam orientation when the cars are equipped with Bending Light systems.

In the first case, the algorithm will get from the CAN the typology of the active beam and will adjust its parameter according to this.

In the second case, we have checked that the addition of fog lamps to low-beam does not change significantly the shape of the low-beam.

In the last case, field tests have shown the robustness of the system towards orientation of the low-beam.

CONCLUSION

We have seen how Dipped Beam headlights and Fog Lamps can be properly activated through tunnel and fog detection performed by a single common front camera. But many other functions associated with lighting could be enhanced by the use of vision based detection.

Indeed, any system which leads to the automation of driver tasks, function enhancement or the provision of additional but relevant information to the driver will enhance driving safety. Vision Based systems and Front and Rear Lighting have numerous uses in Driving Assistance applications. We have listed some of those applications. Interfaces between these systems and future functionalities, are limited only by the imagination of development engineers.

REFERENCES

[1] J.Rebut, B.Fleury. Vision Based Systems for Lighting Automation. 6th International Symposium on Automotive Lighting, Darmstadt University of Technology.

[2] J.Lelevé, J.Rebut. Fog Lamp Automation with Visibility Sensor, the next step of lighting automation. Elektronik im Kraftfahrzeug – VDI 12.Internationales Kongress, Baden-Baden

2006-01-0095

ITS Technology in Automotive -- Who's on First?

Gerald D. Conover
PRC Associates

ABSTRACT

This paper examines the status of important ITS technology developments at major automakers and key Tier One suppliers around the world.

Technology topics include navigation, telematics, vehicle dynamics control, parking aids, adaptive cruise control, lane departure warning, active safety systems, predictive safety systems (e.g., braking assist, collision warning, and collision avoidance), and vehicle-to-vehicle and vehicle-to-roadside communications.

Each company's ITS technical acumen is assessed and compared to its competitors. Leaders in each technical area are suggested.

The paper concludes with postulation of important future trends in automotive ITS.

INTRODUCTION

The whole notion of which organizations or firms are ahead or behind in the development and deployment of ITS products and services is almost ludicrous. After all, ITS is supposed to bring on a host of social and economic benefits, not the least of which are reductions in traffic incidents and deaths.

But the world is a competitive place. Each weekend, thousands of young men and women go onto the fields of sport to compete against one another, rack up the highest score and be declared the winner – or in some cases, the champion.

And so it is with ITS. Like any human pursuit, some people are compelled to measure their accomplishments against those of others – in similar agencies or competing companies – to see who is biggest and best.

The auto industry has been highly competitive for over a hundred years, so it is logical – almost predestined – that automakers and suppliers should peer out of their headquarters at one another to try to figure out who has done the most with ITS. Some popular ways to count success around the world's auto industry are (1) the number of new applications of technology or (2) sales volumes in either units sold or dollars (or yen or euros) of revenue.

We prefer to look at the number of different applications of the various ITS technologies to measure the mettle of automakers and suppliers.

THE FRAMEWORK

To bring some order to the world of automotive ITS applications, we propose the following analytical framework:

	Autonomous	Connected
Driver Assistance	• GPS Navigation • Adaptive Cruise Control • Park Assist • Night Vision (Vision Enhancement)	• Telematics • Emergency Calling (Collision Notification) • Vehicle Infrastructure Integration – With Other Drivers – With Infrastructure
Vehicle and Traffic Safety	• Lane/Road Departure Warning • Lane Keeping • Sensor Fusion (enabler) • Blind Spot Monitor (Lane Change Assistance) • Pre-Collision Protection (Forward Collision Warning/Assistance) • Rear Impact Warning • Rear View Television/Obstacle Detection • Peripheral Monitoring • Drowsy Driver Warning	• Intelligent Speed Adaption • Intersection Collision Warning

Figure 1. Analytical Framework

These technology applications and their allocation around the "picture frame" are certainly open to debate. Others will have other frameworks that better suit their respective arguments.

For this analysis the areas of discrimination are (1) use – to aid the driver or to promote safety – and (2) whether the applications stand alone or need to be connected to some infrastructure off the vehicle in order to deliver the expected benefits.

There are several technology applications that have not been included here – electronic stability control and rollover warning or protection, for example. While these applications certainly provide new levels of safety enhancement they represent improvements in vehicle dynamics control rather than in ITS[1] functionality.

GPS NAVIGATION

Over the last fifteen years, on-board vehicle navigation using GPS as the main positioning engine has become essentially ubiquitous in the major auto consuming countries. As China becomes an automotive power, it too is reaching out to GPS navigation as an essential capability for commercial, government and private drivers.

Offering on-board navigation is more a marketing choice for an automaker than a matter of technical capability. Numerous navigation systems – including very capable GPS engines and highly developed routing algorithms – are available from Tier One and Tier Two automotive suppliers (mainly Japanese and European). Excellent maps can be had from American[2], European and Japanese digital geographic information firms.

Navigation systems are universally available in Japan in both premium and everyday automotive brands. Virtually all European premium and many mainstream cars also have navigation systems available. Many are optional extras although there are others installed as standard. Navigation systems are just starting to catch on with American automakers – Chrysler Group, Ford and General Motors all offer navigation system options on some of their cars and light trucks.

ADAPTIVE CRUISE CONTROL

Adaptive Cruise Control[3], or ACC, is the "killer app" for ITS in this decade not only for its own capabilities but also for the other ITS applications that its radar is spawning – pre-collision warning and blind-spot monitoring, to name only two.

ACC uses radar – either microwave or laser (each has its own operational strengths and weaknesses) – to (1) locate a vehicle in the lane ahead, (2) determine the "target" vehicle's distance from our "own" vehicle, and (3) calculate the relative speed between one's own and the target vehicle. These last two dimensions are sometimes referred to as "range" and range-rate."

There are those who would argue that ACC is a safety system and thus belongs in that "pane" of the analytical framework "window." That notion certainly has merit. We chose the driver assist window because of the way ACC is marketed by automakers. They prefer to position ACC as a driver aid in order to avoid potential tort liability from offering a forward-collision-warning system – the promise might be greater than the deliverable.

Although Mercedes made the first offer of ACC to the retail automotive market in Europe in 1999, in fact Jaguar made the first retail delivery of ACC about a month before Mercedes.

In only a few short years ACC has expanded worldwide with offerings on numerous cars and some SUVs in Europe, America and Japan. Virtually all European auto brands offer ACC, mostly on their premium models. Japanese brands offering ACC include Daihatsu, Nissan (including Infiniti), and Toyota (including Lexus). Cadillac is the only Big Three brand to offer ACC – it's a Delphi design based on a Raytheon sensor.

Numerous Tier One suppliers offer turnkey ACC systems including Continental Automotive Systems, Delphi Automotive, Denso, Hitachi, Siemens VDO Automotive, TRW and Valeo (this is only a partial list of ACC suppliers).

Second-generation ACC systems have just come to market. These new embodiments are termed "full-authority" – they operate all the way from highway speeds down to a complete stop. Gen I ACC systems cut out at around 20-30 km/h. The first of these is offered by Mercedes on its 2005 S Class – Continental is the supplier. Several other Tier One suppliers have Gen II ACC systems developed and ready for sale to automakers.

PARK ASSIST

Ultrasonic park assist is a relatively old technology application. Japanese suppliers were "shopping" ultrasonic park assist systems in America in the mid-1970s. First applied to vehicle rear bumpers to mitigate the occurrence of low-speed contact with objects and other vehicles, park assist has quickly moved to front bumpers for added protection in highly styled vehicles where the front edge may not be easily apparent to the driver.

Park assist can be found on almost all vehicle brands around the world, in all major markets. This is another example of marketing decisions setting the automotive product application limits. The technology is in place and well-proven.

There have been some applications of radar to park assist. This is a higher cost approach than ultrasonics for close-distance protection, but some applications use radar to reach an additional several meters back of the vehicle to give earlier identification of potential obstacles. Visteon and some others have fielded this.

Park assist has not been promoted as a safety device by automakers. It has only been implied that pedestrians or small children would benefit from early detection by a slowly backing vehicle. Suppliers have been more aggressive in this regard than have automakers – tort concerns again.

Denso and Toyota were among the first automotive companies to work on "total parking space definition" using several sensors to determine the length and depth of a parking space, then offering guidance to help the driver park in the space safely. Other suppliers, notably

Aisin AW and Continental, have developed systems that will use the parking space data to steer a vehicle into a parking space – the driver still controls accelerator and brakes.

Aisin's Intelligent Parking Assist was jointly developed with Toyota, and helps the driver in all reversing parking operations. By establishing the target parking position, the vehicle's parking movements are accomplished with automatic steering.

The driver need only control the speed of the vehicle. In the Toyota Prius adaptation, this means operating only the brake.

Volkswagen showed a fully automated parking concept vehicle several years ago, but it used an impossibly expensive 360-degree array of radar and ultrasonic sensors as well as a large computer to work the algorithms.

NIGHT VISION

Night vision and vision enhancement technologies have been under development since the late 1980s – several research applications were demonstrated in 1994 as part of Europe's PROMETHEUS program.

Night Vision was #2 on JD Powers' consumer research list of emerging technologies – until price was mentioned. At $1,500, it dropped to #17.

There are two technical approaches to night vision, one using the far infrared spectrum (FIR) and another using near infrared frequencies (NIR).

Numerous suppliers have developed night vision systems. Among them are Siemens VDO, ITT, Delphi (using Raytheon technology), Autoliv (for BMW) and Robert Bosch.

General Motors was the first automaker in the world to offer night vision (FIR) as a regular production option (on some 2000 model year Cadillacs). Although the first-year take rate approached 20% for the $2,250 option, the rate quickly dropped to 2% when it stayed stubbornly stuck. GM dropped night vision from the Cadillac DTS concluding that a business case could not be realized. The system Raytheon developed for Cadillac used an Uncooled Focal Point Array that works well at 72°F. Raytheon used a $20 part to keep the temperature of the array stable, heating or cooling it as necessary.

Toyota has had similar experience with night vision on Lexus, where the percentage of high-end LX470 models shipped with the $1,750 NIR option has dropped from a peak of 26% a few months ago to just 5% recently[4].

Honda has developed what it calls the "world's first Intelligent Night Vision System" which is targeted to reduce night-time pedestrian casualties. The system is available on the Japanese home market Honda Legend.

Honda uses FIR cameras to detect pedestrians in or approaching the vehicle's path and provides the driver with visual and audible warnings. The Intelligent Night Vision System uses images obtained from two far infrared cameras positioned in the lower section of the front bumper to detect the position and movement of heat-emitting objects and determine whether they are in or approaching the vehicle's path. Based on object's size and shape, the algorithms determine if it is a pedestrian.

The latest automakers to jump into the night vision pool are BMW (NIR) and Mercedes (FIR). Shown on the 7 Series and S Class, respectively, the systems are expected to retail in Europe for more than €2,000.

While it is arguable that night vision could be the "next big thing" in automotive features, the price will have to come down by at least half to get to the mainstream kinds of volumes that suppliers and automakers need to fulfill a sustaining business case.

LANE AND ROAD DEPARTURE WARNING

The US National Highway Traffic Safety Administration says single vehicle road departure crashes represent the most serious type of crash on national highways. There were 927,000 single vehicle off-roadway crashes in 2002 and 12,360 of them resulted in fatalities. There are many different causes of these types of crashes, including weather and vision problems, driver impairment, inattention and improper driving behaviors. Roadway departure systems alert drivers when they are drifting out of their lanes and off the roadway – and when they are approaching an upcoming curve at excessive speed[5].

The first, and so far only, commercially available lane departure warning system has been offered by Iteris for commercial vehicles, and via a licensing agreement with Valeo for light vehicles.

The Valeo system installed on Infiniti products (FX, M and Q45 models) recognizes lane markings through the use of a small camera mounted behind the rearview mirror. The camera's signal and the vehicle's speed are sent to the system's microprocessor which combines the information to calculate both the distance between the vehicle and the lane marking and the lateral velocity to the lane marking. If it is determined that the vehicle is leaving the lane, a combination of visual and audible warnings are given. In some embodiments the car's braking systems are activated to help return the vehicle to its original lane.

The Infiniti LDW system is temporarily disabled by driver activation of the vehicle's turn signals, which informs the system's control unit of intended lane changes. The system also features a manual cancel switch, which allows the driver to turn the system off when desired. The system automatically resets when the vehicle is restarted.

On the 2005 Infiniti FX 35, lane departure warning was offered as part of the DVD Mobile Entertainment System with Lane Departure Warning option package priced at $1,750. LDW likely represents only a small fraction of the total package price.

Aisin's Lane Departure Warning System, jointly developed with Toyota, also measures the distance between a car and the white or yellow lane line but with a rear-mounted camera (which is also used by the parking assist system), and alerts the driver with an audible beep if the vehicle is about to cross a highway lane.

LANE KEEPING

Lane keeping is the next big step beyond lane departure warning, Here an electronic "big brother" applies a corrective torque to the vehicle's steering system to bring the car or truck back to the correct driving line automatically.

While no automaker has put a lane keeping system into regular production, there are numerous development programs underway at automaker and supplier laboratories.

One typical lane keeping system is being developed by Continental Automotive Systems. Like lane departure warning, lane keeping determines the vehicle position relative to the lane markings, but offers active support in keeping the vehicle centered on the lane. The driver always retains control – he or she can feel the recommended steering reaction as a gentle movement of the steering wheel, but his or her decision to act or not takes priority.

Mazda's Lane Drive Aid System automatically determines the vehicle's lateral position using a camera and provides steering assistance that helps the driver keep the vehicle in the middle of the lane. When the system judges that the vehicle is in danger of drifting out of the lane, it issues a warning.

Further, the system uses radar sensors on either side of the vehicle to monitor adjacent lanes alongside and aft of the vehicle. If the driver starts to move into a lane without realizing that a vehicle is there, the system issues a Blind Spot Warning.

Mitsubishi's Lane Trace Assist uses an on-board camera to monitor the lane dividing lines and applies a corrective torque to the electric power steering when it senses the vehicle is starting to depart from its lane.

The Lane Keeping Assistance on Toyota's Estima HEV uses electric power steering guided by a video camera that monitors lane markers to assist steering to help keep the vehicle in the intended lane. The system constantly applies the small amount of steering effort required to keep the vehicle near the center of its lane.

SENSOR FUSION

We must take a short detour – a digression – here to talk about sensor fusion. The foregoing discussion of various driver assistance systems has covered applications based on single sensor inputs. While this is the current state of the art, we would be remiss if we didn't say something about the next generation of ITS vehicle sensors with will feature combinations of sensors working like partners to deliver richer arrays of data that drivers and their support systems need.

Denso, for one, has developed additional sensors that detect road conditions and objects ahead of a vehicle. Denso's lidar sensor (laser radar) or millimeter-wave radar sensor is used with Adaptive Cruise Control systems. The millimeter-wave radar sensor is also used in the Pre-Crash Safety Systems, which can help lessen damage in an imminent collision. A vision sensor is used in the Lane Keeping Assist system that helps the driver stay in the center of a lane.

By combining multiple sensors into a single system, more highly accurate safety systems can be created. Combining a millimeter-wave radar sensor and a vision sensor, a sensing system that recognizes the shape, size and type of object can be developed. The radar sensor detects the position and relative velocity of the object, while the vision sensor detects the type and attributes of the object.

As a result, it is possible to accurately identify the positional relationship between the object and the vehicle, as well as the object's relative movement, leading to a safety system that is better tailored to each situation.

As part of the effort to realize even more advanced safety systems, Denso is developing vision processing technology that allows the detection of pedestrians from among multiple objects.

BLIND SPOT MONITORING

Also known as lane change assistance, the goal of the blind spot monitor is to keep a driver from changing lanes when there is another vehicle aft of and to the side of one's own vehicle. This is another PROMETHEUS development that is finally "coming home."

Modern blind spot monitors use radar (some microwave, although laser seems to be increasing in popularity with developers) to look in an area in about a 90 degree arc at each rear corner of a vehicle. If the directional signal is activated, the corresponding radar looks into its assigned area and returns a warning if there is a vehicle in the "blind spot."

Some designs put the sensor in the outside rearview mirrors. This allows for a narrower arc, but increases range requirements. This mounting alternative does give a view into more of the real "blind spot" – the area behind the driver's peripheral vision but ahead of the outside mirror's field of view.

Hella and Siemens VDO, for example, have designed a corner-mounted sensor system, while Mobileye, an Israeli company, has developed a system with the outside mirror mounting position.

Mercedes is evaluating another route with its exterior monitoring system. Cameras integrated into the housings of the outside rearview mirrors monitor traffic to the side of and behind the vehicle when it is parked. If another car or a bicycle is approaching from behind, the system will automatically disable the doors for a brief period to avoid the risk of a collision when they are opened. A warning signal sounds at the same time accompanied by a red danger symbol that illuminates in the mirror glass.

PRE-COLLISION PROTECTION

Current pre-collision warning systems are tied into adaptive cruise control, using the ACC's forward-looking radar to detect potential collision "targets" ahead of one's own vehicle. Typically these systems take several actions to prepare for the potential collision:

- Adjust the seat back angles of the front seats (and in some cases the rear seats) to an angle best suited for "taking" the potential collision,

- Tighten the seat belts,

- Alert the air bags to be prepared to be quickly deployed in the event of a crash, and

- Pre-load the Brake Assist system, if present, so that the brakes can be applied by the driver with maximum force.

Toyota claims to be the first automaker to have developed a radar-based collision safety system – it came out with its Pre-crash Safety System in February 2003. The system uses millimeter-wave radar and a camera to detect other vehicles and obstacles on the road ahead and warns the driver when a collision is imminent. In August 2003, Toyota added Pre-crash Brakes to the system that applies the brakes when the driver fails to react in time. In July 2004, it adopted an "image fusion" method, which adds camera-gained image information to information obtained by millimeter-wave radar. Toyota has further advanced its Pre-crash Safety System by adding a feature that monitors the driver's alertness to determine if he or she is looking straight ahead.

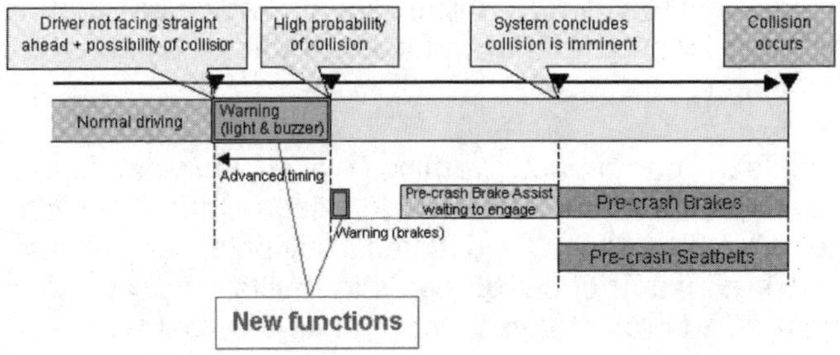

Figure 2. Toyota Pre-Crash Safety System Operation

Honda announced in May 2003 that it had developed the world's first Collision Mitigation Brake System (CMS), which predicts longitudinal collisions and assists brake operation to reduce impact on occupants and vehicle damage. This system determines the likelihood of a collision based on driving conditions, distance to the vehicle ahead, and relative speeds, and uses visual and audio warnings to prompt the driver to take preventive action. It can also initiate braking to reduce the vehicle's speed.

Mercedes' PRE-SAFE system was first announced in Europe in 2001 and came to market in 2003. Initially only adjusting the seat angles and closing the sunroof, the system was quickly expanded to include all the other functions now considered to be part of any pre-crash system.

The evolution of many of these sensor-based detection systems is toward fully automatic collision avoidance and mitigation systems.

REAR IMPACT WARNING AND PROTECTION

As has been demonstrated in the foregoing discussion, most of the attention in longitudinal car-to-car collisions has been on warning the following driver and activating protection systems in his or her vehicle.

While a number of companies have been designing sensor and activator packages to help the occupants of the leading vehicle, Mazda has been the most communicative about its developments via its SensorCar development concept.

Two optical sensors (charge coupled devices or CCDs – really small TV cameras) mounted 2.5 inches apart in the SensorCar's rear bumper monitor surrounding vehicle traffic. The CCD units send their data to a dedicated computer that compares distance, approach angles and closing rates of the other vehicles to determine whether any of them is about to collide with the SensorCar.

If the system determines that a significant rear impact is probable – contact at a closing rate of 6 mph or greater – it sounds an audible alarm from the rear audio speakers and illuminates a warning icon to call attention to the danger.

If the approaching vehicle speed indicates that a collision is imminent, a motorized retractor tightens the front seat belts.

Mazda's rear-impact warning system needs further development and refinement to assure that it screens out all false alarms and detects all potential impacts. Once refined, it could be tied into multiple active safety systems to protect vehicle occupants or avoid accidents entirely.

REAR VIEW TELEVISION

Although closely allied with ultrasonic park assist, rear view TV provides sufficiently more information and lets the driver actually see what objects might pose a danger, or be in danger, when a vehicle is backing. Thus it has been classified as a safety system in this paper.

Rear view TV had its genesis in Japan almost a decade ago – a logical combination of Japanese expertise in making small, rugged television systems with the shared display (for navigation and convenience systems) that had previously taken up residence in the upper center part of the instrument panel. The TV camera is activated when the vehicle is shifted into reverse gear. Nissan, Toyota and Honda quickly jumped on the bandwagon.

Nissan (through its Infiniti brand) was the first Japanese company to bring rear view TV to Western markets. Toyota (through its Lexus channel) and Honda also offer the systems in North America.

The cameras are usually part of a package with other options putting total package prices in the $2,000 to $4,000 range. The Big Three are starting to catch up. A rear view camera system will show up as a regular production option on GM's new 2007 full-size SUVs.

Many Japanese consumer electronics firms offer rear view TV systems in the aftermarket, a trend that is spreading to North America as well. Aftermarket systems are priced between $300 and $700 plus installation.

PERIPHERAL MONITORING

Many automakers are looking at ways to combine the outputs of sensors looking forward, backward and to the sides into a comprehensive system that monitor all around the periphery of the vehicle – hence, the term "peripheral monitoring."

Nissan's Around View Monitor substantially reduces blind spots by displaying a 360-degree view of the area around the vehicle on an instrument panel monitor. The easy-to-understand images displayed in real time are helpful in supporting the driver's maneuvers when parking, by assisting the driver in steering the vehicle easily and accurately into the intended parking space. The system is a further advancement of Nissan's Rear View Monitor, Blind Spot Monitor and Lane Departure Warning applications.

Toyota and Mazda are also experimenting with peripheral monitoring. Image-processing technology enables their systems to detect and warn the driver about children and obstacles within the vehicle's blind spots and to detect and warn the driver about vehicles that are approaching from either side.

Subaru has been researching for at least a decade the use of binocular vision systems for hazard detection and monitoring. Subaru's "eyes" are its frontal recognition sensors, which are adapted from Subaru's Sensor Fusion technology in its Active Driving Assist system. It includes a pair of stereo cameras, as well as a millimeter-wave radar unit from the Legacy Touring Wagon 3.0R.

The stereo camera has been improved as have its recognition algorithms. Processing speed has been accelerated in the new stereo cameras and recognition has been enhanced. In addition, the camera unit and its controller are now packaged together in one module to be more compact and lower cost.

The new stereo camera device can not only detect multiple objects (cars, pedestrians, bicycles), road traffic lines, and conditions (climate changes, light changes, and other conditions), but it also calculates the distance between the car and an object (even at night) as well as the inter-vehicle speed.

DROWSY DRIVER WARNING

Considering the number of traffic incidents and injuries that can be ascribed to driver inattention and drowsiness, it is amazing to see how long it has taken technological solutions to come to fore.

Drowsy driver detection is another of those PROMETHEUS technologies that was demonstrated in vehicles in the mid-1990s. Early systems tried to use changes in the steering wheel reversal rate to predict when a driver was tired (tired drivers correct less often), but these were unable to avoid a high rate of false positive indications (drowsiness was indicated even though the driver was actually alert).

Later experiments tried video detection, using small TV cameras to watch the driver's face the check the location of certain facial features, such as the outboard edges of the eyes and mouth, or eye blink duration and frequency. This technology has continued in development. In the US, Carnegie Mellon University has done extensive work in this area.

The Johns Hopkins University has done work using a 24-GHz transceiver both to illuminate the head and upper torso of the driver. The technique monitors and quantitatively measures several indices, such as the general activity level, the speed, frequency and duration of eyelid closure, the rate of heartbeat and respiration, by analyzing the Doppler components present in the reflected signal.

A drowsy index is calculated based on general activity. As fatigue sets in, this activity will drop below a certain level. A warning can be given at this time notifying the person that he or she is becoming sleepy.

A supplemental index monitors the eye activity for changes associated with increased levels of drowsiness and for eye closure. This second index allows for warnings of increasing intensity as the onset of sleep occurs[6].

Toyota's Pre-Crash Safety System, discussed earlier, comes closest to using sensors to check driver condition, even if Toyota's system determines only head position, not sleepiness or other inattention.

Watching the driver – to detect drowsiness or operation under the influence – is an increasingly popular topic with law enforcement, regulators and automakers because the inattentive or impaired driver is the cause of a large fraction if injury and fatal auto crashes in all developed countries.

Denso is among the leaders among Japanese suppliers for its work on technology that will detect the driver's condition, such as facial recognition, blink and closed eyes detection, and electrocardiograph measurement. Facial recognition identifies an individual by taking a picture with a camera and processing the image.

Blink and closed eyes detection applies different processing to images taken of the driver in order to measure eyelid aperture and detect any lack of attention from sleepiness.

Electrocardiograph measurement is not as far along as the driver monitoring technique, but is envisioned to measure the driver's heart rate through electrodes installed in the steering wheel, then display results on the car navigation monitor or transmit them to an external location such as a physician or family member.

Let's change focus now from autonomous systems to the "connected systems", those that need some electronic link to the roadside or other infrastructure to operate.

TELEMATICS

The telematics industry in Japan in dominated by Toyota and its G-Book, just as General Motors's OnStar dominates in the US.

Toyota recently initiated G-BOOK ALPHA, a more advanced telematics service that consolidates "safety and security", "driving intelligence" and "amusement".

In the event of a traffic accident or medical emergency, the HELPNET service (standard feature) connects users to a dedicated operator and enables summoning of ambulance or other assistance with an onboard microphone. Some new Toyota models come with a system that automatically connects to the operator if the air bags are activated. If there is no response from inside the vehicle, the operator will call for an ambulance.

Optional (e.g., Lexus) G-Security detects breaking into vehicles and tracks vehicle position. For "driving intelligence", the G-BOOK ALPHA service is equipped with a new "G-Route Search" function that combines traffic information from the Vehicle Information and Communication System (VICS) with past statistical data to forecast road traffic conditions and suggest routes that avoid traffic congestion.

The "amusement" area includes Toyota's on-demand car audio system. When vehicles are shipped, encrypted data for more than 10,000 songs are made available on the navigation system's hard drive with a digital rights management system. The customer can then download and purchase a decryption key from a network for the musical pieces that he or she wants to enjoy

Mazda recently adopted Toyota's G-BOOK ALPHA after its own attempt at offering proprietary telematics failed.

Nissan continues to offer its own Telematics system. CARWINGS provides a host of helpful services such as fastest route calculations based on statistical traffic data, real-time traffic updates, weather reports and news. The system supports e-mail notification of the driver's present location, live operator assistance for destination searches and navigation system questions and emergency roadside assistance services, among other services. The current CARWINGS system also provides seamless communication through the use of a Bluetooth-enabled mobile phone.

EMERGENCY CALLING

Also known as Automatic Collision Notification, this is probably one of the most sought-after features from modern telematics systems – the ability to have an on-board mobile phone automatically call emergency services in cases when an air bag deploys.

General Motors added this feature to its OnStar system, receiving wide acclaim from traffic safety professionals and the car and light truck-buying public. GM has, of course, already installed its call centers in North America to handle "ACN" and other calls (but has closed the one center it had previously opened in Europe),

The European Commission has made "eCall" a priority application in its vast new "eSafety" program. In the European vision, eCall is an emergency call either generated manually by vehicle occupants or automatically via activation of in-vehicle sensors when an accident occurs. When activated, the in-vehicle eCall system establishes a voice connection directly with the relevant Public Service Answering Point which is a public authority or a private eCall center. At the same time, a minimum set of data – including key information about the accident such as time, location and vehicle description – is sent to the Public Service Answering Point operator receiving the voice call. The minimum set of data may also contain the link to a potential Service Provider by including its IP address and phone number[7].

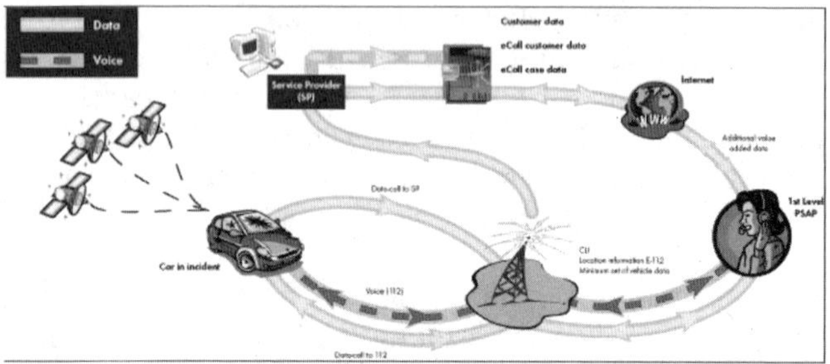

Figure 3. European eCall Network Operation

Mercedes launched its own call-center-based telematics system – TELEAID – which is capable of receiving eCall alerts from vehicles and relaying emergency requests to the appropriate public agencies. Fiat also operates a small telematics call center for its customers in Italy.

Japan has had a more unified approach to emergency calling. The Japanese police have been promoting the Universal Traffic Management Systems (UTMS). The Help System for Emergency Life Saving and Public Safety (HELP) is one of subsystems of UTMS.

Emergency calls from mobile phones have been increasing very rapidly in Japan with the expanding use of mobile phones, and account for more than half the total number of emergency calls. It is difficult to identify the location of a caller and this can delay an emergency vehicle's arrival.

In the HELP system, when an incident occurs while driving, an in-vehicle unit and a cellular phone automatically transmit caller location information obtained from GPS to the operation center, and then automatically activates voice communication.

HELP reduces the time lag from occurrence to reporting of an accident by 40% (from 15 minutes to 9 minutes). All command and control centers of prefectural police headquarters in Japan are equipped to receive location and other information obtained from the HELPNET center. HELP is available everywhere in Japan.

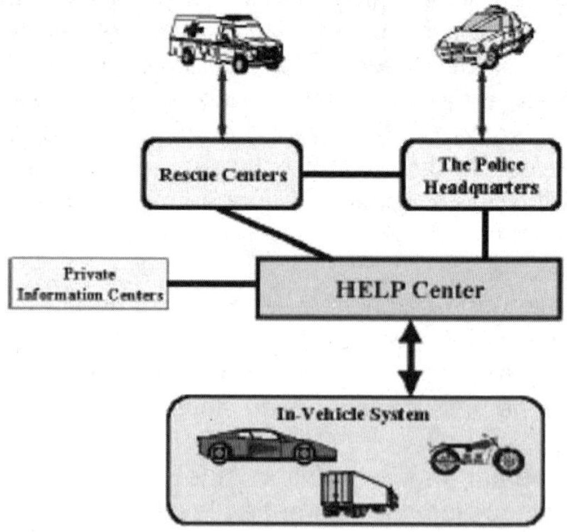

Figure 4. Japanese HELP Emergency Calling System

In order to further improve HELP, automakers in Japan are being encouraged to provide in-vehicle units equipped with the HELP system in all new cars[8].

VEHICLE INFRASTRUCTURE INTEGRATION

VII is a brave (and bold) comprehensive initiative to connect all the cars in the United States with each other and with the roadside (and thus a variety of incident management and emergency services).

The notion behind VII is fairly simple. If vehicles (or their drivers) can be made aware of the intentions of other vehicles (and their drivers) it may be possible to keep these vehicles from running into each other and thus reduce (or eliminate) traffic incidents and the resultant injuries and deaths. Similarly, if vehicles can communicate in real-time with the roadside infrastructure a variety of safety, emergency and convenience features can be made available to the driver and vehicle passengers.

The VII initiative enjoys support from US federal government, a number of trade and research groups, and the principal automakers doing business in North America (both traditional and "new" domestic manufacturers).

Current efforts are focused on determining if the investment necessary to equip new vehicles and the roadway infrastructure with communications is warranted and can be synchronized between the public and private sectors. Studies are underway to achieve at least proof-of-concept for the technology and to develop business cases sufficient to convince public and private sector leaders to invest.

A project to make VII ubiquitous across the United States is probably of greater magnitude than the construction of the Eisenhower Interstate Highway System. No one knows for sure what the total investment would be in a comprehensive network of roadside units that would communicate with and relay messages to vehicles moving on the road. The computer network to process in real time the millions of asynchronous communications between vehicles and infrastructure has yet to be defined.

Nor has anyone figured out how the more than 3,000 road agencies in the US will be convinced to install and operate the roadside units. Perhaps there is a private sector role here.

A similar idea is being pursued in Europe by the Car2Car Consortium among others. The Car2Car Communication Consortium was organized by European vehicle manufacturers and is open to suppliers, researchers and other partners. The Car2Car Communication Consortium wants to improve traffic safety and efficiency by means of inter-vehicle communications.

The Car2Car Consortium hopes to establish an open European industry standard for Car2Car communication systems based on wireless LAN components and to guarantee European-wide inter-vehicle operability. The development of active safety applications is being promoted through the specification, prototyping and demonstration of the Car2Car system. The Consortium also plans to develop realistic deployment strategies and business models to speed-up market penetration.

The radio system for Car2Car is derived from the standard IEEE 802.11 (Wireless LAN). As soon as two or more vehicles are in radio communication range, they connect automatically and establish an ad hoc network. The range of a single Wireless LAN link is limited to a few hundred meters, so every vehicle is also a router that allows sending messages to farther vehicles via multi-hop. The routing algorithm is based on the position of the vehicles and is able to handle fast changes of the ad hoc network topology[9].

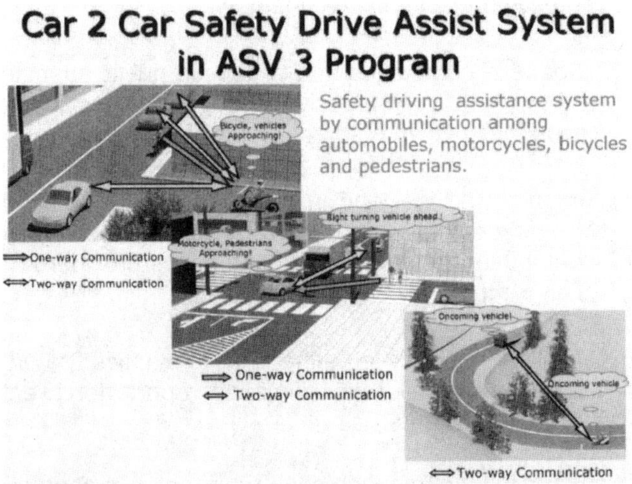

Figure 5. Vision of Car-to-Car Communication in Japan

Japan has integrated the notion of vehicle-to-vehicle and vehicle-to-roadside communication into its Advanced Safety Vehicle program. ASV-3 (the third ASV program) is reaching its conclusion. Demonstrations of the various architectures and technologies are on-going in 2006[10].

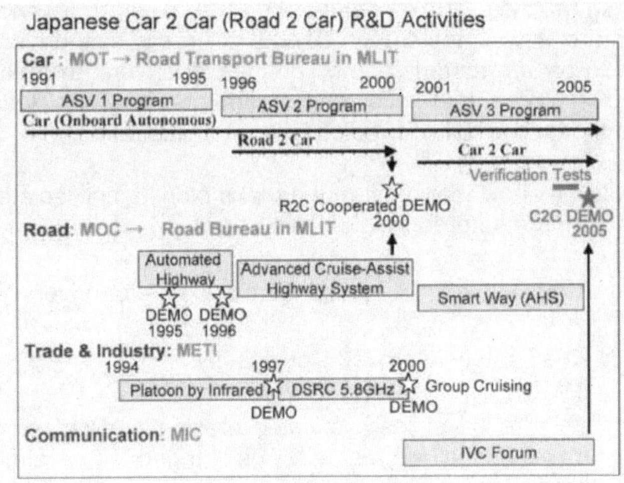

Figure 6. Japanese Car-to-Car R&D Activities

General Motors (Cadillac) and BMW recently demonstrated vehicle-to-vehicle (V2V) communications without benefit of any external communications infrastructure. These respective manufacturers' research cars talked to one-another via an 802.11p WLAN operating in the 5.9 GHz band. Vital information about vehicle location, status (e.g., stopped) and the nearby surroundings (e.g., its raining) were transmitted back to following vehicles so their drivers could take appropriate action. Vehicle location was by GPS, but relative (car-to-car) rather than absolute (on the surface of the planet), so relative positioning error was about one foot.

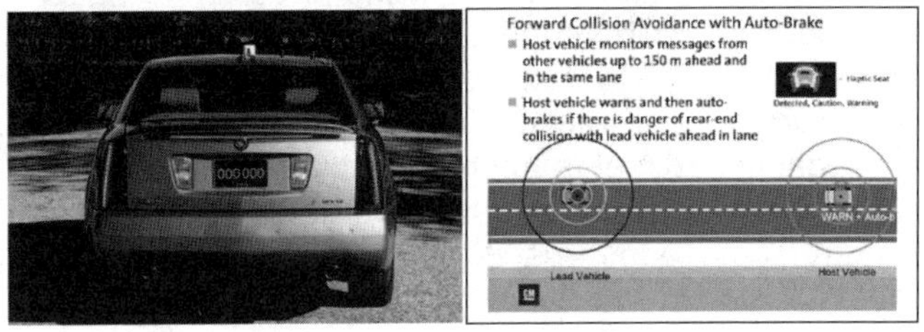

GM equipped one Cadillac with collision avoidance systems that advised the driver when another vehicle was in its blind spot or applied the car's brakes with full authority in case a collision with another V2V-equipped vehicle was eminent.

INTELLIGENT SPEED ADAPTION

Viewed by some as the ultimate automotive invasion by "Big Brother" and by others as a logical and necessary move to improve traffic safety, Intelligent Speed Adaption (or ISA) provides on-board advice to drivers to slow down or in extreme embodiments takes control of the vehicle throttle and actually slows the car or truck down to the posted legal speed limit.

The technology of "smart road signs", capable of transmitting instructions to passing vehicles via some form of short-range communication architecture was part of another of those pesky PROMETHEUS projects. The first practical implementation of ISA was in Sweden where it was tested by 10,000 voluntary test drivers, both private motorists and commercial drivers, in 1999-2002. The trial was a joint venture between local authorities and the Swedish Road Administration.

Results show that most of the trial motorists appreciated the support offered by the ISA system.

- Motorists felt ISA helped them to be better drivers.
- Road safety improved significantly.
- As a result of less repeated braking and stopping, travel time remained unchanged (a slight improvement was noted) despite lower maximum speeds.
- A more even driving speed helped reduce fuel consumption and emissions.
- There was a very high level of acceptance for ISA in urban areas.
- Drivers believed that ISA was the best available measure, along with police surveillance, to solve road safety problems on streets in built-up areas compared with physical measures such as road humps[11].

Other European countries are experimenting with ISA including The Netherlands and the UK. While national auto clubs generally support continued experimentation, they and the automakers are concerned that the technology is still nascent and additional technological and legal impediments need to be overcome before ISA is ready for application as a mandatory traffic control system. These groups do support a rollout in which drivers could opt to volunteer to use.

INTERSECTION COLLISION WARNING

Our final ITS technology application for examination is intersection collision warning. While traffic incidents at intersections are of concern to every traffic agency, they are of particular concern in Japan where many urban intersections can involve small, narrow streets crossing much wider and busier main roadways. In addition, there are many "blind" intersections that are particularly dangerous for crossing vehicular traffic as well as pedestrians.

In the typical embodiment, information on intersections that are without traffic signals is gathered from car navigation system data. Images from the vehicle's cameras are analyzed to detect stop lines and stop signs. Based on the vehicle's speed and distance to the stop line the system determines whether the vehicle is traveling at a speed that will enable it to stop by the time it reaches the stop line.

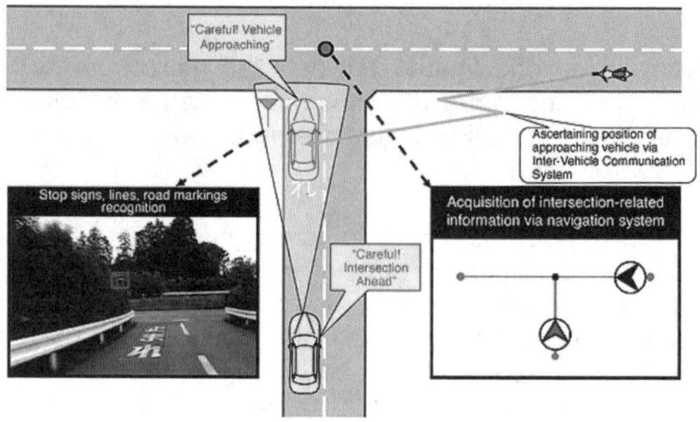

Figure 7. "Smart" intersection with "smart" vehicles

If the vehicle is going too fast, the system delivers an audio warning while signaling the driver to slow down with the application of gentle, intermittent braking.

Once the automobile has come to a stop, the Inter-Vehicle Communication System detects the position of any approaching vehicles and assists the driver in determining whether it is safe to proceed through the intersection[12].

CONCLUSION – WHO IS REALLY "ON FIRST?"

The foregoing discussion paints a very broad picture of which ITS developments that impact cars and trucks are being pursued by whom and where.

There are several general conclusions:

- European automakers, notably those in Germany, are developing and fielding a plethora of automotive safety systems that make use of modern computer and communications technology.
- Japanese companies and Japanese public agencies are working very closely on cooperative systems, those that involve both vehicles and roadways.
- America has the lead in telematics due to General Motors' dedication to its OnStar business unit. The contribution of independent telematics provider ATX is also important.
- Satellite radio is entering the telematics fray by offering real-time traffic situation reports for twenty US metropolitan areas.

This is not to say that each country or region is operating with tunnel vision. On the contrary, there is research (mostly) and development work (some) on every technology application in every region.

There is also a popular notion that some premium vehicles built by European and Japanese companies are "de-contented" when they are exported to North America because "Americans don't understand technology – they are afraid of it." This is not entirely true – for example, Nissan maintains its ITS applications when it sends Infiniti-branded products to America.

When it comes to vehicular applications, there are several conclusions evident:

- Premium vehicles "have all the luck" when it comes to applying ITS technologies. The principal exception to this rule is Ultrasonic Park Assist which is widely applied around the world – because it's cheap.
- One can find similar pricing and application practices with GPS navigation, but in this case its feature content that drives the price. Higher priced, premium vehicles have more features on their navigation systems – color displays, hard-disc drive data storage and route planning algorithms. A small car's navigation system, on the other hand might have a monochrome display, flash card or CD memory and position location.
- European and Japanese premium marques have most of the applications because their domestic buyers are technologically aware and want (and in some cases demand) new safety and convenience enhancing technologies.
- Nissan brings to market a variety of technological wonders – cars and light trucks absolutely laden with multiple, high-capability, high-value ITS applications.

On the supplier side, virtually every Tier One supplier who trades in automotive electronics is developing some ITS systems. In Europe its Continental AG, Siemens VDO Automotive and Valeo. In Japan, the lead is with Denso, Aisin and Hitachi, but many others are also active. The US effort is led by Delphi with the foregoing European and Japanese firms also very active.

If you want to see the future face of new automotive technology in general and ITS in particular, watch Mercedes, Toyota and Honda. These companies have little fear of technological risk – in fact, they seem to revel in it – because at the end of the day it brings them image and, in the long term, image brings customers, revenue and profits.

REFERENCES

[1] ITS is defined in this paper as the application of modern computer and communications technology to road transportation.
[2] In this paper the terms "America" and "American" refer to all of North America – the USA, Canada and Mexico.
[3] Adaptive Cruise Control has also been called "active cruise control" or "intelligent cruise control" in other literature and automotive publicity and sales materials.

[4] *Business Week Online*; September 14, 2005
[5] NHTSA Vehicle Safety Rulemaking and Supporting Research Priorities: Calendar Years 2005-2009 – Update January 2005
[6] The Johns Hopkins University, Applied Physics Laboratory
[7] eCall Toolbox; SCOPE eSafety Observatory; ERTICO
[8] Morita, Masatoshi; "Current Status and Future Plans for HELP"; International Telecommunications Union; March 2005
[9] The Car2Car Consortium
[10] Furukawa, Yoshimi; "Overview of R&D on Active Safety in Japan"; undated (2004 or 2005)
[11] "ISA for increased social responsibility and competitiveness"; Swedish Road Association; undated
[12] "Honda Completes Development of ASV-3 Advanced Safety Vehicles"; Honda press release; September 5, 2005

CONTACT

Gerald Conover is managing director of PRC Associates, an advisor on matters of product, technology and corporate management to firms and agencies in the intelligent transportation systems and services community.

Before founding PRC Associates, Mr. Conover enjoyed 32 years at Ford with assignments in Car Product Development, Manufacturing Operations, and the Technical Staffs. From 1991, his focus was on development and implementation of intelligent transport systems product and supply strategies for Ford and its worldwide affiliates.

Mr. Conover is active in numerous professional organizations including the Society of Automotive Engineers, the Intelligent Transportation Society of America (having served on its Board and Executive Committee), and the Board and Organizing Committee for the ITS World Congress, as well as local and national charitable and community organizations.

Mr. Conover is the 2005 recipient of the SAE Delco Electronics Intelligent Transportation Systems Award.

2005-01-1599

A Navigation Assistance Agent: Online Access to LBS

Wentao Cai and Shengrui Wang
University of Sherbrooke

ABSTRACT

LBS (location-based service) is an important component of navigation assistance systems. Modern onboard devices employ CD-based or DVD-based data storage. In this paper, we are interested in techniques that can be used to build agents for searching and accessing online LBS information. Such agents must be capable of content-based analysis, as most LBS information provided by text in a Web page cannot be easily classified and identified by a keyword search engine. We propose an ontology-based conceptual information retrieval method to perform real-time online LBS information access. The proposed method allows the automatic identification of addresses as structural knowledge through graph matching. Location-based information can then be retrieved and extracted on the basis of addresses: the abundant location-based services provided by YellowPages are an example. A prototype, RouteInfo, has been developed to integrate positioning, LBS information search, address geo-coding and route finding.

INTRODUCTION

In this paper, we report new techniques we have developed for building an agent to perform online LBS access and location-based information database updating. The approach utilizes real-time online search instead of CD-based or DVD-based solutions. The project presented in this paper is part of Auto21 Theme FII – "Construction of an Integrated Navigation Information Infrastructure", supported by NCE Canada (Networks of Centers of Excellence). The goal of Auto21 Theme FII is to design and develop an integrated information system as part of a global information infrastructure to assist navigation, enhance on-board systems for safe driving, and improve access to location-based information [1].

Modern onboard navigation systems provide smarter state-of-the-art solutions to guide driving. The system basically utilizes GPS (Global Positioning System) as the tool for locating a vehicle's position and tracking its path. It integrates digital road maps and information on points of interest. However, updating road map and points of interest data is a costly process. Information providers usually update their products annually by producing new versions. When a driver decides to go to a new city, he has to buy the CD containing the city's information for the current year. Although this solution is feasible, drivers may still not be able to access the most up-to-date information from onboard CDs or DVDs.

On the other hand, the development of wireless telecommunications heralds an era of mobile computing, with ubiquitous location-awareness becoming a significant feature. As Hightower et al [2] explain, "ubiquitous location-awareness is a requirement for certain telecommunication or mobile applications that use location information." This notion also suggests new developments in the field of navigation assistance. In this context, onboard devices will be more intelligent and connectible through wireless networks and ubiquitous computation. When a driver is on the road, such techniques make online access to information portals possible.

LBS is emerging in the industry along with the notion of ubiquitous location-awareness. It involves the ability to find the geographical location of a mobile device and provide services based on this location information. Examples of location-based services might include finding the closest restaurant to a traveler. When the end user passes by a shopping mall, the closest restaurant will be found and its information transmitted to the user by means of unsolicited commercial email or a short message. Obviously, this idea can also be applied in navigation assistance to help the driver find roadside services or points of interest. However, the problem of constructing LBS information infrastructure is far from being solved by industrial and academic researchers. Retrieving, updating and storing large amounts of location-based data all pose significant challenges. On the other hand, the large and growing collection of texts on the Web constitutes a valuable pool of location-based information, most of it up-to-date data. Modern information retrieval (IR) and information extraction (IE) approaches can help in providing access and collecting location-based data via the Internet.

Address identification can be used to achieve location-based information extraction, as much location-based information can be retrieved from Web on the basis of corresponding postal addresses. For example, www.yellowpages.ca and www.411.ca provide a large and valuable database containing abundant services with their addresses. In this context, address extraction from the Web and related content-based information retrieval technology are portals for the automatic updating and retrieval of location-awareness information via the Web in database warehousing applications. In addition, the postal address itself can be projected onto a digital map by address geo-coding techniques. Hence, the online location-based information search agent can also be (part of) a solution to the data updating problem.

In this paper, we propose a method for retrieving online location-based information in real time. The proposal employs ontology-based conceptual information retrieval combined with graph matching to perform address identification from Web pages. A prototype, the RouteInfo system, has been developed and evaluated. Section 2 illustrates the framework for implementation of the RouteInfo system. Section 3 introduces our proposal to achieve online address extraction from Web pages. Section 4 briefly presents the implementation of the RouteInfo prototype system. And finally, Section 5 gives the conclusion.

FRAMEWORK OF THE ROUTEINFO SYSTEM

The RouteInfo system proposes a system framework for the implementation of a new-generation onboard device, applying online information extraction techniques. In this solution, we focus on the problem of extracting postal address structures from Web pages. Postal address extraction is an information extraction task. It identifies possible address concepts in plain text and fits the information into a tabular structure.

The system is composed of eight modules which are run in successive phases. In order, they are: the positioning module, the geo-filtering module, the Web crawling module, the tag filtering module, the address extracting module, the address geo-coding module, the LBS information ranking module and, finally, the route finding module, as illustrated in Figure 1.

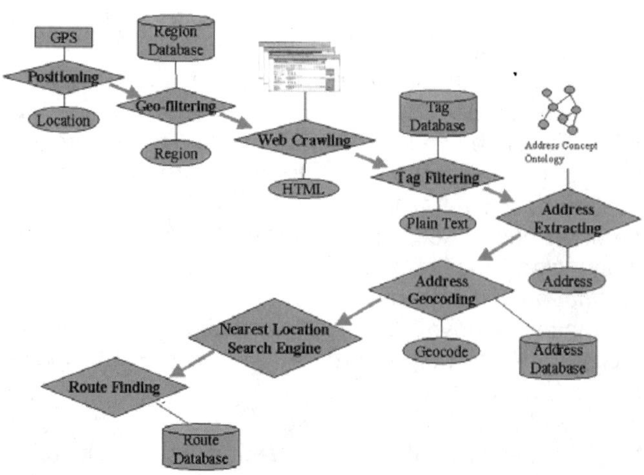

Figure 1: Overview of the RouteInfo system framework

POSITIONING MODULE

The positioning module locates the moving vehicle and retrieves its geographic latitude-longitude coordinates. Many systems have been designed and developed to achieve this goal, such as the magnetic compass, the sextant, radio systems, and most recently, the innovative invention known as the GPS system. The basic functions of this module are to provide the latitude-longitude information of the moving vehicle, track its path, and also communicate with the information system running in the background.

GEO-FILTERING MODULE

Geo-filtering processes the geographic coordinates of a moving vehicle and generates search criteria for the system. The main goal of this module is to reduce the data search depth to meet some performance requirement. For example, in the prototype, we apply www.yellowpages.ca as a location-based service Web database. The database is indexed by city and business category. The more precise the region determined by the vehicle's location, the less data (contained in the response Web page) will be retrieved. If the location can be positioned in a city such as "Toronto East", a set of suitable keywords will be created by the module and passed to the Web crawler. In this context, maintaining the geo-filtering module requires a region boundary database. For each geographic coordinate input, the module will compute the region in which the given input is contained.

WEB CRAWLING MODULE

Web crawling is the basic portal for most Internet-based information search applications. It is responsible for intelligently and automatically gathering data from the Web via batches of links and URLs. A Web crawling component can traverse the Web with tree-search capability. It downloads the Web page of a given URL, records underlying links extracted from the current Web page, and then picks up the most relevant (highest rank) URL to perform repeated new searches.

TAG FILTERING MODULE

Tag filtering eliminates HTML tags from the Web page and outputs the plain text which contains only HTML content. It is also responsible for converting plain text into the uniform format used in the system, for example, transforming all lowercase characters into uppercase letters. This function operates by maintaining a file that records all HTML tags and special URL encoding for some commonly used characters, such as "<BODY>", "<\BODY>", "%7E" (encoding of character "~"). When an input Web page supplied by the Web crawling module enters this component, a word-by-word search will be carried out. Each identified HTML tag will be discarded and each string encoding commonly used characters will be restored to its usual inscriptive form.

ADDRESS EXTRACTION MODULE

The address extraction module takes address candidates from the plain text produced by the tag filtering module and fits these candidates into a tabular and easily understandable address structure. This is the main segment that distinguishes our system from traditional CD-based or DVD-based onboard devices. We propose an ontology-based conceptual information retrieval approach combined with graph matching and structure mapping methods to automatically identify possible address structures in a Web page. First, address concepts and their relations are identified. Next, all of the segments extracted from the plain text are transformed into their graph representations. Graph similarity measurement and node mapping are then performed to evaluate these segment candidates. Finally, possible address data is identified and decomposed into individual elements.

ADDRESS GEO-CODING MODULE

Address geo-coding assigns a latitude-longitude coordinate to an address. It is a basic component in the GIS field since the address itself is the most common form of geographic information. After we extract addresses for LBS information from a Web page, the addresses should be mapped (or located) on the digital map. This process requires the TIGER-format [3] GIS database. It contains street lines and their corresponding information, which includes range of street numbers from start point to end, street name, street type, direction, city, etc.

LBS INFORMATION RANKING MODULE

LBS information ranking assigns a score to each identified piece of location-based service data and orders the address list relative to the driver's request. (In the prototype system, we only implement the nearest location search.) The module can also utilize information ranking techniques which combine distance and other factors. For example, when a driver wants a hotel that is nearby but also cheap, he may consider the nearest 3-star hotel to be the best response from the system. It is also possible to import recommendation systems such as [4] to provide reasonable suggestions on the basis of the driver's tastes.

ROUTE FINDING MODULE

Route finding provides an efficient route planning strategy to guide the driver from the start point to the end goal. It utilizes graph-based traverse methods to find paths in complex modern road networks. This is a very important feature in a navigation system, especially for drivers who are lost. Yahoo! Map [5], Microsoft MapPoint [6] and MapQuest [7] provide online route-finding interfaces and most onboard device producers also integrate such functions into their products. Our previous research proposed an efficient, improved route-finding algorithm in real time for hierarchical road networks [19].

ADDRESS EXTRACTION

OVERVIEW

Address extraction from the Web is actually an IE problem. This process scans textual content in the Web page, identifies possible lexical address descriptions, and finally labels text segments as understandable address structures. As shown in Figure 2, after the Web page is retrieved, the HTML file is converted into plain text, and possible address candidates in the document are extracted and fit into a tabular structure.

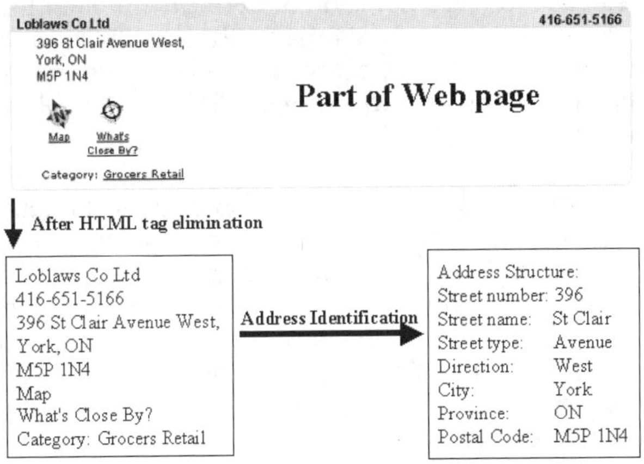

Figure 2: Illustration of address extraction

The process of information extraction has three major steps. First, the system extracts individual "facts" from the text of a document through local analysis. Second, it infers new and related facts. Finally, all the discovered facts are integrated and translated into the required output format. Most IE applications employ information retrieval techniques to accomplish their first step, since the individual "fact"-finding problem is a data retrieval process.

In the postal address domain, an address itself is a knowledge structure. It includes suite (or apartment) information, municipal location, and regional position, as shown in Figure 3. Based on this observation, address extraction should consider appropriate knowledge structure information. For example, a text segment "Kingston Street will be under construction from June 9 to July 15" is not a valid address even though "Kingston" and "Street" are concepts (name entities) in the postal address domain. On the other hand, a text segment like "Loblaws supermarket, located at 125 Kingston Street, Toronto" contains the address descriptor "125 Kingston Street, Toronto".

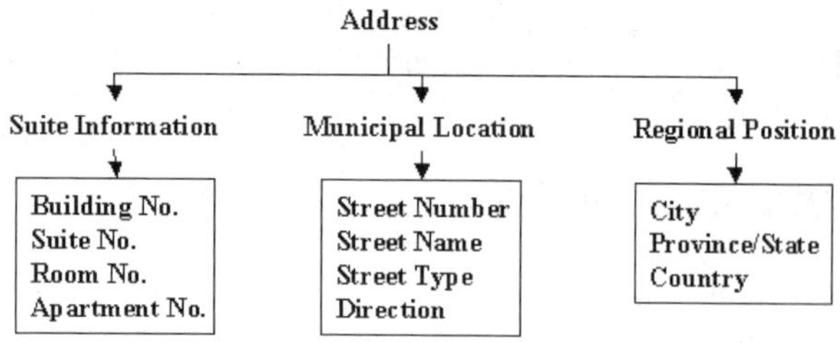

Figure 3: Postal address structure

However, postal address inscriptions are much more diverse than the general description given above. A real mailing address can be written as "Suite 113, 100 Kingston Street, Toronto, ON" or "100 Kingston Street, Suite 113, Toronto, ON", or even "Suite 113, ABC Plaza, Kingston Street, Toronto, ON", in which "ABC Plaza" is a substitution for "100 Kingston Street". On the other hand, not all address elements have to appear in a real address. For example, some addresses have no suite information. The above address does not contain a "direction" description.

Vocabulary poses another set of problems. Language use may cause semantic misunderstandings due to synonyms (different words for the same meaning) and polysemy (the same word with different meanings). In the synonym case, for example, "Street" is often written as its short form "St", "St." or "Str"; "West" is often abbreviated as "W". As illustrations of polysemy, "Quebec" is a province in Canada, but it is also a city name in the province of Quebec; "Ontario" is a province in Canada but it may be a street name in some city; "Sherbrooke" may also appear as a city name or a street name.

Current information retrieval tools mostly use the well-studied method of keyword-based search. This approach encounters significant vocabulary problems [8, 9] and also leads to low precision and recall. On the other hand, content-based information retrieval is a new extensive generation of modern IR approaches, which "combines search technologies and knowledge about query and user context into a single framework in order to provide the most appropriate answer for a user's information needs" [10]. Since this approach simulates humans' understanding of documents, it is recognized as a promising direction in the IR, IE and knowledge discovery fields. Nevertheless, significant effort is still required in order to apply content-based IR approaches to the postal address domain.

Much recent research on content-based information retrieval focuses on conceptual analysis of unstructured texts on the Web. In such conceptual information retrieval systems, researchers tend to utilize the domain ontology as a conceptual structure to accomplish concept extraction by combining human knowledge and computing techniques. Since computers do not treat documents as explicit knowledge but rather as words, mapping the words onto a set of predefined concepts (knowledge) is one way to discover textual underlying meanings. By way of a definition, an ontology specifies a conceptualization of a particular knowledge domain [11], in which each concept is formalized as a node in the ontology and a relationship between concepts is represented by an edge linking concept nodes.

The main advantages of an ontology are that it conceptualizes domain knowledge and avoids vocabulary problems in concept space. Since edges in the ontology describe concept relations, domain knowledge is represented by means of a set of concepts and their connections. Each concept contains two basic elements, one being its inscription and the other its meaning in the domain. In this context, synonyms correspond to distinct nodes with different inscriptions and equivalent concept meanings, while polysemy involves separate nodes with the same inscription and distinct concept meanings.

Some approaches, such as those in [12, 13, 14], suggest applying the concept space model to represent documents, a notion inspired by the classic vector space (bag-of-words) model. Each document is normalized to a concept-element vector and the value of each element is determined by the concept frequency. An ontology or thesaurus is used to merge synonyms and other related syntax. The main advantage of these approaches is that the concept space is so simple that well-studied statistical and clustering methods can be applied to satisfy the automatic indexing requirement for quick-search purposes. However, a common vector cannot exhibit the relationship among concepts. In other words, its usefulness for further knowledge discovery and automatic reasoning is limited. Philosophers and linguists have found that graph structures are a better way to represent human knowledge.

Conceptual graphs [15] and semantic networks are academic efforts towards machine understanding. Based on these notions, graph-based document representation can easily preserve implicit knowledge in the context of texts. However, transforming plain texts into graphs is not an easy task, since concepts or their relationships (in other words, propositions) have to be identified automatically. Graph matching in general is also a difficult problem because most of the approaches are NP-complete. These two problems obstruct the application of graph structures in information retrieval.

OUR PROPOSAL

An ontology is a directed graph, in the straightforward sense that a document can be described as a subgraph of the predefined ontology after concepts in the document are identified and mapped onto this ontology. The matching problem for such graphs is relatively simple, as comparing concepts corresponds to node similarity in the graph. In view of this, approximate graph matching algorithms can be applied to speed up indexing and clustering performance.

Ontology Construction

Ontologies play an increasingly important role in real world modeling in the artificial intelligence literature. Gruber [16] states that an ontology is "a specification of a conceptualization". Such a conceptualization can be defined as a structure *<D, R>*, where *D* is a domain and *R* represents relevant relations on *D*. Based on this view, the ontology itself is actually a set of concepts in a specific domain and defines underlying relations between these concepts.

The concept set in the ontology of the postal address domain is actually a gazetteer, in which each concept can be described as a duple *c=(inscription,meaning)*, where *inscription* corresponds to the lexical inscription form of the concept and *meaning* is the syntactic sense of the concept. For example, the word "Sherbrooke" will be transformed into two concepts: "street_name: Sherbrooke" and "city: Sherbrooke", as "Sherbrooke" can be actually both a street name and a city name. The top-level ontology in the postal address domain is the abstract understanding of a real mailing address, as shown in Figure 4. The concepts here are the basic entities and general descriptors. On the other hand, factual concepts located in the lower level of the ontology graph are the instances of street name, street type, direction, city and province.

In the address domain, concepts are linked together by means of their semantic relations, which can be classified as vertical and horizontal relationships. These are as follows:

(1) The **PartOf** relation (vertical relationship) organizes the concepts according to a decomposition hierarchy. For instance, *municipal location* can be composed into *street-number*, *street-name*, *street-type*, etc. Figure 4 gives a PartOf relation segment for a top-level ontology in the address domain.

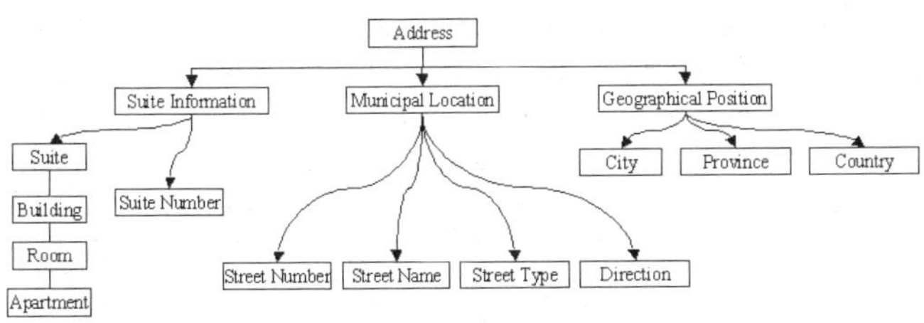

Figure 4: PartOf relation segment for a top-level ontology in the address domain

(2) The **InstanceOf** relation (vertical relationship) provides a specific instance of the concept being defined. For example, *Northeast* is an instance of *Direction*, *Toronto* is an instance of *city*. Figure 5 gives an InstanceOf relation segment for the *Direction* concept.

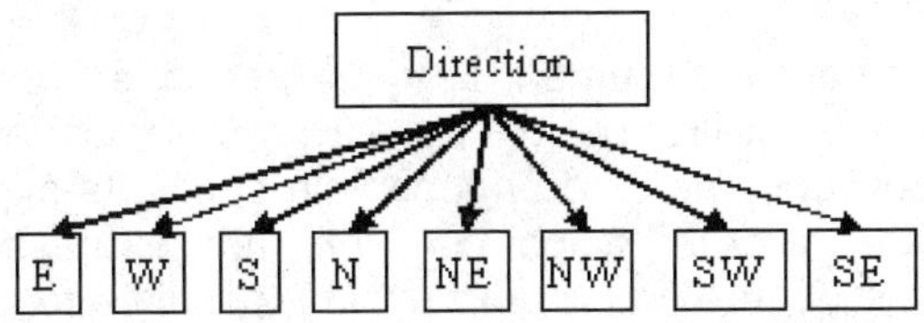

Figure 5: InstanceOf relation segment for the concept *Direction*

(3) The **Similar** relation (horizontal relationship) gives a set of concepts that are similar to the concept being defined. Figure 6 gives a Similar relation segment for the concept *NE*.

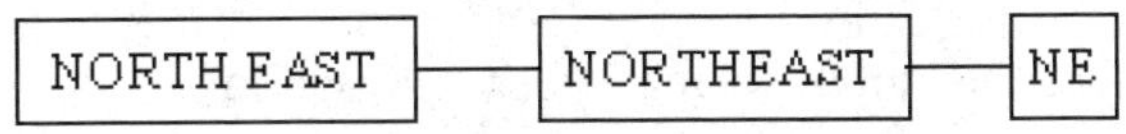

Figure 6: Similar relation segment for the concept *NE*

(4) The **SyntacticNeighbor** relation (horizontal relationship) defines the neighborhood relation when two concepts are linked together in the document, either in the same sentence or two adjacent sentences. For example, in "20 Jutland Road, Etobicoke, Ontario", "Jutland" is SyntacticNeighbor of "Road", and "Road" is SyntacticNeighbor of "Jutland" and "Etobicoke". Figure 7 shows the SyntacticNeighbor relation in the address domain, giving all of the syntactic-neighboring relations in this address expression.

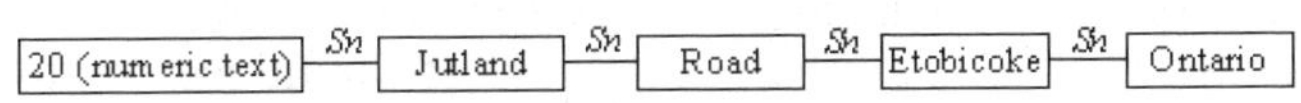

Figure 7. The SyntacticNeighbor relation in the address domain

When a concept is entered in the ontology, relations are determined. Therefore, the intentional definition of an ontology is represented by the following:

$$G_o = (N, E) \qquad (1)$$

where G_o is the ontology graph; N is the set of concept nodes corresponding to

$$N = (n, d) \qquad (2)$$

where *n* is the inscription form of the concept and *d* is the description of the concept (explaining the meanings of the concept); and E is the set of edges linking concept nodes to represent relationships. It is a 4-tuple

$$E = (Pa, In, Si, Sn) \qquad (3)$$

where *Pa* is the PartOf relation, *In* is the InstanceOf relation, *Si* is the Similar relation and *Sn* is the SyntacticNeighbor relation.

Concept Identification

To represent a document using a predefined ontology, concepts must first be identified from unstructured text. However, documents do not contain concepts explicitly, but rather words. Once concepts are expressed by language (words and grammar), it is possible to identify them in text by analyzing phrases [14]. Since it is very important to deduce implicit concepts in the context, we can use the following rules with regard to the relationship categories mentioned above.

***Rule 1**:* The SyntacticNeighbor relation can be identified if two concepts are contiguous in the document. For example, the phrase "Maple Street in Canada" indicates that the concept "Maple" is SyntacticNeighbor of the concept "Street"; the concept "Street" has SyntacticNeighbor "Maple" but not "Canada".

***Rule 2**:* If a concept is an instance of its parent node, that parent node is also identified. For example, in Figure 2, if the concept "East" is spotted, the "direction" concept should be picked out.

***Rule 3**:* If a concept is found, its similar sibling concepts must be identified. For example, in Figure 3, when the concept "NE" is identified, its similar siblings "NORTHEAST" and "NORTH EAST" will also be picked out.

***Rule 4**:* If an identified concept has more than one meaning, all concept nodes corresponding to the concept are highlighted and their parent nodes are also picked out. For example, "Sherbrooke" can be treated as both "street_name" and "city". If "Sherbrooke" is identified in the document, both "street_name:Sherbrooke" and "city:Sherbrooke" are identified, and their InstanceOf relation parent nodes "street name" and "city" are also picked out.

***Rule 5**:* The SyntacticNeighbor relation will be transferred from the child node to its parent node, following the InstanceOf relation edge. For example, in the phrase "Maple Street in Canada", we know that "Maple" and "Street" are syntactic neighbors, "Maple" is a child node of "street_name" under the InstanceOf relation (in other words, "Maple" is an instance of "street_name"), and "Street" is a child node of "street_type" under the InstanceOf relation. We can also determine that "street_name" and "street_type" are syntactic neighbors.

For example, given the phrase (text segment) "*20 TORONTO ROAD ETOBICOKE ON*", we identify "*20*" (numeric text) as a possible instance of "suite_number" or "street_number", "*TORONTO*" as a possible instance of both "street_name" and "city", "*ROAD*" as an instance of "street_type" (its synonym "*RD*" is also picked out), "*ETOBICOKE*" as being in the same situation as "*TORONTO*", and finally "*ON*" as an instance of "province" (its synonym "*ONTARIO*" is also picked out). After identification, the general concepts (or, we may say, abstract descriptors), "suite_number", "street_number", "street_name", "street_type", "city", "province" are also determined, with their relations. The ontology graph of this text segment will be constructed as in Figure 8, following the above five rules.

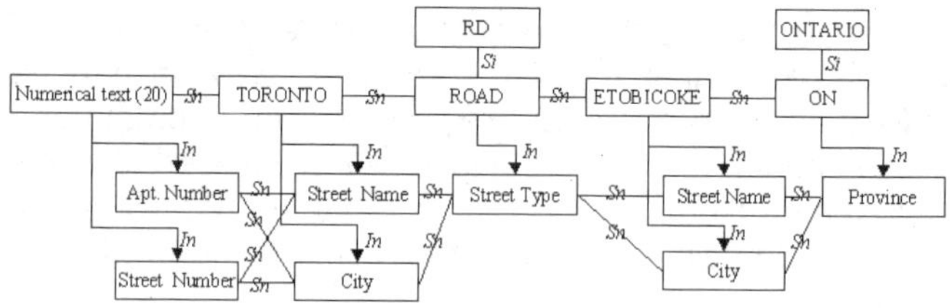

Figure 8: Ontology graph of the phrase "*20 TORONTO ROAD ETOBICOKE ON*"

In the graph, the label "Si" is a Similar relation edge, "Sn" is a SyntacticNeighbor relation edge, "In" is an InstanceOf relation edge.

Graph Matching

Graph matching provides a way of computing similarity and reconciling common concept nodes (node-to-node mapping) between knowledge structures. For postal address extraction, if a graph of a text segment in the document is more similar to the predefined template graph of an address structure, this text segment is more likely to be a real address. Through node-to-node mapping, ambiguous nodes will be disambiguated by coherent correspondences. The mapping results are then used to fill out the tabular address structure after the real address is found.

To perform graph matching, we utilize two definitions, for the template graph and the abstract descriptor subgraph. The template graph is the predefined knowledge (graph structure) of address structure which presents all address elements and their SyntacticNeighbor relations, as in Figure 9. An abstract descriptor subgraph is the subgraph of general concepts in the text segment graph. Based on human analysis of postal address structure, it concentrates on general concepts extracted from a text segment graph to represent abstract knowledge of the text. For example, a real address "100 Kingston St, Toronto, ON" can be represented as a StreetNumber(100)-StreetName(Kingston)-StreetType(St)-City(Toronto)-Province(ON) structure. Here, we call the general concept "StreetName" as the abstract descriptor of the "Kingston" concept, the general concept "StreetType" as the abstract descriptor of the "St" concept, etc. After the concepts in a text segment are identified, their abstract descriptors (InstanceOf or PartOf parent of top-level concept nodes) can be induced along InstanceOf and PartOf relation edges, as shown in Figure 10.

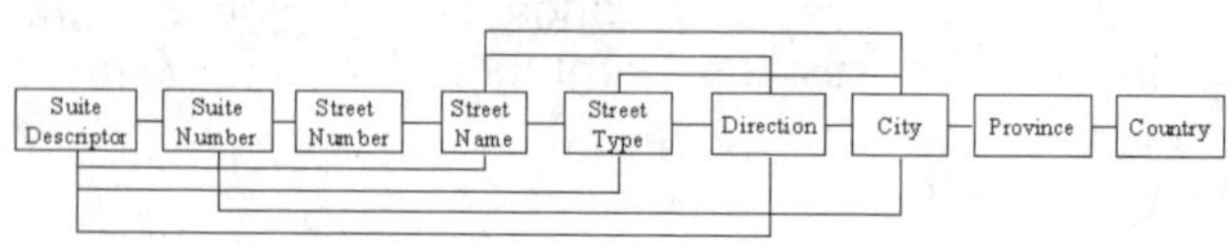

Figure 9: Template graph in the address domain

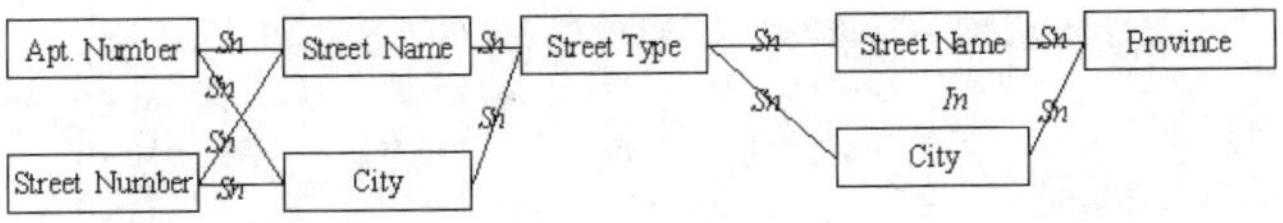

Figure 10: Abstract descriptor subgraph of the phrase "20 TORONTO ROAD ETOBICOKE ON"

Graph similarity measurement in the IR field has received considerable attention from researchers such as [17, 18]. Most of their proposals define graph similarity based on the similarity between concepts and the similarity between relations, corresponding to separate node and edge comparisons. In the address domain, however, the graph similarity problem is relatively simple. After a segment of text in the specified document is transformed into an ontology graph, the closer its abstract descriptor subgraph to the template, the more likely it is that the segment is an address structure. Based on this consideration, the similarity between two graphs can be defined by the following formula:

$$sim = \frac{N_c(G,G_T) + E_c(G,G_T)}{N(G_T) + E(G_T)} \qquad (5)$$

where $N_c(G,G_T)$ is the number of nodes shared by the text segment's abstract descriptor subgraph G and the template graph G_T, $E_c(G,G_T)$ is the number of edges common to G and G_T, $N(G_T)$ is the number of nodes in graph G_T, and $E(G_T)$ is the number of edges in G_T.

For the example illustrated in Figure 8 for the text segment "20 TORONTO ROAD ETOBICOKE ON", if we compare its abstract descriptor subgraph (Figure10) with the template graph (Figure 9) and prune off duplicated elements (for instance, by regarding the two "street_name" nodes as a single "street_name", and the two edges connecting "street_name" and "street_type" as one edge), we can determine that

$$\begin{cases} N_c(G,G_T) = 6 \\ E_c(G,G_T) = 7 \\ \mathrm{N}(\mathrm{G_T}) = 9 \\ \mathrm{E}(\mathrm{G_T}) = 15 \end{cases} \qquad (6)$$

We can then derive the similarity between the two graphs as 0.54167.

After the graph similarity comparison, structure mapping is performed to analyze possible address candidates and decompose them into tabular structures. In our method, structure mapping utilizes a brute-force enumeration procedure. We eliminate the edges that are in the abstract descriptor graph but not in the template graph (these edges are false links between address elements which may be caused by word polysemy and ambiguity). Then, we find a path along SyntacticNeighbor edges in the abstract descriptor subgraph, subject to the following conditions: (1) each instance concept node is mapped to a unique abstract descriptor node; (2) no abstract descriptor node is duplicated. For example, in the graph of the text segment in Figure 8, a path (drawn as a heavy line) can be determined as in Figure 11.

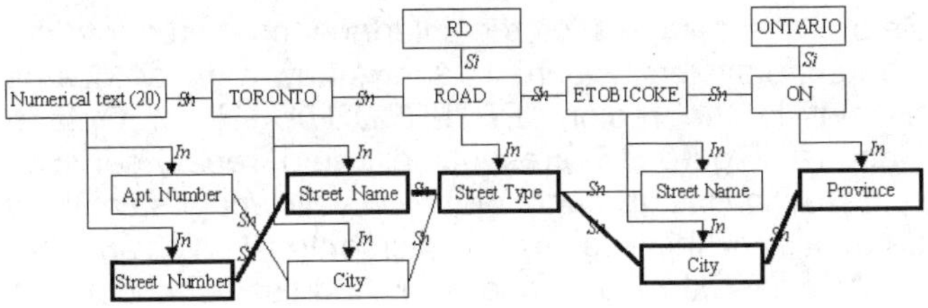

Figure 11: Determine a path by applying structure mapping

THE ROUTEINFO SYSTEM - PROTOTYPE

We implemented the RouteInfo system as a prototype to present our proposal for the infrastructure of a navigation information system and evaluate the suggested methods applied in the main phases. In the system, ontology construction for the address domain utilized the GIS database of DMTI Canada, which provides digital maps and all instance concepts, such as "street_name", "street_type", "direction" and "city", used in Ontario, Canada. We used www.yellowpages.ca as a test Web database of points of interest.

In the prototype, the four main procedures are designated as RI_WebCrawler, RI_AddressExtractor, RI_AddressGeocoder and RI_RouteFinder. The data flow of the system is illustrated in Figure 13.

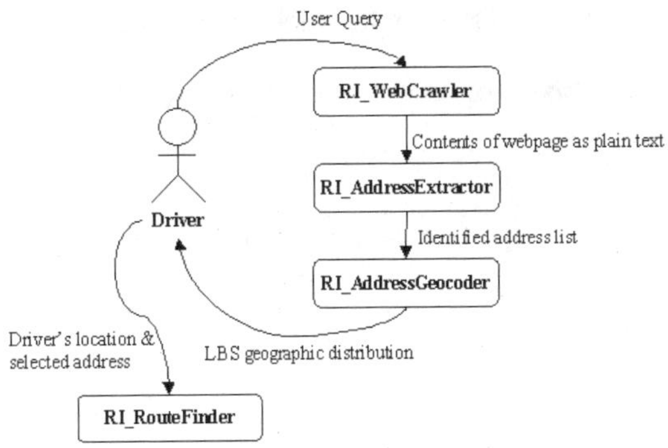

Figure 13: Data flow of the RouteInfo system

The procedure RI_WebCrawler implements the Web crawling and tag filtering functions. After the driver's region and location-based information category are determined, RI_WebCrawler outputs the document corpus which is found on the www.yellowpages.ca website in a plain text format. The procedure RI_AddressExtractor receives the document corpus, extracts possible address candidates and fits them into understandable address structures. It produces an address list and passes it to the procedure

RI_AddressGeocoder. RI_AddressGeocoder performs lookup in the TIGER-format GIS database, matches addresses and assigns latitude-longitude geo-codes. Following the geo-coding process, the data will be fed back to the driver on his digital map. The procedure RI_RouteFinder independently suggests a reasonable route from the driver's location to his chosen destination.

Below are samples of the interface produced by the RouteInfo system. Figure 14 shows how a driver locates himself in the region "PETERBOROUGH" of Ontario Canada. Figure 15 presents all auto repair services retrieved online through the www.yellowpages.ca Web database for this region. It implements RI_WebCrawler, RI_AddressExtractor and RI_AddressGeocoder in combination. Figure 16 exhibits a reasonable path from the driver's location to his goal, "887 WEBBER AVENUE".

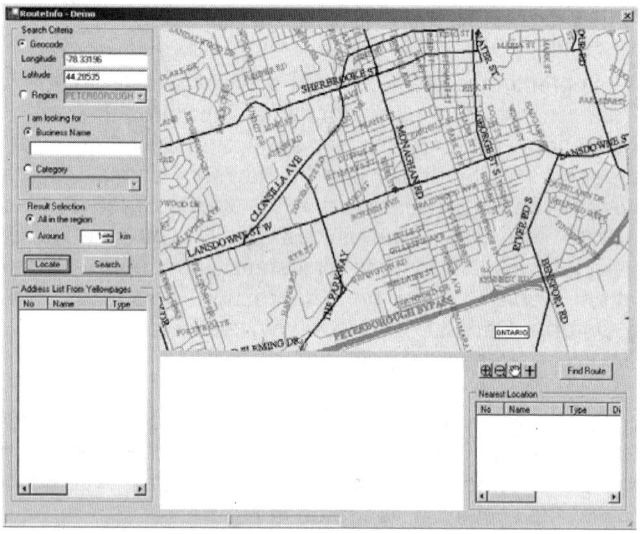

Figure 14: Driver's location in current region

Figure 15: All auto services identified by yellowpages

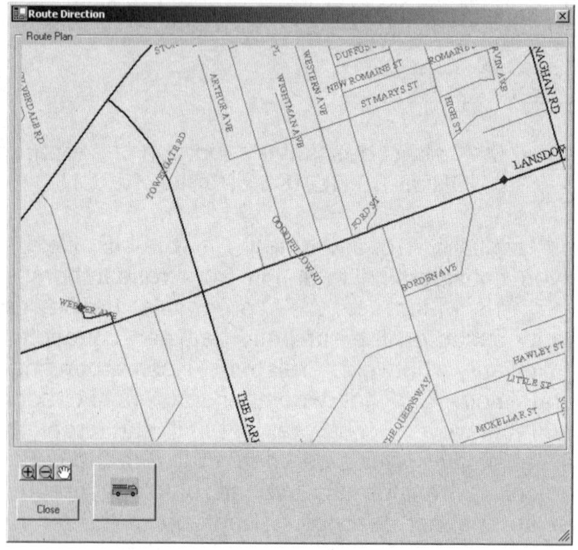

Figure 16: Route plan from driver's location to his destination

CONCLUSION

This paper makes two major contributions. One is the formulation and construction of a new generation navigation system architecture involving modern information and telecommunications technologies. The data, such as roadside services or points of interest, can be retrieved directly from the Web by applying information extraction approaches. The thrust of such an architecture is to enhance the capacity for location-awareness information integration and fusion in the field of assisted navigation. Drivers do not have to update data in their onboard devices annually or region by region. The proposed search agent makes it possible for drivers to access updated LBS information available online. It can help to reshape the way in which LBS data is updated and delivered by distributed information portals. The second contribution of this work, and also its core technical contribution, is address identification from the Web, which helps in extracting location-awareness information by postal addresses. The technique can be utilized not only in onboard navigation devices, but also in geo-marketing and other applications of location-based services. Furthermore, it may be extended to lightweight knowledge extraction simply by changing the domain ontology. However, a suitable noise elimination method is required to reduce the error rate. Another problem is that the concept identification process cannot separate two joined address phrases. For example, "20 Portland Blvd Sherbrooke Quebec 100 King Street Cockville Quebec" (two joined addresses) will be regarded as one address segment.

ACKNOWLEDGMENTS

This research is support by a grant from Canadian Network of Centers of Excellence on Automobiles of 21st century (NCE Auto21). The authors would like to thank all staff of the Auto21 Committee for their support and encouragement. The authors are also grateful to Dr. Qingshan Jiang, professor of Computer Science at Xiamen University, China, for his academic suggestions on the research.

REFERENCES

1. Research Profile, http://www.auto21.ca/.
2. J. Hightower and G. Borriello, Location Systems for Ubiquitous Computing, IEEE Computer Society, vol. 34, 2001.
3. TIGER: **T**opologically **I**ntegrated **G**eographic **E**ncoding and **R**eferencing system, The Census Bureau of the United States, http://www.census.gov/geo/www/tiger/.
4. M. Brunato and R. Battiti, A Location Broker and Mobility-Aware Recommendation System, Universita di Trento, 2002.
5. YAHOO! Map, http://maps.yahoo.com.
6. MapPoint, http://www.microsoft.com/mappoint/default.mspx.
7. MapQuest, http://www.mapquest.com.
8. H. Chen, Collaborative Systems: Solving the vocabulary problem, IEEE Computer, Special Issue On CSCW, vol. 27, no. 5, 1994.
9. G. W. Furnas, The Vocabulary Problem In Human-System Communication, Communications of the ACM, vol. 30, no. 11, 1987.
10. University of Massachusetts Amherst, Challenges in Information Retrieval and Language Modeling, Report of a Workshop Held at the Center for Intelligent Information Retrieval, ACM SIGIR, vol. 37, no. 1, 2003.
11. N. Guarino, Formal Ontology and Information Systems, in Proceedings of the 1st International Conference on Formal Ontology In Information Systems, 1998.
12. H. Chen and B. R. Schatz, Semantic retrieval for the NCSA Mosaic, in Proceedings of the 2nd International World Wide Web Conference, 1994.
13. H. Chen, J. Martinez, T. Ng and B. R. Schatz, A Concept Space Approach to Addressing the Vocabulary Problem in Scientific Information Retrieval: An Experiment on the Worm Community System, Journal of the American Society for Information Science, vol. 48, 1997.
14. S. Loh, L. K. Wives and J. P. M. de Oliveira, Concept-Based Knowledge Discovery in Texts Extracted from the Web, ACM SIGKDD Explorations, vol. 1, no. 1, 2000.
15. J. Sowa, Conceptual Structures: Information Processing in Mind and Machine, Addison-Wesley, 1984.
16. T. Gruber, Toward Principles for Design of Ontologies Used for Knowledge Sharing, International Journal of Human and Computer Studies, vol. 43, no. 5.
17. J. Zhong, H. Zhu, J. Li and Y. Yu, Conceptual Graph Matching for Semantic Search, in Proceedings of the 10th International Conference on Conceptual Structures, ICCS 2002, Lecture Notes in Artificial Intelligence 2393, Spinger-Verlag, 2002.
18. M. Montes-y-Gomez, A. Gelbukh, A. Lopez-Lopez and R. Baeza-Yates, Flexible Comparison of Conceptual Graphs, Lecture Notes in Computer Science 2113, Spinger-Verlag, 2001.
19. W. Cai, S. Wang, Q. Jiang and J. Li, A Practical Implementation of Route Finding, in Proceedings of the 4th International Symposium on Mobile Mapping Technology, March 2004.

CONTACT

Wentao Cai received the BSc degree in computer science from Jilin University, China. He has been involved in the Auto 21 – Theme FII research project since 2002. From 1999 to 2001, he was a software architect and developer in the navigation assistance industry in China. He is pursuing a master's degree in computer science at the Department of Computer Science of the University of Sherbrooke, Quebec, Canada. His interests focus on information retrieval, information extraction, data mining and GIS. His email address is Wentao.Cai@Usherbrooke.ca.

Dr. Shengrui Wang is a full professor at the Department of Computer Science, University of Sherbrooke, Quebec, Canada. His research interests include pattern recognition, data mining, image processing, databases, geographical information systems and navigation systems. He is the co-leader of the project FII-02 (Construction of an integrated navigation infrastructure) in Theme F of NCE AUTU 21. His main research focus in this project is development of new techniques for building online access to location-based services and for updating geospatial information systems for navigation. His email address is Shengrui.Wang@Usherbrooke.ca.

2005-01-0433

Comparison of Visual-Manual and Voice Interaction With Contemporary Navigation System HMIs

Dean P. Chiang, Aaron M. Brooks and David H. Weir
Dynamic Research, Inc.

ABSTRACT

Typically, driver interactions with in-vehicle devices such as navigation systems have been accomplished using a visual-manual interface. As a result of recent advances in technology, voice activated interfaces are being introduced, which reduce or eliminate the need for manual inputs and related visual scanning. This paper compares driver use of contemporary examples of the 2 different types of interface for several types of navigation destination entry tasks based on over-the-road evaluations. These data include glance behavior, HMI interactions (manual inputs, etc.), driver/vehicle response and performance including lane deviations, and subjective ratings. In general, the results show that, for a given task, the example contemporary voice activated systems result in fewer glances, shorter glance durations, fewer entry steps, improved driver/vehicle performance, and improved subjective ratings for ease of task accomplishment and mental workload.

INTRODUCTION

Navigation systems have become popular in-vehicle devices in recent years. Typically, these have been used by the driver with visual-manual interaction, involving a touch screen or other HMI to provide for the manual entry of a destination or other request, and to display the search progress and results. Recently, technological advances have allowed alternative voice interfaces to be introduced. With a voice interface, the driver makes a verbal request or instruction to the system, and the system responds with audio feedback and a visual display of the requested navigational information. This can be supplemented by some visual, or visual-manual, interaction.

Evaluations of voice-based HMIs and comparisons of voice and visual-manual interactions with in-vehicle devices have been reported in the past, but the literature is relatively sparse. A significant portion of it focuses on issues related to cellular phones, and how hand-held usage compares to hands-free usage. In other published comparisons the tasks are generally short in duration (such as radio tuning or cruise control setting), and typically do not reflect contemporary technology. One exception is a recent study reported by Itoh, et al. (Ref 1) where various tasks were examined in a driving simulator using voice and visual-manual entry. For a task involving destination entry using a contemporary navigation system, their results indicated that voice entry had several benefits over visual-manual entry, including lower mental workload, smaller lateral lane displacement, and shorter total glance time.

The results of recent over-the-road (OTR) evaluations of several destination entry methods using a contemporary voice activated navigation system interface are reported herein. Comparisons are made with the results using alternative visual-manual entry methods, and with previously reported results from an OTR study of street address destination entry with a similar visual-manual navigation system (Ref 2).

EXPERIMENTAL SETUP

The driver subjects entered destinations using the voice-audio interface (mode) of a navigation system while driving an instrumented vehicle on city streets and on an urban freeway. The destination entry commands, related manual entries or actions, and associated eye movements were recorded and videotaped and later reduced to obtain entry and response timing, eye fixations, entry errors, and other data. The driver's view of the roadway, and vehicle lane position were videotaped. The subjects also made equivalent entries using the visual-manual mode of the example navigation system.

Two experiments were accomplished. Experiment 1 involved destination entries as a point of interest by Category (e.g., nearest bank, golf course, airport) and by Phone Number (e.g., 310-212-5211). Experiment 2 involved destination entries by Address (street name, street number, and city name).

Ten driver subjects participated in the Experiment 1 evaluation, as summarized in Table 1. All of the drivers were novice users of the navigation system. The driver sample included 7 males and 3 females, 5 of whom were engineers. A somewhat different group of 10 Ss participated in Experiment 2.

Table 1. Driver Subject Characteristics

Occupation	Gender	Age	Exp
Writer	M	29	1
Producer	F	29	1
Engineer	M	29	1
Engineer	M	34	2
Administrator	F	34	2
Engineer	M	35	2
Engineer	M	38, 39	1, 2
Engineer	M	40, 41	1, 2
Draftsperson	M	41	2
Salesperson	F	45, 46	1, 2
Engineer	M	46	1
Homemaker	F	46	2
Administrator	F	48	2
Engineer	M	49	1
Teacher	F	50	2
Manager	F	53	1
Retired (Police Officer)	M	57	1

Five of the drivers in Experiment 2 (3 M and 2 F) also participated in the previous visual-manual entry study reported in (Ref 2).

The Experiment 2 evaluation used a 2005 Acura RL equipped with the Acura Navigation System. The navigation display was located relatively high in the center console of the instrument panel, as shown in Fig 1. In the voice mode, all drivers were able to speak to the system and hear the audio replies, comfortably, from their normal seating position and posture. Voice entries and commands were initiated with a Talk Button on the steering wheel spoke. Some error correction required use of the Back Button. Otherwise, the interactions were limited to voice only, and the visual-manual entry mode using the Interface Dial was not used when the voice mode was being evaluated. The destination category, phone number, or address to be entered was displayed on a card fixed to the steering hub.

The Experiment 1 evaluation used a 2004 Accord equipped with a similar navigation system. Visual-manual entries were made using a touch screen rather than an Interface Dial.

Vehicle instrumentation consisted of video cameras and recording. Two small cameras were mounted on the side mirrors and angled down to view the roadway lane markers, and record lateral lane position. A mini camera was mounted on top of the dashboard, above the navigation display, pointed towards the face of the subject to record eye movements. A fourth camera was mounted between the driver and passenger seats, pointing down at the navigation unit to view manual driver actions and the visual display. Voice commands and audio replies were recorded, also. The camera outputs were combined by a quad splitter, a timer overlay was superimposed, and the final video image and the audio were displayed on a monitor and recorded on a VCR.

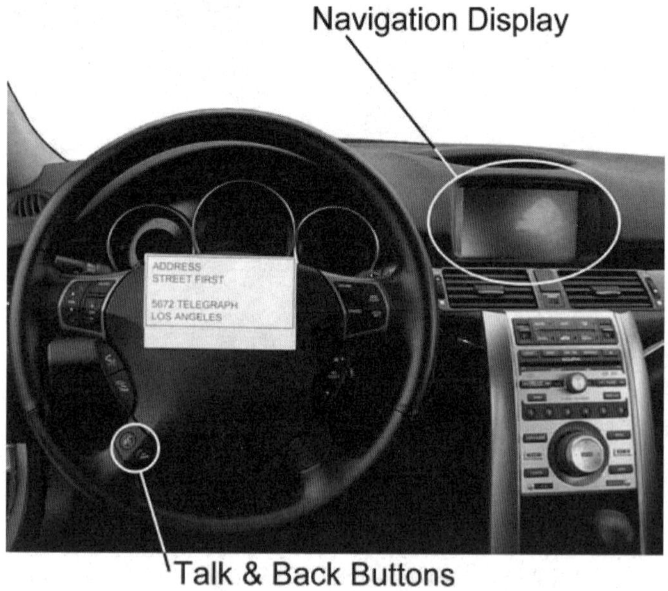

Figure 1. Driver's View of Instrument Panel

PROCEDURE FOR DESTINATION ENTRY

In Experiment 1 using the voice mode, once the "Enter destination" menu is displayed, destination entry is initiated by saying "PLACES." For the category entry mode, the next step is to say "CATEGORY," followed by a category such as "SHOPPING" or "BANKING." Next a subcategory such as "PET FOOD" or "ATM" can be spoken. The system then gives 4 options: Place Name by Keyword, Sort by Distance to Travel, City Vicinity, or Place Name. In this experiment, Sort by Distance to Travel was used. The nearest location is then selected from a list and the destination is then confirmed.

For the phone number voice entry mode in Experiment 1, after saying "PLACES" the user says "PHONE NUMBER." The phone number is then entered by saying the numbers as a continuous string of digits. The phone number is then confirmed and finally the destination is confirmed.

In normal use, if a voice command is not recognized, the user can select the category or option from the screen using the visual-manual mode. Similarly, in normal use of the system, the user can switch to a visual-manual mode if a word or number is not recognized. But this was not done in either Experiment 1 or 2 when the voice mode was being used.

In Experiment 2 all destinations were entered using the "By Address, Street First" method. This means that the full address of a destination was entered, with the street name spoken first in the voice mode, followed by the address number and the city name.

Once the "Enter destination" menu is displayed, address entry is initiated by saying "ADDRESS." The next step is to say "STREET," pause, and then say the street name. The screen will then display selected street choices, and the correct one is entered by saying the number.

The street number is then entered by saying the numbers as a continuous string of digits. It is not necessary to say "NUMBER." If the street number is not recognized, it can be said 1 number at a time.

After the street and number are selected, the screen will then display a list of possible city choices, and the correct city is selected from the list by saying the number.

Saying "OK" completes the voice entry process. Each voice interaction is initiated using a Talk Button on the steering wheel.

A corresponding series of steps was used in Experiment 1 with the visual-manual interface. The visual-manual mode data from Ref 2 that are compared with the Experiment 2 voice mode results were also obtained using a corresponding series of steps.

The destinations in Experiment 2 used for the practice trials and the evaluation trials represented an average level of difficulty for the task. The street names were chosen based on their length and typicality. They are also the same destinations used in the previous visual-manual study (Ref 2). The numerical addresses were chosen to be 4 digits in length, which was felt to be typical. Within a given address, a particular digit only appeared once.

For the city selection in Experiment 2, the location of the destination city was consistent within the practice and evaluation trials. The city displayed initially was neither the current city the car was in nor the desired destination city. In general, the destination cities and addresses were not on the study driving route, but were in nearby cities and locations in the greater Los Angeles area.

The overall study route is shown in Fig 2. It consisted of city streets and freeways in the Torrance, California area. The 2 city streets routes (Vermont and Normandie) were 1.1 miles long, connected by streets approximately 0.5 miles long. Both streets were 2 lanes in each direction, and the subjects drove in the left lane at 40 mph (64 km/h). The urban freeway sections were 6 miles in length, and the subjects looped back to the original entry point. The freeways were 4 lanes in each direction, and subjects drove in the second lane from the right at 65 mph (105 km/h) or with traffic. The route was driven on weekdays either in the morning (9:30 - 11:30 am), or in the afternoon (1:30 - 3:30 pm). In general, the 2 sessions had similar traffic conditions. No sessions were scheduled on Friday afternoon because traffic was typically heavier at that time. The evaluations took place only in good weather and on dry roads.

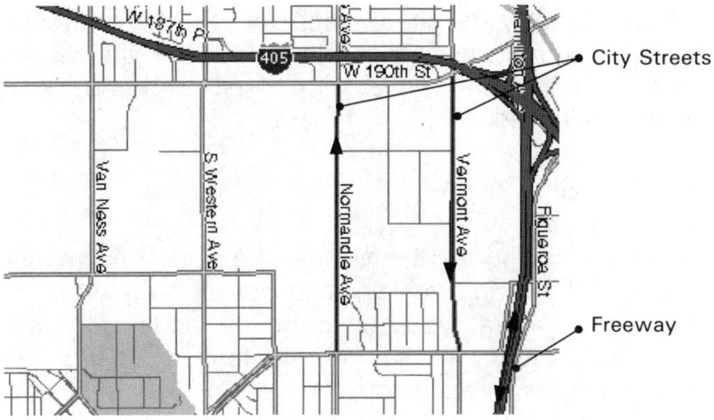

Figure 2. Study Routes

EXPERIMENTAL PROCEDURE

In both Experiments 1 and 2, the subjects began by reviewing pertinent sections of the navigation system user's manual, and receiving introductory instructions. Then subjects sat in the driver's seat and adjusted it. The experimenter in the passenger seat explained the use of the navigation system. The drivers were told that their primary task was to maintain the vehicle speed, maintain a safe following distance, and keep the vehicle in the lane. The navigation entry task was described as less important, and the drivers were told that there was no hurry and that they did not have to enter the destinations quickly. As noted above, the various destinations were not immediately ahead on the OTR driving study route. If a driver did not feel comfortable or safe at any time during a destination entry sequence, that run was aborted, which rarely occurred.

The drivers first did 3 practice trials with the vehicle parked. Most subjects were generally familiar with the area. After driving the study route loop one time, subjects were given 2 practice destinations to enter while driving, one on each stretch of road. The practice trial destinations were different from the evaluation trials, but were entered in the manner described above. Subjects could ask questions during the practice trials. The same practice trials were used for each subject, and they were always shown in the same order.

After the practice trials, the subjects did 3 evaluation trials on the city streets, with one trial on a given road section. In order to eliminate possible ordering effects, 2 groups were used. Group A entered the evaluation destinations in the order 1-2-3, while Group B entered the destinations in the order 3-2-1. After completing the 3 trials on the city streets, the driver stopped the vehicle and filled out a subjective rating form. Then the subjects were directed to the freeway. They first drove the freeways to become familiar with the route. On the second loop, the subjects entered the evaluation destinations. After completing the 3 evaluation trials and exiting the freeway, they filled out another subjective rating form. Subjects were then directed back to the starting point. The entire procedure took approximately

2 hours for one subject to complete. For Experiment 1 this procedure was done twice, once for the visual-manual mode and once with voice with the order counterbalanced.

RESULTS

The data comprised the videos, the audio recordings, and the driver and vehicle response and performance measures. Data reduction from the videos for each destination entry with the voice mode included the start and end times for each entry step, the number of spoken voice commands, the number of individual letter or number voice entries (if used), the number of repeated (not recognized or not understood) voice commands, and the number and duration of eye fixations. These were calculated on a per trial basis and then averaged. Eye movement data consisted primarily of the individual fixation times on each of several "targets" within the driver's field of view, and the percentage of total fixation times on those targets. Similar analysis was accomplished with the data from the visual-manual entry runs.

The following definitions adapted from Ref 3 are used with the eye movement data:

- Target - the forward road scene, the navigation system display, or other.
- Fixation time - the duration of a fixation at 1 target. It does not include the transition time to or from the target.
- Glance duration - fixation time plus the transition to the target. Also called glance time.
- Total glance time - the sum of the individual glance times on 1 target for a destination entry.
- Transition - a change in eye fixation location from 1 target to another.
- Total task time - total time from initiation to completion of destination entry.

RESULTS FOR EXPERIMENT 1

As described above, Experiment 1 involved destination entries by Category and Phone Number.

The average number of entry steps for each mode for a given destination entry trial are shown in Table 2. A voice entry step consisted of a spoken word or group of words spoken together. If a word or phrase had to be repeated before the interface recognized or understood it, that was considered as an additional entry step. A visual-manual entry step consisted of a finger press. Mispresses are included in the number of entry steps. The number of required entry steps is the same for Category for the 2 modes, but less for Phone Number because all the digits in a phone number comprised 1 entry in the voice mode. The minimum number of entry steps in the Category method was 7. For Phone Number, the minimum number of entry steps for voice was 5, and for visual-manual it was 14.

Table 2. Mean Number of Entry Steps per Trial for PLACES Method

Mode	Category		Phone Number	
	City Street	Freeway	City Street	Freeway
Voice	7.1	7.2	5.3	5.4
Visual-manual	7.7	7.2	15.0	15.1

The entry error rates are compared in Table 3. The values shown are the average number of errors per trial. A visual-manual entry error was typically a mispress. A voice entry error resulted from either the user saying the wrong word, or the user saying the right word and the interface misinterpreting it. Again, if the subject had to repeat a voice entry several times before the system recognized a word or number, that was treated as several entries, but not several errors. The overall entry error rates are small (approximately 1 error every 6 trials), and there does not appear to be a systematic difference between voice and visual-manual. Although still very infrequent (1 error in 3 trials), the comparatively high error rate (.35) for the Phone Number with voice mode on the freeway probably arose from the voice recognition step. In particular, inputs by 1 subject in 1 trial were not well understood, perhaps due in part to the noisy freeway environment.

Table 3. Mean Number of Entry Errors per Trial for PLACES Method

Mode	Category		Phone Number	
	City Street	Freeway	City Street	Freeway
Voice	0.00	0.05	0.15	0.35
Visual-manual	0.20	0.15	0.15	0.20

The statistical distribution of the single glance durations are compared in Fig 3. The glances related to voice entry are shorter overall. This is shown by the average single glance durations (sec) in Table 4. The mean visual-manual mode glances are all about the same. The voice entry related glances tended to be shorter, and those related to Phone Number entry were shorter than those for Category.

Table 4. Mean Single Glance Durations for PLACES Method

Mode	Category		Phone Number		Overall
	City Street	Freeway	City Street	Freeway	
Voice	0.93	0.99	0.73	0.71	0.89
Visual-manual	1.10	1.02	1.08	1.04	1.06

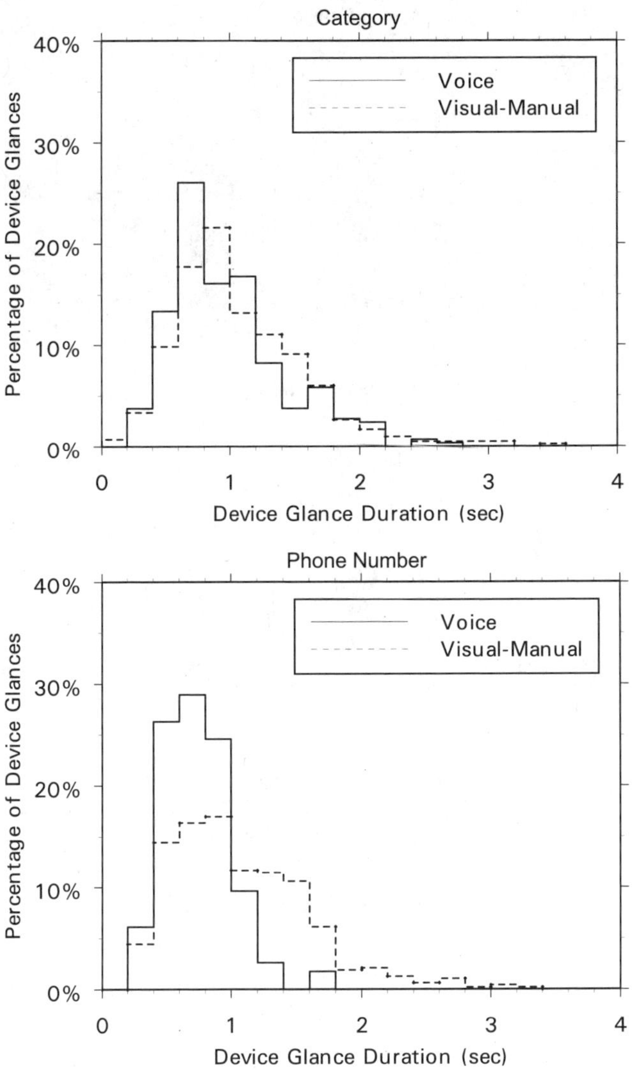

Figure 3. Comparison of Single Glance Durations for PLACES Method

While the average single glance times are not dissimilar, the number of glances to the interface for an entry trial differs greatly between voice and visual-manual, as might be expected. This is shown in Table 5.

Table 5. Mean Number of Glances to Interface per Trial for PLACES Method

Mode	Category		Phone Number	
	City Street	Freeway	City Street	Freeway
Voice	7.7	7.0	3.1	2.6
Visual-manual	10.7	10.2	11.0	12.6

The average total glance time per entry trial generally corresponds to the number of glances per trial. This is shown in Table 6 which gives the mean total glance times (sec) per trial. The voice mode results in much shorter total glance times per entry trial, and the Phone Number method is much shorter than by Category.

Table 6. Mean Total Glance Times per Trial for PLACES Method

Mode	Category		Phone Number	
	City Street	Freeway	City Street	Freeway
Voice	7.2	6.9	2.3	1.8
Visual-manual	11.8	10.3	11.8	13.1

The driver's allocation of visual attention to the road ahead, the navigation interface, and to other targets is summarized in Table 7. This shows that much less time is spent looking at the interface when the voice entry mode is used.

Table 7. Total Glance Time Percentages for PLACES Method

Entry Method	Route	Mode	Road	Navi	Other
Category	City Street	Voice	76	17	7
		Visual-manual	45	48	7
	Freeway	Voice	79	15	6
		Visual-manual	51	45	4
Phone Number	City Street	Voice	76	7	17
		Visual-manual	40	52	8
	Freeway	Voice	79	5	16
		Visual-manual	42	50	8

Total task times (sec) for Experiment 1 are summarized in Table 8. Task times with the voice mode are comparatively long, mainly because of system delays, and primarily due to the voice recognition step. While waiting for the voice mode to respond, the driver is generally looking at the road or other targets in the visual field as shown in Table 7. In effect, the secondary task (navi entry) attentional workload is reduced by spreading it over a longer interval.

Table 8. Mean Total Task Times for PLACES Method

Mode	Category		Phone Number	
	City Street	Freeway	City Street	Freeway
Voice	41	43	33	36
Visual-manual	24	23	23	28

The effect of entry mode on lateral lane keeping performance is shown in Table 9. Lane position was measured with down-looking video. The variance about the mean lane position for each of the 120 entry trials for a given mode was calculated for a 20 second interval which included that entry trial. The variances are generally small. The differences in the pooled variances between voice and visual-manual entry modes can be examined with a simple F-test of the variance ratios.

Assuming a lane position bandwidth of approximately 0.3 rad/sec, each of the variances (representing thirty 20 second trials) shown in Table 9 has about 60 statistical degrees of freedom. In 2 of the 4 cases the lane position variances are seen to be significantly smaller with the voice mode, and in the other 2 cases the differences are not significant at the 95% confidence level.

Table 9. Lane Keeping Performance for PLACES Method

Mode	Category (m^2)		Phone Number (m^2)	
	City Street	Freeway	City Street	Freeway
Voice	0.015	0.021	0.015	0.009
Visual-manual	0.025	0.015	0.020	0.017
Variance ratio	1.67*	1.40	1.33	1.89*

* Significantly different at 95% level.

Subjective rating data were obtained using the rating scales shown in Figs 4 and 5. The bars represent the mean ratings over all Ss, and the 1 standard deviation variations are denoted by the tick marks. Figure 4 shows that the primary driving task was rated easier when voice entry was used, and the subjective mental effort was also lower, as shown in Fig 5.

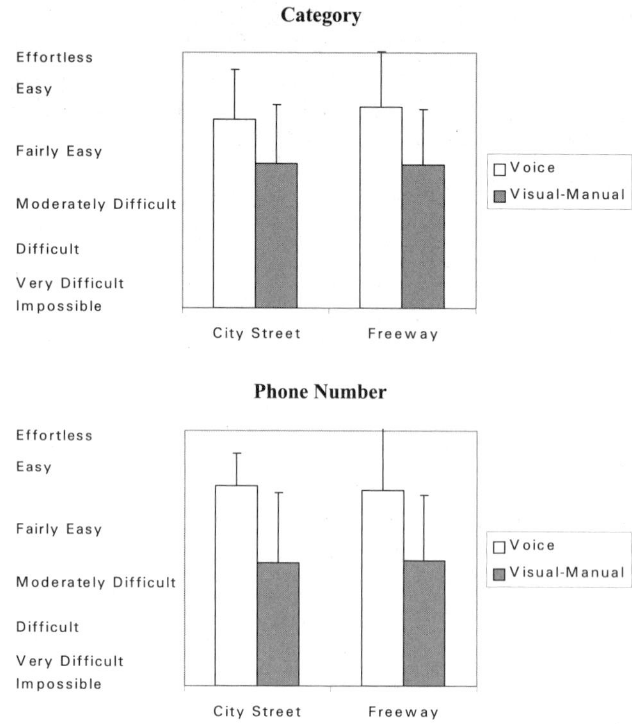

Figure 4. Ratings for Ease of Performing Driving Task for PLACES Method

RESULTS FOR EXPERIMENT 2

As described above, Experiment 2 involved destination entries by Address (street name, street number, and city name). The results of this recent study using a voice interaction HMI are presented below. These results are compared with the results of a similar address destination entry study that used a visual-manual touch screen interface, reported 4 years ago (Ref 2). Both studies used similar entry addresses, the same over-the-road driving routes, and 5 of the 10 driver subjects were common to both evaluations. Lane keeping performance measures and statistics were not obtained in Ref 2, so that comparison is not available for the Experiment 2 results.

The data for several trials (out of 60) in Experiment 2 are not reported here, because those trials involved a larger number of repeat entries where the voice entry was apparently not recognized nor understood by the voice engine. Since the purpose of this effort was to compare the 2 modes of entry and not to evaluate the efficacy of the voice engine, per se, the influence of these outliers was not felt to be relevant to this study's objective. Nevertheless, the reported mean single glance durations (Table 12) and the glance time percentages (Table 15) would be largely unaffected if these outlying data points were included.

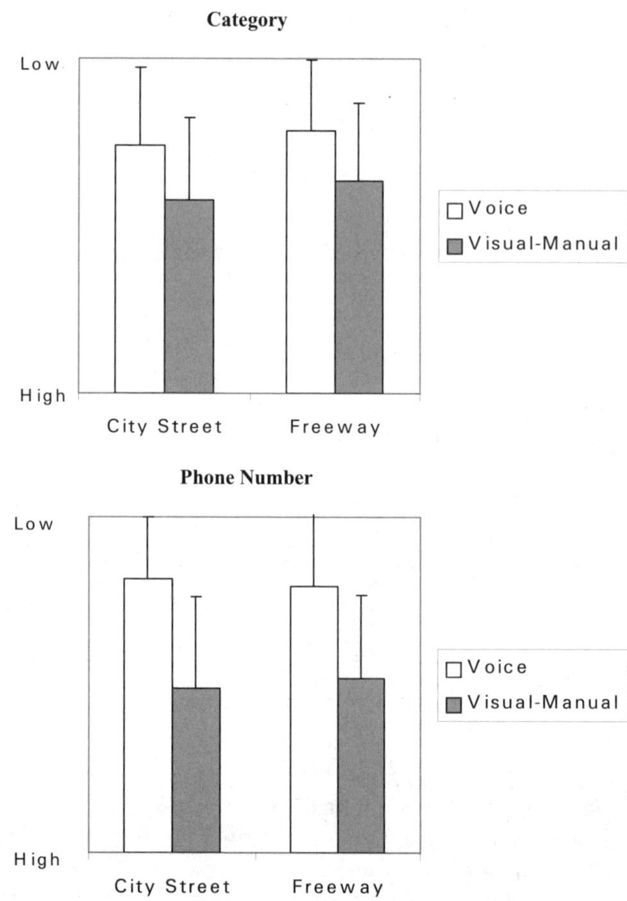

Figure 5. Ratings for Overall Mental Effort for PLACES Method

The average number of entry steps for each interface for a given destination entry trial are shown in Table 10. An entry step for the visual-manual interface (Ref 2) involved pressing the touchscreen (a keystroke), usually one (or sometimes 2) of these was accomplished in 1 glance. A voice entry step typically consisted of a spoken word or a group of words or digits spoken together. The minimum number of entry steps for the voice interface was 7, and it was 15 for the visual-manual interface. The number of entry steps with the visual-manual interface was greater, because each letter had to be entered separately until the word was recognized.

Table 10. Mean Number of Entry Steps per Trial for ADDRESS Method

Interface	City Street	Freeway
Voice	9.2	8.5
Visual-manual	17.1	17.4

The average number of errors per trial is shown in Table 11. As in Experiment 1, a visual-manual error was typically a mispress, and a voice entry error was saying the wrong word(s) or the interface misinterpreting the correct word. The overall error rates are small, and there is not a large difference in the data between the Experiment 2 (voice) and Ref 2 (visual-manual) interfaces. As in Table 3, the somewhat higher observed error rate with the voice interface on the freeway may be due to the noisy freeway environment.

Table 11. Mean Number of Entry Errors per Trial for ADDRESS Method

Interface	City Street	Freeway
Voice	0.58	0.46
Visual-manual	0.60	0.33

The statistical distribution of the single glance durations from Experiment 2, and for all the glances in the database from which Ref 2 was prepared (not just those with 1 or 2 keystrokes) are shown in Fig 6. Again, the glances related to voice entry are shorter overall, and this is shown by the mean values (sec) in Table 12.

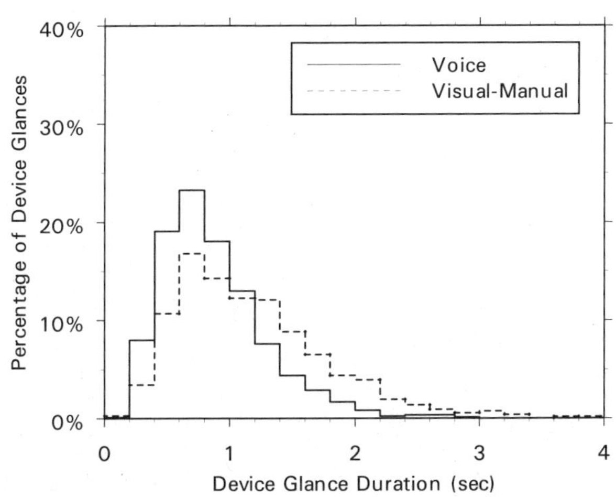

Figure 6. Comparison of Single Glance Durations for ADDRESS Method

Table 12. Mean Single Glance Durations for ADDRESS Method

Interface	City Street	Freeway
Voice	0.88	0.86
Visual-manual	1.24	1.12

The number of glances to the respective Experiment 2 and Ref 2 interfaces per entry trial are shown in Table 13. The number of glances with voice entry is not markedly lower than for visual-manual in these results. By comparison with Table 10, it can be seen that there are typically a number of unnecessary glances to the interface in the voice mode. These glances are typically brief, and they may reflect lack of familiarity with the system on the part of the subject. Nevertheless, the total fixation time (sec) and the percentage time on the Navi are much lower as shown in Tables 14 and 15, because the glance durations are shorter.

Table 13. Mean Number of Glances to Interface per Trial for ADDRESS Method

Interface	City Street	Freeway
Voice	16.3	14.8
Visual-manual	17.9	18.9

Table 14. Mean Total Fixation Time per Trial for ADDRESS Method

Interface	City Street	Freeway
Voice	11.9	10.4
Visual-manual	19.3	18.1

The driver's allocation of visual attention to the road ahead and other targets, and the navigation interface is summarized in Table 15. The visual-manual percentages are a little different from those reported in Ref 2, because they are based on glance times, not fixation times, and they include all the data in the Ref 2 database. Also, the small percentage of "other target" data in Ref 2 has been added to the road column in this Table.

Table 15. Total Glance Time Percentages for ADDRESS Method

Route	Interface	Road/Other	Navi
City Street	Voice	79	21
	Visual-manual	37	63
Freeway	Voice	80	20
	Visual-manual	40	60

Total task times (sec) for Experiment 2 are summarized as the "Voice" entry in Table 16. Total task times for the comparison visual-manual interface are also shown in Table 16, based on the mean total entry times reported in Ref 2. Although the number of entry steps is less with the voice mode, as shown in Table 10, the task times with the voice mode are relatively long mainly because of system delays, primarily in the voice recognition step. The task time may be lengthened further if the system does not recognize or understand a voice command or entry and it has to be repeated. As shown in Table 15, the corresponding glance time percentages to the navi interface are comparatively small, so the secondary task attentional workload rate during the task is reduced by comparison even though the task times are longer.

Table 16. Mean Total Task Times for ADDRESS Method

Interface	City Street	Freeway
Voice	68	60
Visual-manual	34	34

The subjective rating data reported in Ref 2 for the visual-manual task use the scale "Ease of Performing the Entry Task." The mean ratings using this scale for the 2 different interfaces are shown in Fig 7. The data show the voice mode rated as somewhat easier, and both are rated at least fairly easy.

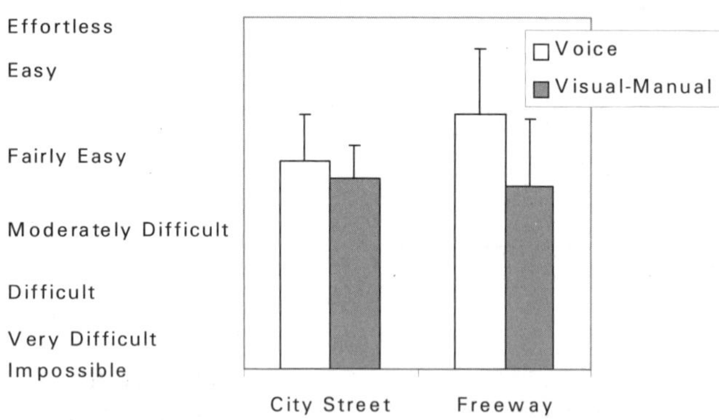

Figure 7. Ease of Performing the Entry Task for ADDRESS Method

DISCUSSION

In general, the results show that, for a given task and by comparison with a typical visual-manual interface, the example recent contemporary voice activated system results in fewer glances, shorter glance durations, a higher percentage of time looking at the road, improved driver/vehicle performance, and improved subjective ratings for ease of task accomplishment and mental workload.

REFERENCES

1. Itoh, K., et al. "Evaluation of a Voice-Activated System Using a Driving Simulator," SAE 2004-01-0232, Warrendale, PA, 2004.
2. Chiang, D.P., et al. "An Experimental Study of Destination Entry with an Example Automobile Navigation System," SAE 2001-01-0810, Warrendale, PA 2001.
3. Definitions and Experimental Measures Related to the Specification of Driver Visual Behavior Using Video Based Techniques, SAE J2396, Warrendale, PA, 1999.

CONTACT

Dean P. Chiang, Technical Director
Dynamic Research, Inc.
355 Van Ness Avenue
Torrance, CA 90501
310-212-5211
e-mail: info@dynres.com

2002-01-0759

Rearview Camera Based Parking Assist System with Voice Guidance

Shoji Hiramatsu, Akihito Hibi, Yu Tanaka, Toshiaki Kakinami, Yoshifumi Iwata and Masahiko Nakamura
Aisin Seiki Co., Ltd.

ABSTRACT

A newly developed parking assist system, which is based on rear view camera, is disclosed.

System features include 'parallel parking aid' with voice guidance message along with several guidelines superimposed onto the rear view camera image. Voice guide message helps driver understand appropriate timing for each procedure of parallel parking. The system was designed to let driver follow the system by voice message rather than visual guide information through the screen for safety reason.

The guide algorism is designed under 'two turns' parking maneuvers so that required longitudinal parking space becomes minimal. A key development of this system, which is to design the guide algorism to avoid collision to adjacent vehicle during parallel parking operation, is also discussed in this paper.

User can select either 'parallel guide' or 'normal (such as garage parking)' mode through touch screen switch on display surface. Wide field of view color camera gives sufficient viewing area for drivers.

Our MPU based new control unit enables wide deployment of the system to any vehicle types by writing vehicle dependent data individually to nonvolatile memory in ECU fabrication line.

This paper introduces the development of the technology and system features including some test results of the system function also.

INTRODUCTION

Generally the novice drivers or the drivers who seldom drive are not good at parking operation and backward driving. Particularly they tend to think that it is difficult to park their car in parallel with the roadside. Further, recently many vehicles are equipped with the rear view camera, however such camera is mainly used for confirming the safety of the scene behind the vehicle so not used for the purpose of reducing the driving efforts for the driver.

We have developed a parking assist system with multiple referenced lines superimposed on image projection of the rear view camera giving the driver various useful information for maneuvering the vehicle during the parking operation or the backward driving.

The system also includes calculation of parallel parking course avoiding the collision with an adjacent vehicle, and a voice guidance as stronger HMI.

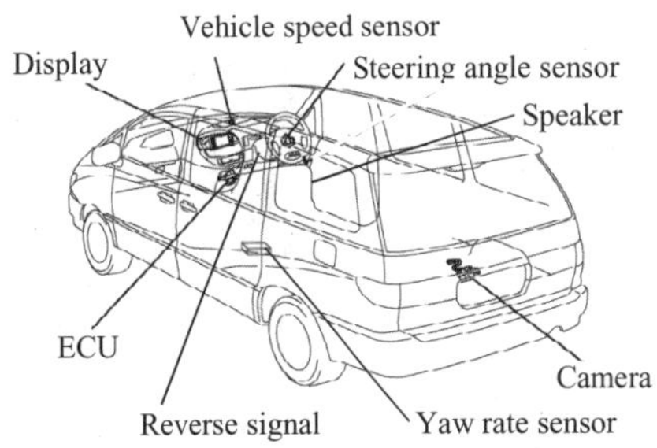

Fig. 1 Actual Vehicle Installation

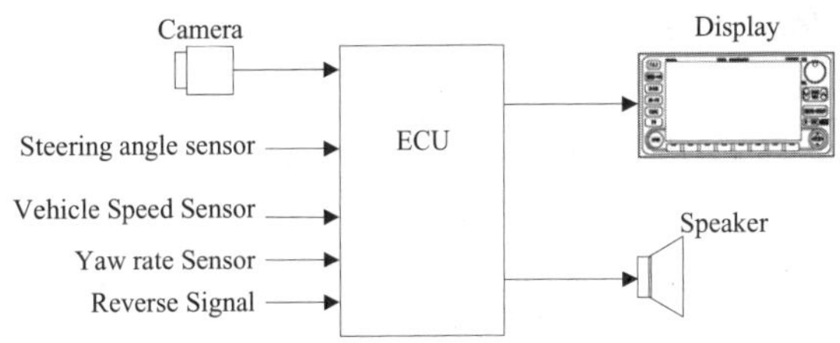

Fig. 2 System Block Diagram

SYSTEM CONSTRUCTION

Fig.1 shows the actual vehicle installation. The System Block Diagram is shown in Fig.2. The system consists of a rear view camera (hereinafter called just a camera), steering angle sensor, vehicle speed sensor, display, speaker, yaw rate sensor and ECU (Electronic Control Unit). The camera is installed on the upper portion of the rear license plate.

Table.1 shows a specification of the camera.

Table.1 Specification of Camera

Item	Spec.
Imaging device	1/4 inch CCD
Pixel (Hor. x Vert.)	512 x 492
Output signal	NTSC, right and left inverted image
Field of View (H. x V.) deg.	131 x 96
Power source	6V, 200mA (max.)

SYSTEM OPERATION

Upon detecting the reverse gear position, the parking assist ECU activates the camera to display the rear view scene. A couple of useful guiding lines for maneuvering vehicle are shown in accordance with the selected operation mode of parking assist ECU.

Basically following two operating modes are available, one is a normal mode for backward driving such as garage parking, and the other is a parallel parking guidance mode having voice guidance.

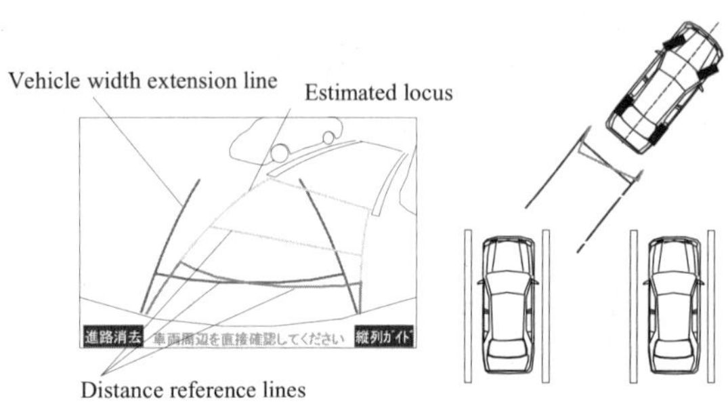

Fig. 3 Normal Mode (scene 1)

User can select one of those operating modes by using the touch switch on the LCD monitor.

NORMAL MODE

Fig.3 shows an example of the normal mode being displayed and showing top view of the scene. In this mode, the estimated locus indicating the backing up path of own vehicle in response to the current steering angle, the vehicle width extension lines indicating the present direction of the own vehicle, and the distance reference lines (0.5, 1.0m) indicating the distance from the bumper of the own vehicle are superimposed on the image shown by camera.

Driver should place the vehicle directing the vehicle in backward to the parking position and shift in reverse.

Adjust the steering angle directing the estimated locus toward the parking lot on the display.

Then drive backward keeping the steering angle fixed until both right and left line of the vehicle width extension line and the parking lot lines become parallel and then drive will back up by returning the steering wheel straight to the center position (Fig.4).

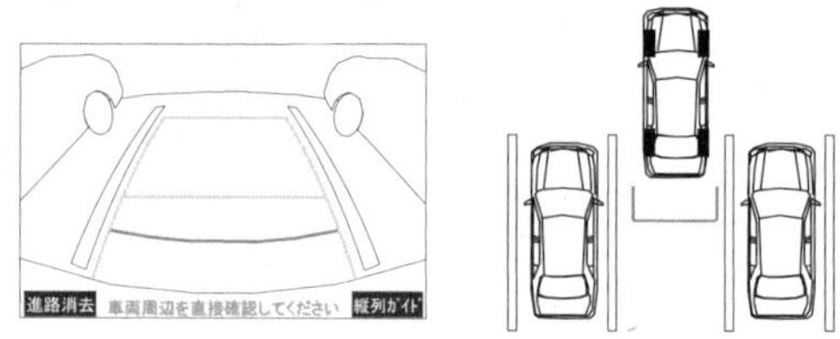

Fig. 4 Normal mode (scene 2)

PARALLEL PARKING GUIDANCE MODE

In parallel parking guidance mode, the guidance information are changed in accordance with the driver's operation and/or vehicle movement with voice guidance according to each condition.

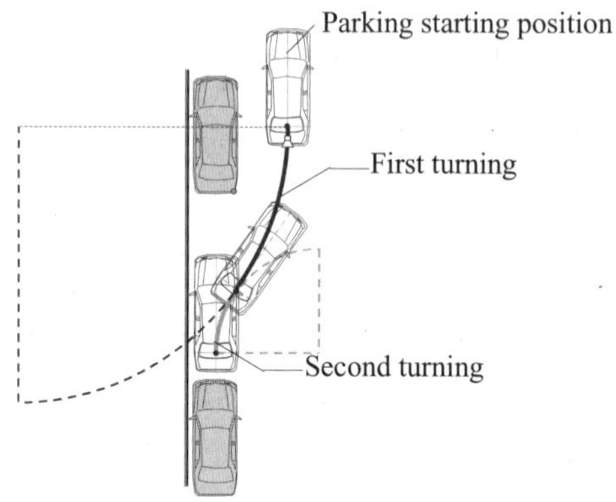

Fig. 5 Two circular turning model

The parallel parking course is determined by "two circular turning model" consists of consecutive two turns. The two circular turning model is shown in Fig.5.

(1) Adjusting of the parking starting position

First of all the vehicle should be placed at distance of 1 m from the forward parked vehicle, in parallel therewith.

Then reverse gear will be selected and back up until the vertical pole shown on the display comes to the rear end of the forward parked vehicle.

Fig.6 shows an example of the displayed image and a top view of the scene.

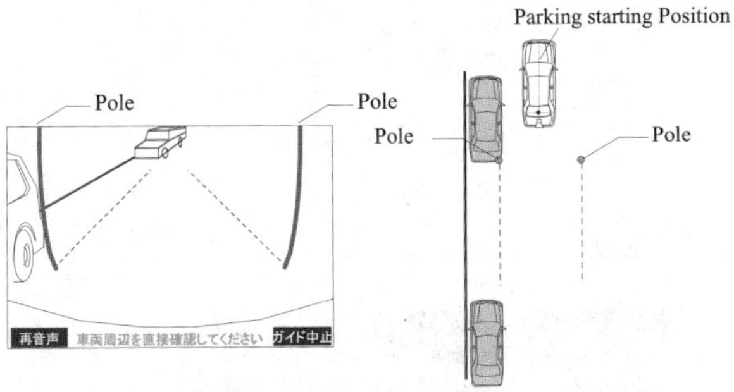

Fig. 6 Adjusting of the parking starting position

(2) Setting of the target parking position

The "parking frame" indicating the target parking position appears on the display as the steering wheel is turned, moves according to the steering wheel angle. Placing this "parking frame" at the final target position to park will determine both target parking position and the steering angle for the first turn at the same time. Fig.7 shows an example of the display and a top view of the scene.

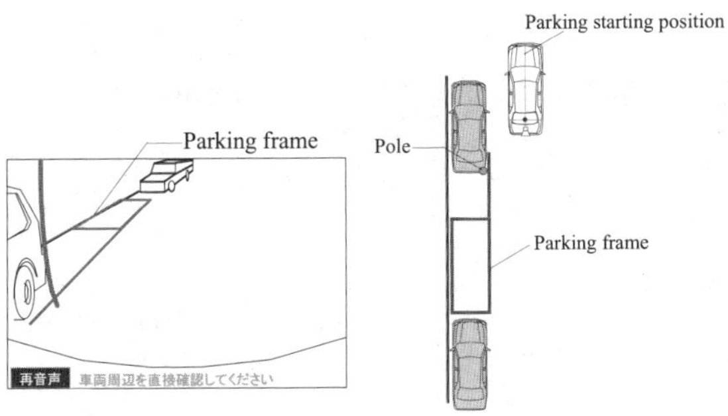

Fig. 7 Setting of the target parking position

(3) First turn and steering wheel operation

After setting the target parking position by turning the steering wheel, the driver moves the vehicle backward keeping the steering at the set angle fixed. In order to avoid the driver stares the display, no estimated locus is shown during this backing up operation.

The system traces the actual vehicle movement by yaw rate sensor at the first turning operation. When the vehicle approached to the roadside, the "parking guide line" appears. The driver stops the vehicle at the position so that the "parking guide line" comes to the roadside and turns the steering wheel

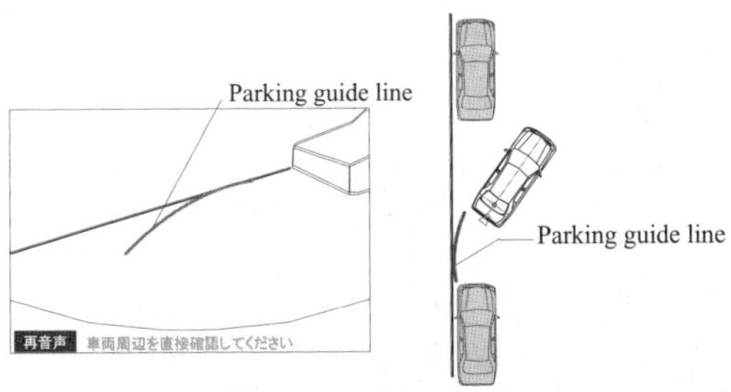

Fig. 8 Parking guide line

fully in another direction. Fig.8 shows an example of the display and a top view of the scene.

(4) Second turn

After the driver turns the steering wheel fully, the guide lines are shown on the display same as explained in normal mode. The driver can back up until the vehicle becomes in parallel with the roadside.

CALCULATION OF PARALLEL PARKING COURSE

The parallel parking is made by two circular turning model. The second turning is made with the minimum turning radius to be able to park the vehicle in the minimum parking space determined by the own vehicle's specification (Fig.9).

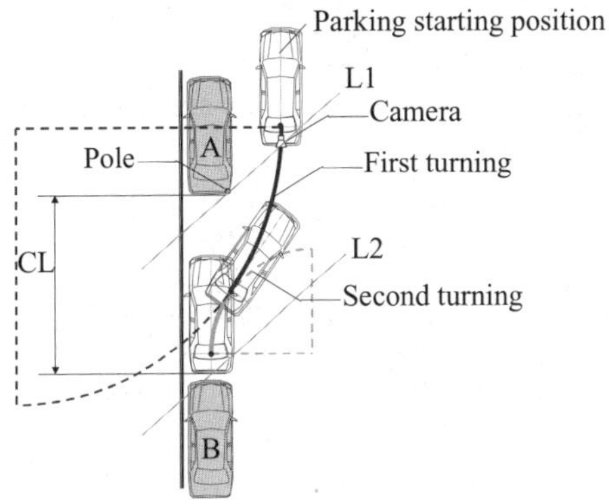

Fig. 9 Parallel parking course

Once adjust the pole to the rear right end of forward parked vehicle A on the display, we can describe the direction of the rear right end of vehicle A to the camera position by straight line L1. Moreover, the target parking position is decided on straight line L2 which is parallel to straight line L1, and pass the point at constant distance CL behind from the rear end of vehicle A. We can find a radius of the 1st turning circle that comes in touch with the 2nd turning circle from the parking starting position.

By defining the CL to be greater than the minimum necessary space for parking determined by each vehicle specification, the parking course can be set not to be in contact with the right rear end of the vehicle A at second turn.

Actual CL is determined with considering dispersion of each vehicle characteristics and driver's operation.

2D-3D PERSPECTIVE PROJECTION

Fig.10 shows a relation between the image coordinates and world coordinates. The point $\mathbf{X}=[X,Y,Z]^{\mathrm{T}}$ of the world coordinates is projected to the point $\mathbf{x}=[x,y]^{\mathrm{T}}$ of the image coordinates with calculation by equation (1) with vector expression.

$$\mathbf{x} = \mathbf{P}\begin{bmatrix}\mathbf{X}\\ \mathbf{1}\end{bmatrix} \qquad \mathbf{P} = \mathbf{C}[\mathbf{R}|\mathbf{T}] \qquad (1)$$

wherein,

$\mathbf{P}$ is 3×4 homogenous camera projection matrix, $\mathbf{C}$ is intrinsic parameter of the camera, $\mathbf{R}$ is rotation component and $\mathbf{T}$ is translation component of extrinsic parameter of the camera. In this system, $\mathbf{C}$ and $\mathbf{T}$ uses design value but

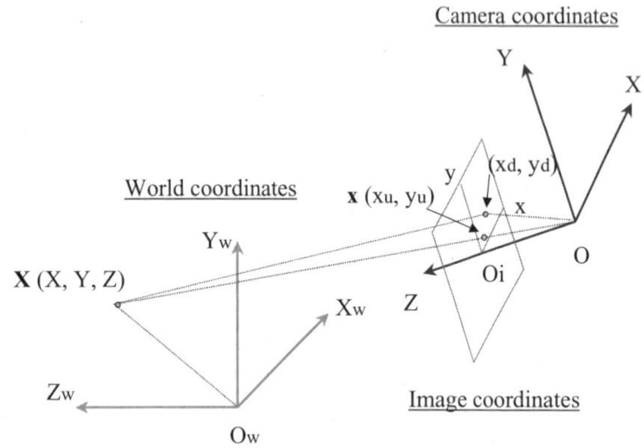

Fig.10 2D-3D perspective projection with image distortion

$\mathbf{R}$ uses actual measured value by a method explained later since the assembling tolerance between the camera principal axis and vehicle body cannot be ignored and varies for every vehicle.

The system adopts the wide field of view lens and the image is distorted as a shape of barrel (Fig.11). The distortion is added to the image coordinates so that the guide lines may correspond with the image.

The coordinates projected to the image coordinates by the equation (1) is added with a distortion in response to the distance D' from the lens center by using the equation (2) to indicate the guide lines which are matched with the distorted image.

$$D = \sum_{i=1}^{6} d_i \cdot D'^{i} \qquad (2)$$

wherein,

D :Distance from the lens center (distorted image)

D' :Distance from the lens center (undistorted image)

$d_{1\sim6}$: Distortion coefficient

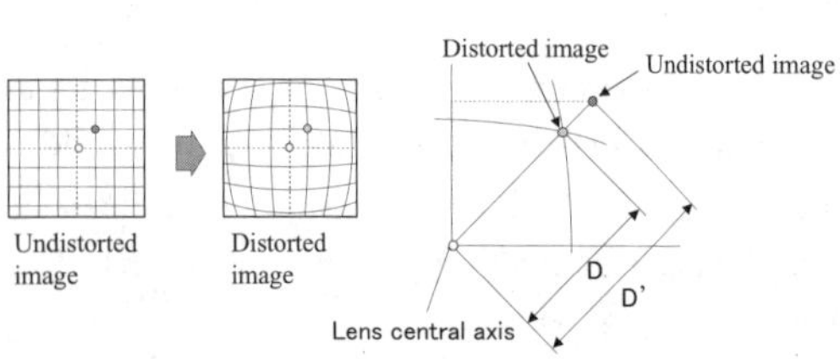

Fig.11 Inverse distortion correction

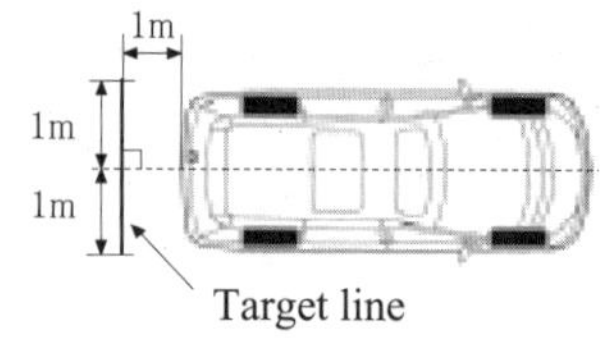

Fig.12 Target line for calibration

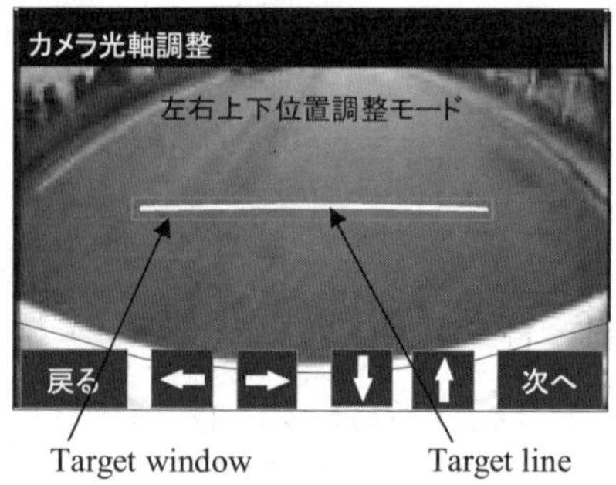

Fig.13 Example of display of Camera calibration

HIGHLY ACCURATE SUPERIMPOSING

The difference between the principal axis direction of CCD camera and the principal direction of the vehicle is as much as about ± 2.0 degrees due to cost constraints. However the required accuracy of this system is ±1.0 degree or less. Accordingly, the target line for camera calibration is set on the road surface at rearward of the vehicle, and the rotation component of the extrinsic camera parameters is corrected.

As shown in Fig.12, a 2-meters-long target line (1m each at right and left from vehicle center) is set on the road surface 1m behind the vehicle and as shown in Fig.13, the role, tilt and pan angle are adjusted by moving the target window on display to the target line.

Compared with the mechanical method of adjusting the camera angle. This approach enables quick and easy but very accurate optical adjustment in vehicle assembly line. Particularly eliminating the need of mechanical adjustment is a great benefit for mass production lines.

EVALUATION RESULTS

About garage parking, accuracy of this system is same as the system described in [1].

Table.2 shows the evaluation results of the parallel parking operation given by fifty panel members.

The evaluation results show overall improvement compared with the one without the developed system and dispersion was also small.

The designed distance from the roadside after completion of parking was set to be 200mm. The result of evaluation shows approximately the same value as the designed distance.

Table.2 Evaluation results

		With System	Without System
Time for parking (second)	AV.	81.18	93.75
	SD.	29.10	58.54
The times of turning steering wheel	AV.	2.0	9.1
	SD.	0	5.5
Distance from road side after parking completion (mm)	AV.	202.89	90.83
	SD.	90.42	250.47

CONCLUSION

The parking assist system using rear view camera with calculation of parallel parking course avoiding the collision with an adjacent vehicle, minimum times steering operation, distortion correction of the parking guide lines, high accuracy image superimposing by measurement of principal axis has been developed.

By using these technologies used in this system, we wish to realize a system with safely and easy to park and in addition, we wish to apply such technologies to more ITS applications.

REFERENCES

[1] H. Satonaka *et.al.* "Development of Back Guide Monitor", TOYOTA Technical Review Vol.50 No.1, Jun 2000.

[2] Y. Tsai: "A versatile camera calibration technique for high-accuracy 3D machine vision metrology using off-the-shelf TV cameras and lenses", Journal of Robotics and Automation Vol.3, pp.323-344, 1987.

[3] O. Faugeras: "Three Dimensional Computer Vision, A Geometric Viewpoint", MIT Press, Cambridge, Massachusetts, 1993.

[4] E. Paromtchik, C. Laugier: "Autonomous Parallel Parking of a Nonholonomic Vehicle", Proceedings of the Intelligent Vehicles Symposium pp.13-18, 1996.

PART V
DRIVER/VEHICLE INTERFACES

2005-01-0436

Mind-on-the-Drive: Real-Time Functional Neuroimaging of Cognitive Brain Mechanisms Underlying Driver Performance and Distraction

Richard A. Young
General Motors Corp.

Li Hsieh, Francis X. Graydon, Richard Genik II, Mark D. Benton and Christopher C. Green
Wayne State University Medical School

Susan M. Bowyer, John E. Moran and Norman Tepley
Henry Ford Hospital

ABSTRACT

How do in-vehicle telematics devices influence mind-on-the-drive? We determined the spatio-temporal properties of the brain mechanisms during a simple visual event detection and motor response in a validated driving-like protocol. We used the safe and non-invasive brain imaging methods of functional magnetic resonance imaging (fMRI) and Magnetoencephalography (MEG) to locate the essential brain activated structures and their corresponding temporal dynamics. This study sets the foundation for determining the fundamental brain mechanisms by which secondary tasks (such as cell phone use) may affect the responses to visual events in a laboratory setting. Improved knowledge of the brain mechanisms underlying selective attention in such driving-like situations may give rise to methods for improving mind-on-the-drive.

INTRODUCTION

An essential issue for human factors research is to examine and evaluate the design of human-machine interfaces for the safe and efficient operation of complex equipment under multitasking conditions [1], [2]. In driving, multitasking is required for primary tasks that have to be performed (steering, braking, navigation), as well as secondary tasks that are elective (e.g. cell phone use). Little is known about the brain mechanisms underlying primary driving tasks, much less during secondary tasks. The scientific goal of this study was to set a foundation for determining the neural basis of mental attention shifts that may underlie some driver errors, which includes driver distraction.

Behavioral metrics have been established for measuring on-road driver performance while doing secondary tasks in a vehicle (Angell, Young, Hankey and Dingus [3]; CAMP [4]). These metrics typically involve direct measurements of vehicle behavior (e.g. lane and speed deviations, braking time, headway to preceding vehicle, etc.). Indirect measures such as eyes-off-road time and subjective workload have also been made in these same studies. Laboratory methods for collecting data that is predictive of on-road driver performance have been developed and validated in these same studies. It is relatively straightforward to use analysis of video recordings to determine how long the eyes are on or off the road during secondary tasks. However, it is not as simple to determine whether a driver's mind is on the drive using such purely behavioral measures.

Some event-detection methods have shown initial promise in measuring mind-on-the-drive. Martens and van Winsum [5] and Olsson and Burns [6] used a peripheral light mounted on a headset to which a driver responds with a hand switch whenever the light turns on. Angell et al. [3] extended these methods by using a central as well as peripheral light mounted on the hood and left outside mirror of the vehicle, respectively. The reaction times and miss rates to the events are measured by the press of a foot switch whenever a light is seen. This technology has shown some initial promise for measuring mind-on-the-drive in some on-road driving experiments [9]. There has also been some limited progress in the difficult task of predicting on-road event-detection variables from even validated static laboratory methods [3], much less non-validated static methods. However, purely behavioral methods for evaluating event detection have inherent limitations.

Drivers might not respond to an event for three separate reasons. First, the driver may make an eye movement to a location sufficiently far from the event such that light from the event does not enter the driver's eyes (*eyes-off-road*). Second, the light from the event or visual stimulus may enter the eyes, but the contrast or movement may not exceed the sensory threshold such that neural messages are sent from the eyes to the brain. Third, the light might enter the driver's eyes and neural messages be sent from the eyes to the brain, but the brain might not perceive the event (*cognitive blindness*). The third reason is also termed *looked-but-did-not-see,* in*attention blindness* or *change blindness*. This effect can occur whether an eye movement does or does not precede or follow the missed event. Every combination of these effects is logically possible: eyes and mind might both be *off* the road, both be *on* the road, or one or the other only. Indeed, it is well established from cognitive and neurophysiological studies that visual detection is affected by both top-down cognitive attentional effects and bottom-up sensory effects (Posner and Raichle [7]; Corbetta and Shulman [8]). Indeed, it is well established that the "spotlight of attention" can be independently directed to any part of the visual field, and improve stimulus detection, independently of gaze location. Because of this independence, and also because gaze patterns cannot discriminate between sensory and attentional effects, gaze patterns alone are not a sufficient indicator of mind-off-road. Therefore, the current study was undertaken to establish direct physiological methods for measuring mind-on-the-drive. Our objective is to set the foundation for elucidating the neural mechanisms underlying attentional effects of secondary tasks on driver event detection performance.

The notion that event detection is independently affected by attention and gaze variables is supported by principal component analysis of multivariate on-road driver performance data while doing secondary tasks (Young and Angell [9]). Glance variables such as eyes-off-road time, number of glances and mean glance duration have the same positive loadings as event-detection variables on an *overall driver demand* dimension, accounting for 61 percent of the total variance in driver performance while doing secondary tasks in the vehicle. That is, more eyes-off-road time is associated with more missed events and longer reaction times. But glance variables are *oppositely* loaded with event detection variables for the second driver performance dimension (interpreted as *low-workload-but-high-inattentiveness*, accounting for 17 percent of variance). That is, some secondary tasks even with driver's eyes mostly on the road have relatively higher missed event rates and longer reaction times. This dimension identifies tasks that make drivers more inattentive to outside events than expected, given that their eyes are on the road.

Like glance behavior, self-reports of attention to the road (e.g. subjective situation awareness metrics) may also not be adequate measures of mind-off-road. Subjective metrics assume that drivers are aware of being distracted –yet drivers may be unaware that they are missing things on the road [10], [11]. What driver has not carefully looked to both sides before entering an intersection, only to be startled by an oncoming vehicle that was in the field of view but not seen? What driver has not been alerted by someone else to an unnoticed impending event in their vehicle path? Some drivers may be unaware that they are capable of missing events directly in front of their eyes (that is, they are blind to change blindness [12]). It is unclear how measurements of eye movements can account for cases where someone is looking right at something and does not see or react to it [2]. In a simulator experiment, Greenberg et al. [13] asked participants to pay attention to a driving scene, and to detect and respond to visual events at different locations in their visual field. Participants were also asked to perform secondary tasks such as answering a phone and carrying on a conversation. Their study found missed events for incoming calls that were not explainable by eye movements: "Drivers were actually looking out the windshield and still failed to detect events occurring directly in front of their vehicle." Huettel et al. [14] using a change-blindness visual paradigm during fMRI concluded that "Detection of change, when transient visual cues are not present, requires activation of extrastriate visual regions and frontal regions responsible for eye movements." That is, with no transient visual sensory cues, the brain must engage eye movements in a search strategy to detect a change in a visual scene.

Glance behavior in simulators, although different than on-road glance behavior, can predict on-road glance behavior via linear regression analysis [3]. Unfortunately, on-road event-related behavior is difficult to predict from static event behavior, as shown in the same studies. The reasons why on-road event variables do not bear a simple relationship to static measurements are not yet fully known. The current study takes an event protocol that has extensive behavioral data collected both statically and dynamically (Angell et al. [3]). Any data collected in it can therefore be related to both static and on-road studies. This study is the first we are aware of that uses the same protocol in a brain imaging study as in static and dynamic vehicle testing studies.

The knowledge gained may help understand how the brain performs in dual-task situations in general [15]. In particular, such knowledge may help explain how the performance of secondary tasks such as conversing on a telematics system may affect reaction times or miss rates to events in laboratory simulator studies [13], [16], but not have a determinable effect on real-world crashes severe enough to deploy an air bag (Young [17]). Such knowledge may also allow a more precise determination of which secondary tasks have appreciable effects on real-world driving performance [18], [19], and which do not.

OBJECTIVES AND PARADIGM

The immediate research objective is to determine the underlying location and dynamics of the neural mechanisms that underlie event detection in a driving-like scenario. The applied objective is to determine better methods for assessment-related behavior that can lead to more effective on-road predictions from laboratory data.

The basic paradigm has been previously applied to the study of the effect of secondary tasks on driving in simple static simulators and on-road studies [3]. When extended to include secondary tasks in the brain-imaging environment, this project will help fulfill its long-range scientific objective to help determine the neural basis of mental attention shifts that underlie driver errors during the performance of secondary tasks in the vehicle (i.e., driver distraction).

Two questions are key: (1) What brain systems are activated and when during normal driving? (2) What changes in this baseline brain activity are induced by secondary non-driving tasks? To answer the first question, we used functional Magnetic Resonance Imaging (fMRI) at the Wayne State Medical School Transportation Imaging Laboratory to identify activated brain structures in a simple driving-like paradigm. This paradigm has been validated with on-road and static vehicle driver performance data [3]. We also used Magnetoencephalography (MEG) at Henry Ford Hospital to determine the temporal dynamics of those pathways in the same driving-like paradigm. We report here a preliminary answer to the first question, particularly with regard to a simple light event detection and response reflex. To answer the second question, we intend to add an auditory-verbal secondary task (cell phone conversation) to the event detection and response task in the same driving-like paradigm. We will then assess the spatio-temporal brain changes and compare them to the baseline established in this study.

Both the fMRI and MEG experiments reported here used a behavioral paradigm that has been well validated to predict on-road behavior for many major driving performance metrics [3], despite its simplicity and low cost compared to elaborate driving simulators. It uses digitized videos of real-world driving scenes, recorded during daylight hours in the summer while driving on various roads and highways in southeast Michigan. The scenes were shot from the inside of a vehicle looking outward, as near to the driver's point of view as practical, using a high-quality video camera [20]. The interior windows of the vehicle were shielded (except for the windshield) to prevent reflections and glare.

Small light events are superimposed at the bottom or to the left of the driving video when shown to the participants, at unpredictable times. The participants are asked to respond when they see a light event by pressing a foot switch in a braking-like manner. We typically use a forward light on the hood of the vehicle, and a peripheral light on the left-side driver's mirror, in on-road and laboratory studies [3]. We use a left-foot switch similar to an old-style headlamp dimming switch in the road studies, and a standard brake pedal operated by the right foot in the static laboratory. We used similar forward and peripheral lights in the MEG experiments reported here, with a right foot pedal. We used a single forward event light in the fMRI studies, and a button operated by the right hand, rather than a foot pedal.

Previous studies have used a single peripheral light with a hand switch, [5], [6], [21]. These studies, combined with studies [3], [4], conclusively demonstrate that simple light detection tasks when used with appropriate parameters and conditions in a driving context can provide a highly sensitive measure for workload variations induced by traffic, the road environment, driving experience, human-vehicle interface complexity or secondary task difficulty. Although successful at predicting overall workload variations, the predictive ability of static event light detection measures for specifically predicting effects on crash rates in real-world driving (e.g. Young [17]), has yet to be shown.

FMRI EXPERIMENT

Functional Magnetic Resonance Imaging (fMRI) is a technique for localizing brain activity by non-invasively measuring the magnetic fields related to blood flow associated with neural activation [22]. Its strengths are that it measures these responses with millimeter spatial resolution, correlates function and anatomy, and is safe and non-invasive. We used whole-brain fMRI to identify the key brain systems involved in visual event detection and response during a limited form of simulated driving.

In the first published fMRI study of simulated driving, Walter et al. [23], using a computer driving game, found two areas of perceptual-motor activation: sensorimotor cortex and cerebellar regions.

Calhoun et al. [24], using a validated computer-generated driving scenario, used independent component analysis to identify specific spatio-temporal brain components involved in driving: (1) vigilance (spatial attention); (2) error monitoring and inhibition (motivation and risk assessment); (3) high-order visual/motor integration and low-order visual; (4) motor control (fine and gross), and (5) visual monitoring. During the simulated driving scenario, brain regions associated with vigilance and spatial attention (e.g. fronto-parietal cortex) decreased their involvement during driving, and those associated with error monitoring and inhibition (e.g. anterior cingulate cortex) showed an exponential decrease during driving. The other components increased in activation while driving.

A joystick simulation study by Toyota of a car-following task during fMRI [25] found activity in cerebellum (visual feedback during smooth tracking of the preceding car); basal ganglia, thalamus, premotor cortex (movement selection); and a premotor-parietal network (visuo-motor coordination). Their study also found that "Task performance was negatively correlated with anterior cingulate activity, consistent with the role of this region in error detection and response selection."

This previous work on more complex forms of simulated driving included more interactive components such as acceleration, deceleration, navigation control or car-following. We were mainly interested in isolating and identifying the brain systems activated during a specific but relatively simple driving behavior, namely visual event detection and response, in the context of immersion in a real-life driving visual scene.

FMRI METHODS

Data were acquired with a 1.5 Tesla Siemens Sonata whole-body MRI scanner (Fig. 1) equipped with a head volume coil. Functional imaging methods were used (see [26], [27], [28] for parameters). Data were analyzed offline using Statistical Parametric Mapping software (http://www.fil.ion.ucl.ac.uk/spm/).

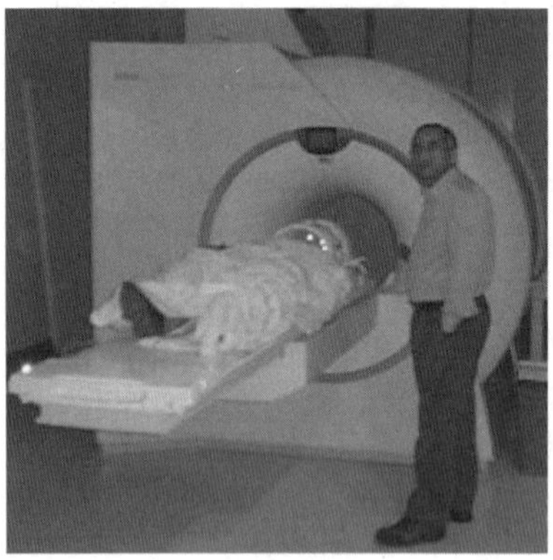

Figure 1. The 1.5 Tesla fMRI scanner at Wayne State Medical School.

Stimuli

Real-world driving scenes were shown through magnetically shielded liquid-crystal display goggles (Resonance Technologies, Northridge, CA). The participant's ears were insulated from intermittent magnet activation noise with headphones (Fig. 2). A microphone allowed communication between the participant and experimenters at all times.

Each screen of the goggles subtended approximately 30 degrees of visual field. The goggles gave a more immersive experience than viewing a projection screen or video monitor, because no visual stimuli other than the driving scene could be seen. No driving sounds accompanied the video.

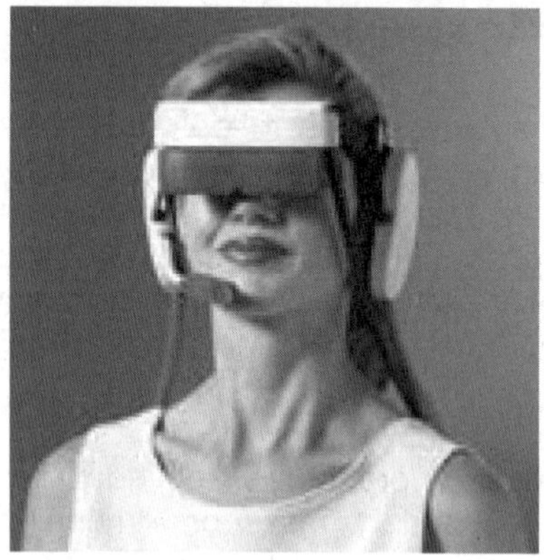

Figure 2. Illustration of immmersive video goggles, microphone and earphones used in fMRI experiments.

For each trial of this task, a small red light event was presented through the liquid-crystal display (LCD) goggles and was shown in the bottom center of the screen just below the driving scene (see Fig. 3). This event was an analog of the light-emitting diode (LED) light placed on the front of the hood of the vehicle in our static and dynamic studies [3]. The participant was asked to press a button with his right index finger as soon as the event was detected. Each light terminated after two seconds.29 The inter-event interval range was two to five seconds with a mean of three and a half seconds. The events were presented at unpredictable time intervals in the inter-event range to prevent participants from anticipating the events. (The vehicle study events [3] were similar except they had a three- to six-second inter-event interval, a peripheral and central light, and a foot pedal that turned off the light when depressed.) The reaction time and percent misses to the event lights were recorded for all stimuli. Participants were free to direct their eyes and visual attention to any spatial location in the driving scene at will. Eye movements were not recorded, but the pilot experiments used a small video camera in the goggles that could display the eye on a screen in the control room, and the eyes appeared to move about during the road scenes as would be expected, rather than to remain fixated at one location. The red light was still visible in the field of view for any possible rotation of the eyes, assuming the eyes were open. Also, the red light was presented in the LCDs for both left and right eyes to ensure they would be out of the blind spot for at least one eye for any eye rotation. The red light persisted long enough (two seconds) that it could still be seen either before or after any eye blink.

Task Conditions

In the main experiment, the participant's brains were imaged during three task conditions: (1) EVENT - the event light alone; (2) VIEW - the driving video alone; and (3) DUAL - the driving video and the event light together (see Fig. 3). In the VIEW and DUAL conditions while viewing the real-life driving scene, participants were asked to imagine driving without overt motor responses such as moving the arms or head. (Indeed, they were asked to remain still to the extent possible, to minimize head movement artifacts in the fMRI.) A finger press and eye movements constituted the only overt motor activity during the task conditions.

Figure 3. Screen shots of the driving video and target visual events presented to subjects during the EVENT task (condition 1, top panel), the simulated driving VIEW task (condition 2, middle panel), or the DUAL task (condition 3, bottom panel). Each of these task conditions alternated four times with a blank screen with a crosshair in the center for each participant (see Fig. 4).

It should be noted that the DUAL task condition implemented here is not a dual task condition in the usual sense of a primary driving task and a secondary non-driving task. The DUAL condition here is the analog of two *primary* driving-like tasks: viewing the roadway and responding to events. It is intended to set the foundation for later experiments (not reported here) of the neural effects of a *secondary* task (e.g. cell phone usage) on a *primary* event detection brain response, in the context of a driving-like scenario.

Recording Methods

Each of the three scanning sessions consisted of four, 40-second blocks of one of the conditions described above, with each block alternated with a 40-second baseline period during which participants fixated on a centrally placed crosshair (baseline fixation condition), producing 360 seconds or six minutes of time for each session (Fig. 4) [30].

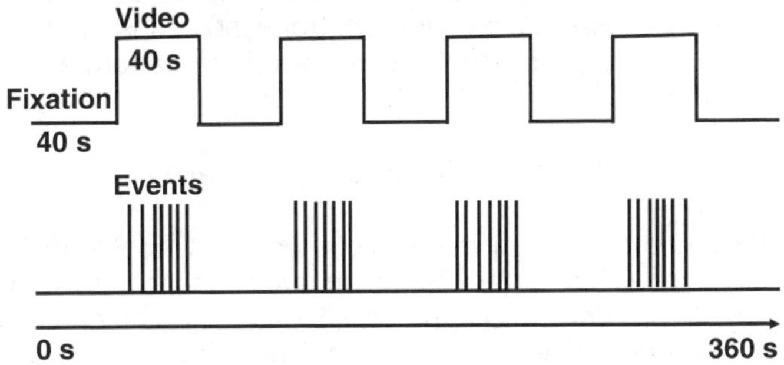

Figure 4. "Boxcar" design, or alternating blocks of baseline fixation (40 seconds) followed by task condition 1, 2, or 3 (40 seconds), followed by baseline, etc. for four blocks (360 seconds). The event lights presented in conditions 1 and 3 are illustrated in the line below.

Participants received seven visual events during each block of the event task in the EVENT and DUAL conditions 1 and 3, representing a total of 28 events over the course of each of those two conditions. All three task conditions were presented to each participant, with the order of the three conditions counterbalanced across participants.

Six normal right-handed volunteers (three male and three female, 22-28 years old) participated in the experiment. All participants had normal or corrected vision. The data were pooled across the six participants for each of the three conditions. The level of activation for each of the three conditions was compared with the activation of the fixation baseline. A separate comparison was made of condition 3 vs. condition 2. The score at each three-dimensional volume element (*voxel*) for each condition was evaluated for statistical significance using the *t*-test with threshold at $p < 0.05$, corrected for multiple comparisons.

BLOCK-RELATED FMRI RESULTS

Multiple neural systems were associated with block-averaged analysis of all three conditions, when compared to fixation baseline (for details, see [26], [27], [28]).

1. EVENT Task vs. Baseline (Crosshair Fixation)

The event light and hand response condition alone (Fig. 3, top panel, condition 1) showed clearly identifiable brain responses to the event light in visual cortex and the motor response in primary motor cortex and supplementary motor area, when compared to the baseline condition (brain image not shown).

This condition was a control to show that the well-known visual and motor brain areas connected with a simple visual-motor reflex such as a hand response to a light event could be detected and measured with the fMRI method. A counterpart in real-world driving would be implausible: sitting in a stationary vehicle pressing a brake pedal in response to a stoplight on a black field of view. For such reasons, this control condition is not run in our on-road or static vehicle driver performance experiments [3].

2. VIEW Task vs. Baseline (Crosshair Fixation)

Viewing the driving video without the event light (VIEW condition 2, Fig. 3, middle panel), vs. baseline activated large brain areas, including visual, parietal and temporal cortex and frontal areas, including BA6 (brain image not shown). In particular, these activations involved statistically significant activation increases in the left precentral gyrus, left superior parietal lobe, left supramarginal gyrus, left inferior frontal gyrus, visual cortex, cerebellum, anterior cingulate gyrus, and basal ganglia. Activation of these brain regions suggested a greater role for motor coordination and control, vigilance, preparatory motor processes, and the regulation of the temporal aspects of specific motor responses.

Indeed, the dynamic brain activation patterns could be viewed in real time on a monitor in the control room using the custom real-time fMRI software TurboFIRE [31], [32], [33], [34]. During pilot experiments a large increase in brain activation of one participant was noted by the experimenters at the same time as the video showed passing an 18-wheel truck (Fig. 3, bottom panel). When questioned after the trial, the participant reported that he had concerns about passing such large trucks in his everyday driving. This observation, although anecdotal, confirmed the objective observations that the driving video actively engaged more than just visual cortex in participants' brains. In fact, it was consistent with the fMRI activations seen in active driving in a simulator [24].

Viewing the driving video by itself is used both as a task to contrast with the baseline crosshair fixation condition, and again as a control condition to contrast with the DUAL task condition (see below). As proof that VIEW is a driving-like task it is noted that the large brain activations in motor as well as vigilance regions (not just visual regions) indicated that participants were actively immersed in the driving scene as intended; that is, they were making covert mental responses consistent with overt driving behavior even though they did not make body movements such as turning a steering wheel or rotating the head. The VIEW counterpart in real-world driving would be simply driving down the road without having to respond to external events or doing a secondary task. This condition is run in our on-road and laboratory driver performance tests as a practice trial [3].

3. DUAL Task vs. Baseline (Crosshair Fixation)

Viewing the driving scene while responding to the red light (Fig. 3, grey square at bottom of panel 3), when compared to baseline, activated similar brain areas as in conditions 1 and 2, but with additional activation in motor cortex.

The detailed increases in activation vs. baseline are shown in Fig. 5 as the lighter shaded areas (see *t*-score scale at bottom of Fig. 5). These areas indicate statistically significant changes in activation.

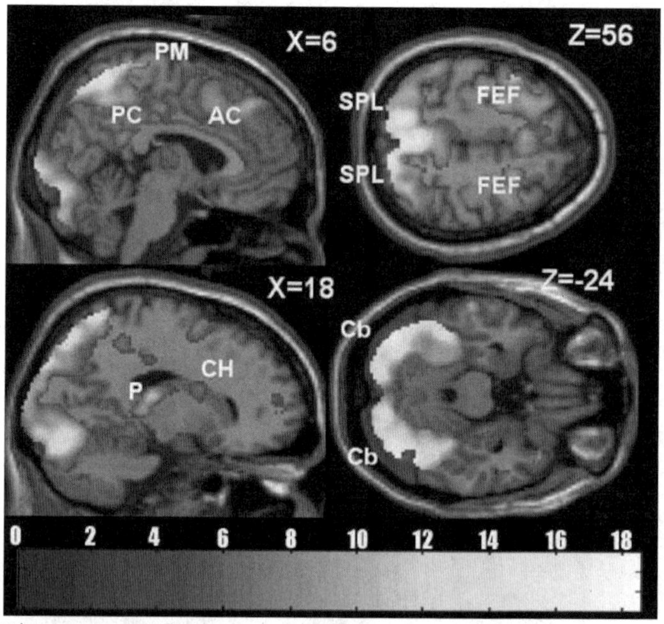

Figure 5. Brain response to DUAL task (video + event) vs. brain response to baseline. The left two images show side views of the brain at different "slices" of a vertical plane. The right two images show top views of the brain at different "slices" of a horizontal plane. There is widespread activation from the driving video plus event task compared to baseline. Key: **PM** (medial pre-motor and also some motor), **PC** (precuneus), **AC** (anterior cingulate). SPL (superior parietal lobule), **FEF** (frontal eye fields and some pre-motor), **P** (pulvinar), **CH** (caudate head), **Cb** (posterior cerebellum). Color scale at bottom is *t*-score for the comparison of brain activation vs. baseline.

These regions are again part of neural systems involved in low and higher level visual processing (Brodmann's Area (BA) 17-19, lingual and fusiform gyri, pulvinar), preparatory motor responses (BA 6 and BA 8), motor control/coordination (cerebellum, basal ganglia), as well as attention-related processing (anterior and posterior cingulate cortex, inferior and superior parietal lobules, temporal-occipital junction and the area of the frontal eye fields). Several of these regions are identified with letter codes in Fig. 5. Other noteworthy sites of activation were observed in the inferior temporal gyri and medial temporal sites (parahippocampal gyrus, uncus).

Average driver performance data collected in a vehicle parked in a garage with a television monitor showing the same driving scene as used here, and with similar event lights, is predictive of on-road driving performance [3].

4. DUAL Task vs. VIEW Task

A comparison was made of the brain responses of the DUAL task (condition 3, Fig. 3, bottom panel) to the brain responses to the VIEW task (condition 2, Fig. 3, middle panel). Each of these task conditions was alternated with the baseline crosshair. But the response to the DUAL task could be compared to the VIEW task through mathematical analysis. This comparison reflects the areas of activation specific to the event task, when done in the context of viewing a driving video, vs. the effects of the video alone. This comparison of the brain activations of DUAL vs. VIEW tasks is shown in Fig. 6 as the colored regions, all of which were statistically significant.

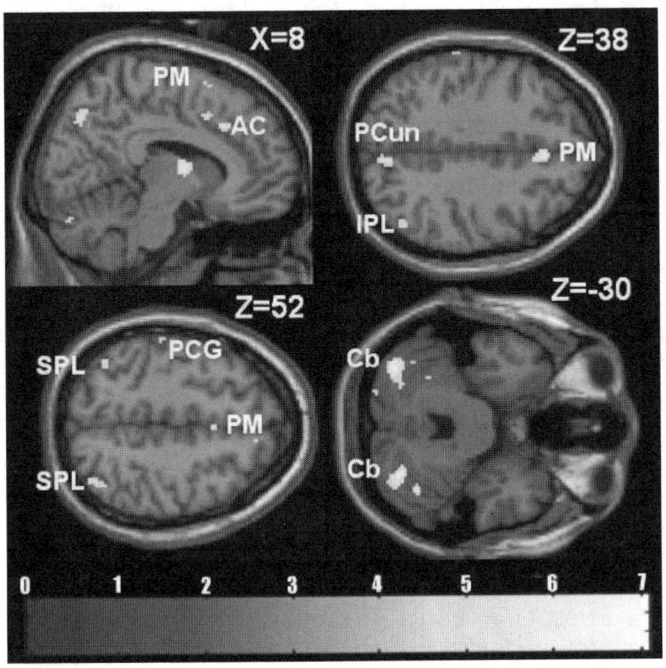

Figure 6. Increase in brain activation (colored regions) to DUAL task vs. brain activation from VIEW task. The top left image shows a side view of the brain at one slice of a vertical plane. The remaining images show top views of the brain at different slices of a horizontal plane. Key: **PM** (medial pre-motor), **AC** (anterior cingulate). **PCun** (precuneus), **IPL** (inferior parietal lobule), **PM** (medial pre-motor), **SPL** (superior parietal lobule), **PCG** (post central gyrus), **PM** (medial pre-motor), **Cb** (posterior cerebellum). Color scale at bottom is *t*-score for the comparison in brain activations.

The areas activated presumably reflect the brain activation specific to the EVENT task when performed in a simulated driving context, while controlling for the effect of the video. That is, the colored regions in Fig. 6 indicate the brain regions recruited specifically for the event detection and response task when performed in a behavioral state evoked by viewing a video of a real-world driving scene from the driver's point of view.

This comparison produced a different activation pattern than the previous three comparisons. The visual and motor activation was either increased or decreased depending on the brain area, as compared to the event detection task alone (condition 1) vs. baseline. Additionally, there was increased activation in left parietal cortex.

In general, the activations were restricted to smaller volumes than in the DUAL task vs. baseline comparison (Fig. 6 has less colored area than Fig. 5). Also, the activations were not as strong: Fig. 6 has a smaller upper range of *t*-values (7) than Fig. 5 (18). This contrast reveals brain activations *specific* to event detection during driving-like behavior are identified in Fig. 6, apart from the effects of the video by itself (condition 2), event detection by itself (condition 1), or their combination (condition 3).

In particular, the comparison of the DUAL task vs. VIEW task in Fig. 6 shows there was reduced activation (compared to DUAL task vs. baseline in Fig. 5) of several fronto-parietal regions, as well as cortical and sub-cortical regions of the motor system seen in Fig. 5 (pre-motor cortex, cerebellum, and basal ganglia). Several of the regions with reduced activation compared to DUAL vs. baseline are identifiable in Fig. 6. Other significant decreases in brain activation from controlling for the activation from the video task itself were centered on prefrontal regions in the superior frontal gyrus (region SPL in Fig. 6, left bottom brain image), known to be involved in higher level cognitive functioning. Again, the fact that these areas continue to show activation after contrasting them with the activation from the video alone, suggest they are involved in the event detection task *during* brain responses activated by the video.

In short, we compared the brain responses to viewing the driving video with event detection, to without event detection. This comparison indicates a frontal-parietal network, including occipital and thalamus regions, is associated with event detection in the context of a driving-like scenario. These areas strongly suggest brain involvement in coordinating visual attention, attentional control, stimulus processing, response selection and motor execution during the event detection task in this scenario; more specifically than in the event task by itself, or the video by itself.

For an analogy to real-world driving, this scenario is the equivalent of comparing (a) driving while responding to a visual event such as a brake or traffic light vs. (b) just driving. On-road data show that responding to event lights plus driving has a somewhat higher workload demand via most driver performance metrics than just driving [3] as would be expected from common sense. The more specific activations seen in Fig. 6, when compared to Fig. 5, suggest specific brain regions that should be looked at in later work studying the effects of secondary tasks on event detection in the context of driving.

Behavioral Event Analysis

There were few misses of any lights in these experiments, consistent with on-road studies of baseline driving with similar protocols for the event lights as used here [3]. The mean success rate for the DUAL task condition 3 was 100 percent (no misses). The mean success rate for the EVENT task condition 1 was 98 percent, not a statistically significantly difference. The mean response time for the DUAL task (condition 3) was 611 milliseconds, while that for the EVENT task alone (condition 1) was slightly faster at 550 milliseconds, indicating a small dual task deficit of 61 milliseconds (DF 5; $t = -2.68$, $p < 0.05$). (It should be cautioned that this result is for only six participants and may not hold up for larger sample sizes.) The neural mechanisms producing this small time difference cannot be reliably determined from fMRI studies with their slower time scales compared to MEG imaging. However, it is interesting to note that the larger amount of brain activation in the DUAL task condition 3 (Fig. 5) actually was associated with slower reaction times than the more restricted activation from just the event light task by itself (condition 1, not shown).

Again for analogs with on-road driving, this scenario is equivalent to comparing driving plus responding to roadway events (condition 2) vs. responding to events with nothing else visible except the event light (condition 1). We have not explicitly tested this comparison in our static or on-road driving studies [3], because we have had no reason for testing a participant's response to the lights against a black field of view (which would not be feasible on-road anyway). But it is plausible that a slightly faster response might be expected to a light event in a black vs. complex visual background.

EVENT-RELATED FMRI RESULTS

A second analysis method (Hsieh et al. [35]) used event-related analysis methods in the brain software program SPM99. This method analyzed the same fMRI data that was analyzed in conditions 1 and 3 above with event data. Condition 2 had no event data and so could not be analyzed with this method.

Event-related analysis provides a close-up window to look at the brain activity with a fine-grain and more precise perspective than block analysis. The event-related method time locks the participant's brain responses according to the red light events (see Fig. 4 bottom), rather to the blocks of the different conditions (Fig. 4 top). There is no need to compare each condition to the baseline brain activity with the crosshairs alone, as in the block-analysis method.

Fig. 7 shows the brain responses to the EVENT (red light detection) task using the event-related analysis of the brain data. Here we observe increased brain activations of the left precentral gyrus, left superior parietal lobe, left inferior frontal gyrus and cingulate gyrus. These areas are known to be recruited for focus attention, stimulus processing, response decision and motor execution.

Fig. 8 shows the brain responses to the DUAL task (driving video with red light detection task) when analyzed with event-related analysis. This analysis showed similar neural networks as the boxcar analysis presented earlier: large fronto-parietal networks, thalamus, claustrum and cerebellum. This event-related analysis confirms, in the DUAL task, the recruitment of neural systems known to be involved in visuo-motor multimodal processing and integration.

An additional task condition was examined for four of the six subjects. This fourth task condition (not discussed in the block-analysis method described above) consisted of the DUAL condition in one 40-second block, followed by the VIEW condition in the next 40-second block, and so forth for four repetitions. There was no central crosshair baseline block in this task condition. This fourth condition was added to more directly determine the areas of activation specific to the event task in the context of viewing a driving video vs. the effects of the driving video itself. This direct DUAL vs. VIEW task condition was designed to answer the same question as the DUAL vs. VIEW *post-hoc* analysis in the block analysis method – to examine the event detection task in a driving context, but now more directly controlling for the effects of the video itself.

Fig. 9 shows that using event-related analysis, this condition showed the activation of mechanisms for attentional executive control that included the anterior cingulate gyrus, left motor cortex and the middle/superior frontal areas in the right hemisphere. This fourth task condition used in the event-related analysis also confirms the block analysis in that the DUAL task, when compared with the video viewing by itself, recruits neural systems known to be involved in visuo-motor multimodal processing and integration and increased attention demand.

The consistent findings of the block-related and event-related analysis approaches validate the results reported here using functional MRI methodology for the investigation of high-level, multitasking activities such as simulated driving and event detection.

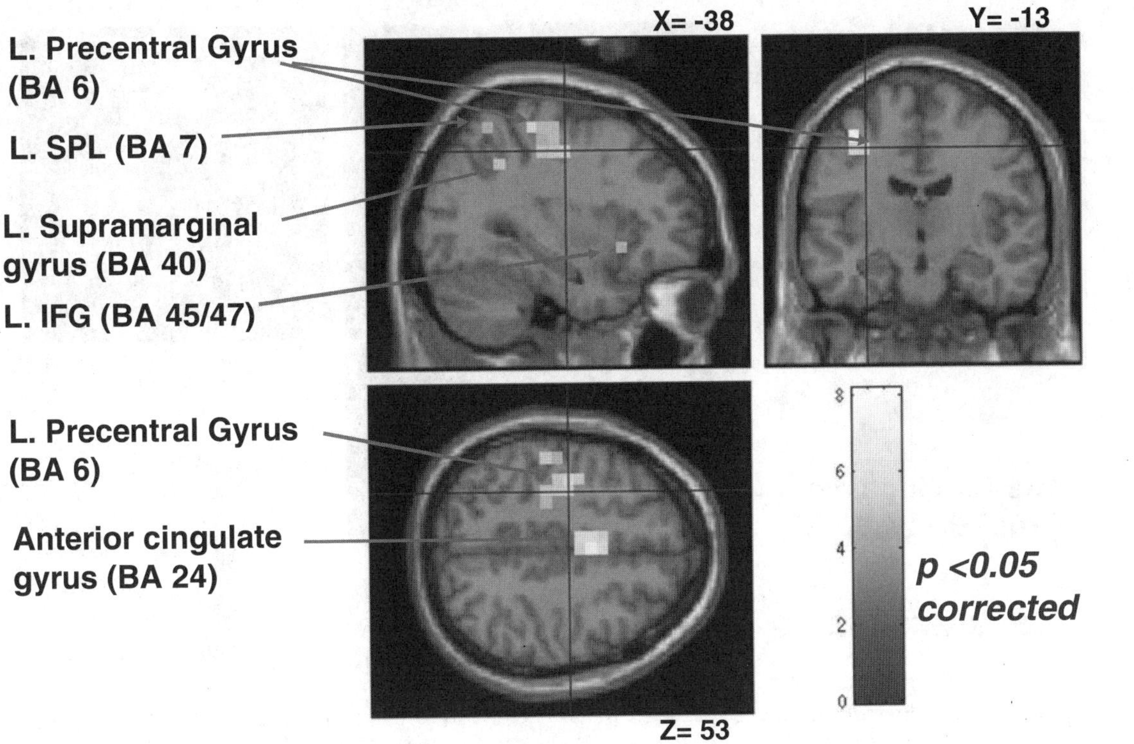

Figure 7. **L. Precentral Gyrus**: finger press from right hand. **L. SPL (BA7)** (superior parietal lobe) and **L. supramarginal gyrus**: sensorimotor integration and higher cortical function (such as monitoring and manipulation). **L. IFG (BA45/47)**: higher cortical function (i.e., executive function), such as decision making, monitoring and selective attention. **Anterior cingulate gyrus**: attention, workload and task demand.

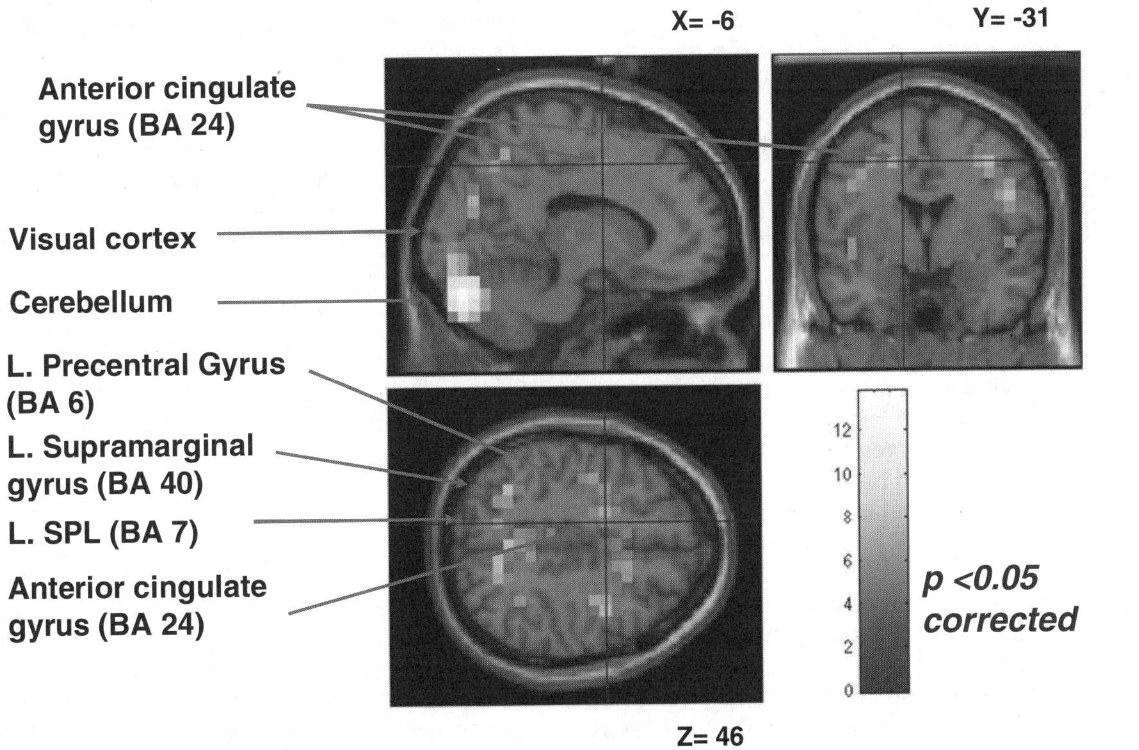

Figure 8. **L. Precentral Gyrus**: finger press from right hand. **L. SPL (BA7)** (the superior parietal lobe) and **L supramarginal gyrus**: sensorimotor integration and higher cortical function (such as monitoring and manipulation). L. IFG (BA45/47): higher cortical function (i.e., executive function), such as decision-making, monitoring and selective attention. **Anterior cingulate gyrus**: attention, workload and task demand. **Visual cortex (BA18/19)**: visual sensory function. **Cerebellum**: motor sequencing, temporal coordination.

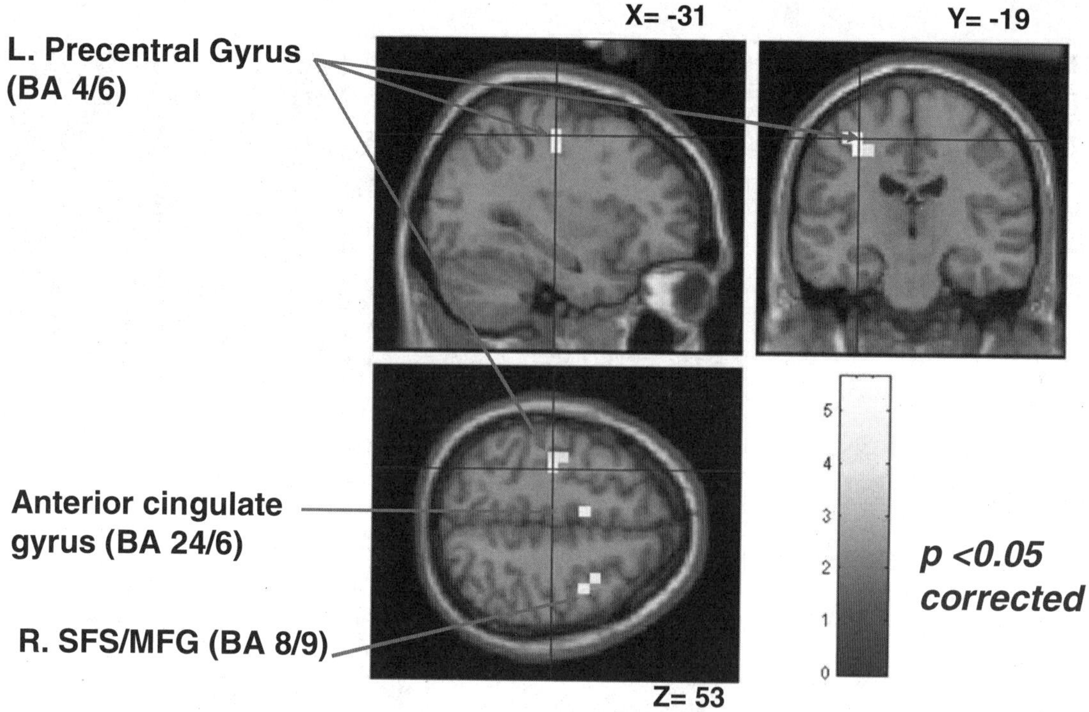

Figure 9. **L. Precentral Gyrus**: finger press from right hand. **Anterior cingulate gyrus**: attention, workload and task demand. **R. Superior Frontal sulcus (BA8)**: frontal eye field. **R. middle frontal gyrus (BA9)**: visuo-spatial monitoring and working memory.

FMRI DISCUSSION

The goal of these fMRI experiments was to identify the spatial neural correlates of a common driving behavior, namely visual event detection, performed as part of a limited simulated driving protocol. The results are in accord with what is well known about the spatial aspects of brain function, e.g., motor cortex activity with manual activity, visual cortex activity increase with complex imagery, Brain areas associated with higher brain functions were also identified, as elicited by the driving video.

In particular, we found evidence for the involvement of multiple brain regions while participants detected and responded to target visual events that appeared in real-world driving scenes used to simulate driving. These brain areas make up widespread and interconnected cortical as well as cortico-sub-cortical anatomical brain networks. In particular, the frontal and parietal cortical regions identified are known components of several large-scale brain systems important during neural processes that include not only visual attention, but also attention control, stimulus processing, motor selection and responses. The interaction of the frontal and parietal systems is thought to control how, what and where we pay attention in our visual environment. These interrelated neural activities are necessary during key driving tasks and behaviors in general, and visual event detection and response in particular. We interpret these findings as reflecting interrelated neural processes associated with visual attention, attention control and allocation, stimulus processing, response selection, execution and timing, all of which are critical during driving. The use of functional neuroimaging techniques such as fMRI is an important technique in the investigation of complex multitasking behaviors such as simulated driving.

The spatial networks identified with fMRI are a required foundation for MEG experiments that can then determine the temporal dynamics of those networks. In particular, fMRI determined the spatial locations of the brain mechanisms involved in the visuo-motor reflex arc giving rise to the foot response to an event light in this paradigm. The timing relationships of those brain mechanisms can then be revealed through MEG experiments, because of the higher temporal resolution capabilities of MEG. The combination of fMRI and MEG experiments in understanding the spatio-temporal properties of the basic reflex arc is required for the eventual study of the neural basis of how secondary activity (such as in auditory-vocal pathways) might influence the timing of primary visual event detection and response reflex pathways. It is logically necessary to understand the neural dynamics of normal behavior, before possible changes to that behavior from secondary activity can be understood. This approach can also be extended to study other neural mechanisms underlying impaired driving, as potentially influenced by factors such as aging, alcohol, brain injury, drugs, fatigue and inexperience.

MEG EXPERIMENT

Magnetoencephalography (MEG) is a technique for localizing sources of electrical activity within the human brain by non-invasively measuring the magnetic fields arising from such activity. Its strengths are similar to fMRI in that it correlates function and anatomy, and is safe and non-invasive with no risk to participants. However, it improves on fMRI in achieving millisecond temporal resolution at the expense of lower spatial resolution.

The variability of MEG data is low. Studies of within-subject variability of temporal, spatial, and strength of neuronal activation have been conducted using repeated runs [36], [40]. Bolander et al. [37] found the variability of source location induced by the rescaling to a common MRI brain was approximately five millimeters. In short, while amplitudes of activity can vary significantly, the timing and location of imaged brain activation is stable from run to run and across individuals.

In this study MEG scans were performed using the same limited automobile driving simulation paradigm as the fMRI experiments. The main objective was to determine if MEG imaging can identify the dynamics of the cortical regions involved in primary driving-like tasks during this simple driving simulation paradigm. The secondary objective was to combine MEG and fMRI data to create a high-resolution space-time "movie" of neural activity in the conscious human brain during simulated driving and event detection, to serve as a foundation for the future investigation of the effect of secondary tasks.

MEG METHODS

A 148-channel whole-head Neuromagnetometer (Magnes WH2500 4-D Neuroimaging) was used to measure magnetic fields from the heads of four females and one male between 30 and 55 years of age, all of whom possessed a current driver's license. Measurements were taken inside a magnetically shielded room located in the Neuromagnetism Laboratory at Henry Ford Hospital. The participant lay comfortably on a bed inside the room. The Neuromagnetometer helmet containing the detector array was placed around the participant's head in close proximity to the skull surface (Fig. 10).

<u>Stimulus-Response</u>

A mirror angled at 45 degrees was placed in front of the participants' eyes so they could view the real-world driving scene on the screen (the same video as in the fMRI experiment). The driving scene was projected into the shielded room and onto a large viewing screen via a system of mirrors. Two red light-emittting diodes (LEDs) were affixed to the viewing screen, one in the lower central region, and the second one on the left side of the screen. Fig. 11 shows a mirror image of the participant's view.

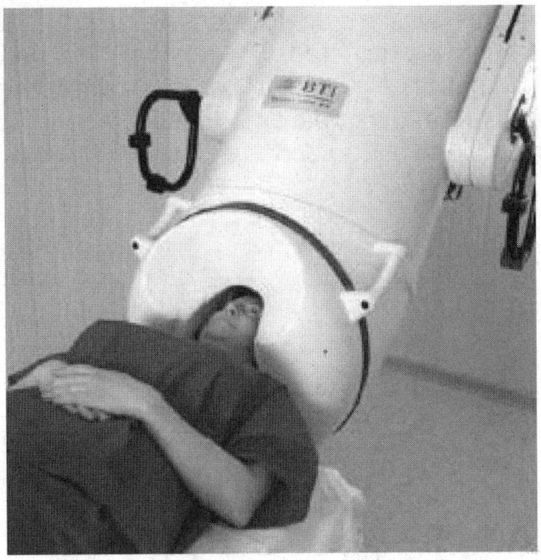

Figure 10. MEG Neuromagnetometer at Henry Ford Hospital Neuromagnetism laboratory, with participant in place.

Figure 11. Typical driving scene with superimposed light events in the MEG experiment. This view is a mirror image of the final image as seen by the participant, so the light event at the right was actually to the left in the participant's view.

LEDs were randomly activated. Participants pushed a mocked-up brake pedal with their right foot to turn the light off.

While in a supine position each participant attended to surrounding vehicle activity, traffic signals, signs and city scenery in a driving video projected directly in front of him/her. At random intervals either the central or peripheral red light stimulus was turned on and the participant was required to detect the light and push the foot pedal. Subsequent pedal activation turned the light off and produced an audible click sound. For the duration of time between turning the light on, to pedal push, a trigger high code was recorded simultaneously with the MEG data. A different trigger code was used for central and peripheral lights. There were 40 red light stimuli during each study. The test was repeated three times to obtain a total of 120 pedal activation events.

The participant was asked to press the foot pedal as soon as a light was detected. The reaction time between turning the light on and pedal push is shown in Fig. 12 for 40 events from participant # 1. On average the pedal is pushed between 0.5-1 second.

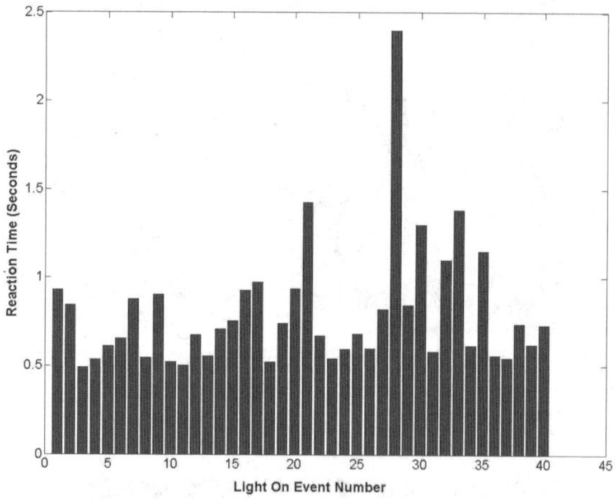

Figure 12. Participant #1's reaction times to the 40 red light events. The highest bar is the longest reaction time, about 2.4 seconds.

The video, lights and foot pedal responses were similar to the methods in laboratory studies validated as predictive of on-road driving behavior [3]. The participant was asked to avoid excessive eye blinks and body movements during data collection. Each participant was monitored by video camera and two-way audio during the time he/she was in the shielded room.

<u>Data Analysis</u>

All MEG brain data were band-pass filtered 0.1 to 100 Hertz (Hz), then digitally sampled at 508 Hz. Data collection runs lasted four minutes and included brain responses to 40 brake pedal pushes in response to the red lights. Each participant performed three runs. The timing of the lights and pedal pushes were recorded as coded events on a trigger event data channel that was simultaneously recorded with the MEG data (Fig. 12). In post processing, windows of MEG data extending from –500 to +500 milliseconds of each pedal push were extracted, forward and backward filtered 1-50 Hz and averaged to obtain a single epoch of data.

All 120 pedal push events from the three runs were averaged for each subject to enhance the signal-to-noise of the MEG data used for imaging the sequence of brain electric activation.

Fig. 13 displays participant #1's averaged MEG data for each of the 148 spatial brain channels. Each line is the brain activation averaged across the 40 pedal push events for a given spatial channel.

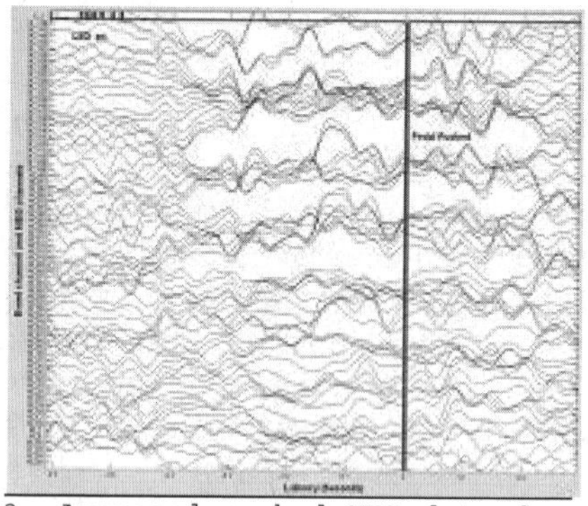

Figure 13. Averaged evoked MEG data for participant #1 for all 148 channels (vertical axis). The horizontal axis is time in seconds compared to the foot pedal responses, which are aligned at the vertical dark line at t = 0.

MEG localizations were performed using the MR-FOCUSS imaging technique (Moran et al. [38]; Moran [39]; Bowyer et al. [40], [41]). Brain imaging results of the five participants were combined into a single brain activation sequence by rescaling the *x,y,z* coordinates of imaged activity of each participant to match a common MRI head model.

MEG RESULTS

Spectral frequency analysis of the MEG data of the five participants demonstrated the data consisted of two major spectral components. The sequence of brain activation was primarily composed of activity in the 1 to 20 Hz band. The other major component was a 28 Hz frequency that was imaged primarily in the right motor and premotor cortex. In some participants this second component was quite prominent.

For all five participants, bilateral orbital-frontal gyrus activation was greatest at light onset and pedal activation. Significant activation of the anterior cingulate gyrus was imaged between 450 to 400 milliseconds prior to the pedal push as well as 100 to 200 milliseconds after. Significant activation of motor and premotor cortex was observed between 180 milliseconds and 50 milliseconds prior to pedal push. Visual cortical activity was imaged during the time interval 500 to 200 msec before the pedal push, and 100 milliseconds after the pedal push turned the light off (cortical OFF response).

Fig. 14 displays the overlay of the 148 channels of MEG data for participant #1; arrows point to the MEG responses associated with the imaged brain responses in Figs. 15-17. For this participant, brain activation in the primary visual cortex to the light onset was significant within the range of 600 to 450 milliseconds prior to the pedal push (see "lights on" in Fig. 14). This activity was followed within 10 milliseconds by superior frontal and anterior cingulate gyrus activation. Motor activity at minus 270 milliseconds in the precentral gyrus (see Fig. 15B) corresponds to foot and leg control motor activity required to depress the pedal (0 milliseconds). This action turned the light off, creating a visual evoked cortical response +95 milliseconds later in the occipital cortex (Fig. 15C). A bilateral response in the auditory cortex (not shown) was observed at +111 milliseconds as a result of a slight click noise from the pedal push.

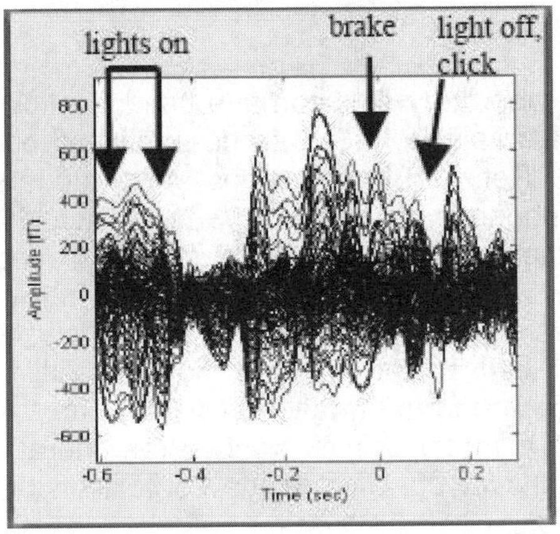

Figure 14. Superimposed MEG channels of Fig. 13 with major events marked. Time traces aligned at brake response $t = 0$ on horizontal axis. Vertical axis is amplitude of brain response.

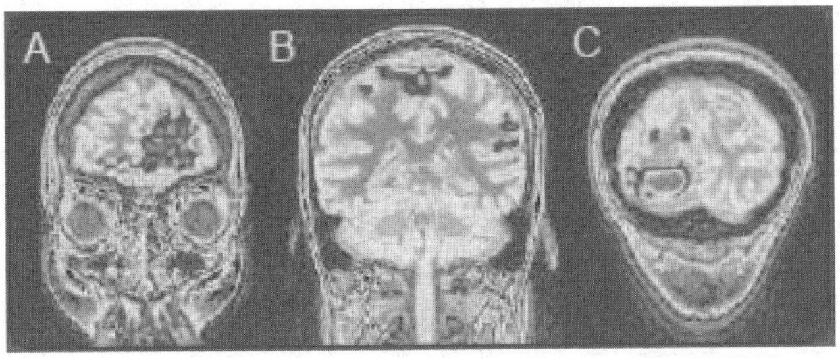

Figure 15. Darker brain areas indicate MR-FOCUSS localizations of activity in (A) the left prefrontal lobe at 300 milliseconds prior to the pedal press, followed by (B) activity in the motor cortex 180 milliseconds prior, followed by (C) visual cortex activation at 80 milliseconds after the pedal press, corresponding to the visual cortex response to the light turning off.

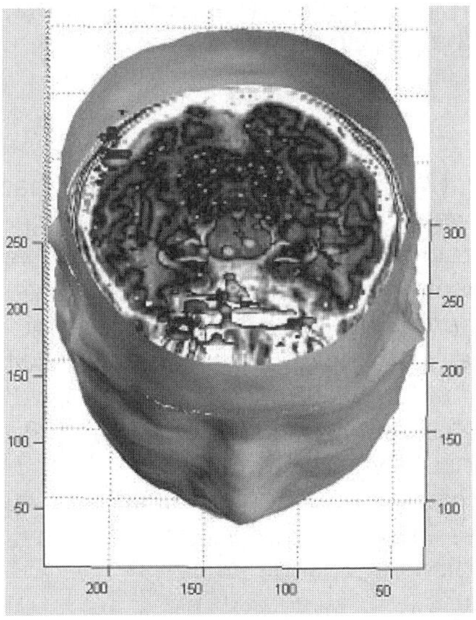

Figure 16. First frame from video of participant at 612 milliseconds before the pedal press, with MRI image of head and brain superimposed.

Fig. 16 shows activation of one participant's brain at 612 milliseconds prior to the pedal press. The lighter areas near the front of the brain indicate activation in frontal cortex regions after the light but before the pedal press.

Fig. 17 is a shading-coded display of the spatial pattern of magnetic fields associated with this brain activation as viewed from the top of a flattened view of the MEG recording array. The darker area near the bottom right of the brain image now represents locations where magnetic field lines are leaving the array and the darker area in the upper right represents locations where the magnetic fields are returning to the array. The areas of deep shading on opposite sides of the brain correspond to strong magnetic field signals of opposite polarity

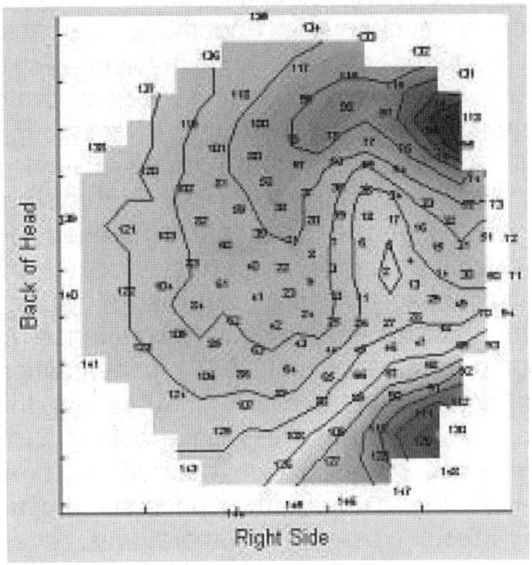

Figure 17. Contour map of the image in Fig. 16 viewed from the top of the head. The darker areas on the right indicate early activation in the frontal cortex.

In summary, the high temporal resolution of MEG imaging allows the time and sequence of activation to be determined for regions involved in this task performance. In particular, transient activation of the occipital (visual) cortex was observed after the light was turned on (ON response) and after the light was turned off (OFF response), as seen for example in single-unit recordings from visual cortex (Young, Lesperance and Meyer [42]; Young and Lesperance [43]). Motor activation was detected during eye movements to the light source and prior to foot movement. Imaged motor activity correlated with known visual motor and leg/foot motor cortex locations. The left pre-frontal region (Fig. 15A) is known to be involved in higher-order condition decision-making, such as that required in the decision to make a foot response. Frontal and parietal networks (Fig. 15A,B) were significantly active at multiple latencies throughout this task performance. The orbital frontal gyrus was likely active throughout the run while attending to the driving scene.

MEG DISCUSSION

These MEG findings suggest driving-like tasks recruit neural systems known to be involved in visual-motor multimodal processing and integration, and reveal the dynamics of those neural systems. Similar to fMRI findings (Fig. 5), activity is first seen in anterior cingulate, followed by prefrontal activity, then activity in the cortical motor areas, giving rise to the foot press. Following the foot press, activation was seen in the visual cortex corresponding to the event light turning off.

GENERAL DISCUSSION

Visual event detection and response performed as part of a limited simulated driving setup engages multiple interconnected cortical and sub-cortical neural systems working in dynamic patterns, as observed with the brain imaging techniques used here. The spatial and temporal properties of brain mechanisms underlying a simple driving-related stimulus-response mechanism were identified using fMRI and MEG. The use of brain imaging in investigating the dynamics of neural processing regions activated during simulated driving and event detection and response is quite promising. This work lays the basic foundation needed to understand the neural basis of effects on event detection and response of secondary tasks, aging, alcohol, brain injury, drugs, fatigue, and inexperience. In particular, imaging studies of cell phone conversation tasks using the foundation laid here may reveal the dynamic cortical networks underlying the effects of such tasks on driver event detection as reported in some simulator studies [13]. It is important to understand what underlies such effects as seen in laboratories, even though the available real-world data indicates that telematic conversations are not a causative factor in crashes serious enough to cause air bag deployments (Young [17]).

ON-ROAD VALIDATION

The fMRI and MEG studies reported here were careful to use behavioral protocols that have been previously validated as predictive of on-road driving (Angell et al. [3]).44 Laboratory experiments using methods that have not been validated may make driving predictions that are not necessarily borne out in real-world driving, giving rise to false positive and false negative errors. A *false positive* error, also called *false alarm*, exists in a driving context when a laboratory or simulator experiment predicts, incorrectly, that it has found a problem in real-world driving, where none exists in reality. A *false negative* error, also called a *miss*, exists in a driving context when a laboratory or simulator experiment predicts, incorrectly, that a problem was not detected when, in fact, it is a problem in real-world driving.

False Positives?

Several studies have generalized to real-world driving with no published data regarding on-road validation of their protocols or results. In our opinion, this could lead to possible "false alarms" for real-world driving.

One fMRI study using a dual-task condition of mental rotation and auditory sentence comprehension concluded that "a complex conversation may put an end to careful driving" even in experienced drivers (Just et al. [45], their p. 425). However, no data on conversations or driving were tested or examined in the study. Moreover, the authors state regarding their own data: "The behavioral measures indicated that the dual tasks were performed without compromising accuracy in either task" and "...both tasks were being performed with a high degree of conscientiousness" (Just et al. [45], their p. 420).

Other behavioral laboratory studies have used joysticks [46], [47] or simulators [16], [48] with no published on-road validation. Ref. [16] concludes that drivers engaged in cell-phone conversations "...may actually exhibit greater impairments (i.e., more accidents and less responsive driving behavior) than legally intoxicated drivers." Ref. [48] states on the basis of results [49] "that cell phone conversations result in impoverished encoding of information necessary for the safe operation of a motor vehicle." However, there a number of questions which arise in the context of this study's findings [50].

In short, in our opinion, non-validated laboratory methods may produce false alarms for real-world driving. A real-world study of millions of customer calls to an advisor was the first analysis of a real-world database that had extensive and actual information about whether a crash serious enough to deploy an air bag occurred at the same time a conversation via telematics was occurring [17]. This study found only two crashes out of 8.1 million calls that occurred while a driver was speaking with a service advisor. It was determined later that there were other underlying causes behind both crashes. Little effect of conversation *per se* on actual driving performance was also seen by Schreiner et al. [51] in an on-road study of voice-activated dialing with a voice-recognition system. Drivers maintained their speed, remained in their lane and scanned their driving environment (checked mirrors, etc.) similarly to how they would during normal driving.

False Negative?

A simulator experiment with college students found that "when participants were legally intoxicated, neither accident rates, nor reaction time to vehicles braking in front of the participant, nor recovery of lost speed following braking differed significantly from baseline" (Strayer et al. [16], their p. 29). In our opinion, this result is inconsistent with numerous simulator, closed-road, and fMRI studies ([52], [53], [54], [55], [56], [57], [58], [59], [60]). It is also inconsistent with real-world data: in 2003, about 275,000 injuries and 17,013 fatalities or 40 percent of all fatalities in motor vehicle traffic crashes were estimated to be alcohol-related [61].

MEDICAL BENEFITS

The medical consequences of severe motor vehicle crashes are well known. However, the medical importance of motor vehicle crashes is not always explicit in rankings of the major causes of death. Anderson and Smith [62] state, "Motor vehicle accidents are not rankable causes of death...though they can be identified using the standard mortality tabulation lists. Were they included in the rankings...motor vehicle accidents would rank eighth." The National Highway Traffic Safety Administration (NHTSA) estimates that driver inattention may be responsible for 25 percent to 30 percent of all police-reported traffic crashes, or about 1.2 million crashes per year in the U.S. [63], [64]. NHTSA is currently focusing mainly on the areas of seat belt use and impaired driving (Runge [65]), but also has some naturalistic studies of crashes in progress (Neale et al. [66]). There is some resource support from NIH and NHTSA for compromised driving studies [67], [68]. It is well known, however, that most crashes happen in broad daylight on open roads with little traffic, with no discernible cause other than generic driver error. While it is commonly understood that drivers at all times have responsibility for safe operation of their vehicle, it would be useful if state and federal governments increased funding priorities to understanding the fundamental neural mechanisms involved in driver attention. It might prove feasible to enhance mind-on-the-drive for all drivers (normal and impaired) if there were a scientific understanding of what mind-on-the-drive actually was.

AUTOMOTIVE BENEFITS

A scientific understanding of the neural basis of mind-on-the-drive has the potential to improve on-road predictions of those task and stimulus features that might lead to mind-off-the-drive in on-road driving. Such work may enhance guidelines for designers of in-vehicle telematics systems as to what should or should not be done in secondary in-vehicle devices so that drivers may maintain high awareness of the road situation. The field of human-vehicle interaction commonly focuses on improving usability of primary driver interfaces, knowledge that does not necessarily transfer to improving usability of navigation and telematics devices that must be attended to only as a secondary priority. In short, a better understanding of the fundamental neural dynamics underlying cognitive attentional factors in driving should lead to a more rapid creation of an in-vehicle environment that maximizes situation awareness of the roadway, while enhancing usability of in-vehicle devices and customer satisfaction.

This analysis of the underlying neural processes may guide the development of integrative cognitive models through which we can better comprehend and investigate driving as a complex human activity (Groeger [69]). The brain imaging techniques when used in conjunction with simple yet validated driving-like protocols offer those engaged in the investigation of driving behavior and performance a complementary tool to existing methodologies involving purely behavioral on-road and laboratory experimental paradigms. This new approach of direct brain measurement opens up a major new field of transportation research, as well as extending current investigations of the neural basis of attentional mechanisms underlying multitasking behavior. Such fundamental knowledge may aid automotive manufacturers in designing safer and more efficient driver interfaces, as well as help educate the general public on their personal responsibilities to keep mind-on-the-drive.

CONCLUSIONS

1. The major brain pathways involved in a simple visual-motor reflex in a driving-like paradigm have been identified using fMRI imaging techniques.
2. The dynamics of those brain pathways have been identified using MEG imaging techniques.
3. The driving-like paradigm used here has been validated for predicting on-road driver performance variables, although static predictions for dynamic event-related variables still need further development compared to other driver performance measures.
4. This study sets a foundation for determining how secondary tasks such as telematics conversations may influence the dynamics of visual-motor reflex pathways, at least in a laboratory setting.
5. This study may lead to potential medical benefits for patients with driving impairments due to attention-deficit hyperactivity disorder (ADHD) or traumatic brain injury.
6. This work may lead to guidelines for the automotive industry and the general public on how to improve driver performance.

ACKNOWLEDGMENTS

We thank Leslie Ash, Yow-Ren Chiang, Dan Fitzgerald, Kunxiu Gao, Roger Hersberger, Zhaid Latif and Shauna Macmillan of Wayne State Medical School for technical support on this project. We thank Stefan Posse for technical and administrative guidance and support during the initial phases of this project, and comments on the manuscript. We thank Sandi Nagel for the references to ADHD and driving. We thank GM Photographic Design for videotaping and digitizing the driving scenes. We thank James Young for assistance in word processing, Linda Angell for continuing support and encouragement, and Vince Calhoun for comments on the manuscript. The research at Wayne State Medical School was supported by an unrestricted gift from the GM Foundation. The research at Henry Ford Hospital was supported by NIH/NINDS Grant RO1-NS30914.

REFERENCES

[1] M. B. Russo, H. Sing and S. Santiago, "Visual neglect: occurrence and pattern in pilots in a simulated overnight flight," *Aviation, Space, and Environmental Medicine.* vol. 75, no. 4, pp. 323-332, 2004.

[2] G. Underwood, P. Chapman, N. Brocklehurst, J. Underwood and D. Crundall, "Visual attention while driving: sequences of eye fixations made by experienced and novice drivers," *Ergonomics*, vol. 46, no. 6, pp. 629-646, 2003.

[3] L. S. Angell, R. A. Young, J. M. Hankey and T. A. Dingus, "An evaluation of alternative methods for assessing driver workload in the early development of in-vehicle information systems," in SAE Proceedings 2002-01-1981, May 2002, http://www.sae.org/servlets/productDetail?PROD_TYP=PAPER&PROD_CD=2002-01-1981.

[4] CAMP, "Driver workload metric project. Crash avoidance metrics partnership second annual report," U.S. Department of Transportation, National Highway Traffic Safety Administration DOT HS 809 663, 2003, http://www-nrd.nhtsa.dot.gov/pdf/nrd-12/CampII.pdf.

[5] M. H. Martens and W. van Winsum, "Measuring distraction: the peripheral detection task," U.S. Department of Transportation, National Highway Traffic Safety Administration, 2000, http://www-nrd.nhtsa.dot.gov/departments/nrd-13/driver-distraction/Papers20034.htm#A34.

[6] S. Olsson and P. C. Burns, "Measuring driver visual distraction with a peripheral detection task," U.S. Department of Transportation, National Highway Traffic Safety Administration, 2000, http://www-nrd.nhtsa.dot.gov/departments/nrd-13/driver-distraction/Papers20006.htm#A6.

[7] M. I. Posner and M. E. Raichle, "Precis of images of mind," *Behavioral and Brain Sciences,* vol. 18, no. 2, pp. 327-383, 1995.

[8] M. Corbetta and G. Shulman, "Control of goal-directed and stimulus-driven attention in the brain," *Nature Reviews Neuroscience*, vol. 3, pp. 215-229, 2002.

[9] R. A. Young and L. S. Angell, "The dimensions of driver performance during secondary tasks," in *Driving Assessment 2003: Proceedings of the Second International Symposium on Human Factors in Driver Assessment, Training, and Vehicle Design*, 2001, http://ppc.uiowa.edu/driving-assessment/2003/Summaries/Downloads/Final_Papers/PDF/25_Youngformat.pdf.

[10] R. A. Rensink, J. K. O'Regan and J. J. Clark, "To see or not to see: the need for attention to perceive changes in scenes," *Psychological Science*, vol. 8, no. 5, pp. 368-373, 1997.

[11] J. DiVita, R. Obermayer, W. Nugent and J. M. Linville, "Verification of the change blindness phenomenon while managing critical events on a combat information display," *Human Factors: The Journal of the Human Factors and Ergonomics Society*, vol. 46, no. 2, pp. 205-218, 2004.

[12] D. T. Levin, N. Momen, S. B. Drivdahl and D. J. Simons, "Change blindness blindness: the metacognitive error of overestimating change-detection ability," *Visual Cognition*, vol. 7, nos. 1, 2, and 3, pp. 397–412, 2000.

[13] J. Greenberg, L. Tijerina, R. Curry, B. Artz, L. Cathey, P. Grant, D. Kochhar, K. Kozak, and M. Blommer, "Evaluation of driver distraction using an event detection paradigm," presented at TRB 82nd Annual Meeting, Washington, D.C, 2003.

[14] S. A. Huettel, G. Güzeldere and G. McCarthy, "Dissociating the neural mechanisms of visual attention in change detection using functional MRI," *Journal of Cognitive Neuroscience*, vol. 13, no. 7, pp. 1006-1018, 2001.

[15] M. Sohn, S. Ursu, J. R. Anderson, V. A. Stenger and C. S. Carter, "The role of prefrontal cortex and posterior parietal cortex in task switching," *Proceedings of the National Academy of Sciences*, vol. 97, no. 24, pp. 13448–13453, Nov. 2000.

[16] D. L. Strayer, F. A. Drews, and D. J. Crouch, "Fatal distraction? A comparison of the cell-phone driver and the drunk driver," in *Driving Assessment 2003: Proceedings of the Second International Symposium on Human Factors in Driver Assessment, Training, and Vehicle Design,* 2003, http://ppc.uiowa.edu/driving-assessment/2003/Summaries/Downloads/Final_Papers/PDF/5_Strayerformat.pdf.

[17] R. A. Young, "Association between embedded cellular phone calls and vehicle crashes involving air bag deployment," in *Driving Assessment 2001: Proceedings of the First International Symposium on Human Factors in Driver Assessment, Training, and Vehicle Design*, 2001, http://ppc.uiowa.edu/driving-assessment/2001/Summaries/Driving%20Assessment%20Papers/81_young-richard.htm.

[18] J. C. Stutts, D. W. Reinfurt, L. Staplin and E. A. Rodgman, "The role of driver distraction in traffic crashes," AAA Foundation report, May 2001, http://www.aaafoundation.org/pdf/distraction.pdf.

[19] J. C. Stutts, J. R. Feaganes, E. A. Rodgman, C. Hamlett, T. Meadows, D. W. Reinfurt, K. Gish, M. Mercadante and L. Staplin, "Distractions in everyday driving," AAA Foundation for Traffic Safety, Washington, DC, 2003, http://www.aaafoundation.org/pdf/DistractionsInEverydayDriving.pdf.

[20] For functional imaging, a complete cockpit and driver interface simulation, with real-time effects on the driving scene through steering or braking, is not necessarily required. For normal adults, the brain responses for any learned complex behavior can be elicited through the introduction of a critical mass of sensory cues. Also, foot or hand responses to lights, for example, exercise neural correlates of visual event detection and subsequent motor

activation, both integral parts of driving behavior. That is, the same activation patterns elicited in the simple task are components of similar tasks in more complex assignments

[21] C. J. D. Patten, A. Kircher, J. Östlund and L. Nilsson, "Using mobile telephones: cognitive workload and attention resource allocation," *Accident Analysis and Prevention*, vol. 36, no. 3, pp. 341-350, 2004.

[22] Strictly speaking, fMRI does not localize neuronal activation by measuring magnetic fields arising from blood flow, but rather through a complicated chain of mechanisms: fMRI signals reflect changes in signal dephasing due to changes in blood susceptibility that are secondary to changes in blood flow and oxygen extraction during neuronal activation.

[23] H. Walter, S. C. Vetter, J. Grothe, A. P. Wunderlich, S. Hahn and M. Spitzer, "The neural correlates of driving," *NeuroReport*, vol. 12, pp. 1763-1767, 2001.

[24] V. Calhoun, J. Pekar, B. McGinty, T. Adali, T. Watson and G. Pearlson, "Different activation dynamics in multiple neural systems during simulated driving," *Human Brain Mapping*, vol. 16, no. 3, pp. 158-167, 2002.

[25] Y. Uchiyama, K. Ebe, A. Kozato, T. Okada, N. Sadato, "The neural substrates of driving at a safe distance: a functional MRI study," *Neuroscience Letters*, vol. 352, no. 3, pp. 199-202, 2003.

[26] F. X. Graydon, R. A. Young, D. Fitzgerald, L. Hsieh, S. Macmillan, C. Green and S. Posse, "Neural correlates of event detection and responding during a limited form of simulated driving using fMRI," presented at *Society for Neuroscience 33rd Annual Meeting*, New Orleans, La, Nov. 2003.

[27] F. X. Graydon, R. J. Genik II, M. D. Benton, R. A. Young, L. Hsieh and C. Green, "Visual event detection during simulated driving: identifying the neural correlates with functional neuroimaging," presented at *Human Brain Mapping 2004*, Budapest, Hungary, June 2004.

[28] F. X. Graydon, R.A. Young, M. D. Benton, R. J. Genik II, S. Posse, L. Hsieh and C. Green, "Visual event detection during simulated driving: identifying the neural correlates with functional neuroimaging," *Transportation Research Part F: Psychology and Behaviour*, vol. 7,issues 4-5, July-Sept., pp. 271-286, 2004.

[29] In the on-road paradigm in Ref. 3 and the MEG paradigm reported here, the light terminated after the driver depressed the brake pedal, not after 2 seconds as in the fMRI method reported here. (The fMRI method required a fixed light offset time because of early technical limitations.) Our later on-road and fMRI paradigms are consistent with the MEG paradigm, which terminates the light with a brake pedal push or after 3.5 seconds if the driver does not respond. However, reaction time is measured from the light onset, not the light offset. Almost all non-miss response times in the fMRI experiments here were less than 2 seconds (mean across 7 subjects and 8 conditions = 502.1 msec, standard deviation 103.8 sec., $n = 56$). Also the lights are delivered via goggles in the fMRI experiments within a 30 deg. field of view, and so they are always visible no matter what the eye position. The shorter 2 second light duration could therefore not have increased the potential for a miss. Also, it is well known that eye movements away from the road in on-road studies are typically less than 2 seconds. Therefore the fMRI behavioral results and on-road behavioral results would not be expected to be affected by this difference.

[30] This design is known as a "boxcar" analysis, because average brain responses are taken across the stimulus blocks, and compared to the brain responses during the control blocks. The boxcar analysis contrasts with an event-based analysis, in which averages are taken across events, as reported later in this paper for fMRI and MEG.

[31] D. Gembris, J. G. Taylor, S. Schor, W. Frings, D. Suter and S. Posse, "Functional MR imaging in real-time using a sliding-window correlation technique," Magnetic Resonance in Medicine, vol. 43, pp. 259-268, 2000.

[32] T. Eickermann, W. Frings, F. Hossfeld, S. Posse and G. Goebbels, "Supercomputer-enhanced functional MR tomography of the human brain utilizing the NIC-GMD gigabit net," *IEEE Concurrency*, vol. 8, no 1, 2000.

[33] K. Mathiak and S. Posse, "Evaluation of motion and realignment for functional magnetic resonance imaging in realtime," Magnetic Resonance in Medicine, vol. 45, no. 1, pp. 167-171, 2001.

[34] S. Posse, F. Binkofski, F. Schneider, D. Gembris, W. Frings, U. Habel, J. B. Salloum, K. Mathiak, S. Wiese, V. Kiselev, T. Graf, B. Elghawaghi and T. Eickermann, "A new approach to measure single-event related brain activity using real-time fMRI: Feasibility of sensory, motor and higher cognitive tasks," *Human Brain Mapping*, vol. 12, no. 1, pp. 25-41, 2001.

[35] L. Hsieh, Y. Chiang, F. X. Graydon, R. A. Young, C. C. Green, D. Fitzgerald, S. Macmillan, L. Ash and S. Posse, "Neural correlates of event detection and distraction during a driving task using event related fMRI," presented at Cognitive Neuroscience Society 11th Annual Meeting, San Francisco, Calif., April 2004, http://www.taramillerevents.com/cns/.

[36] Temporal differences are less than 10 milliseconds from run to run during language processing. Strength of neuronal activation tended to be weaker in a second run, compared to the first, by about 30 percent. Between-subject variability of primary cortical responses was less than eight milliseconds in a control group of 18 subjects. Amplitudes of primary visual cortex responses

were 17 nanoAmp-meters as quantified by an Equivalent Current Dipole model of activation.
[37] H. Bolander, J. E. Moran, V. Nagesh, K. M. Mason, S. M. Bowyer, G. L. Barkley, and N. Tepley, "MEG localization errors associated with a realistic cortical model," in *Biomag 2002: Proceedings 13th International Conference on Biomagnetism*, 2002, pp. 743-745.
[38] J. E. Moran, S. M. Bowyer and N. Tepley, "Multi-Resolution FOCUSS source imaging of MEG Data," *Human Symposium Brain and Heart, NFSI, Biomedizinische Technik*, vol. 46, no. 2, pp. 112-114, 2001.
[39] J. Moran, "MR-FOCUSS. MEG_tools user manual," (unpublished) 2004, http://rambutan.phy.oakland.edu/~meg/meg_tools_user_manual.ZIP.
[40] S. M. Bowyer, J. E. Moran, K. M. Mason, J. E. Constantinou, B. J. Smith, G. L. Barkley and N. Tepley, "MEG localization of language specific cortex utilizing MR-FOCUSS," *Neurology*, vol. 62a, pp. 2247-2255, 2004.
[41] S. M. Bowyer, L. Hsieh, J. E. Moran, Y. R. Chiang, R. A. Young and N. Tepley, "Neural correlates of event-related distractions during a driving task," in *Biomag 2004: Proceedings of the 14th International Conference on Biomagnetism*, 2004, pp. 215-216.
[42] R. A. Young, R. M. Lesperance and W. W. Meyer, "The Gaussian Derivative model for spatial-temporal vision: I. Cortical model," *Spatial Vision*, vol. 14, nos. 3 and 4, pp. 261-319, 2001, http://hometown.aol.com/ryoungup2/GD1_final.pdf.
[43] R. A. Young and R. M. Lesperance, "The Gaussian Derivative model for spatial-temporal vision: II. Cortical data," *Spatial Vision*, vol. 14, nos. 3 and 4, pp. 321-389, 2001, http://hometown.aol.com/ryoungup3/GD2_final.pdf.
[44] It was not the intention here to report on-road validation results for these stimuli. There are some slight differences between the static methods here and those of Reference [3]: participants lie down rather than sit up, and cannot move their heads. Also, the current study reports only "primary" driving tasks – watching a road scene, and responding to events. It is thus similar only to the "baseline" driving conditions in Reference [3].The current study is intended to lay the foundation for brain imaging experiments that study the effect of secondary tasks on the brain responses for primary driving-like behaviors.
[45] M. A. Just, R. A. Carpenter, T. A. Keller, L. Emery, H. Zajac and K. R. Thulborn, "Interdependence of nonoverlapping cortical systems in dual cognitive tasks," *NeuroImage*, vol. 14, no. 2, pp. 417-426, Aug. 2001.
[46] D. L. Strayer and W. A. Johnston, "Driven to distraction: dual-task studies of simulated driving and conversing on a cellular phone," *Psychological Science*, vol. 12, pp. 462-466, 2001.
[47] D. L. Strayer, F. A. Drews, R. W. Albert, and W. A. Johnston, "Cell phone induced perceptual impairments during simulated driving," in *Driving Assessment 2001: Proceedings of the First International Symposium on Human Factors in Driver Assessment, Training, and Vehicle Design*, 2001,http://ppc.uiowa.edu/drivingassessment/2001/Summaries/Driving%20Assessment%20Papers/03_Strayer_David.htm.
[48] D. L. Strayer, J. M. Cooper and F. A. Drews, "What do drivers fail to see when conversing on a cell phone?" Human Factors and Ergonomics Society, New Orleans, La., September 2004.
[49] Ref. [48] placed 30 simulated objects along a simulated roadway, with 15 objects visible during a simulating driving condition, and 15 visible during simulated driving plus conversing on a hands-free cell phone condition. In a post-test, the 30 objects were paired against other simulated objects not previously presented, and 64 subjects had to indicate which object in each pair was the one seen while driving. After "correcting for guessing" using an unspecified method, ref. [48] reports in the first case that the mean corrected probability of recognizing the object as having been on the roadway was 0.21 for simulated driving alone, and 0.16 for simulated driving plus conversation. Ref. [48] in the second case considered only those objects fixated for at least 100 milliseconds by 32 subjects in which eye movements had been measured. It found that only 61 percent of the 30 objects met this criterion. The probabilities after correcting for guessing were reported as 0.25 and 0.15 for the single and dual task conditions in this second case of fixated objects only.
[50] Ref. [48] did not report the numbers of simulated objects correctly recognized in the single or dual task simulated driving condition for either case in [49]. But the difference in the number of simulated objects recognized in the two conditions can be estimated from the numbers in [49], even without knowing the method used for correcting for guessing. In the first case in [49], the difference in probabilities 0.21 and 0.16 for the two conditions is 0.05. Because there were 15 objects in each condition, it can be estimated that about 0.75 fewer objects (0.05 times 15) were recognized in the dual task than single task condition in this first case. In the second case in [49], only 61 percent of the total objects met the fixation criterion. Of the 15 objects in each simulated driving condition, it can be estimated that only about 9.1 objects (0.61 times 15) met the fixation criterion. In this second case, the difference in probabilities 0.25 and 0.15 for the two conditions is 0.10. Therefore of the 9.1 objects analyzed in each condition, it can be estimated that about 0.91 fewer objects (0.10 times 9.1) were recognized in the dual task condition than in the single task condition. In sum, the effect of conversation on the recognition of simulated objects on the side of the road after a simulated

seven mile drive [48] may be estimated from the calculations [49] to be about one simulated object.

[51] C. Schreiner, M. Blanco and J. M. Hankey, "Investigation of driving behavior changes associated with manual and voice-activated phone-dialing in a real-world environment," in *Proceedings of the ITS America 14th Annual Meeting and Exposition*, April 2004.

[52] V. B. McGinty, R. A. Shih, E. S. Garrett, V. D. Calhoun and G. D. Pearlson, "Assessment of intoxicated driving with a simulator: A validation study with on-road driving," in *Proceedings Human Centered Transportation Simulation Conference*, Iowa City, IA, Nov. 2001.

[53] V. D. Calhoun, J. J. Pekar and G. D. Pearlson, "Alcohol intoxication effects on simulated driving: exploring alcohol-dose effects on brain activation using functional MRI," *Neuropsychopharmacology*, pp. 1-11, 2004.

[54] V. D. Calhoun, D. Altschul, V. McGinty, R. Shih, D. Scott, E. Sears and G. D. Pearlson, "Alcohol intoxication effects on visual perception: an fMRI study," *Human Brain Mapping*, vol. 21, no. 1, pp. 15-26, Jan. 2004. Erratum in: Human Brain Mapping, vol. 21, no. 4, pp. 298-299, April 2004.

[55] D. A. Attwood, R. D. Williams and H. D. Madill, "Effects of moderate blood alcohol concentrations on closed-course driving performance," *Journal of Studies on Alcohol*, vol. 41, pp. 623-634, 1980.

[56] D. K. Damkot, "Alcohol influences: A comparison of on-road driving behavior with instrumented car and laboratory research," *Ergonomics*, vol. 19, p. 380, 1976.

[57] A. Crancer Jr., J. M. Dille, J. C. Delay, J. E. Wallace, and M. D. Haykin, "Comparison of the effects of marijuana and alcohol on simulated driving performance," *Science*, vol. 164, pp. 851-854, 1969.

[58] R. W. Hansteen, R. D. Miller, L. Lonero, L. D. Reid and B. Jones, "Effects of cannabis and alcohol on automobile driving and psychomotor tracking," *Annals of the New York Academy of Sciences*, vol. 282, pp. 240-256, 1976.

[59] M. Linnoila, "Effect of drugs and alcohol on psychomotor skills related to driving," *Annals of Clinical Research*, vol. 6, pp. 7-18, 1974.

[60] O. J. Rafaelsen, P. Bech, J. Christiansen, H. Christrup, J. Nyboe and L. Rafaelsen, "Cannabis and alcohol: effects on simulated car driving," *Science,* vol. 179, pp. 920-923, 1973.

[61] National Highway Traffic Safety Administration (2003). www-nrd.nhtsa.dot.gov/pdf/nrd-30/NCSA/PPT/2003AA.Release/pdf.

[62] R. N. Anderson and B. L. Smith, "Deaths: leading causes for 2001," *National Vital Statistics Reports*, vol. 52, no. 9, 2003, http://www.cdc.gov/nchs/data/nvsr/nvsr52/nvsr52_09.pdf.

[63] M. Sundeen, "Along for the ride: reducing driver distractions," Final report of the driver focus and technology forum, Denver, Colo.: National Conference of State Legislatures, 2002, http://www.ncsl.org/programs/transportation/drivdistract.htm.

[64] L. R. Shelton, "Statement before the Subcommittee on Highways and Transit, Committee on Transportation and Infrastructure, U.S. House of Representatives," May 9, 2001, http://www.nhtsa.dot.gov/nhtsa/announce/testimony/distractiontestimony.html.

[65] J. Runge, "Minutes of the 102nd Meeting of the National Advisor Council on Alcohol Abuse and Alcoholism," February 2003, http://www.niaaa.nih.gov/about/min2-03.htm.

[66] V. L. Neale, S. G. Klauer, R. R. Knipling, T. A. Dingus, G. T. Holbrook and A. Petersen, "The 100-car naturalistic driving study: Phase I – experimental design," DOT HS 808 536, December 2002, http://www-nrd.nhtsa.dot.gov/pdf/nrd-12/100CarPhase1Report.pdf.

[67] NCSDR/NHTSA Expert Panel on Driver Fatigue and Sleepiness, "Drowsy driving and automobile crashes," National Heart, Lung, and Blood Institute, 1998, http://www.nhlbi.nih.gov/health/prof/sleep/drsy_drv.pdf.

[68] V. D. Calhoun, V. McGinty, J. J. Pekar, T. Watson and G. D. Pearlson, "Investigation of Marinol (THC) effects upon fMRI activation during active and passive driving using independent component analysis and SPM," *NeuroImage*, vol. 13, S388, 2001.

[69] J. A. Groeger, *Understanding Driving: Applying Cognitive Psychology to a Complex Everyday Task* Hove, U.K.: Psychology Press, 2000.

CONTACT

E-mail: richard.a.young@gm.com

DEFINITIONS, ACRONYMS, ABBREVIATIONS

CAMP: Crash-Avoidance Metrics Partnership

fMRI: functional Magnetic Resonance Imaging

LCD: Liquid-Crystal Display

LED: Light-Emitting Diode

MRI: Magnetic Resonance Imaging

MEG: Magnetoencephalography

NIH: National Institutes of Health

NHTSA: National Highway Traffic Safety Administration

2004-01-0282

Visual User Interfaces for Telematics

Randy Carroll, Brett Hackleman, Philippe Krief and Paul VanderLei
International Business Machines Corporation, Inc.

ABSTRACT

The term "telematics" is now used to cover a large spectrum of in-vehicle functionality. This functionality has a correspondingly large spectrum of human-machine interface (HMI) needs. These HMI needs range from "headless" functions that require no user interaction at all, to complex functions with rich graphical or voice recognition interfaces. This paper describes the visual elements of a modern telematics system and design problems and the trade-offs that must be made in an automotive environment.

INTRODUCTION

The telematics human-machine interface (HMI) spectrum of needs can range from no direct interaction at all, like remote engine diagnostic data access, to a simple LCD touch screen pushbutton interface appropriate for quickly accessing functions and data, to a rich graphical interface such as advanced navigation applications. This spectrum is made multi-dimensional by other HMI techniques and augmentations, such as hard buttons and lights, haptic devices, text-to-speech and voice recognition.

In this paper, we will focus our attention on the requirements of the visual elements of a modern telematics system and the design problems and trade-offs that must be made in an automotive environment. To start, we will examine the typical display and input needs of a spectrum of representative telematics functions. We will then expand on this by extracting the HMI requirements imposed by the domain and the particular set of functionality. Next we will map this information to the leading graphics systems, comparing the capabilities of each graphics system to the requirements and the subsequent impact to the total system in terms of functionality, device resource utilization, deployment characteristics, life-cycle maintenance, necessary developer skills, and overall visual impact and style.

Finally, we will discuss how these needs are met by using a straightforward graphics system such as the P3ML framework that is part of the IBM® WebSphere® Device Developer product.

TELEMATICS HMI BACKGROUND

USAGE SEGMENTATION

We will use Telematics in a generic sense for the functionality gained by having a multi-purpose computer in the vehicle. In its broadest sense, telematics simply means any of a wide range of vehicle-related functions that can be of service to the complete spectrum of interested parties. One way of viewing this set of functions is to categorize them into three groups.

Occupant Functions

This is the most frequently discussed area of telematics, and is the favorite of the popular press. This category ranges from critical functions such as safety and security to some of pure enjoyment such as infotainment. It would also include other functions like navigation capabilities and hands-free phone usage.

Owner Functions

This is a nascent area for the private car owner, but is already vitally important to commercial vehicle owners. This set of functions would assist the owner in a wide spectrum of needs, including tracking the vehicle to enable optimum usage, gathering vehicle operating data to assist in maintaining the vehicle, and gathering vehicle information to help ensure safe and optimal operation of the vehicle.

Vehicle Functions

This is an area of telematics that is beginning to receive a lot of attention from vehicle manufacturers because it can show an immediate business payback in terms of customer satisfaction and lower costs. This category includes straightforward usages such as maintenance tracking of the vehicle, vehicle diagnostics for prediction and resolution of problems, collecting vehicle data for analysis, and accumulating and analyzing data on trends from numerous similar vehicles. This can be useful in fleet maintenance, but it is becoming recognized as an especially powerful way to lower future manufacturing and subsequent warranty costs.

Communications

All of these functions are typically enhanced through the use of wireless technology to connect the vehicle to back-end servers for content, increased processing power, and services.

Summary

As we have shown, the HMI needs vary widely, depending on the particular function and the specific implementation. The total HMI functional requirements of the system are naturally driven, therefore, by the set of particular functions chosen for the device. For our purposes, we will assume what is considered to be the current functional norm that largely consists of three elements. The first element has as a base OnStar® functionality[1], the second an assortment of diagnostic and prognostic functions, and the third element is a range of higher level functions such as navigation, vehicle compartment controls, multimedia controls, communications, and various driver information and notification.

TELEMATICS FUNCTIONAL HMI NEEDS

GRAPHICS SUPPORT

As you can see from the functions provided by the telematics device, the required graphics support is not very complex. The primary support needed is:

- Capability to render artwork in some standard bitmap format
- Capability to render text in an assortment of languages
- Capability to do very simple draw-a-line type functions

There is probably only one window (or logical function) being viewed at a time. Unlike a desktop computer, the screen is usually not large enough to accommodate multiple windows, so there is little need for the concept of stacking windows.

A telematics unit usually does not have a mouse or even a substitute-pointing device. It also does not have a traditional keyboard. This means that many of the standard desktop widgets like drop down combo boxes and text entry fields make no sense for telematics. Instead, the widgets must be simple and intuitive, like the hardware controls elsewhere in the vehicle.

LOCATION

As the in-vehicle computer is used by the vehicle occupants for a wide variety of purposes, it is typically given a mid-dashboard location. This is considered the most precious space in the vehicle cockpit and is allocated very conservatively. Since it usually takes the location traditionally allocated for the vehicle's music system, it will likely be required to include that additional function.

SIZE

Quite often it is only single or double DIN, that is, seven inches wide by two or four inches high. Since the total in-vehicle computer HMI is limited to a single or double DIN space, the display is consequently smaller yet. This is much smaller than a typical laptop display which can be twelve inches wide or larger.

TOUCH INPUT

Touch input is a very popular and convenient way to interact with a user. It can be a very nice way to allow the user to interact directly with icons or other artwork on the display, encouraging the illusion that the user is interacting with an actual physical button or switch. It can also be a very flexible way to have "soft buttons" or buttons that appear only when required and are labeled as needed by the current controlling application.

Touch technology also has some limitations that can be challenging. Since touch input is inherently limited to a touch pad hot spot that is a reasonable size for a human finger, there is, therefore, a limited number of hotspots possible on the display. This limits the size of the underlying corresponding graphic, and in the end is another boundary for how much information can be displayed at one time.

INFORMATION DENSITY/CLARITY

Despite its diminutive size, the display must be large enough to convey the desired information quickly to lessen the impact on driver attention. This has many design implications as to the amount of information displayed, the size of the font, and the design of any touch input on the display.

RESOLUTION

A typical display size is one-quarter VGA or 320 pixels wide by 240 pixels high. This is a small physical bound for all information and touch-sensitive input.

BUTTON INPUT

We have discussed soft buttons, but obviously the application must also interact with the physical buttons and switches of the overall HMI. These are typically located on the dashboard, center console, and steering wheel.

[1] This includes things such as personal calling, virtual advisor, airbag deployment notification, emergency services, MED-NET, roadside assistance, concierge services, stolen vehicle tracking, AccidentAssist, remote door unlock, route support, RideAssist, information/convenience services.

COLOR DEPTH

The decision on color depth can be important for several reasons. First and foremost, the typical functions we have described do not have a requirement for high color depth. With increased color depth comes memory consumption, not only on the display memory of course, but this is also true for every piece of artwork and interaction with the display. Finally, greater color depth can have a dramatic effect on subsequent hardware cost and performance. Designers should take care to fully evaluate whether anything more than eight-bit color is truly necessary before deciding on more color depth.

TELEMATICS HIGH LEVEL HMI NEEDS

BRANDING

Unlike most electronics sold today, vehicles are very high-value assets with an extended life. During that long life the vehicle owner will always attribute a significant part of the joy of the vehicle's driving experience to the brand of the vehicle. This is especially important to the higher end, higher cost vehicles. It is crucial for the OEMs to control every aspect of the vehicle experience such that it is not only high quality, but is attributable to their brand in unique ways. The HMI needs to reinforce the brand wherever possible so that it is instantly recognizable as that brand.

Branding influences not only background graphics, but also the angle of orientation of visual elements, non-rectangular element shapes, the shading and special element animation. Manufacturers also want tight control over the precise layout of the interface. Unlike a web browser that dynamically lays out the content to best fit the window, the layout of a branded telematics interface should be specific and intentional.

USER EXPERIENCE

A telematics system should have a graphical interface like that of other vehicle systems, not a desktop computer. It needs to look and feel more like the hardware controls normally associated with vehicle interiors.

This has several implications. As discussed above, there is likely only one window (or logical function) presented on the display at a time. Each screen should therefore have a straightforward and focused purpose, and should even encourage the illusion that the currently displayed screen is a dedicated, hard physical display and not merely a rectangle of multi-color dots. This illusion is also encouraged by the design of the artwork employed. It should not be a simple rectangular box like a normal workstation HMI, but rather should be a carefully crafted artistic interface that reinforces the look of that brand and employs all manner of graphic art techniques such as 3D and shading to encourage the user's acceptance that this display is a piece of hardware.

CROSS-PLATFORM

A telematics user interface is required to minimize dependency on specific hardware. This can promote portability of applications across a family of different telematics products and vehicle platforms.

It also has implications at product development time. Optimally, the HMI should be developed on the designer's workstation of choice and deployed later on any number of target platforms. Not only does this reduce development time and cost, but it also allows the same user interface to be adapted and customized across different products.

PLATFORM-SPECIFIC

However, the converse of this design point should also be true. Unlike web content presented on an indeterminate desktop computer, telematics HMI screens should be optimized for the specific characteristics of the telematics display. The screens should match the color depth and pixel proportions. The locations of the various screen elements should be specified explicitly, not determined at run time. This again enhances the perception of the display being a hardware device.

SEPARATION OF CONCERNS

A telematics user interface requires not only skilled programming, but also skilled graphics design. Clean separation between function (screen and logic) from the graphics design allows parallel development and allows programmers and graphics designers to focus on the areas that match their skills. It also means that the graphics can change without affecting the logic implementation and vice versa.

FLEXIBILITY

Telematics systems can span a broad range of input and output hardware, so the user interface development tools should be flexible enough to accommodate a wide variety of input and output devices.

It is also important that a telematics user interface be field upgradeable. This allows vendors to introduce new functionality on a system, to re-skin the user interface, and to fix bugs in the field.

DYNAMIC CONTENT

Content presented to the user on a telematics system is often dynamic. That is, the content is downloaded from a specific service gateway to the system. This can include functions such as reading email, checking news, weather and traffic information and purchasing new system functionality.

Using HTML for the dynamic content format limits the ability of the designer to specify the precise layout of the content because HTML does not support that capability. Also, it requires that certain activities be performed with a web browser HMI. As an alternative, it should be possible to download dynamic content that, when presented, looks the same as the static portions of the vehicle's user interface, providing a seamless user experience despite the dynamic nature of the content. Ideally, viewing local weather forecasts would not require an on-board weather application, but would also be more precisely laid out and more branded and stylized than a web browser displaying weather in HTML.

MEMORY CONSTRAINTS

A typical telematics system has a limited amount of memory. It makes sense to minimize the memory consumed by the user interface graphics and the supporting classes.

SURVEY OF CURRENT GRAPHICS SYSTEMS

HISTORICAL

Although there are a number of graphics systems available on the market today, very few are suitable for automotive use due to their cost, hardware requirements, or other limitations. Graphics systems tend to be either based on open standards or proprietary.

We will focus on those graphics systems that are capable of running on a wide range of computing operating systems. This allows the Tier 1 or OEM supplier to choose which operating system best fits its needs or to delay the choice of operating system until late in the development cycle.

AWT/SWING

The Abstract Widget Toolkit (AWT) graphics system was developed for building applications for a traditional desktop computing system. AWT windows are rectangular, and feature a toolbar with the window title and buttons for resizing or closing the window. AWT employs native widgets (such as text fields, drop-down lists, etc), so they will look different depending on which windowing environment they are running on (Windows®, Mac OS®, X). Typically user input is accomplished using a mouse and keyboard.

The AWT framework was developed first and foremost for the desktop environment, and this is reflected in the memory requirements. Often the base AWT libraries use more memory than most telematics devices have for the entire software stack – OS, Java™ Virtual Machine (JVM), graphics system and all applications!

The Swing graphical framework sits on top of the AWT and provides lightweight widgets that do not change based on the windowing environment – they will always look the same. However, this functionality raises the memory requirements even further beyond that required by the AWT, making it unrealistic for embedded applications.

QT®

QT (and QT/e, the embedded flavor of QT) is a native graphics system that runs on a wide range of target operating systems including Linux, Mac OS, and Windows). It is written in C++, but can be accessed from Java using a thin Java Native Interface (JNI) wrapper. It is similar to AWT in that it uses native widgets, and is primarily used to create applications for traditional computing systems with a windowing environment. The default user input devices are the mouse and keyboard. QT/e applications are cross-platform, but require a recompile of the source code.

QT/e was designed for embedded use, so it has a small memory footprint. It is well suited for embedded devices requiring a windowing environment, such as those for automation or Internet appliances. However, QT/e misses the mark for automotive use because of its similarity to traditional computer applications – rectangular size, window bars, etc.

J2ME - MIDP

The Mobile Information Device Profile (MIDP) was designed for use on devices such as cell phones and entry level PDAs. It assumes the device will have a dot matrix LCD panel capable of displaying monochrome or color text and images. The display resolution is typically very small, from 80-by-100 pixels to 94-by-240 pixels. User input is usually limited to the phone keypad and soft keys (i.e.: hard pushbuttons aligned with text labels on the LCD screen).

MIDP is well suited for cell phones and PDAs with a very limited user interface. The APIs were developed through the Java Community Process (JCP), and reflect the domain requirements and experience associated with cell phone applications. Unfortunately this means the API set is very cell phone-oriented, and lacks some of the functionality needed for telematics applications. For example, MIDP does not support the Java Native Interface, which is often used to interface device drivers or a speech recognition system. The MIDP graphics system was designed to fit the "lowest common denominator" cell phone, which makes it too limiting for most telematics displays.

AWT, Swing, QT/e, and MIDP are well suited for a number of domains; however, closer examination reveals that none of these is adequate for fulfilling the requirements of a modern telematics system. This was the conclusion of several joint projects between IBM and various Tier 1 and OEM suppliers in the past, and it drove the development of a new graphics system called P3ML.

P3ML

P3ML is an acronym for "Portable, Positional, Painting Markup Language." This describes the three basic premises of P3ML.

PORTABLE

P3ML is 100% Java, which means it will run on any computing platform with a Java Virtual Machine (JVM). It is capable of running on a wide range of lower-level graphics layers. An application written in P3ML will move seamlessly across a wide range of platforms, without any code changes or even a recompile.

POSITIONAL

P3ML is a markup language. The source code is an XML 1.0-compliant file that describes the layout of the HMI. The format of this file is very similar to HTML in that all elements are described with tags, and each tag has a set of associated attributes that can be used to configure the element. However, unlike HTML, P3ML tags also have attributes to describe their exact position on the screen. Whereas an HTML browser is responsible for positioning all elements described in the source file, a P3ML browser relies on the position information contained in the P3ML source file.

PAINTED

This is another term for bitmap-based, which means that a P3ML HMI is constructed from a set of bitmaps. A close comparison in HTML is an image map with a JavaScript controller, however this comparison breaks down quickly. In P3ML, each bitmap element can be linked with a P3ML tag, which gives that element its behavior. We will discuss this more in a later section.

WHY P3ML?

So, what are the attributes of P3ML which are more suitable for the automotive domain than the other graphics systems available today?

P3ML was developed from the ground up for embedded systems, driven largely from the requirements gathered from several telematics projects between IBM and various automotive suppliers and researchers. It has a small memory footprint, and runs on a wide range of telematics hardware platforms.

BRANDING & USER EXPERIENCE

Being bitmap-based, every visible element can be customized by graphics design artists to match the vehicle branding and interior color scheme. 3-D shading can be used to create a very stylized user interface that fits with the hardware in the vehicle. P3ML elements look and feel the same on every platform, regardless of the hardware, operating system, or windowing environment they run on. The entire user experience can be designed to be intuitive, not intimidating like a traditional computer.

USER INPUT

The primary input device for P3ML is typically a touch screen. However, it also has built-in support for soft and hard buttons as well as mouse, keyboard input, voice recognition system, and speech synthesis.

DISPLAY SIZE AND COLOR DEPTH

P3ML supports a wide range of output displays, ranging from 100-by-100 pixels to full VGA. It also supports up to 32-bit color.

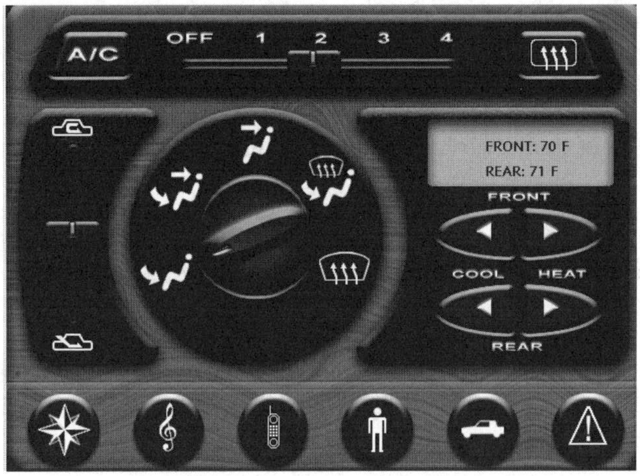

SEPARATION OF CONCERNS

Using XML to describe the HMI layout and tags provides a significant advantage during application development. The XML file is very similar to HTML, which means a graphic designer does not need to know how to program to build a very sophisticated HMI. With AWT, Swing or QT/e, the graphics designer must know how to program Java or C++ before he/she can build or view the HMI. Not so with P3ML – just write the XML file using a simple text editor (or XML editor) and then open it in the P3ML viewer. By cleanly separating the graphics design from the system logic, the graphics designers and software engineers can work in parallel.

FLEXIBILITY

Another advantage of using XML as the P3ML "source code" is that the resulting applications are very flexible. New sub-applications can be easily inserted into the framework during development or after deployment. Applications can have different "skins", without changing a line of embedded source code.

CROSS-PLATFORM

The P3ML framework is a pure Java implementation, so it is extremely portable across a wide range of hardware, operating systems, and low-level graphics drivers. All software can be designed, written and tested on a development workstation before running it on the actual hardware device, and the look and feel remains true to the designer's intent.

Such a system also allows the OEM to scale the telematics functions across a wide range of automotive platforms and vehicle types (economy to luxury). P3ML applications can move easily between them, reducing development costs, support costs, etc.

DYNAMIC CONTENT

Unlike a widget-based system like AWT, P3ML screens need not be created by Java source code. That is, a P3ML screen is described by a P3ML document and displayed on a P3ML viewer. In this way, P3ML is more like a web browser, only displaying P3ML content instead of HTML content, but it is not constrained by the inherent web browser interface.

One of the advantages to this is that a P3ML application does not need to switch to a browser mode to present dynamic content that is downloaded from some external server. This means that even screens downloaded from external servers can seamlessly integrate with the static on-board parts of the application.

A good example of this is location-based services, whereby the telematics unit informs the vehicle occupants of available retail services nearby. Without P3ML, an application typically has two choices for how to present location-based services. One would be using a dedicated application that obtains only the raw data describing the nearby services from an off-board server and presents it using the pre-defined widgets available to it, typically labels and lists. The second option would be to use a web browser to dynamically lay out HTML content from the off-board server.

P3ML provides a third option in which the off-board server serves content as P3ML instead of HTML. Because P3ML content is richer and more specific than HTML, the location-based services can be presented using branded graphics and widgets that fit seamlessly with the on-board portions of the application.

P3ML ELEMENTS

<area>	An <area> element defines a rectangular area. All elements defined in the area are positioned relative to the top left corner of this area. Commonly used to help group other elements.
<button>	A <button> is a rectangular area that can be defined by two main states (i.e., "ON" and "OFF") and one optional intermediate state (i.e., when the button is pressed). A bitmap and/or a colored label can describe each of these three states.
<canvas>	A <canvas> element defines a rectangular area where the display, mouse, and key events are, respectively, delegated to a DisplayListener, MouseListener, and KeyListener respectively. The <canvas> element opens the door to directly access the graphic APIs offered by the underlying graphics layer.
<deckOfCards>	A <deckOfCards> element defines a rectangular area containing several cards but displaying only one card at a time. This tag is generally used to load the same P3ML page with several sub-pages at one time (e.g., as opposed to using the <frame> element).
<frame>	A <frame> element defines a rectangular area whose contents are described in a separate P3ML file. One of the most efficient uses of the <frame> element is to separate the main document listener from the sub-listeners.
<img>	An <img> element defines a passive area described by a bitmap. Unlike a <button> element, an <img> element does not support any state and does not fire any events. Generally, this element is used to provide bitmap decoration around the active elements.
<label>	A <label> element defines a passive area described by a label. Unlike a <button> element, a <label> element does not support any state.
<list>	A <list> element defines a rectangular area that vertically or horizontally visualizes a list of contained <li> elements.
<sensitive>	A <sensitive> element defines a sensitive rectangular area. This area is invisible; it does not draw anything. However, it allows you to specify a hyperlink event that is sent to the

	document listener if a user clicks it.
<slidingArea>	A <slidingArea> element defines a rectangular area where the unique contained element (the cursor) can slide in one or two dimensions. As a result of this motion, the listening application receives a hyperlink event describing the new position in terms of percentage or pixels.
<switch>	A <switch> element defines an area where the content changes dynamically depending on where the user clicks. This element is often used to describe a rocker button.
<textField>	A <textField> element defines a text field to type in. Text can be entered via a physical keyboard or a software keyboard displayed on the screen.

The supported tags provide most of the functionality needed for very complex applications, however, it is possible to add or modify tags if a new application requires it.

The portable graphics layer also provides a mechanism for plug-ins – such as scalable vector graphics, streaming video, HTML browsing, navigation engines, etc. - to co-exist with screens rendered in P3ML.

P3ML EXAMPLE

The best way to learn P3ML is to build a simple application and experiment with the various tags available. To demonstrate the development process, we will present a sample application for climate control.

CLIMATE CONTROL SCREEN

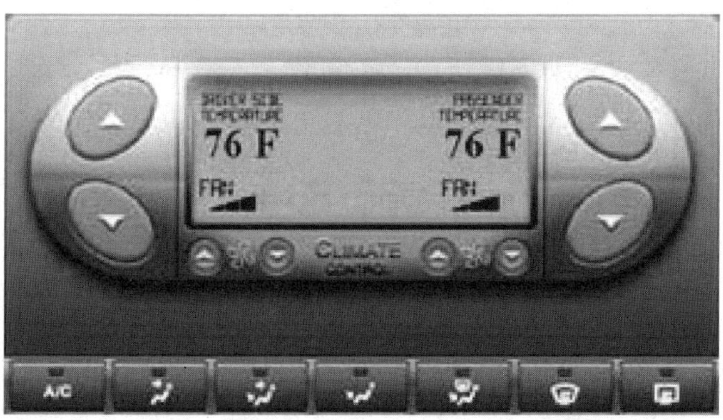

The climate control screen consists of two parts; the main application window and a button bar. The button bar is designed for alignment with a row of soft keys, and the contents of this bar usually change based on the state of the active screen. The main application window contains a number of P3ML elements: images, buttons, labels, and a switch (used to change the fan level images).

The first step to building such an HMI involves both the graphics designer and the programmer. Together they discuss the general behavior of the user interface, mapping the functionality to the application requirements.

After agreeing on the general contents of the screen, the graphics designer can begin working on the layout, graphics, shading, etc. This work can be done using whatever graphics tool the designer prefers. Once the bitmaps are ready, the graphics designer then creates the P3ML using any XML or text editor. This is a simple process:

First, we must define this as a P3ML file and set the background image:

```
<?xml version="1.0"?>
<p3ml>
<body id="Climate"
       width="640"
       height="350"
       background="art/background.gif">
```

Next we define the temperature and fan level button elements:

```
<!-- Temperature buttons -->
<!--(Driver side/ Passenger side) -->

<button
       onsrc="art/leftTempInc down.gif"
       offsrc="art/leftTempInc.gif"
       mask="art/leftTempInc mask.gif"
       href="driverSideTempIncrement"
       x="53"
       y="51"/>

<button
       onsrc="art/leftTempDec down.gif"
       offsrc="art/leftTempDec.gif"
       mask="art/leftTempDec mask.gif"
       href="driverSideTempDecrement"
       x="53"
       y="134"/>

<button
       onsrc="art/rightTempInc down.gif"
       offsrc="art/rightTempInc.gif"
       mask="art/rightTempInc mask.gif"
       href="passengerSideTempIncrement"
       x="500"
       y="51"/>

<button
       onsrc="art/rightTempDec down.gif"
       offsrc="art/rightTempDec.gif"
       mask="art/rightTempDec mask.gif"
       href="passengerSideTempDecrement"
       x="500"
       y="134"/>

<!-- Fan buttons -->
<button
```

```
        onsrc="art/leftFanInc down.gif"
        offsrc="art/leftFanInc.gif"
        href="driverSideFanIncrement"
        x="162"
        y="194"/>

<button
        onsrc="art/leftFanDec down.gif"
        offsrc="art/leftFanDec.gif"
        href="driverSideFanDecrement"
        x="227"
        y="194"/>

<button
        onsrc="art/rightFanInc down.gif"
        offsrc="art/rightFanInc.gif"
        href="passengerSideFanIncrement"
        x="373"
        y="194"/>

<button
        onsrc="art/rightFanDec down.gif"
        offsrc="art/rightFanDec.gif"
        href="passengerSideFanDecrement"
        x="438"
        y="194"/>
```

We use simple label elements to display the temperature values. The “id” attribute values will be used later, when we want to modify the label text at run time.

```
<label
        id="DriverSideTemperature"
        text="76 F"
        fontname="H1"
        x="177"
        y="91"/>

<label
        id="PassengerSideTemperature"
        text="76 F"
        fontname="H1"
        labelhalign="right"
        x="340"
        y="91"/>
```

To display the fan level, we use the <switch> tag. This allows us to specify an image for each of the possible states. This makes it very easy to control from Java, as we'll see later.

```
<!-- left fan level display -->
<switch
        id="DriverSideFan"
        x="173"
        y="141"
        width="64"
        height="44"
        background="art/fanLevel0.gif"
        state="3">

        <img src="art/fanLevel0.gif"
              id="0"/>
        <img src="art/fanLevel1.gif"
              id="1"/>
        <img src="art/fanLevel2.gif"
              id="2"/>
        <img src="art/fanLevel3.gif"
              id="3"/>
        <img src="art/fanLevel4.gif"
              id="4"/>
</switch>

<!-- right fan level display -->
<switch
        id="PassengerSideFan"
        x="392"
        y="141"
        width="64"
        height="44"
        background="art/fanLevel0.gif"
        state="3">

        <img src="art/fanLevel0.gif"
              id="0"/>
        <img src="art/fanLevel1.gif"
              id="1"/>
        <img src="art/fanLevel2.gif"
              id="2"/>
        <img src="art/fanLevel3.gif"
              id="3"/>
        <img src="art/fanLevel4.gif"
              id="4"/>
</switch>
```

Finally, we build the button bar displayed on the bottom of the screen. This is simply a row of button elements:

```
<!-- lower button bar -->
<area
        y="300"
        background="art/menu_background.gif>

        <button
              id="ac"
              onsrc="art/ac down.gif"
              offsrc="art/ac.gif"
              href="airConditioningToggle"/>

        <button
              id="Upper"
              onsrc="art/ventUpper down.gif"
              offsrc="art/ventUpper.gif"
              href="ventSetUpper"
              x="93"/>

        <button
              id="Upper-Lower"

        onsrc="art/ventUpperLower down.gif"
        offsrc="art/ventUpperLower.gif"
        href="ventSetUpperLower}"
        x="184"/>

        <button
              id="Lower"
              onsrc="art/ventLower down.gif"
              offsrc="art/ventLower.gif"
              href="ventSetLower"
              x="275"/>

        <button
              id="Lower-Windshield"
              onsrc="art/WLower down.gif"
              offsrc="art/WLower.gif"
              href="ventSetLowerWindshield"
              x="366"/>

        <button
```

```
            id="Windshield"
            onsrc="art/ventW down.gif"
            offsrc="art/menu/ventW.gif"
            href="ventSetWindshield"
            x="457"/>

      <button
            id="defrost"
            onsrc="art/ventDef down.gif"
            offsrc="art/ventDef.gif"
            href="Defrost"
            x="548"/>
</area>

</body>
</p3ml>
```

That's it! After the graphics designer has created the bitmaps and P3ML file, the file can be rendered to ensure the layout is correct. The easiest way to do this is from within IBM's WebSphere Device Developer (WSDD) IDE. WSDD has full support for P3ML, and includes syntax highlighting, incremental compiling, and an integrated P3ML viewer. All without writing a line of Java code!

RENDERING THE SCREEN FROM JAVA

The first step in building a standalone P3ML application is to create a P3ML viewer. The viewer is responsible for displaying the P3ML file after it has been parsed.

```
public void launch() {
      IViewer viewer =
            new BmgP3mlViewer(640, 300);

      viewer.installHtmlFonts();
      viewer.show();

      URI uri = new URIonClass(
            ClimateSample.class,
            "p3ml/climate.p3ml");
            viewer.render(uri);
            viewer.start();
}
```

This is all the code necessary to display the P3ML file, but obviously the user interface will only be useful once we have coupled it with the underlying application logic.

LISTENING FOR EVENTS

Next we'll add the necessary code to receive events from the climate control screen. To do this, we need to modify our launch code slightly:

```
      viewer.render(uri, this);
```

This API assumes we implement the DocumentListener interface, which contains a single method:

```
public void handleEvent(HyperlinkEvent e);
```

This method will be called whenever a user event is generated. On our climate control screen, an event will be triggered when any of the buttons are pressed. To determine which button was pressed, we'll check the hyperlink event reference. This reference will correspond to the "href" attribute for the button that was pressed. Here's how we would catch one of the button events:

```
public void handleEvent(HyperlinkEvent e)
{
      if (e.getRef().equals(
            "driverSideFanIncrement"))
      {
            System.out.println("FAN UP!");
            doDriverSideFanIncrement();
      }
}
```

UPDATING P3ML ELEMENTS

Now that we're receiving events from the GUI, let's try updating the fan level when the "driver side fan up" button is pressed. To do this, we need to get a reference to the element we wish to modify, the "DriverSideFan" switch element. This is where the "id" attribute comes into play. Once we have our ISwitchElement object, we can increment the state and refresh the element.

```
public void doDriverSideFanIncrement() {
      IRenderingArea rendering =
            viewer.getRenderingArea);

      <!-- get switch element -->
      ISwitchElement fanLevel =
            (ISwitchElement)
                  rendering.getElement(
                  "DriverSideFan");

      <!-- increment the state value, it
           is stored as a string -->

      int MAX STATE NUM = 5;
      int state = Integer.parseInt(
                  fanLevel.getState());

      state = (state + 1) % MAX_STATE_NUM;

      fanLevel.setState(
            Integer.toString(state));

      fanLevel.refresh();
}
```

Now, when we press the "driver side fan up" button, the fan level displayed will increase. It is a straightforward task to enable the remaining buttons and labels using the same process.

CONCLUSION

Hopefully we have made the case that the choice of the graphics system employed for your design should be carefully considered by weighing a wide assortment of needs.

Taking a hard look at the real requirements of the anticipated application set must drive the selection. Does your navigation application really need 32-bit color, Java Swing, Java 3D and a hardware graphics accelerator or can its function be accomplished with a robust bitmap functionality and some simple line drawing capability? Remember you are not deciding this for just one device but for potentially millions of devices. Any thoughtful cost savings here will be amply rewarded for years, so start small and grow grudgingly.

Equally important considerations, though, are the non-functional needs, since they comprise an area that is quite often not given the importance it deserves. Foremost is the flexibility and robustness of the graphics support. It must be able to easily accommodate critical functionality such as the look and feel of physical controls, a branding capability via skins, and upgradeability.

It must, in fact, thrive on change. Since this device is a "connected" device, its software must play by web paced change rates. When the next "killer" app appears, it must be quickly and easily accommodated. Yet more than that, flexibility of change is the norm and is needed so that you can build up a family of applications that are appropriate for an entire product line from small and simple to luxury and complex with minimal software impact. It must also accommodate change inherent in any single production model itself as the functionality and vendors evolve over time. It must embrace the software as it evolves from prototype, to trials, to production, to upgradeability in the field.

Finally, the flexibility of how you work should be accommodated also. It should allow for fragmenting the problem along the lines of the skills needed – software engineers can concentrate on the application logic and HMI experts and graphic artists can concentrate on their work with minimal hindrance from each other.

P3ML FUTURE

P3ML is working its way through the vehicle manufacturing supply chain of OEMs and Tier 1s as higher function telematics designs work their way towards production.

Although there are currently no suitable standards for the automotive Telematics space P3ML is likewise gaining attention in standards bodies and will hopefully be adopted in some form in the future.

CONTACT

Randy Carroll has a B.S. / M.S. in Computer Science from the University of Kentucky and an MBA from Wake Forest. He has spent 28 years roaming the spectrum of computing, but his heart remains in embedded systems. He now spends his time working on telematics-oriented projects.

(rwcarroll@us.ibm.com)

Brett Hackleman has a degree in Computer Engineering from North Carolina State University. As part of the Embedded Java Enablement Team, he works with automotive customers implementing telematics solutions.

(bhackleman@us.ibm.com)

Philippe Krief has a PhD in Computer Science from Paris VIII University, France. He has been involved in object-oriented projects, prototyping environments and HMI paradigms and design for 19 years. He is the project lead of the P3ML project.

(pjkrief@fr.ibm.com)

Paul VanderLei has a Master's Degree in Computer Science from Arizona State University. He has worked in object-oriented software and HMI design for 23 years across a wide variety of business domains ranging from pacemaker control to retail banking and from vehicle assembly line control to in-vehicle telematics.

(pvlei@us.ibm.com)

2003-01-0124

ACE Driving Simulator and Its Applications to Evaluate Driver Interfaces

Vivek Bhise
University of Michigan- Dearborn

Edzko Smid
Oakland University

James Dowd
Collins & Aikman

ABSTRACT

A fixed base driving simulator called the VVDS (Virtual Vehicle Driving Simulator), its operating procedure and software system have been developed by a team of automotive suppliers (called ACE -- Advanced Cockpit Enabler) for quick evaluations of early working prototypes of driver interfaces. The system is designed to provide quick feedback to the product designers in early concept generation and validation phases of new automotive HMI architecture strategies and interfaces of various in-vehicle devices. The simulator consists of a reconfigurable cab with quick-change attachments to mount various controls and displays in package positions. A number of drivers are asked to drive the simulator and perform a number of tasks when prompted by pre-recorded voice commands. The entire data collection and data analysis procedure is developed such that new experiments can be configured, implemented and analyzed quickly and with the least amount of a human analyst's involvement. The system generates reports showing graphs of driver behavior, performance measures (e.g. driver inputs and outputs as functions of time, number of glances, total visual time, lane position standard deviation, velocity standard deviation, etc.) and subjective impressions of drivers (e.g. ratings on work load, control operating feel, surface tactile feel of control surfaces, etc.) for different tasks associated in operating/using various in-vehicle controls and displays.

The paper presents the description of the simulator system, illustrations on its evaluation procedure and results of two experiments conducted to evaluate different radio designs by involving different radio and non-radio tasks (such as increase/decrease radio volume, adjust base and treble, select/seek/tune a given radio station, change CD track, eject a CD and insert a new CD, answer a cell phone, dial a phone number, etc.).

PURPOSE

To provide a quick method to measure usability and customer feedback on alternate driver interface concepts.

INTRODUCTION

With the rapid advances in information technologies, a number of safety, communication and comfort-convenience features are being developed by various inventors for incorporation in future vehicles. Incorporation and operation of these new features involves designing interfaces, i.e. controls and displays, in the already crowded cockpits. Minimizing complexity of these interfaces is critical to assure that the driver is not overloaded. The complexity of many of the driver interfaces has increased to the point that it is simply not possible for a design team to develop the interfaces through the team interactions and "gut feel". A tool is needed to evaluate various driver interface proposals. The VVDS was developed for this purpose. It allows testing of early working prototypes of different driver interfaces in various simulated driving situations and provides automated data collection for quick feedback to the designers.

Figure 1. Aluminum Framed Cab

The ACE project, created and managed under the leadership of Collins & Aikman, include the following three basic teams: a mechanical team, an electrical team and an HMI (Human Machine Interface) team. Each team involves cross-functional co-located engineers and designers from a group of seven automotive interior suppliers, an auto manufacturer, and two universities. The teams develop different proposals for developing improved and cost efficient cockpit systems and their related driver interfaces. Working prototypes of promising designs are made and refined with the data obtained from testing in the VVDS. More detailed description of the ACE HMI process is available in *(1)*.

Use of a simulator for quick evaluations has a number of advantages. Some key advantages of using the simulator are:

- Precise repetition of driving test situation so that behavior of many drivers can be observed and recorded.
- Safety- The elimination of possibility of accidents and injuries to the test subjects.
- Quick feedback to the designers and engineers
- Generally less costly than testing on an actual highway

DESCRIPTION OF THE DRIVING SIMULATOR

The simulator consists of: a) an aluminum framed vehicle buck with front seats, a fully adjustable steering column with steering wheel and stalk controls, and an aluminum channel framework to mount instrument panel, door and console mounted controls, b) a large 3.5 m wide and 3 m high screen mounted at 3 m distance from the driver's eye, c) an overhead mounted video projector for projection of the driving scene, d) driving scene generator SGI computer with the driving simulation software, e) three PCs to issue voice commands to the driver and collect data on lane position, velocity, hands off the wheel time, and f) a synchronized video camera to record driver's eye glances. (See Figures 1, 2 and 3).

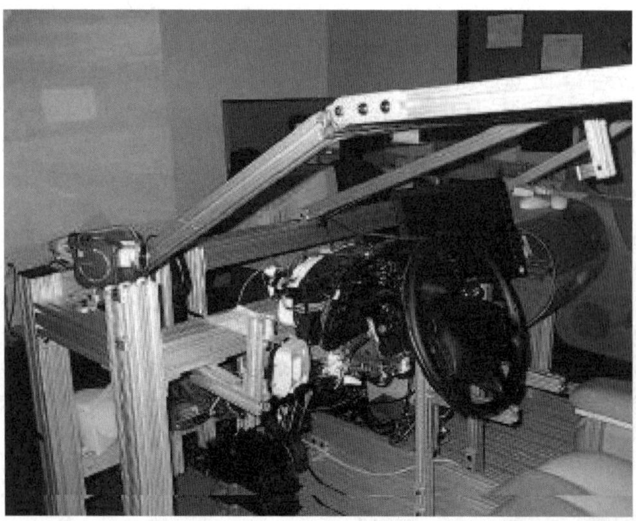

Figure 1. Aluminum Framed Cab

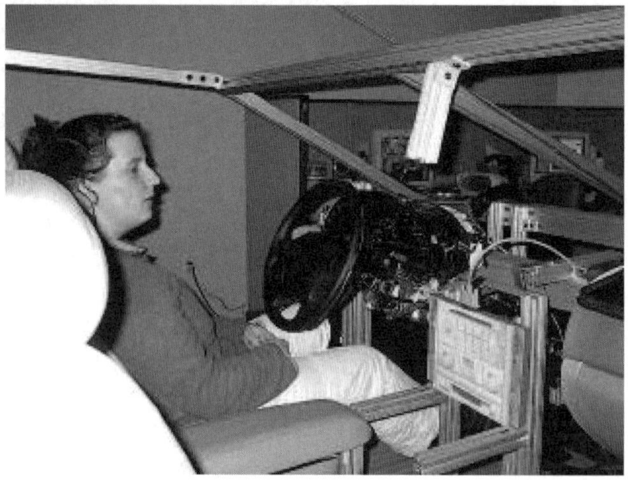

Figure 2. Driver in the Cab with a Prototyped Radio and Climate Control Unit

Figure 3A. Driver's Visual Screen (Rural undivided highway)

Figure 3B. Driver's Visual Screen (Urban Streets)

Figure 3B. Driver's Visual Screen (Urban Streets)

The buck is made to resemble the interior of an actual vehicle. All interior components can be easily relocated for optimization. This setup enables us to optimize a cockpit at a much lesser expense compared to testing on an actual vehicle.

The driving simulator uses an SGI server and a number of Windows based PC's to run applications and collect data. The SGI server simulates the interactive driving environment based on the Virtual Vehicle Simulating Software (VVSS) originally developed in Oakland University for suspension testing *(2, 3, 4)*. The MATLAB and Simulink software provides data collection and processing capabilities.

Hardware Setup

The VVSS environment consists of a Silicon Graphics high performance computer for rendering the virtual scenery (see Figure 4). This host station provides network services for 3 PC workstations on the Local Area Network (LAN) to interact on-line with the simulation execution.

The human-in-the-loop capability is provided by PC-1, which is configured to capture the driver inputs for steering, throttle and brake. These driver inputs are sent to the simulation execution through the LAN using Matlab/Simulink design interface. PC-1 also monitors the lane deviation from the road median, and generates engine sound corresponding to the speed of the virtual vehicle.

The vehicle location is monitored by PC-2. When the driver reaches certain pre-programmed locations in the scenery, PC-2 will issue verbal task commands through the audio system.

Driver information is provided through a conventional automotive cluster, which is controlled by PC-3. This workstation also maintains a truth signal for hands-on-the-wheel and eyes-on-the-road. PC-3 is equipped with a multi-channel analog and digital input/output card.
A fourth workstation is used to record digital video data on disk of the driver subject. This information is later used to confirm hands-on-the-wheel and eyes-on-the-road information.

Unique about the VVSS is that it utilizes custom automotive commercial hardware that is provided by Collins & Aikman. The VVSS can be easily adapted to any other hardware for driver inputs.

Software

All the data from PC's 1-3 is logged and stored in one Matlab binary file. Matlab is used to conduct primary analysis on the data by using a script file that generates an HTML document that includes graphic plots and charts. Together with the observation sheets and the rating scales, this information then provides the basis for the higher-level driver performance evaluation and HMI quality assessment.
The configuration of the VVSS is displayed in Figure 4.
The mathematical dynamics model of the vehicle contains 24 degrees of freedom and has over 90 states.
A special feature of the simulation environment is the multi-access modularity through the LAN.

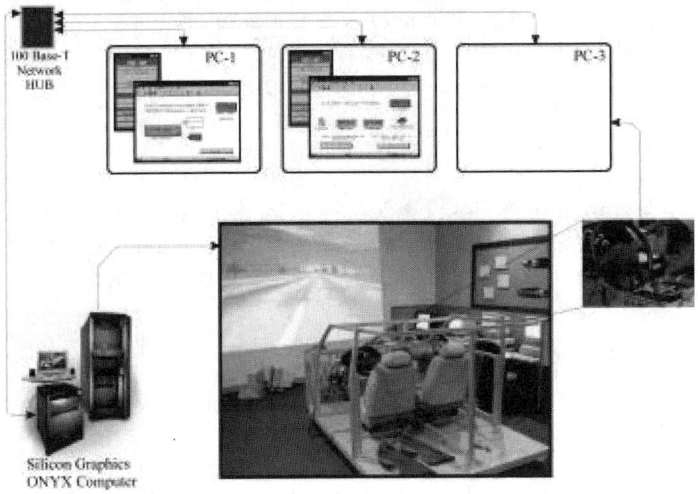

Figure 4. Hardware Configuration

Access to the state values of the mathematical model is implemented through a directional vector table. This allows for external host stations to replace the states of the system by virtually replacing part of the mathematical model. For example, the suspension height of the left front wheel is represented as a state in the vehicle dynamics model. An external model for suspension can be activated, that will replace the model formulation of the left front suspension height and insert a run-time value, derived from the other states and inputs. Elsewhere in the vehicle model where left front suspension height is used to derive other states, this new value from the external model will be used.
Likewise, also the driver input model, vehicle behavior and additional scenery characteristics are accessible for monitoring and altering the driving simulator models. This feature of the VVSS is exploited for the HMI evaluation process described in this paper.

Test Scenarios

In order to develop test scenarios, there is a dedicated scenario manager. The scenario manager stores the route, positions and tasks, and the association for each of the experiment laps in a single file. Each test consists of 6 trips (or laps)—first 2 practice trips followed with the next 4 trips for evaluations runs.

Each trip consists of a course route through the virtual scenery of approximately 20 minutes. The trajectory contains an average number of turns, stop signs, traffic lights, intersections and so on. Associated with the course are a series of assigned locations in the trajectory, which are used to trigger tasks. These locations are stored in the scenario manager. In addition to the course, there are an independent number of task definitions defined in the scenario manager. The task definitions consist of a name and a sound file, which contains the task description. The scenario manager contains an association matrix that defines which task is to be executed at which location for which experiment.

Test Procedure

A standardized test procedure is incorporated to minimize time required to set-up the simulator to conduct evaluation of driver interfaces. The standardized test procedure involves:

1. Pre-Test Procedure
   - Each subject is given basic information on the test.
   - The subject signs a consent form.
   - The subject is asked to fill-out a demographic information form.
   - The subject is given a reaction time test to determine his/her information processing rate in a choice decision situation, vision tests, and his/her relevant anthropometric characteristics (e.g. stature, weight) are measured.

2. Familiarization:
   - The experimenter shows all controls (primary and secondary controls and displays (including feedback LEDs, sounds, etc.), HVAC, Radio, etc.) to the subject.
   - The subject is asked to adjust seat, steering wheel and pedals to his/her preferred settings.
   - The experimenter checks to assure that hands-off-the-wheel measurements work properly.
   - The experimenter makes sure that the "engine sound" is turned on.
   - The experimenter adjusts lighting to avoid any discomforting/disturbing glare from internal or external light sources.
   - Each subject is then asked to drive the simulator for at least 5 minutes before any data collection commences (subjects unfamiliar with the simulator are given longer time until they feel comfortable with the simulator driving).

3. Driving Tests and Data Collection
   - The experimenter provides more specific driving instructions about performing selected tasks involving usage of certain interior controls/displays.

Sample Driver Instructions:

This study will investigate driver performance in operating the driving simulator while performing secondary tasks. You will be asked to drive the simulator through several routes. During these routes we will give you verbal instructions for you to operate different controls in the vehicle.

Keep in mind that your primary task is to keep the vehicle in control and maintain the proper speed and lane position. Your performance on the primary task will be measured. Drive in the left lane (closest to the yellow line) at all times, even when making turns. The recommended speed is 35 to 40 mph. You should attempt to maintain this speed as closely as possible at all times during the drive. You should also maintain your lane position so that the vehicle does not cross the lane boundaries. Just as you drive a car, you should try to minimize the vehicles' lateral -- i.e. left/right movement, and maintain a stable position.

It is important that you always keep your hands in the location that the experimenter tells you on the steering wheel, except when you will need to reach and operate controls to perform the instructed tasks. There are wires on the steering wheel. They are not energized and you cannot receive a shock through them.

The test consists of six laps. The first two laps are practice laps; the other four are experimental laps. Each lap takes 15-20 minutes and the whole test is about 2 hours. You may take breaks between the laps and if at any time you have questions or wish to stop participating in this experiment for any reason, please feel free to notify the experimenter.

   - Pre-recorded instructions are played to enable the subject to practice performing each task. This is conducted in a random order and in a static condition to assure that they are familiar with the driver interface.

   - Each subject is then asked to drive six laps on a pre-selected driving course. During each lap the subjects is asked to perform 8 different tasks. When the subject arrives at each pre-selected location, verbal instructions from pre-recorded audio files are automatically played through a computer's sound system.

   - The experimenter observes the subject and fills out a pre-developed form to record subject's behavior, control operation errors and ratings for each task.

A video camera records the facial behavior of the driver during the complete test. This video data are used to measure eye-movement and eyes-on-the-road information (see Figure 5).

During each lap, the 3 PC's create three data files, each containing the time data and associated log of the driving behavior and vehicle outputs. The data files contain the local time of the PC during the simulation, the synchronized reference time of the simulation environment and the application data associated with each PC. The X-Y position of the vehicle is collected from the driving simulator. The throttle, brake and steering angle are captured from the human driver interface, and the task number is generated from the scenario manager. The lane deviation is computed by comparing the current X-Y position of the vehicle with a pre-recorded center-lane trajectory.

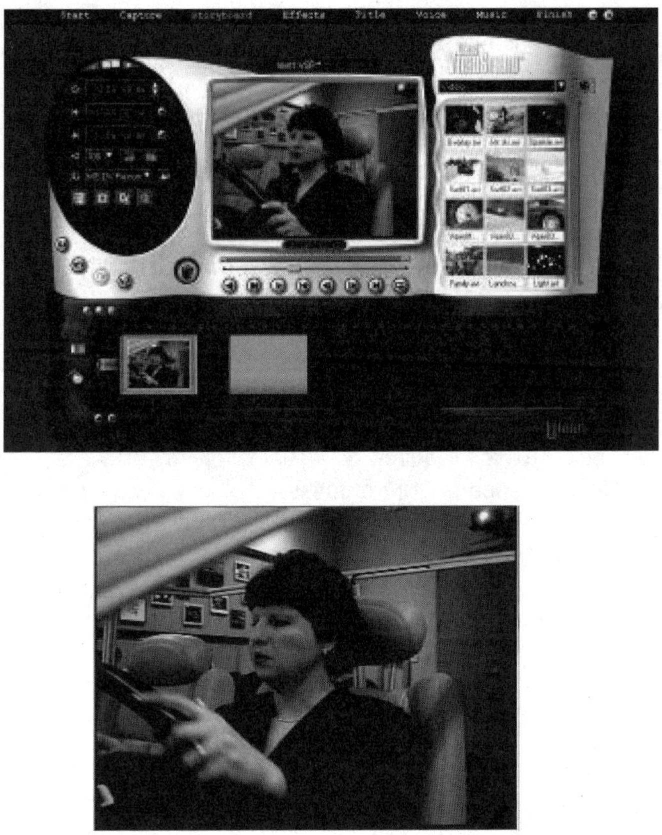

Figure 5. Illustrations of Video Data Collected to Obtain Driver Eye Glance Data

This provides a running difference between the actual and the desired lane position. The hands-on-the-wheel signal is generated from an electrical touch-contact on the steering wheel, and the eyes-on-the-road signal is generated by a push button from an external observer. The external observer is dedicated to push a button whenever the driver is not directly looking at the road in the scenery. The local time is automatically stored from Simulink along with the logged application data. The reference time from the VVSS is also considered as application data. Immediately after the experiment, the 3 data files are collected and consolidated in a special Matlab array format, and stored as the complete experimental data from the test.
In the next section, this data will be subjected to a report generation tool, which extracts the relevant driver performance information from the data in a useful format for further analysis.

Automatic Report Generation

Report generation is conducted by post-processing the collected data files in Matlab. A script is designed that will interpret and analyze the data files and generate 196 graphs and an associated HTML document. This document contains a table of contents, all the graphs and the support documentation for the data. It also contains the scenario definition, task definition and test subject information for the current test
The report generator provides graphs for lane deviation and vehicle velocity, both in actual form and standard deviation and averaged standard deviation.
The final stage of the report generation consists of the additional appendix with documentation on the current test scenario configuration and test subject data.
During this process of the report generation, an additional table is being generated with statistical values for lane deviation and vehicle velocity. Based on pre-defined threshold values for this data, a total count is accumulated per each task. This count provides an indication for the amount of driver distraction for the particular task. The total count of the test provides an indication of the quality of the prototype interface in terms of minimizing the driver distraction during task execution. More details on the report generation are provided in (*5*).

STUDY 1: DRIVING SIMULATOR STUDY

This study was conducted to get baseline data on a production radio and to compare the data with a new prototyped radio. Twelve drivers (8 males and 4 females, ages 16-48) participated in this study. Figure 6 shows a picture of the production radio (called Radio 1). Figure 7 shows a prototyped radio that is somewhat similar to the actual prototyped radio (called Radio 2) used for the actual evaluation. To maintain confidentiality the picture of the Radio 2 is not presented here.

Figure 6. Production Radio (Radio 1) Used for Evaluation

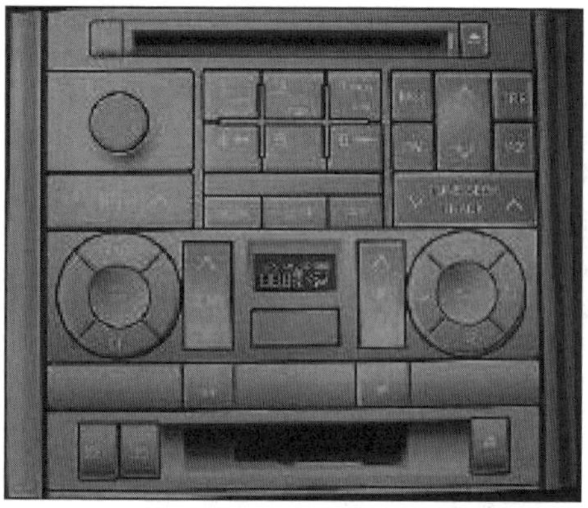

Figure 7. An Illustration of a Prototyped Interface of a Radio and Climate Control Unit

Procedure:

After familiarization with the vehicle controls, and a 20-minute simulator and test route familiarization, each driver drove six complete laps on the test course. A lap consisted of an eight-mile rural 2-lane road, which took about 15 minutes to complete. Sixteen locations were pre-selected on the test route. In any given lap, the test drivers were asked to perform eight of the sixteen randomly selected in-vehicle tasks. The instructions for each of the sixteen tasks (described below) were recorded in voice files, which were played when a subject arrived at each pre-selected location. The tasks were so arranged that during each successive two laps (i.e. laps 1 and 2, laps 3 and 4, and laps 5 and 6), all the sixteen tasks were presented. Thus, by the time the drivers performed the tasks in laps 5 and 6, they had already experienced in performing all the tasks (i.e. performing each task at least two times in the first 4 laps). All the 12 subjects performed exactly the same tasks, except half the subjects were tested with a production radio (referred as Radio 1) and other half used a prototype radio (referred as Radio 2) with similar functionality. Both the Radio 1 and Radio 2 had a CD player (located higher up), a rotary volume control and six preset stations. The following instructions were provided through pre-recorded audio files at the initiation of each task:

Task 1: Press FM (push button) and select preset 6 (push button).
Task 2: Press CD (push button), eject CD in the radio, and insert the "Billboard Top Hits" CD.
Task 3: Press FM, listen to the first three presets, and then select the music of your choice.
Task 4: Adjust the bass and treble to your liking.
Task 5: What is the answer to the following math problem: Five plus nine, minus six, times twenty-three?
Task 6: Press CD, seek track 4.
Task 7: Press FM, tune to 95.5.
Task 8: Turn volume up.
Task 9: Find the cell phone, and dial your home phone number backwards.
Task 10: Press FM, tune to 107.5.
Task 11: Turn the volume down.
Task 12: Press FM, tune to 93.1.
Task 13: Press FM, seek to 105.1.
Task 14: Press CD, seek to track 2.
Task 15: Press CD, eject the CD in the radio, and insert the "Paula Abdul" CD.
Task 16: Ring....Ring.....Ring (Answer the cell phone when it rings).

The cell phone used for Tasks 9 and 16 was kept on front passenger's seat. The phone did not have a flipping door to access the keys. These two cell phone tasks along with Task 5 (which required no visual involvement) were used as reference or control tasks.

Data Collection and Analyses:

The outputs of the simulator runs were recorded in computer files. The files consisted of time and distance based values of lane position, velocity, pedal positions and steering wheel angle. In addition, the driver's face was video taped using a digital video camera, which was synchronized with simulator data. The eye glance data were reduced manually from the digital video files. The experimenter also kept track of any control operational errors (e.g. long looks at the controls, pushed wrong button, etc.) and erratic vehicle maneuvers (e.g. lane deviations, slowed down, etc.). The data were processed to obtain values of the following performance measures for each task performed by each subject in each lap.

Performance Measures:

Number of glances: Total number of glances made away from the forward road scene to perform a given task of operating an in-vehicle device.

Total eye time: Total time spent in glances made away from the forward road scene to perform a given task of operating an in-vehicle device. (Sum of eye glances in seconds)

Total visual time: Total time elapsed between the beginning of the first glance and the end of the last glance made in performing a task (measured in seconds).

Lane position standard deviation: standard deviation of lane position (measured in meters) obtained from 90 lane position data samples (which included: 5 samples/sec x 6-second time interval x 3 6-second intervals) over an 18 seconds interval measured from the location at which the verbal instruction was given to perform a task.

Velocity standard deviation: standard deviation of velocity (measured in m/sec) obtained from 90 velocity data samples (which included: 5 samples/sec x 6-second time interval x 3 6-second intervals) over 18 seconds interval measured from the location at which the verbal instruction was given to perform a task.

Driving Performance Score: Number of erratic events in the 18-second interval (defined above). Erratic events were defined by: 1) when the lane position standard deviation in any of the first three 6-second intervals (following the verbal instructions) exceeded 0.6 m, or
2) when the velocity standard deviation in any of the first three 6-second intervals (following the verbal instructions) exceeded 1.8 m/sec. The values 0.6 m and 1.8 m/sec were determined by the authors to represent high likelihood of traffic hazards due to lane intrusions and sudden slow downs in traffic streams respectively.

Results:

Figures 8 and 9 provide summaries of eye glance based data obtained from the video recording of the drivers' faces during the 16 tasks. The data show that simple tasks such as using preset stations and volume up/down are performed in less than 2 eye glances and total visual time of about 2 secs. Whereas, complex visual tasks such as tuning to a desired station or adjusting sound base and treble took about 4 to 9 eye glances and about 9 to 18 secs of total visual time. The tasks of ejecting a CD, retrieving a new CD from a CD case and inserting it was very demanding taking about 4-5 glances and about 10-15 secs of total visual time.

Figures 10, 11, 12 and 13 show the effect of the radios, i.e. the differences due to the radios 1 and 2 on the four measures. The data plotted in these figures are from the last two laps (laps 5 and 6) where the subjects had the most familiarity with the tasks.

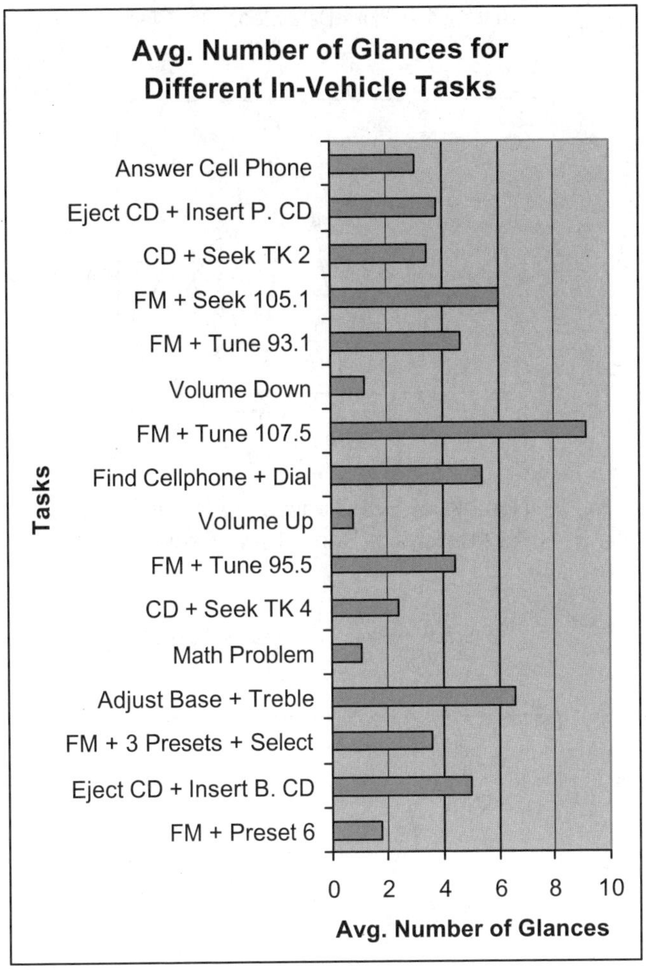

Figure 8. Average Number of Glances Made in Performing the 16 Tasks (from data combined over the evaluation of both radios).

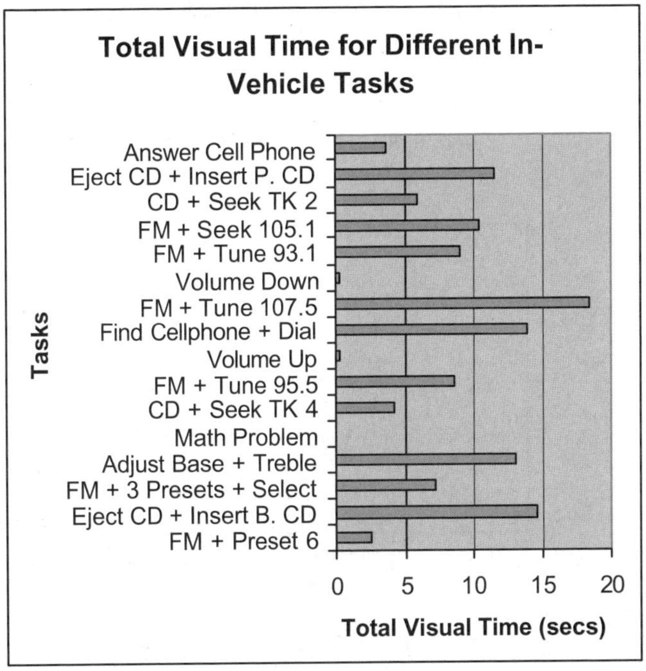

Figure 9. Average Total Visual Time for the 16 Tasks (from data combined over the evaluation of both radios).

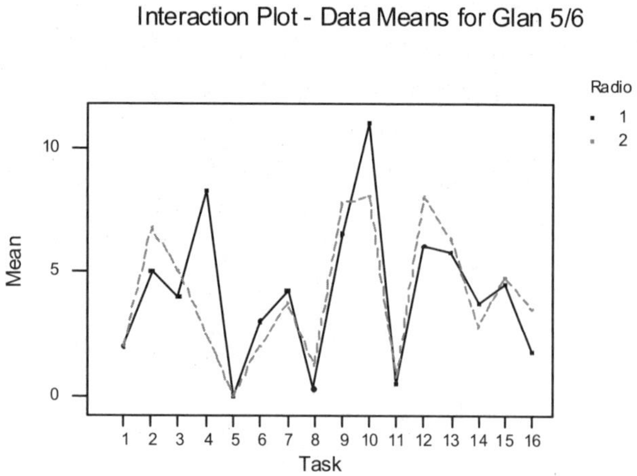

Figure 10. Number of Eye Glances Made during the Evaluations of Radio 1 and Radio 2.

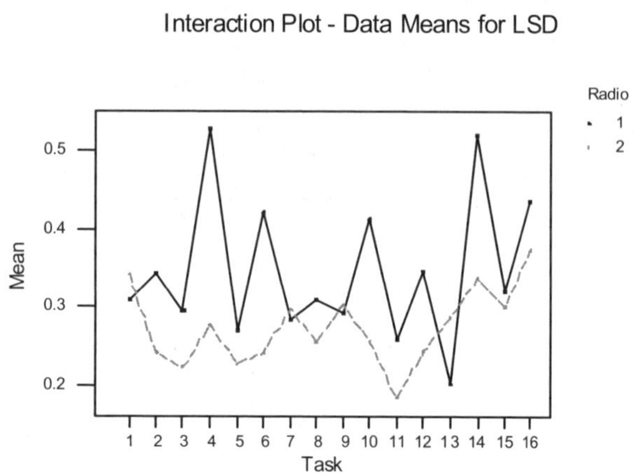

Figure 11. Lane Position Standard Deviation (measured in meters) during the Evaluations of Radio 1 and Radio 2.

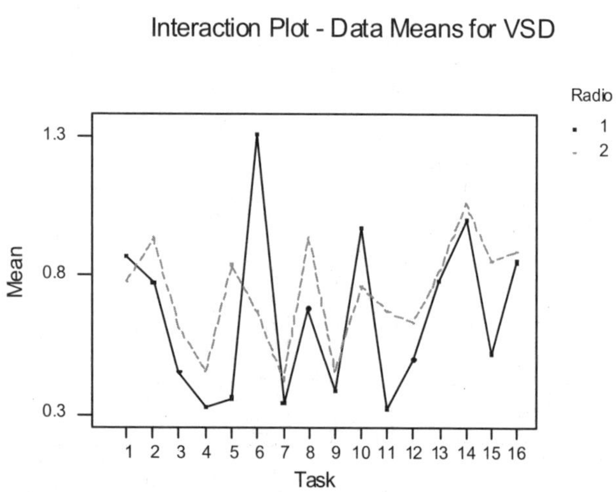

Figure 12. Velocity Standard Deviation (measured in meters) during the Evaluations of Radio 1 and Radio 2.

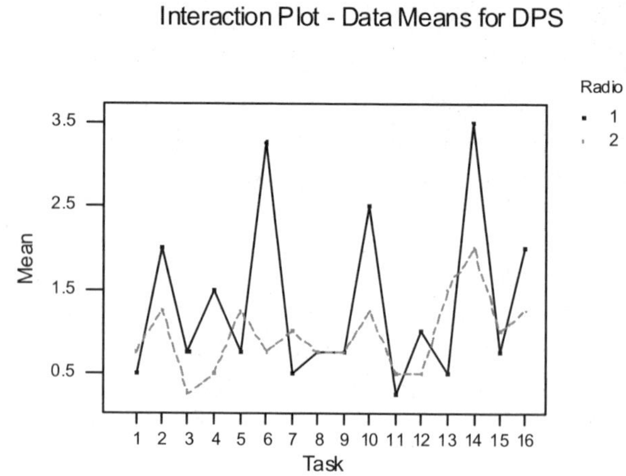

Figure 13. Driving Performance Measures for the Evaluations of Radio 1 and Radio 2.

The data presented in the above figures showed that tasks using Radio 2 were easier to perform than with Radio 1. The figures also show that Tasks 5, 9, and 16 which were not related to the radio operation, in general, did not show significant differences in values of the corresponding measures.

STUDY 2: EVALUATION OF TWO RADIOS

In this study, the driving simulator was used to evaluate an additional radio called Radio 3 using the same 16 tasks (described earlier) and 5 additional subjects. The photograph of the radio is provided in Figure 14.

Figure 14. Photograph of Radio 3 Used in Study 2

Since the eye glance data was not available for Radio 3, only the standard deviation of lane position and velocity data were processed. Figures 15 and 16 present comparison of the data obtained from testing with Radio 3 with Radio 1. The ANOVA tests on the measures showed that the differences between radios were significant at p=.0005.

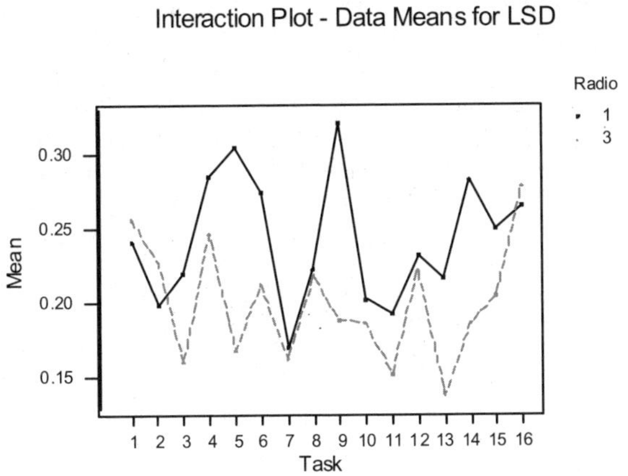

Figure 15. Lane Position Standard Deviation (measured in meters) during the Evaluations of Radio 1 and Radio 3.

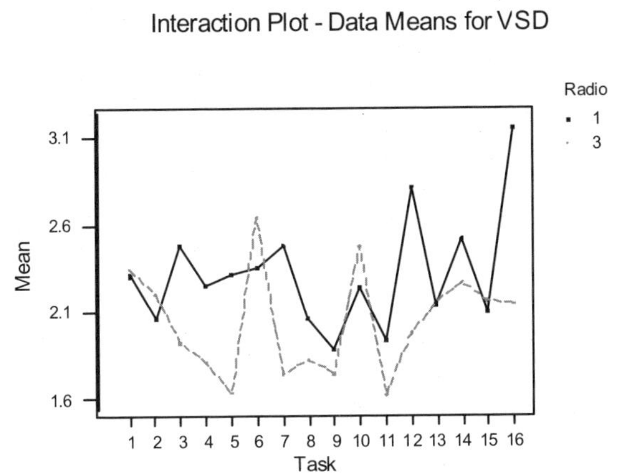

Figure 16. Velocity Standard Deviation (measured in meters) during the Evaluations of Radio 1 and Radio 3.

CONCLUSIONS

The simulator and the HMI evaluation process provided a very powerful method to evaluate tasks associated with new in-vehicle devices and to compare the measures obtained from the tests with similar data obtained from the evaluation of other in-vehicle devices. The evaluation results of Radio 1, Radio 2 and Radio 3 presented in this paper illustrate that the simulator is an excellent HMI evaluation tool to evaluate differences in different interface designs. Recently, two on-road studies in actual vehicles were conducted using the same procedure. In general the data obtained in the simulator showed similar characteristics to the driver behavior observed on the public roads (*6*). In future, the simulator will be used to evaluate various alternate designs of different centerstack mounted devices, reconfigurable displays and multi-function controls at different locations (e.g. on steering wheel, instrument panel, stalks, etc.).

AKNOWLEDGEMENTS

The authors wish to acknowledge and thank the following members of the ACE team for their support and technical assistance during this project: Collins & Aikman (formerly Textron Automotive Company), Sanyo FMS Audio Sdn. Bhd., Nippon Seiki International, Ltd., Douglas Autotech Corporation, Valeo Switch and Detection Systems, KSR International Company, Alcoa Fujikura, Ltd., University of Michigan-Dearborn and Oakland University. We also would like to thank Mr. Scott Davis for his support and persistence throughout the projects and the students for their efforts and enthusiasm.

REFERENCES

1. Bhise, V., Dowd, J., Davis, S. and Smid, E. A Comprehensive HMI Evaluation Process for Automotive Cockpit Design. SAE Paper number 2003-01-0126. To be presented at the SAE Annual Congress, Detroit, Michigan, March 2003.

2. G. E. Smid, "Virtual Vehicle Systems Simulation. A modular approach in real-time". Ph.D. thesis, Department of Electrical and Systems Engineering, Oakland University, 1999.

3. G. E. Smid, Ka C. Cheok, K. Kobayashi. Simulation of Vehicle Dynamics using Matrix-Vector Oriented Calculation in Matlab. Proceedings of CAINE '96, pp 115-120. ISCA, Orlando FL, December 1996.

4. G. E. Smid and Ka C. Cheok. Multi-Computer Real-Time Simulation of Vehicle Control Systems. Proc. of the 7th International Conference on Intelligent Systems (ICIS '98), Paris July 12-15 1998.

5 Smid, E., Dowd, J. and Bhise, V. Design and Implementation of a Driving Simulator Facility for the Optimization of Human-Machine Interface. To be presented at the Transportation Research Board for a presentation at the Annual Meeting in January 2003.

6. Bhise, V., Dowd, J. and Smid, E., Driver Behavior While Operating In-vehicle Devices. To be presented at the Annual Meeting of the Transportation Research Board, Washington, D. C., January 2003.

2003-01-0293

Infrared Night Vision Systems and Driver Needs

Kåre Rumar
The University of Michigan

ABSTRACT

Night vision enhancement systems (NVES), which use infrared (IR) cameras, are designed to supplement the visibility provided by standard headlamps. There are two main NVES systems: active, near infrared (NIR) systems, which require an IR source but give a complete picture of the scene in front of the driver, and passive, far infrared (FIR) systems, which do not need an IR source but only enhance relatively warm objects (such as people and animals). There are three main display alternatives: a head-up display (HUD) superimposed on the direct view of the road, a HUD just above the dashboard but separated from the direct view, and a conventional display somewhere in the dashboard.

This paper analyzes what a NVES should do to improve night visibility based on night crash statistics, driver vision and visibility conditions in night driving, driver tasks and behavior, and the options offered by various technological approaches. Potential problems with using NVES are also discussed. The six main questions that need to be answered concerning NVES are: **What** kind of information should be presented? To **whom** should the information be presented? **Which** technological approach should be used? **When** should the information be presented? **How** should the information be presented? **Where** should the information be presented?

BACKGROUND

Since the development of automobile headlights, the limited visibility offered to drivers in night traffic has been a problem. The present headlighting system suffers from one major drawback–the low-beam system. The low-beam system is a compromise between good illumination and limited glare. The result is that neither visibility nor glare is as good as drivers would like.

Many efforts have been made to achieve good illumination without causing glare. Intelligent (adaptive) headlights improve the situation, but do not solve it. Other technologies, such as ultraviolet headlights and polarized headlights, have given results that are more promising. Both are capable of creating illumination without causing glare, and make use of direct driver vision. But both also have drawbacks, which so far have prevented their introduction.

Consequently, researchers and manufacturers have turned to systems using radiation outside the range of the human visual system. This is not a new idea. The first products were made for military purposes–to see the enemy in dark conditions. However, the purpose and applications are different for military and civilian night vision systems. Advancements in technology have now made these concepts more attractive and more realistic for wider implementation (Tsimhoni and Green, 2002).

In Night-Vision Enhancement Systems (NVES) based on infrared (IR) technology, the radiation used may be IR emitted by relatively warm stimuli (a passive system) or it may be IR emitted by illuminators and reflected from the stimuli (an active system). The radiation is detected by special sensors (cameras), processed, and presented to the driver on a display. The display might be a head-up display (HUD) presented as a contact analogue (i.e., a partially transparent display with the camera view superimposed on the direct view of the road), a HUD just above the dashboard but separated from the direct view, or a conventional, nontransparent display (a head-down display, HDD) somewhere in the dashboard. The screen might be on the windshield itself (in the case of a HUD), a separate conventional screen on top of the dashboard, or a conventional screen integrated into the dashboard. NVES can no doubt increase driver vision in night driving considerably. But there are also potentially negative effects of NVES (Rumar, 2002).

PROBLEMS AND METHODOLOGY

In order to be effective as a safety technology, NVES has to offer advantages in visibility during night driving without introducing disproportionate risks. The two problem areas that this paper addresses are:

- What should be the purpose of NVES? Which visibility problems should NVES try to reduce? How should the image be presented to the driver?
- What could be the potential risks in using NVES and how serious are these risks?

The approach in this paper is to attempt to clarify the role that NVES should play in night driving by analyzing existing knowledge concerning: night traffic characteristics, crashes and risks in night driving, and driver visual performance.

Summaries and conclusions are presented in italics at the end of each of the following sections.

NIGHT DRIVING PROBLEMS

The assumption is that NVES will not replace direct driver vision, but will supplement the direct vision that the driver has through the windshield with additional information. The goal is to find support for the specific use of NVES that will give the most needed and least harmful additional information.

The assumption here is that NVES will complement existing headlights and street lighting. NVES will not replace direct driver vision, but supplement it. Consequently, the task of future NVES is probably to enhance specific parts of the forward night scene. The goal is to find support for the specific form of NVES that will provide additional information that is the most needed and the least distracting or misleading.

The proportion of motorized traffic volume that occurs during the dark period of the day varies from country to country. Typical figures for industrialized countries, including the U.S., are 20 to 25% (NSC, 2000). In very densely populated and highly developed regions such as Japan, night traffic constitutes about 40% of the total traffic volume. However, because crash rates are higher at night (in general two to three times higher) and crash severity is higher at night (Langwieder, 1995; Weber et al., 2001), the number of people killed and injured in night traffic is disproportionately high. A typical figure for highly industrialized countries, like the U.S., is one third of all fatalities.

NVES primarily addresses crashes that are caused by darkness. According to Sullivan and Flannagan (2002), such crashes primarily involve collisions between vehicles and pedestrians (which are about four times higher in darkness). Other crash types typical of night traffic are single vehicle crashes, collisions between vehicles and bicycles, collisions between vehicles and animals, and rear-end collisions between vehicles (Moore and Rumar, 1999). However, factors other than darkness itself seem to play a larger role in these non-pedestrian crashes. The main factors that co-vary with darkness are drunk and/or fatigued drivers and greater presence of wild animals.

At illumination levels typical for night traffic, driver visual performance is considerably decreased. The two major causes of this reduction are lowered contrast sensitivity and increased glare sensitivity. The result is that the visibility distances drivers have in normal night driving situations on two-lane rural roads are often unsafe considering the speed at which they drive.

Older drivers constitute a special problem group in night traffic (Rumar, 1998a). They rate night driving as one of the most difficult driving situations, and try to avoid it as much as possible. Studies show that drivers over 65 have considerably shorter visibility distances in night traffic than do younger drivers. In studies by Blanco et al. (2001) and Flannagan et al. (2000), young drivers had about 20% longer visibility distances. However, the main impairment for the older drivers seems to be target detection, not visual guidance. Table 1 summarizes realistic seeing distances for younger and older drivers based on a large number of experiments around the world.

A rule of thumb based on reaction distances and braking distances at normal speeds on rural roads is that the minimum visibility distance that gives the driver an opportunity to detect and identify the object and to choose an appropriate action is about 150 m. As shown in Table 1, most low-beam conditions and even a few high beam conditions do not meet this criterion.

Visibility of horizontal targets, such as the road surface and road markings, is considerably shorter (Rumar and Marsh, 1998). The visibility of the road surface varies with the diffuse reflectivity of the road (from wet asphalt to snow covered road). It is up to 100 m on low beams and up to 300 m on high beams.

Leibowitz and Owens (1997) suggest that driver's visual performance in night driving is based on two rather separate functions: visual guidance (mainly peripheral vision) and target recognition (mainly central vision). Target detection and recognition are seriously impaired in night driving, while visual guidance is less impaired. This difference in degradation is the major explanation for why drivers tend to overdrive their visibility distances in night driving. They choose speed according to their always-sufficient visual guidance and do not take into consideration the very rarely experienced poor object-detection distances.

Many persons, even experts in the area, believe that street lighting eliminates the visibility problems that are so obvious in dark rural areas. This is probably due to confusion between visibility of the road and visibility of objects. Introducing street lighting normally solves the poor visibility of the road itself. But visibility of objects is only partly solved by street lighting.

From the perspective of formal models of human performance, an important aspect of driving is that it is a self-paced task where choice of speed is the only means by which drivers can regulate the demands placed on them. At nighttime, however, drivers are incapable of regulating their speed in a safe way. According to

Leibowitz and Owens (1977), and Rumar (1998b), the main reason for this seemingly irrational behavior is that drivers do not receive enough feedback about the very short visibility distances of dark objects. They match their speed to the visual guidance, which is not as impaired as obstacle visibility.

This compensatory driver behavior is relevant for the development of NVES because if already good visibility visual guidance is improved further without improving the inferior visibility of obstacles, the risk is that drivers will overdrive their visibility even more. Studies carried out by Kallberg (1993) support this argument. He found that when visual guidance along a road was improved by the installation of side post delineators, drivers increased their speed to such an extent that safety was in fact impaired instead of improved.

Based on this analysis of driver tasks and driver behavior, NVES should be used primarily to enhance visibility of objects on the road, not visibility of the road itself.

Table 1
Detection distances to dark vertical objects, typical for current night driving in realistic conditions.

Condition	Low beams with oncoming low beams		High beams with no oncoming headlights	
	Young drivers	Older drivers	Young drivers	Older drivers
Dark objects	40 – 60 m	30 – 50 m	150 – 300 m	120 – 250 m
Bright objects	60 – 100 m	50 – 80 m	250 – 500 m	200 – 400 m
Dark objects with retroreflectors	100 – 200 m	80 – 160 m	350 – 700 m	300 – 600 m

IR TECHNOLOGIES: POSSIBILITIES AND PERFORMANCE

The infrared spectrum starts near the upper end of the visual sensitivity range at 780 nm and ends at about 16000 nm. The longer wavelengths represent heat radiation. The two parts of the spectrum most relevant for NVES are:

- Near infrared (NIR), approximately 780 to 3000 nm, requiring both infrared sources and infrared sensors (active systems)
- Far infrared (FIR), approximately 6000 to 16000 nm, requiring only infrared sensors, sensing the heat wave lengths from the targets (passive systems)

Presently only one manufacturer produces and sells a car with an IR NVES. That is GM, offering the Cadillac DeVille with an FIR system. Other manufacturers are expected to follow shortly. Considerable research on NVES has been carried out.

The Cadillac sensor is placed in the grill. This may be compared to the positioning of the sensors in four prototype NVES. The Autoliv sensor (FIR-HUD) is placed at the lower end of the windshield (Autoliv, 2002), the Jaguar camera (NIR-contact analogue) is placed just above the head of the driver (Ståhl et al., 1994), the Renault camera (NIR-contact analogue) is placed at the inside rearview mirror (Augello, 1993), and the Daimler-Chrysler camera (NIR-HDD) is placed high above the driver's eyes (DaimlerChrysler, 2000).

The pictures presented in the HUDs are monochrome. The driver may easily modify the brightness of both the NIR and the FIR screens. It could be fairly easy to switch the polarity (negative or positive contrast). It would be an advantage if the driver could modify the contrast in the picture. Also, most systems allow the drivers to adjust the position of the virtual picture to match their respective eye heights.

The NIR systems offer pictures that correspond closely to the normal scene. The visibility of everything is enhanced. The resolution is normally superior to the FIR resolution. However, one of the problems is that oncoming headlights and retroreflective road signs create glare (blooming) on the screen. Fluery (2002) discusses methods to neutralize the blooming when using NIR.

The FIR systems offer pictures that do not look like the normal visual scene through the windshield. The reason is that the FIR systems are mainly sensitive to relatively hot or warm objects. Humans, animals, and hot parts of vehicles (e.g., engine exhausts and radiators) are very visible, while road signs, road markings, the road itself, and the horizon have a lower visibility level. The difference between the FIR picture and the real scene may create confusion and misperceptions. A special problem is that because the visibility of the relatively cold background is reduced, drivers may have problems correctly perceiving the positions of targets in the road scene.

The NIR picture will be easier to interpret than the FIR picture partly because the relative contrasts in the visual field will not differ too much from those in direct vision, and partly because the resolution of the NIR systems is superior. On the other hand, NIR systems normally suffer from glare-related problems, which the FIR systems do not have.

The location of the sensor or camera is critical for obtaining an acceptable picture of the road scene. If the sensor or camera is positioned low (e.g., in the grill), the perspective of the road will be less than ideal, especially when driving on vertical curves. It is acceptable to position the sensor at the driver eye height, and it is preferable to place it above the driver's eyes. Another aspect of camera position is that a lower position is more exposed to dirt. Glass interferes with the FIR wavelengths and the camera cannot be placed, for example, behind the windscreen. This is an advantage for the NIR camera, which may be placed in an area behind the windshield cleared by the wipers.

The display itself offers a limited field of vision, normally 10 to 15 degrees horizontally and less than 5 degrees vertically. It is questionable if such a limited field of view is sufficient for normal driving (Mortimer, 1997). If the goal is to cover a wider field of vision, then the picture has to be scaled down. In contact analogue displays, the scale must of course be 1:1. But in NVES with separate screens the scale can be reduced to cover a wider field of view. A wider field of view has been tested and was preferred by drivers (Hollnagel, 2002). The two fields of view compared in his study were 12 and 18 degrees (corresponding to downscaling of 1:1.5 and 1:2). Of course, the resolution in the picture will suffer from downscaling, but that should not be serious if identification of the visual targets is not considered critical.

Based on this analysis of the technical possibilities it may be concluded that the available technology can do most of what we would like it to do. Technology poses no major problems for the development of NVES. The problem is what we want it to do. The current cost of NVES is a problem for most buyers of passenger cars.

ESTIMATES OF NVES VISIBILITY AND SAFETY POTENTIALS

There are very few studies of the general safety benefits of NVES. Lunenfeld and Stephens (1991) estimated that NVES could reduce night crash fatalities by 20 to 25 percent. However, it is unclear how they reached that conclusion. Färber (1993), giving large weight to the risk for compensatory driver behavior, estimated the crash reduction to vary from +1 percent to -25 percent.

There are several recent studies of visibility distances provided by NVES. Gish et al. (2002) used a Cadillac system in a field experiment and reported considerable visibility improvements for young drivers. Compared to visibility with standard low beams, young drivers increased their visibility distances in the presence of oncoming glare by 65 to 150 m when using NVES. Many of the older drivers did not use the NVES. There are indications that the main reason that use of NVES may be difficult for older drivers is the fact that the systems create dual tasks, which in general cause problems for older subjects. They probably avoid the dual-task situation by not using the NVES, in spite of the fact that they are the driver group that would benefit most from using it.

Blanco et al. (2001) report that an FIR system offers about 250 m visibility distance to most warm objects. Martinelli and Boulanger (2000), using the Cadillac FIR system, report pedestrian visibility distances of 300 m, although they do not provide a description of test conditions. Hollnagel (2002), in a simulator study of an Autoliv FIR system, reports obstacle (pedestrian, dog, etc.) visibility of 400 to 700 m.

Driver subjective evaluations of NVES have been carried out in a number of studies (Gish et al., 2002; Barham, 2001; Buttner and Klapper, 2002; Ståhl et al., 1994; Hollnagel, 2002). The results varied, but a majority was of the opinion that the NVES was useful when driving on straight, unfamiliar, unlit, and/or rural roads. The general opinion was that the system was easy to use and that the distraction potential would not be a major problem.

Hollnagel (2002) also obtained generally positive evaluations. He compared two fields of view (12 and 18 degrees horizontally) and found that the larger field of view was preferred. He also received several complaints that the display was hiding parts of the direct visual scene and about the identification and positioning of objects.

If we compare NVES visibility with the visibility offered by the present low-beam system with opposing low beams, we can say that NVES visibility is normally much better (e.g., Blanco et al., 2001). If we compare NVES visibility with the visibility offered by the present high-beam systems, we can say that they are often equally good.

NVES can offer substantially improved visibility conditions. Most drivers are positive about NVES and would like to have them in their cars. Consequently, the net safety effect of NVES will be determined by the user friendliness of the system (especially for older drivers) and the potential risks of the systems (such as increased speed, increased workload, increased distraction, and cognitive capture).

POTENTIAL RISKS WITH NVES

NVES using separate screens introduce a new dimension to night driving. The driver has to view the direct scene but must also scan the display intermittently. There are at least two problems associated with the new driving situation. One is for the driver to adapt his or her visual scanning behavior, and the other is for the driver to learn what is shown and what is not shown in the NVES display.

A way out of the problems with dual fixation tasks could be to let the technical system handle the signal detection, for instance by comparing the real-life picture with the enhanced-visibility picture and to signal the driver to scan the display only when a critical object is present. That would require image processing functions. The signal detection task would then be taken over by the technical system and the driver would not have to scan the display if nothing was there. On the other hand, such a solution would introduce new problems related to the reliability of the warnings and to false alarms—a critical issue with all warning systems.

If the NVES offers a high quality, complete picture, there are indications that drivers would prefer driving by primarily using the display rather than the direct visual scene. One of the few eye movement studies carried out with NVES (Meitzler et al., 2001) indicates such driver preferences.

A related scanning problem associated with NVES (both contact analogue HUD and separate HUD) could be cognitive capture. This means that the focus on the HUD might attract so much attention that the chances of detecting obstacles and events that occur outside this view (e.g., a cyclist approaching from the side) would be considerably reduced. There is some experimental evidence for this hypothesis (Bossi et al., 1994; Lee and Triggs, 1976). Using a contact analogue NIR system, drivers showed a reduced number of glances in the rearview mirror when using the NVES. The reduction was 15 to 20%. That could be an indication of cognitive capture and/or increased workload. However, it could also be a consequence of getting used to a new system.

Another scanning problem associated with the FIR system is that the direct view and the display picture look so different. Due to this conflict, there may be problems with interpreting the display picture. These interpretation problems, in turn, could increase the distraction caused by the display. There are reports (Foyle et al., 1990; Gish et al., 2002) of drivers who focus too much of their attention on the interpretation of the object and lose contact with the direct visual scene.

A general safety concern when part of the driving task is simplified is how drivers will react to this change. As discussed earlier, compensatory reactions often lead to increased speed. But the reaction may also be decreased attention or effort. In all cases, a compensatory reaction might result in reductions in the safety effect of the measure in question. Several studies have examined the effect of NVES on a driver's choice of speed, but the results are not conclusive. Some indicate no change in speed, while others show an increase in speed as a result of using NVES.

Increased workload is another central issue when considering the potentially negative effects of NVES. Again, the results from experimental studies are inconclusive. Ward et al. (1994), using a Jaguar NIR contact analogue HUD, report significantly increased workload when driving with NVES. The two variables that increased markedly were mental effort and mental demand.

The dual scanning tasks created by a separate display create an increased workload for the driver. It may be that the inconclusive effects of NVES on speed are caused by the additional workload, which may decrease speed, counteracting a tendency for the improved visibility to increase speed.

The analysis in this section indicates that older drivers constitute a special problem concerning NVES, especially for systems with separate displays. Another potential problem concerns the time needed to get comfortable with the system (the learning time). The potential risks of NVES suggest that the presentation of enhanced visual information to the driver should be designed to take into account the following concerns:

- *Not to increase speed*
- *Not to cause too much distraction*
- *Not to cause too much cognitive capture*
- *Not to increase workload too much*
- *To be useful to older drivers*

CONCLUSIONS

The development of NVES is potentially promising. NVES is able to meet both the requirements of drivers and of society, which are sometimes different. However, the optimal designs have not yet been determined. The estimates of traffic safety effects of NVES have a large range (predicted changes in accidents vary from plus 1%

to minus 25% [Lunenfeld and Stephens, 1991; Färber, 1993]), partly because of differing estimates of potential risk factors.

Some of the potential risks have not been fully investigated. Presentation of the enhanced visibility picture on a separate screen creates a number of problems because of the necessity for dual scanning. There are indications that this will influence attention to the primary task and increase driver workload and distraction. Many older drivers show low motivation and/or capacity to use NVES, though they would benefit more from it than younger drivers. The effect of NVES on driver choice of speed is inconclusive. If speed is increased, it might eliminate most of the potential safety benefit. However, there are indications that if road visibility is not enhanced as much as obstacle visibility drivers will not increase their speed when using NVES.

Much of the analysis speaks in favor of a NVES that primarily enhances obstacles and only enhances enough of the road to make it possible for the driver to position the detected objects in the road scene. Analyses of crash risk indicate that it is primarily human and perhaps animal obstacles that should be enhanced. The scene presented must be wide enough to cover curves and crossings, to include approach and crossing behavior of humans and animals. This probably means a field of view of at least 20 degrees.

Table 2 lists the main questions facing the future development of NVES, as well as alternatives and suggested answers, based on the discussion of current research knowledge reviewed in this report. Table 2 illustrates at least two things – the large number of alternatives available, and the fact that the best solution for one NVES purpose is not necessarily the best solution for another purpose. For example, if we want to enhance pedestrians for all drivers, an FIR system with part-time presentation, warning, and icons on a separate HUD display seems to be preferred. If we want to enhance the road and road signs for older drivers, an NIR system with full time presentation and full sensor image on a contact analogue display may be best.

Behind questions 4 and 5 is the signal detection problem. If a reliable technical system for detecting the relevant signals could be designed, the scanning task and the workload of the driver would be substantially reduced. The driver would then only have to react to a warning signal by scanning the display or by slowing down. According to Roper and Howard (1938), a warning alone would increase detection distance by a factor of two, without any displayed vision enhancement system. However, such a system might introduce new problems of false security (leading to reduced attention) and false alarms (leading to reduced usage).

There seems to be no doubt that NVES has a considerable visibility and safety potential. The total effect will depend very much on how well potential risks can be avoided. The optimal design of NVES is yet to be determined.

ACKNOWLEDGMENTS

Appreciation is extended to the members of the University of Michigan Industry Affiliation Program for Human Factors in Transportation Safety for support of this research. The current members of the Program are: AGC America, Autoliv, Automotive Lighting, Avery Dennison, BMW, DaimlerChrysler, DBM Reflex, Denso, Exatec, Federal-Mogul, Fiat, Ford, GE, Gentex, General Motors, Guardian Industries, Guide Corporation, Hella, Honda, Ichikoh Industries, Koito Manufacturing, Labsphere division of X-Rite, Lang-Mekra North America, LumiLeds, Magna International, Mitsubishi Motors, Nichia America, North American Lighting, OSRAM Sylvania, Pennzoil-Quaker State, Philips Lighting, PPG Industries, Reflexite, Renault, Samlip, Schefenacker International, Solutia Performance Films, Stanley Electric, Toyota Technical Center USA, Valeo, Vidrio Plano, Visteon, 3M Personal Safety Products, and 3M Traffic Control Materials

Information about the Industry Affiliation Program is available at: http://www.umich.edu/~industry/

CONTACT

Kåre Rumar can be contacted at:

rumar@umich.edu

Table 2
The six main questions concerning implementation of NVES, possible alternatives, and suggested answers.

Questions	Alternatives	Suggested Answers
1. **What** kind of information should be presented?	The obstacles and/or the road with markings and/or road signs	Mainly warm objects but with enough road information for contrast
2. To **whom** should the information be presented?	To professional and/or private drivers To younger and/or older drivers	To all drivers (including older drivers)
3. **Which** technology should be used?	Heat sensitive FIR or generally sensitive NIR	Primarily FIR, maybe merged with radar or NIR information
4. **When** should the information be displayed?	Always (full time) or warning when target present or when asked for (part time)	If possible, warning when critical target is present
5. **How** should the information be presented?	As full image or as icons (of obstacle, signs, or road), maybe with a warning	If possible, icons for selected critical targets
6. **Where** should the information be displayed?	In a contact analogue display, in a separate HUD, in a HDD, or just a nonvisual warning	Separate HUD about 5 degrees below driver line of vision (or just the warning)

REFERENCES

1. Augello, D.J. (1993). Description of three PROMETHEUS demonstrators having potential safety effects. In, Proceedings of the 13th International Technical Conference on Experimental Safety Vehicles, Paris, France, November 4-7, 1991 (pp. 209-212).
2. Autoliv (2002). Annual Report 2001. Stockholm, Sweden: Autoliv Inc.
3. Barham, P. (2001). The effect of an infrared driver support system on driver behaviour. In, D. Harris (Ed.), Engineering Psychology and Cognitive Ergonomics: Vol. 5. Aerospace and Transportation Systems (pp. 407-413). Hants, England: Ashgate Publishing Company.
4. Blanco, M., Hankey, J.M., and Dingus, T.A. (2001). Evaluating new technologies to enhance night vision by looking at detection and recognition distances of non-motorists and objects. In, Proceedings of the Human Factors and Ergonomics Society 45th Annual Meeting (pp. 1612-1616).
5. Bossi, L., Ward, N., and Parkes, A. (1994). The effect of simulated vision enhancement systems on driver peripheral target detection and identification. Ergonomics and Design, 4, 192-195.
6. Buttner, C. and Klapper, S. (2002). Far infrared vision. Presented at the Conference on Vehicle and Infrastructure Improvement in Adverse Conditions and Night Driving, Rouen, France.
7. DaimlerChrysler (2000). Improving night vision. In, DaimlerChrysler Internet News, April 5, 2000. Stuttgart, Germany: DaimlerChrysler AG.
8. Flannagan, M.J., Sivak, M., Traube, E.C., and Kojima, S. (2000). Effects of overall low-beam intensity on seeing distance in the presence of glare. Transportation Human Factors, 2 (4), 313-330.
9. Fleury, B. (2002). Near infra red vision. Presented at the Conference on Vehicle and Infrastructure Improvement in Adverse Conditions and Night Driving, Rouen, France.
10. Foyle, D.C., Brinker, M.S., Staveland, L.E., and Sanford, B.D. (1990). Human object recognition as a

function of display parameters using television and infrared imagery. Society for Information Display International Symposium Digest of Technical Papers, 2l, 269-272. Anaheim, California.

11. Färber, B. (1993). Determining information needs of the driver. In A. Parkes and S. Franzen (Eds.), Driving future vehicles. Washington, D.C.: Taylor and Francis.
12. Gish, K.W., Shoulson, M., and Perel, M. (2002). Driver behavior and performance using an infrared night vision enhancement system. Presented at the 81st Annual Meeting of the Transportation Research Board. Washington, D.C.: Transportation Research Board.
13. Hollnagel, E. (2002). Personal communication.
14. Kallberg, V.P. (1993). Reflector posts—Signs of danger? Transportation Research Record, 1403, 57-66.
15. Langwieder, K. (1995) Accident types and risks in night traffic (in German). Proceedings from the First Conference on Progress in Automotive Lighting (PAL). Darmstadt, Germany. 105-113.
16. Lee, P.N.J. and Triggs, T.J. (1976). The effects of driving demand and roadway environment on peripheral visual detection. In, Proceedings of the 8th Australian Road Research Board Conference, 1976.
17. Leibowitz, H.W. and Owens, D.A. (1997). Nighttime driving accidents and selective visual degradation. Science, 197, 422-423.
18. Lunenfeld, H. and Stephens, B. W. (1991). Human factors considerations in the development of an IVHS system: night vision enhancement. In, Institute of Transportation Engineers Sixty-First Annual Meeting, Compendium of Technical Papers (pp. 120-124). Washington, D.C.: Institute of Transportation Engineers.
19. Martinelli, N.S. and Boulanger, S.A. (2000). Cadillac DeVille thermal imaging night vision system. In, Human Factors in 2000: Driving, Lighting, Seating Comfort, and Harmony in Vehicle Systems (#SP-1539). Warrendale, PA: Society of Automotive Engineers.
20. Meitzler, T., Lane, K., Bryk, D., Sohn, E.J., Jusela, D., Ebenstein, S., Smith, G., and Rodin, Y. (2001). Eyetracker analysis of fixation points using an IR HUD in an automobile. International Journal of Vehicle Design (Special Issue), 26 (4), 374-384.
21. Moore, D.W. and Rumar, K. (1999). Historical Development and Current Effectiveness of Rear Lighting Systems (Report No. UMTRI-99-31). Ann Arbor, MI: The University of Michigan Transportation Research Institute.
22. Mortimer, R.G. (1997). Some errors in the application of human factors data in traffic safety: Actual and potential problems. In, Proceedings of the 41st Annual Meeting of the Association for the Advancement of Automotive Medicine (pp. 185-198). Des Plaines, IL: Association for the Advancement of Automotive Medicine.
23. NSC (National Safety Council) (2000). Injury Facts (2000 edition). Itasca, IL: Author.
24. Roper, V.J and Howard, E.A. (1938) Seeing with motor car headlamps. Illuminating Engineering Society, 47, 129-134.
25. Rumar, K. (1998a). Vehicle lighting and the aging population (Report No. UMTRI-98-9). Ann Arbor, MI: The University of Michigan Transportation Research Institute.
26. Rumar, K. (1998b). Some unconventional thoughts on visual enhancement. In, Proceedings of the 16th International Technical Conference on the Enhanced Safety of Vehicles (ESV) (Invited Speakers Executive Panel) (pp. 137-140), May 31 – June 4, 1998. Windsor, Ontario.
27. Rumar, K. (2002) Night vision enhancement systems: What should they do and what more do we need to know? (Report No. UMTRI-2002-12). Ann Arbor, MI: The University of Michigan Transportation Research Institute.
28. Rumar, K. and Marsh, D.K. (1998). Lane markings in night driving: A review of past research and of the present situation (Report No. UMTRI-98-50). Ann Arbor, MI: The University of Michigan Transportation Research Institute.
29. Ståhl, A., Oxley, P., Berntman, M., and Lind, L. (1994). The use of vision enhancements to assist elderly drivers. In, Towards an intelligent transport system, Proceedings of the First World Congress on Applications of Transport Telematics and Intelligent Vehicle-Highway Systems, November 30 – December 3, 1994. Paris, France.
30. Sullivan, J.M. and Flannagan, M.J. (2002). Characteristics of pedestrian risk in darkness (Report No. UMTRI-2001-33). Ann Arbor, MI: The University of Michigan Transportation Research Institute.
31. Tsimhoni, O. and Green, P.S. (2002). Night vision enhancement systems for ground vehicles (report No. UMTRI-2002-5). Ann Arbor, MI: The University of Michigan Transportation Research Institute.
32. Ward, N.J., Stapleton, L., and Parkes, A.M. (1994). Behavioural and cognitive impact of night-time driving with HUD contact analogue infra-red imaging. In, Proceedings of the 14th International Technical Conference on Enhanced Safety of Vehicles (ESV) (pp. 319-324), May 23-26, 1994. Munich, Germany.
33. Weber, T. and Plattfaut, C. (2001). Virtual night drive. In, Proceeding of the Conference on Progress in Automotive Lighting (pp. 1062-1069). Darmstadt, Germany: Darmstadt University of Technology, September 25 – 26, 2001.

2003-01-0123

New Cockpit Human-Machine-Interface Concept

Luc Jansseune
Siemens VDO Automotive

ABSTRACT

More and more features in today's vehicles put increasing demands on the driver's ability to process information, operate functions and simultaneously concentrate on driving. This necessitates simplifying and optimizing the human-machine-interface (HMI).

Therefore, Siemens VDO has developed a cockpit study, "Breeze", showing a new, ergonomic HMI concept in an attractive design.

The number of switches is minimized by implementing a force feedback switch, allowing intuitive operation of several functions via a menu system displayed on a 10 inch monitor. Specific driver functions are operated by mulit-function keys in the steering wheel with a secondary display. The turn indicator is operated by squeezing the steering wheel grips. Vibration elements are activated in dangerous situations to alert the driver. Additional features include flat panel loudspeakers and instrumentation with 3D-effect

Many technical details are presently under development, however, some solutions are already in production.

INTRODUCTION

Onboard functionality is increasing : multi media & telematic applications, driver assisted systems, navigation systems, etc....

At the same time traffic density is increasing.

The future HMI should simplify the operations and avoid as much as possible the driving distraction to enable a safe use of the onboard functions.

If no improved HMI is put in place, legislation will avoid further development from car information systems.[1] See already the bad experiences from the cellular phone usage while driving.

The dialogues should be more and more intelligent and multi modal (different in- and output devices : controls, graphics, speech,...). The interface should adapt to the situation and driver.

Cognitive engineering is becoming a key-competence for the new HMI-concepts. Adaptation of the dialogues in function of the driving situation and user habits is already under development.

COCKPIT HMI

An appropriate HMI should be based on new suitable In-/output technologies and modes.

The development from the technologies and modes is going hand in hand with the development of the HMI itself

In new HMI-concepts, functions are distinguished between direct accessible functions and hidden functions. Direct accessible functions are for example indicators, headlamps, warning lights, volume, temperature, etc. These functions will still get separated operating device. Other functions can be looked up in menu's.

NEW HMI MODES

The following minimum modes are mostly required in modern cars:

Cluster

The cluster is generally at the driver side, but sometimes in the middle. The Speedometer is the real minimum that should stay permanently visible for the driver. All other information's can be re-configurable. Which means that electronic display can replace light signals and needle displays more and more. In the re-configurable part, new information can now appear related to navigation and driver assistant systems.

In addition to the cluster, head up displays (HUD) are increasing the safety and comfort. The HUD is currently limited to high end cars and is only used for simple information such as: speed, navigation arrows or driver assistant warnings.

Steering wheel controls

Minimum functions around the steering wheel are indicator lights, horn, wipers,... Nowadays some Multimedia functions are accessible in a redundant way on or under the steering wheel. Except the classical stalks, new input technologies are introduced. Multi-function keys integrated in the steering wheel allow in a very ergonomic way, without big distraction, to navigate through menu-functions.

Pressure sensors in the steering wheel can be used as input device.

Vibrators in the steering wheel can be used as warning output device.

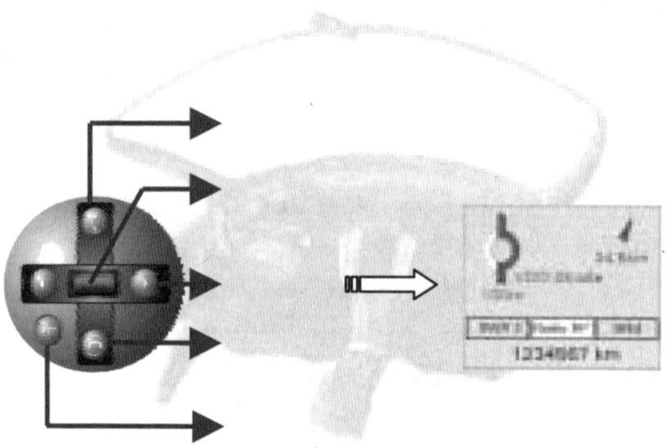

Fig 1: picture integrated multi-function keys

Central input device (CID)°

The CID is mostly used to navigate through menu's displayed on the central display. The position of the CID is in the middle either in the dashboard or close to the armrest.

Today the turn-push button is the most used device and is already in serial production. The version with programmable torque-feedback (haptic feeling) is improving the blind operation. End stops of the menu, different menu grids, favored menu points can be felt in the torque feedback of the knob. The feeling of quick scrolling through long tables (e.g. phone lists), can be given by torque impulses, without really turning the knob.

Other technologies for the CID, such as the touchpad, are under evaluation. The touchpad needs another interaction philosophy. Handwriting, combined with possible speech output, allows a 100% blind input and thus inputs with an improved safety. Comparative user tests are done on a driving simulator between a touchpad and a turn-push configuration. The results were talking for the touchpad. Customer acceptance is still an open issue.

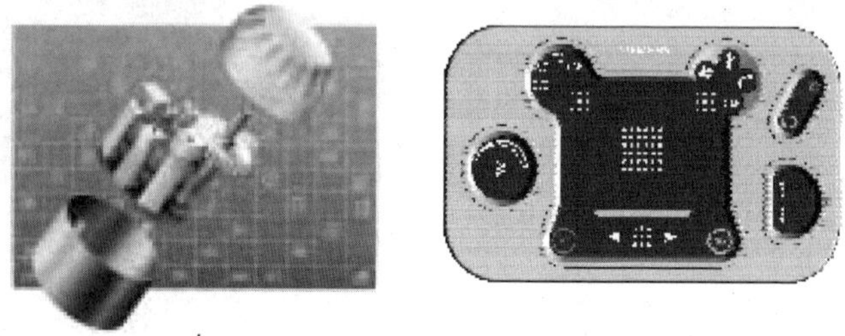

Fig 2 picture left rotary force feedback switch (turn-push); right automotive touchpad

Touch-screens are an alternative solutions, already used in some high end cars. A touch-screen offers very intuitive solution. At one hand, the touch-screen should easily be touchable and thus close to the user. At the other hand, the screen should be in the vision field far away from the eyes to avoid refocusing.

Central display.

The central display is used to display all multimedia functions, telematics, HVAC settings, diagnostics, rearview camera's, car-body and safety settings, etc. Resolution , size and colors are depending on the car-version.

Controls

Complementary to the CID; a minimum of controls for direct accessible functions will remain. E.g. : volume and temperature, warning, etc. Number and configuration depends strongly on OEM. These buttons can be clustered in the middle part of cockpit so that they are also accessible for the passenger.

Speech

Speech in- and output has a big potential for safety and comfort improvement of the HMI. In consequence, speech as HMI-technology will find a larger market penetration. The speech recognizer and also the dialogue are under permanent optimization. Speech is a redundant in/output device. Intelligent dialogue managers , using speech, offer an optimal HMI-concept.

SAFETY THE CHALLENGE FOR HMI

As already mentioned in the introduction safety become a major issue for a good HMI-concept.

According the principle of dual tasking, the driving task is considered as the primary task and all other tasks (e.g. related to multi-media) are secondary tasks. Understanding diagram is assuming a constant driving workload. With increasing secondary task demand, the user can treat the information till he is getting into saturation. At this saturation point the driving performance is decreasing which is becoming dangerous.

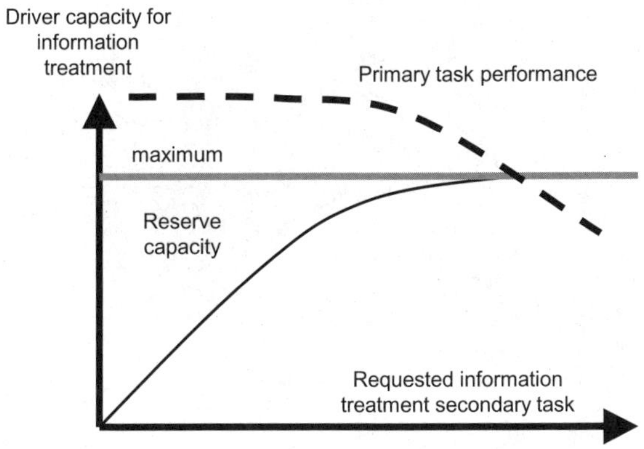

Fig 3 diagram: capacity for information treatment driver versus requested performance secondary task at constant driving workload [2]

With increasing information flow coming from new applications (MM, telematics,...), an intelligent dialog manager has to avoid an overload of the driver. But also a long under-loaded time, leading to driver drowsiness, should be avoided.

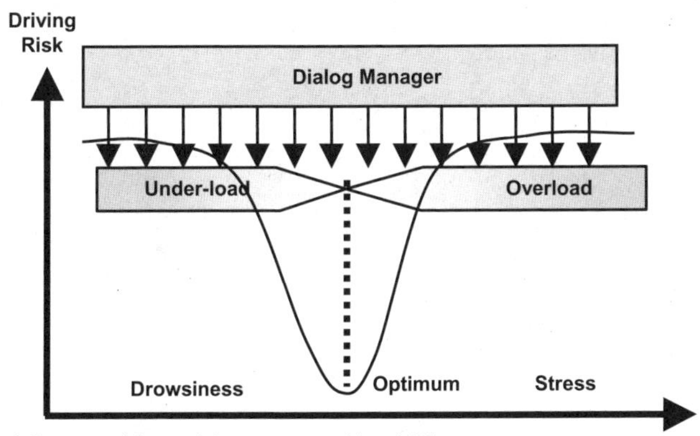

Fig 4 diagram driver risk versus workload [3]

Adaptive behavior can manage the above mentioned problems and will also increase the comfort of the driver.

The main parameters for HMI adaptation are the driving condition estimator (DCE) , driver habit observer (DHO) and intention manager (IM)

The DCE is based on the available car-information (sensors and navigation system) processed in a neuronal network. The output is information about the driving complexity and situation like: city, motorway, rain, approaching curves or cross sections, distance to other cars, traffic, etc. Under difficult driving conditions incoming messages will be reduced and graphical presentations will be simplified to the essential.

The DHO needs a driver identification linked to possible formal stored data. This data will permanently be updated by analyzing the most used menu functions and selections. The menu presentation will be adapted to the user habits so that distraction time while searching will reduce.

Based on situation and possible habits, the IM chooses or prioritizes to most probable menu selection items in the causal network.

THE "BREEZE" COCKPIT STUDY

Fig 5 Picture of the BREEZE model

A new fresh wind in cockpit design. The "BREEZE" cockpit study is illustrating an already big step towards cockpit HMI-simplification and ergonomic improvement without adaptive behavior..

Although "Breeze" offers the driver numerous possibilities up to and including mobile Internet access, the cockpit concept features smooth and clear surface areas that are only interrupted by a main controller and required switch for the hazard lights. The driver can fully concentrate on the road because all main functions are controlled directly from the steering wheel with the innovative new design. This is made possible by two multi-function roller switches that are integrated at thumb-level in the steering wheel., allow the driver to easily navigate through the menus of the on-board system. By manipulating the cylindrical switch with a slight touch to the left or right press buttons, the cursor responds in the corresponding direction.

Siemens VDO designers have added another new feature that is comprised of integrated finger trays hidden at the back of the steering wheel. The driver can activate the indicator lights by applying pressure on these areas corresponding with the left and right hand. Pressure on both finger trays simultaneously activates the hazard lights. Just as the headlights are controlled by a running light assistant, the windshield wipers are activated by a rain sensor and the control elements for interior illumination are moved into the door, rendering the traditional steering arm a relic of the past, in the cockpit of the future.

Two new vibration elements are integrated into the steering wheel, which provide a new dimension of safety by alerting the driver to potentially dangerous driving situations. For example, a subtle vibration in the steering wheel can be activated if the on-board computer registers excessive increase in vehicle speed, insufficient distance between other vehicles on the road, or the vehicle drifting out of its lane.

All other comfort, navigation and entertainment functions of the Siemens VDO cockpit concept can be controlled by a rotating actuator on the center console which, using alternating variable torque-feedback and varying grids, allows for tactile feedback. The system's large, appealing graphics and 10-inch monitor are designed around the driver's needs for intuitive navigation through the menu.

The cockpit concept features new surface speakers that are seamlessly integrated into the cockpit and are invisible to the eye. Instead of large speaker membranes, deep housings and obtrusive decorative grids, this sound system technology only requires small, exciters hidden on the inside of the cockpit. They cause large areas such as air ducts, or the instrument panel to vibrate, converting the cockpit itself into a large-area speaker membrane. This design approach opens tremendous space in the cockpit, allowing designers and mechanical engineers more freedom in cockpit design.

The control elements, which are comprised of a steering wheel with integrated control functions and the controller located in the center column. The instrument display unit is located on the steering column and comprises a speedometer and an adaptive cruise control. The unit features three-dimensional illumination that presents a pearl-colored lighting effect, and provides an interesting contrast to the white illumination of the numbers.

.

CONCLUSION

Many of the technical details of the cockpit concept design study are still in the initial phases of development, however, some solutions are already in production.

The BREEZE shows already the possible HMI simplification and ergonomic improvements.

Considering the adaptive HMI, a lot of process is already achieved and first applications for serial production are excepted around 2008.

Through design studies like the Breeze, Siemens VDO Automotive continues to demonstrate its ability to bring sophisticated design and innovative technology into high-quality standard products

REFERENCES

[1] USA Today, Roland Berger & Partners

[2] Engineering psychology and human perfomance (1984) scott foresman & Co

[3] ATA conference 2001, TRW HMI benchmarking

2002-01-0441

Versatile Human Interface Utilizing the "Windows CE for Automotive" OS for Vehicle Computing Applications

Kenneth A. Schmitt and Raymond P. Ernst, Jr.
Yazaki North America

ABSTRACT

Recent trends in automotive electronics point towards a growing demand for sophisticated electrical & electronic systems in new vehicles. These systems are being implemented into vehicles at an ever-increasing rate and demanding more of the driver & passenger's attention to control and operate them. The incorporation of digital network buses, such as MOST, Media Oriented Systems Transport, builds the digital data infrastructure in the vehicle for some of these systems, while other systems exist in "stand alone" non-network configurations. Consequently, considerable attention must be given to the constraints around the control of each system in such a way that it is natural, intuitive and non-distracting for the driver / passengers, while at the same time is flexible enough to handle the application of additional network devices in a "Plug & Play" fashion. This paper will explore these constraints and discuss some of the approaches that are possible when utilizing the "Windows CE for Automotive" operating system for in-vehicle computing applications.

INTRODUCTION

Vehicle networks, such as MOST, are bringing a number of new devices into the car. These devices provide entertainment, information awareness and driving assistance to the driver and passengers. Along with these devices comes a very large problem, utilizing all these devices without creating a burden for the driver.

Yazaki North America, YNA, is researching and developing a vehicle infotainment network that integrates digital audio/video and can address the concerns of usability of these high tech devices and minimize the driver distraction issues. YNA is solving these issues in its advanced product development department with the use of Microsoft's Windows CE for Automotive.

VEHICLE COMPUTING APPLICATIONS

The car of tomorrow will have many devices in it. The driver and passengers will need to interact with them. These devices may include navigation, hands free cell phones, audio/video entertainment (video cassette players and DVD players), video game systems, and the list goes on. Now with all these devices comes a complex issue with using them while driving. This is where the need for a highly integrated device for controlling and interfacing to these information and entertainment devices.

There are a couple of ways the device control can be handled. The traditional method is switches and knobs. This is somewhat easy to design and relatively low cost. The usability is somewhat difficult for the driver, many buttons and knobs to distinguish from. YNA is solving this problem by developing a multimedia vehicle platform, an in-vehicle computer, to solve these issues. This in-vehicle computer, that has been dubbed MVP – Multimedia Vehicle Platform, can control any device on a MOST network. YNA has developed application software to handle the control of these devices in one central location and provide a user-friendly interface to the operator. This system has been built from the ground up with trying to leverage "off the shelf" software components as much as possible.

THE SOFTWARE SOLUTION

This solution utilizes a common computing platform ruggedized for automotive use along with software to perform the functions of a human machine interface, HMI. The software can be either embedded software or high-level software with the use of an operating system. Our goal here is to leverage "off the shelf" software components to minimize our development. So we started our development with operating system software and high-level development tools.

"What OS is best for this application"? To answer this we need to look at the requirements of this application.

- A graphical user interface
- Multimedia capability
- Open system for 3rd party application development
- Hardware supported
- Device driver availability

- Application Programming Interface, API
- OS Stability
- Are there real time requirements?

For the MVP project at YNA, we selected Microsoft's Windows CE for Automotive, WCEfA. For this project, WCEfA met all our requirements and allowed us to get a system up and running with relative ease. It provides many APIs, has device driver support for almost any type of third party hardware, its an open system based on the Windows programming model and also offers automotive centric APIs to boost the robustness of the OS.

The use of an operating system also brings in the issues of being an open system. By open system we are talking about the ability for the end user to install third party applications. With an open system, there is no guarantee that every application will be rock solid, i.e. it will not crash. WCEfA addresses this with a component called the Critical Process Monitor, CPM. This component acts as a watchdog over applications and monitors their resource usage. If it discovers that it's taking too much CPU time, the CPM has the authority to kill the application and restart it. If the situation is severe enough, it can re-boot the system automatically. It also monitors system resources and notifies all the applications when they are getting low. From this notification, applications can clean up their unused resources and stabilize the operating environment.

Another important factor that we looked at in WCEfA is power management. The typical PDA relies on a backup battery to keep memory alive. Backup batteries of this nature are not acceptable in automotive applications. WCEfA supports a zero current draw shutdown state by flushing memory pages to flash before current loss. Upon revival, the OS restores itself by retrieving the saved information from flash and returning it into the state it was in before the shutdown occurred.

NETWORK CONNECTIVITY

In order for an in-vehicle computer like MVP to control many different entertainment devices in a car, you need to have a common connection between them. YNA is a leader in MOST networking technology. YNA's MVP utilizes a MOST ring to control entertainment devices such as CD/DVD Players, AM/FM Radios, Entertainment Displays, Audio Amplifiers, and many others.

Why MOST? MOST stands for Media Oriented Systems Transport. It is an emerging standard for in-vehicle multimedia data for entertainment. MOST offers a purely digital solution for audio and video data. This information can be streamed to any point in the car with zero EMI interference. The audio/video streams are fully routable to any device or devices. MOST is a tight standard controlled by the MOST Cooperation. The MOST Cooperation is an organization of automotive manufacturers and suppliers working together to achieve a true multimedia network infrastructure standard.

YNA has a four-layer approach to vehicle networking, segregating vehicle network devices into 4 functional areas. The lowest layer is the power distribution network. This layer is the electrical distribution system for the vehicle, handling the main power, the junction block and fusing. All this is interconnected through wiring harnesses. The next layer is the chassis network, which handles the power train, chassis control, steering control, ABS brakes and other critical safety systems. The typical protocol on a chassis network is CAN. The third layer is the body network. This layer is less critical and handles devices like lighting, HVAC, some power features and basic displays. This is a relatively low to medium speed network for control data. Typical protocols used on this layer are J1850, CAN, LIN, etc. The final layer on our network architecture is the information/entertainment network. This is a digital high-speed network. Typical protocols that are used on this type of network are D2B, MOST, and IEEE-1394. Its primary use is for streaming audio/video data for entertainment and other information, such as traffic alerts, brought in by wireless devices. Figure 1 illustrates these four layers and the connectivity between them with gateways.

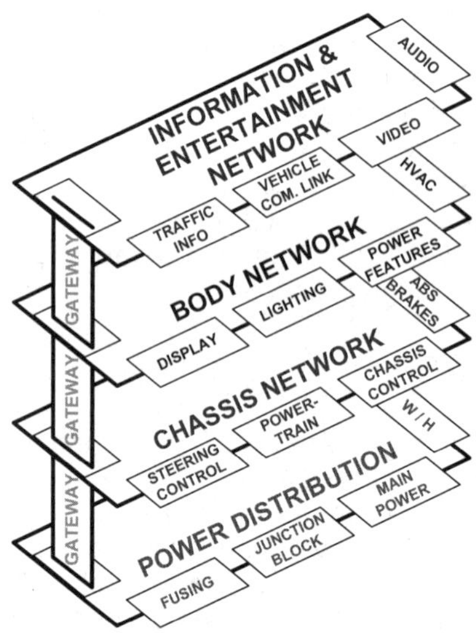

Figure 1

The gateway is a connection point between the network layers to allow communication and control between them. It can also be considered as an information sharing point. The gateway also acts as a firewall between the layers to safeguard the critical systems from any rouge actions. YNA also uses another type of gateway for multimedia applications. This multimedia gateway can be used to connect video game systems, camcorders, or any type of audio/video source into the

MOST network. This type of gateway helps us abstract the automotive constraints from the consumer electronic devices. It allows any consumer device to interact with the entertainment system in the vehicle.

THE INTERFACE

So far we have discussed the needs of an OS for application development and connectivity with devices that need to have an interface to control them. An In-Vehicle computer, such as MVP, can bring this all together into a human machine interface, HMI. In this discussion, we will refer to HMI as an interface that bridges the gap between a human and a machine. It is the operator interface to the devices on our MOST network.

One of the most challenging issues when developing an HMI is designing the user interface in a way that does not distract the driver. What type of things takes a drivers attention away from driving? Small text to read on a small display, cluttered displays with many objects on them, many knobs that are close together, ... In designing our HMI for MVP we have tried to keep these issues in mind and design a methodology that would keep us from rendering such screens. We've replaced many knobs and switches with the use of software type buttons on a touch screen. Now to keep these software type buttons easy and friendly to use, we've made sure that the graphic items representing the buttons are large and the spacing between them is adequate enough. We've also minimized the touch to several areas to reduce confusion and miss-presses. The following figure demonstrates our main interface.

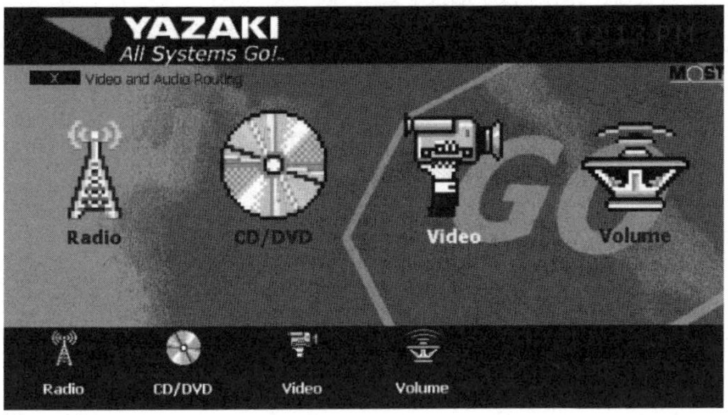

Figure 2

In this particular screen shot, Figure 2, there are 4 touch zones to launch the Radio, CD Player, Video Player and Volume Control applications. Icons are arranged in a horizontal manner and only in one row. This reduces the amount of concentration of finding the area to touch. Figure 3 shows the screen of the radio application. The idea here is limited use of touch points to reduce the amount of time the driver has to focus on touching a screen element.

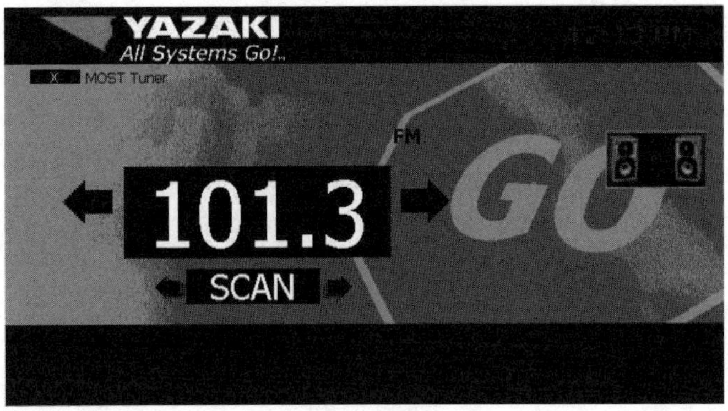

Figure 3

The screen shot in Figure 4 makes use of consumer electronic video devices. These devices are connected to a multimedia gateway and their audio/video is put on to the MOST network. This screen provides the connectivity of the consumer video device to a MOST network display. The user can route the video from any video source on the network to any entertainment display in the vehicle.

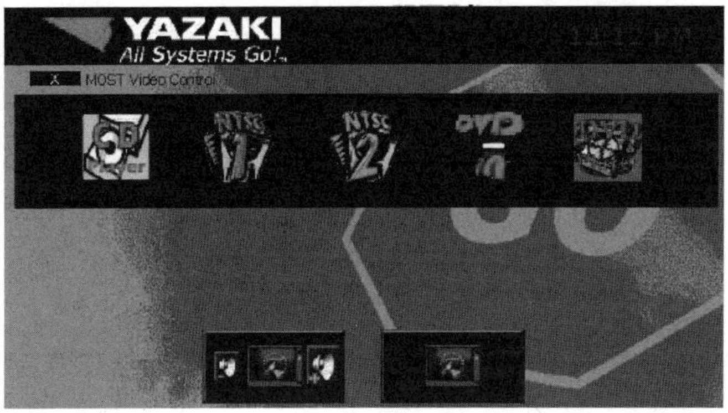

Figure 4

ALTERNATIVE INTERFACES

There are also other solutions to driver distraction. Speech recognition is becoming a popular method for command and control applications. The user speaks a command to the car rather than reaching forward to make an interaction with an HMI element. There are two main speech recognition types, discrete and continuous. In a discrete speech recognition environment, the driver would have to speak a command wait for acceptance notification then speak the next command. This can become tedious and causes the driver to pause between speech commands and listen for an acceptance response. This still requires some driver attention to think and process information to get the task done. Now the continuous speech engines provide more flexibility by allowing the user to speak the commands in a phrase and the speech engine does the work of parsing the commands and performing the operation. The user involvement is only to speak a phrase rather than several commands.

Speech engines are becoming more robust and are adapting to the noisy environment of a vehicle. Work still needs to be done with special microphones to pre-process an audio signal before speech processing can occur. The pre-processing is done by passing the audio signal through a digital signal processor, DSP, to remove noise, perform echo cancellation, beam forming and various other filters.

Another complement to speech recognition is text to speech. This allows an in-vehicle computer to speak information back to the driver rather than having the driver read it. This can be a very effective way of communicating information to the driver without the driver taking their eyes off the road. The text to speech feature can also enhance features of an in-vehicle computer. In today's Internet world, people can get access to information in the form of news, stocks, weather, and any information any time anywhere. The in-vehicle computer can be equipped with wireless communication services to provide this type of content to the driver.

CONCLUSION

The automobiles of today and tomorrow are becoming increasingly complex with the technology push of mobile computing. Yazaki North America is looking at ways to resolve this automotive dilemma by working with companies like Microsoft to develop and effective operating system for automotive use. Microsoft is making strong efforts in bringing a common OS to an automotive space and adapting it to fit its new use. Yazaki North America is designing with Windows CE for Automotive to launch its in-vehicle computing product development.

The use of consumer audio/video electronics and Internet devices in vehicles are driving the need for an infotainment network. The use of these devices and networks are making the long drive productive by entertaining the passengers and informing the driver. They are providing robust connectivity by abstracting the automotive constraints away from the consumer electronics. Microsoft's Windows CE for Automotive has helped us build our in-vehicle computer's human machine interface to help bridge this gap between automotive systems and consumer electronics.

ACKNOWLEDGMENTS

Windows CE for Automotive is a trademark of the Microsoft Corporation.

CONTACT

Kenneth A. Schmitt, Supervisor – Advanced Technologies, Yazaki North America, Canton, MI, kschmitt@yazaki-na.com

Raymond P. Ernst, Jr. – Chief Engineer – Advanced Technologies, Yazaki North America, Canton, MI, rernst@yazaki-na.com.

ADDITIONAL SOURCES

1. MOST – www.mostcooperation.com
2. WCEfA – www.microsoft.com/automotive
3. Yazaki North America – www.yazaki-na.com

DEFINITIONS, ACRONYMS, ABBREVIATIONS

API: Application Program Interface

CAN: Control Area Network

CPM: Critical Process Monitor

CPU: Central Processing Unit

HMI: Human Machine Interface

Infotainment: Information and Entertainment

MOST: Media Oriented Systems Transport

OS: Operating System

PDA: Personal Data Assistant

WCEfA: Microsoft's Windows CE for Automotive

YNA: Yazaki North America

2001-01-0359

Using Cluster Analysis for Deriving Menu Structures for Automotive Mobile Multimedia Applications

Mona L. Toms, Mark A. Cummings-Hill and David G. Curry
Delphi Delco Electronics Systems

Scott M. Cone*
*Veridian Engineering (under contract)

ABSTRACT

This paper describes the cluster analysis technique and how it can be used to support menu interface design for in-vehicle multimedia applications. Cluster analysis and similar types of classifying techniques have proven effective for developing simple menu interfaces. This paper extends the use of the cluster analysis technique to a more complex system that consists of 201 generic functions. These functions are representative of those being incorporated into near-term multimedia products. Study results show promise for using cluster analysis as a tool for incorporating the user's organizational structure into the design of a complex menu architecture. Cluster analysis may also benefit the automotive menu designer by providing a means for partitioning menu tasks into chunkable units that can be easily accessed by the driver in single glances.

INTRODUCTION

Research on automotive user interfaces is investigating effective ways for managing multiple subsystems or applications associated with in-vehicle mobile multimedia systems. It is expected that the content of in-vehicle products will flourish over the next several years as related technologies (e.g., navigation, telematics, on-request entertainment) mature and become more affordable. Since panel real estate is already at a premium, the use of multiple display interfaces is not a viable option. One alternative is a hierarchical menu implemented on an integrated display/control unit such as a multi-function display (MFD). A principal advantage of an MFD implementation is the flexibility it provides in user interface design. By allowing programmable keys to change functions as the information on the display changes, more functions can be implemented within an MFD system without taking up the highly-valued real estate on the vehicle center console.

Designing an effective hierarchical menu system for an automotive application, however, presents some major challenges. Menu designs must be optimized so that the driver can easily accomplish the desired task while controlling the vehicle. If improperly designed, the driver/operator can either become easily confused as to where a particular piece of information or control is located within the menu structure or lost within the intricacies of the menu itself. Another challenge confronting the automotive interface designer is the potential increase in workload resulting from an expansion of the driver's task inventory. Not only does the driver need to continuously control the vehicle while simultaneously monitoring the road and external events, but he or she is now faced with managing a potentially complex information and control interface. In addition, overly complex interfaces can draw the driver's attention "head-down" for extended periods, diverting the driver from attending to external events or stimuli in the environment (e.g., the road or other vehicles on it).

Menu interfaces for automotive environments must promote a rapid search and selection process where the user intuitively knows where to find and activate a specific menu item within the menu structure. In the automobile environment, a "look around and stumble across" search strategy will cost the driver valuable time that is needed for monitoring events outside the vehicle. The time constraints imposed by the driving task and environment must be a major consideration in user interface design. According to the guidelines provided by most states, drivers should maintain a separation of 2.0 seconds between themselves and preceding vehicles. Research has indicated that for safe vehicle operation, vehicle separation distance should be no less than 1.4 seconds. An acceptable limit for single glance duration inside the vehicle is on the order of 1 second or less when traveling on congested roadways and not more than 2 seconds during less demanding travel [1].

Designing an effective interface that is intuitive to the user becomes even more difficult considering that the driving population is highly diverse. Drivers will differ significantly on factors such as age, driving experience, computer familiarity, and understanding of a multimedia system, all which can affect user expectation of system behavior. This problem is exacerbated by the fact that the menus for such systems are often designed by engineers who organize them from the perspective of compatibility with electronic and software subsystem design, rather than in accordance with the end user's understanding of the device's functionality.

MENU INTERFACE DEVELOPMENT ISSUES

Developing menu interfaces for automotive applications involves many of the same issues found in other types of multi-tasking environments (e.g., aircraft cockpits). These issues generally center on requirements for attention to be time-shared so that the driver/operator can easily switch between the task of controlling the vehicle and that of interacting with in-vehicle interfaces. One way this can be accomplished in menu design is providing an intuitive menu architecture that corresponds to operator's expectations and the demands of the environment.

It has been well established that the menu interface is assessed on the basis of how well it maps the cognitive processes of the user when interacting with the menu system. These cognitive processes consist of: searching for information, encoding the meaning of alternatives, assessing the alternatives, making a choice and effecting a response. Together these processes represent the user's mental model for how menu selection works [2]. Within this model, the organizational content of the interface must be congruent to the operator's internal organization of the task domain, closely matching the operator's conceptual relationships between menu items [3].

Empirical evidence has shown that when the user interface is designed to model the operator's conceptual organization, the interface becomes easier to use. Developing an intuitive "I know where to look" menu interface reduces the incidence of driver "head down time" traversing the wrong path trying to find a particular menu item.

PRIOR RESEARCH

Empirical research and guidelines for constructing menu interfaces have addressed many aspects of menu system development. For example, research on screen formatting and syntactical issues (where to place information and what to call it) has shown that human performance improves when menu options are: familiar, consistent, and concise; have highly discriminative options; and use verb phrases. Other studies have investigated issues associated with menu depth (e.g., number of menu layers) versus menu breadth (e.g., number of options per menu page). For example, research by Lee and MacGregor [4] suggested that the preferred number of options per menu panel over a wide range of conditions should be 4 to 8. Papp and Roske-Hofstrand [5]; however, found that grouping options into categories on a menu page can significantly expand this number. In another study, Fisher, Yungkurth, and Moss [6] found that using optimally nested menu hierarchies minimizes the average time for accessing a set of terminal options in deeper menu structures. It is important to note that all of these studies were conducted in a single-task environment, and the applicability to the dual task driving environment is not clear. The optimal breadth and depth issue is largely unexplored territory in dual-task situations.

Research and design guidance on improving operator search strategies within menu hierarchies generally has been very broad in nature, primarily because hierarchical structures are specific to the functional requirements of a particular system. While a guideline might state, "organize menu pages according to the user's model of system tasks," it may not provide specific guidance as to *how* this can be accomplished for a particular system. While various applications may have similar tasks, gray areas exist as to where particular functions should reside within a menu hierarchy.

Research has shown that when cluster analysis techniques are used for structuring command [7] or information retrieval [8] menus, user performance improves. For example, McDonald *et al.* [7] found that users learned menus more quickly when Multi-dimensional scaling and cluster analysis techniques were used to construct a menu of word processing functions. Lewis research [9] also showed improved user performance when the results of a cluster analysis was used to construct a menu interface for 69 oscilloscope functions.

CLUSTERING STRATEGIES

Menu design must also consider the clustering approach of the menu hierarchy. The clustering of functions into categories can occur in either a top-down or bottom-up manner. In a top-down approach, the designer identifies first-order (macro) categories that are repeatedly divided into progressively smaller subcategories until menu items are represented at their lowest level. This approach is conceptually driven in that items are discriminated along categorical boundaries and conceptual dimensions. The top-down approach emphasizes the *differences* between functions rather than their similarities. The greater the designer's system-wide perspective, the greater the likelihood of using top-down clustering. In a bottom-up approach, the designer first identifies all menu items. Similar menu items are then clustered into groups with other conceptually similar items and those groups are repeatedly combined into larger and larger (macro) groups. The bottom-up approach is data-driven, emphasizing *similarities* between items rather than their differences. The greater the knowledge of surface detail and specific options, the higher the likelihood of using a bottom-up clustering approach.

The clustering approach that is selected is often a function of user expertise and perspective. Top-down and bottom-up strategies draw upon different aspects of menu organization, which result in different hierarchical structures. Some research [10] has found that bottom-up methodologies result in larger terminal clusters, more cohesive groups and greater menu depth than do top-down methodologies. Computer programming techniques emphasize a top-down approach to provide a more streamlined structure. However, the perspective of the end user is usually at the level of specific operations and commands, not at higher-level processes. For these reasons, it is important to consider the operator's bottom-up processes when organizing menu items within a hierarchical structure.

TECHNIQUES FOR IDENTIFYING CONCEPTUAL ORGANIZATION

In designing a menu system, it is necessary to develop a taxonomy of tasks defined in terms of the components that the user thinks about in formulating a course of action. Research [11] has found improved performance when menus are designed according to the user's cognitive understanding of the similarity of task elements which can be represented as coordinates in physical space. One technique for identifying the user's conceptual organization is through the use of professional expertise and experience with the system. Disadvantages of this technique are that it is highly subjective and fails to capture the diverse organizational structures that exist within the user population, particularly that of the novice user. Multidimensional scaling and cluster analysis techniques provide a formal approach to identifying the conceptual organization of the typical user and can be helpful in identifying differences across different subsets of users. Both of these approaches are consistent with theoretical models of the mind as an associative network of concepts and assume that the user's mental organization is reflected in the pattern of judged similarity/dissimilarity among items [12].

Multidimensional Scaling

Multidimensional (MDS) scaling is a large family of procedures that can be used to assist the designer in visualizing and understanding data relationships more clearly. The general methodology used in MDS is to obtain subjective estimates of the relatedness of all pairs of menu items. The data are typically gathered by having respondents give simple unidimensional responses (e.g., menu item #1 is more similar to menu item #5 than to menu item #3). Statistical analyses then place menu items as coordinates in a physical space with dimensions that represent psychological factors. These dimensions are assumed to have some semantic meaning that captures the user's cognitive structure of the task. For example, functions may be semantically related because they have similar actions, operate within the same database, and/or are performed sequentially. Menus may then be laid out according to different semantic spaces based upon the psychological distances among the menu items. Semantic clustering methods using multi-dimensional scaling are generally limited to a small set of items since the number of pairwise ratings required in even moderate sets of items can be prohibitive.

Cluster Analysis

Cluster analysis provides a means for empirically classifying items or objects into groups. Because of the limited number of observations that can be used in multi-dimensional scaling programs, cluster analysis can often be more effectively used to generate an initial clustering of observations [13]. The homogenous clusters derived from the cluster analysis can then become a unit for analysis using an MDS procedure.

Hierarchical clustering statistical procedures involve the construction of tree-like structures called dendritic representations. The two major types of hierarchical clustering procedures are agglomerative and divisive. In agglomerative methods, each task item starts out in its own cluster. In subsequent steps, the two closest task items (and possibly a third) are combined into a new aggregate cluster, reducing the number of clusters by at least one. Eventually all individual items are combined into one large cluster. The divisive clustering method proceeds in the opposite direction, starting with one cluster, and then in succeeding steps breaking it apart into separate clusters on the basis of their dissimilarity. Lewis [9] used the Clique Optimization technique for generating hierarchical structures to represent similarity data; however, unlike the well-known hierarchical structuring clustering algorithms, the Clique Optimization technique alternates between the divisive and agglomerative steps rather than using just one or the other.

Clusters identified by the analysis are typically based on two properties: internal cohesion and external isolation [13]. Internal cohesion implies that objects/items within the same cluster are similar to one another. External isolation implies that the objects/items in one cluster are separated from objects/items in another cluster by some form of empty space. The differences among the various algorithms used in cluster analysis are primarily due to the metrics that are used for calculating similarities between objects and for combining objects into clusters. Because each algorithm uses slightly different criteria for forming clusters, the number and type of clusters formed can be different. Two common metrics for measuring object similarity are correlation coefficients and distance measures. Euclidean distance (the square root of the sum of the squared distances over all variables) is perhaps the most common metric used for cluster analysis, although the use of correlation coefficients can provide an excellent alternative metric for further analysis. One of the major drawbacks of the use of the correlation coefficient is its lack of sensitivity to the magnitude of differences between the variables [14]. These may be important when considering menus with disparate functions such as would be the case in the automotive multimedia domain.

Two commonly used methods for combining objects into clusters are the average-linkage-between-groups method and Ward's method. The average-linkage between-groups method combines clusters so that the average distance between all cases in the resulting cluster is as small as possible. Ward's method calculates the means of all variables within each cluster, then calculates the squared Euclidean distance to the cluster mean of each case, and finally sums across all cases. The average linkage method tends to be biased toward the production of clusters with approximately the same variance; whereas Ward's method is biased towards producing clusters that are relatively small and have equal number of objects [13].

METHODOLOGY

The methodology for performing cluster analysis is straightforward in practice and can be performed early in the design process since only functional descriptions (rather than physical products) are required. The following paragraphs detail an expansion of a technique that Delphi has used successfully in the past for developing menu structures [12,15].

PARTICIPANTS

A total of 60 participants, 40 males and 20 females, participated in the study. All participants were Delphi employees, summer interns, or retired employees with ages ranging from 16 to 63 years. The only requirement was that they had no prior experience with developing the functional requirements or user interfaces for in-vehicle communication, navigation, or multimedia systems. No distinction was made between technical or non-technical backgrounds (prior in-house studies did not find any major differences between these two groups).

STIMULI

The stimuli for the analysis consisted of 201 slips of paper (1 1/2 in x 8 in) with a task description written on each slip of paper which the subjects were asked to sort into stacks of related functions. The descriptions consisted of generic tasks that one might perform when using a future in-vehicle communication, navigation, or multimedia system. Careful consideration was given to wording of each task description, so that study participants would base their assessments more on the semantic rather than the syntactic attributes of the task. However, for some tasks, these two attributes were complementary. Subject participants were also instructed to pay close attention to the actions that were described and not simply the words that were used to describe them. They were asked to imagine actually performing the tasks so that task attributes could be more realistically assessed before deciding on their grouping category.

PROCEDURE

Each subject was given a stack of 201 slips of paper (randomly ordered). Each slip of paper had a generic task description on it of a possible menu item of an automotive system. Subjects were instructed to sort task items into stacks of similar items based on their own criteria for similarity. They could make as many separate stacks as they cared to, as long as each stack contained at least two task items. After sorting, they were instructed to go back, review their work, and move tasks from one stack to another if upon further reflection they decided that the task description would fit better in a different stack. This was designed to accommodate any changes the user might have in sorting strategies over the course of the study. If a stack contained a large number of task items (relative to other stacks), they were also asked to assess whether that stack could possibly be better subdivided into smaller stacks. However, if they thought the stack could not be further subdivided, then the stack in question remained intact. Upon completion of the sorting task, subjects were instructed to staple the items together within each stack and write a short description on the top slip of paper explaining their reasons for grouping those tasks together. The table below illustrates an example of task descriptions that were used in the procedure.

Table 1. Sample Task Descriptions

1. Access weather information for a particular location.
2. Add to a voice memo.
3. Display turn-by-turn route guidance.
4. Select a radio station by its programming type.
5. Adjust the relative sound between the right and left sides of the car.

ANALYSIS

The data preparation process for submitting to the SPSS cluster analysis statistical package involved developing a matrix for each subject that contained all unique combinations of task item pairs, a total of 20,100 cells. Duplicate combinations (e.g., task items 1,3 and 3,1) and same task items (e.g. 3,3 combinations) were not considered. Each cell within each individual matrix was then coded "1" if the two items had been sorted into the same stack or "0" if not. Individual matrix cell values were then summed across subjects to produce a group matrix. For example, if five subjects grouped task item #1 and task item #3 into the same group, then the value of "5" was placed in the group matrix cell at the intersection of task item #1 and task item #3. This group matrix was then submitted to the SPSS cluster analysis procedure.

The agglomerative clustering procedure in SPSS was chosen as the clustering method to use in this procedure because it was most representative of the sorting task based on item similarity (performed by study participants). It is also representative of the bottom-up strategy commonly used by the end user when accessing a specific menu item. The method of average linkage between groups was chosen as the method for determining cluster groups, since it provides the least amount of variance within each cluster and is not prone to the creation of smaller, same-size clusters that are more characteristic of the Ward method. It is important that the user's conception of task categories is modeled without imposing any constraints from the clustering algorithm itself.

The major outputs of the hierarchical cluster analysis in SPSS are: an agglomeration schedule, proximity matrix, and cluster membership. The agglomeration schedule displays the cases or clusters combined at each stage, the distances between the cases or clusters being combined, and the last cluster level at which a case (or variable) is joined the cluster level. The proximity matrix gives the distances or similarities between items. Cluster membership displays the cluster to which each case is assigned at one or more stages in the combination. Cluster membership also allows for a single solution or a range of cluster solutions to be shown in the statistic output.

Fusion coefficients, produced in the agglomeration schedule, provide an index of the relative distance of items being joined at each stage of the clustering process. Because larger fusion coefficients indicate more distance (less similarity) between task items, a large jump in the magnitude of fusion coefficients (a knee in the curve) indicates an optimal number of clusters. Fusion coefficients can also be plotted against the number of clusters. A marked flattening of the graph indicates that little information is being used to form clusters [11]. Figure 1 illustrates this effect, which shows the optimal number of clusters for this data set to be 18-20. A review of the clusters membership would reveal the contents of each of these clusters.

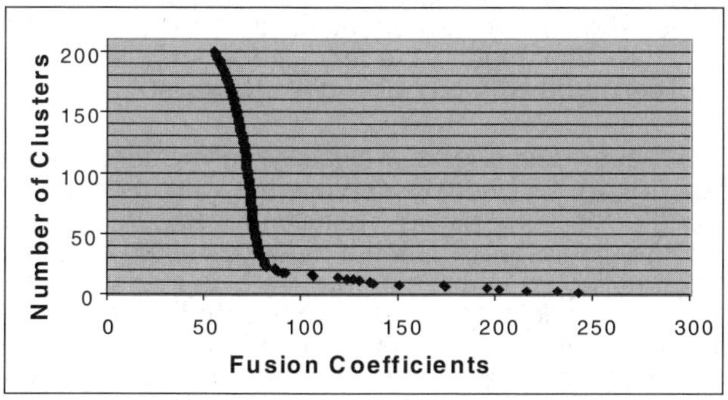

Figure 1. Fusion coefficients for 1 to 200 solutions

Another important output of the SPSS cluster analysis program are the dendrograms (or tree graphs) which graphically depict how clusters are formed during the build-up process. Figure 2 illustrates a portion of the dendrogram output for 201 tasks, and shows a nine (A1-9), a four (B1-4), and a three cluster (C1-3) solution.

APPLICATION TO HMI DESIGN

The outputs of the cluster analysis can provide the framework for constructing an intuitive hierarchical menu system. The fusion coefficient graph provides an excellent starting point for identifying the main items for system applications. As shown in Figure 1, the optimal number of clusters is 18-20 (curve flattens), suggesting that the subjects view the multimedia system as having 18-20 distinct applications. Ideally this would indicate 18-20 dedicated buttons so that each application could be directly accessed. However, the limited real estate of an in-vehicle display/control unit would generally prohibit putting all, but the primary (important and frequently used) applications, on a dedicated controls for direct user access. The other secondary applications

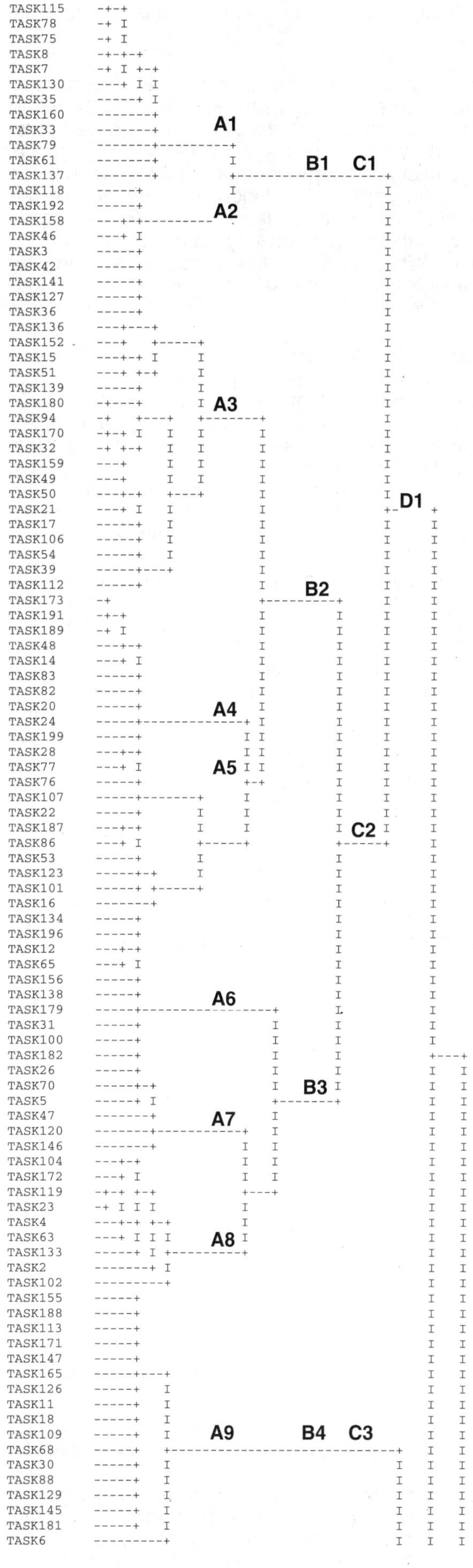

Figure 2. Partial Dendrogram for 201Task Sort

could then be grouped as menu options on a main menu.

Identifying an appropriate menu label is as important to the automotive menu design as matching its contents to the user's organizational structure since the driver must quickly decide whether or not a desired menu item fits within a particular category. Menu labels should be descriptive and capture the functional attributes of the category contents. If a label can not be easily determined, subject rationales for grouping should be examined. While tedious, this process can provide valuable insights into subjects' clustering strategies and grouping conventions.

Two other useful outputs cluster analysis are cluster memberships and dendrograms. Cluster membership identifies the functions that are grouped together within each cluster. Dendrograms illustrate these clusters graphically in a hierarchical tree structure that depicts varying levels of cluster solutions. From these outputs, the human factors interface designer can make decisions on the most practical cluster grouping to implement from a hardware and menu architecture perspective. For example, if the hardware real estate allows for no more than eight dedicated buttons; then in the SPSS program, the cluster membership can be set to be eight or a range of solutions that encompasses eight. Upon review of the dendrogram and cluster membership outputs, the designer can then determine if the eight cluster solution provides a good breakout of functions. If not, other cluster solutions within the dendrogram tree structure will need to be examined. Figure 2 shows three possible cluster solutions that may be employed: (1) A1-9, (2) B1-4, and (3) C1-3.

The dendrogram is especially useful for guiding the development of a menu hierarchy of functions and subfunctions. (On an MFD, these functions/subfunctions could then be accessed with reconfigurable keys that change function according to the application.) The dendrogram tree structure provides the interface designer with a model for representing information in smaller discrete task units, that chunks information in a logical units as viewed by the user. Figure 3 illustrates the A3 cluster depicted in Figure 2.

```
TASK136   ---+---+
TASK152   ---+   +----A3.1
TASK15    ---+-+ I
TASK51    ---+ +-+         I
TASK139   -----+           I
TASK180   -+---+           I
TASK94    -+   +--A3.2.1.-------+ A3
TASK170   -+-+ I   I       I
TASK32    -+ +-+   I       I
TASK159   ---+     I       I
TASK49    ---+     I       I
TASK50    ---+-+   +--A3.2
TASK21    ---+ I   I
TASK17    -----+   I
TASK106   -----+   I
TASK54    -----+   I
TASK39    -----+--
TASK112   -----+  A3.2.2
```

Figure 3. Partial Dendrogram depicted in Figure 2

As shown, the A3 cluster can be delineated into A3.1 and A3.2 subclusters. Within the A3.2 cluster, smaller clusters can be delineated: A3.2.1 and A3.2.2. These two smaller cluster units can then be displayed as discrete task units (assuming that it does not violate other menu criteria). If the screen is large enough, this may be accomplished with a screen layout that separates 3.2.1 tasks into two discrete units (tasks 159, 49) and (tasks 139, 180, 94, 170, 32), using such grouping techniques as color coding or spacing. The same delineation scheme can also be used if display screen is limited with such user-controlled pacing techniques as paging or creating a submenu layer.

By displaying tasks as logical units, the menu architecture can efficiently step the driver through the interface and support an optimum chunking strategy that accommodates driver glance times. If the menu architecture does not support chunkable units, the driver may interact with the interface using an inefficient chunking strategy that results in longer or more frequent glances inside the vehicle.

CONCLUSION

A vehicle menu system must promote quick and intuitive searches when the driver/operator is navigating the menu hierarchy so that he or she is more focused on controlling the vehicle than on managing a complex interface. Grouping menu items in a hierarchical menu structure to promote an effective search so that the task matches user expectation is difficult. For example, the designer must address: conflicting classifications, overlapping categories, extraneous menu items, and unfamiliar technical jargon. In addition, each person will most likely have a slightly different model for how menu items should be represented, thus a perfect menu structure that matches every user's knowledge of the application domain probably does not exist.

This paper describes the cluster analysis technique and how it can be used to capture the driver's conceptual model for organizing functions of an in-vehicle multimedia system. Such a model can then be used for constructing an intuitive menu interface that supports the driver's expectation as to where to find a particular function without "roaming" the interface. By assisting designers in structuring the cognitive content of an interface, the cluster technique facilitates the menu selection process, supports a variety of search styles, matches the task to be performed by the user, as well as, capitalizes on the user's prior experience with similar types of systems. It can also support displaying tasks as chunkable units that accommodate driver glance time inside the vehicle. The cluster analysis technique can accommodate a wide range of functional and hardware requirements for similar types of in-vehicle systems.

The cluster analysis technique, however, is not a cookbook nor a panacea for effective menu interface design. The results of the cluster analysis technique must be applied prudently, as there are many aspects that must be considered in constructing a menu system, such as function priorities, syntax, and format. In fact, one of the disadvantages with using cluster analysis for the creation of menu categories is that it does not provide a mechanism for accommodating overlapping clusters. Also this extended use of the cluster analysis technique should be validated to quantify its usefulness in the design of complex menu architectures. We are currently investigating other techniques such as those that may be used to identify those areas where certain menu items can fall in either two or more clusters, indicating areas in the menu hierarchy where redundancy may be of benefit to the user.

CONTACT

Mona L. Toms
mona.l.toms@delphiauto.com

REFERENCES

1. Dingus, T., Antin, J., Hulse, M, and Wierwille,W. (1989). Attentional demand requirements of an automobile moving-map navigational system, *Transportation Research, A23(4),* 301-315.
2. Norman, K., (1991). *The Psychology of Menu Selection.* Norwood, New Jersey, Ablex Publishing Corporation.
3. Wickens, C.D., (1984). *Engineering Psychology and Human Performance,* Columbus, Ohio, Charles E. Merrill Publishing Company.
4. Lee, E. and MacGregor, J., (1985), Minimizing user search time in menu retrieval systems, *Human Factors, 27,* 157-162.
5. Roske-Hofstran, R.J. & Papp, K.R., (1986). Cognitive networks as a guide to menu organization: An application in the automated cockpit, *Ergonomics,* 29, 1301-1311.
6. Fisher, Yungkurth and Moss, (1990). Optimal menu hierarchy design: syntax and semantics, *Human Factors, 32 (6), 665-683.*
7. McDonald, J.A., Stone, J.D., Liebelt, L.S., and Karat, J. (1982). *Evaluation of methods for structuring the user system Interface, Proceedings of the Human Factors Society 41th Annual Meeting,* 551-554
8. Hollands, J.G. & Merike, PM. (1987). Menu organization and user expertise in information search tasks, *Human Factors, 29,* 577 -586.
9. Lewis, S. (1991). Cluster analysis as a technique to guide interface design, *International Journal of Man-Machine Studies, 35*, 251-265.
10. Chin, J.P., (1987). Top-down and bottom-up menu design. *Proceedings of the Second International Symposium on Human-Computer Interaction*, 144-147.
11. McDonald, J.E., Dayton, T., & McDonald, D.R., (1988). Adapting menu layout to tasks, *International Journal of Man-Machine Studies, 28*, 417-435.
12. Kleiss, J., (1997). Identifying user's conceptual organization of menu functions in an automotive electronic navigation product., *Proceedings of the Human Factors Society 41th Annual Meeting,* 944-948.
13. Hair, J.F., Anderson, R.E., Tatham, R.L. (1987). *Multivariate Data Analysis.,* New York, New York, MacMillian Publishing Company.
14. Alderferer, M.S. and Blashfield, R.K. (1986). *Cluster Analysis.* Beverly Hills, CA., Sage Publications, Inc.
15. Kleiss, J. and Witt, G. (2000). Identifying Control Groupings and Menu Structures for Advance Automotive Systems Using Psychological Clustering and Scaling Techniques. *Human Factors in 2000: Driving, Lighting, Seating Comfort, and Harmony in Vehicle Systems,* SP-1539, 1-9.

2001-01-0356

Evaluation Method for Verbal Interface While Driving from the Viewpoint of Safety

Shin-ichi Kojima, Yuji Uchiyama, Hiroyuki Hoshino and Takero Hongo
Toyota Central R&D Labs., Inc.

ABSTRACT

This study proposes an evaluation method for a verbal interface while driving. In this method, the reaction time is measured and the rate of the delayed reaction time trial is used as an index. We have designed a new reaction time test procedure that contains stimulus, perception, attention, choice and response. Based on results of an actual vehicle experiment, we indicate that our method has better examination capability than using the average reaction time as an index and that we can find the time that tends to delay the reaction during a verbal task by processing the delayed reaction time trial.

INTRODUCTION

Recently, information systems such as a navigation system are increasing in a vehicle, and a verbal interface has been used gradually. To evaluate such a voice operation or voice dialog, subjective usability or the total time of operation were used as an index. However, the index of an effect on driving is necessary from the viewpoint of safety, so we have developed the evaluation method using such an index.

As studies that relate to the effect of verbal interface on driving, there were many studies about the effects of a mobile telephone on driving behavior. They reported an increase in the variation of lateral position on a road [1], an increase in the reaction time to the preceding vehicle's brake lamp, an increase in the rate of reaction time trial more than 1 second [2], and so on. We consider that the variation of lateral position on a road isn't suitable as an index of the effect of verbal interface while driving, because we can drive with both arms at the time of using a verbal interface unlike a mobile telephone. The increase in the reaction time was reported frequently, but there was a report that the effect of voice dialog wasn't statistically significant [3][4], therefore, it isn't clear whether it can be used as an index.

In this paper, we propose a new evaluation method of measuring the delayed reaction time for a verbal interface while driving, and show the validity of the method based on the results of an actual vehicle experiment.

EVALUATION METHOD

The outline of the evaluation method is as follows.

1. Reaction time to the LED lighting installed in a vehicle is measured.
2. Reaction time is measured many times, and the rate of the delayed reaction time trial is used as an index.
3. The time that tends to delay the reaction during voice dialog is found by processing the delayed reaction time trial.

The detailed description is as follows.

We have adopted the reaction time because car accidents by the forward carelessness have recently increased. In the recent studies, the reaction time task was that subjects responded as early as possible to the lighting of the inner lamp or the brake lamp of the preceding vehicle. This measuring method contained stimulus, perception and response. However, during the actual driving scene, if drivers perceived something on the road, they attend to what they perceived, and choose what to do. Therefore, we have designed a new measuring method by adding the processes of perception, attention and choice. In this method, the reaction time to the LED lighting installed in a vehicle is measured. Figure 1 shows the position of LED's and a switch. LED's are installed in a position of the peripheral visual field of a driver. An upper LED and a lower LED are close, so a driver cannot choose which LED was turned on if he doesn't turn his eyes on the LED. Pairs of LED's are installed right and left not to concentrate driver's attention on the specific pair of LED's. The reaction time task is as follows. One of four LED's is turned on at a time, then the subject answers which LED was turned on by the up-down switch. Stimulus is the LED light. Perception is to perceive the LED turned on. Attention is to turn his eyes to the LED. Choice is to choose the lit LED. Response is to push the up-down switch.

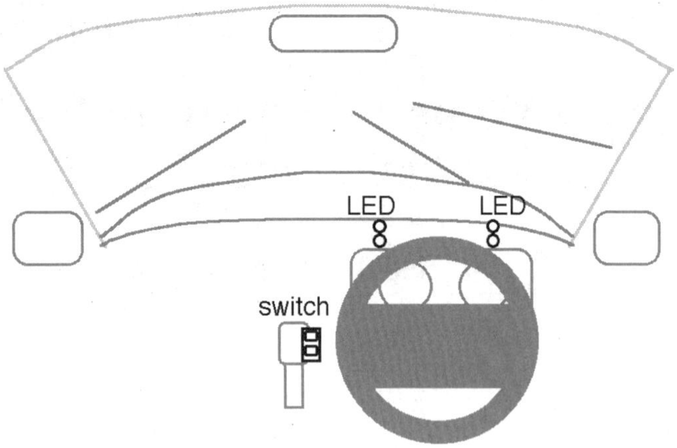

Fig.1 Position of LED and switch

Figure 2 shows the reaction time histogram that measured while driving. The left curve is the distribution of the normal reaction time, and it is usually a normal distribution. On the other hand, the right distribution is the delayed reaction time in some reason, and the type of distribution is unknown. When a verbal interface was used while driving, we found that the delayed reaction increased more than the case that it wasn't used. Therefore, we have considered that the rate of the delayed reaction trial can be used as an index.

In the following, we describe how to calculate the threshold of the delayed reaction time. A fixed value like 1 second cannot be adopted as the threshold of the delayed reaction time, because the distribution of the normal reaction time is altered with a person. Also, "an average + 3SD" of the reaction time cannot be adopted as the threshold, because the deviation from the normal distribution is large. We measure the reaction time under the condition when the vehicle is stopping, and adopt "an average + 3SD under the stopping condition" of the reaction time as the threshold of the delayed reaction time. We have confirmed separately this threshold calculating method give a good result.

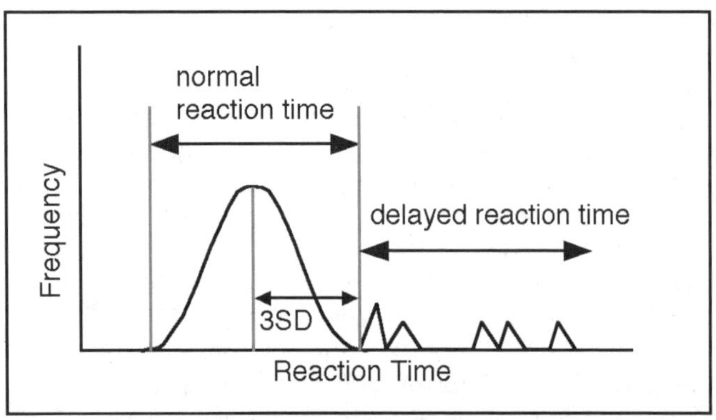

Fig.2 Reaction time histogram while driving

If there are the delayed reaction time trials caused by the effect of the voice dialog, we can find the time that tends to delay the reaction during the voice dialog by processing the delayed reaction time trial.

The horizontal axis of Figure 3 is the time during a verbal task, and the line segment of the delayed reaction time can be drawn like this figure. After drawing all the line segment of the delayed reaction time, a histogram of an appropriate interval can be plotted. The time for a peak in this histogram is the time where the most of the delayed reaction time trials are there. In other words, the reaction during a verbal task tends to be delayed in that time.

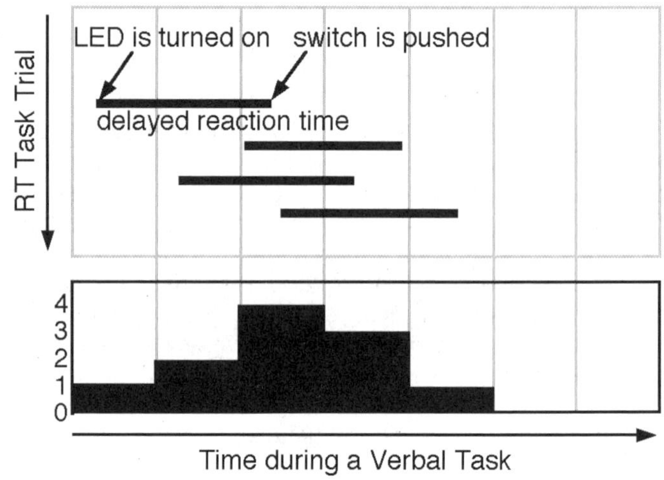

Fig.3 How to process the delayed reaction time trial

We experimented with an actual vehicle to verify the validity of this method.

EXPERIMENT

SUBJECTS – Four male subjects of the thirties participated in this experiment. Two subjects were experienced persons of the verbal task that is explained later, and they had been fully accustomed to the task. The rest had not experienced the verbal task, so they practiced three sets of each condition in advance.

APPARATUS – The experiment was done using an actual vehicle. LED's and a switch for a reaction time task were installed. (Fig.1) Pairs of LED were installed on the dashboard at a distance of 25cm from right to left, and up-down switch was installed near the gearshift. The program in the personal computer controlled the reaction time task and verbal task, and it recorded the time when LED was turned on and the time when switch was pushed. The front scene was recorded in VTR. The subject's eye movements were monitored by a non-contact eye-tracking system and they were overwritten on VTR.

DRIVING COURSE – The driving course was the general path of the inside of our company. The speed limit was 25 km/h, and the time to drive one lap was approximately 8 minutes. There were few other cars, and there were four slow curves and twelve right or left turns.

REACTION TIME TASK – One of four LED's was turned on at a time, then the subject answered by the up-down switch which LED was turned on. The lighting interval of the LED was 6 seconds, and the LED was turned off when a subject pushed the switch. If a subject didn't push the switch, the LED was turned off 2 seconds after turning on.

VERBAL TASKS – The verbal task was simulated by the memory task of listening to words and answering orally. Two memory tasks called the delayed digit recall (DDR) and the free recall (FR) were used to show that this evaluation method could be applied to various tasks. Figure 4 shows the time chart of the delayed digit recall. An experimenter read aloud a one-digit number at a fixed interval, and the subject listened to the number and answered the number that was previously stated. In this experiment, the speech synthesis software in the personal computer read the number, and the reading interval was 2.3 seconds.

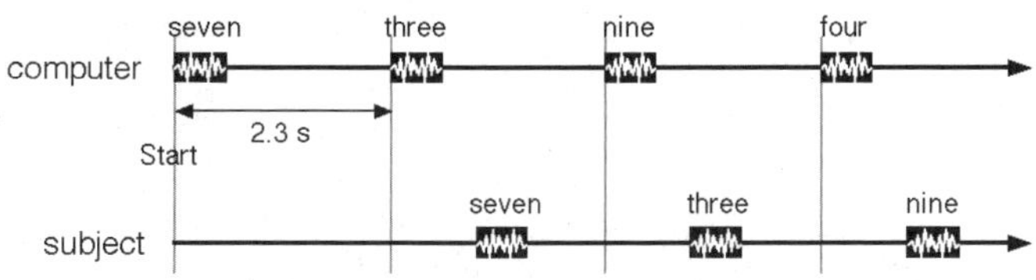

Fig.4 Time chart of delayed digit recall

Figure 5 shows the time chart of the free recall. An experimenter read aloud five nouns at a fixed interval, and the subject repeated them one by one at every beep sound after listening to five nouns. A subject was permitted to answer in the different orders from the heard order. Same as DDR, the speech synthesis software in the personal computer read the nouns. The reading interval was 1.6 seconds and the interval of beep sound was 2.2 seconds.

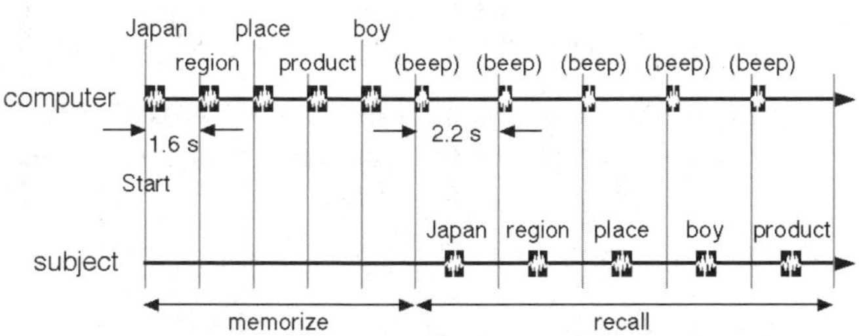

Fig.5 Time chart of free recall

CONDITION – The experimental condition was the following.

1. Stop and do a reaction time task. [stop]
2. Drive and do a reaction time task. [no verbal task]
3. Drive and do a reaction time task and do a verbal task (FR) [FR]
4. Drive and do a reaction time task and do a verbal task (DDR) [DDR]

The [stop] condition time was 4 minutes, and the other conditions were approximately 8 minutes. The day and order were changed, and each condition was done eight times.

DATA PROCESSING – First, the reaction time data that was mistaken was removed, and then the delayed reaction time data was sorted using the VTR according to the cause of the delayed reaction time. Only the delayed reaction time data that was caused by the verbal task was processed.

RESULTS

Figure 6 shows an example of the reaction time histogram of a [no verbal task] condition and an [FR] condition of a certain subject. There is a threshold near 1000ms. The left part of the distribution is the normal reaction time, and the right part is the delayed reaction time. By adding the verbal task, the peak of normal reaction time shifted rightward and the number of the delayed reaction time trial increased. This means that the average reaction time and the rate of the delayed reaction time trial increased by adding the verbal task.

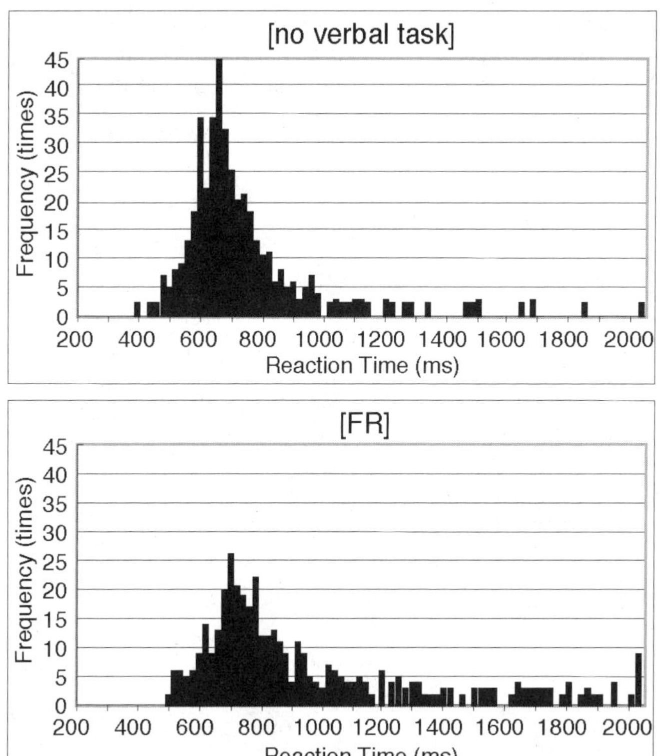

Fig.6 Comparison of reaction time histogram

Figure 7 shows a graph for the rate of the delayed reaction time trial of all the subjects. (Average and standard deviation) It shows that the rate of the delayed reaction time trial increased due to the verbal task. The difference between the [no verbal task] condition and the [FR] condition was statistically significant. ($p<0.05$) And the differences between the [no verbal task] condition and the [DDR] condition were statistically significant, too. ($p<0.05$)

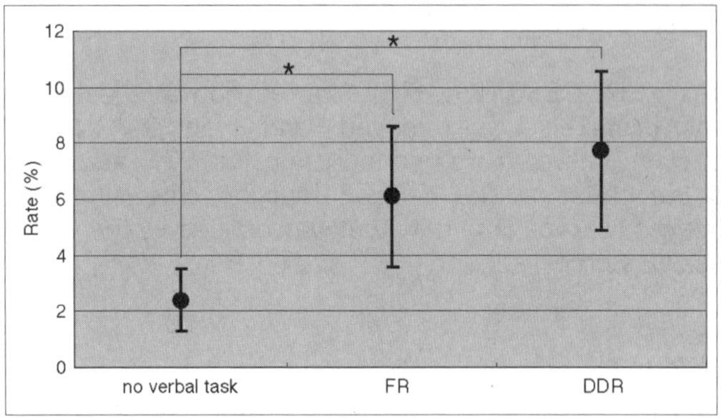

Fig. 7 Rate of delayed reaction time trial (N=4) *:$p<0.05$

Figure 8 shows a graph for the average reaction time of all the subjects. It shows that the average of reaction time increased due to the verbal task. However, the difference between the conditions was not statistically significant.

From the above results, we found out that the examination capability of the method using the rate of the delayed reaction time trial as an index was better than the method using the average reaction time.

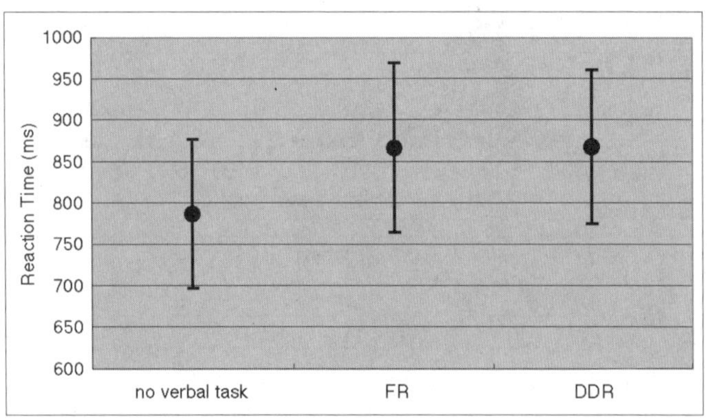

Fig.8 Average of reaction time (N=4)

The following is the processed result of the delayed reaction time trial of the DDR and the FR.

Figure 9 shows an example of the processed result of the FR of a certain subject. The reading time by the personal computer is shown by the vertical dotted line. The first 8 seconds is a period of memorizing, and the rest is a period of recalling. This subject tended to delay the reaction in the recalling time. As for this, the other subjects were the same.

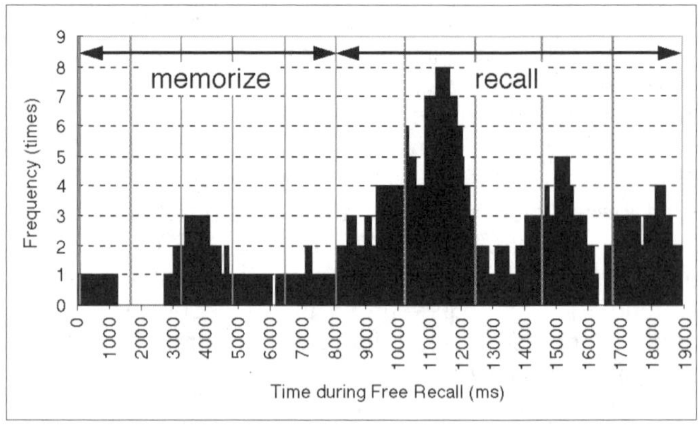

Fig.9 The time that tends to delay the reaction during a free recall

Figure 10 shows an example of the processed result of the DDR of a certain subject. To know the time when the subject answered, the voice data were overwritten. The first part of the voice data is computer's number reading, and the second part is subject's answering. There was a peak at the answering or slightly before the answering. That was the time when this subject tended to delay the reaction.

It was reported that the mental load is greater while talking than while hearing [5]. This result provided proof for the validity of our method.

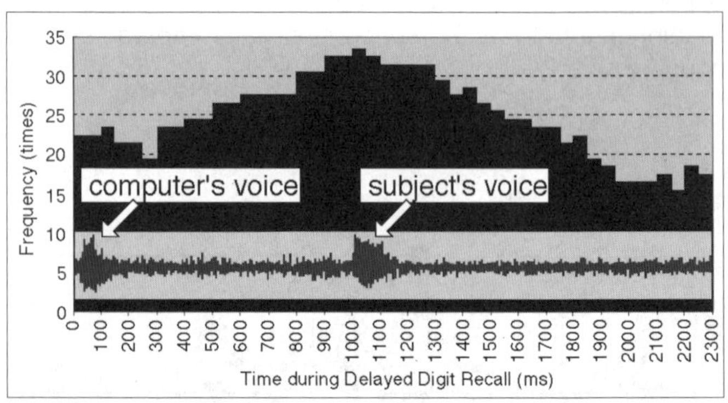

Fig.10 The time that tends to delay the reaction during a delayed digit recall

CONCLUSION

We have developed a new evaluation method for verbal interface while driving from the viewpoint of safety. This evaluation method includes the following characteristics.

- The reaction time task has been designed that contains the processes of stimulus, perception, attention, choice and response.
- An evaluation index is the rate of the delayed reaction time trial, and the examination capability of this method using this index is better than the method using the index of the average reaction time.
- The time that tends to delay the reaction time during a verbal task can be found by processing the delayed reaction time trial.

REFERENCES

1. Stein, A. C. et al., A simulator study of the safety implications of cellular mobile phone use. 31st Annual Proceedings American Association for Automotive Medicine, pp.181-200. 1991.
2. Investigation research about the effect which portable telephone exerts on driving behavior. Japan Safe Driving Center.
3. Brookhuis, K. A. et al., The effects of mobile telephoning on driving performance. Accid. Anal. & Prev. Vol23, No.4, pp.309- 316. 1991.
4. The research of the problem that relates to the portable telephone use and operation while driving vehicle. Roberto A. Tokunaga et al. JSAE, 976. pp.195-198. 1997-10.
5. Kahneman, D. et al., Perceptual deficit during a mental task. Science. Vol.157, pp.218-219. 1967.

CONTACT

skojima@mosk.tytlabs.co.jp

2001-01-0054

Amount of Information Acquired by Reading Display Information Repeatedly

Kazumoto Morita and Ichiro Sakamoto
Traffic Safety and Nuisance Research Institute

ABSTRACT

When a driver views the display device, there are two ways to read the information displayed: repeatedly diverting his attention to the display device for short periods of time or reading the information through, all at one time. The authors investigated differences in the amount of information retained for both of these reading methods by carrying out experiments indoors. This experiment showed that even when the amount of time that the subject was actually viewing the display was the same, the amount of data acquired by the subject from reading the display repeatedly was greater than the amount of information acquired by reading the display through at one time.

INTRODUCTION

The use of car navigation systems that provide route guidance has increased dramatically in recent years. Although these navigation systems make driving more convenient, there is also a concern because drivers take their eyes off the road in order to read the display indications [1]. Thus, the less time drivers spend looking at the devices the safer the driving is. According to a study by the authors regarding eye fixation on navigation systems while driving on city streets, drivers look at them for an average of about 1 second, including the transition time involved in redirecting their line of sight between the road and the navigation device [2]. The conclusion is that drivers can take their eyes off the road to look at the device for this short period without any sense of anxiety. However, since the information displayed can not normally be read in the short time of 1 second, drivers look repeatedly at the monitor. The question then arises as to whether there is a difference in the amount of information acquired when looking at the device repeatedly for a short time or continuously for a longer time. For example, is there a difference in the amount of information acquired when looking twice for only 1 second or once for 2 seconds?

The current study presents the results of a laboratory experiment conducted to clarify this question. Also, to investigate the effects of age, young and elderly groups of subjects were used in the study.

EXPERIMENTAL METHODS

EXPERIMENT OUTLINE - The experiment was conducted under fluorescent ceiling lights in a room cut off from outside light. The position of the head was fixed by having subjects place their chins on a chin rest (height 1.00 m), and they gazed at a personal computer monitor set up in front of them (Figure 1). The distance between the subjects' eyes and the display monitor was 0.75 m.

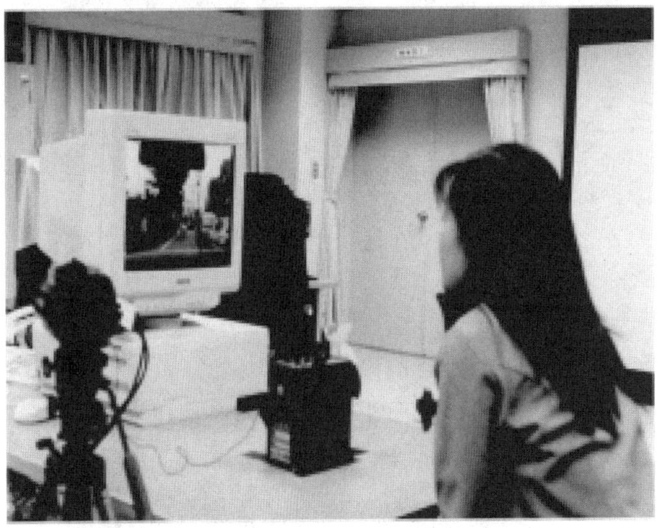

Fig.1 An observer watching PC display screen

During the experiment, the subjects were instructed to read groups of place names displayed on the monitor as quickly and accurately as possible. After the display was finished, subjects were to respond orally with the place names they had read. The number of place names that subjects could recite at this time was investigated.

DISPLAY METHODS - The information displayed was groups of 10 place names. One hundred place names were selected from Tokyo, Japan and the surrounding region. Using these 100 place names, 69 place name groups consisting of 10 names each were prepared in advance. In addition, 11 place name groups were prepared for a practice experiment. Each place name group contained 7 names written with 2 Japanese characters and 3 names written with 3 Japanese characters. Figure 2 shows a sample of the name groups displayed. Here, each place name was positioned on the screen with general consideration of its actual geographical relationship to the other place names. However, since a limited number of names was selected, the precise positional relation could not be reproduced.

Fig.2 A sample of place name groups

Fig.3 A sample of road traffic conditions displayed during display intervals

The following experimental conditions for the display time were used:

(1) Continuous display.
(2) Repeated display for 0.5 seconds with one-second intervals.
(3) Repeated display for 0.5 seconds with two-second intervals.
(4) Repeated display for one second with one-second intervals.
(5) Repeated display for one second with two-second intervals.

Here the 1- or 2-second intervals were assumed to be the time the driver would view the traffic conditions on the road ahead after redirecting his or her line of sight from the navigational device [2]. During the 1- or 2-second display interval, videotaped road traffic conditions were shown on the monitor (Figure 3).

The same type of videotaped road traffic conditions were shown for 5 seconds before the start and for 3 seconds after the completion of the displays of the place name groups. The display of road traffic conditions to the subjects was intended to reproduce actual driving conditions, and also to prevent an afterimage of the display remaining in the subjects' sensory information storage after the place name display had been removed [3]. The video used to show road traffic conditions was taken before the experiment from the inside of a moving car to the road ahead, and then recorded by personal computer.

In addition, before and after the place name groups were displayed, a dark screen was shown for 0.17 seconds each as the assumed transition time of the line of sight. The dark screen for the transition time of the line of sight was adopted based on the idea that input of visual information would be impossible due to rapid eye movement (i.e., so-called saccadic movement). The 0.17 seconds required for the transition time of the line of sight was based on the results of the authors' earlier studies [4].

Screening was done with video software capable of editing 30 frames per second. For example, for a 0.17-second image display, 5 frames (5/30 = 0.17 seconds) were used.

There were 7 display times for the continuous display mentioned in experimental condition (1) above: 0.3 seconds, 0.5 seconds, 1.0 second, 1.5 seconds, 2.0 seconds, 3.0 seconds, and 5.0 seconds. Under conditions (2) and (3), the images were displayed according to 5 different repetitions of 2, 3, 4, 6, or 10 times each. Thus, the total amount of time the subjects viewed the displays (total display time) was 1.0, 1.5, 2.0, 3.0, or 5.0 seconds, respectively. Under conditions (4) and (5), the number of repetitions was 2, 3, or 5 (total display time of 2.0 seconds, 3.0 seconds, or 5.0 seconds).

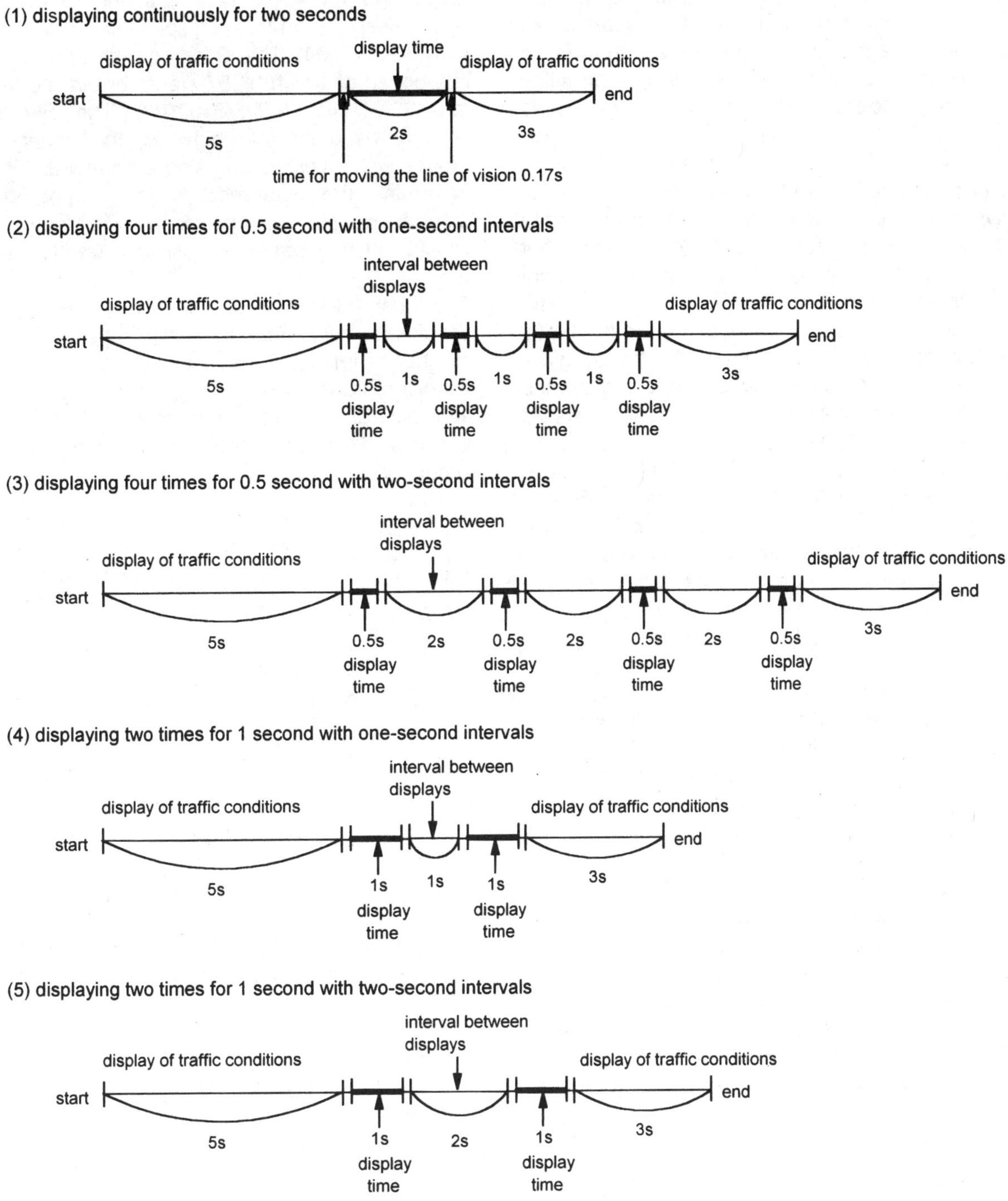

Fig.4 Five display methods for a total display time of two seconds

In total, then, there were 23 different experimental conditions. Each was repeated 3 times, for a total of 69 different trials, which corresponded to the 69 place name groups mentioned above.

As an example, a total display time of 2.0 seconds would mean the following 5 different display methods (Figure 4):

(1) Continuous display for 2 seconds.
(2) Displaying four times for 0.5 seconds with one-second intervals.
(3) Displaying four times for 0.5 seconds with two-second intervals.
(4) Displaying two times for 1.0 second with one-second intervals.
(5) Displaying two times for 1.0 second with two-second intervals.

The aim of the experiment was to determine whether or not there were differences in the number of place names read even when the total display time was the same.

In real life situations, drivers read not only each place name but also try to grasp the geographical relationships between the places when reading navigation information; however, to make quantitative comparison according to a given experimental condition simpler, the information analyzed was limited to the number of place names in the present study.

OTHER EXPERIMENTAL CONDITIONS – In actual driving, drivers look intentionally in the direction of the display. Therefore, the place name groups were not displayed unexpectedly on the monitor in the present experiment. To forewarn subjects, a buzzer (beeping sound) sounded from 0.5 to 0.3 seconds before the place name display. Furthermore, before every trial the examiner informed the subject of how many seconds the names would be displayed and how many repetitions there would be. In these ways we endeavored to raise the subjects' awareness when reading the place names, which is thought to approach the actual conditions under which a driver reads instructions from a navigational device. While approaching an intersection where the driver should turn right or left, for example, the driver is alerted by sounds coming from the car, and he or she then takes this chance to view the device and confirm the instructions.

The place name groups were shown in black characters against a white background. The size of the characters on the monitor was 6 mm vertically, since most navigation devices on the market use characters of about 5–6 mm in height. The brightness in the test room was such that there was a horizontal illuminance of about 1,200 *lx* in the subject head area.

The young group included 16 subjects in their twenties (8 males, 8 females; mean age 25.8 years, S.D. ± 2.3 years). In the elderly group, there were 16 subjects aged 65 years or older (8 males, 8 females; mean age 67.8 years, S.D. ± 1.8 years). Since each of the experimental conditions was repeated 3 times, each subject underwent 69 trials. For each experimental condition there were 3 trials by the 16 subjects, so a total of 48 data were obtained in each group.

A practice experiment was conducted before the actual experiment to familiarize the subjects with the test procedure. In addition, subjects were given appropriate breaks during the experiment.

The display information and subjects' oral responses during the experiment were videotaped. When the examiner could not fully understand a subject's oral recall of the place names, the response was confirmed by video after the experiment.

EXPERIMENTAL RESULTS

CORRECT RESPONSE RATE - Subjects were shown 10 place names × 69 trials × 16 people, for a total of 11,040 names per group. From this total number, the young group responded with 4,277 names, of which 4,186 were correct responses (correct response rate 97.9% = 4,186/4,277*100). The elderly group gave a total of 3,870 responses of which 3,597 were correct (correct response rate 92.9% = 3,597/3,870*100). The difference in the correct response rate between the young and elderly groups was investigated using a normal distribution test to determine the difference in the proportion of correct responses. The young group was found to have a significantly higher correct response rate ($p < 0.05$).

The incorrect responses varied over the 23 experimental conditions, but no characteristic trends were found in the number of incorrect responses according to experimental condition. Data were not sufficient to allow detailed analysis of incorrect responses. Accordingly, further analysis of correct responses was done to ensure strict accuracy.

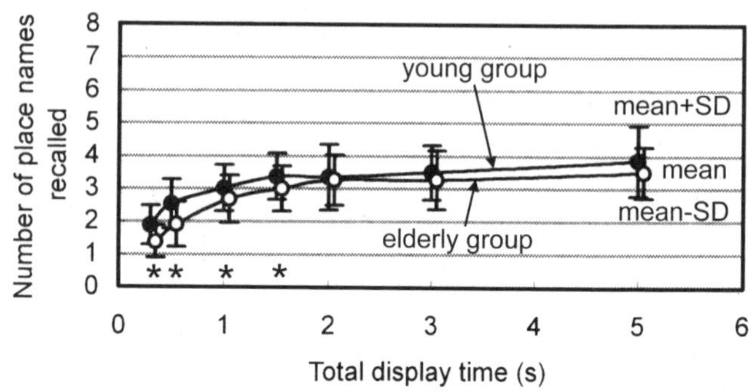

Fig.5 Number of place names recalled in case of continuous display

ANALYSIS OF TOTAL DISPLAY TIME – In this section the results will be analyzed according to the total display time.

<u>Continuous display</u> - Figure 5 shows the mean number and standard deviation of place names recalled from continuous displays. With continuous displays, the display time itself is the total display time. The closed circles in the figure indicate the data from the young group, and the open circles that from the elderly group.

In the young group, the mean number of responses was 1.9 when the total display time was 0.3 seconds, and 3.9 when the total display time was 5 seconds. In the elderly group, the mean number of responses was 1.4 with a total display time of 0.3 seconds and 3.5 with a total display time of 5 seconds. An asterisk (*) in a figure indicates an experimental condition for which *t* test revealed a significant difference ($p < 0.05$) between the number of place names recalled by the young and elderly groups (this also holds for Figures 5–9). The young group recalled a significantly greater number of names than the elderly group with 4 of the 7 different total display times.

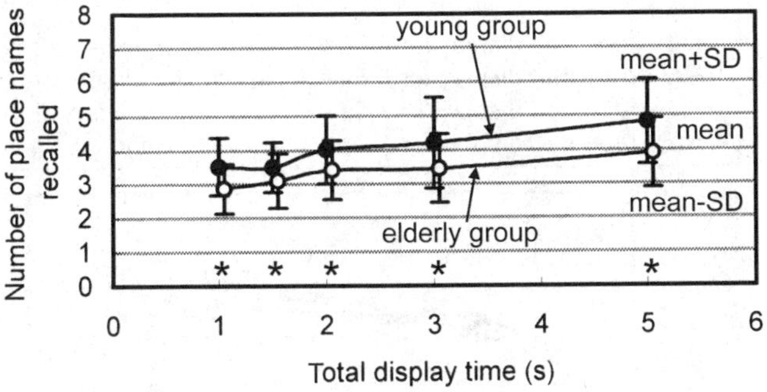

Fig.6 Number of place names recalled
(repeated display for 0.5s with one-second intervals)

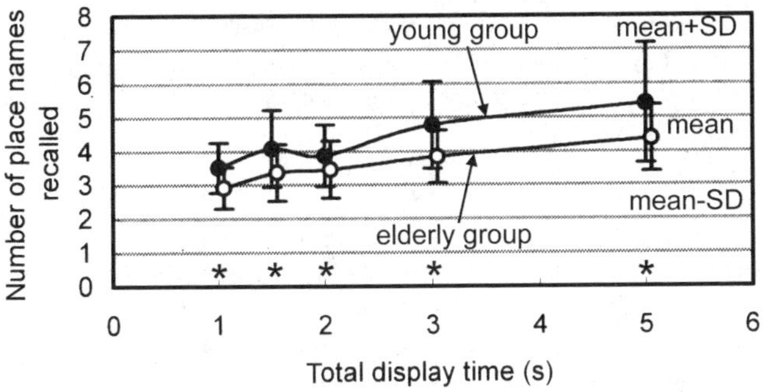

Fig.7 Number of place names recalled
(repeated display for 0.5s with two-second intervals)

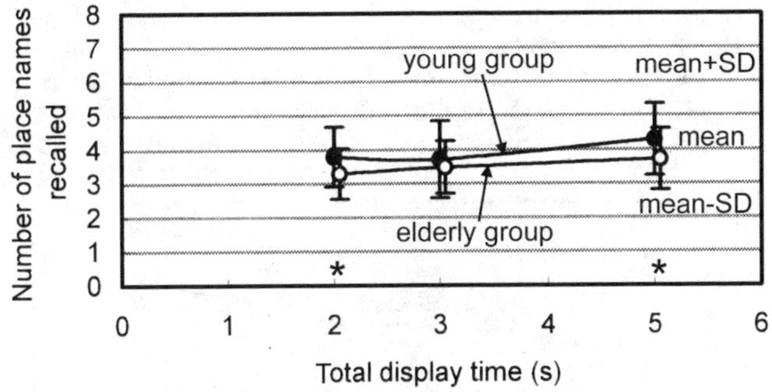

Fig.8 Number of place names recalled
(repeated display for 1.0s with one-second intervals)

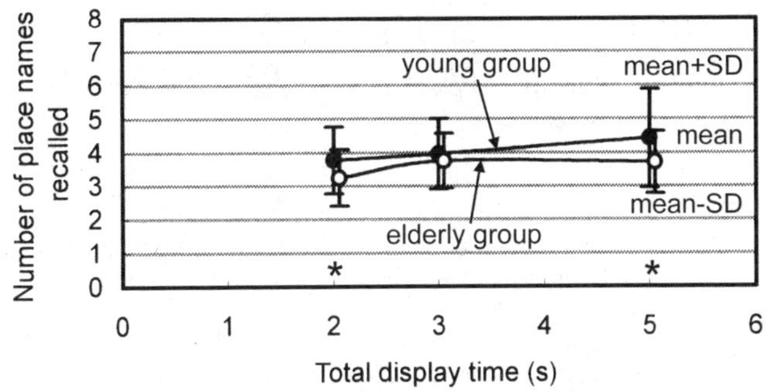

Fig.9 Number of place names recalled
(repeated display for 1.0s with two-second intervals)

Repeated displays of 0.5 seconds - The results with repeated displays of 0.5 seconds and intervals of 1 second between displays are shown in Figure 6 and those with intervals of 2 seconds between displays in Figure 7. In both figures under all conditions, the young group responded with a significantly greater number of names than the elderly group.

Figures 6 and 7 were compared using *t* test with a significance level of 5% to investigate whether there was a significant difference in the number of place names recalled according to the time interval between displays. In the young group, a significantly greater number of names was recalled with 2-second intervals than 1-second intervals when the total display time was either 1.5 seconds or 3.0 seconds. There was no significant difference with the other 3 total display times. Similarly, with the elderly group a significantly greater number of names was recalled with 2-second intervals than 1-second intervals when the total display time was 3.0 seconds or 5.0 seconds. No significant difference was found with the other 3 total display times.

Repeated displays of 1.0 second - The results when displays were shown for 1 second with intervals of 1 and 2 seconds are given in Figures 8 and 9, respectively. The asterisks (*) in both figures indicate a significantly greater number of place names recalled by the young group than the elderly group with total display times of 2.0 or 5.0 seconds.

Judging from the results with continuous displays and repeated displays of 0.5 seconds, in addition to those with repeated displays of 1.0 second, it may be concluded that the young group acquired a greater amount of information than the elderly group.

Figures 8 and 9 were compared using *t* test to investigate whether there was a difference in the number of place names recalled depending on the length of the interval between displays. No significant difference was found in either the young or elderly subjects between the 1- and 2-second display intervals with any of the 3 different total display times ($p < 0.05$).

Therefore, considering the results including those with 0.5 second displays described above, there appears to be little difference in the number of place names recalled with either 1 or 2 second intervals between displays.

Comparison of differences according to display conditions - Figure 10 summarizes the mean number of recalled place names indicated thus far in the young group. A greater number of place names was recalled with repeated displays of 1 second than with continuous displays. Moreover, the number of place names recalled with repeated displays of 0.5 seconds clearly tended to be greater.

The number of place names recalled by the elderly group is shown in the same way in Figure 11. Although the

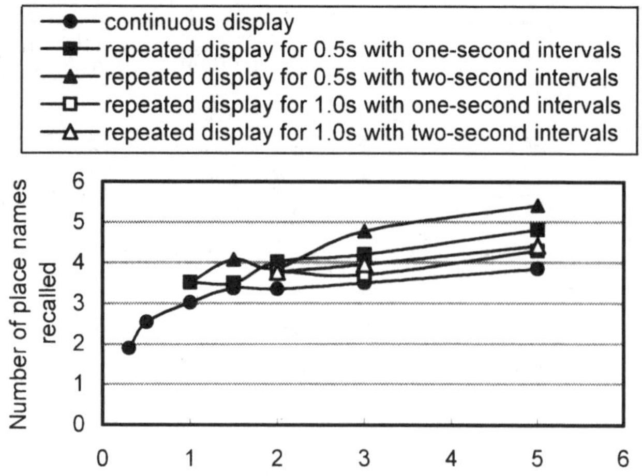

Fig.10 Number of place names recalled with respect to total display time (young group)

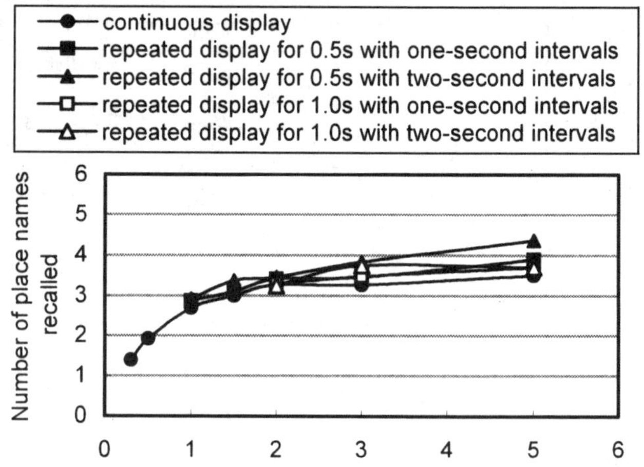

Fig.11 Number of place names recalled with respect to total display time (elderly group)

Table 1 Test results of differences according to the display conditions with significance level of 5% (young group)
(A greater number of place names were recalled under the display conditions in the left column than in the right column.)

(1) For a total display time of 1.0 second

0.5 s display repeated twice (one-second intervals)	>	Continuous display
0.5 s display repeated twice (two-second intervals)	>	Continuous display

(2) For a total display time of 1.5 seconds

0.5 s display repeated three times (two-second intervals)	>	Continuous display
0.5 s display repeated three times (two-second intervals)	>	0.5 s display repeated three times (one-second intervals)

(3) For a total display time of 2.0 seconds

0.5 s display repeated four times (one-second intervals)	>	Continuous display
0.5 s display repeated four times (two-second intervals)	>	Continuous display
1.0 s display repeated two times (one-second intervals)	>	Continuous display
1.0 s display repeated two times (two-second intervals)	>	Continuous display

(4) For a total display time of 3.0 seconds

0.5 s display repeated six times (one-second intervals)	>	Continuous display
0.5 s display repeated six times (two-second intervals)	>	Continuous display
1.0 s display repeated three times (two-second intervals)	>	Continuous display
0.5 s display repeated six times (two-second intervals)	>	0.5 s display repeated six times (one-second intervals)
0.5 s display repeated six times (two-second intervals)	>	1.0 s display repeated three times (one-second intervals)
0.5 s display repeated six times (two-second intervals)	>	1.0 s display repeated three times (two-second intervals)

(5) For a total display time of 5.0 seconds

0.5 s display repeated ten times (one-second intervals)	>	Continuous display
0.5 s display repeated ten times (two-second intervals)	>	Continuous display
1.0 s display repeated five times (one-second intervals)	>	Continuous display
1.0 s display repeated five times (two-second intervals)	>	Continuous display
0.5 s display repeated ten times (one-second intervals)	>	1.0 s display repeated five times (one-second intervals)
0.5 s display repeated ten times (two-second intervals)	>	1.0 s display repeated five times (one-second intervals)
0.5 s display repeated ten times (two-second intervals)	>	1.0 s display repeated five times (two-second intervals)

number of names recalled was greater with repeated displays than with continuous displays, the difference was not as striking as in the young group.

A *t* test (significance level of 5%) for each total display time was used to determine whether or not there was a difference in number of place names depending on display conditions. The combinations of display conditions between which there was a significant difference are shown in Table 1 (young group) and Table 2 (elderly group). Here, a greater number of place names were recalled under the display conditions in the left column of the table than in the right column.

Table 2 Test results of differences according to the display conditions with significance level of 5% (elderly group)
(A greater number of place names were recalled under the display conditions in the left column than in the right column.)

(1) For a total display time of 1.0 second
(No applicable item under this display condition)

(2) For a total display time of 1.5 second

0.5 s display repeated three times (two-second intervals)	>	Continuous display

(3) For a total display time of 2.0 second
(No applicable item under this display condition)

(4) For a total display time of 3.0 second

0.5 s display repeated six times (two-second intervals)	>	Continuous display
1.0 s display repeated three times (two-second intervals)	>	Continuous display
0.5 s display repeated six times (two-second intervals)	>	0.5 s display repeated six times (one-second intervals)
0.5 s display repeated six times (two-second intervals)		1.0 s display repeated three times (one-second intervals)

(5) For a total display time of 5.0 second

0.5 s display repeated ten times (one-second intervals)	>	Continuous display
0.5 s display repeated ten times (two-second intervals)	>	Continuous display
0.5 s display repeated ten times (two-second intervals)	>	0.5 s display repeated ten times (one-second intervals)
0.5 s display repeated ten times (two-second intervals)	>	1.0 s display repeated five times (one-second intervals)
0.5 s display repeated ten times (two-second intervals)	>	1.0 s display repeated five times (two-second intervals)

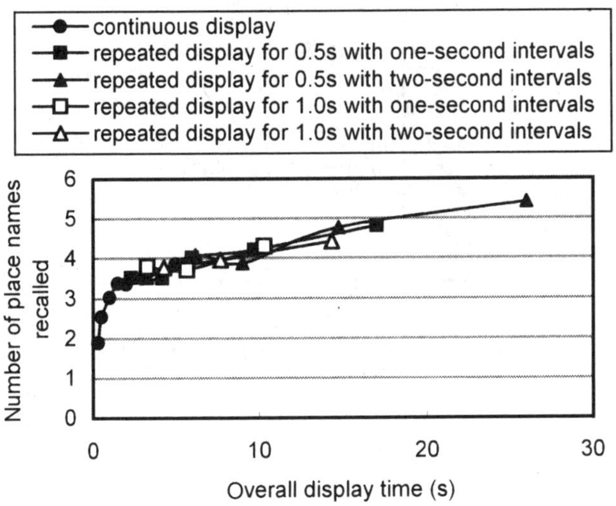

Fig.12 Number of place names recalled with respect to overall display time (young group)

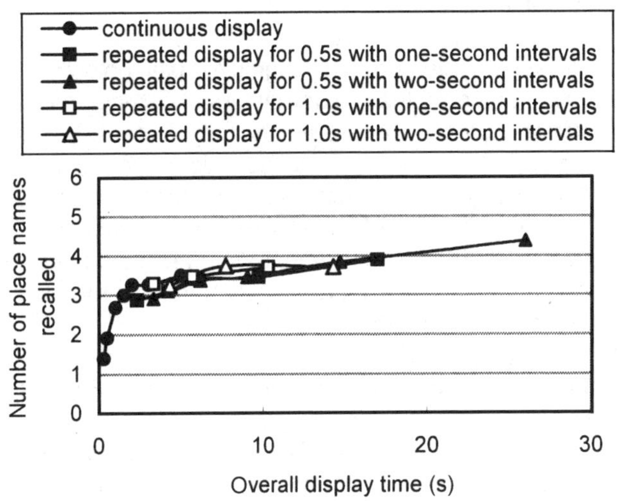

Fig.13 Number of place names recalled with respect to overall display time (elderly group)

As seen in the results for young subjects in Table 1, a significantly greater number of place names was recalled with repeated displays than with continuous displays. A comparison of names recalled with repeated displays of 0.5 seconds and 1.0 second revealed no significant difference when the total display time was 2.0 seconds, while in many cases there was a significant difference when the total display time was 3.0 or 5.0 seconds.

Table 2 shows the results for the elderly group. There were several conditions under which the number of names recalled was greater with repeated as opposed to continuous displays, but the differences were not as striking as in the young group.

In conclusion, it appears that in general drivers acquire a greater amount of information by glancing repeatedly at a display for short times than by gazing at it for a longer time.

THE ANALYSIS OF OVERALL DISPLATY TIME - Overall display time is defined as the time from the start of the displays until all displays are completed. The results for these times were evaluated. The overall display time is obtained by adding to the total display time the 1- or 2-second intervals between displays and the time the monitor is dark to simulate the transition time of the line of sight. The minimum overall display time was 0.3 seconds under the condition of a single continuous display of 0.3 seconds, and the maximum was 26.0 seconds under the condition of 0.5-second displays with 2-second intervals and 10 repetitions. In the latter, adding the total display time of 5.0 seconds, the 9 display intervals (2 seconds × 9) and 18 transition times of the line of sight (5/30 seconds × 18) makes an overall display time of 26.0 seconds. Under continuous display conditions, the total (summed) display time equals overall display time.

Figure 12 (young group) shows the number of place names recalled under each display condition in relation to overall display time. The number of names recalled under each display condition fall along a line on a graph. In Figure 13 (elderly group), the numbers of place names recalled also nearly fall along a line on a graph.

Given the range of the present display conditions, therefore, we can see that the number of place names recalled is obtained uniformly by the overall display time rather than the total display time. Thus, it is surmised that in both the young and elderly subjects the time in which the place names are not being displayed is used as effectively in acquiring information as if the names were still displayed on the screen.

DISCUSSION

In models of memory in cognitive psychology, it is generally thought that external inputs enter sensory information storage, after which they enter short-term memory. Rehearsal then takes place in short-term memory, and part of the information is transferred to long-term memory [3]. In addition, working memory has also been assumed [5]. In the present study, however, working memory will be considered a part of short-term memory for the sake of simplicity [6].

Looking at the experimental results shown in Figures 12 (young group) and 13 (elderly group), there is a rapid rise in the number of place names recalled up to about 3 names (until an overall display time of about 1.5 seconds), but after that the names recalled increase only slowly even as overall display time is lengthened. Recall of up to 3 names is processed in short-term memory, and so the increase in acquired information is marked. Above that amount, however, any information input exceeds the capacity of short-term memory, and it is assumed that part of this information is therefore transferred to long-term memory. As a result, the increase in acquired information is gradual. It is likely that this process continues even during the display intervals when the place name groups are not being displayed. Thus, the number of names recalled is not determined by the actual display time, but instead is determined uniformly with the overall display time. When recalling place names, the subjects are assumed to be responding with the names remaining in short-term memory and those that have been transferred to long-term memory.

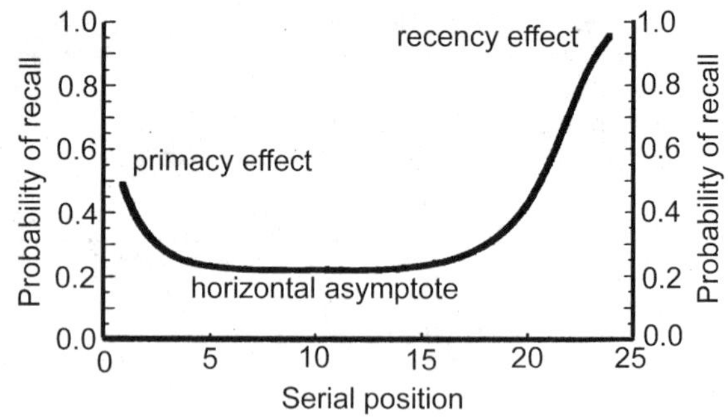

Fig.14 Model of serial position effect of free recall for 24-word list (based on Murdock's study [7])

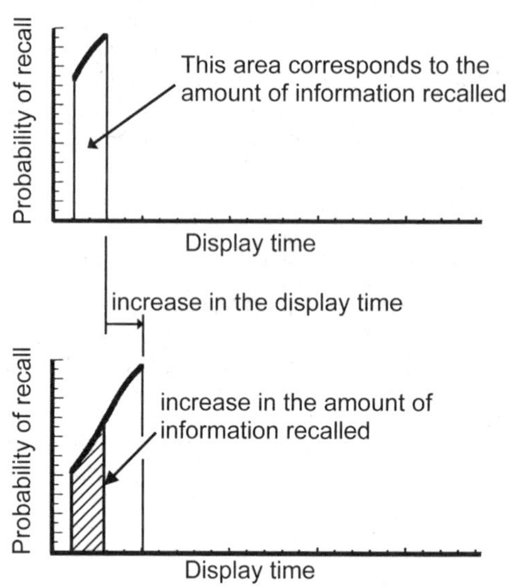

Fig. 15 A model of the increase in number of place names recalled in the region of short-term memory

The relationship between short-term and long-term memory is briefly discussed below. Murdock [7] presented the model illustrated in Figure 14 for the serial position effect of free recall. In this figure, the probability of recall is the highest for the most recently acquired memories (recency effect), followed by for memories acquired first (primacy effect). The recency effect is related to short-term memory and the primacy effect and horizontal asymptote to long-term memory.

In the present experiment, the subjects looked at the 10 place names one at a time rather than all at once. Inferring from the results of Murdock, the following explanation is reasonable: When the display time is short, the input can be processed in short-term memory, and the increase in the amount of information acquired during the display time is striking. The reason for this, as shown by the simple model in Figure 15, is that information is processed in the

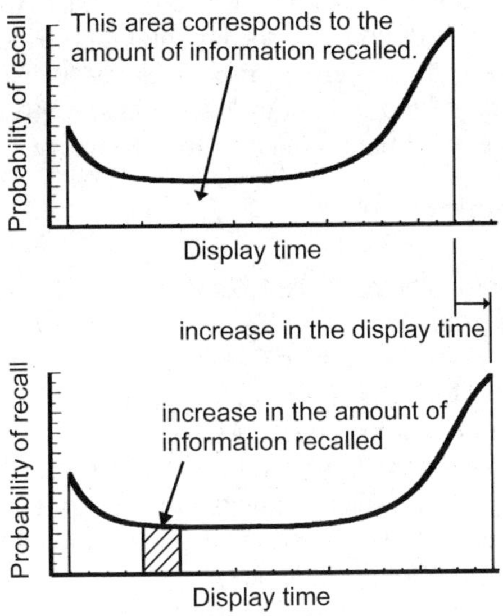

Fig. 16 A model of the increase in number of place names recalled in the region of long-term memory

range of the recency effect in Figure 14, for which there is a high probability of recall.

However, as the display time becomes longer, the region of the horizontal asymptote that is dependent on long-term memory appears as in Figure 16. Figure 16, like Figure 15, is a simplified model. Assuming that the region of the primacy and recency effects are the same, the level of increase in the amount of information acquired when the display time becomes longer is dependent on the horizontal asymptote where the probability of recall is low. As is understood from a comparison with Figure 15, the increase in the amount of information acquired is small. Thus, when information is transferred to long-term memory, there is a gradual increase in the amount of information acquired.

Here, if the number of place names recalled is shown again for the region in which the overall display time is greater than 2 seconds, where the increase in information acquired becomes gradual, it appears as shown in Figure 17 (young group) and Figure 18 (elderly group). The data in both these figures are from all repeated display experimental conditions and continuous displays of 3.0 and 5.0 seconds. A regression analysis with an overall display time of x seconds and y number of place names recalled reveals a high linear relation between number of place names recalled and overall display time in both young and elderly subjects. The regression equations for each are as follows:

Young group... $y = 3.36 + 0.0823x$ ($r = 0.966$).
Elderly group... $y = 3.03 + 0.0535x$ ($r = 0.907$).

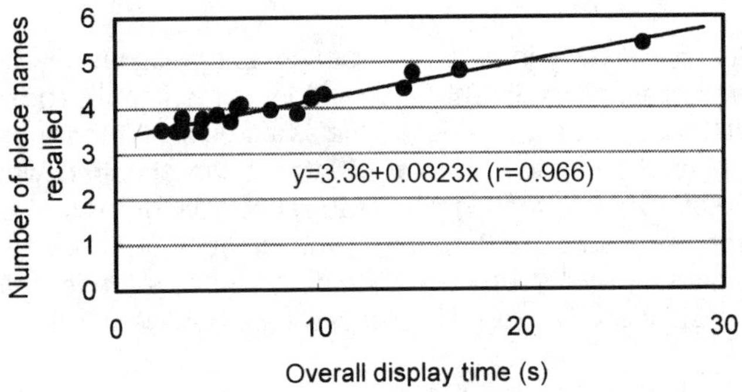

Fig.17 Number of place names recalled for overall display time greater than 2 seconds (young group)

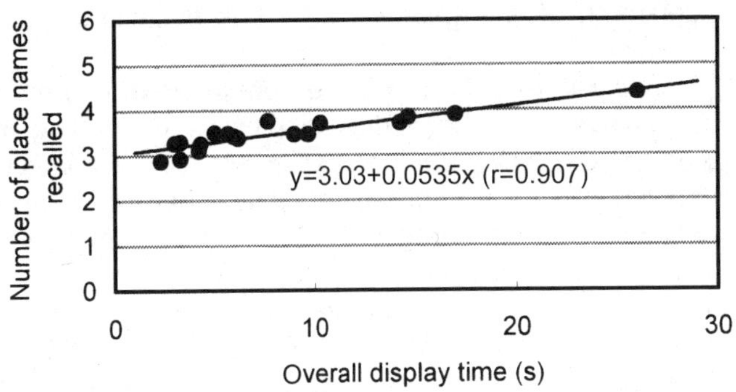

Fig.18 Number of place names recalled for overall display time greater than 2 seconds (elderly group)

The coefficient for the overall display time in the regression equation is 0.0823 for the young group and 0.0535 for the elderly group. Thus, both the transfer of information to long-term memory when the amount of information input exceeds the capacity of short-term memory, and the replay of memories from long-term memory when responding, appear to occur more often in young than in elderly people.

Finally, one should note that in the present study road traffic conditions were displayed on the monitor during the intervals when the place names were not being shown. However, since our experiment was in laboratory conditions, it may be assumed that there was less psychological burden on the subjects. When actually driving a car on the road, information input from the road conditions ahead is processed while driving, so the rehearsal of information from other sources and judgments of its significance in short-term memory during that time are suppressed to that extent. In this situation the amount of information acquired from that displayed on the navigation system would decrease, and one may assume that as a result the number of place names recalled could not be uniformly obtained in line with the overall display time.

CONCLUSION

Reading display information from an automobile navigation system was simulated in an indoor experiment, and an attempt was made to determine whether or not there was a difference in the amount of information acquired when the display information was read repeatedly or for a single time. A possible difference in the amount of information acquired by young and elderly people was also investigated. The following results were obtained.

(1) The amount of information acquired when subjects viewed a display repeatedly was greater than when viewed a single time, even when the actual time looking at the display was the same.

(2) Young subjects had a higher correct response rate and acquired more information than elderly subjects.

(3) An analysis based on the time from the start to the end of displays, (i.e., the overall display time including the time when the place names were not displayed), showed that the number of place names recalled definitely corresponded with the overall display time. The reason is thought to be that information processing in short-term memory and the transfer of information to long-term memory continued to function even during the time the names were not displayed, so this time was used effectively in information acquisition.

However, the above findings were obtained during a simulated reading from a car navigation system, in which the experimental conditions were within a display time range of 0.3 to 5.0 seconds and display intervals of 1 or 2 seconds. These results were also obtained when the subjects were under no special psychological burden during the display intervals. Thus, no conclusion can be drawn immediately as to whether these findings would be the same with other display times and display intervals. In particular, it may be expected that the number of place names would not correspond so closely with overall display time if, during the display intervals when the place names were not shown, the subjects were made to perform some kind of task that suppressed the processing of displayed information in short-term memory.

REFERENCES

1. Kazumoto Morita, Jinichi Mashiko and Takeo Okada : "Usage Situation of In-Vehicle Navigation Devices in Japan," Report of Traffic Safety and Nuisance Research Institute, No.28, pp.9-15 (2000)
2. Kazumoto Morita, Jinichi Mashiko, Takeo Okada and Ichiro Sakamoto : "Analysis of Glances at the Display Screen of In-Vehicle Navigation Systems," Report of Traffic Safety and Nuisance Research Institute, No.29, pp.17-24 (2000) (in Japanese)
3. Geoffrey R. Loftus and Elizabeth F. Loftus : "Human Memory :The Processing of Information," Lawrence Erlbaum Associates, Inc., Publishers (1976)
4. Kazumoto Morita, Jinichi Mashiko, Takeo Okada and Kazuo Matsushima : "Factor Analysis of the Time Required to Read the Name of the Destination among Place Names Displayed by In-Vehicle Navigation Devices," Proceedings of the ninth International Pacific Conference on Automotive Engineering, pp.55-60 (1997)
5. Alan Baddeley : "Working memory," Science, Vol.255, pp.556-559 (1992)
6. Shintaro Funahashi : "Short-term Memory and Working Memory," Brain Medical, Vol.10, No.1, pp.61-67 (1998) (in Japanese)
7. Bennet B. Murdock Jr. : "The Serial Position Effect of Free Recall," Journal of Experimental Psychology, 64-5, pp.482-488 (1962)

2000-01-3075

The Driving Need for Human Factors in the Car of the Future

David J. Wheatley
Motorola Labs, User Centered Research Group

ABSTRACT

The car of the future will be very different from that which we know today – no longer just a mechanical transportation device, but a mobile communications and entertainment platform providing many new functions and services to the occupants.

The use of cellular telephones whilst driving is already a source of major concern and further legislation regarding phone usage will undoubtedly be forthcoming. The future will also add display based navigation, internet access, e-commerce and other location dependent services which will increase the drivers cognitive load. We will also see driver assistance systems such as adaptive cruise control, collision avoidance warnings and vision enhancement systems which will change the driving task and could potentially reduce cognitive load almost to the level of autopilot monitoring.

As the nature of the in-vehicle activity therefore evolves from being a perceptual-motor driving task to that of a communications and vigilance task (set against a background of infotainment services) then we can not only anticipate emergent behaviors but will also see a new need for the management of multimodal information presentation to the driver according to his driving circumstances and indeed, personal preferences. Consequently driving could be as different from what we know today, as today is from the time of leather helmets and driving goggles.

The aim of this presentation is to provide an overview of the major human factors and safety issues which these new systems are raising and which will be fundamental to their effective and safe use as well as to their commercial viability and success.

INTRODUCTION

There was a time when driving a car involved wrestling with heavy and unresponsive steering, using strong leg muscles to operate heavy brakes, paying attention to avoid potholes in the road and double de-clutching. But that of course was a long time ago when life and cars were both much simpler than they are today. Back then cars were relatively simple mechanical devices whose primary purpose was that of transporting people and their luggage from A to B – what some classic car enthusiasts and purists might call "the good old days".

But both life and cars are far more complex today and the latter at least are on the threshold of becoming much more complex still – and will likely change the nature of driving much more than we have seen thus far. We now have abs, traction control, cruise control, adaptive cruise control – in the upmarket models additionally active suspension, night vision, parking assistance and so on - and of course just about everything is power assisted. Though we are still a very long way from actually automating the driving task, many of these technological developments (whose safety benefits incidentally have been very substantial and worthwhile) have gradually changed the nature of the driving task. The in-vehicle environment has also changed substantially – built in video to keep the kids entertained, navigation systems to help avoid getting lost, emergency call and breakdown for peace of mind, information services to the vehicle, cellular telephones to keep in touch and of course, the cup holders necessitated by the drive-thru concept.

But both the evolutionary changes to the driving task and the changes to the in-vehicle environment have at least one thing in common – they both act to place barriers between the driver (and of course the passenger) and the external world. In the "good old days" when driving was more of a seat of the pants experience – the noise level, the wind in the hair, the bumps in the road – this was how the driver sensed the outside world. Not today – he is coccooned in a comfortable, smooth and quiet air-conditioned environment where any sensing of the external environment has to occur through some sort of interface such as the speedometer, thermometer and various warning lights for low traction etc. The importance of these various interfaces is becoming greater at the same time as they are becoming more complex. Just as the technical developments in the vehicle have made it much easier to drive, increases in traffic density and road system complexity have made it more difficult. As a consequence the drivers attention is directed more towards the external vehicle environment and less towards the internal environment.

But there is one thing that has changed little if at all over this period – and that is this driver, the fallible human being whose perceptual and cognitive capacity is not increasing year on year to keep up to speed with the information with which he is bombarded. Though there is still a cognitive demand involved in driving there are different things which are now demanding the drivers attention and this is creating the driving need to pay serious attention not just to traditional physical ergonomics in the vehicle but increasingly to the psychological and cognitive issues with which the driver will have to contend in this information rich future mobile environment.

THE USE OF CELLULAR TELEPHONES IN THE VEHICLE

The problems that these new types of in-vehicle activity will bring are not imagined – we are witnessing right now the response to safety questions raised about the use of mobile telephones whilst driving [8]. Applying a physical ergonomics type of approach to this issue would clearly tell us that there is a finite limit to what a driver can do – he only has a finite number of hands, fingers and feet with which to operate controls. And one of the first major studies into the use of cellular telephones in the vehicle carried out in Japan in 1996 [1] confirmed that this was the case. This study investigated 129 motor vehicle crashes in which use of a cellular telephone was involved and found that 16% of the drivers were conversing on the phone at the time of the crash, 32% were dialling, 5.4% were hanging up the phone and 42% were responding to a call. The large proportion of crashes related to handling the telephone (74%) may be a reflection of the fact that, at that time, 94% of the telephones sold in Japan were hand-held models. The conclusion therefore was that the major safety risk was due to the physical demands of reaching for the phone in the glove box or bag, and physically opening the flip cover and dialling the number.

At the time of this study, handsfree telephone systems were not common and the mobile phones in use were often flip phones without repertory dialling facilities which were often not cradled within reach of the driver. It was a relatively straightforward and logical step to conclude from these results that a handsfree interface to a cradled telephone would solve many, if not all of these problems and mitigate the potential safety hazards.

But this was not the case. The more recent study carried out by Redelmeier and Tibshirani in Toronto during 1994 and 1995 [2] concluded that there were still possible safety issues arising from the use of cellular telephones which were not due solely to the physical handling of the device. They concluded that talking on a cellular telephone quadrupled the risk of a collision and that it was the high cognitive load of being involved in conversation which was a significant hazard. They concluded also that the increased likelihood of accidents persisted even after the call had been completed. In other words the drivers attention was still, to an extent, focused on the verbal interaction and not on the task of driving. The use of handsfree systems might address the physical elements but not these cognitive elements.

It is the same sort of logic which is creating the widely held belief that verbally interacting with the in-vehicle functions by means of a voice interface will adequately address the concerns over cognitive demands on the driver. Unfortunately this is not entirely the case either. This has been shown by a recent study carried out at the University of Iowa [3] in which subjects were required to listen to email messages whilst driving in a simulator. The cognitive demand of listening to the verbalised information led to an increase of 30% in the reaction time to the brake lights of a leading vehicle. Even if the use of a voice interface were to be the best solution to the problem of accessing information functions in the vehicle – it is clear that the technology, particularly speech recognition, is not yet sufficiently robust and flexible to deliver a reliable and easy to use interface – by itself it is increasing the cognitive load on the driver rather than reducing it.

DESKTOP COMPUTING IN THE VEHICLE

The use of cellular telephones in the vehicle is just the beginning of an information revolution in the vehicle and the issues that have been raised by this will be even more critical in the context of the additional functions which are starting to be commonplace in high end vehicles. Functions such as navigation, email and internet access, various information functions as well as those valuable functions clearly targeted at increasing safety and security, such as ecall, breakdown call and automatic notification of airbag deployment. Though attention is being paid to the user interfaces of these devices most, if not all of those currently on the market, derive their user interface principles largely from human factors efforts in the desktop computing environment. The visual displays are often multi-colored, visually rich and frequently use softkeys for menu selection – this is fine for the desktop but not the best approach for using a system in the vehicle where such interaction is not the primary task. Quite simply, many of them represent a visual distraction and one thing that most seem to have in common today is that their usability is generally extremely poor. Perhaps we should consider whether there is a place here for a completely different approach to the user interaction with such systems which is specifically tailored to the unique situation of in-vehicle system interaction.

THE COMPUTER SCREEN AS AN IN-VEHICLE USER INTERFACE

This does not suggest that we therefore ignore all of the learning that has been accrued from research and evaluation of desktop systems, but there are certainly many differences with future in-vehicle systems which need to be considered;

1] Fundamentally, as I have previously stated, the interaction with in-vehicle information systems is a secondary task – driving is the primary task and one which is also safety critical. Though this can be addressed to some extent by "locking out" some or all functions and services when the vehicle is moving or in drive – this approach has the side-effect of seriously limiting the potential value of those functions.

2] Secondly, the user population is very broad, encompassing a very wide range of age, language, educational and driving experience. Though this is also true of desktop computer users there is more time to learn a system or application and the consequences of making a mistake are not so great.

3] Thirdly, it is not valid to assume that potential users have experience with or indeed any interest in computer technology.

4] Fourthly drivers are likely to expect any in-vehicle system to be as intuitive and easy to use as the vehicle itself. The car is not the sort of place to store instruction manuals and even if it were, most people would not read them. It is also unreasonable to expect users to take part in any training course to operate their infotainment system.

What this is suggesting is that the user interface between the driver and the variety of navigation, infotainment and driver assistance systems which are likely to be available in the coming years, is a matter which should receive special attention. And if this transition from a perceptual motor task to one which is more akin to a vigilance and monitoring task is going to be successful and viable then the motor manufacturers, system suppliers and content providers need to collaborate to a much greater extent than hitherto.

THE HUMAN FACTORS CHALLENGES AHEAD

There are a number of fundamental human factors challenges which need to be addressed in the coming years for in vehicle information, navigation, collision avoidance and other such systems to be safe, simple and easy to use. As well as the technological and legal challenges along the way, these human factors issues also need to be seriously addressed to successfully manage the transition from the vehicle as a mechanical transportation device to that of a mobile information and communications platform.

FUNCTIONALITY

Once wideband wireless communications are available to an in-vehicle device there is the potential for a vast number of new functions and services to be delivered. Marketing forces will undoubtedly come into play to exploit these to their maximum – almost certainly, in some cases without consideration being given to the user environment and the primary task demands in that environment. A degree of responsibility will need to be exercised, with the support of reliable human factors data, regarding the appropriateness of various functions and activities when associated with the driving task. For example; verbally presented turn by turn directions are clearly information which supports and should enhance safe driving. At the other extreme there are potential location based events such as trivial and intrusive advertisements when passing close to certain stores or restaurants or movie viewing. Inbetween these extremes are a range of possible functions whose benefits are less clearly defined and whose impact on driving safety must be established.

Many functions and services which pose hazards by unnecessarily distracting the driver could be perfectly acceptable, even desirable for front seat passengers. There are major challenges not only in defining what and when functions should be available but also to whom and how these are presented.

SYSTEMS INTEGRATION

As these different systems start to proliferate, there will additionally be a variety of auditory alerts and alarms as well as visual and probably haptic information presented to the driver. These could be alerting him to anything from an incoming email message to an imminent and life threatening forward collision. In order to ensure that these signals are correctly perceived, understood and acted upon, systems integration is needed within a vehicle. The driver/system interaction must be considered as a whole to avoid the presentation of competing, confusing or non-prioritised information.

INTUITIVE IN USE

The car driver does not expect to, nor does he read an instruction manual neither to learn how to operate the vehicle or the radio, entertainment system or HVAC. The expectation (but not always the reality) is that this is all obvious and sufficiently consistent between different manufacturers that he can work out any small differences. The same will be expected of future in-vehicle systems. Many navigation systems currently available are notoriously difficult and complex to use, are expensive and often give little advantage over using a traditional paper map [4]. Not only does this affect customer take up but can also be a significant safety hazard by adding to rather than alleviating the cognitive load on the driver.

EMERGENT BEHAVIORS

Emergent behaviors are new and potentially unforeseen human behavior patterns which result from the introduction of new technology or systems or which arise from the interaction effects of existing systems. For example some research has suggested that the use of cruise control leads to later braking when approaching behind a slowing vehicle – possibly due to a slight reluctance to go through the process of turning it off temporarily only to turn it on again. A potential example related to Adaptive Cruise Control (ACC) could be an even greater reluctance to brake when approaching behind a slowing vehicle or not braking at all if the driver believes that the ACC will do it for him. If the system happens to be turned off or not available, for instance in a rental car, then clearly this can be very dangerous. Long term experimental studies of driver assistance and other systems will be essential for the prediction of these kinds of emergent behaviors.

MULTIMODAL INFORMATION PRESENTATION

As the amount of information presented to the driver increases other modes of presentation will be utilised. There are already a number of chimes and dings to tell him about open doors and safety restraints. There are likely to be still more indicating upcoming turn manouvre, insufficient headway, vehicle in blind spot, lane deviation and any number of events such as incoming traffic information or email message. In order to avoid overloading the drivers visual capability the auditory and proprioceptive channels are starting to be used. Research needs to be done to determine the associative meaning of auditory icons, spoken commands or haptic events. Particularly for those events which are infrequent, for example an auditory alarm for forward collision warning; the alarm stimulus must be perceived, correctly interpreted, and must elicit the appropriate response within an extremely short time span. For an FCW warning which statistically could only occur once every 25 years or so [5] the driver needs to immediately and instinctively know what it means – there is no time to think about or interpret the meaning of the alarm and there will have been no opportunity to reinforce the associative meaning without increasing the frequency of false alarms and thereby reducing the effectiveness and credibility of the function.

Similarly cross modal information presentation will add a new dimension of complexity. Information may be presented simultaneously through more than one sensory channel and any apparent discrepancy between the associative meaning of multiple simultaneous signals will greatly increase reaction time and reduce effectiveness.

COGNITIVE LOAD MANAGEMENT

Although the concerns about the use of cellular telephones whilst driving center on the high cognitive load of the interaction, the driving task is in fact subject to both extremes of cognitive load. There are also times when the cognitive load is too low – typified by the drowsy driver who lacks situational awareness and may even fall asleep at the wheel. An integrated in-vehicle system could provide some opportunities to moderate these extremes by managing events temporally so as to even out the demand and maintain a required cognitive level closer to the optimum. Lack of integration of potentially competing systems cannot enable this to occur [6]. An example of this might be an incoming telephone call coinciding with and masking, a verbal navigation instruction at the same time as an alert regarding lane deviation.

PERSONALISATION AND PREFERENCES

Once the systems within the vehicle begin to be digital, many hitherto impossible functions and features start to be possible. For example personalisation and customisation of the car has long been a tradition though this has largely been applied to the exterior rather than the interior and has not generally touched upon the dashboard or on the information presented to the driver. It is also a one-time customisation and does not permit changes to be made frequently or in response to changes in preferences. Integrated in vehicle systems have the potential to enable personalisation, such as choosing, within limits, what information is provided to the driver by the vehicle, in what form it is presented and even when it is presented. Family members who share use of the same vehicle could well have different preferences. There are also significant cost benefits to the auto manufacturers who have additional opportunities for personalisation at the point of sale as well as the potential for a more rapid rollout of model updates for instance by the release of software updates to increase the features and functions of a vehicle – these could even be downloaded wirelessly.

BETWEEN VENDOR STANDARDISATION

I have referred to several potential future in vehicle systems - clearly those which are most crucial are those which directly affect safety. Most of us will have had the experience, usually in rental cars, of being totally unable to find the trunk release or the lightswitch or flashing the lights when we intended to turn on the windshield wipers. These are not new functions, they have been in cars for many years yet standardisation of the location and operation of many driving controls still appears to be almost non-existent beyond the steering wheel and pedals. Perhaps it is only mechanical necessity that is driving this consistency and there will be attempts to move these as soon as robust drive by wire systems permit. Similarly, if there is inconsistency between the incoming email alert between different makes and models of cars then the result could be annoyance or even inconvenience. The result is more likely to be injury or death if there is a lack of standardisation of collision warning alarms for example. Standardisation and consistency will therefore be an essential not a desirable element of safety related systems.

INDUSTRY COLLABORATION

The word convergence has frequently been used to allude to the coming together of computing with telecommunications. What will be happening in this future is the three way convergence of computing and telecommunications within the automobile. For the business opportunities that this convergence offers to be successfully exploited, will require a huge degree of collaboration not only within the auto industry but also between players in the computing and communications industry with wireless service providers, content providers, internet companies and many more. In fact a market report recently issued in the UK reported that "Partnering, collaboration and product positioning will be key to addressing the telematics opportunity" [7]

THE WAY FORWARD

The aim of this presentation has been to provide an overview of the major human factors and safety issues which new driver information and assistance systems are generating. These factors will be fundamental to their effective and safe use and to their commercial viability and long term success. The fundamental factors which should drive the way forward and make these systems both safe and acceptable are ;

• Driving a vehicle is not the same as operating a desktop computer so do not assume that information should be presented in the same way.

• Consider the whole driver/system interface – if subsystems are developed independently and separately there could be similar or confusing or competing alerts and alarms.

• Use real human factors research to better understand how, when and through which sensory modality they should be presented.

• Determine the instinctive or intuitive meaning associated with various sounds and exploit the potential of voice interaction with the vehicle.

• The presentation of any safety critical information in the vehicle should be consistent within and between manufacturers, consistent over time and ideally internationally.

• New relationships and collaborations will need to be established between companies who have not traditionally worked together if the true potential of these future systems are to be delivered to the man in the street, or in his car.

CONCLUSIONS

Many new driver assistance and information systems will be appearing in the cars of the future and there is much that we can potentially learn from experiences in the aircraft industry – about glass cockpits and speech synthesis, about haptic displays and vibrating sticks. What I personally hope we will not learn too much about from this is about automation, autopilots and the removal of control from the driver. The automobile is not quite like other industrial products but is one with which we human beings tend to have a special relationship unlike any other manufactured artifact. The task of driving is also one which is perceived quite differently from other tasks. As the nature of the in-vehicle environment evolves into a more information rich and electronic future, it is important to ensure that some of the pleasures of driving and some of the pleasures of car ownership remain whilst fully exploiting the safety benefits and business opportunities which these future systems can offer.

REFERENCES

[1] "An Investigation of the Safety Implications of Wireless Communications in Vehicles" *NHTSA Report*

[2] "Association between Cellular Telephone calls and Motor Vehicle Collisions". Redelmeier, D.A. & Tibshirani, R.J. *The New England Journal of Medicine* 336, 2, 1997, pp. 453 – 458.

[3] "Does a Speech-Based Interface for an In-vehicle Computer Distract Drivers ?" Lee J.D., Brown T.L., Caven B., Haake S., Schmidt K, Dept. of Industrial Eng., University of Iowa – unpublished report – May 2000.

[4] "When you Absolutely, Positively Have to get There... Eventually" *Autoweek,* Jan 3, 2000 pp 15 – 21.

[5] "In Vehicle Collision Avoidance Support under adverse Visibility Conditions – Warnings" in Y Ian Noy – Ergonomics and Safety of Intelligent Driver Interfaces 1997 (Mahwah; Lawrence Erlbaum) pp 221-230

[6] "Beyond the Desktop – and into your Vehicle" Wheatley D.J. *CHI2000 Development Consortium,* Den Haag, Netherlands, April 1-7 2000 - Extended Abstracts pp 43–44.

[7] "In Car Telematics Terminals Market 2000-2006" Strategy Analytics, Strategy Advisory Service, London, Feb 2000

[8] "Death by Distraction" , Kobe G. – Automotive Industries, May 2000 pp 30-37.

2000-01-0818

Human-Machine-Interfaces of Car Computing Devices

Peter Roessger
Computer Aided Animation GmbH, Germany

ABSTRACT

Existing driver information systems (DIS) include navigation, radio, telephone, television etc. The addition of computer functions like internet or word-processing turns DIS into car computing devices (CCD), often called CarPCs. Due to the high mental and visual load of driving, solutions matching the human factors needs of the driving environment have to be developed.

A usability study testing four different existing DIS was conducted. It is possible to transfer the results to future CCD. The visual channel should not be stressed by CCD. Applications running in car have to use acoustic and haptic channels for information transfer between driver and system.

INTRODUCTION

DIS are systems based on digital information processing, that provide drivers with information during the journey. This includes travel computers, navigation systems, and multifunctional integrated system like the Siemens IDIS or the Mercedes Comand. Car audio systems are no DIS by means of this definition.

CCD (or CarPCs) are DIS with additional features like office, e-mail, or internet. This extension of functionality impacts the need for new user interface concepts. Analytical and experimental approaches are necessary to get the knowledge for improving the human machine interface (HMI) of DIS.

COMPUTERWOLRD VERSUS CARWORLD

In DIS and CCD meet computer-world and car-world. Both have restrictions and singularities. Chances and possibilities, including well known standards, of the computer-world face the restrictions of the vehicle cockpit. Human factors experts state [1], that if you add a computer to a car, you get a computer. This means that cars are handy devices, but if you add some digital information processing, it changes to hard to handle.

In the computer world, work with the computer is usually the main task, at least at the moment when it is done. That means, the working person can use all mental and visual capacities to operate the system. Time restrictions are kept to a minimum. Hard- and software, and with it the user interface, is more or less standardized. Easy available rules [2], style guides [3, 4], and official standards on the ergonomics of computer work [5] exist as well as theoretical background and long term experience [6]. There is (or at least should be) enough space on desktops to place a proper sized screen and a standard keyboard plus other input devices such as a mouse or a trackball.

In a vehicle the main task still and definitely is and will be driving, even if the driver in command changes to a driver in control. That means that only limited mental and visual capacities are available for using a CCD. The high visual load while driving [7] and the need to control the car manually leave only a little spare capacity for communicating with a CCD. Most traffic situations do not allow attention anywhere else than on the traffic. There are only small windows in time to use a CCD, leading to strict time restrictions. Input devices, screen layouts, and use-philosophies differ clearly between the manufacturers. The technological development of the equipment is so fast, that on the ergonomics side hardly any experience has been collected. In addition, inside a car, there is only limited space for input and output devices. That leads to small output devices, monochromatic LED-displays or screens sized up to 7 inches. Input devices have to be reduced in size and number as well.

CCD are physically placed in the car world, but they have the functionality of a member of the computer world. The more functions are integrated in the DIS, the more complex they become, the more office- or internet-applications run on them, the more they move to the computer side.

Solutions for passenger-information-systems, which are DIS and CCD only accessible by passengers, are already presented [8] Figure 1. From the human factors point of view they present the less difficult and less interesting side, being just computer world devices placed in a car. The main focus should be set to CCD with office and internet applications for drivers. These systems are in development at the moment. The modification of computer-style-guides for car-installed-systems and the fitting of input- and output devices to the special circumstances of driving could be the major point of automotive human factors research.

Figure 1. Brabus Business Concept [8]

TOOLS TO ANALYSE HUMAN FACTORS OF DIS

The development of DIS requires a constant generation and flow of human factors knowledge. To achieve this, easy to handle and fast to use tools should be available.

One way to analyze a DIS is to have a look at the system itself, how the information input is organized, how the output. How many input devices are used, what kind of screen? A tool supporting this could be a simple protocol to write the information plus an algorithm to extract the knowledge by giving values. A second way is to study the user, his behavior and feelings about the system. The analysis of mistakes is a good way, as well as interviews with owners of a particular system or with naive users after being confronted with a DIS. The first approach is an analytical one, the second more or less empirical.

ANALYTICAL TOOLS – On the analytical side two tools exist. An established tool is the Analysis-Protocol for DIS. This paper contents 21 pages. The first part is the analysis of the DIS in general, the subsystems and functions included, the characteristics of the user interface, or the general philosophy of the user interface. Here general philosophy means: is it a one twist-push-button system, touch-screen, speech input or something else. Number, size, tactile feedback and position of the input devices are noted. Depth and width of the menu-tree is noted, as well as dialogue principles, kind of speech used and so on. On the output side size, position, colors, fonts and so on are in focus. If speech output is provided, questions are on understandability, selection of words, and correct presentation time are answered.

The second part gets into the single applications running in the DIS, e.g. telephone, radio or navigation. Information input and the output are analyzed. The number input-steps is counted, e.g. for the input of a navigation target or a phone number. In addition on each single page is space to collect the personal opinion of the analyzer. This, at the end, leads to a first judgement by an expert and an idea of the strong and the weak points of the system and its interface. Advantages of this tool are the fast results, the direct generation of an opinion by an expert for an expert (or, as usually applied, a group of experts) and the possibility to store information for a later analysis. Disadvantages are the high dependency of the results on the expert making the analysis and the exclusion of the user's view.

The second analytical tool available is a checklist with 250 items, being tested at the moment. The items were generated from literature. Computer style guides were used [e.g. 2], just like DIS-style guides [9, 10] or scientific publications [11, 12]. A second resource for items was the Analysis-Protocol for DIS. After the analysis of some DIS with clearly different user interfaces (Lexus Touch-screen System, Blaupunkt RNS II, Mercedes Comand, Nissan Birdview) items allowing statements on the pros and cons of each system were extracted. The third item-resource was a row of discussions among human factors engineers, developers and users made at CAA. This checklist has the advantages of the Analysis-Protocol for DIS, plus a higher reliability and more independence from personal views of experts. Disadvantage is the low flexibility of checklists compared to free protocols. And, again, the user's view is not included in the judgement.

EMPIRICAL TOOLS – Empirical research is necessary to get the user's point of view into the assessment of DIS. To collect data on an empirical basis, a guide line for semi-structured interviews was developed. It contains 5 questions, beginning with: How did you like the system tested? Why do you like/dislike it? Can you imagine to purchase this system? and ending with Tell me the three things you like most on the system! and Tell me the three things you like less on the system! The latest step of tool evolvement is a questionnaire (for details see below).

USABILITY STUDY ON EXISTING DIS

A usability study of existing DIS was conducted to get information about users views on human factors of DIS. It had two major goals. One was to develop and test a questionnaire, the other one was to get information on the usability of the systems, to generate a knowledge base for the development of future systems.

QUESTIONNAIRE ON THE HUMAN FACTORS OF DIS – A questionnaire development usually begins with the collection and the generation of an item-space (Figure 2). An item-space is build by identifying the relevant facts on the research object. Each component of the item-space will be transformed into one or more items. They will be connected with a rating scale to build the 0.9 version of the questionnaire. To get to a 1.0 version additional tests on reliability and validity of the tool are made in developmental steps following.

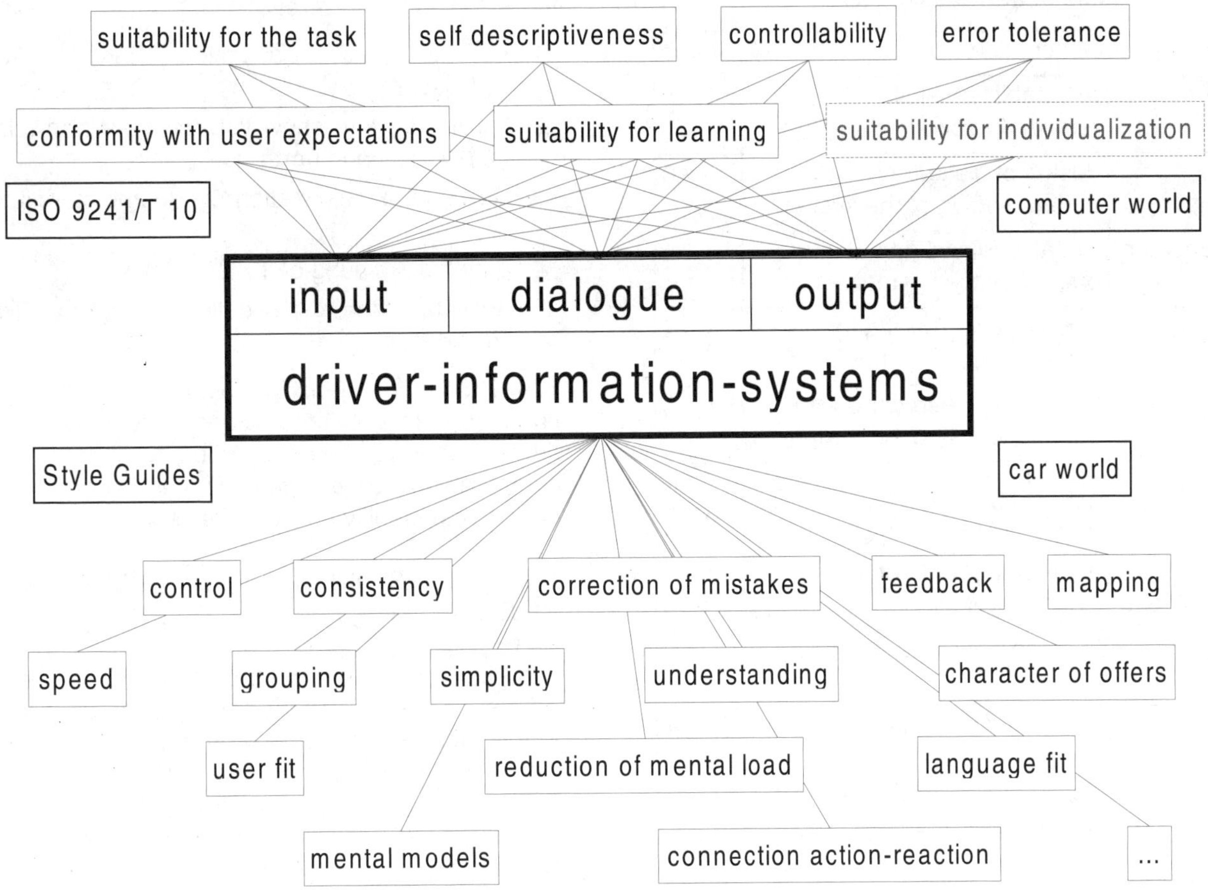

Figure 2. Item-space for the questionnaire

Here the first set of items represented the influence of the computer-world. Basis was ISO 9241-10 [5]. The mentioned factors of the dialogue (suitability for the task, self-descriptiveness, controllability, conformity with user expectations, error tolerance, suitability for individualization, suitability for learning) were adapted for the assessment of DIS human factors. Suitability for learning was renamed and reinterpreted to learnability. DIS should be easy to learn. The idea that the process of learning is desirable, which is the idea behind suitability for learning, is not appropriate for DIS. Suitability for individualization was not included because today's DIS are not personalizable. If individual configurations are possible one day, items on that should be included in the questionnaire. For each factor of ISO 9241-10 one item was generated for the input, the dialogue, and the output.

Items representing the car-world were generated from literature. Main sources were [9], [10], [13], and [14]. Major points were extracted to the item-space. For each element of the item-space one or two items were generated.

A group of four human factors experts made the precise wording of the items. They were presented to 12 novices. They were non-technical colleagues (secretaries, members of the marketing and so on) at the company. A discussion was made on the understandability and the fit between item and asked content. Final wording and selection (to reduce content doubles) were made by the experts. At the end of this process 47 items were left. A five point rating scale was added. The sequence of items was randomized.

To provide a fast and easy interpretation of the data at this early stage items were grouped on a content but not on a statistical bases. These groups were similar to the components of the item-space. The were called parameters (Table 1). Some items belong to one parameter, some to more than one.

Table 1. Parameters of the questionnaire

parameter	Description	items
anthropometric human factors	reachability, visibility, regulation powers	5
cognitive human factors	design of dialogue, understanding of the system	8
sensoric human factors	visual, acoustic and tactile outputs of the system	5
controllability	controllability, having the system in one's hands	4
suitability for the task	relation between costs and benefits of using the system	3
learnability	aspects of learning the system	4
error tolerance	handling of mistakes	3
self descriptiveness	understandability of the system by itself	6
language fit	fit of the system language with the user	3
consistency	similarity of the system with itself, homogeneity	4
feedback	time fit, understandability and task fit of the feedback	3
speed	speed of the system	3
colors	like and dislike of colors of input and output	2
acceptance	like and dislike of the system, prices	9

METHOD OF THE STUDY – The method used in the study was the frontal confrontation. Naive users had to solve five tasks with the systems unknown to them. Help was not provided at all. This method allows to analyze mistakes. It shows problems of the systems best. And it is not unrealistic. Often rental cars have a DIS, someone with out any experience enters one and should be able to use at least the major functions with out any help.

Data was collected with objective and subjective methods. A questionnaire was presented after each system, the interview was made after solving the tasks with the last system. The actions of the users were recorded on video. The number of subjetcs´ failures was counted for each system and every task.

33 subjects took part in the study, 10 of them female. 4 already had experience with a DIS, but not with one of the tested. They were recruited with advertisements in teleTraffic (a magazine dealing with telematics, navigation, and DIS, usually read by user, developers, and vendor of these systems) and in the Stuttgarter Zeitung (a major, high-level newspaper read in the region).

Each subject had to solve the same five tasks with every system. The tasks were:

1. Activate the navigation target "München, Königsplatz"
2. Let the system show you the map and change the map direction to north-up
3. Turn on the radio station SWR3 and store it under no. 1
4. Play the 3rd song of the 2nd CD
5. Activate the navigation target "Hannover, Towncentre"

Four DIS were tested. The follow up of the systems was changed from subject to subject. The tasks were always presented in the same order to provide maximum comparability between the systems (by paying the price of no comparability between the tasks).

THE DRIVER INFORMATION SYSTEMS IN THE STUDY

The Alfa Romeo 166 with Siemens IDIS – The Siemens IDIS in the version provided by Alfa Romeo (IDIS) (Figure 3) includes audio components, telephone, navigation, a trip computer and some parts of the climate equipment. Subsystems are selected with hardkeys positioned under the screen. Navigation in menus and letter inputs for the navigation target is realized with a central twist and push-button. A screen-layout, providing major information from the whole system, can be reached from any point by pressing MAIN. The screen is black, fonts and symbols are green. Speech output is given for navigation.

Figure 3. Siemens IDIS in the Alfa Romeo 166 (Siemens AG)

The BMW Navigation System – The BMW Navigation System (BMW) (Figure 4) includes audio components, television, telephone, and navigation. Input controls are a central twist and push button plus some hard-keys. The output devices are a color screen and speech for navigation information. The activation of the subsystems is sometimes realized with hard-keys, sometimes with soft-keys. Navigation in menus is possible with a central twist and push button. The selection of letters for navigation inputs and the activation of different options is realized with it as well. The MENU button brings the user back to the main menu from any point. The integration of the audio components is weak. It is possible to get audio information (selected radio-station or CD) on the screen, but the inputs are made with separate hard-keys. Background color of the screen is blue, fonts are white or black, depending on the status of information given.

Figure 4. DIS of a BMW 5xx (BMW AG)

The Lexus Voice Navigation System – The Lexus Voice Navigation System (VNS) was installed in a Lexus IS200 (Figure 5). This system has major differences compared with the others. The system itself only includes navigation, the audio components are realized in a more or less traditional manner. A telephone is not included. The input device is a remote control placed between the seats. It includes a joy-stick with a twist element plus four push buttons, including a o.k.-button. Inputs for the navigation targets are made with the joy stick. The output is a color screen placed high on the dashboard.

Figure 5. The Lexus Voice Navigation System [15]

The Mercedes Comand System – The Mercedes Comand System (Comand) (Figure 6) includes audio-components, television, telephone, and navigation. The subsystems are activated by hard-keys. They are placed above the screen. Navigation in menus and letter input is possible with a twist and push button. Some functions are realized as soft-keys, some are on the 2 way-whip around the central twist and push button. The output is realized by a medium sized screen. Colors (yellow and blue) are used consistently to divide between different areas of the screen. Night-design is provided by using complementary colors.

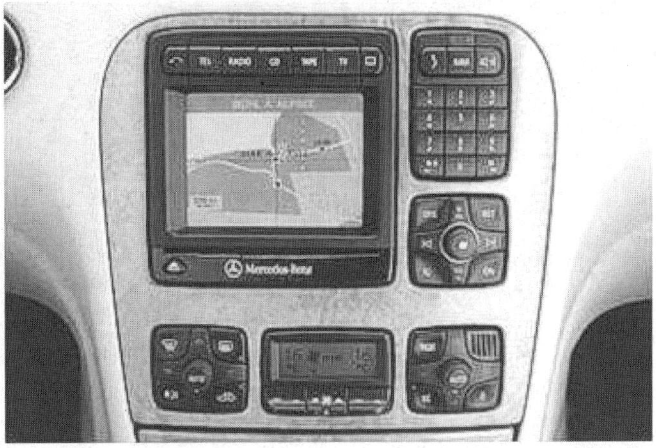

Figure 6. The Mercedes Comand (DaimlerChrysler AG)

RESULTS OF THE STUDY

Subjective Results – To get information on the questionnaire, the relationship of the items with each other, correlations were calculated between them. Highest correlations were found between all items on acceptance. the same goes for all items on learnability, conformity with user expectations and handling of mistakes. A cluster analysis shows more or less the same results.

The correlations between acceptance and the other parameters were calculated to find out about the major influences on acceptance (Figure 7). Consistency has the highest correlation, cognitive human factors (hf) the second. The lowest are mistakes and speed.

The questionnaire is still under construction, so here are only some major results presented. In the overall rating (mean of all items) and for acceptance the Mercedes Comand gained the best results, followed by the Lexus VNS, the Alfa Romeo IDIS and the BMW Navi. The results fail statistical significance. For anthropometric hf Mercedes Comand and Lexus VNS were better than BMW Navi and Alfa Romeo IDIS.

In the interview the inputs of the Alfa Romeo IDIS got good results, as well as the internal organization of the system. The position in the car (too deep, well hidden behind the gear stick, hard to reach) and the German-English language mix were mentioned as negatives. The inputs of the BMW Navi were good, the knobs were a bit too soft, providing only poor tactile feedback. The internal organization, the structure of the menu and the low connection between audio and the rest of the system were mentioned negative. The screen was medium readable, the fonts a bit too small. The inputs of the

Lexus VNS, a remote control placed between the front seats with a joy-stick, were discussed controversially, the internal organization did not match the users expectations. The position of the screen near the line of sight was appreciated by most of the subjects, as well as the bright colors. The Mercedes Comand was good to understand and the less difficult to use in the study. Font size was big enough, the screen colors well accepted by the subjects.

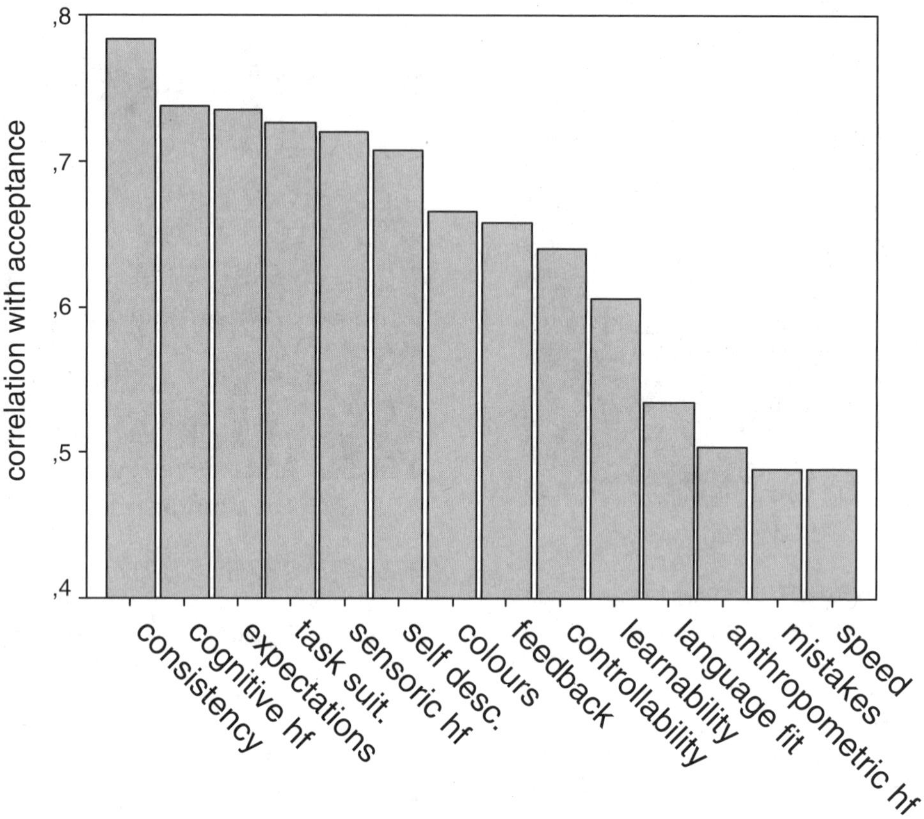

Figure 7. Correlation between the questionnaire parameters and acceptance

Objective Results – The videos have not been analyzed so far. Tools and results will be published soon. More than 22 % of the tasks were not solved by the subjects. The system with the most failures is the Lexus VNS. With the Comand the subjects were most successful (Table 2).

Table 2. Relative failures of the subjects

task	IDIS	BMW	VNS	Comand	∅
1	18.2 %	15.1 %	30.3 %	33.3 %	24.2 %
2	33.3 %	6.1 %	24.2 %	33.3 %	24.2 %
3	33.3 %	27.3 %	30.3 %	18.2 %	27.2 %
4	15.1 %	27.3 %	3.03 %	0 %	11.4 %
5	15.1 %	45.5 %	42.4 %	0 %	25.8 %
∅	23.0 %	24.2 %	26.0 %	17.0 %	22.6 %

DISCUSSION OF THE RESULTS – The questionnaire has to be developed. Some more items have to be added, especially in the area of screen design and language outputs. Some highly correlating items, e.g. for learnability, can be cancelled. In replication experiments the tool has to show its validity and reliability.

Most important for the acceptance of DIS is consistency. This matches the demands of most experts [e.g. 2]. Subjects are irritated if functions change from one subsystem to another. In some submenus of the Lexus VNS an action is activated by choosing the point in the menu, in some the extra O.K. button has to be pressed. In the BMW Navi navigation, television, telephone etc. are activated via the screen and the main button, just the audio components are used with separated input devices, although partly displayed on the screen. The consistency of the main button leads to positive judgements on the navigation subsystem of the BMW Navi. All input actions are made with the same device in the same way.

Cognitive human factors are very important for the acceptance of DIS. This parameter represents the internal structure of the device. At first sight most of the systems are designed well under a cognitive hf point of view. Closer looks show hard to understand and even harder to find submenus. Some DIS force decisions at a point of the input process, where they were not expected.

During the navigation input process of the Lexus VNS a decision has to be made, weather to go to the town center, a junction, an address, or a point of interest. This decision has to be made before entering the name of a town, which is counter rotating to the usual way of thinking.

The Mercedes Comand and the Alfa IDIS have hardkeys for the subsystems (navigation, CD, telephone etc.). This showed the single functions of the systems at first sight and made the access to other subsystem easy and fast.

Conformity with user expectations deals with the fit between user mental models and the system-model. The ratings for the tested DIS were low. The existing systems do not pick the users up where they are. Naive users expect a stronger guidance and more help by the DIS. Users do not think in technical structures, but in goals to reach. HMI of DIS represent the technical side of the system, not the goals of the users.

Suitability for the task deals in main with the relationship between costs and benefits. Users are sensitive to inappropriate input operations. The subsystem for word inputs (e.g. towns for navigation) of the Mercedes Comand irritated some subjects, because it was not possible to move the cursor the way they wanted to. This resulted in bad ratings for the system. All in all most subjects said, that all the systems are too hard to use, so the costs for getting information are higher than the benefits.

Self-descriptiveness was missed by most of the subjects. Help-buttons, on line help and a clear naming of submenus and functions were the demands. Colors were missed by most users as far as the input devices were concerned. The colors of the Mercedes Comand were not attractive but useful, because they were used consistently to distinguish between screen areas. Feedback was divided into two different parts, the direct feedback as an information about the running dialogue and feedback about the state of the system, e.g. route calculation vs. route guidance. The first kind of feedback was acceptable for most of the users, the second kind not so much. The remaining calculation time was not shown by the Mercedes Comand, the Alfa IDIS and the BMW Navi. The display of remaining time in the Lexus VNS was wrong. Controllability was on an medium level, the audio screens of the BMW Navi turned to standard screens after a time out. This leaves novice users with a feeling of reduced controllability. The good news is: all subjects believe, they are able to learn the systems, if not with a trial and error strategy, then with the manual.

The language fit of the Alfa Romeo IDIS was rated quite poor, the mix of German and English expressions was rejected by most of the subjects. The other side of that represents the Mercedes Comand, no English expressions were used at all. This leads sometime to some bulky menu names, but was rated positively by the subjects. Anthropometrics were extremely poor for the Alfa Romeo IDIS, the position of the system was too low and behind the gear stick. The position of the Lexus VNS screen was rated very good. It was near the line of sight, very high in the car. The input device, a remote control with a joystick, was very much under discussion. Some found it to be the best in principle, some rated it worst in the study. All had in common, that the look & feel of the remote control was cheap. The joystick was to soft and inaccurate. Mistakes could usually be handled well, the speed of the system was rated as far too slow.

IMPLICATIONS FOR CAR COMPUTING DEVICES

Empirical data on human factors and usability is available for DIS. CCD add a new dimension to the in car environment. With this new human factors problems raise. Applications and programs fitting well with the office environment are brought to vehicles. The technology push in this area is hard to stop, so the ergonomic community has to escort the development. At this early stage connected with a fast evolvement of new applications and an enormous raise of technological possibilities the knowledge about DIS has to be projected to CCD. All human factors parameters (see above) should be realized well in CCD.

There will be a discussion about the reduction of functions of CCD while driving, maybe speed dependent. This may lead to an increase in safety, but to a decrease in acceptance by the users. Imagine a business man, having spent 10.000US$ for a CCD, and not being able to make a telephone call while driving! If CCD fail human factors standards, legal activity will cut the developmental work and reduce the integration of new technologies in vehicles. Only well designed and easy to use systems, matching the human abilities, will have a chance to be accepted by users and by non users.

COMMUNICATION CHANNELS – Major point of all thinking about designing a driver suitable interface for CCD is the correct choice of communication channels. Due to the high visual demands which driving tasks have, the major focus during the development of user interfaces has to be set to the reduction of visual load.

Reduction of visual load can be achieved by using information transmission channels other than the visual. On the input side, language input is strongly recommended, although technical problems are not solved to completeness now. On the technical side developmental work has to be done on the reduction of background noise disturbances. Human factors research is necessary to fit the verbal dialogue to user expectations. Easy to realize would be a dialogue guided by the system, leaving just "yes" and "no" answers to the driver. This would make dialogues very unhandy. Best fit for the user would be a system understanding natural language. For the near future an compromise between the two will be realized. Human factors research has to provide knowledge about style and structure of speech based dialogues between user and machine.

Language input will work well for navigation in menus, choosing applications or controlling basic functions. The selection of telephone-numbers or addresses will not be too much of a problem either. The text input, writing letters, e-mails, calendar-notes and so on, will also work with language after the solution of the remaining technical and human factors problems.

A much more complex problem is navigation in the internet. Graphical pages need a strong visual feedback, which makes the in-car use difficult. For this, human factors engineers and internet designers have to cooperate, because the design of the CCD reaches its limits quickly. Available internet pages must be reduced in their graphical parameters, providing the content acceptable for drivers.

All outputs should be given acoustically, either as language or as tones. This includes the marking of time windows for aural inputs with beeps and the offering of choices by language. It has to be easily possible to repeat any output at any time.

If inputs cannot be made aurally, haptic feedback on inputs should be provided by using different switches or knobs. Tactile feedback of the status in necessary. Fingertip-information makes, at least for long-time-users, the use with a minimum of visual load possible. All input devices should be grouped under functional not under technological criteria.

If visual attention is needed to obtain information, the relevant outputs should be presented in a form way to read and near the line of sight. In this way fixation times, saccadic movements and visual load can be reduced. Colors should be used to group information and to emphasize most important information.

The development of style-guides for CCD should be enforced, useful basis are [9] and [14]. PC-style-guides have to be modified, but can serve as information resources. Since DIS technology is more and more available for all, ergonomic interfaces become an distinguishing feature.

DIALOGUE WITH A CCD – Office and internet applications as they are used in the PC-world fit perfectly with passenger needs, but they are not suitable for drivers. PC interfaces have to be at least adapted to drivers´ needs. Probably completely new interfaces have to be developed.

Analytical research has to be done about the needs of the user. Which are the functions of CCD needed and used by owners? What do they expect if they purchase a CCD? Is it really necessary to provide full Excel and SPSS functionality in an car? Or is some word-processing, writing and receiving mails and faxes, a calendar, and a organization function enough?

All kind of word-processing, producing or receiving mail, letters and so on should be shifted to the acoustic channel. This requires a modification of PC programs. More than one window on the screen will not be handable for the driver. The input and the output process should be handled and lead by the system as far as possible.

Internet pages as known from the office environment need high visual attention. They include banners, optical hyperlinks, tables, and graphics. Most of these pages are hard to read even under office conditions. The manipulation of these sites by using links spread all over the page requires input devices not suitable for cars. New site designs have to be developed. The Wireless Application Protocol (WAP) shows a way. WAP is a protocol that leads to WML, a language similar to HTML. WAP is used to bring internet contents to cellular phones via the GSM channel. Internet contents are reduced to the minimum to make them readable on the small and often monochromatic displays of these devices. In addition the reduction raises the speed of information transport. The results are pure text pages with the possibility of using hyperlinks to get new information. The use of WAP for cars could be one solution. On the other hand, the reduction to pure text is not the optimum for internet in CCD, reading is not the optimal way to get information to the driver. An acoustical channel should be added to the protocol as well as the presentation of information with simple graphical elements like icons. The optical output should be much more structured than it is in WAP. Driver or driving related internet pages should be available in a version that fits the driving environment, more structured than WAP pages, less optical than usual sites.

A SUGGESTION FOR A CCD INTERFACE – A prototype for a CCD, called CAA CarPC was developed. This prototype was realized to show the technological possibilities and the some human factors solutions. The system provides the complete functionality, navigation, audio components, telephone, teleconferencing, internet access, e-mail, office, seat-positioning, climate control etc. It is based on an Intel^{TM} processor and works with Windows Embedded NT^{TM}.

Figure 8 shows the input devices of the CAA CarPC. The round button in the middle is a twist knob with a push function, allowing the navigation in menus. The subsystem buttons are on top, the help button on the right, and the back button at the bottom. On the left two up and down bottons are positioned. The whole object has a diameter of about 4 inches, so it is large enough be handled while driving. Every button has a different shape, providing blind use for experts. Tactile feedback fits conditions while driving.

Figure 8. Input devices of a CarPC (CAA)

The CarPC is a system with a high consistency, all menus have the same functionality, the choice in submenus on the left, a jump to the right part of the screen by pushing the main button. There is the possibility of activating a function. The organization of the menus will be reorganized during the next months by applicating users models. They will be recorded with a combination of multi dimensional scaling and cluster analysis. The input devices make offers to the user, they clearly indicate what the system can do.

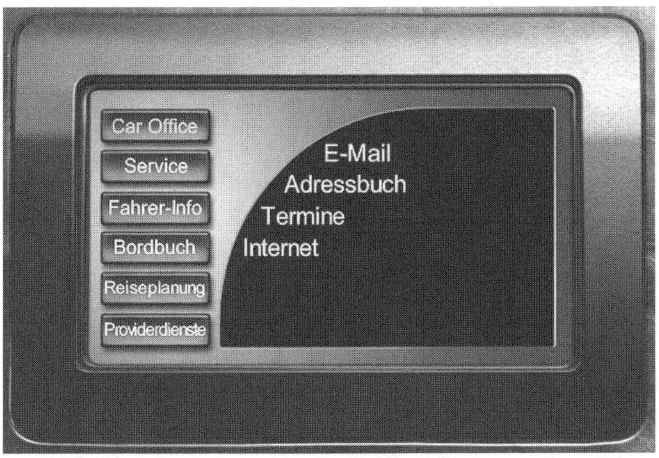

Figure 9. The screen of a CarPC (CAA)

The screen of the CarPC (Figure 9) is a 7" display. It is clearly divided into two sections. On the left side are submenus of the second level, on the right commands, or choices, e.g. radio-stations or CDs. Colors are used for different submenus, the radio has another one than the CD-player or the navigation system. Font-size is large enough, the font-type is well readable. The output is reduced to the necessary. Speech output is provided for navigation information, speech input for creating text, dialing telephone numbers, and choosing e-mails.

CONCLUSION

CCD will come, internet and office will be part of in car information processing. The driver will spent mental capacities on the systems. The benefits of an information have to be higher than the costs to get it. All human factors aspects should be considered. If the realization of any of it fails, the systems might not be accepted, or the costs of using them will be higher than the benefits. The PC standards (Windows etc.) do not match the needs inside a car. They were made for office workers, not for drivers. Solutions fitting the car-world have to be developed.

Do not expect to ever get the optimal user interface for a CCD too many influences needing contrary solutions exist. To find a good or very good solution, invite a sample of users and test, test, test.......

REFERENCES

1. Cooper, A. (1999). *The Inmates are Running the Asylum*. Indianapolis: SAMS.
2. Schumacher, R.M. (1995). *Ameritech Graphical User Interface Standards and Design Guidelines*. Ameritec Cooperation. http://www.ameritec.com, Download at Jan, 12th, 1999.
3. Microsoft. (1992). *The Windows Interface: An Application Design Guide*. PC28921-0692.
4. Apple Computer Inc. (1987). Human Interface Guidelines: The Apple Desktop Interface. Reading, MA: Addison-Wesley.
5. ISO 9241 - 10 (1996). *Ergonomic Requirements for Office Work with Visual Display Terminals. Dialogue Principles*. Berlin: Beuth Verlag.
6. Carayon, P. (1992). A Longitudinal Study of Job Design and Worker Strain: Preliminary Results. In: Quick, J.C., Murphy, L.R. & Hurrell, J.J., *Stress and Well-Being at Work: Assessments and Interventions for Occupational Mental Health*. Washington, D.C.: American Psychological Association.
7. Fastenmeier, W. (1995). Die Verkehrssituation als Analyseeinheit im Verkehrssystem. In: Fastenmeier, W. (Ed.) *Autofahrer und Verkehrssituation* (27-28) Cologne: Verlag TÜV Rheinland.
8. Brabus (1999), http://www.brabus.com/homee.htm, Nov. 30th, 1999.
9. Dingus, T., Hulse, M., Jahn, S. Alves-Foss, J., Confer, S., Rice, A., Roberts, I., Hanowski, R., & Sorenson, D. (1996). *Development of Human Factors Guide Lines for Advanced Traveller Information Systems and Commercial Vehicle Operations: Literature Review*. Federal Highway Administration, Report No. FHWA-RD-95-153.

10. Green, P. (1997). *Human Factors of In-Vehicle Driver Information Systems: An Executive Summary.* Federal Highway Administration, Report No. FHWA-RD-95-014.

11. Hamberger, W., Cremers, R. & Willumeit, H.P. (1998). Verbesserung der aktiven Fahrzeugsicherheit durch fortschrittliche Navigationssysteme. In: Willumeit, H.P. & Kolrep, H.: *Wohin führen Unterstützungssysteme?* (182-194). Sinzheim: Pro Universitate.

12. Peters, H. (1997). User-Centred Design of In-Vehicle Information Systems – requirements for Development and Testing. In: *VDI-Berichte 1317, Der Mensch im Verkehr (93-103).* Düsseldorf: VDI-Verlag GmbH.

13. Green, P., Levison, W., Paelke, G. & Serafin, C. (1995). *Preliminary Human Factors Design Guidelines for Driver Information Systems.* Federal Highway Administration, Report No. FHWA-RD-94-087.

14. Campbell, J.L., Carney, C., & Kantowitz, B.H. (1998). *Human Factors Design Guide Lines for Advanced Traveller Information Systems (ATIS) and Commercial Vehicle Operations (CVO).* Federal Highway Administration, Report No. FHWA-RD-98-057.

15. Rößger, P. & Smyrek, U. (1999). Bestens bedient. *Teletraffic,* No.9/10.

CONTACT

Dr.-Ing. Peter Roessger, CAA GmbH, Raiffeisenstr. 34, 70794 Filderstadt, Germany

mail to: p.roessger@caa.de

http://www.caa.de

2001-01-3286

Driver Eye Movement During a Route Navigation Information Search

Guangyan Li[*] and Helen Middleton
Institute for Automotive and Manufacturing Advanced Practice (AMAP), University of Sunderland

ABSTRACT

In-vehicle route navigation systems are used by an increasing number of drivers throughout the world. These systems are intended to assist the driver in the driving task by providing real-time navigational instructions. However, most route navigation systems appear to have been developed on the basis of technical features, rather than from a usability/human factors viewpoint, causing concerns over their safety implications, especially for older drivers.

An experimental study was carried out to test drivers' preference of markers in an electronic map display. This was done by analysing drivers eye fixation and movement during information searching in a number of route navigation tasks. The study indicates that, in order to find the 'correct' road during a navigational search, participants adopt visual search strategies in which they tend to fixate, initially on text road identification markers, followed by glances to numeric and symbolic road markers. There was also significant interaction between marker type and map orientation for their influences on eye fixation. It is anticipated that by taking the driver preference for road marker type into consideration in the design of in-vehicle route displays, the system will be used more efficiently.

INTRODUCTION

A variety of in-vehicle route navigation systems are now available and are used by an increasing number of drivers throughout the world. These systems are intended to assist the driver by providing route guidance information, enabling travel to a selected destination via the most efficient route (Ashby and Parkes, 1993), thus reducing travel time and cost. It has also been suggested that by reducing decision making and potential stress, more attention will be available for the primary driving tasks, thereby improving safety (Warnes et al., 1993; Dingus and Hulse, 1993).

Systems currently available for route navigation range from static in-vehicle route guidance systems, through to the more advanced dynamic systems. Within these categories there are numerous variations regarding the type of information used to calculate the route, timing of information delivery, method by which information is presented, and mode of presentation. For example, static route guidance systems calculate the optimal route between starting point and destination but do not take traffic conditions into account. They provide only autonomous, pre-trip navigation instructions such as distance and direction to destination, with no additional navigational guidance during the trip. Whilst, dynamic route guidance systems use traffic congestion information at various levels, by predicting recurrent traffic congestion or analysing real time traffic information, for example, to provide optimal route guidance (Eby and Kostyniuk, 1999). More advanced systems such as Advanced Traveller Information Systems (ATIS) have information regarding vehicle position (using the Global Positioning System or GPS) which enables them to provide the driver with turn by turn or map-based, verbal and/or visual instructions during the course of navigation.

Previous studies investigating the performance of ATIS generally suggest that there are considerable advantages to using navigational assistance. Several studies have shown that drivers using in-vehicle route navigation systems make shorter, more efficient trips, and are involved in fewer near crashes than drivers using conventional maps and instructions (Eby et al., 1997; Fastenmeier et al., 1994; Inman et al., 1995; Parkes et al., 1991; Schofer et al., 1996). Eby and Kostyniuk's (1999) study showed no difference in travel time to destination between drivers using dynamic or static route guidance systems, although drivers considered autonomous guidance information less helpful for finding destinations than turn-by turn instruction on-route.

In-vehicle navigation systems present the driver with visual and/or auditory information. However, driving is often characterised as a task that is 90% visual in nature (Sivak, 1995) and this raises concerns regarding potential additional workload associated with screen based route guidance information (Verwey, 1989, 1993; Dingus et al., 1993). It has been proposed that the auditory resource is under utilised in the driving environment (Jackson, 2000) and several auditory interfaces have been developed to convey route guidance information. Research has shown that well-designed verbal guidance is easier than written words or symbols for drivers to process (Verwey, 1993), and is actually prefered by drivers (Street et al., 1985; Burnett & Joyner, 1996). However, Jackson (2000) suggests that route guidance instructions currently in use may actually inhibit the development of cognitive maps and prevent the normal development of mental representations of the area. To be most effective, Jackson (2000) proposes that route guidance should be expressed

[*] Now at Human Engineering Ltd., Shore House, 68 Westbury Hill, Westbury-On-Trym, Bristol BS9 3AA UK

in terms of what the driver actually sees at decision points such as road junctions, and that cognitive maps might be strengthened by linking turn information to salient features and land marks in the immediate environment.

As stated previously, research concerning in-vehicle route navigation systems to date has been focused predominantly around broad issues regarding the type of information used, timing of information presentation, method and mode of presentation, and system performance. More specific aspects of information presentation, such as the most efficient display format for road identification markers still appear to be not well understood. There is a need for information regarding driver's preferences, and the effects of road identification marker type during the dynamic interactions associated with route navigation in the driving task.

There is extensive evidence in the psychological literature to suggest that written road name markers would be easily processed and thus preferred by drivers. For example, word identification is a relatively automatic process (Rayner and Sereno, 1994; Eysenk and Keane, 1996), thus reading is unavoidable and quick. Evidence is provided by the 'Stroop' colour identification task (Stroop, 1935; Cheeseman and Merikle, 1984) in which participants attempt to name the ink colour in which words are printed as rapidly as possible. Naming speed is slowed when the words are conflicting colour names. The 'Stroop effect' suggests that word meaning is extracted even when subjects are attempting not to process it. However, the conclusion that word identification occurs automatically is based mainly on studies using very familiar words, and it is possible that relatively rare words (such as the names of destinations) that are unfamiliar to the driver may not be processed automatically.

Numbers and symbols are increasingly being used on road signs, vehicle controls, and on in-vehicle route navigation interfaces. Symbols are generally used because they are more compact than either associated words or abbreviations, and are considered to provide a means of communication independent of language (Green, 1993). Road sign symbols can be recognised at a smaller visual angle than text signs, and several studies have shown that symbols are at least two times more legible than the text equivalent (Jacobs et al, 1975; Paniati, 1988; Babbitt et al, 1990). However, studies comparing response times for symbols and text on road signs have been contradictory. For example, Dewar and Ells (1974) and Dewar et al. (1979) found road signs with text elicited quicker response times than symbolic signs, but Ells and Dewar (1979) found that symbolic signs elicited a quicker response.

The development of in-vehicle route navigation and similar technologies has created a need for research methodologies with an emphasis on user centred design (Wochinger and Boehm-Davis, 1997). For example eye movement analysis can be a useful tool for probing the cognitive processes underlying behaviour, and have been described as "a window on cognition" (Yarbus, 1967). The measurement of eye movements has been used in many information acquisition contexts and can play an important role in route navigation interface evaluation.

Within the concept of visual information display, Li and Oliver (2000) studied the effects of electronic map complexity and orientation (mental rotation) on driver responses for efficient road identification. The aim of their study was to find out if an in-vehicle information display with reasonable complexity level, combined with little need for mental rotation, would result in faster response time and less error for route identification.

In the present study, driver preference for markers in an electronic map display was investigated. Road maps were designed in a similar way to those reported in Li and Oliver (2000), but with road names in text as well as numbers and the patterns of the maps represented by symbols with arrows indicating the direction of the 'correct' route. Three types of road markers (numeric, text, and symbols) were presented simultaneously to each participant on the same map display and drivers eye movements were recorded/analysed during a number of route navigation tasks using an eye tracking and video analysis system.

An area of interest approach was taken to the eye movement analysis in this study. The method involves dividing the interface into defined areas containing individual road markers. Fixation time and transitions into and from the areas specified were recorded for analysis.

To the authors knowledge few studies have been conducted that use eye movement analysis to assess drivers preference for road markers when using an electronic map display. Therefore, the present study has opened a new door to the understanding of driver's information search strategies when searching through an electronic map display.

METHOD

PARTICIPANTS

Twelve participants took part in the study. Eight were male and four were female. Their mean age was 36.92 (Range=25-55, SD=9.09). The participants were an opportunity sample of staff, students and visitors at the Institute for Automotive and Manufacturing Advanced Practice. All participants were drivers.

APPARATUS

Two PC's, a projector, a screen and an eye-tracking and video analysis system were used for the trial.

PC1: The first PC was a desk top eye movement analysis workstation with a 17-inch monitor, connected to a head mounted eye-tracking device with colour scene camera. The system included a real-time pupil/corneal reflection tracking board, video overlay facility, curVid cursor (indicating point of regard and data overlay into scene image), iView for Windows 3.x/Win9x acquisition and analysis software, and the Observer Video-Pro system for the analysis of CurVid output.

PC2: The second PC was a Viglen 486 with a 14-inch monitor. This had 16 MB RAM, 0.5 GB hard drive, and Windows 98. This system was connected to a projector in order to present experimental instructions and stimulus.

Projector: An Epsom EMP 700 projector was connected to PC2 to project the experimental instructions and stimuli onto the screen.

Screen: The screen was a standard 1.10m x 1.10m white projection screen positioned for viewing at a distance of 2m from the participant.

Eye tracking and video analysis system: An eye tracking system with head mounted optics (iView: Tracksys Ltd., Nottingham, UK), was used to record participants point of regard. The eye tracker works on the corneal reflection technique, which involves directing a light source onto the pupil of the eye via a clear mirror. The position of the resulting pupil threshold and corneal reflection are recorded via a head mounted camera directed at the eye. The displacement of the corneal reflection is mathematically related to the eye movement, making it possible to continuously monitor and record driver eye movements (point of regard). The instructions and stimuli as viewed by the participant are recorded by a second head mounted camera.

Point of regard was viewed as a moving cursor on a video overlay of the experimental stimuli. Viewing behaviour was then coded using a video analysis system installed on PC1 (Observer Video-Pro: Tracksys Ltd., Nottingham, UK), making it possible to conduct an analysis of areas of interest, and fixations (frequency/duration/percentage).

MATERIALS

Power Point slides were used to present the instructions and the experimental stimuli to the participants.

EXPERIMENTAL INSTRUCTIONS

The experimental instructions were presented on a set of power point slides. On each slide a written instruction was presented regarding the road that the participant was required to look for when viewing navigational information. The road information was presented in both text and numeric form; e.g., "You are looking for Stoke Road/A35". Great care was taken to select road names that would be unfamiliar to participants in order to control for the word familiarity effect (Eysenck and Keane, 1996). Position of road information type was counterbalanced to control for order effects. For example, the road name was presented first followed by the road number on half of the total number of slides, the road number was presented first followed by the road name on the remaining slides, and order of presentation was randomised.

EXPERIMENTAL STIMULI

The experimental stimuli were also presented on a set of power point slides. The slides were designed to simulate the type of information available to drivers during route navigation. On each slide three identical representations of a junction were displayed simultaneously. One junction had route navigation information in text, one had numeric and one symbolic. Position on the slide of each type of information was randomised between slides to control for positional effects and to facilitate active information search.

Route navigation information was also presented at three levels of complexity and at three different orientations, an identical design feature as reported in Li and Oliver (2000). For example, for complexity level one, one junction and two road names are presented, for complexity level two, two junctions and three names are presented. The map orientations included upright (no mental rotation), 90° rotation to either side and 180° rotation.

EXPERIMENTAL DESIGN

The experimental design was within subjects, controlling factors for map complexity (3 levels), orientation (3 levels) and type of eye fixation (4 types: text, numeric, symbolic and elsewhere). The participant's eye fixation was recorded and then analysed as percentage of time spent looking at different types of stimuli within each slide. Eye fixation as total duration for each slide show and the frequency of fixation changes between markers were also recorded.

PROCEDURE

The participant was seated at a high-adjustable chair with its height adjusted to the subject's preference and the viewing distance set at 2m. The eye-tracking system was then fitted and adjusted for good image quality and position. A standard training was given prior to the trial to familiarise the participant with the procedure and tasks that they would need to perform. The participant then started the test session with an instruction slide. After reading the instruction, the participant pressed a key to start a slide show containing three maps, each showing the same route guidance information using either text, numeric or symbolic markers. The participant was required to identify the correct road exit, based on the information sources presented, and give the answer, as quickly and accurately as possible, by saying which road exit he/she should take (for example, "second left", "third right", or "straight forward"). After the road was identified and the answer was given, the participant pressed a key to stop the slide show. Following a short pause (4 seconds) another instruction was presented followed by the next map display. No time limit was set for the task. Participant verbal response was scored by the experimenter as correct or incorrect on an experimental score sheet and the participant's eye movements/fixations were continuously recorded during the trial. The whole session (36 pairs of instructions and slide shows) lasted between five to ten minutes, including the short pauses between slide shows.

RESULTS

The data of the twelve participants eye fixation time (expressed as percentage of total duration) was analysed using ANOVA and the results are shown in Table 1.

Table 1. ANOVA results of the effects of map design factors on percentage of total eye fixation.

	df	MS	F	p-level
Complexity	2	238.13	15.183	$p \leq 0.001$
Orientation	2	269.11	9.076	$p \leq 0.001$
Fixation type	3	29704.07	8.008	$p \leq 0.001$
Subject	11	234.37	1.405	-
Orientation x Fixation type	6	919.57	4.025	$p \leq 0.01$

Figure 1 shows the percentage of total eye fixation time for different types of navigational stimuli, which indicates that the participants spent longer looking at the maps marked by text (road names) as compared to other types of information sources. Further analysis with Post hoc comparisons indicated that there was a significant difference in eye fixation between text and numeric references ($p \leq 0.05$), between text and symbolic references ($p \leq 0.001$), and between numeric and symbolic references ($p \leq 0.001$). Figure 2 shows the interaction between type of references/map markers and map rotation for their effects on eye fixation.

For the effect of map complexity on eye fixation, although the effect was significant, the change in overall fixation time due to complexity or orientation was small (within a range of 0.5-1.0 seconds).

Participant responses were scored and error rate was zero.

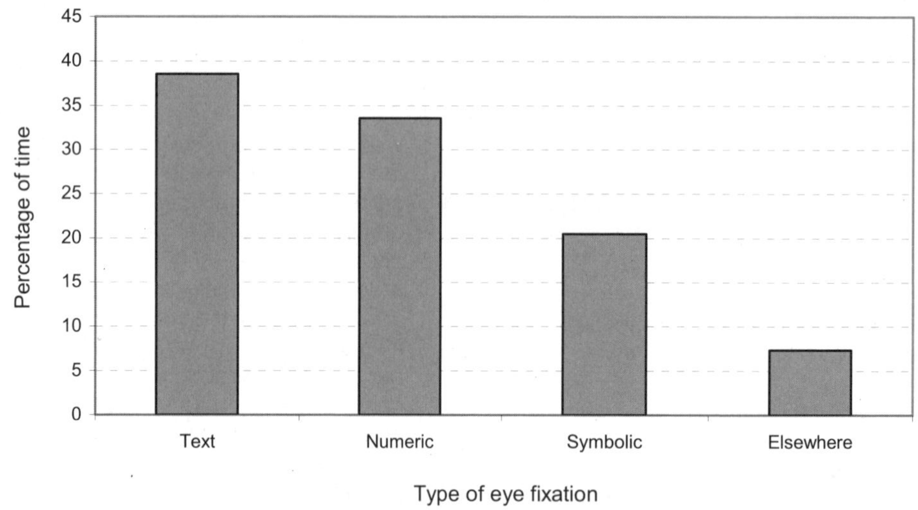

Figure 1. Effects of marker type on eye fixation

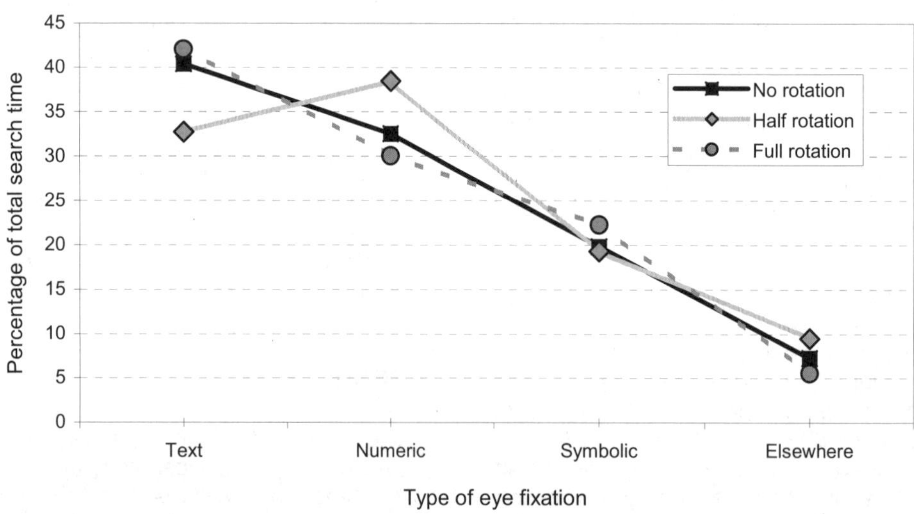

Figure 2. Interaction between marker type and map orientation for eye fixation

DISCUSSION

In the present study driver preferences for markers in a simulated electronic map display were investigated. The findings of this research show that the participants used the maps marked with text or the name of the road more often than any other type of information. This conforms with evidence in the psychological literature which suggests that word identification is a relatively automatic process (Rayner and Sereno, 1994; Eysenk and Keane, 1996), automatic processes are unavoidable and quick, and that word meaning is extracted even when participants attempt not to process it (Stroop, 1935; Cheeseman and Merikle, 1984). However, this was somewhat beyond the designer's expectations due to extensive evidence to suggest that a well designed symbol should be easily recognised (Olson, 1993), and that symbolic information is easily processed by drivers (Jacobs et al, 1975; Ells and Dewar, 1979; Paniati, 1988; Green, 1993; Babbitt et al, 1990). Thus, it might be expected that drivers would use symbolic or numeric information more often in order to navigate efficiently.

It was noticed during the trials that the participants tended to start their navigation by searching the road names first and then confirm their findings by checking the symbolic or numeric sources. One explanation for this could be that drivers fixated upon text first because this process was automatic and unavoidable. This was followed by a confirmation strategy using the other information that was available to them. It is also possible that the particular search strategies adopted by participants were the result of the way in which instructions were presented. For example, in each trial the participants were given the instructions with road names and road numbers at the same time. These were randomised to counterbalance order effects, but navigation information was presented in text, numeric and symbolic form and this could have resulted in a priming effect, producing a bias towards text and numeric based search strategies. An alternative would have been to present the experimental instructions to participants verbally. However, there is no way of giving a symbolic verbal instruction without providing the participant with the answer to the task.

This study also suggests that the participants, who were all experienced drivers, may have become used to utilising and searching for road names in words during their normal driving practice, thus the navigational system should be designed to accommodate their needs and custom.

The significant interaction between marker type and map orientation (as shown in Figure 2) indicates that the variation of eye fixation time depends on both the type of markers/references and their orientation (need for mental rotation). When the markers were presented either upright (no rotation) or upside down (full rotation), for example, the subjects looked at the text marker longer than any other marker types. when the markers were half-rotated, however, the subjects tended to use numeric reference more often. The findings suggest that, in the design of in-vehicle navigation systems, these two design factors (marker type and orientation) need to be carefully considered and balanced. For example, if the information is to be presented in text, it is better shown in an upright format; if the map is sometimes rotated to either side, numerical reference is more preferable. However, the interactions between these design factors appear to be complex and need to be studied further.

The present study noted that, as the result of varying map complexity from 'level 1' to 'level 3' as defined in this study, the magnitude of variation in total duration of eye fixation for information search within each slide was not great. This was in agreement with previous findings which showed that the change in map complexity resulted in significant changes in driver response time mainly when the complexity level was above level 3 (Li and Oliver, 2000). It needs to be noted that in the present study, the participants had several references for getting the same information, which might have counter-balanced the changes in map complexity level or orientation. Also, there were no time restraints regarding task completion, error rate was zero, and the task was designed as an investigation of visual search as opposed to performance. It is possible that driver's preference for road marker type may differ when searching for route navigation information, with maps of different complexity and orientation, under time pressure. Therefore, it is suggested that this research be taken further in future studies to include performance and eye movement, using simulated real traffic scenarios.

CONCLUSION

Most route navigation systems have been developed on the basis of technical development rather than on safety, user acceptance and other human factor issues (Wochinger and Boehm-Davis, 1997). This has led to concerns over safety, especially for older drivers (FHWA, 1995), and there have been demands for an increased emphasis on user centred design principles in the development of in-vehicle navigation systems. The findings of this study have provided further understanding with regard to driver preference and requirements for route markers in the context of route navigation in the driving task.

The results of this study suggested that, in designing the navigational systems, priority should be given in the order of text, numeric and symbolic references. Although there is an issue regarding the way the instruction was given before the participants started their route search, it is highly probable that it has become a common practice or custom that people tend to use road names for their route search. It has also been found useful to provide drivers with a symbolic reference guide in order for them to confirm their finding, before deciding which way to go.

REFERENCES

Ashby, M.C. and Parkes, A.M., 1993, Interface design for navigation and guidance. In: Driving Future Vehicles, (eds. A.M. Parkes and S. Franzen), London: Taylor & Francis, 295-310.

Babbit Kline, T.J., Ghali, L.M. Kline, E.W. and Brown, S., 1990, Visibility distance of highway signs among young, middle-aged, and older observers: Icons are better than text, *Human factors*, 32, (5) 609-20.

Burnett, G.E. and Joyner, S.M., 1996, Vehicle Navigation Systems: getting it right from the driver's perspective, *Journal of navigation,* 49 (2) 174-177.

Burnett, G.E. and Joyner, S.M., 1997, An assessment of moving map and symbol-based route guidance systems. In: Ergonomics and Safety of Intelligent Driver Interfaces, (ed. Y. Ian Noy), Mahwah, NJ: Lawrence Erlbaum Associates, 115-136.

Cheeseman, J., & Merikle, P.M., 1984, Priming with and without awareness. *Perception and Psychophysics,* 36, 387-395.

Dewar, R.E. and Ells, J.G., 1974, Comparison of three methods for evaluating traffic signs, *Transportation Research Record*, 503, 38-47.

Dewar, R.E., Ells, J.G., and Munday, G., 1976, Reaction time as an index of traffic sign perception, *Human factors*, 18(4), 381-92.

Dingus, T.A. and Hulse, M.C., 1993, Some human factors design issues and recommendations for automobile navigation information systems. Transportation Research, IC (2), 119-131.

Eby, D.W and Kostyniuk, L.P., 1999, An on road comparison of In-Vehicle Navigation Assistance systems, *Human Factors,* Vol. 41, No.2, pp. 295-311.

Eby, D.W., Kostyniuk, L.P., Christoff, C., Hopp, M.L., and Streff, F.M., 1997, *An on- the-road comparison of in-vehicle navigation assistance systems: The FAST-TRACK troika study* (Report No. UMTRI-97-05). Ann Arbour, MI: University of Michigan Transportation Research Institute.

Ells, J.G. and Dewar, R.E., 1979, rapid comprehension of verbal and symbolic traffic sign messages, *Human factors,* 21(2), 161-8.

Eysenk, M.W. and Keane, M.T., 1996, *Cognitive Psychology*: A Students Handbook, Psychology Press, Erlbaum (UK).

Fastenmeier, W., Haller, R., and Lerner, G., 1994, A preliminary safety evaluation of route guidance comparing different MMI concepts. In *Proceedings of the 1st World Congress on Applications of Transport Telematics and Intelligent Vehicle Highway Systems (pp. 1750-1757).* Boston: Artech House.

Federal Highway Administration (FHWA), 1995, Spatial ability and advanced traveller information system route guidance. FHWA-RD-95-125.

Green, P., (1993), Design and evaluation of symbols for automobile controls and display. In: *Automotive ergonomics,* (eds. Peacock, B. and Karwowski, W.), London: Taylor and Francis.

Inman, V., Sanchez, R., Porter, C., and Bernstein, L., 1995, *TravTek evaluation: Yoked driver study.* (Report No. FHWA-RD-94-139). Washington, DC: Federal Highway Administration.

Jackson, P.G., 2000, Driven to distraction: in search of better ways to present Route Guidance information, In, *Paper presented at the PACTS (Parlimentry Advisory Committee for transport Safety)* Conference: Transport Telematics and Road Safety: How many stand to benefit?- October 1996.

Jacobs, R.J., Johnston, A.W. and Cole, B.L., 1975, The invisibility of alphabetic and symbolic traffic signs, *Australian Road Research,* May, 5 (7), 68-87.

Li, G. and Oliver, S., 2000, The effect of electronic map complexity and orientation on driver response time and error rate for road identification. In: Human-System Interaction: Education, Research and Application in the 21st Century, (Eds. D. de Waard, C. Weikert, J. Hoonhout and J. Ramaekers), Maastricht: Shaker Publishing BV, 293-302.

Olson, P.L., 1993, Vision and Perception, In: *Automotive ergonomics,* (eds. Peacock, B. and Karwowski, W.), London: Taylor and Francis.

Parkes, A.M., Ashby, M.C., and Fairclough, S.H., 1991, The effects of different in-vehicle route information displays on driver behaviour. In: *Proceedings of the 1991 Vehicle Navigation and Information Systems Conference* (pp. 61-70). Warrendale, P.A: Society of Automotive Engineers.

Paniati, J.F., 1988, Legibility and comprehension of traffic sign symbols, *Proceedings of the Human Factors Society-32nd Annual Meeting,* 568-72, Santa Monica, CA: Human Factors Society.

Rayner, K., & Sereno, S.C., 1994, Eye movements in reading: Psycholinguistic studies. In: M.A. Gernsbacher (Ed.), *Handbook of Psycholinguistics.* New York: Academic Press.

Schofer, J.L., Koppelman, F.S., Webster, R.G., Berka, S., and Peng, T., 1996, *Field test of the effectiveness of ADVANCE dynamic route guidance on a suburban arterial street network* (ADVANCE Project Document No. 8463.01). Evanston, IL: Northwestern University transportation Center.

Sivak, M., 1995, The information that drivers use: is it indeed 90% visual? (keynote address). *Sixth International Conference on Vision in Vehicles,* Derby, UK.

Streeter, L.A. Vitello, D., and Wonsiewicz, S. (1985) How to tell people where to go: comparing navigational aids, *International Journal of Man/Machine Studies,* 22 (4) 549-562.

Stroop, J.R., 1935, Studies of interference in serial verbal reactions. *Journal of Experimental Psychology,* 18, 643-662.

Verwy, W.B., 1989, Simple in-car route guidance information from another perspective: modality versus coding, *Conference record of papers presented at the First vehicle Navigation and Information Systems Conference*, Toronto, Ontario, Canada, September 11-13, 1989.

Verwy, W.B., 1993, Further evidence for benefits of verbal route guidance instructions over symbolic spatial guidance instructions. *In: Proceedings of the 4th IEEE-IEE Vehicle Navigation and Information Systems Conference*, Ottawa, Ontario.

Warnes, A.M., Fraser, D.A., Hawken, R.E. and Sievey, V., 1993, Elderly drivers and new road transport technology. In: Driving Future Vehicles, (Eds. A.M. Parkes and S. Franzen), London: Taylor & Francis, 99-117.

Wochinger, K. and Boehm-Davis, D., 1997, Navigational preference and driver acceptance of advanced traveler information systems. In: Ergonomics and Safety of Intelligent Driver Interfaces, (ed. Y. Ian Noy), Mahwah, NJ: Lawrence Erlbaum Associates, 345-362.

Yarbus, A.L., 1967, *Eye movements and vision.* New York: Plenum.

PART VI
FUTURE TRENDS

2006-01-1426

Security Needs for the Future Intelligent Vehicles

Michael Jenkins and Syed Masud Mahmud
Wayne State University

ABSTRACT

The need for active safety, highway guidance, telematics, traffic management, cooperative driving, driver convenience and automatic toll payment will require future intelligent vehicles to communicate with other vehicles as well as with the road-side infrastructure. However, inter-vehicle and vehicle to roadside infrastructure communications will impose some security threats against vehicles' safety and their proprietary information. To avoid collisions, a vehicle should receive messages only from other authentic vehicles. The internal buses and electronics of a vehicle must also be protected from intruders and other people with malicious intents. Otherwise, a person can inject incorrect messages into an authentic vehicle's internal communication system and then make the vehicle transmit wrong information to the other vehicles within the vicinity. Such an event may have catastrophic consequences. Thus, a detailed study of the security needs of the future vehicles is very important.

In this paper, we will present the results of a comprehensive study related to various types of security threats against a vehicle's electronic communication system. The paper will identify various types of security attacks against a vehicle's electronic system. The paper will also address various issues that are related to the design of secure microcontrollers, secure electronic modules, secure communications through the vehicle's internal buses and privacy-protected secure peer-to-peer communications.

INTRODUCTION

There has been much interest in recent years to extend the functionality of vehicles to include active safety, traffic management, telematics, drive-by-wire, multimedia, remote diagnostics and software uploads, etc. Many of the proposed systems rely on wireless ad hoc networks and involve communications between a source vehicle and a target entity (inter-vehicle communications), where the target entity might be another vehicle or a roadside structure. Information from other vehicles, such as speed, acceleration, and position, will be provided either to the driver or to an active system like by-wire. Decisions are made based on this information. While these systems will improve the driving experience through enhanced safety, communications, and convenience, the once isolated vehicle will now be subject to threats and attacks that were not readily possible before.

Leaving the ad hoc network unprotected or easily hacked opens the door for attackers to broadcast false signals, repeat a legitimate broadcast at a later time, or block network signals (denial-of-service) altogether. Any of these situations could result in accidents.

Attacks on in-vehicle networks are possible through remote or physical access. Denial-of-service attacks are created on some in-vehicle networks if the network is flooded with high-priority messages (CAN), or through the introduction of malicious sleep frames (FlexRay and LIN). Other in-vehicle network attacks exist that would make the network inoperable [1].

In addition, vehicle controller software might be acquired through interception of software uploads and flash access code, or physical access of code storage locations. Disassembly and reverse engineering techniques applied to executables uncover the source code and might reveal one or several C-language vulnerabilities, opening the way for malicious code. Most PC users are familiar with software attacks by computer viruses, worms, Trojan horses, etc. The results range from slower execution of programs and the alteration of files, to stolen passwords and confidential information, and to denial-of-service. While much harm can come from these activities, it pales in comparison to the life-threatening situations that could arise if the software on fast-moving vehicles is compromised.

This paper is a survey of security threats and attacks on future intelligent vehicle systems and gives a general outline of what needs to be done to secure future systems. The paper is organized as follows. The next section defines secure communications, looks at security mechanisms including encryption techniques, and finally general attack types. Following that is a brief look at what constitutes a future vehicle electrical system. The electrical system is broken down into inter-vehicle communications, in-vehicle networks, and control modules. The section titled Security Threats and Attacks investigates potential and documented threats and attacks on the electrical system. Following that, a general list of needs is presented to foster secure vehicle communications and information. Finally, the Conclusion offers a brief overview of the paper.

SECURE COMMUNICATIONS, SECURITY MECHANISMS, AND ATTACK TYPES

SECURE COMMUNICATIONS

There are a number of aspects to what constitutes a secure communication [2]. Secure communications should insure that the data received is exactly the same as the data sent (**data integrity**), with no modifications, insertions, deletions, or replay. The identities of the communicating parties should be verified (**authentication**). The data should be protected from unauthorized parties (**data confidentiality**). A communication system should be available (**availability**) and access limited (**access control**) to authorized users. Finally, some means to prove that the transmitting entity sent a message and the receiving entity received the message is desired (**nonrepudiation**).

SECURITY MECHANISMS

Security can be achieved through both software and hardware. To achieve secure communications, mechanisms include encipherment, digital signatures, access control, data integrity, authentication exchange, traffic padding, routing control and notarization. Of all these methods, encipherment covers most of what constitutes a secure communication.

Encipherment, or the use of cryptographic algorithms to protect and obscure data, can be grouped into three different classes [3, 4].

- **Symmetric ciphers** involve the use of a secret key to encrypt data by a sender. The original message is known as plaintext and the encrypted message is called ciphertext. The ciphertext message is sent to a receiver who uses the same secret key to decrypt the message and retrieve the original plaintext message. Symmetric ciphers are faster to code and decode and are used to protect the transmission of large amounts of data. Key management becomes an issue since both parties share the same key. Examples of symmetric ciphers include the stream and block ciphers AES, 3DES, DES, and RC4.
- **Asymmetric ciphers**, also known as public-key algorithms, use a public key known to all parties for encryption and a private key for decryption. This class of ciphers is used to initiate sessions (authentication), to digitally sign messages, and for key exchange. Asymmetric ciphers tend to be slow to execute due to the more intense computational algorithms employed in their execution. Some examples are RSA and Diffie-Hellman.
- **Secure Hash algorithms** convert messages into unique fixed length messages. Each message has a unique fingerprint. Hashes are used for Message Authentication Codes (MACs) to enhance data integrity. Some examples include MD5 and SHA.

ATTACK TYPES

Attacks can be either passive or active [2]. A passive attack involves monitoring communications with no alteration of data, otherwise known as **eavesdropping**. Listening to phone conversations or traffic analysis to discover sensitive information like passwords or credit card information are examples.

Active attacks involve the manipulation of data. These attacks include **masquerade**, **replay**, **modification of messages**, and **denial-of-service**. A masquerader pretends to be someone they are not and broadcasts false messages. When proper authentication of communications is not in place, this becomes an issue. Replay involves the capture of a legal transmission and the replay of that transmission at a later time to disrupt the system. Replay becomes important in transmissions in which something was true at a particular point in time but not afterwards. Modification of messages modifies, inserts or deletes data. Finally, denial-of-service renders communication impossible. Jamming of signals is just one example of this type of attack.

Attacking encrypted messages is accomplished through **cryptanalysis** and **brute-force** attacks. Cryptanalysis relies on knowledge of the algorithm used and perhaps some sample plaintext-ciphertext pairs or some knowledge of probable keys. A brute-force attack tries every possible key on a piece of ciphertext until readable plaintext appears. With the use of supercomputers, brute-force attacks are not improbable.

FUTURE VEHICLE SYSTEMS

In this paper, the future vehicle electrical system of concern is divided into three separate systems. The first system, termed the **inter-vehicle communication** system, is used for vehicle communications outside of the vehicle. These systems include the **ad hoc networks**, as well as **vehicle positioning systems**. The second system is the **in-vehicle network** used for communications between vehicle modules. These networks include CAN, LIN, FlexRay, and MOST, among others. The last system, the vehicle **module**, includes the controller with its sensors and actuators. While many controllers have built-in CAN controllers, we choose to separate the two functions.

INTER-VEHICLE COMMUNICATIONS

Ad Hoc networks

Ad hoc networks are short-range, often temporary networks that do not require a base station or infrastructure to enable communications and support nodes that are in motion. This makes them ideal for vehicle communications between other vehicles and to short-range roadside structures. This paper examines three ad hoc systems that are potential candidates for vehicle network use.

- **Dedicated Short Range Communications** (**DSRC**) [5] is a short-range wireless technology proposed for mobile, ad hoc networks by the Crash Avoidance Metrics Partnership Vehicle Safety Communications Consortium, consisting of BMW, DaimlerChrysler, Ford, GM, Nissan, Toyota, and VW, along with the U.S. Department of Transportation. DSRC operates in the 5.9 GHz band and has a range of 1000 m. It supports various communication types including one-way from and to the vehicle, two-way, point-to-point and point-to-multipoint communications. The latter includes the ability to broadcast messages from a vehicle to the environment. In addition, it has the shortest latency (< 100 ms) between communications of any current wireless technology, although this figure is based on encryption-less communication.
- **Bluetooth** is a short-range wireless technology used today in wireless handsets, wireless connections to a LAN or peripheral devices, and the synchronization of PDA devices with PCs [6]. Current and proposed vehicle applications include hands-free use of cell phone and control of lights, radio, wipers, etc., remote start of engine, remote monitoring of various parameters including tire pressure, and automatic toll payment. Class 1 Bluetooth-enabled devices have a documented range of 100 m and the more common Class 2 devices have a documented range of 10 m, although experiment has shown a more extended distance. Bluetooth operates in the 2.4 GHz ISM (industrial, scientific, and medical) band and supports two-way and point-to-point communications. Bluetooth has a published latency of 3-4 seconds, although with established networks research has shown that value to be 30 milliseconds.
- The **IEEE 802.11** standard was designed as a wireless extension to the wired Ethernet standard (IEEE 802.3). IEEE 802.11 became known as WiFi, for "Wireless Fidelity". WiFi systems can operate in an infrastructure mode, where a wireless device connects to a wired base station, or in ad hoc mode ("peer-to-peer"). Currently there are four versions of 802.11. The table 1 shows the four versions with specifications.

WiFi Specifications			
Specification	**Max Speed (Mb /s)**	**Frequency Band**	**Compatibility With**
802.11b	11	2.4 GHz	b
802.11a	54	5 GHz	a
802.11g	54	2.4 GHz	b, g
802.11n	100	2.4 GHz	b, g, n

Table 1: WiFi Specifications

The maximum range for this technology is 1000 m and it supports both two-way and point-to-point communications. Table 2 below compares the three technologies.

		Wireless Technologies		
		DSRC	**Bluetooth**	**IEEE 802.11**
Capabilities	**Security**	No	Yes	Yes
	Range	1000 m	100 m	1000 m
	Two-Way	Yes	Yes	Yes
	Point-to-point	Yes	Yes	Yes
	Point-to-multipoint	Yes	No	No
	Latency	200 μs	2-3 s 30 ms	3-5 s

Table 2: Wireless Technologies

Vehicle positioning systems

Vehicle positioning systems assist drivers with exact location, driving distances to prospective locations, and route planning. In addition, GPS systems can provide very accurate time information.

- **Global Positioning Systems** (**GPS**) are radio-based navigation systems that offer three-dimensional position, velocity and time information for all sorts of vehicles. 24 low-power emitting satellites make up the system as well as 5 ground stations. GPS works by accurately measuring the time that it takes to receive radio signals from 3 of the 24 satellites and, through the process of trilateration, determining where in space the receiver is.
- A proposed position system, called **verifiable multilateration** [7-9], uses ground-based towers,

similar to cell towers, and trilateration to determine the exact position of a vehicle. This technique uses distance bounding, a method that measures the time between sending and receiving a signal from a tower to a vehicle and also uses digital signatures to prove that the vehicle in question is *x* meters from the tower.

IN-VEHICLE BUS SYSTEMS

Vehicle Buses

There are several vehicle buses in use. This paper looks at four that are in use currently

- The **Local Interconnect Network** (**LIN**) [10] is a low-cost, single wire sub network used for power doors, windows, and mirrors as well as light and rain sensors, or anywhere where bandwidth and safety-criticality are not issues. LIN was introduced in vehicles in the year 2001. LIN has data rates of up to 20 kBit / s, uses a single master that polls up to 16 slaves and thus eliminates collisions, and has the capacity for synchronization of nodes. In addition, LIN provides a special sleep mode controlled by sleep and wakeup messages, and uses checksums and parity bits for error checking.
- The pervasive **Controller Area Network** (**CAN**) [11] has become the most common vehicle bus since its introduction in 1986 at the SAE World Conference in Detroit. Modules utilizing CAN range in complexity and safety-criticality from medium (park assist module) to high (engine and transmission control, antilock brakes). The CAN bus has a multi-master architecture where messages are prioritized according to their message ID, with the lowest numbered ID having the highest priority. This method (Carrier Sense Multiple Access / Collision Avoidance (CSMA/CA)) guarantees collision-free transmissions. CAN also offers error detection chiefly through the so-called Cyclic Redundancy Check (CRC) field and with parity bits, as well as a mechanism for detection and disconnection of faulty controllers.
- **FlexRay** and **Time-Triggered CAN** [12] were introduced in order to meet the demands of very high safety critical applications, such as the by-wire systems. They use the Time Division Multiple Access (TDMA) method that utilizes synchronous nodes and fixed time slots for every node. Within a time slot, some asynchronous activity with priority access similar to CAN is also reserved for less time-critical messages. These protocols feature higher data rates (10 Mbit / s) and error tolerance using CRC, channel redundancy, and, within FlexRay, a bus guardian that detects and handles logical errors.
- **Medium Oriented System Transport** (**MOST**) [13] is a serial bus that offers up to 24 Mbit /s bandwidth and is used chiefly with fiber optics to transfer voice, audio, and video. Like the TDMA methods above, MOST offers both synchronous and asynchronous data transmissions. MOST uses sender and receiver addresses and has a control channel that allows devices to request and release one of the 60 data channels. Errors are handled by an internal system that detects errors using parity bits, status flags, and CRC, and disconnects faulty nodes.

Table 3 compares the various in-vehicle buses.

Bus	LIN	CAN	FlexRay	MOST
Architecture (Single or Multi Master)	Single	Multi	Multi	Multi
Access Control	Pollin g	CSMA/ CD	TDMA	TDM
Transfer Mode (Synchronous Asynchronous)	S	A	S and A	S and A
Data Rate Mb/s	.02	1	10	24

Table 3: In-Vehicle Bus Specifications

MODULES

Module controllers vary in size and complexity [14]. Some modules, like engine control modules, perform thousands of calculations based on numerous sensors and calibrations, have high throughput requirements, have many safety-critical functions, and large software program sizes. On the other hand, modules, like tire pressure modules, have low performance requirements.

Likewise, there are numerous hardware chips available. System-on-chip designs offer CPU, memory, and sometimes CAN transceivers on one chip. These designs make it more difficult to monitor internal bus activity except through invasive techniques. Other systems rely on external memory to the CPU as well as external peripherals and are more challenging to secure.

SECURITY ATTACKS

INTER-VEHICLE COMMUNICATIONS ATTACKS

Ad Hoc Networks

As of this writing, no aspects of secure communications (authentication, data confidentiality, etc.) are in place for **DSRC** [5], so almost any scenario is possible. The following examples underscore the need for secure communications with vehicle-to-vehicle and vehicle-to-roadside structure communications.

- A **masquerade** can occur if an attacker broadcasts false information from a trusted roadside structure or other vehicle. For instance, consider a situation where an accident occurred ahead of another vehicle and the accident is out-of-sight of that vehicle (say over a hill and at night). An attacker broadcasts messages from a trusted roadside structure to the vehicle that the way ahead is clear. Trusting that information, the vehicle proceeds ahead without slowing down and an accident occurs.

- **Replay** can occur in the following scenario. Suppose at a particular location and point in time, a vehicle broadcasts a legitimate signal to vehicles behind it that the way is clear. An attacker records this message. Later at night the road freezes and the attacker rebroadcasts the message at the same point to other vehicles behind it. Again, the vehicles trust the information and proceed without slowing down.
- An example of a **modification of message** attack follows. Suppose that a roadside structure broadcasts the message "Accident ahead but afterwards the way is clear". A vehicle, the attacker, receives this message. The attacker in turn rebroadcasts the message to vehicles behind it but leaves out "Accident ahead but afterwards".
- Jamming the wireless network is a form of a **denial-of-service** attack. Sabotaging roadside structures are other ways of disrupting or denying service.
- If financial transactions are involved, say in toll collection, payment for location-based services, etc., **eavesdropping** will most certainly be involved to gain credit card or password information.

Bluetooth has security mechanisms in place. However, there have been documented attacks.

- One of the main vulnerabilities with Bluetooth resides with the PIN [6]. The PIN, usually a 4-digit number, is a small number that can easily be hacked using brute force techniques. In "Cracking the Bluetooth PIN" [15], Yaniv Shaked and Avishai Wool described both passive and active methods for obtaining the PIN. Using a Pentium III, 450 MHz and a Pentium IV 3 GHz HT computer, they demonstrated that the PIN could be revealed in 0.3 and 0.06 seconds respectively.
- The normally short-ranged Bluetooth class 2 devices (10 m) can be extended to a distance of one mile by using directional antennas. This method, known as Bluetooth sniping, makes attacking these devices easier.
- A Bluetooth virus was created by a group of virus writers known as 29a and presented to anti-virus groups. It was written as a proof-of-concept experiment. The virus requires that the user download software to the device and has not propagated "in the wild".

The former security mechanism for **IEEE 802.11 wireless LANs**, the so-called Wired Equivalent Privacy or WEP, proved to have weaknesses [16] and was subsequently attacked [17]. This attack was a direct cryptanalysis attack on the stream cipher RC4. The result of this successful attack eventually lead to an improved mechanism based on the block cipher Advanced Encryption Standard (AES) known as WiFi Protected Access 2 (WPA2). As of this writing, there are no reported successful breaches of AES-based security.

Vehicle Positioning Systems

GPS satellites emit low-power signals. With the use of a GPS simulator an attacker (masquerade attack) could overpower the signal and send false signals [7]. A modification of message attack occurs if any Δt is added or subtracted from a legal signal and transmitted to the environment, thus falsifying exact position data. Lastly, denial-of-service is achieved through jamming the selective frequencies.

IN-VEHICLE BUS SYSTEM ATTACKS

Vehicle bus systems are vulnerable to attacks from the vehicle owner, garage personnel, and third parties. Buses are completely exposed and, with the proper equipment, eavesdropping and masquerading may be possible. Current communication between controllers is unencrypted, with no peer-to-peer authorization, and documentation on bus structure and protocols is readily available. The following details specific threats to the buses discussed above [1].

- There are a number of means to shut down or limit accessibility (denial-of-service) to **LIN** networks. One method disables the master and thus cripples the network. Another method introduces sleep message frames. Moreover, modifying the message field responsible for time synchronization (SYNC) renders nodes that rely on time synchronization inoperable.
- The most common type of attack on **CAN** is denial-of-service. This is achieved by continually transmitting high-priority messages (low numbered message ID), thus effectively jamming the network. Moreover, introducing malicious code that sets or posts error flags related to a specific controller would disable it through the CAN mechanism that locates and disconnects faulty controllers.
- **FlexRay** also has its vulnerabilities that can deny service to nodes. The network can be rendered inoperable if more than *n/3* SYNC messages are introduced within one communication cycle, where *n* is the number of FlexRay nodes. The bus guardian feature can be used, as in CAN, to disable specific controllers when malicious error frames are introduced. Also, like LIN, denial-of-service can be achieved through directed sleep frames.
- Disabling the timing master in a **MOST** network would effectively shutdown the network. In addition, continuous bogus channel requests would be a denial-of-service attack for other nodes that want bus access. Moreover, for asynchronous data transmissions, denial-of-service attacks similar to

CAN are feasible by flooding the network with high-priority messages.

MODULES

Modules are as physically accessible as the vehicle bus and can be attacked both through software and hardware. Attacks can occur with non-encrypted, as well as encrypted devices.

Software Attacks

The very nature of software makes it vulnerable to attacks. Software **complexity** and **changeability** are two reasons. For real-world programs, the complexity of the software translates to the increased likelihood of a bug or threat [18-20]. Changing and updating software is a common occurrence to introduce new functionality or to fix bugs. This process leaves the software open to attacks, particularly if remote software uploads are an available feature.

Attacking software generally requires some knowledge of the source code to find and exploit vulnerabilities [19]. Should the executable become available, hackers have a variety of tools available to reverse engineer the code. A **debugger** is a software program that attaches itself to other software programs and allows control of those programs. Debuggers allow stepping, setting breakpoints, and viewing variables and memory. Debuggers are available in two types: the user-mode type for debugging applications and the more powerful kernel-mode type for device drivers and operating systems. **Disassemblers** convert machine code to assembly code. Since assembly is device specific, the tool must understand the device's assembler. **Decompilers** convert machine code to assembler or source code. Decompilers have the same requirements as disassemblers but in addition must know the source language.

Moreover, most embedded software for vehicles is written in the C and C++ languages. There are many **C-language vulnerabilities**, some of which, if exploited, can result in crashing a program (denial-of-service) or transferring control to malicious code (worms. viruses). A partial list [20] of C-language vulnerabilities include: generic logic errors; misused C functions like strcpy, sprintf, and strcat; format stings; generic incorrect bounds checking; loop constructs; off-by-one vulnerabilities; non-null termination issues; skipping beyond a null-terminated byte; signed comparison vulnerabilities; integer-related overflows; different-sized integer comparisons; double free vulnerabilities; and out-of-scope memory usage.

A type of malicious code that affects low-level system functionality is a **kernel rootkit**. Kernel rootkits are loadable modules or drivers (executables) providing complete access to system functionality, including the ability to read and write to memory.

Hardware Attacks

Hardware attacks can be classified as either invasive or non-invasive. Invasive attacks physically open a device to gain access to system internals. Examples of invasive attacks include micro-probing and reverse engineering. On the other hand, non-invasive attacks do not destroy the device but use other means (side-channel attacks) such as timing analysis, power analysis, fault induction, and electromagnetic analysis to gain secure information. Side-channel attacks are similar to a thief breaking into a house through a window rather than a multi-locked door (cracking the cryptographic algorithm through cryptanalysis).

- Invasive **micro-probing** techniques are used with system-on-chip designs to discover the general layout of the chip as a precursor for non-invasive techniques or to simply read internal bus messages. The first step is to remove the outer coating of the chip packaging (de-package) using a fuming acid. Afterwards, successive layers of the chip are de-packaged and observed through microscopy. All processor internals such as the instruction decoder, data and memory buses, ALU, ROM, memory boundaries, etc. are discovered. Values on buses and interfaces to components are analyzed with manual micro-probing or e-beam microscopy. While this technique may not reveal all necessary information, it is useful for certain non-invasive techniques explained below.
- In "Cipher Instruction Search Attack on the Bus-Encryption Security Microcontroller DS5002FP", Markus Kuhn [21] describes a non-invasive **physical** attack on the DS5002FP processor. This processor uses bus encryption for data and software that is stored externally in SRAM. The attack, similar to a brute-force attack, uses special hardware to present guessed encrypted machine instructions to the processor, repeatedly reset the processor, and observe the CPU reaction. The object is to discover the encrypted CPU instructions like MOV and NOP, as well as the address of a parallel port. Once discovered, memory dumps are output in plaintext to the port. This information is then disassembled and the protected software revealed.
- The **timing analysis** attack is a side-channel attack that analyzes the time that a processor takes to perform cryptographic computations [22] and involves predictions about the key value. The technique presumes that a key value is presented, bit-by-bit, to the crypto hardware or software and that the computation time per bit is non-constant. In this case two operations exist, one for a value of 0 for the bit and one where the value is 1. The attacker measures the time for a set of inputs (bit value 0 and 1) and then measures the correlation between the measured time and the estimated time for each input. The actual value used should show the strongest correlation. After that, subsequent key values are presented.

- The **power analysis** attack, also a side-channel attack, is similar to timing analysis, but uses the correlation between computations performed for key evaluation and the current drawn by the device [23]. This attack assumes that the power consumption of the micro is largely because of gate transitions and the parasitic capacitance of internal wiring. Power consumption increases with a greater number of state transitions and if transitions are occurring at larger gates or greater capacitive loads. The attack involves presenting a large number of key values to the processor and collecting power traces with each key.
- **Electromagnetic analysis** attacks are similar to both timing and power analysis attacks [24]. This attack measures the electromagnetic radiation emitted by a micro and has been shown to reveal protected information. Since the internal structure of the device is necessary for an electromagnetic attack, invasive techniques are used prior to employing this technique.
- Boneh, DeMillo, and Lipton [25] showed that attacks are possible on cryptographically protected processors through **fault induction**. An induced fault is a flipped bit in a register caused by random hardware glitches such as power transients, high temperature, static electricity, magnetic field, etc. The attacks exposed the key values for RSA, RSA based on the Chinese Remainder Theorem, Fiat-Shamir, and Schnorr's algorithms.

NEEDS FOR SECURING VEHICLE COMMUNICATION AND INFORMATION

The attacks on various vehicle systems mentioned above underscore the need for both communication and information security. The following lists many of those needs.

- Inter-vehicle communications authentication to identify legitimate sources. These sources include other vehicles and roadside structures.
- Inter-vehicle communications encryption for data confidentiality. While not all messages sent to and from other vehicles and roadside structures need encryption [26], some sensitive information does. Financial transactions, password protection and software uploads are examples.
- Inter-vehicle communications data integrity to insure that the data sent and the data received are the same.
- A firewall or gateway between inter-communication networks and in-vehicle networks to screen messages that are sent and received, route incoming messages to the appropriate place, and possibly encrypt and authenticate outgoing messages.
- Use of in-vehicle bus encryption for confidentiality. In addition, if new encryption keys are passed to vehicle modules by some controlling source, bus encryption prevents eavesdropping.
- The ability to change encryption keys and some form of key management. Brute force attacks can potentially break any encryption key. Changing keys regularly protects the system from this type of attack.
- The failure of a system, either through some defect, a natural disturbance, or malicious behavior, such as signal jamming, is an issue. Providing some system redundancy for safety-critical applications is a means to assure reliability and system robustness.
- Nonrepudiation, or the proof that a message was sent by an entity and received by another, is useful for recreating the scene of an accident or proof of responsibility in an accident. Data recorders can be used for this situation.
- Awareness and elimination of software vulnerabilities in embedded system code and techniques to impede reverse engineering and disassembly should executables fall into the hands of hackers.
- Module authentication protects against the illegal insertion of controllers within a vehicle system. Trusted modules broadcasting false information endanger both the host vehicle and other vehicles that rely on that information.
- Tamper resistant module hardware guarantees that encryption keys, code, and sensitive data are not readily available to hackers. Methods exist that address each of the physical and side-channel attacks described above, including message blinding, randomized clock signals, data-masking, reduction of signal amplitudes, the introduction of noise in power measurement data, aggressive shielding techniques, non-localized internal chip component layouts, and sensors to monitor and respond to environmental changes.

CONCLUSION

The brave new world of future intelligent vehicles promises another level of vehicle performance in the area of safety, traffic management, highway guidance, remote repair, and driver convenience. However, these improvements open the door for attacks not just on inter-vehicular communications, but also with the rest of the communication and information system. This paper investigated the meaning of secure communications, the potential and real threats and attacks on future vehicle systems, and the security needs for those systems. For future work, the authors intend to address the issues outlined above and create a coherent vehicle system that considers security for all future intelligent vehicle needs.

REFERENCE

1. M. Wolf, A. Weimerskirch, and C. Paar, "Security in Automotive Bus Systems". 2004, Available from: http://www.escrypt.com/escrypt_engl/download/Sichere_Bussysteme_escar04.pdf.

2. W. Stallings, *Cryptography and Network Security*, 3rd ed., NJ: Pearson Education, 2003.
3. R. J. Spillman, *Classical and Contemporary Cryptology*, 1st ed., Upper Saddle River, NJ: Pearson Prentice Hall, 2005.
4. B. Schneier, *Applied Cryptography: Protocols, Algorithms, and Source Code In C*, 2nd ed., New York: John Wiley & Sons, Inc., 1996.
5. The Crash Avoidance Metrics Partnership Vehicle Safety Communications Consortium, "Vehicle Safety Communications Project Task 3 Final Report Identify Intelligent Vehicle Safety Applications Enabled by DSRC", Tech. Rep. DOT HS 809 859.
6. S. M. Mahmud. "Bluetooth Technology", 2005 July 12, 2005 Available from: http://ece.eng.wayne.edu/~smahmud.
7. J. Hubaux, S. Capkun, and J. Luo, "The Security and Privacy of Smart Vehicles". *IEEE SECURITY & PRIVACY*, Available from: http://lcawww.epfl.ch/Publications/luo/HubauxCL04.pdf.
8. M. Raya, and J. Hubaux, "Security Aspects of Inter-Vehicle Communications", presented at 5th Swiss Transport Research Conference, Monte Verità / Ascona, March 2005, Available from: http://infoscience.epfl.ch/getfile.py?docid=5377&name=RayaH05A&format=pdf&version=1.
9. J. Luo, and J. Hubaux, "A Survey of Inter-Vehicle Communication", EPFL, Tech. Rep.
10. LIN Consortium, "*LIN Specification Package*", Revision 2.0, Munich, Germany, 2003.
11. K. Etschberger, *Controller Area Network Basics, Protocols, Chips, and Applications*, 1st ed., Weingarten, Germany: IXXAT Press, 2001.
12. FlexRay Consortium, "*FlexRay Communications System Protocol Specification*", Version 2.1, 2005.
13. MOST Corporation, "*MOST Specification*", Rev 2.4, Karlsruhe, Germany, 2005.
14. T. Denton, *Automobile Electrical and Electronic Systems*, Third: SAE International, 2004.
15. Y. Shaked, A. Wool. "Cracking the Bluetooth PIN". in International Conference On Mobile Systems, Applications And Services. 2005. Seattle, Washington: ACM Press, Available from: http://portal.acm.org/citation.cfm?id=1067170.1067176.
16. S. Fluhrer, I. Mantin, and A. Shamir, "Weaknesses in the Key Scheduling Algorithm of RC4", presented at Eight Annual Workshop on Selected Areas in Cryptography, August 2001, Available from: http://www.drizzle.com/~aboba/IEEE/rc4_ksaproc.pdf.
17. A. Stubblefirel, J. Ioannidis, and A. D. Rubin, "Using the Fluhrer, Mantin, and Shamir Attack to Break WEP", AT&T Labs, Tech. Rep. TD-4ZCPZZ, 2001.
18. G. Hoglund, G. McGraw, *Exploiting Software*, 1st ed., Boston: Addison Wesley, 2004.
19. K. Kaspersky, *Hacker Disassembling Uncovered*, 1st ed.: A-List, 2003.
20. J. Koziol, D. Litchfield, D. Aitel, C. Anley, S. Eren, N. Mehta, R. Hassell, *The Shellcoder's Handbook, Discovering and Exploiting Security Holes*: Wiley, 2004.
21. M. G. Kuhn, "Cipher Instruction Search Attack on the Bus-Encryption Security Microcontroller DS5002FP". *IEEE TRANSACTIONS ON COMPUTERS*, 1998, Available from: http://www3.informatik.uni-erlangen.de/Publications/Articles/kuhn_ToC.pdf.
22. P. C. Kocher, "Timing attacks on implementations of Diffie-Hellman, RSA, DSS, and other systems". *Advances in Cryptology – CRYPTO'96*, 1996, Available from: http://www.cryptography.com/resources/whitepapers/TimingAttacks.pdf.
23. P. Kocher, J. Jaffe, and B. Jun. "Differential Power Analysis". in Advances in Cryptology - Crypto 99 Proceedings. 1999: Springer-Verlag.
24. M. G. Kuhn, R. Anderson, "Soft Tempest: Hidden Data Transmission Using Electromagnetic Emanations". *Proc. Int. Wkshp. on Information Hiding* 1998, Available from: http://www.cl.cam.ac.uk/~mgk25/ih98-tempest.pdf.
25. D. Boneh, R. DeMillo, R. J. Lipton, "On the Importance of Eliminating Errors in Cryptographic Computations". *Journal of Cryptology*, 2001, Available from: http://www.springerlink.com/(bqots0mra0zffjeos0sq11n4)/app/home/contribution.asp?referrer=parent&backto=issue,3,5;journal,20,37;linkingpublicationresults,1:100359,1.
26. M. El Zarki, S. Mehrotra, G. Tsudik, and N. Venkatasubramanian, "Security Issues in a Future Vehicular Network". *European Wireless*, Available from: http://www.ics.uci.edu/~dsm/papers/sec001.pdf.

CONTACT

Syed Masud Mahmud, Ph.D.
Associate Professor
Department of Electrical and Computer Engineering
Wayne State University
Detroit, MI 48202
Phone: (313) 577-3855
Fax: (313 577-1101
Email: smahmud@eng.wayne.edu

Michael Jenkins
Ph.D. Student at Wayne State University
Department of Electrical and Computer Engineering
Wayne State University
Detroit, MI 48202
Email: mbj5@dcx.com

2006-01-1329

Reliable Dynamic Discovery Service-Based JINI for the Next Generation Vehicle Network

Rami Baroody, Nizar Al-Holou and Utayba Mohammad
University of Detroit Mercy

ABSTRACT

Vehicles are becoming part of the Internet, either as a terminal in a mobile network, as a network node or as a moving sensor (providing environmental, car status or video information). Interest of vehicles' passengers in location-based information is steadily growing. Moreover drivers and passengers may like to receive information about traffic jams or accidents in their vicinity, or chat with other vehicle's passengers. Enabling communication among automobile nodes (cars) is not a straightforward task. Such nodes form an extremely dynamic ad hoc network, and this presents some technical challenges. One essential characteristic of such networks is that the available services are in principle unknown to a node. A Dynamic Discovery Service (DDS) protocol to discover nodes is needed. The DDS-based Jini system is the middleware for service-oriented computing in wired and wireless networks and may operate well in a static environment where all components don not change their initial locations. However, it may not always function in a dynamic networking environment, such as ad hoc networks that are formed dynamically by mobile nodes. Thus, the provision of services in the network is unreliable. In this paper, we investigate problems that can occur when mobility is considered in the current Jini-based system and propose reliable approaches to overcome these problems and enable us to use Jini in the mobile environment.

I. INTRODUCTION

Electronics are used in automobiles to improve vehicle performance, serviceability, pollution control, product differentiation, reliability, safety, and convenience. As customers continue to demand additional functions and features in their automobiles, (e.g., navigation systems, intelligent highway system supports, automated collision avoidance systems, Internet access, remote diagnostics), a need arises for a large number of devices, such as smart sensors, mobile phones, hands-free devices and various computers to be deployed in future cars. These devices need to be interconnected at appropriate network speed with appropriate protocols that will allow automobiles to be able to perform these functions at a reasonable cost and with high reliability and availability. Future cars will support computing facilities and will be expected to communicate with other cars and with the fixed network. Future developments in the automobile domain will also include the utilization of new communication technologies. The major goals are to provide increased automotive safety, to achieve smooth traffic flow on the roads, and to improve the convenience of vehicles' passengers by providing them with information and entertainment. Introducing new technological features in automobiles, such as DDS-based Jini, becomes of major importance in the case of mobile automobile networks. DDS is a system in which clients search through registries to first discover and then invoke services supporting the capabilities they require. DDS-based Jini consists of three main entities: lookup services, service providers, and users [1]. Service providers are generally required to register their services to lookup services in a form of the proxy. Users request their necessary services to the corresponding lookup services. Lookup services then send the service proxy to users so that users can be offered the wanted services from service providers. This system may operate well in a static environment where all the components are not changing their initial locations in a network topology. However, the system might not always work in a dynamic networking environment such as ad hoc networks that are formed dynamically by mobile nodes [2]. Mobility is at the core of the three problems that can occur in the Jini system. Three possible problems are the absence of lookup service, incorrect information about the service provider, and poor service provider selection. In this paper, we investigate problems that can occur when mobility is considered in the Next Generation Vehicle Network (NGVN) DDS-based Jini system and propose reliable approaches for adapting to the mobility of its components. In Section II, the NGVN architecture is introduced. Section III presents the basic communication schemes and their functionality in future vehicular networks. Section IV will then introduce our approach in detail. Section V discusses service discovery in ad hoc networks. Section VI introduces reliable DDS-based Jini for ad hoc network. Finally, Section VII concludes this paper.

II. NEXT GENERATION VEHICLE NETWORK ARCHITECTURE

In automobiles, many sub-systems need extensive interaction for information exchange. For example, an engine management system and transmission controller may work closely together for proper gear change. These kinds of interactions are becoming so numerous that the traditional view of vehicle electronics as independent sub-systems may not be adequate [3-5]. The concept of local area network (LAN) has been introduced in automobiles to improve communications and interactions among different electronics systems. In applying a LAN to automotive electronics systems, an optimal protocol has been adopted for each system, and each system may run different protocols that satisfy the data rate for their applications. Multiple sub-networks (CAN, MOST and the Internet protocol) have been introduced [6-10]. However, these approaches have failed to adequately address and exploit the emerging Internet technologies and services. The main goal of the NGVN project is to design and implement a mobile website for each vehicle such that it is as universally accessible (with appropriate security mechanisms) as any contemporary website. Such a website would allow one to access dynamic information about the vehicle, such as speed, internal temperature, and fuel supply, in almost real time, within the automobile. This data is obtained from sensors and other mechanisms placed around the car and connected to the in-car networks. Figure 1 shows the Basic NGVN architecture that is broadly divided into four logical domains [11]:

- The User Interface Domain provides the required communication interfaces to enable all devices (e.g., Cellular, PDA, Laptop) used by a mobile user to interact and exchange information with the NGVN information services

- The Network Interoperability Domain provides all the functions required in order to achieve, seamless interaction and exchange of data among different networks such as different types of cellular networks GPRS [9], CAN [7], and MOST [8].

- The Mobility Support Domain enables ubiquitous access to the vehicle website, allowing users with Internet access to interact with the passengers in the vehicle by visiting the vehicle website.

- The Auto Information Domain provides the next generation of auto applications and services targeted towards auto users as well as manufacturers. This domain will utilize the services offered by an Auto Dynamic Discovery to be developed in this project to support the current and emerging auto information and entertainment services.

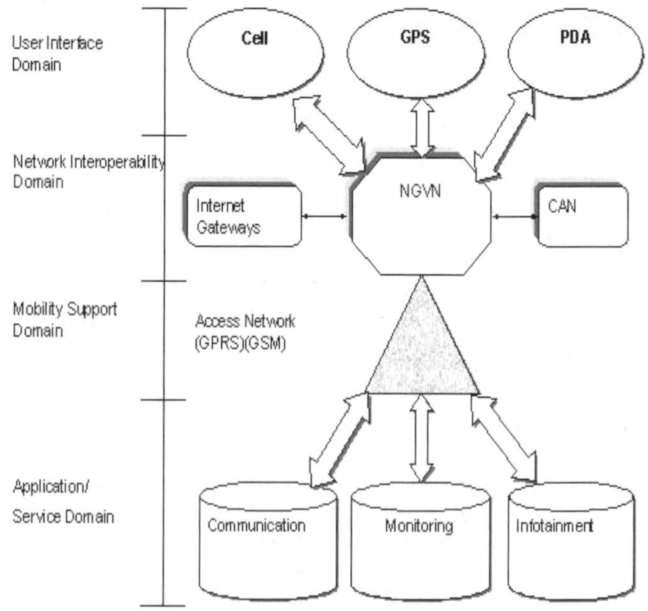

Figure 1: NGVN – Basic Architecture

III. COMMUNICATION IN NGVN

The key design requirements for NGVN are the capability to distribute locally relevant data and the satisfaction of the needs of drivers and passengers of vehicles for location-dependent information and services. Vehicles are able to communicate either directly or using intermediate vehicles as relaying nodes (Figure 2). Vehicles are able to communicate with distant Internet gateways using multi-hop communication. In order to discover and access Internet resources, we need an adequate DDS and communication architecture for Internet integration, as described in the following section.

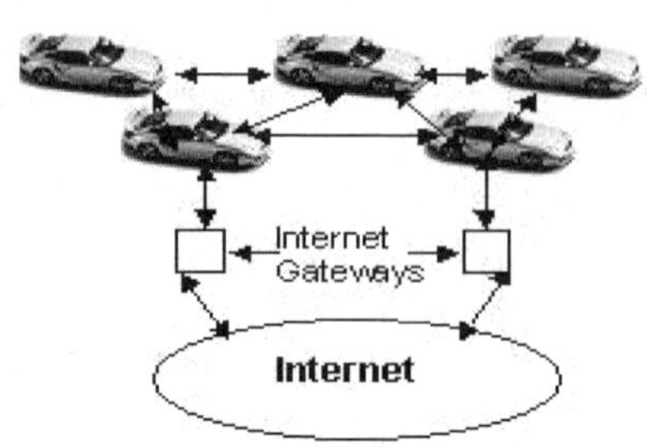

Figure 2: Future Vehicular Communication Scenario

RELATED WORK

1) Service Discovery Protocols: Configuring and using mobile devices could be very inconvenient in large-scale networks. For example, a new user would have to configure his mobile device manually to print a document on the nearest printer. This problem is resolved by service discovery protocols. These protocols enable users, mobile devices, and applications to discover services in a network with minimal prior knowledge. Several service discovery protocols are available currently, including the Service Location Protocol (SLP), Universal Plug and Play (UPnP), Jini, and Salutation [12, 13]. Jini is described below in order to illustrate the basic mechanisms of service discovery protocols.

JINI

Jini technology has been developed by Sun Microsystems as an extension of the Java programming language. It addresses the issue of how devices connect with each other in order to form a simple ad hoc network (a Jini "community"), and how these devices provide services to other devices in this network. Jini consists of architecture and a programming model. Each Jini device is assumed to have a Java Virtual Machine (JVM) running on it. The Jini architecture principle [13] is similar to that of SLP. Devices and applications register with a Jini network using two processes called Discovery and Join. To join a Jini network, a device or application places itself into the lookup table on a lookup server, which is a database for all services on the network (similar to the directory agent in SLP). Besides pointers to services, the lookup table in Jini can also store Java-based program code for these services. This means that services may upload device drivers, interfaces, and other programs that help the user access the service. When a client wishes to utilize the service, the object code is downloaded from the lookup table to the JVM of the client. Whereas a service request in SLP returns a service URL, the Jini object code offers direct access to the service using an interface known to the client. This code mobility replaces the necessity of pre-installing drivers on the client. The Jini specifications are open source and may be used freely. However, Sun charges a licensing fee for commercial use. A reference implementation may be downloaded at http://www.sun.com/jini. The Jini code can be implemented in 46K of Java binaries. Due to its portability and flexibility, we developed a DDS based on Jini technology, a new protocol to discover services in future vehicular ad hoc networks. The following section describes it in more detail.

IV. NGVN DYNAMIC DISCOVERY SERVICE

At the Computer Networking Laboratory, a proof-of-concept prototype of the NGVN has been implemented using Java and Jini Lookup Services [14-15], as well as DDS technology. This project adopts the current prototype to implement the required auto NGVN Internet services. Figure 3 illustrates the architecture of a NGVN DDS, which consists of 6 components: Network Service Proxy, Network Service Attributes, Service Manager, Lookup Service, Service Templates and Access Control Manager. These components, their roles in the system, and their interaction to provide DDS system functionality are described in the following subsections.

NETWORK SERVICE PROXY

NGVN information services access automotive information and entertainment services through objects called *proxies*, which provide all the code needed to connect to a particular network service. Proxies are analogous to device drivers as they allow an application program to interact with a service while encapsulating it from the implementation details of that service. However, unlike device drivers, which are typically installed by a system administrator before the device can be used, proxies are carried by the services themselves, and are dynamically downloaded by the clients when they invoke a particular network service. Client applications do not have to know the implementation details of these proxies and they do not have to be "compiled in" when the applications are written. These proxy objects typically communicate over the network with the backend portion of the service using whatever protocols are supported by the backend system.

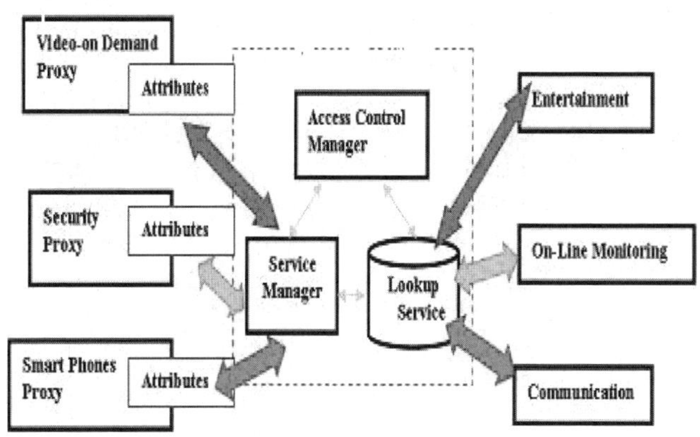

Figure 3: DDS Architecture

NETWORK SERVICE ATTRIBUTES

Attributes are Java objects that are attached to service proxies. Services attach these attributes when they publish their proxies, and NGVN services or clients can search for proxies by looking for certain attribute patterns. Attributes are used to associate descriptive information and state with a service. Attributes are important to distinguish between similar services (i.e., services that implement the same interface). Name, address, and location are some of the standard attributes that are associated with services. But sometimes we need to create our own attributes to reveal service-specific information. There are some attributes which are static, like name, that do not change often with time, but there are some attributes, like state, that are dynamic and can be updated by the service itself. These changes have to be reflected in all the lookup services that the proxy object is registered with, to ensure that clients have access to the most updated services. Figure 4 details the DDS architecture.

SERVICE MANAGER

The service manager maintains updated information about available NGVN services. The service manager detects changes in the service attributes and compares them it against threshold values. If the threshold is exceeded, it updates this information in all the lookup services where the proxy object had previously registered. The services can also have properties, which are not service attributes. These properties can be dynamic and come into effect during the service lookup process. The service manager tracks these dynamic properties and helps the client by providing the most updated values of these dynamic properties.

LOOKUP SERVICE

The lookup service is a special service that keeps track of all other NGVN services in the community. When a provider of a NGVN service wishes to make itself available, it "publishes" its proxy by storing it in a lookup service. Clients (NGVN users) can then connect to the lookup service and ask what services are available. The lookup service can also inform interested parties when new services appear or when services leave the community through remote events [16-18]. Lookup services announce their existence using the multicast announcement protocol. In multicast announcement, interested parties listen on well-known multicast addresses for announcements about the existence of lookup services. Periodically all lookup services send a multicast message to this address. Once an interested party has received an announcement of the existence of a service, it can ask it for its service proxy. It contacts the lookup service using the direct unicast connection, and the lookup service replies with the proxy object that the client can use to communicate with it. The lookup service is the main module in the DDS.

SERVICE TEMPLATES

Service templates are Java objects that NGVN clients use to construct their search criteria. The service template matching system is extremely flexible, and services can be found based on the set of attributes associated with them using type-based and content-based attribute matching rules. NGVN users/clients are the consumers of services. These clients discover the lookup service using the multicast request protocol. Once clients find the lookup service, they search it for services that implement particular services with certain attributes, using templates to construct their search criteria. The client downloads the service proxy and then uses it for communication with the service.

ACCESS CONTROL MANAGER (ACM)

Every lookup service has an ACM that maintains and updates the list of NGVNs (cars that have subscribed to certain NGVN services) that can access the services. When the clients try to download the proxy object from the lookup service, the ACM checks the list to see if the client is authorized to use the service. If the client is authorized, the ACM allows the proxy to be downloaded; otherwise, an "access denied" message is sent back to the NGVN client. The client can make a request of the lookup service, which in turn requests the service for access. If the service accepts the request, it updates the access control list through the ACM. Thus, the ACM provides security in the DDS architecture.

DYNAMIC LOOKUP

In traditional architectures, services are registered with the lookup service once during a session and continue to use the resources till they are freed explicitly. However, these architectures do not reflect the dynamic characteristics in the system, which is very important in the NGVN mobile environment. Two methods have been developed to achieve dynamic lookup: Dynamic Update and Dynamic Filtering. In the Dynamic Update scheme, the service manager detects changes in the service attributes and compares them with certain threshold values. These threshold values determine that the Jini Lookup Service does not support any inequality matching (like greater than, less than, or logical operators) for the attribute values. This is a very rigid constraint in our application. In the dynamic filtering scheme, properties of services that change frequently with time are maintained separately and not defined as service attributes. The service manager can retrieve functionalities to retrieve the current values of the dynamic properties when requested by the client.

V. SERVICE DISCOVERY IN AD HOC NETWORKS

Intensive research in Ad Hoc Networks is taking place. In general, Ad Hoc networks are architectures that can be rapidly deployed without pre-existence of any fixed infrastructure. A critical functionality in these networks is service distribution. Finding a particular service or resource (e.g. gateway to reach the fixed network, proxy or registry server, etc) out of thousands of accessible services and devices is already difficult. Thus, to implement it in a mobile dynamic environment is challenging. A service distribution mechanism for Ad Hoc networks must find services without relying on a centralized directory server. At the same time, it should minimize message overhead and should be able to deal with the high dynamics and changing topology of these networks [16]. Current solutions found in service architectures assume a fairly stable network since they are based on centralized service registries. However, these architectures do not adequately solve all the problems that may arise in a dynamic environment; as a result, frequent disconnections inherent in Ad Hoc networks may lead to inconsistency of data in centralized service directories. DDS protocols such as JINI [17], UpnP [18], Salutation [19], OSGi [20], and SLP [21] focus on application layer services without considering connectivity as an essential service since it is granted by default in fixed networks. Moreover, these protocols are based on central directories. Other architectures for service distribution in Ad Hoc networks offer some solutions based on mesh or tree structures built from multicasting. To solve the problem that arises from a central directory concept, a reliable DDS has been proposed.

VI. PROPOSED ALGORITHM TO PROVIDE RELIABLE DDS FOR NGVN IN MOBILE AD HOC NETWORK (MANET)

Jini is a distributed service-oriented model developed by Sun Microsystems. Services in a Jini system can be hardware devices, software components or a combination of the two. A Jini system has three types of entities; service providers, lookup services and users. Service provider multicasts a request for a lookup service or directly request a remote lookup service known to it *a priori*. Once the handle to a lookup service has been obtained, the service provider registers a proxy object and its attributes with the lookup service. The proxy object serves as client-side handlers to the actual service. The user makes a request for some service by specifying a Java type (or interface that the desired service must implement) and desired attributes. Matching is done based on type and values. Once a candidate service is found, the proxy object registered by the service provider is copied to the client using Remote Message Invocation (RMI). Clients use the proxy object to interact with the service. This system may operate well in a static environment where all the components are not changing their initial locations in a network topology. However, this may not always be true in a dynamic networking environment such as ad hoc networks that are formed dynamically by mobile nodes.

Mobility is at the core of DDS-based Jini's function problems. We believe at least three problems can occur when mobility is considered in the current Jini system. These possible problems are

1. The absence of lookup service.
2. Incorrect information about service provider.
3. Clients disappear.

We present the mobility of lookup services. When the lookup service moves or disappears as shown in Figure 4, Jini system may not work correctly because it does not consider mobility in its current specification. The effect of moving the service provider is depicted in Figure 5. When the service provider moves, the information about the service previously registered into the lookup service becomes stale. If there are clients using the service, they cannot be served any more due to the absence of the service provider. Figure 6 depicts the effect of moving users. When users move away from their current position, any available service provided by service provider number. 1 will no longer be available. Instead, a new service provider, no. 2, is now closer to the users. Therefore, the user should be able to change its connection to service provider no. 2. Looking to each problem more in detail shows how those problems with Jini can be solved. We will outline methodology to overcome these problems and allow us to use Jini in dynamic environment such as Mobile Ad Hoc Network (MANET).

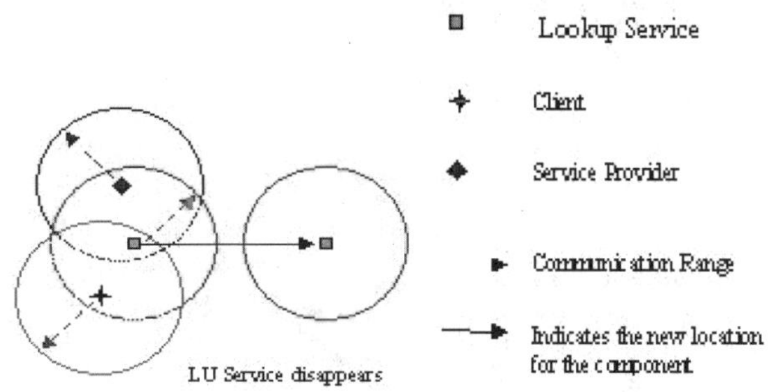

Figure 4 Lookup service disappears

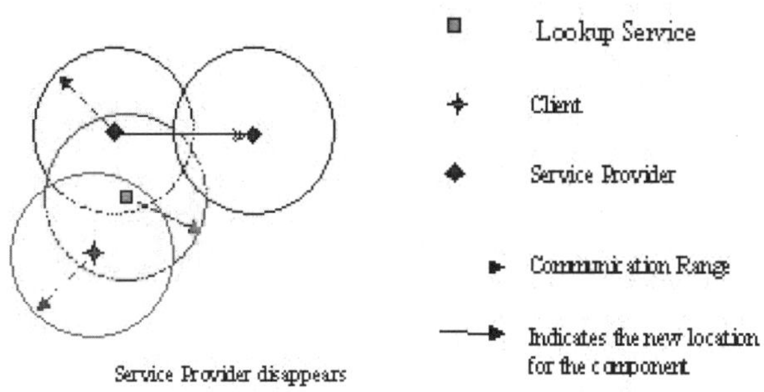

Figure 5 Service Provider disappears

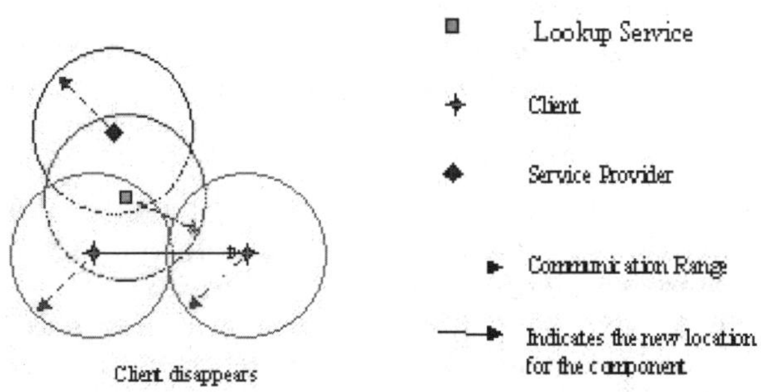

Figure 5 Client disappear

THE ABSENCE OF LOOKUP SERVICE

Any node detecting the absence of lookup service floods a message to inform its neighbors. The message has a hop count field in its header, which increases whenever it is forwarded by intermediate nodes. The message will eventually reach the edge nodes of the network as shown in figure 6. Then these edge nodes will reply with a message that contains the current hop counts to the initial sender. On receiving multiple reply messages, the sender selects the largest hop counts and elects the intermediate node that is located in the half of the largest hop counts. The elected intermediate node is requested to repeat the same operation, until it can calculate the network size. This step attempts to locate the lookup service in the middle of the network. The elected intermediate notifies the elected node of the election information, and the elected node performs the function of lookup service. Figure 7 depict the flow chart for the lookup service election algorithm.

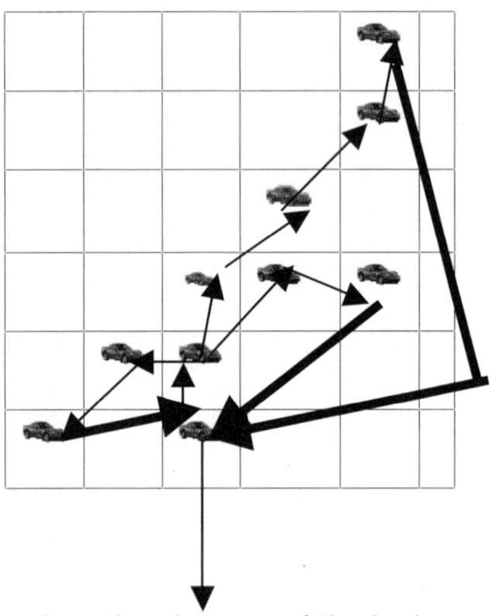

Figure 6 Car1 detects the absence of the lookup service and floods a message to the entire network

INCORRECT INFORMATION ABOUT SERVICE PROVIDER

Service providers always inform the lookup service in the DDS-based Jini of their presence through leasing mechanisms. However, the lookup service may not have the correct information about service providers within the leasing time. The service provider informs the look up service of its presence periodically before the leasing time is ended. If the service provider moves away, the lookup service will not receive the message from the service provider in a determined period. In this case the lookup service sends the query message to the service provider in order to verify if the service provider is still available. If there is no reply from the service provider, the lookup service recognizes the absence of the service provider, and it will drop the proxy. Figure 8 depicts the flow chart for absence of the service provider.

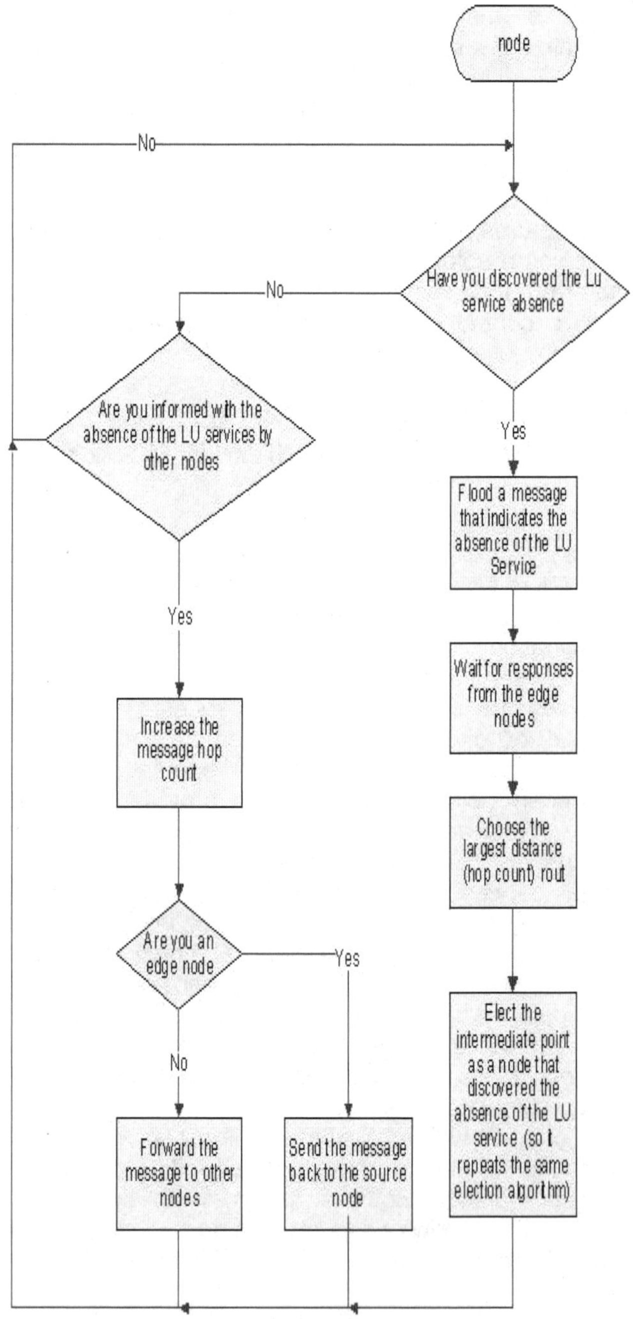

Figure 7 Flow chart for Look up service disappearance

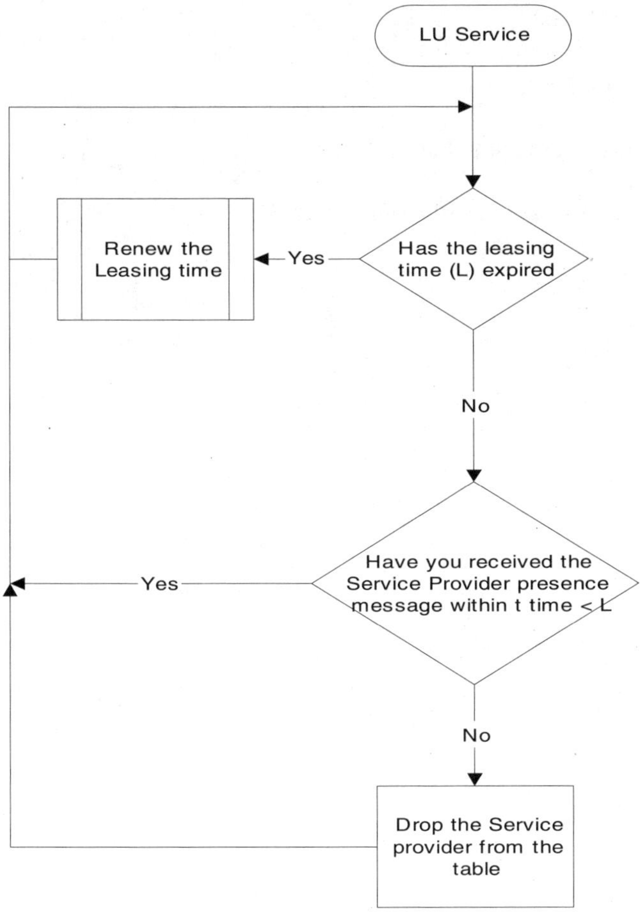

Figure 8 Flow chart for Service Provider disappearance

CLIENT DISAPPEAR

When the connected user moves away, the user no longer can be offered the service. In this case, the user will look for lookup service and request the service needed. The user can be provided the service, not from the beginning, but from the stopped point. Since the user is mobile, the service state can deteriorate and other service providers' service state can improve along with the mobility, then the user stops the existing connection and connects with a better service provider.

VII. CONCLUSION

An effective service discovery is necessary to provide the knowledge of available services to devices in dynamic ad hoc network. We investigate problems that can occur when mobility is considered in the current Jini-based system and propose methodology to overcome these problems and enable us to use Jini in the mobile environment. We conclude that it is imperative to have a service discovery mechanism that is not a burden on the infrastructure and at the same time, highly available to devices and clients anytime anywhere regardless of device and network characteristics. We are currently working to implement the proposed algorithm by modifying the existing Jini and adding new functions to it. The implementation will be tested on Ad hoc On-Demand Vector routing protocol in windows XP environment.

REFERENCES

[1] Wen-Hsien Tseng and Hsing Mei "Inter-Cluster Service Lookup Based on Jini," Proceedings of the 17th IEEE International Conference on Advanced Information Networking and Applications, Xian, China, March 2003, pp. 84-89.

[2] Radu Handorean and Gruia-Catalian Roman, "Service Provision in Ad Hoc Networks" Proceedings of the 5 International Conference on Coordination Models and Languages, 2002, pp.207-219.

[3] Syed Musbahuddin, Syed Mahmud, and Nizar Al-Holou "Development and Performance Analysis of a Data Reduction Algorithm for Automotive Multiplexing" *IEEE Transaction on Vehicular Technology, January 2001, Vol. 50, Number 1, pp. 162-169.*

[4] Nizar Al-Holou and Syed Musbahuddin "Availability Modeling of Hierarchical Distributed Processing Systems," International Journal of Modeling and Simulation, International Association of Science and Technology for Development (IASTED), Vol. 19, Number 2, August 1999, pp. 137-143.

[5] Syed Musbahuddin, Nizar Al-Holou, and Syed Mahmud "Data Reduction Algorithm for Automotive Applications" *SAE 1998 Transactions, Section 6 - Vol. 107, pp. 1667-1670.*

[6] Friedrick H. Phail and David Arnet "In-Vehicle Networking-Serial Communication Requirements and Directions SAE paper 8603901998.

[7] Bosch "CAN Specification." ver2.0, Robert Bosch GmbH, Stuttgart 1991.

[8] R. Tappe, C. Thiel, R. Konig. "MOST Media Oriented Systems Transport." Elektronik. July 2000.

[9] U. J¨ornsson et. al, *MIPMANET – Mobile IP for Mobile Ad Hoc Networks* Proc. ACM International Symposium on Mobile Ad Hoc Networking and Computing , Boston, USA, August. 2000.

[10] Rami Baroody, Nizar Al-Holou, and Salim Hariri "Development of Car Intranet Infrastructure" Detroit, MI SAE Technical Paper Series Series, Paper # 02-0438_112801 March 2002, pp.61-66.

[11] Rami Baroody, Mansoor Mahfoud Nizar Al-Holou, and Salim Hariri. "Design the Next Generation Auto Network (NGANet)" 2nd Annual Intelligent Vehicles Systems Symposium, June 2002, pp. 101-106.

[12] C. Lee and S. Helal *Protocols for Service Discovery in Dynamic Mobile Networks* Int. Journal of Computer Research, Special Issue on Wireless Systems and Mobile Computing, 2002.

[13] G. G. Richard III, *Service Advertisement and Discovery: Enabling Universal Device Cooperation*, IEEE Internet Computing, Sep./Oct. 2000.

[14] Erik Guttman, and James Kempf, "Automatic Discovery of Thin Servers: SLP, Jini and the SLP-Jini Bridge" *IEEE*, Los Alamitos, CA, pp. 722-727.

[15] W. Keith Edwards. Core Jini, Second Edition, Prentice Hall, 2001, ISBN 0-13-089408-7.

[16] J. Costa Requena, Raimo Kantola, and Nicklas Beijar: Mobility and Network Management in Ad Hoc Networks, IASTED International Conference, Communication Systems and Networks (CSN 2002), September 9-12, 2002,

[17] Sun Microsystems, Inc, "JiniTM Architecture Specification" Version 1.2, <URL: http://www.sun.com/jini/. December 2001>

[18] Universal Plug and Play Forum, "Universal Plug and Play Technology UPnP", <URL: http://www.upnp.org/>.

[19] Salutation Consortium. "The Application Programmer's Interface of the Salutation Architecture" <URL: http://www.salutation.org/>.

[20] Open Services Gateway Initiative (OSGi), "OSGi - The Managed Services Specification" <URL: http://www.osgi.org/>.

[21] E. Guttman, C. Perkins, J. Veizades, M. Day, "Service Location Protocol, Version 2" RFC 2608, IETF, June 1999.

CONTACT

Rami Baroody

Rbaroody@gmail.com

Professor: Nizar Alholou

Alholoun@udmercy.edu

2006-01-0478

The Future of Digital Broadcast –More Than Just Crystal Clear Sound

Michael Weber and Matthias Unbehaun
BMW Group

ABSTRACT

Digital radio broadcast systems, like HD-Radio™ and Satellite Radio, provide crystal clear sound. However, since they are essentially bits and bytes, they could also be used for distributing traffic and weather information or any other supplementary information. Due to considerably enhanced compression techniques, digital broadcast systems could also carry surround sound, which significantly improves the sound perception. Integration of the digital tuners in an automotive environment are mainly through MOST ring topologies, which allow flexibly adding different tuner modules depending on customer preferences and standards used in different markets. This paper aims at providing a more detailed insight into the aforementioned trends and developments, with a specific focus on premium segment automobiles.

INTRODUCTION

BMW engineers continually strive for retaining our position in offering *best-in-class* sound systems in today's premium segment automobiles. Sources like CD or DVD do in fact deliver appropriate high-quality input for such sound systems. However, analog radio broadcast, such as AM or FM, suffers from noise and fading and therefore does not live up to the sound quality that our customers expect from a premium HiFi audio system.

Digital radio broadcast systems considerably improve the sound quality. In 2004, BMW integrated Sirius Satellite radio as the first factory-fit fully digital broadcast system. The service offering, comprising a large number of commercial, advertisement-free radio programs, is very much appreciated by our customers.

This success encouraged us to launch HD-Radio™ in our new 2006 models of the 7 and 6 series vehicles. BMW is the first company offering such a factory-fit solution for HD-Radio™. The main difference of HD-Radio™ compared to the satellite systems is that it piggybacks a digitally modulated signal onto the analog radio broadcast without impairing its quality. This simulcast approach solves the issue of backwards compatibility, so that customers with an analog-only tuner can still receive the program. The digital signal provides CD quality for an FM network, whereas quality improvements in an AM network are comparable to that of an analog FM broadcast.

With the rapid market acceptance of the digital satellite systems and HD-Radio™, the USA currently leads the digitalization of radio broadcast worldwide. How much such developments can trigger the –thus far quite slow– progress of e.g. DAB in Europe, remains to be seen. Experience shows that *content is king*. Customers fall for better and more services, not for the appeal of an optimal technical solution. The digital radio market in the USA is an example par-excellence, which should guide the decision and policy makers in Europe.

THE IMPORTANCE OF THE RADIO IN A CAR

A BMW internal customer study shows that AM/FM radio is still the preferred entertainment source on short or spontaneous trips. Whenever a longer trip is considered, the usage of CD is on par with the AM/FM radio. Such results indicate that the radio still is the primary medium for entertainment and information in a car. Thus, new broadcast services do have a great potential and should be able to benefit from the wide acceptance of the traditional car radio.

USING DIGITAL BROADCAST NETWORKS FOR DISTRIBUTING DATA SERVICES

Digital radio systems are essentially a stream of bits and bytes and can thus be used for distributing any kind of digitized information, which is of interest to a large number of customers within the broadcast coverage region.

Traffic information services are an example par-excellence. Today, comprehensive and detailed information is gathered in most European countries, either by commercial service providers or by public authorities. Up till now, such information was either disseminated via cellular carriers or broadcast using RDS-TMC, a digital subcarrier modulated atop the FM radio with a capacity of about 100bps. The former approach is simply too costly if a large number of customers should be served (see Fig. 1), whereas the latter reaches its capacity limits in some heavily trafficked areas in Europe.

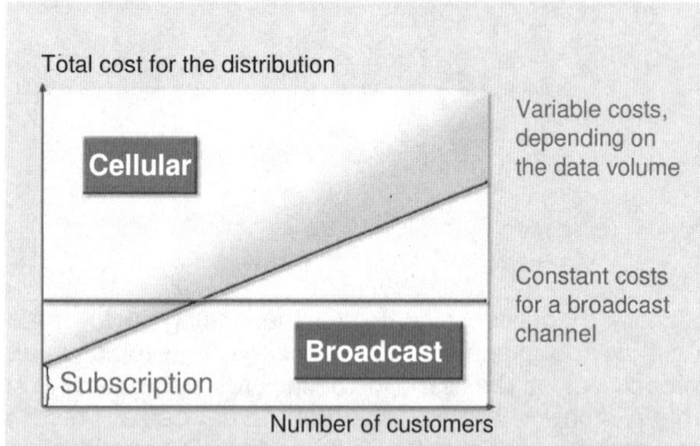

Fig. 1: Cost structure for distributing traffic information services via a broadcast network and a cellular carrier.

RDS-TMC is still the best carrier for traffic information and the majority of European telematics service providers rely heavily on it. However, looking at the extensibility of RDS-TMC, there are certainly some limitations in throughput and code space for the type of applications we envisage for the future. The obvious long-term migration path is using digital broadcast as a carrier for advanced traffic information and telematics services. Recent activities in Germany[1], involving car manufacturers (Audi, BMW, DaimlerChrysler and Volkswagen), 1st tier suppliers (Blaupunkt, SiemenVDO), network providers (Deutsche Telekom) and public broadcasters (WDR) show an increasing interest in extending the use of digital broadcast networks beyond the traditional distribution of radio programs.

Nevertheless, even with the use of digital broadcast networks, the range of possible services is limited to typical multicast applications. Other telematics services, such as the SOS button, breakdown call, remote diagnostics, etc. do require cellular networks. Hybrid networks, using a broadcast network as forward and a cellular system as return channel, are conceivable, but difficult to integrate. However, recent research shows that the combination of cellular and broadcast systems can yield substantial cost savings even for typical multicast applications [1].

[1] See also www.mobile-info.org for further details.

DAB AS THE PREFERED CHOICE FOR TELEMATICS SERVICES IN EUROPE

Various digital broadcast systems are operational, or being built, in Europe. Specifically DVB-T (terrestrial) and DVB-S (satellite) enjoy fast growing popularity, specifically in Germany. However, despite very high data rates and ample capacity in DVB networks, coverage is the main issue that precludes their use for telematics services[2]. DVB-T will, even in the distant future, likely not reach complete geographical coverage. Further, the reception of DVB-T signals in the car[3], even at moderate speeds, is far from trivial due to the higher-order modulation schemes used in the air interface.

DRM, the digital successor of the AM radio in Europe, is still in the making and standards are not settled yet. However, BMW sees great potential in the DRM system, particularly as it offers superb sound quality compared to the traditional AM radio. However, the strongly fluctuating propagation conditions and coverage of DRM, which follows various temporal patterns and suffers from the impact of the global weather situation, makes the reception of DRM signals somewhat difficult to predict.

This leaves DAB as the preferred migration path towards future traffic information and telematics services in Europe. Reliable reception, even in cars traveling at very high speeds, and relatively low integration costs both speak for DAB. Networks are either already in place (e.g. area coverage in Germany is said to be around 95%) or being built up.

TRAFFIC INFORMATION BROADCAST TO LAY THE FOUNDATION FOR INTELLIGENT NAVIGATION

Traffic information is not only important for informing the driver about the global traffic situation (see Fig. 2 for an example), but also vital for the proper functioning of in-car navigation systems.

Fig. 2: Typical traffic information (shown here in a prototype implementation) displayed on the navigation screen.

The calculation of the optimal route uses a static map database, typically on a DVD that is sold together with

[2] Note the difference between area and population coverage. For telematics services, complete geographic coverage is essential in order to reach all vehicles on any road.

[3] BMW does offer now optional DVB-T modules for TV reception. However, TV reception is disabled whenever the vehicle is moving. Therefore, reception in a moving vehicle is not relevant in this context.

the navigation system. Only with the up-to-date information that is provided from the digital radio receiver can the route calculation continually reevaluate the routing against the road network performance and optimize the route (e.g. by circumnavigating traffic jams or roads with temporarily limited throughput) whenever necessary. Only such tight integration (see Fig. 3) of two seemingly unrelated modules –the car radio and the navigation system– allows sophisticated telematics services, which in turn are a prerequisite for coping with the problems we face in the future due to the continuously increasing road traffic.

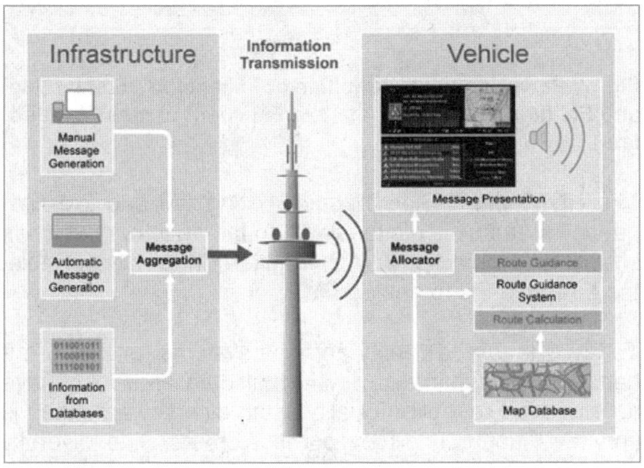

Fig. 3: Broadcasting traffic information – information chain from the source to the integration with the in-car navigation system.

However, not only cost and capacity advantages favor digital broadcast networks for distributing traffic information and telematics services. Latency is yet another factor.

Safety is one of the key motivations for customers to purchase telematics services. One such safety-related service is the Local Hazard Warning, for which an example is shown in Fig. 4. These messages must be broadcast fast and reliably to all drivers in the vicinity of the problem spot. Digital broadcast networks provide such a high-speed and reliable data channel to facilitate these services.

Fig. 4: Local hazard warning (shown here in a prototype implementation).

To that end, digitizing our radio networks offers not only superior sound, but also facilitates intelligent navigation and helps improve traffic safety.

ENHANCED SOUND QUALITY – DISCRETE 5.1 SURROUND SOUND

Beyond the CD-quality sound, as it is delivered by today's digital broadcast systems, emerges a trend that has already taken a foothold in the home entertainment segment: discrete surround sound. Our top-HiFi entertainment systems in the new 5, 6 and 7 series models feature 13 speakers, which are placed such that a near-optimum listening environment for reproducing discrete surround sound is given (see Fig. 5).

Besides the truly fascinating surround effects while listening to live recordings of sports events, classical music, or operas, surround sound has one important advantage in the context of sound reproduction in a car. While stereo sound limits the sound equalization to optimizing only for a single listening position (typically the driver's seat), surround sound expands a larger zone with near-optimum sound perception. Therefore, all passengers can enjoy a more structured and feature-rich sound.

The surround sound encoding needs to be backwards compatible to existing stereo receivers. Therefore, a down-mix from 5.1 to 2 channels (the compatible stereo sound) is performed. The differential information, which is needed to reconstruct the discrete 5.1 signal at the receiver, is sent through a separate, synchronized data channel, which in the case of DAB can be piggybacked onto the audio signal. Details about the coding scheme are given in [2].

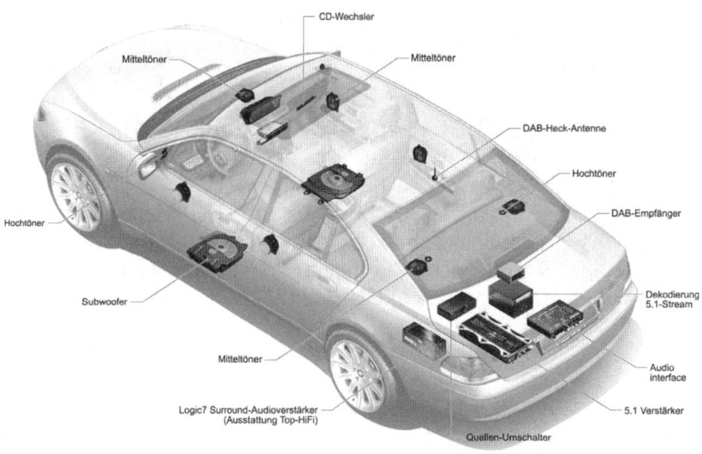

Fig. 5: Prototype surround sound reception system, based on DAB technology with an enhanced audio codec.

INTEGRATION OF DIGITAL TUNER IN OUR VEHICLES

All digital tuners are integrated as slave devices on a MOST bus ring topology [3] as shown in Fig. 6. This allows flexible partitioning of our options. The master contains the audio controller and HMI software. The optional iDrive is connected via CAN-bus to the master. Audio data as well as traffic information is transferred via MOST bus into the specific sub systems.

This so called external-box-strategy is best suited for options that are new in the market. When take rates increase an integration of digital tuners into the master is planned.

Disregarding of further options or different master devices, the digital tuner devices are carry over parts. Therefore, BMW is able to have a fast rollout of new options for our customers into all of our car lines.

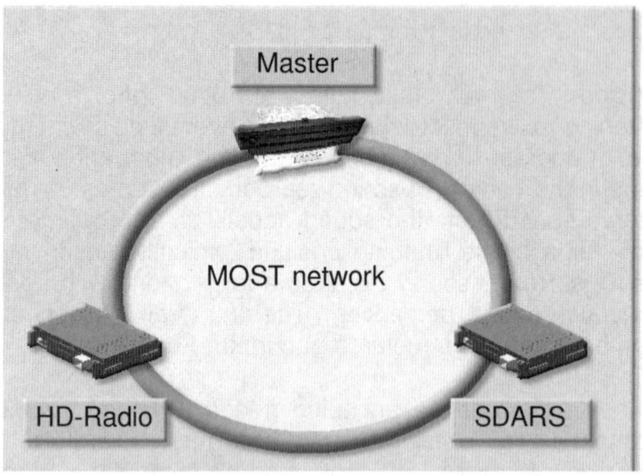

Fig. 6: Configuration of different options by adding MOST-compatible devices to the MOST network.

MAINTAINING COMPATIBILITY OF AM/FM ANTENNAS INTEGRATING HD-RADIO™

This section is intended to give a brief summary of a joint project of iBiquity, BMW and Visteon to make the HD-Radio™ System compatible with switching diversity antenna systems.

THE EFFECT OF FM SWITCHING DIVERSITY TO HD-RADIO™

Besides upcoming DRM in Europe, HD-Radio™ is the only broadcast service reusing the existing AM/FM band. Thus, no new antenna system has to be developed for integration of HD-Radio™.

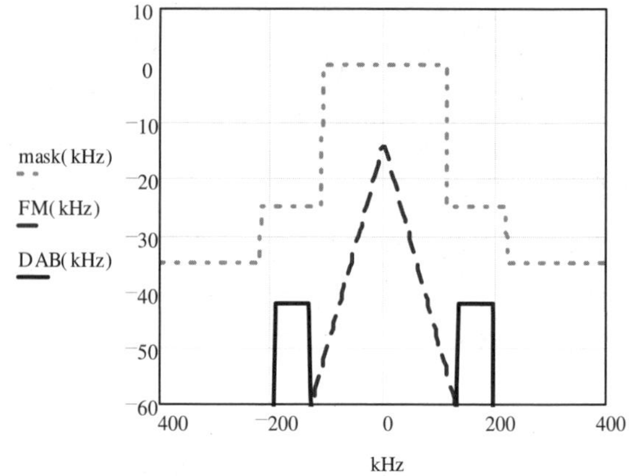

Fig. 7: Power spectral densities of FM analog (dashed line) and FM digital (solid line) below FM spectral mask (dotted line).

The HD-Radio™ Signal uses existing AM and FM Frequencies adding a digital signal to the spectrum which is shown for FM in fig. 7. If the digital FM is not available, the tuner blends to analog FM.

Today, we have diversity antenna systems for FM to enhance FM reception quality in multipath areas. To have an improved reception quality using diversity antennas is very well appreciated by our customers. The diversity system switches between 4 antennas to have the best FM reception. The system is shown in fig. 8.

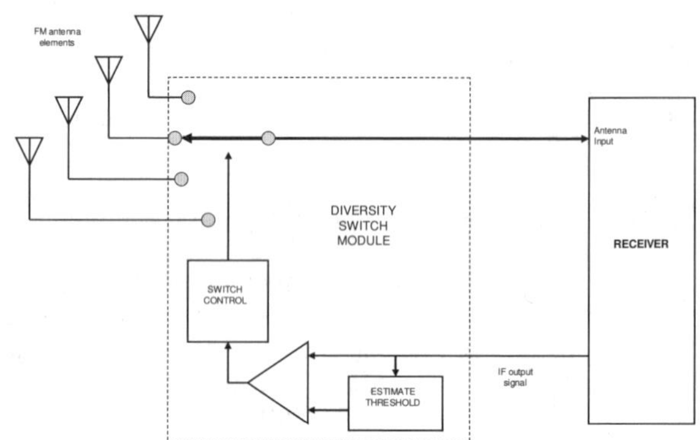

Fig. 8: Functional diagram of switching diversity antenna system, based on an IF feedback of the receiver which provides the quality rating of the signal. The diversity controller switches between 4 antennas.

Having the backward compatibility of HD-Radio™, our customers expect an analog FM reception performance at diversity level. Because HD-Radio™ blends between analog and digital reception, we had to investigate the impact of the diversity system to the digital reception mode. Of particular concern was the effect of diversity switching step transients on the coherent reference signal used for digital reception. It was important to ensure, that the diversity system would work for HD-Radio™ in the Hybrid digital mode shown in fig. 7.

BMW was the first OEM performing intensive field testing together with iBiquity and Visteon to investigate the influence of a switching diversity to HD-Radio™ reception. Whereas first field tests showed no significant impact using a switching diversity, we observed in areas of NYC experienced degraded digital performance caused by severe multipath resulting in excessive antenna switching.

Fig. 9 shows that, whereas the diversity antenna system improves reception quality for the FM-analog mode, the FM Hybrid digital mode was significantly degraded in the severe multipath test in NYC.

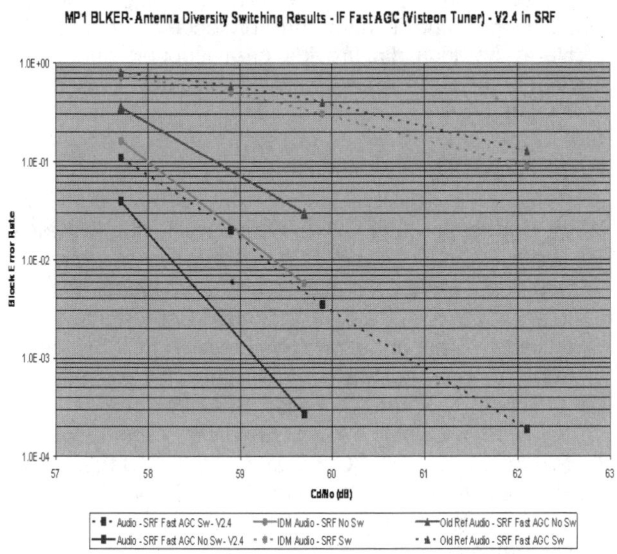

Fig. 9: BER with respect to diversity and non-diversity antenna systems: solid lines (non-diversity mode) indicate a much better BER than dotted lines (diversity mode) at the same SNR level.

After analyzing the entire system, the main root cause was identified:

- The HD-Radio™ System was designed to cope with typical fading effects of a car at about 85 mph maximum speed. Linear FIR filters were originally used in the coherent reference estimation for subsequent digital demodulation.
- The switching of the diversity system causes much faster step transients to the signal than fadings at any vehicle speed. Thus, the filter algorithm was not fast enough to follow the transients and had to be modified. Fig. 10 shows the impact of switching diversity to the signal. Fig. 11 shows the insufficient level of signal estimation by the linear FIR filters, where the step transients were incorrectly smoothed.

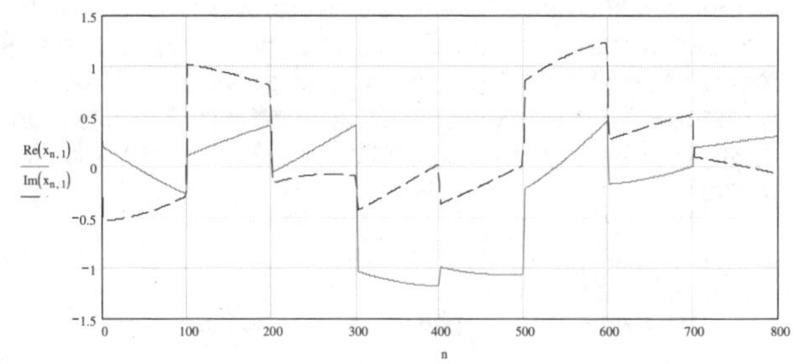

Fig. 10: The fast switching diversity corrupts the signal.

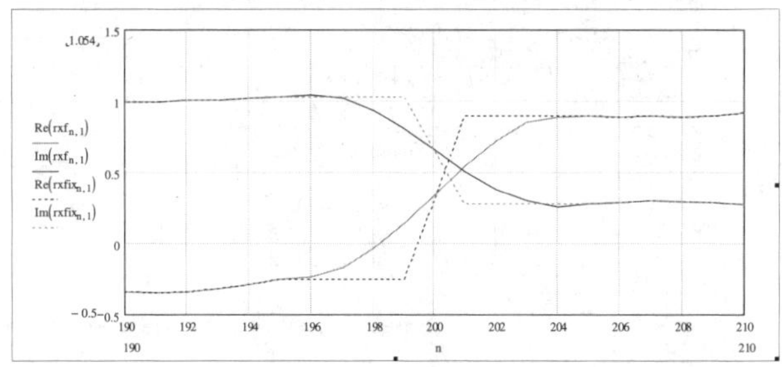

Fig. 11: The linear FIR filter (solid lines) does not estimate the transient step functions (dashed lines) well enough.

NEW FILTERING TO COPE WITH SWITCHING DIVERSITY

To be able to correct the coherent reference data stream, the linear FIR filters were replaced by median filters. Thus, the fast step transient information in the coherent reference as shown in fig. 12 could be preserved.

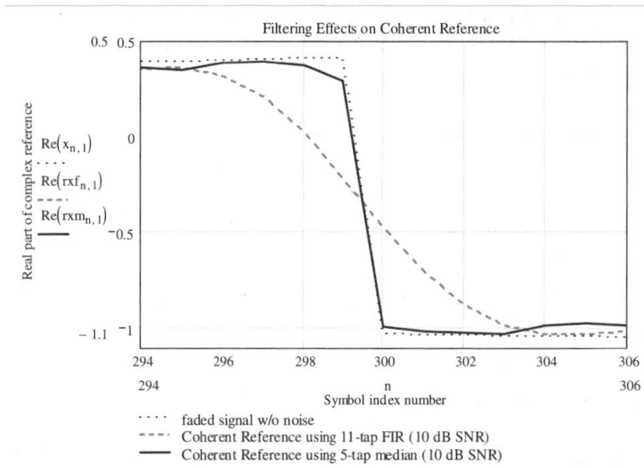

Fig. 12: Replacing FIR by median filter to preserve transient information (dotted line): the estimation of the median filter (solid line) is significantly better than the estimation of the linear FIR filter (dashed line).

Further modifications to the digital signal processing path were also done to cope with our fast active gain control of the tuner.

The final results of fig. 13 show that the new filtering and further modifications have a significantly improved reception performance. The BER using a switching diversity is much lower than without a switching diversity. Thus, we transferred the advantages of a switching diversity from analog FM reception to digital FM reception of HD-Radio™.

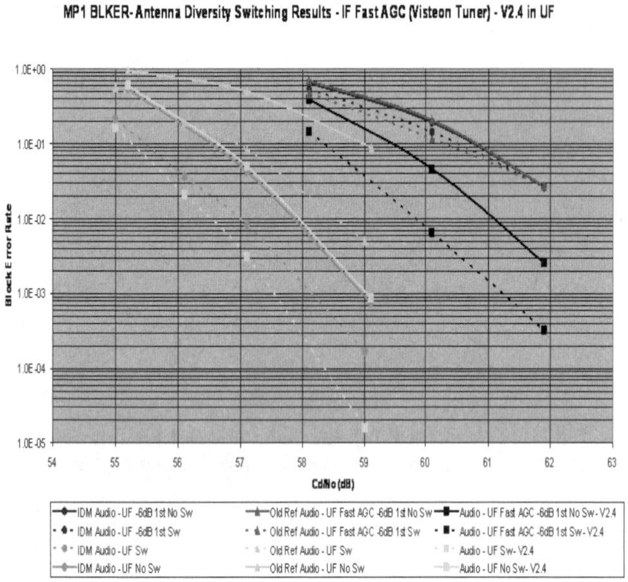

Fig. 13: Improvement of reception quality using switching diversity: the dashed lines show significantly lower BER using diversity compared to the solid lines showing the non-diversity mode.

Thus, the final optimization exploits of benefits of diversity switching in the Hybrid Digital mode, as well as driving at higher speeds than 85 mph, which may be interesting for a HD-Radio™ roll out in other countries.

CONCLUSION

We see many different digital broadcast standards arising worldwide over the next years. The tuner devices should be integrated as slaves in a MOST bus. As soon as take rates rise, the chip industry hopefully will have more tightly integrated solutions. A software controlled tuner combining all standards must be the future target. However, antennas and the analog path prior to digitization will always require significant space since they represent a distributed antenna system in a car, not to be compared with any handheld multistandard receiver. In a car, we should strive for intelligent integration solutions as shown in case of HD-Radio™. Instead of modifying existing diversity components in every car line of all OEMs, we optimized the digital signal processing path in the HD-Radio™ chip set. We not only saved costs by avoiding a change of the antenna system, but the reception quality in digital Hybrid mode was also improved.

ACKNOWLEDGMENTS

We would like to thank both iBiquity and Visteon for their close cooperation in numerous projects. Further, BMW of North America did provide great support during the development and rollout phase of our digital radio products in the USA.

REFERENCES

[1] M. Unbehaun, J. Hu, R. German, A. Heindl, R. Kates, *'Traffic modelling and cost optimization for transmitting traffic messages over a hybrid broadcast and cellular network'*, in Proc. 8th Intl. IEEE Conference on Intelligent Transportation Systems (ITSC'05), Sept. 2005, Vienna, Austria

[2] J. Herre, P. Kroon, C. Faller, S. Geyersberger, *'Spatial Audio Coding – an Enabling Technology for Btrate-efficient and Compatible Multi-Channel Audio Broadcasting'*, Proc. Intl. Broadcast Convention (IBC) 2004, Amsterdam, The Netherlands

[3] www.mostcooperation.com

CONTACT

For further information please contact Michael Weber, Michael.weber@bmw.de.

DEFINITIONS, ACRONYMS, ABBREVIATIONS

DAB: Digital Audio Broadcast

DRM: Digital Radio Mondiale

DVB-T/S: Digital Video Broadcast – Terrestrial/Satellite

BER: Bit Error Rate

MOST: Media Oriented System Transport

2006-01-0167

A Virtualization Architecture for Next Generation In-Car Infotainment Applications

David N. Kleidermacher
Green Hills Software, Inc.

ABSTRACT

Despite the demand for an increasingly rich infotainment environment in cars, the pressure for reduced space, weight, and cost remains steadfast. Although a PC-like environment with office and internet applications is desired, incompatible requirements, including real-time performance, fast start-up times, and bullet-proof security cannot be achieved with legacy PC operating systems alone. A real-time, secure microkernel with virtualization technology can be used to enable these incompatible requirements on a single computer, thereby keeping size, weight, and cost in check. Applications requiring fast start-up, real-time, or security can be run directly on the microkernel, while multiple legacy PC operating systems and applications, can be run in their own virtual environments.

INTRODUCTION

This paper will present an overview of systems software technical requirements for use in next-generation in-car digital infotainment applications, and explain how a virtualization architecture provides an ideal solution to these varied requirements while still minimizing size, weight, power, and production cost – a strict business requirement for automotive systems. The virtualization architecture will be described in detail, focusing on how it addresses the stated requirements and why it is in general a promising new technology in this space.

OFFICE IN THE CAR

Microsoft Windows XP has found its way into some high end infotainment systems, such as the BMW 7 series Individual. With Windows in the car, the passenger now has access to a familiar office environment, including electronic mail, office applications such as spreadsheets and word processors, and an Internet browser. Bringing the office into the car is a natural progression for next generation infotainment systems, to meet consumers' insatiable demand for more features, capabilities, and connectivity. Although BMW has proven that desktop Windows can be used in an infotainment system, we do not have proof that Windows can be used effectively in low or even mid-range infotainment platforms.

Traditionally, infotainment systems have relied on real-time operating systems to provide instant-on access, real-time response, and bullet-proof reliability. Windows is unable to meet these requirements. Therefore, in order to add Windows and its suite of office applications into the infotainment system, designers can either choose to forgo the aforementioned robustness requirements, or they can choose to provide two independent hardware systems: one running Windows on an automotive-grade PC, and another running a traditional infotainment processor (such as a Freescale MPC5200 or an Analog Devices Blackfin) that hosts the applications that have instant-on, real-time and/or high-reliability requirements.

Neither option is desirable. Separate hardware systems effectively double the size, weight, power, and production cost of the infotainment system. While this may be acceptable on a 7 series BMW, it is not a good solution for most of the market. Relying on Windows for all of the infotainment applications is similarly not a good choice. Passengers will not tolerate the "blue screen of death" in response to turning on the radio in an automobile for which they have paid tens of thousands of dollars.

A better solution involves running both the real-time operating system and Windows on the same infotainment processor, but to do so in a way that guarantees an absolutely secure partitioning between the Windows environment and the real-time operating system and its natively executing critical applications. Before we describe this architecture in detail, we will look a little further into aspects of the next generation infotainment system for which a secure, real-time system is needed and where a desktop operating system like Windows is not appropriate.

REAL-TIME RESPONSE

One of the key requirements of multimedia infotainment systems is a high quality audio/visual experience. On home PCs, the sheer power of the microprocessor often makes up for the lack of real-time responsiveness of Windows. Next generation in-car systems, which typically use lower powered microprocessors than those found in the home or office, will depend more on the ability of the operating system to guarantee real-time response because the microprocessor may be loaded with more simultaneously-executing, resource-demanding applications. Researchers at Carnegie Mellon University have studied latency problems associated specifically with audio: "Latency is the stumbling block for music software, and the OS is often the cause of it."[1]

SCHEDULING

Consider a scenario where an occupant is requesting directions from the navigation system while simultaneously playing a DVD for children in the rear of the car. The navigation data processing requires much of the available CPU time but the occupant does not require an immediate response (a few seconds may be typical and expected). On the other hand, the processing of the audio and video samples must occur on time in order to avoid choppiness.

In this example, a real-time operating system can strictly prioritize the audio and video processing above the navigation processing to ensure a high quality DVD experience. A slight delay in the navigation result, due to this prioritization, is not likely to be noticed. In contrast, desktop operating systems like Windows often use heuristic scheduling algorithms that attempt to dole out CPU time "fairly". While fairness-based scheduling is often good for human-user interactive applications, this style of scheduling does not actually provide a guaranteed response; even one bad guess by the operating system can adversely affect the multimedia experience.

INTERRUPT LATENCY

When a process executes a system call, and the kernel is modifying internal data structures to accomplish the request, preemption is disabled by the kernel in order to ensure that another process cannot be context switched in and execute a system call which could access these internal data structures while they are in an inconsistent state. The problem with this approach is that high priority interrupt processing can be delayed while the kernel disables preemption on behalf of potentially lower priority requests (Figure 1). Even simple, self-described "real-time operating systems" can disable interrupt processing in hundreds of locations. In one study of a real-time operating system's interrupt latency, researchers found that some of the disabling sequences contained triply nested loops with estimated execution times of more than 25,000 cycles [2].

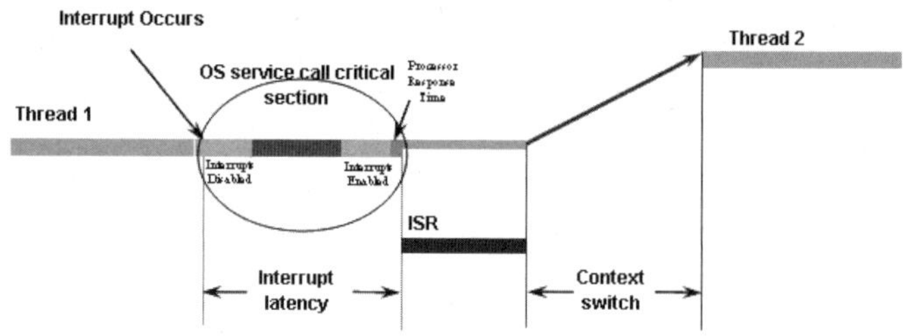

Figure 1

This problem is exacerbated by more complicated, monolithic operating systems such as Windows. The worst case response time for the high priority interrupt source (e.g. the audio device) cannot be determined, and thus the quality of the user experience cannot be guaranteed. It is well known that desktop operating systems which exhibit good overall throughput have large preemption latencies on the order of milliseconds [3], enough to derail a low latency device should its interrupt fire at an inopportune time.

A better architecture for guaranteed real-time response is to never disable interrupts in system calls. By always taking the highest priority interrupt, the kernel ensures smooth performance of the time-critical audio/visual devices. Handling of lower priority requests is postponed. The kernel must be configurable enough to prioritize interrupt handling appropriately. When a high priority process is awakened to perform some I/O handling, the kernel's scheduler should automatically inhibit lower priority interrupts from delaying this processing.

Consumers pay top dollar for upgraded audio systems and expect a concert performance every time they get in the car. Because Windows lacks real-time behavior, sound playback can sometimes be interrupted, with audible clicks and pops, when the system is juggling other CPU-intensive operations such as loading a large Office document. Windows simply cannot ensure the flawless audio/visual experience that the car passenger expects.

RELIABILITY AND SECURITY

Although we expect Windows to crash occasionally, automobile passengers expect the radio and other traditional components to never fail. In fact, a failure in one of these components is liable to cause an expensive visit to the repair shop. Even worse, a severe design flaw in one of these systems may result in a recall that wipes out the profit on an entire vintage of cars.

Exacerbating the reliability problem is a new generation of security threats: bringing Internet into the car exposes it to all the viruses and worms that target networked Windows-based computers.

New Windows flaws are being discovered all the time. A recent worm affected the United States Congress, CNN, and the New York Times [4]. Unlike organizational IT departments, the car does not have a system administrator to enforce security upgrade policies. And we all know that security vulnerabilities will continue to be found in Windows, and there is no guarantee that a flaw can be patched before it is used to perpetrate an attack. The automobile passenger may not complain about office applications going down, but loss of the complete infotainment system will result in irate customers and increased cost for the automobile manufacturer.

Although a networked Windows environment can be infected with malicious software, a robust architecture can limit the damage of such infiltration and ensure that critical services remain unaffected.

MEMORY PROTECTION

A fundamental requirement for robust infotainment systems is memory protection. The operating system utilizes memory protection hardware of the microprocessor to isolate unrelated infotainment functions. Malicious code is unable to crash an application or the operating system by corrupting memory. Similarly, an errant pointer caused by a programming error in one application cannot affect another application executing in a separate protected process.

GUARANTEED RESOURCES

Despite memory protection, malicious code can still take down a critical application by starving it of resources. Most operating systems employ a central store for memory resources. As protected processes ask for new resources (e.g. heap memory, threads, etc.), the operating system allocates these resources from the central store. An errant or malicious application can request too many resources, causing the central store to be depleted and critical applications to fail when they attempt to obtain their required resources (Figure 2). A similar denial of service attack can occur with CPU time. A malicious process can spawn multiple "confederate" processes that soak up the CPU time, keeping critical applications from accomplishing their tasks.

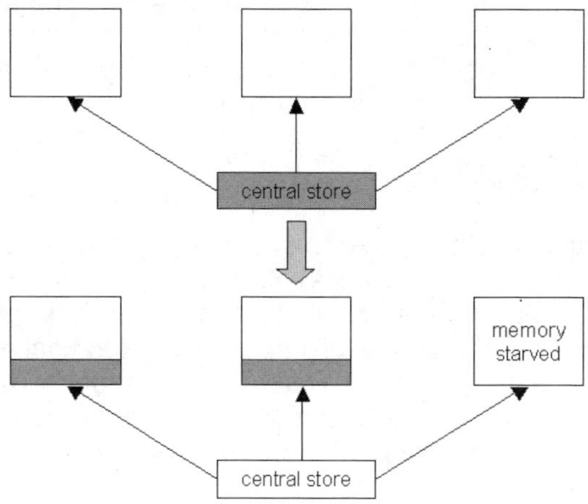

Figure 2

It is possible to architect an operating system such that these critical resources are partitioned according to individual application requirements. An infected process can exhaust its own quota of resources, but it cannot possibly affect the quota of resources held by critical applications (Figure 3).

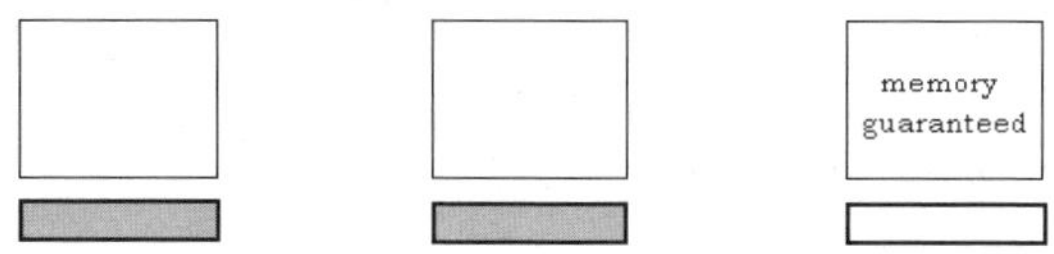

Figure 3

Despite the compelling security advantage of partitioning, one of its potential drawbacks from a usability perspective is the static nature of quotas. Some complex systems may have varying resource requirements during their lifetimes and may not have enough memory for the union of all the desired quotas. To address this, a partitioning operating system must provide the capability for system designers to create a trusted resource manager that can export memory to, and reclaim memory from, applications on demand. The system designer must be able to specify which critical applications can connect to the resource manager. Malicious software imported into new processes will not have access to the resource manager and are therefore governed by their quotas. Partitioning coupled with a resource manager enables system designers to obtain flexibility where needed and security where it is essential.

SECURITY THROUGH SIMPLICITY

As infotainment systems become increasingly complex, integrating more applications from more vendors, the risk of security and robustness problems increases. The operating system controlling the bare hardware, however, is the most critical component: whereas a security flaw in an application can make that application unusable, a security flaw in the operating system can be fatal for the entire infotainment system.

Monolithic Architectures

Monolithic operating systems contain system software, such as networking stacks, file systems, and complex device drivers, that all run in supervisor mode (Figure 4) and provide a plethora of opportunities for hackers to find and exploit vulnerabilities. Examples of monolithic operating systems are Windows, UNIX, and Linux. Most consumers are aware of security flaws discovered in these operating systems.

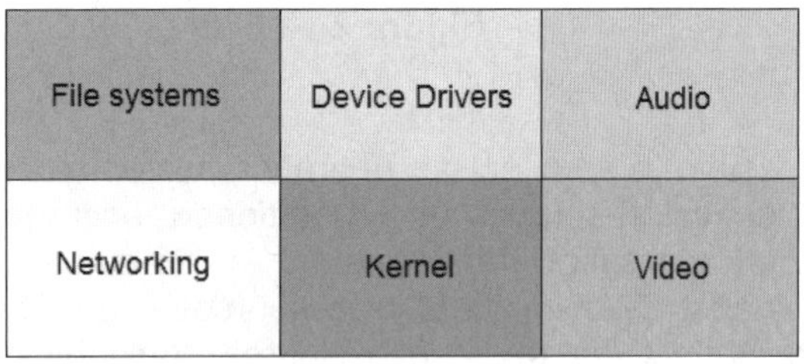

Figure 4 - Monolithic OS

Microkernel Architectures

Microkernel operating systems provide a better architecture for security. A microkernel operating system runs only a minimal set of critical system services, such as thread management, exception handling, and interprocess communication, in supervisor mode (Figure 5) and provides an architecture that enables complex systems software to run in user mode where they are permitted access only to the resources deemed appropriate by the system designer. A virus in one component can not cause damage to a critical device because the infected component simply does not have access to that resource. Because the microkernel is simple, it can be more easily modeled and verified.

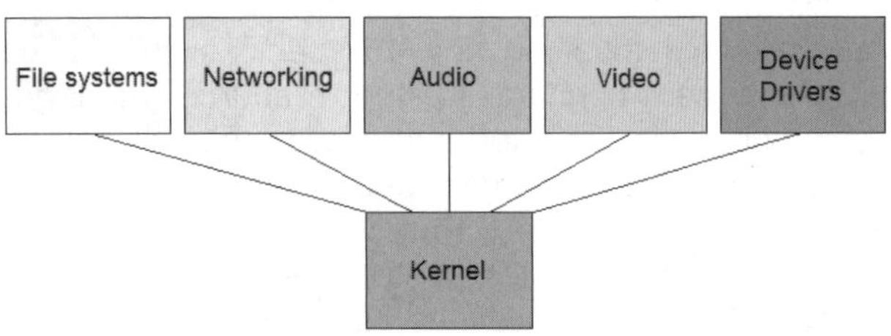

Figure 5 - Microkernel OS

COMMON CRITERIA

Common Criteria is the internationally recognized standard for security evaluation. Common Criteria specifies evaluation assurance levels (EAL), 1 through 7. The higher the EAL for a product, the less likely the product contains security flaws. EAL 7 requires formal modeling of the software and a formal mathematical proof that the software upholds its security functional requirements. As the assurance level increases, the development and life-cycle process requirements (e.g. design, configuration management, testing, maintenance, flaw remediation) become increasingly rigorous.

Windows has achieved an EAL-4 evaluation. The higher EALs, 5 through 7, are required in order to have any reasonable assurance about security. An NSA analyst said it best when he described EAL-4 as "secure as long as nothing is connected to it."[5] It is simply not possible to achieve high assurance with legacy monolithic operating systems. Not only are they too complex, but they lack a fundamental security architectural design. Systems not designed for high assurance cannot have high assurance retrofitted. According to Common Criteria: "EAL4 is the highest level at which it is likely to be economically feasible to retrofit to an existing product line."[6] Not even Microsoft, with its practically unlimited financial resources, can find and remove all of the security flaws in Windows.

In contrast, there is an ongoing effort to evaluate secure, real-time operating systems at the highest levels of assurance (EAL6/7) of the Common Criteria [7].

SOLUTION: A HYBRID ARCHITECTURE

Clearly, we cannot depend on Windows to control all aspects of the infotainment and telematics systems. Windows cannot boot fast enough, cannot guarantee a real-time, flawless quality of service for audio and other staple functions, and is not reliable and secure enough for automotive platforms. Therefore we need a hybrid architecture in which Windows and office applications can peacefully coexist with a real-time, secure kernel and its critical applications.

SURVEY OF OTHER HYBRID ENVIRONMENTS

RTLinux

RTLinux and RTAI are the familiar hybrid real-time and general purpose processing environments in the Linux world. In these architectures, Linux executes as a thread (typically the idle thread) under control of the real-time executive [8]. System designers can include both real-time and general purpose software on a single microprocessor by creating real-time threads and using the real-time API for the real-time portions of the system and the Linux API and Linux processes running under control of the Linux kernel for the general purpose parts of the system. The main drawback of these implementations is that the real-time executive and components run in the same memory space as the Linux kernel and share access to the supervisor mode of the processor. Thus, there is no secure separation between the real-time components and the non-real-time components. In essence, the entire system is subject to the security assurance level attainable by the Linux operating system. This assurance level is relatively low compared to operating systems designed from the ground up for security and reliability.

VxWin

Kuka Controls is a company that has developed a hybrid real-time and general purpose processing system, called VxWin [9], in which the real-time portion is the VxWorks real-time operating system and threads running under its control, and the general purpose processing system is Windows XP or Windows XP Embedded. VxWin suffers from a similar limitation as RTLinux: the VxWorks kernel and the Windows kernel both share supervisory control of the system (Figure 6). Although VxWin configures VxWorks in a protected space that Windows should not access directly or accidentally, this protection does not provide any high level of assurance against unauthorized tampering of the system. Since the Windows kernel runs at ring 0 (supervisor mode in the x86 architecture), Windows can in theory make any modifications to access controls and permissions. In addition, neither Windows nor VxWorks were designed for a high level of security; therefore, this system cannot meet high reliability requirements such as Common Criteria assurance levels above EAL4.

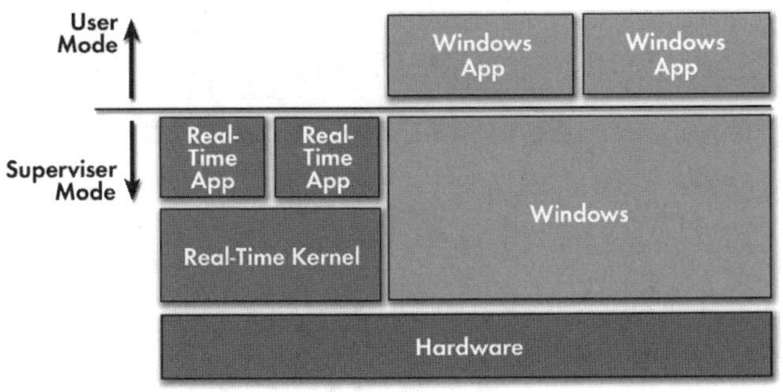

Figure 6 – Inferior hybrid architecture in which general purpose operating system and real-time applications run in supervisor mode

VMware

There are a variety of research and commercial virtual machine (also referred to as a virtual machine monitor) implementations. One of the most well known is VMware, a commercial x86 virtual machine. A virtual machine implementation of the x86-based PC enables one or more additional Windows (or other x86-based operating systems) environments, termed the "guest" operating system, to run simultaneously on the same computer that is controlled by a "host" operating system. In the case of VMware, the host operating system is typically Windows or Linux, although VMware can also run on bare hardware, simultaneously acting as the host operating system and virtual machine [10].

One problem with most of these virtual machines is that they were not themselves designed for a high level of assurance. The implementations are characterized by large bodies of code for which it is not feasible to employ rigorous verification techniques. Thus, they are susceptible to the same sorts of security vulnerabilities that plague other general-purpose commercial software. In addition, these virtual machines often require access to the supervisor mode of the microprocessor in order to achieve their function. Low assurance code running in the supervisor mode of the system provides a rich environment for hackers and Trojan horses. In essence, these approaches suffer from the same problem that native Windows has: they are unable to provide a robust separation between critical and non-critical functions. Furthermore, some implementations employ a single virtual machine to manage multiple concurrent guest operating system environments. Although this approach may provide space optimization possibilities, desirable for a system containing a large number, say tens or hundreds of guest operating system instances, there is a significant reliability tradeoff: a failure in the "shared" virtual machine will take down all of the guest operating systems and their applications. This runs counter to one of the main reasons for employing virtual machines in the first place: to divide the system into independent environments for increased fault tolerance and flexibility.

Paravirtualization

Another approach to virtualization, used in several research endeavors, is "paravirtualization" where the guest operating system is modified in order to improve the ability of the underlying virtual machine to achieve its intended function. Although paravirtualization provides some performance optimization opportunities that traditional system virtualization lacks, the downside of using customized guest operating systems outweigh the benefits when the virtualization solution is being employed in volume automotive applications: there is simply too much overhead required to maintain customized versions of guest operating systems and device drivers that are continually going through release and upgrade cycles.

A NEW VIRTUALIZATION ARCHITECTURE

A better virtualization solution involves using a secure, real-time operating system to run on the bare hardware, and virtual machine monitor (VMM) that runs as an application on top of the real-time operating system. One example of this architecture can be found in the Green Hills Platform for Automotive. In this platform, the secure, real-time component is the INTEGRITY real-time operating system along with native, real-time multimedia and other critical applications. The VMM component is Green Hills' Padded Cell technology which provides a system virtual machine for the x86 and can run Windows and other x86-based desktop environments. However, the architecture presented here could in theory be employed by other secure, real-time operating systems and VMMs, provided they met the requirements described in this paper.

USER MODE VMM

Unlike other commercial virtual machines, Padded Cell runs completely in user-mode along with the guest operating system (e.g. Windows) and its applications. Therefore, none of Windows, its applications, and the virtual machine, itself a complex piece of software, can affect the stability of the real-time, secure components that run directly on top of the real-time microkernel (Figure 7).

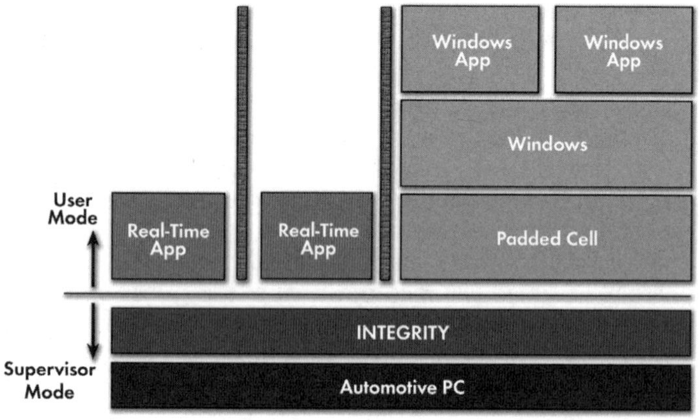

Figure 7 – Real-time, critical applications are securely partitioned from Windows and its applications using a user-mode VMM and secure RTOS

Audio and video applications running under control of the real-time microkernel are guaranteed to perform flawlessly. Because the real-time kernel is optimized for the extremely fast boot times required by automotive systems, instant-on requirements are met (Figure 8).

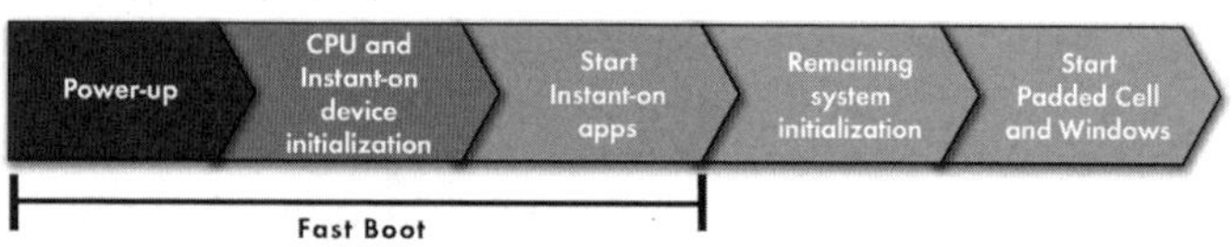

Figure 8 – Fast boot capability ensures that instant-on devices and applications are booted very quickly; Windows initialization can wait

VIRTUAL MACHINE PERFORMANCE

If user-mode execution was the only requirement for a commercial-grade hybrid architecture supporting the secure operation of real-time applications alongside Windows, then one could resort to any number of accurate but slow interpreters or emulators, such as the open source Bochs emulator [11] which provides a faithful representation of the x86/PC architecture and is useful in situations where performance of the guest operating system is not critical.

In order to achieve performance that rivals the behavior of a native system, the virtual machine cannot naively simulate all aspects of the PC architecture. Time critical portions of the guest operating system and applications running under its control must execute at full speed or close to full speed. The general mechanism employed by fast virtual machines such as VMware and Green Hills' Padded Cell is to take advantage of the fact that lots of code running within the guest environment consists of vanilla user-mode instructions that can be safely executed directly. The virtual machine only needs to intercept code that attempts to execute privileged operations such as memory mapping hardware manipulation. Since the guest operating system executes in user-mode under control of the virtual machine, most of these "dangerous" instructions are automatically trapped by the hardware. When such an instruction traps, the kernel suspends the guest operating system thread and notifies the user-mode virtual machine which then performs whatever emulation is necessary to make the guest operating system think that the dangerous instruction was directly executed. This interception is also known as "interposition", as the virtual machine interposes itself between the guest operating environment and the hardware in order to portray the illusion of a true hardware system and to permit a translation between the true hardware and the potentially different virtualized hardware (Figure 9).

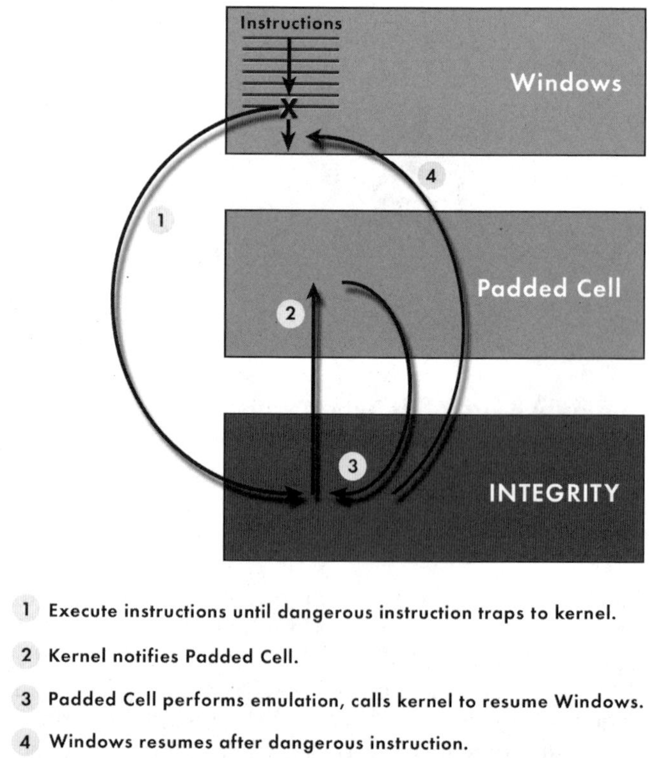

Figure 9 – Secure, high performance virtualization using interposition of VMM and a real-time microkernel

Dangerous instructions that do not cause processor traps are a little more challenging. The virtual machine must detect these instructions before they are executed and ensure that they are safely emulated. There are a variety of techniques for performing this detection. A common method employed is to rewrite the guest operating system code. For example, the virtual machine can replace a dangerous instruction with a trap instruction, thereby guaranteeing that the dangerous code goes through the same path as other privileged instructions that automatically generate exceptions. This rewriting can occur either as a translation step prior to execution of the guest environment or dynamically while the guest is executing.

Note that traps are initially handled by the secure microkernel, since it controls the CPU, and then reflected back into the user-mode VMM. This process adds context switch overhead avoided by VMM implementations that run on bare hardware or in supervisor mode. Therefore, it is essential that the real-time microkernel be capable of very fast, sub-microsecond, context switch times.

VIRTUAL MACHINE DEVICE DRIVERS

Another challenge facing the developers of secure virtual machine technology lies in the handling of I/O devices. In an ideal world, the same set of devices that can be plugged into a PC running Windows can also be plugged into a PC running Windows under a virtual machine. The most common technique for handling guest operating system device drivers is for the virtual machine to intercept device I/O operations and translate them to the host operating system's device driver API. For example, as long as the host operating system supports a WiFi driver, the virtual machine can support WiFi. Furthermore, note that the precise type of device may not be important. Since the virtual machine presents virtual hardware to the guest operating system, the virtual machine can fool most guest operating systems into believing that the Ethernet device in the system is the same Ethernet device which the host operating system happens to support. The problem of supporting devices often reduces to a requirement that the host operating system support at least one type of device in what would otherwise be a large family of similar-function devices. In this manner, virtualization also becomes a useful tool in providing portability of guest operating system environments across disparate hardware platforms.

The proper management of device drivers by the virtual machine and its host operating system is critical to the overall security of the system. Device drivers often use DMA to transfer memory to and from the peripheral and the computer's main memory. The device I/O registers are typically accessed by a device driver running in supervisor mode with unfettered access to physical memory. Any code that runs in supervisor mode must be developed to the highest level of reliability and security, the same as the secure microkernel itself. A rigorous analysis must be used to ensure that the device driver code does not violate the system security policies enforced by the kernel.

If the virtual machine relies on the host operating system for device handling, then the host's device drivers must be secure. On most operating systems, such as Windows, the device driver code was not designed for high assurance and executes completely in supervisor mode. It is not uncommon to find Ethernet drivers that are thousands of lines of code. Furthermore, the virtual machine may use read and write system calls that utilize the host operating system's TCP/IP stack which also resides in the kernel, running in supervisor mode. The same goes for disk drivers and their file systems as well as USB devices and their USB stacks. This adds up to an enormous body of code that cannot possibly be assured to a high level of security and reliability.

The INTEGRITY kernel employs a better architecture for device security. INTEGRITY employs "virtual device drivers" (Figure 10) in which the complex code to manage a device, such as the Ethernet driver and the TCP/IP stack, all run in user mode. The required supervisor code is strictly limited to a simple interrupt service routine that does nothing more than wake up the virtual device driver as well as a simple system call interface that provides secure DMA programming (since we do not want to trust user mode code to program DMA which could in theory access all of physical memory). Moving this complicated device handling code out of supervisor mode means that the device driver cannot affect the security policy enforcement of the kernel. Furthermore, if a device is dedicated for use only by the guest operating system, then the user-mode virtual device driver code need only be assured to the same level as the guest operating system (which, again with Windows, is a relatively low level).

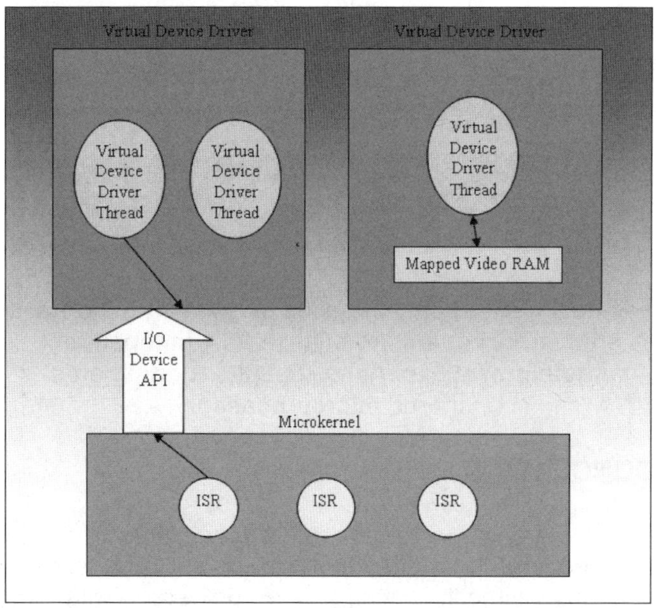

Figure 10 – Virtual device drivers place complicated device management code outside of the secure kernel

This paradigm allows TCP/IP, known to be too complicated for high assurance implementation, to be used in a secure manner. By partitioning the networking software in this manner, hard guarantees can be made that the Ethernet and TCP/IP operation utilized by the virtual machine and guest environment cannot affect the operation of other critical components in the system.

Some devices must be shared between the guest operating system and native applications. For example, the video screen may be used to display a Windows desktop environment within a single window and then a native real-time media player application within another window. If the audio application requires a high level of reliability and security, then the screen management software must itself be assurable to at least the same level of reliability and security. For this reason, the Green Hills Platform for Automotive comes with a high assurance native window manager that can be used to securely partition multiple windows on a shared screen.

A VIRTUAL PC FOR EACH PASSENGER

Using the proposed virtualization architecture, multiple instances of Windows, powered by multiple instances of the virtual machine, can run simultaneously on the same computer. In next-generation infotainment platforms, each passenger has a private video monitor. Without VMM technology, the passengers would have to share a single copy of Windows. Using VMMs, a passenger could even reboot Windows without affecting the second passenger's email session (Figure 11).

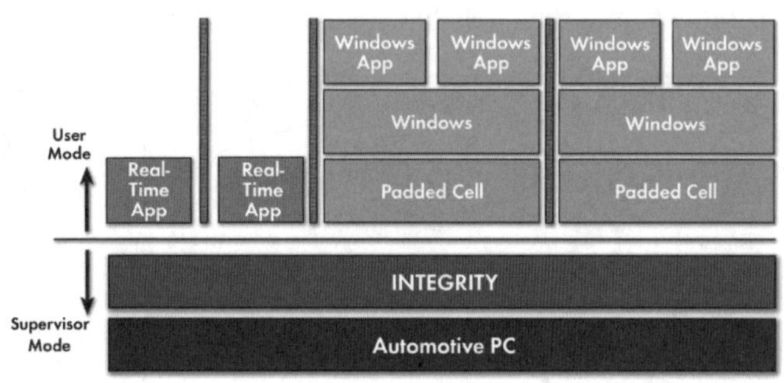

Figure 11 – Multiple instances of VMM and Windows enables occupants to enjoy a fully independent infotainment experience despite running on a shared microprocessor

CONCLUSION

Next-generation systems software architectures are required in order to ensure that future complex, feature-rich infotainment systems are delivered with the reliability, security, real-time performance, and controlled footprint that the automotive industry and consumers alike will demand. Future in-car systems will see a convergence of office functionality with traditional telematics and digital entertainment applications. Bringing these capabilities onto a single compute platform is critical in order to minimize size, weight, power, and production cost. An effective approach involves the coupling of a highly secure, real-time operating system with a high performance, user-mode virtual machine implementation that supports the execution of unmodified Windows binaries and applications.

REFERENCES

1. *Low-latency Music Software Using Off-the-shelf Operating Systems*; Eli Brandt and Roger B. Dannenberg; http://www-2.cs.cmu.edu/~rbd/papers/latency98/latency98.htm
2. *Worst Case Execution Time Analysis, Case Study on Interrupt Latency, For the OSE Real-Time Operating System*; Martin Carlsson; http://www.astec.uu.se/publications/2002/Carlsson-WCET_Exjobb.pdf
3. *Linux extends reach with real-time capabilities*; Charles Murray; http://www.eetimes.com/showArticle.jhtml?articleID=18309476
4. *Worm strikes down Windows 2000 systems*; http://www.cnn.com/2005/TECH/internet/08/16/computer.worm/).
5. Technology Conference; at Green Hills Software, Santa Barbara, CA; 2003
6. *Common Criteria for Information Technology Security Evaluation Version 2.1*; Part 3: Security assurance requirements ; http://csrc.nist.gov/cc/Documents/CC%20v2.1/p3-v21.pdf
7. INTEGRITY-178B Separation Kernel; http://niap.nist.gov/cc-scheme/in_evaluation.html#i
8. *RTLinux – a hard real-time Linux add-on*; http://www.linuxdevices.com/links/LK8662675028.html
9. *VxWin*; http://www.kuka-controls.com/product/vxwin
10. *Virtual Machine* Monitors: *Current Technology and Future Trends*; Mendel Rosenblum and Tal Garfinkel; IEEE Computer, May 2005, p. 44.
11. *Bochs* IA-*32 Emulator Project*; http://bochs.sourceforge.net

CONTACT

David Kleidermacher is vice president of engineering at Green Hills Software where he has been developing real-time operating systems and tools for embedded systems for the past fifteen years. David has a bachelor of science in computer science from Cornell University. Contact David at davek@ghs.com.

2005-01-1345

Operating System Requirements for Use in Next-generation In-car Infotainment Systems

David N. Kleidermacher
Green Hills Software, Inc.

ABSTRACT

Not long ago, an in-dash CD player was considered state-of-the-art for in-car entertainment. Contemporary infotainment and telematics systems include audio, video, voice recognition and synthesis, wireless networking, navigation, internet access, and safety/security features, sometimes running on a single microprocessor. This complexity puts an increasing burden on the microprocessor's operating system. Next-generation infotainment systems require next-generation operating system architectures that can handle this challenge.

INTRODUCTION

This paper will present major operating system challenges in, and propose architectural solutions for, the next-generation infotainment systems environment. We consider real-time response, security, portability, production cost, and a high-quality tools integration to enable efficient development and analysis of these complicated systems.

REAL-TIME RESPONSE

One of the key requirements of multimedia infotainment systems is a high-quality audio/visual experience. On powerful in-home PCs, the sheer power of the microprocessor (now besting 3 GHz) often makes up for the lack of real-time responsiveness of Windows. Next-generation in-car systems will depend more on the ability of the operating system to guarantee real-time response because the microprocessor may be loaded with more simultaneously-executing, resource-demanding applications. Researchers at Carnegie Mellon University have studied latency problems associated specifically with audio: "Latency is the stumbling block for music software, and the OS is often the cause of it."[1]

SCHEDULING

Consider a scenario where an occupant is requesting directions from the navigation system while simultaneously playing a DVD for children in the rear of the car. The navigation data-processing requires much of the available CPU time but the occupant does not require an immediate response (a few seconds may be typical and expected). On the other hand, the processing of the audio and video samples must occur on time in order to avoid choppiness.

In this example, a real-time operating system can strictly prioritize the audio and video processing above the navigation processing to ensure a high quality DVD experience. A slight delay in the navigation result, due to this prioritization, is not likely to be noticed. In contrast, operating systems with a desktop heritage often use heuristic scheduling algorithms that attempt to dole out CPU time "fairly". While fairness-based scheduling is often good for human-user interactive desktop applications, this style of scheduling does not actually provide a guaranteed response; even one bad guess by the operating system can adversely affect the multimedia experience.

INTERRUPT LATENCY

When a process executes a system call, and the kernel is modifying internal data structures to accomplish the request, preemption is disabled by the kernel in order to ensure that another process cannot be context switched in and execute a system call which could access these internal data structures while they are in an inconsistent state. The problem with this approach is that high-priority interrupt processing can be delayed while the kernel disables preemption on behalf of potentially lower-priority requests (Figure 1). Even simple, self-described "real-time operating systems" can disable interrupt processing in hundreds of locations. In one study of a real-time operating system's interrupt latency, researchers found that some of the disabling sequences contained triply-nested loops with estimated execution times of more than 25,000 cycles [2].

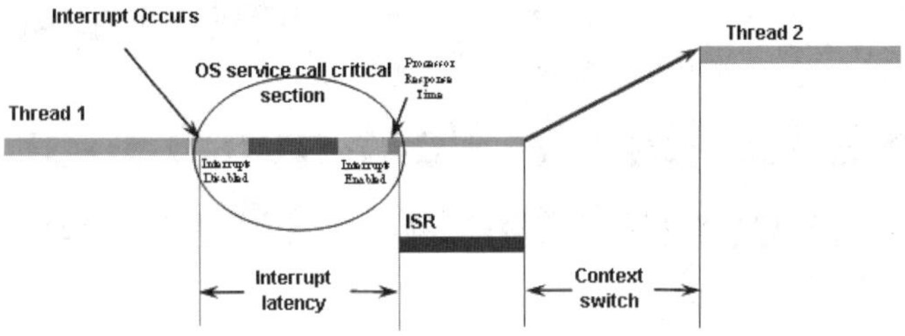

Figure 1

This problem is exacerbated by more complicated, monolithic operating systems. The worst case response time for the high-priority interrupt source (e.g. the audio device) cannot be determined, and thus the quality of the user experience cannot be guaranteed. It is well known that certain operating systems which exhibit good overall throughput have large preemption latencies on the order of milliseconds [3], enough to derail a low-latency device should its interrupt fire at an inopportune time.

A better architecture for guaranteed real-time response is to never disable interrupts in system calls. By always taking the highest-priority interrupt, the kernel ensures smooth performance of the time-critical audio/visual devices. Handling of lower-priority requests is postponed. The kernel must be configurable enough to prioritize interrupt handling appropriately. When a high-priority process is awakened to perform some I/O handling, the kernel's scheduler should automatically inhibit lower-priority interrupts from delaying this processing.

SECURITY

As infotainment systems incorporate internet access and WiFi, security will become a central concern for consumers who know all too well that risk of viruses and other attacks is the price we pay for the convenience of this network connectivity. Although a networked infotainment system can be infected with malicious software, a properly architected operating system can limit the damage of such infiltration and ensure that critical services remain unaffected.

MEMORY PROTECTION

A fundamental requirement for robust infotainment systems is memory-protection. The operating system utilizes memory protection hardware of the microprocessor to isolate unrelated infotainment functions. Malicious code is unable to crash an application or the operating system by corrupting memory. Similarly, an errant pointer caused by a programming error in one application cannot affect another application executing in a separate protected process.

GUARANTEED RESOURCES

Despite memory protection, malicious code can still take down a critical application by starving it of resources. Most operating systems employ a central store for memory resources. As protected processes ask for new resources (e.g. heap memory, threads, etc.), the operating system allocates these resources from the central store. An errant or malicious application can request too many resources, causing the central store to be depleted and critical applications to fail when they attempt to obtain their required resources (Figure 2). A similar denial-of-service attack can occur with CPU time. A malicious process can spawn multiple "confederate" processes that soak up the CPU time, keeping critical applications from accomplishing their tasks.

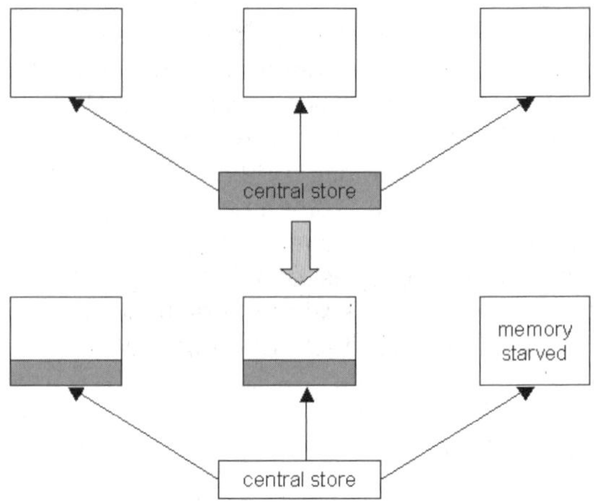

Figure 2

It is possible to architect an operating system such that these critical resources are partitioned according to individual application requirements. An infected process can exhaust its own quota of resources, but it cannot possibly affect the quota of resources held by critical applications (Figure 3).

Figure 3

Despite the compelling security advantage of partitioning, one of its potential drawbacks from a usability perspective is the static nature of quotas. Some complex systems may have varying resource requirements during their lifetimes and may not have enough memory for the union of all the desired quotas. To address this, a partitioning operating system must provide the capability for system designers to create a trusted resource manager that can export memory to, and reclaim memory from, applications on demand. The system designer must be able to specify which critical applications can connect to the resource manager. Malicious software imported into new processes will not have access to the resource manager and are therefore governed by their quotas. Partitioning coupled with a resource manager enables system designers to obtain flexibility where it is needed and security where it is essential.

SECURITY THROUGH SIMPLICITY

As infotainment systems become increasingly complex, integrating more applications from more vendors, the risk of security and robustness problems increases. The operating system, however, is the most critical component since it has direct control of the microprocessor and all of its resources. Whereas a security flaw in an application can make that application unusable, a security flaw in the operating system can be fatal for the entire infotainment system. It follows that use of a secure operating system will increase the overall security and robustness of the infotainment system.

Monolithic Architectures

Monolithic operating systems contain system software, such as networking stacks, file systems, and complex device drivers, that all run in supervisor mode (Figure 4) and provide a plethora of opportunities for hackers to find and exploit vulnerabilities. Examples of monolithic operating systems are Windows, UNIX, and Linux. Most consumers are aware of occasional highly publicized security flaws discovered in these operating systems. What most people may not realize, however, is that many less publicized, yet serious security flaws are being discovered regularly. For example, a quick internet search shows dozens of high-severity Linux security flaws just in the past year; one of the entries is particularly troubling because it reminds us of the fact that no one actually knows how many more flaws are lurking and have yet to be discovered and exploited: "Multiple unknown vulnerabilities in Linux kernel 2.4 and 2.6 allow local users to gain privileges or access kernel memory, as found by the Sparse source code checking tool (CAN-2004-0495)" [4]

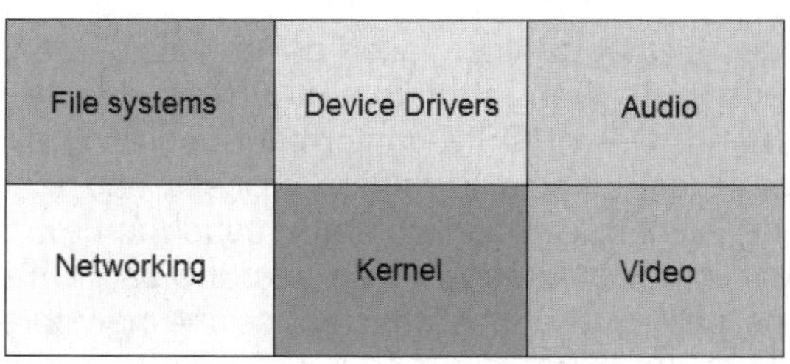

Figure 4 - Monolithic OS

Microkernel Architectures

Microkernel operating systems provide a better architecture for security. A microkernel operating system runs only a minimal set of critical system services, such as thread management, exception handling, and interprocess communication, in supervisor mode (Figure 5) and provides an architecture that enables complex systems software to run in user mode where they are permitted access only to the resources deemed appropriate by the system designer. A virus in one component can not cause damage to the hard drive because the infected component simply does not have access to that resource. Because the microkernel is simple, it can be more easily modeled and verified.

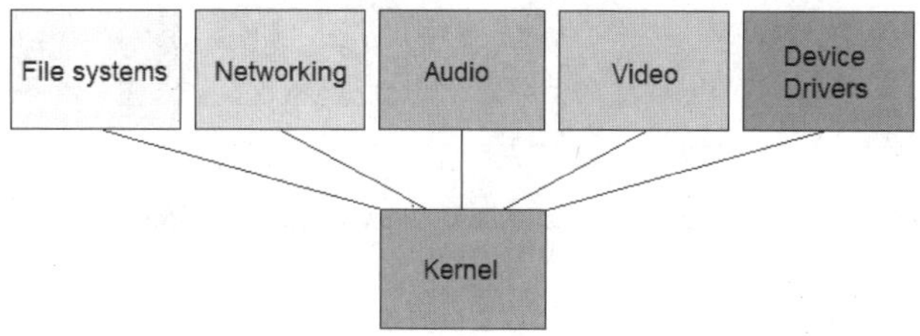

Figure 5 - Microkernel OS

Virtual Device Drivers

Arguably the most important components of the operating system to virtualize are device drivers. Device drivers are frequently compromised by hackers. Monolithic operating systems commonly allow users and processes to dynamically install device drivers into the kernel. A malicious device driver can execute a buffer overflow attack where it intentionally overwrites the runtime stack in order to install malicious code into the kernel. Virtual device drivers prevent these types of attacks because an infiltrated device driver can only harm the process containing the driver, not the kernel itself. In order to facilitate the development of virtual device drivers, the operating system needs to provide a flexible mechanism for I/O control to the virtual driver process. The virtual driver, however, must be provided only access to the specific device resources that the driver is authorized to control (Figure 6).

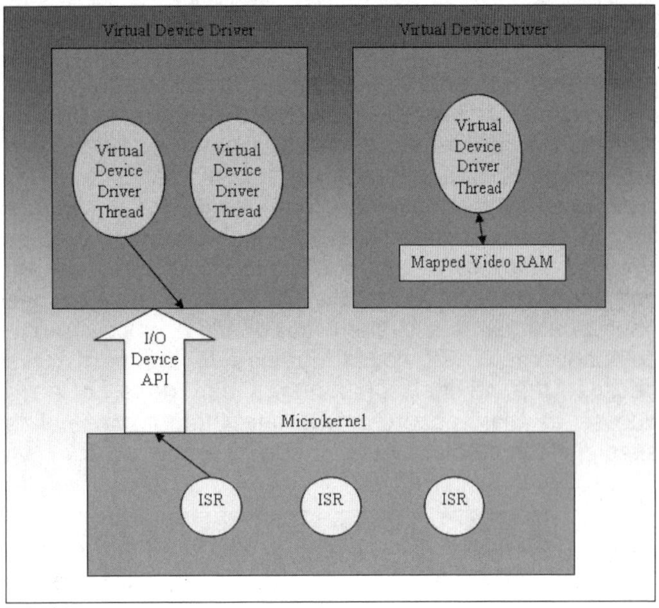

Figure 6 - Virtual Device Drivers

COMMON CRITERIA

Common Criteria is the internationally recognized standard for security evaluation. Common Criteria specifies evaluation assurance levels (EAL), 1 through 7. The higher the EAL for a product, the less likely the product contains security flaws. EAL 7 requires formal modeling of the software and a formal mathematical proof that the software upholds its security functional requirements. As the assurance level increases, the development and life-cycle process requirements (e.g. design, configuration management, testing, maintenance, flaw remediation) become increasingly rigorous.

Linux has achieved an EAL-2 evaluation and Windows has achieved an EAL-4 evaluation. The higher EALs, 5 through 7, are required in order to have any reasonable assurance about security. An NSA analyst said it best when he described EAL-4 as "secure as long as nothing is connected to it."[5] It is simply not possible to achieve high assurance with legacy monolithic operating systems. Not only are they too complex, but they lack a fundamental security architectural design. Systems not designed for high assurance cannot have high assurance retrofitted. According to Common Criteria: "EAL4 is the highest level at which it is likely to be economically feasible to retrofit to an existing product line."[6] Not even Microsoft, with its practically unlimited financial resources, can find and remove all of the security flaws in Windows.

By selecting an operating system with better security, infotainment systems developers also gain a compelling marketing advantage: bragging rights to a more reliable and secure infotainment system that automobile manufacturers and consumers will value.

PORTABILITY

As infotainment systems grow in complexity, integrators will rely increasingly on third parties to provide many of the constituent software packages. Third-party suppliers will, in turn, provide functionality that will be integrated by a variety of systems integrators for all flavors of infotainment systems. Third-party suppliers can get products shipped faster and reach a larger target market if they write their software using open-standard APIs and run on operating systems that support these standards. Conversely, systems integrators can get systems integrated and delivered faster by using an operating system that supports open standards since more third-party software will run unmodified. The universal open standard for operating systems APIs is POSIX.

Recently, the main POSIX standard for operating system APIs, POSIX.1, has been revamped and released as POSIX.1-2001. In addition to many improvements to the API based on years of use and feedback, the new standard comes with a certification program administered by the Open Group that enables operating system vendors to obtain independent acknowledgement of conformance, which in turn gives developers confidence that their POSIX-conformant application code will run unmodified on these operating systems. The list of certified products can be found on the internet [7], and many vendors have announced future plans to obtain certification.

<u>POSIX-like</u>

Infotainment systems developers need to be careful in their use of operating systems that claim to be POSIX-compliant but are not certified conformant. Running POSIX-conformant application code on top of a non-conformant operating system can be problematic. For example, on Linux (which has a POSIX-like API that is not conformant), the **setuid** function only affects the initial thread [8], not the entire process as mandated by POSIX. Consider an application which performs some non-privileged operation (e.g. playing an audio file) whose execution must be logged to a critical log file that only has superuser write permission (e.g. a log of infotainment system usage read by technicians in case of a failure). The application is created setuid root, and when the application starts, it writes an entry to the critical log file, spawns a new thread, lowers the process privilege to that of the caller using setuid, and then proceeds to do the rest of its non-privileged work in the new thread. On a POSIX-conformant operating system, the setuid call affects the entire process and therefore both the initial thread (calling setuid) and the new thread both run in non-privileged mode after the call. On Linux, only the calling thread is affected, so the new thread is actually still running as superuser. A flaw or subversion in the non-privileged code path can now have disastrous repercussions.

PRODUCTION COST

The automotive market is characterized by extreme sensitivity to production cost due to large volumes and intense price competition. One dollar of cost can translate into millions in profit (or loss) over a car's production lifetime. Choice of operating system can have a significant impact on the production cost of the infotainment system and, transitively, the automobile itself.

ROYALTIES

Many commercial operating system vendors charge a royalty for each infotainment unit that embeds the operating system. Although royalty charges may be acceptable in certain industries, high volume, low margin products, such as automotive infotainment systems, are intolerant of this drag on profits.

A better business model for infotainment systems is to charge fixed fees up front for licenses, tools and services that help infotainment systems developers bring their products to market.

FOOTPRINT

Infotainment systems developers are also sensitive to per-unit hardware costs and therefore choose the minimum speed microprocessor and minimum size memory components that can still meet feature requirements. Operating system characteristics can affect the choice of microprocessor memory. Monolithic operating systems with a desktop heritage (e.g. Windows, UNIX, Linux) typically have a significantly larger footprint than operating systems designed and optimized specifically for resource-constrained embedded systems. For example, the INTEGRITY operating system from Green Hills Software occupies as little as 30 KB of ROM and 3 KB of RAM in a minimal configuration. In contrast, a basic Linux profile occupies 4.6 MB of memory [9]. When all of the infotainment applications are added on top of the operating system, the resulting image may require a larger flash device or larger RAM chip. This of course increases per-unit production cost in much the same way as a royalty. Even if everything fits into the desired memory chips, developers will often need to spend significant time configuring, tuning, and making functionality-space tradeoffs in order to stay within size limits.

OS-AWARE TOOLS

Next-generation infotainment systems will consist of many complex software applications controlling the multitude of advanced system capabilities. This software will be created by large teams of programmers. These programmers need next-generation development tools to help develop, comprehend, optimize, and debug these complex applications.

Contemporary programmers use integrated development environments (IDEs) to manage software projects. The IDE contains tools for build management, editing code, compiling, debugging, performance analyzing, and more. Ideally, these tools are integrated not only with each other (e.g. the performance analyzer can display performance analysis information in the context of the debugger's source view) but also with the underlying operating system. Examples of operating system awareness include object state awareness, multi-thread debug, and operating system event analysis.

OBJECT STATE AWARENESS

Infotainment applications are often multi-threaded and synchronize using operating system mutual-exclusion (mutex) primitives, message queues, and other kernel objects. Improper use of these objects can lead to deadlock, priority inversions (depicted in Figure 7), and other failures whose causes are difficult to diagnose within a complex application. The IDE should provide a capability for viewing the state of these kernel objects. For example, if a thread is unexpectedly blocked waiting for a semaphore, then the object state of the semaphore can be displayed. The object state display shows the current thread owner of the semaphore. The developer can then interrogate the state of the thread, perhaps discovering that the owning thread is suspended because of an exception (and thus was unable to release the semaphore). Now the developer can focus on why the owning thread crashed, and so on.

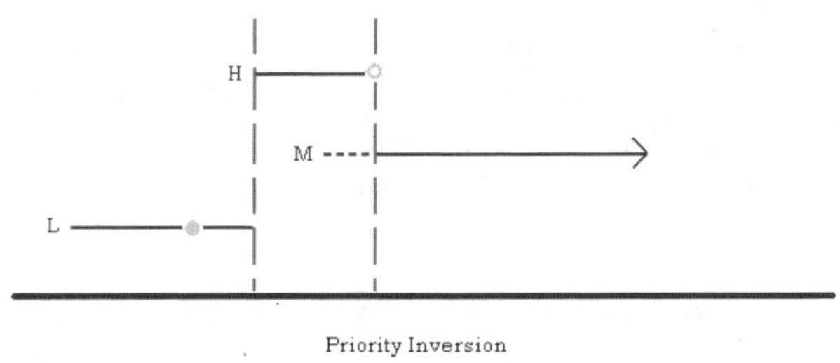

Figure 7

MULTI-THREAD DEBUG

There are a variety of important thread-aware features that the debugger must include in order to help find programming errors in complex multi-threaded applications.

- Ability to debug multiple threads simultaneously, each in its own debug window
- Ability to set breakpoints that affect a single thread, an entire process, or a user-defined group of threads (potentially from multiple processes)
- Ability to set breakpoints that gather data on the target system asynchronously (also known as probes or tracepoints).

- Ability to set a breakpoint that when hit causes another thread, process, or thread group to halt
- Ability to trigger a complete system halt from a breakpoint

What all of these features have in common is providing a fine-grained and precise control over thread execution so that bugs can be diagnosed more efficiently.

Consider an audio system that consists of a low-level audio control application (plays and records audio) and a higher-level audio application (e.g. music player) that interacts with the audio control application. The music player exhibits an intermittent failure in which playback spontaneously and unexpectedly suspends. The developer is able to place a breakpoint in the music player at the execution point at which playback is stopped. The developer suspects that the suspension is caused by a bug in the audio control application and thus adds a trigger to the breakpoint which causes the audio application to stop when the breakpoint is hit. Since the audio control application buffers multiple playback operations, this synchronous trigger is required in order for the developer to examine state at the precise time of the failure, before the audio control application has a chance to handle more buffers whose processing could elide the anomalous state. Subsequent analysis of the state involving the halted audio control threads may show a buffer manipulation error that caused the audio stream to be interrupted.

Tracepoints enable the programmer to set breakpoints at strategic locations in the code without halting threads that hit the breakpoints. Tracepoint locations are conveyed to the operating system by the debugger. When a thread hits this special breakpoint, the operating system handles the exception, stores user-defined data into a buffer, and then immediately resumes the thread. This allows interesting data to be collected in real-time with minimal intrusion. The developer uses the debugger to collect the tracepoint data from the operating system at some later time and analyze the results. Because some failures only manifest when running the system at full speed, this kind of operating system integration with the debugger can prove invaluable.

OS EVENT ANALYSIS

Similar to tracepoints, event logging is a mechanism by which interesting events on the target system can be logged and saved away for future analysis. Operating system level events, such as interrupts, context switches, system calls, and exceptions, are logged to target memory while the system runs at full speed. Unlike tracepoints that are user-defined on the fly, operating system events are pre-instrumented by the operating system developers who understand all of the interesting points of kernel execution. Like tracepoints, event logging does not require user interaction, making it a low-intrusion yet effective analysis technique. When a problem occurs in the infotainment system, the event log can be uploaded to the host computer and analyzed with a powerful graphical user interface (Figure 8). Since the operating system generates the event log, a tight integration between the IDE's event viewer and the operating system is required.

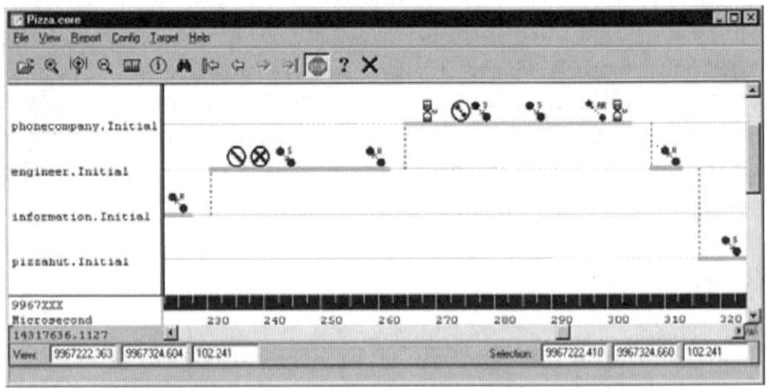

Figure 8 - OS Event Analysis

One of the most famous success stories of using event logging to debug a complex embedded system occurred with the Mars Pathfinder mission in 1997. Soon after landing, the Pathfinder began experiencing system resets that caused loss of scientific data. A failure was captured in an event log and downloaded and analyzed by JPL engineers. The priority inversion bug [10] that was causing the system resets was easy to see in the event viewer. JPL uploaded a software patch to the Pathfinder spacecraft that fixed the problem. Developers of next-generation infotainment systems will find this type of event analysis tool to be critical in understanding system behavior and locating flaws that only manifest at full speed and in the midst of complex system-wide interactions.

TRACE

One of the potential problems with instrumented event analysis and tracepoints is that despite running at full speed, the act of executing the logging code itself can cause subtle timing differences that prevent the manifestation of a bug. In addition, the extra memory overhead of the instrumentation may be prohibitive for resource-constrained systems. Not too long ago, hardware and firmware developers commonly used in-circuit emulators (ICE) to help find problems intolerant of traditional software debugging techniques. One of the most cherished features of the ICE was *trace*. The ICE would record into a trace buffer all instruction and data accessed made by the CPU during its execution. This unprecedented view of execution made some of the most difficult bugs easy to find. Tics Realtime presents several realistic case studies of the use of in-circuit emulator trace to find some insidious bugs [11].

Next-generation hardware trace technology

Unfortunately, ICE technology has not been able to keep up with changes in microprocessor technology, in particular the speed of microprocessors [12]. The good news is that on-chip microprocessor trace is on the uptrend. Many flavors of ARM, PowerPC, and other microprocessors are being outfitted with an on-chip capability to output the same type of instruction and data information to an external hardware debug port. Connecting to on-chip trace ports is much easier, external debug hardware (to collect the trace and transfer it to the IDE) is simpler and less expensive than traditional ICEs, and semiconductor vendors are coming up with clever compression mechanisms that enable the debugging hardware to keep up with high-frequency processors. For example, the latest ARM trace implementation outputs on average only a single byte of instruction trace data for every seven core cycles [13].

Next-generation trace analysis tools

Trace data is historically presented in the IDE as a sequential list of instruction and data accesses. As infotainment systems gain in complexity, large trace buffers are required to store enough history for developers to gain insight into complex sequences of events that led to a failure. But developers are unable to make sense out of a trace listing containing millions of instructions. So the trace tool must mine the trace data to present a higher-level system view of execution. For example, the trace tool can map traced instructions to code functions and show the historical execution path by function name (Figure 9).

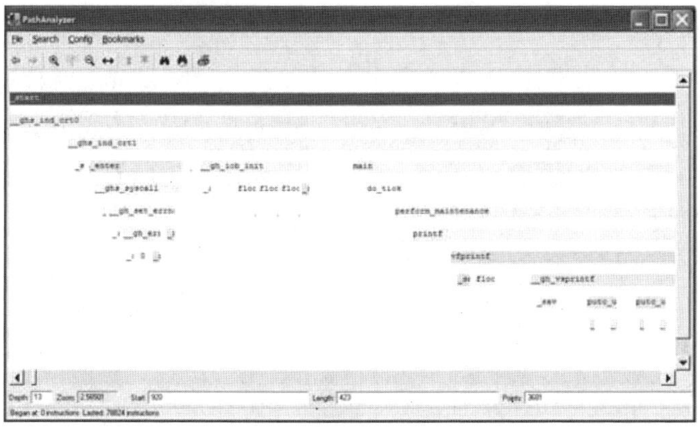

Figure 9 - Execution Path Analysis

If the trace tool is operating system-aware, it can search the trace data for context switches, system calls, and exceptions in order to present the same event analysis display as discussed earlier, except this display is accomplished without any software instrumentation. Some vendors are even using the trace data to drive a virtual multi-threaded debugging session that can run both forwards and backwards in time. A memory corruption can be uncovered simply by setting a watchpoint on the corrupted memory location and running the debugger backwards until the watchpoint is hit. In addition, the debugger can display the values of variables and registers as if the developer was debugging a live system.

CONCLUSION

Next-generation operating system architectures are required in order to ensure that future complex, feature-rich infotainment systems are delivered with the reliability, security, real-time performance, and controlled production cost that the automotive industry and consumers alike will demand. Along with the right operating system, infotainment systems developers need operating system-aware development tools, particularly for debugging and analysis of these complex systems, in order to reduce development cost and time to market.

REFERENCES

1. *Low-latency Music Software Using Off-the-shelf Operating Systems*; Eli Brandt and Roger B. Dannenberg; http://www-2.cs.cmu.edu/~rbd/papers/latency98/latency98.htm
2. *Worst Case Execution Time Analysis, Case Study on Interrupt Latency, For the OSE Real-Time Operating System*; Martin Carlsson; http://www.astec.uu.se/publications/2002/Carlsson-WCET_Exjobb.pdf
3. *Linux extends reach with real-time capabilities*; Charles Murray; http://www.eetimes.com/showArticle.jhtml?articleID=18309476
4. ICAT Metabase - CVE Vulnerability Search Engine; http://icat.nist.gov/icat.cfm
5. Technology Conference; at Green Hills Software, Santa Barbara, CA; 2003
6. *Common Criteria for Information Technology Security Evaluation Version 2.1*; Part 3: Security assurance requirements ; http://csrc.nist.gov/cc/Documents/CC%20v2.1/p3-v21.pdf
7. IEEE POSIX Certification Register; http://get.posixcertified.ieee.org/cert_prodlist.tpl?CALLER=index.tpl
8. *The Native POSIX Thread Library for Linux*; section 8 – Remaining Challenges, p. 16; Ulrich Drepper and Ingo Molnar, Red Hat, Inc.; http://people.redhat.com/drepper/nptl-design.pdf
9. Montavista frequently asked questions; http://www.mvista.com/products/faq.html#q2
10. *What really happened on Mars;* Michael B. Jones; http://research.microsoft.com/~mbj/Mars_Pathfinder
11. *Debugging with an In-Circuit Emulator;* http://concentric.net/~tics/tics0297a.htm
12. *Introduction to In-Circuit Emulators*; section "Practical Realities"; Jack Ganssle; http://www.embedded.com/story/OEG20011126S0065
13. *How CoreSight Technology Gets Higher Performance, More Reliable Product to Market Quicker*; William Orme; http://www.arm.com/pdfs/CoresightWhitepaper.pdf

CONTACT

David Kleidermacher is vice president of engineering at Green Hills Software where he has been developing real-time operating systems and tools for embedded systems for the past fourteen years. David has a bachelor of science in computer science from Cornell University. Contact David at davek@ghs.com.

2005-01-1540

An Adaptive Data-Reduction Protocol for the Future In-Vehicle Networks

Praveen R. Ramteke and Syed Masud Mahmud
Electrical and Computer Engineering Department, Wayne State University

ABSTRACT

The demand for drive-by-wire, pre-crash warnings, telematics and many new features will require very high bandwidth from future in-vehicle networks. One straightforward solution to satisfy the bandwidth requirements of future vehicle networks would be to use a higher bandwidth bus or to use multiple busses. However, the use of a higher bandwidth bus would increase the cost of the network. Similarly, the use of multiple busses would increase the cost and the complexity of the wiring. Another option would be the development of a higher layer protocol to reduce the amount of data to be transferred. This paper presents an adaptive data-reduction algorithm based on the CAN (Controller Area Network) protocol.

INTRODUCTION

As automakers are incorporating more and more advanced features into vehicles, there is a growing need for enhanced processing power. S. Channon and P. Miller [1] estimate that the number of microprocessors per vehicle will increase exponentially and by the end of year 2010, the number of microprocessors in any high-end vehicle will be 250. Also, the application areas that demand more processing power are active safety systems, infotainment (TV, Video, gaming and navigation systems), and drive-by-wire systems. Additionally, functional integration of individual sensors will be necessary for applications such as collision avoidance. These additional functionalities can be achieved by increasing the number of nodes or Electronic Control Modules (ECM's), sensors and actuators that can exchange data among various other nodes in the network. However, the data traffic over the high-speed communication bus, like CAN, will increase significantly with the increase in the number of ECM's. Another important requirement would be to communicate data between the various ECM's in real time for safety-critical applications. Failure to communicate data within a given period of time may lead to degradation in system performance and may put the occupant's life in danger.

In order to address the bandwidth concerns and eliminate message latencies, data-reduction (DR) techniques have been developed which communicate large amounts of data in a short period of time, consuming very less bandwidth. DR techniques have been applied extensively for the task of image compression (e.g. MPEG, JPEG), data compression and digital data transmission.

Due to the safety-critical nature of automotive multiplexing system, selection of an optimum data-reduction technique is imperative to ensure proper system performance. An optimum DR technique can be characterized as the one that consumes the least network bandwidth and has zero message latency. Many DR techniques have been proposed for automotive multiplexing environment. Kempf *et al.* [2] and Michael *et al.* [3] recognized six data reduction algorithms, which could be applied to automotive multiplexing environment. The major drawback of all the DR techniques was that they could only be applied to text-data classes in automotive body electronics [3].

Misbahuddin *et al.*[4] proposed a generalized data-reduction algorithm that could be applied to all data classes found in automotive multiplexing environment. The algorithm is based on the SAE J1939 protocol [5]. This algorithm uses the fact that some of the bytes in the data field of the J1939 message remain constant over a period of time and that many of them change slowly [6]. For example, car speed, wheel speed, gas level, gear position etc. Also, these messages are sent at periodic intervals of time. For example, wheel speed data may be sent every 5 milliseconds and gas level may be indicated every 500 milliseconds. The bit reserved by SAE for future use or *R* bit in the protocol data unit (PDU) within the J1939 message is used to indicate data compression. The *R* bit is set to "1" and "0" to indicate compression and no compression, respectively. Each intelligent control module (ICM) in the multiplexing system consists of a transmit buffer (T_BUF) and a receive buffer (R_BUF). Each ICM keeps a copy of the most recently transmitted message in the T_BUF and a copy of the most recently received message in the R_BUF. Suppose an ICM transmits a message *ri* every *t* time units. The transmitting ICM keeps a copy of message *ri* in its T_BUF. The next time the ICM transmits a message *ri* after *t* time units, the ICM compares the data field of the previous *ri*, saved in the T_BUF, with the current message being transmitted. In the event that two or more of the data bytes of the current transmitted message are of same magnitude as of the message in T_BUF, the transmitting ICM realizes that few of the data bytes have been repeated. The transmitter then initiates a series of steps outlined below, to implement data compression.

1. The transmitter sets the *R* bit or data compression bit (DCB) in the PDU to "1".

2. The transmitter prepares a compression code (CC) to indicate repeated bytes in the recently transmitted message.

3. Each bit in the CC indicates a data byte in the message. The bits in the CC are set to "1" or "0" to indicate a repeated byte or non-repeated byte in the message, respectively. For example, if byte 3 in the message is repeated then bit 3 in CC is set to "1" and so on.

4. The non-repeated bytes are concatenated after the CC in the data field of the message being transmitted over the bus.

At the receiver, the ICM keeps a copy of the most recently received message in its R_BUF to perform decompression. The following steps are involved in data decompression process at the receiving end.

1. The receiver checks the DCB of the received message.

2. If DCB is "1", then the receiver treats the first byte in the data field of the received message as the CC.

3. The receiver retrieves the repeated data bytes by indexing through the R_BUF and fetching bytes whose corresponding bits in the CC have a value "1". For example, byte 3 is fetched if bit 3 in CC is "1".

4. The entire message is recreated using the repeated bytes from R_BUF and non-repeated bytes from the received message.

This algorithm works very well when data bytes within the message remain constant with high probabilities. However, in real life situations, one or more parameters in the message may fluctuate at low rates. For example, during braking, car speed may decrease at a constant rate say 8 miles/sec^2, or during acceleration the speed may increase at 4 miles/sec^2. Under such conditions, the above protocol would transmit the entire length of the data bytes used to represent the particular parameter even though the change in value of the parameter is very less. In the worst-case scenario, if all the parameters in the message change by small amounts, the algorithm would transmit all the eight bytes of the message without leading to any DR. This is highly undesirable since it would lead to high bus utilization and consumption of unnecessary bandwidth.

To overcome this drawback of the previous DR algorithm, we present an Adaptive Data-Reduction (ADR) algorithm. The algorithm is designed to be compatible with the CAN protocol since CAN is the standard protocol used in many present-day automobiles [7]. However, the algorithm can be applied to any SAE J1939 protocol with slight changes in the software. The following section presents the details of the adaptive-data reduction algorithm.

PROPOSED DATA REDUCTION ALGORITHM

The proposed ADR algorithm consists of two parts

- Non-Adaptive data-reduction
- Adaptive data-reduction

The ADR algorithm encompasses some of the desirable features of the DR algorithm presented in [4] with some notable changes.

1. The *R* bit or DCB is ignored.

2. The data field of CAN message is divided into signal fields of varying lengths instead of data bytes. This means that individual signal values in the messages can cross byte boundaries or can be contained in less than one byte.

Point 2 above springs from the fact that all signal values in a message cannot be contained in one byte. For example, on the one hand, engine RPM requires 16 bits and on the other hand, gear position can be indicated using just 3 bits. A clear understanding of the data field format of the CAN message can be obtained from Figure 1. The engine control module generates this message. Engine speed or RPM occupies two data bytes within the message and gas level occupies 7 bits. The following sections explain the details of the ADR technique.

DATA REDUCTION TECHNIQUE

An automotive multiplexing system consists of many nodes interconnected between each other using a high-speed bus. The nodes contain sensors, which periodically communicate to send the change in some parameter values to the Electronic Control Unit (ECU), which in turn ensures optimum operation of the entire vehicle by actuating certain precise operations based on the input parameter values. Additionally, each node transmits and receives a fixed set of messages [8]. We have made the following assumptions for the DR algorithm.

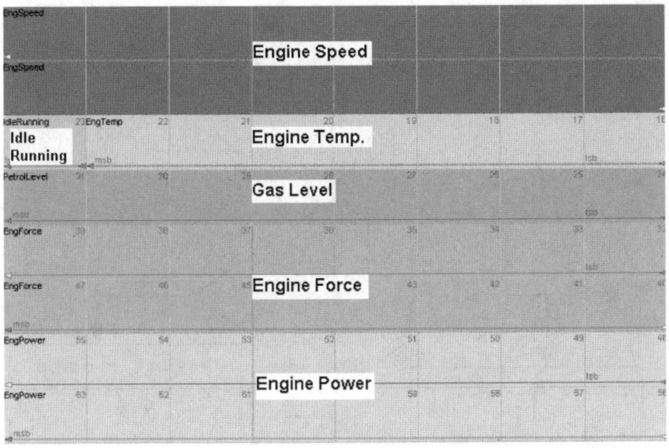

Figure 1. Data field of a CAN message showing various signal fields within the message. Each row indicates a data byte and each column indicates a bit. Some signals within the data field occupy more than a byte where as some others occupy one byte or less.

1. All messages in the system have their compressed version whose individual signal field lengths (in bits) are predefined based on the periodic message transmission rate and rate of change of the signal parameter.

2. The identifiers of the compressed messages differ from the identifiers of their original counterparts by a value of minus one. For example, if the identifier of a normal CAN message is 20, then the identifier of its compressed version would be 19.

3. Each CAN node in the network consists of two buffers called TX_BUF and RX_BUF to store the transmitted and received messages respectively. The TX_BUF and RX_BUF consist of two fields. One field stores the 11-bit (or 29-bit) identifier of the CAN message and another stores its 8-byte data field.

Data Compression

Each CAN node in the network transmits messages at fixed intervals of time depending on the nature of the message being sent. Let us assume that the transmitting unit of each node transmits messages every *t* time units where value of *t* may vary depending on the specific application. A safety critical message will have a very low value for the period *t* when compared to a non-safety critical message.

Assume that a CAN node transmits a message *ci* at time *m.* At time *m,* a copy of the sent message *ci* is stored in the TX_BUF of the transmitting node. When the next *ci* is being transmitted at time $m + t$ time units, a comparison is made between the data fields of the message stored in TX_BUF at time *m* with that of the current message being transmitted at time $m + t$. Depending on the content of the new message, two types of DR techniques can be applied.

1. Non- adaptive DR

2. Adaptive DR

Let us explore the two techniques further.

Non-Adaptive Data-Reduction

This technique is applied for the case when none of the bytes in the data field of the new message *ci* at time $m + t$, change their value since their previous transmission at time *m*. In such a situation, the entire message at time $m + t$ is not transmitted. The receiving node in the network assumes the most recent value of the message *ci* as the current value of the message. However, this technique has a drawback. In the event that none of the signal fields in the message *ci* change their value over a long period of time, the transmitting node will not transmit the message *ci* until it changes its value. To overcome this shortcoming, a copy of the most recent message *ci* is transmitted to the receiving node at every *y* intervals of time where $y >> t$. The value of *y* again depends on the safety-critical nature of the message. In the event of sudden and rapid changes in value of the signals, for example, during hard braking or hard acceleration, normal transmission of CAN messages over the bus resumes till a steady state is reached.

Adaptive Data-Reduction

Adaptive DR is based on the technique of delta modulation or differential pulse code modulation (DPCM) [9] that is widely used in the area digital communications. It is based on the principle that instead of sending the absolute value of a signal at each time instant, only the changes in the signal values from one time instance to another (delta) are transmitted.

To achieve data reduction, the first byte in the data field of the CAN message is used to indicate delta compression. This byte is called the delta compression code (DCC). In the ADR technique, if one or more signal fields in the message *ci* transmitted at time $m + t$ change their value since their previous transmission at time *m*, the transmitting node executes the following series of steps.

1. The transmitting node computes a delta compression code (DCC). A value of “1” in the DCC indicates the delta change in the value of the signal rather than the absolute value. A value of “0” in DCC indicates no change in the value of the signal.

2. Since a copy of the message transmitted at time *m* is stored in TX_BUF, the transmitting node computes differences (deltas) in the value of the corresponding signals in TX_BUF at time *m* with that at time $m + t$.

3. The compressed version of the original CAN message having an identifier whose value is one less than the value of the identifier of the original message is encoded with the delta signal values.

4. The delta-compressed CAN message carrying the delta signals is sent over the CAN bus to the receiving node.

5. In the event that the value of a delta signal exceeds the length of the assigned field, the absolute values of all the signals (i.e. the original CAN message) are transmitted rather than the delta-compressed version of the message. This assumption is based on the fact that a drastic change in the value of a particular signal could reflect a critical condition in which case it would be necessary to communicate absolute values of all signals within the message.

The entire data-compression process is depicted using the flow chart of Figure 3.

Figure 2 shows the format of the data field of the delta-compressed message of Figure 1. The engine module generates this particular message. The first eight bits of the data field are the DCC. The signals within the delta-compressed message occupy half the number of bytes when compared to the original message of Figure 1.

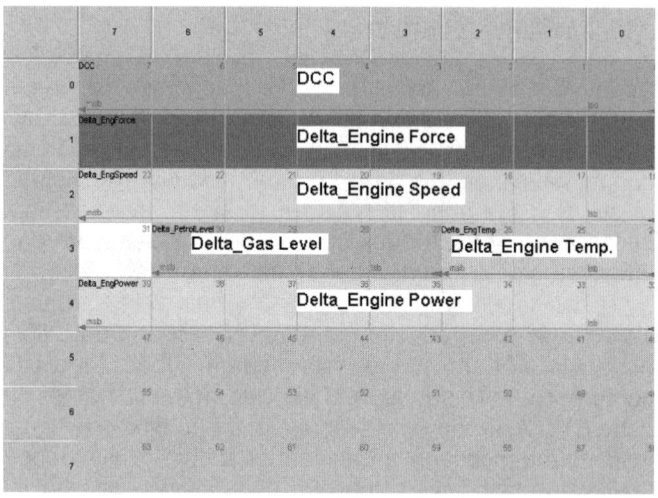

Figure 2. Data field format of delta-compressed message of Figure 1.

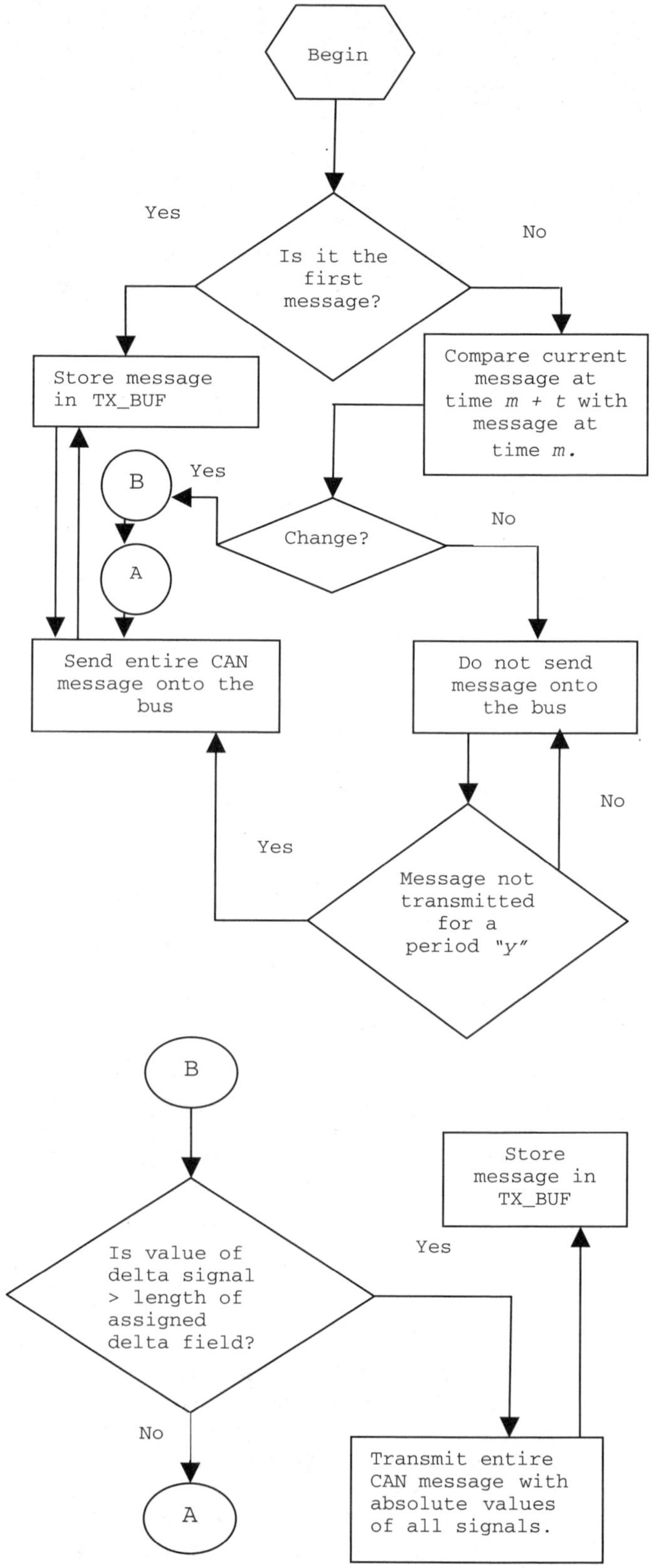

Figure 3. Adaptive data-reduction algorithm

Data-Decompression

The receiving node in the system decompresses the delta-compressed CAN message sent by the transmitter. The following series of steps are executed to perform

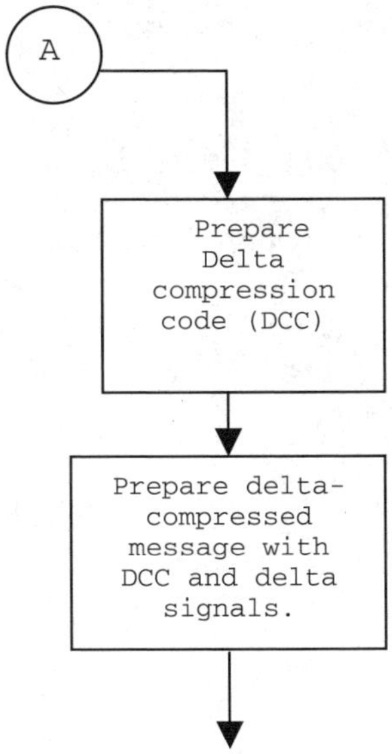

Figure 3. Adaptive data-reduction algorithm continued.

data-decompression. Assuming that a delta-compressed message *Dci* is received,

1. The receiving node checks the identifier of the CAN message *Dci*. If the message is a delta-compressed message, the first byte in the data field of the message is treated as the DCC.

2. The receiver then fetches a copy of the most recently received *ci* from the RX_BUF.

3. The DCC acts as an index to the corresponding signal fields within the delta-compressed message. For example, a value of "1" in the first bit position of the DCC means that the first signal field within the message is a delta signal of the first signal field within the message *ci* from RX_BUF. This delta signal is either added to or subtracted from the corresponding signal field within the message *ci* from RX_BUF to get the new value of the signal.

4. A value of "0" in the DCC means that the corresponding signal has not changed its value since the previous transmission. The absolute value of this signal is fetched from the previous *ci* in RX_BUF.

5. The receiver reconstructs all the signals within the message in a similar fashion.

6. The receiver then updates the RX_BUF with this new message, overwriting the previous *ci*.

The data-decompression process is illustrated graphically below.

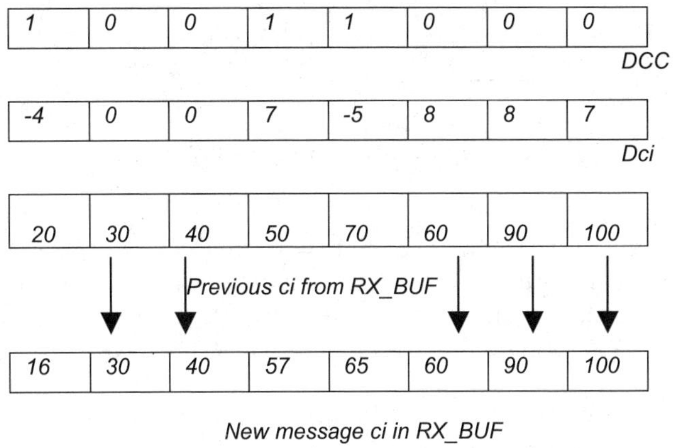

Figure 4. Data-decompression process.

The first row shows the mapping of the bits in the DCC of the received delta-compressed message. The second row is the delta-compressed message *Dci,* which holds delta values of all signal fields within any given message. Third row is the most recent copy of the message *ci* from the RX_BUF. A value of "1" in DCC indicates that the corresponding fields of *Dci* contain the delta values. In this example, delta signals corresponding to a "1" in DCC are -4, 7 and -5. These delta values are then added to the corresponding signal fields of the previous message *ci* in RX_BUF. All other signal fields within the new message retain previous values from the *ci* in RX_BUF. The RX_BUF is then updated with this new message.

The entire data decompression process is depicted in the flow chart of Figure 6. The following section presents simulation results for the presented ADR algorithm.

RESULTS AND DISCUSSIONS

A simulation program has been developed to analyze the performance of the adaptive DR algorithm. The main performance parameters considered are the bus load, message transmission rate (MTR) and the average length of messages (ALM). The simulation model consists of five CAN nodes each of which transmits a predefined set of messages. The distribution of messages among the five nodes is shown in Table I. Their corresponding periodic transmission rates are also included.

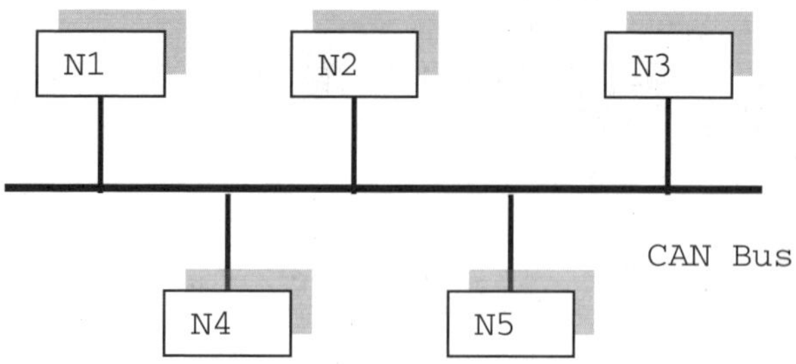

Figure 5. Simulation model consisting of 5 CAN nodes.

The simulation model consisting of 5 CAN nodes is shown in Figure 5. Each of the nodes numbered N1 to N5 consists of the TX_BUF and the RX_BUF to store the transmitted and received messages, respectively.

Table I. Distribution of messages among nodes in the simulation model.

Node Number	Message ID's	Periodic transmission rate (in milliseconds)
1	99 and 100	5
	101 and 102	5
2	200 and 201	5
3	1019 and 1020	50
4	1050 and 1051	500
	1052 and 1053	500
5	272 and 273	500

All message ID's on the left of the message ID column are the ID's of the delta-compressed message. The simulation has been developed to monitor the behavior of the system during three operating conditions.

1. During transient operation of the system i.e. during engine start and acceleration.
2. During steady-state operation i.e. under cruise control, and
3. During hard braking or deceleration.

We will further analyze the performance of the system under these three operating conditions. For the sake of comparison, we will consider the cases when no DR was applied and when non-adaptive and adaptive data-reduction techniques were applied under the three operating conditions. Bus-load, the number of data frames per second or MTR and the average length of messages or ALM have been monitored to evaluate the performance of the ADR algorithm. We will first analyze the system performance under the transient and steady-state conditions.

CASE 1: TRANSIENT AND STEADY-STATE OPERATION

The graphs of Figure 7 through Figure 9 compare the simulation results for the system under transient and steady-state, with no DR and when non-adaptive DR is applied. The variation of different signals within a message (in this case engine data) during transient and steady state is shown in Figure 10. The variation in the MTR is compared in Figure 7.

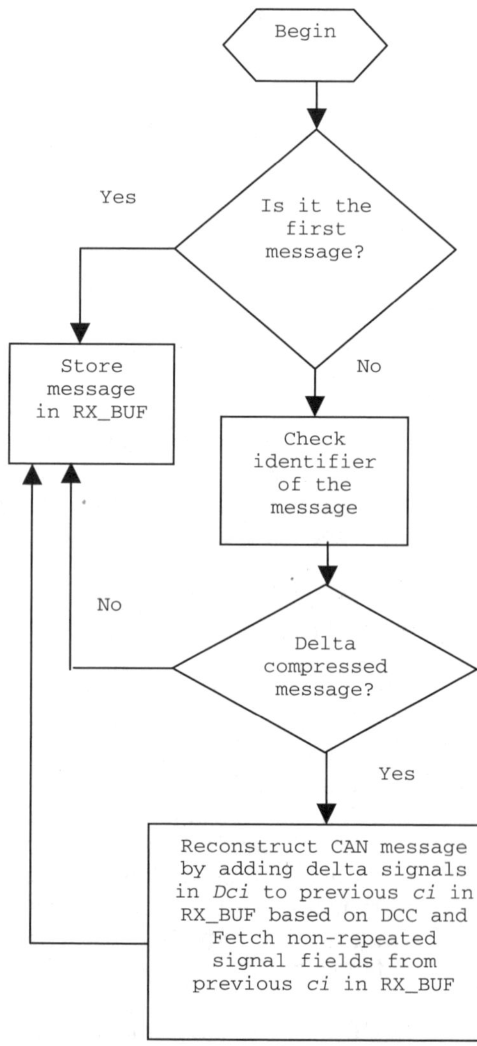

Figure 6. Data-decompression algorithm.

In the transient state, which lasts for sixty seconds after start of simulation, the MTR reaches a peak value of 138 frames/second at time T1 for both the cases, i.e. when no DR is performed and when non-adaptive DR is performed. After the transient period, the system reaches the steady state where all the signals reach a constant value. During the steady state, there is a considerable decrease in the MTR for the case when non-adaptive DR is applied. The MTR falls to 44 frames/second at time T2 reducing the number of message transmissions by 50 in comparison to the case where no DR is used. This gives a compression ratio of 53% over the case when no DR was applied.

The variation in the bus-load is compared in Figure 8. During the transient state, the variation in bus-load is the same for the cases when no DR is performed and when non-adaptive DR is performed. Notable gain in the parameter is made during the steady-state operation where majority of the signals do not vary rapidly from one instance to another and hence the message is not repeated unless there is significant change in its value since the previous transmission. During the steady-state operation, the peak bus-load at time T2 reduced from 18.55% to 7.98% giving a total bandwidth saving of 56% when compared to the case where no DR was applied.

Figure 9 compares the average lengths of the messages (ALM) transmitted between various nodes during the simulation. The ALM remained constant over majority of the simulation run for the two cases when no DR was applied and when non-adaptive DR was applied. However, as the system approached the steady state, minute reductions in the ALM were observed for the case when non-adaptive DR was applied. This is due to the fact that as the system reached the steady state, the small variations in the signals were transmitted in the delta-compressed messages.

CASE 2: HARD BRAKING OR DECELERATION

The performance of the ADR algorithm during the condition of hard braking or deceleration can be analyzed from the graphs of Figure 11 through Figure 13. The variation in MTR during hard braking with no DR and with ADR is compared in Figure 11. During hard braking, the behavior of the system is similar to the behavior during the transient state. The MTR reaches its peak value of 138 frames/second and 137 frames/second at the instance when the brake is applied at time T2, when no DR and when ADR is applied, respectively. There is no significant reduction in the MTR for the case when ADR is applied since the periodic rate of transmission of the delta-compressed messages is similar to the transmission rates of their uncompressed counterparts. After the period of braking, the system again goes to the steady state. The variation of the various signals within a message (in this case engine data) during the application of the brake is shown in Figure 14.

The variation in bus-load is compared in Figure 12. The application of brake leads to the transmission of the delta-compressed messages and hence, the peak bus-load at time T2 increases slightly to a value of 16.97%. A total bandwidth saving of 43% was gained in comparison to the case where no DR was applied.

Figure 13 compares the ALM for the cases when no DR is applied and when ADR is applied. There is a decrease in ALM when ADR is applied since the delta-compressed messages having a smaller duration are transmitted during the application of brakes. The ALM decreases to a value of 0.2 ms at time T2 when brakes are applied giving a total reduction of ((0.30-0.20)/ 0.30)*100= 33% in the ALM when compared to the case when no DR was applied. Table II summarizes the percentage gain in the values of various performance parameters with the application of non-adaptive and ADR algorithms.

Table II. Gain in the values of performance parameters in comparison to the case when no DR was applied to the system.

	% decrease in bus load	% decrease in MTR	% decrease in ALM
Non-adaptive DR	56%	53%	0%
Adaptive DR	43%	0%	33%

CONCLUSION

The performance of an adaptive data-reduction algorithm for future in-vehicle networking applications has been presented. The algorithm is based on the CAN protocol and uses the fact that some of the signals within a CAN message do not change their value from one transmission time instance to another. Another observation is that some of the signal values change by small amounts i.e. during cruise control or deceleration. The algorithm exploits the above two observations to decrease the amount of data traffic to be transmitted over the CAN bus. In the first case, the algorithm refrains from transmitting the repeated messages during successive transmitting instances and in the second case, the algorithm transmits only the delta-change in the value of signals from one transmitting instance to another. The adaptive data reduction (ADR) algorithm generates a delta compression code (DCC) to indicate signals whose corresponding delta values have been transmitted. A dynamic event-based simulation has been developed to analyze the performance of the presented ADR algorithm. The simulation of the algorithm has shown promising results in terms of the reduction in the values of important parameters like message transmission rate (MTR), bus-load and average length of messages (ALM). The reduction in the values of these parameters enables us to cater to the bandwidth requirements of new nodes into the network to provide advanced features like infotainment and active safety etc., without increasing the overall cost of the system.

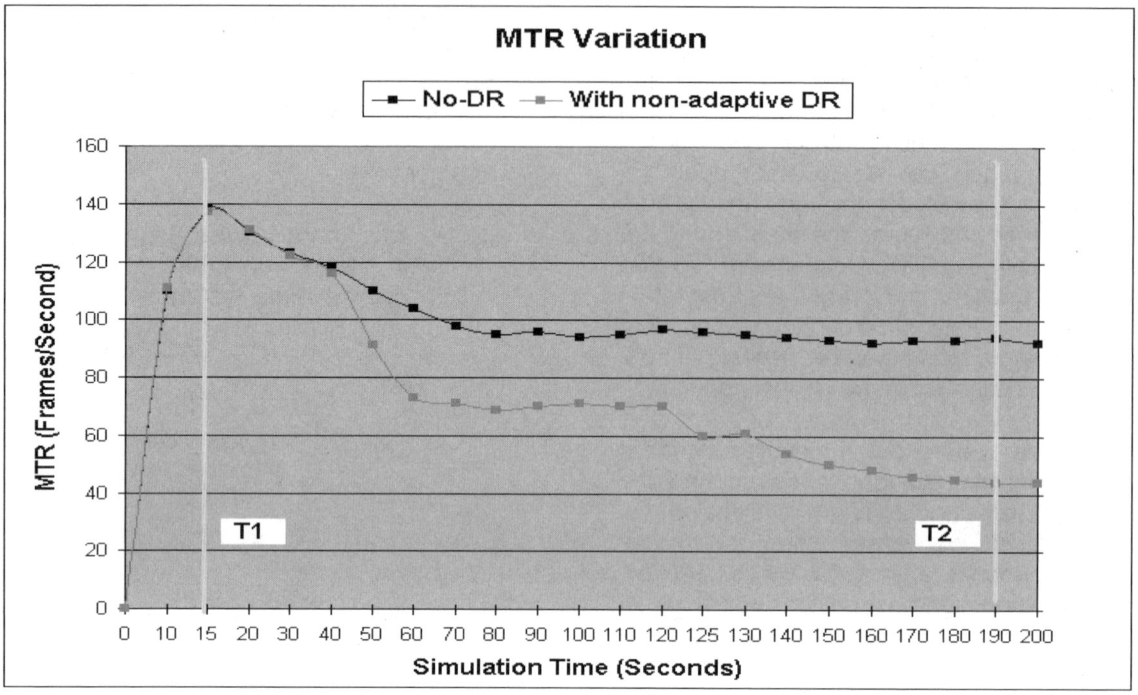

Figure 7. Message transmission rate (MTR) comparison.

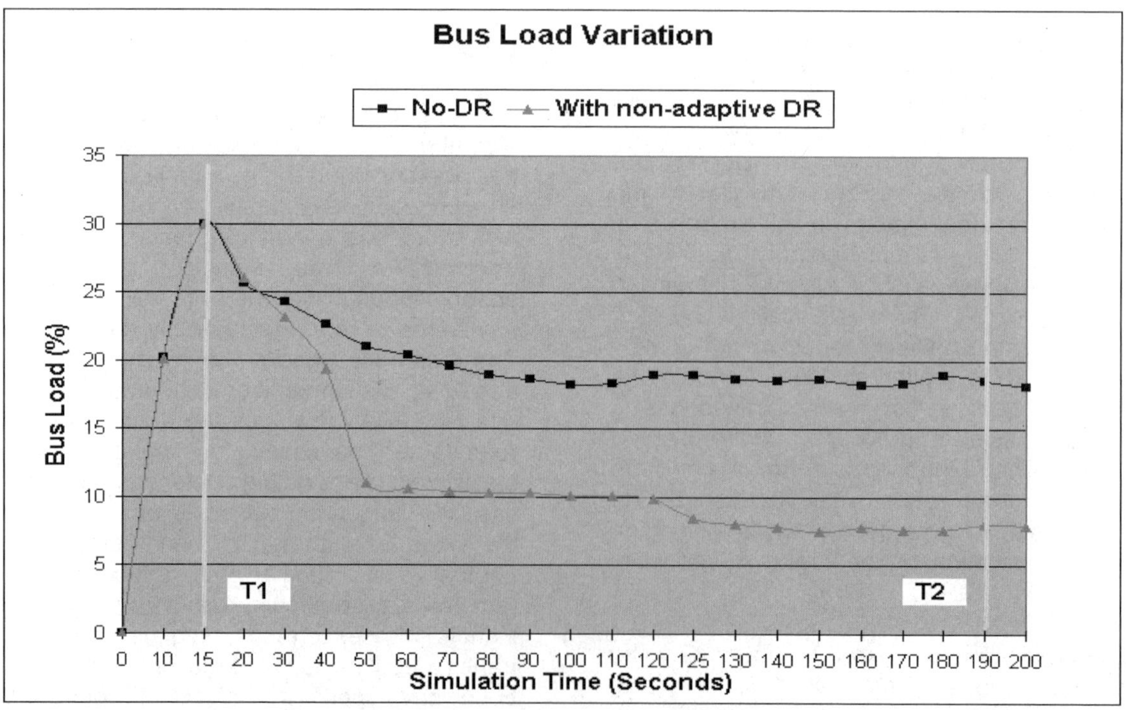

Figure 8. Bus load Comparison.

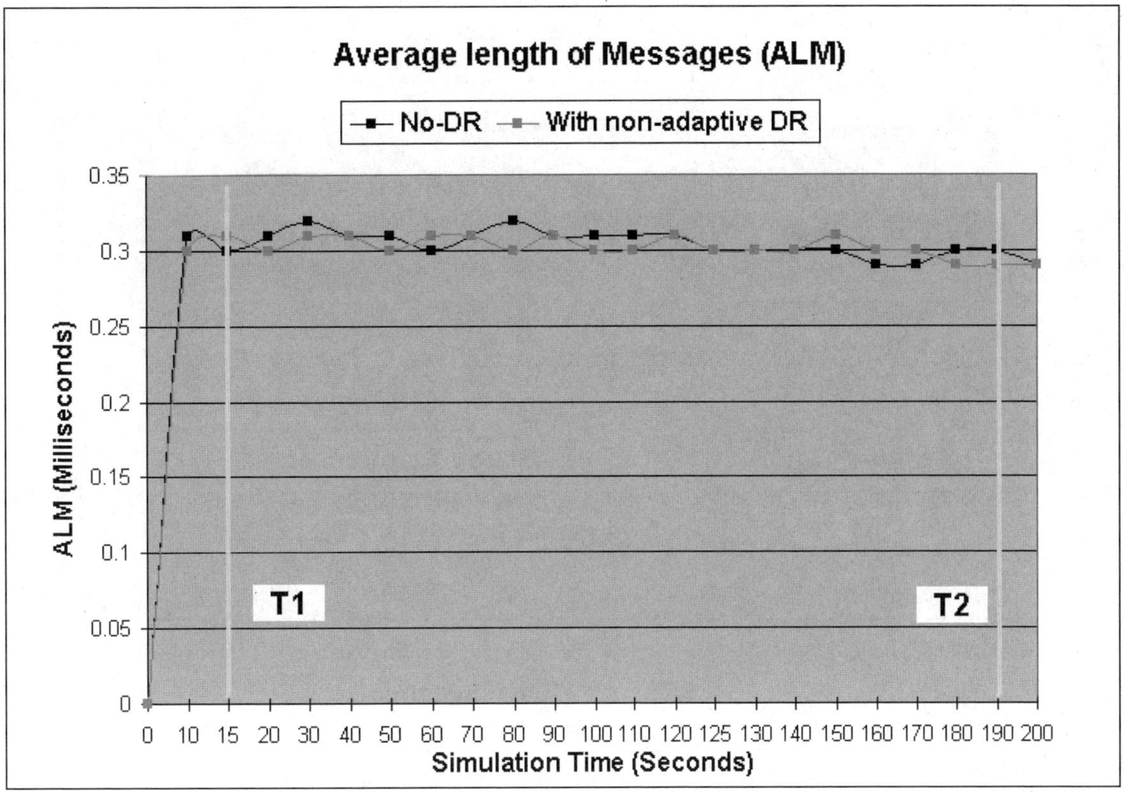

Figure 9. Average message length (ALM) comparison.

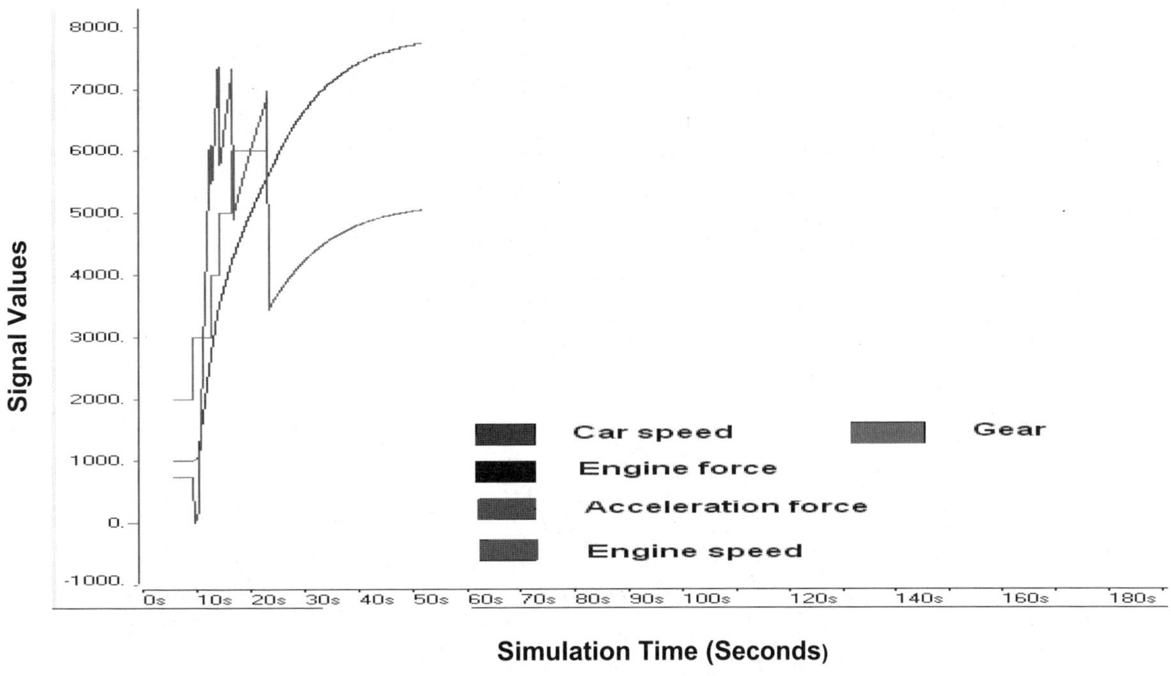

Figure 10. Variation of different signals during transient and steady state.

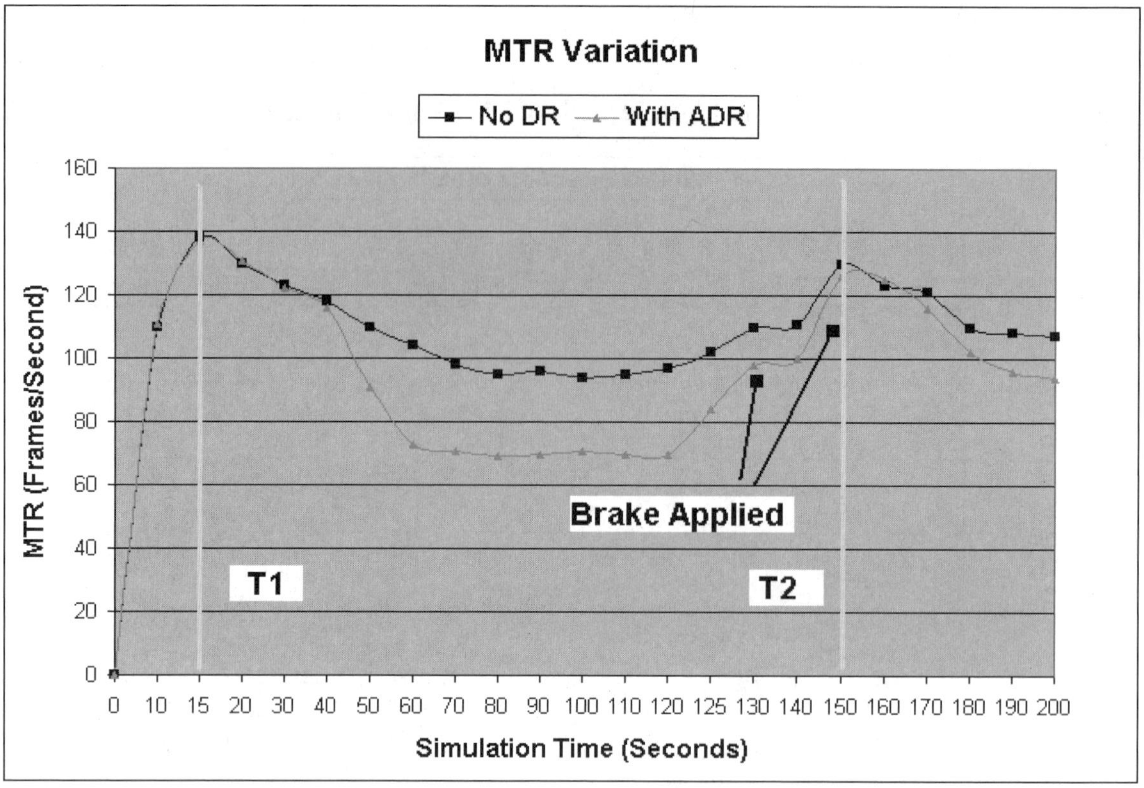

Figure 11. Message transmission rate (MTR) comparison during hard braking.

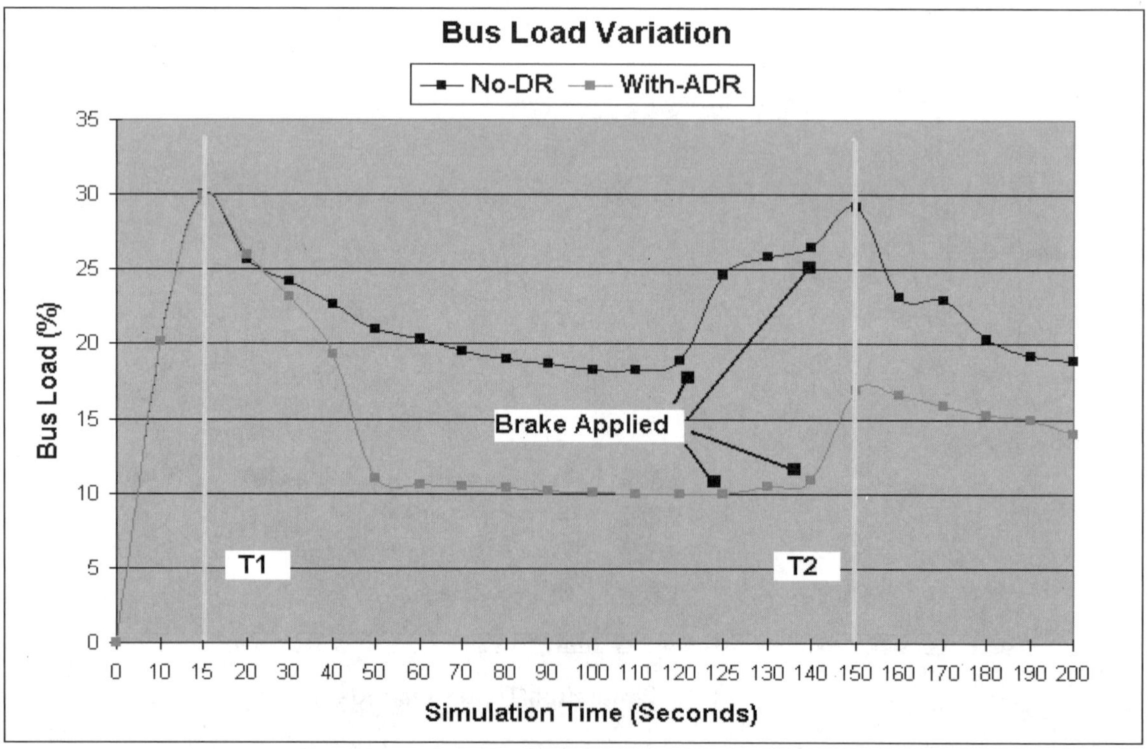

Figure 12. Bus load comparison during hard braking.

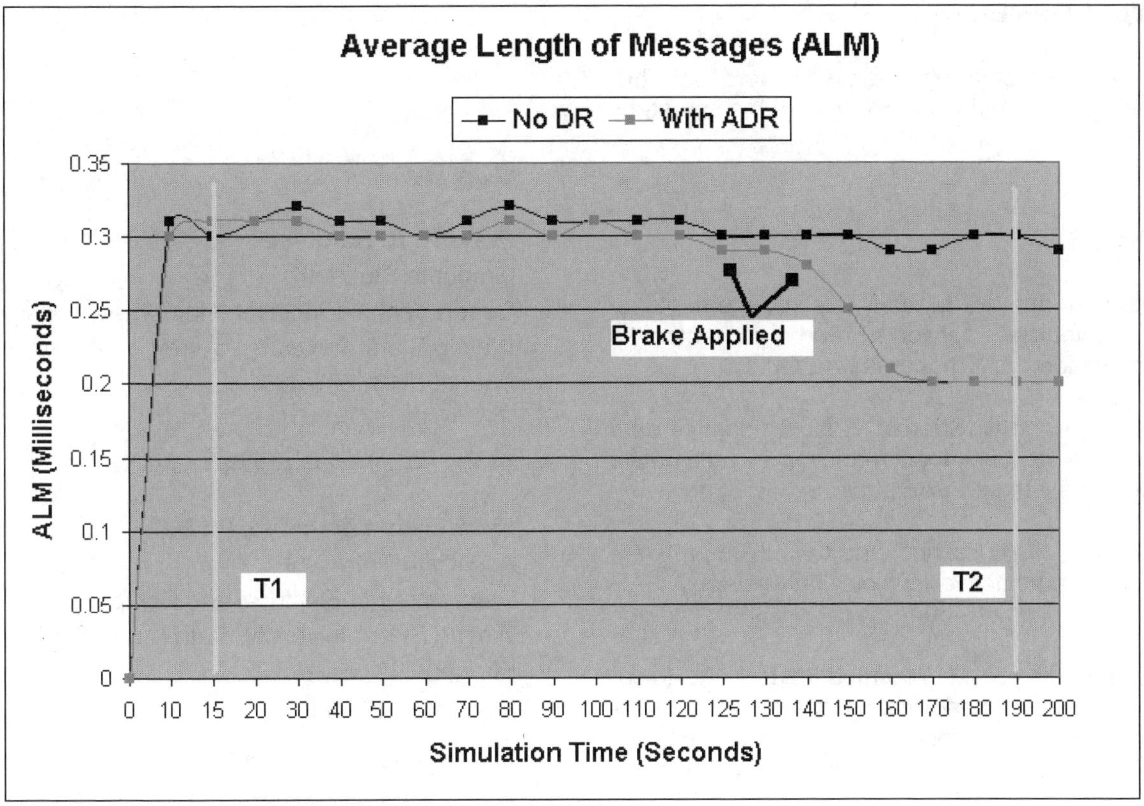

Figure 13. Average message length (ALM) comparison during hard braking.

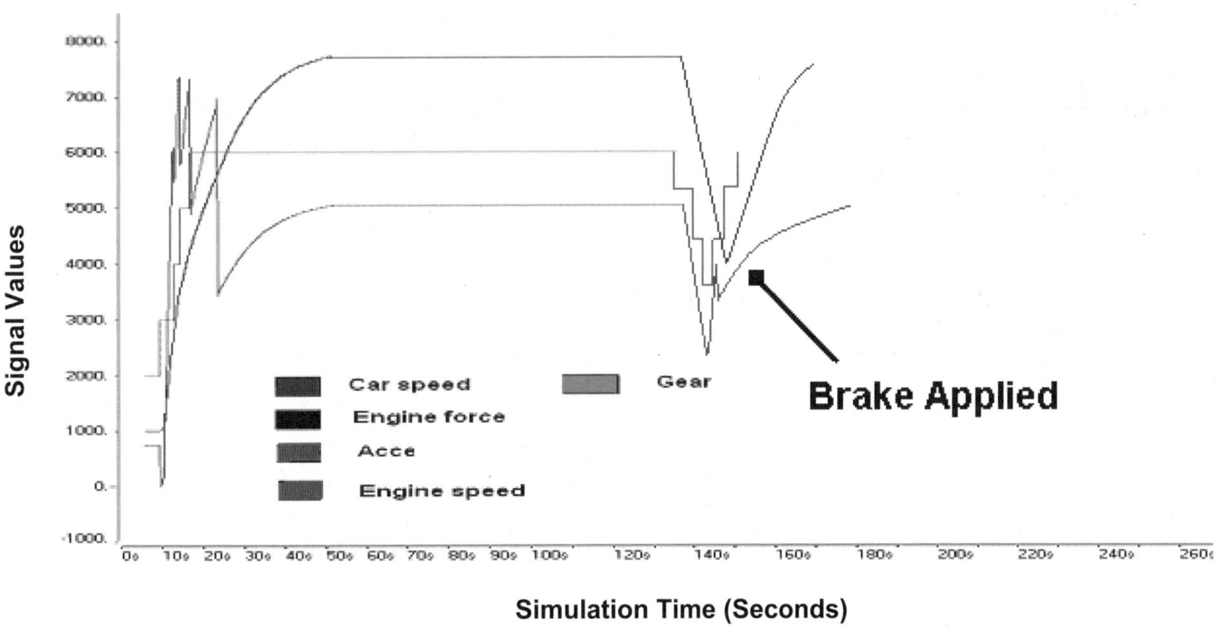

Figure 14. Variation of different signals during transient state, steady state and during hard braking or deceleration.

ACKNOWLEDGEMENTS

I would like to thank Mr. Aakash Arora for his constructive criticism and immense help in the course of this work.

REFERENCES

1. S. Channon and P. Miller, “The requirements of future in-vehicle networks and an example implementation,” SAE paper 2004-01-0206.

2. G. G. Kempf and K. Strenzl, “Robust adaptive data compression for peak-load reduction in automotive multiplexing systems,” SAE paper 941 658, pp. 1-5.

3. G. G. Kempf, M. J. Eckrich, and O. J. Rumpf, "Data reduction in automotive multiplexing systems,” SAE paper 940 135, pp. 45-50.

4. S. Misbahuddin, S. M. Mahmud and N. Al-Holou, “Development and performance analysis of a Data-Reduction algorithm for automotive multiplexing,”, *IEEE Trans. on Vehicular Technology,* Vol. 50, No.1, pp. 162-169.

5. “Recommended practice for serial control and communications vehicle network (Class C),” SAE draft J1939, 1939.

6. SAE recommended practice, “Vehicle application layer,”, SAE J1939/71, Aug. 1994.

7. Bosch, “CAN specification Ver 2.0,” Robert Bosch GmbH, Stuttgart, Germany, 1991.

8. R. Masaki *et al.,* “Development of class C multiplex control IC,”,SAE paper 930 003, 1993.

9. Bill Waggener, "*Pulse Code Modulation Techniques: With Applications in Communications and Data Recording (Electrical Engineering),*" Kluwer Academic Publishers, 15 January, 1995.

CONTACT

Praveen R. Ramteke
Graduate Student
Department of Electrical and Computer Engineering
Wayne State University, Detroit, MI 48202
Phone: (313) 577-3855
Fax: (313) 577-1101
Email: ramteke@wayne.edu

Syed Masud Mahmud, Ph.D.
Associate Professor
Department of Electrical and Computer Engineering
Wayne State University, Detroit, MI 48202
Phone: (313) 577-3855
Fax: (313) 577-1101
Email: smahmud@eng.wayne.edu

2005-01-1531

In-Vehicle Network Architecture for the Next-Generation Vehicles

Syed Masud Mahmud
Department of Electrical & Computer Engineering, Wayne State University

Sheran Alles
Ford Motor Company

ABSTRACT

The demand for drive-by-wire, telematics, entertainment, multimedia, pre-crash warning, remote diagnostic and software update, etc. will significantly increase the complexity of the future in-vehicle communication networks. New types of communication networks will also be necessary to satisfy the requirements of safety and fuel efficiency, and meet the demand for new features. Different sets of vehicle electronic modules will require different types of networks. For example, drive-by-wire and active collision avoidance systems need fault tolerant networks with time-triggered protocols, to guarantee deterministic latencies; multimedia systems need networks with high bandwidth to transfer video files; and body control electronics need low-bandwidth networks to keep the cost down. As the size and complexity of these networks increase, ease of integration has become a major challenge for design engineers. In today's vehicles, there are mainly two networks: a high-speed network for the power train and a low-speed network for the body electronics. Since the complexity of the network is increasing and the demand for bandwidth is growing, future vehicles will require many partitioned networks. The partitioning of the networks will be done based on the locality as well as the functionality of the modules. One of the challenging issues will be the selection of topology to interconnect various in-vehicle partitions of the network. Interconnection among all in-vehicle partitions of the network is necessary for diagnostics and software updates in various modules. One logical approach for interconnecting various partitions of the network would be via a hierarchical bus. This paper shows various types of hierarchical connections among the partitions of in-vehicle networks. Different partitions may use different protocols. For example, one partition may use the CAN protocol, the second partition may use the TTCAN protocol, the third partition may use the LIN protocol, and so on. The hierarchical bus will be using intelligent switches to facilitate the translation of messages from one protocol to another protocol while the messages will be moving from one partition to another partition. This paper discusses the advantages and disadvantages of various types of hierarchical connections in terms of cost, bandwidth, latency, fault tolerance, and many other features. The paper also presents simulation models that can be used to determine the performance of various types of partitions and network topologies.

INTRODUCTION

Automakers are scrambling to implement advanced safety and engine management systems to make vehicles safer and more fuel-efficient, as well as meet growing consumer and government demands. Continuous demands for fuel efficiency mandate "drive-by-wire" systems that eliminate camshafts, power-sapping belt drives and pumps, and a great deal of unnecessary weight. The goal of x-by-wire is to replace nearly every automotive hydraulic/mechanical system with electronics. Electric brakes will replace hydraulics, increasing safety, lowering operating cost and eliminating the use of environmentally hazardous fluids. Steering columns will disappear and will be replaced by electric steering, improving driver safety and making it easy to provide left-hand and right-hand drive models.

The demand for drive-by-wire and many new features such as telematics, entertainment, multimedia, pre-crash warning, remote diagnostic and software update, etc. will significantly increase the complexity of in-vehicle communication networks. New types of communication networks will also be necessary to satisfy the requirements of safety and fuel efficiency, and meet the demand for new features. Different sets of vehicle electronic modules will require different types of networks. For example, drive-by-wire and active collision avoidance systems need fault tolerant networks with time-triggered protocols, to guarantee deterministic latencies; multimedia systems need networks with high bandwidth to transfer video files; and body control electronics need low-bandwidth networks to keep the cost down. As the size and complexity of these networks increase, ease of integration has become a major challenge for design engineers. Major studies are necessary to determine optimal topology for connecting all the in-vehicle networks; to figure out optimal bandwidth required from different types of in-vehicle networks for keeping latencies under certain bounds; and to select appropriate communication protocols for different networks.

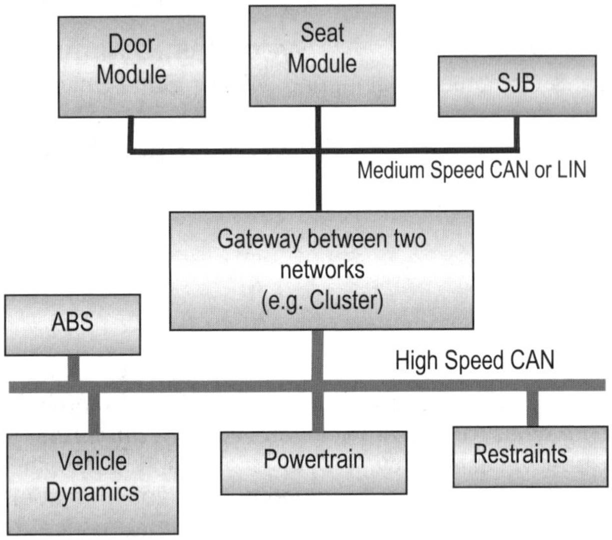

Figure 1: Schematic diagram of a current in-vehicle network.

In this paper, we present various types of in-vehicle network topologies that could be used with various types of networks and protocols to satisfy the requirements for safety, fuel efficiency, diagnostics, comfort and cost.

EVOLUTION OF IN-VEHICLE NETWORK ARCHITECTURE

For the last two decades, automotive companies have been using multiplexing networks in order to reduce wiring harness in vehicles [1-2]. The direct benefit of multiplexing is cost saving. Today's vehicles incorporate many different electronic modules, and have evolved into a distributed processing system. Serial buses are used for interconnecting the electronic modules of a vehicle. Serial buses have been selected due to many advantages of bus-based systems, over other interconnection systems [3]. The advantages of bus-based systems are low cost, lower complexity, greater reliability, better scalability, simpler communication protocols, ease of diagnostics, etc. Networks also enable the partitioning of the various electronic modules depending on function, feature or control location, further reducing cost by impacting the electrical distribution system and control signal (sensor/actuator) routing.

In today's vehicles, two serial buses are used. One bus is used for the powertrain system and the other bus is used for body electronics, as shown in Figure 1. Each bus can be considered as a partition of the in-vehicle network. Thus, today's vehicles have two partitions of networks. But, future vehicles will need many partitions of the in-vehicle network to provide services for various features such as drive-by-wire, multimedia, fuel efficiency, active collision warning/avoidance, etc.

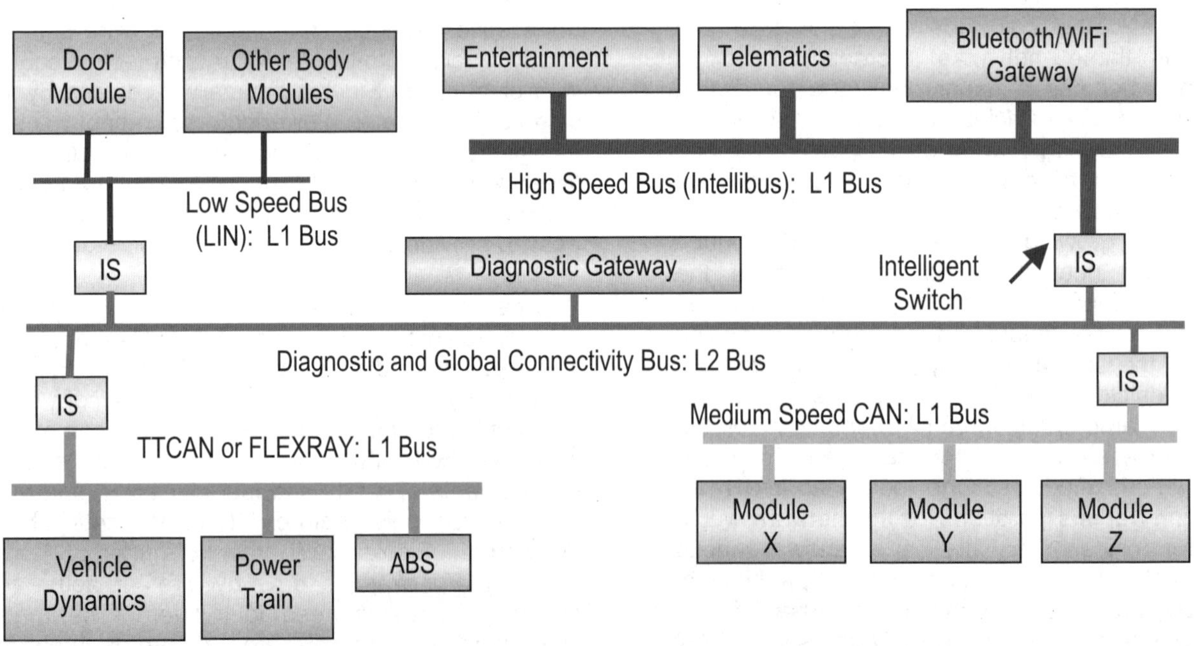

Figure 2: An in-vehicle network with four Level 1 buses, one Level 2 bus and four intelligent switches.

One of the challenging issues will be the selection of an appropriate topology to interconnect various partitions of the in-vehicle network. Interconnection among all partitions of the in-vehicle network is necessary for diagnostics and software updates. Since a bus-based system has many advantages over other interconnection systems, one logical approach would be to use another bus, a hierarchical bus, for connecting all other in-vehicle buses (partitions) together, as shown in Figure 2.

The system shown in Figure 2 has four partitions of the in-vehicle network. Each partition of the network uses a Level 1 bus to interconnect various nodes of the vehicle. Thus, the system shown in Figure 2 has four Level 1 (L1) buses: 1) a low-speed bus for body electronics, 2) a high-speed bus for entertainment, telematics, multimedia, etc., 3) a bus with a time-triggered protocol for the powertrain system and 4) a medium speed bus for other modules of the vehicle. The four L1 buses are connected using a Level 2 (L2) bus. Every L1 bus is connected to the L2 bus using an intelligent switch (IS). The intelligent switch will have a very low-cost microcontroller supporting two protocols: one for an L1 bus and another one for the L2 bus. An IS will act as a node on the L2 bus and also as another node on an L1 bus. The L2 bus, shown in Figure 2, has five nodes: four intelligent switches and a Diagnostic Gateway node. Dealers and mechanics can access different electronic modules of a vehicle via the Diagnostic Gateway module. The architecture shown in Figure 2 allows a very simple way of interconnecting various in-vehicle networks. It's also scalable. The intelligent switches are also simple. The number of intelligent switches, in the system, is equal to the number of partitions in the in-vehicle network.

Though the system shown in Figure 2 is scalable, the number of connections on the L2 bus will be too many if there are too many partitions in the in-vehicle network. The speed of a bus decreases as the number of connections to the bus increases. The speed of a bus also decreases, when its length increases. Figure 3 shows another variation of the system shown in Figure 2. There are only two intelligent switches in Figure 3 compared to four in Figure 2. But the switches of Figure 3 are more complex than those of Figure 2. The switches of Figure 3 make a star connection among three buses: the L2 bus and two L1 buses. Since the number of connections to the L2 bus is less in Figure 3 than in Figure 2, the speed of the L2 bus of Figure 3 will be higher than that of the L2 bus of Figure 2. However, one disadvantage of the architecture of Figure 3 is that it is not as scalable as the architecture shown in Figure 2.

The major problem with the architectures of Figures 2 and 3 is that neither one will tolerate bus faults. If any bus (L2 or L1) fails, then the communication among a group of modules will be disrupted. As a result, the vehicle system will fail to do its intended operations. Communication faults could be of two types: permanent faults and temporary faults. The breakdown of a bus is an example of a permanent fault. Temporary faults can occur due to the presence of momentary noise or high electromagnetic interference for a short time. The presence of a permanent fault will break down communications among many nodes.

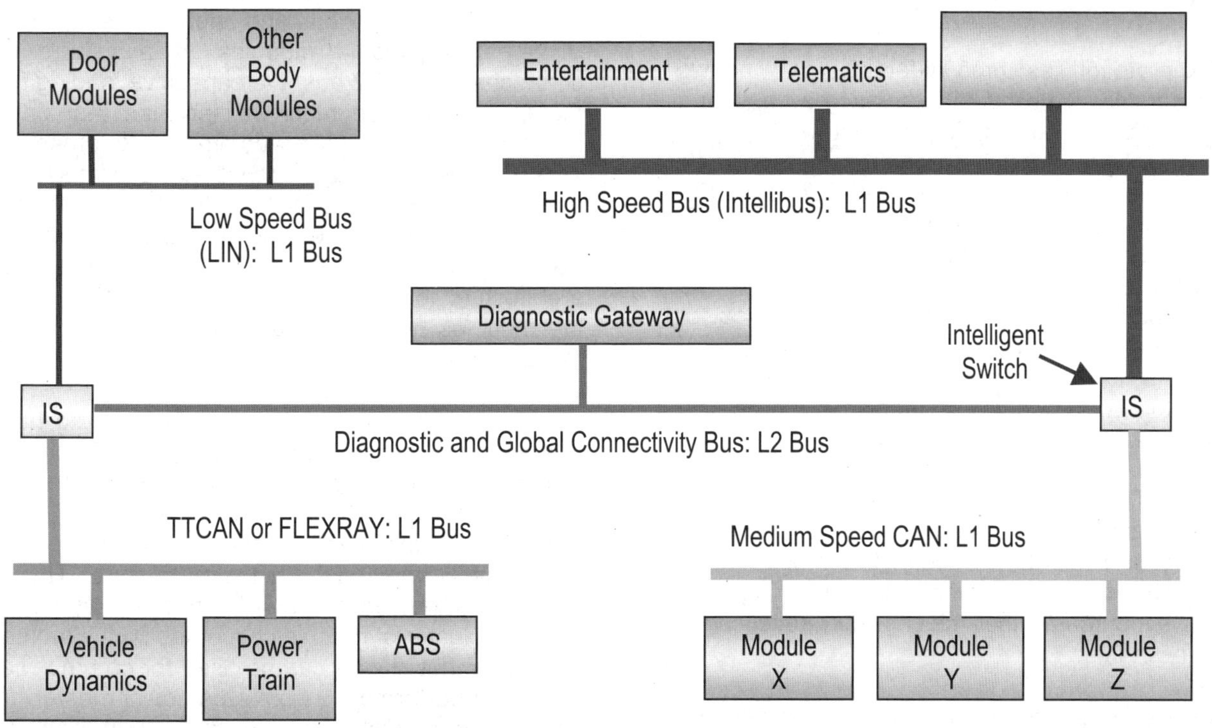

Figure 3: Schematic diagram of an in-vehicle network with four level-1 buses, one level-2 bus and two intelligent switches.

However, the presence of a temporary fault will increase the message latency. High message latencies could be acceptable for non-safety critical messages, but not for safety critical messages. One network partition of Figures 2 and 3 uses a bus with time-triggered protocol, for vehicle dynamics, power train and ABS systems. Since this network partition carries safety critical messages, on time delivery (within certain tolerance) of these messages must be guaranteed even if there are temporary faults.

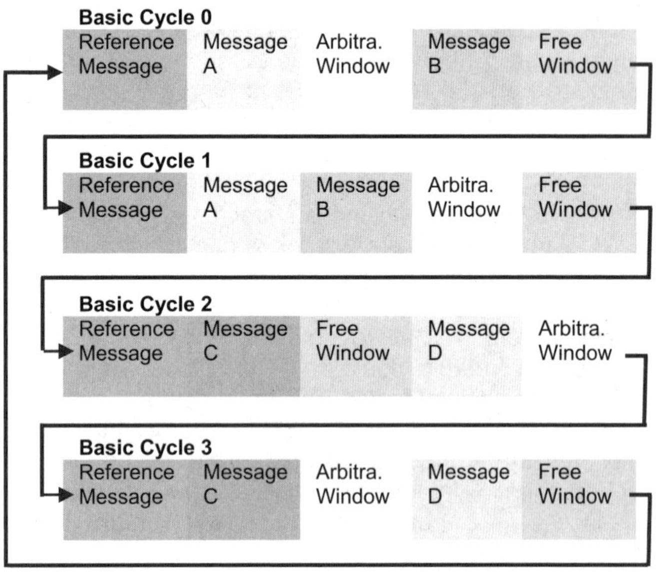

Figure 4: The system matrix of a TTCAN system.

The TTCAN protocol has three different time windows for messages: *exclusive window*, *arbitrating window* and *free window* [4], [5], as shown in Figure 4. Time-triggered messages, which require deterministic latencies, are sent through the *exclusive windows*. For example, Figure 4 shows that fixed windows (exclusive windows) have been reserved for messages A, B, C and D. Event-triggered messages are sent through the *arbitrating windows*. The *free windows* are reserved for future expansion of the system. The sequential flow of messages in a TTCAN system is represented by a matrix called the system matrix, as shown in Figure 4. A system matrix is divided into a number of basic cycles. The first window of a basic cycle is used for a reference message. In a TTCAN system, there is a master node, which is responsible for maintaining a global clock. At the beginning of every basic cycle, the master node sends the global time using a reference message. All other nodes synchronize their clocks after receiving a reference message.

In TTCAN systems, since a message must be delivered within the same time window in which it started, retransmission of the message is not allowed when errors occur within the message. Thus, if a safety critical message could not go through its Exclusive Window due to the presence of errors, it will have to wait until its next Exclusive Window. For example, if Message A could not go through its exclusive window of Basic Cycle 1 (see Figure 4) due to the presence of a temporary fault, then this message can not go until the time of its exclusive window in Basic Cycle 0. Thus, Message A will be delayed by three basic cycles. However, Message A can compete for the bus during an arbitrating window after it failed to go through its own exclusive window, but there is no guarantee that Message A will get the bus during an arbitrating window. If Message A is a safety critical message and if it is delayed by too long, then vehicle's safety will be compromised. Thus, it is desirable to have fault tolerant mechanisms for the transmission of safety critical messages with deterministic latencies.

One way of providing fault tolerant mechanisms is by maintaining additional paths among the nodes. Figure 5 shows a system that will tolerate permanent faults on L1 buses, but the system will work with degraded performance under such faulty conditions. Working with degraded performance may be acceptable for non-safety related systems, but not for powertrain and active collision avoidance/warning systems. In this architecture, if a Level-1 bus connecting a cluster of modules becomes faulty, then the modules of that cluster will have to communicate among themselves using the Level-2 bus. For example, if the TTCAN or FlexRay bus, shown in Figure 5, becomes faulty, then the Vehicle Dynamics, Powertrain and ABS modules will have to use the L2 bus for communicating among themselves. The architecture shown in Figure 5 is scalable and doesn't require any external switches. But, this architecture requires that every electronic module must have two ports: one for the L2 bus and another one for an L1 bus. Since all electronic modules of a vehicle will be connected to the L2 bus, the capacitive loading effect on the L2 bus will be much higher than that on the L1 buses. Thus, for the same communication media (single wire, dual wire, twisted pair, shielded twisted pair, etc.) using copper wire technology, the bandwidth available from the L2 bus will be much less than that available from an L1 bus. Another disadvantage of this architecture is that, since every module has two ports, the modules will be little bit more expensive than those modules that have only one port.

If two-port modules are going to be used to have fault tolerant capabilities for all modules, then Figure 6 shows a better way of connecting the modules at an expense of several three-port intelligent switches. In this architecture, the second port of every module of a cluster is connected by another L1 bus. Thus, every cluster of modules has two L1 buses. Hence, if an L1 bus of a cluster of modules becomes faulty, then another L1 bus of that cluster can be used for communication. If degraded performance from a particular cluster (for non-safety related cluster) is acceptable, then the second L1 bus and the corresponding port of each module of the cluster can be built using low-cost technology. But for safety critical modules, both ports and both L1 buses can be built using the same technology. The Level 2 bus (L2 bus) of the architecture shown in Figure 6 doesn't have too many connections. The total number of connections is equal to the total number of clusters plus another connection for the Diagnostic Gateway. Hence, the bandwidth of the L2 bus will not reduce significantly with the addition of new modules in the vehicle. This architecture is also scalable. Hence, the system can be easily expanded.

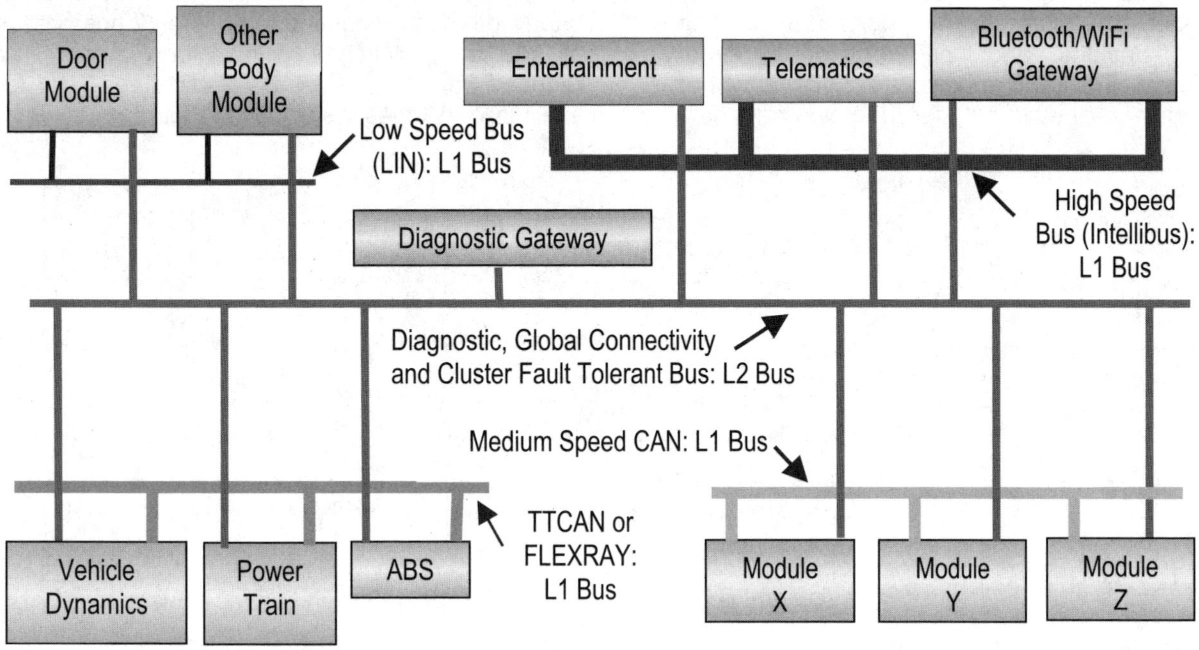

Figure 5: Schematic diagram of a fault tolerant in-vehicle network with four level-1 buses and one level-2 bus.

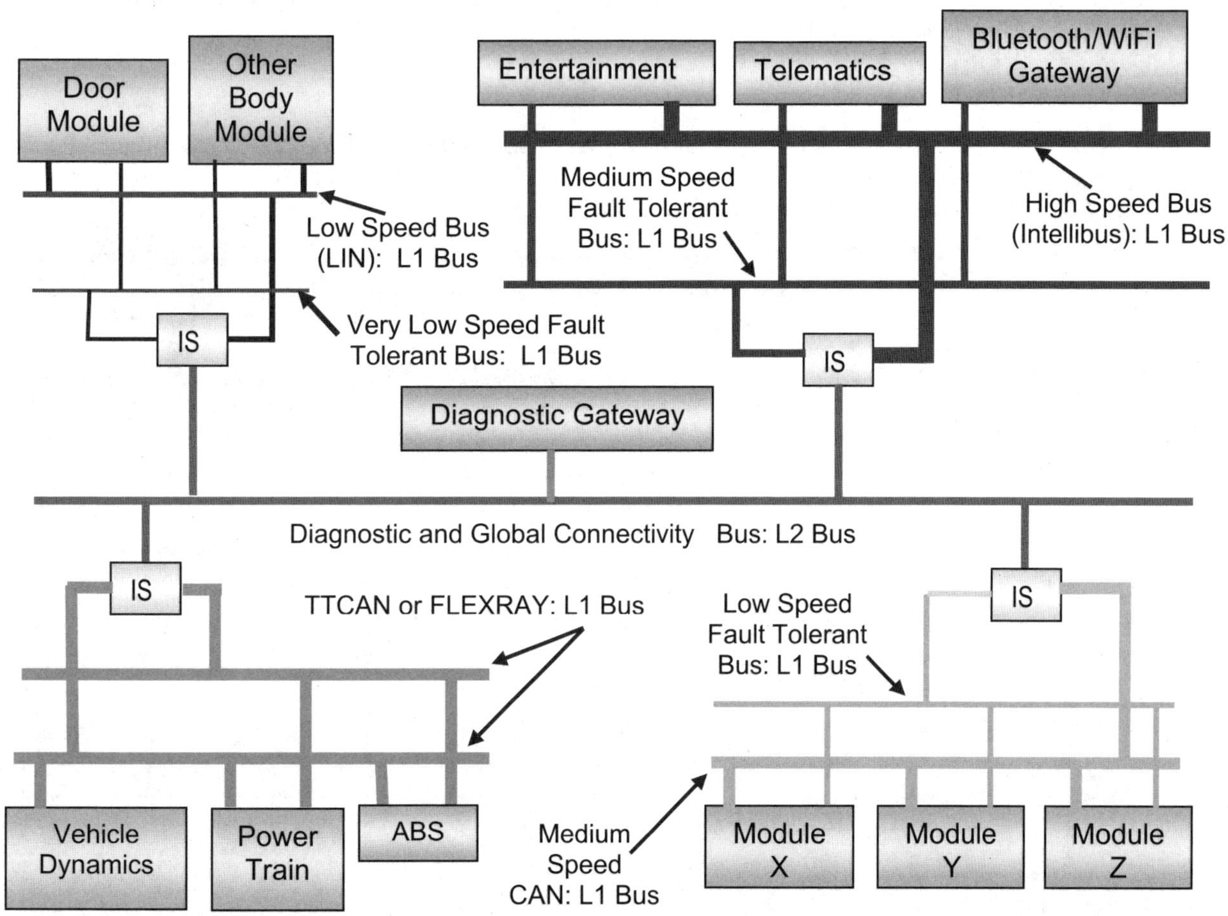

Figure 6: Schematic diagram of a fault-tolerant in-vehicle network with eight level-1 buses, one level-2 bus and four intelligent switches.

The major drawback of the architecture shown in Figure 6 is the cost of dual-port modules and three-port intelligent switches. Since all modules are not safety-critical modules. We can use dual-ports only for the safety-critical modules, and one port for all other modules. Figure 7 shows another architecture where dual-port modules are used only for the powertrain bus.

The architecture shown in Figure 7 is also scalable and doesn't have too many connections on the L2 bus. Thus, the system can be easily expanded, and good bandwidth can be obtained from the L2 bus. The number of intelligent switches, shown in Figure 7, can be reduced from five to two if we use three- and four-port intelligent switches, as shown in Figure 8.

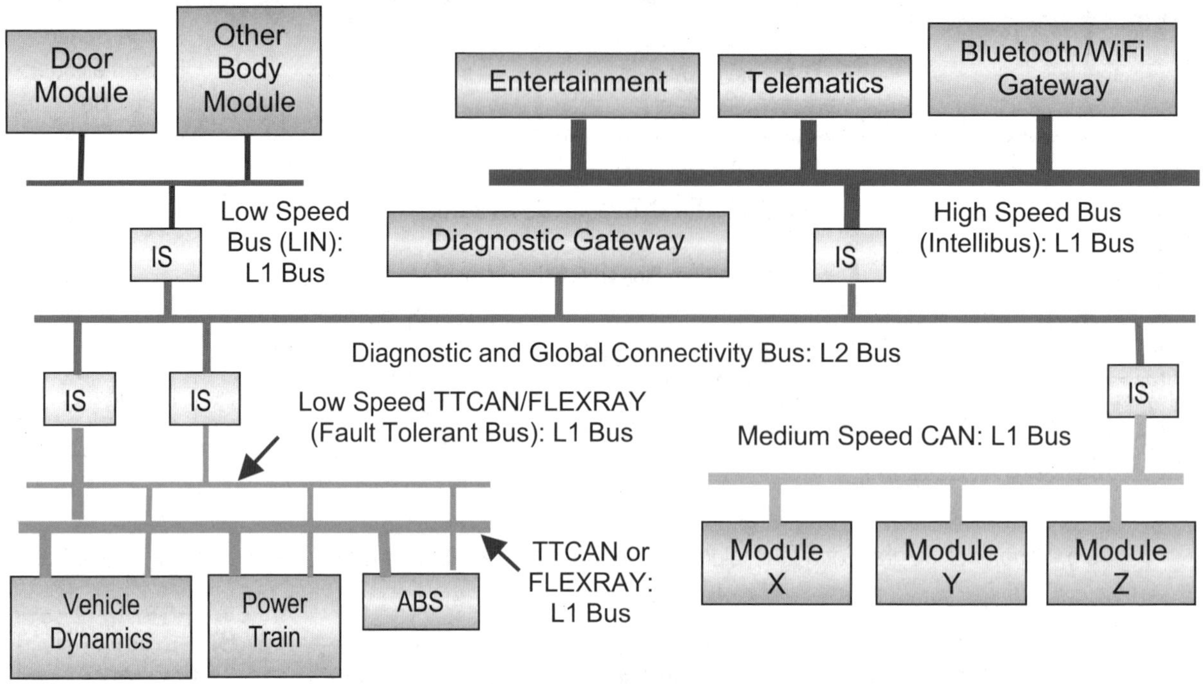

Figure 7: Schematic diagram of a partial fault-tolerant in-vehicle network with five Level 1 buses, one Level 2 bus and five intelligent switches.

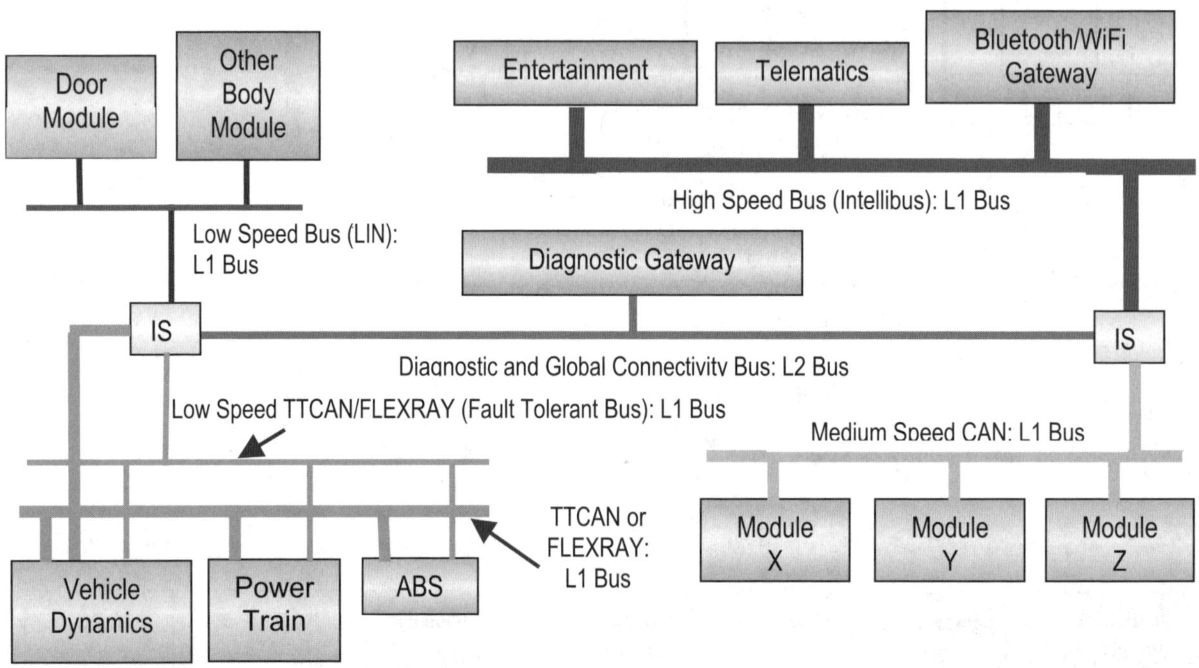

Figure 8: Schematic diagram of a partial fault-tolerant in-vehicle network with five Level 1 buses, one Level 2 bus and two intelligent switches.

FORMING CLUSTERS (GROUPS) OF ELECTRONIC MODULES

The electronic modules of a vehicle can be divided into several groups or clusters. The clusters can be formed based on functionality and locality. This means that the modules that do similar type of work and are located close to each other can be put in one cluster. Each cluster will be provided with at least one Level 1 bus. If there are similar electronic modules both at the front and rear of a vehicle, then the front modules can be put in one cluster and the rear modules can be put in another cluster. This way, other clusters can be formed depending on the locality and functionality of the modules. Then several clusters can be joined together by a Level 2 bus. If the clusters are formed the way it is described here, then each cluster will need a lower speed bus compared to the bus that would have been required otherwise. Since the inter-cluster communications may not be as much as the intra-cluster communications, even a low speed bus can be used as a Level 2 bus to connect the clusters. This approach of forming the clusters will save cost due to the fact that for the same length, a low-speed bus costs less than a high-speed bus.

PERFORMANCE ANALYSIS OF IN-VEHICLE NETWORK ARCHITECTURE

The performance of various partitions of the in-vehicle network as well as the entire network can be determined by developing simulation models. After executing the simulation models on computers, one can determine the minimum requirements for different partitions of the network architecture. Some of these requirements will include minimum processing powers needed from various electronic modules, minimum bandwidth needed from various buses, minimum size of buffers needed in various switches, etc. Computer simulations will also allow us to select the optimal network topology needed to meet the requirements of the next generation vehicles. The next section of the paper describes how simulation models can be developed to study various performance parameters of different partitions of the in-vehicle network.

TYPES OF SIMULATIONS:

Computer simulations can be divided into two types [7]: i) time-based simulation and ii) event-based simulation. In a time-based simulation, the program control loop is associated with time.

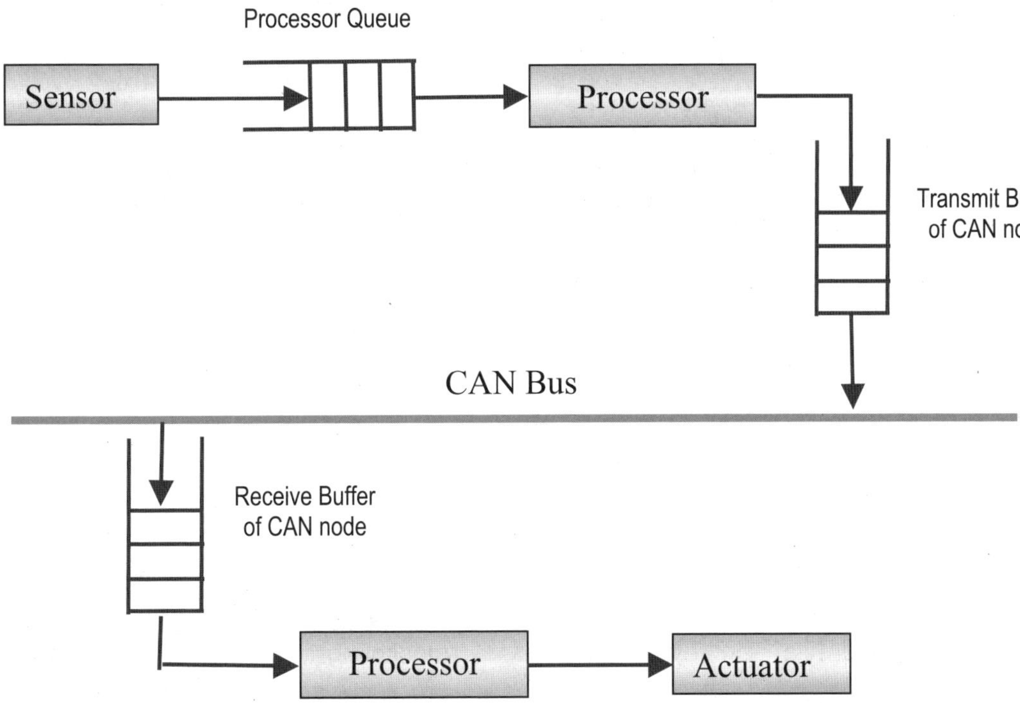

Figure 9: A diagram of information flow from a sensor to an actuator.

For each execution of the main control loop, the simulation clock advances by a fixed time unit. In the case of an event-based simulation, the execution of the main loop represents a single event. The simulation clock is simply advanced by the amount of time since the last event. For asynchronous systems, the event-based simulation is computationally more expensive and accurate than the time-based simulation. But, for synchronous systems, the time-based simulation is as good as the event-based simulation, and it is computationally less expensive than event-based simulation. CAN protocol is an event-based protocol. Thus an event-based simulation tool will be the most appropriate tool for analyzing various performance parameters of a CAN bus. Buses that use time-triggered protocols, such as TTCAN [4], [5] and FlexRay [6], carry both time-triggered and event-triggered messages. The time-based simulation can be used to simulate time-triggered messages and the event-based simulation can be used to simulate event-triggered messages. Thus, a combination of both time- and event-based simulations is necessary to simulate a bus like TTCAN or Flexray.

Various types of commercial tools are available to do different kinds of simulation. However, there could be some problems with commercial tools. For example, using commercial tools, it may not be possible to tune some of the simulation parameters the way we want to tune them. Thus, it might be a better idea to develop a custom simulation tool from the scratch. Using a custom tool we can do simulation in whatever way we want to do.

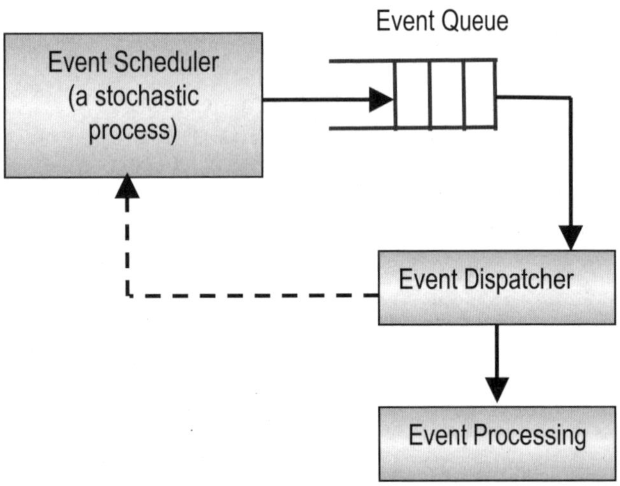

Figure 10: Software model of an event-based simulation.

DEVELOPING AN EVENT-BASED SIMULATION TOOL

Here we explain how to develop a custom event-based simulation tool to meet the requirements of our specific need for the next generation vehicles. In a vehicle system, an event is triggered by a sensor or by the driver's action such as pressing the brake or gas paddle. The event then goes to a processor queue, as shown in Figure 9. If the processor is busy or other events are waiting in the processor queue, then the event stays in the processor queue. Otherwise, the processor starts working on the event immediately. The event, queued in the processor queue, will stay in the queue until the previous events are taken care of by the processor. The processor spends some time (processing time) on an event. After that, the processor tries to send a message through the bus (say CAN bus) connected to the processor. If the bus is available, then the message is immediately sent to the bus. Otherwise, the message is queued in the transmit buffer of the CAN node. The message will go through the bus after the previous messages have been transmitted. After a certain time (transmit time), the message is queued to the receive buffer of the destination CAN node. If the processor at the receiving node is free, then it will immediately process the message. Otherwise, the processor will first take care of other queued messages and then it will process this new message. Figure 9 shows the entire process of information flow from a sensor to an actuator.

Components of the latency of an event:

There is a delay (latency) between the time an event occurs at a sensor or due to a driver's action, and the time an actuator takes an action. The latency has several components as shown by the following equation.

$$latency = t_{PQ} + t_{ps} + t_{TB} + t_{bus} + t_{RB} + t_{pd} \qquad (1)$$

where,

t_{PQ} = *delay at the processor queue*

t_{ps} = *processing time at the source node*

t_{TB} = *delay at the transmit buffer of the source node*

t_{bus} = *transmit time through the bus*

t_{RB} = *delay at the receive buffer of the destination node*

t_{pd} = *processing time at the destination node*

In the simulation model, the value of the delay, t_{PQ}, at the queue of the source processor can be determined by monitoring the arrival and exit times of the event in the processor queue. The value of the processing time, t_{ps}, depends on the type of the processor. This time can be expressed as

$$t_{ps} = T_s + k_s N \qquad (2)$$

Where T_s is a constant time, which represents the constant overhead of the processor at the source node in order to prepare a message. This constant overhead may include

- The time needed by the processor to get out of the main program,
- The time needed by the processor go to the interrupt service routine (assuming that the transmission of a message is interrupt driven),
- The time needed by the processor to check some status bits and set/clear some control bits of the CAN controller,
- The time needed by the processor for some other house keeping operations.

Thus, for a given processor, the value of T_s can be calculated based on its clock frequency and the number of instructions the processor needs to execute to do the abovementioned operations. The parameter k_s, shown in Equation 2, is another constant and N is the number of data bytes in the message. The value of t_{TB} can be determined by monitoring the arrival and exit times of the message in the transmit buffer of the source node. The value of t_{bus} can be expressed as

$$t_{bus} = \frac{M}{S} \qquad (3)$$

Where, M is the total number of bits in the message, and S is the speed of the bus in bits/sec. For example, if the message is a CAN message, then M will include, the start bit, arbitration bits, RTR bit, control bits, data bits, stuff bits, CRC bits, all delimiter bits and the end of frame bits. The value of t_{RB} can be determined by monitoring the arrival and exit times of the message in the receive buffer of the destination node. Like t_{ps}, the value of t_{pd} can be expressed as

$$t_{pd} = T_d + k_d N \qquad (4)$$

Where T_d is a constant time, which represents the constant overhead of the processor at the destination node in order to prepare a message, and k_d is the additional overhead per byte of data in preparing the message.

Simulation Model:

Figure 10 shows the block diagram of an event-based simulation model. In an event-based simulation model, an event is generated by a scheduler. The scheduler generates this event based on some kind of realistic stochastic process. We can develop a stochastic model for a particular event by collecting a large set of real data for that event. For example, the stochastic model of the brake event (pressing the brake paddle by the driver), can be developed by logging the driver's brake activity over a long period of time and collecting similar data from many vehicles.

After generating an event, the scheduler keeps that event in the event queue, as shown in Figure 10. When an event is dispatched from the event queue, another event is generated. This new event is then sent to the event queue. When a new event enters into the event queue, it is sorted within the event queue using the event-time as the sorting key. The new event is then placed at an appropriate point in the event queue. After dispatching an event from the event queue, the event is then sent to the event processing unit. The event processing unit then simulates the event in exactly the same way as a real system would process it.

The stochastic model of an event determines the interarrival time of the event, based on the behavior of the device that generates the event. A synchronous device, such as a time-triggered device, generates events after fixed interval of time. Hence, for a time-triggered system, the interarrival time is fixed. But, an asynchronous device doesn't generate events after fixed interval of time. Most physical asynchronous systems behave like a Poisson process. Thus, we can assume that a non time-triggered device will behave like a Poisson process. The stochastic model of an event will have the appropriate values of the parameters that define the characteristics of the Poisson process of the event. As mentioned earlier, these parameters of the stochastic model for an event can be determined by collecting a large set of field data for that particular event. The model shown in Figure 10 can be used to simulate an event-triggered system with an event-triggered bus (say CAN bus).

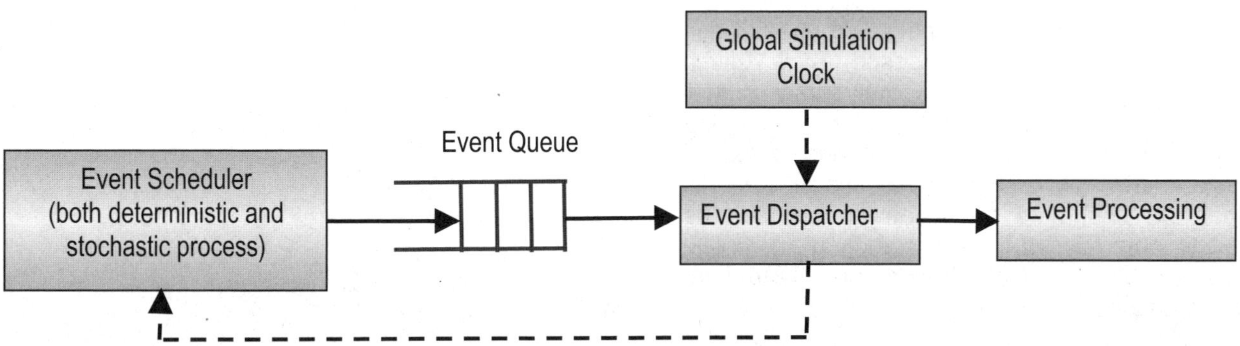

Figure 11: Software model of a combined time- and event-based simulation.

Since both TTCAN and Flexray support time- and event-triggered messages, we can develop the simulation models of these buses by building another layer on the top of the event-based simulation model. Figure 11 shows a software simulation model of a combined time- and event-based system. Here, the event scheduler is a deterministic as well as a stochastic process. In this case, a global simulation clock is maintained to keep the time-triggered events in sync. The frequency of this global simulation clock (software clock) should be at least equal to the highest frequency clock used in the in-vehicle network architecture. This requirement on the software clock will allow us to determine the latency and other performance parameters at a very high resolution (within a clock cycle of the highest frequency clock of the real system). At every global simulation clock pulse, the event queue must be checked. If the event-time of the event at the head of the event queue is less than or equal to the current value of the global simulation clock, then the event will be dispatched from the event queue. The dispatched event will then be checked to determine whether it is a deterministic event or a non-deterministic event. If it is a deterministic event, then the deterministic scheduling process will be used to schedule the next deterministic event. Otherwise, stochastic scheduling process will be used to schedule the next non-deterministic event. The scheduled event, whether deterministic or non-deterministic, will then be sent to the event queue. The event will be placed in the event queue after sorting it with other events in the event queue. The event-time will be used as the key to sort the events in the event queue.

By developing a simulation model, one can determine various performance parameters of the in-vehicle network. These parameters will include, but not limited to are the latency of different types of message, busload, bandwidth, and throughput.

CONCLUSION

In this paper, we discussed various types of topologies and protocols that could be used in the future in-vehicle networks. Due to the complexity of the future in-vehicle networks, many partitions of the network will be required. These partitions must be interconnected together for better diagnostic and software upload purposes. Since safety critical messages need fault tolerant mechanisms, we proposed how such mechanisms can be provided to the safety critical messages. The cost-effective way to compare the advantages and disadvantages of various types of topologies and protocols is by doing realistic simulations. This paper explains, how simulation models can be developed to determine the performance of in-vehicle network systems that will deal with both event- and time-triggered messages.

REFERENCE

1. R. K. Jurgen, "Coming from Detroit: Netwoks on wheel," IEEE Spectrum, pp. 53-59, June 1986
2. J. W. Tuska, "Multiplex wiring with microcomputer control," International Congress & Exposition, SAE paper 840495, Detroit, MI, Feb. 27 - March 2, 1984
3. C. R. Das and Laxmi Bhuyan, "Bandwidth availability of multiple-bus multiprocessors," IEEE Transactions on Computers, Vol. 34, No. 7, pp. 918-926, Oct. 1985.
4. Thomas Fuehrer, Bernd Mueller, Florian Hartwich and Robert Hugel, "Time-Triggered CAN (TTCAN)," Proc. of the SAE 2001 World Congress, Detroit, Michigan, March 5-8, 2001, paper number: 2001-01-0073.
5. Holger Zeltwanger, "Time-Triggered Communication on CAN," Proc. of the SAE 2002 World Congress, Detroit, Michigan, March 4-7, 2002, paper number: 2002-01-0437.
6. Christopher Temple, "Protocol Overview," Notes of FlexRay International Workshop, Detroit, Michigan, March 4, 2003.
7. Michael K. Molloy, "Fundamentals of Performance Modeling," Macmillan Publishing Company, 1989.

CONTACT

Syed Masud Mahmud, Ph.D.
Associate Professor
Department of Electrical and Computer Engineering
Wayne State University
Detroit MI 48202
Phone: (313) 577-3855
Fax: (313) 577-1101
Email: smahmud@eng.wayne.edu

Sheran Alles, Ph.D.
Technical Specialist
ECC Building
20600 Rotunda Dr.,
Ford Motor Company
Dearborn, MI 48124
Phone: (313) 594-0553
Email: salles@ford.com